Civil Procedure

EDITORIAL ADVISORS

Aspen Casebook Series

Civil Procedure

A Coursebook

Fourth Edition

Joseph W. Glannon
Professor of Law
Suffolk University

Andrew M. Perlman
Dean and Professor of Law
Suffolk University

Peter Raven-Hansen
Glen Earl Weston Research Professor of Law Emeritus
George Washington University

Wolters Kluwer

Published by Wolters Kluwer in New York.

Wolters Kluwer Legal & Regulatory U.S. serves customers worldwide with CCH, Aspen Publishers, and Kluwer Law International products. (www.WKLegaledu.com)

To contact Customer Service, e-mail customer.service@wolterskluwer.com, call 1-800-234-1660, fax 1-800-901-9075, or mail correspondence to:

Wolters Kluwer
Attn: Order Department
PO Box 990
Frederick, MD 21705

Printed in the United States of America.

1 2 3 4 5 6 7 8 9 0

ISBN 978-1-5438-2625-8

Library of Congress Cataloging-in-Publication Data

Names: Glannon, Joseph W., author. | Perlman, Andrew M. (Andrew Marcus), author. | Raven-Hansen, Peter, 1946- author.
Title: Civil procedure: a coursebook / Joseph W. Glannon, Professor of Law, Suffolk University; Andrew M. Perlman, Dean and Professor of Law, Suffolk University; Peter Raven-Hansen, Glen Earl Weston Research Professor of Law Emeritus, George Washington University.
Description: Fourth edition. | New York: Wolters Kluwer, [2021] | Series: Aspen casebook series | Includes bibliographical references and index. | Summary: "Casebook for law students in the Civil Procedure course"— Provided by publisher.
Identifiers: LCCN 2020046781 (print) | LCCN 2020046782 (ebook) | ISBN 9781543826258 (hardcover) | ISBN 9781543826265 (ebook)
Subjects: LCSH: Civil procedure—United States—Cases. | LCGFT: Casebooks (Law)
Classification: LCC KF8839.G578 2021 (print) | LCC KF8839 (ebook) | DDC 347.73/5—dc23
LC record available at https://lccn.loc.gov/2020046781
LC ebook record available at https://lccn.loc.gov/2020046782

SUSTAINABLE FORESTRY INITIATIVE
Certified Chain of Custody
Promoting Sustainable Forestry
www.sfiprogram.org
SFI-01681

SFI label applies to the text stock

About Wolters Kluwer Legal & Regulatory U.S.

Wolters Kluwer Legal & Regulatory U.S. delivers expert content and solutions in the areas of law, corporate compliance, health compliance, reimbursement, and legal education. Its practical solutions help customers successfully navigate the demands of a changing environment to drive their daily activities, enhance decision quality and inspire confident outcomes.

Serving customers worldwide, its legal and regulatory portfolio includes products under the Aspen Publishers, CCH Incorporated, Kluwer Law International, ftwilliam.com and MediRegs names. They are regarded as exceptional and trusted resources for general legal and practice-specific knowledge, compliance and risk management, dynamic workflow solutions, and expert commentary.

I dedicate this book to Carol McGeehan.
—J.W.G.

To Lisa, Maya, Brynne, and Talia
—A.M.P.

To Winnie, Erik, and Anna
—P.R-H.

SUMMARY OF CONTENTS

CONTENTS

Chapter 9. Long Arm Statutes 309

Chapter 10. The Constitutional Requirement of Notice and Methods of Service of Process 329

PART IV ■ VENUE

PART V ■ PLEADING

PART VII ■ DISCOVERY

PART IX ■ TRIAL AND PRETRIAL

Chapter 33. Claim Preclusion 1189

Chapter 34. Issue Preclusion: Further Limits to Relitigation 1223

PREFACE

After decades of teaching Civil Procedure, we became convinced that students need a text that offers more than a series of cases followed by dense post-case notes and questions. Simply put, we concluded that students need a *coursebook,* not simply a *casebook.*

Based on this premise, we developed a number of features in this book that should help you to place the material in context. For example, each chapter begins with a brief summary of contents to orient you to the topics covered in the chapter. Moreover, each case begins with an introduction that provides context for the opinion and offers factual and legal background to make the case more accessible. The case introductions also pose questions for you to consider *before* you read each case to help you focus on the important aspects of the opinion.

Following each case, we provide textual notes and questions, but, unconventionally, *we answer almost all of the questions we pose.* We believe that the typical unanswered casebook question is ineffective. If you think that you know the answer, you have no way of confirming it. If you do not know the answer, the authors have lost an opportunity to educate you. Unanswered questions and dense post-case notes that require you to consult outside authorities often produce more frustration than understanding, so we have largely avoided them.

We also have adopted a number of other techniques that make this book more user-friendly. We have written short chapters of manageable scope. We have used a different font and a shaded border for the text of opinions, so you will know when you are reading original material as opposed to our text. For some especially difficult cases, we have inserted bracketed editorial guidance into the case itself. We include multiple choice questions to test your understanding of new concepts and, in keeping with our pedagogical approach, we include our analyses of these questions. We also have adopted another simple feature that our students appreciate: a summary of key concepts at the close of each chapter.

The coursebook will also improve your capacity for legal analysis. For example, by highlighting the subtle distinctions between the best answer to a multiple choice question and "near misses," the coursebook will help you to develop the ability to make fine distinctions in applying complicated concepts. We also offer several detailed questions for more in-depth treatment, followed by a sample "issue analysis" so that you can see how to analyze a sophisticated problem.

We expect that the coursebook will hone your analytical skills, give you a rich understanding of civil procedure, and provide important insights into the role that procedure plays in the American system of justice.

Joseph W. Glannon
Andrew M. Perlman
Peter Raven-Hansen

November 2020

BOOK FEATURES AND CONVENTIONS

This book uses several unique features and conventions, including the following:

Q / A — These icons flag questions and answers for your consideration. We recommend that you try to answer these questions on your own before reading the answers that we supply.

Case reading guidance — We include a boxed, shaded guide to reading each case, which provides important background material and questions that you should try to answer while reading the opinion.

Italicization of terms of art — When we mention a term of art for the first time, we place the word or phrase in italics. Some Latin phrases also consistently appear in italics.

Shaded borders — We use a shaded border to the left of the principal cases to highlight when you are reading the text of a case rather than our own text and to make it easier for you to locate case excerpts during class.

Bracketed editorial inserts — We occasionally include our own explanatory material in the body of an opinion. This material, which appears in the case itself or in an asterisked footnote, is set off in brackets and, if it is more than two lines long, begins with "Eds.—" to make clear that you are reading our text rather than the text of the case.

Internal case citations — We regularly omit internal case citations that appear in the body of an opinion without noting the omission. We have retained citations (without parallel citations) when needed to identify the source of a quotation, and we indicate textual omissions (other than internal case citations) through the use of ellipses.

Footnotes — When we have retained a footnote in a case, we have kept its original Arabic number. We have omitted all other case footnotes without noting the omission. Our own footnotes have asterisks.

Short forms for commonly cited books and treatises — We have adopted short citation forms for certain books and treatises frequently cited in the text, including:

Richard D. Freer, Civil Procedure (4th ed. 2018) is referred to as *Freer.*
James W. Moore et al., Moore's Federal Practice is referred to as *Moore.*
Gene R. Shreve, Peter Raven-Hansen & Charles Gardner Geyh, Understanding Civil Procedure (6th ed. 2019) is referred to as *Shreve, Raven-Hansen & Geyh.*
Charles Alan Wright & Mary Kay Kane, Law of Federal Courts (8th ed. 2017) is referred to as *Wright & Kane.*
Charles Alan Wright & Arthur R. Miller, Federal Practice and Procedure is referred to as *Wright & Miller.*

ACKNOWLEDGMENTS

Writing and updating a book of this size and scope is a major undertaking. We have been fortunate to receive invaluable assistance from Darren Kelly and Tom Daughhetee at The Froebe Group in preparing the Fourth Edition. We are also grateful for the indispensable role played by Carol McGeehan in encouraging and supporting this project through its ten-year gestation period.

Thanks, too, to the many research assistants who assisted us in preparing and revising the book, and to members of the Civil Procedure professoriat who reviewed various chapters and gave us valuable input and advice, and continue to do so. We are especially grateful to Professor Aaron Caplan for his many helpful comments and corrections.

It is common for authors to thank their spouses and families. After writing this book, it is clear why they deserve our thanks. A project of this sort requires efforts above and beyond the usual demands of academic life. We are grateful to our families for their support, patience, and encouragement, and especially to our spouses, Ann Glannon, Lisa Aidlin, and Winnie Raven-Hansen.

We would like to thank the following authors and publishers for kindly granting permission to reproduce excerpts of, or illustrations from, the following material:

Blue Note, Columbia, MO. Copyright © Columbia Daily Tribune. Reproduced by permission. All rights reserved.

Blue Note Jazz Club, New York City. Copyright © 2003 Bernd Jonkmanns / LAIF / Redux. Reproduced with permission. All rights reserved.

Courtroom Interior. Copyright © The Daily Hampshire Gazette.

Dairy Queen restaurant. Copyright © Dairy Queen Corporation. Reproduced by permission. All rights reserved.

Dupont Plaza Hotel Fire, San Juan, Puerto Rico. Copyright © 1986 AP Images. Reproduced by permission. All rights reserved.

Erie Railroad Tracks. Courtesy of the Collection of the Supreme Court of the United States.

Freight Cars. Copyright © Ted Horowitz / Corbis. Reproduced by permission. All rights reserved.

Greyhound Stock Certificate. Courtesy of Greyhound.

Jack Greenberg. Copyright © Columbia Law School. Reproduced by permission. All rights reserved.

Legal Notice in Newspaper. Courtesy of Quincy Patriot Ledger.

Les Avocats Et Les Plaideurs. Daumier, Honore (1808-1879). Excerpt from Le Charivari. Musée des Beaux-Arts, Marseille, France. Copyright © Scala / White Images / Art Resource, NY.

Map of Carter Lake. Courtesy of the City of Carter Lake, Iowa.

Official Portrait of Justice William J Brennan, 1972. WikiMedia Commons.
O.J. Simpson Jury Court Painting. Courtesy of Bill Robles.
Oliver Wendell Holmes, Jr. Courtesy of the Library of Congress.
Pacific Christian Advocate. Courtesy of Willamette University College of Law.
People in Line Outside Courthouse. Copyright © 2009 Birmingham News / AL.com.
Robert Jackson. Courtesy of the Collection of the Supreme Court of the United States.
Ruth Bader Ginsburg. Courtesy of the Collection of the Supreme Court of the United States.
Sandra Day O'Connor. Courtesy of the Collection of the Supreme Court of the United States.
Sonia Sotomayor. Courtesy of the Collection of the Supreme Court of the United States.
Snow Machine on A Ski Slope. Copyright © 2016 Grafton Smith / Getty Images. Reproduced by permission. All rights reserved.
Storage of Government Documents in Warehouse in Maryland. Copyright © 2016 Jim Pickerell / Fotosearch. Reproduced by permission. All rights reserved.
SWAT Team, Dan Pelle, Spokesman Review.
Swimming Pool with A Slide. Copyright © Chiyacat / Dreamstime.com.
Supreme Court of The United States, Building Exterior. Courtesy of the Collection of the Supreme Court of the United States.
Supreme Court of The United States. Courtesy of the Collection of the Supreme Court of the United States.
Sylvester Pennoyer. Courtesy of Oregon Historical Society.
Thurgood Marshall. Courtesy of the Collection of the Supreme Court of the United States.
Tire Valve. Courtesy of Emily Behrendt.
12 Angry Men. Copyright © Moviestore Collection, Ltd. / Alamy Stock Photo. Reproduced by permission. All rights reserved.
United Mine Workers Strike. Copyright © 1963 AP Images. Reproduced by permission. All rights reserved.
Westlaw List of Amicus Briefs. Copyright © 2016 Thomson Reuters. Reproduced by permission. All rights reserved.

Civil Procedure

PART I

Introduction

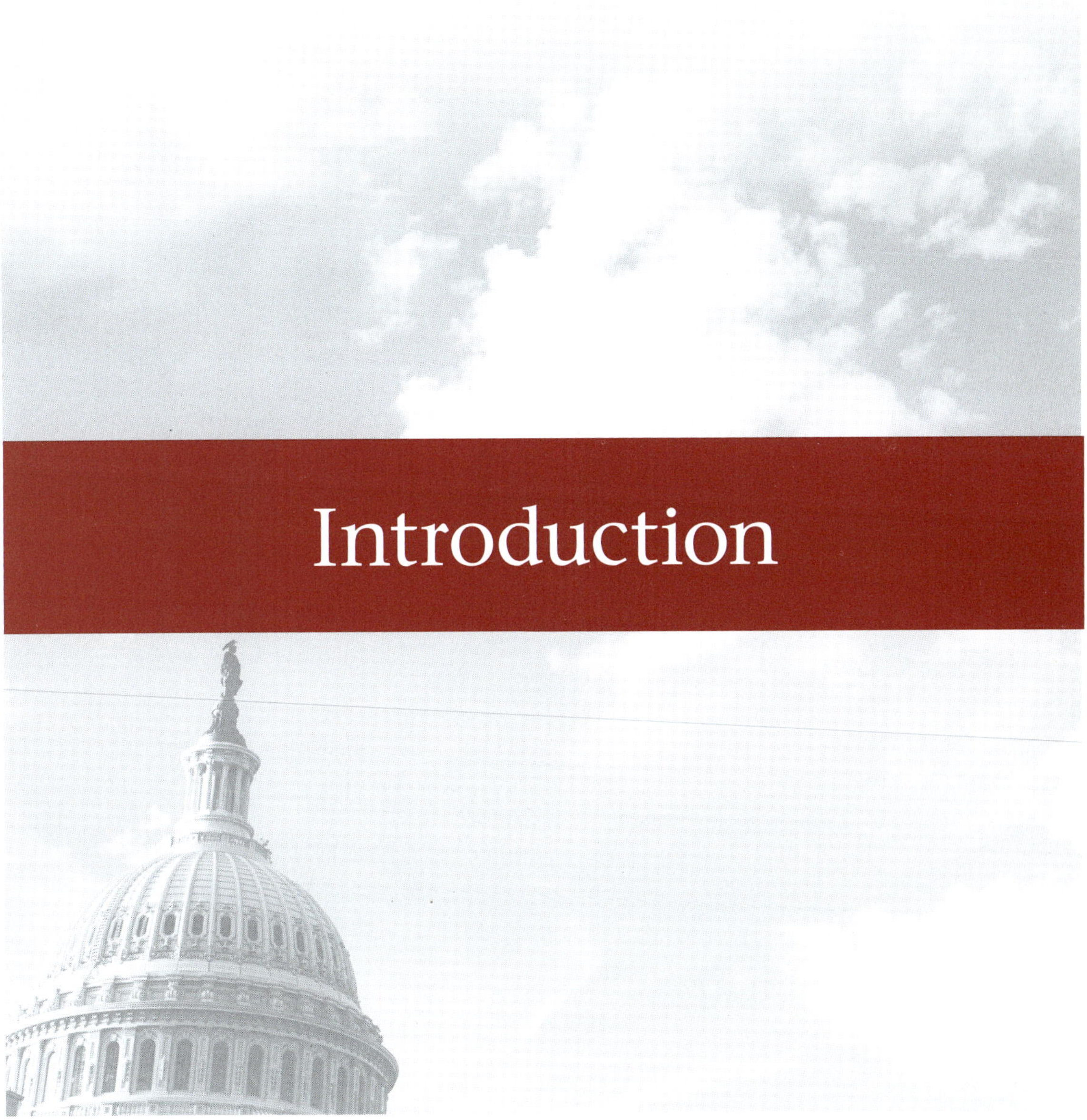

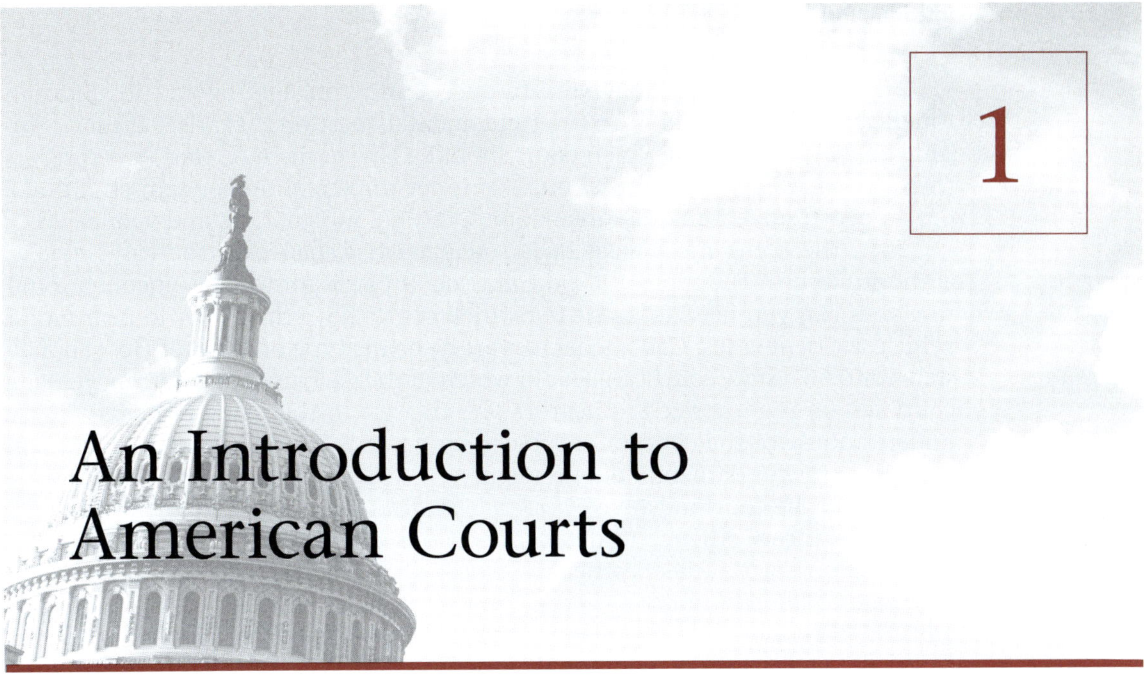

1

An Introduction to American Courts

I. Some Introductory Comments

The purpose of this book is to introduce you to the process of civil litigation in American courts. To help you understand this process, the book includes not only cases—the staple of most first-year courses—but a variety of other materials as well, including explanatory text, multiple choice questions, hypotheticals, and questions for further study.

First-year law casebooks have traditionally tended to "hide the ball," leaving students to struggle with complex problems without much guidance or background. This book starts from a different premise: that you will learn more from class preparation and from class if the coursebook provides explanatory material to accompany the cases. We explain basic principles fully and (departing again from tradition) we answer most of the questions that we pose in our notes. Even with such explanations, much sophisticated material remains for you and your procedure professor to work through in class. A firm grasp of the basics will help you to address the complex issues more effectively.

This chapter and the next introduce basic concepts about litigation in American courts. We then turn to a fundamental question that arises at the beginning of every lawsuit: In which court should a lawyer file (i.e., start) the case? As these chapters indicate, counsel must consider three requirements in choosing a proper court: subject matter jurisdiction, personal jurisdiction, and venue.

First, the court must have *subject matter jurisdiction* over the case, that is, authority to hear the type of dispute at issue. If you want to sue someone for hitting your car, you need to figure out which courts have the power to hear motor vehicle accident cases. Can a federal court hear this type of dispute? How about a state court? If a state court can hear it, which of the various courts within the state court system is authorized to hear it? The answers to these questions require an understanding of the concept of subject matter jurisdiction. Chapters 3 through 5 analyze this fundamental requirement.

Second, the court must have *personal jurisdiction* over the defendant. Lawsuits are a great inconvenience to defendants. Consequently, both the United States Constitution and statutes restrict the power of courts to force a defendant from one state to appear and defend a lawsuit in another. If Stein lives in Colorado and hits Fernandez's car in Denver, can Fernandez sue Stein for his injury in Nebraska? The answer depends on whether the Nebraska court has personal jurisdiction over Stein, that is, the power to force her to appear in a Nebraska court to defend the case. Chapters 6 through 9 introduce the accepted bases on which a court can exercise personal jurisdiction.

Third, the plaintiff must choose a court that is an authorized *venue* for the action under the relevant venue statute. Venue defines which courts within a court system (e.g., the California state court system) can hear a particular suit. If you live in California and have an accident in Los Angeles, can the driver of the other car sue you in a state court in San Francisco? The answer to this question turns on whether the San Francisco court is "a proper venue" under California venue statutes. While personal jurisdiction restricts a court's power over an out-of-state defendant, venue regulates which specific court within a court system may hear a particular case. Chapters 11 and 12 discuss venue and transfers of venue.

After analyzing these three principles that determine where a suit may be brought, we turn to the actual process of litigation. Several chapters analyze *pleadings*, the documents by which parties commence a case and state their positions on the issues in dispute. We then turn to the problem of *joinder*, the rules governing who can be made parties to a single case and the scope of claims that may be asserted in a single action. Several chapters cover pretrial *discovery* of evidence, the process by which parties exchange relevant information before trial. Later chapters cover trial procedure, motions that may resolve a case prior to or during trial, and complex issues involving the substantive law that applies to claims litigated in federal court. The book closes with an examination of *claim preclusion* and *issue preclusion*, two doctrines that limit relitigation of claims or issues resolved in a prior case.

Students, please take note: There is no one way to structure the Civil Procedure course, which is indeed a seamless web. While there is a fairly broad consensus on the core issues that should be covered in the course, procedure teachers often present them in a different order than they appear in this coursebook. So don't be surprised if your professor takes the chapters out of order or, as is frequently the case where the course is allocated fewer credits, does not cover certain chapters at all.

II. The Two American Court Systems

Let's start with some basics. The Framers of the United States Constitution chose to create a federal form of government, in which governmental power is shared between a national government—the federal government—and state governments in each state of the union.

The original states existed long before the Constitution was adopted, and each had its own court system. The Framers saw no reason to abolish these state courts, which functioned well enough in many respects. However, they did see the need for a set of national courts that could hear certain types of cases that implicate national interests or pose significant risks of local bias. Consequently, in Article III of the United States Constitution, they empowered Congress to establish a separate system of federal courts, which co-exists with the courts of the states.

Each of these court systems has *trial courts*, in which cases are litigated through trial, as well as *appellate courts*, which hear appeals from the trial courts within that system. Before we explore the subject matter jurisdiction of state and federal courts, we will look briefly at the structure of state court systems and of the federal court system.

While this coursebook focuses on the state and federal courts, the heading above—*The Two American Court Systems*—is actually a serious misnomer, since there are many more than two systems of courts in the United States. Many American Indian tribes maintain tribal courts, which adjudicate cases involving tribal members and cases arising on Indian reservations. *See generally* William Canby, American Indian Law in a Nutshell 67–69 (6th ed. 2015). In addition, many agencies of both the states and the federal government adjudicate claims related to their administrative roles. For example, state departments of employment frequently adjudicate unemployment claims. State motor vehicle bureaus may administer license revocation proceedings. At the federal level, the Social Security Administration has an adjudicatory division that hears claims for benefits and the National Transportation Safety Board entertains claims involving denial or revocation of pilot licenses. Such administrative agencies are legion, and collectively hear a great many more claims than state and federal courts do. (The Social Security Administration website states that its 1,300 administrative law judges heard almost 800,000 appeals in 2019. *See* www.ssa.gov/appeals (last visited May 28, 2020).) Such bodies—studied in the course on Administrative Law—have their own procedural rules for processing claims,* which may or may not look much like the civil procedure rules that we cover in this book.

* Federal administrative adjudication, for example, usually follows rules of procedure set out in the federal Administrative Procedure Act, 5 U.S.C. §§ 551 et seq.

III. The Structure of State Court Systems

Every state has a set of trial courts, or courts of *original jurisdiction*, in which cases are filed and litigated through final judgment. Since the states establish their own court systems they can call their courts whatever they like, and states have chosen different names and configurations for their courts. For example, in New Jersey and California, the trial courts of general jurisdiction are called superior courts; in Texas, they are called district courts; in Florida, circuit courts; in New York, some of them are, surprisingly, called supreme courts.

In most states, the plaintiff commences litigation by filing a pleading called a *complaint* in the trial court, setting forth her claims against the defendant. The defendant files an *answer* to the complaint setting forth his position on the facts alleged by the plaintiff and any defenses he has to the claims in the complaint. The parties develop the facts relevant to their claims and defenses through *discovery*—the process of production of evidence from opposing parties and witnesses—in the trial court. If the case goes to trial, it will be tried in that court, and a final *judgment* will be entered there for the winning party.

In addition to trial courts of broad jurisdiction, most states also have several specialized trial courts with limited subject matter jurisdiction. Often, there is a probate or family court, which has jurisdiction over estates, guardianships, divorces, child support, and other domestic matters. There may also be a housing court, which handles landlord-tenant cases; a land court, which deals with cases involving interests in or title to real property; a small claims court; or others suited to local needs. Some of our thirstier states have "water courts," which decide the allocation of water resources. While such courts have limited subject matter jurisdiction, they are still *trial* courts, that is, they are the courts in which cases within that court's jurisdiction are filed, litigated, tried, and decided. Lastly, many states have municipal courts that handle relatively minor criminal and civil matters. *See generally* Daniel John Meador & Gregory Mitchell, American Courts 9 (3d ed. 2009).

Q **The creation of state court systems.** The configuration of broad trial courts and specialized courts differs from state to state. Who decides which state courts will exist within a state court system and which trial court will hear which cases? If a lawyer decides to bring a tort case in a New Mexico state court, how would she find out which court within the New Mexico court system has the authority to hear it?

A Each state determines the structure of its state court system for itself. Some state constitutions specify broad aspects of the structure of that state's courts. In most states, the state legislature prescribes the structure of the state courts and determines the subject matter jurisdiction of each court within the state. Thus, counsel should review the New Mexico *statutes* (laws passed by the state legislature) defining the jurisdiction of the various trial courts within the state, to determine which one has statutory authority to hear tort claims. If she sued in a Minnesota court, she would search the Minnesota statutes governing subject matter jurisdiction of its trial courts, and so on.

Every state also has at least one appellate court that hears appeals from trial courts within the state. Typically, a state will have an intermediate appellate court, which hears most appeals from the trial courts. (In a few smaller states, there are only trial courts and a state supreme court, which hears all appeals.) There may be one intermediate appellate court covering the entire state, or there may be several units of the appellate court. Illinois, for example, is divided into five geographic appellate districts, each with its own intermediate appellate court to hear appeals from trial courts within that district. If you appeal a judgment rendered by a trial court in Edwards County, which is within the Fifth Appellate District, your appeal goes to the Appellate Court for the Fifth Appellate District. If you appeal a case tried in Cass County, your appeal would go to the Appellate Court for the Fourth Appellate District.

In states with intermediate appellate courts, litigants usually have a right to appeal to that appellate court. The party who loses the appeal may ask the state's highest court—usually, but not always, called the state supreme court—to take further review of a case. However, in most states the state's highest court is not required to hear such appeals. It chooses whether to grant further review (*appeal by permission* or *discretionary appeal*) and typically does so only in cases that pose novel issues of law or involve important public issues.*

Figures 1–1 and 1–2 illustrate the structure of two state court systems. (There is a good discussion of the structure of state court systems in Daniel John Meador & Gregory Mitchell, AMERICAN COURTS 9–19 (3d ed. 2009).)

Court of Final Review	**Illinois Supreme Court**
	↑
Intermediate Appellate Court	**Illinois Appellate Courts** **(First Appellate Court, Second Appellate Court, etc.)** Five geographic districts within the state, each with its own Appellate Court
	↑
Trial Court	**Illinois Circuit Courts** **(E.g., Circuit Court for Logan County, DeKalb County, etc.)** Twenty-four circuits, organized by county [and several specialized trial courts for particular types of cases]

Figure 1–1: STRUCTURE OF THE ILLINOIS STATE COURT SYSTEM

* State supreme courts may hear direct appeals from the trial courts in some types of cases. The structure and process for taking an appeal are determined by the legislature in each state and vary a good deal from one state to another. A good source on American appellate courts is Daniel John Meador, APPELLATE COURTS IN THE UNITED STATES (2006).

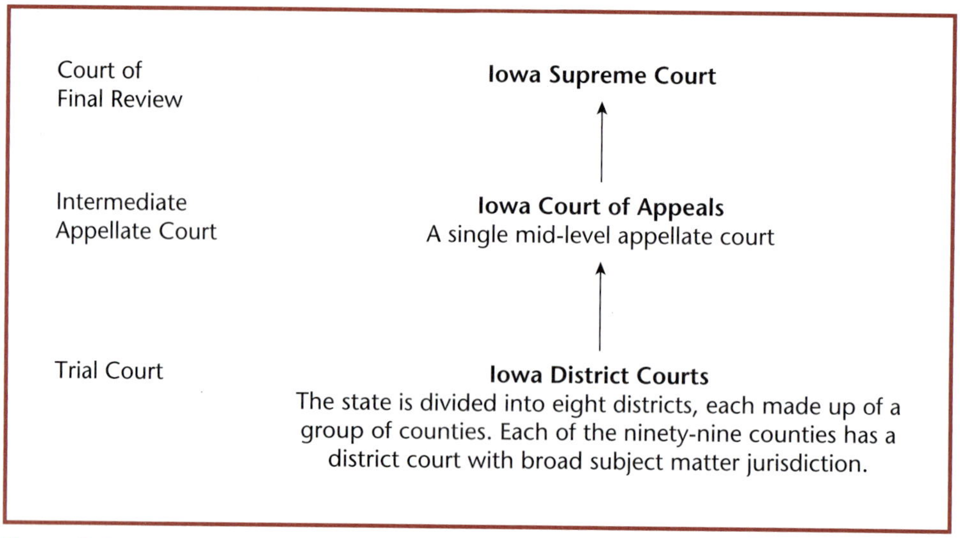

Figure 1–2: STRUCTURE OF THE IOWA STATE COURT SYSTEM

As Figures 1–1 and 1–2 illustrate, the court systems in these two states are not exactly the same, but both systems include trial courts, one or more intermediate appellate courts, and a state supreme court. As the mechanic said when asked how he could work on so many different kinds of cars, "They're all a little bit different, but they're all basically the same."

IV. The Structure of the Federal Court System

Article III, Section 1 of the United States Constitution provides that "[t]he judicial Power of the United States [that is, the federal government], shall be vested in one Supreme Court, and . . . such inferior Courts as the Congress may from time to time ordain and establish." U.S. Const. art. III, § 1. Thus, the United States Supreme Court is created by the Constitution itself. But the decision whether to create "inferior" federal courts, that is, federal trial courts or federal appellate courts below the Supreme Court, is left by Article III, Section 1 for Congress to decide.

Congress might have decided not to create any lower federal courts. If so, all cases would be litigated through trial in state courts. However, the first Congress favored a strong national government and immediately exercised its authority in Article III, Section 1 by creating lower federal courts, in the Judiciary Act of 1789.* Since then Congress has periodically revised the structure and jurisdiction of the lower federal courts, but both federal trial courts and federal appellate courts below the Supreme Court have operated continuously since the First Judiciary Act.

* Judiciary Act of 1789, 1 Stat. 73 §§ 3–4 (1789).

The federal trial courts are called the *federal district courts*. These courts sit in ninety-four federal districts within the United States. Each district comprises a state or part of a state. The federal District of South Carolina, for example, includes the entire state of South Carolina. California, on the other hand, because of its size and the number of cases it generates, is divided into four federal districts, the Northern, Eastern, Central, and Southern Districts of California, with a federal court sitting in each district. Figure 1–3 illustrates the configuration of the federal districts as of 2016.

As the diagram shows, the size of the federal districts varies substantially. For example, the Northern District of California is much smaller than the Eastern District. These district lines have been drawn more with a view to population and the presence of commercial, litigation-generating centers (e.g., San Francisco) than to square mileage. The number of federal judges sitting in each district also varies depending on the caseload of the court.

Like the trial courts of state court systems, the federal district courts are courts of original jurisdiction, that is, they are trial courts, in which cases are filed and litigated through to a final decision. The plaintiff commences the action there; the parties develop the facts through discovery in the district court; if the case goes to trial, it will be tried in the district court, and a final judgment will be entered there for the winning party.

Usually, a federal case ends with the final decision in the federal district court, either after trial or by settlement or dismissal. However, a party who loses in the district court and claims some error in the course of the litigation may appeal from the district court's judgment to one of the federal courts of appeals. Like the federal district courts, the courts of appeals (other than the Federal Circuit)

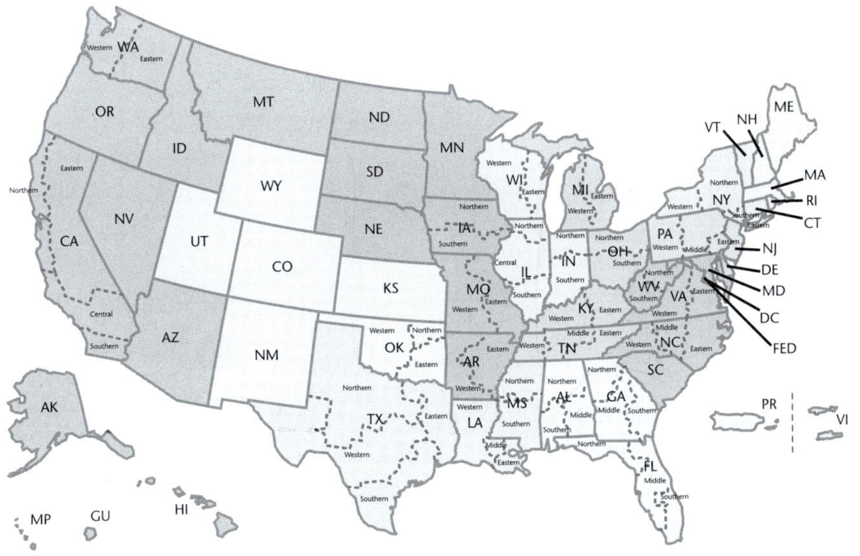

Figure 1–3: GEOGRAPHICAL BOUNDARIES OF UNITED STATES FEDERAL JUDICIAL DISTRICTS

are organized geographically. Each hears appeals from the federal district courts sitting in a group of states. Figure 1–4 illustrates the geographic scope of the federal courts of appeals. For example, if a case is filed, litigated, and decided in the District of Maine, an appeal from the district court's judgment will go to the Court of Appeals for the First Circuit. An appeal from a case decided in the Federal District Court for the Northern District of Illinois goes to the Court of Appeals for the Seventh Circuit, and so on.*

The United States Supreme Court sits at the top of the federal court system. A litigant who loses an appeal in the court of appeals may ask the Supreme Court to review that court's legal rulings. Unlike appeals to the federal courts of appeals, review in the Supreme Court is almost always discretionary, that is, the Court chooses to review only those cases that involve important federal issues or conflicts in lower courts' interpretation of federal law. The Supreme Court only grants certiorari (agrees to review) in a small percentage of the cases in which review is sought—perhaps one to two percent. Thus, the decision of the court of appeals usually ends the case. Figure 1–5 illustrates the relationship of the trial and appellate courts in the federal court system.

The unique role of the United States Supreme Court. We have described two separate court systems, each operating independent of the other. But the United States Supreme Court has a unique role in our federal system. Each state supreme court is the court of last resort for most cases tried in that state's courts. For example, if a case involves the meaning of an Iowa statute, the Iowa Supreme Court,

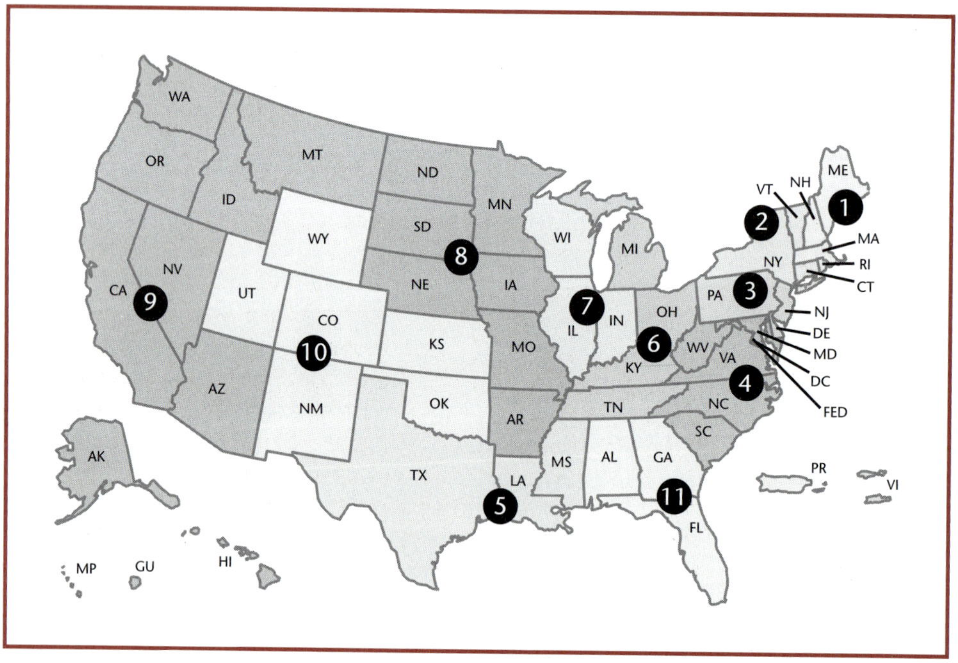

Figure 1–4: GEOGRAPHICAL BOUNDARIES OF THE UNITED STATES COURTS OF APPEALS

* The procedure appellate courts use to consider and decide appeals is described in Chapter 2.

Court of Final Review	**United States Supreme Court** Single court with nine justices. It exercises discretionary review of United States Court of Appeals decisions and some state court decisions. It has original jurisdiction in a few special cases.
	↑
Intermediate Appellate Court	**United States Court of Appeals** Twelve federal appellate courts hear appeals from cases decided in the district courts within their geographic area,* and some decisions by federal administrative agencies.
	↑
Trial Court	**United States District Courts** Ninety-four districts, each covering a state or part of a state. These are courts of "original jurisdiction," in which cases are filed, tried, and decided.

Figure 1–5: THE THREE LEVELS OF THE FEDERAL COURT SYSTEM

as the highest court of Iowa, would be the highest court that could review and determine its meaning. However, when issues of federal law are litigated in a state court case, the losing party may ask the United States Supreme Court to review the state court's decisions on those federal issues. 28 U.S.C. § 1257.

Suppose, for example, that parties litigate a case in an Iowa state court in which the plaintiff seeks to enforce rights under a federal statute. (As we will see, cases involving federal law can usually be litigated in state courts.) The Iowa court holds the federal statute unconstitutional, and the Iowa Supreme Court affirms that holding. The party who lost this case may ask the United States Supreme Court to review the state court's ruling on the constitutionality of the federal statute. This power of the United States Supreme Court to review issues of federal law, whether litigated initially in a state or a federal court, allows the Supreme Court to provide definitive rulings on issues of federal law. Once it does, its rulings will bind all American courts, state and federal.

* The one exception is the United States Court of Appeals for the Federal Circuit. It hears appeals in a potpourri of specialized federal cases (such as patent and trademark cases) from all of the federal district courts and from certain federal agencies as well.

The United States Supreme Court

The Supreme Court, which sits in this imposing edifice in Washington, D.C., is created by Article III of the Constitution. As the highest court of the federal court system, it reviews cases that come to it from lower federal courts throughout the nation. It also has jurisdiction to review cases decided in state courts when those cases raise issues of federal law. Justice Robert Jackson once said of the Court, "we are not final because we are infallible, but we are infallible only because we are final."

The Supreme Court hears oral arguments in the courtroom pictured here. Note the nine chairs behind the "bench" for the nine Justices who sit on the Court.

Frank Santzen, Collection of the Supreme Court of the United States

V. The Subject Matter Jurisdiction of State Courts: General Principles

Subject matter jurisdiction refers to the power of a court to hear disputes of a particular type. For example, not every court can hear a tort case arising from a car accident or a claim for breach of contract. To choose a proper court, a lawyer needs to know which courts have subject matter jurisdiction over the type of claim she wishes to bring.

Suppose you practice law in Massachusetts and a new client, Corey, comes into your office. Corey explains that he is originally from New Hampshire and is currently a student in Boston. He was out one night in Boston and got into a fight with a bartender at a bar called Barristers. Corey claims that the bartender started the fight and that, as a result of the fracas, Corey suffered a broken leg. Corey wants to sue the bartender, who lives in New Hampshire, as well as Barristers, Inc., the corporation that owns the bar, for his injuries.

You learn that Barristers is incorporated in Delaware, has its corporate headquarters in Rhode Island, and owns nine Barristers bars in Massachusetts, one in

Rhode Island, and one in Maine. Corey has a credible story, and you would like to take his case. You prepare a complaint (the pleading that initiates the suit) alleging that the bartender committed a tort by battering Corey. In order to decide where to bring the action, you will have to decide which courts (state or federal) have subject matter jurisdiction over Corey's battery case.

Although the structure of the federal and state court systems is somewhat similar, the subject matter jurisdiction of the courts in the two systems is dramatically different. State courts have broad subject matter jurisdiction over most, though not all, types of cases. But the federal courts are courts of limited subject matter jurisdiction, meaning that they can only hear a narrow range of cases.

For example, federal courts do not have general authority to hear the types of cases you study in your first year of law school, such as contracts, torts, and property cases.* Nor can they hear other categories of cases, such as domestic relations cases, settlement of estates, and state administrative appeals. All of these types of cases, which comprise the great majority of disputes adjudicated every year, are usually left to the state courts.

The extent to which state courts handle the nation's judicial business is illustrated by comparing the number of federal judges to the number of state judges in any state. In 2016, Colorado, for example, had fewer than twenty-five federal district judges and magistrate judges,** but over five hundred state trial judges. Maryland had fewer than thirty federal judges and magistrate judges, but more than three hundred state trial judges. Clearly, the state courts continue to handle the lion's share of litigation today.

The most common subject matter jurisdiction issue in state courts is determining *which* court within the state system has authority to hear a particular dispute. While every state has a trial court with broad jurisdiction, many also have specialized courts that exercise exclusive jurisdiction over certain types of cases. For example, in Massachusetts, the Probate and Family Court has exclusive subject matter jurisdiction over divorce cases, which means you can only file for divorce in that court. MASS. GEN. LAWS ch. 208, § 3. A lawyer bringing a case must figure out which court within the state's court system has subject matter jurisdiction over that type of case.

VI. The Subject Matter Jurisdiction of Federal Courts: General Principles

The basic course in Civil Procedure focuses on the subject matter jurisdiction of the federal courts. This may seem a curious choice, since most litigation is conducted in the state courts. On the other hand, we need to study some system

* Federal courts may hear most such cases if the parties are from different states, under the federal diversity jurisdiction, which we analyze in Chapter 3.

** Magistrate judges are federal judicial officers who handle many pretrial matters in federal litigation. Their decisions are usually subject to review by the district judge. They are not "Article III judges," because they are appointed for a term rather than during good behavior as required in Article III, Section 1.

to illustrate general principles of subject matter jurisdiction. No matter what state you practice law in, there will be a federal court there, exercising the same subject matter jurisdiction as all other federal courts. So it makes sense to use federal courts as an example. In addition, studying federal subject matter jurisdiction sheds a lot of light, by contrast, on the nature of state court jurisdiction.

It is helpful to start by asking why the federal courts have limited (as opposed to general) subject matter jurisdiction. As mentioned earlier, state courts existed before the Constitution was drafted. No one at the Constitutional Convention advocated doing away with state courts. Indeed, the Framers assumed that the vast bulk of judicial business would continue to be handled by the courts of the individual states after adoption of the Constitution.

However, the Framers concluded that federal courts should have the power to hear certain types of cases that implicate national interests. In Article III, Section 2 of the Constitution, the Framers provided that the federal judicial power "shall extend to" these categories of disputes. The wisdom with which they defined the federal jurisdiction is reflected by the fact that the categories of jurisdiction granted in Article III remain essentially intact after more than two hundred years.

> **Article III, Section 2, par. 1.** The judicial Power shall extend to all Cases, in Law and Equity, arising under this Constitution, the Laws of the United States, and Treaties made, or which shall be made, under their Authority;—to all Cases affecting Ambassadors, other public Ministers and Consuls;—to all Cases of admiralty and maritime jurisdiction;—to Controversies to which the United States shall be a Party;—to Controversies between two or more States;—between a State and Citizens of another State;—between Citizens of different States;—between Citizens of the same State claiming Lands under Grants of different States, and between a State, or the Citizens thereof, and foreign States, Citizens or Subjects.

This one short paragraph defines the constitutional scope of the federal courts' subject matter jurisdiction. If a case falls within this list, Congress may (but need not) authorize a federal court to hear it. If it does not—and most types of disputes do not—then the federal courts "lack subject matter jurisdiction" to entertain the case.

Of the nine types of cases listed in Article III, Section 2, two give rise to the vast majority of cases litigated in federal courts today: cases "arising under this Constitution [or] the Laws of the United States" (the *federal question jurisdiction*) and cases between "Citizens of different States" (the *diversity jurisdiction*). Our study of federal subject matter jurisdiction will concentrate on these two categories. Several others, however, are also important, including cases between citizens of a state and foreign citizens, cases involving maritime activities ("Cases of admiralty and maritime jurisdiction"), and cases to which the United States—that is, the federal government—is a party.

As noted above, however, the Constitution leaves it to Congress to decide how much of the Article III subject matter jurisdiction to grant to the lower federal courts. For a federal trial court to hear a case, the type of case must be within the Article III grant, *and* Congress must also authorize the court by statute to exercise jurisdiction over that type of case.

Notes and Questions: Federal Subject Matter Jurisdiction

Q **1. Why these categories?** Consider each type of case listed in Article III, Section 2. Why did the Framers authorize federal courts to hear those cases? In what way does each implicate an important national interest?

A A few of the categories are obvious. The grant of jurisdiction for cases "arising under this Constitution [or] the Laws of the United States" permits federal courts, created by and owing allegiance to the national government, to interpret and apply federal law. The Framers recognized that the new national government could be undermined if it relied solely on state courts to enforce and interpret laws made by the federal government. They also recognized the need for the United States Supreme Court to exercise final authority over the meaning of federal law by reviewing cases that raise federal issues.*

Several categories of jurisdiction in Article III, Section 2 involve cases in which local courts might be biased against out-of-state litigants. For example, the Framers probably created diversity jurisdiction out of concern that state courts might favor the local litigant in a case between an in-state citizen and an out-of-state citizen. Similar concerns led to the provision for federal jurisdiction over cases between two or more states and those between a citizen of a state and a foreign citizen. Although federal judges will almost always be from the state in which they sit, they are appointed during good behavior (basically, life tenure), which insulates them somewhat from local biases. State court judges are elected in many states, leaving them more sensitive to popular opinion and arguably more likely to favor local citizens.

The other categories in Article III, Section 2 involve cases in which the federal government has a direct interest (cases to which the federal government is a party) and cases with a potential impact on foreign relations, such as maritime cases and those involving ambassadors and foreign ministers.

Q **2. The authority of state courts to hear cases within federal court jurisdiction.** If a plaintiff wishes to bring a case that falls within some category in Article III, Section 2, must she sue in federal court or can she choose a state court instead?

A Article III, Section 2 provides that the federal judicial power "shall extend to" the cases listed there. It does not declare that *only a federal court* may hear these categories of cases. The Supreme Court has construed Article III, Section 2 to authorize jurisdiction over the listed categories of cases in the federal courts, *but not to withdraw jurisdiction over such cases from the state courts. Claflin v. Houseman,* 93 U.S. 130, 136 (1876). Thus, generally speaking,

* Remember that Article III, Section 2 defines the constitutional scope of the subject matter jurisdiction of all federal courts, including the Supreme Court.

a case that could be brought in federal court may also be brought in state court. In such cases, the plaintiff determines (as least initially) which court system will hear the case by filing in the court she prefers.

However, there is an important exception to this principle of *concurrent jurisdiction.* While state courts usually have concurrent jurisdiction over cases within the Article III grant, Congress may, in conferring jurisdiction over a particular category of federal cases, provide that those cases may only be heard in federal court. *Gulf Offshore Co. v. Mobil Oil Corp.,* 453 U.S. 473, 478 (1981). Some federal statutes provide for such *exclusive federal jurisdiction.* For example, 28 U.S.C. § 1333 provides that the federal district courts "shall have original jurisdiction, exclusive of the courts of the States" in admiralty and maritime cases. Similarly, 28 U.S.C. § 1338 provides for exclusive federal jurisdiction in patent and copyright cases.

Q **3. Corey's options in a diversity case.** Assume that Corey and Barristers are citizens of different states. In which court systems could Corey file his tort action against Barristers?

A If Corey and Barristers are diverse—citizens of different states—Corey could file the action in federal court, assuming he meets the statutory amount-in-controversy requirement for diversity cases. And because state courts have broad jurisdiction to hear common law claims such as battery claims, he could file it in a state court as well. Below, at note 6, we consider some of the tactical considerations his lawyer might take into account in choosing between the state and federal systems.

Q **4. What is a "law of the United States"?** Harris, a citizen of Wisconsin, wishes to sue Panil, also a citizen of Wisconsin, for violation of a Wisconsin statute, the Wisconsin Employment Discharge Act. Can she bring this case in federal court?

A No. This case doesn't fit into any of the Article III, Section 2 categories. The parties are not diverse. And the claim arises under a Wisconsin statute. That is a law of ***one of*** the states of the Union, but not a law of "the United States," which refers to federal laws made by Congress, regulations promulgated by federal agencies, or in some cases, common law rulings of federal judges.

Q **5. Federal claims in state court.** Assume that Harris wishes to sue Panil under the Federal Age Discrimination in Employment Act (ADEA), a federal statute. However, for tactical reasons, she would like to bring the action in state court. May she do so?

A The fact that a case *could* be brought in federal court does not mean that it has to be. For the most part the jurisdiction is concurrent, that is, the plaintiff has the choice to bring it in federal court or in state court. Congress has not made federal jurisdiction in federal ADEA cases exclusive, so Harris could sue in state court.

However, we will see in Chapter 5 that if a plaintiff brings a case in state court that could have been filed in federal court, the defendant may be able to *remove* it to federal court. That way, if either party wants a federal court to hear a case within federal jurisdiction, the federal court will do so.

6. Tactical considerations in choosing state or federal court. Due to this principle of concurrent jurisdiction, a lawyer will frequently have the choice to file a case in either state or federal court. When that is true, how should she decide which court to choose? Why might she prefer one system over the other for a particular case?

Naturally, a lawyer will choose the court that she believes offers strategic advantages for her case. Scholars refer to such tactical maneuvering—with a hint of disdain—as *forum shopping*. Lawyers, however, will not hesitate to choose between two courts that have proper jurisdiction based on the best interests of their clients.

There are many differences in the practice of state and federal systems that could influence counsel's decision to file a particular suit in state or federal court. Here are a few such considerations.

Convenience. In some parts of the country, the federal court may sit quite far from where the lawyer and client reside. In those circumstances, it might be easier to litigate the case in state court. For example, the state trial court for Lipscomb County sits in Lipscomb, Texas. The federal court for the Northern District of Texas (which includes Lipscomb County) sits in Amarillo. A lawyer from Lipscomb who files in the Lipscomb County court can walk across the street to argue a motion; if she files in the Federal District Court for the Northern District of Texas, she would have to travel 149 miles to argue the same motion.

Familiarity. Frequently, lawyers choose one system over the other because they litigate there frequently and are familiar with the details of practice in that court. A lawyer who regularly files cases in state court in Lipscomb County will tend to choose that court unless there is some clear countervailing reason to sue in federal court.

Jury pools. Federal and state courts usually draw their juries from different geographic areas. State juries are usually selected by county, whereas the federal jury will likely be drawn from a broader geographic area. A civil rights plaintiff in Boston, for example, might prefer the diverse and perhaps more liberal urban jury she would draw in a Suffolk County court to the largely suburban jury she would likely draw in the Federal District Court for the District of Massachusetts.

Speed. An important factor may be the speed with which the system processes cases. A lawyer with a badly injured client may want to get the case to judgment as soon as possible. In a particular state, one system may have a smaller backlog of cases than the other. Although there are exceptions, federal courts have the reputation of resolving cases more quickly than state courts.

Case assignment to one judge. In many federal courts, cases are assigned to a particular judge when they are filed, and that judge will handle the case from start to finish. By contrast, in some state court systems, cases are not assigned. The parties might litigate a motion to dismiss in front of Judge A, argue subsequent discovery motions in front of Judge B, and end up trying the case in front of Judge C, none of whom have any previous acquaintance with the file. If a case involves complex issues, having a judge assigned to handle all phases of the litigation may be preferable.

A plaintiff may also prefer litigating before a federal judge in cases that seek a decision that may prove politically unpopular (such as certain civil rights cases), since life tenure provides federal judges a measure of insulation from majoritarian pressures.

Attorney control. A major trend in the last twenty years is toward more judicial management of cases. Judges, especially in the federal system, hold scheduling conferences and pretrial conferences and set strict deadlines for completion of pretrial tasks. State courts may be more free-wheeling, leaving more control to attorneys in scheduling litigation.

Out-of-state litigants. An out-of-state litigant may prefer to litigate in federal court. Federal judges' life tenure insulates them to some extent from local political pressures. State court judges are frequently elected, and thus, more accountable to local citizens. Since they are human, this may affect their decision making in a case against an out-of-state litigant, consciously or unconsciously. The Framers were sufficiently concerned about the possibility of bias against out-of-state citizens that they created diversity jurisdiction to allay such concerns.

Expertise. Judges in one system or the other may have more experience dealing with a particular type of case. If a case involves sophisticated federal law issues that federal judges regularly handle, the plaintiff's counsel may prefer to file in federal court. For example, federal courts will have more experience hearing cases under federal antidiscrimination laws or cases under the federal civil rights laws. State courts, on the other hand, may have greater expertise in land use or zoning cases.

Other factors. Many other factors may influence the decision. The rules of evidence may differ in state and federal court. The rules of discovery—the process for compelling production of evidence from other parties and witnesses—may differ. The court's power to order parties to appear in the action may differ. One system may use larger juries than the other or allow non-unanimous verdicts.

This list of factors that lawyers consider in choosing between the two systems is certainly not comprehensive, but it highlights the fact that the two systems differ in many practical respects. When a lawyer has a choice, because either system has jurisdiction to hear the case she is bringing, she will consider these and other factors in deciding where to file her case.

VII. American Courts: Summary of Basic Principles

- Every American state has its own court system. The structure of a state court system, and the types of cases that each court within that state may hear, are generally established by statutes enacted by the state legislature.
- Most cases are litigated in state courts. Every state has trial courts with very broad subject matter jurisdiction over most types of common disputes. Most states also have several specialized trial courts, such as probate courts or housing courts, that only hear limited types of cases.
- Each state has an appellate court at the apex of the system, frequently called the state supreme court. Many state court systems also have intermediate appellate courts, which hear most appeals from the trial courts.
- The United States Constitution provides for a separate federal court system. Article III, Section 1 of the Constitution creates the United States Supreme Court, and authorizes Congress to create other federal courts "below" the Supreme Court. Congress has created federal trial courts, called United States District Courts, and intermediate appellate courts, called United States Courts of Appeals, as well as a few specialized courts.
- The United States Supreme Court is the court of last resort in the federal court system. It also may review cases decided by state appellate courts, if those cases present issues of federal law.
- The categories of cases that federal courts may hear under Article III, Section 2 (their subject matter jurisdiction) are quite narrow. These include cases arising under federal law, cases between citizens of different states, cases between citizens and aliens, cases in which the United States is a party, admiralty and maritime cases, and several other narrow types of cases.
- State courts have concurrent jurisdiction over most cases that federal courts are authorized to hear. If both federal and state courts have subject matter jurisdiction over a case, the plaintiff may file in either system.
- There is an exception to this concurrent jurisdiction principle. Congress may provide that federal jurisdiction over a particular type of case is "exclusive of the courts of the states." It has done so for some types of cases, including patent and copyright cases.

2

A Description of the Litigation Process and Sources of Procedural Law

I. Introduction

This chapter provides a look at the Civil Procedure forest before we focus on the trees. It describes the process of a typical case from commencement to final judgment. This overview should give you a sense of how individual topics we study in the course relate to the overall course of litigation.

The second part of the chapter describes sources of law—constitutional provisions, statutes and rules—that govern aspects of civil procedure. An introduction to the sources of law that govern procedural issues and the hierarchical relations among them will help you to understand the materials throughout the book.

II. A Description of the Process of a Civil Case

Only a small subset of disputes turn into lawsuits. The parties resolve most disputes informally or just "deal with it" without involving lawyers or courts. Even where aggrieved parties seek legal advice, they do not usually end up in litigation. With the help of counsel they resolve their disputes through informal negotiation or mediation without filing suit. Even disputes that turn into lawsuits seldom go to trial; most are settled as litigation proceeds.

Below we describe the stages of a typical lawsuit, focusing on procedure in the federal courts. However, litigation procedure in most state courts is quite similar. Figure 2–1 provides a time line that illustrates the stages of a lawsuit.

Pleading Phase	Discovery Phase	Pretrial	Trial	Post-trial	Appeal
P files complaint; D answers or moves to dismiss	Parties investigate facts, take discovery, file and argue motions	Pretrial conference, possible motions for summary judgment or on evidentiary issues	Opening statements, P's evidence/D's evidence, closing statements, instructions to jury, jury deliberates and renders verdict	Judgment entered for winning party, post-trial motions heard	Losing party may appeal errors of law to a higher court

Figure 2–1: TIME LINE OF A TYPICAL CIVIL ACTION

Very few cases proceed through all of these stages of litigation. In 2019, less than 2 percent of cases resolved in the federal district courts actually went to trial.* Most were resolved before reaching the stage of a pretrial conference, by voluntary dismissal, dismissal by the court on various grounds, settlement, or summary judgment. The federal courts resolve many cases, but try very few of them.

A. The Pleading Phase

The complaint. The plaintiff starts a lawsuit (usually acting through her lawyer) by filing a *complaint* against the defendant in court. A complaint sets forth the basic facts that gave rise to the dispute. It then asserts the plaintiff's legal claims (traditionally referred to as *causes of action*)—the legal wrongs the plaintiff asserts that the defendant committed that entitles the plaintiff to a remedy. For example, she might assert a claim for negligence, a claim for child support, a claim for breach of contract, or a claim for violation of an antidiscrimination statute. At the end of the complaint the plaintiff must state the relief she wants from the court. Often, the demand is for money damages but a complaint may seek other remedies such as specific performance (a court order for the defendant to perform obligations under a contract), a divorce, an order invalidating (or upholding) a will, an accounting of profits of a business, or many other types of orders. For an example of a complaint, see p. 441.

Q **Asserting multiple claims.** Janice hired Bornstein to build a garage next to her house and claims that he built it too small. She also claims that his backhoe damaged her shrubbery in the process. Can she sue on both claims in a single suit?

A Under the Federal Rules of Civil Procedure and similar state rules, a plaintiff may assert whatever claims she has against the defendant, so they may all be

* http://www.uscourts.gov/statistics/table/c-4/statistical-tables-federal-judiciary/2019/12/31 (last visited June 1, 2020).

settled in a single litigation. Fed. R. Civ. P. 18(a). The Rules even allow a plaintiff to assert contradictory claims (Claim #1: "We never properly executed the contract so it should be declared invalid." Claim #2: "We had a valid contract and I want damages for breach.").

In Janice's case, her first claim that Bornstein did not build the garage in accordance with their agreement would be for breach of contract. The other, for damage caused by careless conduct in the course of the work, would be a negligence claim. Under the Federal Rules, however, the two may still be pursued in a single lawsuit. In addition, Janice could sue multiple defendants together for a single claim. For example, she could sue Bornstein and Maria, his backhoe driver, as co-defendants on the negligence claim.

After filing the complaint in court, the plaintiff must *serve process* on the defendant, that is, deliver to her a copy of the complaint and a court *summons* ordering the defendant to appear and defend the action. The methods for serving the summons and complaint are prescribed in detail in court rules, because it is important that a defendant receive notice that the action has been commenced. (If the defendant does not find out, she will *default*—fail to respond—and a judgment for the plaintiff may be entered against her.) Typically, rules for service of process require personal delivery to the defendant (or, for a corporate defendant, to an officer of the corporation), delivery to the defendant's home, delivery by mail, or service on an authorized agent of the defendant.

The answer. The defendant must respond to the suit by filing an *answer.* The answer must respond to each allegation made in the complaint, admitting those that are true, denying those the defendant believes untrue, or stating that the defendant does not have sufficient information to admit or deny the allegation. Allegations that are admitted are assumed to be true for purposes of the case; trial preparation will thus focus on those allegations in the complaint that the defendant denies.

The answer may also assert *affirmative defenses.* An affirmative defense asserts that, even if the claim alleged in the complaint is true, the defendant still should not be liable because of additional facts. For example, on a claim for breach of contract, the defendant might raise the affirmative defense that the relevant *statute of limitations* (prescribing how long a party has to sue after a claim arises) had expired. ("Well, maybe I did deliver fewer computers than I was supposed to. But that was four years ago, and the statute of limitations for contract claims has passed, so you can't recover for it now.") Or, she might assert the defense of *release.* ("I admit that I agreed to provide twenty computers, but you later gave me a signed release from that provision of the contract.") In a negligence claim, a defendant might assert that, even if she was negligent in causing the plaintiff's injury, the plaintiff cannot recover under applicable tort law because the plaintiff was more negligent in causing it. ("Even if you can prove that I was partly at fault in causing the collision, you were more negligent, and under our tort law that bars you from recovering damages.") For an (imperfect) example of an answer, see p. 524.

Amending the pleadings. Pleadings are filed early in the parties' preparation of the case. The intensive process of *discovery* and preparing a case for trial takes place after pleading and is likely to lead to new information and new theories that are not reflected in the original complaint and answer. The Federal Rules allow parties to *amend their pleadings*—that is, rewrite them to change the allegations or defenses—quite liberally, although the judge must usually grant leave to amend a pleading. Even well into the case, a party might be granted leave to amend if new information comes to light or a new legal theory surfaces. The rationale for freely allowing amendments is that the trial should reflect the parties' educated understanding of their cases after substantial preparation of the case; they should not be rigidly confined (as the early common law required) to positions asserted at the beginning of the case, before they had fully investigated the relevant facts and law.

B. Early Motion Practice

Parties often ask the court to act by filing a *motion* asking the court to enter an order of some sort. For example, a defendant may have objections to a suit that may prevent the case from going forward. Under Rule 12(b) of the Federal Rules, parties may raise such objections at the beginning of the case, either by asserting them in their answer or by a *pre-answer motion to dismiss* before responding to the complaint. Some of these objections will end the case if the court agrees. For example, a defendant may raise lack of subject matter jurisdiction or personal jurisdiction by a pre-answer motion. Because the court cannot hear a case if it lacks jurisdiction, it will dismiss the case if it agrees with the defendant's objection.

Other preliminary objections may also be raised by pre-answer motion so they can be cleared up before the case proceeds. For example, a defendant may move to dismiss for improper service of process, arguing that he was not served with the summons and complaint by a proper method. If the court agrees that service was improper, it will likely order that the papers be re-served rather than dismiss the case.

A defendant may also file a pre-answer motion arguing that a plaintiff's claim should be dismissed at the outset because it is legally insufficient. Under Federal Rule 12(b)(6), the defendant may move to dismiss a claim for "failure to state a claim upon which relief can be granted." This motion asserts that the conduct alleged in the complaint does not state a recognized legal claim for which the court can grant relief. Because the court cannot grant a remedy for conduct that does not violate a recognized legal right, the defendant argues that the claim should be dismissed without further litigation.

Example: A Rule 12(b)(6) dismissal. Under tort law, an employer may be held liable for an injury caused by its employee's negligence on the job ("in the scope of employment"). But it is not liable for negligence of an employee when he is not at work. Ortega sues Acme Corporation for an accident caused by Pitovsky, an employee of Acme. Ortega alleges that Pitovsky is an Acme employee, that he ran into Ortega while driving to the movies on the weekend and broke Ortega's leg, and demands damages from Acme. Acme moves to dismiss the claim under Rule 12(b)(6). Should the motion be granted?

> While an employer is usually liable for torts committed by its employees in the scope of their employment, it is not liable for their antics on their own time. Acme has no control over Pitovsky's conduct off the job and gets no benefit

from it. Here, it is clear from Ortega's complaint (which alleges that Pitovsky was driving to the movies at the time of the accident) that Acme is not liable for this accident. There would be little point in allowing Ortega to litigate this accident claim against Acme where it is clear that Acme cannot be liable for it. Even if Ortega can prove that Pitovsky negligently injured her, Acme is not liable, since the accident did not take place while Pitovsky was on the job. The motion to dismiss for failure to state a claim should be granted.

C. The Discovery Phase

Discovery is the process of obtaining evidence from witnesses and from other parties to the case through court-enforced procedures. This phase of litigation dominates the experience of litigators today. In most court systems around the world, the production of evidence must be ordered by the judge, who decides when a party or witness will be required to testify or produce documents. In most American courts, however, the rules allow the attorneys for the parties to demand production of relevant documents and testimony without a court order. This discovery system is highly intrusive, often expensive, and is viewed with considerable skepticism by other countries. The rationale for compelling such broad production of evidence is that full understanding of the facts in a case before trial will facilitate efficient trials and lead to settlement of most cases.

The scope of discovery. Under the Federal Rules of Civil Procedure, parties are free to demand production of information and testimony that is relevant to any claim or defense that has been raised in the action. Fed. R. Civ. P. 26(b)(1). Generally, the lawyers run the discovery process, by requesting information from other parties and exchanging it directly.

Although relevant evidence is *presumptively* discoverable under Rule 26(b), the court has authority to regulate and restrict discovery for various reasons. The judge might limit production of relevant evidence because it would be unduly burdensome, it would breach an evidentiary privilege (such as the attorney-client privilege), or because producing it would cost more than the information is likely to be worth. If a party objects to producing information sought by an adversary, it may seek a *protective order* from the court. The court will then determine whether the information is discoverable and may enter an order for production or an order limiting discovery.

The methods of discovery. The Federal Rules require *automatic disclosure* of certain categories of information by the parties at the outset of the case. These items would be routinely sought in discovery anyway, so the process can be shortened by an early mandatory exchange of this information without formal requests. Rule 26 requires the parties to meet at the outset of the case to arrange for this exchange of information about the case, including the documents and witnesses they may use to support their claims and defenses.

The Federal Rules establish further discovery methods that may be used at the discretion of the parties. Rule 33 authorizes parties to send *interrogatories*—that is, questions—about the claims and defenses in the action to other parties. Typically, interrogatories are drafted by one party's lawyer and sent to the opposing party's lawyer. They are answered under oath by the responding party, though the answers are usually drafted by the responding party's lawyer. They may not be used to obtain information from non-party witnesses.

Rule 34 authorizes a party to send *requests for production of documents* to other parties, requesting any documents within the other party's custody or control relevant to issues in the case. Rule 34 requests must specify the documents sought by category (no "give me everything you've got" allowed) so the producing party understands clearly what documents to produce. Such requests may be extremely burdensome and compliance can be costly. This problem is exacerbated by the fact that most documents today are in electronic form. A party may have huge amounts of data responsive to the request, which it must preserve, locate, retrieve, and review. Again, the court may enter orders limiting production, balancing the requesting party's need for information against the burden and expense caused to the responding party. Parties may also make requests under Rule 34 to enter land or inspect tangible things relevant to the case (such as a car involved in a collision). Similar discovery may be obtained from non-parties by subpoena under Rule 45.

Rule 34 requests, like interrogatories, are sent and responded to by the parties without any need for court approval. The receiving party must respond by producing requested documents or stating objections to the requests. If the parties cannot resolve disputes about what should be produced, one of them will seek a ruling from the court. But ideally, this extensive pretrial exchange of information will be conducted by counsel with little court involvement.

The third core discovery tool is the *deposition*, the taking of testimony from a witness under oath. Rule 30 governs deposition practice in detail. The lawyers may take depositions of any witness with relevant information, whether a party to the case or not. Typically, the deposition is taken at the office of the requesting lawyer. A court reporter swears the witness, records the testimony verbatim, and produces a written transcript for both parties.

Q **Discovery tactics.** Why do you think lawyers view the deposition as the most effective discovery device available?

A Because deposition testimony is taken under oath, it "puts a witness on the record" in advance of trial. It also allows counsel to ask a series of questions to follow up on prior answers. The answers will also be spontaneous—the witness is required to reply immediately without coaching from her attorney. A deposition also allows counsel to see the witness in person—probably for the only time before trial—and judge the impression she will make at trial. Tactically, a witness's demeanor and credibility may be as important as what the witness says.

The main drawback of depositions is that they are expensive. The court reporter will charge a substantial fee, and the attorneys will charge for their time to prepare for and take the deposition.

There are other discovery devices as well. Rule 35 authorizes parties to conduct a *medical examination of a party* whose physical or mental condition is at issue in the lawsuit. Unlike the other discovery tools, medical exams require a court order because they are uniquely intrusive on a party's privacy. Parties may also send *requests for admission* to other parties, asking them to admit facts about the issues in the case or the authenticity of documents. Such admissions can narrow the issues litigated at the trial, since issues agreed upon by the parties need not be proved.

During the discovery phase, counsel will also prepare their cases through other means of investigation as well. They will talk to their client, the client's employees, and witnesses willing to be interviewed. They will gather documents. They may use the Internet, Freedom of Information Act requests, private investigators, and any other means they have to learn all they can about the facts. They will also research the legal issues likely to arise and prepare memos and briefs supporting their positions. They will frequently hire experts to help them understand technical issues in a case and often to testify at trial as well.

Example: Distasteful discovery. Zucker went to a popular restaurant, Goliath's, and ordered seafood. It didn't taste right, as he reported to the waiter. Four hours later he became violently ill. Goliath's manager learned of Zucker's illness the next morning and had the three chefs from the night before fill out routine incident reports. Two of the reports (which Goliath's regards as confidential) state that the kitchen was very busy and they think one of the cooks may not have properly prepared the fish during the evening.

Lab tests confirmed that Zucker had food poisoning. He sues Goliath's for negligence in causing his illness. During the discovery phase, Goliath's lawyer schedules a deposition of Riordan, one of the chefs, to take her testimony under oath. She also requests that Goliath's produce for inspection any reports that were done of the incident that night or afterwards. Must Riordan give her testimony at the deposition? Must Goliath's produce the incident reports?

> These discovery requests are clearly within the scope of discovery, since the testimony and documents are relevant to Zucker's food poisoning claim. Yet Goliath's counsel (and probably Riordan as well) would clearly prefer to avoid the deposition and protect the incident reports from discovery, since they may reveal information that strongly supports Zucker's case. However, under the discovery rules, Zucker's counsel has the right to depose witnesses with relevant information and to inspect any documents in Goliath's possession that are relevant to the issues in the case.
>
> As noted above, there are certain objections parties may make to discovery requests, such as attorney-client privilege or the expense of burdensome discovery requests. However, these do not apply here. Nor does the fact that Goliath's ordinarily keeps the reports confidential protect them from discovery. Goliath's will almost certainly have to produce the documents in response to Zucker's requests.

D. Judicial Conferences

Traditionally, judges played a passive role in litigation. The parties prepared their cases, and the court provided a judge to preside at a trial when they wanted one. If disputes arose during the pretrial phase, or parties filed motions in court, a judge would hear the motion or resolve the dispute. But judges did not actively oversee cases during the pretrial stage.

In recent decades, judges have become more involved in managing the pretrial litigation process, particularly in the federal courts. In federal courts today, cases are assigned to a district court judge when filed. That judge handles all matters in that case from filing to final judgment. Federal judges actively manage their cases through conferences with counsel for the parties. Often there will be an early *scheduling conference* to set deadlines for stages in the litigation, such as hearing preliminary motions, automatic disclosure, document production and depositions, filing of motions for summary judgment, or amendment of the pleadings. After the conference, the judge will issue case management orders that set deadlines to structure the stages of pretrial litigation.

Toward the end of the discovery phase, the judge will likely convene a final *pretrial conference*, which may cover any matters relevant to planning the trial. These include defining the issues in dispute, approving exhibits, resolving challenges to the admissibility of evidence, determining what witnesses will testify, exploring the possibility of settlement, resolving pending motions, and ordering the presentation of evidence at the trial. After the final pretrial conference, the judge will issue a final *pretrial order* resolving issues concerning trial procedure and setting the stage for presentation of the case to the jury.

E. Motions for Summary Judgment

As noted above, cases may come to an early end on a motion to dismiss for failure to state a claim. Others are litigated through the discovery phase but still do not end up going to trial if discovery reveals that a party does not have evidence to establish a fact that is essential to recovery. In such cases, the opposing party may move for *summary judgment*.

Example: A case for summary judgment. Ortega sues Acme Company for negligence of Pitovsky, an Acme employee, who drove into her on Main Street. Ortega alleges that Acme is liable for Pitovsky's negligent driving because Pitovsky acted in the scope of his employment for Acme at the time of the accident. Acme's lawyers know that Acme would be liable under negligence law if Pitovsky caused the accident while acting in the scope of employment. Thus, they cannot get the case dismissed for failure to state a claim: Acme would be liable if Ortega proved the allegations in her complaint.

However, Acme is confident that Ortega *cannot prove* that Pitovsky acted in the scope of employment. Acme has clear evidence—Pitovsky's time cards and an affidavit from his supervisor—that he was not working on the day of the accident. This evidence, Acme's lawyers conclude, clearly shows that Pitovsky was *not* on the job at the time of the accident. Unless Ortega can cast doubt on this evidence or provide contradictory proof, Acme must win, since it is not liable for Pitovsky's negligence if he was not on the job at the time of the accident. "Why have a trial," Acme argues, "if the uncontradicted evidence shows that Ortega cannot prove a fact she must prove to recover? My evidence shows that Ortega cannot prove the scope-of-employment allegation." Acme moves for summary judgment and submits this evidence to the court in support of its motion. What should the court do?

Acme's motion challenges Ortega to show that there is a genuine dispute concerning whether Pitovsky was acting in the scope of employment when he had the accident. To do that, she must produce some evidence contradicting Acme's. The court will allow Ortega to submit opposing evidence to show that Pitovsky was acting in the scope of employment at the time of the accident. For example, Ortega might submit her affidavit swearing that the truck Pitovsky was driving at the time of the accident was full of Acme's products. Maybe Ortega can testify that she heard him say, "I'm so sorry, I was in a hurry to finish my deliveries for the day." (Wouldn't Ortega's lawyer love to have that testimony!)

If Ortega produces evidence contradicting Acme's, it will show that there is a dispute about the issue, which should be resolved at trial. Summary judgment should be denied. However, if Ortega cannot produce contradictory evidence—presumably because Pitovsky really wasn't working at the time of the accident—it becomes clear that Ortega cannot prove a fact that she must establish to recover. Thus Acme "is entitled to judgment as a matter of law," and the court may grant summary judgment for Acme. The judgment is "summary" because it is issued by the judge without a trial.

F. Trial

Students often know more about trials than other aspects of Civil Procedure because of depictions of trials in the media. You may not realize, however, that *the right to trial by jury* does not apply to many types of civil cases. If the parties are not entitled to a jury trial, the case will be tried before a judge (called a *bench trial*), and the judge will decide both the factual and legal issues. Even if there is a right to a jury, parties may waive the right for tactical reasons, choosing to try the case before the judge instead.

If a case is tried to a jury, the first step will be to choose the jury through a process called *voir dire*, in which prospective jurors are questioned by the judge or counsel for the parties to assure that they are impartial. Once the jury is chosen, parties typically make opening statements setting forth the proof they expect to submit. The plaintiff then calls and examines her witnesses and submits documents as exhibits. The defendant's counsel may cross-examine the witnesses. After the plaintiff completes her case, the defendant calls and examines his witnesses, subject to cross-examination by the plaintiff's counsel. All questioning is confined by strict rules of evidence, which you will study in the upper-level course in Evidence rather than in Civil Procedure.

Once the parties have submitted their evidence (including any rebuttal witnesses), each party will make a closing statement summarizing her case and arguing why the evidence supports a verdict in her favor. A party may move at this point for *judgment as a matter of law,* arguing that the opponent's evidence on some element of the claim or defense is too weak to allow a verdict in the opponent's favor. If the motion is denied, the judge will then instruct the jury on the legal rules they must apply to the case. (For example, in a contract case, the judge would explain the elements a plaintiff must prove to recover for breach of contract.) The judge will also explain to the jurors how they should consider the evidence, who has the burden of proof on which issues, and how the jury should record their verdict on the verdict form. The jury then deliberates and reaches a verdict.

The Civil Procedure course touches on some procedural matters relevant to trial, including motions for judgment as a matter of law and for a new trial. However, detailed study of the trial process is deferred to the upper-level course in Trial Practice.

G. Post-Trial Motions

Even when a case has been tried and the jury has rendered its verdict, the case is not over. The losing party may make several motions to forestall entry of a judgment against her. She may move for a *new trial*—a do-over—arguing that the first trial was unfair due to erroneous rulings, improper argument, or other problems. She might seek a new trial on the ground that the jury's verdict was so clearly wrong that it represents a miscarriage of justice. She might also move again for judgment as a matter of law, contending that the jury's verdict for her opponent is not rationally supported by the evidence, so that the judge should enter judgment for her instead. As we will see, the judge has the authority to grant such motions in appropriate cases.

When all post-trial motions have been resolved, the judge will order *entry of a judgment* on the verdict. It is this ministerial act of entering a notation of final judgment on the court docket that officially ends a case in the federal district court.

H. Appeal

Entry of a judgment usually ends the case. However, a losing party may file an *appeal* if he is convinced that some legal error at or before trial prejudiced his right to present his case fully in the trial court. Typically, appeals must be filed within a short period of time, often thirty days after entry of judgment, so parties will know if the case is over or will go to the appellate court for review. If an appeal is filed, the appeal may automatically *stay*—postpone—the right to collect the judgment or the party taking the appeal may ask the court to stay enforcement proceedings until the appeal is resolved.

Q **The limited role of appeals.** If a party appeals, is the case retried in the appellate court?

A No. Appellate courts do not retry cases or take further evidence. Their role is to review claims that an error of law was made in processing the case at the trial level, based on a review of the course of the proceedings below. Parties have a right to have their cases handled fairly by the trial court and decided under the right rules of law. Appellate courts are there to assure that the process was fair and the law correctly applied in the trial court. Except in unusual circumstances, they do not second-guess the factual findings of the judge or the jury.

For example, the appellate court would consider whether the jury was given the wrong instruction on the meaning of negligence or whether the trial judge excluded evidence that should have been admitted. It would not usually reconsider the jury's factual findings, such as whether the defendant drove negligently at the time of an accident. Such factual questions are generally for the trier of fact, not issues for appeal.

Appeals are typically heard by a panel of three to seven appellate judges. The panel will review the appellant's claims of error based on a "record of the proceedings below" prepared by the parties. This written record (sometimes called the *record appendix*) will include documents submitted to the trial court relevant to the issues on appeal, such as pleadings, motions, exhibits, briefs, and transcripts of evidence and argument. The *appellant* will submit a brief stating the issues on appeal—the mistakes she claims were made in the trial court—and arguing why those mistakes support her claim for a reversal of the adverse judgment rendered by the trial court. The *appellee* (the party who won below, and opposes the appeal) will file a brief arguing that the trial court's rulings were proper, so that its judgment should be affirmed.

The Procedure on Appeal

Reprinted with permission of the Daily Hampshire Gazette

The role of appellate courts is not to retry the factual issues in a case. Witnesses do not appear, and no new testimony is taken. The appellate court decides the appeal based on a written record showing what happened in the trial court. An appeal asserts that some legal mistake was made in the trial court that prevented a fair resolution of the case in that court. The lawyers for the parties argue the issues on appeal in briefs filed in the appellate court and (often, but not always) at oral argument before a panel of appellate judges, as shown here. The panel will then confer, determine how the issues should be decided, and issue an opinion that both resolves the appeal and explains the governing law. If the court concludes that an error was made in the trial court, it may remand the case to that court to reconsider or retry.

Appellate courts will hear oral argument from counsel for the parties in many cases, but need not if they believe it unnecessary in particular cases. After argument, the panel will meet and decide how the appeal should be resolved. One member of the panel will be designated to write an opinion explaining the appellate court's decision. That judge will draft an opinion and circulate it to the other judges on the panel. If they all agree on the opinion, it will be issued, delivered to the parties, and often published in a court reporter. If one or more members of the panel do not agree with the outcome favored by the majority, they will file a dissenting opinion setting forth their view as to how the case should be resolved.

Most of the opinions you read in law school casebooks are appellate opinions. This gives a distorted view of civil litigation, since only a small minority of trial court decisions are appealed. These opinions reflect only the tip of the litigation iceberg.

I. The Effect of a Judgment on Later Litigation

Litigation is a strenuous and expensive business; few litigants would want to do it more often than necessary. Courts have developed some interesting rules to prevent parties from relitigating a case that has already been litigated and decided. The doctrine of *claim preclusion*, also called *res judicata*, bars a party who has sued a defendant on a claim from suing that defendant again on the same claim, if the first case was decided after a full opportunity to reach the merits.

Q **Two bites at the apple?** Merkle sues Rico for personal injuries she suffered in an auto accident with Rico in June 2016. Could she later sue Rico in a new suit for damage to her car in the same accident?

A Today, most courts would preclude Merkle's second suit, because both the personal injuries and property damage arose out of the same occurrence. Claim preclusion would bar the second action because Merkle already sued Rico for this accident and is not entitled to a second "bite at the apple."

Q **Apples and oranges.** Could Merkle bring a later action against Rico for injuries in a different accident they had in 2015?

A Yes. While both of Merkle's claims are accident claims, they arose out of different occurrences at different times. The fact that she sued Rico for one accident does not bar her from bringing a separate action against Rico for the other.

Q **Issue preclusion distinguished.** Sometimes parties litigate and resolve an *issue* in one case that arises again in a later case. This situation implicates another preclusion principle called *issue preclusion* or *collateral estoppel*. This principle usually precludes parties from relitigating issues that were litigated, decided, and necessary to the judgment in a prior action between the parties.

For example, suppose that Jane wants to sublet her apartment for the summer, but Stamski, her landlord, sues Jane, arguing that her lease does not allow her to sublet. The court holds that the lease gives her the right to sublet. The next summer she decides to sublet again, and Stamski sues again, arguing that the same provision in the lease bars her from subletting. Will Stamski be precluded from relitigating the issue?

A This second case is not barred by claim preclusion, because it arises out of new facts that had not taken place when Stamski sued Jane the first time. But issue preclusion will probably bar Stamski from relitigating the meaning of the lease provision. This issue is the same one that was litigated and decided in the first case. Why should a court allow them to relitigate the issue if it was fairly decided in the prior action? It would waste the parties' and the court's resources to go through this a second time.

Caution! Don't be intimidated by this quick romp through the phases of a lawsuit. This overview is meant to give you a sense of the scope of the litigation process so you can place issues in context as we study them. Later chapters will cover each of these concepts in detail.

III. Sources of Civil Procedure Regulation: Constitutions, Statutes, and Rules

The materials you study in Civil Procedure include a good many rules, statutes, and other provisions of law that regulate the process of litigation. This section explains where these come from, who enacted them, and how they relate to each other. First, consider the types of regulations that govern procedure in the *federal* courts.

The United States Constitution. Certain aspects of civil procedure in the federal courts are governed by provisions of the United States Constitution, which establishes the basic framework of our federal government. For example, Article III includes basic provisions governing the structure and jurisdiction of the federal courts. Article I, Section 8, clause 18 authorizes Congress to make laws "necessary and proper" to implement the federal judicial power. The Fifth and Fourteenth Amendments guarantee parties *due process* before a court can deprive them of life, liberty, or property. The Sixth Amendment guarantees a jury trial, a right to counsel, and other rights in federal criminal cases. The Seventh Amendment guarantees the right to jury trial in some civil cases in federal courts.

Federal statutes governing procedure in the federal courts. Pursuant to Article I, Section 8, clause 18 of the Constitution (the Necessary and Proper Clause) Congress enacts statutes that regulate many aspects of procedure in the federal courts.* Many of these statutes governing federal court procedure are published in Title 28 of the United States Code. Some of these statutes are included in your

* The term "statute" usually refers to an enactment of the highest level legislative body in a government. Congress enacts federal statutes. The state legislature of each state enacts the statutes of that state.

Rules supplement—but only some, so there are frequently gaps in numbering. Here are some examples of statutes that govern various aspects of federal practice.

1. 28 U.S.C. § 133 (appointment and number of federal district judges)
2. 28 U.S.C. §§ 1251–1257 (jurisdiction of the United States Supreme Court)
3. 28 U.S.C. §§ 1291–1296 (jurisdiction of the federal courts of appeals)
4. 28 U.S.C. §§ 1331–1369 (jurisdiction of the federal district courts)
5. 28 U.S.C. §§ 1441–1454 (removal of cases from state to federal court)
6. 28 U.S.C. §§ 1861–1875 (jury selection in federal cases)

The statutes Congress enacts under its constitutional powers cannot contradict the United States Constitution, which by its terms is the "supreme Law of the Land." U.S. Const. art. VI, § 2. For example, the Seventh Amendment guarantees jury trial in certain civil cases, so Congress could not enact a statute barring jury trials in those cases. But Congress may enact statutes pursuant to the Necessary and Proper Clause to regulate procedure in the federal courts in ways consistent with the Constitution. The Constitution establishes the broad outlines of the federal court system; Congress regulates the particulars of practice and procedure in the federal courts by statute. For example, the statutes cited above (28 U.S.C. §§ 1861–1875) set forth procedures for implementing the right to jury trial and thus are consistent with that constitutional right.

The Federal Rules of Civil Procedure. In addition to federal statutes governing federal court practice, Congress has delegated to the United States Supreme Court the power to adopt court rules governing matters of procedure in the federal courts that are not prescribed by statute. *See* 28 U.S.C. §§ 2071–2077 (the "Rules Enabling Act"). The Rules Enabling Act authorizes the Supreme Court to adopt general rules for practice in the federal district courts and the courts of appeals. The Court, in turn, has delegated rule-making to the Judicial Conference of the United States, whose Advisory Committee on Civil Rules, composed of lawyers, judges, and law professors, does the actual work of drafting and recommending rule changes (which is why the Advisory Committee notes are sometimes cited as legislative history). The Advisory Committee's recommendations for rule changes pass through the Judicial Conference to the Supreme Court, and if the Court approves the changes, they are submitted to Congress no later than May 1 of each year. Unless Congress modifies or rejects the rule changes, they become effective on December 1. This basic process has been in place since the Supreme Court adopted the Federal Rules of Civil Procedure in 1938.

The Federal Rules, which you will study closely in Civil Procedure, govern many aspects of day-to-day practice in the district courts that are not governed by statute or the Constitution. Because the Court adopted the Federal Rules pursuant to a delegation of authority from Congress, the Rules have the force of law—in effect, Congress has authorized the Court to write the detailed "laws" governing practice in the federal trial courts. If you thumb through the Federal Rules, you will see that they regulate the entire process described in the first half of this chapter, including filing suit, pleadings, pre-answer and other motions, judicial conferences, discovery, conduct of trial, post-trial motions, and enforcement of judgments. The order of the Rules generally reflects these stages of a lawsuit: Early rules deal with issues such as pleadings and service of process, middle rules with discovery, and later rules with trial and post-trial procedure.

Local rules of federal district courts. There is yet another level of "law making" in the federal courts. Federal Rule 83 authorizes the judges of each federal district to adopt local rules to govern the details of practice in that district.* Such local rules must be consistent with the Federal Rules of Civil Procedure, federal statutes, and constitutional provisions. Local rules govern many details of practice not prescribed by the Federal Rules, federal statutes, or the Constitution. For example, a district's local rules may govern details of district court practice such as the time for filing briefs, impoundment of private material in civil cases, the form of discovery requests, conduct of scheduling conferences, assignment of cases, continuances (postponements) of hearings or trials, electronic filing of documents, and many other aspects of practice. Although you will become familiar with the local rules of the federal districts in your state when you enter practice, local rules will not be covered in detail in your Civil Procedure class.

This hierarchy of types of legal regulation is portrayed in Figure 2–2 below. In reading cases that analyze constitutional provisions, statutes, and rules applicable to the federal courts, keep this hierarchy of authority in mind, and the basic principle that a regulation at each level may supplement but may not contradict sources of regulation above it in the hierarchy.

Here's an example of how these levels of procedural regulation might apply to a single issue. The Seventh Amendment to the United States Constitution guarantees the right to jury trial in many civil cases in the federal courts. Congress could not enact a statute that barred jury trials in those cases, nor could the Supreme Court promulgate a Federal Rule of Civil Procedure that called for a different method of trying those cases. Nor could the federal court for the Western District of Washington (to pick a district at random) adopt a local rule calling for a different mode of trial.

But federal statutes and rules can govern other aspects of jury trial that are not addressed in the Constitution. For example, Congress has enacted statutes governing the qualifications of jurors, an issue not prescribed by the Constitution but consistent with the Seventh Amendment right.** And Rule 38(b) of the Federal Rules of Civil Procedure (adopted by the Supreme Court pursuant to the Rules Enabling Act) prescribes the proper procedure for demanding a jury trial, an issue not addressed by either the Seventh Amendment or any federal statute. Further, a local rule of a federal district might govern details of calling jurors for jury service or specific procedures for claiming a jury trial or examining jurors, details not covered in the Constitution, statutes, or Federal Rules. *See, e.g.*, Local Rules, W.D. Wash. R. 38(b) (specifying method of placing demand for jury trial in a pleading).

Confusion worse confounded. Actually, there is at least one more level of judicial regulation to consider, though it will seldom come up in the materials in this

---

* Analogously, the courts of appeals are authorized to promulgate additional rules applicable in their circuit court. These rules supplement the Federal Rules of *Appellate* Procedure (the rules for procedure in the courts of appeals adopted by the Supreme Court). *See* Fed. R. App. P. 47.

** *See, e.g.*, 28 U.S.C. §§ 1861–1866.

United States Constitution
Ratified by the States

Federal statutes
Enacted by Congress
(must be consistent with constitutional
provisions governing the federal courts)

Federal Rules of Procedure
Adopted by United States Supreme Court
(must be consistent with the congressional
delegation of authority to regulate procedure
in the Rules Enabling Act and with the
federal Constitution)

Local rules
Adopted by individual federal districts
(e.g., the Local Rules for the Eastern District of Arkansas)
(must be consistent with the Federal Rules,
federal statutes, and with the federal Constitution)

Figure 2–2: SOURCES OF PROCEDURAL REGULATION IN FEDERAL COURTS

book. Individual judges often issue "standing orders" specifying procedures they will use in their individual courtrooms. These orders cannot contradict the Constitution, statutes, the Federal Rules, or local rules of the district, but they can fill in further interstices. For example, a judge's standing order might specify how potential jurors will be questioned during voir dire, or when counsel may move to strike a juror, assuming these details are not specified by statute, Federal Rule, or local rule.

Example: Sources of procedural regulation. Federal Rule of Civil Procedure 48(a) provides that a jury shall "begin with at least 6 and no more than 12 members, and each juror must participate in the verdict unless excused [for good cause]." The Federal District Court for the District of Alhambra adopts Local Rule 48.1, which provides that "district judges in the District of Alhambra shall empanel juries of eight (including two alternate jurors in case a juror is dismissed during trial) and shall dismiss the two alternate jurors before the jury deliberates if no other juror has been dismissed." Is the Local Rule valid?

> Only in part. Federal Rule of Civil Procedure 83, adopted by the United States Supreme Court under the Rules Enabling Act, provides that local rules "must be consistent with" the Federal Rules. The provision of Alhambra District Court Local Rule 48.1 calling for eight jurors is consistent with Rule 48 of the Federal Rules, because the Federal Rule allows anywhere from six to twelve jurors. But the provision of the local rule calling for dismissal of alternate jurors is not consistent with Federal Rule 48, which provides that all jurors shall participate in the verdict unless excused for cause. This aspect of the local rule is invalid, since it contradicts the governing Federal Rule.

Regulation of procedure in the state courts. A similar hierarchy of authorities applies in state courts. Certain guarantees in the United States Constitution apply in the state courts as well as federal courts, such as the Fifth Amendment right against self-incrimination. Some aspects of state court practice will be governed by the state's constitution, others by state statute, others by court rules promulgated by the legislature or the state's highest court, and others by rules adopted by a particular court (such as the probate court or housing court) within a state system. Here again, lower-level rules and regulations must be consistent with "higher-level" state statutes and constitutional provisions.

Keep in mind, however, that the Federal Rules, which you will deal with consistently in Civil Procedure, do not govern state court procedure. They are *federal* rules applicable in the federal courts only. Many states, however, have modeled their civil procedure rules on the Federal Rules (another reason to study them in Civil Procedure). As of 1986, twenty-three states had copied them almost verbatim, and two-thirds of the states base their rules substantially on the federal model. *Shreve, Raven-Hansen & Geyh* § 1.03.

IV. The Substance of Procedure and the Problem of Social Justice

A. The Substance of Procedure

This book covers civil procedure (the procedures for resolving civil litigation in the courts), so you might think that it will not focus much on who should win a case under the *substance* of the law. In a sense, this is true. The procedures described in this book are supposed to dictate *how* disputes should be resolved, not *who* should prevail.

That said, throughout the course, you will discover that many procedures have an important effect on who wins and who loses. For example, Chapters 6 through 9 cover personal jurisdiction (the power of a court to require a party to defend an action in a state). If a court's authority to require a party to defend an action is limited, a plaintiff may have to bring a lawsuit in a distant state. This can increase the cost of filing the lawsuit and make it more likely that the lawsuit will not be filed in the first place. This is obviously good news for the would-be defendant. In contrast, expansive personal jurisdiction authority makes it easier for plaintiffs to file a lawsuit in their home states, but it could make defending the action more difficult and expensive for an out-of-state party.

Chapter 13 covers basic pleadings, including how much detail a plaintiff must allege in order to pursue a case against a defendant. The more specificity that plaintiffs are expected to include in their complaints, the more difficult it will be to avoid dismissal at the outset of the case. The reality is that plaintiffs often do not have a lot of information about a defendant's supposed misconduct at the beginning of the lawsuit and typically only learn that information during the discovery process. If the plaintiff must allege the defendant's misconduct with specificity in the complaint, more lawsuits will be dismissed shortly after they are filed and before the opportunity for discovery. In contrast, if plaintiffs can file a complaint with less specificity, defendants might have to spend a lot of time and money litigating cases that have very little merit.

Chapters 21 through 23 cover the subject of discovery. If the parties have limited opportunities to discover evidence that is in the other side's possession, plaintiffs will have more difficulty uncovering the evidence they need to prove their cases. Limitations on discovery thus may increase the likelihood that a plaintiff will lose on summary judgment or at trial. In contrast, discovery is often quite expensive, and liberal discovery rules can impose substantial search and production costs on defendants, making them more likely to settle cases that have little merit just to avoid discovery expenses.

Numerous other procedural rules, depending on how they are written, can similarly offer tactical advantages to one side or another. As you proceed through the course, remain aware of the "substance of procedure"—that is, how procedural concepts affect whether plaintiffs or defendants will prevail. Consider at every turn whether the procedures you study offer the parties a balanced playing field for litigating their cases or whether certain procedural concepts tend to favor one side.

B. Civil Procedure and Social Justice

Another important and often overlooked feature of civil procedure is how lawyer-centric it is: Most procedures used in civil cases have been created by and for lawyers. The assumption is that each side has a lawyer who understands those procedures and can ensure that disputes are resolved on their merits.

The unfortunate reality is that more than 80 percent of people living below the poverty line and a majority of middle-income Americans receive no meaningful legal assistance when facing important civil legal issues, such as child custody, debt collection, eviction, and foreclosure. In other words, they cannot afford a lawyer, and nobody is available to represent them for free. For this reason, U.S. courts are overrun with pro se litigants (i.e., people who represent themselves), and those litigants are frequently denied justice because they do not know how to deal with the court system's many procedural complexities. After all, they don't have the benefit, as you will, of an entire course on civil procedure. Millions of other Americans never even show up in the courts (they "default"), because they cannot obtain counsel and do not know how to represent themselves.

In short, a significant percentage of Americans each year have to deal with critical legal problems, such as eviction or debt collection, without the benefit of a lawyer. Underrepresented communities, particularly communities of color, are disproportionately affected by this reality, and it is critical to keep in mind how the procedural concepts you encounter in this course impact these communities and social justice issues more generally.

Students can easily lose sight of these problems when studying civil procedure because they are appropriately focused on becoming excellent advocates for their future clients. Just do not forget that millions of people every year have to face the civil justice system and the procedures described in this book alone and without any meaningful legal assistance from people like you. The consequences for them and our justice system are profound and deeply troubling.

V. The Litigation Process: Summary of Basic Principles

- Federal litigation commences with the filing and service of pleadings, followed by an intensive phase of automatic disclosure, discovery, motions, and investigation, culminating in a pretrial conference to map out the scope and order of the trial.
- Cases that do not settle are tried to a jury or to a judge. Litigation in the trial court ends with the entry of a judgment for the prevailing party.
- Discovery dominates most litigation practice. It is conducted by the lawyers for the parties, but their discovery requests are backed by the enforcement power of the court under the Federal Rules governing discovery. Most discovery disputes are worked out by the parties. If they cannot agree, the court will control access to proof through orders to produce evidence or protective orders barring inappropriate requests.
- Several different layers of legal regulations govern the litigation process in federal courts. Provisions of the United States Constitution set forth broad structural features of the federal courts. Congress has enacted statutes that regulate many additional aspects of federal court procedure, which must be consistent with constitutional provisions.
- In the Rules Enabling Act, Congress delegated authority to the Supreme Court to regulate procedure in the lower federal courts. The Court has adopted the Federal Rules of Civil Procedure pursuant to that authority. The Rules govern many aspects of pleading, pretrial practice, and trial procedure in the federal courts.
- The judges within each federal district are authorized under Federal Rule 83 (a delegation of the Court's delegation!) to enact local rules governing

details of practice in that district. Local rules supplement the Constitution, statutes, and Federal Rules in regulating local practice, but cannot contradict those sources of procedural regulation.

- Civil procedure has important implications for who wins and who loses. Moreover, the civil litigation system described in this book was created by and for lawyers and, as a result, disadvantages the millions of litigants each year who have critical legal needs but do not have access to meaningful legal assistance.

PART II

Subject Matter Jurisdiction

3

Diversity Jurisdiction in the Federal Courts

I. Introduction

The first two chapters introduced basic principles about civil procedure. This chapter will analyze one category of federal subject matter jurisdiction—jurisdiction over diversity cases—in detail.

The Framers evidently created federal jurisdiction over diversity cases—cases "between citizens of different states" in the language of Article III, Section 2—to provide a neutral forum for cases involving a risk of local bias. When such cases are brought in state court, one litigant or the other will end up litigating in the local courts of the other party's state and may doubt that it will be treated fairly by local judges. The Framers—many of them men* of means—were also concerned that state courts would not adequately protect out-of-state creditors trying to collect debts from local citizens. In many states, judges are elected rather than

* We use the term advisedly—they were all men.

appointed. The Framers likely anticipated more even-handed treatment of out-of-state litigants from federal judges, who are appointed for life by a government with a national perspective. *See generally* Jack H. Friedenthal, Mary Kay Kane & Arthur R. Miller, Civil Procedure § 2.5 (5th ed. 2015). Despite debate on the original rationale for diversity and whether it is still needed, it remains a major category of federal jurisdiction. About a third of cases filed in federal court are based on diversity jurisdiction.

Constitutions establish grand principles, but they cannot cover the details. The phrase "between citizens of different states" in Article III, Section 2 grants diversity jurisdiction in general terms. It has fallen to the federal courts to determine which cases qualify as diversity cases. Here are some major issues that have arisen concerning the meaning of diversity jurisdiction:

- What does it mean for a person to be a citizen of a state? Is it enough to live in a state, to own property there, to visit there? In what state is Corey, from Chapter 1 (p. 12), a citizen? Massachusetts, where he goes to school? Or New Hampshire, where he lived before starting college? What test should courts use to determine state citizenship?
- Is a corporation a citizen of a state? If so, how do we determine a corporation's state citizenship? In Corey's case, of what state or states should Barristers be considered a citizen?
- Suppose the parties are diverse at one point during the litigation, but not at another. For example, suppose that the plaintiff and the defendant are both Utah citizens when an accident takes place, the plaintiff moves to a different state and sues the defendant, and then moves back to Utah while the case is still pending. What date (or dates) should be used in determining diversity?
- Is a case a "diversity case" if Corey, a Massachusetts citizen, sues Barristers, a Rhode Island citizen and the bartender who hit him, who is from Massachusetts? There is some diversity (Corey and Barristers are from different states), but there is not "complete diversity," since there is a Massachusetts plaintiff and a Massachusetts defendant.
- When Congress creates federal district courts, must it authorize them to hear *all* diversity cases, or can Congress grant jurisdiction over *some* diversity cases but not all of them? For example, can Congress require that a minimum dollar amount be in dispute for the federal court to hear a diversity case (an *amount-in-controversy* requirement)?

Case law has clearly answered the last question. The Supreme Court has held that Congress may authorize the federal district courts to hear *some* diversity cases, but not others. *Kline v. Burke Construction Co.*, 260 U.S. 226, 233–34 (1922). And Congress has always limited its grant of diversity jurisdiction. For example, 28 U.S.C. § 1332(a), the statute by which Congress authorizes the federal district courts to hear diversity cases, includes a minimum amount-in-controversy requirement.

> **28 U.S.C. § 1332.** (a) The district courts shall have original jurisdiction of all civil actions where the matter in controversy exceeds the sum or value of $75,000, exclusive of interest and costs, and is between—
>
> (1) citizens of different States;
>
> (2) citizens of a State and citizens or subjects of a foreign state, except that the district courts shall not have original jurisdiction under this subsection of

an action between citizens of a State and citizens or subjects of a foreign state who are lawfully admitted for permanent residence in the United States and are domiciled in the same State;

(3) citizens of different States and in which citizens or subjects of a foreign state are additional parties; and

(4) a foreign state, defined in section 1603(a) of this title, as plaintiff and citizens of a State or of different States.

Under § 1332(a), a case between a citizen of Missouri and a citizen of Arkansas, involving a $25,000 contract claim, could not be brought in federal court based on diversity jurisdiction, because the amount in controversy is below the required amount.

The following materials will explore these and other issues concerning diversity jurisdiction. The problems they explore should help you to appreciate a basic fact about law: that statutes and constitutions cannot anticipate and address all issues that arise in their administration. Consequently, courts must interpret statutes and constitutional provisions to fill in the interstices and elaborate their meaning. This process of construing statutes and constitutions is one of the great creative challenges of judging—and lawyering.

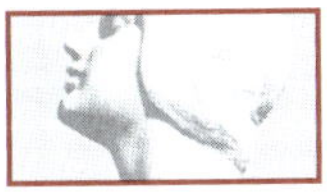

II. State Citizenship of Individuals: The Domicile Test

To determine if a federal court has diversity jurisdiction the federal courts have had to determine the meaning of the term "citizen of a state." This section explores the standard federal courts use to determine an *individual's* (that is, a person's) state citizenship.

Although it is frequently obvious that a person is a citizen of a particular state, it isn't always so. States don't issue passports or grant social security cards, so what legal standard should a court apply to ascertain a person's *state* citizenship? Since neither Article III, Section 2 nor § 1332 answers this question, judges must establish rules of interpretation in individual diversity cases.

READING *GORDON v. STEELE*. In the *Gordon* case below, the court considers how to determine the state citizenship of a student. The court notes that an individual's state citizenship for diversity purposes turns on her domicile. Great, one conundrum exchanged for another. Consider these questions in reading *Gordon*:

- What test for domicile does the court apply?
- What date does it choose for comparing the state citizenship of the parties?
- What factors does it look to in applying the domicile test to the facts of Susan Gordon's life?
- The practical factors seem to point both ways. What do you think is the basic reason that the court concludes that Gordon is domiciled in Idaho?

GORDON v. STEELE

376 F. Supp. 575 (W.D. Pa. 1974)

Knox, District Judge.

The problems of students have lately become numerous with respect to their legal status and the law with respect to them is in a constant state of flux. In recent years, there has been a deluge of litigation with respect to the residence of students for voting purposes. . . . It was inevitable that the federal courts would soon feel the impact of this litigation with respect to problems arising under diversity jurisdiction. . . . Thinking of the courts in this area is probably colored by numerous constitutional and statutory provisions in various states to the effect that no one shall be deemed to have gained or lost a residence by attendance at an institution of higher learning.

The thinking is also colored by the traditional rule that the fact that a college student is supposedly maintained by his or her parents is a strong circumstance indicating no gain of residence in the college town. *See* 44 A.L.R.3d 822 and this is in accord with Restatement of Conflicts of Laws, Section 30, that a minor child has the same domicile as its father. In these days when nearly all the state legislatures have reduced the age of majority to 18, this poses a more pressing problem with respect to college students who can no longer be put off with the explanation that those under 21 are minors and hence continue their residence with their parents. . . .

The plaintiff Susan Gordon is one of those who was benefitted by the provisions of the aforesaid emancipation acts of June 16, 1972. She was born November 20, 1953 and hence was 18 years of age at the time the cause of action herein mentioned arose and was 19 at the time this action was brought, April 10, 1973.

The action is one for malpractice against two physicians and an osteopathic hospital in Erie County, Pennsylvania. All of the defendants are citizens of Pennsylvania. There seems little question that prior to August 9, 1972, the plaintiff was also a citizen of Pennsylvania, residing at 227 Goodrich Street, Erie, Pennsylvania, with her parents and if this continued to be her address, her suit must fail for lack of diversity jurisdiction.

She complains that she suffered an injury to her wrist on February 25, 1972, and there was wrongful diagnosis as to the existence of fractures in the bones by the defendants at that time. She claims that they concluded that there were no such fractures and that as a result she endured continuing pain and disability resulting in hospitalization and medical attention and that her wrist and right hand remain at least partly disabled as the result of the alleged malpractice.

On August 9, 1972, plaintiff enrolled in Ricks College at Rexburg, Idaho where she rented an apartment which she has retained ever since. Defendants on January 21, 1974, moved to dismiss for lack of diversity. Briefs have been filed, arguments held and the court postponed decision on the matter until further depositions of the plaintiff could be taken. The matter is now before the court for disposition.

We approach the problem recognizing, of course, that it is citizenship at the time of filing suit, in this case April 10, 1973, which is controlling. Further, the rule is unquestioned that where plaintiff is challenged on her claim of diversity, the burden is upon her to show by convincing evidence that diversity jurisdiction exists.

As is required in all of such cases, we must reckon up the indicators pointing for and against acquisition of a new domicile for diversity jurisdiction purposes. Defendant claims that the following indicate that plaintiff is still a citizen of Pennsylvania and has not acquired a new residence or citizenship in Idaho:

(1) At the time of application for admission to the college at Rexburg, Idaho, she gave her address as Erie, Pennsylvania.
(2) The college records dated in 1972 show her address as Erie, Pennsylvania. The same is true of the college records dated May 4, 1973.
(3) During summer vacations, she worked in Erie, Pennsylvania.
(4) She held a Pennsylvania Driver's License and had a bank account in Erie.
(5) She came to Erie for Christmas vacations.
(6) While Ricks College is a Mormon Church Institution, the supplemental depositions which were taken at the request of the court indicate that females unlike males are generally not required to participate in the missionary activity of the church and that she has no present intentions of participating in such missionary work which, of course, might take her to any part of the world.

On the other side of the ledger, plaintiff points to the following:

(1) Her expressed intention is not to return to Pennsylvania. This, of course, is a very strong factor in a situation where subjective intent plays a part in determining what is her animo manendi.
(2) She has an apartment in Rexburg which she regards as her residence and this is not sublet during various times of the year but remains hers.
(3) She states she came back to Erie only one summer in 1973 because of her eye problems and that she took eye treatment in Erie and Cleveland.
(4) She claims that her purpose in visiting at Christmas 1973 was to be deposed and for medical appointments. She has not returned to Erie during Spring or Thanksgiving vacations.
(5) Her religious desires as a sincere Mormon are to further her faith and insure that she marries in a Mormon Temple to someone of her faith. At the present time, she has no present plans of marrying anyone but she does desire to marry in her faith and claims that the opportunities for such a marriage in Erie are very small and that she would be unable to marry in a Temple here.
(6) She has introduced exhibits showing that she is a member of the Blue Cross of Idaho, becoming a subscriber in 1972.
(7) She claims she may locate after graduation in any other of the 49 states or abroad. She may, of course, return to Pennsylvania. She, like many other females, has vague intentions of marrying some day but does not know to whom and in such case it is likely that she would follow her husband where his work may take him.

We recognize that the problem of students' residence is not altogether a new one but has concerned the federal courts since Chicago and Northwestern Railway Company v. Ohle, 117 U.S. 123 (1886), where the court held that determinations of a domicile were a matter to be determined by the trier of fact.

The most recent exposition of the law on this subject for our edification by the Third Circuit is found in Krasnov v. Dinan, 465 F.2d 1298 (3d Cir. 1972), from which we quote at length:

> "*It is the citizenship of the parties at the time the action is commenced which is controlling.* Brough v. Strathmann Supply Co., 358 F.2d 374 (3d Cir. 1966). One domiciled in a state when a suit is begun is 'a citizen of that state within the meaning of the Constitution, art. 3, § 2, and the Judicial Code. . . .' "
>
> "*The fact of residency must be coupled with a finding of intent to remain indefinitely.* Proof of intent to remain permanently is not the test. 'If the new state is to be one's home for an *indefinite period of time, he has acquired a new domicile.*' Gallagher v. Philadelphia Transp. Co., *supra*, 185 F.2d (543) at 546. *Where jurisdictional allegations are traversed, as here, 'the burden of showing . . . that the federal court has jurisdiction rests upon the complainants.'* . . . 'In determining whether a party has intended to establish a domicile in the state to which he has moved, the factfinder will look to such circumstances as his declarations, exercise of political rights, payment of personal taxes, house of residence, and place of business.' " . . .
>
> "Applying these principles to the evidence before the factfinder, we cannot construe, as clearly erroneous, its finding that the defendant 'intended to remain in the Commonwealth for an indefinite period of time.' *Because animo manendi is at best a subjective manifestation, Dinan's own declarations of intent are important, as were his explanations of the lack of compulsion in religious order assignments and his failure to obtain a Pennsylvania driver's license.*"

We also have further instruction on this subject in the case in Judge Hastie's opinion in Gallagher v. Philadelphia Transportation Company, 185 F.2d 543 (3d Cir. 1950), in which the lower court was criticized as putting too much emphasis on permanence of the attachment to a given state. We also quote at length from this decision.

> "*The emphasis of the court on the permanence of the anticipated attachment to a state, in our opinion, required too much of the plaintiff. . . .*"
>
> "It is enough to intend to make the new state one's home. It is not important if there is within contemplation a vague possibility of eventually going elsewhere, or even of returning whence one came. If the new state is to be one's home for an indefinite period of time, he has acquired a new domicile. Finally, it is the intention at the time of arrival which is important. The fact that the plaintiff may later have acquired doubts about remaining in her new home or may have been called upon to leave it is not relevant, so long as the subsequent doubt or the circumstance of the leaving does not indicate that the intention to make the place the plaintiff's home never existed."

In the light of the foregoing and in view of the current tendency to treat students 18 years of age and above as emancipated and particularly in view of [the] fact that in this case the plaintiff has rented an apartment in Rexburg and with due regard for Judge Goodrich's statement from his Handbook of the Conflict of Laws that the possibility of eventually going elsewhere or even returning whence one came does not defeat the acquisition of a new domicile, we conclude upon the *facts of this case* considering the student's connection with Idaho and her subjective intention of not returning to Pennsylvania in the foreseeable future that she is a citizen of Idaho for the purpose of diversity jurisdiction and the motion to dismiss must be denied.

Notes and Questions: Applying the Test for State Citizenship

1. The common law concept of domicile. The court holds that Susan Gordon's state citizenship depends upon her domicile. To determine *that,* the court uses a further test, residence with the intent to remain "indefinitely." This test was not created out of whole cloth: The common law concept of domicile has long been used for several purposes. It may, for example, be used to determine the power to exercise personal jurisdiction over a person, to grant a divorce, to impose a tax or to determine the persons entitled to inherit property. *Restatement (Second) of Conflict of Laws* § 11 cmt. c (1989).

2. Losing and gaining a domicile. Courts hold that a person does not lose her old domicile until she acquires a new one, that is, until she goes to another state with the intent to reside indefinitely in the new state. With this corollary of the domicile test in mind, consider the following scenario.

Susan Gordon, after growing up in Pennsylvania, goes to Ricks College, in Idaho, planning to get a two-year nursing degree and return to practice nursing in Pennsylvania. Two months after starting school, she files suit in a Pennsylvania federal district court against Dr. Rodriguez, a Pennsylvania citizen who treated her in Pennsylvania for an injury. She claims jurisdiction based on diversity. The court probably

A. lacks diversity jurisdiction, because Gordon is still domiciled in Pennsylvania.
B. lacks diversity jurisdiction, because the treatment took place in Pennsylvania.
C. has diversity jurisdiction, because she was living in Idaho when she filed the suit.
D. would have diversity jurisdiction, if she brought the action in an Idaho federal court.

Several of the "distractors" (wrong choices) here reflect misconceptions about diversity. **B** is wrong because the court's jurisdiction in a diversity case has nothing to do with *where the claim arose*, only with the state citizenship of the parties. If Kim, from Texas, has an accident with Olsen, from Michigan, in Tennessee, that's a diversity case, since the parties are from different states. The federal court will have subject matter jurisdiction over it whether it is brought in a federal court in Texas or Tennessee or Alaska.

D is also wrong because diversity does not have anything to do with which federal district court the suit is filed in, only whether the plaintiffs and defendants are from different states. **C** fails as well, because a person may be living in a state, but not be domiciled there under the test, if she plans to leave at a definite time. Based on the domicile test, the best answer is **A**. Since Gordon is in Idaho for a definite time only, she did not acquire a new domicile when she went to Ricks College. Thus we look back to her last domicile, Pennsylvania.

With that warm-up, consider where Susan Gordon would be domiciled in the following examples.

A. Susan Gordon goes to Ricks College, planning to get a two-year nursing degree and then move to California to work in a hospital there. Before leaving for Ricks College, she announces to her friends that she is never coming back to Pennsylvania. Two months after starting school, she sues the Pennsylvania doctors.

B. Susan Gordon goes from Pennsylvania to Ricks College, planning to get her degree and practice nursing in Idaho. After three months at college, she decides that she does not like Idaho and will return to Pennsylvania after she completes her degree. The next week she brings the suit.

C. Susan Gordon goes from Pennsylvania to Ricks College, planning to get her degree and practice nursing in California. After three months at college, she decides she likes Idaho and will stay and practice nursing there after she completes her degree. She brings suit a month after she makes that decision.

D. Susan Gordon goes from Pennsylvania to Ricks College, planning to practice nursing after she finishes her degree, but with no plan as to where she will do so. A month after starting school, she sues the Pennsylvania defendants.

A. Pennsylvania. She has not formed a new domicile in Idaho, since she is only in Idaho for a definite period. She hasn't formed one in California either, because she hasn't moved there yet. Ironically, though she swears she will never set foot in Pennsylvania again, she does not lose her Pennsylvania domicile until she forms a new one.

B. Idaho. When Gordon arrived in Idaho planning to stay, she acquired domicile there. Although she now intends to leave Idaho, she won't lose her Idaho domicile until she goes to live in another state with the intent to remain there indefinitely.

C. Idaho. Gordon did not acquire domicile when she moved to Idaho but did when her intent changed while she was living there. The statement quoted in *Gordon* that "[i]t is the intention at the time of arrival which is important" is misleading. Even though Gordon did not form a domicile on the day she moved there, she does form it later when she is living there and decides to stay.

D. Here, Gordon has no clear intent to leave Idaho. She might, but has no definite plan to do so or to do anything else. The better answer is that she acquires domicile in Idaho. This is close to the actual facts of the case.

3. Meaning of "indefinite" intent. What does it mean to intend to remain "indefinitely" in a state? It is often said that this prong of the domicile test is not met if a person goes to a state temporarily, that is, to visit. On the other hand, it is not necessary to intend to remain permanently to meet the test. (How many Americans today could testify that they live in a state permanently?) Often, courts state that it is enough that the party "intend[s] to make the new state home and that the person has no present intention of going elsewhere [to live]." *Wright & Kane* § 26. If so, the person is in the state on an open-ended basis and establishes a new domicile.

Q **4. Applying the test.** In *Holmes v. Sopuch*, 639 F.2d 431 (8th Cir. 1981), the plaintiff, Holmes, had been living in Missouri and working for the federal Defense Mapping Agency. The DMA sent him to a one-year program at Ohio State University during the 1978–79 academic year. He and his wife moved to Ohio, where they leased an apartment for one year. In February 1979, while he was still living in Ohio, he brought a diversity action against two Missouri citizens.

Holmes testified that "after finishing his studies at Ohio State he would obtain the best position available with the DMA and that he never intended Ohio to be his permanent home. Moreover, there is no DMA facility in Ohio which Holmes might have chosen upon the completion of his studies. Holmes also testified that he might have chosen to return to the St. Louis DMA facility." Did Holmes acquire domicile in Ohio?

A The court held that Holmes did not acquire domicile in Ohio during his time there. Although he resided there, he was not there "indefinitely." He intended to leave Ohio at a definite time, since he planned to resume his work for the DMA, and he could only do so by leaving Ohio.

The result would likely have been different if the DMA had a facility in Ohio, and Holmes might have been hired there. In that case, he might have remained in Ohio after the one-year program. Even if there were more DMA offices in other states, it would not be clear that Holmes was going to leave Ohio at a definite time.

Q **5. An alternative formulation of the domicile test.** Some courts may state the domicile test a little differently. "To establish a domicile of choice a person generally must be physically present at the location and intend to make that place his home for the time at least." *Sadat v. Mertes*, 615 F.2d 1176 (7th Cir. 1980). This test is meaningfully different from the intent-to-remain-indefinitely test. How would Holmes's case in note 4 come out under this test?

A Under this test Holmes would become a citizen of Ohio, since he was there "for the time at least." However, most diversity cases have applied the intent-to-remain-indefinitely test. (The *Holmes* court rejected plaintiffs' argument for the alternative test. 639 F.2d at 433–34.) As previously noted, domicile is a common law concept used in many contexts, so it may be applied somewhat differently in one context than another.

6. The date for determining diversity. The *Gordon* court states the long-established rule *(see, e.g., Smith v. Sperling,* 354 U.S. 91, 93 (1957)) that the parties must be diverse on the day the complaint is filed. If the parties are diverse on that date, the case is a proper diversity case, even if the parties were *not* diverse at the time of the events giving rise to the claim, or later in the litigation. In *Leavitt v. Scott,* 338 F.2d 749 (10th Cir. 1964), the plaintiff was from Utah and had an accident with another Utah citizen. He moved to Colorado briefly and brought suit against the defendant. Although he returned to live in Utah after filing suit, the court upheld diversity jurisdiction since the parties were diverse on the date of filing.

If the underlying rationale for diversity is prejudice against an out-of-stater, why determine diversity based on a single day? And why choose the day of filing? Wouldn't the day of trial make more sense? Or why not require the parties to be diverse throughout the litigation? Or on the day the claim arose, a date likely beyond the power of either party to manipulate?

Ultimately, the choice to focus on the parties' domicile on a single day is a matter of administrative simplicity: The court has to know whether it has jurisdiction or not. Choosing the date of filing provides this certainty. Using the date the claim arose would be dubious in cases that arise over a period of time (such as claims for unfair competition or sexual discrimination toward an employee). If the court used the day of trial, a court might process a case through the pretrial stages for a year or more, only to discover (because a party moved) that it no longer had jurisdiction. The day of filing seems a bit arbitrary, but it promotes efficiency by providing a clear test for jurisdiction, which will not change even if the parties later change their domiciles.

7. Evidence of domicile contrasted with the test for domicile. The courts consider a wide variety of evidence in determining a party's domicile. In *Gordon,* the court considers evidence about Susan Gordon's driver's license, her health insurance, her apartment, her religious affiliation, and other facts. Yet these practical facts are not the test itself; they are evidence relevant to applying the test. In some situations most of these facts would point to one state, but the person would still lack the subjective intent to remain there indefinitely.

Consider, for example, a student who graduates from medical school in Indiana and starts a three-year residency at a Texas hospital, planning to return to Indiana to establish a practice. Wouldn't she rent an apartment, join a health plan, get a driver's license, pay local taxes, and do other things suggesting a local affiliation? Probably so, but if it is clear that she plans to leave at a particular point, these indicia would not establish a Texas domicile. It is, after all, the person's intent that is the test. The practical facts described in *Gordon* represent evidence that can be useful—or at times, deceiving—in trying to prove that subjective fact.

Very likely the *Gordon* court's fundamental reason for concluding that Susan Gordon had acquired a domicile in Idaho (though not too clearly articulated in the opinion) was not her Blue Cross membership or her apartment in Rexburg, but the fact that she simply didn't know what she would do after she finished school.

Q **8. Corey's case.** In light of the principles discussed above, what kinds of questions would you want to ask Corey (our battery plaintiff from Chapter 1, p. 12) to determine his state citizenship?

A You would ask him about the practical facts of his life, such as whether he had changed his bank accounts, driver's license, and voting registration. But you would be particularly interested in Corey's plans after school. If he is quite clear that he is going back to New Hampshire or to some third state, he would not acquire domicile in Massachusetts. If he has little or no idea of his future plans, a court would likely conclude that he was in Massachusetts "indefinitely" and therefore a Massachusetts citizen.

Q **9. If diversity exists, which federal district court has jurisdiction?** Gordon brought her suit in the Federal District Court for the Western District of Pennsylvania. Would the diversity analysis be different if she brought it in the Northern District of California? Or the Southern District of Texas?

A No, it wouldn't. The diversity statute, 28 U.S.C. § 1332(a), provides that "the [federal] district courts" shall have jurisdiction over cases between citizens of different states. If the plaintiff and defendant are from different states, *any* federal district court will have diversity jurisdiction over the case. The particular federal district the plaintiff chooses matters in determining whether the court has personal jurisdiction over the defendant or is a proper venue, but is irrelevant in determining whether the court has subject matter jurisdiction over the case. The court has diversity jurisdiction as long as the plaintiff and defendant are citizens of different states (and the amount-in-controversy requirement is met, as we will see later).

Q **10. Diversity cases in state court.** Gordon, from Idaho, brings suit against the Pennsylvania doctors in a state court in Pennsylvania. Would the state court have subject matter jurisdiction over the case?

A Yes. Recall a crucial point made in Chapter 1. The fact that a case could be filed in federal court as a diversity case does not mean that it *must* be filed in federal court. As a general rule, the state courts also have jurisdiction over cases within federal subject matter jurisdiction. Even if Gordon is diverse from the defendants, state courts have broad jurisdiction to hear tort cases as well, and Gordon may have strategic reasons for preferring to sue in state court.

11. Issue analysis: Applying the domicile test. Here's a nice scenario one of the authors used to test domicile on an exam.

> Originally from Massachusetts, Ruggles drifted from one New England state to another, staying for a while and then getting itchy feet and moving on. At one point, he drifted up to New Hampshire, where he took a job on a lobster boat for the summer season. He had a contract to work on the boat for six months. During this period, Ruggles was injured when he was hit by Quan's car. May Ruggles sue Quan, a New Hampshire citizen, in federal court under the diversity jurisdiction?

A suggested analysis. If a student wrote the following analysis of Ruggles's domicile, she would do very well: "To invoke diversity jurisdiction Ruggles would have to be a citizen of a different state than Quan. This turns on where Ruggles is domiciled (that is, the last state he has resided in with the intent to reside indefinitely) on the day he files suit. If, as the question suggests, Ruggles brings suit while he is still working in New Hampshire, he will likely be found a citizen of New Hampshire. True, he is a 'drifter,' tends to move on after a while, and probably will leave New Hampshire at some point. But the question does not indicate that he has any specific plan to do so at a particular time. Although his contract is only for six months, the facts do not suggest that he has any plans as to what he will do at the end of the six months. Presumably, Ruggles's only plan at that point is to see what turns up, and if nothing does, then perhaps he'll move on. If this is so, Ruggles does not have a fixed future plan, is living in New Hampshire on an open-ended basis, and is domiciled in New Hampshire. Consequently, he cannot sue Quan in federal court based on diversity jurisdiction."

III. The Complete Diversity Rule

Another question unanswered by the broad language of Article III, Section 2 is how courts should assess diversity in a case with multiple plaintiffs or defendants. Suppose, for example, that Corey sues both Barristers, Inc. and Brummell, the bartender who hit him. Assume further that Corey is a New Hampshire citizen and Brummell and Barristers are Massachusetts citizens. The case looks like this:

Corey (NH) v. Barristers (MA)
Brummell (MA)

Is this a proper diversity case, even though two of the parties are Massachusetts citizens? Or suppose that Corey and Brummell are both from New Hampshire? Now the case looks like this:

Corey (NH) v. Barristers (MA)
Brummell (NH)

Is this a proper diversity case, even though there is a New Hampshire plaintiff and a New Hampshire defendant?

READING *MAS v. PERRY.* The *Mas* case below addresses the complete diversity rule, as well as the problem of applying diversity jurisdiction to a case involving citizens of another country. In reading *Mas,* note that the court rejects the old common law rule that a woman automatically takes the domicile of her husband. Thus, it must assess the domicile of three parties, the two plaintiffs and the defendant. Consider the following questions in reading *Mas.*

- If Mr. Mas alone sued Perry, could he do so in federal court? Could he do so if he were domiciled in Louisiana?

- Why does the court conclude that Mrs. Mas did not acquire a domicile in Louisiana while there as a student? Is its analysis consistent with *Gordon v. Steele*?
- Note that at the time of *Mas* the amount in controversy was required to exceed $10,000, not $75,000.
- Students often find this case frustrating, because it appears to contradict *Gordon v. Steele*. The *Mas* court concludes that the Mases did not acquire domicile because they were "in Louisiana only as students and lacked the requisite intention to remain there." Consider whether the court adequately explains its conclusion that Mrs. Mas never acquired domicile in Louisiana. And, perhaps, ask yourself why the coursebook authors might include the case if it somewhat "muddies the waters" with regard to the domicile test.

MAS v. PERRY

489 F.2d 1396 (5th Cir. 1974)

AINSWORTH, Circuit Judge:

This case presents questions pertaining to federal diversity jurisdiction under 28 U.S.C. § 1332, which, pursuant to article III, section II of the Constitution, provides for original jurisdiction in federal district courts of all civil actions that are between, *inter alia*, citizens of different States or citizens of a State and citizens of foreign states and in which the amount in controversy is more than $10,000.

Appellees Jean Paul Mas, a citizen of France, and Judy Mas were married at her home in Jackson, Mississippi. Prior to their marriage, Mr. and Mrs. Mas were graduate assistants, pursuing coursework as well as performing teaching duties, for approximately nine months and one year, respectively, at Louisiana State University in Baton Rouge, Louisiana. Shortly after their marriage, they returned to Baton Rouge to resume their duties as graduate assistants at LSU. They remained in Baton Rouge for approximately two more years, after which they moved to Park Ridge, Illinois. At the time of the trial in this case, it was their intention to return to Baton Rouge while Mr. Mas finished his studies for the degree of Doctor of Philosophy. Mr. and Mrs. Mas were undecided as to where they would reside after that.

Upon their return to Baton Rouge after their marriage, appellees rented an apartment from appellant Oliver H. Perry, a citizen of Louisiana. This appeal arises from a final judgment entered on a jury verdict awarding $5,000 to Mr. Mas and $15,000 to Mrs. Mas for damages incurred by them as a result of the discovery that their bedroom and bathroom contained "two-way" mirrors and that they had been watched through them by the appellant during three of the first four months of their marriage.

At the close of the appellees' case at trial, appellant made an oral motion to dismiss for lack of jurisdiction.... The motion was denied by the district court. Before this Court, appellant challenges the final judgment below solely on jurisdictional grounds, contending that appellees failed to prove diversity of citizenship among the parties and that the requisite jurisdictional amount is lacking with respect to Mr. Mas. Finding no merit to these contentions, we affirm. Under section 1332(a)(2), the federal judicial power extends to the claim of Mr. Mas, a citizen of France, against the appellant, a citizen of Louisiana. Since we conclude that Mrs. Mas is a citizen of Mississippi for diversity purposes, the district court also properly had jurisdiction under section 1332(a)(1) of her claim.

It has long been the general rule that complete diversity of parties is required in order that diversity jurisdiction obtain; that is, no party on one side may be a citizen of the same State as any party on the other side. Strawbridge v. Curtiss, 7 U.S. (3 Cranch) 267 (1806). This determination of one's State citizenship for diversity purposes is controlled by federal law, not by the law of any State. As is the case in other areas of federal jurisdiction, the diverse citizenship among adverse parties must be present at the time the complaint is filed. The burden of pleading the diverse citizenship is upon the party invoking federal jurisdiction... and if the diversity jurisdiction is properly challenged, that party also bears the burden of proof....

To be a citizen of a State within the meaning of section 1332, a natural person must be both a citizen of the United States... and a domiciliary of that State. For diversity purposes, citizenship means domicile; mere residence in the State is not sufficient.

A person's domicile is the place of "'his true, fixed, and permanent home and principal establishment, and to which he has the intention of returning whenever he is absent therefrom....'" Stine v. Moore, 5 Cir., 1954, 213 F.2d 446, 448. A change of domicile may be effected only by a combination of two elements: (a) taking up residence in a different domicile with (b) the intention to remain there.

It is clear that at the time of her marriage, Mrs. Mas was a domiciliary of the State of Mississippi. While it is generally the case that the domicile of the wife—and, consequently, her State citizenship for purposes of diversity jurisdiction—is deemed to be that of her husband, we find no precedent for extending this concept to the situation here, in which the husband is a citizen of a foreign state but resides in the United States. Indeed, such a fiction would work absurd results on the facts before us. If Mr. Mas were considered a domiciliary of France—as he would be since he had lived in Louisiana as a student-teaching assistant prior to filing this suit—then Mrs. Mas would also be deemed a domiciliary, and thus, fictionally at least, a citizen of France. She would not be a citizen of any State and could not sue in a federal court on that basis; nor could she invoke the alienage jurisdiction to bring her claim in federal court, since she is not an alien. On the other hand, if Mrs. Mas's domicile were Louisiana, she would become a Louisiana citizen for diversity purposes and could not bring suit with her husband against appellant, also a Louisiana citizen, on the basis of diversity jurisdiction. These are curious results under a rule arising from the theoretical identity of person and interest of the married couple.

An American woman is not deemed to have lost her United States citizenship solely by reason of her marriage to an alien. 8 U.S.C. § 1489. Similarly, we conclude that for diversity purposes a woman does not have her domicile or State citizenship changed solely by reason of her marriage to an alien.

Mrs. Mas's Mississippi domicile was disturbed neither by her year in Louisiana prior to her marriage nor as a result of the time she and her husband spent at LSU after their marriage, since for both periods she was a graduate assistant at LSU. Though she testified that after her marriage she had no intention of returning to her parents' home in Mississippi, Mrs. Mas did not effect a change of domicile since she and Mr. Mas were in Louisiana only as students and lacked the requisite intention to remain there. Until she acquires a new domicile, she remains a domiciliary, and thus a citizen, of Mississippi.[2]

Appellant also contends that Mr. Mas's claim should have been dismissed for failure to establish the requisite jurisdictional amount for diversity cases of more than $10,000. In their complaint Mr. and Mrs. Mas alleged that they had each been damaged in the amount of $100,000. As we have noted, Mr. Mas ultimately recovered $5,000.

It is well settled that the amount in controversy is determined by the amount claimed by the plaintiff in good faith. Federal jurisdiction is not lost because a judgment of less than the jurisdictional amount is awarded. That Mr. Mas recovered only $5,000 is, therefore, not compelling. As the Supreme Court stated in St. Paul Mercury Indemnity Co. v. Red Cab Co., 303 U.S. 283, 288–290:

> [T]he sum claimed by the plaintiff controls if the claim is apparently made in good faith.
>
> It must appear to a legal certainty that the claim is really for less than the jurisdictional amount to justify dismissal. The inability of the plaintiff to recover an amount adequate to give the court jurisdiction does not show his bad faith or oust the jurisdiction. . . .
>
> His good faith in choosing the federal forum is open to challenge not only by resort to the face of his complaint, but by the facts disclosed at trial, and if from either source it is clear that his claim never could have amounted to the sum necessary to give jurisdiction there is no injustice in dismissing the suit.

Having heard the evidence presented at the trial, the district court concluded that the appellees properly met the requirements of section 1332 with respect to jurisdictional amount. Upon examination of the record in this case, we are also satisfied that the requisite amount was in controversy.

Thus the power of the federal district court to entertain the claims of appellees in this case stands on two separate legs of diversity jurisdiction: a claim by an alien against a State citizen; and an action between citizens of different States. We also note, however, the propriety of having the federal district court entertain a spouse's action against a defendant, where the district court already has jurisdiction over a claim, arising from the same transaction, by the other spouse against the same defendant. In the case before us, such a result is particularly desirable. The claims of Mr. and Mrs. Mas arise from the same operative facts, and there was almost complete interdependence between their claims with respect to the proof required and the issues raised at trial. Thus, since the district court had jurisdiction of Mr. Mas's action, sound judicial administration militates strongly in favor of federal jurisdiction of Mrs. Mas's claim.

Affirmed.

---

2. The original complaint in this case was filed within several days of Mr. and Mrs. Mas's realization that they had been watched through the mirrors, quite some time before they moved to Park Ridge, Illinois. Because the district court's jurisdiction is not affected by actions of the parties subsequent to the commencement of the suit, the testimony concerning Mr. and Mrs. Mas's moves after that time is not determinative of the issue of diverse citizenship, though it is of interest insofar as it supports their lack of intent to remain permanently in Louisiana.

Notes and Questions: The Complete Diversity Requirement

1. The "complete diversity" rule. As *Mas* indicates, the diversity statute has been interpreted to require *complete diversity* between all plaintiffs and all defendants. *Strawbridge v. Curtiss*, 7 U.S. 267 (1806). To be a proper diversity case, no plaintiff can be a citizen of the same state as any defendant. The first example before the *Mas* case, between a New Hampshire plaintiff and two Massachusetts defendants, satisfies the requirement. (It would also satisfy the requirement if there were twenty-five, or one hundred, Massachusetts defendants.) But the second case, in which Corey sues a Massachusetts citizen and a New Hampshire citizen, would not be proper because there is a New Hampshire citizen on both sides of the case. There is *minimal diversity* in that case—that is, *someone* on the defendants' side is diverse from the plaintiff—but not the complete diversity that *Strawbridge* requires.

A good way to think about the complete diversity requirement is to imagine that each plaintiff had sued each defendant in a separate action. If they had, would all the cases be proper diversity cases? If so, then there is diversity jurisdiction if they all join in one action. But if the plaintiff could not have sued one of the defendants in federal court under diversity, she cannot add that defendant to the case simply because the other defendants are diverse.

Although the complete diversity rule has been criticized, it makes a certain amount of sense. After all, a New Hampshire plaintiff could not sue a New Hampshire defendant in federal court on the basis of diversity, so why should she be able to bootstrap the case into federal court just because she also sues someone from Massachusetts? At any rate, complete diversity remains the current interpretation of § 1332(a).

2. The "alienage jurisdiction." In *Mas*, Mr. Mas was a citizen of France, suing an American citizen. The Framers authorized federal courts to hear such cases. *See* Article III, Section 2 (allowing federal jurisdiction over cases "between a State, or the Citizens thereof, and foreign States, Citizens or Subjects"). And Congress has authorized such jurisdiction in the diversity statute:

> **28 U.S.C. § 1332.** (a) The district courts shall have original jurisdiction of all civil actions where the matter in controversy exceeds the sum or value of $75,000, exclusive of interest and costs, and is between—. . .
>
> (2) citizens of a State and citizens or subjects of a foreign state, except that the district courts shall not have original jurisdiction under this subsection of an action between citizens of a State and citizens or subjects of a foreign state who are lawfully admitted for permanent residence in the United States and are domiciled in the same State;
>
> (3) citizens of different States and in which citizens or subjects of a foreign state are additional parties. . . .

Under § 1332(a)(2), Mr. Mas could sue Perry in federal court, if his claim meets the amount-in-controversy requirement and he is not a permanent resident domiciled in Louisiana. The question, however, was whether his wife could join with him as a coplaintiff. If she was a citizen of Louisiana, there would not be complete diversity, since she and the defendant would be from the same state. If she was a citizen of

Mississippi, the case would fall under § 1332(a)(3); it would be a case between citizens of different states with a citizen of a foreign state (Mr. Mas) as an additional party.

Q **3. State citizens and national citizens.** Suppose that Mr. Mas was domiciled in Louisiana, that is, he was living there and planning to do so indefinitely. Could he sue Perry in federal court based on diversity?

A Maybe. If Mr. Mas were admitted to the United States for permanent residence and domiciled in Louisiana, the exception in § 1332(a)(2) would bar him from suing Perry under the diversity jurisdiction. The logic for the exception is that Mas would effectively be a local citizen and not at risk of prejudice.

If Mr. Mas had not been admitted for permanent residence, he could sue Perry in federal court based on diversity. It would be a case between a citizen of a state and a citizen of a foreign state.

The exception in 28 U.S.C. § 1332(a)(2) for foreign citizens admitted to the United States for permanent residence was not in the statute at the time that *Mas* was decided. Even if it had been, there is no suggestion that Mr. Mas had been admitted for permanent residence, so he was treated as a foreign citizen under § 1332(a)(2).

4. United States citizens who are not state citizens. Consider the following question, which involves both foreign citizens and U.S. citizens.

Assume that Mr. and Mrs. Mas were both domiciled in Louisiana while in school, but after finishing their degrees they move to France, planning to live there indefinitely. After arriving in France, they bring suit on a state law tort claim against Perry in federal court in Louisiana.

A. The court lacks jurisdiction, because Mrs. Mas is not a citizen of a state or a foreign citizen.
B. The court lacks jurisdiction, because Mrs. Mas remains a citizen of Louisiana.
C. The court has jurisdiction, since neither Mr. Mas nor Mrs. Mas is domiciled in Louisiana.
D. The court has jurisdiction, because Mr. and Mrs. Mas have become foreign citizens. Thus, the case is between a state citizen, Mr. Perry, and citizens of a foreign state.

Let's take these choices in reverse order. **D** is wrong, because Mrs. Mas does not become a citizen of France just by moving there. She is still a U.S. citizen, unless she renounces that citizenship. So it is not a case of a state citizen (Perry) against two French citizens.

C fails as well. To invoke diversity, it is not enough that the Mases are not from Louisiana. The case must fit into a category of jurisdiction in Article III, Section 2. Here, Mrs. Mas is not a citizen of any state, because she is not domiciled in any state (even though she is a U.S. citizen). Mr. Mas, as a foreign citizen, could sue Perry in federal court, but Mrs. Mas cannot join with him because she does not satisfy diversity jurisdiction. Nor is she a citizen of France, since she is still a U.S. citizen.

B is wrong, because Mrs. Mas does not remain a citizen of Louisiana. To be a citizen of Louisiana, she must be a U.S. citizen domiciled in Louisiana. She remains a U.S. citizen after moving to France, but is now domiciled in France, since she is living there with no definite intent to leave.

So **A** is right. Once she moves to France, Mrs. Mas loses her Louisiana citizenship. She remains a U.S. citizen, but she is not a citizen of any state since she is domiciled in France. *See Twentieth Century-Fox Film Corp. v. Taylor*, 239 F. Supp. 913 (S.D.N.Y. 1965) (no diversity jurisdiction in suit against Elizabeth Taylor, a U.S. citizen domiciled in England when suit was commenced, since she was not a state citizen).

Q **5. A follow-up question.** Where could the Mases sue Perry in the last example?

A They could sue him in state court in Louisiana. The subject matter jurisdiction of the state courts in every state is quite broad and would include tort claims such as the Mases' claims against Perry. They could not sue in federal court, for lack of subject matter jurisdiction. They probably could not sue him in France, since he would not be subject to personal jurisdiction there for the Mases' claims.

6. Did the *Mas* court get it right? In *Mas*, the court concluded that Mrs. Mas had not acquired domicile in Louisiana, since she and her husband "were in Louisiana only as students and lacked the requisite intention to remain there." 489 F.2d at 1400. Yet, as the *Gordon* case indicates, a student can acquire domicile in the state where she studies.

In the 1970s, jobs for students finishing graduate school were tough to come by. Let's hypothesize that Mr. and Mrs. Mas, when they sued Perry, would have gratefully accepted academic positions anywhere they could get one (or two). On that assumption, it would seem that their intent was open-ended; they would probably leave Louisiana (since most potential jobs would be in other states) but might not (since presumably some jobs would be there).

On this assumption, the court's conclusion that Mrs. Mas did not acquire domicile in Louisiana seems dubious. The court suggests that Mr. and Mrs. Mas lacked "intent to remain permanently in Louisiana." 489 F.2d at 1400 n.2. Compare *Gordon v. Steele*, which notes the difference between "indefinite" and "permanent" intent, suggesting that a "permanence" test demands too much. If the Mases were willing to stay in Louisiana, they probably were not sure they were leaving at the end of their studies and arguably were Louisiana domiciliaries. In the diversity context, most courts articulate the test in terms of intent to remain indefinitely rather than intent to remain permanently.

Q **7. The consequences of finding that subject matter jurisdiction is lacking.** The opinion in *Mas* was issued by the Fifth Circuit Court of Appeals, responding to defendant Perry's appeal claiming that the federal district court that tried the case had lacked subject matter jurisdiction over it. If the court of appeals had agreed with Perry's argument that the trial court lacked jurisdiction, what would it have ordered?

A There are few truly ineluctable rules in law. One that is close, however, is that a court cannot decide a case if it lacks subject matter jurisdiction. If the court of appeals had concluded that the trial court lacked subject matter jurisdiction over the Mases' case, it would have had to order it dismissed from federal court. As the Seventh Circuit stated in dismissing a case for lack of diversity:

> After eight years in federal court and consideration by four federal judges . . . this case comes before us on appeal. This substantial consumption of federal resources makes it all the more regrettable that we must now order the dismissal of the case

> for lack of subject matter jurisdiction rendering everything that has occurred in those eight years a nullity.

Hart v. Terminex International, 336 F.3d 541, 541–42 (7th Cir. 2003). In *Mas*, the entire course of the litigation, including the completed trial, would have been wiped out if the court of appeals concluded that Mrs. Mas was domiciled in Louisiana, at least as to her claim against Perry. It seems possible that this consequence, in a factually close case, may have influenced the court's analysis.

In the last paragraph of the *Mas* opinion, the court notes that "sound judicial administration" favors hearing Mrs. Mas's claim with Mr. Mas's. This bit of dicta should be approached with caution. In many situations efficiency would be served by hearing a claim along with others but the court will not be able to do so for lack of jurisdiction. Judicial efficiency cannot substitute for a recognized basis of subject matter jurisdiction.

8. The domestic relations exception to diversity jurisdiction. The Supreme Court has long held that the diversity statute does not authorize jurisdiction over domestic relations cases. *See Ankenbrandt v. Richards*, 504 U.S. 689 (1992) (divorce cases); *Markham v. Allen*, 326 U.S. 490 (1946) (probate of an estate). The Court has not held that such cases fall outside the grant of diversity jurisdiction in Article III, Section 2. Rather, *Ankenbrandt* reasoned that the *diversity statute* has long been read to exclude domestic relations matters. This interpretation avoids interference with the administration of state probate or family courts, which handle most family law matters and have specialized resources for doing so. An unstated consideration may also lie behind this exception: "federal judges understandably lack enthusiasm for burdensome, fact-bound, and often protracted domestic relations disputes." *Shreve, Raven-Hansen & Geyh* § 5.04[3] (footnote omitted).

IV. State Citizenship of Corporations and Other Entities

Lawyers representing corporations have generally favored litigating in the federal courts, especially in cases between local citizens and an out-of-state corporation. So the question arose early in the administration of the federal courts whether a corporation could claim to be a "citizen of a state" and invoke federal diversity jurisdiction.

A corporation is an intangible legal entity created under state incorporation laws. It has several advantages as a vehicle for engaging in commercial enterprises. Because the corporation is a separate legal "person," apart from its shareholders, investors in the corporation are generally protected from personal liability beyond the amount they have invested in the company. A corporation is also a self-perpetuating entity; the officers and directors conduct the affairs of the corporation with substantial independence from the investors and can be replaced under the bylaws to ensure continuity of corporate operations. In addition, through the issuance of stock, corporations can raise capital and provide an effective vehicle for many small investors to profit from a single commercial enterprise.

It is doubtful that the Framers had corporations in mind when they authorized jurisdiction over cases between "citizens of different states" in Article III,

Section 2. Corporations were rare in 1787, and it seems odd to think of a corporation—an intangible legal entity—as a "citizen." The Supreme Court initially rejected the idea that a corporation could invoke diversity jurisdiction under Article III, Section 2. *Bank of United States v. Deveaux*, 9 U.S. 61 (1809). Ultimately, however, "[t]he increased use of the corporate device as a means of doing business and the desire of these corporations to resort to the federal courts proved irresistible." *Wright & Kane* § 27, p. 165. In 1844, the Supreme Court reversed itself, holding that a corporation could invoke the diversity jurisdiction of the federal courts. *Louisville, Cincinnati, & Charleston R.R. Co. v. Letson*, 43 U.S. 497 (1844).

Once the Supreme Court held that corporations are state citizens, it had to provide some test for determining the state citizenship of a corporation. Initially, the Court held that corporations would be viewed as citizens of the state in which they were incorporated, that is, the state that grants them their corporate charter, allowing them to operate as a corporation under the laws of the chartering state. *Marshall v. Baltimore & Ohio R.R. Co.*, 57 U.S. 314 (1853). Thus, a corporation incorporated in New Mexico was a New Mexico citizen and could sue parties from states other than New Mexico in federal court under diversity jurisdiction.

This rule prevailed for a century without causing too many problems. Most corporations did business in only one state and incorporated under the laws of that state. So designating them as "local" in the state of incorporation made sense.

However, in the twentieth century, corporations increasingly chose to incorporate in one state even though they conducted their operations in another—or in many others. Many corporations incorporated in Delaware for business reasons, although all their productive activity was conducted elsewhere. Silver Mining Company might incorporate in Delaware to take advantage of the Delaware incorporation laws, even though all of its mines are in Nevada. If so, the *Marshall* rule would treat Silver Mining as a citizen of Delaware, even though it has no employees, activities, or facilities in Delaware. Silver Mining would be diverse from a Nevada citizen, although in every practical sense it is "local" in Nevada if it is local anywhere.

This anomaly led Congress to enact 28 U.S.C. § 1332(c) (now § 1332(c)(1)), which provides that a corporation shall be deemed a citizen of "every State and foreign state by which it has been incorporated and of the State or foreign state where it has its principal place of business." The statute makes corporations "local" in the state where their principal place of business is located, eliminating diversity suits between the corporation and citizens of that state.

Notes and Questions on § 1332(c)(1)

Q **1. Solving one problem....** How does the statute eliminate the anomaly represented by the Silver Mining example?

A The statute makes Silver Mining a citizen of both Delaware *and* Nevada. That is, under § 1332(c)(1) the corporation has dual citizenship. Thus, there is no longer diversity jurisdiction over a case between it and a Nevada citizen.

Q **2. Corporations with large operations in multiple states.** Suppose that Nevada is Silver Mining's principal place of business, but it also has a mine in Wyoming. Is it diverse from a Wyoming citizen?

A Yes. Section 1332(c)(1) refers to "*the* State or foreign state" where the corporation has its principal place of business. (Emphasis supplied.) Courts have interpreted this to mean that a corporation can have only one principal place of business for diversity purposes. Even if a corporation does a great deal of business in other states, it will not be deemed a citizen of those other states. Silver Mining is a citizen of Nevada, but not of Wyoming.

Q **3. Citizenship in the state of incorporation.** Suppose that Silver Mining, which does no business in Delaware, is sued by a Delaware citizen. Is there diversity?

A No. Section 1332(c)(1) makes the corporation a citizen of both its state of incorporation and the state of its principal place of business. Thus, Silver Mining is a citizen of Nevada and of Delaware and is not diverse from either a Nevada or a Delaware citizen. Since Silver Mining has no physical presence or activity in Delaware, this seems anomalous; Delaware citizens will not think of Silver Mining as a local entity. However, incorporation—which for corporations is an act of creation— is such a profound connection to a state that the statute treats corporations as "local" in the state of incorporation as well as the state of their principal place of business.

4. ...but creating other problems. While § 1332(c)(1) alleviates one problem, it creates another. It requires the courts to determine a corporation's "principal place of business." In most cases, choosing the principal place of business is a no-brainer, because the corporation only does business in one state. The local hardware store in Grand Rapids, Michigan or Arlington, Texas, for example, is probably a corporation, doing business only in one location and incorporated in that state. However, in some cases determining a corporation's principal place of business is problematic. Which state should be considered the principal place of business of the corporations described below?

- Olson Corporation manufactures picture frames and mirrors at a factory in Winona, Mississippi. The factory employs 113 people. Olson has bank accounts and handles accounts payable and receivable from Winona. It purchases most of its supplies in Mississippi. Its marketing manager lives in Texas. Its corporate offices are in Chicago, Illinois, at which major financial decisions are made, accounting and taxes are handled and records are kept, corporate officers have their offices, and the board of directors meets. It has thirty-five sales representatives scattered around the country.
- Steadfast Investments, Inc., a financial services company, has offices in seventeen states, from which employees advise individual and corporate clients on investments. It has clients in every state and does most of its business by phone and e-mail. The largest office is in New York. The largest dollar value of investments under management is in California. The headquarters of the company is in Texas. The branch offices are coordinated from the Texas office and administrative functions such as preparing accounting statements and tax returns are handled there. The corporate officers have their offices there.

The lower federal courts struggled with this interpretive problem for fifty years after § 1332(c)(1) was enacted, without guidance from the Supreme Court. Some courts applied a "nerve center" test, under which the corporate headquarters was deemed the corporation's principal place of business. These courts would conclude that Olson's principal place of business was in Illinois and Steadfast's in Texas. Other courts focused on the corporation's daily operations rather than high-level management. In the Olson example, these latter courts would conclude that Mississippi was the corporation's principal place of business, because its daily production activities took place there and people would interact regularly with Olson employees there. The Steadfast example raised particular problems: Not only were the nerve center and the place of daily operations in different states, but the daily operations were widespread. Even if the court used a daily operations test, it still had to choose among various states that might claim to be the center of those operations.

READING *HERTZ CORP. v. FRIEND.* In *Hertz Corporation*, the Supreme Court finally addressed the proper test for a corporation's principal place of business. The Court reviews the history of the application of diversity jurisdiction to corporations and the problem of determining a corporation's principal place of business. And, unequivocally, it resolves this long running interpretive debate among the courts of appeals.

- What test for principal place of business did the lower courts apply to Hertz?
- What test did the Supreme Court endorse?
- What three reasons does it offer in support of its choice?
- How would the Court's test apply to the *Olson* case described immediately above?
- Where would Hertz be more likely to be viewed as "local"—New Jersey or California?

HERTZ CORP. v. FRIEND

559 U.S. 77 (2010)

Justice Breyer delivered the opinion of the Court.

The federal diversity jurisdiction statute provides that "a corporation shall be deemed to be a citizen of any State by which it has been incorporated *and of the State where it has its principal place of business.*" 28 U.S.C. § 1332(c)(1) (emphasis added). We seek here to resolve different interpretations that the Circuits have given this phrase. In doing so, we place primary weight upon the need for judicial administration of a jurisdictional statute to remain as simple as possible. And we conclude that the phrase "principal place of business" refers to the place where the corporation's high level officers direct, control, and coordinate the corporation's activities. Lower federal courts have often metaphorically called that place the corporation's "nerve center." We believe that the "nerve center" will typically be found at a corporation's headquarters.

I

[Eds.—In *Hertz,* two California citizens, Melinda Friend and John Nhieu, sued the Hertz Corporation on a state law wage and hour claim. They brought

the action in state court, but Hertz removed to federal court, claiming that the case was within the federal diversity jurisdiction. Hertz was incorporated in Delaware and argued that its principal place of business (its other state citizenship under 28 U.S.C. §1332(c)(1)) was in New Jersey, where the corporation's headquarters was located. The plaintiffs argued that Hertz's principal place of business was in California, because California had the largest share of Hertz's rental locations, employees and revenue. Whether the case was properly removed thus depended on the meaning of the phrase "principal place of business" in § 1332(c)(1).] . . .

IV

The phrase "principal place of business" has proved more difficult to apply than its originators likely expected. . . .

After Congress' amendment [Eds.—**making corporations citizens of their principal place of business]**, courts were similarly uncertain as to where to look to determine a corporation's principal place of business for diversity purposes. If a corporation's headquarters and executive offices were in the same State in which it did most of its business, the test seemed straightforward. The "principal place of business" was located in that State.

But suppose those corporate headquarters, including executive offices, are in one State, while the corporation's plants or other centers of business activity are located in other States? In 1959 a distinguished federal district judge, Edward Weinfeld, relied on the Second Circuit's interpretation of the Bankruptcy Act to answer this question in part:

> "Where a corporation is engaged in far-flung and varied activities which are carried on in different states, its principal place of business is the nerve center from which it radiates out to its constituent parts and from which its officers direct, control and coordinate all activities without regard to locale, in the furtherance of the corporate objective. The test applied by our Court of Appeals, is that place where the corporation has an 'office from which its business was directed and controlled'—the place where 'all of its business was under the supreme direction and control of its officers.'" *Scot Typewriter Co.,* 170 F. Supp., at 865.

Numerous Circuits have since followed this rule, applying the "nerve center" test for corporations with "far-flung" business activities.

Scot's analysis, however, did not go far enough. For it did not answer what courts should do when the operations of the corporation are not "far-flung" but rather limited to only a few States. When faced with this question, various courts have focused more heavily on where a corporation's actual business activities are located.

Perhaps because corporations come in many different forms, involve many different kinds of business activities, and locate offices and plants for different reasons in different ways in different regions, a general "business activities" approach has proved unusually difficult to apply. Courts must decide which factors are more important than others: for example, plant location, sales or servicing centers; transactions, payrolls, or revenue generation.

The number of factors grew as courts explicitly combined aspects of the "nerve center" and "business activity" tests to look to a corporation's "total activities," sometimes to try to determine what treatises have described as the corporation's "center of gravity." . . .

This complexity may reflect an unmediated judicial effort to apply the statutory phrase "principal place of business" in light of the general purpose of diversity jurisdiction, *i.e.*, an effort to find the State where a corporation is least likely to suffer out-of-state prejudice when it is sued in a local court. But, if so, that task seems doomed to failure. After all, the relevant purposive concern—prejudice against an out-of-state party—will often depend upon factors that courts cannot easily measure, for example, a corporation's image, its history, and its advertising, while the factors that courts can more easily measure, for example, its office or plant location, its sales, its employment, or the nature of the goods or services it supplies, will sometimes bear no more than a distant relation to the likelihood of prejudice. At the same time, this approach is at war with administrative simplicity. And it has failed to achieve a nationally uniform interpretation of federal law, an unfortunate consequence in a federal legal system.

V

A

In an effort to find a single, more uniform interpretation of the statutory phrase, we have reviewed the Courts of Appeals' divergent and increasingly complex interpretations. Having done so, we now return to, and expand, Judge Weinfeld's approach, as applied in the Seventh Circuit. We conclude that "principal place of business" is best read as referring to the place where a corporation's officers direct, control, and coordinate the corporation's activities. It is the place that Courts of Appeals have called the corporation's "nerve center." And in practice it should normally be the place where the corporation maintains its headquarters—provided that the headquarters is the actual center of direction, control, and coordination, *i.e.*, the "nerve center," and not simply an office where the corporation holds its board meetings (for example, attended by directors and officers who have traveled there for the occasion).

Three sets of considerations, taken together, convince us that this approach, while imperfect, is superior to other possibilities. First, the statute's language supports the approach. The statute's text deems a corporation a citizen of the "State where it has its principal place of business." 28 U.S.C. § 1332(c)(1). The word "place" is in the singular, not the plural. The word "principal" requires us to pick out the "main, prominent" or "leading" place. 12 Oxford English Dictionary 495 (2d ed. 1989) (def. (A)(I)(2)). Cf. *Commissioner v. Soliman,* 506 U.S. 168, 174 (1993) (interpreting "principal place of business" for tax purposes to require an assessment of "whether any one business location is the 'most important, consequential, or influential' one"). And the fact that the word "place" follows the words "State where" means that the "place" is a place *within* a State. It is not the State itself.

A corporation's "nerve center," usually its main headquarters, is a single place. The public often (though not always) considers it the corporation's main place of business. And it is a place within a State. By contrast, the application of a more general business activities test has led some courts, as in the present case, to look, not at a particular place within a State, but incorrectly at the State itself, measuring the total amount of business activities that the corporation conducts there and determining whether they are "significantly larger" than in the next-ranking State.

This approach invites greater litigation and can lead to strange results, as the Ninth Circuit has since recognized. Namely, if a "corporation may be deemed a citizen of California on th[e] basis" of "activities [that] roughly reflect California's larger population . . . nearly every national retailer—no matter how far flung its operations—will be deemed a citizen of California for diversity purposes." *Davis v. HSBC Bank Nev., N.A.*, 557 F.3d 1026, 1029-1030 (2009). But why award or decline diversity jurisdiction on the basis of a State's population, whether measured directly, indirectly (say proportionately), or with modifications?

Second, administrative simplicity is a major virtue in a jurisdictional statute. Complex jurisdictional tests complicate a case, eating up time and money as the parties litigate, not the merits of their claims, but which court is the right court to decide those claims. Complex tests produce appeals and reversals, encourage gamesmanship, and, again, diminish the likelihood that results and settlements will reflect a claim's legal and factual merits. Judicial resources too are at stake. Courts have an independent obligation to determine whether subject-matter jurisdiction exists, even when no party challenges it. So courts benefit from straightforward rules under which they can readily assure themselves of their power to hear a case.

Simple jurisdictional rules also promote greater predictability. Predictability is valuable to corporations making business and investment decisions. Predictability also benefits plaintiffs deciding whether to file suit in a state or federal court.

A "nerve center" approach, which ordinarily equates that "center" with a corporation's headquarters, is simple to apply *comparatively speaking*. The metaphor of a corporate "brain," while not precise, suggests a single location. By contrast, a corporation's general business activities more often lack a single principal place where they take place. That is to say, the corporation may have several plants, many sales locations, and employees located in many different places. If so, it will not be as easy to determine which of these different business locales is the "principal" or most important "place."

Third, the statute's legislative history, for those who accept it, offers a simplicity-related interpretive benchmark. The Judicial Conference provided an initial version of its proposal that suggested a numerical test. A corporation would be deemed a citizen of the State that accounted for more than half of its gross income. The Conference changed its mind in light of criticism that such a test would prove too complex and impractical to apply. That history suggests that the words "principal place of business" should be interpreted to be no more complex than the initial "half of gross income" test. A "nerve center" test offers such a possibility. A general business activities test does not.

B

We recognize that there may be no perfect test that satisfies all administrative and purposive criteria. We recognize as well that, under the "nerve center" test we adopt today, there will be hard cases. For example, in this era of telecommuting, some corporations may divide their command and coordinating functions among officers who work at several different locations, perhaps communicating over the Internet. That said, our test nonetheless points courts in a single direction, towards the center of overall direction, control, and coordination. Courts do not have to try to weigh corporate functions, assets, or revenues different in kind, one from the other. Our approach provides a sensible test that is relatively easier to apply, not a test that will, in all instances, automatically generate a result.

Rule? We also recognize that the use of a "nerve center" test may in some cases produce results that seem to cut against the basic rationale for 28 U.S.C. § 1332. For example, if the bulk of a company's business activities visible to the public take place in New Jersey, while its top officers direct those activities just across the river in New York, the "principal place of business" is New York. One could argue that members of the public in New Jersey would be *less* likely to be prejudiced against the corporation than persons in New York—yet the corporation will still be entitled to remove a New Jersey state case to federal court. And note too that the same corporation would be unable to remove a New York state case to federal court, despite the New York public's presumed prejudice against the corporation.

We understand that such seeming anomalies will arise. However, in view of the necessity of having a clearer rule, we must accept them. Accepting occasionally counterintuitive results is the price the legal system must pay to avoid overly complex jurisdictional administration while producing the benefits that accompany a more uniform legal system.

The burden of persuasion for establishing diversity jurisdiction, of course, remains on the party asserting it. When challenged on allegations of jurisdictional facts, the parties must support their allegations by competent proof. And when faced with such a challenge, we reject suggestions such as, for example, the one made by petitioner that the mere filing of a form like the Securities and Exchange Commission's Form 10-K listing a corporation's "principal executive offices" would, without more, be sufficient proof to establish a corporation's "nerve center." Such possibilities would readily permit jurisdictional manipulation, thereby subverting a major reason for the insertion of the "principal place of business" language in the diversity statute. Indeed, if the record reveals attempts at manipulation—for example, that the alleged "nerve center" is nothing more than a mail drop box, a bare office with a computer, or the location of an annual executive retreat—the courts should instead take as the "nerve center" the place of actual direction, control, and coordination, in the absence of such manipulation.

VI

Petitioner's unchallenged declaration suggests that Hertz's center of direction, control, and coordination, its "nerve center," and its corporate headquarters are one and the same, and they are located in New Jersey, not in California. Because respondents should have a fair opportunity to litigate their case in light of our holding, however, we vacate the Ninth Circuit's judgment and remand the case for further proceedings consistent with this opinion.

It is so ordered.

Notes and Questions: Corporate Citizenship for Diversity

Q **1. An anomalous result?** After the *Hertz* case, where is Olson Company's principal place of business under § 1332(c)(1)? (See note 4 on page 63.)

A Olson's principal place of business is in Illinois under *Hertz,* since its corporate headquarters is there. Ironically, very few people in Illinois will know that Olson has its home office in Illinois or think of it as "local" in Illinois. By contrast, Olson may be Winona, Mississippi's largest employer and highly visible due to its local purchases and employees. Under the *Hertz* decision, Olson would be deemed local in Illinois but an outsider in Mississippi. This choice seems at odds with the underlying purpose of diversity jurisdiction, to provide a federal forum for parties likely to suffer prejudice based on the perception that they are "out-of-staters." Olson Company can sue a Mississippi vendor of supplies in federal court, but it could not sue an Illinois citizen in federal court under diversity jurisdiction.

2. The virtue of clear jurisdictional rules. The *Hertz* Court notes that the lower courts' tests for principal place of business had spawned considerable litigation about a procedural issue. Ideally, the Court notes, litigants should spend their time litigating the merits of their dispute, not procedural issues. However, parties often contest issues like subject matter and personal jurisdiction aggressively because they think that they have a better chance of winning on the merits in one court than another, for a variety of tactical reasons.

Sometimes it makes sense to have relatively blunt procedural rules—even if we can think of more finely tuned alternatives—so that the parties will not spend time and money litigating procedural issues. We have already seen one fairly blunt rule—assessing diversity based on the date of filing of the lawsuit. A more nuanced rule might match the underlying policy reasons for diversity jurisdiction more closely, but the day-of-filing rule works well enough in the run of cases. The greater accuracy of a "better" rule may not be worth the increased litigation that comes with a more complex standard.

The *Hertz* Court clearly accepts this premise in opting for the nerve center or corporate headquarters test for principal place of business: "We also recognize that the use of a 'nerve center' test may in some cases produce results that seem to cut against the basic rationale for 28 U.S.C. § 1332." But the test will point to an appropriate state in most cases, and the simpler test (as opposed to the fact-bound center-of-operations test) will reduce litigation and promote predictability.

3. Tougher cases: Corporate activity in multiple states. Prior to *Hertz,* courts struggled to choose a principal place of business when the high-level corporate decision making took place at corporate headquarters in one state, and the daily management and business activity was spread among a number of states. In *Kelly v. United States Steel Co.,* 284 F.2d 850 (3d Cir. 1960), United States Steel Corporation had its corporate headquarters in New York. The corporation filed its tax returns there; the board of directors met there; the executive committee, the finance committee, the corporation's major banking activities and the management of its government securities and pension plan were all centered there; the chairman of the board, the president, the secretary, the treasurer, and general counsel had their offices there. Thus, high-altitude decisions on corporate policy were made in New York.

However, daily management of the corporation's business was delegated to the operation policy committee in Pennsylvania, so that even a nerve center test might point there. All of the executive vice presidents and most of the other vice presidents and their staffs were in Pennsylvania, which also had far more employees and tangible property than New York or any other state. There was also a good deal of business in other states—Pennsylvania accounted for about a third of the productive activity of the corporation. The Third Circuit held that "business by way of activities is centered in Pennsylvania and we think it is the activities rather than the occasional meeting of policy-making Directors which indicate the principal place of business." *Id.* at 854.

After *Hertz,* New York would be U.S. Steel's principal place of business, even though everyone in Pittsburgh knew in 1960 that U.S. Steel was a huge local employer—they even named the local football team the Steelers.

Q **4. Manipulating jurisdiction.** Suppose that Hertz Corporation, intent on suing a New Jersey citizen in federal court, were to move its corporate headquarters to Wisconsin, to "create diversity." Would the parties be diverse?

A Corporations have done this on occasion, and the Court has found diversity satisfied as long as the corporation really did change its citizenship. In *Black & White Taxicab & Transfer Co. v. Brown & Yellow Taxicab & Transfer Co.,* 276 U.S. 518 (1928), a Kentucky corporation dissolved itself and reincorporated in Tennessee to become diverse from a Kentucky corporation. The Supreme Court held that, since it had legally become a Tennessee corporation, it was diverse, and refused to entertain arguments about its motivation for doing so. *Hertz* might be criticized on the ground that it may lead to similar manipulation by small corporations. However, it would rarely make sense for a corporation to uproot its corporate offices and move to another state just to invoke federal jurisdiction in a particular case.

5. More square pegs: Unincorporated associations and other entities. In addition to corporations, a variety of other entities exist for both business and non-business purposes. Some examples are unincorporated associations (such as labor unions, churches, and advocacy groups), partnerships, subsidiaries and divisions of corporations, cooperatives, nonprofit corporations, and professional corporations. State legislatures have authorized even more exotic forms of business organizations, such as limited liability partnerships, limited liability limited partnerships, and others. Section 1332(c)(1) does not specify how such entities are to be treated, so the courts have had to analogize them to corporations or to a collection of individuals in determining their state citizenship. Since these pegs are really neither square nor round, courts inevitably have problems fitting them into either category.

Partnerships and unincorporated associations have been treated as groups of individual litigants, not as corporations. *See Chapman v. Barney,* 129 U.S. 677 (1889) (partnerships); *United Steel Workers of America AFL-CIO v. R.H. Bouligny, Inc.,* 382 U.S. 145 (1965) (unions). Thus, the citizenship of each partner or member of the association is considered in determining whether there is diversity between the partners or members and the parties on the other side of the case. If Monez,

Parker and Shin, a law partnership, sues Local 421 of the Pipefitters Union, an unincorporated association, to collect a legal fee, there would not be diversity if any partner in the law firm was from the same state as any member of the union.

In *Carden v. Arkoma Associates*, 494 U.S. 185 (1990), the Supreme Court considered how to determine the state citizenship of a limited partnership for diversity purposes. A limited partnership has general partners, who conduct the operations of the partnership, and limited partners, who are in effect passive investors akin to corporate stockholders. The Court held that the citizenship of the limited partners had to be considered. *Carden* suggests that the Court will not treat various business entities like corporations for diversity purposes just because they may function like them in some respects. Instead, the Court will rely primarily on how the entity is characterized under state law.

For example, professional corporations such as law firms or medical practice groups that incorporate under professional corporation statutes have been treated as corporations for diversity purposes. *See, e.g., Hoagland v. Sandberg, Phoenix & von Gontard P.C.*, 385 F.3d 737 (7th Cir. 2004). These entities are created under state incorporation statutes, not as common law associations. They are *called* corporations. Even though, in some respects, they operate like partnerships, most courts have concluded that, since they are created as corporate entities, they should be treated like other corporations under 28 U.S.C. § 1332(c)(1). By contrast, federal courts have treated limited liability companies like partnerships, even though they resemble corporations in some respects, because they are not called corporations and resemble limited partnerships. *See, e.g., Harvey v. Grey Wolf Drilling Co.*, 542 F.3d 1077, 1080 (5th Cir. 2008).

Q **6. Applying the test to a partnership.** Rota, a Pennsylvania citizen, sues Matthews, Bernstein, Rollins and Grey, a 120-person law firm with offices in New York City. Her claim is for fraud. Most of the partners live in New York, but ten live in New Jersey and one in Pennsylvania. Is this a diversity case?

A No. The law firm is considered to be a citizen of New York, New Jersey, and Pennsylvania. As a result, there is no complete diversity. Since the claim arises under state law, and there is no diversity jurisdiction, the case must be brought in state court.

7. A perfectly horrible example. In *Hart v. Terminex International*, 336 F.3d 541 (7th Cir. 2003), two Illinois plaintiffs sued several defendants, including Terminex, a limited partnership created under Delaware law. One of the partners in the limited partnership was *itself a partnership*. The parties evidently assumed that Terminex was a Delaware citizen, but since one of the partners of Terminex was a partnership, the citizenship of the partners in that partnership had to be considered in determining diversity! Since several of the partners in the partnership-in-the-partnership were from Illinois, there was no diversity, and the case was dismissed for lack of subject matter jurisdiction after eight years of litigation. The lesson is that applying diversity to modern exotic forms of business entities is a minefield, through which litigants must tread with the utmost care.

8. A rule out of sync with its time. The *Carden* rule treats partnerships, limited liability companies, and other new forms of business organizations as collections of individuals, and therefore as citizens of the state of each member or shareholder, making it increasingly impractical as a test for diversity jurisdiction. One problem is that the membership of such business entities is frequently not a matter of public record, so a plaintiff bringing suit against the entity cannot determine if she is diverse from all members. Another is that the members or shareholders of such organizations are often complex business entities themselves, leading to a complex, multi-level analysis to determine proper state citizenship for diversity. Yet another issue is that there may be many "members" of such entities, and that those members may change—for example, when a shareholder sells her shares. Since jurisdiction is determined by the citizenship of the parties on the day of filing, extensive research may be necessary to determine the members on that date.

These problems have led courts to urge a change in the *Carden* analysis. *See, e.g., Lincoln Beneficial Life Co. v. AEI Life, LLC*, 800 F.3d 99, 111 (3d Cir. 2015), which urged the Supreme Court to reconsider the *Carden* rule. It has also spawned a report by the American Bar Association Section on Litigation recommending that Congress amend 28 U.S.C. § 1332 to provide that an unincorporated association be treated as a citizen of the state in which it has been organized and the state of its principal place of business. *See* ABA Section on Litigation, Proposed Resolution and Report, House Resolution 103B, 2015 ABA Annual Meeting, http://www.americanbar.org/content/dam/aba/administrative/house_of_delegates/resolutions/2015_hod_annual_meeting_103B.docx. Just as twentieth-century business realities led Congress to enact 28 U.S.C. § 1332(c)(1), superseding the early rule that corporations were citizens only of their state of incorporation, perhaps twenty-first-century business practices will lead to a statutory revision of the *Carden* rule.*

Q **9. "Perfecting" diversity.** Jiminez, a Colorado plaintiff, sues three defendants, Kramer and Jost (two individuals from Wyoming) and Delta Corporation, incorporated in Wyoming with a good deal of business in Wyoming and Colorado. Just before trial, Delta moves to dismiss, claiming that Colorado is its principal place of business. The court takes evidence and hears argument on the issue and concludes that Delta is right. Consequently, it is a citizen of both Wyoming (based on incorporation) and Colorado (based on its principal place of business). Must the court dismiss the case?

A The court cannot hear the case as originally framed because there is not complete diversity. However, it need not dismiss the entire suit; it can order Delta dropped as a defendant, thus "perfecting diversity," and continue with the case against the two individual defendants.

In *Caterpillar Inc. v. Lewis,* 519 U.S. 61 (1996), the case was removed to federal court improperly, since there was a non-diverse defendant. Just before trial the non-diverse defendant settled and was dismissed, thus perfecting diversity. The Supreme Court held that the lower court had jurisdiction to try the case and enter a valid judgment, since proper federal jurisdiction existed at the time the judgment was entered. *See also Newman-Green, Inc. v. Alfonso-Larrain*, 490 U.S. 826 (1989) (court of appeals properly ordered non-diverse party dropped to perfect diversity).

These cases seem inconsistent with the established rule that jurisdiction is assessed as of the time of filing. When the *Caterpillar* litigation arrived in the

* However, the Supreme Court reaffirmed the approach of the *Carden* case in 2016. *See Americold Realty Trust v. Conagra Foods, Inc.*, 136 S. Ct. 1012 (2016).

federal court (via removal from state court), the court lacked jurisdiction. However, because the jurisdictional defect was cured before the case went to judgment, the Supreme Court concluded that it made no sense to vacate the judgment and make the parties start over in state court.

> In this case . . . no jurisdictional defect lingered through judgment in the District Court. To wipe out the adjudication postjudgment, and return to state court a case now satisfying all federal jurisdictional requirements, would impose an exorbitant cost on our dual court system, a cost incompatible with the fair and unprotracted administration of justice.

519 U.S. at 77. Based on this reasoning, if the court of appeals in *Mas v. Perry* had concluded that Mrs. Mas was domiciled in Louisiana, it could have dismissed her claim for lack of subject matter jurisdiction and entered judgment against Perry on Mr. Mas's claim.

10. Applying the complete diversity rule. Consider the following question concerning diversity jurisdiction in *Corey v. Barristers*.

> You represent Corey in his bar fight case and would like to file the case in federal court based on diversity jurisdiction. Assume that Corey is a citizen of Massachusetts, based on his domicile there. Barristers is incorporated in Delaware. It owns and operates eight bars in Massachusetts. It also owns and operates one in Rhode Island, two in Connecticut, and one in Maine. Its corporate headquarters is in Rhode Island.
>
> A federal court would
>
> A. have diversity jurisdiction, even if Barrister's principal place of business is in Massachusetts, because Corey is a citizen of Massachusetts and Barristers is a citizen of Delaware.
> B. have diversity jurisdiction, because Corey is a citizen of Massachusetts and Barristers is a citizen of Rhode Island and Delaware.
> C. lack diversity jurisdiction, because both Corey and Barristers are citizens of Massachusetts.
> D. lack diversity jurisdiction, if the suit is brought in Massachusetts, since Corey is domiciled there.

D here is a real dog. It suggests that there is no diversity jurisdiction if the plaintiff is a citizen of the state in which she brings the suit. Not so; to determine diversity we compare the plaintiff's citizenship to that of the defendant, not to the state in which she sues.

A is also based on a misconception. Under § 1332(c)(1), the corporation is a citizen of *both* the state in which it is incorporated and the state of its principal place of business. Corey cannot argue that there is diversity here because he is from Massachusetts and Barristers is from Delaware. If Barristers has its principal place of business in Massachusetts, it is *also* a citizen of Massachusetts. The case would be between a citizen of Massachusetts and a citizen of Delaware *and Massachusetts*, so there would not be complete diversity.

So the answer to this question turns on whether Barristers's principal place of business is in Massachusetts or Rhode Island. Here's the answer we wrote before *Hertz* was decided:

> If the court applies the "headquarters" test, Barristers' principal place of business is Rhode Island, and **B** is the best answer. If it applies the daily activities test, the answer is less clear. Probably, for a business that runs local bars, and has most of them concentrated in one state, the court would focus on where it sells pints, rather than the corporate headquarters. Barristers exists to sell beer and sells considerably more of it in Massachusetts than other states. Thus, Barristers would have more interaction with the citizenry in Massachusetts and would be viewed as local by many more people in Massachusetts. Likely, a court would hold that its principal place of business is Massachusetts, making **C** the best answer.

That answer is now obsolete. Under *Hertz*, Barristers' principal place of business is determined by its headquarters. Since that is in Rhode Island, **B** is the right answer.

V. The Amount-in-Controversy Requirement

Nothing in Article III, Section 2 requires a minimum amount in controversy in diversity cases. However, Congress has chosen to keep minor diversity cases out of federal court by including an amount-in-controversy requirement in the diversity statute. Congress set the requirement at $500 in 1789 and has periodically raised it, most recently to $75,000 in 1996. The amount has been set "not so high as to convert the Federal courts into courts of big business or so low as to fritter away their time in the trial of petty controversies."*

Limiting jurisdiction by an amount-in-controversy requirement creates a paradox for the courts. How is the court to know how much is "in controversy" without trying the case? The plaintiff might claim a million dollars for a slight insult. Or, she might sue for intangible injuries such as pain and suffering, loss of reputation, or emotional distress, which are difficult to value without actually trying facts. Yet the court cannot wait until trial to determine whether it has jurisdiction over the case. Courts need to decide at the outset whether they have jurisdiction; otherwise, they could spend considerable time and resources handling a case, only to decide later that they had no power to do so.

The federal courts need some rule of thumb for assessing at the outset whether the required amount is "in controversy" in such cases. The Supreme Court provided one in *St. Paul Mercury Indemnity Co. v. Red Cab Co.*, 303 U.S. 283 (1938). In *St. Paul Mercury*, the Court held that the plaintiff's claim for more than the required amount will generally be accepted, if it appears to be made in good faith, unless it "appear[s] to a legal certainty that the claim is really for less than the jurisdictional amount." 303 U.S. at 289. Under the *St. Paul Mercury* test, the judge will look at the injuries the plaintiff has alleged in the complaint and ask herself whether it is possible that a jury could award more than $75,000 for those injuries. If it could, then more than $75,000 is in controversy; if not, the case will be dismissed.

* S. Rep. No. 1830, 85th Cong., 2d Sess. p.4 (1958), 1958 U.S.C.C.A.N. 3099, 3101.

The *St. Paul Mercury* test gives the plaintiff the benefit of the doubt. If she will probably recover more than $75,000, but might not, the amount requirement is met. If she probably will *not* recover that much but conceivably could, the amount is met. Only where the judge, looking at the facts and supporting evidence, is convinced that the claim is certainly not worth more than $75,000 will she dismiss for failure to meet the amount requirement.

READING *DIEFENTHAL v. C.A.B.* There's a difference between giving the plaintiff the benefit of the doubt and accepting whatever number the plaintiff's lawyer demands in the complaint—the latter would render the amount-in-controversy requirement a dead letter. The *Diefenthal* case, below, illustrates that difference. In reading *Diefenthal,* keep in mind that at the time it was decided the amount in controversy was required to exceed $10,000.

- In their complaint, the plaintiffs each sought $50,000 in damages. Doesn't that satisfy the amount in controversy?
- What further evidence did the judge in *Diefenthal* want the plaintiffs to submit to demonstrate that the amount requirement was met?
- Why didn't they provide such evidence?

DIEFENTHAL v. C.A.B.

681 F.2d 1039 (5th Cir. 1982)

CLARK, Chief Judge:

Stanley and Elka Diefenthal appeal from the district court's order dismissing their claims against the Civil Aeronautics Board (CAB) and Eastern Airlines. They also petition for review of a CAB order finding that regulating smoking was within the scope of its statutory authorization. We affirm.

I

The Diefenthals purchased first class tickets aboard a flight from New Orleans to Philadelphia on Eastern Airlines. They requested seats in the smoking section and confirmed that their request was granted prior to departure. After they boarded the flight, the Diefenthals were told that the smoking section in first class was filled and that they would have to sit in a no-smoking area if they wished to fly first class. The Diefenthals alleged that in informing them that they could not smoke the flight attendant treated them "brusquely," causing them extreme embarrassment, humiliation and emotional distress.

This relatively trivial incident has given rise to a spate of litigation. The Diefenthals [sued the Civilian Aeronautics Board on various theories and further] alleged that Eastern had breached its contract with them by denying them first class seats in a smoking area and that it had tortiously embarrassed and humiliated them and deprived them of their right to smoke on board the plane. Eastern moved to dismiss the complaint for failure to state a claim on which relief could be granted....

The district court dismissed the Diefenthals' contract and tort claims for lack of diversity jurisdiction. With respect to the contract claim, the district court found that even though the parties were diverse, it could not "conceive by the wildest stretch of the imagination how there could be $10,000.00 damage on the basis of what [the Diefenthals] allege."

With respect to the tort claim, . . . it allowed the Diefenthals to amend their complaint to allege that the actions of Eastern's employees had tortiously humiliated and embarrassed them. The court expressly cautioned the Diefenthals that the jurisdictional amount would again be in question. . . .

The amended complaint alleged that an unknown flight attendant "maliciously, and intentionally treated plaintiffs in a manner calculated to cause plaintiffs serious embarrassment and humiliation." Eastern moved to dismiss the complaint for lack of subject matter jurisdiction. At a hearing on Eastern's motion to dismiss, the district court noted that the Diefenthals had not alleged any physical or emotional damage or loss of reputation. Although the Diefenthals never stated exactly what the flight attendant had said, the court found that it could not "conceive how being told, no matter how abruptly, that you cannot smoke before the few passengers that are in the first class cabin of an airplane can possibly, in the absence of some [physical or emotional] damage . . . entitle [the Diefenthals] to $10,000.00." . . .

IV

The district court dismissed the Diefenthals' contract and tort claims against Eastern for lack of diversity jurisdiction. Even though the parties were diverse, the court found that it could not conceive how the inquiries alleged satisfied the requisite $10,000 limitation. *See* 28 U.S.C. § 1332. The Diefenthals argue that because their request for $50,000 in damages was made in good faith the district court had jurisdiction. We disagree.

Before considering the merits of the Diefenthals' argument, it is important to review the allegations made in their complaint. The plaintiffs initially alleged only that the stewardess had "brusquely" informed them that there were no vacant seats in the first-class smoking section. Because of her manner, they claimed that they were "damaged, embarrassed, humiliated and were deprived of their right to smoke during said flight." During the first hearing on Eastern's motion to dismiss, the district court judge told the Diefenthals' counsel that he doubted highly that the damages alleged amounted to $10,000. . . .

The amended complaint alleged only that a flight attendant "maliciously and intentionally treated plaintiffs in a manner calculated to cause plaintiffs serious embarrassment and humiliation." No physical contact was asserted. The complaint did not allege that any physical or emotional impairment or loss of reputation resulted from the stewardess' actions, nor did it seek punitive damages. It simply alleged that the stewardess' remarks were brusque and intentional and that they had resulted in $50,000 worth of humiliation. When Eastern moved to dismiss for lack of jurisdiction, the Diefenthals did not attempt to support their complaint with affidavits which might have revealed some factual basis of their claim for damages. They simply rested on the unsupported allegation that the stewardess' actions humiliated them.

In *St. Paul Mercury Indemnity Co. v. Red Cab Co.*, 303 U.S. 283, 288 (1938), the Court stated:

> The rule governing dismissal for want of jurisdiction in cases brought in the federal court is that, unless the law gives a different rule, the sum claimed by the plaintiff controls if the claim is apparently made in good faith. It must appear to a legal certainty that the claim is really far less than the jurisdictional amount to justify dismissal.*

The Court, however, also noted that the party invoking the court's jurisdiction bears the burden of "alleg[ing] with sufficient particularity the facts creating jurisdiction" and of "support[ing] the allegation" if challenged. *See id.* at 287 n.10. In order to meet this burden, a party may amend the pleadings, as was done in this case, or may submit affidavits. This procedure provides a court with a basis for making a threshold determination as to whether the jurisdictional amount has been satisfied.

In establishing the jurisdictional amount, Congress intended to set a figure "not so high as to convert the Federal Courts into courts of big business nor so low as to fritter away their time in the trial of petty controversies." Sen. Rep. No. 1830, 85th Cong., 2d Sess. *reprinted in* 1958 U.S. Code Cong. & Ad. News 3099, 3101 (explaining the $10,000 threshold figure). While a federal court must of course give due credit to the good faith claims of the plaintiff, a court would be remiss in its obligations if it accepted every claim of damages at face value, no matter how trivial the underlying injury. This is especially so when, after jurisdiction has been challenged, a party has failed to specify the factual basis of his claims. Jurisdiction is not conferred by the stroke of a lawyer's pen. When challenged, it must be adequately founded in fact.

In the case at bar, the only specific factual incident alleged was that the stewardess had brusquely told the Diefenthals that there were no vacant seats left in the first-class smoking section. The amended complaint merely alleged that the stewardess had intended to humiliate the plaintiffs. It failed to demonstrate how the Diefenthals had suffered anything more than a trivial loss. Even though the Diefenthals were aware that both the court and Eastern questioned the factual basis of their damage claim, they wholly failed to specify that basis.

To a legal certainty, the brusque refusal by a stewardess to permit a passenger to sit in a particular smoking section, even a refusal the requesting passenger asserts was intended to "humiliate," will not justify a damage claim of $10,000.[15] This aspect of the suit is precisely the kind of "petty controversy" that Congress intended the jurisdictional amount to exclude from federal jurisdiction.[16]

In sum, the party invoking the court's jurisdiction has the burden of establishing the factual basis of his claim by pleading or affidavit. This allows the court to test its jurisdiction without requiring the expense and burden of a full trial on the merits. The Diefenthals were put on notice both by the court's own statements

---

*** [Eds.—The word "far" in this quotation is a misquote; the word is "for" in *St. Paul Mercury*.]**

15. Each of the Diefenthals may aggregate his tort and contract claims in order to satisfy the $10,000 jurisdictional minimum. However, because the claims are separate and distinct as to each plaintiff, the two plaintiffs may not add their own individual claims together in order to reach the jurisdictional minimum. . . .

16. At oral argument, the Diefenthal's counsel was hardpressed to explain how the jurisdictional amount was satisfied in this case. His argument rested almost solely on a plea to permit the Diefenthals to prove their claim in court.

and by Eastern's motion to dismiss for lack of jurisdiction, that they needed to show some basis for the amount of damages they claimed. They failed to do so and the district court properly dismissed their claims.

AFFIRMED.

Notes and Questions: The Amount-in-Controversy Requirement

Q **1. Master of her complaint?** How can the court conclude that there is not more than $10,000 in controversy when the plaintiffs have each claimed $50,000 in their complaint?

A Although a plaintiff is given substantial leeway in alleging damages, the damages allegations may be so far-fetched that there is no conceivable way that the damages could exceed the jurisdictional amount. The *Diefenthal* court concludes that, even though the plaintiffs have alleged damages in excess of $10,000, their factual allegations could not support a monetary recovery over $10,000. Thus, "to a legal certainty," the claim is for less and does not meet the amount requirement.

Q **2. But it *is* in good faith!** The language quoted from *St. Paul Mercury* is a little confusing. On the one hand it suggests that the plaintiff's demand will be accepted if it is made in good faith. On the other, it holds that the case should be dismissed if it appears to a legal certainty that the plaintiff could not recover the required amount. Suppose that the Diefenthals really believe that they should each recover $50,000 for the humiliation they suffered, but the judge concludes that it is legally certain that they would only be able to recover less than the required jurisdictional minimum. Should the judge dismiss the case for failure to meet the amount-in-controversy requirement?

A Yes. Although *St. Paul Mercury* talks about good faith, the Diefenthals' genuine belief that they are entitled to a large verdict will not meet the amount requirement. There must be a legal and factual basis for a recovery of the required amount. Even if a plaintiff and her lawyer are convinced that the damages exceed the jurisdictional amount, the case will be dismissed if there is no evidentiary basis to support such an award.

The goal of the amount-in-controversy requirement, as the court notes, is to keep federal courts from frittering away their resources on petty cases. Cases that cannot yield a judgment above the jurisdictional amount should be weeded out at the outset and left to the state courts, no matter how outraged the plaintiffs may be. Toward the end of the opinion the court notes that "this is precisely the kind of 'petty controversy' that Congress intended the jurisdictional amount to exclude from federal jurisdiction." It really is, isn't it? Federal courts have more important things to do than to decide whether the Diefenthals should have been allowed to smoke on their flight or were insulted by the attendant's refusal to let them.

Q **3. Hindsight is 20/20.** Santini sues Chang for serious personal injuries that would support a damage award over the required amount. However, the jury finds that Chang was not negligent and renders a verdict for her. Should the court dismiss the case after trial for failure to meet the amount-in-controversy requirement?

A No. Santini did satisfy the amount requirement. He filed a case that plausibly alleged that Chang was liable for injuries that satisfied the amount requirement. Although he lost the case, it concerned a plausible claim for more than $75,000, so the amount-in-controversy requirement was met. The judge should enter judgment for Chang on the merits.

If the judge dismissed the case for lack of subject matter jurisdiction, Santini could sue Chang again for the same claim: A dismissal for lack of jurisdiction would not bar him from suing again on the same claim. This case has been fully litigated and fairly tried. Santini lost because he couldn't prove his case, not because he failed to allege a colorable claim for more than $75,000.

Similarly, in *Mas v. Perry*, Mr. Mas recovered less than the required amount but certainly had a legitimate argument for more. As long as a reasonable jury could have awarded more than $10,000 to Mr. Mas for this intrusion on his domestic tranquility, the amount requirement was met.

Q **4. Ethical limits on insupportable claims.** The rules that govern the ethical responsibilities of lawyers, as well as court rules governing procedure, bar attorneys from asserting claims that lack a colorable basis in fact or in law. Rule 11(b)(3) of the Federal Rules of Civil Procedure requires that the factual allegations in a complaint "have evidentiary support." Would a complaint alleging that the Diefenthals' claims satisfy the amount-in-controversy requirement meet this standard?

A Perhaps not but given the difficulty of quantifying emotional distress damages, it is unlikely that the court would sanction the Diefenthals' counsel for filing the case in federal court. (There is no indication that the court did so in *Diefenthal.*)

Attorneys are also subject to ethical restraints under rules of professional conduct, usually adopted by the supreme court of the state in which they practice. Most states' rules of professional conduct are modeled on the ABA Model Rules of Professional Conduct. Model Rule 3.1 provides, "A lawyer shall not bring or defend a proceeding, or assert or controvert an issue therein, unless there is a basis for doing so that is not frivolous. . . ." The comment to Rule 3.1 indicates that an action is frivolous if "the lawyer is unable . . . to make a good faith argument on the merits of the action." Unfortunately, just as Rule 11 does not give much guidance as to what qualifies as "evidentiary support," Rule 3.1 provides no specific guidance as to what level of improbability would establish a lack of good faith and subject a lawyer to discipline.

Q **5. Legal certainty.** In *Kahn v. Hotel Ramada of Nevada*, 799 F.2d 199 (5th Cir. 1986), the plaintiff left his suitcase for safekeeping at a hotel, and it was lost. Kahn, a jewelry broker, alleged that it contained some $50,000 in jewelry (the amount at the time had to exceed $10,000). A Nevada statute limited an innkeeper's liability for lost property to $750. The hotel moved to dismiss Kahn's suit for failure to meet the amount-in-controversy requirement. What should the court do?

A The court should dismiss the case for lack of subject matter jurisdiction, since the plaintiff cannot meet the amount-in-controversy requirement. Unless the plaintiff has an argument that the statute is somehow inapplicable, there is a legal certainty that the plaintiff cannot recover more than $750, well below the required amount.

In *Kahn*, the plaintiff could not recover the jurisdictional amount because the applicable *legal remedy* limited damages to a lesser amount. The Diefenthals' case was dismissed because they could not provide a *factual basis* for a damage award above the jurisdictional amount.

6. Taking evidence on the amount-in-controversy issue. While the court must assess the amount in controversy at the outset of the case to determine its jurisdiction, it can look beyond the allegations in the complaint to decide the issue. If the amount requirement is in doubt, the plaintiff might amend her complaint to allege damages more fully or submit affidavits detailing the injuries or damage she had suffered, with supporting documentation such as medical bills. The court could even take live testimony at a hearing on the issue if necessary.

In *Diefenthal*, the Diefenthals did amend their complaint, but the amended version basically alleged the same confrontation and humiliation as the first complaint. Although the judge had challenged them to do so, the Diefenthals did not produce any supporting evidence to show that they might recover more than the jurisdictional amount. Such evidence might include bills for resulting medical treatment, lost wages or business opportunities, or some other concrete injury for which a jury could award sufficient damages.

Although the judge may look at evidence to determine whether the amount requirement is met, that does not mean that she determines the amount of the plaintiff's damages. The judge decides, under *St. Paul Mercury*, whether the evidence of the plaintiff's injuries could possibly support a jury verdict over the required amount. If it might, the amount requirement is met and the court has subject matter jurisdiction, even if the judge, were she the fact finder, might award less than the required amount.

In some states, a plaintiff is not allowed to ask for a specific dollar figure in a complaint that seeks damages for intangible, "non-economic" losses, such as pain and suffering, emotional distress, or loss of reputation. *See, e.g.*, Wa St. § 4.28.360. While this appears to make it difficult to determine whether the amount requirement is met, it really has little impact. Whether the complaint demands a specific amount or not, the judge must resolve the amount-in-controversy issue by looking at *the nature of the plaintiff's injuries*, not at a number at the end of the complaint.

Q **7. Corey's case.** What would you want to find out from Corey (our bar-fight plaintiff) in order to decide whether his case will meet the amount-in-controversy requirement?

A You need to know *the facts* about Corey's injuries to determine whether a jury could award more than $75,000 in damages. You will need to question Corey about his physical and psychological injuries, obtain copies of his medical bills, obtain an opinion from his doctor about any permanent disability from his injury. Before filing in federal court, you should consider whether the evidence you have gathered could credibly support a claim for more than $75,000. After gathering this damages evidence, draft a short memo stating what documents and testimony you would submit to convince the court that a demand for more than $75,000 is supportable, should Barristers move to dismiss for failure to meet the amount requirement. If you do that and are left with the kind of flimsy support the Diefenthals presented, file the case in state court, where there is likely no minimum amount required.

VI. Aggregating Claims to Meet the Amount Requirement

A separate problem arises in determining the amount in controversy where one or more parties assert separate claims. Essentially, courts have held that a single plaintiff may aggregate—add together—any separate claims she has against a single defendant to meet the amount-in-controversy requirement, even if the claims are unrelated. But coplaintiffs cannot add their claims together to reach the amount requirement, or add amounts demanded from different defendants.

Consider whether the amount requirement is met in the cases below. Assume that the parties are diverse and that the amounts demanded are supportable on the evidence.

A. P sues D for $20,000 for an accident claim, $30,000 for libel, and $40,000 for a contract breach.
B. P sues D1 for $40,000 and D2 for $60,000, in a single action arising from a single business dispute.
C. P sues D1 for $120,000 and D2 for $60,000, in a single action arising from a single business dispute.
D. P1 sues D for $50,000. P2 joins as a coplaintiff, asserting a claim against D for $60,000 in the action, arising from the same business dispute.

A. The amount requirement is met. A single plaintiff suing a single defendant may add together any claims she has against the defendant to meet the amount requirement, even if they are unrelated.

B. The amount requirement is not met. A plaintiff may not add claims against different defendants to meet the amount requirement (absent a common and undivided interest—see note 3 on page 83).

C. P meets the amount requirement against D1 but not against D2. She cannot add the two claims together. She is suing D1 for more than the jurisdictional amount, so that claim is proper. But her claim against D2 does not meet the amount requirement and cannot be aggregated with the claim against D1. D2 will have to be dropped from the suit.

D. No good. Neither plaintiff meets the amount requirement independently. The plaintiffs cannot add their claims together to reach the $75,000 plus threshold.

Notes and Questions: Aggregation of Claims

1. A straightforward multiple choice question, finally. Here's a question to drive home these somewhat arbitrary rules.

In which of the following cases is the amount-in-controversy requirement met as to all claims?

A. Adams sues Bickel for $40,000 for slander, and for $50,000 for an unrelated breach of contract.
B. Adams sues Bickel for $60,000 for injuries in an auto accident. Rajiv joins as a coplaintiff, claiming $50,000 from Bickel for his injuries in the same accident.
C. Lopez sues Alou for $50,000 for losses he suffered in a business deal. He also sues Antoine, as a codefendant in the same action, for $60,000 in losses Antoine caused in the same deal.
D. The amount requirement is not met in any of these cases.

The amount requirement is met in **A**, since a plaintiff may add her claims together to reach the $75,000 plus threshold, even if they are unrelated. But courts have not allowed separate plaintiffs, each with an insufficient claim, to join together in a single action and aggregate their claims to meet the requirement. So, in **B**, neither Adams nor Rajiv meets the amount requirement. Nor have courts allowed a plaintiff to aggregate claims against separate defendants, as Lopez has tried to do in example **C**. So **A** takes the prize.

While these aggregation rules have been criticized (*see Wright & Kane* § 36), there is a certain logic to them. In **B**, Adams could not meet the amount requirement if he sued Bickel alone; why should he be able to do so simply because Rajiv has a claim against Bickel too? Similarly, in **C**, Lopez couldn't sue Alou alone under § 1332, since he does not claim more than $75,000. Why should he be allowed to simply because he has a claim against Antoine as well?

2. An exception: The second plaintiff tags along. Consider this variation: P1 sues D for $150,000. P2 joins as a coplaintiff, asserting a claim for $60,000 in the action, arising from a single business dispute. Using the every-tub-on-its-own-bottom logic described in the previous note, courts traditionally denied jurisdiction over the claim by a plaintiff like P2 who did not sue for the jurisdictional amount. The same principle was applied in class actions, in which representatives of a class of similarly situated persons sue on behalf of the class. In *Zahn v. International Paper Co.*, 414 U.S. 291 (1973), some members of the class met the amount requirement in a class action lawsuit, but others did not. The Supreme Court held that the district court had no jurisdiction over the claims of those class members seeking less than $10,000.01.

The answer in this scenario has been changed by the enactment of 28 U.S.C. § 1367, the supplemental jurisdiction statute. Under that statute, the second plaintiff in this example may tag along, since the first plaintiff's claim meets the amount requirement. *See Exxon Mobil Corp. v. Allapattah Servs., Inc.*, 545 U.S. 546 (2005). To appreciate the logic for this exception, you need to study the concept of supplemental jurisdiction, which we analyze later in the book. For now just remember that this exception exists.

3. "Common undivided interests." In some narrow circumstances, plaintiffs may sue on a joint interest or a claim that is in some sense "indivisible." Suppose that Kaufman and Polk are the beneficiaries of a trust and First Federal Savings Bank is the trustee. Kaufman and Polk sue First Federal, claiming that its improper investment of their funds led to a loss of $80,000. Here, Kaufman and Polk each have an interest in the common fund managed by the bank, but they have not suffered separate losses. If they win, the full $80,000 will be restored to the trust; if they lose, nothing will. In such cases the full amount is in controversy. *See, e.g., Hyde v. First & Merchants Nat'l Bank*, 41 F.R.D. 527 (W.D. Va. 1967). Although the value of Kaufman's and Polk's individual interests have been diminished by only $40,000, they could both sue the bank in federal court under § 1332.

Cases involving the common undivided interest exception are relatively rare. In most cases involving multiple plaintiffs, each asserts a separate right to recover her own damages, even if their claims arise from the same underlying events. In the typical motor vehicle tort case, for example, each injured party has her own claim for damages, which she may pursue separately or in a joint action with other plaintiffs. Because her claim is independent of other claims arising from the accident, the usual aggregation rules apply.

Q **4. Determining the amount in controversy where either or both defendants might be liable.** Everett, a passenger in Lipmann's car, is injured when Lipmann's car collides with Ritter's. She sustains $100,000 in injuries and sues both Lipmann and Ritter for negligence. Under applicable tort law, whichever defendant is found negligent would be fully liable for her injuries. If both are found negligent, both would be liable to pay her full damages. (Of course, if she collected $100,000 from Lipmann she could not then collect *another* $100,000 from Ritter, but she could demand payment of the full amount from either defendant.) Does she meet the amount-in-controversy requirement?

A Here, either defendant may end up incurring a judgment for more than $75,000. If the jury finds that the accident was Lipmann's fault, Lipmann will be liable for $100,000. If they find that it was Ritter's fault, Ritter will be liable for $100,000. If they find it was due to the negligence of both defendants, they may (depending on local law) both be liable for $100,000. So either *might* be liable for more than $75,000.

Of course, either might escape liability entirely. Or, *both* might escape liability, if the jury finds that neither was negligent. But either might be liable for more than the jurisdictional amount, which is all that is required.

The same result would follow in a case in which the plaintiff sues two defendants in the alternative. If Cornwell is hit by a car but is unsure whether it was driven by Jeckle or Hyde, she might sue them both for injuries worth $120,000. Either *might* be liable (if found to be the driver) but both will not be liable, only the defendant who was driving. Cornwell meets the amount requirement against each.

5. The effect of a counterclaim in assessing the amount requirement. While the result is not entirely settled, it appears that a counterclaim cannot be aggregated with the plaintiff's claim to meet the amount requirement. Suppose, for example, that P sues D for $30,000 and D counterclaims from $65,000. Adding the two together to meet the amount requirement would be inconsistent with the general principle that a court's jurisdiction must be assessed based on the original complaint. If the court considered the counterclaim, the defendant would be able to choose federal court or avoid it, depending on her response to the complaint. If she wanted to be in federal court, she could answer, asserting the counterclaim. If she did not, she could simply move to dismiss for lack of subject matter jurisdiction, without filing an answer. Thus, the better view is that a counterclaim should not be aggregated with the plaintiff's claim to reach the required amount in controversy. *See generally Wright & Miller* § 3706.

6. Issue analysis: Fuzzy's Furs. Here's an amount-in-controversy issue from an old midterm that drove some of our students crazy.

Jane buys a coat, allegedly mink, from Fuzzy's Furs for $40,000. She later learns it is worthless muskrat fur. She sues Fuzzy's for compensatory damages. In Count I of her complaint, she alleges that Fuzzy's defrauded her, by deliberately selling her the muskrat coat as mink. In Count II, she alleges that Fuzzy's was negligent in selling her the coat, since it should have realized that the coat was not really mink. Is the amount-in-controversy requirement met?

A suggested analysis. Jane has sought relief based on two legal theories, fraud and negligence. Presumably, she could not prove both; either Fuzzy's intentionally defrauded her or negligently sold her muskrat for mink. Whichever theory she proves, the jury (absent a claim for punitive damages not given in the question) will be instructed to award her the damages she has suffered due to the tort. Her loss is one coat worth $40,000. This does not meet the amount requirement.

The same would be true if she *could* recover on both theories. As long as she is seeking only compensatory damages, the amount will be determined by asking what loss Jane has suffered, not how many legal wrongs Jane's lawyer chooses to call it. If her loss is $40,000, Jane does not meet the amount-in-controversy requirement in § 1332.

VII. The Constitutional Scope of Diversity Jurisdiction Compared to the Statutory Grant of Diversity

As we have seen, Article III, Section 2 sets forth the types of cases that federal courts can hear. If a case is not on the Article III list, the federal courts don't have subject matter jurisdiction over it. However, it does not necessarily follow that, if a case *is* within a category of the Article III subject matter jurisdiction, a federal court always will have the authority to hear it.

Recall that Article III, Section 1 creates the United States Supreme Court and empowers Congress to create lower federal courts. Because Congress did not have to create lower federal courts at all, the Supreme Court has held that it may create them and give them less than all of the potential jurisdiction authorized by Article III:

> By § 2 of [Article III] it is provided that the judicial power shall extend to certain designated cases and controversies, and, among them, "to controversies...between citizens of different states...." The effect of these provisions is not to vest jurisdiction in the inferior courts over the designated cases and controversies, but to delimit those in respect of which Congress may confer jurisdiction upon such courts as it creates. Only the jurisdiction of the Supreme Court is derived directly from the Constitution. Every other court created by the general government derives its jurisdiction wholly from the authority of Congress. That body may give, withhold, or restrict such jurisdiction at its discretion, provided it be not extended beyond the boundaries fixed by the Constitution. The Constitution simply gives to the inferior courts the capacity to take jurisdiction in the enumerated cases, but it requires an act of Congress to confer it.

Kline v. Burke Construction Co., 260 U.S. 226, 233–34 (1922). In other words, the Constitution delimits the outer bounds of the cases that the lower federal courts may be authorized to hear, but it is up to Congress to directly bestow jurisdiction on the lower federal courts. "When it comes to jurisdiction of the federal courts, truly, to paraphrase the scripture, Congress giveth, and Congress taketh away." *Senate Select Committee v. Nixon*, 366 F. Supp. 51, 55 (D.D.C. 1973).

Consequently, determining whether a federal district court can hear a case entails two questions. First, is the case within the constitutional grant of federal subject matter jurisdiction in Article III, Section 2? And if it is, has Congress passed a statute actually conveying jurisdiction over the case to the federal district courts?

Visually, the relation between Article III and federal jurisdictional statutes is represented below, in Figure 3–1:

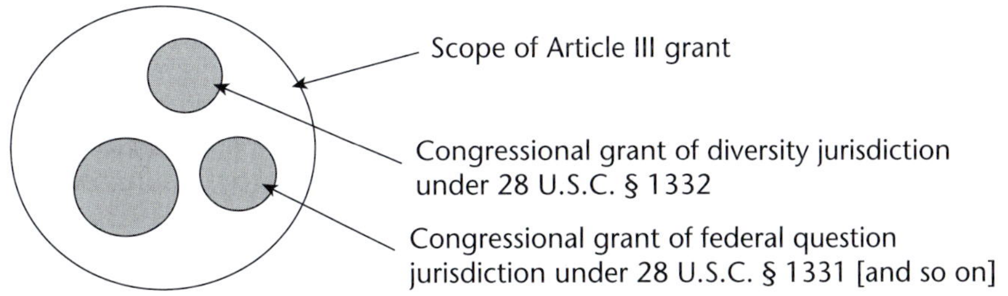

Figure 3–1: RELATION OF ARTICLE III GRANT OF JURISDICTION TO FEDERAL JURISDICTIONAL STATUTES

Congress has never authorized the federal trial courts to hear *all* of the cases listed in Article III, Section 2. Rather, it has granted some cases in these categories to the federal district courts. For example, the grant of diversity jurisdiction in 28 U.S.C. § 1332 imposes several limits that are not found in Article III:

1. **The amount-in-controversy requirement.** Nothing in Article III, Section 2 requires a diversity case to meet a minimum amount in controversy.

That section simply refers to "cases between citizens of different states." Congress has imposed the amount requirement to exclude minor diversity cases from federal court. A case between an Oregon citizen and an Idaho citizen for $35,000 is within the *constitutional* grant of diversity jurisdiction because it is a case between citizens of different states. But Congress has not authorized federal district courts to hear that case, since it is for less than $75,000.01. Congress *could* authorize federal courts to hear it, since it is within the constitutional grant.

2. **The complete diversity requirement.** *Strawbridge v. Curtiss*, 7 U.S. 267 (1806), held that a diversity case can only be brought in federal court if there is complete diversity between all plaintiffs and all defendants, that is, no plaintiff is a citizen of the same state as any defendant. For many years, it was unclear whether *Strawbridge v. Curtiss* interpreted the phrase "citizens of different states" in Article III, Section 2, or the same phrase in the diversity statute. That was an important question. If *Strawbridge* interpreted Article III, the complete diversity rule would be a constitutional restriction and could only be changed by constitutional amendment. But if *Strawbridge* construed the statute, that statute could be amended to authorize jurisdiction even if there was not complete diversity.

   In *State Farm Fire and Casualty Co. v. Tashire*, 386 U.S. 523 (1967), the Supreme Court held that *Strawbridge* interpreted the diversity statute, not Article III, Section 2. *Tashire* held that a case is a proper diversity case under Article III, Section 2 as long as there is minimal diversity—that is, at least one plaintiff is from a different state than at least one defendant. Thus, if Adams, from Massachusetts, sues Madison, from Virginia, and Gerry, from Massachusetts, the case is "between citizens of different states" under Article III, Section 2. But it could not be brought in federal court, because it is not authorized by the diversity statute. *Strawbridge* is still the governing interpretation of 28 U.S.C. § 1332(a).

Notes and Questions Comparing the Constitutional and Statutory Scope of Diversity Jurisdiction

Q **1. Two levels of analysis.** Casey, a New Mexico citizen, sues Lopez, from Utah, for $20,000 for injuries suffered in an auto accident. The suit is for negligence, a state tort claim. Is this case within the Article III, Section 2 grant of diversity jurisdiction to the federal district courts? Can the federal district court hear it?

A Casey's case is a proper diversity case under Article III, Section 2, since the parties are from different states. So there is a constitutional basis for a federal court to hear Casey's case. However, Article III, Section 2 does not directly grant diversity jurisdiction to the federal district court—Congress does, within the limits set by Article III. Congress has not authorized the federal district courts to hear diversity cases unless more than $75,000 is in controversy. The federal court cannot hear Casey's case, even though it is, constitutionally speaking, a proper diversity case.

Q **2. Deep-sixing the amount-in-controversy requirement.** Suppose that Congress decided to allow all diversity cases to be heard in federal court. Could it eliminate the amount-in-controversy requirement, that is, amend § 1332(a) by striking out the language "where the amount in controversy exceeds the sum or value of $75,000" from the statute?

A Certainly. Article III authorizes federal courts to hear all diversity cases, without regard to the amount in controversy. It is 28 U.S.C. § 1332(a) that limits diversity cases to those involving more than $75,000. If Congress struck the amount-in-controversy language from the statute, it would expand the *statutory* diversity jurisdiction, but the jurisdiction conferred would still be within the constitutional grant.

3. Raising the amount-in-controversy requirement. The question below considers the extent of Congress's control over the amount-in-controversy requirement.

Congress, fed up with the crowded dockets of the federal district courts, decides to raise the amount-in-controversy requirement in diversity cases to $10 million. Could it do so?

A. Yes, because Congress can make any changes it wants to the federal district courts' subject matter jurisdiction.
B. Yes, because Congress can limit the federal district courts' exercise of jurisdiction over cases authorized in Article III, Section 2.
C. No, because a $10 million requirement would leave too many people at risk of state court bias against outsiders.
D. No, because Article III, Section 2 authorizes jurisdiction over diversity cases without regard to the amount in controversy between the parties.

The correct answer is **B**. **A** is wrong because Congress cannot make *any* changes it wants in the subject matter jurisdiction of the federal district courts. Congress could not authorize jurisdiction over cases that are not within the constitutional grant in Article III, Section 2 (e.g., all divorce cases). That would grant jurisdiction beyond that authorized in the Constitution. However, Congress can limit the federal district courts' jurisdiction more narrowly than the Framers did in Article III. It could grant *no* diversity jurisdiction if it wants. Thus **C** is wrong. **D** is wrong, too. The fact that there is no amount-in-controversy requirement in Article III, Section 2 does not mean that Congress cannot impose one.

4. Comparing the statutory and constitutional scope of diversity jurisdiction.

Casey, a New Mexico citizen, wishes to sue Lopez, from Utah, and Ming, from New Mexico, for injuries suffered in an auto accident. Her claim is for more than $75,000. Which of the following statements is correct?

A. A federal court has statutory, but not constitutional authority to hear the case.
B. A federal court has constitutional, but not statutory authority to hear the case.
C. A federal court has neither constitutional nor statutory authority to hear the case.
D. A federal court has both constitutional and statutory authority to hear the case.

There is no complete diversity here, since Casey is from the same state as one of the defendants. Since § 1332 is interpreted to require complete diversity, it does not authorize jurisdiction in this case. So **A** and **D** are wrong. However, the *Strawbridge* complete diversity rule is a statutory requirement only. *Tashire* holds that the phrase "between citizens of different states" in Article III, Section 2 only requires that one plaintiff be from a different state than one defendant. Thus, it would be constitutionally permissible for a federal court to hear cases like Casey's case that involve minimal diversity. But there is no statutory authority to hear the case, due to the *Strawbridge* interpretation of § 1332(a). The correct answer is **B**.

5. Jurisdiction based on minimal diversity. Congress has from time to time authorized federal courts to hear cases based on minimal diversity. For example, the Federal Interpleader Act, which authorizes jurisdiction over certain cases involving multiple claimants to the same property, allows federal district courts to hear actions as long as at least two of the claimants are diverse. *State Farm Fire & Casualty Co. v. Tashire*, 386 U.S. 523, 530 (1967). Similarly, the Class Action Fairness Act allows nationwide class actions to be brought in federal court or removed to federal court if any member of the plaintiff class is diverse from any defendant, and the amount in controversy (for the entire class) exceeds $5 million. 28 U.S.C. §§ 1332(d)(2)(A), 1453. *See also* 28 U.S.C. § 1369 (authorizing federal jurisdiction over certain mass disaster cases based on minimal diversity).

VIII. Diversity Jurisdiction: Summary of Basic Principles

- Article III, Section 2 of the Constitution authorizes federal courts to hear cases "between citizens of different states," commonly referred to as diversity jurisdiction.
- The *constitutional* grant in Article III, Section 2 is satisfied as long as there is minimal diversity between the parties, that is, at least one plaintiff is a citizen of a different state than one defendant.
- Article III does not directly confer diversity jurisdiction on the federal district courts. Congress must convey it to them by statute. It may authorize

them to hear all cases within the constitutional grant of diversity, or some, or none.

- The diversity statute, 28 U.S.C. § 1332, is narrower than the Article III grant. It imposes an amount-in-controversy requirement. In addition, *Strawbridge v. Curtiss*, which holds that the statute requires complete diversity, is still the interpretation of § 1332(a). Thus, for most diversity cases § 1332 is only satisfied if no plaintiff is from the same state as any defendant.
- A person—that is, a human being—is a citizen of the state where she is domiciled. To be a state citizen for diversity purposes, she must be a citizen of the United States and be domiciled in a state. Most courts hold that a person's domicile is the last state in which she resided with the intent to remain indefinitely.
- Corporations are also held to be state citizens for diversity purposes. 28 U.S.C. § 1332(c)(1) states that a corporation is a citizen of the state in which it is incorporated and of the state of its principal place of business. Under *Hertz Corp. v. Friend*, the state of the corporation's headquarters will almost always be its principal place of business.
- In determining whether the amount-in-controversy requirement is met, the court assesses whether the plaintiff, if she wins at trial, might recover more than $75,000 from the defendant on the claim that she has alleged. The court will dismiss for lack of subject matter jurisdiction if it appears to a legal certainty that the plaintiff's injuries could not support a recovery of that amount.

4

Federal Question Jurisdiction

I. Introduction

This chapter analyzes a second major category of cases within the sc of Article III, Section 2: cases "arising under this Constitution, the Laws of United States, and Treaties made, or which shall be made under their Authority. The Framers recognized that federal courts, created and administered by the federal government, must have the power to interpret and enforce federal law. Otherwise, the national government could be rendered powerless by hostile state court interpretations of the meaning and constitutionality of federal law. "All governments which are not extremely defective in their organization, must possess, within themselves, the means of expounding, as well as enforcing, their own laws." *Osborn v. Bank of the United States*, 22 U.S. 738, 818–19 (1824).

As noted in Chapter 1, the lower federal courts do not automatically exercise all the jurisdiction described in Article III, Section 2. Congress must bestow that jurisdiction upon them by statute, and may authorize them to hear only some of the cases within the constitutional grant. Interestingly, Congress did not give federal trial courts broad jurisdiction over cases arising under federal law until almost a hundred years after the adoption of the Constitution.* Early statutes authorized the federal trial courts to hear cases arising under *particular* federal statutes—such as the immigration and patent statutes. But most cases arising under federal law still were litigated in the state courts, subject to review in the United States Supreme Court. It was not until 1875 that Congress, fearing that the state courts would not vigorously enforce the federal civil rights statutes enacted during Reconstruction, granted broad jurisdiction over cases arising under federal law to the lower federal courts. Today, 28 U.S.C. § 1331 grants jurisdiction to the federal district court over all cases "arising under the Constitution, laws or treaties of the United States."

Before examining what it means for a case to "arise under" federal law, it may be useful to consider the types of cases that do *not* arise under federal law. Most of the cases you study in the first year of law school are not "federal question" cases. Contracts cases, tort cases, property cases, and most criminal cases, for example, arise under state law. Similarly, domestic relations cases, inheritance cases, and cases under state statutes involve law made by the states rather than the federal government. Unless the parties to such cases are diverse, these cases must be litigated in state court.

In your upper-class years, you will likely take courses that involve federal statutory regimes, such as Labor Law, Environmental Law, Federal Tax, Patent Law, and Securities Law. These courses involve statutes enacted by Congress, not the state legislatures. Suits to enforce those laws arise under federal law, so that federal courts have jurisdiction over them under 28 U.S.C. § 1331.

II. The Constitutional Scope of Federal Question Jurisdiction

The previous chapter emphasized that the constitutional grant of diversity jurisdiction is broad, but the statutory grant in 28 U.S.C. § 1332 has been interpreted much more narrowly. The same is true with regard to arising-under jurisdiction. In *Osborn v. Bank of the United States*, 22 U.S. 738, 823 (1824), Chief Justice Marshall offered an expansive interpretation of the scope of federal question jurisdiction in Article III, Section 2:

> We think, then, that when a question to which the judicial power of the Union is extended by the constitution, forms an ingredient of the original cause, it is in the power of Congress to give the [lower federal courts] jurisdiction of that cause, although other questions of fact or of law may be involved in it.

* Broad federal question jurisdiction was enacted by Congress in 1801, but repealed a year later, "after the electoral triumph of the Jeffersonians who were ever distrustful of the power of the federal government." Jack H. Friedenthal, Mary K. Kane & Arthur R. Miller, CIVIL PROCEDURE 14 (5th ed. 2015).

Although Chief Justice Marshall referred to "the original cause," which might suggest that the plaintiff's original claim must involve a "federal ingredient," this language has been interpreted more broadly. So long as there is a federal ingredient in the action—whether it is introduced by the plaintiff's claims or by a defense asserted in the defendant's answer—*Osborn* holds that Article III, Section 2 grants federal question jurisdiction over the case.

So, for example, if Conway sues Deliso under 42 U.S.C. § 1983, a federal statute that authorizes suits for violation of federal civil rights, the case arises under federal law, since Conway's complaint seeks relief under a federal statute. But if Conway sues Deliso for libel, a state law claim, and Deliso raises the defense that the First Amendment right to freedom of speech protected his statement, that case would also satisfy the constitutional standard for federal question jurisdiction. Under *Osborn,* as long as the "original cause" (the basic suit) involves a question of federal law, the case arises under federal law. Virtually any case in which an issue of federal law is asserted by one of the original parties thus satisfies the *constitutional* definition of federal question jurisdiction.

III. The Statutory Scope of Federal Question Jurisdiction: The Well-Pleaded Complaint Rule

Congress has conveyed the federal question jurisdiction to the federal district courts in 28 U.S.C. § 1331. That statute, like Article III, Section 2, authorizes jurisdiction over "cases arising under" federal law. However, the courts have interpreted this statutory grant of federal question jurisdiction much more narrowly than the constitutional grant.

READING *LOUISVILLE & NASHVILLE RAILROAD CO. v. MOTTLEY.* The classic *Mottley* case, below, established basic doctrine concerning when a case "arises under" federal law under the congressional grant of federal question jurisdiction. As the case illustrates, there is a perplexing distinction between cases that *involve* federal law and cases that *arise under* federal law, as that phrase is used in 28 U.S.C. § 1331.

The *Mottley* Court refers to the "demurrer" filed by the defendant. A demurrer is a procedural device the defendant may use to assert that the plaintiff's complaint is legally insufficient because the law does not provide a remedy for the conduct alleged in the plaintiff's complaint. It challenges the legal adequacy of the claims challenged, not the court's subject matter jurisdiction. Note that the "circuit court" referred to was a federal *trial* court, not a circuit court of appeals.

In reading *Mottley,* consider the following points and questions.

- What did the trial court hold concerning subject matter jurisdiction over the case? (You can infer the answer to this question from the procedural history of the case.)
- What two issues of federal law were presented by the appeal to the Supreme Court?

- How did the Supreme Court rule on these two federal issues, and why?
- The Mottleys made several references to federal law in their complaint. Why did this not suffice to make the case one that "arises under" federal law? What standard did the Court establish for determining when a case arises under federal law?

LOUISVILLE & NASHVILLE RAILROAD CO. v. MOTTLEY

211 U.S. 149 (1908)

Statement by Mr. Justice Moody:

The appellees (husband and wife), being residents and citizens of Kentucky, brought this suit in equity in the circuit court of the United States for the western district of Kentucky against the appellant, a railroad company and a citizen of the same state. The object of the suit was to compel the specific performance of the following contract:

> Louisville, Ky., Oct. 2d, 1871.
>
> The Louisville & Nashville Railroad Company, in consideration that E.L. Mottley and wife, Annie E. Mottley, have this day released company from all damages or claims for damages for injuries received by them on the 7th of September, 1871, in consequence of a collision of trains on the railroad of said company at Randolph's Station, Jefferson County, Kentucky, hereby agrees to issue free passes on said railroad and branches now existing or to exist, to said E.L. & Annie E. Mottley for the remainder of the present year, and thereafter to renew said passes annually during the lives of said Mottley and wife or either of them.

The bill alleged that in September, 1871, plaintiffs, while passengers upon the defendant railroad, were injured by the defendant's negligence, and released their respective claims for damages in consideration of the agreement for transportation during their lives, expressed in the contract. It is alleged that the contract was performed by the defendant up to January 1, 1907, when the defendant declined to renew the passes. The bill then alleges that the refusal to comply with the contract was based solely upon that part of the act of Congress of June 29, 1906 (34 Stat. 584), which forbids the giving of free passes or free transportation. The bill further alleges: First, that the act of Congress referred to does not prohibit the giving of passes under the circumstances of this case; and, second, that, if the law is to be construed as prohibiting such passes, it is in conflict with the Fifth Amendment of the [United States] Constitution, because it deprives the plaintiffs of their property without due process of law. The defendant demurred to the bill. The judge of the circuit court overruled the demurrer, entered a decree for the relief prayed for, and the defendant appealed directly to this court. . . .

Mr. Justice Moody, after making the foregoing statement, delivered the opinion of the court:

Two questions of law were raised by the demurrer to the bill, were brought here by appeal, and have been argued before us. They are, first, whether that part of the act of Congress of June 29, 1906 which forbids the giving of free passes or the collection of any different compensation for transportation of passengers than that specified in the tariff filed, makes it unlawful to perform a contract for transportation of persons who, in good faith, before the passage of the act, had accepted such contract in satisfaction of a valid cause of action against the railroad; and, second, whether the statute, if it should be construed to render such a contract unlawful, is in violation of the 5th Amendment of the Constitution of the United States. We do not deem it necessary, however, to consider either of these questions, because, in our opinion, the court below was without jurisdiction of the cause. Neither party has questioned that jurisdiction, but it is the duty of this court to see to it that the jurisdiction of the circuit court, which is defined and limited by statute, is not exceeded. This duty we have frequently performed of our own motion.

There was no diversity of citizenship, and it is not and cannot be suggested that there was any ground of jurisdiction, except that the case was a "suit . . . arising under the Constitution or laws of the United States." It is the settled interpretation of these words, as used in this statute, conferring jurisdiction, that a suit arises under the Constitution and laws of the United States only when the plaintiff's statement of his own cause of action shows that it is based upon those laws or that Constitution. It is not enough that the plaintiff alleges some anticipated defense to his cause of action, and asserts that the defense is invalidated by some provision of the Constitution of the United States. Although such allegations show that very likely, in the course of the litigation, a question under the Constitution would arise, they do not show that the suit, that is, the plaintiff's original cause of action, arises under the Constitution. In *Tennessee v. Union & Planters' Bank*, 152 U.S. 454, the plaintiff, the state of Tennessee, brought suit in the circuit court of the United States to recover from the defendant certain taxes alleged to be due under the laws of the state. The plaintiff alleged that the defendant claimed an immunity from the taxation by virtue of its charter, and that therefore the tax was void, because in violation of the provision of the Constitution of the United States, which forbids any state from passing a law impairing the obligation of contracts. The cause was held to be beyond the jurisdiction of the circuit court, the court saying, by Mr. Justice Gray (p. 464): "A suggestion of one party, that the other will or may set up a claim under the Constitution or laws of the United States, does not make the suit one arising under that Constitution or those laws." Again, in *Boston & M. Consol. Copper & S. Min. Co. v. Montana Ore Purchasing Co.*, 188 U.S. 632, the plaintiff brought suit in the circuit court of the United States for the conversion of copper ore and for an injunction against its continuance. The plaintiff then alleged, for the purpose of showing jurisdiction, in substance, that the defendant would set up in defense certain laws of the United States. The cause was held to be beyond the jurisdiction of the circuit court, the court saying . . . :

"It would be wholly unnecessary and improper, in order to prove complainant's cause of action, to go into any matters of defense which the defendants might possibly set up, and then attempt to reply to such defense, and thus, if possible, to show that a Federal question might or probably would arise in the course of the trial of the case. To allege such defense and then make an answer to it before the defendant has the opportunity to itself plead or prove its own defense is inconsistent with any known rule of pleading, so far as we are aware, and is improper.

"The rule is a reasonable and just one that the complainant in the first instance shall be confined to a statement of its cause of action, leaving to the defendant to set up in his answer what his defense is, and, if anything more than a denial of complainant's cause of action, imposing upon the defendant the burden of proving such defense.

"Conforming itself to that rule, the complainant would not, in the assertion or proof of its cause of action, bring up a single Federal question. The presentation of its cause of action would not show that it was one arising under the Constitution or laws of the United States.

"The only way in which it might be claimed that a Federal question was presented would be in the complainant's statement of what the defense of defendants would be, and complainant's answer to such defense. Under these circumstances the case is brought within the rule laid down in *Tennessee v. Union & Planters' Bank, supra*. That case has been cited and approved many times since."

...The application of this rule to the case at bar is decisive against the jurisdiction of the circuit court.

It is ordered that the judgment be reversed and the case remitted to the circuit court with instructions to dismiss the suit for want of jurisdiction.

Notes and Questions: The Well-Pleaded Complaint Rule

Q **1. *Osborn* vs. *Mottley*.** Is a case like *Mottley* within the constitutional grant of federal question jurisdiction in Article III, as interpreted in *Osborn v. Bank of the United States*?

A Certainly. The case involved two substantial federal issues, one requiring the interpretation of a federal statute, and the other a question of the constitutionality of that statute. These two federal "ingredients" satisfy Chief Justice Marshall's expansive constitutional test for federal question jurisdiction. If *Osborn*'s constitutional test were the only limit on the federal courts' jurisdiction over federal question cases, the federal court would have had jurisdiction to hear the case. The perplexing problem is that the Court interprets Congress's statutory grant (in the statute that is now § 1331) much more narrowly.

The following oversimplified diagram suggests the relationship between the constitutional scope of federal question jurisdiction and the statutory scope.

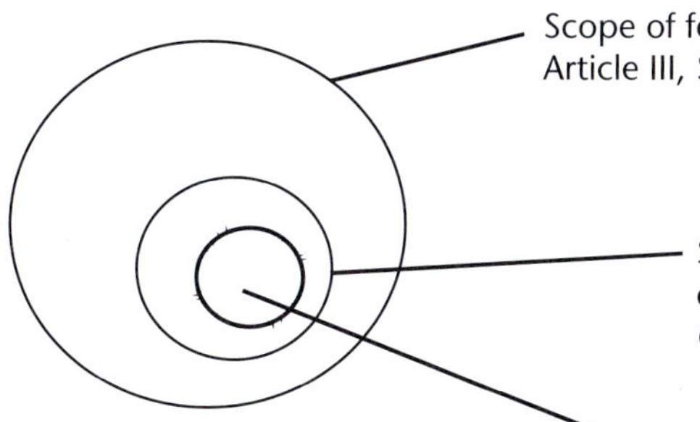

Figure 4–1: CONSTITUTIONAL AND STATUTORY SCOPE OF FEDERAL JURISDICTION

Q **2. The source of the Mottleys' claim.** The holding of *Mottley* requires the federal trial court to look at the claim for relief asserted in the plaintiff's complaint and ask whether that claim "arises under" federal law. What was the source of the Mottleys' right to relief from the railroad?

A The Mottleys could demand renewal of their passes because the railroad had contracted to grant them. If there were no contract, they would have had no right to the passes. If the judge asked them, "Why should I order the railroad to renew these passes?," the Mottleys would have replied, "because they agreed to, in exchange for a release of our right to sue for our injuries. Our courts in Kentucky have always enforced valid contracts." The Court holds that this claim does not support federal question jurisdiction; the statute only grants jurisdiction if the plaintiff's right to sue is based on federal law. The Mottleys' case was based on Kentucky contract law, not federal law.

Q **3. The "well-pleaded complaint" rule.** It is often said that *Mottley* illustrates the *well-pleaded complaint* rule. Under that rule, the case arises under federal law, as that phrase is used in § 1331, if the federal issue appears on the face of the well-pleaded complaint, that is, if a proper complaint, limited to the allegations necessary to state a proper claim for relief, relies on federal law. Suppose the Mottleys' complaint pleaded as follows:

1. In 1871, we entered into an agreement with the defendant railroad, agreeing to accept free passes for life on the railroad in settlement of our personal injury claims for damages.

2. In 1907, the defendant, after annually renewing our passes, refused to do so.
3. The defendant refused to do so on the ground that a recent federal statute, 34 Stat. 584, bars them from doing so.
4. 34 Stat. 584 was not intended to bar renewal of passes granted under contracts entered into before its enactment.
5. If 34 Stat. 584 is construed to bar renewal of passes previously granted, it violates the Fifth Amendment to the United States Constitution, which prohibits the federal government from taking private property without due process of law.
6. Wherefore, the plaintiffs request that the court order the defendant to perform its obligations under the contract, by annually renewing the passes as agreed.

Which of the above paragraphs would be required to state an adequate (i.e., well-pleaded) complaint for breach of contract? Which do not allege elements of a good contract claim?

A Paragraphs 1, 2, and 6 are all the Mottleys needed to include to state a proper claim for breach of contract. These paragraphs allege contract, breach, and a demand for specific performance. And none of these makes reference to federal law. The allegations that raise federal issues are in Paragraphs 3, 4, and 5. Paragraph 3 alleges the railroad's expected defense to the claim—that it refused to renew because it concluded that the federal statute barred it from doing so. This is interesting but not necessary to the Mottleys' statement of their claim for breach of contract. Paragraph 4 denies that the federal statute bars renewing the passes. This responds to the railroad's anticipated defense by denying that it is true. This also goes beyond a statement of the Mottleys' basic cause of action. Paragraph 5 argues that the defense the railroad is likely to raise is invalid for another reason, again anticipating and responding to the defendant's case rather than stating the Mottleys' own claim for relief.

Q **4. The role of *Mottley* in tempering lawyer creativity.** Suppose that the Court had upheld jurisdiction on the ground that the complaint *did* raise federal issues by anticipating the railroad's defenses. How would that affect plaintiffs' pleading strategy in future cases?

A If anticipating federal defenses sufficed to get a case into federal court, creative lawyers who wanted to litigate in federal court would doubtless manage to anticipate one. They would sue in federal court, plead their state law claim, and then allege some federal defense that might be asserted. But suppose the defendant didn't oblige; she answered the complaint raising only state law defenses. Presumably, the case would then have to be dismissed.

A distinct practical advantage of the well-pleaded complaint rule is that it allows a court to decide whether it has federal question jurisdiction based on the complaint alone, without regard to defenses the defendant might raise. Sometimes a defendant will not answer the complaint for a considerable time—for example, she may move to dismiss it on various grounds without filing an answer. Yet the court needs to know whether it has the power to proceed with the case. The *Mottley* rule allows the court to determine its jurisdiction without demanding an immediate answer to the complaint or relying on the plaintiff's representations about likely defenses. Like the day-of-filing rule for determining diversity, it provides a practical rule that serves administrative convenience more than intellectual elegance. *See Franchise Tax Board v. Construction Laborers Vacation Trust*, 463 U.S. 1, 11 (1983) (well-pleaded complaint rule "makes sense as a quick rule of thumb").

The Dubious Practice of Granting Free Passes

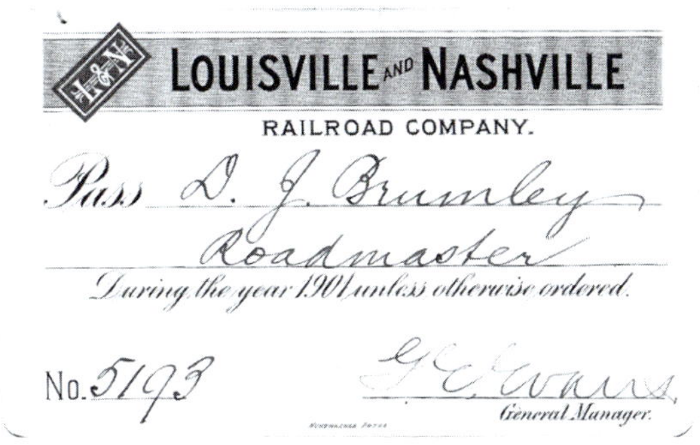

In 1906, Congress passed the Hepburn Act, the statute at issue in *Mottley*. It did not enact the statute to abuse the Mottleys, but to put an end to the widespread and corrupt practice of granting free passes to politicians in a bid to advance the railroads' interests. "All sections of the country complained about the influence railroads exercised over public officials through the universal practice of granting free passes to congressmen, judges, sheriffs, assessors and even town officials.... By 1897 the railroads of North Carolina were giving out 100,000 passes a year at an estimated annual revenue loss of $325,000. Paying passengers found it difficult to conceal their disgust when they found their seatmate to be a 'deadhead,' for they knew they were indirectly paying his passage." John F. Stover, American Railroads 115 (2008).

5. Federal questions and "federal question jurisdiction." Ironically, the only disputed issues in *Mottley* were issues of federal law. First, the parties disputed the meaning of the federal statute: whether it was intended to bar renewal of passes that had been granted before the statute was enacted. Second, they disputed a question arising under the United States Constitution: if the statute *did* bar renewal, whether it deprived the Mottleys of due process under the Fifth Amendment. These issues were litigated below, decided, and appealed by the railroad. Yet, the Supreme Court holds that the case is not a "federal question case"! This may be the law, but it does seem a bit quixotic. As Wright and Kane suggest,

> If the basis for original federal-question jurisdiction is that the federal courts have a special expertness in applying federal law, and that assertions of federal law will be received more hospitably in a federal court, it would seem that the courts should have jurisdiction where there is some federal issue regardless of which pleading raises it.

Wright & Kane § 18.

Despite these arguments, the *Mottley* well-pleaded complaint rule persists, primarily because the rule works quite well as a rough sorting mechanism for cases:

> The policy [of the *Mottley* rule] is a sound one. A litigant who invokes the jurisdiction of the federal court ought to be able to do so with a fair assurance that the case will be determined in that court. He cannot do so if his jurisdictional allegation is, of necessity, no more than a guess as to the strategy his opponent will follow. The time of the court and the lawyers, and the money of the litigants, would be wasted needlessly on the preliminary stages in federal court of a case which is ultimately dismissed. Some protection would have to be given the plaintiff, in a case which is so dismissed, against being barred from a subsequent state action by a state statute of limitations.

American Law Institute, *Study of the Division of Jurisdiction Between State and Federal Courts* 190 (1969). However, we will see that this interpretation of the *federal district courts'* jurisdiction does not limit the authority of the United States Supreme Court itself. In *Mottley*, the Supreme Court held that the federal trial court lacked original jurisdiction, not that the Supreme Court could not review issues of federal law that are asserted as defenses.

6. Creative redrafting. Students always want to know what the Mottleys should have done to fix their pleading problem and get into federal court.

The Mottleys may not have realized that their case, which raised several novel questions of federal law, might fail to satisfy the statutory requirement for federal question jurisdiction. Suppose that after the Supreme Court's decision the federal trial judge gave them the opportunity to amend their complaint to solve the problem. What should they plead to get into federal court?

A. They could not amend the complaint in any way that would satisfy the statutory requirements for federal question jurisdiction.
B. They should amend, stating with more specificity why they know the railroad would raise the federal statute as a defense.
C. They should amend to allege that the railroad has deprived them of their constitutional rights under the Fifth Amendment.
D. They should amend to allege a right to relief under the federal transportation statute itself, not just under the contract.

Students often conclude that the Mottleys' lawyer simply failed to make the right allegations to get into federal court. But you can't make an elephant out of a turtle or a federal violation out of a contract breach.

B is not going to do the trick. The Court says anticipating a defense by the railroad is not sufficient to make a case arise under federal law. So stating the expected defense more clearly, or alleging that you are really sure they will raise it, isn't going to change the fact that you are just anticipating a defense. **C** is a loser too. The railroad hasn't deprived the Mottleys of any constitutional rights; if anyone has it is Congress. The Fifth Amendment grants protection from governmental deprivations without due process, not railroad deprivations. Only their contract protects them from that. And **D** wouldn't work unless the federal statute had created a right to train passes that the Mottleys could enforce. But the statute didn't do that; it barred issuing the passes.

So, it's hard to see how fancy pleading could help the Mottleys. Contract cases just don't arise under federal law (in the *Mottley* sense of that phrase). **A** is the best answer. The Mottleys could not manufacture federal question jurisdiction by clever pleading. Their only source of a right to relief against the railroad was the contract, so their counsel—even after reading the Supreme Court's *Mottley* decision—would not be able to create federal jurisdiction by redrafting their complaint.

7. The "rule of *Tennessee v. Union and Planters' Bank*." Students are often confused by the paragraph toward the end of the *Mottley* opinion that begins, "The only way in which it might be claimed. . . ." What the Court is saying here is, "the only way the case could be construed to arise under federal law would be if we considered anticipated defenses that the plaintiff includes in the complaint and responses to those defenses." However, (as *Mottley* notes) *Tennessee v. Union & Planters' Bank* held that such anticipated defenses and rebuttals cannot be considered in determining whether the case arises under federal law.

Q **8. Deep-sixing *Mottley*.** If you don't like the *Mottley* rule, can you think of a better working rule for deciding whether a case arises under federal law? How about an interpretation of § 1331 that postpones the decision on jurisdiction until the defendant answers, and finds federal question jurisdiction, even if the complaint relied solely on state law, if the answer raises a federal issue? Do you see any problems with that rule?

A One problem with this approach is that defendants don't have to answer a complaint if the court lacks subject matter jurisdiction over the case: They can move to dismiss the case. Even if ordered to answer, a defendant might answer raising only state law defenses, omitting her defenses under federal law. At that point, the court would have to dismiss the case for lack of jurisdiction, since neither the complaint nor the answer would rely on federal law. If the plaintiff then sued in state court, could the defendant assert federal defenses there? Scenarios like this suggest that the *Mottley* rule, though restrictive, has its advantages. It allows efficient and early decision about the federal court's jurisdiction.

Q **9. Expanding the statutory scope of jurisdiction.** Could Congress amend 28 U.S.C. § 1331 to give the federal district courts subject matter jurisdiction over cases like the Mottleys', in which federal law is raised as a defense?

A Yes, it could. A federal defense injects an "ingredient" of federal law into the case. *Osborn v. Bank of the United States*, 22 U.S. 738, 818–19 (1824), held that a case arises under federal law, as that phrase is used in Article III, Section 2, if a federal issue is present in the dispute. Thus, Congress could authorize federal district court jurisdiction based on assertion of a federal defense.

10. The court's obligation to dismiss where subject matter jurisdiction is lacking. Note that in *Mottley* no one—not even the judge—objected to subject matter jurisdiction in the trial court (called at that time the "circuit court"). The Supreme Court, however, raised the issue *sua sponte* (on its own) after the case had been decided in the trial court and reached the Supreme Court on appeal. In dismissing the case, it nullified the entire course of the litigation and left the parties back at square one.

The principle that subject matter jurisdiction may be raised at any stage of the case, and that the court must dismiss whenever it appears that it lacks subject matter jurisdiction, is a fundamental tenet of the federal judicial system. "If the court determines at any time that it lacks subject-matter jurisdiction, the court must dismiss the action." Fed. R. Civ. P. 12(h)(3). Under our Constitution, the federal courts are courts of limited—indeed, very limited—subject matter jurisdiction. If jurisdiction over a case is not within the Article III, Section 2 grant (or if it is proper under Article III but Congress has not enacted a statute authorizing the federal district courts to hear it), the federal court lacks power to hear the case. The federal courts are not free to alter the jurisdictional limits in the Constitution by hearing cases if the parties consent to suit in federal court or fail to raise an objection. "[I]t would be not simply wrong but indeed an unconstitutional invasion of the powers reserved to the states if [the federal] courts were to entertain cases not within their jurisdiction." *Wright & Kane*, p. 27.

IV. Applying *Mottley*: Justice Holmes's Creation Test

Mottley establishes one basic guideline for determining whether a case arises under federal law: The analysis must focus on the allegations in the plaintiff's complaint, not potential defenses the defendant might assert in her answer. Even narrowing our focus to the complaint, however, it can still be problematic to determine whether a case "arises under" federal law. Even where a complaint *refers* to federal law in some way—as the *Mottley* complaint did—the court may conclude that federal law is not sufficiently central to the case to support federal question jurisdiction.

Justice Oliver Wendell Holmes suggested one test for determining whether a suit arises under federal law. Holmes argued that a suit "arises under the law that creates the cause of action." *American Well Works v. Layne*, 241 U.S. 257, 260 (1916). In *Mottley*, for example, the law that created the plaintiffs' cause of action was contract law; thus the suit "arose under" contract law, which is state law. *Mottley* does not satisfy the Holmes test.

Notes and Questions: The Creation Test

1. Two straightforward examples that satisfy the Holmes test. In most cases, the Holmes test works well. Here are two examples in which the Holmes test is satisfied, and courts would hold that each case "arises under" federal law as that phrase is used in 28 U.S.C. § 1331.

- Zander holds a patent on inverse rototurnbuckles. Federal law provides that a patent holder enjoys the right to exclude others from manufacturing a patented device unless the patent holder grants a license to another to do so. Cassevites, without obtaining a license from Zander, begins to make rototurnbuckles. Zander sues to obtain an injunction barring Cassevites from doing so.
- Bluestein, a fifty-five-year old employee of Concept Corp., is fired. He claims that he was fired based on his age and replaced by a younger worker. The federal Age Discrimination in Employment Act bars age discrimination in employment and allows actions for damages for it. Bluestein sues for damages under the Act.

In the first example, it is the federal patent statute that gives the inventor the legal right to exclude others from manufacturing a patented invention and authorizes suits to enjoin others from doing so without permission. Because the federal patent statute "creates" Zander's cause of action, the Holmes test is satisfied. Similarly, in Bluestein's case, the federal age discrimination statute creates a substantive right not to be discriminated against in the workplace because of age and authorizes suits by those who are. Bluestein, as an older worker covered by the statute, demands relief for a violation of that federally created right. In each of these cases, Congress has enacted a federal statute creating a right and authorizing plaintiffs to sue for violation of that right. In each, if the plaintiff stood before the bench and the judge asked, "Why do you think you have a right to relief from the defendant?," the plaintiff's response would be, "because federal law creates such a right, Your Honor." Thus, both cases arise under federal law under the Holmes test.

2. Applying the Holmes test: Some hypotheticals to test the test. The following hypotheticals explore the parameters of the Holmes test. Consider whether each "arises under" federal law.

A. Jones, driving down Interstate 95, a part of the federal interstate highway system, collides with Smith. Jones sues Smith for negligence.

B. Larry Lawstudent borrows $5,000 from Metropolitan Bank, under a federal student loan program. Under the program, banks make loans to students under individual loan agreements with each student. The statute setting up the federal loan program includes a guarantee that, if the student defaults, and the bank cannot collect after diligent efforts, the federal government will assure payment of the outstanding balance. Larry defaults on his loan, and Metropolitan sues him for the amount due.

C. On the facts of example B, assume that Metropolitan is unable to collect from Larry and demands payment from the federal agency administering the loan program. The federal program administrator refuses payment, and Metropolitan sues the agency to collect. (Disregard the possibility that there is federal jurisdiction due to the fact that the United States is a party to the action.)

D. Apex Company has a patent on inverse rototurnbuckles. (Patents are granted by the federal Patent Office under a federal statute.) Allied Manufacturing wants to use Apex's rototurnbuckles as a component of a threshing machine they manufacture. Apex executes a contract that licenses Allied to do so, provided it pays Apex $10 for each turnbuckle it manufactures. Allied falls behind in its payments and Apex sues to collect the balance due.

E. Instead of suing Allied to collect the balance due under the licensing agreement, Apex sues to enjoin Allied from continuing to manufacture the patented rototurnbuckles, arguing that making them without its permission infringes Allied's patent.

F. Ace Tractor Company ships all its tractors via Great Northern Railroad, the only railroad that serves the area where its factory is located. Great Northern notifies Ace that it intends to raise its rates by 20 percent. Ace sues to enjoin the increase on the ground that the new rates exceed those allowed by the federal Interstate Commerce Commission.

G. Danbury is hired by General Hospital on a one-year contract to work on a medical research project. The funding for the project is provided by the National Institutes of Health, a federal agency. She is fired, allegedly for being late too often. She sues for breach of contract.

The first and last of these are straightforward. In **A**, Jones has sued for negligence. It is negligence law—which is state tort law—that creates his right to sue. Although the accident took place on a federal highway, Jones does not seek relief under federal law. If there were a Federal Recovery for Accidents on Interstate Highways Act, authorizing injured parties to sue for such accidents, Jones could sue under that Act and invoke 28 U.S.C. § 1331. But there isn't, and Jones didn't. He sued for negligence, a state law claim. No jurisdiction.

Similarly, in **G**, there is a vague federal aura to the case, since Danbury was working on a federally funded project. But no federal law creates her cause of action; her suit is for breach of contract. There is no jurisdiction under § 1331.

The others are a little harder. Three of the hypotheticals pretty clearly satisfy the Holmes test for jurisdiction. Which are they?

3. The Holmes test and the well-pleaded complaint rule. Students are sometimes confused about the role of the well-pleaded complaint rule and the Holmes test for federal question jurisdiction under 28 U.S.C. § 1331. These are not alternative tests, either of which can be applied to determine whether the case arises under federal law. Rather, *Mottley*'s well-pleaded complaint rule teaches that, in assessing whether a claim arises under federal law, the court will only consider the plaintiff's properly pleaded claim, not any defenses or counterclaims that might be asserted by the defendant. Even if the plaintiff alleges in the complaint that the defendant will rely on federal law as a defense, this allegation will be disregarded, because it is not a proper part of the plaintiff's "well-pleaded" claim, which should only contain those allegations necessary for the plaintiff to state her own claim for relief.

Under the Holmes test, the court considers, as *Mottley* requires, only the well-pleaded allegations of the complaint. The court asks whether those allegations assert a right to relief created by federal law. If they do, the Holmes test is met, and the case will almost always be found to arise under federal law. Thus, the Holmes test accepts *Mottley*'s focus on the allegations in the complaint, and provides a test (though, as we will see, not quite an exclusive test) for determining when those allegations do "arise under" federal law. In other words, the well-pleaded complaint concept tells you where to look, while the Holmes test tells you *what* to look for.

4. State court jurisdiction in federal question cases. Just to reiterate a point made in Chapter 1, consider this item.

Rosario sues Demerest in state court, claiming that Demerest fired him based on his age, a violation of the federal Age Discrimination in Employment Act. The state court should

A. hear the suit.
B. hear the case only if the parties are not diverse.
C. dismiss the case, because it arises under federal law and must be filed in federal court.
D. dismiss the case, unless Congress has expressly authorized bringing such federal claims in state court.

C implies that a state court cannot hear a case that arises under federal law. However, state courts usually may hear cases within the federal subject matter jurisdiction. They have "concurrent jurisdiction" over cases arising under federal law, unless Congress specifies that a particular type of federal claim must be brought in federal court. *Claflin v. Houseman*, 93 U.S. 130 (1876). *See, e.g.*, 28 U.S.C. § 1338(a) (providing that "[n]o State court shall have jurisdiction" over patent cases). So **C** is wrong.

D implies that state courts can only hear federal law claims if Congress specifically authorizes them to do so. That reverses the usual presumption, which is that the jurisdiction is concurrent (i.e., either system may entertain the case) unless Congress restricts a particular category of federal claims to the federal courts. **B** suggests that any case in which the parties are diverse must be heard in federal court. Not so; state courts may hear claims arising under federal law whether the parties are diverse or not. **A** is on the money; the state court can hear the case.

Q **5. Federal question jurisdiction based on a counterclaim.** Suppose that the plaintiff sues a non-diverse defendant on a state law claim. The defendant then asserts a counterclaim—that is, a claim of her own back against the plaintiff—that arises under federal law. For example, Hatfield, a police officer, arrests Malloy, and a scuffle takes place during the arrest. Officer Hatfield sues Malloy for battery for his injuries in the scuffle, and Malloy asserts a counterclaim alleging that Hatfield injured him by using excessive force, an unreasonable seizure under the Fourth Amendment to the United States Constitution. Would the federal court have arising-under jurisdiction over the case?

A

In The Holmes Group, Inc. v. Vornado Air Circulation Systems, Inc., 535 U.S. 826 (2002), the Supreme Court held that a counterclaim cannot be the basis for arising-under jurisdiction.

> we have declined to adopt proposals that "the answer as well as the complaint... be consulted before a determination [is] made whether the case 'ar[ises] under' federal law...." ... It follows that a counterclaim—which appears as part of the defendant's answer, not as part of the plaintiff's complaint—cannot serve as the basis for "arising under" jurisdiction....
>
> Allowing a counterclaim to establish "arising under" jurisdiction would also contravene the longstanding policies underlying our precedents. First, since the plaintiff is "the master of the complaint," the well-pleaded-complaint rule enables him, "by eschewing claims based on federal law,... to have the cause heard in state court."... The rule proposed by respondent, in contrast, would leave acceptance or rejection of a state forum to the master of the counterclaim. It would allow a defendant to remove a case brought in state court under state law, thereby defeating a plaintiff's choice of forum, simply by raising a federal counterclaim. Second, conferring this power upon the defendant would radically expand the class of removable cases, contrary to the "[d]ue regard for the rightful independence of state governments" that our cases addressing removal require.... And finally, allowing responsive pleadings by the defendant to establish "arising under" jurisdiction would undermine the clarity and ease of administration of the well-pleaded-complaint doctrine, which serves as a "quick rule of thumb" for resolving jurisdictional conflicts.... For these reasons, we decline to transform the longstanding well-pleaded-complaint rule into the "well-pleaded-complaint-*or-counterclaim* rule" urged by respondent.

535 U.S. at 831–32.

6. An ironic corollary of the no-counterclaim rule. Interestingly, the *Holmes Group* case involved a counterclaim under the federal patent laws. Because of the holding in *Holmes Group,* a defendant asserting a patent law counterclaim in a state court case would have to litigate the patent claim in the state court. (The federal counterclaim could not be the basis for removing the case to federal court, because under 28 U.S.C. § 1441(a) only cases that may be commenced in federal court may be removed there by the defendant.) This was a bit of a Catch-22; the patent statute has long provided for exclusive federal jurisdiction over patent claims (28 U.S.C. § 1338(a)), but one asserted as a counterclaim in state court could not be removed to federal court.

In 2011 Congress amended Title 28 of the United States Code to address this conundrum. Section 1454(a) now provides that "[a] civil action in which *any party asserts a claim for relief arising under* any Act of Congress relating to patents, plant variety protection, or copyrights may be removed to the district court of the United States for the district and division embracing the place where the action is pending" (emphasis added). A defendant asserting a patent law counterclaim in state court may now remove the case to federal court. However, § 1454 only applies to patent, plant variety, and copyright cases. The basic holding of *Holmes Group* continues to govern most cases involving counterclaims under federal law.

7. Assessing federal jurisdiction in declaratory judgment actions. Federal procedure provides a mechanism for a party who is likely to be sued for a dispute to bring suit itself to determine its rights and liabilities. This civilized device, called a "declaratory judgment," allows a party, before an alleged violation of rights has actually taken place, to bring suit and ask the court to "declare" the rights of the parties. 28 U.S.C. §§ 2201–2202. The declaratory judgment procedure allows a party to know, prior to taking an action that may violate the other party's rights, whether it will do so.

On the facts of the *Mottley* case, for example, the railroad might bring a declaratory judgment action against the Mottleys seeking a declaration that it is barred by the new federal statute from renewing the Mottleys' passes. By doing so, it could obtain a ruling on the legality of its refusal without violating the Mottleys' rights first. If the railroad obtains a declaratory judgment that it is barred from renewing the passes, that judgment will protect it from claims by the Mottleys and discourage other pass holders from suing. If the court holds that the railroad still must renew the passes, at least they know their obligations under the law before violating those obligations.

Interestingly, if the railroad brings suit for a declaratory judgment, its complaint *will rely on federal law,* since it will base its right to the declaratory judgment on the claim that the federal statute bars it from issuing the passes. Arguably, then, the case arises under federal law if the railroad starts the action, but not if the Mottleys do.

The Supreme Court has held, however, that in assessing federal question jurisdiction over an action for a declaratory judgment, the court must ask whether the case would arise under federal law if brought by the party who would ordinarily be the plaintiff seeking a coercive judgment.

> Where the complaint in an action for declaratory judgment seeks in essence to assert a defense to an impending or threatened state court action, it is the character of the threatened action, and not of the defense, which will determine whether there is federal-question jurisdiction in the District Court.

Public Service Commission v. Wycoff, 344 U.S. 237, 248 (1952). In *Mottley,* the plaintiffs in a typical coercive action would be the Mottleys, suing to compel the railroad to renew the passes. If their action does not arise under federal law, then the railroad's should not either. In other words, availability of the declaratory judgment procedure, which reverses the posture of the parties and makes the railroad's defense the basis of the declaratory judgment complaint, should not change the rules for assessing subject matter jurisdiction.

At least we know the rule here: Inverting the parties doesn't make the case arise under federal law. But a good argument can be made that it should change the outcome. When the railroad sues and alleges that it is barred by the federal statute from renewing the passes, we *know* that the federal issue will be litigated. Why should the court ignore that fact and hold that the claim does not arise under federal law? One reason, certainly, is that it would allow the parties to assure federal jurisdiction if they both wanted it. If the plaintiff claimed under federal law, she would sue. If the defendant had a federal defense, it would sue, seeking a declaratory judgment. Another reason is that fairness to the parties suggests that they both should have access to federal court, or neither.

Q **8. Congressional control over federal question jurisdiction.** In the early 1980s, a number of bills were filed in Congress that would have deprived the federal district courts of jurisdiction over cases arising under particular federal statutes or constitutional provisions, such as abortion and school busing cases. What provision in Article III would support the argument that Congress may selectively limit the types of federal question cases the federal district courts may hear?

A As noted earlier, Article III, Section 1 gives Congress the power to "ordain and establish" lower federal courts. But nothing in Article III expressly requires Congress to give the federal trial courts jurisdiction over all the types of cases authorized in Section 2. *See, e.g., Kline v. Burke Construction Co.,* 260 U.S. 226,

233–34 (1922). Congress could authorize jurisdiction over diversity cases but not federal question cases, or admiralty cases but not cases against aliens. The cases also uphold the authority of Congress to limit the jurisdiction of the lower federal courts to a subset of federal question cases, for example, or a subset of diversity cases.

If Congress can pick and choose in this way, it seems to follow that it may make exceptions barring jurisdiction over claims that raise particular issues of substantive federal law. However, constitutional scholars disagree radically on the authority of Congress to restrict federal jurisdiction to advance a particular substantive agenda. *See generally* Erwin Chermerinsky, Federal Jurisdiction § 3.3 (6th ed. 2019). The issue has never been squarely resolved by the Supreme Court.

V. Beyond the Holmes Test: State Law Claims Involving Substantial Questions of Federal Law

If a case satisfies the Holmes test, it will almost certainly be held to arise under federal law for purposes of 28 U.S.C. § 1331. "The 'vast majority' of cases that come within this grant of jurisdiction are covered by Justice Holmes' statement that 'a suit arises under the law that creates the cause of action.'" *Merrell Dow Pharmaceuticals Inc. v. Thompson*, 478 U.S. 804, 808 (1986). It is a fair working guideline that where a plaintiff seeks relief under a federal statute or regulation, the federal court will have jurisdiction under § 1331.

The converse statement, however, is not so ironclad. Some cases in which the plaintiff seeks relief under state law may *still* arise under federal law. The United States Supreme Court has held that a case that asserts a state law claim may satisfy § 1331 if, in order to decide the state law claim, the court will have to resolve a substantial issue of federal law:

> Under our interpretations, Congress has given the lower federal courts jurisdiction to hear, originally or by removal from a state court, only those cases in which a well-pleaded complaint establishes *either* that federal law creates the cause of action *or* that the plaintiff's right to relief necessarily depends on resolution of a substantial question of federal law.

Franchise Tax Board of California v. Construction Laborers Vacation Trust, 463 U.S. 1, 27–28 (1983) (emphasis added). This statement recognizes that sometimes a plaintiff may invoke federal question jurisdiction even though the source of her right to relief is a state law cause of action. This will be true if the resolution of the plaintiff's state law claim "necessarily depends" on the decision of an issue of federal law.

Some Background

***An early case:* Smith v. Kansas City Title & Trust Co.** In *Smith v. Kansas City Title & Trust Co.*, 255 U.S. 180 (1921), the Supreme Court held that a case based on a state law claim could arise under federal law if the plaintiff's case turned on an important federal issue. Smith, a shareholder, sued to enjoin Kansas City Title from investing in certain bonds issued by federal banks. Smith claimed that under its charter Kansas City Title could only invest in valid federal securities and that the bonds in the case were invalid because the federal law authorizing them exceeded Congress's authority under the United States Constitution.

Smith's action was a state law equity proceeding to enjoin a corporation from acting beyond the limits of its charter. But the underlying *ground* for the relief sought was the invalidity of the bonds under the federal Constitution. In order to obtain his injunction, Smith had to establish that investing in the bonds was beyond Kansas City Title's authority. To do that, he had to show that the bonds were invalid; and to show that, he had to show that the federal act authorizing issuance of the bonds was unconstitutional. Because Smith could only win by establishing this proposition of federal law, the Supreme Court held that the federal court had jurisdiction to entertain the action.

The* Smith *exception reaffirmed and articulated. For many years, there was considerable doubt whether *Smith* represented a viable alternative to the Holmes test or a quirky case of little precedential value. However, in 2005 the Supreme Court reaffirmed *Smith* in *Grable & Sons Metal Products, Inc. v. Darue Engineering & Manufacturing*, 545 U.S. 308 (2005). In *Grable*, the federal government had taken real property of Grable's to satisfy a tax liability, and sold it to Darue. Grable later brought an action to quiet title, claiming that notice of the tax taking had not been given properly, so that Darue had not acquired clear title to the property. An action to quiet title arises under state property law, but Grable argued that the federal court had jurisdiction over the case because, to determine whether Darue had acquired good title, the court would have to determine whether proper notice of the seizure had been given under the federal tax code. Thus, to establish the state property law claim, Darue had to prove a proposition of federal law, just as the plaintiff had to in *Smith*.

In *Grable*, the Supreme Court reaffirmed the viability of the *Smith* exception to the Holmes test for arising-under jurisdiction. But the *Grable* court held that only some cases involving embedded federal issues will qualify for arising-under jurisdiction. The Court provided the following guidelines for determining which issues will do so:

> But even when the state action discloses a contested and substantial federal question, the exercise of federal jurisdiction is subject to a possible veto. For the federal issue will ultimately qualify for a federal forum only if federal jurisdiction is consistent with congressional judgment about the sound division of labor between state and federal courts governing the application of § 1331. Thus, *Franchise Tax Bd.* explained that the appropriateness of a federal forum to hear an embedded issue could be evaluated only after considering the "welter of issues regarding the interrelation of federal and state authority and the proper management of the federal judicial system." *Id.*, at 8, 103 S. Ct. 2841. Because arising-under jurisdiction to hear a state-law claim always raises the possibility of upsetting the state-federal line drawn (or at least assumed) by Congress, the presence of a disputed federal issue and the ostensible importance of a federal forum are never necessarily dispositive; there must always be an assessment of any disruptive portent in exercising federal jurisdiction....
>
> These considerations have kept us from stating a "single, precise, all-embracing" test for jurisdiction over federal issues embedded in state-law

> claims between nondiverse parties.... We have not kept them out simply because they appeared in state raiment, as Justice Holmes would have done [under the "creation" test] ... but neither have we treated "federal issue" as a password opening federal courts to any state action embracing a point of federal law. Instead, the question is, does a state-law claim necessarily raise a stated federal issue, actually disputed and substantial, which a federal forum may entertain without disturbing any congressionally approved balance of federal and state judicial responsibilities.

The *Grable* guidelines on the reach of the "*Smith* exception" are somewhat enigmatic (described as an "unruly doctrine" in *Gunn v. Minton,* the case below). The *Gunn* case provides a well-reasoned example of the Court applying those guidelines to an embedded-federal-issue case.

READING *GUNN v. MINTON.* This case involved two lawsuits. The first was a patent infringement case brought in federal court against an alleged infringer. Minton lost that case, because the court held that he had not been entitled to a patent on his invention. Minton then sued his lawyers from the first case for legal malpractice, in state court. He claimed that they had failed to make an argument under federal patent law (the "experimental use" exception) that would have led the court in the prior suit to find his patent valid. He lost on that argument in the state trial court, but on appeal he argued (hey, any port in a storm!) that the trial court had lacked subject matter jurisdiction over the case, because it arose under the federal patent laws. Why? He argued that, in order to prove legal malpractice—a state tort claim—he had to establish that his patent would have been held valid if his lawyers had made the experimental use argument in the prior lawsuit. Thus his case against his lawyers arose under federal law under the *Smith/Grable* exception to the Holmes test: In order to prove his state legal malpractice claim he had to establish a proposition of federal law. And, if the case arose under federal patent law, the state court had no subject matter jurisdiction to hear it, because 28 U.S.C. § 1338(a) makes federal jurisdiction over claims that arise under patent law exclusive to the federal courts.

So the case presented another example of a plaintiff asserting that his state law claim arose under federal law because it required resolution of an embedded federal issue. Note that the "Court of Appeals" referred to in the opinion is the Texas state Court of Appeals, not a federal court of appeals. This case was litigated up through the Texas court system and appealed from the Texas Supreme Court to the United States Supreme Court.

- Why would a federal court lack subject matter jurisdiction over this case under the Holmes test?
- Did the Court agree with Minton that his case required proof of an embedded federal issue?
- What would have been the effect on the workload of the federal courts if this case had been decided the other way? What would be the effect on the opportunity for state courts to decide malpractice cases?
- If the Supreme Court had agreed that the case arose under the federal patent laws, what would it have ordered the Texas state court to do?

GUNN v. MINTON

568 U.S. 251 (2013)

Chief Justice ROBERTS delivered the opinion of the Court.

Federal courts have exclusive jurisdiction over cases "arising under any Act of Congress relating to patents." 28 U.S.C. § 1338(a). The question presented is whether a state law claim alleging legal malpractice in the handling of a patent case must be brought in federal court.

I

In the early 1990s, respondent Vernon Minton developed a computer program and telecommunications network designed to facilitate securities trading. In March 1995, he leased the system—known as the Texas Computer Exchange Network, or TEXCEN—to R.M. Stark & Co., a securities brokerage. A little over a year later, he applied for a patent for an interactive securities trading system that was based substantially on TEXCEN. The U.S. Patent and Trademark Office issued the patent in January 2000.

Patent in hand, Minton filed a patent infringement suit in Federal District Court against the National Association of Securities Dealers, Inc. (NASD) and the NASDAQ Stock Market, Inc. He was represented by Jerry Gunn and the other petitioners. NASD and NASDAQ moved for summary judgment on the ground that Minton's patent was invalid under the "on sale" bar, 35 U.S.C. § 102(b). That provision specifies that an inventor is not entitled to a patent if "the invention was . . . on sale in [the United States], more than one year prior to the date of the application," and Minton had leased TEXCEN to Stark more than one year prior to filing his patent application. Rejecting Minton's argument that there were differences between TEXCEN and the patented system that precluded application of the on-sale bar, the District Court granted the summary judgment motion and declared Minton's patent invalid. . . .

Minton then filed a motion for reconsideration in the District Court, arguing for the first time that the lease agreement with Stark was part of ongoing testing of TEXCEN and therefore fell within the "experimental use" exception to the on-sale bar . . . (describing the exception). The District Court denied the motion.

Minton appealed to the U.S. Court of Appeals for the Federal Circuit. That court affirmed, concluding that the District Court had appropriately held Minton's experimental-use argument waived. . . .

Minton, convinced that his attorneys' failure to raise the experimental-use argument earlier had cost him the lawsuit and led to invalidation of his patent, brought this malpractice action in Texas state court. His former lawyers defended on the ground that the lease to Stark was not, in fact, for an experimental use, and that therefore Minton's patent infringement claims would have failed even if the experimental-use argument had been timely raised. The trial court agreed, holding that Minton had put forward "less than a scintilla of proof" that the lease had been for an experimental purpose. App. 213. It accordingly granted summary judgment to Gunn and the other lawyer defendants.

On appeal, Minton raised a new argument: Because his legal malpractice claim was based on an alleged error in a patent case, it "aris[es] under" federal patent law for purposes of 28 U.S.C. § 1338(a). And because, under § 1338(a), "[n]o State court shall have jurisdiction over any claim for relief arising under any Act of Congress relating to patents," the Texas court—where Minton had originally brought his malpractice claim—lacked subject matter jurisdiction to decide the case. Accordingly, Minton argued, the trial court's order should be vacated and the case dismissed, leaving Minton free to start over in the Federal District Court.

A divided panel of the Court of Appeals of Texas rejected Minton's argument. Applying the test we articulated in *Grable & Sons Metal Products, Inc. v. Darue Engineering & Mfg.*, 545 U.S. 308 (2005), it held that the federal interests implicated by Minton's state law claim were not sufficiently substantial to trigger § 1338 "arising under" jurisdiction. It also held that finding exclusive federal jurisdiction over state legal malpractice actions would, contrary to *Grable*'s commands, disturb the balance of federal and state judicial responsibilities. Proceeding to the merits of Minton's malpractice claim, the Court of Appeals affirmed the trial court's determination that Minton had failed to establish experimental use and that arguments on that ground therefore would not have saved his infringement suit.

The Supreme Court of Texas reversed, relying heavily on a pair of cases from the U.S. Court of Appeals for the Federal Circuit.... The Court concluded that Minton's claim involved "a substantial federal issue" within the meaning of *Grable* "because the success of Minton's malpractice claim is reliant upon the viability of the experimental use exception as a defense to the on-sale bar." 355 S.W.3d, at 644. Adjudication of Minton's claim in federal court was consistent with the appropriate balance between federal and state judicial responsibilities, it held, because "the federal government and patent litigants have an interest in the uniform application of patent law by courts well-versed in that subject matter." *Id.*, at 646....

Justice Guzman, joined by Justices Medina and Willett, dissented. The dissenting justices would have held that the federal issue was neither substantial nor disputed, and that maintaining the proper balance of responsibility between state and federal courts precluded relegating state legal malpractice claims to federal court.

We granted certiorari.

II

"Federal courts are courts of limited jurisdiction," possessing "only that power authorized by Constitution and statute." *Kokkonen v. Guardian Life Ins. Co. of America*, 511 U.S. 375, 377 (1994). There is no dispute that the Constitution permits Congress to extend federal court jurisdiction to a case such as this one, see *Osborn v. Bank of United States*, 9 Wheat. 738, 823–824 (1824); the question is whether Congress has done so.

As relevant here, Congress has authorized the federal district courts to exercise original jurisdiction in "all civil actions arising under the Constitution, laws, or treaties of the United States," 28 U.S.C. § 1331, and, more particularly, over "any civil action arising under any Act of Congress relating to patents," § 1338(a). Adhering to the demands of "[l]inguistic consistency," we have interpreted the phrase "arising under" in both sections identically, applying our § 1331 and § 1338(a) precedents interchangeably. See *Christianson v. Colt Industries Operating Corp.,* 486 U.S. 800, 808–809 (1988). For cases falling within the patent-specific arising under jurisdiction of § 1338(a), however, Congress has not only provided for federal jurisdiction but also eliminated state jurisdiction, decreeing that "[n]o State court shall have jurisdiction over any claim for relief arising under any Act of Congress relating to patents." § 1338(a) (2006 ed., Supp. V). To determine whether jurisdiction was proper in the Texas courts, therefore, we must determine whether it would have been proper in a federal district court—whether, that is, the case "aris[es] under any Act of Congress relating to patents."

For statutory purposes, a case can "aris[e] under" federal law in two ways. Most directly, a case arises under federal law when federal law creates the cause of action asserted. See *American Well Works Co. v. Layne & Bowler Co.,* 241 U.S. 257 (1916) ("A suit arises under the law that creates the cause of action"). As a rule of inclusion, this "creation" test admits of only extremely rare exceptions, see, *e.g., Shoshone Mining Co. v. Rutter,* 177 U.S. 505 (1900), and accounts for the vast bulk of suits that arise under federal law... Minton's original patent infringement suit against NASD and NASDAQ, for example, arose under federal law in this manner because it was authorized by 35 U.S.C. §§ 271, 281.

But even where a claim finds its origins in state rather than federal law—as Minton's legal malpractice claim indisputably does—we have identified a "special and small category" of cases in which arising under jurisdiction still lies. *Empire Healthchoice Assurance, Inc. v. McVeigh,* 547 U.S. 677, 699 (2006). In outlining the contours of this slim category, we do not paint on a blank canvas. Unfortunately, the canvas looks like one that Jackson Pollock got to first. See 13D C. Wright, A. Miller, E. Cooper, & R. Freer, Federal Practice and Procedure § 3562, pp. 175–176 (3d ed. 2008) (reviewing general confusion on question).

In an effort to bring some order to this unruly doctrine several Terms ago, we condensed our prior cases into the following inquiry: Does the "state-law claim necessarily raise a stated federal issue, actually disputed and substantial, which a federal forum may entertain without disturbing any congressionally approved balance of federal and state judicial responsibilities"? *Grable,* 545 U.S., at 314. That is, federal jurisdiction over a state law claim will lie if a federal issue is: (1) necessarily raised, (2) actually disputed, (3) substantial, and (4) capable of resolution in federal court without disrupting the federal-state balance approved by Congress. Where all four of these requirements are met, we held, jurisdiction is proper because there is a "serious federal interest in claiming the advantages thought to be inherent in a federal forum," which can be vindicated without disrupting Congress's intended division of labor between state and federal courts. *Id.,* at 313–314.

III

Applying *Grable*'s inquiry here, it is clear that Minton's legal malpractice claim does not arise under federal patent law. Indeed, for the reasons we discuss, we are comfortable concluding that state legal malpractice claims based on underlying patent matters will rarely, if ever, arise under federal patent law for purposes of § 1338(a). Although such cases may necessarily raise disputed questions of patent law, those cases are by their nature unlikely to have the sort of significance for the federal system necessary to establish jurisdiction.

A

To begin, we acknowledge that resolution of a federal patent question is "necessary" to Minton's case. Under Texas law, a plaintiff alleging legal malpractice must establish four elements: (1) that the defendant attorney owed the plaintiff a duty; (2) that the attorney breached that duty; (3) that the breach was the proximate cause of the plaintiff's injury; and (4) that damages occurred. See *Alexander v. Turtur & Associates, Inc.,* 146 S.W.3d 113, 117 (Tex. 2004). In cases like this one, in which the attorney's alleged error came in failing to make a particular argument, the causation element requires a "case within a case" analysis of whether, had the argument been made, the outcome of the earlier litigation would have been different.... To prevail on his legal malpractice claim, therefore, Minton must show that he would have prevailed in his federal patent infringement case if only petitioners had timely made an experimental-use argument on his behalf.... That will necessarily require application of patent law to the facts of Minton's case.

B

The federal issue is also "actually disputed" here—indeed, on the merits, it is the central point of dispute. Minton argues that the experimental-use exception properly applied to his lease to Stark, saving his patent from the on-sale bar; petitioners argue that it did not. This is just the sort of "'dispute... respecting the... effect of [federal] law'" that *Grable* envisioned. 545 U.S., at 313 (quoting *Shulthis v. McDougal,* 225 U.S. 561, 569 (1912)).

C

Minton's argument founders on *Grable*'s next requirement, however, for the federal issue in this case is not substantial in the relevant sense. In reaching the opposite conclusion, the Supreme Court of Texas focused on the importance of the issue to the plaintiff's case and to the parties before it. 355 S.W.3d, at 644 ("because the success of Minton's malpractice claim is reliant upon the viability of the experimental use exception as a defense to the on-sale bar, we hold that it is a substantial federal issue").... As our past cases show, however, it is not enough that the federal issue be significant to the particular parties in the immediate suit; that will *always* be true when the state claim "necessarily raise[s]" a disputed federal issue, as *Grable* separately requires. The substantiality inquiry under *Grable* looks instead to the importance of the issue to the federal system as a whole.

In *Grable* itself, for example, the Internal Revenue Service had seized property from the plaintiff and sold it to satisfy the plaintiff's federal tax delinquency. Five years later, the plaintiff filed a state law quiet title action against the third party that had purchased the property, alleging that the IRS had failed to comply with certain federally imposed notice requirements, so that the seizure and sale were invalid. *Ibid.* In holding that the case arose under federal law, we primarily focused not on the interests of the litigants themselves, but rather on the broader significance of the notice question for the Federal Government. We emphasized the Government's "strong interest" in being able to recover delinquent taxes through seizure and sale of property, which in turn "require[d] clear terms of notice to allow buyers... to satisfy themselves that the Service has touched the bases necessary for good title." *Id.,* at 315. The Government's "direct interest in the availability of a federal forum to vindicate its own administrative action" made the question "an important issue of federal law that sensibly belong[ed] in a federal court." *Ibid.*

A second illustration of the sort of substantiality we require comes from *Smith v. Kansas City Title & Trust Co.,* 255 U.S. 180 (1921), which *Grable* described as "[t]he classic example" of a state claim arising under federal law. 545 U.S., at 312. In *Smith,* the plaintiff argued that the defendant bank could not purchase certain bonds issued by the Federal Government because the Government had acted unconstitutionally in issuing them. 255 U.S., at 198. We held that the case arose under federal law, because the "decision depends upon the determination" of "the constitutional validity of an act of Congress which is directly drawn in question." *Id.,* at 201. Again, the relevant point was not the importance of the question to the parties alone but rather the importance more generally of a determination that the Government "securities were issued under an unconstitutional law, and hence of no validity." *Ibid.*

Here, the federal issue carries no such significance. Because of the backward-looking nature of a legal malpractice claim, the question is posed in a merely hypothetical sense: *If* Minton's lawyers had raised a timely experimental-use argument, would the result in the patent infringement proceeding have been different? No matter how the state courts resolve that hypothetical "case within a case," it will not change the real-world result of the prior federal patent litigation. Minton's patent will remain invalid.

Nor will allowing state courts to resolve these cases undermine "the development of a uniform body of [patent] law." *Bonito Boats, Inc. v. Thunder Craft Boats, Inc.,* 489 U.S. 141, 162 (1989). Congress ensured such uniformity by vesting exclusive jurisdiction over actual patent cases in the federal district courts and exclusive appellate jurisdiction in the Federal Circuit. See 28 U.S.C. §§ 1338(a), 1295(a)(1). In resolving the nonhypothetical patent questions those cases present, the federal courts are of course not bound by state court case-within-a-case patent rulings.... See *Tafflin v. Levitt,* 493 U.S. 455, 465 (1990). In any event, the state court case-within-a-case inquiry asks what would have happened in the prior federal proceeding if a particular argument had been made. In answering that question, state courts can be expected to hew closely to the pertinent federal precedents. It is those precedents, after all, that would have applied had the argument been made. Cf. *ibid.* ("State courts adjudicating civil RICO claims will ... be guided by federal court interpretations of the relevant federal criminal statutes, just as federal courts sitting in diversity are guided by state court interpretations of state law").

As for more novel questions of patent law that may arise for the first time in a state court "case within a case," they will at some point be decided by a federal court in the context of an actual patent case, with review in the Federal Circuit. If the question arises frequently, it will soon be resolved within the federal system, laying to rest any contrary state court precedent; if it does not arise frequently, it is unlikely to implicate substantial federal interests. The present case is "poles apart from *Grable,*" in which a state court's resolution of the federal question "would be controlling in numerous other cases." *Empire Healthchoice Assurance, Inc.,* 547 U.S., at 700.

Minton also suggests that state courts' answers to hypothetical patent questions can sometimes have real-world effect on other patents through issue preclusion. Minton, for example, has filed what is known as a "continuation patent" application related to his original patent. See 35 U.S.C. § 120; 4A D. Chisum, Patents § 13.03 (2005) (describing continuation applications). He argues that, in evaluating this separate application, the patent examiner could be bound by the Texas trial court's interpretation of the scope of Minton's original patent.... It is unclear whether this is true. The Patent and Trademark Office's Manual of Patent Examining Procedure provides that res judicata is a proper ground for rejecting a patent "only when the earlier decision was a decision of the Board of Appeals" or certain federal reviewing courts, giving no indication that state court decisions would have preclusive effect.... In fact, Minton has not identified any case finding such preclusive effect based on a state court decision. But even assuming that a state court's case-within-a-case adjudication may be preclusive under some circumstances, the result would be limited to the parties and patents that had been before the state court. Such "fact-bound and situation-specific" effects are not sufficient to establish federal arising under jurisdiction. *Empire Healthchoice Assurance, Inc., supra,* at 701.

Nor can we accept the suggestion that the federal courts' greater familiarity with patent law means that legal malpractice cases like this one belong in federal court. See *Air Measurement Technologies,* 504 F.3d, at 1272 ("The litigants will also benefit from federal judges who have experience in claim construction and infringement matters"); 355 S.W.3d, at 646 ("patent litigants have an interest in the uniform application of patent law by courts well-versed in that subject matter"). It is true that a similar interest was among those we considered in *Grable*.... But the possibility that a state court will incorrectly resolve a state claim is not, by itself, enough to trigger the federal courts' exclusive patent jurisdiction, even if the potential error finds its root in a misunderstanding of patent law.

There is no doubt that resolution of a patent issue in the context of a state legal malpractice action can be vitally important to the particular parties in that case. But something more, demonstrating that the question is significant to the federal system as a whole, is needed. That is missing here.

D

It follows from the foregoing that *Grable*'s fourth requirement is also not met. That requirement is concerned with the appropriate "balance of federal and state judicial responsibilities." *Ibid.* We have already explained the absence of a substantial federal issue within the meaning of *Grable*. The States, on the other hand, have "a special responsibility for maintaining standards among members of the licensed professions." *Ohralik v. Ohio State Bar Assn.*, 436 U.S. 447, 460 (1978). Their "interest . . . in regulating lawyers is especially great since lawyers are essential to the primary governmental function of administering justice, and have historically been officers of the courts." *Goldfarb v. Virginia State Bar*, 421 U.S. 773, 792 (1975) (internal quotation marks omitted). We have no reason to suppose that Congress—in establishing exclusive federal jurisdiction over patent cases—meant to bar from state courts state legal malpractice claims simply because they require resolution of a hypothetical patent issue.

* * *

As we recognized a century ago, "[t]he Federal courts have exclusive jurisdiction of all cases arising under the patent laws, but not of all questions in which a patent may be the subject-matter of the controversy." *New Marshall Engine Co. v. Marshall Engine Co.*, 223 U.S. 473 (1912). In this case, although the state courts must answer a question of patent law to resolve Minton's legal malpractice claim, their answer will have no broader effects. It will not stand as binding precedent for any future patent claim; it will not even affect the validity of Minton's patent. Accordingly, there is no "serious federal interest in claiming the advantages thought to be inherent in a federal forum," *Grable, supra*, 13. Section 1338(a) does not deprive the state courts of subject matter jurisdiction.

The judgment of the Supreme Court of Texas is reversed, and the case is remanded for further proceedings not inconsistent with this opinion.

It is so ordered.

Notes and Questions on the "*Smith* Exception"

Q **1. Does the plaintiff's claim in *Gunn* satisfy the Holmes test?**

A No, Gunn's claim for legal malpractice clearly does not "arise under" federal law as construed by Justice Holmes. Minton's claim in *Gunn* was for legal malpractice, a state law tort claim. However, as in *Smith v. Kansas City Title* and *Grable & Sons*, the plaintiff could only prove the state law claim by establishing a point of federal law.

2. Minton's turnabout on subject matter jurisdiction. Note that it was Minton, the plaintiff, who brought suit in the state court and lost, who then argued on appeal that the state trial court had lacked jurisdiction to decide the case. Even though this seems like dubious litigation conduct, courts virtually always consider objections to subject matter jurisdiction. As *Mottley* illustrates, this objection can even be raised on appeal, and may be raised by the court *sua sponte*—that is, without any party raising the point. Had the *Gunn* Court concluded that the case arose under federal law, it would have remanded the case with an order to dismiss it, which would have left Minton free to try again in federal court.

Q **3. The standard for finding federal jurisdiction in embedded-federal-issue cases.** In *Smith* and *Grable* the Court upheld jurisdiction. In *Gunn,* which also involved an embedded state law issue, the Court rejected it. So what is the rule in such cases?

A Under *Grable* and *Gunn,* there is no mechanical rule that will easily resolve these federal-issue-in-a-state-law-claim cases. The court must consider several factors in determining whether the case merits federal jurisdiction.

> Does the "state-law claim necessarily raise a stated federal issue, actually disputed and substantial, which a federal forum may entertain without disturbing any congressionally approved balance of federal and state judicial responsibilities"? *Grable,* 545 U.S., at 314. That is, federal jurisdiction over a state law claim will lie if a federal issue is: (1) necessarily raised, (2) actually disputed, (3) substantial, and (4) capable of resolution in federal court without disrupting the federal-state balance approved by Congress.

Gunn, 133 S. Ct. at 1065. In most cases the first two factors will be met, so the analysis will focus on the last two. A major factor in determining whether the federal issue is "substantial" is the importance of the federal issue to the development of federal law. In *Grable,* the issue of the proper method to serve process in tax foreclosure proceedings could impact many cases and affect title to many properties. In *Gunn,* a decision about whether the lawyers should have made the "experimental use" argument would affect Minton's right to recover malpractice damages, so it was clearly a "substantial" ingredient of the parties' lawsuit. But it was not substantial in terms of defining federal patent law; it raised a factual issue that would have no precedential effect in other cases. The last factor, the potential for disrupting the balance between state and federal courts, is clearly implicated in cases (like *Gunn*) involving matters generally reserved to the states, such as the regulation of lawyers. *Gunn* also emphasized the impact that finding federal jurisdiction would have on the federal courts' docket; upholding jurisdiction in the malpractice case would bring a myriad of state tort cases into federal court. It would also disrupt the traditional federal/state jurisdictional balance, since states have traditionally played the predominant role in regulating the legal profession.

4. Clear jurisdictional rules? In a concurring opinion in *Grable,* Justice Thomas suggested that recognizing jurisdiction in these cases may not be worth the effort involved in making the distinction. "Jurisdictional rules should be clear. Whatever the virtues of the *Smith* standard, it is anything but clear." 545 U.S. at 321. The Court's decision to find jurisdiction in some embedded-federal-issue cases, but not all, will lead to more jurisdictional litigation. Parties anxious to use the federal courts will bring their state law claim in federal court and argue that an embedded federal issue supports jurisdiction. Consequently, federal courts will end up litigating whether they have jurisdiction under the *Grable* guidelines in a good many cases. If the Court had adopted the Holmes test in all cases instead, the rule would be clearer and save a lot of court time and litigation expense for clients. Of course, the justices were aware of this in deciding *Gunn* and *Grable.* Their reaffirmation of the *Smith* exception reflects a judgment that providing a federal forum for some cases presenting important embedded federal issues is sufficiently important to the role of federal courts that it is worth the cost of increased litigation applying the *Grable* guidelines to close cases.

Interestingly, the Court's holding in *Hertz Corp. v. Friend,* 559 U.S. 77 (2010), reflects a different priority in jurisdictional analysis. In *Hertz,* the Court pronounced a bright line rule for determining a corporation's principal place of business for purposes of diversity jurisdiction, emphasizing the importance of having a clear standard for jurisdiction in order to reduce litigation about jurisdiction.

5. Revisiting the substantial federal issues in *Mottley.* Consider the following question, which revisits the Mottleys' dilemma after the Supreme Court's decisions in *Grable* and *Gunn.*

In *Grable,* the Court noted that "in certain cases federal question jurisdiction will lie over state-law claims that implicate significant federal issues." 545 U.S. at 312. Suppose that, just after *Grable* and *Gunn,* the Mottleys sue to renew their passes. (Ignore the fact that they would be 150 years old, please.) The railroad raises the federal statute barring free passes as a defense to the claim. The Mottleys' position (asserted in their complaint) is that the statute does not bar renewal of passes given before its enactment, and that, if it does, it is unconstitutional under the Fifth Amendment. Assume that these issues have never been resolved by the courts.

Given the analysis in *Grable* and *Gunn,* the Mottleys

A. could bring their action in federal court, because their well-pleaded complaint raises issues of federal law.
B. could not bring their action in federal court, because their complaint does not assert a federal claim or require them to establish an important issue of federal law to recover.
C. could not bring their action in federal court, unless the court finds that these are substantial issues of federal law, and entertaining the action will not disrupt the balance between state and federal courts.
D. could bring their action in federal court, because the Mottleys have raised two substantial, unresolved issues of federal law.

To answer this question, you need to understand a basic point about the *Smith* exception: It does not change the fundamental holding of *Mottley* that in assessing federal question jurisdiction, the court must look at the plaintiff's claim without regard to any defenses the defendant may assert (or has asserted). In *Smith, Grable,* and *Gunn,* the plaintiffs had to establish a proposition of federal law in order to recover, even if that proposition was not a direct element of their state law claim. These cases do not displace the *Mottley* principle that jurisdiction must be based on the plaintiff's claims; rather they reaffirm a fairly narrow corollary of the *Mottley* rule. Perhaps we might call it the "well-proved complaint" rule.

A is wrong here because the Mottleys' well-pleaded complaint would still not raise any issue of federal law. The railroad will raise the first federal issue—that the statute bars renewing the passes—as a defense. And the Mottleys would raise the Fifth Amendment argument in rebuttal to that defense. **D** is wrong because, while the Mottleys raised these issues in their complaint, they would not be raised in a *well-pleaded* complaint for breach of contract, just as in the original case. And **C** is wrong because, even if these are substantial federal issues, they are not embedded in the plaintiff's original case.

B, then, is the correct answer. Just as in the original case, the Mottleys' complaint raises only state law issues. After *Grable* and *Gunn*, it would not support jurisdiction under 28 U.S.C. § 1331, because the federal issues here do not have to be established to prove the plaintiff's original claim.

6. An exception for every rule. The Holmes test provides a little solid footing in this slippery jurisdictional morass. If federal law creates the plaintiff's right to sue, the case arises under federal law. It is usually the embedded-federal-issue cases that raise the problems.

But there's even an exception to the Holmes test. *Shoshone Mining Co. v. Rutter*, 177 U.S. 505 (1900), involved a suit to settle a mining claim. A federal statute authorized parties to bring such suits, but provided that they should be decided under local mining customs and statutes. The Holmes test arguably supports jurisdiction in *Shoshone Mining*, since the federal statute authorized the suits. But in another sense, the statute did not "create the cause of action," since the governing substantive standard for deciding the claims was state law. The Supreme Court held that this case did not arise under federal law, even though federal law created the right to sue, because the governing property law rules were provided by state or local law.

This exception also makes good sense. Even though a federal statute authorized the suits in *Shoshone Mining*, virtually all the suits would involve state law issues only. Applying the Holmes test mechanically would arguably bring all of these cases into federal court, without any reason to do so. *Grable* characterized *Shoshone Mining* as "an extremely rare exception" to the Holmes test. 545 U.S. at 317 n.5.

7. The *Bell v. Hood* problem: Suits asserting novel claims to relief under federal law. In *Bell v. Hood*, 327 U.S. 678 (1946), the plaintiffs claimed money damages for violation of their Fourth Amendment rights to be free of unreasonable searches and seizures. The Supreme Court had never held that plaintiffs are entitled to money damages for such violations. The plaintiffs claimed that their complaint arose under federal law, but the defendants argued that the federal court lacked subject matter jurisdiction to hear the case: A case could hardly "arise under" federal law, they argued, if the federal right the plaintiffs assert does not exist.

The Supreme Court held that the *Bell* plaintiffs' claims did arise under federal law, because they *claimed* a right to recover under federal law. There is a difference, the Court suggested, between asserting a right to relief under federal law and convincing the court that that right exists. Clearly, the plaintiffs' complaint asserted a right to relief under federal law and that sufficed to support federal question jurisdiction. True, the court might conclude that the right they claimed did not exist. If so, it should dismiss their claims *on the merits*, not for lack of jurisdiction. That way, the federal court would be able to perform one of its primary functions, defining the contours of federal rights.

On remand in *Bell*, the federal district court exercised federal question jurisdiction over the case and reached the merits. It concluded that the Constitution did not authorize damages for unreasonable searches and seizures. The plaintiffs, although they had asserted a substantial federal claim, failed to convince the court that the federal right they claimed existed. They lost on the merits. Some years later, however, the Supreme Court held that plaintiffs sometimes may recover damages for such violations. *Bivens v. Six Unknown Named Agents of the Federal Bureau of Narcotics*, 403 U.S. 388 (1971).

Q **8. Federal law adopting state standards.** Suppose that Congress passes a statute providing that no federally chartered bank may charge interest rates in excess of those authorized by the law of the state in which it is located. An Oregon federal bank charges Wellington 19 percent interest, which exceeds the 17 percent ceiling set by Oregon law. She sues the bank to enjoin them from charging 19 percent, claiming it exceeds the rate allowed by the federal statute. Does the case arise under federal law?

A The court would probably conclude that this case arises under federal law. Here, Congress has created a federal limit on the interest rate that banks may charge: No bank shall charge more than the legal rate of interest in the state where it is located. Congress might have said, "No bank may charge more than 18 percent." Or, it might have said, "No bank may charge more than the Federal Reserve Bank charges." Instead, it has chosen to define the limit by reference to state law. But it is still a limit established by federal law. Similarly, if a federal statute provided that no manufacturer may sell electrical components failing to meet the standards of Underwriters Laboratory, it would set a federal standard, although that federal standard incorporated private safety standards by reference.

9. Cases raising both federal and state claims. Plaintiffs frequently assert several claims in a single action, some based in federal law and others based in state law. Lowell, a plaintiff roughed up by a police officer during an arrest, might sue under 42 U.S.C. § 1983, a federal statute that authorizes suits for damages for violation of federal constitutional rights. But she also might assert a state tort claim for battery in her complaint based on the same facts.

Lowell's first claim arises under federal law, since she must establish a violation of the federal Constitution (an unreasonable seizure under the Fourth Amendment) in order to recover. But her second claim arises under state law. Should the court throw out the second claim, both claims, or neither?

This is a complex issue, which we address fully in Chapter 20 on "supplemental" jurisdiction. Generally, if the plaintiff asserts a substantial claim that provides a basis for federal court jurisdiction, the federal court will have supplemental jurisdiction over other claims arising from the same facts. In Lowell's case, for example, because the federal civil rights claim gives the federal court a basis for jurisdiction, it may hear the related state law claim for battery as well.

However, supplemental jurisdiction only extends to such state law claims if they arise out of the same underlying events as the federal claim. All of these claims, state and federal, are thought of as a single dispute; as long as one claim gives the federal court a basis for jurisdiction (the § 1983 claim in Lowell's case), the court may hear all claims that arise from that dispute.

10. A reprise on the limits of federal question jurisdiction.

In which of the following cases would the federal district court have subject matter jurisdiction over the case?

A. Gupta, from Kentucky, sues Milinoski, also from Kentucky, claiming a violation of the federal Age Discrimination in Employment Act.
B. Consolidated Widget Company sues Ruggiero for breach of an employment contract. Ruggiero, who is from the same state, counterclaims for damages under the federal Age Discrimination in Employment Act.
C. Erskine, a city councilor, sues the *Times-Union*, the local newspaper, for libel, based on a *Times-Union* story stating that he had fled the scene of an accident. The *Times-Union* claims a privilege under the First Amendment, which bars recovery for libel of a public figure unless the paper acted in reckless disregard of the truth in researching the allegations in the story. Erskine claims that the privilege does not apply because the story made no reference to his public office. Whether the privilege applies in such circumstances is an important, unresolved issue of federal law.
D. Margolis threatens to sue her employer, Petrikas Publishers, claiming that it has failed to make its premises accessible to the disabled, as required by the federal Americans with Disabilities Act. Petrikas brings suit in federal district court for a declaratory judgment that it is not subject to the requirements of the Act.

Let's proceed in order. **A** is a proper federal question case, since Gupta seeks relief under federal law. The fact that he and the defendant are from the same state is irrelevant. A case only needs to meet one category of federal subject matter jurisdiction to be brought in federal court, not two or more.

B is also straightforward. Federal question jurisdiction must be based on the plaintiff's complaint, not an answer or counterclaim. There is no jurisdiction over this case, since Consolidated brings a breach of contract action, and the court cannot base federal question jurisdiction on a counterclaim. **C** turns on a similar principle: The defendant cannot assert federal jurisdiction based on a federal defense, even if it has already been asserted at the time she invokes federal jurisdiction. Although the federal issue is important, this does not mean that the *Smith/Grable* exception applies. In those cases, *the plaintiff* had to establish an important federal issue to recover; federal issues raised by *the defendant* still don't support federal question jurisdiction under 28 U.S.C. § 1331.

D is a little tricky. It involves a declaratory judgment action. In such actions, there is federal question jurisdiction if the case would have arisen under federal law if it had been brought as an ordinary action by the party seeking coercive relief. Here, the plaintiff in a "regular" suit would have been Margolis, seeking injunctive relief to make the property accessible. If Margolis had sued, her claim would have arisen under federal law—the federal Americans with Disabilities Act—so the declaratory judgment action does too.

VI. Article III and Supreme Court Jurisdiction: *Mottley*, Round II

Let's return for a moment to the Mottleys. Recall that they sued the railroad in federal court for their passes and litigated the case all the way up to the United States Supreme Court, only to be told by the justices that the federal trial court never had subject matter jurisdiction over their case.

State courts have very broad subject matter jurisdiction, much broader than that of the federal courts. Thus, the Kentucky state trial court of general jurisdiction (confusingly called the circuit court) had jurisdiction to hear the Mottleys' breach of contract claim. So the Mottleys sued the railroad in the Kentucky Circuit Court, seeking renewal of their passes on the same breach of contract theory. The railroad raised the same two defenses under federal law. The Kentucky Circuit Court heard the case, held that the Mottleys were entitled to renewal of their passes, and entered judgment ordering the railroad to renew them.

The railroad appealed again. Now, however, the railroad was appealing a state trial court decision, so the case went on appeal to the Kentucky Court of Appeals, the highest state court of Kentucky. That court affirmed, holding that the federal statute did not apply to passes issued prior to the passage of the statute. *Louisville & Nashville R.R. Co. v. Mottley*, 133 Ky. 652 (1909).

Now we come to the interesting part. The railroad, having lost again, appealed again to the United States Supreme Court. Recall that the Supreme Court sits at the top of both court systems: The Supreme Court can hear appeals from the appellate courts of the states as well as the federal courts of appeals, if it has subject matter jurisdiction over the appeal. That's how *Gunn v. Minton* reached the Court from the Texas Supreme Court.

Q **So now the question.** Although the Supreme Court had held that it could not hear the appeal the first time the Mottleys' case reached it, the Court took jurisdiction of the appeal from the Kentucky Court of Appeals. How could it have jurisdiction the second time but not the first?

A The answer to this paradox lies in the distinction between the reach of jurisdiction under the Constitution and the reach of jurisdiction under 28 U.S.C. § 1331, by which Congress conveys federal question jurisdiction to the federal district courts. Remember that the lower federal courts derive their jurisdiction from federal statutes. The first *Mottley* decision interpreted the *statutory grant of original jurisdiction* to the federal district courts (in the predecessor to § 1331) to focus on cases in which the plaintiff's claim arises under federal law. Because the Mottleys sued for breach of contract, the federal statute did not authorize the *federal trial court* to exercise jurisdiction over their case.

When the Mottleys' case came to the Court on appeal from the Kentucky courts, the question was whether the case was within *the Supreme Court's appellate jurisdiction*, not the lower federal court's jurisdiction. The Supreme Court derives its power to hear cases directly from Article III, Section 2, which confers appellate jurisdiction upon the Court over most Article III cases. U.S. Const. art. III, § 2, para. 2. However, Article III authorizes Congress to regulate and restrict the Court's appellate jurisdiction. And the federal statute regulating the Supreme Court's jurisdiction over appeals from the state courts (now 28 U.S.C. § 1257)* authorizes the Supreme Court to review a state judgment "where the validity of a treaty or statute of the United States is drawn in question on the ground of its being repugnant to the Constitution, treaties or laws of the United States, or where any title, right, privilege or immunity is specially set up or claimed under the Constitution or the treaties or statutes of . . . the United States. . . ." Nothing in this broad language limits the Court's appellate jurisdiction to cases in which the federal issue is raised by the plaintiff. The railroad's appeal to the Supreme Court was authorized by the statute, since the railroad claimed an "immunity" to the Mottleys' claim under the federal statute barring free passes. And, under *Osborn v. Bank of the United States*, 22 U.S. 738, 823 (1824), the case was within the *constitutional* scope of federal question jurisdiction, since the railroad's defense injected a "federal ingredient" into the case.

The two *Mottley* appeals illustrate the different meanings of the phrase "arising under the Constitution, Laws and Treaties . . . of the United States" in Article III, Section 2 and in § 1331. Congress has limited the grant of federal question jurisdiction to the lower federal courts for practical reasons. "Although the constitutional meaning of 'arising under' may extend to all cases in which a federal question is 'an ingredient' of the action, we have long construed the statutory grant of federal question jurisdiction as conferring a more limited power." *Merrell Dow Pharmaceuticals, Inc. v. Thompson*, 478 U.S. 804, 807 (1986). Even though § 1331 uses the same language as the Constitution, it is interpreted much more narrowly under the *Mottley* rule.

Under Article III, a case is within the federal question jurisdiction as long as it involves a federal issue, whether that issue is raised by the plaintiff or the defendant. In regulating *the appellate jurisdiction of the Supreme Court*, Congress has granted the Supreme Court the right to review cases that turn on federal issues, whether they arise from the original claim or as a defense. Under that broad grant the Court can define and uphold federal law no matter how it arises in a case, under a standard almost as broad as the scope of federal question jurisdiction in Article III, Section 2. (However, as a practical matter, the Supreme Court cannot review very many state court cases. Thus, in many cases, issues of federal law are determined by state courts with no realistic likelihood of review by a federal court.)

What did the Supreme Court hold when it finally reached the merits of the Mottleys' case? The Court concluded that the statute was intended to bar passes

* The version of the statute in force at the time of the *Mottley* appeal, tracing back to the First Judiciary Act of 1789, was quite similar to § 1257.

granted before its enactment and that the statute was constitutional. *Louisville & Nashville R.R. Co. v. Mottley*, 219 U.S. 467 (1911). The Mottleys made some long-standing black letter law, but they lost their case.

VII. Federal Question Jurisdiction: Summary of Basic Principles

- The constitutional grant of federal question jurisdiction in Article III, Section 2 was broadly construed in *Osborn v. Bank of the United States.* So long as a case involves a non-frivolous issue of federal law, whether raised in the original complaint or in a defendant's answer, a federal court may be authorized to hear it.
- The power of Congress to create lower federal courts includes the power to define their jurisdiction by statute. Article III, Section 2 sets the outer limit, but within the scope of Article III, Section 2, Congress may pick and choose, granting federal trial courts less than the full jurisdiction authorized by the Constitution. Thus, Congress may, and has, authorized the federal district courts to hear some cases that arise under federal law, but not others.
- The grant of federal question jurisdiction in 28 U.S.C. § 1331 is considerably more limited than the constitutional scope of federal question jurisdiction under *Osborn*. Under *Mottley*'s well-pleaded complaint rule, the court looks only to the plaintiff's claim in determining whether a case arises under federal law.
- In the vast majority of cases, the Holmes test works to determine whether a case satisfies the *Mottley* requirement. If federal law creates the cause of action that the plaintiff seeks to enforce, the federal court has jurisdiction under 28 U.S.C. § 1331. If the plaintiff seeks recovery on a state law cause of action, it usually does not.
- Occasionally, a case will be held to arise under federal law even though the plaintiff seeks recovery on a state law claim. In cases such as *Grable & Sons Metal Products, Inc. v. Darue Engineering & Manufacturing,* the Supreme Court has recognized that sometimes a plaintiff will have to establish an important proposition of federal law in order to prove a state law claim. Depending on the importance of the federal issue, whether federal jurisdiction would disrupt the allocation of business between state and federal courts, and other prudential factors, a court may find that the federal district court has jurisdiction over the case under 28 U.S.C. § 1331.
- The jurisdiction of the United States Supreme Court is established in Article III, Section 2 and also regulated by federal statute. The statutes authorizing the Court's appellate jurisdiction are much broader than 28 U.S.C. § 1331. Many state court cases that involve issues of federal law may be reviewed by the Supreme Court, even though the federal issue is raised as a defense or in some other posture. Even though such cases do not satisfy the *Mottley* rule, they are within the grant of appellate jurisdiction to the Supreme Court.

5

Removal of Cases from State to Federal Court

I. Introduction: Concurrent Jurisdiction of the State and Federal Courts

Previous chapters have focused on two categories of federal subject matter jurisdiction: diversity and federal question cases. In addition to those categories of cases, Article III, Section 2 of the Constitution also authorizes federal courts to hear cases between states, cases to which the United States is a party, admiralty and maritime cases, and others. However, recall a basic point made earlier: The fact that a case may be heard in federal court does not mean that it must be. Most cases that are within the federal courts' subject matter jurisdiction may also be heard in state courts as well.

For example, if Callahan, from California, wants to sue Colletti, from Oregon, for $200,000 for breach of contract, she may bring that case in federal court under diversity jurisdiction. However, if she prefers to sue in state court, she may bring it there instead. The state and federal courts are said to have *concurrent jurisdiction* over diversity cases. Similarly, if Matsui has a claim against Moreau under the federal Age Discrimination in Employment Act, he could bring that suit in federal court, since the case arises under a federal statute. Once again, however, he does not have to. Because the state courts exercise concurrent jurisdiction over most federal question cases, Matsui may bring the action in either court.

Since the inception of the federal courts, federal removal statutes have authorized defendants sued in state court to remove certain cases to federal court, that is, to take the case out of the state court and refile it in federal court. The rationale for allowing removal is that the defendant should have the same option as the plaintiff to choose a federal court to hear a case that is within federal subject matter jurisdiction. The plaintiff may choose federal court by filing suit there initially. (If she does, the defendant cannot "remove" the case to state court.) If the plaintiff files in state court, the removal statute allows the defendant to choose a federal forum by removing the case to federal court.

II. The Standard for Removal

The basic removal provision, 28 U.S.C. § 1441(a), reflects this premise of equal access—that the defendant should only be entitled to remove a case if the case, as pleaded by the plaintiff, could have been filed initially in federal court by the plaintiff:

> (a) Except as otherwise provided by Act of Congress, any civil action brought in a State court of which the district courts of the United States have original jurisdiction, may be removed by the defendant or the defendants, to the district court of the United States for the district and division embracing the place where such action is pending.

Under § 1441(a), the defendant may remove a case "of which the district courts of the United States have original jurisdiction," that is, cases that the plaintiff could have filed in federal court initially. Even though the plaintiff prefers to litigate the case in state court (we know that she does, because she filed there), the defendant may, in most cases, override that choice by removing the case to federal court. The result is that if either party wants a case within federal jurisdiction to be heard in federal court, the case will be heard there.

READING *AVITTS v. AMOCO PRODUCTION CO.* The *Avitts* case, below, illustrates this basic removal principle. In reading *Avitts*, consider the following questions.

- Why did Amoco, the defendant, think that the case could be removed?
- After it removed the case, what order did the federal district court enter?
- Who appealed to the Fifth Circuit Court of Appeals?
- When did the plaintiff move to remand to state court? (A trick question.)
- How did the appellate court resolve the case?

AVITTS v. AMOCO PRODUCTION CO.

53 F.3d 690 (5th Cir. 1995)

Per Curiam:

This matter comes before the court on a consolidated appeal from interim orders entered by the district court. In 94-60058, Appellants **[Eds.—several other oil companies were defendants along with Amoco]** appeal from the entry of a preliminary injunction requiring them to complete a "phase II" environmental study. In 94-60059, Appellants appeal from an order requiring them to pay approximately $650,000 in interim costs and attorney's fees. We find that the district court lacks subject matter jurisdiction over this action, and therefore vacate the orders of the district court and remand with instructions to remand this action to the state court from which it was removed.

I. BACKGROUND

Appellees originally filed suit in Texas state district court to recover monetary damages for alleged injuries to their property caused by the defendants' oil and gas operations in the West Hastings Field. The matter was removed to the Southern District of Texas on the basis that Appellees' complaint stated,

> It is expected that the evidence will reflect that the damages caused by the Defendants are in violation of not only State law *but also Federal law.*

(emphasis supplied). Despite the nebulous referral to "federal law," the complaint stated no cause of action which could be read to confer federal question jurisdiction on the district court. In fact, in concert with their notice of removal Appellants filed a Fed. R. Civ. P. 12(e) motion for a more definite statement, which *inter alia* stated,

> Plaintiffs claim Defendants violated "State law" and "Federal law" in allegedly causing these spills. However, Plaintiffs fail to specify which State of [sic] Federal laws Defendant allegedly violated. Consequently, Defendants cannot possibly formulate a response or know what defenses may apply.

Although the district court summarily denied Appellants' motion for a more definite statement, Appellees subsequently filed a first amended complaint, this time omitting *all* reference to federal law. Although the Appellees' complaint has been amended several times during the pendency of this litigation, no federal question has ever been stated.[3]

3. Plaintiff's last complaint, the seventh amended complaint, contains state law causes of action for "nuisance," "trespass," "negligence," "breach of contract" and "fraud and misrepresentation" and prays for actual damages in the amount of ten million dollars and exemplary damages in the amount of one hundred million dollars.

II. DISCUSSION

"Any civil action brought in a State court of which the district courts of the United States have original jurisdiction, may be removed by the defendant or the defendants, to the district court of the place where such action is pending." 28 U.S.C. § 1441(a). Original jurisdiction over the subject matter is mandatory for the maintenance of an action in federal court. Subject matter jurisdiction may not be waived, and the district court "shall dismiss the action" whenever "it appears by suggestion of the parties or otherwise that the court lacks jurisdiction of the subject matter."

Original jurisdiction, in non-maritime claims, lies where the conditions of 28 U.S.C. §§ 1331 or 1332 are satisfied. In the present action, the court claims original jurisdiction pursuant to § 1331, also known as federal question jurisdiction. There is no dispute that original jurisdiction does not lie under § 1332, diversity of citizenship, because complete diversity does not exist. Under 28 U.S.C. § 1331, "[t]he district courts shall have original jurisdiction of all civil actions arising under the Constitution, laws, or treaties of the United States."

Plaintiff is generally considered the master of his complaint, and "whether a case arising . . . under a law of the United States is removable or not . . . is to be determined by the allegations of the complaint or petition and that if the case is not then removable it cannot be made removable by any statement in the petition for removal or in subsequent pleadings by the defendant." *Great Northern Ry., Co. v. Alexander,* 246 U.S. 276, 281 (1918). Of course, this does not mean that a plaintiff can avoid federal jurisdiction by simply "artfully pleading" a federal cause of action in state law terms. See *Federated Dept. Stores, Inc. v. Moitie,* 452 U.S. 394, 397 n.2 (1981). However, it is also plain that when both federal and state remedies are available, plaintiff's election to proceed exclusively under state law does not give rise to federal jurisdiction.

In the present case, there is no doubt that Appellees have chosen to pursue only state law causes of action. The only mention of federal law in any of Appellees' complaints was the above mentioned oblique reference to Appellants' violation of unspecified federal laws. No federal cause of action has ever been asserted, and it is plain that removal jurisdiction under 28 U.S.C. § 1441 simply did not exist. The district court had no jurisdiction over the subject matter of the complaint, and the action should have been immediately remanded to state court. . . .

[S]ubject matter jurisdiction was supposedly achieved through Appellees' reference to CERCLA and the Oil Pollution Act of 1990 (OPA) **[Eds.—two federal statutes]** in the Joint Pretrial Order (PTO). Notwithstanding the highly questionable applicability of either of these statutes to the facts and circumstances of this case, adoption of this argument would require us to rewrite the PTO. Under the PTO's plain terms, CERCLA and OPA are offered only as a means to calculate the "Measure of Damages" owed to the Appellees. Appellees never asserted a cause of action under either statute, and subject matter jurisdiction cannot be created by simple reference to federal law. Subject matter jurisdiction can be created only by pleading a cause of action within the district court's original jurisdiction. No such cause of action has *ever* been plead in this matter, and therefore subject matter jurisdiction is plainly absent.

III. CONCLUSION

The district court lacked subject matter jurisdiction over this action and was therefore without authority to enter its orders. The orders of the district court are vacated, and this matter is remanded to the district court with instructions to remand this action to the state court from which it was removed in accordance with 28 U.S.C. § 1447(c).

VACATED and REMANDED.

Notes and Questions: *Avitts v. Amoco Production Co.*

1. The basic premise: Jurisdiction upon removal turns on original federal jurisdiction. For most cases, removal jurisdiction gives defendants the same access to federal court that plaintiffs have. Thus, in deciding whether removal is proper, the court must ask whether the plaintiff (who sued in state court) could have filed the action in federal court. If so, the defendant may usually remove; if not, the case should be remanded to state court.

2. Were the defendants justified in removing the case? It is unclear whether the *Avitts* complaint asserts a federal claim or not. It does claim that the defendants had violated federal law. Amoco's lawyers may have been genuinely uncertain as to whether the complaint stated a federal claim. If so, and if they preferred to litigate in federal court, they would have to remove to avoid waiving the right to do so: If a case is removable, the defendants must remove it within thirty days of receiving the complaint. 28 U.S.C. § 1446(b)(1). So defense counsel may have made an understandable tactical decision to remove the case rather than lose the chance to do so.

3. When did Avitts, the plaintiff, move to remand the case to state court? The opinion contains no indication that Avitts ever moved to remand, and a later opinion in the case explains that Avitts did not. Avitts amended the complaint after removal, and the amended complaint omitted any reference to federal law. Before trial the defendants moved to remand the case to state court for lack of subject matter jurisdiction. Interestingly, the plaintiffs opposed the motion, since things seemed to be going very well for them in federal court. The federal court denied the motion to remand, commenced a nonjury trial, took four days of testimony, and entered an order requiring the defendants to pay more than $600,000 to fund an environmental study and to pay the plaintiffs' attorneys fees.

Conversely, things did not look so good for the defendants, now subject to a burdensome order from the federal court. So, just before trial, *the defendants*—who had removed to federal court—moved to remand for lack of subject matter jurisdiction and Avitts *opposed* the motion to remand!

> After the pre-trial conference, all the defendants moved to dismiss the action on grounds that the district court had no federal question or diversity jurisdiction over any part of the action. Appellees [the plaintiffs] opposed the motion, arguing that the district court had authority to entertain the action under its pendent jurisdiction. Appellees persuaded the district court to deny the motion to dismiss and retain the case in federal court. In fact, the district court embraced the appellees' position and characterized the defendants' jurisdictional arguments as "meritless."

111 F.3d 30, 31 (5th Cir. 1997) (a later decision in the same case).

4. The appellate court's conclusion. Because the judge had entered a final judgment ordering the defendants to do the study and pay the plaintiff's fees, the defendants could—and did—appeal that judgment to the Fifth Circuit Court of Appeals. Ironically, on appeal they challenged the judge's orders on the merits, not his conclusion that the court had federal subject matter jurisdiction. The court of appeals concludes that the *Avitts* complaint only asserted state law claims, so it was improperly removed. Although the complaint included several general references to federal law, Avitts did not sue under any federal statute, nor was there diversity between the parties. Thus, the case could not have been filed originally in federal court and could not be removed under 28 U.S.C. § 1441(a).

There are echoes of *Mottley* here. In *Mottley*, as in *Avitts*, the plaintiffs *referred to* federal law in their complaint, but they did not assert a right to relief under federal law. Just as the Mottleys' right to sue initially in federal court required that they seek relief under federal law, here the right to remove turned on whether Avitts sought relief under federal law. The court concluded that he (and the co-plaintiffs) did not.

Q **5. What became of the order to do an environmental study?** How did the court of appeals rule on the trial court's order to complete the environmental study? What will happen next after the court of appeals' decision?

A With removed cases as well as cases filed initially in federal court, if the court lacks jurisdiction, it cannot proceed. Since the court of appeals concluded that the district court lacked subject matter jurisdiction, it ordered the district court to remand the case to state court. The case will not be dismissed, but remanded—returned to the state court to be litigated there.

Thus, the order for the environmental study was vacated, since the federal district judge had no authority to enter it. Avitts, if not too exhausted to press on, will have to start over in state court.

6. The in-state defendant rule. The removal statute bars removal of a diversity case if any defendant is from the forum state.

> A civil action otherwise removable solely on the basis of the jurisdiction under section 1332(a) of this title [i.e., a diversity case] may not be removed if any of the parties in interest properly joined and served as defendants is a citizen of the state in which such action is brought.

28 U.S.C. § 1441(b)(2). Thus, if Carrera, from Michigan, sues Dempsey, from Texas, in a Texas state court, Dempsey may not remove to federal court. The logic for this exception is that Dempsey is not at risk of prejudice based on his state citizenship, since he has been sued in his home state. If anyone might suffer prejudice based on state citizenship, it would be Carrera, but he has chosen the Texas state court. So there is no need to allow Dempsey the option of removal to federal court.

7. Removal and "forum shopping." A plaintiff may have many reasons for preferring to keep a case in state court. She may view the state judge who is likely to hear the case as favorably inclined toward her case. She may like the discovery rules in the state court. She may be more comfortable with the state court's procedures or rules of evidence. (Some of the tactical considerations that may influence counsel's choice are discussed at the end of Chapter 1.) If the plaintiff prefers state court, naturally, she will sue there. However, under the removal statute, the defendant may be able to second-guess that choice and move the case to federal court. Lawyers can sometimes structure their cases to avoid removal, a form of "forum shopping." Here are some ways that plaintiffs might avoid removal by structuring their cases.

- *Careful pleading.* In *Avitts*, the plaintiffs, who at least initially preferred state court, could have pleaded more carefully by avoiding any reference to federal law in their complaint. They did not actually assert any federal claims, so this would have been appropriate and avoided any argument that the case was removable under federal question jurisdiction.

  A plaintiff with both federal claims and state law claims against a non-diverse defendant can also simply omit the federal claim from the case, avoiding a basis for removal based on federal question jurisdiction. Of course, the plaintiff gives up the chance to recover on the federal claim by failing to plead it. In some cases, lawyers might consider this a proper price to pay to avoid federal court, especially if the federal claim is not a strong one.

- *Joining an in-state defendant.* Plaintiffs may decide to sue a defendant from the forum state in order to prevent removal under the in-state defendant bar in § 1441(b)(2). Suppose that Chang, from Utah, suffers injury after using a drug manufactured by Acme Drug Corporation, incorporated in Delaware with its principal place of business in Pennsylvania. If Chang prefers state court, but sues only Acme, it could remove the case to federal court based on diversity (unless she sues in Pennsylvania or Delaware). However, suppose that Dr. Nathan, a Colorado doctor, prescribed the drug for Chang. If she sued Nathan along with Acme, in Colorado state court, the case would not be removable, since there is an in-state defendant.
- *Joining a non-diverse defendant.* Similarly, a plaintiff may avoid removal by suing a non-diverse defendant. If Chang sued Acme in Pennsylvania, but also sued Dr. Maroni, a Utah doctor who prescribed the drug, the case would remain in state court. To do so, however, she must have a viable claim against Maroni. And, Maroni must be subject to personal jurisdiction in the Pennsylvania action, which is doubtful if she treated Chang in Utah.
- *Limiting the amount requested in a diversity case.* A plaintiff might limit her claim to less than the jurisdictional amount in 28 U.S.C. § 1332(a) or leave out a claim, such as a demand for punitive damages, that would bolster the argument that the amount requirement is met.
- *Fraudulent joinder.* Plaintiffs may be tempted to prevent removal by asserting a claim against an in-state defendant in a diversity case, or against a non-diverse defendant, even if that claim is weak or frivolous. If a defendant believes that the plaintiff has "fraudulently joined" another defendant to prevent removal, without any viable claim against the added defendant, the defendant should remove the case and argue to the federal court that the case is actually a proper diversity case because the other defendant has been fraudulently joined. In this context, "fraudulently joined" means "that the plaintiff cannot state a reasonable or colorable claim for relief under the applicable substantive law against the party whose presence in the action would destroy the district court's subject matter jurisdiction." *Wright & Miller* § 3641.1 (footnote omitted). If the federal court agrees with the defendant, it will order the fraudulently joined defendant dismissed, and take jurisdiction over the case.

In some of these examples, the plaintiff will pay a price to buy the state forum—lower damages, the additional expense and complexity of litigating against another defendant, or forgoing a potentially viable theory of relief. Plaintiffs often conclude, however, that obtaining their preferred forum really matters, so that they are willing to pay that price.

8. Forum shopping: A lawyer's obligation or an abuse of the system? The term "forum shopping" refers to the choice of a court for some strategic advantage that may be important in a particular case. The term has a pejorative flavor, suggesting a low-down, sneaky lawyer trick. Yet lawyers represent clients and seek to advance their legal interests. If a case may be heard in several courts, a strong argument can be made that a lawyer should choose the forum most likely to advance those interests.

Is this kind of tactical maneuvering unethical? Nothing in the rules governing lawyers' conduct prohibits structuring litigation to avoid federal court. Ethical rules prohibit the filing of *frivolous* claims, but if, for example, a plaintiff has a valid claim against a non-diverse party (along with a diverse one), she is entitled to pursue it, even if she is motivated by a desire to avoid federal court. Most lawyers would consider this an acceptable tactical choice in pursuing their client's litigation interests.

9. Probing the limits of §§ 1441(a) and (b). Consider the following multiple choice question.

Which of the following cases may be removed to federal court?

A. Martinez, from Texas, sues Murphy, from Utah, on a state law breach of contract claim, in a Utah state court, for $200,000.
B. Martinez, from Texas, sues Murphy, from Utah, and Mercer, from Nevada, on a state law breach of contract claim, in a Utah state court, for $200,000.
C. Martinez, from Texas, sues Murphy, from Utah, on a claim arising under federal law. She brings the suit in a Utah state court.
D. Martinez, from Texas, sues Hawkins, from Texas, on a state law claim for negligence. Hawkins counterclaims against Martinez for violation of a federal statute. (A counterclaim is a claim asserted by a defendant seeking relief from the plaintiff.)

Section 1441(b)(2) bars removal of the case in **A**. Murphy is sued at home, so he is not at risk of prejudice as an out-of-state litigant and has no need of an alternative federal forum. Martinez, the plaintiff, is the out-of-stater. If he feared bias as an out-of-stater, he could have brought the case in federal court. Evidently, he isn't concerned about that, since he chose the state court.

In **B**, Mercer is an out-of-state litigant who might fear prejudice in the Utah state court. Yet, she cannot remove: Section 1441(b)(2) provides that diversity cases "may not be removed if any of the parties in interest properly joined and served is a citizen of the State in which such action is brought." Here one of the defendants is local, so removal is barred. This doesn't seem fair to Mercer. Isn't it possible that a local jury will shift the blame from Murphy to Mercer? It is possible, but the case still cannot be removed.

The case described in **C** is removable, even though there is an in-state defendant, because it arises under federal law. (Section 1441(a) authorizes removal, since the federal court would have original jurisdiction over the case, and the exception in § 1441(b)(2) does not apply.) This makes sense. Federal courts provide an experienced and hospitable forum for application and interpretation of federal law. If either party wants the federal court to hear a case arising under federal law, she should be able to invoke it.

The last case is not removable. Although Hawkins has injected a federal claim into the case by bringing a federal counterclaim against Martinez, the Supreme Court has held that the "defendant or defendants" language in the removal statute only allows defendants to remove. *Shamrock Oil & Gas Corp. v. Sheets,* 313 U.S. 100 (1941). The *Avitts* court states that removal cannot be based on subsequent pleadings, such as an answer asserting a counterclaim; it must be based on the original pleading. This is consistent with the general premise that defendants may only remove cases that the plaintiff could have brought in federal court. This plaintiff could not have filed in federal court, since she sued a non-diverse defendant on a state law claim.*

10. Specialized removal statutes. This chapter focuses on the general provisions for removal in 28 U.S.C. §§ 1441(a) and (b), 1446, and 1447. There are also various statutes that authorize removal of particular types of cases or by particular defendants. *See, e.g.,* 28 U.S.C. § 1442 (removal of cases against federal officers or agencies); 28 U.S.C. § 1443 (removal of certain civil rights cases); 28 U.S.C. § 1441(d) (removal of cases against foreign states); 28 U.S.C. § 1441(e) (removal of certain multi-party accident cases). There are even a few statutes that *bar* removal of particular types of cases that would otherwise be removable under § 1441. *See, e.g.,* 28 U.S.C. § 1445(a) (barring removal of Federal Employers Liability Act (FELA) cases). For a full discussion, see *Wright & Miller* §§ 3728–3728.2.

III. Procedure for Removal and Remand

A. The "Who, When, Where, and How" of Removal

Who may remove? As already stated, only a defendant may remove. Suppose the plaintiff sues several defendants, and some prefer federal court, while others want to stay in state court? The removal statute provides that a case may be removed by "the defendant or defendants." Based on this language, the Supreme Court held that all defendants must agree to remove. *Chicago, Rock Island & Pacific Railway Co. v. Martin,* 178 U.S. 245 (1900). This requirement has now been codified in 28 U.S.C. § 1446(b)(2)(A) (all defendants who "have been properly joined and served" must join in or consent to removal).

When must the case be removed? A defendant sued in state court must remove to federal court within thirty days of receiving the initial pleading or being

* One exception to this rule applies to patent, copyright, and plant variety cases. 28 U.S.C. § 1454. Section 1454 provides that "[a] civil action in which any party asserts a claim for relief arising under any Act of Congress relating to patents, plant variety protection, or copyrights may be removed to the district court of the United States for the district and division embracing the place where the action is pending" (emphasis added). Under this section, a defendant asserting a patent law counterclaim in state court may remove the case to federal court.

served with process in the action. 28 U.S.C. § 1446(b)(1). If the defendant does not remove within that period, she waives her right to remove. If she has second thoughts later on, it is too late. Thirty days is not very long to consider all the issues that may arise in a case and make an informed tactical choice between state and federal court. However, this short window for removal resolves quickly which court will hear the case, so the parties and the court can proceed with the case without fear that it will be bounced into another court.

Some of the tactical consequences of removing a case (or of not removing it) will be immediately apparent, like the place of the courthouse, how congested the docket is in the state and federal court, and (sometimes) which judge will hear the case in one court or the other. But other tactical consequences may not be apparent at the outset, when counsel have to make the choice to remove or not. Counsel will decide to remove—or not to—based on the information available at the beginning of the case. Yet later developments, unforeseeable at the time of removal, may lead her to wish that she had made the opposite choice.

Example of a notice of removal. The notice of removal below was filed in federal district court in the District of Massachusetts, removing a case from the Massachusetts Superior Court for Essex County to the federal court. It is drafted to demonstrate to the federal court that the requirements for removal of the case are met. It avers:

- (in the caption) that it is filed in the federal district court;
- that the notice is filed within thirty days after receipt of the summons and complaint [paragraph 1];
- that there is complete diversity among the parties [paragraphs 2–6];
- that the amount in controversy requirement is met [paragraph 7];
- that the federal court has original jurisdiction and removal jurisdiction over the case based on diversity [paragraph 8];
- that all documents filed in the state court are provided with the notice of removal [paragraph 9];
- that the plaintiff and the state court will be notified of the removal [paragraph 10];
- that all the defendants consent to removal [preamble and paragraph 11].

United States District Court, D. Massachusetts.

Vicente LARA and Mary Lara, Plaintiffs,
v.
FARREL CORPORATION, Stanley Black & Decker, Inc.,
and Rubber City Machinery Corp., Defendants.
No. 1:13CV12231.

September 9, 2013.

Notice of Removal

Consent to removal of this matter given by: Farrel Corporation, By its attorneys [names omitted]

Rubber City Machinery Corp., By its attorney [name omitted]

Stanley Black & Decker, Inc., By its attorneys [names omitted]

Stanley Black & Decker, Inc. ("Stanley") gives notice of removing this case from the Trial Court of Massachusetts, Superior Court Department, Essex County (Civil Action Number ESCV2013-01120-D) to the United States District Court for the District of Massachusetts. Removal is proper because there is complete diversity of citizenship and the claim of damages by the plaintiffs is in excess of $75,000, the statutory minimum for diversity jurisdiction. In support of removal, Stanley states:

1. Stanley first received a copy of the summons and complaint by certified mail, sent by [attorney's name omitted], on August 13, 2013, less than thirty days from the date of filing this notice of removal. Thus, this Notice of Removal is timely. 28 U.S.C. § 1446(b)(2)(B).

2. The plaintiffs Vicente and Mary Lara reside in and are citizens of the Commonwealth of Massachusetts. (Complaint ¶ 1.)

3. Farrel Corporation is a corporation organized under the laws of Delaware with a principal place of business in Ansonia, Connecticut. (Complaint ¶ 2.)

4. Stanley Black & Decker, Inc. is a corporation organized under the laws of Connecticut with a principal place of business in New Britain, Connecticut.

5. Rubber City Machinery Corp. is a corporation organized under the laws of Ohio with a principal place of business in Akron, Ohio. (Complaint ¶ 4.)

6. There is, therefore, complete diversity between the plaintiffs and defendants. 28 U.S.C. § 1332(c)(1).

7. Plaintiffs allege over $375,000 in damages, including over $25,000 in medical expenses, over $75,000 in lost wages, over $25,000 in reasonably anticipated future medical

expenses, and over $250,000 in other damages. (Civil Action Cover Sheet.) Accordingly, the amount in controversy exceeds $75,000.00, exclusive of interest and costs.

8. Consequently, the Plaintiff's claims are ones over which this Court has original jurisdiction pursuant to 28 U.S.C. § 1332 because there is complete diversity between the plaintiffs and defendants and the amount in controversy exceeds $75,000. The action is therefore removable under 28 U.S.C. § 1441(a).

9. Pursuant to 28 U.S.C. §1446(a), the complaint, summons, and tracking order, which constitute all process, pleadings, and orders served upon Stanley, are attached to this Notice of Removal.

10. Pursuant to 28 U.S.C. §1446(d), the Defendant will promptly give notice of this filing to the plaintiff and will file a copy of this Notice of Removal with the clerk of the Essex County Superior Court Department.

11. All defendants consent to this removal. 28 U.S.C. § 1446(b)(2)(A).

WHEREFORE, Stanley Black & Decker, Inc. respectfully requests that this Court remove to this court the civil action against it now pending in the Superior Court of Massachusetts, Essex County.

Consent to removal of this matter given by:

FARREL CORPORATION, By its attorneys, [signed by attorneys for the defendants]

RUBBER CITY MACHINERY CORP., By its attorney, [signed by attorney for the defendants]

STANLEY BLACK & DECKER, INC., By its attorneys, [signed by attorneys for the defendants]

Removal later in the case. Even if the defendant does not remove a case within thirty days after it is filed, it may sometimes be removed later. Suppose that Carla, a Florida plaintiff, files suit against Marin, a Florida defendant, for assault. Later, Carla's counsel learns that Marin, when he committed the assault, was arresting Carla in the course of his duties as a police officer. At this point counsel realizes that Carla has a federal civil rights claim against Marin for violation of the Fourth Amendment to the United States Constitution, and amends her complaint to add the federal claim.

Marin could not have removed this case as originally filed, since it was a state law tort claim between two Floridians. However, once Carla amends to add a claim under federal law, the case "becomes removable." In such cases, 28 U.S.C. § 1446(b)(3) gives Marin thirty days to remove after receiving the amended pleading. Similarly, Charlene, from Texas, might sue Bobby, from Utah and Jane, from Texas, in state court. After the period for removal has passed, she might drop Jane as a defendant. The case would then become removable based on diversity, and § 1446(b)(3) allows Bobby thirty days to remove it.*

This provision for later removal prevents wily plaintiffs from defeating the right to removal. A plaintiff wishing to avoid federal court could file suit in state court raising only state law claims, let the thirty-day period for removal go by, and then amend her complaint to assert her federal theories of relief. To avoid removal based on diversity, she could sue a non-diverse defendant along with a diverse defendant, let the thirty days run, and then drop the non-diverse defendant. Section 1446(b)(3) removes the temptation to engage in such maneuvering. It is always appropriate to craft civil procedure statutes and rules to discourage such manipulation.

Where should the case be removed to? The defendant cannot remove an action to any federal district she prefers. She must remove it to "the district court of the United States for the district and division embracing the place where such action is pending." 28 U.S.C. § 1441(a). If a state court case is filed in Dane County, which falls within the Western District of Wisconsin, it can only be removed to the Federal District Court for the Western District of Wisconsin. Thus, removal allows the defendant to choose the federal *system*, but does not give her a choice to move the case to a different state. Removal may still change the location of the litigation, however, if the federal district court sits in a city some distance from the county where the state case was filed.

The Geographic Impact of Removal

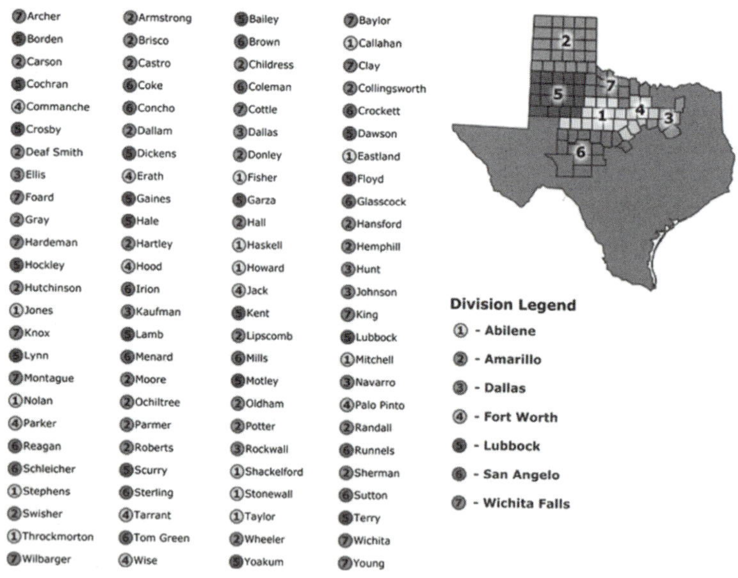

This chart from the website for the Federal District Court for the Northern District of Texas shows the counties within each division of the district. A case removed from any county within Block 2 will go to the Amarillo Division of the Northern District. Although removal is meant to move the case from the state to the federal court system, not to change the location of the litigation, removal often will move litigation to a city some distance from the county where it was filed. A case removed from the state court for Lipscomb County will go to the Amarillo Division sitting in Amarillo, 149 miles from Lipscomb.

* However, diversity cases may not, except in cases of bad faith by the plaintiff, be removed more than one year after commencement. 28 U.S.C. § 1446(c)(1).

B. The Process of Removal

To remove a case to federal court, the defendant files a notice of removal in the federal court and notifies the plaintiff and the state court that she has done so. 28 U.S.C. § 1446(a), (d). The notice should specify the ground on which the case is removable (e.g., that the case arises under a federal statute or is a claim between diverse citizens for more than $75,000) and include a copy of the state court complaint and summons.

Filing a notice of removal *automatically* transfers the case to the federal court—whether it is within the federal court's jurisdiction or not. Thus, the notice of removal in *Avitts* removed the case to the federal district court, even though that court ultimately held that it did not have jurisdiction over it.* When the notice of removal is filed and the state court notified, the state court loses all power to proceed with the case. 28 U.S.C. § 1446(d).

C. Motions to Remand

The defendant removes a case by filing the notice of removal. The plaintiff takes no part in the removal and may not even know about it until the notice of removal has been filed. If she thinks that the case is not removable or that the defendant did not use the proper procedure to remove (for example, that it was removed after the thirty-day period or removed without consent of other defendants), she should move *in the federal court* to remand the action to the state court. 28 U.S.C. § 1447(c). Appropriately, then, the federal court will decide whether the case was properly removed.

Notes and Questions: Removal Procedure

1. Waiving the right to remand based on improper removal. A plaintiff may move to remand for lack of subject matter jurisdiction "at any time before final judgment." 28 U.S.C. § 1447(c). However, other problems with removal (such as a claim that the defendant missed the thirty-day period in § 1446(b)(1) or removed without consent of all defendants) are waived if not raised in the federal court within thirty days. "A motion to remand the case on the basis of any defect other than lack of subject matter jurisdiction must be made within 30 days after the filing of the notice of removal under section 1446(a)." 28 U.S.C. § 1447(c).

The thirty-day period in § 1447(c) is different from that in § 1446(b)(1). Under § 1446(b)(1), the defendant must remove the case within thirty days of receiving the initial pleading in the case. In contrast, under 28 U.S.C. § 1447(c), a party moving to remand based on objections other than lack of subject matter jurisdiction must do so within thirty days after removal. If she does not, the objection is waived.

* That's not so strange, if you think about it. A plaintiff can always file a case in a court that lacks subject matter jurisdiction to hear it. Suppose that Chang, from New York, brings a case in federal court against Borden, from New York, on a state law claim. The federal court lacks jurisdiction over it, but has the authority to hear the motion to dismiss and decide whether it has jurisdiction.

The logic for the thirty-day period under § 1447(c) is that it is important to settle quickly which court is going to hear the case. This requirement also avoids manipulation by the parties. Without it, a party might notice a problem with removal but not raise it... unless things go badly for her later in the federal court.

Q Able sues Baker in state court on a federal claim. Baker removes to federal court thirty-five days after being served with the summons and complaint in the action. Forty days later Able moves to remand based on untimely removal. What will the court do?

A The court will deny the motion. Since removing late is not a jurisdictional defect, Able waives the objection under 28 U.S.C. § 1447(c) if he does not move to remand within thirty days after removal. Section 1447(c) forces Able to raise the problem right away or proceed in federal court. He waives all objections to removal other than a lack of subject matter jurisdiction if he fails to raise them within thirty days.

2. Applying § 1446(b)(3). The question below focuses on the tricky provision for later removal in the second paragraph of 28 U.S.C. § 1446(b)(3). Read that subsection carefully to choose the best answer.

Cannavo, from Oregon, sues Singh, from Minnesota, after he is fired by Singh three months into a one-year contract as an office manager for Singh. He sues in an Oregon state court, seeking $200,000 for breach of contract. Three months later, Cannavo amends the complaint to add a claim under the Americans with Disabilities Act, a federal statute, claiming that Singh failed to make reasonable accommodations for a disability that interfered with his job performance. Two weeks after receiving the amended complaint, Singh removes the case to federal court. Which of the following is correct?

A. Removal is proper under 28 U.S.C. § 1446(b)(3) after the amendment to add the federal claim.
B. Removal is proper under the *Mottley* rule, because Cannavo seeks relief under federal law.
C. Removal is not proper, because three months have gone by since the case was filed in state court.
D. Removal is not proper, because the case could have been removed as originally filed.

A student who didn't read § 1446(b)(3) would probably pick **C**, on the ground that a case must be removed within thirty days of receiving the initial pleading. But §1446(b)(3) is an exception to that, allowing later removal in some situations.

A student who read § 1446(b)(3) too quickly, would probably choose **A**, concluding that the case is now removable, since the amendment added a claim under federal law. Well, it did add a federal claim, but the case was *also* removable as originally filed, and Singh didn't do so. Section 1446(b)(3) allows removal of cases that "become removable" later in the case. *See* 28 U.S.C. § 1446(b)(3) ("If the case stated by the initial pleading is not removable. . . ."). Because Singh could have removed the original case based on diversity, but did not, he waived his right to remove. **D** is right. Ironically, Singh may have been content to litigate a contract claim in state court, but strongly prefer a federal forum once a federal claim is added to the case. However, he will not get one in this case.

Q **3. Removing a case when the state court lacks subject matter jurisdiction.** Congress may make federal jurisdiction over particular claims exclusive. For example, 28 U.S.C. § 1338(a) provides that patent cases must be brought in federal court. Suppose a plaintiff files such a case in state court. May the defendant remove it to federal court?

A For many years, the answer to this question was "no." The logic was that a federal court could not derive jurisdiction upon removal from a court that had no jurisdiction. *See generally Wright & Miller* § 3722. The state court had to dismiss the case, leaving the plaintiff to file a new suit in federal court.

Congress changed this "derivative jurisdiction" rule by enacting 28 U.S.C. § 1441(f), which sensibly provides that such an action may be removed to federal court even though the state court where it was filed lacked jurisdiction over it.

IV. Removal: Summary of Basic Principles

- The state and federal courts exercise concurrent jurisdiction over many types of cases. If there is concurrent jurisdiction, the case may be filed in either state or federal court. The plaintiff chooses the initial forum in such cases by filing in the court she prefers.
- If the plaintiff files a case in state court that could have been filed in federal court, the federal removal statute allows the defendants to remove the case to federal court. 28 U.S.C. § 1441.
- One exception to this principle is the "forum defendant" rule of § 1441(b)(2), which bars removal of a diversity case if any defendant is a citizen of the state in which the suit is brought.
- If a removable case is filed in state court, defendants must remove the case within thirty days or it will remain in state court. If a case is not initially removable, but later becomes removable (by addition of a federal claim or by dropping a non-diverse party), the defendants may remove within thirty days of receiving the pleading or order from which they can first determine that the case has become removable.

- Removal is automatic. Even if the defendant removes a non-removable case, it will be pending in federal court once the notice of removal is filed and the state court is notified. A party who believes that the case was improperly removed or that it is not within the federal court's subject matter jurisdiction should move in the federal court to remand the case.
- Motions to remand for lack of subject matter jurisdiction may be made at any time prior to final judgment in the case. Motions based on other objections, such as a late notice of removal or failure of a codefendant to agree to the removal, must be raised within thirty days after removal. If these non-jurisdictional objections are not asserted within this thirty-day period, they are waived.

PART III

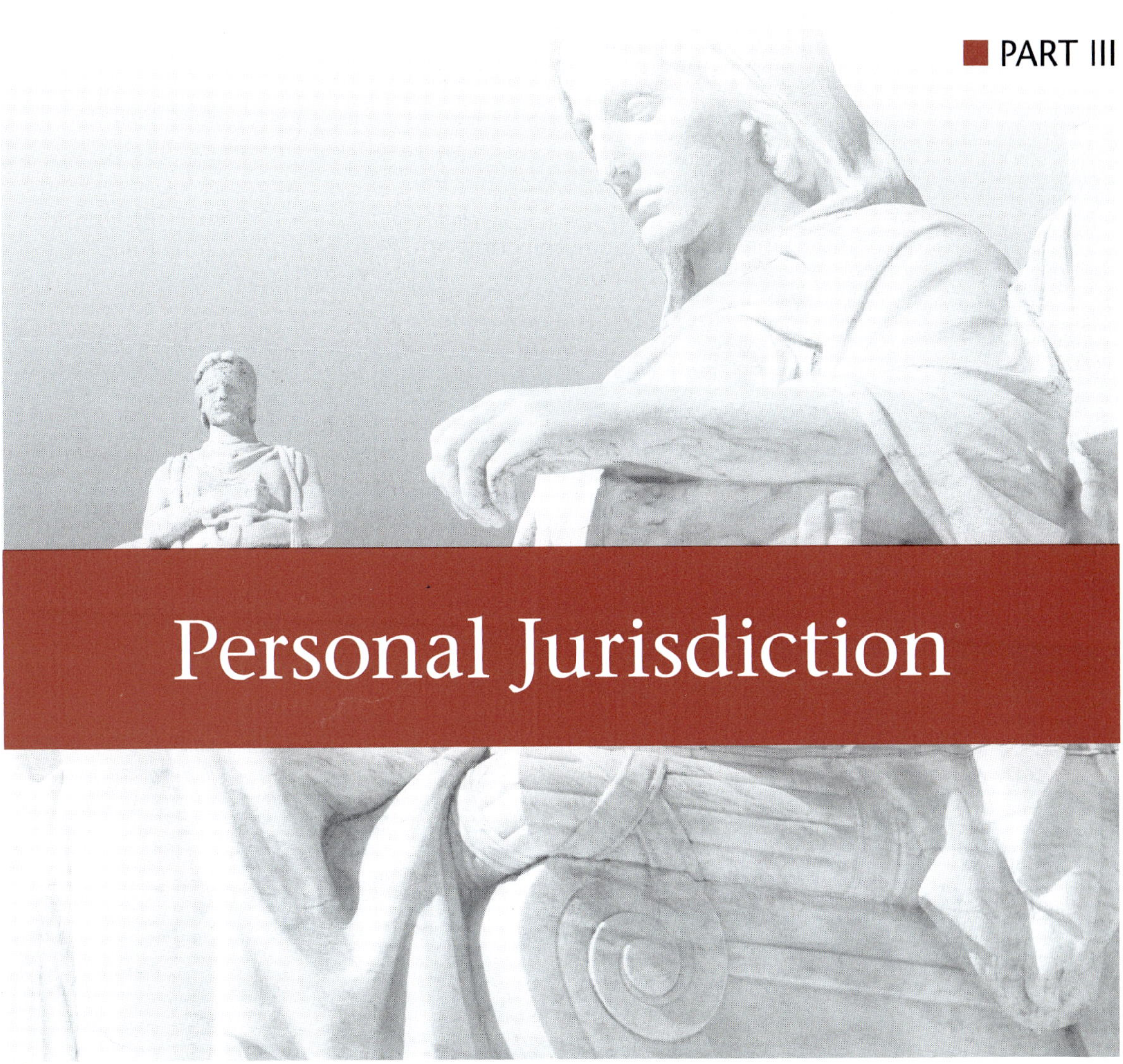

Personal Jurisdiction

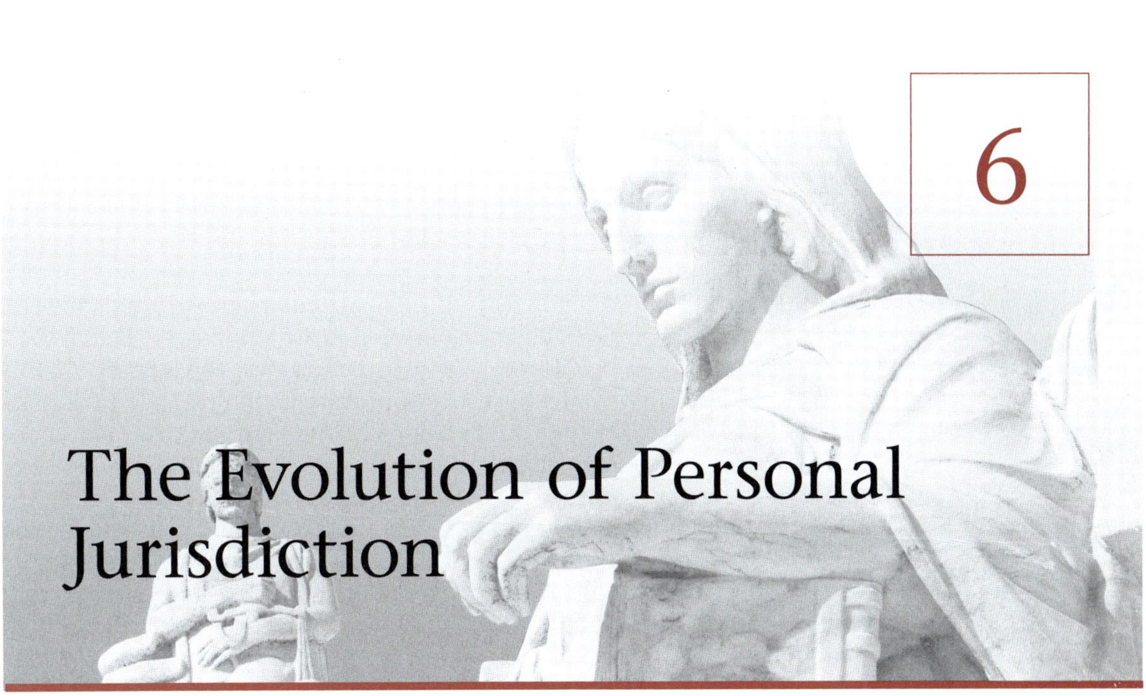

6

The Evolution of Personal Jurisdiction

I. An Introduction to Personal Jurisdiction

In previous chapters, you learned about a fundamental procedural requirement: A court must have subject matter jurisdiction over a case. The present chapter, and the three chapters that follow it, explore an additional requirement: A court must have the authority to require the defendant to appear in the forum and defend the action there. This judicial authority is referred to as *personal jurisdiction*.

To illustrate how personal jurisdiction differs from subject matter jurisdiction, consider a simple example. Imagine that Peter, a Massachusetts citizen, takes a vacation in Alaska and is in a car accident there with Dalia, an Alaskan citizen. Peter suffers injuries in the accident, so after returning home to Massachusetts, Peter asks a lawyer to sue Dalia in Massachusetts state court. As you have learned, subject matter jurisdiction is not a problem in that court. State trial courts have broad power to hear most types of cases, including most tort claims. A lawyer simply needs to determine *which* Massachusetts state trial court has subject matter jurisdiction (e.g., the superior court, the district court, etc.), not *whether* the Massachusetts state courts can hear the case.

But just because there is a Massachusetts state court with subject matter jurisdiction over this *type* of dispute does not mean that the court has the power to force Dalia to defend this case in Massachusetts. Look at the case from Dalia's perspective. She lives in Alaska, drove her car in Alaska, and was involved in an accident in Alaska. Nevertheless, this lawsuit would require her to mount a defense in Massachusetts. Dalia would likely consider it grossly unfair to be dragged into a Massachusetts court to defend this case when neither she nor the case has any connection to Massachusetts.

Dalia would be right. Given the facts of this particular case, a Massachusetts court does not have the power to "exercise personal jurisdiction over" Dalia, even though the court would have subject matter jurisdiction over the lawsuit. As this chapter explains, the United States Constitution imposes important restrictions on a court's authority over defendants. Specifically, the Fourteenth Amendment provides that a state may not deprive a person of property without *due process of law*. Because entering and enforcing a civil judgment can result in a defendant's loss of property (e.g., money damages), a court must use a fair procedure—due process—before entering that judgment. And one element of procedural fairness is ensuring that the court has an appropriate relationship to the claims or the parties. Here, since neither the claim nor Dalia has any connection to Massachusetts, Dalia would be deprived of due process of law if the Massachusetts court asserts jurisdiction over her.

Unfortunately, the Fourteenth Amendment Due Process Clause speaks only in general terms; it does not explain when a court can require an out-of-state defendant to appear and defend an action in the state. As a result, judges and generations of law students have struggled to understand what "due process" means in the personal jurisdiction context. The cases and materials that follow explain what the courts have found.

The cases not only reveal how courts have interpreted the Due Process Clause, but they also illustrate a fascinating feature of the law more generally: It evolves continuously to reflect changes in society. These materials explain why that evolution has taken place and how it has led to the current principles that limit a court's exercise of personal jurisdiction.

II. Early History: *Pennoyer v. Neff*

Pennoyer v. Neff is an early and important case in which the United States Supreme Court tried to define the appropriate limits of a court's power to exercise personal jurisdiction over out-of-state defendants. Some aspects of *Pennoyer* are no longer "good law"—they have been superseded by subsequent cases. Nonetheless, *Pennoyer's* basic premises about a court's authority to exercise personal jurisdiction prevailed for nearly seventy years and, in some respects, still do.

Pennoyer's *procedural history.* The *Pennoyer* opinion is difficult to follow, in part because it describes two related lawsuits. In the first, filed in 1865, J.H. Mitchell sued Marcus Neff in an Oregon circuit court (a state trial level court), alleging that Neff owed Mitchell legal fees. Mitchell could not locate Neff, so pursuant to an Oregon statute, Mitchell tried to notify Neff of the suit by publishing a notice for several consecutive weeks in a local newspaper. Despite the notice, Neff did not appear in court. As a result, the Oregon state court entered a default judgment—a judgment for failing to contest the action—in favor of Mitchell. Mitchell subsequently used that default judgment to obtain a writ of execution (a court order that allowed the sheriff to auction off land that Neff owned in Oregon) to satisfy the civil judgment. Mitchell himself then purchased the land at auction, was given a *sheriff's deed* to the land, and sold the land (for a tidy profit) to Sylvester Pennoyer.

Several years later, Neff returned to Oregon and discovered Pennoyer occupying his land. Neff responded in 1874 by filing a lawsuit against Pennoyer in federal court, claiming that Pennoyer had not acquired a good title to the land and that the land should be returned to Neff. Among other arguments, Neff contended that the original judgment in *Mitchell v. Neff* and the subsequent sheriff's sale of the land were invalid because the state court never acquired jurisdiction over Neff or his property. For this reason, Neff argued that he still owned the land.

The federal court ruled in Neff's favor, and Pennoyer appealed to the Supreme Court, whose opinion appears below. Keep in mind that the opinion deals with Pennoyer's appeal in this second case and not the earlier dispute between Mitchell and Neff.

Terminology. A further bit of useful background involves the distinction between personal jurisdiction (jurisdiction in personam) and in rem jurisdiction. A court has in personam jurisdiction over a defendant if the court has the authority to require the defendant to appear personally and defend the case in the state where the suit was brought. If a court has this type of jurisdiction (i.e., jurisdiction over a "person"), a judgment against the defendant can be satisfied from any assets the defendant owns.

In contrast, in rem jurisdiction involves a court's assertion of control over a defendant's specific *property*, such as real estate or a bank account, that is located within the state where the defendant is sued. Historically, courts frequently asserted in rem jurisdiction over a defendant's assets even if the defendant herself was not subject to personal jurisdiction in the state (i.e., the defendant was not required to appear personally). In these types of cases, the court would issue a *writ of attachment*, ordering the sheriff to attach (assert control of) particular real or personal property that the defendant owned in the forum. Unlike in personam jurisdiction, in rem jurisdiction did not give the court jurisdiction over the defendant personally, but it did subject the defendant's attached property to the power of the court. If the court subsequently upheld the plaintiff's claim, the court could order the attached property sold to satisfy that claim. However, unlike a judgment based on in personam jurisdiction, an in rem judgment did not subject the defendant to orders from the court or entitle the plaintiff to collect the judgment from other property the defendant owned.

Not surprisingly, plaintiffs prefer to establish in personam jurisdiction over a defendant because an in personam judgment may be satisfied out of any of the defendant's assets, not just those assets attached pursuant to the court's in rem jurisdiction. In addition, because the Full Faith and Credit Clause in the Constitution requires state courts to recognize in personam judgments of another state's courts, the plaintiff can take an in personam judgment to another state where the defendant has assets and enforce the judgment there. An in rem judgment, by contrast, only authorizes the sale of the particular property that the court has attached, and the judgment cannot be enforced in other states under the Full Faith and Credit Clause.

READING *PENNOYER v. NEFF.* As you read *Pennoyer*, consider the following questions:

- According to *Pennoyer*, when can a court exercise in personam jurisdiction over a defendant?
- When can a court exercise in rem jurisdiction?
- Which form of jurisdiction was at issue in this case?
- Why does the Court conclude that the state trial court that ordered the sale of Neff's land lacked jurisdiction to do so?

PENNOYER v. NEFF

95 U.S. 714 (1878)

Mr. Justice FIELD delivered the opinion of the court.

This is an action to recover the possession of a tract of land, of the alleged value of $15,000, situated in the State of Oregon .... The defendant [Pennoyer] claims to have acquired the premises under a sheriff's deed, made upon a sale of the property on execution issued upon a judgment recovered against the plaintiff in one of the circuit courts of the State. The case turns upon the validity of this judgment.

It appears from the record that the judgment was rendered in February, 1866, in favor of J.H. Mitchell, for less than $300, including costs, in an action brought by him upon a demand for services as an attorney; that, at the time the action was commenced and the judgment rendered, the defendant therein, the plaintiff here, was a non-resident of the State; that he was not personally served with process, and did not appear therein; and that the judgment was entered upon his default in not answering the complaint, upon a constructive service of summons by publication [in a local weekly newspaper in Oregon for six consecutive weeks].

... The authority of every tribunal is necessarily restricted by the territorial limits of the State in which it is established. Any attempt to exercise authority beyond those limits would be deemed in every other forum, as has been said by this court, an illegitimate assumption of power, and be resisted as mere abuse. In the case against the plaintiff, the property here in controversy sold under the judgment rendered was not attached, nor in any way brought under the jurisdiction of the court. Its first connection with the case was caused by a levy of the execution. It was not, therefore, disposed of pursuant to any adjudication, but only in enforcement of a personal judgment, having no relation to the property, rendered against a non-resident without service of process upon him in the action, or his appearance therein. The court below did not consider that an attachment of the property was essential to its jurisdiction or to the validity of the sale, but held that the judgment was invalid from defects in the affidavit upon which the order of publication was obtained, and in the affidavit by which the publication was proved....

[EDS.—The Court concluded that Neff should have raised the affidavit's defects in the state trial court or by appealing the state court's decision.

Because Neff failed to do so, the Court concluded that the defects could not be raised in the federal court proceeding. Thus, the only argument that was properly before the Court concerned personal jurisdiction.]

... But it was also contended in that court, and is insisted upon here, that the judgment in the State court against the plaintiff was void for want of personal service of process on him, or of his appearance in the action in which it was rendered and that the premises in controversy could not be subjected to the payment of the demand of a resident creditor except by a proceeding *in rem*; that is, by a direct proceeding against the property for that purpose. If these positions are sound, the ruling of the Circuit Court* as to the invalidity of that judgment must be sustained, notwithstanding our dissent from the reasons upon which it was made. And that they are sound would seem to follow from two well-established principles of public law respecting the jurisdiction of an independent State over persons and property. The several States of the Union are not, it is true, in every respect independent, many of the rights and powers which originally belonged to them being now vested in the government created by the Constitution. But, except as restrained and limited by that instrument, they possess and exercise the authority of independent States, and the principles of public law to which we have referred are applicable to them. One of these principles is, that every State possesses exclusive jurisdiction and sovereignty over persons and property within its territory. As a consequence, every State has the power to determine for itself the civil *status* and capacities of its inhabitants; to prescribe the subjects upon which they may contract, the forms and solemnities with which their contracts shall be executed, the rights and obligations arising from them, and the mode in which their validity shall be determined and their obligations enforced; and also to regulate the manner and conditions upon which property situated within such territory, both personal and real, may be acquired, enjoyed, and transferred. The other principle of public law referred to follows from the one mentioned; that is, that no State can exercise direct jurisdiction and authority over persons or property without its territory. Story, Confl. Laws, c. 2. The several States are of equal dignity and authority, and the independence of one implies the exclusion of power from all others. And so it is laid down by jurists, as an elementary principle, that the laws of one State have no operation outside of its territory, except so far as is allowed by comity; and that no tribunal established by it can extend its process beyond that territory so as to subject either persons or property to its decisions. "Any exertion of authority of this sort beyond this limit," says Story, "is a mere nullity, and incapable of binding such persons or property in any other tribunals."

But as contracts made in one State may be enforceable only in another State, and property may be held by non-residents, the exercise of the jurisdiction which

---

*** [Eds.—At the time of Pennoyer, the "Circuit Court" functioned as a federal trial level court. The first paragraph of the opinion also refers to "circuit courts," but the reference there is to the trial level state courts of Oregon. Just be aware that the term "circuit court" had two different meanings.]**

every State is admitted to possess over persons and property within its own territory will often affect persons and property without it. . . .

So the State, through its tribunals, may subject property situated within its limits owned by non-residents to the payment of the demand of its own citizens against them; and the exercise of this jurisdiction in no respect infringes upon the sovereignty of the State where the owners are domiciled. Every State owes protection to its own citizens; and, when non-residents deal with them, it is a legitimate and just exercise of authority to hold and appropriate any property owned by such non-residents to satisfy the claims of its citizens. It is in virtue of the State's jurisdiction over the property of the non-resident situated within its limits that its tribunals can inquire into that non-resident's obligations to its own citizens, and the inquiry can then be carried only to the extent necessary to control the disposition of the property. If the non-resident[s] have no property in the State, there is nothing upon which the tribunals can adjudicate. . . .

If, without personal service, judgments *in personam*, obtained *ex parte* against non-residents and absent parties, upon mere publication of process, which, in the great majority of cases, would never be seen by the parties interested, could be upheld and enforced, they would be the constant instruments of fraud and oppression. Judgments for all sorts of claims upon contracts and for torts, real or pretended, would be thus obtained, under which property would be seized, when the evidence of the transactions upon which they were founded, if they ever had any existence, had perished.

Substituted service by publication, or in any other authorized form, may be sufficient to inform parties of the object of proceedings taken where property is once brought under the control of the court by seizure or some equivalent act. The law assumes that property is always in the possession of its owner, in person or by agent; and it proceeds upon the theory that its seizure will inform him, not only that it is taken into the custody of the court, but that he must look to any proceedings authorized by law upon such seizure for its condemnation and sale. Such service may also be sufficient in cases where the object of the action is to reach and dispose of property in the State, or of some interest therein, by enforcing a contract or a lien respecting the same, or to partition it among different owners, or, when the public is a party, to condemn and appropriate it for a public purpose. In other words, such service may answer in all actions which are substantially proceedings *in rem*. But where the entire object of the action is to determine the personal rights and obligations of the defendants, that is, where the suit is merely *in personam*, constructive service in this form upon a non-resident is ineffectual for any purpose. Process from the tribunals of one State cannot run into another State, and summon parties there domiciled to leave its territory and respond to proceedings against them. Publication of process or notice within the State where the tribunal sits cannot create any greater obligation upon the non-resident to appear. Process sent to him out of the State, and process published within it, are equally unavailing in proceedings to establish his personal liability.

The want of authority of the tribunals of a State to adjudicate upon the obligations of non-residents, where they have no property within its limits, is not denied by the court below: but the position is assumed, that, where they have property within the State, it is immaterial whether the property is in the first instance brought under the control of the court by attachment or some other equivalent act, and afterwards applied by its judgment to the satisfaction of demands against its owner; or such demands be first established in a personal action, and the property of the non-resident be afterwards seized and sold on execution. But the answer to this position has already been given in the statement, that the jurisdiction of the court to inquire into and determine his obligations at all is only incidental to its jurisdiction over the property. Its jurisdiction in that respect cannot be made to depend upon facts to be ascertained after it has tried the cause and rendered the judgment. If the judgment be previously void, it will not become valid by the subsequent discovery of property of the defendant, or by his subsequent acquisition of it. The judgment, if void when rendered, will always remain void: it cannot occupy the doubtful position of being valid if property be found, and void if there be none. Even if the position assumed were confined to cases where the non-resident defendant possessed property in the State at the commencement of the action, it would still make the validity of the proceedings and judgment depend upon the question whether, before the levy of the execution, the defendant had or had not disposed of the property. If before the levy the property should be sold, then, according to this position, the judgment would not be binding. This doctrine would introduce a new element of uncertainty in judicial proceedings. The contrary is the law: the validity of every judgment depends upon the jurisdiction of the court before it is rendered, not upon what may occur subsequently. . . .

The force and effect of judgments rendered against non-residents without personal service of process upon them, or their voluntary appearance, have been the subject of frequent consideration in the courts of the United States and of the several States, as attempts have been made to enforce such judgments in States other than those in which they were rendered, under the provision of the Constitution requiring that "full faith and credit shall be given in each State to the public acts, records, and judicial proceedings of every other State"; and the act of Congress providing for the mode of authenticating such acts, records, and proceedings, and declaring that, when thus authenticated, "they shall have such faith and credit given to them in every court within the United States as they have by law or usage in the courts of the State from which they are or shall be taken." In the earlier cases, it was supposed that [the federal statute concerning full faith and credit] gave to all judgments the same effect in other States which they had by law in the State where rendered. But this view was afterwards qualified so as to make the act applicable only when the court rendering the judgment had jurisdiction of the parties and of the subject-matter, and not to preclude an inquiry into the jurisdiction of the court in which the judgment was rendered, or the right of the State itself to exercise authority over the person or the subject-matter. . . .

Since the adoption of the Fourteenth Amendment to the Federal Constitution, the validity of such judgments may be directly questioned, and their enforcement in the State resisted, on the ground that proceedings in a court of justice to determine the personal rights and obligations of parties over whom that court has no jurisdiction do not constitute due process of law. Whatever difficulty may be experienced in giving to those terms a definition which will embrace every permissible exertion of power affecting private rights, and exclude such as is forbidden, there can be no doubt of their meaning when applied to judicial proceedings. They then mean a course of legal proceedings according to those rules and principles which have been established in our systems of jurisprudence for the protection and enforcement of private rights. To give such proceedings any validity, there must be a tribunal competent by its constitution—that is, by the law of its creation—to pass upon the subject-matter of the suit; and, if that involves merely a determination of the personal liability of the defendant, he must be brought within its jurisdiction by service of process within the State, or his voluntary appearance.

Except in cases affecting the personal *status* of the plaintiff, and cases in which that mode of service may be considered to have been assented to in advance, as hereinafter mentioned, the substituted service of process by publication, allowed by the law of Oregon and by similar laws in other States, where actions are brought against non-residents, is effectual only where, in connection with process against the person for commencing the action, property in the State is brought under the control of the court, and subjected to its disposition by process adapted to that purpose, or where the judgment is sought as a means of reaching such property or affecting some interest therein; in other words, where the action is in the nature of a proceeding *in rem*. . . .

It follows from the views expressed that the personal judgment recovered in the State court of Oregon against the plaintiff herein, then a non-resident of the State, was without any validity, and did not authorize a sale of the property in controversy.

To prevent any misapplication of the views expressed in this opinion, it is proper to observe that we do not mean to assert, by any thing we have said, that a State may not authorize proceedings to determine the *status* of one of its citizens towards a non-resident, which would be binding within the State, though made without service of process or personal notice to the non-resident. The jurisdiction which every State possesses to determine the civil *status* and capacities of all its inhabitants involves authority to prescribe the conditions on which proceedings affecting them may be commenced and carried on within its territory. The State, for example, has absolute right to prescribe the conditions upon which the marriage relation between its own citizens shall be created, and the causes for which it may be dissolved. One of the parties guilty of acts for which, by the law of the State, a dissolution may be granted, may have removed to a State where no dissolution is permitted. The complaining party would, therefore, fail if a divorce were sought in the State of the defendant; and if application could not be made to the tribunals of the complainant's domicile in such case, and proceedings be there instituted without personal service of process or personal notice to the offending party, the injured citizen would be without redress.

Neither do we mean to assert that a State may not require a non-resident entering into a partnership or association within its limits, or making contracts enforceable there, to appoint an agent or representative in the State to receive service of process and notice in legal proceedings instituted with respect to such partnership, association, or contracts, or to designate a place where such service may be made and notice given, and provide, upon their failure, to make such appointment or to designate such place that service may be made upon a public officer designated for that purpose, or in some other prescribed way, and that judgments rendered upon such service may not be binding upon the non-residents both within and without the State. As was said by the Court of Exchequer in *Vallee v. Dumergue*, 4 Exch. 290, "It is not contrary to natural justice that a man who has agreed to receive a particular mode of notification of legal proceedings should be bound by a judgment in which that particular mode of notification has been followed, even though he may not have actual notice of them." Nor do we doubt that a State, on creating corporations or other institutions for pecuniary or charitable purposes, may provide a mode in which their conduct may be investigated, their obligations enforced, or their charters revoked, which shall require other than personal service upon their officers or members. Parties becoming members of such corporations or institutions would hold their interest subject to the conditions prescribed by law.

In the present case, there is no feature of this kind, and, consequently, no consideration of what would be the effect of such legislation in enforcing the contract of a non-resident can arise. The question here respects only the validity of a money judgment rendered in one State, in an action upon a simple contract against the resident of another, without service of process upon him, or his appearance therein.

Judgment affirmed.

[Justice Hunt's dissenting opinion is omitted.]

Notes and Questions: Understanding *Pennoyer*

1. States as independent sovereigns. *Pennoyer* draws heavily on international law concepts that were prevalent at the time, especially the notion that the courts of one nation could not typically exercise jurisdiction over people or property located in another country. Analogously, American judges believed that they should refrain from exercising jurisdiction over people or property located in another state. For example, according to this logic, an Oregon court could not exercise jurisdiction over people or property located in California. The Court put it this way:

> [N]o State can exercise direct jurisdiction and authority over persons or property without [outside of] its territory. The several States are of equal dignity and authority, and the independence of one implies the exclusion of power

> from all others. And so it is laid down by jurists, as an elementary principle, that the laws of one State have no operation outside of its territory, except so far as is allowed by comity; and that no tribunal established by it can extend its process beyond that territory so as to subject either persons or property to its decisions.

2. The *Pennoyer* problem. In *Pennoyer,* the Oregon state court asserted jurisdiction over Neff's Oregon property, so jurisdiction appears to have been consistent with the passage quoted above. What went wrong?

In *Pennoyer,* Mitchell sued Neff in the Oregon state court to recover fees for the work that Mitchell had performed for Neff in Oregon. After Neff defaulted, Mitchell asked the court to order the sale of Neff's Oregon real estate in order to satisfy the default judgment. Why did the Supreme Court conclude that the Oregon state court did not have jurisdiction to order the sale of Mitchell's Oregon property?

A. Neff was not notified in person about the pending lawsuit.
B. Neff was not within the state at the time that the suit began.
C. A and B both had to be satisfied and were not satisfied in this case.
D. The court failed to attach Neff's property before it exercised jurisdiction to resolve Mitchell's claim.

A is incorrect. Although the Court required in-person notice to establish in personam jurisdiction, the Court did not require such notice for in rem jurisdiction. Indeed, at the time of *Pennoyer,* notice by publication or posting was considered to be sufficient for in rem actions. (Constitutional standards have changed considerably in this regard since *Pennoyer* was decided, as you will learn in later chapters.)

B is not right either, because in rem jurisdiction is based on the presence of *the property* in the forum state, not the presence of the defendant. If the land was in Oregon, the court could assert jurisdiction over it, whether Neff was present in Oregon or not. Because neither **A** nor **B** were required, **C** is also wrong.

The real problem with Mitchell's judgment was that he did not provide the court with any basis for jurisdiction *before the court purported to exercise it.* Mitchell filed a suit and got a default judgment, but neither Neff nor his property was before the court. You should have focused on this passage in *Pennoyer*:

> The jurisdiction of the court to inquire into and determine [Neff's] obligations at all is only incidental to its jurisdiction over the property. Its jurisdiction in that respect cannot be made to depend upon facts to be ascertained after it has tried the cause and rendered the judgment. If the judgment be previously void, it will not become valid by the subsequent discovery of property of the defendant, or by his subsequent acquisition of it. The judgment, if void when rendered, will always remain void: it cannot occupy the doubtful position of being valid if property be found, and void if there be none.

Thus, to assert in rem jurisdiction under the *Pennoyer* framework, a court had to assert authority over the property (through attachment) before exercising jurisdiction, not after. In this case, when the Oregon state court entered judgment against Neff, the court did not have control over Neff's property. Seizing the property later, through post-judgment attachment, did not validate the judgment that had been rendered before the court had obtained jurisdiction. For this reason, **D** is the best answer—before a court can exercise in rem jurisdiction, it must first attach the defendant's property. That did not happen here.

3. The distinction between notice and personal jurisdiction. *Pennoyer*'s discussion of notice and personal jurisdiction can be confusing. Certainly, fairness requires that defendants receive adequate *notice* that a lawsuit has been filed against them. But fairness *also* requires that the plaintiff's claims against the defendant have an appropriate connection to the state where the lawsuit was filed; that is, the court must also have *jurisdiction* over the defendant or the defendant's property.

Pennoyer does not clearly explain this distinction between notice and jurisdiction, because at that time there was little need to do so. Under the *Pennoyer* framework, by serving the defendant with process within the forum state (in-state service), the requirements of jurisdiction and notice were satisfied simultaneously. But in subsequent cases (that you will soon read), the Court developed new ways of establishing in personam jurisdiction, making it necessary to clarify this distinction between notice and personal jurisdiction. The following two questions illustrate the differences between notice and jurisdictional requirements.

Q **4. Improper jurisdiction/proper notice.** Imagine that shortly after *Pennoyer* was decided, Paul sued Dora in Massachusetts state court and alleged that Dora breached a contract. Dora lived in Connecticut, so Paul hired a process server who located Dora in Connecticut and personally handed her the complaint and summons. Would the Massachusetts state court have had personal jurisdiction over Dora using the standard set out in *Pennoyer*?

A No. In this case, the defendant received notice of the pending lawsuit in a manner clearly likely to inform her that she had been sued. As a result, notice is proper. But under *Pennoyer*, personal service of process—proper *notice*—did not suffice to establish *personal jurisdiction*. A court only had jurisdiction over persons and property located within its territory, not outside of it. The *Pennoyer* Court put it this way:

> Process from the tribunals of one State cannot run into another State, and summon parties there domiciled to leave its territory and respond to proceedings against them. Publication of process or notice within the State where the tribunal sits cannot create any greater obligation upon the non-resident to appear. Process sent to him out of the State, and process published within it, are equally unavailing in proceedings to establish his personal liability.

Thus, the problem in Dora's case was that she was outside of the state when she was served. Clear notice of the suit was not enough.

Recent cases have established several bases besides physical presence in the state to support personal jurisdiction over out-of-state defendants like Dora. But a court using *only* the logic of *Pennoyer* could not force such a defendant to cross state lines to litigate a case.

Notice to Neff?

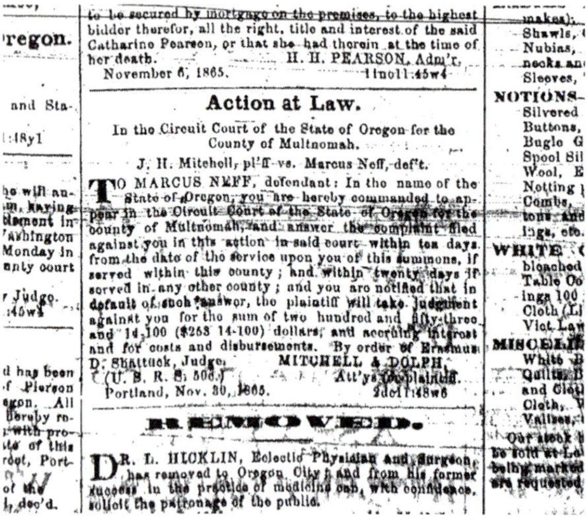
to be secured by mortgage on the premises, to the highest bidder therefor, all the right, title and interest of the said Catharine Pearson, or that she had therein at the time of her death. H. H. PEARSON, Adm'r.
November 6, 1865. 1tno11:45w4

Action at Law.

In the Circuit Court of the State of Oregon for the County of Multnomah.

J. H. Mitchell, pl'ff vs. Marcus Neff, def't.

TO MARCUS NEFF, defendant: In the name of the State of Oregon, you are hereby commanded to appear in the Circuit Court of the State of Oregon for the county of Multnomah, and answer the complaint filed against you in this action in said court within ten days from the date of the service upon you of this summons, if served within this county; and within twenty days if served in any other county; and you are notified that in default of such answer, the plaintiff will take judgment against you for the sum of two hundred and fifty-three and 14-100 ($253 14-100) dollars, and accruing interest and for costs and disbursements. By order of Erasmus D. Shattuck, Judge.
(U. S. R. S. 506.) MITCHELL & DOLPH, Att'ys for plaintiff.
Portland, Nov. 30, 1865. 2dc1:48w6

REMOVED.

DR. L. HICKLIN, Eclectic Physician and Surgeon, has removed to Oregon City; and from his former success in the practice of medicine can, with confidence, solicit the patronage of the public.

Here is the notice that Mitchell's law firm published in the *Pacific Christian Advocate* of J.H. Mitchell's lawsuit against Marcus Neff for $253.14. The notice appeared for six weeks. There is no evidence that Neff ever learned of the suit from this notice.

Q **5. Improper notice?** Assume now that Dora lived in Massachusetts, and Paul's process server nailed a copy of the complaint and summons to the front door of Dora's house. Dora then got the papers when she returned home that day. Would the Massachusetts court have had the authority to require Dora to appear?

A It depends. Unlike the previous example, Dora is now within the Massachusetts court's territory, so personal jurisdiction is clearly available. But whether posting the complaint and summons on the house constituted proper *notice* is another issue.

At the time of *Pennoyer,* the appropriateness of notice by a posting depended on whether the plaintiff sought in personam or in rem jurisdiction. In personam jurisdiction usually required notice by personal service, but notification of the lawsuit by publication (as in *Pennoyer*) or by a posting (as in this case) was often sufficient for in rem actions.

So if Paul were seeking in rem jurisdiction, the notice he offered would have been sufficient at the time of *Pennoyer.* (As explained earlier, the notice requirements for in personam and in rem actions have changed since then.)

But if Paul were seeking to establish in personam jurisdiction after *Pennoyer,* posting the complaint and summons at the house was probably inadequate notice. As the Court explained in *Pennoyer,* "[i]f, without *personal service,* judgments in personam . . . could be upheld and enforced, they would be the constant instruments of fraud and oppression."

This rigid requirement of personal service for in personam jurisdiction is rooted in early English practice. Traditionally, the court would direct the sheriff to arrest the defendant through a court order known as a *capias ad respondendum* and put the defendant into a debtor's prison unless the defendant posted bail. Fortunately, this draconian practice has been replaced by a symbolic seizure of the person through service of process. But the basic concept is still the same: A court has to acquire power over the defendant personally (i.e., in personam jurisdiction) by asserting the court's authority over her. That control now occurs symbolically through service rather than arrest, but it is still necessary before a court can enter a judgment against the defendant personally.

Q **6. Advising plaintiffs after *Pennoyer*.** A key holding in *Pennoyer*—that a court had jurisdiction over people or things within the court's territory—was conceptually tidy, but it had impractical consequences. Suppose, for example, that Danny traveled to Oregon to hire a doctor (Potter) and incurred medical bills there arising from Potter's services. Danny then moved to California and ignored Potter's bills. How would Potter go about asserting his claim for unpaid bills? If you were Potter's lawyer at the time of *Pennoyer*, what would you have advised Potter to do to collect?

A The easiest approach would have been to sue Danny in Oregon and get an in personam judgment there. But to do that, Potter would have had to arrange to serve Danny with process while Danny was present in Oregon. Potter's process server could have waited for Danny to return to the state from California, but Potter could not have been sure that Danny would ever do so. Accordingly, any effort to get an in personam judgment in Oregon would have been unlikely to succeed.

Under the logic of *Pennoyer*, Potter would have had two other options. First, Potter could have sued Danny in Oregon and attached any property that Danny owned in the state. Assuming the attachment took place at the appropriate time, the court would have had the authority to order the sale of the attached property. One problem is that defendants like Danny usually do not leave significant property behind when they leave a state. Moreover, even if a party leaves property in the forum state, a plaintiff can only obtain full relief if the property is worth more than the amount of the judgment. A court with in rem jurisdiction only has the authority to dispose of the attached property, so any damages in excess of the property's value would not be collected.

Another option would have been to sue Danny in California and serve him with process there. That way, the California court would have had in personam jurisdiction over Danny. If Potter obtained a judgment and Danny failed to pay it, the California court could have ordered the sale of Danny's California assets to satisfy the claim. Moreover, under the Full Faith and Credit Clause, Potter could have taken the in personam judgment into any other state and enforced the judgment in states where Danny had property. Unfortunately, you would have had to advise Potter that pursuing claims in other states was (and still is) a more expensive option.

Understandably, Potter would not like this advice. Indeed, it sounds quite unfair to require Potter to litigate in California given that Danny's allegedly wrongful conduct occurred in Oregon and injured Potter in Oregon. This basic problem helps to explain why the Court subsequently developed a different approach to personal jurisdiction in *International Shoe v. Washington*, a case that appears later in this chapter.

7. An intentional exception: Status determinations. Sometimes an opinion is notable for what it does not decide. In *Pennoyer,* the Court went out of its way to say that its decision did not impact how courts should resolve status determinations. For example, when a court grants a divorce, it is essentially granting a status change to the married couple. What *Pennoyer* said—and what is still true today—is that courts can have jurisdiction to grant status changes, such as divorces, even though one spouse cannot be found or served with process. Because the marital status is viewed as a *res*—a type of property right—a court can typically dissolve the marriage if either of the spouses appears in the court and is domiciled in the jurisdiction. (For example, at one time, Nevada considered a spouse to be domiciled in the state after a very short period of residence. As a result, Las Vegas developed a reputation for granting quick divorces.) This exception, however, does not apply if one of the spouses is seeking financial support (e.g., alimony payments) from the out-of-state spouse. In such a case, the court is being asked to do more than grant a status change—it is being asked to require the out-of-state spouse to incur a financial obligation. A court needs in personam jurisdiction over the spouse to impose such an obligation.

8. Prelude to a problem: Consent. Another exclusion appears in the next to last paragraph of the opinion. The Court explained that a state could require out-of-state businesses to appoint in-state agents for service of process as a condition for conducting certain types of business in the state. If a case arose, plaintiffs could obtain personal jurisdiction over the corporation by serving the summons and complaint on the in-state agent. The Court also recognized that individuals could consent to a court's exercise of jurisdiction over them, even if they would otherwise not be subject to jurisdiction.

Pennoyer's Peeve

Oregon Historical Society, Image No. CN014004

Sylvester Pennoyer, pictured here, purchased Marcus Neff's Oregon homestead on the west bank of the Willamette River in Portland, under a sheriff's deed. He lived on the property for eight years but faced eviction after the Supreme Court's decision in *Pennoyer v. Neff.* Although he went on to become Governor of Oregon, Pennoyer remained bitter about the legal system and lambasted the *Pennoyer v. Neff* decision in his inaugural address. (Later he urged impeachment of the entire Supreme Court.) The fascinating background of this case is told in Professor Wendy Perdue's classic article, *Sin, Scandal, and Substantive Due Process: Personal Jurisdiction and* Pennoyer *Reconsidered,* 62 Wash. L. Rev. 479 (1987).

III. Social Change and Doctrinal Rigidity: Problems with the *Pennoyer* Doctrine

The courts gradually recognized that *Pennoyer*'s rigid rules were ill equipped to deal with an increasingly national economy in which both individuals and businesses frequently conducted activities across state lines. At first, the Court tried to work within the *Pennoyer* framework by broadening the two primary methods of establishing personal jurisdiction that were mentioned in the case: consent and in-state presence. It eventually became clear, however, that even with broadened notions of these concepts, the *Pennoyer* doctrine could not deal adequately with society's increasing mobility.

A. Dealing with Interstate Businesses: Stretching the Concepts of Consent and Presence

Before *Pennoyer*, businesses were generally subject to in personam jurisdiction where they were formed. In the years after *Pennoyer*, however, businesses engaged in significantly more interstate activity, and the courts recognized that these businesses should sometimes be held accountable for their conduct in other states as well. Thus, the courts began to accept more liberal consent-based theories of jurisdiction and a broadening of the definition of presence to include "carrying on business" in a forum.

With regard to consent-based theories, states sometimes required companies to consent to personal jurisdiction as a condition of doing business in the state. Because the Supreme Court raised constitutional concerns about these forced consent statutes, *see, e.g., International Textbook Co. v. Pigg*, 217 U.S. 91, 110–11 (1910), courts also began to rely on expanded notions of in-state "presence" as a way to expand their authority to exercise personal jurisdiction. The Supreme Court defined corporate presence expansively: "We are satisfied that the presence of a corporation within a state necessary to the service of process is shown when it appears that the corporation is there carrying on business in such sense as to manifest its presence within the state, although the business transacted may be entirely interstate in its character." *International Harvester Co. v. Kentucky*, 234 U.S. 579, 589 (1914). This shift prompted considerable litigation over whether a corporation was "present" or "carrying on business" in a particular state, but no satisfactory standards for applying these concepts emerged.

B. Dealing with a Mobile Public: *Hess v. Pawloski* and the Fiction of Consent

With the advent of the automobile, people also had become more mobile, requiring a more flexible doctrine for individual defendants as well. *Hess v. Pawloski*, 274 U.S. 352 (1927), illustrates the problem. In *Hess*, a Pennsylvania citizen drove into Massachusetts and injured Pawloski, a Massachusetts citizen. After Hess returned to Pennsylvania, Pawloski sued Hess in Massachusetts state court, asserting personal jurisdiction under the following Massachusetts statute:

> The acceptance by a nonresident of the rights and privileges conferred by section three or four, as evidenced by his operating a motor vehicle thereunder, or the operation by a nonresident of a motor vehicle on a public way in the commonwealth other than under said sections, shall be deemed equivalent to an appointment by such nonresident of the registrar or his successor in office, to be his true and lawful attorney upon whom may be served all lawful processes in any action or proceeding against him, growing out of any accident or collision in which said nonresident may be involved while operating a motor vehicle on such a way, and said acceptance or operation shall be a signification of his agreement that any such process against him which is so served shall be of the same legal force and validity as if served on him personally....

Hess moved to dismiss the case for lack of personal jurisdiction, contending that the statute's fictional consent provision deprived him of due process of law under the Constitution's Fourteenth Amendment.

Despite *Pennoyer*'s prescription that a defendant be served personally within the forum, the Court rejected Hess's argument and concluded that the statute's consent provision was constitutionally acceptable:

> The question is whether the Massachusetts enactment contravenes the due process clause of the Fourteenth Amendment.
>
> The process of a court of one state cannot run into another and summon a party there domiciled to respond to proceedings against him. Notice sent outside the state to a nonresident is unavailing to give jurisdiction in an action against him personally for money recovery. *Pennoyer v. Neff.* There must be actual service within the state of notice upon him or upon some one authorized to accept service for him. A personal judgment rendered against a nonresident, who has neither been served with process nor appeared in the suit, is without validity. The mere transaction of business in a state by nonresident natural persons does not imply consent to be bound by the process of its courts....
>
> Motor vehicles are dangerous machines, and, even when skillfully and carefully operated, their use is attended by serious dangers to persons and property. In the public interest the state may make and enforce regulations reasonably calculated to promote care on the part of all, residents and nonresidents alike, who use its highways. The measure in question operates to require a nonresident to answer for his conduct in the state where arise causes of action alleged against him, as well as to provide for a claimant a convenient method by which he may sue to enforce his rights. Under the statute the implied consent is limited to proceedings growing out of accidents or collisions on a highway in which the nonresident may be involved. It is required that he shall actually receive and [sic] receipt for notice of the service and a copy of the process.... The state's power to regulate the use of its highways extends to their use by nonresidents as well as by residents. And, in advance of the operation of a motor vehicle on its highway by a nonresident, the state may require him to appoint one of its officials as his agent on whom process may be served in proceedings growing out of such use. [This Court has] recognized [the] power of the state to exclude a nonresident until the formal appointment is made. And, having the power so to exclude, the state may declare that the use

> of the highway by the nonresident is the equivalent of the appointment of the registrar as agent on whom process may be served. The difference between the formal and implied appointment is not substantial, so far as concerns the application of the due process clause of the Fourteenth Amendment.

274 U.S. at 355–57.

Understandably, the Court thought that Pawlowski should be able to sue Hess in Massachusetts, even though Hess could not be served in Massachusetts. To reach that result, the Court accepted the theory of implied consent embodied in the statute—that the voluntary act of driving in Massachusetts constituted consent to defend suits in the state arising from that act.

Of course, *Pennoyer* had recognized that a defendant could expressly consent to jurisdiction, but the Court in *Hess* extended that exception dramatically by permitting the type of implied consent described in the Massachusetts statute. Very probably, Hess knew nothing about the statute and did not mean to consent to anything by driving in Massachusetts. *Pennoyer*'s in-state service requirement simply did not fit the realities of the automobile age, so the Court modified the doctrine to reach an acceptable result. The Court admitted as much in a later decision:

> It is true that in order to ease the process by which new decisions are fitted into pre-existing modes of analysis there has been some fictive talk to the effect that the reason why a non-resident can be subjected to a state's jurisdiction is that the non-resident has "impliedly" consented to be sued there. In point of fact, however, jurisdiction in these cases does not rest on consent at all. The defendant may protest to high heaven his unwillingness to be sued and it avails him not. The liability rests on the inroad which the automobile has made on the decision of *Pennoyer v. Neff*. . . . [T]o conclude . . . that the motorist, who never consented to anything and whose consent is altogether immaterial, has actually agreed to be sued . . . is surely to move in the world of Alice in Wonderland.

Olberding v. Ill. Cent. R. Co., Inc., 346 U.S. 338, 340–41 (1953).

C. Other Doctrinal Modifications

The rigidity of *Pennoyer* also led the Court to recognize domicile—the legal term that typically refers to the state where someone is living with the intent to remain indefinitely—as an alternative basis for a court to exercise personal jurisdiction over an individual, even when the lawsuit arose out of conduct that occurred elsewhere. In *Milliken v. Meyer*, 311 U.S. 457 (1940), the Court held that "[d]omicile in the state is alone sufficient to bring an absent defendant within the reach of the state's jurisdiction for purposes of a personal judgment. . . ." *Id.* at 462. This conclusion makes sense. If state citizens can elect lawmakers and enjoy the usual benefits of state citizenship, it is not unreasonable to ask them to accept the "burden" of defending an action in that state as well.

Thus, after *Milliken* and *Hess*, an individual defendant was subject to personal jurisdiction in a state, even if not served within the state's borders, if the defendant was domiciled there or had implicitly consented to personal jurisdiction in the forum. Corporate defendants were also subject to personal jurisdiction under broad consent theories and, later, under liberal notions of "presence" that included "doing business" in the forum.

Ultimately, it became clear that *Pennoyer*'s emphasis on physical presence, even as ameliorated by an expansive understanding of corporate presence and by exceptions like those in *Hess* and *Milliken*, was inadequate as a logical framework for analyzing due process constraints on the exercise of personal jurisdiction. Some fundamentally new approach to the problem was needed.

In *International Shoe v. Washington*, the Court pronounced such a new framework, shifting the analytical focus away from in-state service, presence, and implied consent and toward the defendant's purposeful in-state contacts.

IV. The Modern Era Begins: *International Shoe Co. v. Washington*

During the decades after *Pennoyer*, many judges began to think about the meaning and sources of law in new ways. For example, judges were increasingly skeptical that the law contained a body of immutably "right," scientifically derivable "natural" principles that judges could objectively determine without reference to the real world implications of those principles. Rather, many judges began to believe that at least some legal doctrines are indeterminate and are necessarily interpreted and developed in light of social, political, and economic realities. Judges who adopted this "legal realist" view of law found it easier to move away from formalistic doctrines—such as the rigid presence theory in *Pennoyer*—that did not seem to correspond to the realities of a modern, mobile world. Legal realism arguably played at least some role in the evolution of personal jurisdiction doctrine.

READING *INTERNATIONAL SHOE CO. v. WASHINGTON*. This case illustrates why personal jurisdiction doctrine had become so problematic in light of modern realities. The state of Washington had insisted that International Shoe, a company that was incorporated in Delaware and had its headquarters in Missouri, make contributions to the state of Washington's unemployment fund. International Shoe had no offices or permanent employees in Washington, so it was a stretch to say that the company was "present" there, even using the expansive "presence" concept that courts had developed. At the same time, the Court clearly considered it reasonable to expect International Shoe to defend certain kinds of claims in Washington. Consider the following questions when reading the case:

- Does the Court extend the definition of "presence," or does it choose a new path? If the latter, what is the Court's approach to determining when in personam jurisdiction is constitutionally permissible?
- Pay close attention to which of the defendant's in-state contacts are deemed to be important and how different types of contacts lead to different jurisdictional consequences. In particular, what are the jurisdictional consequences when a defendant has (a) no contacts in the forum; (b) single or limited contacts; and (c) extensive contacts?

INTERNATIONAL SHOE CO. v. WASHINGTON

326 U.S. 310 (1945)

Mr. Chief Justice Stone delivered the opinion of the Court.

The questions for decision are (1) whether, within the limitations of the due process clause of the Fourteenth Amendment, appellant, a Delaware corporation, has by its activities in the State of Washington rendered itself amenable to proceedings in the courts of that state to recover unpaid contributions to the state unemployment compensation fund exacted by state statutes [under the Washington Unemployment Compensation Act] ... and (2) whether the state can exact those contributions consistently with the due process clause of the Fourteenth Amendment.

The statutes in question set up a comprehensive scheme of unemployment compensation, the costs of which are defrayed by contributions required to be made by employers to a state unemployment compensation fund. The contributions are a specified percentage of the wages payable annually by each employer for his employees' services in the state. The assessment and collection of the contributions and the fund are administered by respondents. Section 14(c) of the Act authorizes respondent Commissioner to issue an order and notice of assessment of delinquent contributions upon prescribed personal service of the notice upon the employer if found within the state, or, if not so found, by mailing the notice to the employer by registered mail at his last known address....

In this case notice of assessment for the years in question was personally served upon a sales solicitor employed by appellant in the State of Washington, and a copy of the notice was mailed by registered mail to appellant at its address in St. Louis, Missouri. Appellant appeared specially before the office of unemployment and moved to set aside the order and notice of assessment on the ground that the service upon appellant's salesman was not proper service upon appellant; that appellant was not a corporation of the State of Washington and was not doing business within the state; that it had no agent within the state upon whom service could be made; and that appellant is not an employer and does not furnish employment within the meaning of the statute.

The motion was heard on evidence and a stipulation of facts by the appeal tribunal which denied the motion and ruled that respondent Commissioner was entitled to recover the unpaid contributions. That action was affirmed by the Commissioner; both the Superior Court and the Supreme Court [of Washington] affirmed. Appellant in each of these courts assailed the statute as applied, as a violation of the due process clause of the Fourteenth Amendment, and as imposing a constitutionally prohibited burden on interstate commerce. The cause comes here on appeal, appellant assigning as error that the challenged statutes as applied infringe the due process clause of the Fourteenth Amendment and the commerce clause.

The facts as found by the appeal tribunal and accepted by the state Superior Court and Supreme Court, are not in dispute. Appellant is a Delaware corporation, having its principal place of business in St. Louis, Missouri, and is engaged in the manufacture and sale of shoes and other footwear. It maintains places of business in several states, other than Washington, at which its manufacturing is carried on and from which its merchandise is distributed interstate through several sales units or branches located outside the State of Washington.

Appellant has no office in Washington and makes no contracts either for sale or purchase of merchandise there. It maintains no stock of merchandise in that state and makes there no deliveries of goods in intrastate commerce. During the years from 1937 to 1940, now in question, appellant employed eleven to thirteen salesmen under direct supervision and control of sales managers located in St. Louis. These salesmen resided in Washington; their principal activities were confined to that state; and they were compensated by commissions based upon the amount of their sales. The commissions for each year totaled more than $31,000. Appellant supplies its salesmen with a line of samples, each consisting of one shoe of a pair, which they display to prospective purchasers. On occasion they rent permanent sample rooms, for exhibiting samples, in business buildings, or rent rooms in hotels or business buildings temporarily for that purpose. The cost of such rentals is reimbursed by appellant.

The authority of the salesmen is limited to exhibiting their samples and soliciting orders from prospective buyers, at prices and on terms fixed by appellant. The salesmen transmit the orders to appellant's office in St. Louis for acceptance or rejection, and when accepted the merchandise for filling the orders is shipped f.o.b. ["free on board," meaning that the seller has completed its obligation upon delivery to the carrier of the goods] from points outside Washington to the purchasers within the state. All the merchandise shipped into Washington is invoiced at the place of shipment from which collections are made. No salesman has authority to enter into contracts or to make collections.

The Supreme Court of Washington was of opinion that the regular and systematic solicitation of orders in the state by appellant's salesmen, resulting in a continuous flow of appellant's product into the state, was sufficient to constitute doing business in the state so as to make appellant amenable to suit in its courts. But it was also of opinion that there were sufficient additional activities shown to bring the case within the rule frequently stated, that solicitation within a state by the agents of a foreign corporation plus some additional activities there are sufficient to render the corporation amenable to suit brought in the courts of the state to enforce an obligation arising out of its activities there. The court found such additional activities in the salesmen's display of samples sometimes in permanent display rooms, and the salesmen's residence within the state, continued over a period of years, all resulting in a substantial volume of merchandise regularly shipped by appellant to purchasers within the state....

Appellant ... insists that its activities within the state were not sufficient to manifest its "presence" there and that in its absence the state courts were without jurisdiction, that consequently it was a denial of due process for the state to subject appellant to suit. It refers to those cases in which it was said that the mere solicitation of orders for the purchase of goods within a state, to be accepted without the state and filled by shipment of the purchased goods interstate, does not render the corporation seller amenable to suit within the state. And appellant further argues that since it was not present within the state, it is a denial of due process to subject it to taxation or other money exaction. It thus denies the power of the state to lay the tax or to subject appellant to a suit for its collection.

Historically the jurisdiction of courts to render judgment in personam is grounded on their de facto power over the defendant's person. Hence his presence within the territorial jurisdiction of a court was prerequisite to its rendition of a judgment personally binding him. Pennoyer v. Neff, 95 U.S. 714, 733 (1877). But now that the capias ad respondendum [the arrest of the civil defendant] has given way to personal service of summons or other form of notice, due process requires only that in order to subject a defendant to a judgment in personam, if he be not present within the territory of the forum, he have certain minimum contacts with it such that the maintenance of the suit does not offend "traditional notions of fair play and substantial justice." Milliken v. Meyer, 311 U.S. 457, 463 (1940); see also Hess v. Pawloski, 274 U.S. 352 (1927).

Since the corporate personality is a fiction, although a fiction intended to be acted upon as though it were a fact, it is clear that unlike an individual its "presence" without, as well as within, the state of its origin can be manifested only by activities carried on in its behalf by those who are authorized to act for it. To say that the corporation is so far "present" there as to satisfy due process requirements, for purposes of taxation or the maintenance of suits against it in the courts of the state, is to beg the question to be decided. For the terms "present" or "presence" are used merely to symbolize those activities of the corporation's agent within the state which courts will deem to be sufficient to satisfy the demands of due process. Those demands may be met by such contacts of the corporation with the state of the forum as make it reasonable, in the context of our federal system of government, to require the corporation to defend the particular suit which is brought there. An "estimate of the inconveniences" which would result to the corporation from a trial away from its "home" or principal place of business is relevant in this connection.

"Presence" in the state in this sense has never been doubted when the activities of the corporation there have not only been continuous and systematic, but also give rise to the liabilities sued on, even though no consent to be sued or authorization to an agent to accept service of process has been given. Conversely it has been generally recognized that the casual presence of the corporate agent or even his conduct of single or isolated items of activities in a state in the corporation's behalf are not enough to subject it to suit on causes of action unconnected with the activities there. To require the corporation in such circumstances to defend the suit away from its home or other jurisdiction where it carries on more substantial activities has been thought to lay too great and unreasonable a burden on the corporation to comport with due process.

While it has been held in cases on which appellant relies that continuous activity of some sorts within a state is not enough to support the demand that the corporation be amenable to suits unrelated to that activity, there have been instances in which the continuous corporate operations within a state were thought so substantial and of such a nature as to justify suit against it on causes of action arising from dealings entirely distinct from those activities.

Finally, although the commission of some single or occasional acts of the corporate agent in a state sufficient to impose an obligation or liability on the corporation has not been thought to confer upon the state authority to enforce it, other such acts, because of their nature and quality and the circumstances of their commission, may be deemed sufficient to render the corporation liable to suit. True, some of the decisions holding the corporation amenable to suit have been supported by resort to the legal fiction that it has given its consent to service and suit, consent being implied from its presence in the state through the acts of its authorized agents. But more realistically it may be said that those authorized acts were of such a nature as to justify the fiction.

It is evident that the criteria by which we mark the boundary line between those activities which justify the subjection of a corporation to suit, and those which do not, cannot be simply mechanical or quantitative. The test is not merely, as has sometimes been suggested, whether the activity, which the corporation has seen fit to procure through its agents in another state, is a little more or a little less. Whether due process is satisfied must depend rather upon the quality and nature of the activity in relation to the fair and orderly administration of the laws which it was the purpose of the due process clause to insure. That clause does not contemplate that a state may make binding a judgment in personam against an individual or corporate defendant with which the state has no contacts, ties, or relations. Cf. *Pennoyer v. Neff*, supra.

But to the extent that a corporation exercises the privilege of conducting activities within a state, it enjoys the benefits and protection of the laws of that state. The exercise of that privilege may give rise to obligations; and, so far as those obligations arise out of or are connected with the activities within the state, a procedure which requires the corporation to respond to a suit brought to enforce them can, in most instances, hardly be said to be undue.

Applying these standards, the activities carried on in behalf of appellant in the State of Washington were neither irregular nor casual. They were systematic and continuous throughout the years in question. They resulted in a large volume of interstate business, in the course of which appellant received the benefits and protection of the laws of the state, including the right to resort to the courts for the enforcement of its rights. The obligation which is here sued upon arose out of those very activities. It is evident that these operations establish sufficient contacts or ties with the state of the forum to make it reasonable and just according to our traditional conception of fair play and substantial justice to permit the state to enforce the obligations which appellant has incurred there. Hence we cannot say that the maintenance of the present suit in the State of Washington involves an unreasonable or undue procedure.

We are likewise unable to conclude that the service of the process within the state upon an agent whose activities establish appellant's "presence" there was not sufficient notice of the suit, or that the suit was so unrelated to those activities as to make the agent an inappropriate vehicle for communicating the notice.

It is enough that appellant has established such contacts with the state that the particular form of substituted service adopted there gives reasonable assurance that the notice will be actual. Nor can we say that the mailing of the notice of suit to appellant by registered mail at its home office was not reasonably calculated to apprise appellant of the suit. . . .

Appellant having rendered itself amenable to suit upon obligations arising out of the activities of its salesmen in Washington, the state may maintain the present suit in personam to collect the tax laid upon the exercise of the privilege of employing appellant's salesmen within the state. For Washington has made one of those activities, which taken together establish appellant's "presence" there for purposes of suit, the taxable event by which the state brings appellant within the reach of its taxing power. The state thus has constitutional power to lay the tax and to subject appellant to a suit to recover it. The activities which establish its "presence" subject it alike to taxation by the state and to suit to recover the tax.

Affirmed.

Mr. Justice Black delivered the following opinion.

. . . Certainly a State, at the very least, has power to tax and sue those dealing with its citizens within its boundaries, as we have held before. Were the Court to follow this principle, it would provide a workable standard for cases where, as here, no other questions are involved. The Court has not chosen to do so, but instead has engaged in an unnecessary discussion in the course of which it has announced vague Constitutional criteria applied for the first time to the issue before us. It has thus introduced uncertain elements confusing the simple pattern and tending to curtail the exercise of State powers to an extent not justified by the Constitution.

The criteria adopted insofar as they can be identified read as follows: Due process does permit State courts to "enforce the obligations which appellant has incurred" if it be found "reasonable and just according to our traditional conception of fair play and substantial justice." . . .

[Our prior cases do not mean] that all legislative enactments which this Court might deem to be contrary to natural justice ought to be held invalid under the due process clause. None of the cases purport to support or could support a holding that a State can tax and sue corporations only if its action comports with this Court's notions of "natural justice.". . .

I believe that the Federal Constitution leaves to each State, without any "ifs" or "buts," a power to tax and to open the doors of its courts for its citizens to sue corporations whose agents do business in those States. Believing that the Constitution gave the States that power, I think it a judicial deprivation to condition its exercise upon this Court's notion of "fair play," however appealing that term may be. Nor can I stretch the meaning of due process so far as to authorize this Court to deprive a State of the right to afford judicial protection to its citizens on the ground that it would be more "convenient" for the corporation to be sued somewhere else. . . .

Superimposing the natural justice concept on the Constitution's specific prohibitions could operate as a drastic abridgment of democratic safeguards they embody, such as freedom of speech, press and religion, and the right to counsel.... For application of this natural law concept, whether under the terms "reasonableness," "justice," or "fair play," makes judges the supreme arbiters of the country's laws and practices.... This result, I believe, alters the form of government our Constitution provides....

True, the State's power is here upheld. But the rule announced means that tomorrow's judgment may strike down a State or Federal enactment on the ground that it does not conform to this Court's idea of natural justice. I therefore find myself moved by the same fears that caused Mr. Justice Holmes to say in 1930:

"I have not yet adequately expressed the more than anxiety that I feel at the ever increasing scope given to the Fourteenth Amendment in cutting down what I believe to be the constitutional rights of the States. As the decisions now stand, I see hardly any limit but the sky to the invalidating of those rights if they happen to strike a majority of this Court as for any reason undesirable." *Baldwin v. Missouri,* 281 U.S. 586.

Notes and Questions: Understanding *International Shoe*

1. The shift to contacts. The Court explained that, to determine whether personal jurisdiction exists, a judge must focus on the defendant's contacts with a forum, not simply on whether the defendant is present or doing business there. This shift made sense in light of the practical difficulties that the Court had encountered in applying *Pennoyer.*

2. Two *Shoe* sizes: Specific and general in personam jurisdiction. The Court suggests that there are two ways in which a defendant's contacts with a forum can lead to in personam jurisdiction. First, in personam jurisdiction exists if the claim arises out of the defendant's deliberate contact with the state. This type of personal jurisdiction is now known as *specific in personam jurisdiction* or *specific jurisdiction.*

Second, the Court explains that in personam jurisdiction can exist even if the claim does not arise out of the defendant's in-state contacts, as long as the defendant has ongoing contacts with the state. According to the Court, such contacts exist for corporations when "the continuous corporate operations within a state [are] ... so substantial and of such a nature as to justify suit against it on causes of action arising from dealings entirely distinct from those activities." Similarly, such contacts exist for individuals when they are domiciled in a particular state. *Milliken v. Meyer,* 311 U.S. 457 (1940). Under these circumstances, the defendant is subject to what is now called *general in personam jurisdiction* or *general jurisdiction* and can be sued in the forum even if the claim arose elsewhere.

Q **3. Understanding specific jurisdiction.** Recall Hess's car ride into Massachusetts and assume that Hess visited Massachusetts on just that single occasion. Under *International Shoe,* a Massachusetts court could exercise specific jurisdiction over Hess, because the lawsuit arose directly out of Hess's driving in the state. Under these circumstances, Hess's single contact in Massachusetts was sufficient to give rise to personal jurisdiction there.

Now imagine a different set of facts. Assume that a company called Demo Corporation is incorporated in Pennsylvania and has its principal place of business and all of its employees and facilities in Pennsylvania. Also imagine that Patti and Demo entered into a contract in Pennsylvania and that, after Demo breached the contract, Patti moved to Massachusetts and sued Demo for the breach in her new state. Assume that Demo has had only one contact with Massachusetts: one of its drivers drove through the state to make a delivery in Maine. Can Patti sue Demo in Massachusetts for the contract breach?

A

Although Demo has a contact in Massachusetts (one of its drivers previously entered the state), that contact does not support jurisdiction over Patti's claim. The key to specific jurisdiction is that the plaintiff's claim must arise out of the particular contact that the defendant had in the state. Here, unlike in *Hess*, Demo's act of driving in Massachusetts was *unrelated* to the subject of the lawsuit. Patti's claim concerns an alleged breach of contract, not Demo's drive through Massachusetts. As a result, there is no specific jurisdiction over Demo in Massachusetts for Patti's lawsuit, even though the type of contact is exactly the same as it was in the *Hess* case.

4. An example of general jurisdiction. Assume now that Demo's driver got into an accident while driving in Massachusetts. Would there be personal jurisdiction over Demo in *Pennsylvania* if the accident victim sued Demo there?

A

Yes. Even though there is probably no *specific* jurisdiction in Pennsylvania, there is *general* jurisdiction over Demo in Pennsylvania, because Demo is effectively at home in the state. Thus, both the Massachusetts courts (specific in personam) and Pennsylvania courts (general in personam) would have in personam jurisdiction over Demo in this case.

5. Why contacts? According to the *International Shoe* opinion, a defendant's in-state contacts are important because they imply that the defendant has taken advantage of the benefits and protections of a state's laws. The Court explained the idea this way:

> [T]o the extent that a corporation exercises the privilege of conducting activities within a state, it enjoys the benefits and protection of the laws of that state. The exercise of that privilege may give rise to obligations; and, so far as those obligations arise out of or are connected with the activities within the state, a procedure which requires the corporation to respond to a suit brought to enforce them can, in most instances, hardly be said to be undue.

A second important reason for focusing on contacts is that defendants can control where they direct their activities. This control enables a defendant to predict or limit exposure to suits in a distant forum. For example, defendants can alter their conduct to prevent contact with a particular state, thereby avoiding personal jurisdiction in that forum.

These rationales help to explain the concepts of specific and general jurisdiction. Recall that specific jurisdiction exists when a defendant has only a single or limited in-state contact. Under those circumstances, it seems fair to permit personal jurisdiction only for those claims that actually arise from the defendant's limited activity. If a claim arises out of the defendant's contact, the defendant will have taken advantage of the forum's benefits and protections *and* would have had an opportunity to anticipate and prevent the type of litigation that resulted from the contact. For example, in *Hess*, the defendant could have avoided the risk of being sued for negligent driving in Massachusetts by simply not driving in Massachusetts. By driving in the state, Hess not only took advantage of the benefits and protections that Massachusetts affords its visitors (e.g., driving on its roads), but Hess could have foreseen the consequences of driving in the state.

Similarly, in the context of general jurisdiction, it is reasonable and fair to expect a defendant who is at home in a state to defend a lawsuit there, even when the lawsuit arose out of conduct in another jurisdiction. At some point, the defendant is so integrated into the economic life of the state and the defendant's contacts are so extensive that the defendant should be considered akin to an in-state citizen, who is subject to personal jurisdiction under *Milliken v. Meyer,* 311 U.S. 457 (1940). In this sense, there is an appropriate symmetry between the extent to which the defendant "exercises the privilege of conducting activities within a state" and the extent of the defendant's exposure to lawsuits there.

Q **6. Trying on the *Shoe*.** Would it be constitutional for a court to exercise in personam jurisdiction in the following cases? If so, what type of in personam jurisdiction? Specific or general?

A. Demo (the Pennsylvania company from the earlier note) sends one of its products by mail to Paula, a California citizen. The product injures Paula in California, and she sues Demo in California.

A There would be specific jurisdiction over Demo in California. Demo made a deliberate contact with California (the sending of the package to the state), and the claim arises out of that voluntary contact with the state.

B. Same as A, except that Paula sues Demo in Pennsylvania.

A There would be general jurisdiction over Demo in Pennsylvania because Demo is at home there.

C. Same as A, except that after her injury, Paula moves to Arizona and sues Demo there. Assume that Demo's only contact with Arizona is that it recently sent a catalog to a potential customer in the state.

A There would not be in personam jurisdiction in this case. There is no general jurisdiction, because Demo does not appear to have sufficient contacts with Arizona to be considered at home there. Rather, from what we can tell, Demo merely sent one catalog to the state.

There is also no specific jurisdiction. Although Demo does have a contact in Arizona (it sent the catalog there), the claim does not arise out of that contact. Rather, the claim arises out of Demo's contact with California. As a result, there is no personal jurisdiction in Arizona for this case.

D. Same as C, except that the lawsuit is brought by the Arizona citizen as a result of fraudulent claims in the catalog sent to her in the state.

A Even though Demo's contacts with Arizona are exactly the same as they were in C, there *would be* personal jurisdiction in this case. The key difference is that this claim arises out of Demo's contacts in Arizona, whereas in C, the claim did not.

Q **7. Specific or general jurisdiction in *International Shoe?*** Based on the contacts that International Shoe had with the state of Washington, what type of in personam jurisdiction could have been exercised by a Washington court over International Shoe?

A Surely there would be specific jurisdiction. International Shoe had contacts with Washington through the representatives who sold the company's shoes there. Moreover, the lawsuit arose out of unemployment compensation payments that were owed because of the employment of those sales representatives. The Court wrote: "The obligation which is here sued upon arose out of [International Shoe's] very activities [in the forum]."

The Court also noted that International Shoe's activities in Washington were "neither irregular nor casual. They were systematic and continuous throughout the years in question." However, these activities were probably not sufficient to support general jurisdiction. A corporation can have ongoing contacts with a state, but not enough contacts to support general jurisdiction. *See, e.g., Daimler AG v. Bauman,* 571 U.S. 310 (2014) (making the distinction between having "continuous and systematic contacts" and being "at home" in the forum). Thus International Shoe's limited but ongoing sales in Washington were probably not sufficient to support general jurisdiction in Washington.

8. *Pennoyer* revisited. Consider the following multiple choice question.

Assume that Mitchell sues Neff in Oregon, alleging that Neff hired Mitchell to perform legal services in Oregon and failed to pay Mitchell the resulting legal fees. Also assume that the suit arose after *International Shoe* was decided and that Mitchell found Neff in California and served Neff with process in California. Would it be constitutional for the Oregon court to exercise in personam jurisdiction over Neff?

A. Yes, because Neff was served personally in California.
B. Yes, because Neff had a contact with Oregon, and the claim arose out of that contact.
C. No, because Neff was not served within Oregon's borders.
D. No, because the claim in Oregon is unrelated to Neff's contact with California.

A is incorrect. Serving Neff in California does not, by itself, establish a basis for personal jurisdiction in *Oregon*.

C is wrong as well. After *International Shoe*, a defendant may be sued in a state, even if she is not served personally in the state where the court sits, as long as the claim arises out of her minimum contacts with the state.

D is also wrong. Although the Oregon claim is unrelated to Neff's contacts with California, that's not the issue. The issue is whether Mitchell's claim arises out of Neff's contacts with *Oregon*, the state where Mitchell filed the suit.

The answer, then, is **B**. Neff hired Mitchell in Oregon, and Neff failed to pay Mitchell in Oregon. Mitchell sued Neff for the failure to pay the fees in Oregon. *Neff, therefore, had a contact within Oregon, and Mitchell's claim arose out of that contact.* Thus, if the suit were brought today, the Oregon court could exercise in personam jurisdiction over Neff.

In addition to highlighting how personal jurisdiction doctrine has evolved, this question also illustrates how much clearer the distinction between personal jurisdiction and notice has become. Under *Pennoyer*, the two concepts were integrally linked: Personal service in the forum state sufficed to establish jurisdiction. After *International Shoe*, however, personal jurisdiction now typically turns on whether the defendant had sufficient contacts with the forum state and not on where the defendant was notified or served with process. The issue of whether a defendant is properly notified of the suit is now a separate question subject to different rules and a different constitutional analysis. See Chapter 10.

9. Giving the boot to *Pennoyer*. In some respects, *International Shoe* overrules *Pennoyer*. After *International Shoe*, a court can exercise personal jurisdiction over a defendant even if that defendant was not served within the state, was not domiciled or present in the state, and did not otherwise consent to be sued in the state. Contacts provide a new and independent basis for establishing personal jurisdiction that did not exist under the *Pennoyer* framework.

At the same time, some basic principles from *Pennoyer* remain intact. The territorial authority of a court is still important. For example, a defendant must generally have a contact within the forum state in order to be subject to a lawsuit there. Moreover, some of the basic methods for establishing personal jurisdiction remain effective. For instance, personal service on an individual defendant while the defendant is within the state still supports personal jurisdiction, at least in most circumstances. *Burnham v. Superior Court*, 495 U.S. 604 (1990). Domicile and consent also remain legitimate bases for establishing personal jurisdiction. Finally, the focus on a company's "presence" and whether it is "doing business" in a state has morphed into a conceptually similar doctrine: general jurisdiction. So although *International Shoe* expanded the permissible scope of a court's personal jurisdiction authority, some of the underlying principles and doctrines contained in *Pennoyer* remain good law.

10. Challenging personal jurisdiction (part I): Special appearances and alternatives. Challenges to personal jurisdiction are fairly common, but there is a potential trap waiting for the unwary defendant. Remember that it is possible to establish personal jurisdiction by personally serving defendants while they are within the forum state. So, if a defendant shows up in court to challenge personal jurisdiction, does that mean that the plaintiff can simply serve the defendant while there and thus establish personal jurisdiction?

Special appearance. To avoid this catch-22, courts have long allowed defendants to make a "special appearance" in the court—this is, an appearance for the exclusive purpose of challenging personal jurisdiction. As long as the defendant appears "specially," the plaintiff cannot just serve the defendant while at the courthouse and establish personal jurisdiction. (It is for this reason that the Court in *International Shoe* mentioned that the company had appeared "specially" in the case.)

Special appearances are a helpful procedural device, but courts have interpreted the concept strictly. Typically, if a defendant raises any issue other than personal jurisdiction while making an appearance, the defendant is considered to have waived the personal jurisdiction defense.

Alternatives to special appearance. In recent years, federal courts and a growing number of states have given defendants a bit more leeway to raise personal jurisdiction issues without making a special appearance. For example, in federal court, a defendant can make a motion to dismiss that raises other issues as well. *See* Fed. R. Civ. P. 12(g)–(h). However, even in these jurisdictions, defendants must still raise the personal jurisdiction issue early in the case or risk waiving the defense. *Id.*

Q

11. Easy waiver. Recall from earlier chapters that a party can typically raise subject matter jurisdiction for the first time long after the case has begun, even on direct appeal. Why is personal jurisdiction, unlike subject matter jurisdiction, so easily waived?

A

Subject matter jurisdiction concerns the court's constitutional authority to hear a case. Without that power, the court's decisions can have no legal effect, so the parties have no authority to waive subject matter jurisdiction. In contrast, personal jurisdiction is not a limitation on the court's inherent authority; it is a procedural protection for a party (typically the defendant) under the Fourteenth Amendment Due Process Clause. If a defendant wants to litigate in the state that the plaintiff has chosen, the defendant may waive the procedural safeguard of personal jurisdiction. In other words, personal jurisdiction is a defense that is personal to the defendant, whereas subject matter jurisdiction implicates systemic concerns.

12. Challenging personal jurisdiction (part II): Direct challenges vs. collateral attacks. Direct challenges—challenges in the court where the lawsuit was filed—are not the only way to contest personal jurisdiction. A defendant may also raise personal jurisdiction in a collateral proceeding.

To employ a collateral challenge, the defendant must fail to appear in the court where the plaintiff filed the original lawsuit. This failure to appear eventually results in a default judgment against the defendant. The plaintiff can then take that judgment to a state where the defendant resides or has assets and can ask the court in that state to enforce the judgment under the U.S. Constitution's

Full Faith and Credit Clause. Although courts typically enforce judgments from another state's courts under this Clause, that obligation only exists when the original court entered a valid judgment. In a collateral challenge, the defendant appears in the *enforcing* court and contends that the *original* (i.e., rendering) court's judgment was invalid for lack of personal jurisdiction and should not be enforced.

Q **13. Lawyering strategy: Direct or collateral attack?** Under what circumstances would you advise a client to challenge personal jurisdiction collaterally?

A This tactic is very risky. By not appearing in the court that entered the default judgment, the defendant has waived any opportunity to contest the plaintiff's claim on the merits. Thus, if the defendant's collateral challenge fails, the enforcing court can order the defendant's assets to be sold or transferred to satisfy the default judgment.

Given this risk, a collateral challenge only makes sense if the defendant has no defense (or a very weak defense) to the plaintiff's claims on the merits, the amount at issue is small relative to the amount of money it would cost to mount a defense, and the argument against personal jurisdiction is particularly strong. Under these circumstances, it might make sense for the defendant to default in the original court and let the plaintiff try to enforce the judgment wherever the defendant has assets. If personal jurisdiction in the original court is questionable and the amount at stake is small, the plaintiff might not bother to go to another state to enforce the judgment. In that case, the defendant will have saved the expense of showing up in a distant forum and face a limited risk of having to pay a significant judgment.

14. Appealing adverse rulings on personal jurisdiction. In the federal courts, and in some states, the defendant cannot immediately appeal a trial court's finding that it has personal jurisdiction. In these states, the defendant must wait until the trial court enters a final judgment in the case, which could take years.

There is an obvious problem with this approach. The parties might litigate the entire case only to have the appellate court rule that the trial court did not have personal jurisdiction in the first place. The entire case would then have to be relitigated in a forum that has personal jurisdiction, resulting in an enormous waste of time and money.

To avoid this problem, some states allow a defendant to immediately appeal a trial court's rulings on personal jurisdiction. This process of appealing an issue in the middle of a case is called an *interlocutory appeal*. Although interlocutory appeals solve some problems, they create others. For example, they have the effect of dragging out litigation, because the trial court proceedings may be put on hold (stayed) until the interlocutory appeal is resolved.

15. Big shoes and long arms: The role of long arm statutes. *International Shoe* considers the constitutional scope of personal jurisdiction—the outer limits on a court's authority to assert jurisdiction over an out-of-state defendant. However, the Constitution does not automatically confer personal jurisdiction on the courts of a state; the state legislature does. Each state specifies how expansively its courts can exercise personal jurisdiction, as long as that specification is within constitutional bounds. States typically define the reach of personal jurisdiction in their courts through statutes, often called *long arm statutes*, which specify contacts with the state that allow their courts to assert jurisdiction over the defendant. (States may also authorize personal jurisdiction through other statutes, such as business registration statutes, directors' consent laws, and nonresident motorists' statutes, as in *Hess*.) Thus, a court can exercise personal jurisdiction only if it has the constitutional authority to do so *and* the relevant statute—usually, a long arm statute—authorizes it.

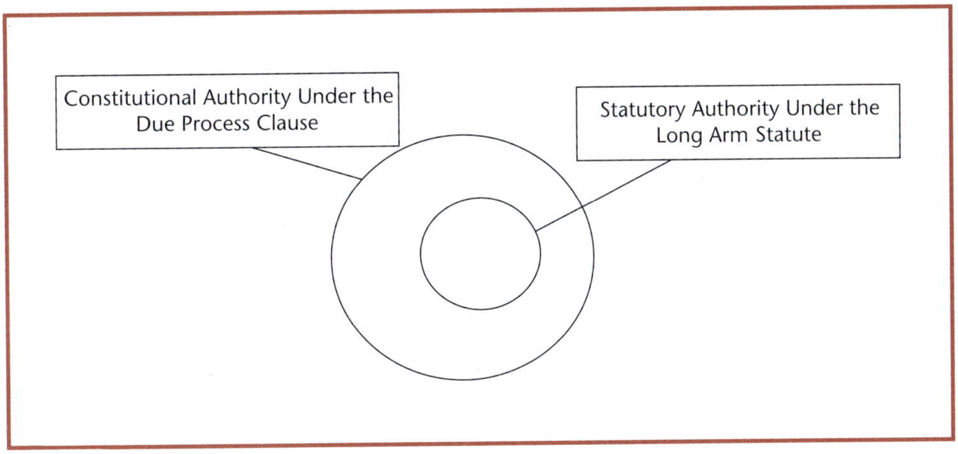

Figure 6–1: LONG ARM STATUTES AND THE CONSTITUTION

We saw a similar relationship between statutes and constitutional authority in the subject matter jurisdiction context. Recall that Congress can pass (and has passed) statutes that give the federal courts less than the full scope of constitutionally permissible subject matter jurisdiction. Congress, however, cannot confer *more* subject matter jurisdiction than the Constitution permits.

As the diagram above demonstrates, long arm statutes work the same way. A court typically does not have personal jurisdiction unless it is both granted in the long arm statute (the inner circle) *and* permitted under the Constitution (the outer circle). A case must fall within both circles for a court to have the authority to hear it.

Because many states' long arm statutes simply give the courts as much personal jurisdiction authority as the Constitution allows, the outer circle and inner circle are the same in those states. Chapter 9 examines those situations where the long arm statute offers less than the full scope of constitutional authority and is thus a smaller circle than the constitutional circle (as in the above diagram). That chapter also describes how this issue is handled in federal courts. In the meantime, Chapters 7 and 8 offer more detail on the size of the outer circle.

V. The Evolution of Personal Jurisdiction: Summary of Basic Principles

- Under *Pennoyer v. Neff*, which reflected nineteenth-century jurisdictional concepts, courts typically only had in personam jurisdiction over a person if she was personally served with the complaint and summons within the forum state. Courts had in rem jurisdiction over property if it was located in the state and was attached prior to adjudication of the claim.

- *Pennoyer*'s rigid doctrine was ill equipped to deal with an increasingly mobile society and the increased scope of interstate corporate activity. Consequently, the Court, in *International Shoe,* shifted its focus from the strict requirement of in-state presence to allow jurisdiction based on a defendant's contacts with the state.
- Courts have identified different ways to establish in personam jurisdiction. If the claim arises out of the defendant's contact, a court has specific jurisdiction over the defendant. If the claim does not arise out of the defendant's contact but the defendant is essentially at home in the state, the court has general jurisdiction.
- The Supreme Court has recognized several other bases for jurisdiction that are constitutionally sufficient. For example, a person is subject to personal jurisdiction where she is domiciled. In addition, a defendant who would otherwise not be subject to personal jurisdiction in a state may waive her objection or consent to jurisdiction.
- Even if personal jurisdiction is consistent with the Due Process Clause, a court typically cannot exercise jurisdiction unless a long arm statute or some other jurisdiction-granting statute or rule authorizes it.

7

Specific In Personam Jurisdiction

I. Introduction

This chapter describes specific jurisdiction in detail and explores many of the ambiguities that arise when courts apply the doctrine. For example, what counts as a contact? When does a claim arise out of a contact? What other factors must a court take into account when determining whether specific jurisdiction is constitutional? And is a contacts-based analysis still viable today, when so much commerce takes place over the Internet? The chapter begins with an elaboration of the concept of a "contact" and explains what counts as a contact in different kinds of cases.

II. What Counts as a Contact?

A. An Early Definition: *McGee v. International Life Insurance Co.*

The test for specific jurisdiction took some time to develop and, in many ways, is still developing. In the decade after *International Shoe*, the Court decided two important cases—*McGee v. International Life Insurance Company*, 355 U.S. 220 (1957), and *Hanson v. Denckla*, 357 U.S. 235 (1958)—that helped to clarify the doctrine at that time. The *McGee* case arguably represents the Court's most liberal approach to specific jurisdiction.

READING *MCGEE v. INTERNATIONAL LIFE INSURANCE CO.* In *McGee*, the Court discusses an insurance company's contacts with California, as well as the plaintiff's and California's interests in having the case heard in a California court. When reading the case, consider the following questions:

- A California statute authorized personal jurisdiction in this case. Why wasn't that the end of the matter?
- Does the Court view minimum contacts as a prerequisite for finding specific jurisdiction? Or does the Court view the insurance company's California contacts as one of several factors that must be considered?
- Was the Court's analysis consistent with the approach adopted in *International Shoe*?

MCGEE v. INTERNATIONAL LIFE INSURANCE CO.

355 U.S. 220 (1957)

Opinion of the Court by Mr. Justice Black, announced by Mr. Justice Douglas.

Petitioner, Lulu B. McGee, recovered a judgment in a California state court against respondent, International Life Insurance Company, on a contract of insurance. Respondent was not served with process in California but by registered mail at its principal place of business in Texas. The California court based its jurisdiction on a state statute which subjects foreign corporations to suit in California on insurance contracts with residents of that State even though such corporations cannot be served with process within its borders.

Unable to collect the judgment in California petitioner went to Texas where she filed suit on the judgment in a Texas court. But the Texas courts refused to enforce her judgment holding it was void under the Fourteenth Amendment because service of process outside California could not give the courts of that

State jurisdiction over respondent. Since the case raised important questions, not only to California but to other States which have similar laws, we granted certiorari. It is not controverted that if the California court properly exercised jurisdiction over respondent the Texas courts erred in refusing to give its judgment full faith and credit. 28 U.S.C. § 1738.

The material facts are relatively simple. In 1944, Lowell Franklin, a resident of California, purchased a life insurance policy from the Empire Mutual Insurance Company, an Arizona corporation. In 1948 the respondent agreed with Empire Mutual to assume its insurance obligations. **[Eds.— International Life essentially bought Empire Mutual's insurance business, becoming a successor in interest.]** Respondent then mailed a reinsurance certificate to Franklin in California offering to insure him in accordance with the terms of the policy he held with Empire Mutual. He accepted this offer and from that time until his death in 1950 paid premiums by mail from his California home to respondent's Texas office. Petitioner, Franklin's mother, was the beneficiary under the policy. She sent proofs of his death to the respondent, but it refused to pay, claiming that he had committed suicide. It appears that neither Empire Mutual nor respondent has ever had any office or agent in California. And so far as the record before us shows, respondent has never solicited or done any insurance business in California apart from the policy involved here.

Since *Pennoyer v. Neff*, this Court has held that the Due Process Clause of the Fourteenth Amendment places some limit on the power of state courts to enter binding judgments against persons not served with process within their boundaries. But just where this line of limitation falls has been the subject of prolific controversy, particularly with respect to foreign corporations. In a continuing process of evolution this Court accepted and then abandoned "consent," "doing business," and "presence" as the standard for measuring the extent of state judicial power over such corporations. More recently in *International Shoe Co. v. State of Washington*, the Court decided that due process requires only that in order to subject a defendant to a judgment *in personam*, if he be not present within the territory of the forum, he have certain minimum contacts with it such that the maintenance of the suit does not offend "traditional notions of fair play and substantial justice."

Looking back over this long history of litigation a trend is clearly discernible toward expanding the permissible scope of state jurisdiction over foreign corporations and other nonresidents. In part this is attributable to the fundamental transformation of our national economy over the years. Today many commercial transactions touch two or more States and may involve parties separated by the full continent. With this increasing nationalization of commerce has come a great increase in the amount of business conducted by mail across state lines. At the same time modern transportation and communication have made it much less burdensome for a party sued to defend himself in a State where he engages in economic activity.

Turning to this case we think it apparent that the Due Process Clause did not preclude the California court from entering a judgment binding on respondent.

It is sufficient for purposes of due process that the suit was based on a contract which had substantial connection with that State. The contract was delivered in California, the premiums were mailed from there and the insured was a resident of that State when he died. It cannot be denied that California has a manifest interest in providing effective means of redress for its residents when their insurers refuse to pay claims. These residents would be at a severe disadvantage if they were forced to follow the insurance company to a distant State in order to hold it legally accountable. When claims were small or moderate individual claimants frequently could not afford the cost of bringing an action in a foreign forum—thus in effect making the company judgment proof. Often the crucial witnesses—as here on the company's defense of suicide—will be found in the insured's locality. Of course there may be inconvenience to the insurer if it is held amenable to suit in California where it had this contract but certainly nothing which amounts to a denial of due process. There is no contention that respondent did not have adequate notice of the suit or sufficient time to prepare its defenses and appear. . . .

The judgment is reversed and the cause is remanded . . . for further proceedings not inconsistent with this opinion.

It is so ordered.

Notes and Questions: Understanding the Reach of *McGee*

Q **1. The interaction of long arm statutes and constitutional analysis.** California's long arm statute subjected "foreign corporations to suit in California on insurance contracts with residents of that State even though such corporations [could not] be served with process within [California's] borders." Given that the statute clearly conferred personal jurisdiction in this case, why did the Court need to discuss the Constitution?

A A court can exercise personal jurisdiction only if the relevant long arm statute authorizes it *and* the Constitution does not prohibit it. (Review the diagram at the end of the previous chapter.) Here, the California statute authorized personal jurisdiction, but the Court still had to determine whether the statute, as applied to the facts of this case, was constitutional.

Q **2. The role of contacts in the analysis.** Under the Court's analysis in *McGee*, must a defendant have contacts in the forum? Or is the existence of a contact merely one of several relevant factors that a court must consider when determining whether specific jurisdiction is constitutional?

A In *McGee,* the Court appeared to conclude that a defendant's deliberate in-state contact (e.g., an offer of insurance to a California resident or the mailing of the reinsurance certificate into California) was merely one factor to consider. The Court concluded that it was also important to analyze the plaintiff's interest in suing in California, the insured's mailing of premiums from California, the availability of witnesses in California, California's interest in providing a remedy, and (as in *International Shoe*) the extent to which the defendant would be inconvenienced.

McGee did not make clear whether all of these considerations bore equal weight or whether some—particularly minimum contacts—were essential. Subsequent cases explain that the defendant's contacts in the state are, in fact, an essential requirement.

3. Contacts as an essential and distinct element of specific jurisdiction. In *Hanson v. Denckla*, 357 U.S. 235 (1958), the Court moved away from *McGee*'s vague, multi-factored analysis and emphasized *International Shoe*'s focus on the defendant's *deliberate* in-state contacts. Using language that is still widely cited today, the Court explained that "it is essential in each case that there be some act by which the defendant purposefully avail[ed] itself of the privilege of conducting activities within the forum State, thus invoking the benefits and protections of its laws." *Id.* at 253.

Critically, *Hanson* made clear that an overall consideration of the forum's connection to the controversy is not a substitute for the existence of minimum contacts. The defendant has to have initiated a contact in the forum state. Absent such a contact, specific jurisdiction does not exist.

4. The traveling insurance policy. In light of *Hanson*'s clarification that a defendant must have contacts with the forum state (i.e., the defendant must purposefully avail itself of the privilege of conducting activities within the forum State), consider the following variation on *McGee*.

Imagine that Lowell Franklin purchased an insurance policy from the International Life Insurance Company while living in North Carolina and that he moved to California only a week before his death. Assume that the beneficiary of the policy, Lulu McGee, had always lived in California. If the insurance company had no other connection to California, would a California court have authority to exercise personal jurisdiction over the insurance company if the company makes a timely objection?

A. No. The California statute does not confer personal jurisdiction in this case.
B. No. Personal jurisdiction in this case would probably be unconstitutional.
C. Yes. The California statute permits personal jurisdiction in this type of case, because the case involves an insurance policy that covered someone who was a California citizen at the time of death.
D. Yes. The statute probably applies here, and its application to this case would be constitutional: Witnesses regarding the cause of McGee's death are in California, and California has an interest in ensuring that one of its citizens recovers on an insurance policy. In addition, Mrs. McGee has an interest in suing in California.

A is incorrect. Arguably, the statute confers jurisdiction in this case, because Franklin moved to California before he died. C, however, is also incorrect. Even though the statute confers jurisdiction in this case, that is not enough. Personal jurisdiction must also satisfy the constitutional requirements of due process, and those requirements are probably not satisfied here. Unlike *McGee*, the defendant in this question does not appear to have purposefully directed any contacts into California. Accordingly, personal jurisdiction would be unconstitutional, regardless of what the long arm statute says.

It is important to understand why **D** is wrong. In *McGee*, it was not entirely clear whether the presence of the plaintiff and the witnesses in California, together with the state's interest in providing redress, sufficed to establish personal jurisdiction. But *Hanson* made the answer clearer: A defendant must have purposeful contacts in the forum state. And in this example, the defendant did not have any such contacts.

In the end, California may be a reasonable place to hear this case given that important witnesses live there and the beneficiary of the policy lives there. But without the defendant's purposeful contacts in California, there is probably no personal jurisdiction. Thus, **B** is the best answer.

B. The Relationship Between Contacts and Reasonableness: *World-Wide Volkswagen v. Woodson*

Hanson made clear that, to establish specific jurisdiction, a plaintiff's claim has to arise out of the defendant's contacts with the forum. But many doctrinal ambiguities remained, several of which were addressed in *World-Wide Volkswagen v. Woodson*.

One ambiguity that existed in these early cases was whether a claim-related contact is always sufficient to establish specific jurisdiction. In other words, if a claim arises out of the defendant's contact with the forum, are there ever any circumstances when specific jurisdiction might nevertheless be unconstitutional? *International Shoe*, *McGee*, and *Hanson* all recognized that other "reasonableness" factors had to be considered in the analysis, but the precise role of those factors was vague.

Another important ambiguity concerned the meaning of "purposeful availment." When precisely does a defendant have a contact with a forum under this standard? For example, does a defendant have a contact with a forum when a consumer buys the defendant's product in one state, takes it into another state, and is injured by it there? The answer has important implications given that consumers frequently bring products across state lines.

READING *WORLD-WIDE VOLKSWAGEN v. WOODSON*. Consider the following questions as you read *World-Wide*:

- Does the Court conclude that the defendants had contacts in Oklahoma?
- What "reasonableness" factors should a court consider when determining whether specific jurisdiction is constitutional?
- Should a court consider the reasonableness of personal jurisdiction separately from whether the defendant had claim-related contacts in the forum? Or is the question of reasonableness inextricably linked to the contacts inquiry?

■ What does Justice Brennan conclude in his dissent regarding the rela-
tionship between contacts and the "reasonableness" factors? Why doe
the outcome in this case turn on whether there is such a relationshi

WORLD-WIDE VOLKSWAGEN v. WOODSO

444 U.S. 286 (1980)

Mr. Justice White delivered the opinion of the Court.

The issue before us is whether, consistently with the Due Process Cla the Fourteenth Amendment, an Oklahoma court may exercise *in personam* jurisdiction over a nonresident automobile retailer and its wholesale distributor in a products-liability action, when the defendants' only connection with Oklahoma is the fact that an automobile sold in New York to New York residents became involved in an accident in Oklahoma.

I

Respondents Harry and Kay Robinson purchased a new Audi automobile from petitioner Seaway Volkswagen, Inc. (Seaway), in Massena, N.Y., in 1976. The following year the Robinson family, who resided in New York, left that State for a new home in Arizona. As they passed through the State of Oklahoma, another car struck their Audi in the rear, causing a fire which severely burned Kay Robinson and her two children.

The Robinsons subsequently brought a products-liability action in the District Court for Creek County, Okla., claiming that their injuries resulted from defective design and placement of the Audi's gas tank and fuel system. They joined as defendants the automobile's manufacturer, Audi NSU Auto Union Aktiengesellschaft (Audi); its importer, Volkswagen of America, Inc. (Volkswagen); its regional distributor, petitioner World-Wide Volkswagen Corp. (World-Wide); and its retail dealer, petitioner Seaway. Seaway and World-Wide entered special appearances, claiming that Oklahoma's exercise of jurisdiction over them would offend the limitations on the State's jurisdiction imposed by the Due Process Clause of the Fourteenth Amendment.

The facts presented to the District Court showed that World-Wide is incorporated and has its business office in New York. It distributes vehicles, parts, and accessories, under contract with Volkswagen, to retail dealers in New York, New Jersey, and Connecticut. Seaway, one of these retail dealers, is incorporated and has its place of business in New York. Insofar as the record reveals, Seaway and World-Wide are fully independent corporations whose relations with each other and with Volkswagen and Audi are contractual only. Respondents adduced no evidence that either World-Wide or Seaway does any business in Oklahoma, ships or sells any products to or in that State, has an agent to receive process there, or purchases advertisements in any media calculated to reach Oklahoma. In fact, as respondents' counsel conceded at oral argument, there was no showing that any automobile sold by World-Wide or Seaway has ever entered Oklahoma with the single exception of the vehicle involved in the present case.

Despite the apparent paucity of contacts between petitioners and Oklahoma, the District Court rejected their constitutional claim and reaffirmed that ruling in denying petitioners' motion for reconsideration. Petitioners then sought a writ of prohibition in the Supreme Court of Oklahoma to restrain the District Judge, respondent Charles S. Woodson, from exercising *in personam* jurisdiction over them. They renewed their contention that, because they had no "minimal contacts" with the State of Oklahoma, the actions of the District Judge were in violation of their rights under the Due Process Clause.

The Supreme Court of Oklahoma denied the writ, holding that personal jurisdiction over petitioners was authorized by Oklahoma's "long-arm" statute. Although the court noted that the proper approach was to test jurisdiction against both statutory and constitutional standards, its analysis did not distinguish these questions, probably because [the Oklahoma statute] has been interpreted as conferring jurisdiction to the limits permitted by the United States Constitution. The court's rationale was contained in the following paragraph:

> "In the case before us, the product being sold and distributed by the petitioners is by its very design and purpose so mobile that petitioners can foresee its possible use in Oklahoma. This is especially true of the distributor, who has the exclusive right to distribute such automobile in New York, New Jersey and Connecticut. The evidence presented below demonstrated that goods sold and distributed by the petitioners were used in the State of Oklahoma, and under the facts we believe it reasonable to infer, given the retail value of the automobile, that the petitioners derive substantial income from automobiles which from time to time are used in the State of Oklahoma. This being the case, we hold that under the facts presented, the trial court was justified in concluding that the petitioners derive substantial revenue from goods used or consumed in this State."

We granted certiorari to consider an important constitutional question with respect to state-court jurisdiction and to resolve a conflict between the Supreme Court of Oklahoma and the highest courts of at least four other States. We reverse.

II

The Due Process Clause of the Fourteenth Amendment limits the power of a state court to render a valid personal judgment against a nonresident defendant. A judgment rendered in violation of due process is void in the rendering State and is not entitled to full faith and credit elsewhere. *Pennoyer v. Neff*, 95 U.S. 714, 732–33 (1878). Due process requires that the defendant be given adequate notice of the suit and be subject to the personal jurisdiction of the court. *International*

Shoe Co. v. Washington, 326 U.S. 310 (1945). In the present case, it is not contended that notice was inadequate; the only question is whether these particular petitioners were subject to the jurisdiction of the Oklahoma courts.

As has long been settled, and as we reaffirm today, a state court may exercise personal jurisdiction over a nonresident defendant only so long as there exist "minimum contacts" between the defendant and the forum State. *International Shoe*, 326 U.S. at 316. The concept of minimum contacts, in turn, can be seen to perform two related, but distinguishable, functions. It protects the defendant against the burdens of litigating in a distant or inconvenient forum. And it acts to ensure that the States through their courts, do not reach out beyond the limits imposed on them by their status as coequal sovereigns in a federal system.

The protection against inconvenient litigation is typically described in terms of "reasonableness" or "fairness." We have said that the defendant's contacts with the forum State must be such that maintenance of the suit "does not offend 'traditional notions of fair play and substantial justice.' " *International Shoe*, 326 U.S. at 316 (quoting *Milliken v. Meyer*, 311 U.S. 457, 463 (1940)). The relationship between the defendant and the forum must be such that it is "reasonable . . . to require the corporation to defend the particular suit which is brought there." 326 U.S., at 317. Implicit in this emphasis on reasonableness is the understanding that the burden on the defendant, while always a primary concern, will in an appropriate case be considered in light of other relevant factors, including the forum State's interest in adjudicating the dispute, see *McGee v. International Life Ins. Co*, 355 U.S. 220, 223 (1957); the plaintiff's interest in obtaining convenient and effective relief, at least when that interest is not adequately protected by the plaintiff's power to choose the forum; the interstate judicial system's interest in obtaining the most efficient resolution of controversies; and the shared interest of the several States in furthering fundamental substantive social policies.

The limits imposed on state jurisdiction by the Due Process Clause, in its role as a guarantor against inconvenient litigation, have been substantially relaxed over the years. As we noted in *McGee*, this trend is largely attributable to a fundamental transformation in the American economy:

> "Today many commercial transactions touch two or more States and may involve parties separated by the full continent. With this increasing nationalization of commerce has come a great increase in the amount of business conducted by mail across state lines. At the same time modern transportation and communication have made it much less burdensome for a party sued to defend himself in a State where he engages in economic activity."

The historical developments noted in *McGee*, of course, have only accelerated in the generation since that case was decided.

Nevertheless, we have never accepted the proposition that state lines are irrelevant for jurisdictional purposes, nor could we, and remain faithful to the principles of interstate federalism embodied in the Constitution. The economic interdependence of the States was foreseen and desired by the Framers. In the

Commerce Clause, they provided that the Nation was to be a common market, a "free trade unit" in which the States are debarred from acting as separable economic entities. But the Framers also intended that the States retain many essential attributes of sovereignty, including, in particular, the sovereign power to try causes in their courts. The sovereignty of each State, in turn, implied a limitation on the sovereignty of all of its sister States—a limitation express or implicit in both the original scheme of the Constitution and the Fourteenth Amendment.

Hence, even while abandoning the shibboleth that "[t]he authority of every tribunal is necessarily restricted by the territorial limits of the State in which it is established," *Pennoyer*, 95 U.S., at 720, we emphasized that the reasonableness of asserting jurisdiction over the defendant must be assessed "in the context of our federal system of government," *International Shoe*, 326 U.S. at 317, and stressed that the Due Process Clause ensures not only fairness, but also the "orderly administration of the laws," *id.*, at 319. As we noted in *Hanson*:

> "As technological progress has increased the flow of commerce between the States, the need for jurisdiction over nonresidents has undergone a similar increase. At the same time, progress in communications and transportation has made the defense of a suit in a foreign tribunal less burdensome. In response to these changes, the requirements for personal jurisdiction over nonresidents have evolved from the rigid rule of *Pennoyer* to the flexible standard of *International Shoe*. But it is a mistake to assume that this trend heralds the eventual demise of all restrictions on the personal jurisdiction of state courts. [Citation omitted.] Those restrictions are more than a guarantee of immunity from inconvenient or distant litigation. They are a consequence of territorial limitations on the power of the respective States."

Thus, the Due Process Clause "does not contemplate that a state may make binding a judgment *in personam* against an individual or corporate defendant with which the state has no contacts, ties, or relations." *International Shoe*, 326 U.S., at 319. Even if the defendant would suffer minimal or no inconvenience from being forced to litigate before the tribunals of another State; even if the forum State has a strong interest in applying its law to the controversy; even if the forum State is the most convenient location for litigation, the Due Process Clause, acting as an instrument of interstate federalism, may sometimes act to divest the State of its power to render a valid judgment. *Hanson*, 357 U.S., at 251.

III

Applying these principles to the case at hand, we find in the record before us a total absence of those affiliating circumstances that are a necessary predicate to any exercise of state-court jurisdiction. Petitioners carry on no activity whatsoever in Oklahoma. They close no sales and perform no services there. They avail themselves of none of the privileges and benefits of Oklahoma law. They solicit no business there either through salespersons or through advertising reasonably calculated to reach the State. Nor does the record show that they regularly sell cars at wholesale or retail to Oklahoma customers or residents or that they indirectly, through others, serve or seek to serve the Oklahoma market. In short, respondents seek to base jurisdiction on one, isolated occurrence and whatever inferences can be drawn therefrom: the fortuitous circumstance that a single Audi automobile, sold in New York to New York residents, happened to suffer an accident while passing through Oklahoma.

It is argued, however, that because an automobile is mobile by its very design and purpose it was "foreseeable" that the Robinsons' Audi would cause injury in Oklahoma. Yet "foreseeability" alone has never been a sufficient benchmark for personal jurisdiction under the Due Process Clause. In *Hanson v. Denckla, supra*, it was no doubt foreseeable that the settlor of a Delaware trust would subsequently move to Florida and seek to exercise a power of appointment there; yet we held that Florida courts could not constitutionally exercise jurisdiction over a Delaware trustee that had no other contacts with the forum State. In *Kulko v. California Superior Court*, 436 U.S. 84 (1978), it was surely "foreseeable" that a divorced wife would move to California from New York, the domicile of the marriage, and that a minor daughter would live with the mother. Yet we held that California could not exercise jurisdiction in a child-support action over the former husband who had remained in New York.

If foreseeability were the criterion, a local California tire retailer could be forced to defend in Pennsylvania when a blowout occurs there; a Wisconsin seller of a defective automobile jack could be haled before a distant court for damage caused in New Jersey; or a Florida soft-drink concessionaire could be summoned to Alaska to account for injuries happening there. Every seller of chattels would in effect appoint the chattel his agent for service of process. His amenability to suit would travel with the chattel. . . .[11]

This is not to say, of course, that foreseeability is wholly irrelevant. But the foreseeability that is critical to due process analysis is not the mere likelihood that a product will find its way into the forum State. Rather, it is that the defendant's conduct and connection with the forum State are such that he should reasonably anticipate being haled into court there. The Due Process Clause, by ensuring the "orderly administration of the laws," *International Shoe*, gives a degree of predictability to the legal system that allows potential defendants to structure their primary conduct with some minimum assurance as to where that conduct will and will not render them liable to suit.

---

11. Respondents' counsel, at oral argument, sought to limit the reach of the foreseeability standard by suggesting that there is something unique about automobiles. It is true that automobiles are uniquely mobile, that they did play a crucial role in the expansion of personal jurisdiction through the fiction of implied consent, e.g., *Hess v. Pawloski*, and that some of the cases have treated the automobile as a "dangerous instrumentality." But today, under the regime of *International Shoe*, we see no difference for jurisdictional purposes between an automobile and any other chattel. The "dangerous instrumentality" concept apparently was never used to support personal jurisdiction; and to the extent it has relevance today it bears not on jurisdiction but on the possible desirability of imposing substantive principles of tort law such as strict liability.

When a corporation "purposefully avails itself of the privilege of conducting activities within the forum State," *Hanson*, 357 U.S., at 253, it has clear notice that it is subject to suit there, and can act to alleviate the risk of burdensome litigation by procuring insurance, passing the expected costs on to customers, or, if the risks are too great, severing its connection with the State. Hence if the sale of a product of a manufacturer or distributor such as Audi or Volkswagen is not simply an isolated occurrence, but arises from the efforts of the manufacturer or distributor to serve directly or indirectly, the market for its product in other States, it is not unreasonable to subject it to suit in one of those States if its allegedly defective merchandise has there been the source of injury to its owner or to others. The forum State does not exceed its powers under the Due Process Clause if it asserts personal jurisdiction over a corporation that delivers its products into the stream of commerce with the expectation that they will be purchased by consumers in the forum State. *Cf. Gray v. American Radiator*, 176 N.E.2d 761 (Ill. 1961).

But there is no such or similar basis for Oklahoma jurisdiction over World-Wide or Seaway in this case. Seaway's sales are made in Massena, N.Y. World-Wide's market, although substantially larger, is limited to dealers in New York, New Jersey, and Connecticut. There is no evidence of record that any automobiles distributed by World-Wide are sold to retail customers outside this tristate area. It is foreseeable that the purchasers of automobiles sold by World-Wide and Seaway may take them to Oklahoma. But the mere "unilateral activity of those who claim some relationship with a nonresident defendant cannot satisfy the requirement of contact with the forum State." *Hanson,* 357 U.S. at 253.

In a variant on the previous argument, it is contended that jurisdiction can be supported by the fact that petitioners earn substantial revenue from goods used in Oklahoma. The Oklahoma Supreme Court so found, drawing the inference that because one automobile sold by petitioners had been used in Oklahoma, others might have been used there also. While this inference seems less than compelling on the facts of the instant case, we need not question the court's factual findings in order to reject its reasoning.

This argument seems to make the point that the purchase of automobiles in New York, from which the petitioners earn substantial revenue, would not occur *but for* the fact that the automobiles are capable of use in distant States like Oklahoma. Respondents observe that the very purpose of an automobile is to travel, and that travel of automobiles sold by petitioners is facilitated by an extensive chain of Volkswagen service centers throughout the country, including some in Oklahoma. However, financial benefits accruing to the defendant from a collateral relation to the forum State will not support jurisdiction if they do not stem from a constitutionally cognizable contact with that State. In our view, whatever marginal revenues petitioners may receive by virtue of the fact that their products are capable of use in Oklahoma is far too attenuated a contact to justify that State's exercise of *in personam* jurisdiction over them.

Because we find that petitioners have no "contacts, ties, or relations" with the State of Oklahoma, the judgment of the Supreme Court of Oklahoma is

Reversed.

Rule: Just b/c defective product goes somewhere doesn't mean that business that sold product can be sued there.

Mr. Justice BRENNAN, dissenting.

. . .

I

The Court's opinions focus tightly on the existence of contacts between the forum and the defendant. In so doing, they accord too little weight to the strength of the forum State's interest in the case and fail to explore whether there would be any actual inconvenience to the defendant. The essential inquiry in locating the constitutional limits on state-court jurisdiction over absent defendants is whether the particular exercise of jurisdiction offends " 'traditional notions of fair play and substantial justice.' " *International Shoe,* 326 U.S. at 316. The clear focus in *International Shoe* was on fairness and reasonableness. The Court specifically declined to establish a mechanical test based on the quantum of contacts between a State and the defendant . . . .

Surely *International Shoe* contemplated that the significance of the contacts necessary to support jurisdiction would diminish if some other consideration helped establish that jurisdiction would be fair and reasonable. The interests of the State and other parties in proceeding with the case in a particular forum are such considerations. . . .

Another consideration is the actual burden a defendant must bear in defending the suit in the forum. Because lesser burdens reduce the unfairness to the defendant, jurisdiction may be justified despite less significant contacts. The burden, of course, must be of constitutional dimension. Due process limits on jurisdiction do not protect a defendant from all inconvenience of travel, and it would not be sensible to make the constitutional rule turn solely on the number of miles the defendant must travel to the courtroom.[1] Instead, the constitutionally significant "burden" to be analyzed relates to the mobility of the defendant's defense. For instance, if having to travel to a foreign forum would hamper the defense because witnesses or evidence or the defendant himself were immobile, or if there were a disproportionately large number of witnesses or amount of evidence that would have to be transported at the defendant's expense, or if being away from home for the duration of the trial would work some special hardship on the defendant, then the Constitution would require special consideration for the defendant's interests. . . .

That considerations other than contacts between the forum and the defendant are relevant necessarily means that the Constitution does not require that trial be held in the State which has the "best contacts" with the defendant. The defendant has no constitutional entitlement to the best forum or, for that matter, to any particular forum. Under even the most restrictive view of *International Shoe,* several States could have jurisdiction over a particular cause of action. We need

1. In fact, a courtroom just across the state line from a defendant may often be far more convenient for the defendant than a courtroom in a distant corner of his own State.

only determine whether the forum States in these cases satisfy the constitutional minimum.

II

. . . I would find that the forum State has an interest in permitting the litigation to go forward, the litigation is connected to the forum, the defendant is linked to the forum, and the burden of defending is not unreasonable. Accordingly, I would hold that it is neither unfair nor unreasonable to require these defendants to defend in the forum State. . . .

[T]he interest of the forum State and its connection to the litigation is strong. The automobile accident underlying the litigation occurred in Oklahoma. The plaintiffs were hospitalized in Oklahoma when they brought suit. Essential witnesses and evidence were in Oklahoma. The State has a legitimate interest in enforcing its laws designed to keep its highway system safe, and the trial can proceed at least as efficiently in Oklahoma as anywhere else.

The petitioners are not unconnected with the forum. Although both sell automobiles within limited sales territories, each sold the automobile which in fact was driven to Oklahoma where it was involved in an accident.[8] It may be true, as the Court suggests, that each sincerely intended to limit its commercial impact to the limited territory, and that each intended to accept the benefits and protection of the laws only of those States within the territory. But obviously these were unrealistic hopes that cannot be treated as an automatic constitutional shield.[9]

An automobile simply is not a stationary item or one designed to be used in one place. An automobile is *intended* to be moved around. Someone in the business of selling large numbers of automobiles can hardly plead ignorance of their mobility or pretend that the automobiles stay put after they are sold. It is not merely that a dealer in automobiles foresees that they will move. The dealer actually intends that the purchasers will use the automobiles to travel to distant States where the dealer does not directly "do business." The sale of an automobile does *purposefully* inject the vehicle into the stream of interstate commerce so that it can travel to distant States. . . .

Furthermore, an automobile seller derives substantial benefits from States other than its own. A large part of the value of automobiles is the extensive, nationwide network of highways. Significant portions of that network have been constructed

---

8. On the basis of this fact the state court inferred that the petitioners derived substantial revenue from goods used in Oklahoma. The inference is not without support. Certainly, were use of goods accepted as a relevant contact, a plaintiff would not need to have an exact count of the number of petitioners' cars that are used in Oklahoma.

9. Moreover, imposing liability in this case would not so undermine certainty as to destroy an automobile dealer's ability to do business. According jurisdiction does not expand liability except in the marginal case where a plaintiff cannot afford to bring an action except in the plaintiff's own State. In addition, these petitioners are represented by insurance companies. They not only could, but did, purchase insurance to protect them should they stand trial and lose the case. The costs of the insurance no doubt are passed on to customers.

by and are maintained by the individual States, including Oklahoma. The States, through their highway programs, contribute in a very direct and important way to the value of petitioners' businesses. Additionally, a network of other related dealerships with their service departments operates throughout the country under the protection of the laws of the various States, including Oklahoma, and enhances the value of petitioners' businesses by facilitating their customers' traveling.

Thus, the Court errs in its conclusion that "petitioners have *no* 'contacts, ties, or relations' " with Oklahoma. There obviously are contacts, and, given Oklahoma's connection to the litigation, the contacts are sufficiently significant to make it fair and reasonable for the petitioners to submit to Oklahoma's jurisdiction.

III

... *International Shoe* inherited its defendant focus from *Pennoyer v. Neff* and represented the last major step this Court has taken in the long process of liberalizing the doctrine of personal jurisdiction. Though its flexible approach represented a major advance, the structure of our society has changed in many significant ways since *International Shoe* was decided in 1945. Mr. Justice Black, writing for the Court in *McGee,* recognized that "a trend is clearly discernible toward expanding the permissible scope of state jurisdiction over foreign corporations and other nonresidents." He explained the trend as follows:

> "In part this is attributable to the fundamental transformation of our national economy over the years. Today many commercial transactions touch two or more States and may involve parties separated by the full continent. With this increasing nationalization of commerce has come a great increase in the amount of business conducted by mail across state lines. At the same time modern transportation and communication have made it much less burdensome for a party sued to defend himself in a State where he engages in economic activity."

As the Court acknowledges, both the nationalization of commerce and the ease of transportation and communication have accelerated in the generation since 1957. The model of society on which the *International Shoe* Court based its opinion is no longer accurate. Business people, no matter how local their businesses, cannot assume that goods remain in the business' locality. Customers and goods can be anywhere else in the country usually in a matter of hours and always in a matter of a very few days.

In answering the question whether or not it is fair and reasonable to allow a particular forum to hold a trial binding on a particular defendant, the interests of the forum State and other parties loom large in today's world and surely are entitled to as much weight as are the interests of the defendant. The "orderly administration of the laws" provides a firm basis for according some protection to the interests of plaintiffs and States as well as of defendants. Certainly, I cannot see how a defendant's right to due process is violated if the defendant suffers no inconvenience.

. . . The conclusion I draw is that constitutional concepts of fairness no longer require the extreme concern for defendants that was once necessary. Rather, as I wrote in dissent from *Shaffer v. Heitner*, 433 U.S., at 220 (emphasis added), minimum contacts must exist "among the *parties*, the contested transaction, and the forum State." The contacts between any two of these should not be determinative. . . . Assuming that a State gives a nonresident defendant adequate notice and opportunity to defend, I do not think the Due Process Clause is offended merely because the defendant has to board a plane to get to the site of the trial....

The Court's opinion ... suggests that the defendant ought to be subject to a State's jurisdiction only if he has contacts with the State "such that he should reasonably anticipate being haled into court there."[18] There is nothing unreasonable or unfair, however, about recognizing commercial reality. Given the tremendous mobility of goods and people, and the inability of businessmen to control where goods are taken by customers (or retailers), I do not think that the defendant should be in complete control of the geographical stretch of his amenability to suit. Jurisdiction is no longer premised on the notion that nonresident defendants have somehow impliedly consented to suit. People should understand that they are held responsible for the consequences of their actions and that in our society most actions have consequences affecting many States. When an action in fact causes injury in another State, the actor should be prepared to answer for it there unless defending in that State would be unfair for some reason other than that a state boundary must be crossed.

In effect the Court is allowing defendants to assert the sovereign rights of their home States. The expressed fear is that otherwise all limits on personal jurisdiction would disappear. But the argument's premise is wrong. I would not abolish limits on jurisdiction or strip state boundaries of all significance; I would still require the plaintiff to demonstrate sufficient contacts among the parties, the forum, and the litigation to make the forum a reasonable State in which to hold the trial.

I would also, however, strip the defendant of an unjustified veto power over certain very appropriate fora—a power the defendant justifiably enjoyed long ago when communication and travel over long distances were slow and unpredictable and when notions of state sovereignty were impractical and exaggerated. But I repeat that that is not today's world. If a plaintiff can show that his chosen forum State has a sufficient interest in the litigation (or sufficient contacts with the defendant), then the defendant who cannot show some real injury to a constitutionality [sic] protected interest should have no constitutional excuse not to appear.[21]

... Accordingly, I would hold that the Constitution should not shield the defendants from appearing and defending in the plaintiffs' chosen fora.

[Dissenting opinions by Justice Marshall and Justice Blackmun are omitted.]

---

18. The Court suggests that this is the critical foreseeability rather than the likelihood that the product will go to the forum State. But the reasoning begs the question. A defendant cannot know if his actions will subject him to jurisdiction in another State until we have declared what the law of jurisdiction is.

21. Frequently, of course, the defendant will be able to influence the choice of forum through traditional doctrines, such as venue or *forum non conveniens*, permitting the transfer of litigation.

Notes and Questions: Understanding *World-Wide Volkswagen*

1. Reaffirming the threshold requirement of contacts. The Court in *World-Wide* reaffirms *Hanson*'s holding that specific jurisdiction is not permissible unless the defendant has had deliberate, voluntary contacts with the state. A strong showing of "reasonableness" does not suffice. The Court put it this way:

> [T]he Due Process Clause "does not contemplate that a state may make binding a judgment *in personam* against an individual or corporate defendant with which the state has no contacts, ties, or relations." *International Shoe*, 326 U.S., at 319. Even if the defendant would suffer minimal or no inconvenience from being forced to litigate before the tribunals of another State; even if the forum State has a strong interest in applying its law to the controversy; even if the forum State is the most convenient location for litigation, the Due Process Clause, acting as an instrument of interstate federalism, may sometimes act to divest the State of its power to render a valid judgment.

In sum, a defendant's contacts with the forum state are an essential requirement, even if personal jurisdiction would nevertheless be fair and reasonable in that state.

2. Contacts are not enough. Contacts are a necessary requirement, but they are not sufficient to establish specific jurisdiction. *World-Wide* explains that, in addition to having contacts with the forum state, "the relationship between the defendant and the forum must be such that it is 'reasonable . . . to require the corporation to defend the particular suit which is brought there' " (quoting *International Shoe*, 326 U.S. at 317). To determine whether jurisdiction is "reasonable" in any given case, *World-Wide* instructs courts to consider several factors:

> Implicit in this emphasis on reasonableness is the understanding that the burden on the defendant, while always a primary concern, will in an appropriate case be considered in light of other relevant factors, including the forum State's interest in adjudicating the dispute; the plaintiff's interest in obtaining convenient and effective relief, at least when that interest is not adequately protected by the plaintiff's power to choose the forum; the interstate judicial system's interest in obtaining the most efficient resolution of controversies; and the shared interest of the several States in furthering fundamental substantive social policies.

Thus, after *World-Wide,* the exercise of specific jurisdiction is constitutional only when (1) the defendant had purposeful or deliberate contacts with the forum state, (2) the plaintiff's claim arose out of those contacts, and (3) personal jurisdiction is reasonable based on a consideration of the factors mentioned above.

Q **3. Foreseeable contacts?** What purposeful contact did the defendants supposedly have in Oklahoma? Why did the Court nevertheless conclude that the defendants did not have any purposeful contacts in Oklahoma? How does Justice Brennan's view differ from the majority's position?

A

The plaintiffs argued that the defendants had contacts in Oklahoma because the defendants should have foreseen that any cars purchased in New York could cause injuries in Oklahoma. The Court rejected this argument. The Court explained that, just because a manufacturer can foresee that a consumer might bring the manufacturer's product into the state and cause injuries there, does not mean that the manufacturer had purposeful contacts in that forum. In this case, two of the defendants—the dealership and regional distributor—did not direct any activity specifically toward Oklahoma. Rather, the plaintiffs made the unilateral decision to drive their car into the state. As a result, the defendants did not have a purposeful contact in Oklahoma.

In his dissent, Justice Brennan appears to concede that *International Shoe* probably supports the majority's conclusion that the defendants did not have purposeful contacts in Oklahoma, but he argues that the Court should revise its approach to personal jurisdiction (yet again) in light of society's increasing mobility. He calls for a test that focuses on more than a defendant's contacts:

> The conclusion I draw is that constitutional concepts of fairness no longer require the extreme concern for defendants that was once necessary. Rather, . . . contacts must exist "among the *parties*, the contested transaction, and the forum State." The contacts between any two of these should not be determinative.

Justice Brennan's test would focus on the overall reasonableness of jurisdiction, which sounds a lot like the approach that the Court appeared to endorse in *McGee* and subsequently rejected in *Hanson.*

Q

4. The problem with foreseeable contacts. The Court concludes that a defendant does not have a contact with a state simply because a consumer unilaterally transports one of the defendant's goods into the forum. Why does the Court believe that a contrary holding would be problematic? How does Justice Brennan respond to the majority's concerns?

A

According to the Court, defendants must have some control over where they subject themselves to a lawsuit. Otherwise, personal jurisdiction would be unfair:

> The Due Process Clause, by ensuring the "orderly administration of the laws" gives a degree of predictability to the legal system that allows potential defendants to structure their primary conduct with some minimum assurance as to where that conduct will and will not render them liable to suit.

Justice Brennan, in contrast, does not believe that due process requires the defendant to have this sort of control:

> Given the tremendous mobility of goods and people, and the inability of businessmen to control where goods are taken by customers (or retailers), I do not think that the defendant should be in complete control of the geographical stretch of his amenability to suit. Jurisdiction is no longer premised on the notion that nonresident defendants have somehow impliedly consented to suit. People should understand that they are held responsible for the consequences of their actions and that in our society most actions have consequences affecting many States. When an action in fact causes injury in another State, the actor should be prepared to answer for it there unless defending in that State would be unfair for some reason other than that a state boundary must be crossed.

Although Justice Brennan's position did not prevail, his view does make a certain amount of sense. Given that travel and communications are relatively easy and inexpensive today, it is reasonable to ask whether a defendant should be permitted to exercise extensive control over where a lawsuit is filed, absent some real evidence of prejudice from litigating in the plaintiff's chosen forum.

Q **5. What if jurisdiction is very, very reasonable?** If the claim had arisen out of the defendants' contacts in Oklahoma, would personal jurisdiction have been fair and reasonable in the state? In other words, would the reasonableness factors have been satisfied?

A Almost certainly. Consider some of the reasonableness factors described above. First, Oklahoma had a strong interest in adjudicating the dispute there, because the accident occurred in Oklahoma. Second, the plaintiffs had a very strong interest in litigating in Oklahoma. Keep in mind that their original destination was Arizona; they stayed in Oklahoma because they had been badly injured. Litigating elsewhere would have been very inconvenient for them. *See* Charles W. Adams, World-Wide Volkswagen v. Woodson—*The Rest of the Story*, 72 Neb. L. Rev. 1122 (1993). And third, many of the witnesses and much of the evidence was in Oklahoma, making it the most efficient location for the resolution of the controversy. Oklahoma, in short, seems like a pretty fair place to litigate this case.

World-Wide demonstrates that no matter how reasonable personal jurisdiction might be, specific jurisdiction does not exist unless the defendant has some kind of contact in the forum. Because the defendants had no such contact, the Oklahoma court's exercise of personal jurisdiction was unconstitutional.

6. Foreseeability vs. certainty. Consider the following scenario.

Imagine that you are a New Mexico citizen and that while traveling in Arizona, you enter a local hardware store looking for a chainsaw. You tell the owner that you intend to bring the chainsaw back to New Mexico, and the owner then sells you the chainsaw. You return to New Mexico, are injured by the chainsaw, and file a lawsuit in New Mexico against the hardware store. Would it be constitutional for the New Mexico court to exercise personal jurisdiction over the store?

A. Yes. Because the customer told the store owner where the chainsaw was being taken, the owner directed a contact to New Mexico.
B. Yes. Regardless of whether the owner knew where the chainsaw was being taken, the owner should have foreseen that a small product like a chainsaw could be used in a neighboring state.

C. No. Although the claim arose out of the defendant's contact with the state, personal jurisdiction would be unfair and unreasonable in this case.
D. No. The claim does not arise out of the defendant's contacts with New Mexico.
E. Yes. Although the store's contact with New Mexico is indirect, the reasonableness factors overcome the weak contacts that exist.

B is incorrect. New Mexico's proximity to Arizona and the product's mobility might make New Mexico a foreseeable locale for the product's use, but the Court held in *World-Wide* that personal jurisdiction is not established simply because the defendant could have foreseen that the product would be used in the forum state.

A is also wrong. It makes no difference that, unlike *World-Wide Volkswagen,* the defendant in this case knew where the product was headed. Again, even if the defendant knew that the product would end up in a particular forum, the Court held that foreseeing where a consumer might take a product does not confer personal jurisdiction. The defendant has to reach into the state more purposefully.

C is wrong for two reasons. First, as just explained, the defendant did not have a contact with New Mexico. And second, several of the reasonableness factors would favor personal jurisdiction in New Mexico. For example, the plaintiff would have an interest in suing in the state where the injury occurred. New Mexico would have an interest in hearing this case as well, because not only was a New Mexico citizen injured, but the injury occurred in the state. The burden on the defendant would be minimal, because Arizona borders New Mexico. In fact, depending on the precise location of the store, a New Mexico court might be closer to the store than an Arizona court! Moreover, witnesses and evidence regarding the accident would be in New Mexico as well.

For these reasons, one might be inclined to select **E**. The reasonableness factors do strongly support New Mexico as a forum. Nevertheless, the Court held in *World-Wide* that personal jurisdiction cannot be established just because the forum is a reasonable location for the lawsuit. In *World-Wide,* Oklahoma was a particularly appropriate place for the plaintiffs' claims to be heard, but the Court nevertheless held that personal jurisdiction was unconstitutional. The Court emphasized that, to establish specific jurisdiction, a plaintiff must show that the claim arises out of the defendant's contact with the forum. In this question, as in *World-Wide,* no such contact existed.

That leaves **D**. There would not be personal jurisdiction here. The defendant did not direct the product to New Mexico, and the defendant did not otherwise avail itself of the privilege of doing business in the state.

Q **7. Lawyering strategy: Rearguing *McGee.*** If Lulu McGee's case arose after *World-Wide* and you represented her, how would you have argued that the California court had personal jurisdiction over the insurance company?

A

After *World-Wide,* the argument in *McGee* would have to be structured around the elements of the specific jurisdiction analysis. First, you should identify the contacts that the insurance company had with California. In particular, the company purposefully sent an offer of insurance to Lowell Franklin in California, and the company also sent a reinsurance certificate to Mr. Franklin in California.

You should then argue that Ms. McGee's claim arose out of those purposeful contacts. You could note that the insurance company's contact with California involved an offer to renew the very policy that was at issue in the lawsuit. There is, therefore, a strong argument that the claim arose out of the defendant's contact with the forum.

Finally, you should argue that it would be fair and reasonable to subject the insurance company to personal jurisdiction in California. Using the five factors identified in *World-Wide,* you should point out that California has a strong interest in adjudicating the dispute, given the insured's and beneficiary's residency in the state. Moreover, as the Court noted in *McGee,* the plaintiff has a strong interest in having this case heard in her home state, given the cost and inconvenience of litigating the case elsewhere. California also would be an efficient place for the litigation, given the presence of witnesses who can testify about the cause of Franklin's death (a crucial fact in the case). Although the insurance company might be inconvenienced to some degree if it had to travel to California, that inconvenience alone is not sufficient to constitute a due process violation.

8. The accidental tourist. Consider the following scenario.

Imagine that during a driving trip from Pennsylvania to Maine, Donald takes a wrong turn and, unbeknownst to him, drives into Vermont. Before Donald discovers his error, his car collides with Penelope's. Penelope sues Donald in Vermont, and Donald moves to dismiss the case for lack of personal jurisdiction. Assuming that Vermont's long arm statute authorizes jurisdiction over the action, the motion should be

A. denied, because the case arises out of Donald's contacts in Vermont.
B. granted. Personal jurisdiction would be unreasonable in this case, even if Donald's accident is considered to be a contact with Vermont.
C. granted. Donald did not purposefully avail himself of the privilege of driving in Vermont because he drove into Vermont by mistake. As a result, he lacked any constitutionally cognizable contacts in Vermont.
D. granted. Not only did Donald lack any contacts in Vermont, but the exercise of personal jurisdiction would be unreasonable under the circumstances.

The goal here is to apply the underlying rationale of the applicable legal principle to come up with the best answer (or argument). Recall that the *World-Wide* Court offered two rationales for a contacts-based analysis: ensuring that courts operate within their territorial authority and preventing unfairness to defendants. Here, Donald did enter Vermont's territory, albeit unintentionally, so the Vermont court would not be overstepping its territorial authority if it asserts that Donald had a contact in the state. Moreover, it certainly seems fair to exercise personal jurisdiction over someone who drove into a state and injured someone there. Using this logic, "purposeful availment" does not mean that Donald had to be aware that he was entering Vermont; all that matters is that Donald purposefully drove his car into an area that happened to be in Vermont. Most courts would find this to be a contact, thus ruling out **C** as the best answer.

The reasonableness part of the inquiry would also be satisfied. Because Donald injured someone while driving in Vermont, a Vermont court would have a strong interest in hearing this case. All of the witnesses would probably be in Vermont, making it the most efficient location for the lawsuit. Also, assuming Penelope is a Vermont citizen, fairness favors Vermont for that reason as well. This reasoning rules out **B** and **D**. Thus, the best answer is **A**.

C. Contacts in Intentional Torts Cases

The United States Supreme Court has decided several personal jurisdiction cases that explore the meaning of a "contact" in intentional torts cases. The questions below are based on three of those cases.

1. Publishing a libelous article. Consider the following multiple choice question.

In *Keeton v. Hustler Magazine, Inc.*, 465 U.S. 770 (1984), Keeton sued *Hustler Magazine*, a nationally circulated publication, for libel in New Hampshire. Although Keeton was a citizen of New York whose only connection to New Hampshire was that the libelous magazine had been distributed there, she sued Hustler in New Hampshire because it was the only state where the statute of limitations for her claim had not yet expired. Keeton's libel claim alleged damages to her reputation in New Hampshire and nationally, though her damages in New Hampshire were relatively small. What would you expect the Court to say about whether there was personal jurisdiction in this case?

A. There isn't personal jurisdiction. Keeton's contacts with New Hampshire were insufficient to give rise to personal jurisdiction there.
B. There isn't personal jurisdiction. Hustler's contacts with New Hampshire—and Keeton's damages there—were insufficient to give rise to jurisdiction.
C. There is personal jurisdiction. The claim arises out of Hustler's contact with the state of New Hampshire.

It's important to see why **A** is wrong. Personal jurisdiction typically has little to do with the plaintiff's contacts with the forum; the focus is on the defendant's contacts. A court might consider the plaintiff's connection with the forum when analyzing the "reasonableness" factors, but even if the plaintiff's connection to the forum is minimal, personal jurisdiction over the defendant will typically exist as long as the claim arises out of the defendant's contact with that forum.

B is wrong because Keeton's reputation was damaged anywhere the magazine was sold. Damages may have occurred elsewhere as well, but she did suffer some damages in New Hampshire. One issue in the case concerned whether Keeton could sue for all of her damages nationwide in New Hampshire, and the Court held that she could. The Court explained that, if libel plaintiffs could not sue for all of their damages in one state, there was a "potential [for a] serious drain of libel cases on judicial resources." *Keeton*, 465 U.S. at 777. Allowing one forum to decide nationwide damages "protect[s] defendants from harassment resulting from multiple suits." *Id.*

Ultimately, the Court concluded as follows:

> [M]onthly sales of thousands of magazines cannot by any stretch of the imagination be characterized as random, isolated, or fortuitous. It is, therefore, unquestionable that New Hampshire jurisdiction over a complaint based on those contacts would ordinarily satisfy the requirement of the Due Process Clause that a State's assertion of personal jurisdiction over a nonresident defendant be predicated on "minimum contacts" between the defendant and the State.

C, therefore, is the best answer.

Q **2. Writing and editing a libelous article.** In *Calder v. Jones*, 465 U.S. 783 (1984), the facts were similar to *Keeton*, but with a twist. A writer and editor wrote an article in Florida about Shirley Jones (one of the stars of the old TV show *The Partridge Family*), who was a California citizen. The article suggested that Jones was such a heavy drinker that she could not fulfill her professional obligations. The *National Enquirer* published the article nationally, including in California. Jones sued the *National Enquirer*, the story's writer, and the story's editor in California, alleging libel and related claims.

Although the *National Enquirer* conceded personal jurisdiction (wisely, given the contemporaneous holding in *Keeton*), the reporter and the editor contested it. Did the California court have personal jurisdiction over them, even though they wrote and edited the article in Florida? What would you expect the Court to say?

A The Court held that California's exercise of personal jurisdiction over the reporter and editor was constitutional. It offered the following reasoning:

> The allegedly libelous story concerned the California activities of a California resident. It impugned the professionalism of an entertainer whose television career was centered in California. The article was drawn from California sources, and the brunt of the harm, in terms both of respondent's emotional distress and the injury to her professional reputation, was suffered in California. In sum, California is the focal point both of the story and of the harm suffered. Jurisdiction over

> petitioners is therefore proper in California based on the "effects" of their Florida conduct in California. *World-Wide Volkswagen*, 444 U.S. 286, 297–298 (1980).
>
> Petitioners argue that they are not responsible for the circulation of the article in California. A reporter and an editor, they claim, have no direct economic stake in their employer's sales in a distant State. Nor are ordinary employees able to control their employer's marketing activity. The mere fact that they can "foresee" that the article will be circulated and have an effect in California is not sufficient for an assertion of jurisdiction ....
>
> [P]etitioners are not charged with mere untargeted negligence. Rather, their intentional, and allegedly tortious, actions were expressly aimed at California. Petitioner South wrote and petitioner Calder edited an article that they knew would have a potentially devastating impact upon respondent. And they knew that the brunt of that injury would be felt by respondent in the State in which she lives and works and in which the *National Enquirer* has its largest circulation. Under the circumstances, petitioners must "reasonably anticipate being haled into court there" to answer for the truth of the statements made in their article. *World-Wide Volkswagen*, 444 U.S. 286, 297 (1980). An individual injured in California need not go to Florida to seek redress from persons who, though remaining in Florida, knowingly cause the injury in California.
>
> Petitioners are correct that their contacts with California are not to be judged according to their employer's activities there. On the other hand, their status as employees does not somehow insulate them from jurisdiction. Each defendant's contacts with the forum State must be assessed individually. In this case, petitioners are primary participants in an alleged wrongdoing intentionally directed at a California resident, and jurisdiction over them is proper on that basis.

465 U.S. at 788–90. Note how the Court distinguishes *World-Wide Volkswagen*. In that case, the dealership and regional distributor did not engage in any conduct that was specifically directed to Oklahoma. In contrast, the *National Enquirer*'s writer and editor intended to direct their conduct (the article and the article's contents) to a California market and even relied on California sources to write the story. Accordingly, they purposefully availed themselves of the privilege of conducting activities in California.

Q **3. The unlucky tourist.** Here's a multiple choice question closely modeled on a more recent United States Supreme Court case, *Walden v. Fiore*, 571 U.S. 277 (2014):

> Dudley, a Georgia citizen, works in security at an airport in Atlanta, Georgia. While at work, Dudley stops Lucky, a Nevada citizen, who was at the airport for a brief layover during his trip home to Nevada after vacationing in Puerto Rico. During the layover, Dudley confiscated a significant amount of cash from Lucky, who claimed to have won it while gambling at a Puerto Rico casino. Lucky returned home to Nevada without his money, while Dudley filed an affidavit in Georgia as part of an effort to have the money forfeited to the government. Assume that Dudley knew that Lucky was on his way home to Nevada at the time Dudley confiscated the money, and also assume that Dudley knew that Lucky was in Nevada at the time Dudley filed his affidavit.

Lucky sues Dudley in Nevada state court, alleging that Dudley's affidavit was knowingly false. Assuming Dudley moves to dismiss the Nevada case on personal jurisdiction grounds, the motion would likely be:

A. Denied, because Dudley knew where Lucky lived at the time of the alleged intentional misconduct and was thus purposefully directing conduct to Nevada.
B. Denied. Even if Dudley did not know where Lucky lived at the time of the alleged intentional misconduct, Dudley could reasonably foresee that his misconduct at a major national airport could result in harm to travelers in their home states.
C. Both A and B are accurate.
D. Granted, because Dudley did not purposefully direct any conduct to Nevada.

This case is a useful companion to *Calder* because each case raises similar issues. In both cases, the defendants knew where the plaintiffs lived at the time of the intentional and allegedly wrongful conduct and were thus expressly aiming their conduct at the plaintiffs in their home states. So, at first blush, one might conclude that both cases should come out the same way (i.e., that personal jurisdiction should be permissible in this case, just as it was in *Calder*).

The Supreme Court, however, disagreed and distinguished these two cases in a unanimous opinion:

> [In *Calder*], we examined the various contacts the defendants had created with California (and not just with the plaintiff) by writing the allegedly libelous story. We found those forum contacts to be ample: The defendants relied on phone calls to "California sources" for the information in their article; they wrote the story about the plaintiff's activities in California; they caused reputational injury in California by writing an allegedly libelous article that was widely circulated in the State; and the "brunt" of that injury was suffered by the plaintiff in that State. 465 U.S., at 788–789. "In sum, California [wa]s the focal point both of the story and of the harm suffered." Id., at 789. Jurisdiction over the defendants was "therefore proper in California based on the 'effects' of their Florida conduct in California." Ibid.
>
> The crux of *Calder* was that the reputation-based "effects" of the alleged libel connected the defendants to California, not just to the plaintiff. The strength of that connection was largely a function of the nature of the libel tort. However scandalous a newspaper article might be, it can lead to a loss of reputation only if communicated to (and read and understood by) third persons. Accordingly, the reputational injury caused by the defendants' story would not have occurred but for the fact that the defendants wrote an article for publication in California that was read by a large number of California citizens. Indeed, because publication to third persons is a necessary element of

> libel, the defendants' intentional tort actually occurred in California. *Keeton*, 465 U.S., at 777 ("The tort of libel is generally held to occur wherever the offending material is circulated"). In this way, the "effects" caused by the defendants' article—i.e., the injury to the plaintiff's reputation in the estimation of the California public—connected the defendants' conduct to California, not just to a plaintiff who lived there. That connection, combined with the various facts that gave the article a California focus, sufficed to authorize the California court's exercise of jurisdiction ....
>
> Applying the foregoing principles, we conclude that petitioner lacks the "minimal contacts" with Nevada that are a prerequisite to the exercise of jurisdiction over him. It is undisputed that no part of petitioner's course of conduct occurred in Nevada. Petitioner approached, questioned, and searched respondents, and seized the cash at issue, in the Atlanta airport. It is alleged that petitioner later helped draft a "false probable cause affidavit" in Georgia and forwarded that affidavit to a United States Attorney's Office in Georgia to support a potential action for forfeiture of the seized funds. Petitioner never traveled to, conducted activities within, contacted anyone in, or sent anything or anyone to Nevada. In short, when viewed through the proper lens—whether the defendant's actions connect him to the forum—petitioner formed no jurisdictionally relevant contacts with Nevada.

Id. at 1123–24. Thus, the answer here is **D**.

D. Contracts as Contacts: *Burger King v. Rudzewicz*

In *Burger King v. Rudzewicz*, 471 U.S. 462 (1985), the Court addressed another important question: When can a contractual relationship give rise to personal jurisdiction in a distant forum?

READING *BURGER KING v. RUDZEWICZ*. Rudzewicz, a Michigan citizen, opened a franchise there after negotiating the key terms of the franchise agreement with Burger King Corporation's district office in Michigan and its headquarters in Florida. The contract stated that the franchise relationship was established in Miami and governed by Florida law. The contract also required all fees and monthly payments to be sent to Florida, although Burger King's Michigan district office conducted day-to-day oversight of operations.

Rudzewicz fell behind on royalty payments and ultimately could not meet his contractual obligations. Burger King terminated the franchise agreement, but Rudzewicz continued to operate the franchise. As a result, Burger King sued Rudzewicz for breach of contract and trademark infringement in federal court in Florida. Rudzewicz challenged personal jurisdiction, and the Court concluded that the Florida court had personal jurisdiction over the Michigan franchisees.

As you read the case, consider the following questions:

- How does the Court determine whether a contract constitutes a contact in a particular state?
- Why did the contract in this case give rise to personal jurisdiction over the defendants in Florida?

BURGER KING v. RUDZEWICZ

471 U.S. 462 (1985)

Justice Brennan delivered the opinion of the Court.

The State of Florida's long-arm statute extends jurisdiction to "[a]ny person, whether or not a citizen or resident of this state," who, *inter alia*, "[b]reach[es] a contract in this state by failing to perform acts required by the contract to be performed in this state," so long as the cause of action arises from the alleged contractual breach. Fla. Stat. § 48.193(1)(g) (Supp. 1984). The United States District Court for the Southern District of Florida, sitting in diversity, relied on this provision in exercising personal jurisdiction over a Michigan resident who allegedly had breached a franchise agreement with a Florida corporation by failing to make required payments in Florida. The question presented is whether this exercise of long-arm jurisdiction offended "traditional conception[s] of fair play and substantial justice" embodied in the Due Process Clause of the Fourteenth Amendment.

issue

I

A

Burger King Corporation is a Florida corporation whose principal offices are in Miami. It is one of the world's largest restaurant organizations, with over 3,000 outlets in the 50 States, the Commonwealth of Puerto Rico, and 8 foreign nations. ... Burger King licenses its franchisees to use its trademarks and service marks for a period of 20 years and leases standardized restaurant facilities to them for the same term. In addition, franchisees acquire a variety of proprietary information concerning the "standards, specifications, procedures and methods for operating a Burger King Restaurant." Id., at 52 ....

In exchange for these benefits, franchisees pay Burger King an initial $40,000 franchise fee and commit themselves to payment of monthly royalties, advertising and sales promotion fees, and rent computed in part from monthly gross sales. Franchisees also agree to submit to the national organization's exacting regulation of virtually every conceivable aspect of their operations ....

Burger King oversees its franchise system through a two-tiered administrative structure. The governing contracts provide that the franchise relationship is established in Miami and governed by Florida law, and call for payment of all required fees and forwarding of all relevant notices to the Miami headquarters. The Miami headquarters sets policy and works directly with its franchisees in attempting to resolve major problems. Day-to-day monitoring of franchisees, however, is conducted through a network of 10 district offices which in turn report to the Miami headquarters.

The instant litigation grows out of Burger King's termination of one of its franchisees.... The appellee John Rudzewicz, a Michigan citizen and resident, is the senior partner in a Detroit accounting firm. In 1978, he was approached by Brian MacShara, the son of a business acquaintance, who suggested that they jointly apply to Burger King for a franchise in the Detroit area. MacShara proposed to serve as the manager of the restaurant if Rudzewicz would put up the investment capital; in exchange, the two would evenly share the profits. Believing that MacShara's idea offered attractive investment and tax-deferral opportunities, Rudzewicz agreed to the venture.

Rudzewicz and MacShara jointly applied for a franchise to Burger King's Birmingham, Michigan, district office in the autumn of 1978. Their application was forwarded to Burger King's Miami headquarters, which entered into a preliminary agreement with them in February 1979. During the ensuing four months it was agreed that Rudzewicz and MacShara would assume operation of an existing facility in Drayton Plains, Michigan. MacShara attended the prescribed management courses in Miami during this period, and the franchisees purchased $165,000 worth of restaurant equipment from Burger King's Davmor Industries division in Miami. Even before the final agreements were signed, however, the parties began to disagree over site-development fees, building design, computation of monthly rent, and whether the franchisees would be able to assign their liabilities to a corporation they had formed. During these disputes Rudzewicz and MacShara negotiated both with the Birmingham district office and with the Miami headquarters.[7] With some misgivings, Rudzewicz and MacShara finally obtained limited concessions from the Miami headquarters, signed the final agreements, and commenced operations in June 1979. By signing the final agreements, Rudzewicz obligated himself personally to payments exceeding $1 million over the 20-year franchise relationship.

The Drayton Plains facility apparently enjoyed steady business during the summer of 1979, but patronage declined after a recession began later that year. Rudzewicz and MacShara soon fell far behind in their monthly payments to Miami. Headquarters sent notices of default, and an extended period of negotiations began among the franchisees, the Birmingham district office, and the Miami headquarters. After several Burger King officials in Miami had engaged in

7. Although Rudzewicz and MacShara dealt with the Birmingham district office on a regular basis, they communicated directly with the Miami headquarters in forming the contracts; moreover, [the appellate record reflects] they learned that the district office had "very little" decisionmaking authority and accordingly turned directly to headquarters in seeking to resolve their disputes.

prolonged but ultimately unsuccessful negotiations with the franchisees by mail and by telephone, headquarters terminated the franchise and ordered Rudzewicz and MacShara to vacate the premises. They refused and continued to occupy and operate the facility as a Burger King restaurant. . . .

B

Burger King commenced the instant action in the United States District Court for the Southern District of Florida in May 1981 . . . [and] alleged that Rudzewicz and MacShara had breached their franchise obligations . . . by failing to make the required payments "at plaintiff's place of business in Miami, Dade County, Florida," and also charged that they were tortiously infringing [Burger King's] trademarks and service marks through their continued, unauthorized operation as a Burger King restaurant. . . . Rudzewicz and MacShara entered special appearances and argued, *inter alia*, that because they were Michigan residents and because Burger King's claim did not "arise" within the Southern District of Florida, the District Court lacked personal jurisdiction over them. The District Court denied their motions after a hearing, holding that, pursuant to Florida's long-arm statute, "a non-resident Burger King franchisee is subject to the personal jurisdiction of this Court in actions arising out of its franchise agreements." . . .

After a 3-day bench trial, the court again concluded that it had "jurisdiction over the subject matter and the parties to this cause." Finding that Rudzewicz and MacShara had breached their franchise agreements with Burger King and had infringed Burger King's trademarks and service marks, the court entered judgment against them, jointly and severally, for $228,875 in contract damages. The court also ordered them "to immediately close Burger King Restaurant Number 775 from continued operation or to immediately give the keys and possession of said restaurant to Burger King Corporation," found that they had failed to prove any of the required elements of their counterclaim, and awarded costs and attorney's fees to Burger King.

Rudzewicz appealed to the Court of Appeals for the Eleventh Circuit. A divided panel of that Circuit reversed the judgment, concluding that the District Court could not properly exercise personal jurisdiction over Rudzewicz. . . .

Burger King appealed the Eleventh Circuit's judgment to this Court . . . . [W]e grant the petition and now reverse.

II

A

The Due Process Clause protects an individual's liberty interest in not being subject to the binding judgments of a forum with which he has established no meaningful "contacts, ties, or relations." *International Shoe Co. v. Washington*, 326 U.S., at 319. By requiring that individuals have "fair warning that a particular activity may subject [them] to the jurisdiction of a foreign sovereign," *Shaffer v.*

Heitner, 433 U.S. 186 (1977) (Stevens, J., concurring in judgment), the Due Process Clause "gives a degree of predictability to the legal system that allows potential defendants to structure their primary conduct with some minimum assurance as to where that conduct will and will not render them liable to suit," *World-Wide Volkswagen Corp. v. Woodson*, 444 U.S. 286, 297 (1980).

Where a forum seeks to assert specific jurisdiction over an out-of-state defendant who has not consented to suit there, this "fair warning" requirement is satisfied if the defendant has "purposefully directed" his activities at residents of the forum, *Keeton v. Hustler Magazine, Inc.*, 465 U.S. 770, 774 (1984), and the litigation results from alleged injuries that "arise out of or relate to" those activities. Thus "[t]he forum State does not exceed its powers under the Due Process Clause if it asserts personal jurisdiction over a corporation that delivers its products into the stream of commerce with the expectation that they will be purchased by consumers in the forum State" and those products subsequently injure forum consumers. *World-Wide Volkswagen Corp. v. Woodson, supra*, 444 U.S., at 297–298. Similarly, a publisher who distributes magazines in a distant State may fairly be held accountable in that forum for damages resulting there from an allegedly defamatory story. And with respect to interstate contractual obligations, we have emphasized that parties who "reach out beyond one state and create continuing relationships and obligations with citizens of another state" are subject to regulation and sanctions in the other State for the consequences of their activities. *Travelers Health Assn. v. Virginia*, 339 U.S. 643, 647 (1950).

We have noted several reasons why a forum legitimately may exercise personal jurisdiction over a nonresident who "purposefully directs" his activities toward forum residents. A State generally has a "manifest interest" in providing its residents with a convenient forum for redressing injuries inflicted by out-of-state actors. *McGee v. International Life Insurance Co.*, 355 U.S. 220, 223 (1957). Moreover, where individuals "purposefully derive benefit" from their interstate activities, it may well be unfair to allow them to escape having to account in other States for consequences that arise proximately from such activities; the Due Process Clause may not readily be wielded as a territorial shield to avoid interstate obligations that have been voluntarily assumed. And because "modern transportation and communications have made it much less burdensome for a party sued to defend himself in a State where he engages in economic activity," it usually will not be unfair to subject him to the burdens of litigating in another forum for disputes relating to such activity. *McGee v. International Life Insurance Co.*, supra, 355 U.S., at 223.

Notwithstanding these considerations, the constitutional touchstone remains whether the defendant purposefully established "minimum contacts" in the forum State. Although it has been argued that foreseeability of causing injury in another State should be sufficient to establish such contacts there when policy considerations so require, the Court has consistently held that this kind of foreseeability is not a "sufficient benchmark" for exercising personal jurisdiction. *World-Wide Volkswagen Corp. v. Woodson*, 444 U.S., at 295. Instead, "the foreseeability that is critical to due process analysis . . . is that the defendant's conduct and connection with the forum State are such that he should reasonably anticipate being haled into court there." Id., at 297. In defining when it is that a potential defendant should "reasonably anticipate" out-of-state litigation, the Court frequently has drawn from the reasoning of *Hanson v. Denckla*, 357 U.S. 235 (1958):

> "The unilateral activity of those who claim some relationship with a nonresident defendant cannot satisfy the requirement of contact with the forum State. The application of that rule will vary with the quality and nature of the defendant's activity, but it is essential in each case that there be some act by which the defendant purposefully avails itself of the privilege of conducting activities within the forum State, thus invoking the benefits and protections of its laws."

This "purposeful availment" requirement ensures that a defendant will not be haled into a jurisdiction solely as a result of "random," "fortuitous," or "attenuated" contacts, or of the "unilateral activity of another party or a third person." Jurisdiction is proper, however, where the contacts proximately result from actions by the defendant himself that create a "substantial connection" with the forum State. Thus where the defendant "deliberately" has engaged in significant activities within a State, or has created "continuing obligations" between himself and residents of the forum, he manifestly has availed himself of the privilege of conducting business there, and because his activities are shielded by "the benefits and protections" of the forum's laws it is presumptively not unreasonable to require him to submit to the burdens of litigation in that forum as well.

Jurisdiction in these circumstances may not be avoided merely because the defendant did not physically enter the forum State. Although territorial presence frequently will enhance a potential defendant's affiliation with a State and reinforce the reasonable foreseeability of suit there, it is an inescapable fact of modern commercial life that a substantial amount of business is transacted solely by mail and wire communications across state lines, thus obviating the need for physical presence within a State in which business is conducted. So long as a commercial actor's efforts are "purposefully directed" toward residents of another State, we have consistently rejected the notion that an absence of physical contacts can defeat personal jurisdiction there.

Once it has been decided that a defendant purposefully established minimum contacts within the forum State, these contacts may be considered in light of other factors to determine whether the assertion of personal jurisdiction would comport with "fair play and substantial justice." *International Shoe Co. v. Washington*, 326 U.S., at 320. Thus courts in "appropriate cases" may evaluate "the burden on the defendant," "the forum State's interest in adjudicating the dispute," "the plaintiff's interest in obtaining convenient and effective relief," "the interstate judicial system's interest in obtaining the most efficient resolution of controversies," and the "shared interest of the several States in furthering fundamental substantive social policies." *World-Wide Volkswagen Corp. v. Woodson*, 444 U.S., at 292. These considerations sometimes serve to establish the reasonableness of jurisdiction upon a lesser showing of minimum contacts than would otherwise be required.

On the other hand, where a defendant who purposefully has directed his activities at forum residents seeks to defeat jurisdiction, he must present a compelling case that the presence of some other considerations would render jurisdiction unreasonable. Most such considerations usually may be accommodated through means short of finding jurisdiction unconstitutional. For example, the potential clash of the forum's law with the "fundamental substantive social policies" of another State may be accommodated through application of the forum's choice-of-law rules. Similarly, a defendant claiming substantial inconvenience may seek a change of venue. Nevertheless, minimum requirements inherent in the concept of "fair play and substantial justice" may defeat the reasonableness of jurisdiction even if the defendant has purposefully engaged in forum activities. *World-Wide Volkswagen Corp. v. Woodson*, 444 U.S., at 292. . . .

B

(1)

Applying these principles to the case at hand, we believe there is substantial record evidence supporting the District Court's conclusion that the assertion of personal jurisdiction over Rudzewicz in Florida for the alleged breach of his franchise agreement did not offend due process. At the outset, we note a continued division among lower courts respecting whether and to what extent a contract can constitute a "contact" for purposes of due process analysis. If the question is whether an individual's contract with an out-of-state party *alone* can automatically establish sufficient minimum contacts in the other party's home forum, we believe the answer clearly is that it cannot. The Court long ago rejected the notion that personal jurisdiction might turn on "mechanical" tests, *International Shoe Co. v. Washington*. . . . Instead, we have emphasized the need for a "highly realistic" approach that recognizes that a "contract" is "ordinarily but an intermediate step serving to tie up prior business negotiations with future consequences which themselves are the real object of the business transaction." *Hoopeston Canning Co. v. Cullen*, 318 U.S. 313, 316–17 (1943). It is these factors—prior negotiations and contemplated future consequences, along with the terms of the contract and the parties' actual course of dealing—that must be evaluated in determining whether the defendant purposefully established minimum contacts within the forum.

In this case, no physical ties to Florida can be attributed to Rudzewicz other than [his business partner's] brief training course in Miami. Rudzewicz did not maintain offices in Florida and, for all that appears from the record, has never even visited there. Yet this franchise dispute grew directly out of "a contract which had a *substantial* connection with that State." *McGee v. International Life Ins. Co.*, 355 U.S. 220, 223 (1957) (emphasis added). Eschewing the option of operating an independent local enterprise, Rudzewicz deliberately "reach[ed] out beyond" Michigan and negotiated with a Florida corporation for the purchase of a long-term franchise and the manifold benefits that would derive from affiliation with a nationwide organization. Upon approval, he entered into a carefully structured

20-year relationship that envisioned continuing and wide-reaching contacts with Burger King in Florida. In light of Rudzewicz' voluntary acceptance of the long-term and exacting regulation of his business from Burger King's Miami headquarters, the "quality and nature" of his relationship to the company in Florida can in no sense be viewed as "random," "fortuitous," or "attenuated." Rudzewicz' refusal to make the contractually required payments in Miami, and his continued use of Burger King's trademarks and confidential business information after his termination, caused foreseeable injuries to the corporation in Florida. For these reasons it was, at the very least, presumptively reasonable for Rudzewicz to be called to account there for such injuries....

Moreover, we believe the Court of Appeals [which found no personal jurisdiction] gave insufficient weight to provisions in the various franchise documents providing that all disputes would be governed by Florida law. The franchise agreement, for example, stated:

> "This Agreement shall become valid when executed and accepted by BKC at Miami, Florida; it shall be deemed made and entered into in the State of Florida and shall be governed and construed under and in accordance with the laws of the State of Florida. The choice of law designation does not require that all suits concerning this Agreement be filed in Florida."

The Court of Appeals reasoned that choice-of-law provisions are irrelevant to the question of personal jurisdiction, relying on *Hanson v. Denckla* for the proposition that "the center of gravity for choice-of-law purposes does not necessarily confer the sovereign prerogative to assert jurisdiction." This reasoning misperceives the import of the quoted proposition. The Court in *Hanson* and subsequent cases has emphasized that choice-of-law *analysis*—which focuses on all elements of a transaction, and not simply on the defendant's conduct—is distinct from minimum-contacts jurisdictional analysis—which focuses at the threshold solely on the defendant's purposeful connection to the forum. Nothing in our cases ... suggests that a choice-of-law *provision* should be ignored in considering whether a defendant has "purposefully invoked the benefits and protections of a State's laws" for jurisdictional purposes. Although such a provision standing alone would be insufficient to confer jurisdiction, we believe that, when combined with the 20-year interdependent relationship Rudzewicz established with Burger King's Miami headquarters, it reinforced his deliberate affiliation with the forum State and the reasonable foreseeability of possible litigation there. As Judge Johnson argued in his dissent below, Rudzewicz "purposefully availed himself of the benefits and protections of Florida's laws" by entering into contracts expressly providing that those laws would govern franchise disputes.[24] ...

24. In addition, the franchise agreement's disclaimer that the "choice of law designation does not *require* that all suits concerning this Agreement be filed in Florida," App. 72 (emphasis added), reasonably should have suggested to Rudzewicz that by negative implication such suits *could* be filed there ....

(2)

... The Court of Appeals also concluded ... that the parties' dealings involved "a characteristic disparity of bargaining power" and "elements of surprise," and that Rudzewicz "lacked fair notice" of the potential for litigation in Florida because the contractual provisions suggesting to the contrary were merely "boilerplate declarations in a lengthy printed contract." 724 F.2d, at 1511–1512, and n.10 .... [T]he District Court found that Burger King had made no misrepresentations, that Rudzewicz and MacShara "were and are experienced and sophisticated businessmen," and that "at no time" did they "ac[t] under economic duress or disadvantage imposed by" Burger King. Federal Rule of Civil Procedure 52(a) requires that "[f]indings of fact shall not be set aside unless clearly erroneous," and neither Rudzewicz nor the Court of Appeals has pointed to record evidence that would support a "definite and firm conviction" that the District Court's findings are mistaken. To the contrary, Rudzewicz was represented by counsel throughout these complex transactions and ... was himself an experienced accountant "who for five months conducted negotiations with Burger King over the terms of the franchise and lease agreements, and who obligated himself personally to contracts requiring over time payments that exceeded $1 million." Rudzewicz was able to secure a modest reduction in rent and other concessions from Miami headquarters; moreover, to the extent that Burger King's terms were inflexible, Rudzewicz presumably decided that the advantages of affiliating with a national organization provided sufficient commercial benefits to offset the detriments ....

III

Because Rudzewicz established a substantial and continuing relationship with Burger King's Miami headquarters, received fair notice from the contract documents and the course of dealing that he might be subject to suit in Florida, and has failed to demonstrate how jurisdiction in that forum would otherwise be fundamentally unfair, we conclude that the District Court's exercise of jurisdiction ... did not offend due process. The judgment of the Court of Appeals is accordingly reversed, and the case is remanded for further proceedings consistent with this opinion ....

key:

Justice Stevens, with whom Justice White joins, dissenting.

In my opinion there is a significant element of unfairness in requiring a franchisee to defend a case of this kind in the forum chosen by the franchisor. It is undisputed that appellee maintained no place of business in Florida, that he had no employees in that State, and that he was not licensed to do business there....

Throughout the business relationship, appellee's principal contacts with appellant were with its Michigan office....

Judge Vance's opinion for the Court of Appeals for the Eleventh Circuit adequately explains why I would affirm the judgment of that court. I particularly find the following more persuasive than what this Court has written today: ...

"Given that the office in Rudzewicz' home state conducted all of the negotiations and wholly supervised the contract, we believe that he had reason to assume that the state of the supervisory office would be the same state in which Burger King would file suit. Rudzewicz lacked fair notice that the distant corporate headquarters which insulated itself from direct dealings with him would later seek to assert jurisdiction over him in the court of its own home state....

"Just as Rudzewicz lacked notice of the possibility of suit in Florida, he was financially unprepared to meet its added costs. The franchise relationship in particular is fraught with potential for financial surprise. The device of the franchise gives local retailers the access to national trademark recognition which enables them to compete with better-financed, more efficient chain stores. This national affiliation, however, does not alter the fact that the typical franchise store is a local concern serving at best a neighborhood or community. Neither the revenues of a local business nor the geographical range of its market prepares the average franchise owner for the cost of distant litigation....

"The particular distribution of bargaining power in the franchise relationship further impairs the franchisee's financial preparedness. In a franchise contract, 'the franchisor normally occupies [the] dominant role.' ...

"We discern a characteristic disparity of bargaining power in the facts of this case. There is no indication that Rudzewicz had any latitude to negotiate a reduced rent or franchise fee in exchange for the added risk of suit in Florida. He signed a standard form contract whose terms were non-negotiable and which appeared in some respects to vary from the more favorable terms agreed to in earlier discussions. In fact, the final contract required a minimum monthly rent computed on a base far in excess of that discussed in oral negotiations. Burger King resisted price concessions, only to sue Rudzewicz far from home. In doing so, it severely impaired his ability to call Michigan witnesses who might be essential to his defense and counterclaim....

"Jurisdiction under these circumstances would offend the fundamental fairness which is the touchstone of due process."

Accordingly, I respectfully dissent.

Notes and Questions: Personal Jurisdiction in Contracts Cases

1. The context of contracts. In *Burger King,* the Court held that a party to a contract is not necessarily subject to personal jurisdiction in a state where one of the parties to the contract resides. Rather, a court must look to the circumstances of the commercial relationship—the negotiation of the contract, the provisions in the contract itself, and ensuing experience under the contract—to assess jurisdiction. Relevant factors include whether negotiations were directed to the forum state, whether the contract involved obligations in the forum state, the duration of the contractual relationship, and others. The majority held that the factors weighed in favor of jurisdiction in this case.

2. Have it your way: Choice of law provisions and forum selection clauses. Parties to a contract can agree in advance that, if a dispute arises, the parties will litigate any disagreements under the law of a particular state. The contract at issue in *Burger King* included such a provision, quoted above in Part IIB(1) of the Court's opinion.

This provision is known as a *choice of law* clause, because it chooses a particular body of state contract law to govern the interpretation of the contract. A choice of law provision is usually binding, but the courts of the state whose law is chosen do not necessarily have personal jurisdiction over the defendant. That's why the Court in *Burger King* did not assume that personal jurisdiction existed in Florida simply because the contract specified that Florida law should apply to any case arising out of the contract. As you will learn later in the book, courts in one state frequently apply the law of another jurisdiction, so just because the contract specified that Florida law would govern any disputes did not mean that such disputes would have to be resolved in the Florida *courts*. Nevertheless, the *Burger King* Court viewed a choice of law clause as a relevant factor in the analysis, because such a clause suggests that the defendants purposely availed themselves of the benefits of the state specified in the clause. In sum, a Florida choice of law clause added weight to the argument that the defendants purposefully availed themselves of the benefits of doing business in Florida, but it was not conclusive.

A different and more important contract provision for personal jurisdiction purposes is a *forum selection clause*. Such provisions often require that any dispute arising out of the contract be litigated in a particular state (e.g., Florida). In fact, many contracts contain forum selection clauses, thus reducing the likelihood of litigation over personal jurisdiction issues. Courts generally enforce these provisions, as long as they select a forum with a reasonable relation to the parties or the transaction. *See, e.g., Carnival Cruise Lines, Inc. v. Shute,* 499 U.S. 585 (1991). Enforcing these clauses is reasonable, as they reflect a kind of consent to personal jurisdiction that the courts have upheld since *Pennoyer.* Interestingly, in *Burger King,* the lawyers had not included a forum selection clause in the contract, apparently because such clauses were not enforceable under Michigan franchise laws.

3. Personal jurisdiction in federal court. The lawsuit in *Burger King* was originally filed in a Florida federal court, but the Court discussed personal jurisdiction as if the case had been filed in a Florida state court. Why?

> There is a long answer to this question, which is covered in Chapter 9, but for now, the short answer suffices. Federal Rule of Civil Procedure 4(k)(1)(A) permits a federal court to exercise personal jurisdiction only if the "defendant ... is subject to the jurisdiction of a court of general jurisdiction in the state where the district court is located." (General jurisdiction here refers to the court's subject matter jurisdiction, not to general in personam jurisdiction.)
>
> Put simply, in most cases, a federal court can exercise personal jurisdiction over a defendant if the courts of the state in which the federal court sits could do so under the state's long arm statute and the Fourteenth Amendment Due Process Clause. For example, in general, a federal district court in Boston may exercise personal jurisdiction over a defendant if a Massachusetts *state* court would have been able to exercise personal jurisdiction over that defendant if the claim been filed in the state court. So in *Burger King,* this means that the

federal district court in Florida had to analyze personal jurisdiction the same way a Florida state court would, including an examination of the Florida long arm statute and a due process analysis.

4. Review Questions: Subject Matter and Personal Jurisdiction. At this point, it is worth reviewing the basic distinction between personal and subject matter jurisdiction. Consider the following two questions.

Distinctions between subject matter and personal jurisdiction (part I). Paula, a California citizen, sues David, an Illinois citizen, in federal district court in California. Paula alleges that while she was living in Illinois, David shot off fireworks that set Paula's house on fire. Assume that Paula's claim is based on a state law cause of action and that the alleged damages exceed $75,000. Also assume that David has never set foot in California and that California's long arm statute reaches as far as the Constitution allows. David moves to dismiss for lack of personal and subject matter jurisdiction. Which of the following statements is the most accurate?

A. The court cannot hear the case because it lacks subject matter jurisdiction.
B. The court cannot hear the case because it lacks personal jurisdiction.
C. The court cannot hear the case because it lacks both personal and subject matter jurisdiction.
D. The court can hear the case because it has subject matter jurisdiction and personal jurisdiction.
E. The court can hear the case because it has subject matter jurisdiction, even though it lacks personal jurisdiction.

A and **C** are incorrect, because there is subject matter jurisdiction (diversity jurisdiction). The suit is between citizens of different states, and the claim exceeds $75,000. **D** is incorrect because David has no contacts whatsoever with California, so there is no basis for the California court to exercise personal jurisdiction here. **E** is wrong for an important reason: a court cannot hear a case simply because it has subject matter jurisdiction. If a defendant challenges personal jurisdiction, the court must find that it has personal jurisdiction as well.

Because the court lacks personal jurisdiction but has subject matter jurisdiction, **B** is the answer.

Distinctions between subject matter and personal jurisdiction (part II). Instead of bringing her lawsuit in California federal court, Paula files suit in Illinois state court. In this case, however, Paula alleges damages of only $50,000. Assuming the Illinois long arm statute reaches as far as the Constitution allows and David makes all relevant motions to dismiss, the court

A. cannot hear the case because it lacks subject matter jurisdiction.
B. cannot hear the case because it lacks personal jurisdiction; even though David is from Illinois, Paula now lives in California and no longer has any contacts with Illinois.

C. cannot hear the case because it lacks both personal and subject matter jurisdiction.
D. can hear the case because it has subject matter jurisdiction and personal jurisdiction.

A and **C** are wrong. There is subject matter jurisdiction in this case, even though the amount in controversy is less than $75,000, because state courts are not subject to the $75,000 amount-in-controversy requirement. (The case may have to be filed in a particular type of state court, but there is little doubt that subject matter jurisdiction would be proper in the Illinois state court system.) **B** is wrong because personal jurisdiction typically concerns the defendant's contacts with the forum, not the plaintiff's. In this case, not only did the claim arise out of David's contacts with Illinois, but David lives in Illinois. For both of those reasons, the court would have personal jurisdiction. Thus, the answer is **D**.

E. Contacts Through the "Stream of Commerce": *Asahi Metal Industry Co. v. Superior Court of California*

To appreciate the problem in *Asahi*, consider the facts of an earlier case, *Gray v. American Radiator & Standard Sanitary Corp.*, 176 N.E.2d 761 (Ill. 1961). In *Gray*, Titan Valve was an Ohio company that manufactured safety valves for water heaters. Titan sold its valves to a Pennsylvania company, American Radiator, that used the valves as component parts in water heaters. American Radiator then sold the water heaters in a number of states, including in Illinois. Mrs. Gray, an Illinois citizen, purchased the water heater in Illinois and was injured after the water heater exploded there. She sued Titan and American Radiator in Illinois for negligence. The question was whether the Illinois court had personal jurisdiction over Titan.

Gray presents what has become known as a "stream of commerce" problem. A manufacturer makes a component part in one state and sells it to a company in another. The latter company then incorporates the component into a larger product and distributes (or sells to a wholesaler who redistributes) the final product in another state. The "stream of commerce" looks like this:

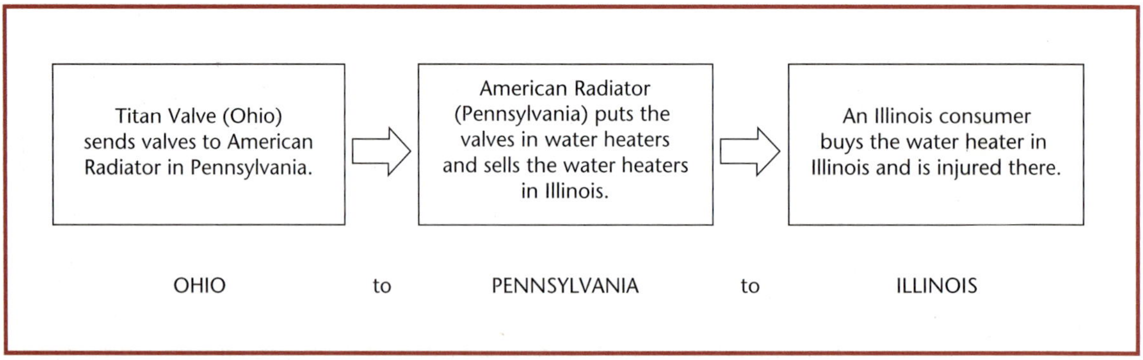

Figure 7–1: ILLUSTRATING *GRAY v. AMERICAN RADIATOR & STANDARD SANITARY CORP.*

In *Gray*, the Illinois Supreme Court concluded that a component part manufacturer is subject to personal jurisdiction in a state where its component is ultimately sold, even though the component part manufacturer did not sell the component directly into that state:

> [A company like the defendant] enjoys benefits from the laws of [Illinois], and it has undoubtedly benefitted, to a degree, from the protection which our law has given to the marketing of hot water heaters containing its valves. Where the alleged liability arises, as in this case, from the manufacture of products presumably sold in contemplation of use here, it should not matter that the purchase was made from an independent middleman or that someone other than the defendant shipped the product into this State. . . . As a general proposition, if a corporation elects to sell its products for ultimate use in another State, it is not unjust to hold it answerable there for any damage caused by defects in those products.

Id. at 766.

Keep in mind that *Gray* was an Illinois Supreme Court decision, so it was not binding precedent for courts outside of Illinois. Indeed, after *Gray*, there was considerable disagreement about the viability of the stream of commerce theory. Moreover, even in states (like Illinois) that accepted the stream of commerce theory, there were many other questions that remained unanswered. For example, what if Titan Valve had manufactured the entire water heater, instead of just the valve, and sold the water heater through a wholesaler in Pennsylvania? Should the stream of commerce theory apply to that situation? Would the seller be subject to jurisdiction if its product was resold into the state by a wholesaler, and the manufacturer did not even know that the wholesaler was selling in that state?

Tire Valves and Trade

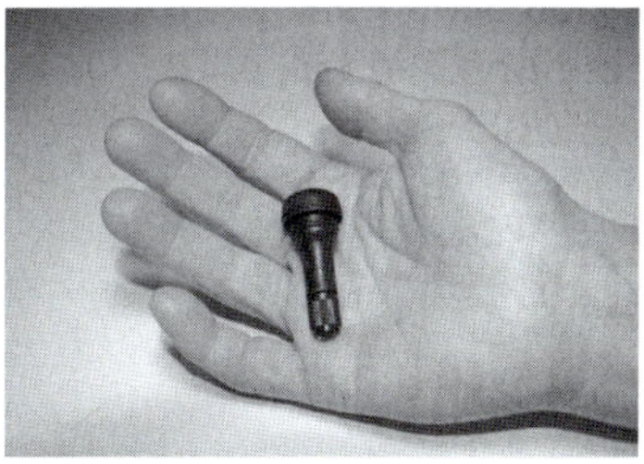

Photo by Emily Behrendt.

Your authors are not experts on motorcycle tires, so this tire valve may not be exactly the same as the tire valve at issue in *Asahi*. But it is a tire valve. As the photo suggests, it is hardly a massive import item. A cardboard box might contain about 500 of them, each costing about 27 cents. This may offer some perspective on the extent of Asahi's "purposeful availment" in the California market.

READING *ASAHI METAL INDUSTRY CO. v. SUPERIOR COURT OF CALIFORNIA*. In *Asahi*, the United States Supreme Court addressed the stream of commerce theory, but it did not speak with one voice. The decision contains several opinions, with justices agreeing only as to certain parts of Justice O'Connor's opinion. Remember that only those parts of an opinion that receive the support of five justices are binding precedent. Opinions or parts of an opinion that receive fewer than five votes are *not* the law and merely reflect the views of individual justices.

- Which parts of Justice O'Connor's opinion received five votes and are binding precedent?
- Does her opinion make law on the stream of commerce issue? If not, what is the law on this issue after *Asahi*?
- Why does the Court reverse the California Supreme Court?

ASAHI METAL INDUSTRY CO. v. SUPERIOR COURT OF CALIFORNIA

480 U.S. 102 (1987)

Justice O'Connor announced the judgment of the Court and delivered the unanimous opinion of the Court with respect to Part I, the opinion of the Court with respect to Part II-B, in which The Chief Justice, Justice Brennan, Justice White, Justice Marshall, Justice Blackmun, Justice Powell, and Justice Stevens join, and an opinion with respect to Parts II-A and III, in which The Chief Justice, Justice Powell, and Justice Scalia join.

issue

This case presents the question whether the mere awareness on the part of a foreign defendant that the components it manufactured, sold, and delivered outside the United States would reach the forum State in the stream of commerce constitutes "minimum contacts" between the defendant and the forum State such that the exercise of jurisdiction "does not offend 'traditional notions of fair play and substantial justice.'" *International Shoe Co. v. Washington,* 326 U.S. 310, 316 (1945) (quoting *Milliken v. Meyer,* 311 U.S. 457, 463 (1940)).

I

On September 23, 1978, on Interstate Highway 80 in Solano County, California, Gary Zurcher lost control of his Honda motorcycle and collided with a tractor. Zurcher was severely injured, and his passenger and wife, Ruth Ann Moreno, was killed. In September 1979, Zurcher filed a product liability action in the Superior Court of the State of California in and for the County of Solano. Zurcher alleged that the 1978 accident was caused by a sudden loss of air and an explosion in the rear tire of the motorcycle, and alleged that the motorcycle tire, tube, and sealant were defective. Zurcher's complaint named, *inter alia,* Cheng Shin Rubber Industrial Co., Ltd. (Cheng Shin), the Taiwanese manufacturer of the tube. Cheng Shin in turn filed a cross-complaint seeking indemnification from its codefendants and from petitioner, Asahi Metal Industry Co., Ltd. (Asahi), the manufacturer of the tube's valve assembly.* Zurcher's claims against Cheng Shin and the other defendants were eventually settled and dismissed, leaving only Cheng Shin's indemnity action against Asahi.

California's long-arm statute authorizes the exercise of jurisdiction "on any basis not inconsistent with the Constitution of this state or of the United States." Asahi moved to quash Cheng Shin's service of summons, arguing the State could not exert jurisdiction over it consistent with the Due Process Clause of the Fourteenth Amendment.

In relation to the motion, the following information was submitted by Asahi and Cheng Shin. Asahi is a Japanese corporation. It manufactures tire valve assemblies in Japan and sells the assemblies to Cheng Shin, and to several other tire manufacturers, for use as components in finished tire tubes. Asahi's sales to Cheng Shin took place in Taiwan. The shipments from Asahi to Cheng Shin were sent from Japan to Taiwan. Cheng Shin bought and incorporated into its tire tubes 150,000 Asahi valve assemblies in 1978; 500,000 in 1979; 500,000 in 1980; 100,000 in 1981; and 100,000 in 1982. Sales to Cheng Shin accounted for 1.24 percent of Asahi's income in 1981 and 0.44 percent in 1982. Cheng Shin alleged that approximately 20 percent of its sales in the United States are in California. Cheng Shin purchases valve assemblies from other suppliers as well, and sells finished tubes throughout the world.

In 1983 an attorney for Cheng Shin conducted an informal examination of the valve stems of the tire tubes sold in one cycle store in Solano County. The attorney declared that of the approximately 115 tire tubes in the store, 97 were purportedly manufactured in Japan or Taiwan, and of those 97, 21 valve stems were marked with the circled letter "A", apparently Asahi's trademark. Of the 21 Asahi valve stems, 12 were incorporated into Cheng Shin tire tubes. The store contained 41 other Cheng Shin tubes that incorporated the valve assemblies of other manufacturers. An affidavit of a manager of Cheng Shin whose duties included the purchasing of component parts stated: " 'In discussions with Asahi regarding the purchase of valve stem assemblies the fact that my Company sells tubes throughout the world and specifically the United States has been discussed. I am informed and believe that Asahi was fully aware that valve stem assemblies sold to my Company and to others would end up throughout the United States and in California.' " An affidavit of the president of Asahi, on the other hand, declared that Asahi " 'has never contemplated that its limited sales of tire valves to Cheng Shin in Taiwan would subject it to lawsuits in California.' " The record does not include any contract between Cheng Shin and Asahi.

trial court: (PJ)

Primarily on the basis of the above information, the Superior Court denied the motion to quash summons, stating: "Asahi obviously does business on an international scale. It is not unreasonable that they defend claims of defect in their product on an international scale."

---

* [Eds.—In an indemnity action, a defendant (in this case, Cheng Shin) asserts that someone else (in this case, Asahi) is the responsible party and should reimburse the defendant for any damages that the defendant has to pay to the plaintiff.]

The Court of Appeal of the State of California issued a peremptory writ of mandate commanding the Superior Court to quash service of summons. The court concluded that "it would be unreasonable to require Asahi to respond in California solely on the basis of ultimately realized foreseeability that the product into which its component was embodied would be sold all over the world including California."

The Supreme Court of the State of California reversed and discharged the writ issued by the Court of Appeal. The court observed: "Asahi has no offices, property or agents in California. It solicits no business in California and has made no direct sales [in California]." Moreover, "Asahi did not design or control the system of distribution that carried its valve assemblies into California." Nevertheless, the court found the exercise of jurisdiction over Asahi to be consistent with the Due Process Clause. It concluded that Asahi knew that some of the valve assemblies sold to Cheng Shin would be incorporated into tire tubes sold in California, and that Asahi benefited indirectly from the sale in California of products incorporating its components. The court considered Asahi's intentional act of placing its components into the stream of commerce—that is, by delivering the components to Cheng Shin in Taiwan—coupled with Asahi's awareness that some of the components would eventually find their way into California, sufficient to form the basis for state court jurisdiction under the Due Process Clause.

We granted certiorari, and now reverse.

II

A

The Due Process Clause of the Fourteenth Amendment limits the power of a state court to exert personal jurisdiction over a nonresident defendant. "[T]he constitutional touchstone" of the determination whether an exercise of personal jurisdiction comports with due process "remains whether the defendant purposefully established 'minimum contacts' in the forum State." *Burger King v. Rudzewicz*, 471 U.S. 462, 474 (1985). Most recently we have reaffirmed the oft-quoted reasoning of *Hanson v. Denckla* that minimum contacts must have a basis in "some act by which the defendant purposefully avails itself of the privilege of conducting activities within the forum State, thus invoking the benefits and protections of its laws." *Burger King*, 471 U.S., at 475. "Jurisdiction is proper . . . where the contacts proximately result from actions by the defendant *himself* that create a 'substantial connection' with the forum State." *Ibid.*

Applying the principle that minimum contacts must be based on an act of the defendant, the Court in *World-Wide Volkswagen* rejected the assertion that a *consumer's* unilateral act of bringing the defendant's product into the forum State was a sufficient constitutional basis for personal jurisdiction over the defendant. It had been argued in *World-Wide Volkswagen* that because an automobile retailer and its wholesale distributor sold a product mobile by design and purpose, they could foresee being haled into court in the distant States into which their customers might drive. The Court rejected this concept of foreseeability as an insufficient basis for jurisdiction under the Due Process Clause. The Court disclaimed, however, the idea that "foreseeability is wholly irrelevant" to personal jurisdiction, concluding that "[t]he forum State does not exceed its powers under the Due Process Clause if it asserts personal jurisdiction over a corporation that delivers its products into the stream of commerce with the expectation that they will be purchased by consumers in the forum State." *World-Wide Volkswagen v. Woodson,* 444 U.S. 286, 297–98 (1980). The Court reasoned:

> When a corporation "purposefully avails itself of the privilege of conducting activities within the forum State," it has clear notice that it is subject to suit there, and can act to alleviate the risk of burdensome litigation by procuring insurance, passing the expected costs on to customers, or, if the risks are too great, severing its connection with the State. Hence if the sale of a product of a manufacturer or distributor . . . is not simply an isolated occurrence, but arises from the efforts of the manufacturer or distributor to serve, directly or indirectly, the market for its product in other States, it is not unreasonable to subject it to suit in one of those States if its allegedly defective merchandise has there been the source of injury to its owners or to others.

Id. at 297.

In *World-Wide Volkswagen* itself, the state court sought to base jurisdiction not on any act of the defendant, but on the foreseeable unilateral actions of the consumer. Since *World-Wide Volkswagen,* lower courts have been confronted with cases in which the defendant acted by placing a product in the stream of commerce, and the stream eventually swept defendant's product into the forum State, but the defendant did nothing else to purposefully avail itself of the market in the forum State. Some courts have understood the Due Process Clause, as interpreted in *World-Wide Volkswagen,* to allow an exercise of personal jurisdiction to be based on no more than the defendant's act of placing the product in the stream of commerce. Other courts have understood the Due Process Clause and the above-quoted language in *World-Wide Volkswagen* to require the action of the defendant to be more purposefully directed at the forum State than the mere act of placing a product in the stream of commerce.

The reasoning of the Supreme Court of California in the present case illustrates the former interpretation of *World-Wide Volkswagen.* The Supreme Court of California held that, because the stream of commerce eventually brought some valves Asahi sold Cheng Shin into California, Asahi's awareness that its valves would be sold in California was sufficient to permit California to exercise jurisdiction over Asahi consistent with the requirements of the Due Process Clause. The Supreme Court of California's position was consistent with those courts that have held that mere foreseeability or awareness was a constitutionally sufficient basis for personal jurisdiction if the defendant's product made its way into the forum State while still in the stream of commerce.

Other courts, however, have understood the Due Process Clause to require something more than that the defendant was aware of its product's entry into the forum State through the stream of commerce in order for the State to exert jurisdiction over the defendant. In the present case, for example, the State Court of Appeal did not read the Due Process Clause, as interpreted by *World-Wide Volkswagen,* to allow "mere foreseeability that the product will enter the forum state [to] be enough by itself to establish jurisdiction over the distributor and retailer." In *Humble v. Toyota Motor Co.,* 727 F.2d 709 (CA8 1984), an injured car passenger brought suit against Arakawa Auto Body Company, a Japanese corporation that manufactured car seats for Toyota. Arakawa did no business in the United States; it had no office, affiliate, subsidiary, or agent in the United States; it manufactured its component parts outside the United States and delivered them to Toyota Motor Company in Japan. The Court of Appeals, adopting the reasoning of the District Court in that case, noted that although it "does not doubt that Arakawa could have foreseen that its product would find its way into the United States," it would be "manifestly unjust" to require Arakawa to defend itself in the United States.

We now find this latter position to be consonant with the requirements of due process. The "substantial connection," between the defendant and the forum State necessary for a finding of minimum contacts must come about by *an action of the defendant purposefully directed toward the forum State.* The placement of a product into the stream of commerce, without more, is not an act of the defendant purposefully directed toward the forum State. Additional conduct of the defendant may indicate an intent or purpose to serve the market in the forum State, for example, designing the product for the market in the forum State, advertising in the forum State, establishing channels for providing regular advice to customers in the forum State, or marketing the product through a distributor who has agreed to serve as the sales agent in the forum State. But a defendant's awareness that the stream of commerce may or will sweep the product into the forum State does not convert the mere act of placing the product into the stream into an act purposefully directed toward the forum State.

Assuming, *arguendo,* that respondents have established Asahi's awareness that some of the valves sold to Cheng Shin would be incorporated into tire tubes sold in California, respondents have not demonstrated any action by Asahi to purposefully avail itself of the California market. Asahi does not do business in California. It has no office, agents, employees, or property in California. It does not advertise or otherwise solicit business in California. It did not create, control, or employ the distribution system that brought its valves to California. There is no evidence that Asahi designed its product in anticipation of sales in California. On the basis of these facts, the exertion of personal jurisdiction over Asahi by the Superior Court of California exceeds the limits of due process.

B

The strictures of the Due Process Clause forbid a state court to exercise personal jurisdiction over Asahi under circumstances that would offend " 'traditional notions of fair play and substantial justice.' " *International Shoe,* 326 U.S., at 316 (quoting *Milliken,* 311 U.S., at 463).

We have previously explained that the determination of the reasonableness of the exercise of jurisdiction in each case will depend on an evaluation of several factors. A court must consider the burden on the defendant, the interests of the forum State, and the plaintiff's interest in obtaining relief. It must also weigh in its determination "the interstate judicial system's interest in obtaining the most efficient resolution of controversies; and the shared interest of the several States in furthering fundamental substantive social policies." *World-Wide Volkswagen*, 444 U.S., at 292.

A consideration of these factors in the present case clearly reveals the unreasonableness of the assertion of jurisdiction over Asahi, even apart from the question of the placement of goods in the stream of commerce.

Certainly the burden on the defendant in this case is severe. Asahi has been commanded by the Supreme Court of California not only to traverse the distance between Asahi's headquarters in Japan and the Superior Court of California in and for the County of Solano, but also to submit its dispute with Cheng Shin to a foreign nation's judicial system. The unique burdens placed upon one who must defend oneself in a foreign legal system should have significant weight in assessing the reasonableness of stretching the long arm of personal jurisdiction over national borders.

When minimum contacts have been established, often the interests of the plaintiff and the forum in the exercise of jurisdiction will justify even the serious burdens placed on the alien defendant. In the present case, however, the interests of the plaintiff and the forum in California's assertion of jurisdiction over Asahi are slight. All that remains is a claim for indemnification asserted by Cheng Shin, a Taiwanese corporation, against Asahi. The transaction on which the indemnification claim is based took place in Taiwan; Asahi's components were shipped from Japan to Taiwan. Cheng Shin has not demonstrated that it is more convenient for it to litigate its indemnification claim against Asahi in California rather than in Taiwan or Japan.

Because the plaintiff [Cheng Shin] is not a California resident, California's legitimate interests in the dispute have considerably diminished. The Supreme Court of California argued that the State had an interest in "protecting its consumers by ensuring that foreign manufacturers comply with the state's safety standards." The State Supreme Court's definition of California's interest, however, was overly broad. The dispute between Cheng Shin and Asahi is primarily about indemnification rather than safety standards. Moreover, it is not at all clear at this point that California law should govern the question whether a Japanese corporation should indemnify a Taiwanese corporation on the basis of a sale made in Taiwan and a shipment of goods from Japan to Taiwan. The possibility of being haled into a California court as a result of an accident involving Asahi's components undoubtedly creates an additional deterrent to the manufacture of unsafe components; however, similar pressures will be placed on Asahi by the purchasers of its components as long as those who use Asahi components in their final products, and sell those products in California, are subject to the application of California tort law.

World-Wide Volkswagen also admonished courts to take into consideration the interests of the "several States," in addition to the forum State, in the efficient judicial resolution of the dispute and the advancement of substantive policies. In the present case, this advice calls for a court to consider the procedural and substantive policies of other *nations* whose interests are affected by the assertion of jurisdiction by the California court. The procedural and substantive interests of other nations in a state court's assertion of jurisdiction over an alien defendant will differ from case to case. In every case, however, those interests, as well as the Federal interest in Government's foreign relations policies, will be best served by a careful inquiry into the reasonableness of the assertion of jurisdiction in the particular case, and an unwillingness to find the serious burdens on an alien defendant outweighed by minimal interests on the part of the plaintiff or the forum State. "Great care and reserve should be exercised when extending our notions of personal jurisdiction into the international field." *United States v. First National City Bank*, 379 U.S. 378, 404 (1965) (Harlan, J., dissenting).

Considering the international context, the heavy burden on the alien defendant, and the slight interests of the plaintiff and the forum State, the exercise of personal jurisdiction by a California court over Asahi in this instance would be unreasonable and unfair.

III

Because the facts of this case do not establish minimum contacts such that the exercise of personal jurisdiction is consistent with fair play and substantial justice, the judgment of the Supreme Court of California is reversed, and the case is remanded for further proceedings not inconsistent with this opinion.

It is so ordered.

Justice Brennan, with whom Justice White, Justice Marshall, and Justice Blackmun join, concurring in part and concurring in the judgment.

I do not agree with the interpretation in Part II-A of the stream-of-commerce theory, nor with the conclusion that Asahi did not "purposely avail itself of the California market." I do agree, however, with the Court's conclusion in Part II-B that the exercise of personal jurisdiction over Asahi in this case would not comport with "fair play and substantial justice." This is one of those rare cases in which "minimum requirements inherent in the concept of 'fair play and substantial justice' . . . defeat the reasonableness of jurisdiction even [though] the defendant has purposefully engaged in forum activities." *Burger King Corp. v. Rudzewicz*, 471 U.S. 462, 477–478 (1985). I therefore join Parts I and II-B of the Court's opinion, and write separately to explain my disagreement with Part II-A.

Part II-A states that "a defendant's awareness that the stream of commerce may or will sweep the product into the forum State does not convert the mere act of placing the product into the stream into an act purposefully directed toward the forum State." Under this view, a plaintiff would be required to show "[a]dditional conduct" directed toward the forum before finding the exercise of jurisdiction over the defendant to be consistent with the Due Process Clause. I see no need for such a showing, however. The stream of commerce refers not to unpredictable currents or eddies, but to the regular and anticipated flow of products from manufacture to distribution to retail sale. As long as a participant in this process is aware that the final product is being marketed in the forum State, the possibility of a lawsuit there cannot come as a surprise. Nor will the litigation present a burden for which there is no corresponding benefit. A defendant who has placed goods in the stream of commerce benefits economically from the retail sale of the final product in the forum State, and indirectly benefits from the State's laws that regulate and facilitate commercial activity. These benefits accrue regardless of whether that participant directly conducts business in the forum State, or engages in additional conduct directed toward that State. Accordingly, most courts and commentators have found that jurisdiction premised on the placement of a product into the stream of commerce is consistent with the Due Process Clause, and have not required a showing of additional conduct.

The endorsement in Part II-A of what appears to be the minority view among Federal Courts of Appeals represents a marked retreat from the analysis in *World-Wide Volkswagen*. In that case, "respondents [sought] to base jurisdiction on one, isolated occurrence and whatever inferences can be drawn therefrom: the fortuitous circumstance that a single Audi automobile, sold in New York to New York residents, happened to suffer an accident while passing through Oklahoma." *World-Wide Volkswagen*, 444 U.S. at 295. The Court held that the possibility of an accident in Oklahoma, while to some extent foreseeable in light of the inherent mobility of the automobile, was not enough to establish minimum contacts between the forum State and the retailer or distributor. The Court then carefully explained:

> "[T]his is not to say, of course, that foreseeability is wholly irrelevant. But the foreseeability that is critical to due process analysis is not the mere likelihood that a product will find its way into the forum State. Rather, it is that the defendant's conduct and connection with the forum State are such that he should reasonably anticipate being haled into Court there." *Id.*, at 297.

The Court reasoned that when a corporation may reasonably anticipate litigation in a particular forum, it cannot claim that such litigation is unjust or unfair, because it "can act to alleviate the risk of burdensome litigation by procuring insurance, passing the expected costs on to consumers, or, if the risks are too great, severing its connection with the State." *Ibid.*

To illustrate the point, the Court contrasted the foreseeability of litigation in a State to which a consumer fortuitously transports a defendant's product (insufficient contacts) with the foreseeability of litigation in a State where the defendant's product was regularly *sold* (sufficient contacts). The Court stated:

> "Hence if the *sale* of a product of a manufacturer or distributor such as Audi or Volkswagen is not simply an isolated occurrence, but arises from the efforts of the manufacturer or distributor to serve, *directly or indirectly,* the market for its

> product in other States, it is not unreasonable to subject it to suit in one of those States if its allegedly defective merchandise has there been the source of injury to its owner or to others. The forum State does not exceed its powers under the Due Process Clause if it asserts personal jurisdiction over a corporation that delivers its products into the stream of commerce *with the expectation that they will be purchased by consumers* in the forum State." *Id.*, at 297–298 (emphasis added).

The Court concluded its illustration by referring to *Gray v. American Radiator*, a well-known stream-of-commerce case in which the Illinois Supreme Court applied the theory to assert jurisdiction over a component-parts manufacturer that sold no components directly in Illinois, but did sell them to a manufacturer who incorporated them into a final product that was sold in Illinois.

The Court in *World-Wide Volkswagen* thus took great care to distinguish "between a case involving goods which reach a distant State through a chain of distribution and a case involving goods which reach the same State because a consumer . . . took them there." *Id.*, at 306–307 (Brennan, J. dissenting). The California Supreme Court took note of this distinction, and correctly concluded that our holding in *World-Wide Volkswagen* preserved the stream-of-commerce theory.

In this case, the facts found by the California Supreme Court support its finding of minimum contacts. The court found that "[a]lthough Asahi did not design or control the system of distribution that carried its valve assemblies into California, Asahi was aware of the distribution system's operation, and it knew that it would benefit economically from the sale in California of products incorporating its components." Accordingly, I cannot join the determination in Part II-A that Asahi's regular and extensive sales of component parts to a manufacturer it knew was making regular sales of the final product in California is insufficient to establish minimum contacts with California.

Justice Stevens, with whom Justice White and Justice Blackmun join, concurring in part and concurring in the judgment.

The judgment of the Supreme Court of California should be reversed for the reasons stated in Part II-B of the Court's opinion. While I join Parts I and II-B, I do not join Part II-A for two reasons. First, it is not necessary to the Court's decision. An examination of minimum contacts is not always necessary to determine whether a state court's assertion of personal jurisdiction is constitutional. Part II-B establishes, after considering the factors set forth in *World-Wide Volkswagen*, that California's exercise of jurisdiction over Asahi in this case would be "unreasonable and unfair." This finding alone requires reversal; this case fits within the rule that "minimum requirements inherent in the concept of 'fair play and substantial justice' may defeat the reasonableness of jurisdiction even if the defendant has purposefully engaged in forum activities." *Burger King*, 471 U.S., at 477–478. Accordingly, I see no reason in this case for the plurality to articulate "purposeful direction" or any other test as the nexus between an act of a defendant and the forum State that is necessary to establish minimum contacts.

Second, even assuming that the test ought to be formulated here, Part II-A misapplies it to the facts of this case. The plurality seems to assume that an unwavering line can be drawn between "mere awareness" that a component will find its way into the forum State and "purposeful availment" of the forum's market. Over the course of its dealings with Cheng Shin, Asahi has arguably engaged in a higher quantum of conduct than "[t]he placement of a product into the stream of commerce, without more. . . ." Whether or not this conduct rises to the level of purposeful availment requires a constitutional determination that is affected by the volume, the value, and the hazardous character of the components. In most circumstances I would be inclined to conclude that a regular course of dealing that results in deliveries of over 100,000 units annually over a period of several years would constitute "purposeful availment" even though the item delivered to the forum State was a standard product marketed throughout the world.

Sandra Day O'Connor

Collection of the Supreme Court of the United States

Sandra Day O'Connor (1930–) spent her early years on a ranch in rural Arizona. A natural student, she graduated third in her Stanford Law School class—behind William Rehnquist, later Chief Justice of the United States Supreme Court. Although she served as an editor on the Stanford Law Review, she faced gender discrimination—the large California firms did not offer her a job except as a legal secretary. She became a county attorney and later returned to Arizona, where she served as Assistant Attorney General, was elected to the state Senate, and later served as a trial judge and appellate judge on the Arizona Court of Appeals, acquiring experience in all three branches of the state government.

In 1981, President Reagan nominated her as the first female justice of the United States Supreme Court. Justice O'Connor served on the Court for twenty-five years, earning a reputation as a restrained and pragmatic jurist who provided the deciding vote in some of the Court's most important cases.

In *Asahi*, Justice O'Connor tackles a complex problem that is still not clearly resolved: Should a foreign manufacturer whose product reaches the United States through the "stream of commerce" be subject to personal jurisdiction in a state court for claims arising from an injury allegedly caused there by the product?

Notes and Questions: Understanding *Asahi* and the Stream of Commerce

1. A stream of opinions. What does the Supreme Court actually hold regarding the stream of commerce method of establishing personal jurisdiction? Consider this multiple choice question.

Trellis Industries is a Delaware corporation with its principal place of business in Delaware. Trellis makes laptop batteries, which are used as components in computers manufactured by Nectarine Computer, Inc., a Delaware corporation with its principal place of business in Massachusetts. Trellis ships its batteries to Nectarine's factory in Massachusetts, knowing that Nectarine incorporates the batteries into its computers for thousands of sales in every United States jurisdiction. Trellis does not send its batteries to any other company; it does not deal directly with Nectarine's customers; and it engages in no other business-related activities outside of the state of Delaware.

Eugene (an Idaho citizen) buys a computer from Nectarine, which is shipped to him from Nectarine's plant in Massachusetts. The computer catches on fire, causing Eugene to lose all of his valuable data. Eugene sues Nectarine and Trellis in Idaho state court, alleging that the fire was due to a defective Trellis battery. Trellis moves to dismiss for lack of personal jurisdiction. Assuming Idaho's long arm statute reaches as far as the Constitution allows, which of the following statements most accurately describes what the United States Supreme Court has held in this type of case?

A. The Idaho state court has personal jurisdiction over Trellis.
B. The Idaho state court would not have personal jurisdiction over Trellis, because Trellis lacks sufficient contacts with Idaho.
C. The Idaho state court would not have personal jurisdiction because Trellis lacks sufficient contacts with Idaho and because the exercise of personal jurisdiction would be unfair and unreasonable.
D. The United States Supreme Court has left unresolved whether the Idaho state court would have personal jurisdiction over Trellis.
E. The United States Supreme Court has left unresolved whether Trellis has sufficient contacts with Idaho, but the Supreme Court has held that the exercise of personal jurisdiction would be unfair in this type of case.

Let's start with the Court's analysis of the stream of commerce issue. Remember that an opinion is not the law unless it receives five votes. Three justices joined Part II-A of Justice O'Connor's opinion, which said that, in this type of case, a contact does not exist simply because the defendant's component part ended up in the state through the stream of commerce. The defendant must direct activity into the state, and there is no evidence that Trellis engaged in this extra step in Idaho beyond the stream of commerce. Thus, four justices of the Supreme Court (Justice O'Connor and the three justices who joined Part II-A) believed that the answer should be **B**. Without a fifth justice to join the opinion, however, this view is not the law.

Justice Brennan also wrote an opinion that three justices joined. His opinion concluded that, in this type of case, a defendant establishes a contact in a state if the defendant's product is regularly sold there as a result of the stream of commerce and the defendant is aware that sales take place there. These four justices would presumably have chosen answer **A**. Once again, though, this opinion falls one vote short of announcing the law, so **A** is not the answer.

Justice Stevens, who would have been the deciding vote, gave us a hint as to what his approach would be. He suggested that courts should focus on factors such as the volume of the defendant's sales in the state and the hazardous nature of the product at issue. He concluded, however, that the Court did not need to decide the stream of commerce issue because the case could be decided on "reasonableness" grounds. As a result, the issue of whether a contact can be established via the stream of commerce is still unresolved. Thus, you can also rule out **C**.

C is also wrong for another reason, which turns on the Court's analysis of the reasonableness factors. The Court's analysis of those factors in *Asahi* turned heavily on the absence of any domestic parties. The parties in this question, however, are entirely domestic, so this case has a much stronger connection to Idaho than the *Asahi* litigation had to California. The plaintiff in this question lives in Idaho, was injured in Idaho, and (unlike the original plaintiff in *Asahi*) is still involved in the case. Because the reasonableness factors would not rule out personal jurisdiction here, **E** is also not the best answer. Therefore, the answer is **D**—the Court has left this issue largely unresolved.

2. A drying stream? The Court appeared ready to offer a more definitive answer to the question posed in note 1 when it granted certiorari in *McIntyre Machinery, Ltd. v. Nicastro*, 564 U.S. 873 (2011). McIntyre Machinery, Ltd. was a United Kingdom company that sold a variety of machines, including a metal shearing machine, in the United States through an independently owned distributor in Ohio. The distributor sold one of McIntyre's shearing machines to a company in New Jersey, and one of the company's employees (the plaintiff, Robert Nicastro) severed four fingers while operating the machine. Nicastro sued McIntyre in New Jersey state court, and the New Jersey Supreme Court, relying heavily on the stream of commerce doctrine, held that McIntyre was subject to personal jurisdiction in New Jersey.

The United States Supreme Court reversed, but to the disappointment of professors, students, and lawyers, the Court did not resolve the stream of commerce issue. Justice Kennedy, joined by Justices Roberts, Scalia, and Thomas, essentially endorsed Justice O'Connor's view in *Asahi* and concluded that a defendant must direct some kind of activity to the forum. According to these four justices, a mere expectation or hope that a product will be sold in a jurisdiction is insufficient to give rise to personal jurisdiction there. Because there was no evidence that McIntyre directed any activity to New Jersey, these four Justices reasoned that the New Jersey courts could not exercise personal jurisdiction over McIntyre.

Justice Breyer, joined by Justice Alito, wrote a concurring opinion, agreeing that McIntyre's contacts in New Jersey were insufficient to give rise to personal jurisdiction. These justices expressly declined, however, to decide the scope of the stream of commerce doctrine, suggesting instead that the Court take up the issue in a different case that "implicate[s] modern concerns," such as a case arising in the Internet context. In the meantime, Justice Breyer was unwilling to make any "broad pronouncements" about the stream of commerce doctrine and rested his conclusion on the narrow ground that McIntyre's isolated contacts in New Jersey did not give rise to personal jurisdiction. He explained that, if the facts had been different (e.g., if McIntyre had a regular flow of business in New Jersey), New Jersey might have had personal jurisdiction over McIntyre. In this sense, Justice Breyer's opinion largely mirrors Justice Stevens's opinion in *Asahi*, which suggested that the volume of sales in a particular state might be a relevant consideration. In sum, six justices concluded that personal jurisdiction was improper in this case, but only four of those justices were willing to make a general pronouncement about the scope of the stream of commerce doctrine.

Finally, Justice Ginsburg, joined by Justices Sotomayor and Kagan, dissented. Justice Ginsburg's opinion has much in common with Justice Brennan's opinion in *Asahi* in that it endorses a rather permissive stream of commerce doctrine. In particular, Justice Ginsburg reasoned that, when a manufacturer seeks to sell its product in "several States, it is reasonable 'to subject it to suit in [any] one of those States if its allegedly defective [product] has there been the source of injury.' " *McIntyre Machinery*, 564 U.S. at 899 (Ginsburg, J., dissenting) (quoting *World-Wide Volkswagen*). Applying that principle to McIntyre, Justice Ginsburg concluded that the company had treated the United States as a single market and had hoped that its distributor would sell machines throughout the United States, including in New Jersey, where there happened to be a sizeable potential market for McIntyre's products. Accordingly, she believed that personal jurisdiction should have been proper in New Jersey.

So what does this all mean? There is a rule—the so-called *Marks* rule—that says that "when a fragmented Court decides a case and no single rationale explaining the result enjoys the assent of five Justices, the holding of the Court may be viewed as that position taken by those Members who concurred in the judgments on the narrowest grounds." *Marks v. United States*, 430 U.S. 188, 193 (1977). Here, the narrowest rationale for the holding is that, in a stream of commerce fact pattern, a single isolated sale in the forum is not sufficient for personal jurisdiction. *See, e.g., Ainsworth v. Moffett Engineering, Ltd.*, 716 F.3d 174, 178 (5th Cir. 2013) (interpreting *McIntyre* this way after applying the *Marks* rule). This means that, as in *Asahi*, the Court once again failed to definitively resolve when contacts through the stream of commerce will give rise to personal jurisdiction when there are more than "isolated" sales in the jurisdiction. *Id.* Because the question in note 1 specifies that there are thousands of sales by Nectarine in Idaho, *McIntyre* does not produce a clear answer. In short, the answer to the multiple choice question in note 1 is still **D**.

Q **3. Lawyering in the face of ambiguity.** Imagine that you are asked to represent Trellis Industries in the case described in note 1. In light of *Asahi* and *McIntyre*, what would you argue to the Idaho court to convince it that Trellis should not be subject to specific jurisdiction?

A Your goal should be to convince the court to adopt the approach articulated by Justice O'Connor in *Asahi* and Justice Kennedy in *McIntyre*. That approach offers the most protection to a component part manufacturer like Trellis, because it requires a defendant to have directed some kind of activity to the forum state beyond the mere sale of another company's product (here, Nectarine's) containing the defendant's component part. The Idaho court would not be obligated to adopt this position, because this view did not receive majority support in either *Asahi* or *McIntyre*. But a lower court typically has to take some position on the issue, so you would need to convince the court to adopt the reasoning that Justice O'Connor offered in *Asahi* or that Justice Kennedy supplied in *McIntyre*.

In contrast, if you represent the plaintiff, you should try to convince the court to adopt the position articulated by Justice Brennan in *Asahi* or Justice Ginsburg in *McIntyre*.

To convince the court to choose your preferred approach, you might consider making public policy arguments of the sort the justices made in *Asahi* and *McIntyre*. For example, if you represent the defendant, you might point out that a liberal approach to the stream of commerce analysis is problematic because it would mean that defendants would have little control over where they are subject to personal jurisdiction. After all, even if a defendant may be aware that its component part (e.g., a touch screen) is being incorporated into a final product (e.g., a mobile phone) by another company and being sold in a far-flung state, the component part maker typically has little, if any, real control over where the final product is sold. Without that control, it seems fundamentally unfair to subject a defendant to personal jurisdiction.

On the other hand, if you represent the plaintiff, you might argue that this lack of control is simply the cost of doing business in a modern economy. If companies benefit financially from sales around the country, those companies should have to accept the occasional lawsuit in a far-flung state, even if they had little control over the location of the ultimate sale. Personal jurisdiction would not be unfair, one might argue, given the financial benefits of sales in the forum and how easy it is today to travel to other states to defend suits there.

Given the strength of these competing views, it is not surprising that lower courts have split on the issue. Some courts have adopted Justice O'Connor's stream of commerce "plus" approach. (These courts are now also likely to cite Justice Kennedy's opinion in *McIntyre*.) Others have adopted Justice Brennan's pure stream of commerce theory (i.e., agreeing with *Gray*). (These courts are now also likely to cite Justice Ginsburg's opinion in *McIntyre*.) Still others have agreed with the middle ground position that Justice Stevens implicitly endorsed in *Asahi* and that Justice Breyer appears to follow in *McIntyre*, which focuses (at least in part) on the volume of the defendant's products that flow into the state. And still other courts have avoided taking sides. For example, when a court finds that a defendant has had a contact with the forum that would satisfy Justice O'Connor's/Justice Kennedy's test, the court can be relatively sure that the Supreme Court would find jurisdiction under any test. Thus, the court can simply find that personal jurisdiction exists without having to adopt any particular approach.

Q **4. Distinguishing the "stream of commerce" from foreseeability.** In *World-Wide Volkswagen*, the consumer took the car from New York to Oklahoma, and the Court concluded that the seller of the car was not subject to personal jurisdiction in Oklahoma. How is the theory of personal jurisdiction that the Court rejected in *World-Wide Volkswagen* different from the "stream of commerce" theory?

A In *World-Wide Volkswagen*, the product entered the forum state (Oklahoma) as a result of the *consumer's* conduct. In contrast, in *Asahi*, the component part was not taken to California by a consumer. Rather, Asahi sold the component to Cheng Shin, the tube manufacturer, and Cheng Shin sent its tubes to

California. Similarly, in *McIntyre*, McIntyre sent the machine from the United Kingdom to an independently owned distributor in Ohio, who then sold the machine to a company in New Jersey.

There are important differences between a consumer's movement of a product, on the one hand, and the movement of a product through the supply chain (the "stream of commerce"), on the other. First, when a product moves through the supply chain, the manufacturer of the product has more control over where that product ends up. For example, Asahi knew that Cheng Shin was selling tire tubes in California, so Asahi could have avoided the forum by refusing to sell tubes to Cheng Shin. In contrast, a retailer has no control over where a consumer transports a product after it is purchased. For example, in *World-Wide*, the defendants had no control over where the Robinsons drove the car after it was purchased in New York. Because courts have emphasized the importance of a defendant's ability to control where it is subject to personal jurisdiction, *World-Wide* presents a less compelling case for personal jurisdiction than a case involving sales through the stream of commerce.

That said, one might argue that this "control" distinction is illusory. After all, as explained in the immediately preceding note, component part manufacturers typically do not have much control over where their products are ultimately sold by other companies "downstream." For example, Trellis may sell its components to Nectarine, but Trellis probably has no power to tell Nectarine where it can (or cannot) sell its products. The only control Trellis may have is whether to sell its products to Nectarine at all. The problem is that, if Nectarine is Trellis's primary (or exclusive) customer, Trellis does not really have much of a "choice" about selling to Nectarine. Thus, if control is the touchstone for the personal jurisdiction analysis, there may not be much of a difference as a practical matter between the theory rejected in *World-Wide* and the "stream of commerce" theory endorsed by Justice Brennan in *Asahi* and Justice Ginsburg in *McIntyre.*

Another possible distinction between the two theories of personal jurisdiction is that companies like Asahi and McIntyre profited from the sale of goods "downstream" in ways that the car dealership and regional distributor in *World-Wide Volkswagen* did not. For example, McIntyre clearly profited from the sale of its product in New Jersey. In contrast, the car dealership and regional distributor in *World-Wide* did not receive any financial benefit from the Robinsons driving their car through Oklahoma. For this reason, personal jurisdiction may seem fairer in a case like *McIntyre* than in *World-Wide.*

In sum, there are some differences between *World-Wide* and the "stream of commerce" cases. Whether those differences are sufficiently significant that they warrant a different outcome for purposes of personal jurisdiction is still an open question.

Q **5. Explaining the reversal.** The Court did not conclusively determine whether Asahi had contacts in California, so why did the Court reverse the California Supreme Court?

A The Court ultimately concluded that the reasonableness factors had not been satisfied. Those factors include an examination of "the burden on the defendant, the interests of the forum State, and the plaintiff's interest in obtaining relief. [A court] must also weigh in its determination 'the interstate judicial system's interest in obtaining the most efficient resolution of controversies; and the shared interest of the several States in furthering fundamental substantive social policies.' "

Here, the burden on the defendant is significant given the defendant's foreign locale. Even more critical is California's limited interest in this case, given that it no longer involves a California citizen. Moreover, the third-party plaintiff (Cheng Shin), a foreign company, has no particular reason to have this case heard in California. Although the applicable law in the United States might be more plaintiff-friendly than Taiwan's law, it is not clear that California law (as opposed to Taiwanese law) would apply to the claim between these two foreign companies in light of the choice of law analysis that the California court would have to apply. And even if there is a difference between the law that would apply in the California court and the law that would apply in Taiwan, those differences do not mean that California should hear this case. American tort law is generally the most liberal in the world, so if a plaintiff could establish personal jurisdiction over a defendant simply because American tort law is more favorable than another country's tort law, virtually any foreign defendant could be subjected to personal jurisdiction in the United States in a tort case.

In addition, because the indemnification dispute involves the relationship established in Asia between two foreign companies, a California forum could not resolve this case any more efficiently than a Taiwanese or Japanese court. In fact, some relevant evidence and important witnesses are likely to be in Taiwan or Japan, where the component and the product were manufactured. Finally, it is not clear what domestic social policies would be advanced by having this case heard in California.

Q **6. Exploring the tributaries.** Consider the following variations on *Asahi*. Would the reasonableness factors be satisfied in these cases?

A. Zurcher sues Asahi directly for his injuries. Asahi moves to dismiss Zurcher's claim for lack of personal jurisdiction.

A A court would probably *not* dismiss Asahi on reasonableness grounds in this example. If Zurcher had sued Asahi directly, many of the reasonableness factors would have cut the other way. The plaintiff would have had a strong interest in a California forum; without it, Zurcher would have had to go to Japan to sue for his California accident! For similar reasons, California would have had a much stronger interest in this case. Students often conclude that *Asahi* stands for the proposition that it would be unfair to force a foreign defendant to litigate a case in this country, but the Court's opinion in Part II-B stands for a much narrower proposition.

Of course, just because the reasonableness factors would be satisfied in this version of the case does not mean that personal jurisdiction would have existed. The court would still need to determine whether Asahi had any contacts in the forum that gave rise to the claims. We know that Justice O'Connor (and the three justices who joined her opinion in *Asahi*) would still conclude that Asahi lacked the requisite contacts in California to be subject to personal jurisdiction there.

B. Zurcher's case with Cheng Shin does not settle, but the facts otherwise remain the same (i.e., Zurcher did not sue Asahi directly). Asahi then moves to dismiss Cheng Shin's claim on personal jurisdiction grounds.

A Zurcher is still in this case, so California would have a stronger interest in this hypothetical case than it did in the real case. On the other hand, California does not have much of an interest in Cheng Shin's third-party claim over Asahi. Although the outcome here is not entirely clear, it is likely that a court would recognize the value of resolving the third-party claim at the same time as Zurcher's claim against Cheng Shin and would find the reasonableness factors to be satisfied.

Q **7. Lawyering strategy: Advising a component part manufacturer.** Imagine that you represent a component part maker that wants to limit where it can be sued. The company has asked you to devise a business plan that will ensure that it is subject to in personam jurisdiction in the smallest number of states. What would you advise the company to do?

A With regard to possible lawsuits against your client by the manufacturer of the ultimate product (e.g., for contract-related claims), you could advise the client to include a forum selection clause in the contract with that manufacturer.

With regard to lawsuits by consumers, one possibility is to advise your client never to deal directly with them. You could suggest that the company sell its components only to the manufacturer of the final product and that it not advertise or engage in other business-related activity outside of its home state. By following this advice, the client will not likely be subject to specific jurisdiction where the customers buy the finished product under Justice O'Connor's (or Justice Kennedy's) stream of commerce theory.

Your client also could avoid being subject to specific jurisdiction under Justice Stevens's (and Justice Breyer's) approach by ensuring that consumer goods containing the company's components are not sold in large numbers in any state. But that doesn't sound like much of a business plan.

Of course, the most important advice for your client would be that, even if it follows your instructions, it may still find itself litigating a case against a consumer in a distant forum because of the current ambiguity in the reach of the stream of commerce theory. That answer may be frustrating to a client, but the client should know the risks and the unsettled nature of the law.

III. The "Arises Out of" Element

So far, we have glossed over two ambiguities regarding the meaning of the "arises out of" element. The first ambiguity relates to how a court determines whether a particular claim arises out of a contact. The second is whether a court can establish personal jurisdiction over all claims in a case, as long as one claim arises out of the defendant's contact with the forum.

A. Determining When a Claim Arises Out of a Contact

At the time this edition of the book went to press in early 2021, the Supreme Court had not yet offered clear guidance on when a claim "arises out of" a contact. The question, however, is squarely presented in *Ford Motor Co. v. Mont. Eighth Jud. Dist. Court*, 443 P.3d 407 (Mont. 2019), *cert. granted*, __ U.S. __, 140 S. Ct. 917 (2020). In that case, the Court appears ready to announce its approach to the issue. In the meantime, lower courts have developed several distinct approaches to determining whether a claim arises out of the defendant's contacts.

One common approach is the "evidence" test. According to this test, a claim arises out of the defendant's in-state contacts only if "the defendant's forum contact provides evidence of one or more elements of the underlying claim." *See* Linda Sandstrom Simard, *Meeting Expectations: Two Profiles for Specific Jurisdiction*, 38 Ind. L. Rev. 343, 349 (2005).

A second common approach is the "but for" test. Under the "but for" framework, a claim arises out of a contact if the claim would not have arisen but for the defendant's contact with the state. *Id.* at 356.

The Supreme Court has not yet endorsed an "arises out of" test, but it has ruled out one option: a "sliding scale." *Bristol-Myers Squibb Co. v. Superior Court of California*, 582 U.S. __, 137 S. Ct. 1773 (2017). Under a "sliding scale" approach, the strength of the needed relationship between the defendant's in-state contacts and the plaintiff's claim would vary according to how extensive the defendant's contacts are in the forum. *Id.* at 1778 (quoting *Bristol-Myers Squibb Co. v. Superior Court of California*, 377 P.3d 874, 889 (2016)). For example, if a defendant has extensive contacts in the forum (but not enough to establish general jurisdiction), the plaintiff would only need to demonstrate a very loose relationship between the defendant's contacts and the plaintiff's claim. In contrast, if a defendant has only a single contact in the forum, the plaintiff would need to demonstrate a much stronger relationship between the contact and the claim.

The Court rejected the "sliding scale" approach in *Bristol-Myers Squibb*. The Court was concerned that, by allowing personal jurisdiction over a defendant with extensive contacts in the forum without showing that the plaintiff's claim arose out of those contacts, a sliding scale would allow for a "loose and spurious form of general jurisdiction." *Id.* at 1781. In short, the Court has made clear that the "arises out of" test for specific jurisdiction should not vary depending on the extensiveness of the defendant's contacts in the forum.

Bristol-Myers Squibb is helpful, but it does not resolve the key question: What must the requisite connection actually be between a plaintiff's claim and the defendant's contacts in the forum? If the necessary relationship is not supposed to vary according to the extensiveness of the defendant's contacts in the forum, what sort of relationship between the contacts and the claim must exist? The answer is not entirely clear, but the "but for" and "evidence" tests can offer some analytical guidance. Let's have a look at how to apply them.

Q **1. Satisfying either test.** Hotel Alaska operates a hotel in Alaska. The hotel's marketing department in Anchorage regularly sends advertising materials through the mail to businesses around the country. These advertisements describe the hotel's low corporate rates and beautiful facilities. One Massachusetts business, People Tech, receives the advertisement and engages in some telephone negotiations with the hotel about room rates. After agreeing to a special corporate rate for People Tech's employees, the company books a convention at the Hotel Alaska.

When People Tech employees arrive at the Hotel Alaska, they discover that the hotel does not look anything like the photographs in the glossy advertisement. The facilities are in poor condition, and the convention is a disaster. People Tech subsequently files a lawsuit in Massachusetts for consumer fraud against Hotel Alaska. Hotel Alaska moves to dismiss on personal jurisdiction grounds. Does the court have personal jurisdiction?

A Yes. The Hotel Alaska directed a contact into Massachusetts (the advertisement), and the lawsuit is about the truthfulness of that advertisement. Under either of the commonly used approaches, the claim arises out of the in-state contact. The advertisement (the contact with Massachusetts) would be essential evidence regarding the consumer fraud claim (i.e., the advertisement would be offered as evidence in support of the consumer fraud claim), so it would satisfy the evidence test. Moreover, it would also satisfy the "but for" test; the claim would not have arisen but for the defendant's contact with Massachusetts.

Q **2. Satisfying only one test.** Now assume that the facilities were as advertised, and People Tech began to send many employees to the hotel. During one of these business trips, a People Tech employee drowns in the hotel's swimming pool. The decedent's family sues the hotel in Massachusetts, claiming that the hotel's negligence caused the tragic accident. The hotel contests personal jurisdiction. Should the court grant *this* motion?*

A The answer depends on which approach to "arises out of" the court adopts. Under the evidence test, the issue is whether the hotel's contact with Massachusetts (the advertisement) is essential evidence of the claim. Unlike the first case, where the advertisement was used as evidence to support the claim of fraudulent advertising, the claim here turns on whether the hotel was negligent in its maintenance of the swimming pool. The advertisement offers no evidence regarding any element of that claim, so if a court adopts this approach, it would likely conclude that personal jurisdiction does not exist.

By contrast, the "but for" test would probably support personal jurisdiction. In particular, this claim would not have arisen but for the hotel's attempt to solicit business in Massachusetts. Courts applying this more liberal standard would probably uphold personal jurisdiction over the hotel in Massachusetts.

Q **3. Satisfying neither test?** Now assume that the person who drowned was an employee of People Tech, but that she was staying at the hotel on

* These facts are loosely based on *Nowak v. Tak How Investments, Ltd.*, 94 F.3d 708 (1st Cir. 1996).

vacation, not for business, and that she had heard about the hotel from another People Tech employee who had stayed there on business. Would there be personal jurisdiction over the hotel in this case?

A

As in the second example, the evidence test would not be satisfied here. The advertisement (the only Massachusetts contact) offers no evidence regarding whether the hotel was negligent.

In contrast, the "but for" test might be satisfied. It appears that the employee went to the hotel because colleagues at People Tech had stayed there on business and had recommended it. In that case, the employee would not have stayed at the hotel but for the hotel's original advertisement in Massachusetts.

At some point, however, the causal link between the contact and the claim becomes so attenuated that personal jurisdiction is problematic. One possible argument against personal jurisdiction is that this claim is too far removed from the initial contact to form a basis for personal jurisdiction even under the "but for" test. Alternatively, one could argue that even if this situation satisfies the "but for" test, a court should reject personal jurisdiction on the ground that it would be unfair under the "reasonableness" factors. Regardless of the particular approach that a court adopts, it seems likely that a court would not exercise personal jurisdiction in a case like this one.

B. The Focus on Claims, Not Cases

Another common question is whether a court can establish personal jurisdiction over all claims in a case if only one claim arises out of the defendant's contact with the forum. Imagine, for example, that in the Hotel Alaska case, People Tech brings a single lawsuit but alleges two claims. First, it alleges that the hotel's advertising material was fraudulent. Second, it alleges negligence; because the employee who drowned in the pool was important to People Tech, the hotel's negligence caused People Tech to lose substantial income. Is there personal jurisdiction over both claims?

Fortunately, the answer to this question is clearer. Aside from a very limited and controversial exception involving a narrow category of federal claims, a court must have personal jurisdiction over *each* individual claim by *each* individual plaintiff. A court cannot typically assert personal jurisdiction over the entire case simply because the court has personal jurisdiction over one of the claims. See, e.g., *Bristol-Myers Squibb.* This means that, although there is personal jurisdiction over the fraudulent advertising claim, the court would not necessarily have personal jurisdiction over the negligence claim. People Tech would have to demonstrate that each claim arises out of the defendant's contacts. If it cannot do so and if People Tech wants to litigate both claims in a single court, People Tech will have to file its lawsuit in Alaska.

1. Claims by multiple plaintiffs. In light of this background on the "arises out of" element, try your hand at the following multiple choice question.

A single lawsuit is filed in California state court on behalf of 86 California residents and 592 residents of 33 other states, alleging 13 violations of California law against a pharmaceutical company (Pharma) that is incorporated in Delaware and has its principal place of business in New York.

The lawsuit includes products liability, negligent misrepresentation, and misleading advertising claims based on the sale of Pharma's drug, Plavix. Pharma sold millions of Plavix pills in California each year, but only to the California-based plaintiffs (i.e., not to the nonresident plaintiffs). The nonresident plaintiffs instead purchased Plavix in their home states.

Assume that Plavix was designed and manufactured outside of California and that the nonresident plaintiffs did not obtain Plavix through California physicians or from any other California source. Also assume that the nonresident plaintiffs did not allege that they incurred injuries from Plavix in California or were treated for their injuries there.

Pharma moves to dismiss the claims by the nonresident plaintiffs on personal jurisdiction grounds. (Pharma concedes that personal jurisdiction exists as to the plaintiffs who are California residents.) Is there specific jurisdiction over Pharma with regard to the claims by the nonresident plaintiffs?

A. Yes, because Pharma has extensive contacts in California through the sale of Plavix there and the nonresidents' claims are related to those contacts.
B. Yes, but only if the court uses the "but for" test for specific jurisdiction.
C. Yes, but only if the court uses the "evidence" test for specific jurisdiction.
D. Yes, because the nonresidents' claims are related to the residents' claims, over which personal jurisdiction is conceded.
E. No, because the nonresidents' claims do not arise out of Pharma's contacts in the forum.

These are essentially the facts of *Bristol-Myers Squibb,* and for the reasons set out in that case, personal jurisdiction does not exist as to the nonresidents' claims. **A** is incorrect because it essentially applies a "sliding scale" test. As mentioned earlier, the Court has rejected the idea that a looser standard for specific jurisdiction exists when a defendant has extensive contacts in a forum. **B** is incorrect because the "but for" test would not be satisfied here; nothing that allegedly happened in California was a "but for" cause of the injuries sustained by the nonresident plaintiffs. **C** is wrong because none of Pharma's activities in California would provide material evidence in support of the claims of the nonresident plaintiffs. Although one could imagine a set of facts where the nonresident plaintiffs need to rely on evidence of injuries to California residents to show that Pharma was on notice about the dangerousness of its product, no such facts appear in the question. Finally, **D** is wrong because there must be personal jurisdiction over each plaintiff's claim; the existence of personal jurisdiction over one claim by one plaintiff does not necessarily mean that there is personal jurisdiction over other claims by the same plaintiff or claims by other plaintiffs who suffered the same or similar injuries. That leaves E. The claims by the nonresident plaintiffs do not arise out of any contacts by Pharma in California using any of the standard tests for "arises out of."

Q **2. A jurisdictional puzzle.** Assume you are the lead counsel for the plaintiffs in *Bristol-Myers Squibb* and want to avoid bringing dozens of separate lawsuits in the various states where the non-California plaintiffs reside. In which state courts, if any, would that be possible?

A You could bring a single lawsuit in any state where Bristol-Myers Squibb (BMS) is subject to general jurisdiction. As you will learn in the next chapter, that would be where BMS has its place of incorporation or principal place of business. In BMS's case, this happens to be Delaware and New York respectively.

IV. Back to the Future: Does the Internet Pose a New Challenge for Personal Jurisdiction Doctrine?

Personal jurisdiction doctrine evolved considerably after *Pennoyer* in response to society's increased mobility, and the doctrine faces similar challenges today. This time, instead of cars, courts have to struggle with a new form of interstate activity: the Internet. Although the United States Supreme Court has not yet tackled this issue, an increasing number of lower courts have addressed personal jurisdiction in the Internet context. The following case nicely illustrates the various issues that arise when trying to apply existing doctrine to a digital world.

READING *BURDICK v. SUPERIOR COURT.* The defendant (an Illinois resident) posted allegedly defamatory comments on Facebook about the plaintiffs (who were California residents). The question is whether the Facebook posts, which originated in Illinois, constituted a contact in California, given that the defendant knew that the plaintiffs resided there when posting the allegedly defamatory material. As you read the case, consider the following questions:

- Under what circumstances does Internet activity, such as a social media post, constitute a contact in a state? Is it enough for the defendant to know where a plaintiff resides at the time of the post? If not, what other factors are relevant when determining whether a defendant's social media communications constitute a contact in a state?
- Is it necessary to adopt a new approach to personal jurisdiction in order to resolve cases of this sort? Or is the existing *International Shoe* framework capable of resolving these cases?

BURDICK v. SUPERIOR COURT

233 Cal. App. 4th 8 (2015)

FYBEL, J.

INTRODUCTION

. . .

The plaintiffs in this case—John Sanderson and George Taylor (together, Plaintiffs **[EDS.—both California residents]**)—sued Douglas Burdick, an Illinois resident, for defamation and other intentional torts, based on an allegedly defamatory posting made by Burdick on his personal Facebook page while he was in Illinois. The respondent court denied Burdick's motion to quash service of summons for lack of personal jurisdiction, and Burdick has challenged that ruling by petition for writ of mandate or prohibition. **[EDS.—Normally, a party has to wait for a final judgment before appealing. A denial of a motion to quash service is not a final judgment, because the case continues after such a denial. But California allows a party to seek an interlocutory appeal (an appeal in the middle of the case) in limited circumstances, and this is one of those cases.]** . . .

ALLEGATIONS, JURISDICTIONAL FACTS, AND PROCEDURAL HISTORY

I. Allegations of the Complaint

Plaintiffs filed a verified complaint and a verified first amended complaint (the Complaint), naming as defendants Nerium International, LLC (Nerium International), Nerium Biotechnology, Inc. (Nerium Biotechnology), Nerium SkinCare, Inc. (Nerium SkinCare), Jeff Olson, and Burdick. The Complaint asserted six causes of action against Burdick, [including libel per se, defamation, slander and other intentional torts]. . . .

The Complaint alleged the following:

Nerium International and Nerium SkinCare are incorporated in Texas, and Nerium Biotechnology is incorporated in Canada. The Nerium Entities are involved in the research, development, advertising, marketing, and sale of a skin care product called NeriumAD. . . .

Olson is the chief executive officer of Nerium International, and Burdick is "another high-level and highly compensated representative of Nerium International and is the company's Corporate Consultant." Plaintiffs are physician-scientists and entrepreneurs. . . .

In June 2012, Plaintiffs began to question the science behind NeriumAD and published blog entries questioning its safety and efficacy and criticizing Nerium International's multilevel marketing organization. "In response to Plaintiffs' questioning of the science behind NeriumAD and criticisms of the Nerium organization,

Defendants engaged in a campaign of harassment and defamation against Plaintiffs to destroy their reputations using false and misleading information." . . .

Burdick, as his part of the campaign of harassment, in November 2012, posted on his Facebook page an announcement that "more scandalous information would be revealed regarding the 'Blogging Scorpions.' " The Facebook posting announcement stated that within a short period of time, new information would be posted on " '[w]hy he uses multiple social security numbers' and 'how many times he has been charged with domestic violence.' " Burdick posted those statements on Facebook "in his capacity as Corporate Consultant for Nerium International" and a person reading those statements would reasonably understand they referred to Sanderson or Taylor.

II. Motion to Quash Service of Summons

Burdick filed a motion to quash service of summons (the motion to quash), based on lack of personal jurisdiction. With the motion to quash, Burdick submitted his own declaration stating he is an independent contractor for Paradiselife, Inc., an Illinois corporation with its principal place of business in Illinois, through which he provides consulting services to Nerium International. Burdick declared he has been a resident of Illinois since 1971. He has never lived in California; maintained an office or been employed in California; had a bank account, safe deposit box, or mailing address in California; owned or leased real property in California; had employees in California; been a party to a contract with a person or entity in California; or held any licenses or certifications issued by any governmental agency or unit in California. Burdick declared he posted and later removed the allegedly defamatory Facebook posting from his personal Facebook page while he was in the State of Illinois.

Plaintiffs filed opposition to the motion to quash, which included a declaration (with exhibits) from Sanderson and a declaration from Plaintiffs' counsel. Sanderson declared that Burdick posted defamatory material on his "publicly-available Facebook wall." Among the exhibits attached to Sanderson's declaration was a print copy of the allegedly defamatory Facebook posting made by Burdick. That posting did not mention Sanderson or Taylor by name, but referred to a "Blogging scorpion, liar, terrorist, pretencer, amateur, wanna-be, con artist." . . . More to come shortly about the Truth and Facts about this 'Blogging Scorpion[ ]', things like: [(1)] Why he lost his medical license (yes we have the documents directly from the Medical Board of California) [(2)] Why he personally uses multiple social security numbers [(3)] How many times has he been charged with domestic violence [(4)] Why he makes medical claims about his product that is not FDA approved (yes we have the video of him making these medical claims publically) [(5)] And much much more! Stay tuned as we reveal the 'REAL' truth behind this 'Blogging Scorpion'."

The respondent court issued a minute order denying the motion to quash. After finding that all of Plaintiffs' claims against Burdick arose out of the Facebook posting, the respondent court concluded he was subject to personal jurisdiction under the "effects" test of *Calder v. Jones*. . . .

III. Writ Proceedings

Burdick filed a petition for peremptory writ of mandate/prohibition to challenge the respondent court's order denying his motion to quash service of summons. . . .

DISCUSSION

I. General Principles of Personal Jurisdiction

California courts may exercise jurisdiction over nonresidents "on any basis not inconsistent with the Constitution of this state or of the United States." (Code Civ. Proc., § 410.10.) . . .

A nonresident defendant may be subject to specific jurisdiction if three requirements are met: (1) the defendant has purposefully availed itself of forum benefits with respect to the matter in controversy; (2) the controversy is related to or arises out of the defendant's contacts with the forum; and (3) the exercise of jurisdiction would comport with fair play and substantial justice.

II. May California Exercise Specific Personal Jurisdiction over Burdick?

May specific jurisdiction be exercised over Burdick, an Illinois resident, based on his conduct related to the lawsuit, that is, his posting of the allegedly defamatory statements on his personal Facebook page? When, as in this case, intentional torts are alleged, "[a] forum State's exercise of jurisdiction over an out-of-state intentional tortfeasor must be based on intentional conduct by the defendant that creates the necessary contacts with the forum." (*Walden v. Fiore* (2014), 571 U.S. at p. —, 134 S. Ct. at p. 1123.)

A. The Effects Test

1. Calder

The respondent court concluded, and Plaintiffs argue, that Burdick is subject to specific jurisdiction under the effects test. The starting point for understanding the effects test is the United States Supreme Court decision in *Calder, supra,* 465 U.S. 783. In that case, Shirley Jones, a well-known actress living in California, brought a libel suit in California against a reporter and an editor for an allegedly defamatory article published in the National Enquirer, a national weekly publication with a circulation of about 600,000 in California. Both the reporter and the editor worked for the National Enquirer at its headquarters in Florida. . . .

The United States Supreme Court held that jurisdiction over the reporter and the editor in California was proper "based on the 'effects' of their Florida conduct in California." (*Calder, supra,* 465 U.S. at p. 789.) Those effects were felt in California because, the court explained, "[t]he allegedly libelous story concerned the California activities of a California resident. It impugned the professionalism of an entertainer whose television career was centered in California. The article was drawn from California sources, and the brunt of the harm, in terms both of respondent's emotional distress and the injury to her professional reputation, was suffered in California." (*Id.* at pp. 788–789.) "In sum," the court concluded, "California is the focal point both of the story and of the harm suffered." (*Id.* at p. 789.) The court noted too the intentional acts of the reporter and the editor "were expressly aimed at California" in that they wrote or edited an article "they knew would have a potentially devastating impact upon respondent" and "knew that the brunt of that injury would be felt by respondent in the State in which she lives and works and in which the National Enquirer has its largest circulation." (*Id.* at pp. 789–790.)

2. "Express Aiming" and Pavlovich

Courts have struggled with the import of *Calder* and have not applied the effects test uniformly. Most courts have agreed, nonetheless, that "merely asserting that a defendant knew or should have known that his intentional acts would cause harm in the forum state is not enough to establish jurisdiction under the effects test." (*Pavlovich v. Superior Court* (2002) 29 Cal.4th 262, 270–271.)

To narrow the potentially broad scope of *Calder* courts have interpreted the effects test as having an express aiming requirement and requiring the plaintiff to show (1) the defendant committed an intentional tort; (2) the plaintiff felt the brunt of the harm caused by that tort in the forum state such that the forum state was the focal point of the plaintiff's injury; and (3) the defendant expressly aimed the tortious conduct at the forum state such that the forum state was the focal point of the tortious activity. To satisfy the third prong, the plaintiff must show "the defendant knew that the plaintiff would suffer the brunt of the harm caused by the tortious conduct in the forum, and point to specific activity indicating that the defendant expressly aimed its tortious conduct at the forum." (*Id.* at p. 266.) . . .

3. Effects Test and the Internet-Based Defamation

Although *Pavlovich* made "express aiming or intentional targeting" (*Pavlovich,* supra, 29 Cal. 4th at p. 273) part of California personal jurisdiction law, it was not a defamation case. Courts in other jurisdictions, which have considered *Calder* and the effects test in defamation actions arising out of Internet posts and advertising, have held the "mere posting of information or advertisements on an Internet website does not confer nationwide personal jurisdiction." (*Remick v. Manfredy* (3d Cir. 2001) 238 F.3d 248, 259, fn. 3.) . . .

As summed up in *Gorman v. Jacobs* (E.D. Pa. 2009) 597 F. Supp. 2d 541, 548: ". . . Simply (a) knowing that the plaintiff is in the forum state, (b) posting negative statements about the plaintiff's forum-related activities, and (c) referring to the forum in one's writing will not suffice to satisfy the *Calder* effects test."

4. Walden

Recently, in *Walden, supra,* 571 U.S. ___, 134 S. Ct. 1115 the United States Supreme Court readdressed the personal jurisdiction analysis for intentional torts. . . .

The court confirmed that "[f]or a State to exercise jurisdiction consistent with due process, the defendant's suit-related conduct must create a substantial connection with the forum State." (*Id.* at p. 1121.) The court emphasized two concepts related to this principle. "First, the relationship must arise out of contacts that the 'defendant himself' creates with the forum State." (*Id.* at pp. 1121–1122.) The plaintiff's contacts with the forum "cannot be 'decisive.' " (*Id.* at p. 1122.) "Second, our 'minimum contacts' analysis looks to the defendant's contacts with the forum State itself, not the defendant's contacts with persons who reside there." (*Id.* at p. 1122.) The defendant's conduct "must form the necessary connection with the forum State that is the basis for its jurisdiction over him." (*Id.* at p. 1122.)

. . . After reviewing the nature of the contacts in *Calder,* the Supreme Court concluded: "The crux of *Calder* was that the reputation-based 'effects' of the alleged libel connected the defendants to California, not just to the plaintiff. The strength of that connection was largely a function of the nature of the libel tort. However scandalous a newspaper article might be, it can lead to a loss of reputation only if communicated to (and read and understood by) third persons. [Citations.] Accordingly, the reputational injury caused by the defendants' story would not have occurred but for the fact that the defendants wrote an article for publication in California that was read by a large number of California citizens. Indeed, because publication to third persons is a necessary element of libel [citation], the defendants' intentional tort actually occurred *in* California. [Citation.] In this way, the 'effects' caused by the defendants' article—*i.e.,* the injury to the plaintiff's reputation in the estimation of the California public—connected the defendants' conduct to *California,* not just to a plaintiff who lived there. That connection, combined with the various facts that gave the article a California focus, sufficed to authorize the California court's exercise of jurisdiction." (*Walden,* 134 S. Ct. at pp. 1123–1124.) The defendants in *Calder* " 'expressly aimed' " their intentional conduct at California because they knew the National Enquirer had its largest circulation in California and the article would " 'have a potentially devastating impact' there." (*Walden,* 134 S. Ct. at p. 1124, fn. 7.) . . .

B. Application of the Effects Test of Calder, Pavlovich, *and* Walden

Walden is not a defamation case, and the Supreme Court made clear that commission of intentional torts via the Internet presented some "very different questions" which it left "for another day." (*Walden, supra,* 134 S. Ct. at p. 1125, fn. 9.) Nonetheless, *Walden*'s essential teachings and its interpretation of *Calder* directly apply to this case. *Walden* teaches that the correct jurisdictional analysis focuses on (1) the defendant's contacts with the forum, not with the plaintiff, and (2) whether those contacts create "the relationship among the defendant, the forum, and the litigation" necessary to satisfy due process. (*Walden,* 134 S. Ct. at p. 1126.) And, "[t]he proper question is not where the plaintiff experienced a particular injury or effect but whether the defendant's conduct connects him to the forum in a meaningful way." (*Id.* at p. 1125.)

It is undisputed Burdick has no direct contacts with California. He is an Illinois resident, has never resided or worked in California, has never owned or leased property in the state, and, by all accounts, has been in the state only twice. He is a consultant for Nerium International, a Texas corporation which markets products throughout the country. The only conduct which might connect Burdick in a meaningful way with California was the allegedly defamatory posting on his Facebook page. As the trial court found, all of Plaintiffs' claims arise out of that posting.

. . .

The question under *Walden* is whether Burdick's "suit-related conduct"—the posting and removal of the allegedly defamatory Facebook post—created a "substantial connection" between Burdick and California. It is undisputed Burdick posted and removed that Facebook posting while he was in his home state of Illinois. Although it can be inferred from the posting itself that Burdick knew Plaintiffs resided in California and understood they would suffer any injury here, his knowledge that the posting could harm California residents is not enough in itself to support jurisdiction. The substantial connection required by *Walden* is not created by Plaintiffs having suffered injury in California: "The crux of *Calder* was that the reputation-based 'effects' of the alleged libel connected the defendants to California, not just to the plaintiff." (*Walden, supra,* at 134 S. Ct. at pp. 1123–1124.)

We agree with those cases holding that merely posting on the Internet negative comments about the plaintiff and knowing the plaintiff is in the forum state are insufficient to create minimum contacts. *Calder, Pavlovich,* and *Walden* emphasize the difference between conduct directed at the plaintiff and conduct directed at the forum state itself: Those cases require, in addition to intentional conduct causing harm to a forum resident, evidence the nonresident defendant expressly aimed or intentionally targeted his or her intentional conduct at the forum state. Plaintiffs did not produce evidence to show Burdick's personal Facebook page or the allegedly defamatory posting was expressly aimed or intentionally targeted at California, that either the Facebook page or the posting had a California audience, that any significant number of Facebook "friends," who might see the posting, lived in California, or that the Facebook page had advertisements targeting Californians. Sanderson declared that Burdick's Facebook page was "publicly-available," but that fact would mean it would have been less likely Burdick had intentionally targeted California as opposed to any other jurisdiction.

. . . Burdick declared he made the allegedly defamatory posting on his personal Facebook page while he was in Illinois. Neither Burdick's Facebook page nor the allegedly defamatory posting had a California focus like the defamatory article in *Calder.* The posting was about NeriumAD—a product sold throughout the country—and its critics. No evidence was presented that Burdick's Facebook page had its widest circulation, i.e., the greatest number of Facebook friends, in California, that Burdick expressly aimed his intentional conduct at California, or that Burdick knew the posting would cause harm connecting his conduct to California and not only to Plaintiffs.

. . . Plaintiffs did not produce evidence that Burdick expressly aimed or intentionally targeted his intentional conduct at California, rather than at them personally, and therefore failed to meet their burden of demonstrating facts justifying the exercise of personal jurisdiction over Burdick.

. . .

Notes and Questions: Understanding Personal Jurisdiction and the Internet

1. Analyzing personal jurisdiction in the Internet context. The key in these Internet cases seems to be—as it is in other personal jurisdiction cases—whether the defendant intentionally directed activity into the state and whether that activity gave rise to the cause of action in the case.

But what does it mean to intentionally direct Internet-related activity into a state? Analogizing to Supreme Court cases involving intentional torts (especially *Calder* and *Walden*), the *Burdick* court says that "merely posting on the Internet negative comments about the plaintiff and knowing the plaintiff is in the forum state are insufficient to create minimum contacts." There must be "evidence [that] the nonresident defendant expressly aimed or intentionally targeted his or her intentional conduct at the forum state."

So what more would Burdick have to do to establish a contact in California beyond knowing that the plaintiffs resided there? The court hints at an answer when it notes that Burdick's personal Facebook page was not expressly aimed at California and that neither his Facebook page nor the posting in question had a California audience. The court also noted that Burdick did not have a significant number of Facebook "friends" in California and that there was no evidence that Burdick's Facebook page had advertisements targeting Californians. In other words, Burdick might have had a contact in California if he had a large number of California Facebook friends, expressly noted in his post that the plaintiffs were in California and were engaged in misconduct there, or (perhaps) used hashtags in his post to generate viewers in California (e.g., #CaliforniaCrooks). No single factor would be decisive, but simply knowing that the subject of the social media post is in California is not enough to constitute a contact there. Burdick's post would have to target California more directly.

2. New wine in old bottles? Commentators have offered different predictions as to whether the Internet will produce new jurisdictional principles or simply require an application of existing doctrine to a new form of communication. *Compare* Martin H. Redish, *Of New Wine and Old Bottles: Personal Jurisdiction, the Internet, and the Nature of Constitutional Evolution,* 38 Jurimetrics J. 575 (1998) (suggesting that the Internet poses a problem for existing doctrine because of its unusual characteristics), *with* Catherine Ross Dunham, *Zippo-ing the Wrong Way: How the Internet Has Misdirected the Federal Courts in Their Personal Jurisdiction Analysis,* 43 U.S.F L. Rev. 559 (2011) (criticizing efforts to create new doctrinal approaches to personal jurisdiction in the Internet context); Allan R. Stein, *Personal Jurisdiction and the Internet: Seeing Due Process Through the Lens of Regulatory Precision,* 98 Nw. U. L. Rev. 411, 411 (2004) (arguing that the "Internet does not pose unique jurisdictional challenges"). It seems fair to say that most of the cases applying jurisdictional doctrine to the Internet look more like variations on a theme than a new jurisdictional construct. Given that *Calder* and other personal jurisdiction cases translate reasonably well to the Internet context, *International Shoe* seems secure, at least for the time being.

V. Issue Analysis

The following fact pattern appeared on one author's exam. A suggested analysis of the issues follows the question.

A. The Question

Burroughs Farm is a Canadian corporation that grows Christmas trees on a farm in Ontario, Canada, just north of the New Hampshire border. Each fall, Burroughs employees cut a new crop of trees and ship them to customers throughout the New England states.

Last fall, in late November, Rosales, the firm manager, received a call from Mistletoe Farms, a Massachusetts nursery that was a good customer for Burroughs's trees. Mistletoe needed an extra delivery of trees right away and asked Burroughs if it could fill the order for a premium price. Rosales agreed to do so but had a problem with delivering the trees because all of Burroughs's trucks were out making deliveries. So, Rosales called LeMarque, a Canadian friend who had a Canadian farm west of Burroughs, and asked if he would deliver the trees with his truck. LeMarque agreed to do so, being paid by the hour, and arrived the next morning to collect the trees. Brown, a Burroughs employee, loaded the trees on LeMarque's truck, which had wooden panel sides to hold the trees in place. The load was a big one, and the sides bulged a bit. Rosales noticed the bulge but gave LeMarque permission to proceed. She told LeMarque to drive through the nearby checkpoint on the Ontario/New Hampshire border and then south through New Hampshire. However, LeMarque had had a recent run-in with the police and was afraid that he might have trouble crossing into the United States. He knew a dirt road that ran off of his farm directly into Vermont without going through a Customs checkpoint, so he took that instead.

Twenty miles into Vermont the load on the truck seemed to shift. LeMarque wasn't sure the load was stable, so after checking the load, he called Rosales at the farm for advice. LeMarque told Rosales that he was in Vermont, headed due south. Rosales was annoyed to learn that LeMarque had gone through Vermont, but Rosales told LeMarque that the load was well secured and that LeMarque should continue on his current route. Five miles farther down the road one of the side rails on the truck broke, spilling trees into the roadway. Hidalgo, a Vermont citizen, drove into the trees and was seriously injured.

Hidalgo brought a negligence action in a Vermont state court against driver LeMarque; Burroughs Farm; the farm's manager, Rosales; and the farm's employee and loader, Brown. The lawsuit sought $200,000 in damages. After all of the defendants were properly served in Canada, all four defendants moved to dismiss Hidalgo's claims for lack of personal jurisdiction.

How should the court rule on the four motions? Assume that the relevant long arm statute authorizes the exercise of personal jurisdiction to the limits of due process under the Fourteenth Amendment.

B. A Suggested Analysis

Let's start with LeMarque's motion to dismiss. LeMarque purposefully drove into Vermont, and doing so was a deliberate contact with the state. Moreover, this claim arose directly out of that contact. Finally, all of the so-called reasonableness factors are satisfied here: Vermont has a strong interest in adjudicating the dispute there, because the accident occurred in Vermont; Hidalgo has a very strong interest in litigating in Vermont, where he is a citizen and was injured; and many of the witnesses and much of the evidence would be in Vermont, making it the most efficient location for the resolution of the controversy. Personal jurisdiction over LeMarque in Vermont would therefore be constitutional regardless of where LeMarque is now or where he was when he was served.

Brown's motion to dismiss is also straightforward, but with the opposite outcome. Brown loaded the trees in Ontario, but she did nothing to reach into Vermont to engage in activities there. She could probably foresee that LeMarque might drive the trees through Vermont—an easy alternate route from Ontario to Massachusetts. But foreseeing that LeMarque would reach into Vermont is not the same as Brown purposefully reaching into Vermont herself. *See World-Wide Volkswagen*. Because Brown had not engaged in any deliberate activity in Vermont, her motion to dismiss should be granted. (The result would be the same even if LeMarque had told Brown that LeMarque intended to drive through Vermont. The contact is still LeMarque's, not Brown's.)

The motion of the corporation, Burroughs Farm, is slightly more difficult to resolve, but it also should not be granted. Burroughs is not an in-state Vermont corporation (it is incorporated and has its farm in Ontario), so there is no basis for general in personam jurisdiction over Burroughs in Vermont.

But what about specific jurisdiction? When LeMarque drove through the state, he was working for Burroughs. His contacts in the course of working for the corporation will be attributed to the corporation. After all, other than incorporating in a state, a corporation can only make contacts with a state through those who conduct its activities, and that is what LeMarque did when he drove through Vermont. Even if Rosales didn't want LeMarque to go that way, LeMarque was still conducting Burroughs's business, so LeMarque's contact will subject both him and Burroughs Farm to personal jurisdiction for Hidalgo's claim.

The hardest issue is whether Rosales's motion should be granted. She had told LeMarque to drive through New Hampshire, not Vermont. LeMarque's decision to go through Vermont was his choice, not a deliberate contact by Rosales with Vermont. Thus, LeMarque's initial decision to drive through Vermont would not subject Rosales to personal jurisdiction for Hidalgo's claim. If the load had collapsed before LeMarque called Rosales, Rosales would be dismissed for lack of personal jurisdiction.

But that's not what happened. Here, the accident occurred after Rosales's conversation with LeMarque and his request for further instructions. During that call, Rosales told LeMarque that *he should proceed with driving the trees through Vermont*. Though it is a close question, I conclude that this instruction means that Rosales was purposefully directing activity in Vermont and thus has a contact there. Rosales knew that LeMarque was in Vermont and that, by instructing him to continue his journey there, Rosales would be imposing a risk on persons in

Vermont. It is hard to see how this instruction to LeMarque to continue on his path is different from Rosales telling LeMarque to drive through Vermont in the first place.

Rosales will claim that she never did anything in Vermont; she just answered a call from an employee who shouldn't have been there in the first place. Yet at the point Rosales ordered LeMarque to proceed, she was directing LeMarque's activity in Vermont and therefore had a purposeful contact there.

There may also be some debate about whether Rosales's contact in Vermont gave rise to Hidalgo's claim. The "but for" test would probably be satisfied, because the accident would not have happened but for Rosales's instruction to LeMarque to continue on his journey. (Rosales, for example, could have called a tow truck and ordered LeMarque to end his trip. She instead instructed LeMarque to continue his trip.) The evidence test is also likely satisfied. During the call, Rosales reiterated the safety of the truck, and LeMarque is likely to use Rosales's assertion as a defense against Hidalgo's claim. In particular, LeMarque is likely to argue that he is not at fault because he was relying on Rosales and the other defendants to secure the trees for transport and had been assured that the truck was safely loaded. Thus, Rosales's telephone conversation with LeMarque constitutes a contact with Vermont and that contact gave rise to Hidalgo's claim.

Finally, the reasonableness factors are satisfied here for the same reason that they were satisfied in the context of LeMarque's motion. Accordingly, Rosales's motion should be denied, and she should be subject to personal jurisdiction in Vermont.

VI. Specific Jurisdiction: Summary of Basic Principles

- A defendant is subject to specific jurisdiction if the defendant has purposeful contacts with the forum, the claim arises out of those contacts, and the exercise of personal jurisdiction would be fair and reasonable.
- All three requirements must be satisfied. Even if personal jurisdiction would be fair and reasonable in a particular forum, specific jurisdiction does not exist unless the claim arises out of the defendant's contacts in the forum. Similarly, contacts with the forum by themselves are not sufficient to confer specific jurisdiction unless the claim arose out of those contacts and jurisdiction is reasonable under the circumstances.
- A contact exists when defendants have purposefully availed themselves of the privileges and benefits of conducting activities in a particular forum. A plaintiff's or third party's contact with the forum is not sufficient to confer personal jurisdiction over the defendant. In some cases, like those involving the Internet or the "stream of commerce," the definition of a contact is still unclear.
- The Supreme Court has not yet articulated a clear standard for determining when a claim "arises out of" the defendant's contacts. Lower courts have

developed a range of approaches to this problem, including an "evidence" test and a "but for" test.

- In assessing whether personal jurisdiction would be fair under the third part of the test, a court must consider at least five factors: the burden on the defendant, the interests of the forum state, the plaintiff's interest in obtaining relief, the interstate judicial system's interest in obtaining the most efficient resolution of controversies, and the shared interest of the several states in furthering fundamental substantive social policies.
- If a claim arises out of a defendant's contacts, a court will very likely conclude that personal jurisdiction is established, even if some of the reasonableness factors are not satisfied.

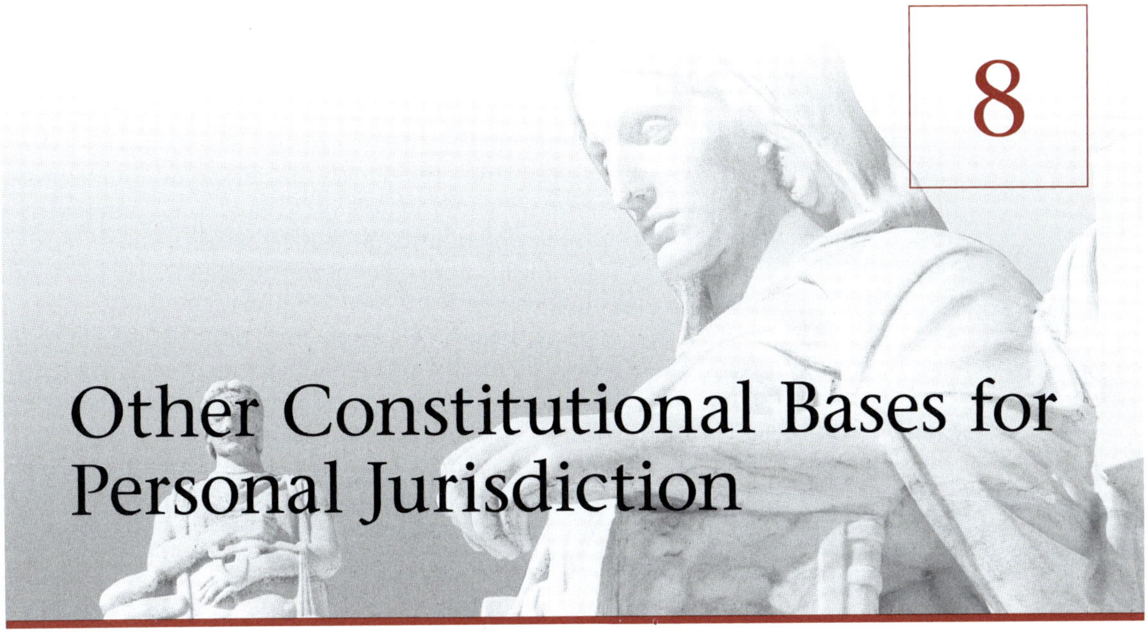

8

Other Constitutional Bases for Personal Jurisdiction

I. Introduction

Specific jurisdiction offers one basis for establishing personal jurisdiction, but there are a number of constitutionally permissible alternatives, including general in personam jurisdiction, quasi in rem jurisdiction, in rem jurisdiction, transient presence (also known as "tag" jurisdiction), consent, and waiver. This chapter covers those doctrines.

II. General In Personam Jurisdiction: *Daimler AG v. Bauman*

A. Distinguishing Specific and General Jurisdiction

The last chapter explained that a court can exercise specific jurisdiction over a defendant when the plaintiff's claim arises out of the defendant's deliberate in-state contacts and the exercise of jurisdiction is consistent with traditional notions of fair play and substantial justice. Under these circumstances, the claim is "specific" to the defendant's in-state contacts.

In contrast, general jurisdiction allows courts to exercise personal jurisdiction over a defendant for claims having nothing to do with the defendant's contacts in the forum. This "general" personal jurisdiction authority, however, comes with a catch. Before a court can exercise it, defendants must have much more extensive contacts in the forum state. "Minimum" contacts do not suffice.

This distinction raises an obvious question: How much more extensive do the contacts need to be before a court can exercise general jurisdiction? The Supreme Court has held that, for corporate defendants, the contacts must be sufficiently extensive that the defendant is "essentially at home in the forum State." *Goodyear Dunlop Tires Operations, S.A. v. Brown*, 564 U.S. 915, 919 (2011). Analogously, when the defendant is an individual, the requisite contacts exist wherever the individual is domiciled. *Goodyear*, 564 U.S. at 921. The chart below illustrates this basic distinction between specific and general jurisdiction.

	Specific Jurisdiction	**General Jurisdiction**
Requirements for Establishing This Form of Jurisdiction	Each of the claims must arise out of the defendant's deliberate contacts with the forum ("minimum contacts"), and the exercise of jurisdiction must otherwise be consistent with traditional notions of fair play and substantial justice	The defendant's contacts are sufficiently extensive that the defendant would be considered "at home" in the state (for corporations) or domiciled there (for individuals)*
Claims over Which the Court's Personal Jurisdiction Extends	Only those claims arising out of the defendant's in-state contacts	Any claim that the plaintiff has against the defendant

FIGURE 8–1: DISTINGUISHING SPECIFIC AND GENERAL JURISDICTION

For example, imagine that Damage, Inc. is incorporated and has its principal place of business in Ohio. Assume that Peter is injured in Indiana by a product

* Until recently, there was some disagreement over whether general jurisdiction requires an examination of the so-called reasonableness factors discussed in the previous chapter. In the case excerpted below, the Supreme Court offered some clarity, explaining that "[w]hen a corporation is genuinely at home in the forum State, . . . any second-step inquiry [into the reasonableness of personal jurisdiction] would be superfluous." *Daimler AG v. Bauman*, 571 U.S. 117, 139 n.20 (2014). Thus, an analysis of the reasonableness factors is not necessary in this context.

that Damage designed, manufactured, and sold only in Indiana. Also assume that, instead of suing in Indiana, Peter sues Damage in *Ohio*, because Peter recently moved to that state. The Ohio court does not have specific jurisdiction over this claim, because the claim does not arise out of anything that Damage did in Ohio.

But there is an alternative to specific jurisdiction: *general jurisdiction*. Because Damage's corporate headquarters and principal place of business are in Ohio, Damage is essentially "at home" there. The Ohio court can thus exercise personal jurisdiction over any claim that a plaintiff might have against Damage, even a claim (such as Peter's) that arose entirely in Indiana.

B. Why Is General Jurisdiction Fair?

Personal jurisdiction exists to protect a party's constitutional right to due process, and that right is violated when a party is forced to litigate in an unfair forum. Indiana would be a fair forum in the above example, because that is where the defendant's contacts gave rise to the plaintiff's injuries.

But why is it also fair for an *Ohio* court to exercise personal jurisdiction over Damage? The answer isn't entirely clear, even after the *Daimler* case, below. One possible answer is that, if a corporate defendant is effectively "at home" in the forum state (as Damage is in Ohio, based on its incorporation and principal place of business there), it is not much of a burden to defend a case there, even if the case arose elsewhere. Personal jurisdiction also appears to make sense under these circumstances for reasons that trace back to *Pennoyer*. Namely, a court has the authority to exercise jurisdiction over people and property within the court's territory. A corporation that is "at home" in a state is arguably "within" the state for jurisdictional purposes. The same can be said for individuals who are domiciled in the forum.

C. General Jurisdiction over Corporations

The doctrine of general jurisdiction as applied to corporations is simply stated: General jurisdiction exists wherever the corporation is "at home." The term "at home," however, is not self-defining, as the following case makes clear.

READING *DAIMLER AG v. BAUMAN*. *Daimler* is one of the few modern United States Supreme Court cases to discuss general jurisdiction in any detail. As a result, the Court has to refer back to two older cases and a more recent one to explain the concept.

In one older case, *Perkins v. Benguet Consolidated Mining Co.*, 342 U.S. 437 (1952), the president of a company maintained an office in Ohio from which he conducted company-related activities, such as keeping corporate files and holding directors' meetings. The Court concluded that the company, which was based in the Philippines, "[had] been carrying on in Ohio a continuous and systematic, but limited, part of its general business" and that what we now call general jurisdiction was "reasonable and just." *Id.* at 438.

In contrast, in *Helicopteros Nacionales de Colombia, S.A. v. Hall*, 466 U.S. 408 (1984), the corporate defendant had a number of contacts in Texas, including "sending its chief executive officer to Houston for a contract-negotiation session; accepting into its New York bank account checks drawn on a Houston bank; purchasing helicopters, equipment, and training services from [a Texas company] for substantial sums; and sending personnel to ... facilities in Fort Worth for training." *Id.* at 416. Nevertheless, the Court concluded that those contacts were not sufficiently continuous or systematic to warrant subjecting the company to general jurisdiction in Texas. In sum, regular contacts were not enough; the contacts had to be more extensive.

Finally, in *Goodyear Dunlop Tires Operations, S.A. v. Brown*, 564 U.S. 915 (2011), the Supreme Court considered whether a North Carolina court could exercise general jurisdiction over three foreign subsidiaries of Goodyear on the grounds that those subsidiaries manufactured tires that were sold in North Carolina. (The suit did not arise out of those North Carolina sales, so the only basis for personal jurisdiction in North Carolina over the subsidiaries was general jurisdiction.) The Court concluded that it was unconstitutional to exercise general jurisdiction under these circumstances, reasoning that general jurisdiction is appropriate only when a corporation is "at home" in the forum state and that the foreign subsidiaries were most certainly not "at home" in North Carolina. *Goodyear Dunlop Tires Operations, S.A. v. Brown*, 564 U.S. 929 (2011).

Goodyear was the first case in which the Supreme Court emphasized the "at home" formulation, and many people wondered whether it reflected a tightening of the general jurisdiction doctrine. Prior to *Goodyear*, most courts had assumed that general jurisdiction existed if the defendant merely had "continuous and systematic" contacts in the forum state. The *Goodyear* Court seemed to signal that "continuous and systematic" contacts were no longer sufficient for general jurisdiction and that general jurisdiction required a more extensive connection to the state (i.e., that the company had to be effectively "at home" in the forum state).

Fortunately, the Court decided another case—*Daimler AG v. Bauman*—not long after *Goodyear*, and it sheds more light on this issue. Consider the following questions as you read *Daimler*:

- When is a company considered to be "at home" in a state for purposes of general jurisdiction?
- Is the "at home" test narrower than the "continuous and systematic" contacts test? If so, how?
- What contacts did Daimler have in California? Why does the answer to this question turn on Daimler's relationship to one of its subsidiaries?
- Why were Daimler's contacts insufficient to subject it to general jurisdiction in California?

Ruth Bader Ginsburg

Collection of the Supreme Court of the United States

Ruth Bader Ginsburg (1933-2020) was born and raised in New York City. She attended Cornell University, where she graduated first in her college class. She entered Harvard Law School in 1956, one of nine women in an entering class of 500. Continuing an impressive procession of "firsts," she was the first woman invited to join the Harvard Law Review. When her husband took a job in New York City, she transferred to Columbia, where she was invited to join the Columbia Law Review—making her the first woman to serve on two major law reviews. She shared first place in her Columbia Law School class.

After law school, she clerked for Judge Edmund Palmieri of the United States District Court for the Southern District of New York, after United States Supreme Court Justice Felix Frankfurter declined to appoint her as a law clerk because of her gender. She then returned to Columbia to serve as director of the Columbia Law School Project on International Procedure. There, she learned Swedish in order to coauthor a book on judicial procedure in Sweden. She then taught law at Rutgers from 1963 to 1972 and at Columbia, where she became the first woman tenured on the law faculty, from 1972 until 1980.

While at Rutgers, Justice Ginsburg co-founded the Women's Rights Law Journal, the first law journal to focus exclusively on women's rights, and during her Columbia years she coauthored the first law school casebook on gender discrimination. She also cofounded the Women's Rights Project of the American Civil Liberties Union, and became General Counsel of the ACLU in 1973. In that capacity, she argued six major gender discrimination cases before the United States Supreme Court.

She was nominated to the United States Court of Appeals for the District of Columbia Circuit in 1980 by President Jimmy Carter, and to the United States Supreme Court by President Bill Clinton in 1993. She passed away in 2020 after serving 27 years on the Court. Doubtless, as a veteran teacher and student of Civil Procedure, she relished the chance to create civil procedure law in cases like *Daimler* (below).

DAIMLER AG v. BAUMAN

571 U.S. 117 (2014)

Justice GINSBURG delivered the opinion of the Court.

This case concerns the authority of a court in the United States to entertain a claim brought by foreign plaintiffs against a foreign defendant based on events occurring entirely outside the United States. The litigation commenced in 2004, when twenty-two Argentinian residents filed a complaint in the United States District Court for the Northern District of California against DaimlerChrysler Aktiengesellschaft (Daimler), a German public stock company, headquartered in Stuttgart, that manufactures Mercedes–Benz vehicles in Germany. The complaint alleged that during Argentina's 1976–1983 "Dirty War," Daimler's Argentinian subsidiary, Mercedes–Benz Argentina (MB Argentina) collaborated with state security forces to kidnap, detain, torture, and kill certain MB Argentina workers, among them, plaintiffs or persons closely related to plaintiffs. Damages for the alleged human-rights violations were sought from Daimler under the laws of the United States, California, and Argentina. Jurisdiction over the lawsuit was predicated on the California contacts of Mercedes–Benz USA, LLC (MBUSA), a subsidiary of Daimler incorporated in Delaware with its principal place of business in New Jersey. MBUSA distributes Daimler-manufactured vehicles to independent dealerships throughout the United States, including California.

The question presented is whether the Due Process Clause of the Fourteenth Amendment precludes the District Court from exercising jurisdiction over Daimler in this case, given the absence of any California connection to the atrocities, perpetrators, or victims described in the complaint. Plaintiffs invoked the court's general or all-purpose jurisdiction. California, they urge, is a place where Daimler may be sued on any and all claims against it, wherever in the world the claims may arise. For example, as plaintiffs' counsel affirmed, under the proffered jurisdictional theory, if a Daimler-manufactured vehicle overturned in Poland, injuring a Polish driver and passenger, the injured parties could maintain a design defect suit in California. Exercises of personal jurisdiction so exorbitant, we hold, are barred by due process constraints on the assertion of adjudicatory authority.

In *Goodyear Dunlop Tires Operations, S.A. v. Brown*, 564 U.S. __ (2011), we addressed the distinction between general or all-purpose jurisdiction, and specific or conduct-linked jurisdiction. As to the former, we held that a court may assert jurisdiction over a foreign corporation "to hear any and all claims against [it]" only when the corporation's affiliations with the State in which suit is brought are so constant and pervasive "as to render [it] essentially at home in the forum State." *Id.*, at __ (slip op., at 2). Instructed by *Goodyear*, we conclude Daimler is not "at home" in California, and cannot be sued there for injuries plaintiffs attribute to MB Argentina's conduct in Argentina.

I

In 2004, plaintiffs (respondents here) filed suit in the United States District Court for the Northern District of California, alleging that MB Argentina collaborated with Argentinian state security forces to kidnap, detain, torture, and kill plaintiffs and their relatives during the military dictatorship in place there from 1976 through 1983, a period known as Argentina's "Dirty War." Based on those allegations, plaintiffs asserted claims under the Alien Tort Statute, 28 U.S.C. § 1350, and the Torture Victim Protection Act of 1991, 106 Stat. 73, note following 28 U.S.C.

§ 1350, as well as claims for wrongful death and intentional infliction of emotional distress under the laws of California and Argentina. The incidents recounted in the complaint center on MB Argentina's plant in Gonzalez Catan, Argentina; no part of MB Argentina's alleged collaboration with Argentinian authorities took place in California or anywhere else in the United States.

Plaintiffs' operative complaint names only one corporate defendant: Daimler, the petitioner here. Plaintiffs seek to hold Daimler vicariously liable for MB Argentina's alleged malfeasance. Daimler is a German *Aktiengesellschaft* (public stock company) that manufactures Mercedes–Benz vehicles in Germany and has its headquarters in Stuttgart. At times relevant to this case, MB Argentina was a subsidiary wholly owned by Daimler's predecessor in interest.

Daimler moved to dismiss the action for want of personal jurisdiction. Opposing the motion, plaintiffs submitted declarations and exhibits purporting to demonstrate the presence of Daimler itself in California. Alternatively, plaintiffs maintained that jurisdiction over Daimler could be founded on the California contacts of MBUSA, a distinct corporate entity that, according to plaintiffs, should be treated as Daimler's agent for jurisdictional purposes.

MBUSA, an indirect subsidiary of Daimler, is a Delaware limited liability corporation. MBUSA serves as Daimler's exclusive importer and distributor in the United States, purchasing Mercedes–Benz automobiles from Daimler in Germany, then importing those vehicles, and ultimately distributing them to independent dealerships located throughout the Nation. Although MBUSA's principal place of business is in New Jersey, MBUSA has multiple California-based facilities, including a regional office in Costa Mesa, a Vehicle Preparation Center in Carson, and a Classic Center in Irvine. According to the record developed below, MBUSA is the largest supplier of luxury vehicles to the California market. In particular, over 10% of all sales of new vehicles in the United States take place in California, and MBUSA's California sales account for 2.4% of Daimler's worldwide sales.

The relationship between Daimler and MBUSA is delineated in a General Distributor Agreement, which sets forth requirements for MBUSA's distribution of Mercedes–Benz vehicles in the United States. That agreement established MBUSA as an "independent contracto[r]" that "buy[s] and sell[s] [vehicles] . . . as an independent business for [its] own account." App. 179a. The agreement "does not make [MBUSA] . . . a general or special agent, partner, joint venturer or employee of DAIMLERCHRYSLER or any DaimlerChrysler Group Company"; MBUSA "ha[s] no authority to make binding obligations for or act on behalf of DAIMLERCHRYSLER or any DaimlerChrysler Group Company." *Ibid.*

After allowing jurisdictional discovery on plaintiffs' agency allegations, the District Court granted Daimler's motion to dismiss. Daimler's own affiliations with California, the court first determined, were insufficient to support the exercise of all-purpose jurisdiction over the corporation. Next, the court declined to attribute MBUSA's California contacts to Daimler on an agency theory, concluding that plaintiffs failed to demonstrate that MBUSA acted as Daimler's agent.

The Ninth Circuit at first affirmed the District Court's judgment. Addressing solely the question of agency, the Court of Appeals held that plaintiffs had not shown the existence of an agency relationship of the kind that might warrant attribution of MBUSA's contacts to Daimler. Judge Reinhardt dissented. In his view, the agency test was satisfied and considerations of "reasonableness" did not bar the exercise of jurisdiction. Granting plaintiffs' petition for rehearing, the panel withdrew its initial opinion and replaced it with one authored by Judge Reinhardt, which elaborated on reasoning he initially expressed in dissent.

Daimler petitioned for rehearing and rehearing en banc, urging that the exercise of personal jurisdiction over Daimler could not be reconciled with this Court's decision in *Goodyear*. Over the dissent of eight judges, the Ninth Circuit denied Daimler's petition.

We granted certiorari to decide whether, consistent with the Due Process Clause of the Fourteenth Amendment, Daimler is amenable to suit in California courts for claims involving only foreign plaintiffs and conduct occurring entirely abroad. 569 U.S. __ (2013).

II

Federal courts ordinarily follow state law in determining the bounds of their jurisdiction over persons. See Fed. Rule Civ. Proc. 4(k)(1)(A) (service of process is effective to establish personal jurisdiction over a defendant "who is subject to the jurisdiction of a court of general jurisdiction in the state where the district court is located"). Under California's long-arm statute, California state courts may exercise personal jurisdiction "on any basis not inconsistent with the Constitution of this state or of the United States." Cal. Civ. Proc. Code Ann. § 410.10 (West 2004). California's long-arm statute allows the exercise of personal jurisdiction to the full extent permissible under the U.S. Constitution. We therefore inquire whether the Ninth Circuit's holding comports with the limits imposed by federal due process.

III

In *Pennoyer v. Neff*, 95 U.S. 714, 24 L. Ed. 565 (1878), decided shortly after the enactment of the Fourteenth Amendment, the Court held that a tribunal's jurisdiction over persons reaches no farther than the geographic bounds of the forum. See *id.*, at 720 ("The authority of every tribunal is necessarily restricted by the territorial limits of the State in which it is established."). In time, however, that strict territorial approach yielded to a less rigid understanding, spurred by "changes in the technology of transportation and communication, and the tremendous growth of interstate business activity." *Burnham v. Superior Court of Cal., County of Marin*, 495 U.S. 604, 617 (1990) (opinion of Scalia, J.).

"The canonical opinion in this area remains *International Shoe*, in which we held that a State may authorize its courts to exercise personal jurisdiction over an out-of-state defendant if the defendant has 'certain minimum contacts with [the State] such that the maintenance of the suit does not offend "traditional notions of fair play and substantial justice.' " *Goodyear,* 564 U.S., at __ (slip op., at 6) (quoting *International Shoe,* 326 U.S., at 316)....

International Shoe's conception of "fair play and substantial justice" presaged the development of two categories of personal jurisdiction. The first category is represented by *International Shoe* itself, a case in which the in-state activities of the corporate defendant "ha[d] not only been continuous and systematic, but also g[a]ve rise to the liabilities sued on." 326 U.S., at 317. *International Shoe* recognized, as well, that "the commission of some single or occasional acts of the corporate agent in a state" may sometimes be enough to subject the corporation to jurisdiction in that State's tribunals with respect to suits relating to that in-state activity. *Id.,* at 318. Adjudicatory authority of this order, in which the suit "aris[es] out of or relate[s] to the defendant's contacts with the forum," *Helicopteros Nacionales de Colombia, S.A. v. Hall,* 466 U.S. 408, 414, n.8, 104 S. Ct. 1868, 80 L. Ed. 2d 404 (1984), is today called "specific jurisdiction." See *Goodyear,* 564 U.S., at __ (slip op., at 7).

International Shoe distinguished between, on the one hand, exercises of specific jurisdiction, as just described, and on the other, situations where a foreign corporation's "continuous corporate operations within a state [are] so substantial and of such a nature as to justify suit against it on causes of action arising from dealings entirely distinct from those activities." 326 U.S., at 318. As we have since explained, "[a] court may assert general jurisdiction over foreign (sister-state or foreign-country) corporations to hear any and all claims against them when their affiliations with the State are so 'continuous and systematic' as to render them essentially at home in the forum State." *Goodyear,* 564 U.S., at __ (slip op., at 2); see id., at __ (slip op., at 7); *Helicopteros,* 466 U.S., at 414, n.9.[5]

Since *International Shoe,* "specific jurisdiction has become the centerpiece of modern jurisdiction theory, while general jurisdiction [has played] a reduced role." *Goodyear,* 564 U.S., at __ (slip op., at 8) (quoting Twitchell, The Myth of General Jurisdiction, 101 Harv. L. Rev. 610, 628 (1988)). *International Shoe*'s momentous departure from *Pennoyer*'s rigidly territorial focus, we have noted, unleashed a rapid expansion of tribunals' ability to hear claims against out-of-state defendants when the episode-in-suit occurred in the forum or the defendant purposefully availed itself of the forum.

Our post-*International Shoe* opinions on general jurisdiction, by comparison, are few. "[The Court's] 1952 decision in *Perkins v. Benguet Consol. Mining Co.* remains the textbook case of general jurisdiction appropriately exercised over a

---

5. Colloquy at oral argument illustrated the respective provinces of general and specific jurisdiction over persons. Two hypothetical scenarios were posed: *First,* if a California plaintiff, injured in a California accident involving a Daimler-manufactured vehicle, sued Daimler in California court alleging that the vehicle was defectively designed, that court's adjudicatory authority would be premised on specific jurisdiction. See Tr. of Oral Arg. 11 (Daimler's counsel acknowledged that specific jurisdiction "may well be ... available" in such a case, depending on whether Daimler purposefully availed itself of the forum). *Second,* if a similar accident took place in Poland and injured Polish plaintiffs sued Daimler in California court, the question would be one of general jurisdiction. See *id.,* at 29 (on plaintiffs' view, Daimler would be amenable to such a suit in California).

foreign corporation that has not consented to suit in the forum." *Goodyear*, 564 U.S., at ___ (slip op., at 11). The defendant in *Perkins*, Benguet, was a company incorporated under the laws of the Philippines, where it operated gold and silver mines. Benguet ceased its mining operations during the Japanese occupation of the Philippines in World War II; its president moved to Ohio, where he kept an office, maintained the company's files, and oversaw the company's activities. *Perkins v. Benguet Consol. Mining Co.*, 342 U.S. 437, 448 (1952). The plaintiff, an Ohio resident, sued Benguet on a claim that neither arose in Ohio nor related to the corporation's activities in that State. We held that the Ohio courts could exercise general jurisdiction over Benguet without offending due process. *Ibid.* That was so, we later noted, because "Ohio was the corporation's principal, if temporary, place of business." *Keeton v. Hustler Magazine, Inc.*, 465 U.S. 770, 780, n.11 (1984).[8]

The next case on point, *Helicopteros*, 466 U.S. 408, arose from a helicopter crash in Peru. Four U.S. citizens perished in that accident; their survivors and representatives brought suit in Texas state court against the helicopter's owner and operator, a Colombian corporation. That company's contacts with Texas were confined to "sending its chief executive officer to Houston for a contract-negotiation session; accepting into its New York bank account checks drawn on a Houston bank; purchasing helicopters, equipment, and training services from [a Texas-based helicopter company] for substantial sums; and sending personnel to [Texas] for training." *Id.*, at 416. Notably, those contacts bore no apparent relationship to the accident that gave rise to the suit. We held that the company's Texas connections did not resemble the "continuous and systematic general business contacts . . . found to exist in *Perkins*." *Ibid.* "[M]ere purchases, even if occurring at regular intervals," we clarified, "are not enough to warrant a State's assertion of in personam jurisdiction over a nonresident corporation in a cause of action not related to those purchase transactions." *Id.*, at 418.

Most recently, in *Goodyear*, we answered the question: "Are foreign subsidiaries of a United States parent corporation amenable to suit in state court on claims

---

8. Selectively referring to the trial court record in *Perkins* (as summarized in an opinion of the intermediate appellate court), Justice Sotomayor posits that Benguet may have had extensive operations in places other than Ohio. **[Eds.—We have omitted Justice Sotomayor's concurrence.]** Justice Sotomayor's account overlooks this Court's opinion in *Perkins* and the point on which that opinion turned: All of Benguet's activities were directed by the company's president from within Ohio. See *Perkins v. Benguet Consol. Mining Co.*, 342 U.S. 437, 447–448 (1952) (company's Philippine mining operations "were completely halted during the occupation . . . by the Japanese"; and the company's president, from his Ohio office, "supervised policies dealing with the rehabilitation of the corporation's properties in the Philippines and . . . dispatched funds to cover purchases of machinery for such rehabilitation"). . . . Given the wartime circumstances, Ohio could be considered "a surrogate for the place of incorporation or head office."

Justice Sotomayor emphasizes *Perkins'* statement that Benguet's Ohio contacts, while "continuous and systematic," were but a "limited . . . part of its general business." 342 U.S., at 438. Describing the company's "wartime activities" as "necessarily limited," *id.*, at 448, however, this Court had in mind the diminution in operations resulting from the Japanese occupation and the ensuing shutdown of the company's Philippine mines. No fair reader of the full opinion in *Perkins* could conclude that the Court meant to convey anything other than that Ohio was the center of the corporation's wartime activities.

unrelated to any activity of the subsidiaries in the forum State?" 564 U.S., at __ (slip op., at 1). That case arose from a bus accident outside Paris that killed two boys from North Carolina. The boys' parents brought a wrongful-death suit in North Carolina state court alleging that the bus's tire was defectively manufactured. The complaint named as defendants not only The Goodyear Tire and Rubber Company (Goodyear), an Ohio corporation, but also Goodyear's Turkish, French, and Luxembourgian subsidiaries. Those foreign subsidiaries, which manufactured tires for sale in Europe and Asia, lacked any affiliation with North Carolina. A small percentage of tires manufactured by the foreign subsidiaries were distributed in North Carolina, however, and on that ground, the North Carolina Court of Appeals held the subsidiaries amenable to the general jurisdiction of North Carolina courts.

We reversed, observing that the North Carolina court's analysis "elided the essential difference between case-specific and all-purpose (general) jurisdiction." *Id.*, at __ (slip op., at 10). Although the placement of a product into the stream of commerce "may bolster an affiliation germane to specific jurisdiction," we explained, such contacts "do not warrant a determination that, based on those ties, the forum has general jurisdiction over a defendant." *Id.*, at __ (slip op., at 10–11). As *International Shoe* itself teaches, a corporation's "continuous activity of some sorts within a state is not enough to support the demand that the corporation be amenable to suits unrelated to that activity." 326 U.S., at 318. Because *Goodyear*'s foreign subsidiaries were "in no sense at home in North Carolina," we held, those subsidiaries could not be required to submit to the general jurisdiction of that State's courts. 564 U.S., at __ (slip op., at 13).

As is evident from *Perkins*, *Helicopteros*, and *Goodyear*, general and specific jurisdiction have followed markedly different trajectories post-*International Shoe*. Specific jurisdiction has been cut loose from *Pennoyer*'s sway, but we have declined to stretch general jurisdiction beyond limits traditionally recognized. As this Court has increasingly trained on the "relationship among the defendant, the forum, and the litigation," *Shaffer*, 433 U.S., at 204, i.e., *specific* jurisdiction, general jurisdiction has come to occupy a less dominant place in the contemporary scheme.[11]

IV

With this background, we turn directly to the question whether Daimler's affiliations with California are sufficient to subject it to the general (all-purpose) personal jurisdiction of that State's courts. In the proceedings below, the parties agreed on, or failed to contest, certain points we now take as given. Plaintiffs have never attempted to fit this case into the *specific* jurisdiction category. Nor did plaintiffs challenge on appeal the District Court's holding that Daimler's own

11. As the Court made plain in *Goodyear* and repeats here, general jurisdiction requires affiliations "so 'continuous and systematic' as to render [the foreign corporation] essentially at home in the forum State." 564 U.S., at __ (slip op., at 2), *i.e.*, comparable to a domestic enterprise in that State.

contacts with California were, by themselves, too sporadic to justify the exercise of general jurisdiction. While plaintiffs ultimately persuaded the Ninth Circuit to impute MBUSA's California contacts to Daimler on an agency theory, at no point have they maintained that MBUSA is an alter ego of Daimler.

Daimler, on the other hand, failed to object below to plaintiffs' assertion that the California courts could exercise all-purpose jurisdiction over MBUSA.[12] We will assume then, for purposes of this decision only, that MBUSA qualifies as at home in California.

A

In sustaining the exercise of general jurisdiction over Daimler, the Ninth Circuit relied on an agency theory, determining that MBUSA acted as Daimler's agent for jurisdictional purposes and then attributing MBUSA's California contacts to Daimler. The Ninth Circuit's agency analysis derived from Circuit precedent considering principally whether the subsidiary "performs services that are sufficiently important to the foreign corporation that if it did not have a representative to perform them, the corporation's own officials would undertake to perform substantially similar services." 644 F.3d, at 920 (quoting *Doe v. Unocal Corp.*, 248 F.3d 915, 928 (C.A.9 2001); emphasis deleted).

This Court has not yet addressed whether a foreign corporation may be subjected to a court's general jurisdiction based on the contacts of its in-state subsidiary. Daimler argues, and several Courts of Appeals have held, that a subsidiary's jurisdictional contacts can be imputed to its parent only when the former is so dominated by the latter as to be its alter ego. The Ninth Circuit adopted a less rigorous test based on what it described as an "agency" relationship. Agencies, we note, come in many sizes and shapes: "One may be an agent for some business purposes and not others so that the fact that one may be an agent for one purpose does not make him or her an agent for every purpose." 2A C.J.S., Agency § 43, p. 367 (2013) (footnote omitted).[13] A subsidiary, for example, might be its parent's agent for claims arising in the place where the subsidiary operates, yet not its agent regarding claims arising elsewhere. The Court of Appeals did not advert to that prospect. But we need not pass judgment on invocation of an agency theory in the context of general jurisdiction, for in no event can the appeals court's analysis be sustained.

The Ninth Circuit's agency finding rested primarily on its observation that MBUSA's services were "important" to Daimler, as gauged by Daimler's hypothetical readiness to perform those services itself if MBUSA did not exist. Formulated this way, the inquiry into importance stacks the deck, for it will always yield a pro-jurisdiction answer: "Anything a corporation does through an independent contractor, subsidiary, or distributor is presumably something that the corporation

---

12. MBUSA is not a defendant in this case.

13. Agency relationships, we have recognized, may be relevant to the existence of *specific* jurisdiction . . . .

would do 'by other means' if the independent contractor, subsidiary, or distributor did not exist." 676 F.3d, at 777 (O'Scannlain, J., dissenting from denial of rehearing en banc). The Ninth Circuit's agency theory thus appears to subject foreign corporations to general jurisdiction whenever they have an in-state subsidiary or affiliate, an outcome that would sweep beyond even the "sprawling view of general jurisdiction" we rejected in *Goodyear.* 564 U.S., at __ (slip op., at 12).

B

Even if we were to assume that MBUSA is at home in California, and further to assume MBUSA's contacts are imputable to Daimler, there would still be no basis to subject Daimler to general jurisdiction in California, for Daimler's slim contacts with the State hardly render it at home there.

Goodyear made clear that only a limited set of affiliations with a forum will render a defendant amenable to all-purpose jurisdiction there. "For an individual, the paradigm forum for the exercise of general jurisdiction is the individual's domicile; for a corporation, it is an equivalent place, one in which the corporation is fairly regarded as at home." 564 U.S., at __ (slip op., at 7). With respect to a corporation, the place of incorporation and principal place of business are "paradig[m] ... bases for general jurisdiction." *Id.*, at 735. Those affiliations have the virtue of being unique—that is, each ordinarily indicates only one place—as well as easily ascertainable. Cf. *Hertz Corp. v. Friend*, 559 U.S. 77, 94 (2010) ("Simple jurisdictional rules ... promote greater predictability."). These bases afford plaintiffs recourse to at least one clear and certain forum in which a corporate defendant may be sued on any and all claims.

Goodyear did not hold that a corporation may be subject to general jurisdiction *only* in a forum where it is incorporated or has its principal place of business; it simply typed those places paradigm all-purpose forums. Plaintiffs would have us look beyond the exemplar bases *Goodyear* identified, and approve the exercise of general jurisdiction in every State in which a corporation "engages in a substantial, continuous, and systematic course of business." Brief for Respondents 16–17, and nn.7–8. That formulation, we hold, is unacceptably grasping.

As noted, the words "continuous and systematic" were used in *International Shoe* to describe instances in which the exercise of *specific* jurisdiction would be appropriate. See 326 U.S., at 317 (jurisdiction can be asserted where a corporation's in-state activities are not only "continuous and systematic, but also give rise to the liabilities sued on").[17] Turning to all-purpose jurisdiction, in contrast, *International Shoe* speaks of "instances in which the continuous corporate operations within a state [are] so substantial and of such a nature as to justify suit ... *on causes of action arising from dealings entirely distinct from those activities.*" *Id.*, at 318 (emphasis added). See also Twitchell, Why We Keep Doing Business With

17. *International Shoe* also recognized, as noted above, that "some single or occasional acts of the corporate agent in a state ..., because of their nature and quality and the circumstances of their commission, may be deemed sufficient to render the corporation liable to suit." 326 U.S., at 318.

Doing-Business Jurisdiction, 2001 U. Chi. Legal Forum 171, 184 (*International Shoe* "is clearly not saying that dispute-blind jurisdiction exists whenever 'continuous and systematic' contacts are found."). Accordingly, the inquiry under *Goodyear* is not whether a foreign corporation's in-forum contacts can be said to be in some sense "continuous and systematic," it is whether that corporation's "affiliations with the State are so 'continuous and systematic' as to render [it] essentially at home in the forum State." 564 U.S., at ___ (slip op., at 2).[19]

Here, neither Daimler nor MBUSA is incorporated in California, nor does either entity have its principal place of business there. If Daimler's California activities sufficed to allow adjudication of this Argentina-rooted case in California, the same global reach would presumably be available in every other State in which MBUSA's sales are sizable. Such exorbitant exercises of all-purpose jurisdiction would scarcely permit out-of-state defendants "to structure their primary conduct with some minimum assurance as to where that conduct will and will not render them liable to suit." *Burger King Corp.*, 471 U.S., at 472 (internal quotation marks omitted).

It was therefore error for the Ninth Circuit to conclude that Daimler, even with MBUSA's contacts attributed to it, was at home in California, and hence subject to suit there on claims by foreign plaintiffs having nothing to do with anything that occurred or had its principal impact in California.[20] ...

* * *

For the reasons stated, the judgment of the United States Court of Appeals for the Ninth Circuit is

Reversed.

[Justice Sotomayor's concurring opinion is omitted.]

---

19. We do not foreclose the possibility that in an exceptional case, see, *e.g., Perkins*, a corporation's operations in a forum other than its formal place of incorporation or principal place of business may be so substantial and of such a nature as to render the corporation at home in that State. But this case presents no occasion to explore that question, because Daimler's activities in California plainly do not approach that level. It is one thing to hold a corporation answerable for operations in the forum State, quite another to expose it to suit on claims having no connection whatever to the forum State.

20. ... General jurisdiction ... calls for an appraisal of a corporation's activities in their entirety, nationwide and worldwide. A corporation that operates in many places can scarcely be deemed at home in all of them. Otherwise, "at home" would be synonymous with "doing business" tests framed before specific jurisdiction evolved in the United States....

Justice Sotomayor would reach the same result, but for a different reason. Rather than concluding that Daimler is not at home in California, Justice Sotomayor would hold that the exercise of general jurisdiction over Daimler would be unreasonable "in the unique circumstances of this case." In other words, she favors a resolution fit for this day and case only. True, a multipronged reasonableness check was articulated in *Asahi*, 480 U.S., at 113–114, but not as a free-floating test. Instead, the check was to be essayed when *specific* jurisdiction is at issue. First, a court is to determine whether the connection between the forum and the episode-in-suit could justify the exercise of specific jurisdiction. Then, in a second step, the court is to consider several additional factors to assess the reasonableness of entertaining the case. When a corporation is genuinely at home in the forum State, however, any second-step inquiry would be superfluous....

Notes and Questions: Understanding *Daimler* and General Jurisdiction over Corporations

Q **1. There's no place like home.** When is a corporation "at home" for purposes of general jurisdiction?

A According to the Court, a corporation is considered to be "at home" wherever it has its principal place of business or place of incorporation. In footnote 19, the Court explains that a corporation might also be "at home" in other jurisdictions under "exceptional" circumstances and cites *Perkins* as such a case. In *Perkins*, the company's principal place of business was overseas (in the Philippines), but because World War II had a devastating effect on the company's properties there, the company's president directed the company's rehabilitation from an Ohio office. (Footnote 8 contains additional details.) Given these exceptional circumstances, general jurisdiction existed over the company in Ohio, even though its principal place of business and state of incorporation were elsewhere.

Q **2. A more difficult test?** Prior to *Daimler*, many courts had assumed that general jurisdiction existed wherever a corporation had continuous and systematic contacts. Is the "at home" test narrower or broader than the "continuous and systematic" contacts test? Why?

A The "at home" test is narrower and more difficult to satisfy. A corporation may have "continuous and systematic" contacts in many states but not be "at home" in any of them. Consider, for example, Wal-Mart. It has continuous and systematic contacts in numerous states as a result of its substantial retail presence in those jurisdictions. But just because Wal-Mart has dozens of stores in a particular state (and thus may have continuous and systematic contacts there) does not mean that Wal-Mart is "at home" in the sense of having its principal place of business or place of incorporation in those jurisdictions. Nor is there any basis to conclude that an exceptional circumstance exists that would warrant general jurisdiction in a state that happens to have a lot of Wal-Marts.

This shift in approach probably means that large companies are now subject to general jurisdiction in fewer (and for companies like Wal-Mart, far fewer) states than when the test was "continuous and systematic contacts." Of course, a company like Wal-Mart may still be subject to specific jurisdiction for claims that arise out of Wal-Mart's conduct in a particular state, but general jurisdiction is now more difficult to establish.

Q **3. Why it matters.** After *Daimler*, a company can be sued in a state where its contacts give rise to the claim (specific jurisdiction) or where it has its principal place of business or place of incorporation (general jurisdiction). That seems to give a plaintiff a lot of options. So when will this change in general jurisdiction doctrine matter?

A One answer is that it will matter in cases like *Daimler*, where the defendant is a foreign company that has its principal place of business and place of incorporation abroad and when the claims against the company arise out of conduct that occurred abroad. In that situation, there is no place within the United States where specific jurisdiction is possible, so if the plaintiff wants to sue in the United States, general jurisdiction is the only option.

Another answer is that the new approach makes recovery for injuries more inconvenient when the plaintiff is injured in a state other than where the plaintiff lives. Imagine, for example, a citizen of Nevada taking a vacation in New York and getting hit by a Home Depot truck while visiting there. She returns home to Nevada and sues Home Depot in Nevada. Assume Home Depot has 50 stores in Nevada but that its place of incorporation and principal place of business are elsewhere. Before *Daimler*, this suit probably could be heard in Nevada, at least as a matter of personal jurisdiction. Home Depot most likely would be found to have continuous and systematic contacts in Nevada as a result of its substantial retail presence there. It is probably not, however, "at home" in Nevada, so the plaintiff will have to litigate elsewhere. (As a practical matter, this would likely be the outcome even if personal jurisdiction is appropriate in Nevada because of a different concept called "venue." That topic is discussed in detail in Chapters 11 and 12.)

There are a number of recent examples of cases and rules that make litigating a case a bit more difficult for plaintiffs, and *Daimler* is arguably part of this larger trend. Keep an eye out for other examples of this development throughout the book.

4. Daimler's contacts: The Daimler/MBUSA distinction. Like many companies, Daimler consists of multiple corporate entities. The particular defendant contesting personal jurisdiction in this case is the parent company, Daimler AG. Daimler AG doesn't have a physical presence in California, so personal jurisdiction over the company turns on its relationship with its subsidiary, MBUSA. MBUSA is Daimler AG's exclusive U.S. importer and distributor. MBUSA purchases Mercedes-Benz cars from Daimler AG in Germany, imports the cars into the United States and then distributes the vehicles to independent dealerships located throughout the country. Although MBUSA has multiple California facilities, MBUSA's place of incorporation is Delaware and its principal place of business is New Jersey.

One important doctrinal question is whether MBUSA's contacts in California should be attributable to Daimler. The Court explains that there has been some disagreement over the extent to which a subsidiary's contacts with a forum should be attributable to the parent corporation. For example, some courts have held that the imputation of contacts to an affiliated company is limited to situations where the corporate entities are not genuinely distinct from each other, such as when the typical corporate formalities between or among the entities are not observed. *Daimler AG v. Bauman*, 571 U.S. 117, 134-35 (2014). In contrast, in this case, the Ninth Circuit adopted a more liberal doctrine and concluded that a subsidiary's contacts in a forum are attributable to the parent if the parent and the subsidiary merely have a particular kind of agency relationship. *Id.* The Court declines to resolve this debate, but notes that this issue typically arises when there is an attempt to establish specific jurisdiction over a parent corporation as a result of the subsidiary's contacts in the forum state. *See Daimler AG*, 571 U.S. at 135 n.13.

The Court then goes on to say that, even if it were possible to establish general jurisdiction over a parent company as a result of the parent's relationship with its subsidiary in the forum state, there is no basis for doing so under the particular facts of this case. The Court explains that, "[e]ven if we were to assume that MBUSA is at home in California, and further to assume MBUSA's contacts are imputable to Daimler, there would still be no basis to subject Daimler to general jurisdiction in California, for Daimler's slim contacts with the State hardly render it at home there." *Daimler AG*, 571 U.S. at 136.

In a concurring opinion, Justice Sotomayor takes issue with this analysis. She contends that the Court should have focused on the magnitude of the defendant's contacts in the forum, not on the *relative* magnitude of those contacts:

> Until today, our precedents had established a straightforward test for general jurisdiction: Does the defendant have "continuous corporate operations within a state" that are "so substantial and of such a nature as to justify suit against it on causes of action arising from dealings entirely distinct from those activities"? *International Shoe Co. v. Washington*, 326 U.S. 310, 318 (1945). In every case where we have applied this test, we have focused solely on the magnitude of the defendant's in-state contacts, not the relative magnitude of those contacts in comparison to the defendant's contacts with other States.

Daimler AG, 571 U.S. at 149–50 (Sotomayor, J., concurring).

In sum, a majority of the Court was willing to assume for the sake of argument that MBUSA was "at home" in California and that its contacts should be attributable to Daimler, but the Court nevertheless concluded that Daimler's connection to California relative to its contacts elsewhere in the world were still too slim to warrant general jurisdiction.

Q **5. Why not specific jurisdiction?** Given that the Court was willing to assume that Daimler had contacts in California through MBUSA, why were those contacts insufficient for specific jurisdiction?

A Even if Daimler is considered to have contacts in California through its subsidiary, the plaintiffs' claims did not arise out of those contacts under two commonly used tests. For example, none of Daimler's contacts in California were a "but for" cause of the plaintiffs' injuries, which occurred in South America. Moreover, none of Daimler's contacts in California offered evidence concerning any element of the plaintiffs' claims. Because the "arising out of" requirement was not satisfied here, specific jurisdiction was not an option.

6. A scholarly take on specific and general jurisdiction. Some scholars have suggested that general and specific jurisdiction should be thought of as merely two points on a sliding scale of personal jurisdiction. *See, e.g.*, William M. Richman, Review Essay, *Part I—Casad's Jurisdiction in Civil Actions: Part II—A Sliding Scale to Supplement the Distinction Between General and Specific Jurisdiction*, 72 Cal. L. Rev. 1328, 1340–41 (1984) (reviewing Robert C. Casad, Jurisdiction in Civil Actions (1983)). According to this view, courts should require more contacts as the relationship between the claim and the contacts becomes attenuated. For example,

thin

if a claim is somewhat related to the contacts (but not related enough to confer specific jurisdiction) and the contacts are not sufficiently extensive to confer general jurisdiction, personal jurisdiction should nevertheless be permissible if the contacts are "regular." The diagram below illustrates this idea.

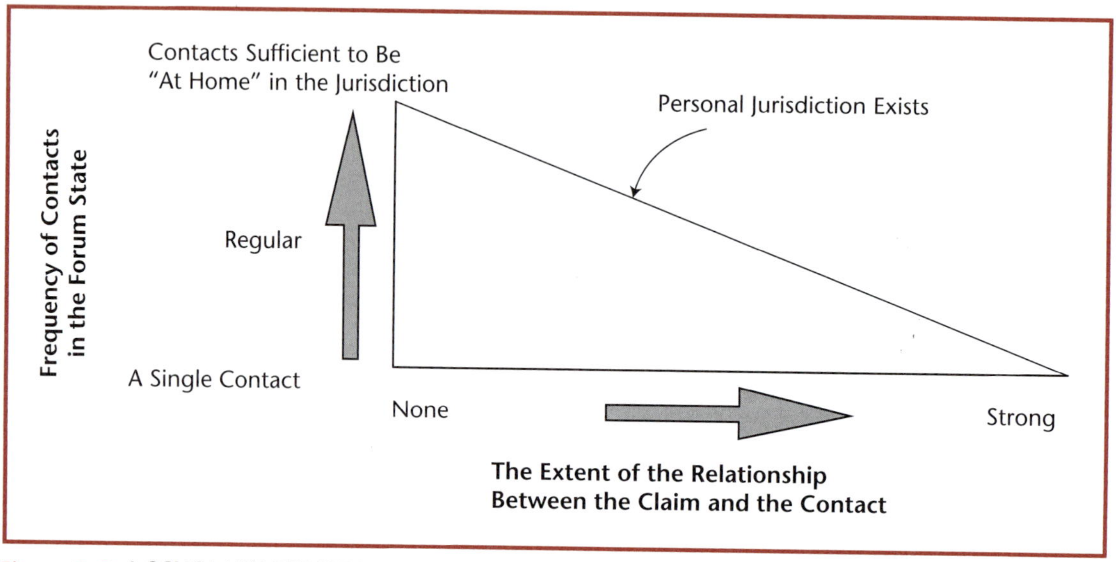

Figure 8–2: A SCHOLAR'S PERSPECTIVE ON PERSONAL JURISDICTION

This view of personal jurisdiction may help to conceptualize the relationship between specific and general jurisdiction, but the Supreme Court has rejected the use of a sliding scale as a matter of doctrine. *Bristol-Myers Squibb Co. v. Superior Court of California*, 582 U.S. __, 137 S. Ct. 1773 (2017) (rejecting a "sliding scale" for personal jurisdiction). This means that a plaintiff must establish either specific jurisdiction (by showing that the claim arises out of the defendant's contacts) or general jurisdiction (by showing that the defendant is "at home" in the forum). There is no middle ground that would allow for personal jurisdiction over defendants who have substantial contacts in the forum that are only loosely related to the claim.

Consider an example. Nagel, a California citizen, suffers injuries in New York after purchasing a product there manufactured by Detrius Corp. Nagel returns home and sues Detrius in California state court. Assume that Detrius sells thousands of units of the same product in California but has its principal place of business and place of incorporation in New York. Under these circumstances, Nagel's claim does not "arise out of" Detrius's contact in California, so there is no specific jurisdiction in California. Moreover, Detrius has its place of incorporation and principal place of business in New York, so Detrius is not subject to general jurisdiction in California. Although Nagel's claim is loosely related to Detrius's substantial contacts in California (i.e., the claim involves a Detrius product that is frequently sold there) and could plausibly support personal jurisdiction under a sliding-scale approach, the Court has rejected the idea that there is some middle ground between specific and general jurisdiction. For this reason, Detrius would not be subject to personal jurisdiction in California for purposes of Nagel's case.

7. "McQuestion": Personal jurisdiction and the national franchise. Consider the following question.

> Penelope suffers third-degree burns from hot coffee purchased at a McDonald's in Florida. Upon returning to her home in Georgia, Penelope sues McDonald's in a Georgia state court for negligence, alleging that the store sold excessively hot coffee and caused her to suffer damages. Assume that the Georgia long arm statute reaches as far as the Constitution allows and that McDonald's is incorporated in Delaware, has its principal place of business in Illinois, and has seventy-five stores in Georgia. If McDonald's moves to dismiss the case on personal jurisdiction grounds, the court will probably
>
> A. grant the motion. Even under the most liberal definition of "arising out of," this case does not arise out of any contact that McDonald's had with Georgia.
> B. deny the motion. The state court has the authority to hear all state law claims as a matter of subject matter jurisdiction.
> C. grant the motion. McDonald's has its principal place of business and place of incorporation outside of Georgia, so a Georgia court cannot exercise general jurisdiction in Georgia. And for the reasons set out in A, there is no specific jurisdiction.
> D. deny the motion, because the court would likely have general jurisdiction over McDonald's in Georgia.

B is incorrect. Personal and subject matter jurisdiction are two distinct requirements. Just because the court has subject matter jurisdiction does not mean that it has personal jurisdiction.

A is partially correct in that specific jurisdiction does not exist here. But specific jurisdiction is not the only way to establish personal jurisdiction.

That leaves **C** and **D**. Until the Court decided *Daimler* in early 2014, we believed that **D** was the probable answer to this question, reasoning that McDonald's had "continuous and systematic" contacts with the forum state through its numerous restaurants there. Although *Goodyear* had made us more tentative about that answer because of the Court's reference in that case to the "at home" concept, we still thought that the answer was **D**. Now, however, *Daimler* makes **C** the best answer. *Daimler* makes clear that the "at home" concept means that general jurisdiction typically exists over corporations only where they are incorporated or have their principal place of business. Here, that would be Illinois and Delaware. Although the Court suggested that a corporation may in "exceptional" circumstances be "at home" in other states as well, such as in *Perkins* (where the Philippines company directed its business from Ohio due to the devastating effects of World War II), McDonald's does not seem to present such an exceptional case. After all,

McDonald's has substantial connections with just about every U.S. jurisdiction; its contacts with Georgia do not seem unusual or exceptional given the nature of its operations.

D. General Jurisdiction over Individuals: Domicile

In *Daimler*, the Court reaffirmed *Goodyear*'s holding that general jurisdiction exists over corporations where they are "at home." Analogously, "[f]or an individual, the paradigm forum for the exercise of general jurisdiction is the individual's domicile." *Goodyear*, 564 U.S. at 924. That is, individuals are subject to general jurisdiction wherever they are domiciled. *Milliken v. Meyer*, 311 U.S. 457, 462 (1940).

General jurisdiction over a corporation and general jurisdiction over an individual are quite similar, but there is at least one important difference. A company may be subject to general jurisdiction in several different states simultaneously (e.g., in its place of incorporation, its principal place of business, and perhaps (in exceptional circumstances) a limited number of other jurisdictions as well). In contrast, individuals have only one domicile for purposes of personal jurisdiction.

To summarize, if the lawsuit has nothing to do with the forum state and the defendant is an individual, the defendant can still be subject to general jurisdiction if the defendant is domiciled there.* If the lawsuit has nothing to do with the forum state and the defendant is a company, the company can still be subject to general jurisdiction if the company is "at home" there.

III. In Rem and Quasi In Rem Jurisdiction: *Shaffer v. Heitner*

A. Distinguishing In Personam and In Rem/Quasi In Rem Jurisdiction

A court with in personam jurisdiction has the power to require a defendant to pay a money judgment. In contrast, a court with in rem and quasi in rem jurisdiction has much narrower authority—the power to control and determine the ownership of specific property, such as a parcel of land or a bank account. A court with in rem jurisdiction can declare the true owner of specific property relative to everyone in the world, whereas a court with quasi in rem jurisdiction can declare which of the *litigants* has the better claim to the property without determining whether the winner is the true owner relative to everyone else in the world.

An example will help to explain these distinctions. Imagine that Larry, an Arkansas citizen, purchases swampland in Florida. Carrie claims that she is the

* The definition of "domicile" in this context is not necessarily the same as the definition of "domicile" for diversity jurisdiction purposes. Some courts, however, have held that the word has the same meaning in both situations.

rightful owner of that swampland and that the land was sold to Larry without her permission. Thus, Carrie brings a claim in Florida state court, asking the court to declare that the land belongs to her and not Larry. When she files her suit, Carrie asks the court to issue an attachment order. In the case of real estate, such as the swampland here, the attachment order is typically filed at the registry of deeds (or the equivalent body that keeps real estate records) to give notice to potential buyers that Carrie has a claim pending that might affect Larry's ownership of the property.

By attaching the property at the outset of Carrie's case, the Florida court establishes quasi in rem jurisdiction—the power to determine who owns the swampland as between Carrie and Larry. Note that the court is exercising quasi in rem jurisdiction, not in rem jurisdiction, because the court is only determining whether Carrie or Larry has the better claim to the property, not who should own the land relative to other potential claimants elsewhere in the world.

Recall that, in *Pennoyer*, the Court explained why this process of attachment is an important prerequisite for in rem and quasi in rem jurisdiction:

> [In the absence of attachment,] the validity of the proceedings and judgment [would] depend upon the question whether, before the levy of the execution, the defendant had or had not disposed of the property. If before the levy the property should be sold, then ... the judgment would not be binding. This doctrine would introduce a new element of uncertainty in judicial proceedings.

Pennoyer v. Neff, 95 U.S. 714, 728 (1878). Notably, although the attachment can give the Florida court in rem or quasi in rem jurisdiction to determine who owns Larry's property, the court's power does not extend to any other property that Larry may own, either in Florida or elsewhere. Unlike in personam jurisdiction, which can result in a personal judgment against a defendant like Larry and affect any assets that he has, the Florida court in this case only has quasi in rem jurisdiction—the power to determine the ownership of Larry's swampland and nothing more.

B. Other Types of Attachment

It is important to distinguish the kind of attachment used to establish in rem and quasi in rem jurisdiction from two other common forms of attachment: a post-judgment attachment and a prejudgment attachment for security.

A post-judgment attachment—also known as a *garnishment*, especially when referring to wages—is used to collect on a judgment that the defendant refuses to pay. Imagine, for example, that Patty sues Donald for negligence in Texas, where Donald is subject to in personam jurisdiction, and a jury awards Patty money damages. Donald decides not to appeal, and after the judgment is final, Donald refuses to pay Patty. Initially, Patty can ask a Texas court to attach any assets that Donald owns in Texas, such as bank accounts or real estate. In the latter case, the court can even order the sale of Donald's real estate to ensure that Donald satisfies the judgment against him. The court could also garnish Donald's wages, ordering a portion of each paycheck to be paid to Patty. Moreover, if Donald does not have sufficient assets in Texas to satisfy the full value of the judgment, Patty can take the Texas judgment to another state where Donald does have adequate assets and ask that state's courts to attach Donald's assets there. Under most circumstances, the other state's courts are bound by the Constitution's Full Faith and Credit Clause to enforce the Texas judgment by ordering the attachment of Donald's property. This form of attachment, however, is not the exercise of in rem or quasi in rem jurisdiction; it is simply a method by which a winning litigant can collect on a judgment entered by a court that had in personam jurisdiction over the defendant.

A *prejudgment attachment for security* permits a court to attach a defendant's assets when there is a concern that the defendant might dissipate those assets to prevent the satisfaction of a future judgment. For example, while a case is pending and before a judgment has been entered, a defendant might try to transfer assets to another country, transfer them to a third party, or take other measures designed to prevent the plaintiff from collecting any future judgment. A prejudgment attachment removes the defendant's control over those assets and ensures that they are available to satisfy a judgment in the event that the plaintiff wins the case.

In sum, a court's power to "attach" property can serve three unrelated functions. It can be a necessary step to gaining in rem or quasi in rem jurisdiction (jurisdictional attachment); it can be a method to reach the assets of a party who refuses to pay a judgment (post-judgment attachment/garnishment); or it can be a method to prevent the disappearance of assets while a case is pending (prejudgment attachment for security).

C. Taking Attachment to the Extreme: *Harris v. Balk*

One potential problem with attachment as a means of obtaining in rem or quasi in rem jurisdiction is that it can be taken to an extreme. Consider, for example, the unusual case of *Harris v. Balk*, 198 U.S. 215 (1905). Harris, a North Carolina citizen, owed money to Balk, another North Carolina citizen. At the same time, Epstein, a Maryland citizen, claimed that Balk owed Epstein money. (See the diagram below.)

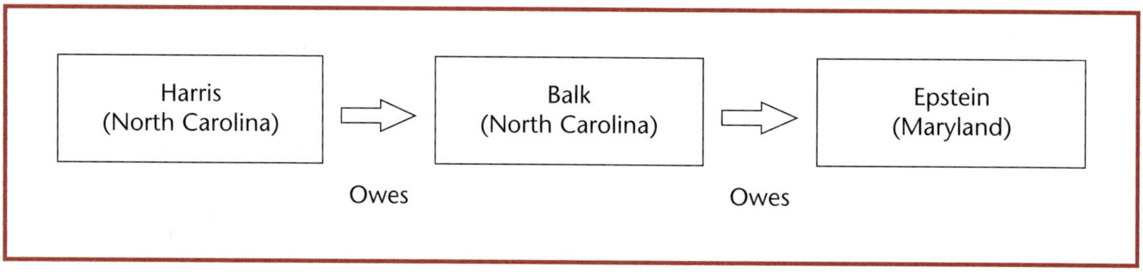

Figure 8-3: AN ILLUSTRATION OF *HARRIS v. BALK*

When Harris traveled to Maryland to conduct some business, Epstein asked a Maryland court to issue a writ of attachment against Harris in the form of a summons to appear in court, which the sheriff delivered to Harris while he was in Maryland. Epstein claimed that because Harris owed money to Balk and Balk owed money to Epstein, Epstein could use the writ of attachment against Harris as a way to obtain jurisdiction over the debt that Harris owed to Balk. A Maryland court agreed and issued a judgment in Epstein's favor, ordering Harris to pay Epstein. Harris subsequently paid the amount of the judgment.

Balk subsequently sued Harris in North Carolina for the amount that Harris owed to Balk. Harris defended the action by claiming that he no longer owed the money to Balk because Harris had been forced to pay Balk's debt to Epstein as a result of the Maryland action. The case involved other nuances, but the ultimate question was whether the Maryland court had the authority to exercise quasi in rem jurisdiction by "attaching" Harris's debt to Balk by serving Harris while he was in Maryland.

The United States Supreme Court upheld the exercise of jurisdiction, using logic that appeared to be supportable under *Pennoyer*. *Pennoyer* had held that a court could exercise in rem or quasi in rem jurisdiction as long as the asset at issue was within the state and attached at an appropriate time. In *Harris*, that is precisely what happened. The asset—Harris's debt to Balk—was in Maryland (because that's where Harris was), making the debt attachable while Harris was visiting there. Here is a poetic version of the holding:

> Harris had a little debt, and to Balk that debt was owed;
> And everywhere that Harris went, the debt was sure to go.
> It followed him to Baltimore, and there it was attached;
> To establish jurisdiction, and then reduced to cash.
> And Mr. Epstein took that cash and stuffed it in his boot
> But Mr. Balk tried to recoup, by filing his own suit.
> Too late, too late the Court declares, your lawsuit is foreclosed
> The judgment was a valid one, as every first year knows.*

The problem, of course, is that *International Shoe* subsequently overruled *Pennoyer* in several important respects. But did *International Shoe* overrule the *Pennoyer* Court's treatment of in rem and quasi in rem jurisdiction? Or did the Court simply alter the analysis for in personam jurisdiction? These questions remained unanswered for more than thirty years after *International Shoe* was decided.

D. Addressing *International Shoe*'s Unanswered Question: *Shaffer v. Heitner*

The Court's opinion in *International Shoe* transformed how courts analyzed in personam jurisdiction by forcing courts to look at a defendant's in-state contacts, but the Court did not state explicitly whether it had changed the analysis for in rem or quasi in rem jurisdiction. As a result, courts did not know whether they could still exercise in rem or quasi in rem jurisdiction over an asset—like the "asset" in *Harris*—simply because that asset could be found within the forum and attached at an appropriate time or whether the contacts framework applied to in rem/quasi in rem jurisdiction as well. The Court finally resolved this ambiguity in *Shaffer*.

---

* **[Eds.—Thanks to Professor Allan Ides for giving us permission to publish his creation.]**

A Basis to Adjudicate?

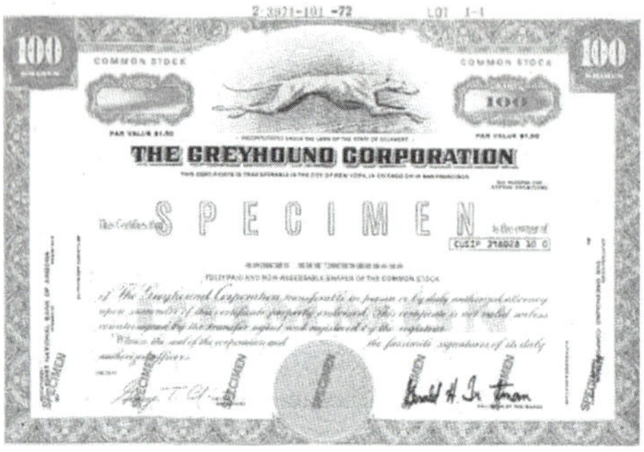

Reprinted with permission of Greyhound

Under *Pennoyer,* a court could exercise jurisdiction based on the presence of a defendant's *property* in the forum state, even if the debtor was not subject to personal jurisdiction in that state. For example, if the debtor left a car in the state or a piece of land, the court could seize and sell that property to satisfy the absconding debtor's debts. But suppose the defendant owns stock in a corporation. Can the asset be seized in an in rem action simply because the stock is deemed "present" in the state under a local statute? This is the central question in *Shaffer.*

READING *SHAFFER v. HEITNER.* Consider the following questions as you read this complicated case.

- Does the Court conclude that the minimum contacts inquiry of *International Shoe* applies to in rem and quasi in rem jurisdiction? How does the Court reach its conclusion?
- How does the Court apply the new approach to in rem and quasi in rem jurisdiction to the facts of this case?
- After this case, are the concepts of in rem and quasi in rem jurisdiction obsolete?

SHAFFER v. HEITNER

433 U.S. 186 (1977)

Mr. Justice Marshall delivered the opinion of the Court.

The controversy in this case concerns the constitutionality of a Delaware statute that allows a court of that State to take jurisdiction of a lawsuit by sequestering any property of the defendant that happens to be located in Delaware. Appellants contend that the sequestration statute as applied in this case violates the Due Process Clause of the Fourteenth Amendment both because it permits the state courts to exercise jurisdiction despite the absence of sufficient contacts among the defendants, the litigation, and the State of Delaware and because it authorizes the deprivation of defendants' property without providing adequate procedural safeguards. We find it necessary to consider only the first of these contentions.

I

Appellee Heitner, a nonresident of Delaware, is the owner of one share of stock in the Greyhound Corp., a business incorporated under the laws of Delaware with its principal place of business in Phoenix, Ariz. On May 22, 1974, he filed a shareholder's derivative suit in the Court of Chancery for New Castle County, Del., in which he named as defendants Greyhound, its wholly owned subsidiary Greyhound Lines, Inc.,[1] and 28 present or former officers or directors of one or both of the corporations. In essence, Heitner alleged that the individual defendants had violated their duties to Greyhound by causing it and its subsidiary to engage in actions that resulted in the corporations being held liable for substantial damages in a private antitrust suit and a large fine in a criminal contempt action. The activities which led to these penalties took place in Oregon.

Simultaneously with his complaint, Heitner filed a motion for an order of sequestration of the Delaware property of the individual defendants pursuant to Del. Code Ann., Tit. 10, § 366 (1975).[4] This motion was accompanied by a supporting affidavit of counsel which stated that the individual defendants were nonresidents of Delaware. The affidavit identified the property to be sequestered as

> "common stock, 3% Second Cumulative Preferenced Stock and stock unit credits of the Defendant Greyhound Corporation, a Delaware corporation, as well as all options and all warrants to purchase said stock issued to said individual Defendants and all contractural (sic) obligations, all rights, debts or credits due or accrued to or for the benefit of any of the said Defendants under any type

1. Greyhound Lines, Inc., is incorporated in California and has its principal place of business in Phoenix, Ariz.

4. Section 366 provides:

"(a) If it appears in any complaint filed in the Court of Chancery that the defendant or any one or more of the defendants is a nonresident of the State, the Court may make an order directing such nonresident defendant or defendants to appear by a day certain to be designated.... The Court may compel the appearance of the defendant by the seizure of all or any part of his property, which property may be sold under the order of the Court to pay the demand of the plaintiff, if the defendant does not appear, or otherwise defaults. Any defendant whose property shall have been so seized and who shall have entered a general appearance in the cause may, upon notice to the plaintiff, petition the Court for an order releasing such property or any part thereof from the seizure. The Court shall release such property unless the plaintiff shall satisfy the Court that because of other circumstances there is a reasonable possibility that such release may render it substantially less likely that plaintiff will obtain satisfaction of any judgment secured. If such petition shall not be granted, or if no such petition shall be filed, such property shall remain subject to seizure and may be sold to satisfy any judgment entered in the cause. The Court may at any time release such property or any part thereof upon the giving of sufficient security.

"(b) The Court may make all necessary rules respecting the form of process, the manner of issuance and return thereof, the release of such property from seizure and for the sale of the property so seized, and may require the plaintiff to give approved security to abide any order of the Court respecting the property.

"(c) Any transfer or assignment of the property so seized after the seizure thereof shall be void and after the sale of the property is made and confirmed, the purchaser shall be entitled to and have all the right, title and interest of the defendant in and to the property so seized and sold and such sale and confirmation shall transfer to the purchaser all the right, title and interest of the defendant in and to the property as fully as if the defendant had transferred the same to the purchaser in accordance with law."

> of written agreement, contract or other legal instrument of any kind whatever between any of the individual Defendants and said corporation."

The requested sequestration order was signed the day the motion was filed. Pursuant to that order, the sequestrator[6] "seized" approximately 82,000 shares of Greyhound common stock belonging to 19 of the defendants, and options belonging to another 2 defendants. These seizures were accomplished by placing "stop transfer" orders or their equivalents on the books of the Greyhound Corp. So far as the record shows, none of the certificates representing the seized property was physically present in Delaware. The stock was considered to be in Delaware, and so subject to seizure, by virtue of Del. Code Ann., Tit. 8, 169 (1975), which makes Delaware the situs of ownership of all stock in Delaware corporations.[9]

All 28 defendants were notified of the initiation of the suit by certified mail directed to their last known addresses and by publication in a New Castle County newspaper. The 21 defendants whose property was seized (hereafter referred to as appellants) responded by entering a special appearance for the purpose of moving to quash service of process and to vacate the sequestration order. They contended that the *ex parte* sequestration procedure did not accord them due process of law and that the property seized was not capable of attachment in Delaware. In addition, appellants asserted that under the rule of *International Shoe*, they did not have sufficient contacts with Delaware to sustain the jurisdiction of that State's courts.

The Court of Chancery rejected these arguments in a letter opinion which emphasized the purpose of the Delaware sequestration procedure:

> "The primary purpose of 'sequestration' as authorized by 10 Del. C. § 366 is not to secure possession of property pending a trial between resident debtors and creditors on the issue of who has the right to retain it. On the contrary, as here employed, 'sequestration' is a process used to compel the personal appearance of a nonresident defendant to answer and defend a suit brought against him in a court of equity. It is accomplished by the appointment of a sequestrator by this Court to seize and hold property of the nonresident located in this State subject to further Court order. If the defendant enters a general appearance, the sequestered property is routinely released, unless the plaintiff makes special application to continue its seizure, in which event the plaintiff has the burden of proof and persuasion."

---

6. The sequestrator is appointed by the court to effect the sequestration. His duties appear to consist of serving the sequestration order on the named corporation, receiving from that corporation a list of the property which the order affects, and filing that list with the court. For performing those services in this case, the sequestrator received a fee of $100 under the original sequestration order and $100 under the alias order.

9. Section 169 provides:

> "For all purposes of title, action, attachment, garnishment and jurisdiction of all courts held in this State, but not for the purpose of taxation, the situs of the ownership of the capital stock of all corporations existing under the laws of this State, whether organized under this chapter or otherwise, shall be regarded as in this State."

This limitation on the purpose and length of time for which sequestered property is held, the court concluded, rendered inapplicable the due process requirements enunciated in *Sniadach v. Family Finance Corp.*, 395 U.S. 337 (1969) [and other similar Supreme Court cases]. The court also found no state-law or federal constitutional barrier to the sequestrator's reliance on Del. Code Ann., Tit. 8, § 169 (1975). Finally, the court held that the statutory Delaware situs of the stock provided a sufficient basis for the exercise of *quasi in rem* jurisdiction by a Delaware court.

On appeal, the Delaware Supreme Court affirmed the judgment of the Court of Chancery. . . . The court's analysis of the jurisdictional issue is contained in two paragraphs:

> "There are significant constitutional questions at issue here but we say at once that we do not deem the rule of *International Shoe* to be one of them. . . . The reason of course, is that jurisdiction under § 366 remains . . . *quasi in rem* founded on the presence of capital stock here, not on prior contact by defendants with this forum. Under 8 Del. C. § 169 the 'situs of the ownership of the capital stock of all corporations existing under the laws of this State . . . [is] in this State,' and that provides the initial basis for jurisdiction. Delaware may constitutionally establish situs of such shares here, . . . it has done so and the presence thereof provides the foundation for § 366 in this case. . . .
>
> "We hold that seizure of the Greyhound shares is not invalid because plaintiff has failed to meet the prior contacts tests of *International Shoe*." *Id.*, at 229.

We noted probable jurisdiction.[12] We reverse.

II

The Delaware courts rejected appellants' jurisdictional challenge by noting that this suit was brought as a *quasi in rem* proceeding. Since *quasi in rem* jurisdiction is traditionally based on attachment or seizure of property present in the jurisdiction, not on contacts between the defendant and the State, the courts considered appellants' claimed lack of contacts with Delaware to be unimportant. This categorical analysis assumes the continued soundness of the conceptual structure founded on the century-old case of *Pennoyer v. Neff*, 95 U.S. 714 (1878). . . .

[Eds.—The Court summarized *Pennoyer*, including the premise that a court only has power over persons or things within its territory and no power over persons or things outside of the court's territory. The Court then summarized some of the pragmatic problems that arose from this premise prior to *International Shoe*, including the advent of automobiles and proliferation of corporations.]

---

12. Under Delaware law, defendants whose property has been sequestered must enter a general appearance, thus subjecting themselves to *in personam* liability, before they can defend on the merits. Thus, if the judgment below were considered not to be an appealable final judgment, appellants would have the choice of suffering a default judgment or entering a general appearance and defending on the merits. . . . Accordingly, "consistent with the pragmatic approach that we have followed in the past in determining finality," we conclude that the judgment below is final within the meaning of § 1257.

[The Court explained that, after *International Shoe*,] the relationship among the defendant, the forum, and the litigation, rather than the mutually exclusive sovereignty of the States on which the rules of *Pennoyer* rest, became the central concern of the inquiry into personal jurisdiction. The immediate effect of this departure from *Pennoyer*'s conceptual apparatus was to increase the ability of the state courts to obtain personal jurisdiction over nonresident defendants.

No equally dramatic change has occurred in the law governing jurisdiction *in rem*. There have, however, been intimations that the collapse of the *in personam* wing of *Pennoyer* has not left that decision unweakened as a foundation for *in rem* jurisdiction. Well-reasoned lower court opinions have questioned the proposition that the presence of property in a State gives that State jurisdiction to adjudicate rights to the property regardless of the relationship of the underlying dispute and the property owner to the forum. The overwhelming majority of commentators have also rejected *Pennoyer*'s premise that a proceeding "against" property is not a proceeding against the owners of that property. Accordingly, they urge that the "traditional notions of fair play and substantial justice" that govern a State's power to adjudicate *in personam* should also govern its power to adjudicate personal rights to property located in the State.

Although this Court has not addressed this argument directly, we have held that property cannot be subjected to a court's judgment unless reasonable and appropriate efforts have been made to give the property owners actual notice of the action. This conclusion recognizes, contrary to *Pennoyer*, that an adverse judgment *in rem* directly affects the property owner by divesting him of his rights in the property before the court. . . .

It is clear, therefore, that the law of state-court jurisdiction no longer stands securely on the foundation established in *Pennoyer*. We think that the time is ripe to consider whether the standard of fairness and substantial justice set forth in *International Shoe* should be held to govern actions *in rem* as well as *in personam*.

III

The case for applying to jurisdiction in rem the same test of "fair play and substantial justice" as governs assertions of jurisdiction *in personam* is simple and straightforward. It is premised on recognition that "[t]he phrase, 'judicial jurisdiction over a thing,' is a customary elliptical way of referring to jurisdiction over the interests of persons in a thing." Restatement (Second) of Conflict of Laws § 56. This recognition leads to the conclusion that in order to justify an exercise of jurisdiction *in rem*, the basis for jurisdiction must be sufficient to justify exercising "jurisdiction over the interests of persons in a thing."[23] The standard for determining whether an exercise of jurisdiction over the interests of persons is consistent with the Due Process Clause is the minimum-contacts standard elucidated in *International Shoe*.

---

23. It is true that the potential liability of a defendant in an *in rem* action is limited by the value of the property, but that limitation does not affect the argument. The fairness of subjecting a defendant to state-court jurisdiction does not depend on the size of the claim being litigated.

This argument, of course, does not ignore the fact that the presence of property in a State may bear on the existence of jurisdiction by providing contacts among the forum State, the defendant, and the litigation. For example, when claims to the property itself are the source of the underlying controversy between the plaintiff and the defendant,[24] it would be unusual for the State where the property is located not to have jurisdiction. In such cases, the defendant's claim to property located in the State would normally indicate that he expected to benefit from the State's protection of his interest. The State's strong interests in assuring the marketability of property within its borders and in providing a procedure for peaceful resolution of disputes about the possession of that property would also support jurisdiction, as would the likelihood that important records and witnesses will be found in the State.[28] The presence of property may also favor jurisdiction in cases such as suits for injury suffered on the land of an absentee owner, where the defendant's ownership of the property is conceded but the cause of action is otherwise related to rights and duties growing out of that ownership.

It appears, therefore, that jurisdiction over many types of actions which now are or might be brought *in rem* would not be affected by a holding that any assertion of state-court jurisdiction must satisfy the *International Shoe* standard.[30] For the type of *quasi in rem* action typified . . . [in] the present case, however, accepting the proposed analysis would result in significant change. These are cases where the property which now serves as the basis for state-court jurisdiction is completely unrelated to the plaintiff's cause of action. Thus, although the presence of the defendant's property in a State might suggest the existence of other ties among the defendant, the State, and the litigation, the presence of the property alone would not support the State's jurisdiction. If those other ties did not exist, cases over which the State is now thought to have jurisdiction could not be brought in that forum.

Since acceptance of the *International Shoe* test would most affect this class of cases, we examine the arguments against adopting that standard as they relate to this category of litigation.[31] Before doing so, however, we note that this type of case also presents the clearest illustration of the argument in favor of assessing assertions of jurisdiction by a single standard. For in cases such as . . . this one, the only role played by the property is to provide the basis for bringing the defendant into court. Indeed, the express purpose of the Delaware sequestration procedure is to compel the defendant to enter a personal appearance. In such cases, if a direct assertion of personal jurisdiction over the defendant would violate the Constitution, it would seem that an indirect assertion of that jurisdiction should be equally impermissible.

---

24. This category includes true *in rem* actions and the first type of *quasi in rem* proceedings.

28. We do not suggest that these illustrations include all the factors that may affect the decision, nor that the factors we have mentioned are necessarily decisive.

30. We do not suggest that jurisdictional doctrines other than those discussed in text, such as the particularized rules governing adjudications of status, are inconsistent with the standard of fairness.

31. Concentrating on this category of cases is also appropriate because in the other categories, to the extent that presence of property in the State indicates the existence of sufficient contacts under *International Shoe*, there is no need to rely on the property as justifying jurisdiction regardless of the existence of those contacts.

The primary rationale for treating the presence of property as a sufficient basis for jurisdiction to adjudicate claims over which the State would not have jurisdiction if *International Shoe* applied is that a wrongdoer "should not be able to avoid payment of his obligations by the expedient of removing his assets to a place where he is not subject to an in personam suit." Restatement § 66, Comment a.

This justification, however, does not explain why jurisdiction should be recognized without regard to whether the property is present in the State because of an effort to avoid the owner's obligations. Nor does it support jurisdiction to adjudicate the underlying claim. At most, it suggests that a State in which property is located should have jurisdiction to attach that property, by use of proper procedures, as security for a judgment being sought in a forum where the litigation can be maintained consistently with *International Shoe*. Moreover, we know of nothing to justify the assumption that a debtor can avoid paying his obligations by removing his property to a State in which his creditor cannot obtain personal jurisdiction over him. The Full Faith and Credit Clause, after all, makes the valid *in personam* judgment of one State enforceable in all other States.

It might also be suggested that allowing *in rem* jurisdiction avoids the uncertainty inherent in the *International Shoe* standard and assures a plaintiff of a forum.[37] We believe, however, that the fairness standard of *International Shoe* can be easily applied in the vast majority of cases. Moreover, when the existence of jurisdiction in a particular forum under *International Shoe* is unclear, the cost of simplifying the litigation by avoiding the jurisdictional question may be the sacrifice of "fair play and substantial justice." That cost is too high.

We are left, then, to consider the significance of the long history of jurisdiction based solely on the presence of property in a State. Although the theory that territorial power is both essential to and sufficient for jurisdiction has been undermined, we have never held that the presence of property in a State does not automatically confer jurisdiction over the owner's interest in that property. This history must be considered as supporting the proposition that jurisdiction based solely on the presence of property satisfies the demands of due process, but it is not decisive. "[T]raditional notions of fair play and substantial justice" can be as readily offended by the perpetuation of ancient forms that are no longer justified as by the adoption of new procedures that are inconsistent with the basic values of our constitutional heritage. The fiction that an assertion of jurisdiction over property is anything but an assertion of jurisdiction over the owner of the property supports an ancient form without substantial modern justification. Its continued acceptance would serve only to allow state-court jurisdiction that is fundamentally unfair to the defendant.

We therefore conclude that all assertions of state-court jurisdiction must be evaluated according to the standards set forth in *International Shoe* and its progeny.

---

37. This case does not raise, and we therefore do not consider, the question whether the presence of a defendant's property in a State is a sufficient basis for jurisdiction when no other forum is available to the plaintiff.

IV

The Delaware courts based their assertion of jurisdiction in this case solely on the statutory presence of appellants' property in Delaware. Yet that property is not the subject matter of this litigation, nor is the underlying cause of action related to the property. Appellants' holdings in Greyhound do not, therefore, provide contacts with Delaware sufficient to support the jurisdiction of that State's courts over appellants. If it exists, that jurisdiction must have some other foundation.

Appellee Heitner did not allege and does not now claim that appellants have ever set foot in Delaware. Nor does he identify any act related to his cause of action as having taken place in Delaware. Nevertheless, he contends that appellants' positions as directors and officers of a corporation chartered in Delaware provide sufficient "contacts, ties, or relations," *International Shoe*, 326 U.S. at 319, with that State to give its courts jurisdiction over appellants in this stockholder's derivative action. This argument is based primarily on what Heitner asserts to be the strong interest of Delaware in supervising the management of a Delaware corporation. That interest is said to derive from the role of Delaware law in establishing the corporation and defining the obligations owed to it by its officers and directors. In order to protect this interest, appellee concludes, Delaware's courts must have jurisdiction over corporate fiduciaries such as appellants.

This argument is undercut by the failure of the Delaware Legislature to assert the state interest appellee finds so compelling. Delaware law bases jurisdiction, not on appellants' status as corporate fiduciaries, but rather on the presence of their property in the State. Although the sequestration procedure used here may be most frequently used in derivative suits against officers and directors, the authorizing statute evinces no specific concern with such actions. Sequestration can be used in any suit against a nonresident and reaches corporate fiduciaries only if they happen to own interests in a Delaware corporation, or other property in the State. But as Heitner's failure to secure jurisdiction over seven of the defendants named in his complaint demonstrates, there is no necessary relationship between holding a position as a corporate fiduciary and owning stock or other interests in the corporation. If Delaware perceived its interest in securing jurisdiction over corporate fiduciaries to be as great as Heitner suggests, we would expect it to have enacted a statute more clearly designed to protect that interest.

Moreover, even if Heitner's assessment of the importance of Delaware's interest is accepted, his argument fails to demonstrate that Delaware is a fair forum for this litigation. The interest appellee has identified may support the application of Delaware law to resolve any controversy over appellants' actions in their capacities as officers and directors. But we have rejected the argument that if a State's law can properly be applied to a dispute, its courts necessarily have jurisdiction over the parties to that dispute.

> "[The State] does not acquire . . . jurisdiction by being the 'center of gravity' of the controversy, or the most convenient location for litigation. The issue is personal jurisdiction, not choice of law. It is resolved in this case by considering the acts of the [appellants]." *Hanson v. Denckla*, 357 U.S. 235, 254 (1958).

Appellee suggests that by accepting positions as officers or directors of a Delaware corporation, appellants performed the acts required by Hanson. He notes that Delaware law provides substantial benefits to corporate officers and directors, and that these benefits were at least in part the incentive for appellants to assume their positions. It is, he says, "only fair and just" to require appellants, in return for these benefits, to respond in the State of Delaware when they are accused of misusing their power.

But like Heitner's first argument, this line of reasoning establishes only that it is appropriate for Delaware law to govern the obligations of appellants to Greyhound and its stockholders. It does not demonstrate that appellants have "purposefully avail[ed themselves] of the privilege of conducting activities within the forum State," *Hanson, supra,* at 253, in a way that would justify bringing them before a Delaware tribunal. Appellants have simply had nothing to do with the State of Delaware. Moreover, appellants had no reason to expect to be haled before a Delaware court. Delaware, unlike some States, has not enacted a statute that treats acceptance of a directorship as consent to jurisdiction in the State. And "[i]t strains reason ... to suggest that anyone buying securities in a corporation formed in Delaware 'impliedly consents' to subject himself to Delaware's ... jurisdiction on any cause of action." Appellants, who were not required to acquire interests in Greyhound in order to hold their positions, did not by acquiring those interests surrender their right to be brought to judgment only in States with which they had had "minimum contacts."

The Due Process Clause "does not contemplate that a state may make binding a judgment ... against an individual or corporate defendant with which the state has no contacts, ties, or relations." *International Shoe,* 326 U.S., at 319. Delaware's assertion of jurisdiction over appellants in this case is inconsistent with that constitutional limitation on state power. The judgment of the Delaware Supreme Court must, therefore, be reversed.

It is so ordered.

Mr. Justice Powell, concurring.

I agree that the principles of *International Shoe* should be extended to govern assertions of *in rem* as well as *in personam* jurisdiction in a state court. I also agree that neither the statutory presence of appellants' stock in Delaware nor their positions as directors and officers of a Delaware corporation can provide sufficient contacts to support the Delaware courts' assertion of jurisdiction in this case.

I would explicitly reserve judgment, however, on whether the ownership of some forms of property whose situs is indisputably and permanently located within a State may, without more, provide the contacts necessary to subject a defendant to jurisdiction within the State to the extent of the value of the property. In the case of real property, in particular, preservation of the common-law concept of *quasi in rem* jurisdiction arguably would avoid the uncertainty of the general *International Shoe* standard without significant cost to " 'traditional notions of fair play and substantial justice.' "

Subject to the foregoing reservation, I join the opinion of the Court.

Mr. Justice Stevens, concurring in the judgment.

The Due Process Clause affords protection against "judgments without notice." *International Shoe*, 326 U.S. at 324 (opinion of Black, J.). Throughout our history the acceptable exercise of *in rem* and *quasi in rem* jurisdiction has included a procedure giving reasonable assurance that actual notice of the particular claim will be conveyed to the defendant. Thus, publication, notice by registered mail, or extraterritorial personal service has been an essential ingredient of any procedure that serves as a substitute for personal service within the jurisdiction.

The requirement of fair notice also, I believe, includes fair warning that a particular activity may subject a person to the jurisdiction of a foreign sovereign. If I visit another State, or acquire real estate or open a bank account in it, I knowingly assume some risk that the State will exercise its power over my property or my person while there. My contact with the State, though minimal, gives rise to predictable risks.

Perhaps the same consequences should flow from the purchase of stock of a corporation organized under the laws of a foreign nation, because to some limited extent one's property and affairs then become subject to the laws of the nation of domicile of the corporation. As a matter of international law, that suggestion might be acceptable because a foreign investment is sufficiently unusual to make it appropriate to require the investor to study the ramifications of his decision. But a purchase of securities in the domestic market is an entirely different matter.

One who purchases shares of stock on the open market can hardly be expected to know that he has thereby become subject to suit in a forum remote from his residence and unrelated to the transaction. As a practical matter, the Delaware sequestration statute creates an unacceptable risk of judgment without notice. Unlike the 49 other States, Delaware treats the place of incorporation as the situs of the stock, even though both the owner and the custodian of the shares are elsewhere. Moreover, Delaware denies the defendant the opportunity to defend the merits of the suit unless he subjects himself to the unlimited jurisdiction of the court. Thus, it coerces a defendant either to submit to personal jurisdiction in a forum which could not otherwise obtain such jurisdiction or to lose the securities which have been attached. If its procedure were upheld, Delaware would, in effect, impose a duty of inquiry on every purchaser of securities in the national market. For unless the purchaser ascertains both the State of incorporation of the company whose shares he is buying, and also the idiosyncrasies of its law, he may be assuming an unknown risk of litigation. I therefore agree with the Court that on the record before us no adequate basis for jurisdiction exists and that the Delaware statute is unconstitutional on its face.

How the Court's opinion may be applied in other contexts is not entirely clear to me. I agree with Mr. Justice Powell that it should not be read to invalidate *quasi in rem* jurisdiction where real estate is involved. I would also not read it as invalidating other long-accepted methods of acquiring jurisdiction over persons with adequate notice of both the particular controversy and the fact that their local activities might subject them to suit. My uncertainty as to the reach of the opinion, and my fear that it purports to decide a great deal more than is necessary to dispose of this case, persuade me merely to concur in the judgment.

Mr. Justice BRENNAN, concurring in part and dissenting in part.

I join Parts I-III of the Court's opinion. I fully agree that the minimum-contacts analysis developed in *International Shoe* represents a far more sensible construct for the exercise of state-court jurisdiction than the patchwork of legal and factual fictions that has been generated from the decision in *Pennoyer.* It is precisely because the inquiry into minimum contacts is now of such overriding importance, however, that I must respectfully dissent from Part IV of the Court's opinion....

I ... would approach the minimum-contacts analysis differently than does the Court. Crucial to me is the fact that appellants voluntarily associated themselves with the State of Delaware, "invoking the benefits and protections of its laws," *Hanson*, 357 U.S. at 253, by entering into a long-term and fragile relationship with one of its domestic corporations. They thereby elected to assume powers and to undertake responsibilities wholly derived from that State's rules and regulations, and to become eligible for those benefits that Delaware law makes available to its corporations' officials. While it is possible that countervailing issues of judicial efficiency and the like might clearly favor a different forum, they do not appear on the meager record before us;[8] and, of course, we are concerned solely with "minimum" contacts, not the "best" contacts. I thus do not believe that it is unfair to insist that appellants make themselves available to suit in a competent forum that Delaware might create for vindication of its important public policies directly pertaining to appellants' fiduciary associations with the State.

Thurgood Marshall

Collection of the Supreme Court of the United States

Thurgood Marshall (1908–1993) was raised in Baltimore and graduated from Lincoln University and Howard University School of Law. As general counsel for the NAACP (National Association for the Advancement of Colored People), he argued thirty-two civil rights cases in the United States Supreme Court, including the landmark *Brown v. Board of Education* case challenging segregation in public schools. He later served on the Second Circuit Court of Appeals and as Solicitor General of the United States. He was appointed in 1967 as the first Black justice on the United States Supreme Court. The University of Maryland Law School, which had denied Marshall admission because of his race in 1930, named its law library for him in 1980.

In *Shaffer v. Heitner,* Justice Marshall, writing for the Court, reconceptualizes the basis and limits of in rem jurisdiction, concluding that the traditional doctrine "supports an ancient form without substantial modern justification."

8. And, of course, if a preferable forum exists elsewhere, a State that is constitutionally entitled to accept jurisdiction nonetheless remains free to arrange for the transfer of the litigation under the doctrine of *forum non conveniens.*

Notes and Questions: Understanding *Shaffer* and In Rem/Quasi In Rem Jurisdiction

Q **1. The answer under *Pennoyer*.** If the Court had applied the *Pennoyer* approach to in rem/quasi in rem jurisdiction, would the Delaware courts have had quasi in rem jurisdiction over the executives' stock?

A Probably. Remember that, under *Pennoyer*, a court could exercise in rem or quasi in rem jurisdiction as long as the asset was located within the forum state and was attached at an appropriate time. In *Harris v. Balk*, this view was taken to an extreme. The Court concluded that an asset—Harris's debt to Balk—was present in Maryland because Harris was physically within the state.

These precedents suggest that the stock in *Shaffer* was property that could support in rem or quasi in rem jurisdiction. The stock was considered to be physically present in Delaware, and the sequestration statute provided for its attachment. Under the pre-*Shaffer* framework, therefore, quasi in rem jurisdiction probably would have been constitutionally permissible.

Q **2. Understanding the holding.** What is the Court's new approach to in rem/quasi in rem jurisdiction, and why did the Court change the doctrine?

A The Court's holding appears just before Part IV of the opinion: "We therefore conclude that all assertions of state-court jurisdiction must be evaluated according to the standards set forth in *International Shoe* and its progeny." This sentence suggests that courts now have to employ a contacts-based inquiry when analyzing assertions of in rem or quasi in rem jurisdiction.

The Court cites several reasons for this conclusion, but one important explanation is that the exercise of jurisdiction over a person's property is effectively an exercise of jurisdiction over the owner: "The fiction that an assertion of jurisdiction over property is anything but an assertion of jurisdiction over the owner of the property supports an ancient form without substantial modern justification. Its continued acceptance would serve only to allow state-court jurisdiction that is fundamentally unfair to the defendant." Since a court in an in rem or quasi in rem action is, in effect, exercising jurisdiction over the defendant personally, the plaintiff must show that the defendant would be subject to either specific or general jurisdiction in the forum.

Q **3. Applying the *International Shoe* standard.** The Court holds that the plaintiff has to show that the directors are subject to personal jurisdiction under the *International Shoe* contacts analysis. Why is there no personal jurisdiction using that framework?

A The plaintiff's claims concerned the executives' alleged misconduct in Oregon, not Delaware, so there does not appear to be a basis for specific jurisdiction. Even if the stock certificates somehow constituted a contact in

Delaware, the Court concluded that this case did not arise out of those contacts. Thus, the Court concluded that personal jurisdiction in this case would be unconstitutional.

In his dissent, Justice Brennan argues that a company's executives are always exercising powers granted by Delaware and, critically, performing their corporate duties subject to Delaware law and regulations. According to this view, the alleged misconduct had a very strong connection with Delaware and should therefore have given rise to specific jurisdiction there.

Q **4. A legislative drafting challenge.** Imagine that you are a legislator in Delaware, and you want to write a statute that is consistent with *Shaffer* but that would give the Delaware courts personal jurisdiction over out-of-state directors whose companies are incorporated in Delaware. Would such a statute be constitutional? If so, how would you write the statute?

A There are several ways for a court to obtain personal jurisdiction, and one of them is consent. If Delaware wants all executives of Delaware-incorporated companies to be subject to personal jurisdiction in Delaware, it can enact a statute specifying that, when someone accepts a director-level position with a Delaware-incorporated company, they subject themselves to personal jurisdiction in Delaware for any claims that relate to their work as a director. (Recall the statute in *Hess v. Pawloski*, which provided that drivers subjected themselves to personal jurisdiction in Massachusetts for any claims that arose out of their driving in the forum.)

As the Court notes, some states have adopted such statutes: "Delaware, unlike some States, has not enacted a statute that treats acceptance of a directorship as consent to jurisdiction in the State." Not surprisingly, Delaware passed a similar statute after the Court's decision in *Shaffer*, Del. Code Ann. tit. 10, § 3114(a)–(b), and the statute survived a subsequent constitutional challenge. *Armstrong v. Pomerance*, 423 A.2d 174 (Del. 1980).

5. The new approach to quasi in rem jurisdiction (part I).

Pietra has a claim against Donnor, a California citizen, that arose out of a car accident that occurred in California. Pietra is a citizen of North Carolina and asks a North Carolina court to attach a money market account that Donnor owns in the state and that he opened while visiting the state. Pietra then seeks to litigate the car accident case in North Carolina, resigning herself to recover only the funds in Donnor's North Carolina money market account. Assume Donnor's North Carolina account is completely unrelated to Pietra's underlying claim against Donnor, and assume that Donnor does not otherwise have contacts with North Carolina sufficient to subject him to in personam jurisdiction in the state. Under these facts, most courts would probably

A. not exercise quasi in rem jurisdiction because Donnor lacks sufficient contacts with the state.

B. not exercise quasi in rem jurisdiction because this basis for jurisdiction was eliminated by the Supreme Court's *Shaffer* opinion.
C. exercise quasi in rem jurisdiction as long as the state court attached Donnor's account at an appropriate time in the case.
D. exercise in personam jurisdiction because the Supreme Court has eliminated the distinction between quasi in rem and in personam jurisdiction.

Under *Pennoyer*, **C** would have been the answer. As long as the property was in the forum state and attached before the judgment, a court typically would have had jurisdiction under the old framework. But *Shaffer* held that it is now necessary to engage in a contacts-based inquiry for in rem and quasi in rem cases.

Students frequently choose **B**, but that is also wrong. The Court did not eliminate quasi in rem jurisdiction; the Court simply held that this form of jurisdiction must be analyzed using a contacts-based analysis.

D is wrong, because even if there is no longer much, if any, distinction between the constitutional requirements of quasi in rem and in personam jurisdiction (there is still some debate about whether there may be some minor distinctions between the two), there is no basis for in personam jurisdiction in this case. Namely, there is no evidence that this claim arose out of any contacts that Donnor had in North Carolina, so a contacts-based analysis does not support jurisdiction here.

A is the best answer: There is no specific jurisdiction, so there is likely no quasi in rem jurisdiction.

6. The new approach to quasi in rem jurisdiction (part II).

Pietra has a claim against Donnor, a California citizen, that arose out of an injury that Pietra suffered while jogging on a rental property in North Carolina that Donnor owned. Pietra sues Donnor in North Carolina and asks the North Carolina court to attach Donnor's property at the outset of the case in an attempt to establish quasi in rem jurisdiction. Donnor's property is valuable enough to cover Pietra's damages if she wins. Assume that Donnor purchased the property only to rent it out and has never been to North Carolina. (Donnor purchased the property from California.) Donnor has no other contacts with North Carolina. Donnor moves to dismiss the case for lack of personal jurisdiction. Under these facts, most courts would probably

A. grant the motion, because Donnor has never been to North Carolina.
B. deny the motion, because this case arises out of Donnor's contacts with North Carolina.
C. deny the motion, because Donnor is at home in North Carolina and is thus subject to general jurisdiction there.
D. grant the motion, because this case does not arise out of Donnor's contacts with North Carolina.

Shaffer tells us that we must ask whether personal jurisdiction would exist using the *International Shoe* contacts framework. To answer that question, we have to ask whether Donnor has any contacts in North Carolina sufficient to give rise to jurisdiction. He does. He rents out North Carolina land for a profit, and the claim arises out of activity that took place on that property.

Recall *McGee*, where the Court said that personal jurisdiction was permissible in California over a Texas insurance company because the company sought to renew the insurance policy of an insured in California *through the mail*. The Court did not hold that the insurance company had to visit California. **A**, therefore, is incorrect; Donnor can be subject to personal jurisdiction in North Carolina even though he has never visited the state.

C is incorrect. To establish general jurisdiction over an individual, the individual must be domiciled in the forum state, and Donnor is most certainly not domiciled in North Carolina.

That leaves **B** and **D**. This case does, in fact, arise out of Donnor's contacts with North Carolina. The case involves an injury that occurred on Donnor's North Carolina property, so this case arises directly out of the contact that Donnor had in the state. **B**, therefore, is the best answer. The Court said in *Shaffer*: "The presence of property may also favor jurisdiction in cases such as suits for injury suffered on the land of an absentee owner, where the defendant's ownership of the property is conceded but the cause of action is otherwise related to rights and duties growing out of that ownership."

IV. "Transient Presence" Jurisdiction: *Burnham v. Superior Court*

Imagine that Potter sues Dalia, a Pennsylvania citizen, in Hawaii for a claim that arose out of an incident that occurred in Arkansas. Assume that Dalia has never set foot in Hawaii and that the case has nothing at all to do with Hawaii. Shortly after the case is filed, Dalia takes her first trip to Hawaii and is served with process (i.e., a copy of the complaint and a summons to appear in the case that Potter filed in Hawaii) while there. Does the Hawaii court now have personal jurisdiction over Dalia?

During the *Pennoyer* era, the answer was yes. In personam jurisdiction typically existed whenever a person was served with process while physically present in the forum state, and that is precisely what happened when Dalia visited Hawaii.

International Shoe held that personal service of the defendant in the forum state is no longer required. But even if personal service in the forum state is no longer *necessary* to establish personal jurisdiction, *International Shoe* did not resolve whether personal service in the forum is still *sufficient* to confer personal jurisdiction. In other words, is a defendant like Dalia still subject to personal jurisdiction in Hawaii because she was served with process while visiting the state on a temporary ("transient") basis?

One might argue that, if Dalia's visit to Hawaii had nothing to do with the case, the answer should be "no." The Court said in *Shaffer* that "all assertions of state-court jurisdiction must be evaluated according to the standards set forth in *International Shoe* and its progeny." That is, all assertions of personal jurisdiction should be evaluated using the contacts framework, and in this case, the Hawaii court would have neither specific nor general jurisdiction over Dalia. That seems straightforward enough. When the Court said, "all," it must have meant "all." Right?

READING *BURNHAM v. SUPERIOR COURT.* In the divorce action at issue in *Burnham*, one spouse (Mrs. Burnham) sought custody of her children as well as financial support from her husband (Mr. Burnham). To grant these requests, which would affect Mr. Burnham's parental rights and his pocketbook, the court needed to have personal jurisdiction over Mr. Burnham. As you read this case, consider the following questions:

- Why did Mr. Burnham's temporary physical presence in California suffice for personal jurisdiction?
- How does the Court distinguish its earlier decision in *Shaffer*?
- Will a defendant's temporary physical presence in a state always suffice to establish personal jurisdiction? If not, when does it suffice?

BURNHAM v. SUPERIOR COURT

495 U.S. 604 (1990)

Justice Scalia announced the judgment of the Court and delivered an opinion in which The Chief Justice and Justice Kennedy join, and in which Justice White joins with respect to Parts I, II-A, II-B, and II-C.

The question presented is whether the Due Process Clause of the Fourteenth Amendment denies California courts jurisdiction over a nonresident, who was personally served with process while temporarily in that State, in a suit unrelated to his activities in the State.

I

Petitioner Dennis Burnham married Francie Burnham in 1976 in West Virginia. In 1977 the couple moved to New Jersey, where their two children were born. In July 1987 the Burnhams decided to separate. They agreed that Mrs. Burnham, who intended to move to California, would take custody of the children. Shortly before Mrs. Burnham departed for California that same month, she and petitioner agreed that she would file for divorce on grounds of "irreconcilable differences."

In October 1987, petitioner filed for divorce in New Jersey state court on grounds of "desertion." Petitioner did not, however, obtain an issuance of summons against his wife and did not attempt to serve her with process. Mrs. Burnham, after unsuccessfully demanding that petitioner adhere to their prior agreement to submit to an "irreconcilable differences" divorce, brought suit for divorce in California state court in early January 1988.

In late January, petitioner visited southern California on business, after which he went north to visit his children in the San Francisco Bay area, where his wife resided. He took the older child to San Francisco for the weekend. Upon returning the child to Mrs. Burnham's home on January 24, 1988, petitioner was served with a California court summons and a copy of Mrs. Burnham's divorce petition. He then returned to New Jersey.

Later that year, petitioner made a special appearance in the California Superior Court, moving to quash the service of process on the ground that the court lacked personal jurisdiction over him because his only contacts with California were a few short visits to the State for the purposes of conducting business and visiting his children. The Superior Court denied the motion, and the California Court of Appeal denied mandamus relief, rejecting petitioner's contention that the Due Process Clause prohibited California courts from asserting jurisdiction over him because he lacked "minimum contacts" with the State. The court held it to be "a valid jurisdictional predicate for *in personam* jurisdiction" that the "defendant [was] present in the forum state and personally served with process." We granted certiorari.

II

A

The proposition that the judgment of a court lacking jurisdiction is void traces back to [early English opinions]. . . . In *Pennoyer v. Neff,* we announced that the judgment of a court lacking personal jurisdiction violated the Due Process Clause of the Fourteenth Amendment as well.

To determine whether the assertion of personal jurisdiction is consistent with due process, we have long relied on the principles traditionally followed by American courts in marking out the territorial limits of each State's authority. That criterion was first announced in *Pennoyer v. Neff,* in which we stated that due process "mean[s] a course of legal proceedings according to those rules and principles which have been established in our systems of jurisprudence for the protection and enforcement of private rights," 95 U.S. 714, 733 (1878), including the "well-established principles of public law respecting the jurisdiction of an independent State over persons and property." *Id.,* at 722. In what has become the classic expression of the criterion, we said in *International Shoe Co. v. Washington,* that a state court's assertion of personal jurisdiction satisfies the Due Process Clause if it does not violate " 'traditional notions of fair play and substantial justice.' " Since *International Shoe,* we have only been called upon to decide whether these "traditional notions" permit States to exercise jurisdiction over absent defendants in a manner that deviates from the rules of jurisdiction applied in the 19th century. We have held such deviations permissible, but only with respect to suits arising out of the absent defendant's contacts with the State.[1] See, *e.g., Helicopteros Nacionales de Colombia v. Hall*, 466 U.S. 408, 414 (1984). The question we must decide today is whether due process requires a similar connection between the litigation and the defendant's contacts with the State in cases where the defendant is physically present in the State at the time process is served upon him.

B

Among the most firmly established principles of personal jurisdiction in American tradition is that the courts of a State have jurisdiction over nonresidents who are physically present in the State. The view developed early that each State had the power to hale before its courts any individual who could be found within its borders, and that once having acquired jurisdiction over such a person by properly serving him with process, the State could retain jurisdiction to enter judgment against him, no matter how fleeting his visit. That view had antecedents in English common-law practice, which sometimes allowed "transitory" actions, arising out of events outside the country, to be maintained against seemingly nonresident defendants who were present in England. Justice Story believed the principle, which he traced to Roman origins, to be firmly grounded in English tradition: "[B]y the common law[,] personal actions, being transitory, may be brought in any place, where the party defendant may be found," for "every nation may . . . rightfully exercise jurisdiction over all persons within its domains." J. Story, Commentaries on the Conflict of Laws §§ 554, 543 (1846).

Recent scholarship has suggested that English tradition was not as clear as Story thought. Accurate or not, however, judging by the evidence of contemporaneous or near-contemporaneous decisions, one must conclude that Story's understanding was shared by American courts at the crucial time for present purposes: 1868, when the Fourteenth Amendment was adopted. . . .

Decisions in the courts of many States in the 19th and early 20th centuries held that personal service upon a physically present defendant sufficed to confer jurisdiction, without regard to whether the defendant was only briefly in the State or whether the cause of action was related to his activities there. Although research has not revealed a case deciding the issue in every State's courts, that appears to be because the issue was so well settled that it went unlitigated. Most States, moreover, had statutes or common-law rules that exempted from service of process individuals who were brought into the forum by force or fraud, or who were there as a party or witness in unrelated judicial proceedings. These exceptions obviously rested upon the premise that service of process conferred

1. . . . It may be that whatever special rule exists permitting "continuous and systematic" contacts, to support jurisdiction with respect to matters unrelated to activity in the forum applies *only* to corporations, which have never fitted comfortably in a jurisdictional regime based primarily upon "de facto power over the defendant's person." *International Shoe,* 326 U.S. at 316. We express no views on these matters—and, for simplicity's sake, omit reference to this aspect of "contacts"-based jurisdiction in our discussion.

jurisdiction. Particularly striking is the fact that, as far as we have been able to determine, *not one* American case from the period (or, for that matter, not one American case until 1978) held, or even suggested, that in-state personal service on an individual was insufficient to confer personal jurisdiction. Commentators were also seemingly unanimous on the rule.

This American jurisdictional practice is, moreover, not merely old; it is continuing. It remains the practice of, not only a substantial number of the States, but as far as we are aware *all* the States and the Federal Government—if one disregards (as one must for this purpose) the few opinions since 1978 that have erroneously said, on grounds similar to those that petitioner presses here, that this Court's due process decisions render the practice unconstitutional. We do not know of a single state or federal statute, or a single judicial decision resting upon state law, that has abandoned in-state service as a basis of jurisdiction. Many recent cases reaffirm it.

C

Despite this formidable body of precedent, petitioner contends, in reliance on our decisions applying the *International Shoe* standard, that in the absence of "continuous and systematic" contacts with the forum, a nonresident defendant can be subjected to judgment only as to matters that arise out of or relate to his contacts with the forum. This argument rests on a thorough misunderstanding of our cases.

The view of most courts in the 19th century was that a court simply could not exercise *in personam* jurisdiction over a nonresident who had not been personally served with process in the forum. *Pennoyer v. Neff,* while renowned for its statement of the principle that the Fourteenth Amendment prohibits such an exercise of jurisdiction, in fact set that forth only as dictum and decided the case (which involved a judgment rendered more than two years before the Fourteenth Amendment's ratification) under "well-established principles of public law." Those principles, embodied in the Due Process Clause, required (we said) that when proceedings "involv[e] merely a determination of the personal liability of the defendant, he must be brought within [the court's] jurisdiction by service of process within the State, or his voluntary appearance." We invoked that rule in a series of subsequent cases, as either a matter of due process or a "fundamental principl[e] of jurisprudence."

Later years, however, saw the weakening of the *Pennoyer* rule. In the late 19th and early 20th centuries, changes in the technology of transportation and communication, and the tremendous growth of interstate business activity, led to an "inevitable relaxation of the strict limits on state jurisdiction" over nonresident individuals and corporations. *Hanson v. Denckla,* 357 U.S. 235, 260 (1958) (Black, J. dissenting). States required, for example, that nonresident corporations appoint an in-state agent upon whom process could be served as a condition of transacting business within their borders and provided in-state "substituted service" for nonresident motorists who caused injury in the State and left before personal service could be accomplished. We initially upheld these laws under the Due Process Clause on grounds that they complied with *Pennoyer*'s rigid requirement of either "consent," see, e.g., *Hess v. Pawloski*, 274 U.S. 352 (1927), or "presence." As many observed, however, the consent and presence were purely fictional. Our opinion in *International Shoe* cast those fictions aside and made explicit the underlying basis of these decisions: Due process does not necessarily *require* the States to adhere to the unbending territorial limits on jurisdiction set forth in *Pennoyer.* The validity of assertion of jurisdiction over a nonconsenting defendant who is not present in the forum depends upon whether "the quality and nature of [his] activity" in relation to the forum renders such jurisdiction consistent with " 'traditional notions of fair play and substantial justice.' " Subsequent cases have derived from the *International Shoe* standard the general rule that a State may dispense with in-forum personal service on nonresident defendants in suits arising out of their activities in the State. As *International Shoe* suggests, the defendant's litigation-related "minimum contacts" may take the place of physical presence as the basis for jurisdiction. . . .

Nothing in *International Shoe* or the cases that have followed it, however, offers support for the very different proposition petitioner seeks to establish today: that a defendant's presence in the forum is not only unnecessary to validate novel, nontraditional assertions of jurisdiction, but is itself no longer sufficient to establish jurisdiction. . . .

The short of the matter is that jurisdiction based on physical presence alone constitutes due process because it is one of the continuing traditions of our legal system that define the due process standard of "traditional notions of fair play and substantial justice." That standard was developed by *analogy* to "physical presence," and it would be perverse to say it could now be turned against that touchstone of jurisdiction.

D

Petitioner's strongest argument, though we ultimately reject it, relies upon our decision in *Shaffer v. Heitner*. In that case, a Delaware court hearing a shareholder's derivative suit against a corporation's directors secured jurisdiction quasi in rem by sequestering the out-of-state defendants' stock in the company, the situs of which was Delaware under Delaware law. Reasoning that Delaware's sequestration procedure was simply a mechanism to compel the absent defendants to appear in a suit to determine their personal rights and obligations, we concluded that the normal rules we had developed under *International Shoe* for jurisdiction over suits against absent defendants should apply—viz., Delaware could not hear the suit because the defendants' sole contact with the State (ownership of property there) was unrelated to the lawsuit.

It goes too far to say, as petitioner contends, that *Shaffer* compels the conclusion that a State lacks jurisdiction over an individual unless the litigation arises out of his activities in the State. *Shaffer*, like *International Shoe*, involved jurisdiction over an *absent defendant*, and it stands for nothing more than the proposition that when the "minimum contact" that is a substitute for physical presence consists of property ownership it must, like other minimum contacts, be related to the litigation. Petitioner wrenches out of its context our statement in *Shaffer* that "all assertions of state-court jurisdiction must be evaluated according to the standards set forth in *International Shoe* and its progeny." When read together with the two sentences that preceded it, the meaning of this statement becomes clear:

> "The fiction that an assertion of jurisdiction over property is anything but an assertion of jurisdiction over the owner of the property supports an ancient form without substantial modern justification. Its continued acceptance would serve only to allow state-court jurisdiction that is fundamentally unfair to the defendant.
>
> "We *therefore conclude* that all assertions of state-court jurisdiction must be evaluated according to the standards set forth in *International Shoe* and its progeny." *Ibid.* (emphasis added).

Shaffer was saying, in other words, not that all bases for the assertion of *in personam* jurisdiction (including, presumably, in-state service) must be treated alike and subjected to the "minimum contacts" analysis of *International Shoe*; but rather that *quasi in rem* jurisdiction, that fictional "ancient form," and *in personam* jurisdiction, are really one and the same and must be treated alike—leading to the conclusion that *quasi in rem* jurisdiction, i.e., that form of *in personam* jurisdiction based upon a "property ownership" contact and by definition unaccompanied by personal, in-state service, must satisfy the litigation-relatedness requirement of *International Shoe*. The logic of *Shaffer*'s holding—which places all suits against absent nonresidents on the same constitutional footing, regardless of whether a separate Latin label is attached to one particular basis of contact—does not compel the conclusion that physically present defendants must be treated identically to absent ones. As we have demonstrated at length, our tradition has treated the two classes of defendants quite differently, and it is unreasonable to read *Shaffer* as casually obliterating that distinction. *International Shoe* confined its "minimum contacts" requirement to situations in which the defendant "be not present within the territory of the forum," and nothing in *Shaffer* expands that requirement beyond that.

It is fair to say, however, that while our holding today does not contradict *Shaffer*, our basic approach to the due process question is different. We have conducted no independent inquiry into the desirability or fairness of the prevailing in-state service rule, leaving that judgment to the legislatures that are free to amend it; for our purposes, its validation is its pedigree, as the phrase "*traditional notions* of fair play and substantial justice" makes clear. *Shaffer* did conduct such an independent inquiry, asserting that " 'traditional notions of fair play and substantial justice' can be as readily offended by the perpetuation of ancient forms that are no longer justified as by the adoption of new procedures that are inconsistent with the basic values of our constitutional heritage," *Shaffer*, 433 U.S. at 212. Perhaps that assertion can be sustained when the "perpetuation of ancient forms" is engaged in by only a very small minority of the States. Where, however, as in the present case, a jurisdictional principle is both firmly approved by tradition and still favored, it is impossible to imagine what standard we could appeal to for the judgment that it is "no longer justified." While in no way receding from or casting doubt upon the holding of *Shaffer* or any other case, we reaffirm today our time-honored approach. For new procedures, hitherto unknown, the Due Process Clause requires analysis to determine whether "traditional notions of fair play and substantial justice" have been offended. But a doctrine of personal jurisdiction that dates back to the adoption of the Fourteenth Amendment and is still generally observed unquestionably meets that standard.

III

A few words in response to Justice Brennan's opinion concurring in the judgment: It insists that we apply "contemporary notions of due process" to determine the constitutionality of California's assertion of jurisdiction. But our analysis today comports with that prescription, at least if we give it the only sense allowed by our precedents. The "contemporary notions of due process" applicable to personal jurisdiction are the enduring "*traditional* notions of fair play and substantial justice" established as the test by *International Shoe*. By its very language, that test is satisfied if a state court adheres to jurisdictional rules that are generally applied and have always been applied in the United States.

But the concurrence's proposed standard of "contemporary notions of due process" requires more: It measures state-court jurisdiction not only against traditional doctrines in this country, including current state-court practice, but also against each Justice's subjective assessment of what is fair and just. Authority for that seductive standard is not to be found in any of our personal jurisdiction cases. It is, indeed, an outright break with the test of "traditional notions of fair play and substantial justice," which would have to be reformulated "*our* notions of fair play and substantial justice."

The subjectivity, and hence inadequacy, of this approach becomes apparent when the concurrence tries to explain *why* the assertion of jurisdiction in the present case meets its standard of continuing-American-tradition-*plus*-innate-fairness. Justice Brennan lists the "benefits" Mr. Burnham derived from the State of California—the fact that, during the few days he was there, "[h]is health and safety [were] guaranteed by the State's police, fire, and emergency medical services; he [was] free to travel on the State's roads and waterways; he likely enjoy[ed] the fruits of the State's economy." Three days' worth of these benefits strike us as powerfully inadequate to establish, as an abstract matter, that it is "fair" for California to decree the ownership of all Mr. Burnham's worldly goods acquired during the 10 years of his marriage, and the custody over his children. We dare-say a contractual exchange swapping those benefits for that power would not survive the "unconscionability" provision of the Uniform Commercial Code. Even less persuasive are the other "fairness" factors alluded to by Justice Brennan. It would create "an asymmetry," we are told, if Burnham were *permitted* (as he is) to appear in California courts as a plaintiff, but were not *compelled* to appear in California courts as defendant; and travel being as easy as it is nowadays, and modern procedural devices being so convenient, it is no great hardship to appear in California courts. The problem with these assertions is that they justify the exercise of jurisdiction over *everyone, whether or not* he ever comes to California. The only "fairness" elements setting Mr. Burnham apart from the rest of the world are the three days' "benefits" referred to above—and even those, do not set him apart from many other people who have enjoyed three days in the Golden State (savoring the fruits of its economy, the availability of its roads and police services) but who were fortunate enough not to be served with process while they were there and thus are not (simply by reason of that savoring) subject to the general jurisdiction of California's courts. In other words, even if one agreed with Justice Brennan's conception of an equitable bargain, the "benefits" we have been discussing would explain why it is "fair" to assert general jurisdiction over Burnham-returned-to-New-Jersey-after-service only at the expense of proving that it is also "fair" to assert general jurisdiction over Burnham-returned-to-New-Jersey-*without*-service—which we *know* does not conform with "contemporary notions of due process."

There is, we must acknowledge, one factor mentioned by Justice Brennan that *both* relates distinctively to the assertion of jurisdiction on the basis of personal in-state service *and* is fully persuasive—namely, the fact that a defendant voluntarily present in a particular State has a "reasonable expectatio[n]" that he is subject to suit there. By formulating it as a "reasonable expectation" Justice Brennan makes that seem like a "fairness" factor; but in reality, of course, it is just tradition masquerading as "fairness." The only reason for charging Mr. Burnham with the reasonable expectation of being subject to suit is that the States of the Union assert adjudicatory jurisdiction over the person, and have always asserted adjudicatory jurisdiction over the person, by serving him with process during his temporary physical presence in their territory. That continuing tradition, which anyone entering California should have known about, renders it "fair" for Mr. Burnham, who voluntarily entered California, to be sued there for divorce—at least "fair" in the limited sense that he has no one but himself to blame. Justice Brennan's long journey is a circular one, leaving him, at the end of the day, in complete reliance upon the very factor he sought to avoid: The existence of a continuing tradition is not enough, fairness also must be considered; fairness exists here because there is a continuing tradition.

While Justice Brennan's concurrence is unwilling to confess that the Justices of this Court can possibly be bound by a continuing American tradition that a particular procedure is fair, neither is it willing to embrace the logical consequences of that refusal—or even to be clear about what consequences (logical or otherwise) it does embrace. Justice Brennan says that "[f]or these reasons [*i.e.*, because of the reasonableness factors enumerated above], as a rule the exercise of personal jurisdiction over a defendant based on his voluntary presence in the forum will satisfy the requirements of due process." The use of the word "rule" conveys the reassuring feeling that he is establishing a principle of law one can rely upon—but of course he is not. Since Justice Brennan's only criterion of constitutionality is "fairness," the phrase "as a rule" represents nothing more than his estimation that, *usually*, all the elements of "fairness" he discusses in the present case will exist. But what if they do not? Suppose, for example, that a defendant in Mr. Burnham's situation enjoys not three days' worth of California's "benefits," but 15 minutes' worth. Or suppose we remove one of those "benefits"—"enjoy[ment of] the fruits of the State's economy"—by positing that Mr. Burnham had not come to California on business, but only to visit his children. Or suppose that Mr. Burnham were demonstrably so impecunious as to be unable to take advantage of the modern means of transportation and communication that Justice Brennan finds so relevant. Or suppose, finally, that the California courts lacked the "variety of procedural devices," that Justice Brennan says can reduce the burden upon out-of-state litigants. One may also make additional suppositions, relating not to the absence of the factors that Justice Brennan discusses, but to the presence of additional factors bearing upon the ultimate criterion of "fairness." What if, for example, Mr. Burnham were visiting a sick child? Or a dying child? Since, so far as one can tell, Justice Brennan's approval of applying the in-state service rule in the present case rests on the presence of *all* the factors he lists, and on the absence of any others, every different case will present a different litigable issue. Thus, despite the fact that he manages to work the word "rule" into his formulation, Justice Brennan's approach does not establish a rule of law at all, but only a "totality of the circumstances" test, guaranteeing what traditional territorial rules of jurisdiction were designed precisely to avoid: uncertainty and litigation over the preliminary issue of the forum's competence. It may be that those evils, necessarily accompanying a freestanding "reasonableness" inquiry, must be accepted at the margins, when we evaluate *non*traditional forms of jurisdiction newly adopted by the States. But that is no reason for injecting them into the core of our American practice, exposing to such a "reasonableness" inquiry the ground of jurisdiction that has hitherto been considered the very *baseline* of reasonableness, physical presence.

The difference between us and Justice Brennan has nothing to do with whether "further progress [is] to be made" in the "evolution of our legal system." It has to do with whether changes are to be adopted as progressive by the American people or decreed as progressive by the Justices of this Court. Nothing we say today prevents individual States from limiting or entirely abandoning the in-state-service basis of jurisdiction. And nothing prevents an overwhelming majority of them from doing so, with the consequence that the "traditional notions of fairness" that this Court applies may change. But the States have overwhelmingly declined to adopt such limitation or abandonment, evidently not considering it to be progress. The question is whether, armed with no authority other than individual Justices' perceptions of fairness that conflict with both past and current practice, this Court can compel the States to make such a change on the ground that "due process" requires it. We hold that it cannot.

Because the Due Process Clause does not prohibit the California courts from exercising jurisdiction over petitioner based on the fact of in-state service of process, the judgment is

Affirmed.

Justice WHITE, concurring in part and concurring in the judgment.

I join Parts I, II-A, II-B, and II-C of Justice Scalia's opinion and concur in the judgment of affirmance. The rule allowing jurisdiction to be obtained over a nonresident by personal service in the forum State, without more, has been and is so widely accepted throughout this country that I could not possibly strike it down, either on its face or as applied in this case, on the ground that it denies due process of law guaranteed by the Fourteenth Amendment. Although the Court has the authority under the Amendment to examine even traditionally accepted procedures and declare them invalid, *e.g., Shaffer v. Heitner*, 433 U.S. 186 (1977), there has been no showing here or elsewhere that as a general proposition the rule is so arbitrary and lacking in common sense in so many instances that it should be held violative of due process in every case. Furthermore, until such a showing is made, which would be difficult indeed, claims in individual cases that the rule would operate unfairly as applied to the particular nonresident involved need not be entertained. At least this would be the case where presence in the forum State is intentional, which would almost always be the fact. Otherwise, there would be endless, fact-specific litigation in the trial and appellate courts, including this one. Here, personal service in California, without more, is enough, and I agree that the judgment should be affirmed.

Justice BRENNAN, with whom Justice MARSHALL, Justice BLACKMUN, and Justice O'CONNOR join, concurring in the judgment.

I agree with Justice Scalia that the Due Process Clause of the Fourteenth Amendment generally permits a state court to exercise jurisdiction over a defendant if he is served with process while voluntarily present in the forum State.[1] I do not perceive the need, however, to decide that a jurisdictional rule that " 'has been immemorially the actual law of the land,' " automatically comports with due process simply by virtue of its "pedigree." Although I agree that history is an important factor in establishing whether a jurisdictional rule satisfies due process requirements, I cannot agree that it is the *only* factor such that all traditional rules of jurisdiction are, *ipso facto*, forever constitutional. Unlike Justice Scalia, I would undertake an "independent inquiry into the ... fairness of the prevailing in-state service rule." I therefore concur only in the judgment.

I

I believe that the approach adopted by Justice Scalia's opinion today—reliance solely on historical pedigree—is foreclosed by our decisions in *International Shoe* and *Shaffer*. In *International Shoe*, we held that a state court's assertion of personal

1. I use the term "transient jurisdiction" to refer to jurisdiction premised solely on the fact that a person is served with process while physically present in the forum State.

jurisdiction does not violate the Due Process Clause if it is consistent with " 'traditional notions of fair play and substantial justice.' "[2] In *Shaffer*, we stated that "*all* assertions of state-court jurisdiction must be evaluated according to the standards set forth in *International Shoe* and its progeny." 433 U.S., at 212 (emphasis added). The critical insight of *Shaffer* is that all rules of jurisdiction, even ancient ones, must satisfy contemporary notions of due process. No longer were we content to limit our jurisdictional analysis to pronouncements that "[t]he foundation of jurisdiction is physical power," and that "every State possesses exclusive jurisdiction and sovereignty over persons and property within its territory." *Pennoyer*, 95 U.S. at 722. While acknowledging that "history must be considered as supporting the proposition that jurisdiction based solely on the presence of property satisfie[d] the demands of due process," we found that this factor could not be "decisive." 433 U.S., at 211–212. We recognized that " '[t]raditional notions of fair play and substantial justice' can be as readily offended by the perpetuation of ancient forms that are no longer justified as by the adoption of new procedures that are inconsistent with the basic values of our constitutional heritage." *Id.*, at 212. I agree with this approach and continue to believe that "the minimum-contacts analysis developed in *International Shoe* . . . represents a far more sensible construct for the exercise of state-court jurisdiction than the patchwork of legal and factual fictions that has been generated from the decision in *Pennoyer*." *Shaffer*, 433 U.S. at 219 (Brennan, J., concurring in part and dissenting in part).

While our *holding* in *Shaffer* may have been limited to *quasi in rem* jurisdiction, our mode of analysis was not. Indeed, that we were willing in *Shaffer* to examine anew the appropriateness of the *quasi in rem* rule—until that time dutifully accepted by American courts for at least a century—demonstrates that we did not believe that the "pedigree" of a jurisdictional practice was dispositive in deciding whether it was consistent with due process. We later characterized *Shaffer* as "abandon[ing] the outworn rule of *Harris v. Balk* that the interest of a creditor in a debt could be extinguished or otherwise affected by any State having transitory jurisdiction over the debtor." *World-Wide Volkswagen Corp v. Woodson*, 444 U.S. 286, 325–326 (1980). If we could discard an "ancient form without substantial modern justification" in *Shaffer*, we can do so again. Lower courts, commentators, and the American Law Institute all have interpreted *International Shoe* and *Shaffer* to mean that *every* assertion of state court jurisdiction, even one pursuant to a "traditional" rule such as transient jurisdiction, must comport with contemporary notions of due process. Notwithstanding the nimble gymnastics of Justice Scalia's opinion today, it is not faithful to our decision in *Shaffer*.

2. Our reference in *International Shoe* to " 'traditional notions of fair play and substantial justice,' " meant simply that those concepts are indeed traditional ones, not that, as Justice Scalia's opinion suggests, their specific *content* was to be determined by tradition alone. We recognized that contemporary societal norms must play a role in our analysis.

II

Tradition, though alone not dispositive, is of course *relevant* to the question whether the rule of transient jurisdiction is consistent with due process.[7] Tradition is salient not in the sense that practices of the past are automatically reasonable today; indeed, under such a standard, the legitimacy of transient jurisdiction would be called into question because the rule's historical "pedigree" is a matter of intense debate. The rule was a stranger to the common law and was rather weakly implanted in American jurisprudence "at the crucial time for present purposes: 1868, when the Fourteenth Amendment was adopted." For much of the 19th century, American courts did not uniformly recognize the concept of transient jurisdiction, and it appears that the transient rule did not receive wide currency until well after our decision in *Pennoyer.*

. . . I find the historical background relevant because, however murky the jurisprudential origins of transient jurisdiction, the fact that American courts have announced the rule for perhaps a century (first in dicta, more recently in holdings) provides a defendant voluntarily present in a particular State *today* "clear notice that [he] is subject to suit" in the forum. *World-Wide Volkswagen*, 444 U.S. at 297. Regardless of whether Justice Story's account of the rule's genesis is mythical, our common understanding *now*, fortified by a century of judicial practice, is that jurisdiction is often a function of geography. The transient rule is consistent with reasonable expectations and is entitled to a strong presumption that it comports with due process. "If I visit another State, . . . I knowingly assume some risk that the State will exercise its power over my property or my person while there. My contact with the State, though minimal, gives rise to predictable risks." *Shaffer*, 433 U.S., at 218 (Stevens, J., concurring in judgment). . . .

By visiting the forum State, a transient defendant actually "avail[s]" himself, *Burger King Co. v. Rudzewicz*, 471 U.S. 462, 476 (1985), of significant benefits provided by the State. His health and safety are guaranteed by the State's police, fire, and emergency medical services; he is free to travel on the State's roads and waterways; he likely enjoys the fruits of the State's economy as well. Moreover, the Privileges and Immunities Clause of Article IV prevents a state government from discriminating against a transient defendant by denying him the protections of its law or the right of access to its courts. Subject only to the doctrine of *forum non conveniens*, an out-of-state plaintiff may use state courts in all circumstances in which those courts would be available to state citizens. Without transient jurisdiction, an asymmetry would arise: A transient would have the full benefit of the power of the forum State's courts as a plaintiff while retaining immunity from their authority as a defendant.

The potential burdens on a transient defendant are slight. " '[M]odern transportation and communications have made it much less burdensome for a party

---

7. I do not propose that the "contemporary notions of due process" to be applied are no more than "each Justice's subjective assessment of what is fair and just." Rather, the inquiry is guided by our decisions beginning with *International Shoe*, and the specific factors that we have developed to ascertain whether a jurisdictional rule comports with "traditional notions of fair play and substantial justice." This analysis may not be "mechanical or quantitative," *International Shoe*, 326 U.S. at 319 but neither is it "freestanding," or dependent on personal whim. Our experience with this approach demonstrates that it is well within our competence to employ.

sued to defend himself' " in a State outside his place of residence. *Burger King,* 471 U.S., at 474 (quoting *McGee v. International Life Ins. Co.,* 355 U.S. 220, 223 (1957)). That the defendant has already journeyed at least once before to the forum—as evidenced by the fact that he was served with process there—is an indication that suit in the forum likely would not be prohibitively inconvenient. Finally, any burdens that do arise can be ameliorated by a variety of procedural devices [such as inexpensive discovery options, motions to dismiss, and motions for summary judgment, among others]. For these reasons, as a rule the exercise of personal jurisdiction over a defendant based on his voluntary presence in the forum will satisfy the requirements of due process.[14]

In this case, it is undisputed that petitioner was served with process while voluntarily and knowingly in the State of California. I therefore concur in the judgment.

Justice STEVENS, concurring in the judgment.

As I explained in my separate writing, I did not join the Court's opinion in *Shaffer,* because I was concerned by its unnecessarily broad reach. The same concern prevents me from joining either Justice Scalia's or Justice Brennan's opinion in this case. For me, it is sufficient to note that the historical evidence and consensus identified by Justice Scalia, the considerations of fairness identified by Justice Brennan, and the common sense displayed by Justice White, all combine to demonstrate that this is, indeed, a very easy case.* Accordingly, I agree that the judgment should be affirmed.

Notes and Questions: Understanding *Burnham* and "Transient Presence" Jurisdiction

1. Does "all" mean "all"? A central question in *Burnham* was whether the holding in *Shaffer*—that "all assertions of state-court jurisdiction must be evaluated according to the standards set forth in *International Shoe*"—should be applied to transient presence jurisdiction.

14. . . . I note, moreover, that the dual conclusions of Justice Scalia's opinion create a singularly unattractive result. Justice Scalia suggests that when and if a jurisdictional rule becomes substantively unfair or even "unconscionable," this Court is powerless to alter it. Instead, he is willing to rely on individual States to limit or abandon bases of jurisdiction that have become obsolete. This reliance is misplaced, for States have little incentive to limit rules such as transient jurisdiction that make it *easier* for their own citizens to sue out-of-state defendants. That States are more likely to expand their jurisdiction is illustrated by the adoption by many States of long-arm statutes extending the reach of personal jurisdiction to the limits established by the Federal Constitution. Out-of-staters do not vote in state elections or have a voice in state government. We should not assume, therefore, that States will be motivated by "notions of fairness" to curb jurisdictional rules like the one at issue here. The reasoning of Justice Scalia's opinion today is strikingly oblivious to the *raison d'être* of various constitutional doctrines designed to protect out-of-staters, such as the Art. IV Privileges and Immunities Clause and the Commerce Clause.

* Perhaps the adage about hard cases making bad law should be revised to cover easy cases. **[EDS.—Footnote in original.]**

Justice Scalia and three other justices concluded that the *Shaffer* opinion really meant to say that assertions of in personam, quasi in rem, and in rem jurisdiction had to meet the *International Shoe* standard, not that *International Shoe* applied to *other* bases for personal jurisdiction, like transient presence. These justices reasoned that transient presence jurisdiction was well established historically, so the use of that form of jurisdiction was clearly consistent with "traditional" notions of fair play and substantial justice.

Justice Brennan and three other justices agreed with Justice Scalia that personal jurisdiction existed in this particular case, but they disagreed as to the reasoning. These justices thought that *Shaffer* meant what it said: "All" assertions of personal jurisdiction, including transient presence, had to be analyzed using the *International Shoe* standard. Nevertheless, these justices believed that the *International Shoe* standard was satisfied here. They reasoned that Mr. Burnham had contacts with California, including visiting his children and using the state's roads, so transient presence jurisdiction was fair in this case.

The tie-breaking ninth justice, Justice Stevens, concluded that Justice Scalia's focus on history and Justice Brennan's focus on fairness were both strong arguments for finding personal jurisdiction in this case and that there was no need to decide between the two rationales. In short, all nine justices concluded that transient presence jurisdiction existed here, but they disagreed about the reasoning.

2. Transient presence in the corporate context. *Burnham* affirms that jurisdiction based on transient presence survives *Shaffer*, but does it apply to companies? For example, can a plaintiff obtain personal jurisdiction over an out-of-state corporation by serving the company's executive while she's traveling in the forum?

Courts have consistently held that a plaintiff cannot obtain personal jurisdiction over a corporation by serving an officer of that company who happens to be in the forum state. *See, e.g., James Dickinson Farm Mortgage Co. v. Harry*, 273 U.S. 119, 122 (1927) (holding that "[j]urisdiction over a corporation of one state cannot be acquired in another state or district in which it has no place of business and is not found, merely by serving process upon an executive officer temporarily therein, even if he is there on business of the company"). This approach makes sense given that a corporation has a legal status that is distinct from the legal status of its employees.

In contrast, partnerships do not have a legal status that exists independently of the individual partners. Recall that, for diversity jurisdiction purposes, a partnership is considered to be a citizen of every state where an individual partner is domiciled. Because a partnership does not have a status independent from the partners themselves, it is constitutionally permissible for a court to exercise personal jurisdiction over a partnership if one of the partners is served within the forum state. *See, e.g., First American Corp. v. Price Waterhouse LLP*, 154 F.3d 16, 19 (2d Cir. 1998). Notably, this power exists only if a state has authorized it under a long arm provision, and not all states have done so. *See, e.g., Shank/Balfour Beatty, Inc. v. Int'l Brotherhood of Elec. Workers Local 99*, 497 F.3d 83, 94 (1st Cir. 2007).

Q **3. Another legislative drafting challenge.** Recall the McDonald's example from earlier in this chapter. Penelope suffers third-degree burns from a McDonald's coffee that she purchased in Florida. Upon returning to her home in Georgia, Penelope sues McDonald's in a Georgia state court for negligence, alleging that the store sold excessively hot coffee and caused her to suffer damages. McDonald's is incorporated in Delaware and has its principal place of business in Illinois. As discussed earlier, McDonald's is not at home in Georgia, so it is not subject to general jurisdiction there. Are there any other ways to subject McDonald's to personal jurisdiction in Georgia? What kind of statute would have to exist? (Hint: Think back to Delaware's legislative solution after *Shaffer*.)

A The answer turns once again on consent. Many states require companies that do business in the forum to appoint an in-state agent for service of process. (See one such example in Chapter 9, section II, note 3.) If such a statute exists and a plaintiff wants to sue the company in that forum, the plaintiff can serve the in-state agent that the company had previously designated. This process is unlike the service of the transient executive described in note 2, because in this case, the company itself consents to being sued in the forum by appointing an in-state agent. There is no such corporate consent when an executive simply happens to travel through the forum. In short, a corporate registration statute could arguably require a company to consent to general jurisdiction in the forum as a condition of registering to do business there.

The reason that this authority is only arguable is that *Daimler* made clear that general jurisdiction is constitutionally permissible only when a company has its principal place of business and place of incorporation in the forum. It is not yet clear whether a state has the constitutional authority to require a company to consent to general jurisdiction as a condition of doing business in the state. *See, e.g., Brown v. Lockheed Martin*, 814 F.3d 619, 640–41 (2d Cir. 2016) (raising, but not deciding, the question of whether a statute that confers general jurisdiction under these circumstances is constitutional in light of the holding in *Daimler*); *In re Asbsestos Prods. Liab. Litig.*, 384 F. Supp. 3d 532, 540–41 (E.D. Pa. 2019) (holding that such a statute is now unconstitutional).

4. An exception: Transient presence by fraud or duress. *Burnham* makes clear that transient presence jurisdiction remains a viable option under many circumstances. Nevertheless, courts have recognized some exceptions, such as when a defendant is served with process after being coaxed into the state by fraud or duress. *See Burnham v. Superior Court*, 495 U.S. 604, 613 (1990). For example, in *Terlizzi v. Brodie*, 329 N.Y.S. 2d 589 (N.Y. App. Div. 1972), a court held that personal jurisdiction was improper because the out-of-state defendants, who were served outside of a Broadway theater, had been lured into New York by a call promising them two tickets to a show. There are also cases denying jurisdiction based on in-state service if a defendant is visiting the state in connection with another piece of litigation.

V. Issue Analysis: The Sky's the Limit?

Justice Stevens thought that *Burnham* presented an easy case, but lower courts have had a hard time applying the decision to more difficult fact patterns. For a good example of such a case, consider the question below, which has appeared in various forms on many professors' final exams and on at least one bar exam. Try writing out an answer before looking at the suggested analysis. This is not only good practice, but many students who read the suggested analysis before writing out their own answers mistakenly think, "Oh yeah. I would have written that." Prove it!

A. The Question

Pangea, a Nevada citizen, suffers injuries in Maine after colliding with a car driven by Denny, a Maine citizen. Pangea returns home to Nevada and sues Denny in Nevada state court. Assume Denny has never set foot in Nevada, but shortly after Pangea files her lawsuit, Denny flies to California to visit some relatives. While flying over Nevada's airspace, another passenger (a process server) serves Denny with Pangea's complaint and a summons to appear in the Nevada court. Denny moves to dismiss the case on personal jurisdiction grounds. Explain whether Denny's motion should be granted and why you have reached that conclusion. Be sure to identify reasonable counterarguments and explain why you have found them to be unpersuasive.

B. A Suggested Analysis

The court should grant Denny's motion. Under these facts, the only two possible ways to establish personal jurisdiction are specific jurisdiction and transient presence jurisdiction. Neither doctrine is likely to apply here.

To establish specific jurisdiction, the defendant must have a purposeful contact in the forum, the claim must arise out of that contact, and personal jurisdiction must be reasonable. In this case, Denny has no contacts in Nevada other than the flight, so the flight is the only plausible basis for specific jurisdiction. The problem is that, even if the flight is considered to be a purposeful contact in Nevada, this case has nothing to do with the flight. Because the claim does not arise out of any contact that Denny has had in Nevada, specific jurisdiction does not exist here.

There is a stronger but ultimately unpersuasive argument in favor of transient presence jurisdiction. Transient presence jurisdiction exists when the defendant is served personally with process while in the forum state. Traditionally, courts have exercised personal jurisdiction under these circumstances, and the Supreme Court made clear in *Burnham* that courts continue to have this power today. Thus, at first blush, transient presence jurisdiction appears to exist here: Denny was present in Nevada when served with process.

A closer examination of *Burnham*, however, makes this reasoning unconvincing. Four justices in that case upheld the doctrine of transient presence jurisdiction on the grounds that it has existed for centuries and that it is, therefore, "consistent with traditional notions of fair play and substantial justice." In defining what is traditionally fair and reasonable, the *Burnham* Court focused heavily on the voluntariness of the defendant's presence in the state. For example, Justice Scalia noted that a defendant who is "*voluntarily* present in a particular State has a 'reasonable expectatio[n]' that he is subject to suit there" (emphasis added). Similarly, Justice White assumed that personal jurisdiction would generally exist when the defendant was served while in the forum, at least "where presence in the forum State is intentional." This logic suggests that transient presence jurisdiction is *not* consistent with traditional notions of fair play and substantial justice when defendants are physically present in a state *without* their knowledge or intent.

In this case, there is no evidence that Denny intended to enter Nevada or that he knew the plane would fly over Nevada. Although it is quite likely that such a flight would pass over Nevada, Denny had probably not given it any thought. The airline, the pilot, and air traffic controllers make these decisions, not the passengers. For this reason, Denny's entry into Nevada air space was neither intentional nor voluntary. Accordingly, transient presence jurisdiction should not apply here.

The conclusion would be the same under the rationale offered in Justice Brennan's opinion in *Burnham*, which was joined by three other justices. These justices contended that a court should ask whether the defendant took advantage of the state's services and could have expected to be subjected to suit there. In this case, Denny arguably took advantage of Nevada's services, such as the air traffic control facilities that helped guide his plane safely through Nevada airspace. Using this reasoning, it may appear that Denny should be subject to personal jurisdiction. The better argument, however, is that an airline passenger does not take advantage of a state's resources just because the passenger's pilot relied on an air traffic control tower in the state. A greater level of purposefulness should be required. Indeed, in finding that Mr. Burnham took advantage of California's resources, Justice Brennan's opinion observed that Mr. Burnham had been "served with process while voluntarily and knowingly" present in California. In other words, Justice Brennan's opinion (like Justice Scalia's) implied that the defendant had to "knowingly" enter the forum state. As explained earlier, Denny did not do so in this case.

For these reasons, I conclude that the court should grant Denny's motion.

Comments on the suggested analysis. This suggested analysis is not necessarily the right answer or the answer that a majority of courts would give. In fact, one pre-*Burnham* decision held that transient presence jurisdiction could exist under facts very similar to those presented here. *Grace v. MacArthur*, 170 F. Supp. 442 (E.D. Ark. 1959). For a question like this one, though, your answer is less important than your reasoning. You need to identify the right issue (i.e., whether transient jurisdiction applies), explain why existing case law (e.g., *Burnham*) does not definitively resolve the issue, and analyze how existing precedents could be used to make various arguments regarding the issue at hand.

Law students often have a hard time with this kind of ambiguity, typically because they are accustomed to being asked to find the "right" answer to questions. The reality is that many legal questions are not so straightforward, and you will encounter many ambiguities on law school exams and throughout your careers. You need to be able to identify those ambiguities and analyze them. When you hear people say that law school trains you to "think like a lawyer," this is often what they mean.

VI. Consent and Waiver

This chapter describes alternatives to specific jurisdiction, including general jurisdiction, in rem/quasi in rem jurisdiction, and "transient presence." There are also two other common ways of establishing personal jurisdiction: consent and waiver.[1]

A. Consent

There are several ways for a party to consent to personal jurisdiction. First, and most obviously, a defendant can affirmatively decide not to raise the issue. Courts typically do not address personal jurisdiction *sua sponte* (on their own), so if a defendant wants to litigate in a court that lacks personal jurisdiction, the defendant can simply appear in court and not raise the issue.

Second, parties can consent to personal jurisdiction through their conduct. For example, by filing a claim, a plaintiff consents to the court's exercise of personal jurisdiction over any counterclaims that the defendant might allege against the plaintiff. *Adam v. Saenger*, 303 U.S. 59, 67 (1938) (holding that "[t]here is nothing in the Fourteenth Amendment to prevent a state from adopting a procedure by which a judgment in personam may be rendered in a [counterclaim] against a plaintiff in its courts ...").

Third, defendants can consent to personal jurisdiction before a lawsuit occurs. For example, contracts often contain "forum selection clauses," which specify where the parties will litigate any claims that might arise from the transaction. Thus, a contract may contain a provision like this one: "any dispute arising under or in connection with the agreement or related to any matter which is the subject of the agreement shall be subject to the exclusive jurisdiction of the state and/or federal courts located in New York, New York." Courts typically enforce these clauses if they were the result of an arm's length bargain, even when personal jurisdiction would not otherwise have existed over the defendant in the specified forum.

Similarly, some statutes provide that, by engaging in certain forum-related conduct, a party implicitly designates someone in the state to accept service of process on the party's behalf for particular types of claims. For example, the Massachusetts statute in *Hess v. Pawloski*, 274 U.S. 352 (1927), stated that out-of-state drivers authorized the registrar of the department of motor vehicles to

1. To make matters a bit confusing, the words "consent" and "waiver" are not uniformly understood to refer to two different concepts. Some view the two words as synonyms for a party's voluntary relinquishment of a right and instead refer to "forfeiture" to describe the failure to raise an issue in a timely way. For example, the United States Supreme Court recently noted that "[t]he terms waiver and forfeiture—though often used interchangeably by jurists and litigants—are not synonymous. '[F]orfeiture is the failure to make the timely assertion of a right[;] waiver is the 'intentional relinquishment or abandonment of a known right.' " *Hamer v. Neighborhood Housing Servs.*, 583 U.S. __, __, 138 S. Ct. 13, 17 n.1 (2017) (quoting two earlier cases). Regardless of one's preferred terminology, the basic point is that there are two distinct concepts—intentional relinquishment of an objection to personal jurisdiction (what we refer to above as "consent") and the failure to raise the objection at an appropriate time (what we refer to above as "waiver" but is sometimes referred to as "forfeiture").

accept service of process on the driver's behalf for any claims that arose due to that person's in-state driving. Similarly, after *Shaffer*, Delaware used the concept of implicit consent to expand the scope of personal jurisdiction over officers and directors of Delaware corporations. The statute specified that, by becoming an officer or director of a Delaware-incorporated company, an individual implicitly authorized the corporation's registered agent to accept service of process on the officer's or director's behalf. Del. Code Ann. tit. 10, § 3114(a)–(b) (2010). Officers and directors of Delaware companies are thus subject to suit in Delaware for their company-related activities, even when those activities might not otherwise subject them to personal jurisdiction in Delaware (e.g., under the facts of *Shaffer*).

B. Waiver

Waiver is similar to consent, except that waiver typically results from a party's failure to raise an issue within a specified time or in a proper manner. In federal court, Rules 12(g)–(h) of the Federal Rules of Civil Procedure describe the procedures that a defendant must follow to avoid waiving a personal jurisdiction defense. Some states have adopted a similar approach, and other states require a defendant to make a "special appearance," where the defendant appears in the court at the outset of the case for the sole purpose of contesting personal jurisdiction.

A court can also deem a party to have waived personal jurisdiction if the party fails to comply with court orders. In *Insurance Corp. of Ireland v. Compagnie des Bauxites de Guinee*, 456 U.S. 694, 706 (1982), a party failed to comply with court-ordered discovery that was designed to determine whether personal jurisdiction existed. As a sanction, the trial court ruled that the defendant had waived the personal jurisdiction defense. The Supreme Court affirmed the sanction, concluding that, "[b]y submitting to the jurisdiction of the court for the limited purpose of challenging jurisdiction, the defendant agree[d] to abide by that court's determination on the issue of jurisdiction." *Id.*

Waiver and consent are common alternatives to the usual methods of establishing personal jurisdiction. It is important to remember, however, that a party cannot consent to or waive a court's *subject matter* jurisdiction.

VII. Other Constitutional Bases for Personal Jurisdiction: Summary of Basic Principles

- There are several alternatives to specific jurisdiction, including general jurisdiction, in rem/quasi in rem jurisdiction, "transient presence," consent, and waiver.

- General jurisdiction allows a plaintiff to sue the defendant "generally" for any claims that the plaintiff might have, no matter where they arose, but only if the defendant is "at home" in the forum state.

- A company typically is "at home" in states where it has its principal place of business or place of incorporation. It may also be "at home" in other jurisdictions under limited circumstances.
- An individual is typically subject to general jurisdiction in the state where she is domiciled.
- In rem and quasi in rem jurisdiction are now analyzed using the minimum contacts formula of *International Shoe.*
- An individual is usually subject to personal jurisdiction in any state where she is served personally while physically present in that forum, assuming she is in the forum voluntarily.
- A party can waive personal jurisdiction or consent to it, such as by failing to raise the issue in a timely manner, deciding not to raise the issue, or accepting a contract with a forum selection clause.

9

Long Arm Statutes

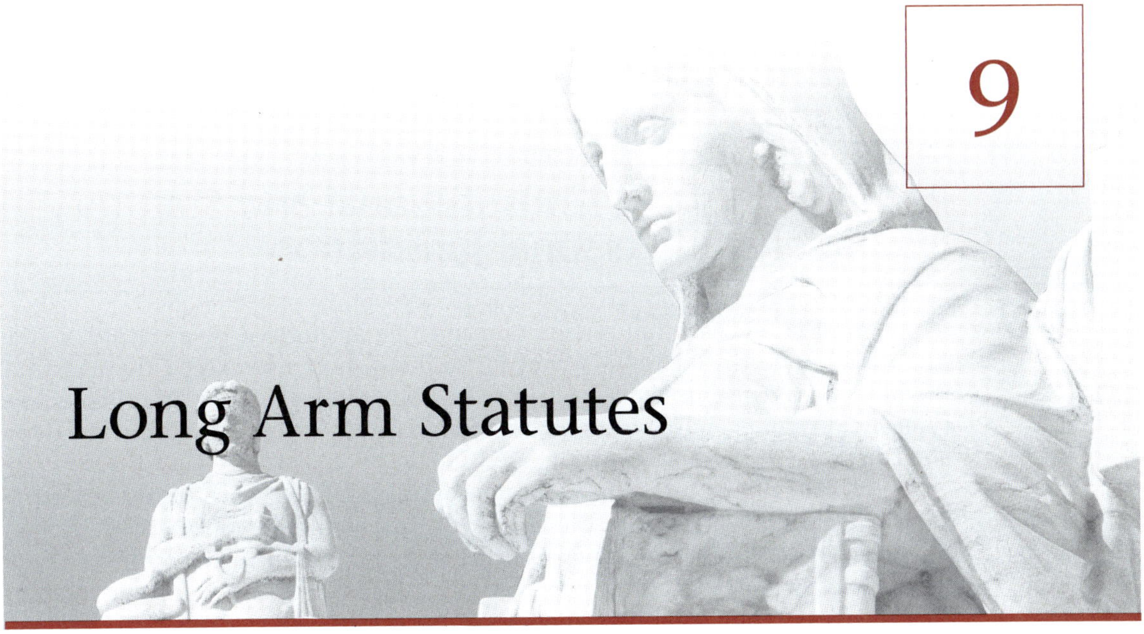

I. Introduction

The last three chapters examined the constitutional limits on a court's authority to exercise personal jurisdiction. The present chapter explains a critical limitation on this authority: A court cannot exercise personal jurisdiction in every instance where it would be constitutional to do so. The Due Process Clause places a *limit* on a court's power to exercise personal jurisdiction, but the Due Process Clause does not give a court the *authority* to exercise that power.

A court's authority to exercise personal jurisdiction is usually granted in *long arm statutes*. Through these statutes, each state's legislature determines how much personal jurisdiction its courts should have (i.e., how far the "long arm" of the courts should reach). This authority is limited by the Constitution, but without this statutory (or sometimes rule-based) authorization, a court typically cannot exercise personal jurisdiction. This chapter explains the relationship between long arm provisions and the constitutional limitations on personal jurisdiction described in the previous three chapters.*

II. Distinguishing Constitutional and Statutory Limitations on Personal Jurisdiction

In most cases, personal jurisdiction must be authorized by a statute or rule (the inner circles in Figure 9–1), but jurisdiction must not exceed the constitutional limits of the Due Process Clause (the outer circle). A court, in other words, typically cannot exercise personal jurisdiction unless a case falls within the darkened areas.

Most states have more than one long arm provision, with each conferring some (but usually not all) of the authority that would be constitutionally permissible. These states often have a statute, referred to in the diagram as an *enumerated act* long arm statute, that contains a list of common in-state contacts that give rise to personal jurisdiction in the forum. As the diagram suggests, these enumerated act statutes are often written broadly and confer considerable authority to exercise personal jurisdiction. (Note 2 below contains an example of such a statute.)

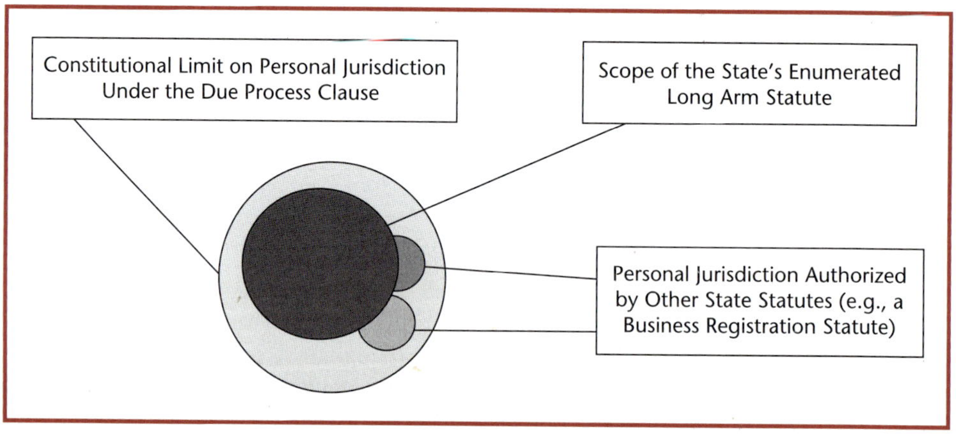

Figure 9–1: LONG ARM STATUTES AND THE CONSTITUTION

A few states have adopted long arm provisions that confer on courts as much authority to exercise personal jurisdiction as the Constitution allows. For example, California's long arm statute provides that "[a] court of this state may exercise jurisdiction on any basis not inconsistent with the Constitution of this state or

* Many long arm provisions take the form of statutes, so this chapter and many cases refer to "long arm statutes." Just be aware that there are also rules, including rules of civil procedure, that address a court's long arm authority, so it is more accurate to refer to this chapter's topic as one related to "long arm provisions." We use the word "statute" to conform to the usual terminology.

of the United States." CAL. CIV. PROC. CODE § 410.10. In California, therefore, the diagram looks different. The long arm statute circle is the same as (and completely overlaps with) the circle representing the constitutional limits on a court's authority to exercise personal jurisdiction.

Notes and Questions: Distinguishing Constitutional and Statutory Limitations on Personal Jurisdiction

Q **1. Constitutional limits and statutory authority.** Imagine that Darwin, a Florida citizen, sent a shipment of computers to Ohio. Peggy, an Ohio citizen, bought one of the computers in Ohio and brought it back to her house, where it short-circuited and caused a fire. Peggy sues Darwin in Ohio state court and serves Darwin with process in Florida. Darwin moves to dismiss on personal jurisdiction grounds. Will the court deny this motion?

A The correct answer here is "maybe." This case arose out of Darwin's contacts in Ohio, so personal jurisdiction would be *constitutional* there. We still need to know, however, whether Ohio has a long arm provision that authorizes personal jurisdiction in this type of case.

2. A typical enumerated act long arm statute. Ohio has a fairly typical enumerated act statute, which is drawn largely from the Uniform Interstate and International Procedure Act:

OHIO REVISED CODE ANN. § 2307.382. PERSONAL JURISDICTION

(A) A court may exercise personal jurisdiction over a person who acts directly or by an agent, as to a cause of action arising from the person's:

(1) Transacting any business in this state;

(2) Contracting to supply services or goods in this state;

(3) Causing tortious injury by an act or omission in this state;

(4) Causing tortious injury in this state by an act or omission outside this state if he regularly does or solicits business, or engages in any other persistent course of conduct, or derives substantial revenue from goods used or consumed or services rendered in this state;

(5) Causing injury in this state to any person by breach of warranty expressly or impliedly made in the sale of goods outside this state when he might reasonably have expected such person to use, consume, or be affected by the goods in this state, provided that he also regularly does or solicits business, or engages in any other persistent course of conduct, or derives substantial revenue from goods used or consumed or services rendered in this state;

(6) Causing tortious injury in this state to any person by an act outside this state committed with the purpose of injuring persons, when he might reasonably have expected that some person would be injured thereby in this state;

> (7) Causing tortious injury to any person by a criminal act, any element of which takes place in this state, which he commits or in the commission of which he is guilty of complicity.
>
> (8) Having an interest in, using, or possessing real property in this state. . . .

OHIO REV. CODE ANN. § 2307.382.

Applying the statute to the facts from question 1, it appears likely that the statute authorizes personal jurisdiction under section (A)(1). Peggy's cause of action arises from Darwin's transaction of business (i.e., the sale of computers) in the state. Thus, the statute authorizes personal jurisdiction. Moreover, because the case arises out of Darwin's in-state contacts, the case does not exceed the constitutional limits on a court's authority to exercise personal jurisdiction. Accordingly, the court would probably deny the motion to dismiss.

3. Specialized long arm provisions. In addition to enumerated act long arm statutes, many states also authorize personal jurisdiction through specialized provisions that are designed to apply to a relatively narrow range of cases. For example, some states authorize personal jurisdiction in directors' consent laws and nonresident motorists' statutes.

Recall the *Hess* case, which involved a nonresident motorist statute that authorized personal jurisdiction over out-of-state defendants who caused an in-state car accident. It provided as follows:

> The acceptance by a nonresident of the rights and privileges conferred by section three or four, as evidenced by his operating a motor vehicle thereunder, or the operation by a nonresident of a motor vehicle on a public way in the commonwealth other than under said sections, shall be deemed equivalent to an appointment by such nonresident of the registrar or his successor in office, to be his true and lawful attorney upon whom may be served all lawful processes in any action or proceeding against him, growing out of any accident or collision in which said nonresident may be involved while operating a motor vehicle on such a way, and said acceptance or operation shall be a signification of his agreement that any such process against him which is so served shall be of the same legal force and validity as if served on him personally.

Hess v. Pawloski, 274 U.S. 352, 354 (1927) (quoting MASS. GEN. LAWS ch. 431, § 2 (1923)).

Other statutes confer personal jurisdiction under similarly narrow circumstances. For example, after the Supreme Court decided *Shaffer*, Delaware adopted a statute that authorized personal jurisdiction over nonresident officers of Delaware companies in cases arising from the officer's exercise of corporate responsibilities. DEL. CODE ANN. tit. 10, § 3114(b). Similarly, Ohio has a business registration statute that authorizes courts to exercise personal jurisdiction over corporations that have registered to do business in the state:

> (B) To procure . . . a license [to do business in Ohio], [a] corporation . . . shall file with the secretary of state an application in such form as the secretary of state prescribes, verified by the oath of any authorized officer of such corporation, setting forth . . .

> (5) The appointment of a designated agent and the complete address of such agent;
>
> (6) The irrevocable consent of such corporation to service of process on such agent so long as the authority of such agent continues and to service of process upon the secretary of state in the events provided for [elsewhere in the Code] . . . .

OHIO REV. CODE ANN. § 1703.04(B)(5)–(6). In essence, if a corporation wants to do business in Ohio, it must consent to the appointment of an agent who can accept service of process. This appointment effectively subjects the company to personal jurisdiction in Ohio. That said, and as discussed in note 3 after the *Burnham* case in Chapter 8, there is now some debate about whether such a statute is constitutional. *See, e.g., Brown v. Lockheed Martin*, 814 F.3d 619, 640–41 (2d Cir. 2016) (raising, but not deciding, the question of whether a statute that confers general jurisdiction over a corporation under these circumstances is constitutional in light of the holding in *Daimler AG v. Bauman*, 571 U.S. 117 (2014)).

To summarize, two conditions must generally be satisfied before a court can exercise personal jurisdiction. First, personal jurisdiction must be authorized by a long arm provision, such as an enumerated act statute (like OHIO REV. CODE ANN. § 2307.382, a specialized provision (like OHIO REV. CODE ANN. § 1703.04(B)(5)), or a catchall provision like California's. And second, personal jurisdiction must be constitutionally permissible.

4. Common law personal jurisdiction? Normally, a court can exercise personal jurisdiction only if there is an applicable statute or rule that authorizes it. This is especially true when the basis for personal jurisdiction is specific jurisdiction. (Indeed, the prefatory language of Ohio's enumerated act statute refers to claims "arising from" activities in Ohio.)

But what if the basis for personal jurisdiction is "tag" (transient presence) jurisdiction, as in *Burnham*? Does a statute or rule have to authorize this basis for jurisdiction as well? There is some support for the notion that a court has inherent common law authority to exercise "tag" jurisdiction even if a statute or rule does not authorize it. *See, e.g., Schinkel v. Maxi-Holding, Inc.*, 565 N.E.2d 1219, 1222–23 (Mass. App. Ct. 1991) (stating that "[t]here is no need to predicate [personal] jurisdiction . . . on the long-arm statute" because the defendant was served personally within the state); Kevin M. Clermont, *Principles of Civil Procedure* § 4.2(B)(2)(a) (2d ed. 2009) (explaining that "a state court must be authorized by state statute to exercise the various bases of jurisdictional power, except for the bases of presence and consent which were recognized at common law").

The argument for such common law authority is that "tag" jurisdiction has existed for centuries, even though statutes never provided for it. In contrast, specific jurisdiction (exercising jurisdiction over defendants who are *outside* of the state) grew out of the Supreme Court's decision in *International Shoe* and is thus not part of a court's common law authority. Therefore, a statute or rule must explicitly authorize specific jurisdiction.

General jurisdiction is probably like specific jurisdiction and needs to be authorized by statute. Although there is some debate on the point, it is largely moot as a practical matter. Most states have statutes that either require businesses to designate an agent for service of process, like the Ohio provision cited in note 3, or have another relevant long arm provision that applies to defendants who are "doing business" in the state. Moreover, although Ohio's enumerated act statute primarily concerns specific jurisdiction, section (A)(4) confers personal jurisdiction where there is a tortious injury in the state and the defendant "regularly does or solicits business, or engages in any other persistent course of conduct, or derives substantial revenue from goods used or consumed or services rendered in this state."

5. Overextending a long arm? Consider the following scenario.

Imagine that Ohio adds a new provision to its long arm statute, specifying that "a defendant is subject to personal jurisdiction in Ohio if the plaintiff resides in the state." Percy, an Ohio citizen, visited Georgia and was in a car accident with Donnor, a Georgia citizen. Donnor has never left Georgia and has no contacts in any other state. Percy returns home to Ohio and sues Donnor in Ohio state court. Donnor is properly served in Georgia, and Donnor immediately moves to dismiss the case on personal jurisdiction grounds (i.e., Donnor does not waive the issue). The court should

A. grant the motion because the exercise of personal jurisdiction is unconstitutional.
B. deny the motion because the long arm statute authorizes personal jurisdiction, and personal jurisdiction in this case is constitutional.
C. deny the motion because, although personal jurisdiction would not be constitutional on these facts, Ohio has authorized personal jurisdiction under its long arm statute.
D. grant the motion because personal jurisdiction is not authorized by the long arm statute.

In this case, as in most cases involving personal jurisdiction, a court must ask: (1) whether the facts fit within a provision of the state's long arm statute, and (2) whether the exercise of personal jurisdiction is constitutional.

The first part of the analysis is clearly satisfied here. The long arm statute confers personal jurisdiction in all cases where the plaintiff is an Ohio resident, and Percy is both the plaintiff and a resident of Ohio. Because the statute authorizes personal jurisdiction in this case, we can rule out **D.**

The second part of the analysis turns on whether it would be constitutional for the court to exercise personal jurisdiction over Donnor. In this case, it clearly would not. Donnor has no contacts in Ohio, so personal jurisdiction in this case is impermissible under the Due Process Clause. **B**, therefore, is wrong.

C is wrong because the court cannot typically exercise personal jurisdiction unless the statute authorizes it *and* personal jurisdiction is constitutional. Because the exercise of personal jurisdiction would be unconstitutional here, the court must grant the motion. **A**, therefore, is the best answer.

The case looks like the diagram in Figure 9–2.

A court can hear some cases under this hypothetical statute. For example, if Donnor came to Ohio and hit Percy while there, the statute would confer personal jurisdiction, and jurisdiction would be constitutional. Such a case would fall in the darkened area of the diagram.

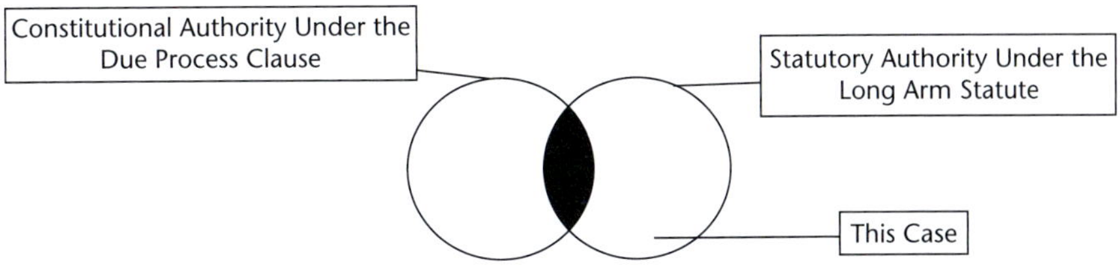

Figure 9–2: **AN UNCONSTITUTIONAL APPLICATION OF A LONG ARM STATUTE**

6. Shortening a long arm. Consider the following scenario.

Imagine now that Ohio passes a statute that says that "a defendant is subject to personal jurisdiction in Ohio only if the defendant resides in Ohio." Assume that Ohio repeals its enumerated act long arm statute and repeals all other possible bases for personal jurisdiction. Now imagine that Davis, a Wisconsin citizen, visits Ohio, gets drunk at a bar, and recklessly collides with Percy, an Ohio citizen, while in Ohio. Percy suffers serious injuries and sues Davis in Ohio state court. Davis is served at home in Wisconsin. Davis immediately moves to dismiss the case on personal jurisdiction grounds. The court should

A. grant the motion because the exercise of personal jurisdiction would be unconstitutional.
B. deny the motion because the long arm statute is unconstitutionally narrow.
C. deny the motion because personal jurisdiction is constitutional in this case.
D. grant the motion because personal jurisdiction is not authorized by the long arm statute.
E. both A and D are correct.

The first step is to see whether the statute authorizes personal jurisdiction. It does not. The statute clearly limits the court's personal jurisdiction to cases where the defendant resides in Ohio. In this case, the defendant resides in Wisconsin, so the court cannot exercise personal jurisdiction. Certainly, personal jurisdiction would be *constitutional* here because this case arises out of Davis's in-state contacts. The court, however, must also be authorized to exercise specific jurisdiction, and in this case, it isn't. C, therefore, is wrong, because constitutionality is only one part of the analysis.

Most courts would not reach the constitutional analysis in this case because the statute clearly does not apply here. Courts prefer to avoid constitutional issues whenever possible, so if a statute resolves an issue, a court will usually end its analysis there. Students and lawyers, however, are well advised *not* to take this approach. When analyzing a long arm issue (or any other legal issue for that matter), be sure to consider plausible fallback (alternative) arguments that might favor your position and have support in the record. In this case, that means analyzing both the statutory and constitutional dimensions of the problem, even if the statute resolves the issue. Indeed, a judge (or professor) may not agree with your statutory analysis, so your client (or your grade) may suffer if you fail to consider the constitutional question as well.

B is wrong because states have extensive authority to control the personal jurisdiction of their courts. If a state wants to confer only a small fraction of the authority that the Constitution would otherwise permit, it may do so.

A is wrong, because personal jurisdiction *would* be constitutional here. The case arises out of Davis's conduct in Ohio. (That makes **E** wrong as well.)

D, therefore, is the answer. The court cannot exercise personal jurisdiction because the statute does not authorize it. The case looks like this:

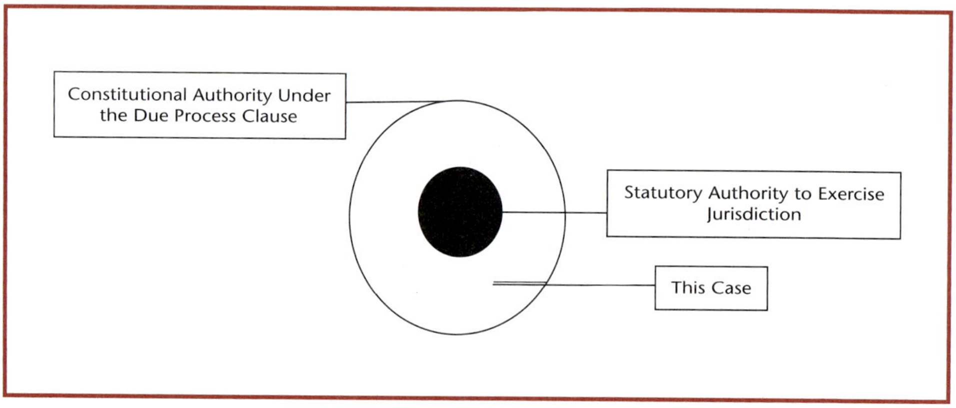

Figure 9–3: A LACK OF STATUTORY AUTHORITY

The statute is constitutional, but the statute does not confer personal jurisdiction in every case where it would be constitutional to do so. The present case falls in that gap between what the statute confers and what the Constitution would allow, making personal jurisdiction impermissible in this case. (Some students wonder if this means that the plaintiff cannot sue the defendant. Not at all. It just means that the plaintiff cannot sue the defendant in *Ohio*. The plaintiff can still sue the defendant in *Wisconsin*.)

7. Taking it to the limit. Note 5 offers an example of a long arm statute that is unconstitutionally broad. Note 6 offers a statute that is constitutional, but narrower than the full authority that would be constitutionally permissible. But there's also a third possibility: a statute that confers personal jurisdiction to the full extent that the Constitution allows, no more and no less.

Many states have statutes that are written this way. *See McIntyre Machinery, Ltd. v. Nicastro*, 564 U.S. 873, 903 n.8 (2011) (citing twenty-seven such jurisdictions). As mentioned earlier, California's long arm statute provides that "[a] court of this state may exercise jurisdiction on any basis not inconsistent with the Constitution of this state or of the United States." CAL. CIV. PROC. CODE § 410.10. In such cases, the two circles in the diagram above would be identical—the long arm statute circle would completely overlap with the constitutional limits of personal jurisdiction under the Due Process Clause. In these states, the personal jurisdiction analysis collapses into a single question: Would the exercise of personal jurisdiction be constitutional?

It is not entirely clear why more states have not adopted statutes of this sort. One reason appears to be historical. States added new bases for personal jurisdiction to their statutes as the law on personal jurisdiction evolved, thus creating a hodgepodge of different provisions, much like Ohio's enumerated act statute.

Another possible reason is that state legislatures want their courts to hear only those cases that have a particularly strong connection to the forum. By limiting their courts' personal jurisdiction through enumerated act statutes, states can free their courts from having to hear cases that have only a tenuous connection to the state. Keep in mind, though, that there are substantive policy implications of making this choice. It means that plaintiffs, especially individuals with fewer resources, may opt not to pursue an otherwise meritorious action because of the cost and inconvenience of litigating in another jurisdiction. In this sense, long arm statutes (like so many other aspects of civil procedure) have important substantive effects on the outcome of a dispute. In short, states need not—and many do not—authorize their courts to hear every case in which personal jurisdiction would be constitutional, and that choice can have significant consequences for litigants.

III. Interpreting Long Arm Statutes

State long arm statutes define how much personal jurisdiction authority the courts of that state may exercise. Some of these statutes (such as California's) reach as far as the Constitution allows, but because many of them do not, courts frequently have to interpret the reach of a state's long arm provision.

Two Blue Notes

The Blue Note—New York City

Bernd Jonkmanns / Laif / Redux

The Blue Note—Columbia, Missouri

Columbia Daily Tribune

In the *Bensusan* case, below, the New York Blue Note sues the Missouri Blue Note for trademark infringement. The court considers whether a local jazz cabaret in Columbia, Missouri, "committed a tortious act" in New York by posting its billings on its website in Missouri. In analyzing the New York long arm statute, the court considers this hypothetical case: Would a New Jersey assailant commit a tortious act in New York under the statute if she lobbed a bazooka shell across the Hudson River and hit a tourist at Grant's Tomb?

READING *BENSUSAN RESTAURANT CORP. v. KING*. The *Bensusan* case offers a fairly typical example of how a court interprets a long arm statute. Although this is a federal case, a federal district court usually applies the long arm statute of the state in which that district court sits. Fed. R. Civ. P. 4(k)(1)(A). Since this case was filed in a New York federal district court, the court had to interpret the New York long arm statute. Focus on the wording of New York's enumerated act long arm statute. The relevant provisions, which the court does not quote in full, are as follows:

> [A] court may exercise personal jurisdiction over any non-domiciliary, or his executor or administrator, who in person or through an agent: . . .
>
> 2. commits a tortious act within the state, except as to a cause of action for defamation of character arising from the act; or
> 3. commits a tortious act without the state causing injury to person or property within the state, . . . if he . . . expects or should reasonably expect the act to have consequences in the state and derives substantial revenue from interstate or international commerce. . . .

- What is the statutory ambiguity that the court must resolve?
- How does the court resolve that ambiguity?

BENSUSAN RESTAURANT CORP. v. KING

126 F.3d 25 (2d Cir. 1997)

Van Graafeiland, Circuit Judge:

Bensusan Restaurant Corporation, located in New York City, appeals from a judgment of the United States District Court for the Southern District of New York dismissing its complaint against Richard B. King, a Missouri resident, pursuant to Fed. R. Civ. P. 12(b)(2) for lack of personal jurisdiction. We affirm.

Columbia, Missouri is a small to medium size city far distant both physically and substantively from Manhattan. It is principally a white-collar community, hosting among other institutions Stephens College, Columbia College and the University of Missouri. It would appear to be an ideal location for a small cabaret featuring live entertainment, and King, a Columbia resident, undoubtedly found this to be so. Since 1980, he has operated such a club under the name "The Blue Note" at 17 North Ninth Street in Columbia.

Plaintiff alleges in its complaint that it is "the creator of an enormously successful jazz club in New York City called 'The Blue Note,'" which name "was registered as a federal trademark for cabaret services on May 14, 1985." Around 1993, a Bensusan representative wrote to King demanding that he cease and desist from calling his club The Blue Note. King's attorney informed the writer that Bensusan had no legal right to make the demand.

Nothing further was heard from Bensusan until April 1996, when King, at the suggestion of a local web-site design company, ThoughtPort Authority, Inc., permitted that company to create a web-site or cyberspot on the internet for King's cabaret. This work was done in Missouri. Bensusan then brought the instant action in the Southern District of New York, alleging violations of sections 32(1) and 43(a) of the Lanham Act [concerning trademarks], 15 U.S.C. §§ 1114(1) & 1125(a), and section 3(c) of the Federal Trademark Dilution Act of 1995, 15 U.S.C. § 1125(c), as well as common law unfair competition.

In addition to seeking trebled compensatory damages, punitive damages, costs and attorney's fees, Bensusan requests that King be enjoined from [using the mark "The Blue Note," including on the website]. . . .

The web-site describes King's establishment as "Mid-Missouri's finest live entertainment venue, ... [l]ocated in beautiful Columbia, Missouri," and it contains monthly calendars of future events and the Missouri telephone number of King's box office. Initially, it contained the following text:

> The Blue Note's CyberSpot should not be confused with one of the world's finest jazz club Blue Note, located in the heart of New York's Greenwich Village. If you should ever find yourself in the big apple give them a visit.

This text was followed by a hyperlink that could be used to connect a reader's computer to a web-site maintained by Bensusan. When Bensusan objected to the above-quoted language, King reworded the disclaimer and removed the hyperlink, substituting the following disclaimer that continues in use:

> The Blue Note, Columbia, Missouri should not be confused in any way, shape, or form with Blue Note Records or the jazz club, Blue Note, located in New York. The CyberSpot is created to provide information for Columbia, Missouri area individuals only, any other assumptions are purely coincidental.

The district court dismissed the complaint in a scholarly opinion that was published in 937 F. Supp. 295 (1996). Although we realize that attempting to apply established trademark law in the fast-developing world of the internet is somewhat like trying to board a moving bus, we believe that well-established doctrines of personal jurisdiction law support the result reached by the district court.

In diversity or federal question cases the court must look first to the long-arm statute of the forum state, in this instance, New York. If the exercise of jurisdiction is appropriate under that statute, the court then must decide whether such exercise comports with the requisites of due process. Because we believe that the exercise of personal jurisdiction in the instant case is proscribed by the law of New York, we do not address the issue of due process.

The New York law dealing with personal jurisdiction based upon tortious acts of a non-domiciliary who does not transact business in New York is contained in sub-paragraphs (a)(2) and (a)(3) of CPLR § 302, and Bensusan claims jurisdiction with some degree of inconsistency under both sub-paragraphs. Because King does not transact business in New York State, Bensusan makes no claim under section 302(a)(1). The legislative intent behind the enactment of sub-paragraphs (a)(2) and (a)(3) best can be gleaned by reviewing their disparate backgrounds. Sub-paragraph (a)(2), enacted in 1962, provides in pertinent part that a New York court may exercise personal jurisdiction over a non-domiciliary who "in person or through an agent" commits a tortious act within the state. The New York Court of Appeals has construed this provision in several cases. In *Feathers v. McLucas,* 209 N.E.2d 68 (N.Y. 1965), the Court held that the language "commits a tortious act *within* the state," as contained in sub-paragraph (a)(2), is "plain and precise" and confers personal jurisdiction over non-residents *"when they commit acts within the state." Feathers* adopted the view that CPLR § 302(a)(2) reaches only tortious acts performed by a defendant who was physically present in New York when he performed the wrongful act. The official Practice Commentary to CPLR § 302 explains that "if a New Jersey domiciliary were to lob a bazooka shell across the Hudson River at Grant's tomb, Feathers would appear to bar the New York courts from asserting personal jurisdiction over the New Jersey domiciliary in an action by an injured New York plaintiff." C302:17. The comment goes on to conclude that:

> As construed by the *Feathers* decision, jurisdiction cannot be asserted over a nonresident under this provision unless the nonresident commits an *act* in this state. This is tantamount to a requirement that the defendant or his agent be physically present in New York. . . . In short, the failure to perform a duty in New York is not a tortious act in this state, under the cases, unless the defendant or his agent enters the state.

The Court of Appeals adhered to the *Feathers* holding in [two other cases. In one,] . . . it said:

> The failure of a man to do anything at all when he is physically in one State is not an "act" done or "committed" in another State. His decision not to act and his not acting are both personal events occurring in the physical situs. That they may have consequences elsewhere does not alter their personal localization as acts.

In *Harvey v. Chemie Grunenthal, G.m.b.H,* 354 F.2d 428, 431 (2d Cir. 1965), we held that this construction of sub-paragraph (a)(2) should be followed. Numerous lower courts, both state and federal, have arrived at the same conclusion.

In 1990, Judge McLaughlin, who wrote the above-quoted commentary on section 302(a)(2), further evidenced his belief that the commentary correctly interpreted the statute when he quoted its substance in *Twine v. Levy,* 746 F. Supp. 1202, 1206 (E.D.N.Y. 1990). As recently as 1996, another of our district judges flatly stated: "To subject non-residents to New York jurisdiction under § 302(a)(2) the defendant must commit the tort while he or she is physically in New York State."

. . . [W]e recognize that the interpretation of sub-paragraph (a)(2) in the line of cases above cited has not been adopted by every district judge in the Second Circuit. However, the judges who differ are in the minority. In the absence of some indication by the New York Court of Appeals that its decisions . . . , as interpreted and construed in the above-cited majority of cases, no longer represent the law of New York, we believe it would be impolitic for this Court to hold otherwise.

Applying these principles, we conclude that Bensusan has failed to allege that King or his agents committed a tortious act in New York as required for exercise of personal jurisdiction under CPLR § 302(a)(2). The acts giving rise to Bensusan's lawsuit—including the authorization and creation of King's web site, the use of the words "Blue Note" and the Blue Note logo on the site, and the creation of a hyperlink to Bensusan's web site—were performed by persons physically present in Missouri and not in New York. Even if Bensusan suffered injury in New York, that does not establish a tortious act in the state of New York within the meaning of § 302(a)(2). *See Feathers*, 209 N.E.2d 68....

For all the reasons above stated, we affirm the judgment of the district court.

Notes and Questions: State Long Arm Statutes in Action

Q **1. Framing the issue.** Which long arm provision was at issue in this case, and what was the ambiguity?

A The court focused primarily on subsection (a)(2) of the New York long arm statute, which confers personal jurisdiction over an out-of-state defendant who "commits a tortious act within the state."

The ambiguity concerns the meaning of the phrase "tortious act." Does a tortious act occur where the plaintiff is injured? Or does the tortious act occur where the defendant's harmful act was initiated? The plaintiff's allegations would satisfy the first test, because the alleged injuries occurred in New York. But the allegations do not satisfy the latter test, because the defendant's alleged wrongful conduct took place in Missouri.

Q **2. The court's rationale.** Why did the court adopt the view that a "tortious act" occurs where the defendant's harmful act took place?

A Courts interpret statutory provisions through various methods, usually beginning with the statute's plain language. If the plain language is ambiguous, courts rely on precedents (if any), refer to the underlying rationales for the statute, consider the legislative history of the statute, and assess the public policy consequences of a particular interpretation. There are so many methods of statutory interpretation that entire books and law school courses are dedicated to the subject.

In *Bensusan*, the court relied primarily on New York case law, referring to a number of cases that have interpreted the New York long arm statute to mean that the defendant's conduct must have occurred in New York.

Another factor supporting the court's conclusion is that subsection (3) provides for personal jurisdiction over acts occurring "without [outside of] the state." Given the existence of another provision that appears to govern out-of-state acts, the logical inference is that subsection (2) is designed to cover in-state acts. (The court rejects subsection (3)'s applicability because that provision requires the defendant to derive substantial revenue from interstate commerce, and there is no evidence that the defendant's business drew revenue from outside of Missouri.)

This conclusion is by no means the only plausible one. As the court acknowledges, courts from other states have interpreted similar statutory language to cover out-of-state acts causing in-state injuries. These courts often observe that a tort does not exist until there is an injury, so the site of the injury is the location where the "tortious act" occurred. *See, e.g., Gray v. American Radiator and Standard Sanitary Corp.*, 176 N.E.2d 761, 762–63 (Ill. 1961) (concluding that the long arm statute conferred personal jurisdiction over an out-of-state component manufacturer because the component injured someone inside of the forum). This logic suggests that the tortious act in this case occurred in New York, where the plaintiff was injured. This reasoning is plausible (and has been adopted by courts interpreting similar provisions in other states), but the *Bensusan* court implicitly rejected it.

Q **3. The constitutionality of personal jurisdiction over the Blue Note.** The court concluded that the long arm statute did not apply here, so the court did not reach the constitutional question. (Recall that courts prefer to avoid constitutional questions.) But what if the statute had applied to this case? Would personal jurisdiction have been constitutional over the Blue Note in New York? Which line of cases would you examine to predict the court's ruling on this issue?

A Recall the *Burdick* case in Chapter 7. That case suggests that personal jurisdiction over a defendant for Internet-based conduct is constitutional only if the defendant intended to serve or attract an in-state audience. *See, e.g., Young v. New Haven Advocate*, 315 F.3d 256, 263 (4th Cir. 2002) (finding that personal jurisdiction would be unconstitutional over a newspaper that published an allegedly defamatory story on the Internet unless there was evidence that the newspaper's website was "designed to attract or serve [an] . . . audience [in the forum state]"). In this case, there does not appear to be any evidence that the Missouri establishment intended to attract or serve a New York audience, so even if New York's long arm statute covered these facts, there is a good argument that the statute would be unconstitutional as applied.

4. Unconstitutional applications of long arm statutes. Imagine that the court had concluded that the long arm statute applied to this case but that the exercise of personal jurisdiction was nevertheless unconstitutional. Would the court strike down the statute as unconstitutional or simply refuse to apply the statute in this particular case? Typically, courts take the latter approach. If a statute is constitutional in most instances, courts prefer to leave the statute intact and hold that the statute is unconstitutional "as applied" to the facts of the case.

5. A bazooka fired from New Jersey. Consider the following scenario.

The court in *Bensusan* refers to a hypothetical case in which an irate citizen of New Jersey fires a bazooka at New York, hitting an unsuspecting New Yorker. Imagine that the injured New Yorker sues the New Jersey defendant in New York state court. Assuming that the defendant moves to dismiss the case on personal jurisdiction grounds and that the New York long arm statute is the same as described in *Bensusan*, the court would probably

A. deny the motion because personal jurisdiction would be constitutional in this case.
B. grant the motion because personal jurisdiction would be unconstitutional in this case.
C. grant the motion because the long arm statute does not authorize personal jurisdiction in this case.
D. deny the motion because the long arm statute applies to these facts, and personal jurisdiction would be constitutional.

Personal jurisdiction would be constitutional here. The defendant engaged in conduct that was directed at New York, so the defendant clearly had a contact in the forum. Moreover, the claim arose out of that contact, making the exercise of personal jurisdiction constitutional. **B**, therefore, is wrong.

Although personal jurisdiction is constitutional, **A** is an incomplete answer because the case must also fit within an applicable long arm statute. According to *Bensusan*, subsection (2) of the long arm statute requires the defendant's act to have occurred in New York. In the bazooka case, it didn't. Moreover, subsection (3) does not apply here, because there is no evidence that the defendant derived substantial revenue from New York. Thus, **D** is probably incorrect.

Given the weight of New York authority described in *Bensusan*, a New York state court would likely conclude that the long arm statute does not authorize personal jurisdiction in this case because the acts giving rise to the injury did not take place in New York. Accordingly, **C** is the best answer.

IV. Long Arm Provisions in Federal Courts

In *Bensusan*, the federal district court interpreted New York's long arm statute. Why didn't the federal court apply a federal long arm statute? The answer is surprisingly complicated.

A. Distinguishing the Fourteenth and Fifth Amendments' Due Process Clauses

Courts usually look to the Fourteenth Amendment Due Process Clause to determine whether a particular forum should be allowed to exercise personal jurisdiction over a defendant. Notably, the Fourteenth Amendment applies to the states, not the federal government: "No *State* shall ... deprive any person of life, liberty, or property, without due process of law ..." (emphasis added).

A *federal* court's power is usually limited by the Fifth Amendment Due Process Clause. That clause, although very similar to the Fourteenth Amendment version, has been interpreted to permit the federal court to exercise much more personal jurisdiction authority than the state courts are permitted under the Fourteenth Amendment. *See Republic of Panama v. BCCI Holdings (Luxembourg), S.A.*, 119 F.3d 935 (11th Cir. 1997) (discussing the differences between Fourteenth and Fifth Amendment analyses of personal jurisdiction and identifying some disagreements about the precise limitations on personal jurisdiction under the Fifth Amendment).

The reason for this distinction between federal and state court authority is that a court's power to exercise personal jurisdiction turns to a significant degree on the territory controlled by the sovereign for which the court acts. Unless a defendant has the requisite contacts inside that court's territory, a court typically does not have the power to exercise personal jurisdiction over that defendant. For state courts, this logic means that a defendant must have the requisite contacts within the state.

A federal court, in contrast, is a United States court, so it can probably exercise personal jurisdiction if a defendant has the requisite contact anywhere in the *entire United States*. For example, according to this reasoning, it would be constitutional for an Oregon federal court to assert personal jurisdiction over a Florida defendant in a federal question case, even if that defendant never had any contacts in Oregon. As long as the Florida defendant had a contact within the United States, that contact would be sufficient to establish personal jurisdiction in any federal court.*

But if federal courts have such broad constitutional authority to exercise personal jurisdiction, why do federal courts (like the court in *Bensusan*) usually look to the long arm statutes of the states in which they sit? Put another way, why do federal courts usually have the same authority to exercise personal jurisdiction as the local state courts?

The answer is that the Fifth Amendment, like the Fourteenth Amendment, does not automatically confer on a court the power to exercise personal jurisdiction. Typically, a long arm provision must confer that authority.

B. The Federal Long Arm Provision: Rule 4(k)(1)(A)

The long arm provision that applies in most federal cases is Rule 4(k)(1)(A) of the Federal Rules of Civil Procedure. It states that personal jurisdiction exists over a "defendant who is subject to the jurisdiction of a court of general jurisdiction

---

* There is some authority for the notion that the reasonableness factors that are used to analyze the Fourteenth Amendment Due Process Clause should also be used in the Fifth Amendment due process context. See, e.g., Wendy Perdue, Aliens, the Internet, and "Purposeful Availment": A Reassessment of Fifth Amendment Limits on Personal Jurisdiction, 98 Nw. U. L. Rev. 455, 468 n.85 (2004) (noting the disagreement).

in the state where the district court is located."* Put simply, a federal court can usually exercise personal jurisdiction over a defendant only if the courts of the state in which that federal court sits could do so. As the diagram illustrates, Rule 4(k)(1)(A) dramatically limits the scope of a federal court's authority to exercise personal jurisdiction.

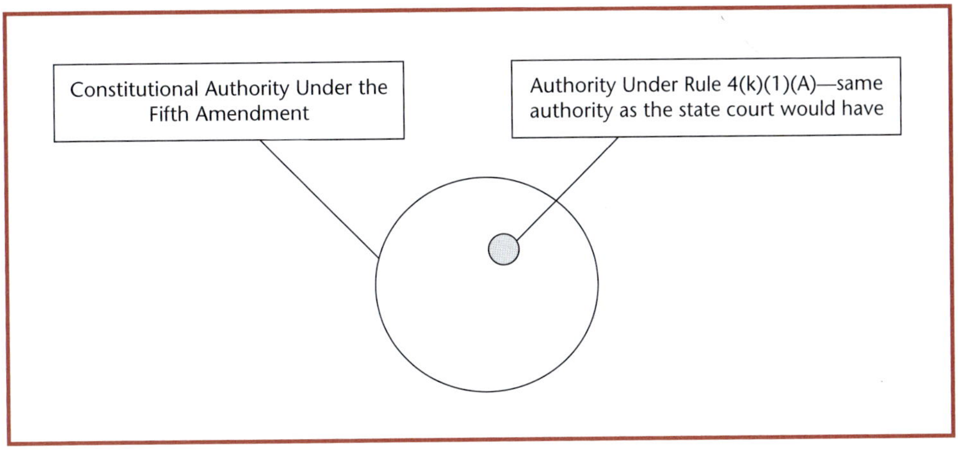

Figure 9–4: PERSONAL JURISDICTION IN FEDERAL COURT

Without the Rule, personal jurisdiction would be easier to establish in federal court, so more plaintiffs might decide to sue there instead of state court, thus placing a larger burden on the federal court system. Moreover, without the Rule, defendants might have to defend themselves in distant federal courts that have very little connection to the lawsuit. Such long distance litigation might pass muster under the Fifth Amendment, but it does not seem fair as a matter of public policy.

Rule 4(k)(1)(A) also has the benefit of being easy to apply. For example, it specifies that a federal district court in Portland, Oregon can exercise personal jurisdiction over a defendant only if an Oregon state court can do so. That means that the Oregon federal court has to analyze personal jurisdiction in precisely the same way as an Oregon state court does: determine whether the case falls within Oregon's long arm statute and, if so, whether personal jurisdiction would be consistent with the *Fourteenth* Amendment Due Process Clause.

This symmetry between state and federal court authority neutralizes personal jurisdiction as a forum shopping tool. Without that symmetry, a party might choose federal court simply because it has broader authority to exercise personal jurisdiction than the state court in which that federal court sits. The Rule also makes life easier for law students and lawyers, because in most cases, the analysis is the same in federal and state cases.

* The rule makers unnecessarily tortured lawyers and law students by using the phrase "general jurisdiction." The context clearly means general subject matter jurisdiction (i.e., state courts that can hear a wide range of claims as a matter of subject matter jurisdiction), not general in personam jurisdiction.

C. Examples of Broader Authority in Rule 4(k)

The analysis is the same in *most* cases, but not in *all* cases. For example, Rule 4(k)(1)(C) provides an exception to Rule 4(k)(1)(A), stating that a federal court may exercise broader jurisdiction whenever the court is authorized to do so under a federal statute.

There are a few statutes that confer this broader authority. For example, federal law authorizes nationwide personal jurisdiction in bankruptcy cases. *See, e.g.*, Fed. R. Bankr. P. 7004(f) ("If the exercise of jurisdiction is consistent with the Constitution and laws of the United States, serving a summons or filing a waiver of service in accordance with this rule ... is effective to establish personal jurisdiction over the person of any defendant with respect to a case under the [Bankruptcy] Code or a civil proceeding arising under the [Bankruptcy] Code ..."). Some statutes that provide for nationwide service of process, such as in securities litigation, are also construed as congressional grants of nationwide personal jurisdiction. *See, e.g., Pinker v. Roche Holdings, Ltd.*, 292 F.3d 361, 369 (3d Cir. 2002) (stating that "[w]here Congress has spoken by authorizing nationwide service of process ... , as it has in the Securities Act, the jurisdiction of a federal court need not be confined by the defendant's contacts with the state in which the federal court sits"). These statutes, unlike Rule 4(k)(1)(A), permit the federal courts to exercise the full reach of personal jurisdiction authorized by the Fifth Amendment Due Process Clause (i.e., they can assert personal jurisdiction over defendants with relevant contacts anywhere in the country).

In addition, Rule 4(k)(2) provides that, for claims arising under federal law, the service of "a summons or filing a waiver of service establishes personal jurisdiction over a defendant if: (A) the defendant is not subject to jurisdiction in any state's courts of general jurisdiction; and (B) exercising jurisdiction is consistent with the United States Constitution and laws." This means that personal jurisdiction is proper in federal question cases involving foreign defendants when no state can exercise personal jurisdiction, but only if the federal court's exercise of personal jurisdiction is consistent with the Fifth Amendment—that is, only if the defendant has a sufficient contact with the United States.

Finally, Rule 4(k)(1)(B)—often referred to as the "bulge" rule—also confers broader personal jurisdiction authority. This Rule provides that, if a defendant has been joined pursuant to Rule 14 (a third-party claim) or Rule 19 (for necessary and indispensable parties), the defendant is subject to personal jurisdiction in federal court as long as the defendant is served within one hundred miles of the federal courthouse. Jurisdiction exists even if the service occurs in another state and even if the applicable state long arm statute would not otherwise reach that defendant.

V. Long Arm Statutes: Summary of Basic Principles

- A court can usually exercise personal jurisdiction only if: (1) a long arm provision authorizes it and (2) personal jurisdiction is constitutional. One possible exception to this general rule is "tag" jurisdiction, which appears to exist as part of a court's common law authority.

- Many state long arm provisions do not confer the full constitutional authority to exercise personal jurisdiction, so courts often have to interpret the scope of applicable long arm provisions. These provisions commonly appear in enumerated act statutes that confer personal jurisdiction in only specific types of cases.

- Some states, like California, authorize their courts to exercise personal jurisdiction to the full extent that the Constitution allows, making an analysis of the long arm provision unnecessary.

- If a court concludes that a long arm provision authorizes personal jurisdiction in a case, but the exercise of personal jurisdiction would be unconstitutional, a court will refuse to exercise personal jurisdiction in that case.

- Federal courts have more expansive personal jurisdiction authority under the Fifth Amendment Due Process Clause than state courts have under the Fourteenth Amendment. Nevertheless, Rule 4(k)(1)(A) provides that, in most cases, a federal court may only exercise personal jurisdiction if a state court in the state where the federal court sits could do so.

- Congress has passed some rules and statutes that authorize federal courts to exercise nationwide jurisdiction. For example, Congress has authorized federal courts to exercise personal jurisdiction to the full extent that the Constitution allows under the Fifth Amendment in certain kinds of cases, such as in bankruptcy cases. Under those statutes, federal courts can probably exercise personal jurisdiction as long as a defendant has a relevant contact somewhere in the United States.

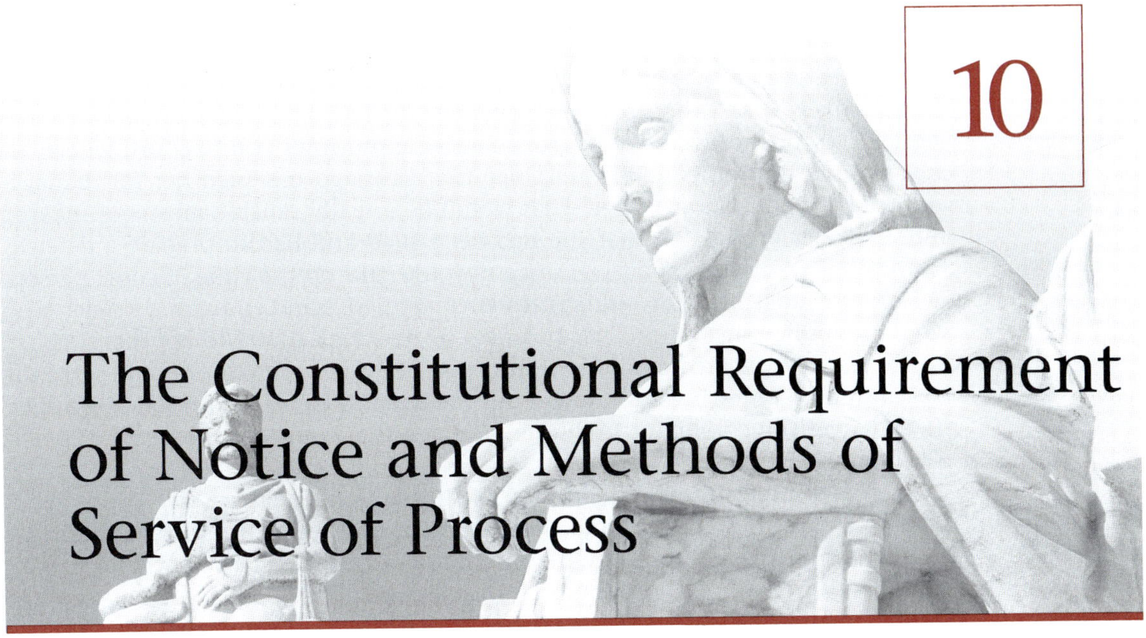

10

The Constitutional Requirement of Notice and Methods of Service of Process

I. Introduction

Even if a defendant's contacts in a state suffice to subject her to personal jurisdiction there, the court must assert jurisdiction over her by an order to appear and defend the action. This is usually accomplished through service of process, delivery to the defendant of the initial papers in the action. Service of process fulfills two functions: It formally asserts the court's authority over the defendant and it informs her of the case so she can prepare to defend it. In this chapter, we address one notice issue that is fundamental—what methods of service of process are constitutionally sufficient to provide notice—and one that is technical—the specific methods that statutes and court rules authorize litigants to use to inform defendants that they have been sued.*

* The term "service of process" is also used to refer to delivery of a court order (a subpoena) to a witness to testify or provide documents. *See, e.g.*, Fed. R. Civ. P. 45. The term may also refer to delivery of copies of motions, discovery documents and other papers in the case to the other parties—papers generated later in the case, after pleading. *See* Fed. R. Civ. P. 5.

Courts might use all sorts of methods to inform the defendant that she has been sued and that the court intends to adjudicate her rights. Some of these would be more likely than others to actually convey the bad news to her. If Santiago sues Ressler, the court officers might arrest Ressler and bring her into court, where the judge would announce in a loud voice that Santiago has sued her for damages and read the complaint to her. That would be a really reliable means of making sure that Ressler realized that she had been sued and had to prepare a defense. However, it would be expensive, since it would take up the time of court personnel and the judge. And it would greatly inconvenience and embarrass Ressler, who would be pulled away from her business or personal affairs to appear in court. Surely, less complicated methods of informing Ressler of the case should serve the basic function of letting her know about the lawsuit. For example, sending a sheriff to deliver the complaint to Ressler, along with a court order to appear, seems like it ought to do the trick.

Perhaps something even simpler will provide adequate notice. How about mailing the court summons and the complaint to Ressler by registered mail? Or calling her on the phone? Or e-mailing her a pdf of the documents? Or just an e-mail saying "I've sued you in Albion District Court." Or publishing notice of the lawsuit in the newspaper? Or just filing the papers with the court, which could post a list of new lawsuits, including the names of all defendants, on a bulletin board at the clerk's office?

If there were no Due Process Clause, courts could establish whatever rules they liked for serving process on the defendant in a lawsuit. But there are Due Process Clauses in both the Fifth Amendment (applicable to federal courts) and the Fourteenth Amendment (applicable to state courts), which impose constitutional constraints on methods of service of process.

II. *Mullane v. Central Hanover Bank*: The Constitutional Standard for Adequate Notice

The federal Constitution bars the states and the federal government from taking a person's life, liberty, or property without due process of law. U.S. Const. amends. V, XIV. When a court enters a judgment against a defendant, it interferes with the defendant's liberty or property, so it must act in accordance with due process of law in reaching its decision. This broad phrase encompasses several protections for litigants, including the requirement that the court have personal jurisdiction over the defendant and that it use fair judicial procedures in processing the case and reaching a decision. Certainly, one component of fair procedure is the commonsense requirement that the defendant be adequately informed that the court intends to adjudicate her rights. *Mullane v. Central Hanover Bank & Trust Co.*, the case below, articulates basic constitutional standards for adequate methods of service of process.

READING *MULLANE v. CENTRAL HANOVER BANK & TRUST CO.* Some background on the common trust fund device will help you to understand *Mullane*. The common trust fund allowed banks to invest the assets of many small trusts in one fund, achieving economies of scale and minimizing expenses. Each individual trust would then share in the earnings or losses in proportion to the amount it invested in the common fund.

The New York statute authorizing common trust funds required banks to obtain court approval of the financial accounts of a common trust fund, to assure that the bank was administering the funds properly. If the court approved the accounts, its judgment would bind anyone with an interest in the trust; consequently a beneficiary who thought the Bank had invested unwisely, depleting the common trust fund (and hence, the value of the beneficiary's interest) would be barred from suing the Bank for mismanagement. Thus, the accounting could deprive a beneficiary of property—her right to sue the Bank for misfeasance. Hence, the Fourteenth Amendment Due Process Clause required adequate notice of the action to those with an interest in the fund.

Giving individual notice to all those with an interest in a common trust fund like the one in *Mullane* would be almost impossible. Any individual trust might call for payment of the income to A, then to A's spouse after her death, and then to their children. The trust might provide that if A survives her spouse, the income and principal will be paid to the children at A's death, or, if any child dies, to that child's children. If she dies childless, it might provide that the income and principal will go to siblings or parents, or, if they predecease A, then to A's heirs. So a lot of people may have "contingent interests" in the trusts—they might be entitled to the income or principal of the trust at some point in the future. In *Mullane*, the Bank estimated that about 5,000 people might have interests in the commingled trusts and that the expense of hiring investigators and lawyers to identify all interested persons would make it financially impossible to use the common trust fund device.

In reading *Mullane*, consider these questions:

- How did the Bank notify persons with an interest in the trusts?
- Why did it use that method of notice?
- Why did the Court hold that different types of notice were required for different categories of persons with an interest in the trusts?
- Did the Court approve notice by publication for any persons with an interest in the trusts?

Because *Mullane* is a complex opinion, we have inserted some editorial comments in brackets to act as guideposts along the way.

MULLANE v. CENTRAL HANOVER BANK & TRUST CO.

339 U.S. 306 (1950)

Mr. Justice Jackson delivered the opinion of the Court.

This controversy questions the constitutional sufficiency of notice to beneficiaries on judicial settlement of accounts by the trustee of a common trust fund established under the New York Banking Law, Consol. Laws, c. 2. The New York Court of Appeals considered and overruled objections that the statutory notice contravenes requirements of the Fourteenth Amendment and that by allowance of the account beneficiaries were deprived of property without due process of law. The case is here on appeal under 28 U.S.C. § 1257.

Common trust fund legislation is addressed to a problem appropriate for state action. Mounting overheads have made administration of small trusts undesirable to corporate trustees. In order that donors and testators of moderately sized trusts may not be denied the service of corporate fiduciaries, the District of Columbia and some thirty states other than New York have permitted pooling small trust estates into one fund for investment administration.... The income, capital gains, losses and expenses of the collective trust are shared by the constituent trusts in proportion to their contribution. By this plan, diversification of risk and economy of management can be extended to those whose capital standing alone would not obtain such advantage.

[Eds.—Here the Court describes the common trust fund device, and the particular fund established by the Bank to jointly manage a group of small trusts.]

Statutory authorization for the establishment of such common trust funds is provided in the New York Banking Law. Under this Act a trust company may, with approval of the State Banking Board, establish a common fund and, within prescribed limits, invest therein the assets of an unlimited number of estates, trusts or other funds of which it is trustee. Each participating trust shares ratably in the common fund, but exclusive management and control is in the trust company as trustee, and neither a fiduciary nor any beneficiary of a participating trust is deemed to have ownership in any particular asset or investment of this common fund. The trust company must keep fund assets separate from its own, and in its fiduciary capacity may not deal with itself or any affiliate. Provisions are made for accountings twelve to fifteen months after the establishment of a fund and triennially thereafter. The decree in each such judicial settlement of accounts is made binding and conclusive as to any matter set forth in the account upon everyone having any interest in the common fund or in any participating estate, trust or fund.

In January, 1946, Central Hanover Bank and Trust Company established a common trust fund in accordance with these provisions, and in March, 1947, it petitioned the Surrogate's Court for settlement of its first account as common trustee. During the accounting period a total of 113 trusts, approximately half inter vivos and half testamentary, participated in the common trust fund, the gross capital of which was nearly three million dollars. The record does not show the number or residence of the beneficiaries, but they were many and it is clear that some of them were not residents of the State of New York.

[Eds.—The Bank was required by the New York statute to provide notice of the account settlement procedure to those with an interest in the fund. Note how it gave notice of the settlement action.]

The only notice given beneficiaries of this specific application was by publication in a local newspaper in strict compliance with the minimum requirements of N.Y. Banking Law § 100-c(12): "After filing such petition [for judicial settlement of its account] the petitioner shall cause to be issued by the court in which the petition is filed and shall publish not less than once in each week for four successive weeks in a newspaper to be designated by the court a notice or citation addressed generally without naming them to all parties interested in such common trust fund and in such estates, trusts or funds mentioned in the petition, all of which may be described in the notice or citation only in the manner set forth in said petition and without setting forth the residence of any such decedent or donor of any such estate, trust or fund." Thus the only notice required, and the only one given, was by newspaper publication setting forth merely the name and address of the trust company, the name and the date of establishment of the common trust fund, and a list of all participating estates, trusts or funds.

At the time the first investment in the common fund was made on behalf of each participating estate, however, the trust company, pursuant to the requirements of § 100-c(9), had notified by mail each person of full age and sound mind whose name and address was then known to it and who was "entitled to share in the income therefrom . . . [or] . . . who would be entitled to share in the principal if the event upon which such estate, trust or fund will become distributable should have occurred at the time of sending such notice." Included in the notice was a copy of those provisions of the Act relating to the sending of the notice itself and to the judicial settlement of common trust fund accounts.

[Eds.—Because many persons with contingent interests in the common trust fund would probably not receive notice of the accounting, the New York statute provided an alternative means of protecting the interests of such persons.]

Upon the filing of the petition for the settlement of accounts, appellant was, by order of the court pursuant to § 100-c(12), appointed special guardian and attorney for all persons known or unknown not otherwise appearing who had or might thereafter have any interest in the income of the common trust fund; and appellee Vaughan was appointed to represent those similarly interested in the principal. There were no other appearances on behalf of any one interested in either interest or principal.

Appellant appeared specially, objecting that notice and the statutory provisions for notice to beneficiaries were inadequate to afford due process under the Fourteenth Amendment, and therefore that the court was without jurisdiction to render a final and binding decree. Appellant's objections were entertained and overruled, the Surrogate holding that the notice required and given was sufficient. A final decree accepting the accounts has been entered, affirmed by the Appellate Division of the Supreme Court, and by the Court of Appeals of the State of New York.

The effect of this decree, as held below, is to settle "all questions respecting the management of the common fund." We understand that every right which beneficiaries would otherwise have against the trust company, either as trustee of the common fund or as trustee of any individual trust, for improper management of the common trust fund during the period covered by the accounting is sealed and wholly terminated by the decree.

[Eds.—Mullane, as special guardian for the income beneficiaries, argued that the action was "in personam," because it would affect the right of each investor to sue the bank for negligence. Thus, he argued, personal jurisdiction

must be obtained over each investor. The bank argued that the action was "in rem," because the trust was before the court, so that it could settle rights of all claimants to the trust assets before it. The Court, however, refused to make the due process standard for adequate notice turn on the in rem/in personam distinction.]

We are met at the outset with a challenge to the power of the State—the right of its courts to adjudicate at all as against those beneficiaries who reside without the State of New York. It is contended that the proceeding is one in personam in that the decree affects neither title to nor possession of any res, but adjudges only personal rights of the beneficiaries to surcharge their trustee for negligence or breach of trust. Accordingly, it is said, under the strict doctrine of *Pennoyer v. Neff*, 95 U.S. 714, the Surrogate is without jurisdiction as to nonresidents upon whom personal service of process was not made.

Distinctions between actions in rem and those in personam are ancient and originally expressed in procedural terms what seems really to have been a distinction in the substantive law of property under a system quite unlike our own. The legal recognition and rise in economic importance of incorporeal or intangible forms of property have upset the ancient simplicity of property law and the clarity of its distinctions, while new forms of proceedings have confused the old procedural classification. American courts have sometimes classed certain actions as in rem because personal service of process was not required, and at other times have held personal service of process not required because the action was in rem.

Judicial proceedings to settle fiduciary accounts have been sometimes termed in rem, or more indefinitely quasi in rem, or more vaguely still, "in the nature of a proceeding in rem." It is not readily apparent how the courts of New York did or would classify the present proceeding, which has some characteristics and is wanting in some features of proceedings both in rem and in personam. But in any event we think that the requirements of the Fourteenth Amendment to the Federal Constitution do not depend upon a classification for which the standards are so elusive and confused generally and which, being primarily for state courts to define, may and do vary from state to state. Without disparaging the usefulness of distinctions between actions in rem and those in personam in many branches of law, or on other issues, or the reasoning which underlies them, we do not rest the power of the State to resort to constructive service in this proceeding upon how its courts or this Court may regard this historic antithesis. It is sufficient to observe that, whatever the technical definition of its chosen procedure, the interest of each state in providing means to close trusts that exist by the grace of its laws and are administered under the supervision of its courts is so insistent and rooted in custom as to establish beyond doubt the right of its courts to determine the interests of all claimants, resident or nonresident, provided its procedure accords full opportunity to appear and be heard.

[Eds.—The Court notes that approval of the accounts may deprive trust beneficiaries of property by cutting off their right to sue the Bank for mismanagement that depletes the value of the trusts.]

Quite different from the question of a state's power to discharge trustees is that of the opportunity it must give beneficiaries to contest. Many controversies have raged about the cryptic and abstract words of the Due Process Clause but there can be no doubt that at a minimum they require that deprivation of life, liberty or property by adjudication be preceded by notice and opportunity for hearing appropriate to the nature of the case.

In two ways this proceeding does or may deprive beneficiaries of property. It may cut off their rights to have the trustee answer for negligent or illegal impairments of their interests. Also, their interests are presumably subject to diminution in the proceeding by allowance of fees and expenses to one who, in their names but without their knowledge, may conduct a fruitless or uncompensatory contest. Certainly the proceeding is one in which they may be deprived of property rights and hence notice and hearing must measure up to the standards of due process.

[Eds.—Now the Court gets down to the business of reconciling two values: the Bank's and the investors' interest in making it practical to use common trust funds, and the investors' interest in adequate notice of the settlement proceeding.]

Personal service [i.e., in-hand delivery] of written notice within the jurisdiction is the classic form of notice always adequate in any type of proceeding. But the vital interest of the State in bringing any issues as to its fiduciaries to a final settlement can be served only if interests or claims of individuals who are outside of the State can somehow be determined. A construction of the Due Process Clause which would place impossible or impractical obstacles in the way could not be justified.

Against this interest of the State we must balance the individual interest sought to be protected by the Fourteenth Amendment. This is defined by our holding that "The fundamental requisite of due process of law is the opportunity to be heard." *Grannis v. Ordean*, 234 U.S. 385, 394. This right to be heard has little reality or worth unless one is informed that the matter is pending and can choose for himself whether to appear or default, acquiesce or contest.

The Court has not committed itself to any formula achieving a balance between these interests in a particular proceeding or determining when constructive notice may be utilized or what test it must meet. Personal service has not in all circumstances been regarded as indispensable to the process due to residents, and it has more often been held unnecessary as to nonresidents. We disturb none of the established rules on these subjects. No decision constitutes a controlling or even a very illuminating precedent for the case before us. But a few general principles stand out in the books.

[Eds.—The Court next expounds the basic constitutional standard for adequate notice.]

An elementary and fundamental requirement of due process in any proceeding which is to be accorded finality is notice reasonably calculated, under all the circumstances, to apprise interested parties of the pendency of the action and afford them an opportunity to present their objections. *Milliken v. Meyer*, 311 U.S. 457. The notice must be of such nature as reasonably to convey the required information, and it must afford a reasonable time for those interested to make their appearance. But if with due regard for the practicalities and peculiarities of the case these conditions are reasonably met the constitutional requirements are satisfied. "The criterion is not the possibility of conceivable injury, but the just and reasonable character of the requirements, having reference to the subject with which the statute deals." *American Land Co. v. Zeiss*, 219 U.S. 47.

But when notice is a person's due, process which is a mere gesture is not due process. The means employed must be such as one desirous of actually informing the absentee might reasonably adopt to accomplish it. The reasonableness and hence the constitutional validity of any chosen method may be defended on the ground that it is in itself reasonably certain to inform those affected, or, where conditions do not reasonably permit such notice, that the form chosen is not substantially less likely to bring home notice than other of the feasible and customary substitutes.

[Eds.—The court discusses here the problems with "constructive" service of process by publication.]

It would be idle to pretend that publication alone as prescribed here, is a reliable means of acquainting interested parties of the fact that their rights are before the courts. It is not an accident that the greater number of cases reaching this Court on the question of adequacy of notice have been concerned with actions founded on process constructively served through local newspapers. Chance alone brings to the attention of even a local resident an advertisement in small type inserted in the back pages of a newspaper, and if he makes his home outside the area of the newspaper's normal circulation the odds that the information will never reach him are large indeed. The chance of actual notice is further reduced when as here the notice required does not even name those whose attention it is supposed to attract, and does not inform acquaintances who might call it to attention. In weighing its sufficiency on the basis of equivalence with actual notice we are unable to regard this as more than a feint.

Nor is publication here reinforced by steps likely to attract the parties' attention to the proceeding. It is true that publication traditionally has been acceptable as notification supplemental to other action which in itself may reasonably be expected to convey a warning. The ways of an owner with tangible property are such that he usually arranges means to learn of any direct attack upon his possessory or proprietary rights. Hence, libel of a ship, attachment of a chattel or entry upon real estate in the name of law may reasonably be expected to come promptly to the owner's attention. When the state within which the owner has located such property seizes it for some reason, publication or posting affords an additional measure of notification. A state may indulge the assumption that one who has left tangible property in the state either has abandoned it, in which case proceedings against it deprive him of nothing, or that he has left some caretaker under a duty to let him know that it is being jeopardized. . . .

In the case before us there is, of course, no abandonment. On the other hand these beneficiaries do have a resident fiduciary as caretaker of their interest in this property. But it is their caretaker who in the accounting becomes their adversary. Their trustee is released from giving notice of jeopardy, and no one else is expected to do so. Not even the special guardian is required or apparently expected to communicate with his ward and client, and, of course, if such a duty were merely transferred from the trustee to the guardian, economy would not be served and more likely the cost would be increased.

This Court has not hesitated to approve of resort to publication as a customary substitute in another class of cases where it is not reasonably possible or practicable to give more adequate warning. Thus it has been recognized that, in the case of persons missing or unknown, employment of an indirect and even a probably futile means of notification is all that the situation permits and creates no constitutional bar to a final decree foreclosing their rights.

[Eds.—Next, the Court applies the basic constitutional standard to various classes of persons with an interest in the trusts.]

Those beneficiaries represented by appellant whose interests or whereabouts could not with due diligence be ascertained come clearly within this category. As to them the statutory notice is sufficient. However great the odds that publication will never reach the eyes of such unknown parties, it is not in the typical case much more likely to fail than any of the choices open to legislators endeavoring to prescribe the best notice practicable.

Nor do we consider it unreasonable for the State to dispense with more certain notice to those beneficiaries whose interests are either conjectural or future or, although they could be discovered upon investigation, do not in due course of business come to knowledge of the common trustee. Whatever searches might be required in another situation under ordinary standards of diligence, in view of the character of the proceedings and the nature of the interests here involved we think them unnecessary. We recognize the practical difficulties and costs that would be attendant on frequent investigations into the status of great numbers of beneficiaries, many of whose interests in the common fund are so remote as to be ephemeral; and we have no doubt that such impracticable and extended searches are not required in the name of due process. The expense of keeping informed from day to day of substitutions among even current income beneficiaries and presumptive remaindermen, to say nothing of the far greater number of contingent beneficiaries, would impose a severe burden on the plan, and would likely dissipate its advantages. These are practical matters in which we should be reluctant to disturb the judgment of the state authorities.

Accordingly we overrule appellant's constitutional objections to published notice insofar as they are urged on behalf of any beneficiaries whose interests or addresses are unknown to the trustee.

As to known present beneficiaries of known place of residence, however, notice by publication stands on a different footing. Exceptions in the name of necessity do not sweep away the rule that within the limits of practicability notice must be such as is reasonably calculated to reach interested parties. Where the names and post office addresses of those affected by a proceeding are at hand, the reasons disappear for resort to means less likely than the mails to apprise them of its pendency.

The trustee has on its books the names and addresses of the income beneficiaries represented by appellant, and we find no tenable ground for dispensing with a serious effort to inform them personally of the accounting, at least by ordinary mail to the record addresses. Certainly sending them a copy of the statute months and perhaps years in advance does not answer this purpose. The trustee periodically remits their income to them, and we think that they might reasonably expect that with or apart from their remittances word might come to them personally that steps were being taken affecting their interests.

We need not weigh contentions that a requirement of personal service of citation **[Eds.—That is, in-hand delivery.]** on even the large number of known resident or nonresident beneficiaries would, by reasons of delay if not of expense, seriously interfere with the proper administration of the fund. Of course personal service even without the jurisdiction of the issuing authority serves the end of actual and personal notice, whatever power of compulsion it might lack. However, no such service is required under the circumstances. This type of trust presupposes a large number of small interests. The individual interest does not stand alone but is identical with that of a class. The rights of each in the integrity of the fund and the fidelity of the trustee are shared by many other beneficiaries. Therefore notice reasonably certain to reach most of those interested in objecting is likely to safeguard the interests of all, since any objections sustained would inure to the benefit of all. We think that under such circumstances reasonable risks that notice might not actually reach every beneficiary are justifiable. "Now and then an extraordinary case may turn up, but constitutional law, like other mortal contrivances, has to take some chances, and in the great majority of instances, no doubt, justice will be done." *Blinn v. Nelson, supra*, 222 U.S. at page 7.

The statutory notice to known beneficiaries is inadequate, not because in fact it fails to reach everyone, but because under the circumstances it is not reasonably calculated to reach those who could easily be informed by other means at hand. However it may have been in former times, the mails today are recognized as an efficient and inexpensive means of communication. Moreover, the fact that the trust company has been able to give mailed notice to known beneficiaries at the time the common trust fund was established is persuasive that postal notification at the time of accounting would not seriously burden the plan.

In some situations the law requires greater precautions in its proceedings than the business world accepts for its own purposes. In few, if any, will it be satisfied with less. Certainly it is instructive, in determining the reasonableness of the impersonal broadcast notification here used, to ask whether it would satisfy a prudent man of business, counting his pennies but finding it in his interest to convey information to many persons whose names and addresses are in his files. We are not satisfied that it would. Publication may theoretically be available for all the world to see, but it is too much in our day to suppose that each or any individual beneficiary does or could examine all that is published to see if something may be tucked away in it that affects his property interests. We have before indicated in reference to notice by publication that, "Great caution should be used not to let fiction deny the fair play that can be secured only by a pretty close adhesion to fact." *McDonald v. Mabee*, 243 U.S. 90, 91.

We hold the notice of judicial settlement of accounts required by the New York Banking Law § 100-c(12) is incompatible with the requirements of the Fourteenth Amendment as a basis for adjudication depriving known persons whose whereabouts are also known of substantial property rights. Accordingly the judgment is reversed and the cause remanded for further proceedings not inconsistent with this opinion.

Reversed.

Notes and Questions on *Mullane v. Central Hanover Bank*

1. The holding of *Mullane*. What exactly did the *Mullane* case hold? Consider the question below. (Yes, we answer our question with a question, a typical law school ploy.)

In *Mullane v. Central Hanover Bank & Trust Co.*, the Supreme Court held that

A. every person with a current right to income from the trust is entitled to at least mail notice of the proceeding.
B. every person whose name and address could be ascertained through investigation must be given individual notice of the proceeding.
C. any person whose interests might be affected by the proceeding must be given notice by in-hand service of process.
D. due to the large number of persons whose interests might be affected by the proceedings, notice by publication was sufficient on the facts of the case.
E. None of the above is true.

A is not right. The court did hold that the bank must provide mail notice to current income beneficiaries whose names and addresses were in its files. That is easy to do and cheap. But since these trusts were established, the right to current income may have shifted to new beneficiaries if new children were born, or married, or the settlor of the trust died or for other reasons. *Mullane* recognized that requiring the bank to do legal and factual research to identify and locate such persons was impracticable, since the expense of doing so would eat up the profits of the trust. So some current beneficiaries, whose names and addresses would not be in the bank's records, did not have to receive individual notice.

B also fails, for the same reason. It suggests that the bank would have to conduct an investigation to determine all persons having an interest in the combined trusts and give them individual notice. The *Mullane* opinion declines to impose that heavy a burden on the bank.

C is also inaccurate: *Mullane* did not require any beneficiary to be served in-hand. The opinion approved service by mail on known beneficiaries for whom the bank had addresses in its files.

D is also not entirely right. *Mullane* held that publication notice sufficed as to many persons with an interest in the proceeding, but not as to all. For those whose names were in the bank's files, at least notice by mail was constitutionally required. Notice by publication would not constitute due process for those beneficiaries, because a better method of notice was readily available. But *Mullane* upholds notice by publication under the New York statute (together with the appointment of the guardians required by the statute) as constitutionally sufficient to notify beneficiaries whose names and addresses were not known to the bank.

So, the prize goes to **E**.

Q **2. Service by the book.** In *Mullane*, the method of service of process for the accounting procedure was set forth in detail in the New York statute governing common trust funds. The bank, in seeking approval of its accounts, complied with the statutory procedures. So what's the problem?

A The problem is that state notice statutes must specify a method of notice that is constitutionally sufficient under the Due Process Clause of the Fourteenth Amendment. The method used must both be authorized by the applicable statutes or rules governing service in the particular court and also meet constitutional standards. So, the fact that a statute authorizes a particular method of service does not automatically make it proper. This is similar to the relation between a state long arm statute and the Fourteenth Amendment; even if a long arm statute authorizes personal jurisdiction, it cannot be exercised if it would exceed due process limits.

New York Banking Law § 100-c(6), dealing with settlement of common trust funds, now contains detailed requirements for mail notice to various categories of persons of whom the bank has knowledge and who might have an interest in the trusts.

3. The point reiterated: A statute that failed to pass constitutional muster. *Greene v. Lindsey*, 456 U.S. 444 (1982), involved service of process in an eviction action. A Kentucky statute authorized the sheriff to deliver the notice to the tenant, or, if no one was home, to post the papers on the tenant's door. This statute was challenged by tenants in federal court, claiming that the statutory method of serving process "did not satisfy the minimum standards of constitutionally adequate notice described in *Mullane v. Central Hanover Bank & Trust Co.*" 456 U.S. at 447.

The Supreme Court agreed with the tenants' argument. The problem was that many such notices did not reach the defendants whose tenancies were at risk.

> As the process servers were well aware, notices posted on apartment doors... were "not infrequently" removed by children or other tenants before they could have their intended effect. Under these conditions, notice by posting on the apartment door cannot be considered a "reliable means of acquainting interested parties of the fact that their rights are before the courts."

456 U.S. at 453–54 (citing *Mullane*, 339 U.S. at 315). The other side of the constitutional coin was that a reliable and inexpensive means of enhancing the likelihood of actual notice was available: dropping a second copy of the papers in the U.S. mail addressed to the tenant at the rental address. Because the method used was not sufficiently likely to reach the tenants and an easy means of providing more effective service was available, the Court held the statutory posting procedure constitutionally inadequate under *Mullane*.

4. And another... In *Jones v. Flowers*, 547 U.S. 220 (2006), an Arkansas statute authorized notice in a tax sale proceeding by certified mail to the owner of the property, followed by publication if the letter was returned unclaimed. The Supreme Court, in a closely divided opinion, held this notice inadequate under *Mullane*.

> [W]e conclude...that someone who actually wanted to alert Jones that he was in danger of losing his house would do more when the attempted notice letter was returned unclaimed, and there was more that reasonably could be done.

547 U.S. at 238. The majority relied in part on the extent of the deprivation involved—sale by the court of the defendant's real estate—and in part on the fact that several additional steps would be likely to give actual notice of the taking, including the posting of notice on the property or regular mail notice to the occupant of the property. 547 U.S. at 222. *See also Mennonite Board of Mission v. Adams*, 462 U.S. 791 (1983) (statute authorizing notice of sale of property by publication and posting held unconstitutional under *Mullane*).

Q **5. Is "last and usual" service constitutional?** Federal Rule 4(e)(2)(B) allows service by leaving the summons and complaint (if the defendant is a person) at the defendant's dwelling house with a person of suitable age and discretion residing therein. However, some states allow service of process by leaving copies of the summons and complaint at the defendant's "last and usual place of abode" without the additional requirement of leaving them with a person residing there. *See, e.g.*, Mass. R. Civ. P. 4(d)(1). What is the argument that this method of service is unconstitutional under *Mullane*?

A This provision appears to allow service by simply slipping papers under the door. This is considerably less likely to assure actual notice than delivery to a person. (Indeed, it would appear that this rule would be met by posting the papers on the defendant's door—the procedure rejected in *Greene*.) The papers might somehow get lost or picked up by someone else. At the same time, there is a convenient means of improving the likelihood of actual notice: mailing copies to the defendant at the address.

This provision has been in effect in Massachusetts for many years, but counsel may be wise to use one of the other methods authorized in the Rule (such as personal delivery) to avoid the risk of a constitutional challenge. For a rule that avoids the constitutional problem, see Ind. R. Trial Proc. Rule 4.1(B), which requires mailing the summons to the defendant after leaving the summons and complaint at her usual place of abode. *See also* Kan. Stat. Ann. § 60-303(d)(1)(C) (requiring mail notice that summons and complaint have been left at the usual place of abode).

6. So, how must notice be given to satisfy the Due Process Clause? It would be nice to give a single, simple answer to this question, but the types of proceedings, types of defendants, and the circumstances in which notice is attempted vary too much to allow one. The means required by due process must vary with the circumstances. Thus, *Mullane* establishes a broad constitutional standard rather than providing a mechanical answer. The standard Justice Jackson suggests is an eminently sensible one:

> [W]hen notice is a person's due, process which is a mere gesture is not due process. The means employed must be such as one desirous of actually informing the absentee might reasonably adopt to accomplish it.

Justice Robert Jackson

Collection of the Supreme Court of the United States

Justice Robert Jackson (1892–1954) was raised in New York State. He never went to college. He apprenticed in a law office, attended one year of law school and passed the New York bar at the age of 21. He became an eminent practitioner and an advisor to President Franklin D. Roosevelt. During the Roosevelt administration he served in the Justice Department, was appointed Solicitor General of the United States, then Attorney General of the United States, where he aggressively pursued the policies of the New Deal. He was appointed to the Supreme Court in 1941. He also served as the chief prosecutor at the Nuremberg trials, at which Nazi officials were prosecuted for war crimes during World War II. His opinion in *Mullane*—like several other classics he penned on procedural issues—reflects his good judgment and grasp of the practicalities of law practice.

7. Adequate service in an ordinary case. Johnson sues Fuentes, an individual who owes her some money. Based on the discussion of constitutional standards in *Mullane,* which of the following methods would you expect the court to find constitutionally adequate?

1. in-hand service (i.e., personal delivery) of the summons and complaint on Fuentes by a sheriff;
2. in-hand service of the summons and complaint on Fuentes by Johnson;
3. mailing of the summons and complaint to Fuentes at his home address by certified mail;
4. mailing of the summons and complaint to Fuentes at his home address by first-class mail;
5. publication of notice of the filing of the action in a local newspaper for three weeks in a row;
6. posting of notice of the suit on a bulletin board in front of the courthouse in which the case is filed.

Personal delivery of the papers notifying Fuentes of the suit and his duty to defend it is the best possible form of notice. The person giving notice physically confronts the defendant and hands him papers delivering the bad news.

This is about as good as notice gets, so 1 and 2 should pass constitutional muster.*

Methods 3 and 4 use the U.S. mail to give notice. Justice Jackson's opinion suggests that this is generally constitutionally proper where the papers are mailed to a current address for the defendant.

However, method 5 is constitutionally defective if Johnson can do something better. Surely a businessperson trying to contact a customer would not publish a notice in the paper, if she had an address for the customer. As *Mullane* suggests, publication is a hit-or-miss proposition that no one would use if they had surer alternatives. It may be constitutionally sufficient if nothing better can be done but otherwise it will not suffice. Posting a notice at the courthouse (6) is also a chancy means of reaching the defendant. (If you wanted to ask him to pay back a loan, you wouldn't use this method, would you?) Again, unless nothing better is feasible—because you have no idea where Fuentes is—this is constitutionally deficient. As a working rule, service by mail and personal delivery are constitutionally acceptable but publication notice is not, unless other means have failed.

Q **8. Reasonable investigation?** Marino is in an accident with Malewicz. He exchanges information with Malewicz at the accident scene. Later, he brings an action against Malewicz and serves him by mail, but the mailing comes back "undeliverable." Based on the analysis in *Mullane*, may Marino now serve Malewicz by publication?

A Probably not. In *Mullane*, the Court approved publication notice to various persons with interests in the trusts, even though the Bank might have found their names and addresses after some investigation. But in *Mullane*, there were many parties with a remote interest in the fund, and circumstances provided other protections for the interests of those absent beneficiaries: Those who did get notice had the same interest in making sure that the Bank had managed the combined fund appropriately, and two special guardians were appointed to protect those interests as well.

Here, there is only one person to be located and served, so the expense of trying to locate him would be less than in *Mullane*. And, absent personal notice, Malewicz will very likely not learn of the case and protect his rights. Since publication is likely to be a mere gesture, the reasonableness analysis articulated in *Mullane* clearly calls for more effort to find Malewicz. *See, e.g., Gaeth v. Deacon*, 964 A.2d 621 (Me. 2009) (rejecting publication notice despite aggressive efforts to locate the defendant).

III. Implementing the Due Process Standard: Statutes and Rules Governing Service of Process

As the first part of this chapter states, service on the defendant must be both constitutionally sufficient and authorized by a statute or rule of the court

* Fed. R. Civ. P. 4(c)(2) bars service of process by a party, perhaps to avoid physical confrontations by the parties. However, nothing in *Mullane* suggests that this prudential limit is constitutionally required.

system in which the case is filed. When you enter law practice and are first asked to serve process on a defendant, you won't engage in original constitutional speculation about what might be a proper method of doing so. You will turn to the rules of procedure or state statutes governing service of process in the court in which you are filing suit. Those statutes have been around for a long time, were drafted with constitutional constraints in mind, and have probably withstood constitutional challenges or been amended to assure that they will. In addition, service must be made in a manner authorized by the applicable rules or statutes: You cannot just use any method you like as long as it meets due process standards.

Every state has either court rules or state statutes setting forth the permissible methods of service of process in the courts of that state. For actions brought in federal court, the proper procedures for service of process are set forth in Rule 4 of the Federal Rules of Civil Procedure. We will explore the federal methods as a model; many state procedures are quite similar. First, we cover some basic points.

A. Some Practicalities of Service: Who, What, and When?

What gets served on the defendant? Under Federal Rule 4(c)(1), the complaint and a summons must be served together on the defendant. The complaint is the plaintiff's initial pleading, setting forth her claims against the defendant. The summons is an official order of the court, commanding the defendant to appear and defend the action or suffer default. (The contents of a proper summons are prescribed in detail in Rule 4(a).) Thus, the complaint apprises the defendant of the claims against her and the summons orders her to answer those claims.

Who serves process on the defendant? One might reasonably expect that the court would take charge of notifying the defendant that she has been sued. Generally, however, the duty to serve process is delegated to the plaintiff. Federal Rule 4(c)(1) provides that "[t]he plaintiff is responsible for having the summons and complaint served" on the defendant. The plaintiff does not serve it herself, however. Rule 4(c)(2) provides that "[a]ny person who is at least 18 years old and not a party may serve a summons and complaint." The plaintiff's lawyer could do it herself, but more likely she will hire a private process server to do so or a sheriff or deputy sheriff authorized to serve process. If service by mail is authorized, however, counsel probably will do so.

When must service be made? The complaint and summons must be served after the complaint is filed. *See* Fed. R. Civ. P. 4(b) (summons issued after filing of the complaint). Rule 4(m) provides that the court must dismiss an action if service is not made on the defendant within ninety days after filing, or order service to be made within a specified time. If the plaintiff shows good cause for the failure to make service, the court must grant an extension of the time to make service "for an appropriate period." *Id.* If no good cause is shown, Rule 4(m) still authorizes the court to extend the time for service, but it has the discretion to dismiss instead. Dismissal for failure to make timely service would not bar the plaintiff from filing a new action, but the plaintiff would have to pay a new filing fee and would risk statute of limitations problems in refiling.

B. Serving Natural Persons Under the Federal Rules

Federal Rule 4(e) provides four methods to serve the summons and complaint on an individual defendant (i.e., a person). The process server may

- deliver the papers to the defendant personally ("in-hand service") wherever she can find the defendant. Fed. R. Civ. P. 4(e)(2)(A).
- leave the summons and complaint at the defendant's "dwelling or usual place of abode with someone of suitable age and discretion who resides there." Fed. R. Civ. P. 4(e)(2)(B).
- deliver the summons and complaint to an agent of the defendant authorized by appointment or by law to receive service of process. Fed. R. Civ. P. 4(e)(2)(C).
- follow the rules for service of process of the state where the federal court sits or of the state in which service of process is made. Fed. R. Civ. P. 4(e)(1).

The last provision gives a plaintiff several alternatives to the three methods specified in Rule 4(e)(2). Suppose that Arnett sues Costa in federal court in Kentucky. Costa resides in Arkansas but is subject to jurisdiction in the Kentucky action because the case arises out of an accident that took place in Kentucky. Federal Rule 4(e)(1) allows Arnett to serve Costa under the rules for service of process that apply in the Kentucky courts or, if she is serving Costa in Arkansas, to use the Arkansas rules for service of process.

C. Serving Corporations and Other Entities Under Federal Rule 4

Rule 4(h) prescribes methods for serving a "corporation, partnership or association." The term "association" covers a wide variety of groups that may be sued under a common name, including labor unions, church groups, political groups, and other unincorporated entities. Service can be made by

- delivering a copy of the summons and complaint to an officer, a managing agent, or a general agent of the entity. Fed. R. Civ. P. 4(h)(1)(B).
- delivering the papers to an agent authorized by law or by appointment to receive service of process. Fed. R. Civ. P. 4(h)(1)(B). This does not refer to a general business agent but one specifically empowered to receive service. For example, many states have statutes authorizing service of process on the state's Secretary of State for actions against corporations doing business within the state. *See, e.g.,* Fla. Stat. Ann. § 48.181 (2010); Ga. Code Ann. § 9-11-4(e)(1)(A) (2010).
- serving process under state rules for serving corporations, in either the state where the federal court sits or in the state where service is made. Fed. R. Civ. P. 4(h)(1)(A).

The last provision is a little confusing. Fed. R. Civ. P. 4(h)(1)(A) provides that service may be made "in the manner prescribed by Rule 4(e)(1) for serving an individual." This appears to authorize service by the means permitted under state law for serving a person. But it can't mean that—you can't deliver the papers to a corporation "personally" nor can you leave them at a corporation's dwelling house. Rather, this means that, analogous to service on individuals, the plaintiff may invoke state service rules for serving a corporation.*

Q **Service on other entities.** Your firm is bringing a federal civil action against the City of Denver, the Federal Small Business Administration, and Penny & Wright, a law firm. You are asked to determine how to serve the summons and complaint on each of these entities. Under Rule 4, how should you serve process on these defendants?

A To answer a question like this, it makes sense to start by looking at the Federal Rules. Students desperately resist looking at them, but as you gain experience in practice you will come to appreciate how many questions they answer about procedure. Rule 4 specifies methods for service on each of these defendants:

City of Denver: You should deliver a copy of the summons and complaint to the city's chief executive officer. Fed. R. Civ. P. 4(j)(2)(A). (A little research will likely confirm that this is the mayor.) Or, you can use a method authorized by Colorado law for serving process on a local government. *See* Fed. R. Civ. P. 4(j)(2)(B).

Federal Small Business Administration: You would do research to confirm this, but it certainly appears that the Small Business Administration is a federal agency. If so, Fed. R. Civ. P. 4(i)(2) applies. Under that provision, you must serve the United States (see the provisions for doing so in Fed. R. Civ. P. 4(i)(1)) and send a copy of the summons and complaint by registered or certified mail to the agency.

Penny & Wright: The law firm is likely a partnership or a corporation. Thus, you would use one of the methods provided in Fed. R. Civ. P. 4(h).

That wasn't so bad, actually.

Q **A comedy of errors: Some practice in applying the service rules.** Consider whether service of process is proper in each of the following cases under Federal Rule 4 (disregard the possibility of using state service rules).

A. Hugo, the plaintiff, serves the defendant Hyde, an individual, by delivering the summons and complaint to her himself.

A No good. Hugo, as a party, is not authorized to serve process himself. Fed. R. Civ. P. 4(c)(2).

B. Hugo serves Hyde by having a private process server deliver the complaint to Hyde at her office.

A Still no good. Hugo did not have a copy of the summons delivered with the complaint. Fed. R. Civ. P. 4(c)(1).

* While this proposition seems utterly self-evident, it is hard to find cases that state it—perhaps because it is self-evident. *See Duckworth v. GMAC Ins.*, No. CIVA 2: 09CV214-P-A N.D. Miss. Apr. 14, 2010 (2010 WL 1529392) ("Rule 4(e)(1), however, also allows for service pursuant to state law. The court, therefore, must review state law regarding proper service of process on a corporation.").

C. Hugo sues Jekyll and Hyde, two unrelated individuals. He serves process by having the process server deliver two copies of the summons and complaint to Jekyll at his home.

A Process has been properly served on Jekyll, but not on Hyde. Each defendant must be served separately, unless Jekyll is Hyde's agent for service of process.

D. Hugo serves Jekyll by having a process server leave the summons and complaint at his house with Jack, a friend of Jekyll who is in town for a convention.

A This also does not comply with Rule 4(e). If service is made at the defendant's dwelling, it must be left with a person of suitable age and discretion who resides there. A visiting conventioneer would probably not qualify. Fed. R. Civ. P. 4(e)(2)(B).

E. Hugo serves Jekyll by having a process server leave the summons and complaint with Jekyll's wife Jane at the restaurant she runs.

A Fails again. If the process server delivered the papers to Jane at Jane and Hugo's home, this would comply with Rule 4(e)(2)(B), but that rule does not allow service on Jane at some other location.

F. Hugo sues Jane's Restaurant Corporation and serves process by having the process server deliver the summons and complaint to Child, a pastry chef at Jane's restaurant.

A Another flop. A corporation may be served by delivering the papers to a "managing or general agent" of the corporation, but it is doubtful that a pastry chef has the kind of authority that fits this definition. Fed. R. Civ. P. 4(h)(1)(B).

G. Hugo sues Jane's Restaurant Corporation, which owns a restaurant in Minnesota, in Minnesota federal court. The process server delivers the summons and complaint to Jane, president of Jane's, while she is visiting her mother in Wisconsin.

A No problem. A corporation may be served by delivering the papers to an officer. Fed. R. Civ. P. 4(h)(1)(B). The Rule does not require that the officer be in any particular place when she receives service.

H. Hugo sues Jekyll and hires Moth, a lazy process server, to serve process on Jekyll. Moth drops the papers down the sewer and files an affidavit with the court attesting that he served the papers on Jekyll personally.

A This ploy is common enough to have its own name, "sewer service." Clearly, it is inadequate (and illegal) and cannot support a valid judgment. As a plaintiff's lawyer, you will want to develop a relationship with a reliable process server to avoid this risk.

D. Service on Parties Outside the United States

Litigation, like so much else these days, is "going global." Foreign defendants are frequently sued in United States courts and must be served with process. Court rules or statutes typically provide a number of methods for making international service. Rule 4(f) provides several methods for serving process on individual defendants in other countries in federal cases. Service may be made

- as provided by international agreements, such as the Hague Convention on the Service Abroad of Judicial and Extrajudicial Documents. Fed. R. Civ. P. 4(f)(1). Many countries, including the United States, have signed the Hague Convention, which provides a mechanism for sending the documents to a designated Central Authority in the country where service is to be made, which then completes service on the defendant.
- using the methods for service of process in the country where service is made. Fed. R. Civ. P. 4(f)(2)(A). This method requires researching the procedural rules of that country, which can be difficult, especially when those rules are in a different language.
- by personal delivery, unless prohibited by the law of the country where service is made. Fed. R. Civ. P. 4(f)(2)(C)(i). Again, it may be difficult to ascertain whether personal service is allowed there.
- by a form of mail requiring a signed receipt, unless prohibited by the law of the country where service is made. Fed. R. Civ. P. 4(f)(2)(C)(ii).
- by seeking instructions from an appropriate authority in the country where service is made through a letter of request. Fed. R. Civ. P. 4(f)(2)(B).
- by seeking a court order for alternative means of service. Fed. R. Civ. P. 4(f)(3). (Federal district courts are not likely to be receptive to such requests, however, from plaintiffs who have not tried one of the other permissible methods.)

Similarly, state court procedural rules and statutes specify methods for service on defendants outside the United States. *See, e.g.,* Alaska R. Civ. P. 4(d)(13), which closely tracks the options under Federal Rule 4(f).

E. Avoiding Technicalities: Waiver of Service of Process

Federal Rule 4 offers a simple and inexpensive alternative to formal service of process. Under Fed. R. Civ. P. 4(d), the plaintiff may ask the defendant to waive formal service. The plaintiff sends the defendant a notice of the action with two copies of the waiver form, the complaint, and a prepaid envelope for returning the waiver. Fed. R. Civ P. Rule 4(d)(1). Defendants have a duty to avoid the costs of formal service. If they do not return the waiver, they must pay the costs of formal service, including the attorneys' fees for any motion to collect those costs. The rule also offers an enticement to defendants to waive service: It gives them sixty days to answer instead of the usual twenty-one. Fed. R. Civ. P. 4(d)(3).*

* The waiver procedure under Rule 4(d) may also be used for foreign defendants. *See* Fed. R. Civ. P. 4(d)(1)(F) and (3).

Q **Duty unfulfilled.** Alice, counsel for Chang in a federal action, sends Fuentes, the defendant, two copies of a waiver form, a stamped return envelope, and the complaint, in compliance with Rule 4(d)(1). The thirty-day period for returning the waiver goes by and she does not get back the waiver form. What should she do next?

A The clear implication of Rule 4(d) is that, if the waiver is not returned, the plaintiff must serve process through the formal means in Rule 4. *See* Rule 4(d)(2)(A), which makes the non-complying defendant responsible for the costs of service.

Q **A trap for the unwary.** Under the law of some states, the statute of limitations is satisfied by service of process on the defendant within the statutory period, rather than by filing the complaint with the court. Assume that is true of Chang's case. On January 1, five days before the statute of limitations expires on the plaintiff's tort claim against Fuentes, Alice sends Fuentes a request to waive service together with the summons and complaint and return envelope. Fuentes receives it on January 4, two days before the statute runs, and returns it on January 24, twenty days later. Alice files it with the court two days later, on January 26. When Fuentes answers the complaint, he asserts as a defense that the claim is barred by the passage of the statute of limitations. How should the court rule? *See* Rule 4(d)(4).

A The court should accept the defense and dismiss the claim. Rule 4(d)(4) provides that "these rules apply as if a summons and complaint had been served at the time of filing the waiver." Under this rule, service was completed on Fuentes on January 26, when the waiver was filed with the court, eighteen days after the limitations period ran. Although Fuentes received the summons and complaint before the limitations period ran, service is not complete by waiver until it is filed. So he was not served on time.

Note, however, that returning the waiver only waives the duty to serve process under Rule 4. It does not waive any other objection the defendant may have, such as an objection to jurisdiction or venue.

This provision, that service is effective upon filing the waiver, avoids difficult factual issues about when the defendant received the papers, which plaintiff will not know. It clearly suggests, however, that if the limitations period is about to run, counsel should not use the waiver procedure since Fuentes might not return the waiver form at all or return it too late to meet the limitations period.

The provisions governing waiver of service were added to Federal Rule 4 in 1993. Although many states' rules of civil procedure are modeled on the Federal Rules, it appears that many have not amended their rules to allow for waiver of service of process. For one that has, see Va. Code Ann. § 8.01-286.1, adopted in 2005.

Q **Possibilities for manipulation.** Galleraga is sued by O'Hara for breach of contract in federal court. O'Hara serves the summons and complaint on Galleraga, but service does not comply with any of the methods authorized in Rule 4. Galleraga answers the complaint and begins discovery. Six months later, after the statute of limitations has passed, Galleraga moves to dismiss the action, arguing that she was not properly served with process, and that the court cannot acquire jurisdiction over the defendant without proper service. Assuming that the court agrees that service was improper, what will the court do?

A You can see how a defendant might engage in serious manipulation if she could keep this objection in her pocket and raise it later to get rid of the case. Here, for example, O'Hara might be unable to refile the action if it was dismissed after six months, since the limitations period has passed. To avoid such tactical maneuvering, the Federal Rules provide that objections to service of process must be raised early in the litigation either by a pre-answer motion or in the answer to the complaint. *See* Fed. R. Civ. P. 12(g)–(h). If the objection is not timely raised, it is waived.

IV. Service of Process in State Courts

The Federal Rules provisions for service of process do not apply in the state courts; every state provides methods for service of process in its courts by statute or court rule. Of course, such provisions, like those for service in federal court, must comply with the due process standard of *Mullane*. This section illustrates state methods of service, based on a divorce case filed in a New York state court.

1. Service methods for divorce cases under New York law. New York has a special provision for service of process in divorce cases, which provides in part:

> A judgment shall not be rendered in favor of the plaintiff upon the defendant's default in appearing or pleading, unless either (1) the summons and a copy of the complaint were personally delivered to the defendant; or (2) the copy of the summons (a) personally delivered to the defendant, or (b) served on the defendant pursuant to an order directing the method of service of the summons in accordance with the provisions of section three hundred eight or three hundred fifteen of the civil practice law and rules, shall contain such notice [sic].

N.Y. Dom. Rel. Law § 232(a). Note that this section allows service—if personal delivery is not possible—through various methods specified in § 308 of the Civil Practice Law and Rules (referred to in the *Baidoo* opinion as "CPLR"). Section 308 provides in part:

> Personal service upon a natural person shall be made by any of the following methods:
>
> 1. by delivering the summons within the state to the person to be served; or
>
> 2. by delivering the summons within the state to a person of suitable age and discretion at the actual place of business, dwelling place or usual place of abode of the person to be served and by either mailing the summons to the person to be served at his or her last known residence or by mailing the

> summons by first class mail to the person to be served at his or her actual place of business in an envelope bearing the legend "personal and confidential" and not indicating on the outside thereof, by return address or otherwise, that the communication is from an attorney or concerns an action against the person to be served, such delivery and mailing to be effected within twenty days of each other . . . or
>
> 4. where service under paragraphs one and two cannot be made with due diligence, by affixing the summons to the door of either the actual place of business, dwelling place or usual place of abode within the state of the person to be served and by either mailing the summons to such person at his or her last known residence or by mailing the summons by first class mail to the person to be served at his or her actual place of business in an envelope bearing the legend "personal and confidential" and not indicating on the outside thereof, by return address or otherwise, that the communication is from an attorney or concerns an action against the person to be served, such affixing and mailing to be effected within twenty days of each other . . .
>
> 5. in such manner as the court, upon motion without notice, directs, if service is impracticable under paragraphs one, two and four of this section.*

2. A hierarchy of service methods. Note that § 232(a) establishes a preferred method of service in divorce actions—by personal delivery of the summons and complaint to the defendant under § 232(a)(1), or personal delivery of the summons under § 232(a)(2)(a). If service is made by personal delivery, no order from the court is required. If personal delivery is not possible (for example, if the defendant avoids service or her whereabouts are unknown), § 232(a) authorizes service under one or more of the alternative methods in § 308, as ordered by the court.

- by delivering the summons to a person of suitable age and discretion at the defendant's place of business or residence *and* mailing the summons to the defendant's place of business. § 308(2) *or*
- by affixing the summons to the door of the defendant's place of business, dwelling place or place of abode within the defendant's state of domicile *and* by mailing to the person's last known residence or actual place of business *or*
- in a manner ordered by the court if other methods are "impracticable"

If an alternative method is used, the court must approve that method, again to assure that service is likely to provide actual notice. The court can consider the circumstances and enter an appropriate order for service either through one of the methods specified in § 308 or through another method likely to provide actual notice of the action to the defendant, or through a combination of methods.

These provisions differ in some respects from the methods of service specified in Federal Rule 4, and in some respects are more stringent. (Remember,

* N.Y. C.P.L.R. 315, cited in § 232(a), also authorizes service by publication "if service cannot be made by another prescribed method with due diligence."

however, that Federal Rule 4 authorizes use of methods of service of process permitted by either the state where the action is pending or the state where service is made, *in addition to* the service methods specified in Rule 4. Fed. R. Civ. P. 4(e)(1) and 4(h)(1)(A).)

The *Baidoo* case below applies these New York statutory provisions for service of process in a divorce case.

READING *BAIDOO v. BLOOD-DZRAKU.* This case was filed in state court, so the New York statutes governing methods of service of process reviewed above apply, not the Federal Rules. Because the defendant could not be served by personal delivery, the court reviews other methods available under New York law. Consider the following questions in reading *Baidoo.*

- If the plaintiff cannot serve the defendant in person, what must she do to make proper service?
- Did the *Baidoo* court consider the constitutional standards of *Mullane* as well as the New York service statutes in deciding whether to authorize service via Facebook?
- What concerns did the *Baidoo* court have about authorizing service by social media?
- Why did the court reject service of process through publication, a time-honored last resort for notifying a defendant of an action?

BAIDOO v. BLOOD-DZRAKU

5 N.Y.S.3d 309 (N.Y. Sup. Ct. 2015)

Matthew F. Cooper, J.

As recently as 10 years ago, it was considered a cutting-edge development in civil practice for a court to allow the service of a summons by email. Since then, email has all but replaced ordinary mail as a means of written communication. And while the legislature has yet to make email a statutorily authorized method for the service of process, courts are now routinely permitting it as a form of alternative service.

The past decade has also seen the advent and ascendancy of social media, with websites such as Facebook and Twitter occupying a central place in the lives of so many people.[2] Thus, it would appear that the next frontier in the developing law of the service of process over the Internet is the use of social media

2. The "many" includes the 157,000,000 people in the United States who, according to Facebook's 2014 fourth quarter shareholder report, check their Facebook accounts each day. It does not, by and large, include the members of the New York State Judiciary, who have been advised that they should be wary of using social network sites (see Advisory Comm on Jud Ethics Op 08-176 [2009]; Advisory Comm on Jud Ethics Op 13-39 [2013]; see also Richard Raysman & Peter Brown, Judicial and Attorney Misuse of Social Media Can End Careers, NYLJ, Mar. 10, 2015 at 5, col 1).

sites as forums through which a summons can be delivered. In this matrimonial action, the issue before the court, by way of plaintiff wife's ex parte application, is whether she may serve defendant husband with the divorce summons solely by sending it through Facebook by private message to his account.

The standard method—or perhaps better stated, the method of first resort—for serving the summons in a divorce action is personal delivery to a defendant (Domestic Relations Law § 232 [a]). This reflects the great emphasis that this state places on insuring that a person who is being sued for divorce—a proceeding that can have immeasurable financial and familial consequences—be made aware of and afforded the opportunity to appear in the action. The problem with personal service, of course, is that in order for it to be accomplished, a plaintiff must be able to locate the defendant. Even where a defendant's whereabouts are known, there are times when it is logistically difficult, if not impossible, for a process server to gain the close proximity necessary for personal delivery.

Fortunately, the Domestic Relations Law provides a remedy for a person who is seeking a divorce but faces the prospect of being unable to effect personal service. Domestic Relations Law § 232 permits plaintiffs to request permission to utilize one of the alternative methods allowed under the Civil Practice Law and Rules that does not require "in-hand" delivery to the defendant. One such method, often referred to as "substitute service," involves delivering the summons to a person of "suitable age and discretion" at the defendant's "actual place of business, dwelling place or usual place of abode" (CPLR 308 [2]). Another method, known as "nail and mail" service, requires affixing the summons to the door of a defendant's "actual place of business, dwelling place or usual place of abode" (CPLR 308 [4]), and then, as with "substitute service," mailing a copy to the defendant's "last known residence" or "actual place of business." A third method is "publication service," where the summons is printed in a newspaper designated by the court and which can be granted upon a showing that "service cannot be made by another prescribed method with due diligence" (CPLR 315).

Additionally, pursuant to CPLR 308 (5), a court, upon a plaintiff's ex parte application, may direct the manner by which service is to be made. This allows a court to go beyond any of the specifically prescribed methods of service and devise a method that fits the particular circumstances of the case. An application for alternative service under CPLR 308 (5) can be granted only upon a sufficient showing that personal service, "substitute service," or "nail and mail" service would prove "impracticable." Case law, in accordance with well-established constitutional principles, further imposes the requirement that the method devised by the court be one that is "reasonably calculated, under all the circumstances, to apprise [the defendant] of the pendency of the action" (*Hollow v Hollow*, 193 Misc 2d 691, 696 [Sup Ct, Oswego County 2002], quoting *Mullane v Central Hanover Bank & Trust Co.*, 339 U.S. 306, 314 [1950]).

In the instant application, plaintiff asks the court to find that service of the divorce summons via a social media site, in this case Facebook, constitutes an appropriate form of alternative service under CPLR 308 (5). Moreover, contending that she has no other way to reach defendant, she requests that this judicially-crafted method of service be designated the only means by which notice of the divorce action is given. In order for her application to be granted, plaintiff must first demonstrate that she is unable to have the summons personally served on defendant, the method of service initially prescribed by Domestic Relations Law § 232 (a). Next, she must show that it would be "impracticable" to serve him by "substitute service" on a person of suitable age and discretion (CPLR 308 [2]) or by using "nail and mail" (CPLR 308 [4]). Finally, she must show that sending the summons through Facebook can reasonably be expected to give him actual notice that he is being sued for divorce.

Plaintiff has easily met the requirement of demonstrating that she will be unable to effect personal service on defendant. Although the parties married in 2009, they never resided together, and the last address plaintiff has for defendant is an apartment that he vacated in 2011. Plaintiff has spoken with defendant by telephone on occasion and he has told her that he has no fixed address and no place of employment. He has also refused to make himself available to be served with divorce papers. As detailed in her attorney's affirmation, the investigative firms that plaintiff hired to assist in locating defendant have all been unsuccessful in their efforts, the post office has no forwarding address for him, there is no billing address linked to his prepaid cell phone, and the Department of Motor Vehicles has no record of him. Inasmuch as plaintiff is unable to find defendant, personal delivery of the summons to him is an impossibility.

Similarly, plaintiff has shown that it would be an exercise in futility to attempt the two alternative service methods provided for by CPLR 308. Both "substitute service" and "nail and mail" service require knowledge of the defendant's "actual place of business, dwelling place or usual place of abode" (CPLR 308 [2], [4]). The record establishes that plaintiff has been unsuccessful in obtaining either a business or home address for defendant, even though she has diligently sought that information. As a result, she has met her burden of demonstrating that it would be impracticable to attempt to serve defendant by either of these methods ....

Having demonstrated a sound basis for seeking alternative service pursuant to CPLR 308 (5), plaintiff must now show that the method she proposes is one that the court can endorse as being reasonably calculated to apprise defendant that he is being sued for divorce. This hurdle poses a number of challenges. First, there are only a handful of reported decisions, mostly from federal district courts, that have addressed the issue of service of process being accomplished through social media, with there being an almost even split between those decisions approving it and those rejecting it. Second, as will be further discussed, the cases permitting such service have done so only on condition that the papers commencing the lawsuit be served on the defendant by another method as well. Thus, in seeking permission to effectuate service of the divorce summons by simply sending it to defendant through a private Facebook message, plaintiff is asking the court, already beyond the safe harbor of statutory prescription, to venture into uncharted waters without the guiding light of clear judicial precedent.

Consideration must also be given to the fact that the way plaintiff proposes to provide defendant with notice of the divorce represents a radical departure from the traditional notion of what constitutes service of process. Even decisions from as recently as 2012 and 2013 have referred to the use of Facebook messaging for the purpose of commencing a lawsuit as being a "novel concept" (*PCCare247 Inc.*, [No. 12. 7189(PAE)] 2013 WL 841037 *5 [S.D.N.Y. Mar. 7, 2013] [permitting it as a supplemental method of service]) and "unorthodox to say the least" (*Fortunato*, 2012 WL 2086950, *2 [S.D.N.Y. June 7, 2012] [rejecting it as a means of service]).

That a concept is new to the law is something that may very well require a court to exercise a high degree of scrutiny and independent legal analysis when judicial approval is sought. But a concept should not be rejected simply because it is novel or nontraditional. This is especially so where technology and the law intersect. In this age of technological enlightenment, what is for the moment unorthodox and unusual stands a good chance of sooner or later being accepted and standard, or even outdated and passé. And because legislatures have often been slow to react to these changes, it has fallen on courts to insure that our legal procedures keep pace with current technology .... As noted by the United States Court of Appeals for the Ninth Circuit in *Rio Props., Inc. v Rio Intl. Interlink* (284 F.3d 1007, 1017 [9th Cir. 2002]), one of the earliest cases authorizing service of process by email, the "broad constitutional principle" upon which judicially-devised alternative service is based "unshackles ... courts from anachronistic methods of service and permits them entry into the technological renaissance."

In the final analysis, constitutional principles, not the lack of judicial precedent or the novelty of Facebook service, will be ultimately determinative here. The central question is whether the method by which plaintiff seeks to serve defendant comports with the fundamentals of due process by being reasonably calculated to provide defendant with notice of the divorce. Or more simply posed: If the summons for divorce is sent to what plaintiff represents to be defendant's Facebook account, is there a good chance he will receive it?

In order for the question to be answered in the affirmative, plaintiff must address a number of this court's concerns. The first is that the Facebook account that plaintiff believes is defendant's might not actually belong to him. As is well known, the Facebook profile somebody views online may very well belong to someone other than whom the profile purports it to be. This has led courts to observe that "anyone can make a Facebook profile using real, fake, or incomplete information, and thus, there is no way for the Court to confirm whether the Facebook page belongs to the defendant to be served." ... As a result, this court required plaintiff to submit a supplemental affidavit to verify that the Facebook account she references is indeed that of the defendant. Plaintiff submitted such an affidavit, to which she annexed copies of the exchanges that took place between her and defendant when she contacted him through his Facebook page, and in which she identified defendant as the subject of the photographs that appear on that page. While it is true that plaintiff's statements are not absolute proof that the account belongs to defendant—it being conceivable that if plaintiff herself or someone at her behest created defendant's page, she could fabricate exchanges and post photographs—plaintiff has nevertheless persuaded the court that the account in question does indeed belong to defendant.

The second concern is that if defendant is not diligent in logging on to his Facebook account, he runs the risk of not seeing the summons until the time to respond has passed. Here too, plaintiff's affidavit has successfully addressed the issue. Her exchanges with defendant via Facebook show that he regularly logs on to his account. In addition, because plaintiff has a mobile phone number for defendant, both she and her attorney can speak to him or leave a voicemail message, or else send him a text message alerting him that a divorce action has been commenced and that he should check his account (*WhosHere, Inc.*, [No. 1:13-cv-00526-AJT-TRJ] 2014 WL 670817, *4 [E.D. Va. Feb. 20 2014] ["[C]ourts have taken into consideration whether defendant already possessed either knowledge of suit or that he may be the subject to a suit"]).

The third concern is whether a backup means of service is required under the circumstances. Although, as was discussed, other court decisions have endorsed using Facebook as a means of service, they have done so only where Facebook was but one of the methods employed, not the only method. As the court stated in *PCCare247 Inc.* (2013 WL 841037, *5), "[t]o be sure, if the [plaintiff] were proposing to serve defendants only by means of Facebook, as opposed to using Facebook as a supplemental means of service, a substantial question would arise whether that service comports with due process." In that case, and as well as in *WhosHere, Inc.*, the other federal court decision authorizing Facebook service, the court stressed that it was allowing the use of a social media site only in conjunction with notice being sent to the defendants by email. In *Noel B.* (2014 N.Y. Misc. LEXIS 4708 at 4) [No. F00787-13/14B, Fam. Ct. Sept. 12], the only decision from a state court permitting service via Facebook, the petitioner was required to mail a copy of the child support summons and petition to the respondent's "previously used last known address."

Here, plaintiff does not have an email address for defendant and has no way of finding one. Nor does she have a street address for defendant that could constitute a viable "last known address"; defendant's last known address dates back at least four years and the post office confirmed that defendant no longer resides there and he has left no forwarding address. Thus, plaintiff has a compelling reason to make Facebook the sole, rather than the supplemental, means of service, with the court satisfied that it is a method reasonably calculated to give defendant notice that he is being sued for divorce.

Before granting plaintiff leave to serve defendant via Facebook, a method of alternative service judicially-devised pursuant to CPLR 308 (5), there is one remaining question that should be addressed: Why use Facebook as either the sole or the supplemental means of service in the first place when there is a statutorily prescribed method of service readily available? That method is service by publication, something that is specifically authorized under CPLR 315. After all, publication is not only expressly sanctioned by the CPLR, but it is a means of service of process that has been used in New York in one form or another since colonial times. Even today, it is probably the method of service most often permitted in divorce actions when the defendant cannot be served by other means.

The problem, however, with publication service is that it is almost guaranteed not to provide a defendant with notice of the action for divorce, or any other lawsuit for that matter .... In divorce cases brought in New York County, plaintiffs are often granted permission to publish the summons in such newspapers as the *New York Law Journal* or the *Irish Echo*. If that were to be done here, the chances of defendant, who is neither a lawyer nor Irish, ever seeing the summons in print, either in those particular newspapers or in any other, are slim to none. The dangers of allowing somebody to be divorced and not know it are simply too great to allow notice to be given by publication, a form of service that, while neither novel nor unorthodox, is essentially statutorily authorized non-service. This is especially so when, as here, there is a readily available means of service that stands a very good chance of letting defendant know that he is being sued.

Moreover, the court will not require publication in any newspaper even as a backup method to Facebook. Although a more widely circulated newspaper, like the New York Post or the Daily News, might reach more readers, the cost, which approaches $1,000 for running the notice for a week, is substantial, and the chances of it being seen by defendant, buried in an obscure section of the paper and printed in small type, are still infinitesimal.

Under the circumstance presented here, service by Facebook, albeit novel and nontraditional, is the form of service that most comports with the constitutional standards of due process. Not only is it reasonably calculated to provide defendant with notice that he is being sued for divorce, but every indication is that it will achieve what should be the goal of every method of service: actually delivering the summons to him.

In light of the foregoing, plaintiff is granted permission to serve defendant with the divorce summons using a private message through Facebook. Specifically, because litigants are prohibited from serving other litigants, plaintiff's attorney shall log into plaintiff's Facebook account and message the defendant by first identifying himself, and then either including a web address of the summons or attaching an image of the summons. This transmittal shall be repeated by plaintiff's attorney to defendant once a week for three consecutive weeks or until acknowledged by the defendant. Additionally, after the initial transmittal, plaintiff and her attorney are to call and text message defendant to inform him that the summons for divorce has been sent to him via Facebook.

Notes and Questions: State Service

1. An eye on the *Mullane* basics. In *Baidoo*, the court of course analyzes the methods for service authorized under § 308 of the Civil Practice Law and Rules, the New York service of process statute. But the court also considers whether the alternative form of service it orders satisfies the core constitutional standard in *Mullane*:

> The central question is whether the method by which plaintiff seeks to serve defendant comports with the fundamentals of due process by being reasonably calculated to provide defendant with notice of the divorce. Or more simply posed: If the summons for divorce is sent to what plaintiff represents to be defendant's Facebook account, is there a good chance he will receive it?

5 N.Y.S.3d at 714. Technology may change, but the court rightly keeps the focus on the underlying value emphasized in *Mullane*, the likelihood of providing actual notice of the action to the defendant.

2. Considering the alternatives. N.Y. C.P.L.R. § 308 authorizes various alternatives to the preferred method of personal delivery. The *Baidoo* court reviews each option and concludes that none of them are reasonably likely to provide actual notice, while notification on Facebook probably will reach the defendant. Judges crafting such orders for service under § 308(5) will likely order service in several ways—perhaps mail, service at a place of business, and publication as well. In *Baidoo*, Judge Cooper also orders service through multiple methods—Facebook posting, messages to Facebook, and calls and texts to the defendant's cell phone.

As *Baidoo* notes, some cases have refused to allow service through Facebook. The court in *Joe Hand Promotion, Inc. v. Shepard*, No. 4:12cv1728 SNLJ, 2013 WL 4058745 (E.D. Mo. Aug. 12, 2013), rejected Facebook service on the ground that relevant state law mandated publication notice where the defendant could not be found. *Fortunato v. Chase Bank USA, N.A.*, No. 11 Civ. 6608 (JFK), 2012 WL 2086950 (S.D.N.Y. June 7, 2012), rejected it on the ground that the account may have been posted by someone other than the defendant. *But see WhosHere, Inc. v. Orun*, No. 1:13-cv-00526-AJT-TRJ, 2014 WL 670817 (E.D. Va. Feb. 20, 2014) (Facebook service approved along with e-mail service). Generally, the cases turn on whether the facts adduced by the plaintiff convince the court that the suggested service methods are likely to actually reach the defendant.

3. Alternatives to alternative service? In light of the *Baidoo* case, consider whether the motion should be granted in the following case.

Harris sues Budovsky for breach of contract in a New York court. The provisions of N.Y. C.P.L.R. § 308 apply to service of process in the action. Harris does not have a current home address for Budovsky; she knows he has moved but not where he now resides. She has been told that Budovsky travels a lot for his work, but has an office at a store near the corner of Fifth Avenue and 34th Street in New York City. She isn't sure that this is true or which store it is. During negotiations for the contract Harris had communicated regularly with Budovsky through Facebook. She moves for an order from the court allowing her to serve Budovsky via Facebook, citing *Baidoo* as authority for using this procedure for service. The court will likely

A. grant the motion, if Harris submits an affidavit attesting to the facts given above.
B. grant the motion, but only if Harris has made reasonable efforts to locate the store where Budovsky works and failed to do so.
C grant the motion if Harris can convince the court that Budovsky regularly uses his Facebook account.
D. deny the motion because Harris has not sufficiently explored other methods of serving Budovsky.

For sure, choose **D**. Section 308 authorizes service "as the court . . . directs" if service is "impracticable" under the methods in § 308(1), (2), or (4). It does not allow the court to go straight to an alternative method of service whenever the plaintiff argues that it is likely to provide actual notice to the defendant. On these facts, the court would surely require Harris to make further inquiries to find a home address or a business address—or both—for Budovsky. If post office regulations require forwarding of mail after a patron moves, Harris may be able to serve the papers on Budovsky by mail. She may be able to find a current address for him with a bit of research or by hiring an investigator. An investigator might well locate Budovsky's place of work with the information Harris has. And there's always the manifold resources of the Internet. The court will almost certainly require greater efforts by Harris to comply with the methods specified in §§ 308(1), (2), or (4) to serve Budovsky before authorizing Facebook service. Harris's motion to serve via Facebook looks like an effort to avoid more extensive efforts to locate Budovsky, rather than the only viable option for serving an elusive defendant. Motion denied.

Q **4. But do the New York service provisions authorize service of process through social media?** Generally, service of process must both comport with the constitutional standard of *Mullane* and be authorized by the statutes or rules applicable in the relevant court. The New York service statutes do not expressly authorize service through social media; in ordering service through Facebook, isn't the judge ignoring the limits on service methods under New York law?

A Although service through social media is not a specified method for service under § 308 of the New York Civil Practice Law and Rules, § 308(5) authorizes the court to order an alternative method of service where the specifically authorized methods are not reasonably calculated to provide actual notice, or have failed to reach the defendant. This fallback provision allows the court to craft a different method of service—or multiple methods—in an effort to provide actual notice to the defendant.

5. Service by publication as a last resort. If the defendant cannot be located, so that none of the methods of service specified in the relevant court's service-of-process rules is likely to provide actual notice, the plaintiff will typically apply to the court for an order authorizing service through alternative means. In New York, such a frustrated plaintiff would (as the *Baidoo* plaintiff did) seek an order under § 308(5) of the Civil Practice Law and Rules. *See also* N.Y. C.P.L.R. § 315, which authorizes service by publication "if service cannot be made by another prescribed method with due diligence." In many cases, courts will order service of process by publication in a newspaper if no alternative exists, or all have been tried without success. Publication would seldom suffice under *Mullane* as the first and only means of service, but where nothing else has worked, such "substituted service" is probably constitutionally sufficient.

However, counsel will be well advised to exhaust all other practical means of notice before seeking notice by publication. In *Gaeth v. Deacon*, 964 A.2d 621 (Me. 2009), plaintiff's counsel made herculean efforts to find the defendant. He conducted computer searches, mailed the papers to an address for the defendant, and attempted service by the sheriff. Finally, he obtained an order from the court for service by publication. The Maine Supreme Court still granted relief from judgment, on the ground that publication was not sufficient in light of other options plaintiff's counsel might have explored to give actual notice to the defendant. The court suggested, for example, that counsel might have hired an Internet web searching service, published notice in the area where the defendant had last resided, or used college records to try to locate members of the defendant's family.

The *Baidoo* court rejected service by publication on practical grounds. Judge Cooper somewhat iconoclastically characterizes this centuries-old practice as "essentially statutorily authorized non-service" (5 N.Y.S.3d at 715) because publication in local or specialized papers would be unlikely to provide actual notice, and publication in more widely circulated papers would be too expensive given the small likelihood that it would actually reach the defendant.

Reasonable Notice?

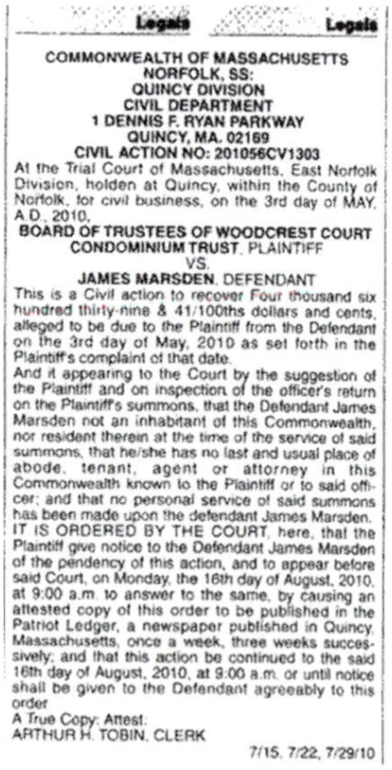

Legals Legals

COMMONWEALTH OF MASSACHUSETTS
NORFOLK, SS:
QUINCY DIVISION
CIVIL DEPARTMENT
1 DENNIS F. RYAN PARKWAY
QUINCY, MA. 02169
CIVIL ACTION NO: 201056CV1303

At the Trial Court of Massachusetts, East Norfolk Division, holden at Quincy, within the County of Norfolk, for civil business, on the 3rd day of MAY, A.D., 2010,

BOARD OF TRUSTEES OF WOODCREST COURT CONDOMINIUM TRUST, PLAINTIFF
VS.
JAMES MARSDEN, DEFENDANT

This is a Civil action to recover Four thousand six hundred thirty-nine & 41/100ths dollars and cents, alleged to be due to the Plaintiff from the Defendant on the 3rd day of May, 2010 as set forth in the Plaintiff's complaint of that date.

And it appearing to the Court by the suggestion of the Plaintiff and on inspection of the officer's return on the Plaintiff's summons, that the Defendant James Marsden not an inhabitant of this Commonwealth, nor resident therein at the time of the service of said summons, that he/she has no last and usual place of abode, tenant, agent or attorney in this Commonwealth known to the Plaintiff or to said officer; and that no personal service of said summons has been made upon the defendant James Marsden.

IT IS ORDERED BY THE COURT, here, that the Plaintiff give notice to the Defendant James Marsden of the pendency of this action, and to appear before said Court, on Monday, the 16th day of August, 2010, at 9:00 a.m. to answer to the same, by causing an attested copy of this order to be published in the Patriot Ledger, a newspaper published in Quincy, Massachusetts, once a week, three weeks successively; and that this action be continued to the said 16th day of August, 2010, at 9:00 a.m. or until notice shall be given to the Defendant agreeably to this order

A True Copy: Attest:
ARTHUR H. TOBIN, CLERK

7/15, 7/22, 7/29/10

Reprint with permission of The Patriot Ledger

The snippet here from a local newspaper includes publication notice of a lawsuit. In *Mullane*, Justice Jackson suggests that notice of this sort, tucked in the back pages of a local newspaper, will seldom satisfy constitutional standards for adequate notice. "Chance alone brings to the attention of even a local resident an advertisement in small type inserted in the back pages of a newspaper, and if he makes his home outside the area of the newspaper's normal circulation the odds that the information will never reach him are large indeed." 339 U.S. at 315.

6. Alternative means of service in federal court. Federal Rule 4 does not contain a provision like § 308, authorizing the federal district judge to order service by publication or other alternative methods. However, Rule 4 also authorizes service through the methods available in the state where the court sits or where service is made. *See, e.g.*, Fed. R. Civ. P. 4(e)(1). Thus, if the *Baidoo* case had been in federal court, the federal judge could similarly have crafted an order for alternative means of service under N.Y. C.P.L.R. § 308(5). *See Webster Industries, Inc. v. Northwood Doors, Inc.*, 244 F. Supp. 2d 998, 1005–10 (N.D. Iowa 2003) (describing state methods for service available in federal action under both Minnesota and Iowa rules of civil procedure).

7. The effect of actual notice to the defendants. Suppose that service of process does not actually reach the defendant, but she learns in some other manner that the action has been filed. This might happen, for example, if the plaintiff's lawyer sent a courtesy copy of the complaint to defendant's counsel, or if a third party learns of the suit and tells the defendant or her lawyer. May the defendant object based on lack of service "by the book"?

Most courts do not view a judgment as valid, even if the defendant actually receives notice of the action, unless service is made in compliance with the applicable service rules or statutes. Courts view proper service of process—delivery of the papers by a method authorized by statute or rule and that is constitutionally proper—as necessary to acquire personal jurisdiction over a defendant. *Moore's Federal Practice* § 4.03[3][a].

The Federal Rules clearly contemplate that a defendant may object to service even though she actually learns that she has been sued: Rule 12(b)(4) and (5) authorize defendants to move to dismiss an action based on improper service of process or insufficiency of the process (the summons). To make the motion, the defendant would of course have to know that the case had been filed.

This principle seems unduly fastidious: The purpose of proper service, after all, is to inform the defendant he has been sued; if it is clear that the defendant has received service, shouldn't that suffice? Virginia has an interesting statute, Va. Code Ann. § 8.01-288 (2010), which provides as follows:

> Except for process commencing actions for divorce or annulment of marriage or other actions wherein service of process is specifically prescribed by statute, process which has reached the person to whom it is directed within the time prescribed by law, if any, shall be sufficient although not served or accepted as provided in this chapter.

Shouldn't every state (and the Federal Rules) have a statute like this, validating service as long as the defendant receives actual notice? (Note that it does not relax standards for service in divorce cases.) Perhaps not; the statute might create more problems than it solves. If there are not clear rules about how service is properly made and when it has been completed, there are likely to be difficult disputes about what the defendant knew and when. Particularly if the date of service is crucial to meet the applicable statute of limitations, these requirements should be clearly spelled out and consistently applied. And if ignoring the rules carries no penalties as long as actual notice is received, there is much less incentive to follow them in the future, even though they often reflect the legislature's judgments about what service is best.

8. Proper service, but no notice. Suppose that Jarboe serves process on Fuentes by a means that is authorized by statute and constitutionally sufficient, but Fuentes still does not find out about the suit. Perhaps Jarboe mails the summons and complaint to Fuentes at Fuentes' home address, a method authorized by the local statutes and usually constitutionally sufficient under *Mullane*. But, for one reason or another, the defendant does not get the papers. Perhaps one of Fuentes' kids brings in the mail, but throws out the court papers with the recycling. Or the kid puts the envelope on a cabinet and the envelope falls behind it.

Service was properly made here, but Fuentes still does not know that he has been sued. When Fuentes finds out about the default judgment, he will doubtless move for relief from judgment under Fed. R. Civ. P. 60(b). Jarboe has a credible argument that the judgment should stand because he complied with the rules of service and the method was acceptable under due process standards. But the defendant still did not learn about the case and did not have a chance to defend it. A practical judge is almost always going to grant relief from the judgment in this situation, even though service was done by the book. Few judges are willing to see the defendant lose the chance to defend a suit when she never knew it had been filed. *See Restatement (Second) of Judgments* § 65 (judgment rendered without adequate notice may be avoided).

Consequently, the plaintiff has as much interest as the defendant in assuring that service both complies with the service statute or rule and actually informs the defendant of the action. The plaintiff will rarely win a case because the defendant defaults for lack of notice. More likely, the defendant will later learn of the action and move to set aside the entry of default or default judgment, and the motion will be granted. Consequently, the failure to achieve actual notice will more likely lead to delay than to an enforceable judgment for the plaintiff.

9. Service of later filings in civil actions. This chapter has focused on service of the original complaint and summons, because initial service of process serves the crucial function of giving notice that an action has been filed. All subsequent papers filed in the action must also be served on all parties in the action, including later pleadings, motions, trial memoranda, and many other documents. Later documents may be served on the other lawyers rather than the parties, and under Rule 5 may be served by first class mail. Fed. R. Civ. P. 5(b)(1), (b)(2).

All federal courts now accept electronic service and filing of court papers after the initial complaint. *See* http://www.uscourts.gov/news/2012/05/17/all-federal-courts-now-accepting-electronic-filing. For an example of local rules implementing electronic filing, see United States District Court for the Eastern District of Texas, Local Rule CV-5, which mandates electronic filing of court documents in most cases. In the Eastern District of Texas, as in other jurisdictions with rules of this type, all attorneys admitted to practice before the court must register with the clerk as users of the court's electronic filing system and receive a user log-in and password that allows them access to the court's Case Management/Electronic Case Files (CM/ECF) System. Under CV-7, all motions, responses, replies, and proposed orders, if filed electronically, must be submitted in searchable and editable Portable Document Format (PDF). All other documents should be submitted as a searchable PDF whenever possible. Local Rule CV-5 provides that receipt by the filing party of a Notice of Electronic Filing, sent automatically by e-mail from the court, is proof of service of the document on all counsel who have consented to electronic service by registering for the CM/ECF System with the clerk.

In 2016, the Committee on Rules of Practice and Procedure of the Judicial Conference of the United States proposed amendments to Fed. R. Civ. P. 5 that would have made electronic filing of papers after the complaint mandatory in most cases in the federal courts.

> Electronic filing has matured. Most districts have adopted local rules that require electronic filing, and allow reasonable exceptions as required by the former rule. The time has come to seize the advantages of electronic filing

> by making it generally mandatory in all districts for a person represented by an attorney.

Preliminary Draft of Proposed Amendments to the Federal Rules of Appellate Procedure, Bankruptcy, Civil and Criminal Rules, http://www.uscourts.gov/rules-policies/proposed-amendments-published-public-comment, p. 209.

Despite this prediction, a 2018 amendment to Rule 5 did not mandate electronic service in the federal district courts. Instead amended Rule 5 continues to authorize electronic service upon parties who have consented to it. Fed. R. Civ. P. 5(b)(2)(E). If the parties have agreed to electronic service, the PACER system automatically serves documents filed electronically on all parties to the action:

> Service is made by the system in the form of an automatically generated notice of electronic filing, which includes a hyperlink to where the filed document may be viewed and downloaded, that is sent to the attorneys representing other parties involved in the case if the attorneys are registered with the system. Local rules vary regarding whether pro se litigants may register to use the CM/ECF system to make and receive service.

Wright & Miller § 1147.

Federal Rule 45 (and similar state rules) include separate provisions for service of subpoenas. A subpoena is a court order to a person who is not a party to the litigation to appear to give testimony or produce documents. Subpoenas must be served by "delivering a copy to the named person," Fed. R. Civ. P. 45(b)(1), which suggests personal in-hand service. However, not all courts read this phrase to require in-hand service. *See, e.g., Hall v. Sullivan*, 229 F.R.D. 501, 503–06 (D. Md. 2005) (approving service by Federal Express).

V. The Relation of Service of Process to Personal Jurisdiction

As noted above, a court cannot acquire personal jurisdiction over the defendants without proper service of process. However, it does not follow that, if the defendant is properly served, the court will have personal jurisdiction over her. Service and personal jurisdiction are separate though related principles. Personal jurisdiction requires that the defendant have an appropriate relationship to the state that makes it fair to require her to defend there. Service of process fulfills a separate due process requirement, providing notice of the suit to the defendant so she can appear and defend.

Consider the following questions to help clarify this distinction:

A. Danziger, who lives in Georgia, sues Alioto, from Florida, for injuries in an auto accident they had in Florida. Danziger files the suit in a Georgia federal court. Alioto has no contacts with Georgia. Danziger's counsel arranges for service of process on Alioto in Florida. A Florida process server goes to Alioto's machine shop in Florida and hands her the summons and complaint in the action. Is service of process on Alioto proper? Does the court have personal jurisdiction over Alioto?

A Service is proper under Fed. R. Civ. P. 4(e)(2)(A), which allows service on a defendant by personal delivery. It does not specify that personal delivery must be at any particular place, so handing the papers to Alioto at the shop is proper service. However, the Georgia court lacks any basis to exercise personal jurisdiction over Alioto. The accident took place in Florida, and the example indicates that Alioto has no other contacts that might support personal jurisdiction over her in Georgia.

B. Danziger files suit for his injuries in the accident in a Florida federal court. He serves process by publishing notice of the action in a newspaper in the county where the action is pending for three weeks in a row. Is service of process on Alioto proper? Does the court have personal jurisdiction over Alioto?

A Here, the Florida court could exercise personal jurisdiction over Alioto because the suit arises out of her contact with Florida—driving in the state. However, publication was almost certainly insufficient as a means of notifying Alioto of the suit. Even if a Florida statute authorizes service by publication, *Mullane* suggests that publication notice is only proper if nothing better can be done to provide actual notice to the defendant. Presumably, Danziger and Alioto exchanged papers after the accident, so Danziger's attorney has an address for Alioto. He could attempt service by mail, if authorized by Florida service statutes, or he could serve under Fed. R. Civ. P. 4(e)(2)(A) or (B) at Alioto's home.

C. Danziger files suit for his injuries in the accident in a Georgia federal court. He serves process on Alioto by having the process server deliver the summons and complaint to Alioto at her hotel while Alioto is visiting Atlanta. Is service of process on Alioto proper? Does the court have personal jurisdiction over Alioto?

A Service is proper under Rule 4(e)(2)(A). In-hand service is as good as it gets as a means of providing actual notice of the action. And there probably is personal jurisdiction over Alioto based on in-hand service within the state. In *Burnham v. Superior Court*, 495 U.S. 604 (1990), the Supreme Court upheld jurisdiction based on in-hand service within the forum state. The Court did not hold that this would always suffice to support jurisdiction, but it frequently will.

The point is that you must always analyze these two due process requirements separately. Both must be satisfied, and satisfying one does not satisfy the other.

Q **But didn't *Pennoyer* say courts couldn't do this?** Didn't the Supreme Court say in *Pennoyer v. Neff* that "[p]rocess from the tribunals of one State cannot run into another State, and summon parties there domiciled to leave its territory and respond to proceedings against them"? 95 U.S. at 727. How can a court in one state serve process on a defendant in another state and require that defendant to come into the forum state and defend a lawsuit, without contradicting this statement?

A Yes, *Pennoyer* did say that. But that statement in *Pennoyer* is no longer true. After *International Shoe*, an Oregon court can require a defendant from California to come into Oregon and defend a claim that arises out of the defendant's minimum contacts with Oregon. And, adequate notice can be given even if it is delivered to the defendant in another state. Handing the summons and complaint to the defendant is an excellent way of telling her she has been sued, whether you do it in Oregon or California.

If Pennoyer sued Neff today in an Oregon court for breach of a contract Neff made with him in Oregon, the court would have personal jurisdiction over Neff because hiring Mitchell in Oregon is a minimum contact that gave rise to the claim. And, under *Mullane*, mailing the summons and complaint to Neff in California (if authorized by Oregon service of process rules) would be a constitutionally proper means of letting Neff know about the case.

VI. Notice and Service: Summary of Basic Principles

- Due process of law requires (among other things) that a defendant be properly notified that an action has been commenced against her, so that she can appear and defend the action. The methods of providing such notice are referred to as "service of process."
- In *Mullane v. Central Hanover Bank & Trust Co.*, the Supreme Court held that notice must be given by a means "reasonably calculated, under all the circumstances, to apprise interested parties of the pendency of the action and afford them an opportunity to present their objections."
- Generally, publication alone is not sufficient under *Mullane* unless nothing better can be done. Usually something more than publication can be done. Personal delivery and mail service are generally upheld, though mail might be insufficient in some circumstances.
- Every court system has a detailed set of procedures, set forth in court rules or state statutes, governing service of process. In addition to being constitutionally sufficient, service must comply with the statutes or rules applicable in the court in which the case is filed.
- A court does not have personal jurisdiction over the defendant just because process has been properly served. And service may be improper even if there is a valid basis for exercising personal jurisdiction over the defendant. Each requires a separate analysis.
- The term "service of process" is often used to refer to the delivery of litigation papers or orders other than the summons and complaint to the defendant. Often, court rules or statutes specify other, less elaborate, means of serving these later papers in the action.

PART IV

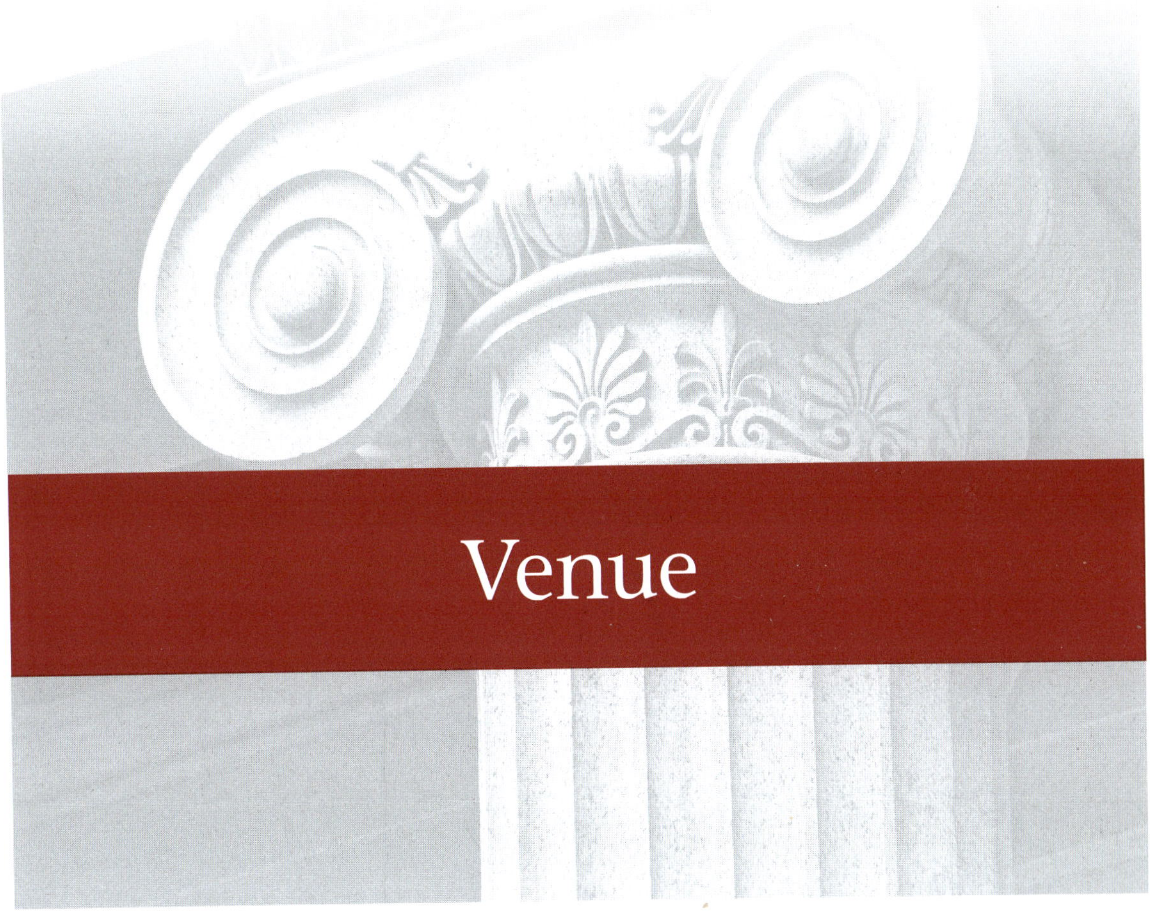

Venue

11

Basic Venue: Statutory Allocation of Cases Within a Court System

I. An Introduction to Venue

Previous chapters explained that a trial court must have subject matter jurisdiction over the type of case that the plaintiff has filed as well as personal jurisdiction over the defendant. This chapter describes another requirement: A court must also be a proper *venue*.

A. Venue Basics

Venue refers to the particular court within a court system where a plaintiff can file a lawsuit. For example, in the federal court system, each federal district is a distinct venue that covers a specific geographic area, such as the Western District of Missouri, the Northern District of Iowa, or the District of Utah. Figure 11–1 shows each of the ninety-four districts (venues) in the federal court system as well as the territory covered by each United States Court of Appeals. For example, the United States Court of Appeals for the Ninth Circuit covers a number of western states, and each of those states has at least one federal district court. The more populous states (such as California) have more than one federal district (i.e., more than one possible venue).

State court systems are also divided by territory, often by counties or municipalities. For example, in Ohio, the general trial court is called the court of common pleas, and each county has its own court. Overall, there are eighty-eight common pleas courts in Ohio, giving plaintiffs eighty-eight possible venues for filing most types of cases.

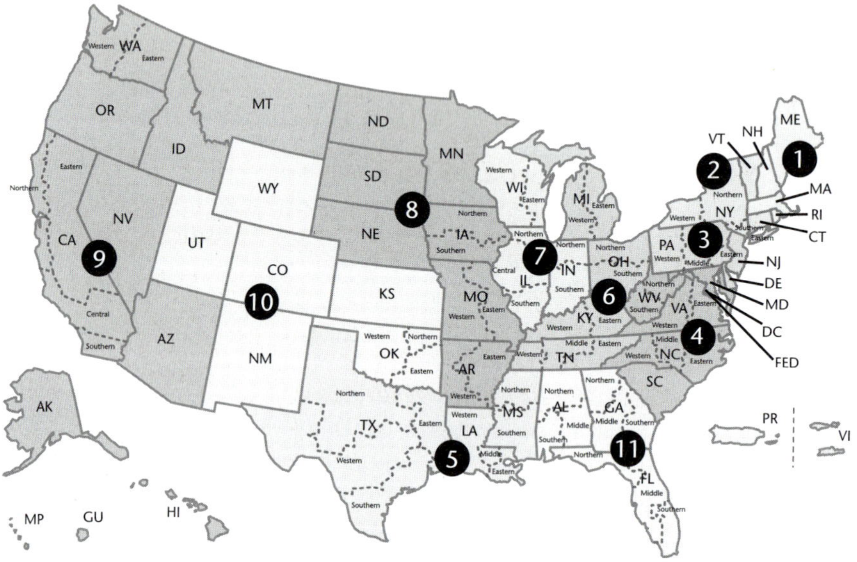

Figure 11–1: **FEDERAL VENUES**

B. The Purpose of Venue

Venue requirements exist to ensure that a case is litigated in a court that is conveniently located and has some connection to the lawsuit or to one or both of the parties. Venue overlaps with personal jurisdiction in that both concepts often consider the defendant's relationship to the forum, but venue is neither constitutionally compelled nor focused exclusively on the defendant's interests.

For example, consider a car accident that occurred in Manhattan, New York (which is located within the Southern District of New York), between Powers, a citizen of Connecticut, and Doris, a New Jersey citizen. Assume that Powers has suffered serious injuries and sues Doris in federal court in Buffalo (which is in the Western District of New York) for damages in excess of $75,000. The federal court would have subject matter jurisdiction over this case because it is between citizens of different states and the amount in controversy exceeds $75,000. Moreover, there would be personal jurisdiction over Doris in New York (and thus in any federal or state court located in New York), because this case arose out of Doris's in-state contacts. Thus, the federal court for the Western District of New York would have subject matter jurisdiction over the dispute (diversity jurisdiction) and personal jurisdiction over the defendant (specific in personam).

The problem is that Buffalo is four hundred miles away from the place of the accident and from where either party lives. To prevent cases like Powers's from proceeding in a court that has nothing to do with the case (but that happens to have subject matter and personal jurisdiction), Congress has passed venue statutes. These statutes define which federal districts are proper venues and try, in a general way, to restrict litigation to courts that are convenient given the facts of the case and the location of the parties.

C. Distinguishing Venue, Subject Matter Jurisdiction, and Personal Jurisdiction

Venue differs from subject matter and personal jurisdiction in several important respects. First, unlike subject matter and personal jurisdiction, the Constitution does not restrict a plaintiff's choice of venues. The Constitution limits a federal court's subject matter jurisdiction under Article III and a court's authority to exercise personal jurisdiction under the Due Process Clause, but the Constitution has nothing to say about venue.

Second, restrictions on a plaintiff's choice of venue are designed to ensure that the location of the suit is reasonable and convenient given the location of the evidence, the witnesses, and the defendant. In contrast, subject matter jurisdiction is designed to limit a court's power to hear a particular type of dispute, and personal jurisdiction doctrine is designed to ensure that litigation in a particular state is fair to the defendant. Although fairness to the defendant is a concern for both venue and personal jurisdiction, fairness to the defendant is personal jurisdiction's primary concern. In contrast, venue statutes often require an examination of the plaintiff's, the witnesses', and the court's connections to the case.

Finally, personal jurisdiction focuses on whether a state as a whole is a fair location in which to force the defendant to litigate, whereas venue turns on whether a particular court *within* a state is a convenient location for the suit. For example, in Powers's case, the Western District of New York was a fair location as a matter of personal jurisdiction because the case arose out of Doris's contacts in the state of New York. But the Western District of New York is not a proper *venue*, because all of the events that relate to the suit occurred in the Southern District of New York.

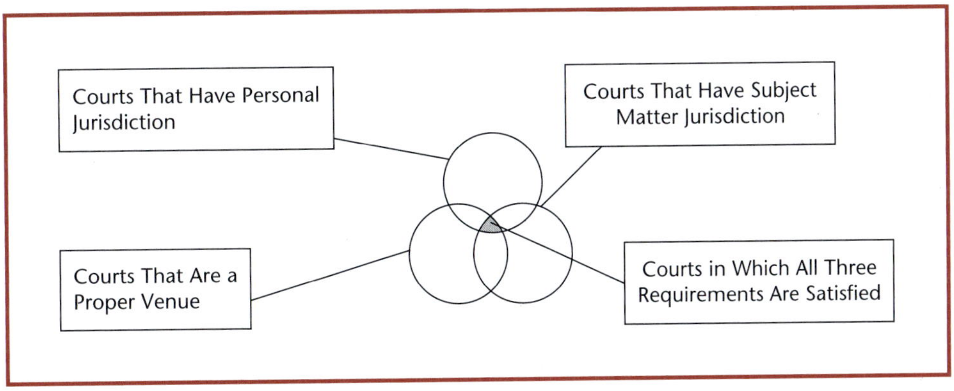

Figure 11–2: THREE REQUIREMENTS FOR FILING A LAWSUIT

In sum, a court must not only have subject matter jurisdiction and personal jurisdiction; the court must also be a proper venue. Thus, a court can only hear cases falling within the small shaded area in Figure 11–2, where all three circles overlap.

D. State Venue Statutes

This chapter focuses primarily on the statutes that govern venue in the federal courts, but states have their own venue statutes as well. These state statutes tend to recognize a larger number of proper venues than the general federal venue statute. For example, as explained below, the general federal venue statute does not authorize venue in a federal district simply because the plaintiff resides there, though many state statutes authorize venue on that basis. *See Shreve, Raven-Hansen & Geyh* § 6.01[2]. Just be aware that, in state court, you have to review the applicable state venue statutes, which are similar (but not identical) to the general federal venue statute.

II. The General Federal Venue Statute

For most federal cases, 28 U.S.C. § 1391(b) defines which federal districts are proper venues. The statute provides as follows:

> (b) Venue in general.—A civil action may be brought in—
>
> (1) a judicial district in which any defendant resides, if all defendants are residents of the State in which the district is located;
>
> (2) a judicial district in which a substantial part of the events or omissions giving rise to the claim occurred, or a substantial part of property that is the subject of the action is situated; or
>
> (3) if there is no district in which an action may otherwise be brought as provided in this section, any judicial district in which any defendant is subject to the court's personal jurisdiction with respect to such action.

These provisions have several noteworthy features. First, if there is any district where the action could be brought under *either* subsection (1) or (2), subsection (3) does not apply. Because of the breadth of subsections (1) and (2), subsection (3) applies to relatively few cases (typically only when the claims arise abroad). Accordingly, most of this chapter focuses on subsections (1) and (2).

Second, for any particular case, several venues may be proper. Just as more than one court may have subject matter or personal jurisdiction, more than one court may be a proper venue.

Finally, keep in mind how the statute furthers the interests of convenience and efficiency. Subsection (1) assumes that defendants will not be greatly inconvenienced by having to defend a case in a federal court that is located in a state where all of the defendants reside. For example, in Powers's case, Doris is from New Jersey. Under § 1391, the federal district court in New Jersey would be an appropriate venue because it would be relatively easy for Doris to defend the case there. Moreover, this court would have an interest in resolving a dispute involving a New Jersey defendant.

Subsection (2) recognizes that, if a district is located where "a substantial part of the events or omissions giving rise to the claim occurred," the district is likely to be an efficient and convenient forum for the lawsuit. For example, Powers's case arose out of an accident that occurred in Manhattan, so the Southern District of New York (which encompasses Manhattan) is a proper venue under subsection (2). This makes sense because the evidence and the witnesses are likely to be located in that district.

In sum, subsection (1) tells us that the District of New Jersey is a proper venue, and subsection (2) tells us that the Southern District of New York is a proper venue. Thus, Powers can file the lawsuit in either district, at least as a matter of venue. On the other hand, the Western District of New York is *not* a proper venue. That district does not satisfy subsection (1) or subsection (2), and because there are two proper venues, subsection (3) does not apply.

Notes and Questions: The General Federal Venue Statute

1. Focusing on districts, not states. Recall that venue, unlike personal jurisdiction, focuses on connections to specific federal districts, not to entire states. With that reminder, try the following question.

Reconsider Powers's Manhattan car accident, which involved Powers, a citizen of Connecticut, and Doris, a New Jersey citizen. Recall that Powers had suffered serious injuries and sued Doris in federal court in Buffalo (which is in the Western District of New York) for damages in excess of $75,000. But now change one fact. Assume that Doris, the only defendant, is not a resident of New Jersey, but rather a resident of Albany, New York, which is located in the Northern District of New York. Powers, the Connecticut plaintiff, wants to file her claim in federal court. In which districts would venue be proper?

A. Any federal district court in New York.
B. The Northern District of New York only.
C. The Southern District of New York only.
D. The Northern District and Southern District of New York only.
E. The Northern District of New York and the District of Connecticut only.
F. The Northern District of New York, the Southern District of New York, and the District of Connecticut only.

According to subsection (1), venue is proper in "a judicial district in which any defendant resides, if all defendants are residents of the State in which the district is located." Here, there is only one defendant, so "all defendants are residents of the State in which the district is located." Critically, the focus here is on the "judicial district" where Doris resides and not on the *state* where she resides. In this case, Doris resides in Albany, which is in the Northern District of New York. So although Doris is subject to personal jurisdiction anywhere in New York, venue is proper under subsection (1) only in the Northern District of New York.

The plaintiff's Connecticut home is irrelevant for venue purposes; subsection (1) focuses only on the *defendant's* state of residence, so **E** and **F** are wrong.

B is not the answer, because we must also consider subsection (2). The accident occurred in Manhattan, which is in the Southern District of New York, so the Southern District is "a judicial district in which a substantial part of the events or omissions giving rise to the claim occurred." Because the Northern District of New York is a proper venue under subsection (1) and the Southern District of New York is a proper venue under subsection (2), the answer is **D**.

2. Multiple defendants. Try this variation, which includes an additional defendant.

> Now imagine that the Manhattan car accident involved Powers (a resident of Connecticut), Doris (a resident of Albany, New York), and Donald (a resident of Buffalo, New York, which is in the Western District of New York). Powers wants to sue both Doris and Donald in federal court, alleging that they both caused the accident. Where is venue proper in this case?
>
> A. The Northern District of New York, the Southern District of New York, and the Western District of New York only.
> B. The Southern District of New York only.
> C. Any federal district in New York, including the Eastern District of New York.
> D. None of the above is correct.

Start with subsection (1). All defendants are residents of New York, so venue is proper in any district in New York in which a defendant resides. In this case, that means that both the Western District of New York (where Donald resides) and the Northern District of New York (where Doris resides) are proper venues. Of course, the Southern District is also a proper venue under subsection (2) for the reasons explained earlier. Thus, the answer here is **A**.

3. Multiple defendants redux. This variation adds some complexity. Read subsection (1) closely.

> Now imagine the same facts as in the previous example, except that Donald is a resident of Vermont. Where is venue proper in this case?
>
> A. The Northern District of New York, the Southern District of New York, and the District of Vermont.
> B. The Southern District of New York only.
> C. The Southern District of New York and the Northern District of New York only.
> D. None of the above is correct.

Start with subsection (1) and ask whether "all defendants are residents" of the same state. In this case, they are not. Doris resides in New York, and Donald resides in Vermont. Thus, there is no proper venue under subsection (1).

Now look at subsection (2). The Southern District of New York is still proper under that subsection, and there does not appear to be any other district where a substantial part of the events or omissions giving rise to the claim occurred. Accordingly, the Southern District of New York is the only proper venue. **B** is the answer.

4. Districts and divisions. Some federal districts are divided into different "divisions" that are located in different cities. For example, the Northern District of Illinois has courts located in an Eastern Division (Chicago) and a Western Division (Rockford). The Chicago and Rockford courts are both in the same district (i.e., the Northern District of Illinois), but they are located in different cities. The federal venue statutes are concerned with districts, not divisions, but be aware that these additional choices within districts sometimes exist and are often governed by local rules.

III. The Meaning of "Resident" Under Subsection (1)

Subsection (1) uses the word "resident," which can have different meanings depending on whether a litigant is an individual, a corporation, or a non-corporate entity.

A. The Definition of "Resident" for Individuals

The preceding hypotheticals assumed that each party's residence was clear. But what if a party's residence is ambiguous? For example, if Doris had a home in two different states, where would her "residence" be under subsection (1)?

For some time, there was disagreement as to the answer, but in 2011, Congress resolved the matter by amending 28 U.S.C. § 1391(c)(1). The statute now provides that "for all venue purposes . . . a natural person, including an alien lawfully admitted for permanent residence in the United States, shall be deemed to reside in the judicial district in which that person is domiciled." Thus, for purposes of interpreting subsection (1), a person will be considered to reside in the state where she is domiciled. The case law suggests that most courts will apply the concept of "domicile" in much the same way as they do in the context of diversity jurisdiction. (See the discussion of this issue in Chapter 3.)

B. The Definition of "Resident" for Corporations and Other Entities

Where do corporate and non-corporate entities "reside" for venue purposes? Sections 1391(c)(2) and (d) offer guidance:

(c) Residency.—For all venue purposes—

. . .

(2) an entity with the capacity to sue and be sued in its common name under applicable law, whether or not incorporated, shall be deemed to reside, if a defendant, in any judicial district in which such defendant is subject to the court's personal jurisdiction with respect to the civil action in question and, if a plaintiff, only in the judicial district in which it maintains its principal place of business.

. . .

(d) Residency of corporations in States with multiple districts.—For purposes of venue under this chapter, in a State which has more than one judicial district and in which a defendant that is a corporation is subject to personal jurisdiction at the time an action is commenced, such corporation shall be deemed to reside in any district in that State within which its contacts would be sufficient to subject it to personal jurisdiction if that district were a separate State, and, if there is no such district, the corporation shall be deemed to reside in the district within which it has the most significant contacts.

In general, therefore, entities reside in every federal district where they would be subject to personal jurisdiction if that district were their own state. To make sense of this definition, we offer a few examples below.

Notes and Questions: Venue in Cases Against Corporations and Other Entities

Q **1. Determining where entities reside.** Peggy, a South Carolina resident, sues Devo Corp. in federal court. Peggy alleges that Devo manufactured a product that injured Peggy at her home in South Carolina. Devo manufactured the product in Sacramento, California, in the Eastern District of California, and mailed it from Sacramento to Peggy's home in South Carolina, after Peggy placed an order from there via the Internet. In addition to accepting Internet orders that are processed in Sacramento, Devo has five stores in Los Angeles, which is in the Central District of California. Assume that Devo has its place of incorporation in Delaware and its principal place of business in San Diego, which is in the Southern District of California. Also assume that Devo has no contacts in any district not mentioned here. Identify every district where venue would be proper.

A Start with subsection (1). There is a single defendant, Devo Corp., so venue will be proper in every district where Devo "resides." Sections 1391(c) and 1391(d)(2), when read together, provide that a corporate defendant resides (for venue purposes) in any district where it would be subject to personal jurisdiction if that district were viewed as its own state.

In this case, Devo would be subject to general jurisdiction in the districts where it is incorporated and has its principal place of business—the District of Delaware and the Southern District of California, respectively. Devo would be subject to specific jurisdiction in two districts. First, Devo sent the allegedly defective product to South Carolina, so specific jurisdiction would be proper there. There also would be specific jurisdiction in the Eastern District of California because the case arose out of the manufacturing of a product there. Because Devo is subject to personal jurisdiction in each of these districts, Devo is considered to "reside" in each of these districts for purposes of subsection (1). In sum, venue is probably proper in the Southern District of California, the District of Delaware, the District of South Carolina, and the Eastern District of California.

In contrast, the Central District of California is probably not a proper venue, even though Devo has a significant presence there. None of the stores located there gave rise to this particular claim, and after *Daimler*, it seems reasonably clear that these stores do not constitute a sufficient presence to subject Devo to general jurisdiction.

But wait a minute. Isn't Devo subject to general jurisdiction everywhere in California given that its principal place of business is in San Diego (in the Southern District of California)? Devo is, indeed, subject to general jurisdiction in California, but remember that venue requires that we look at each district as if it were a "separate State." Devo Corp. has no contacts in the Northern District of California, so if the Northern District were considered a separate state, Devo would not be subject to personal jurisdiction there. Similarly, although Devo has contacts in the Central District of California (where it has stores), Devo would not be subject to personal jurisdiction in the Central District if the Central District were considered a separate state. Accordingly, venue is not proper in either the Northern or Central Districts of California.

This distinction between venue and personal jurisdiction makes sense, given that the two concepts serve different purposes. Personal jurisdiction protects the defendant, whereas venue focuses on the overall convenience and efficiency of litigating in a particular district. Put another way, it may be fair as a matter of personal jurisdiction to require Devo to defend the lawsuit anywhere in California, but only certain federal districts offer a reasonably convenient location for the lawsuit given the location of the parties, the witnesses, and the evidence.

Finally, under subsection (2), venue would be proper in the District of South Carolina, because that is where the product malfunctioned and Peggy was injured. The Eastern District of California is also likely a proper venue under this subsection because the product was manufactured there. Of course, those two districts are already proper venues under subsection (1), so this subsection does not authorize any additional venues on these facts.

Q **2. Subsection (1) and multiple corporate defendants.** Imagine that Company 1 has its place of incorporation and principal place of business in Idaho and that Company 2 has its place of incorporation in Idaho, but its principal place of business in North Dakota. (Each state has only one federal district.) If a plaintiff sues both companies in the same lawsuit in federal court, would there be a proper venue under subsection (1)?

A | Corporate defendants only need one shared district of residence under § 1391(c) to satisfy subsection (1), and in this case, there is one: the District of Idaho. Company 1 resides there, as does Company 2.

3. The corporate vs. non-corporate entity distinction. Until recently, 28 U.S.C. § 1391(c) applied only to corporations, so courts had no clear authority for determining the residence of non-corporate entities, such as partnerships. In 2011, Congress resolved the ambiguity by amending § 1391(c) so that the statute now explicitly applies to both corporations and non-corporate entities. Although this amendment offers much needed clarity, it is inconsistent with the way courts treat non-corporate entities when analyzing diversity jurisdiction. In that context, non-corporate entities are treated as citizens of every state in which one of their members is domiciled. There does not appear to be a sound conceptual reason for treating non-corporate entities differently in these two situations. The dichotomy appears to be a product of historical circumstances—the law in these two areas developed separately over a long period of time—rather than the result of some conceptually coherent approach to the status of legal entities.

IV. The Meaning of "Substantial Part" Under Subsection (2)

READING *UFFNER v. LA REUNION FRANCAISE.* Subsection (2) authorizes venue wherever "a substantial part of the events or omissions giving rise to the claim occurred." When is an event or omission sufficiently "substantial" to satisfy subsection (2)? In some cases, the answer is clear, but in many cases, as in *Uffner*, it is not. Consider the following questions as you read this case:

- How does the court interpret the phrase "substantial part" in this case?
- Why does the court conclude that the events off the coast of Puerto Rico were a sufficiently substantial part of the case to authorize venue in Puerto Rico?

UFFNER v. LA REUNION FRANCAISE

244 F.3d 38 (1st Cir. 2001)

Torruella, Chief Judge.

Plaintiff-appellant Daniel L. Uffner, Jr. filed this diversity suit in federal district court in the District of Puerto Rico against his insurance issuer and underwriters for wrongful denial of an insurance claim. Defendants-appellees La Reunion Francaise, S.A. ("La Reunion"), T.L. Dallas & Co. Ltd. ("T.L. Dallas"), and Schaeffer

& Associates, Inc. ("Schaeffer") filed motions to dismiss for lack of subject matter jurisdiction, failure to state a claim, and improper venue. The district court granted the motions based upon lack of personal jurisdiction and improper venue. For the reasons stated below, we vacate the district court's dismissal and remand the case for further proceedings.

BACKGROUND

La Reunion is a French insurance company which provides vessels with marine insurance coverage and has its principal place of business in Paris, France. T.L. Dallas, a marine underwriting manager based in Bradford, England, specializes in insuring yachts and represents La Reunion in the placement of marine insurance policies. Finally, Schaeffer is an underwriting agent located in the State of Georgia that places yacht policies in the United States (including Puerto Rico) for T.L. Dallas. Together, these three entities issued and underwrote a marine policy for Uffner's sailing yacht, *La Mer,* in a cover note dated March 18, 1997.

On June 14, 1997, Uffner departed from Fajardo, Puerto Rico on a voyage to St. Thomas, U.S. Virgin islands. When he was positioned near Isla Palominos, a small island approximately one mile off the coast of Puerto Rico, a fire broke out in the engine room, forcing Uffner to abandon the vessel. The yacht subsequently sank in the same location. Shortly thereafter, Uffner contacted his insurance broker, International Marine Insurance Services ("IMIS") to file a claim for the loss of the boat. After a series of written communications and telephone calls between IMIS and appellees, the claim was denied due to the alleged absence of a "current out-of-water survey."

Uffner filed this suit on June 12, 1998, claiming damages for a bad-faith denial of an insurance claim. La Reunion and T.L. Dallas filed separate motions to dismiss based on lack of subject matter jurisdiction, failure to state a claim upon which relief can be granted, and improper venue. Schaeffer filed a motion joining these motions to dismiss on the same grounds. Uffner timely opposed all motions.

On September 20, 1999, the district court dismissed Uffner's complaint without prejudice, concluding that the court lacked personal jurisdiction over appellees and that venue did not lie in Puerto Rico. Uffner moved the court to reconsider its ruling and requested leave to amend the complaint in order to assert admiralty jurisdiction as an alternative basis for subject matter jurisdiction. The court denied both motions on December 10, 1999, and this appeal followed.

DISCUSSION

The district court dismissed appellant's complaint on two grounds. First, the court concluded that pursuant to the provisions of the Puerto Rico Long-Arm statute, appellees lacked sufficient minimum contacts with the forum to be subject to personal jurisdiction therein. In addition, the court determined that the suit involved a contract claim unrelated to the District of Puerto Rico, making it an improper forum for litigation. We review the court's legal conclusions supporting the dismissal *de novo.*

A. Personal Jurisdiction

In their motions to dismiss, appellees argued that the court lacked subject matter jurisdiction, Fed. R. Civ. P. 12(b)(1), that Uffner failed to state a claim for which relief could be granted, Fed. R. Civ. P. 12(b)(6), and that venue was improper, Fed. R. Civ. P. 12(b)(3). None of the parties raised any objection to personal jurisdiction. *See* Fed. R. Civ. P. 12(b)(2). Nevertheless, the court itself raised and disposed of the motion on this ground. In doing so, it overlooked the provisions of Fed. R. Civ. P. 12(g), which states that "[i]f a party makes a motion under this rule but omits therefrom any defense or objection then available to the party which this rule permits to be raised by motion, the party shall not thereafter make a motion based on the defense or objection so omitted. . . ." Rule 12(h)(1)(A) provides, in turn, that "[a] defense of lack of personal jurisdiction over the person is waived . . . if omitted from a motion in the circumstances described in subdivision (g). . . ." Fed. R. Civ. P. 12(h)(1)(A). By failing to include a 12(b)(2) argument in their motion to dismiss, appellees waived this defense in the district court.

Once a party has waived its defense of lack of personal jurisdiction, the court may not, *sua sponte,* raise the issue in its ruling on a motion to dismiss. This is so because, since personal jurisdiction may be acquired through voluntary appearance and the filing of responsive pleadings without objection, the court has no independent reason to visit the issue.[1] Furthermore, such a prohibition avoids prejudicing the plaintiff, who has not had an opportunity to respond to the issue before the court, and promotes the purpose of Rules 12(g) and (h). There is no evidence here that the Rule 12(b)(2) defense was unavailable to appellees at the time they filed their answer. Nor is this merely a case of a litigant improperly characterizing a substantive argument for lack of personal jurisdiction under a different subsection. Rather, appellees simply failed to raise the issue in their motion to dismiss and thereby consented to the court's jurisdiction. Since the court was not at liberty to nullify appellees' consent, we conclude that the district court erred in dismissing the complaint for lack of personal jurisdiction.

B. Venue

Due to its focus on personal jurisdiction, the district court dealt only perfunctorily with the issue of whether venue was proper in the district of Puerto Rico. Specifically, the court found that the appellant's claim sounded in contract rather than tort. As such, the court observed, the claim was wholly unrelated to Puerto Rico: the "triggering event" was the denial of the claim and "[t]he issue at bar is the interpretation of the contract." The court also noted that the contract was

1. Unlike subject-matter jurisdiction, which is a statutory and constitutional restriction on the power of the court, *see* U.S. Const. art. III, § 1, personal jurisdiction arises from the Due Process Clause and protects an individual liberty interest. *Ins. Corp. of Ir., Ltd. v. Compagnie des Bauxites de Guinee,* 456 U.S. 694. The ability to waive this right thus reflects the principle that "the individual can subject himself to powers from which he may otherwise be protected." *Id.* at 703 n.10.

neither negotiated nor formed in Puerto Rico. Finally, according to the court, the occurrence of the fire in Puerto Rican waters was "a tenuous connection at best."

To begin, the distinction between tort and contract is immaterial to the requirements for venue set forth in the general venue statute, 28 U.S.C. § 1391(a). . . .*

There is no dispute that § 1391(a)(1) is inapplicable in this case. The question, then, is whether "a substantial part of the events . . . giving rise to the claim occurred" in Puerto Rico.

Prior to 1990, § 1391(a) provided venue in "the judicial district . . . in which the claim arose." 28 U.S.C. § 1391(a) (1988). Congress amended the statute to its current form because it found that the old language "led to wasteful litigation whenever several different forums were involved in the transaction leading up to the dispute." The pre-amendment statute also engendered a plethora of tests to determine the single venue in which the claim "arose." By contrast, many circuits have interpreted the legislative history of the 1990 amendment as evincing Congress's recognition that when the events underlying a claim have taken place in different places, venue may be proper in any number of districts. We look, therefore, not to a single "triggering event" prompting the action, but to the entire sequence of events underlying the claim.

In so doing, we consider the following acts: (1) appellant, a resident of the Virgin Islands, obtained an insurance policy for his yacht, *La Mer*;[5] (2) the insured vessel caught fire and sank in Puerto Rican waters; (3) appellant filed a claim with appellees through his insurance broker demanding payment for this loss; and (4) the claim was ultimately denied because it was allegedly not covered by the policy. Though this is merely a skeletal outline of events leading to the claim, for purposes of this appeal, we need just establish that the sinking of *La Mer* was one part of the historical predicate for the instant suit.[6] It is the only event, however, that occurred in Puerto Rico. For venue to be proper in that district, therefore, the loss of *La Mer* must be "substantial."

Appellees argue that Uffner's complaint alleges a bad faith denial of his insurance claim, not that the loss itself was due to their fault or negligence. Consequently, they reason, the sinking of the vessel cannot be considered "substantial." It is true, as the district court pointed out, that the legal question in the suit is "whether [an out-of-water survey] was necessary under the terms of the insurance contract." Resolving this issue does not require an investigation into how, when, or why the accident occurred. In this sense, the sinking of Uffner's yacht is not related to the principal question for decision.

However, an event need not be a point of dispute between the parties in order to constitute a substantial event giving rise to the claim. *Cf. Woodke v. Dahm,* 70

---

* **[Eds.—Section 1391 was amended in 2011. The provisions that previously appeared in § 1391(a) now appear in 1391(b).]**

5. As far as the record suggests, this contract was drafted in France, underwritten in England, and issued to appellant through Georgia.

6. In considering "events or omissions" for purposes of venue, we decline to adopt the Eighth Circuit's approach, which looks only at the acts of the defendant. Instead, we join those courts that have chosen a more holistic view of the acts underlying a claim.

F.3d 983, 986 (8th Cir. 1995) (requiring that the event itself be "wrongful" in order to support venue). In this case, Uffner's bad faith denial claim alleges that the loss of his yacht was covered by the contract and the payment due to him wrongfully denied. Thus, although the sinking of *La Mer* is itself not in dispute, the event is connected to the claim inasmuch as Uffner's requested damages include recovery for the loss. We conclude that, in a suit against an insurance company to recover for losses resulting from a vessel casualty, the jurisdiction where that loss occurred is "substantial" for venue purposes.

We add that our conclusion does not thwart the general purpose of statutorily specified venue, which is "to protect the defendant against the risk that a plaintiff will select an unfair or inconvenient place of trial." *Leroy v. Great W. United Corp.*, 443 U.S. 173 (1979). First, appellees have not alleged—either below or on appeal—that continuing the suit in the district of Puerto Rico would confer a tactical advantage to appellant or prejudice their own case in any way. We also highlight the absence of a forum-selection clause in the insurance policy indicating appellees' preferred forum for litigation. Finally, appellees conceded at oral argument that they would not object to litigating in the Virgin Islands, suggesting that traveling to the Caribbean would not be unduly burdensome. We therefore hold that venue properly lies in the district of Puerto Rico.

CONCLUSION

Appellees have suggested that venue is proper in the Virgin Islands or in Georgia. We do not address these possibilities since, as we have already noted, § 1391 contemplates that venue may be proper in several districts. In this case, Puerto Rico is at least one of them.

The judgment of the district court is **vacated** and the case **remanded** for further proceedings.

Notes and Questions: Understanding Substantiality Under Subsection (2)

Q **1. Defining substantiality.** How does the court define the word "substantial," and how does the definition support the court's conclusion that venue is proper in Puerto Rico?

A The court asserts that, as long as what happened in the district was an important part of the "sequence of events" or "historical predicates" giving rise to the case, venue is proper in that district. In this case, a significant "historical predicate" for the claim was the sinking of the plaintiff's boat in Puerto Rico. Without that event, there would be no claim, thus making the District of Puerto Rico a proper venue under subsection (2). For this reason, the court concluded that "in a suit against an insurance company to recover for losses resulting from a vessel casualty, the jurisdiction where that loss occurred is 'substantial' for venue purposes."

2. Other approaches. There are other plausible and narrower ways of interpreting subsection (2). For example, the court notes that the Eighth Circuit has adopted an interpretation of "substantial" that requires the defendant to have been responsible for the forum-related event and the event to "be a point of dispute between the parties."

Under this narrower approach, venue would have been improper in Puerto Rico for two reasons. First, the defendant did not engage in any act or omission in Puerto Rico. Second, the key issue in the case and the only "point of dispute" was whether an out-of-water survey was necessary under the policy—an issue having nothing to do with Puerto Rico or the sinking of the ship. That issue required an interpretation of the policy that "was drafted in France, underwritten in England, and issued to [the plaintiff] through Georgia." Under this standard, therefore, a district in Georgia would have been a proper venue, but not the District of Puerto Rico.

3. Resolving ambiguities. When a statute or other authority contains an ambiguity, courts and good lawyers frequently ask how the premise of the doctrine would be furthered by reaching a particular outcome. The *Uffner* court engages in such an inquiry here, noting that Puerto Rico appears to be a convenient and reasonable location for the lawsuit, especially given that the defendants were willing to litigate in the nearby Virgin Islands. By focusing on venue's underlying concern for convenience, the court is able to make sense of a statutory ambiguity like the meaning of the word "substantial."

V. The Fallback Provision

Subsection (3) applies to those rare cases where neither subsection (1) *nor* subsection (2) specifies a proper venue. In such a case, and *only* in such a case, a court can "fall back" to subsection (3) to find a proper venue. Such a case most commonly arises when the events giving rise to the suit occurred outside of the United States. Consider the following example.

Q **A case that triggers subsection (3).** There is a three-car accident in Toronto, Canada, involving Pieter (a Michigan resident), Dolly (a Minnesota resident), and Dirk (an Oregon resident). Pieter sues Dolly and Dirk in the federal district of Minnesota based on diversity jurisdiction. Where is venue proper?

A There are no proper venues under subsection (1) because the defendants reside in different states. There are also no proper venues under subsection (2) because all of the significant events giving rise to the suit occurred in Canada.

Because there are no proper venues under either subsection (1) or subsection (2), we must look to the fallback provision in subsection (3). Under that provision, venue is proper in "any judicial district in which any defendant is subject to the court's personal jurisdiction with respect to such action." So venue is proper in either the District of Minnesota, where Dolly is subject to personal jurisdiction, or the District of Oregon, where Dirk is subject to personal jurisdiction.

Of course, even if venue is proper in the District of Minnesota (for example), Pieter still has a problem. Dirk is an Oregon resident, so there is no personal jurisdiction over him in Minnesota. Thus, Pieter may be forced to pursue his claim separately against Dirk in Oregon unless he can establish personal jurisdiction over Dirk in Minnesota some other way. One such possibility is to have Dirk served with process if he happens to visit there. Another possibility is that Dirk might consent to or waive personal jurisdiction in Minnesota.

VI. Specialized Venue Statutes

Section 1391(a) specifies where venue is proper in all civil actions "except as otherwise provided by law." That's an important exception. What law might "otherwise provide" for venue?

It turns out that Congress has passed a number of specialized venue statutes that apply in certain types of cases. For example, under 28 U.S.C. § 1402, tort claims against the federal government can be brought where the plaintiff resides or where the incident at issue occurred. Copyright and patent infringement claims also have specialized venue rules. 28 U.S.C. §§ 1400(a)–(b).

The statute governing employment discrimination cases (often referred to as Title VII) also has a commonly cited specialized venue rule:

> Such an action may be brought in any judicial district in the State in which the unlawful employment practice is alleged to have been committed, in the judicial district in which the employment records relevant to such practice are maintained and administered, or in the judicial district in which the aggrieved person would have worked but for the alleged unlawful employment practice, but if the respondent is not found within any such district, such an action may be brought within the judicial district in which the respondent has his principal office....

42 U.S.C. § 2000e-5(f)(3). This specialized venue statute is exclusive, meaning that it replaces the general venue provisions in § 1391. In contrast, some specialized venue statutes are supplemental and thus authorize venues in *addition* to the venues authorized in § 1391. To know whether a particular statute is exclusive or supplemental, it is often necessary to look at the case law interpreting it.

There is one other important statute that functions as a specialized venue provision. The removal statute, 28 U.S.C. § 1441(a), requires removal of a state case to the federal district that covers the geographic area where the state court sits. A defendant cannot remove a case to any other federal district. In this sense, the removal statute is a specialized venue statute, conferring venue on only a single court for removal purposes. Thus, the usual venue statutes do not apply to cases removed from state to federal court. Of course, there is another way to get the case to a different federal venue *after* removal. It's called *transfer*, a subject to which we turn in the next chapter.

VII. Basic Venue: Summary of Basic Principles

- The word "venue" refers to the particular court within a court system where a lawsuit can be brought. In federal court, each federal district is a distinct venue. In state court, venues are often defined by counties or municipalities.
- Absent consent or waiver, a court cannot hear a case unless it is brought in a proper venue.
- Venue in federal cases is governed by federal venue statutes, which ensure that cases are brought in districts that have some logical connection to the case or the parties.
- The general federal venue statute, 28 U.S.C. § 1391, applies in most federal cases. Section 1391(b) provides for venue in "(1) a judicial district in which any defendant resides, if all defendants are residents of the State in which the district is located"; and "(2) a judicial district in which a substantial part of the events or omissions giving rise to the claim occurred, or a substantial part of property that is the subject of the action is situated." Subsection (3), which confers venue in "any judicial district in which any defendant is subject to the court's personal jurisdiction with respect to such action," is used only if there is no proper venue anywhere in the United States under subsections (1) and (2).
- More than one venue may be proper under 28 U.S.C. § 1391.
- To determine where entities reside for purposes of subsection (1), a court looks to § 1391(c), which says that an entity resides in a district where it would be subject to personal jurisdiction if that district were its own state.
- There is a split of authority on the meaning of "substantial" in subsection (2). Some courts define it to mean that the defendant engaged in a forum-related event that produced "a point of dispute between the parties." Other courts have interpreted it more broadly to include any event—whether caused by the defendant or another party—that was a part of the sequence of events giving rise to the claim.
- Specialized venue statutes apply to claims against the federal government, employment discrimination cases, racketeering cases, copyright and patent infringement matters, and other types of claims. Specialized venue statutes either replace 28 U.S.C. § 1391 or supplement the venues that § 1391 specifies.

12

Challenges to Venue: Transfers and Dismissals

I. Introduction

Imagine that your client, Carol, is sued in the United States District Court for the Southern District of New York. You determine that the Southern District of New York is a proper venue, but Carol lives and works in Alexandria, Virginia, as do most of the witnesses to the events that gave rise to the claims. Moreover, your office is located in Virginia.

Under these circumstances, Carol probably will want to litigate in the Eastern District of Virginia, the district encompassing Alexandria, Virginia. That court is not only more convenient for her and the witnesses, but it will also be less expensive for Carol to litigate there. She will not have to travel to New York (or pay you to travel to New York) for court appearances or pay for local counsel in New York.*

* Lawyers are usually permitted to litigate a case in a state where they are not licensed to practice by filing a motion for admission *pro hac vice* (for purposes of this case). Courts typically grant these motions, but they often require the out-of-state lawyer to affiliate with an in-state attorney. This in-state attorney, who is referred to as "local counsel," ensures that the out-of-state lawyer understands unusual features of local law and procedure.

This scenario arises with some regularity. Most of your clients will want to litigate lawsuits where it is most convenient for them (and least convenient for their opponents). For this reason, motions to transfer a case from one venue to another are fairly common. This chapter explains when a court will grant these transfer motions and venue-related motions to dismiss.

II. Statutory Transfers and Dismissals in Federal Court

There are generally two types of venue-related motions. First, and most obviously, a defendant can make a motion that asserts that the case was filed in an improper venue. If the motion has merit, 28 U.S.C. § 1406 authorizes a judge to dismiss the case or transfer it to a federal venue where the suit could have been brought:

28 U.S.C. § 1406. CURE OR WAIVER OF DEFECTS

(a) The district court of a district in which is filed a case laying venue in the wrong division or district shall dismiss, or if it be in the interest of justice, transfer such case to any district or division in which it could have been brought.

The second type of motion concerns a case like Carol's. It contends that, although venue is proper in the court where the lawsuit was filed, there is a more appropriate federal district (or division) where the case should be litigated. If the judge agrees, a separate statute—28 U.S.C. § 1404—authorizes the court to transfer the case to that other district:

28 U.S.C. § 1404. CHANGE OF VENUE

(a) For the convenience of parties and witnesses, in the interest of justice, a district court may transfer any civil action to any other district or division where it might have been brought or to any district or division to which all parties have consented.

There is one more wrinkle. Even though no statute authorizes a federal court to dismiss a case that was filed in a proper venue, the federal courts (and most state courts) have retained their common law authority to grant such dismissals. This is called a *forum non conveniens* dismissal, which is a Latin phrase meaning "inconvenient forum."

To summarize, if a plaintiff files a lawsuit in an improper venue, a party can move to dismiss the case or transfer it pursuant to § 1406. If the case is filed in a proper venue, a party can move to transfer it pursuant to § 1404 or dismiss it pursuant to the doctrine of forum non conveniens. The first part of this chapter focuses on the three motions that are authorized by statute, and the last part of this chapter explains forum non conveniens. For now, the chart below summarizes these various options.

	Cases Filed in the Wrong Venue	Cases Filed in the Correct Venue
Motions to Transfer	28 U.S.C. § 1406	28 U.S.C. § 1404
Motions to Dismiss	28 U.S.C. § 1406 and Federal Rule 12(b)(3)	Forum non conveniens (a common law doctrine)

Figure 12–1: **OPTIONS FOR CHALLENGING VENUE**

A. Transfers and Dismissals Under § 1406

Section 1406 authorizes a federal district court to dismiss a case that was filed in an improper federal venue or transfer it to a federal venue where the suit could have been brought (if such a venue exists). Despite the apparent simplicity of these options, the statute leaves open several important questions.

Notes and Questions: Transfers and Dismissals Under § 1406

Q **1. Dismiss or transfer?** Suppose that a plaintiff files a lawsuit in the District of Nevada, but the only proper venue is the District of Utah. Under these circumstances, § 1406 and Federal Rule 12(b)(3) authorize the federal court to grant a motion to dismiss the case. As an alternative, § 1406 authorizes the judge to transfer the case if doing so is "in the interest of justice." Which option should the court select?

A A transfer is usually in the "interest of justice," because a transfer will save the plaintiff the time and expense of having to refile the claim in another forum. If the transferor court decides to transfer the case, it can simply send the case file to the clerk of another federal district court and tell the parties to litigate in that court (the transferee court) instead. In contrast, if the court dismisses the case, the plaintiff has to refile the case in a proper venue, pay a filing fee, and ensure proper service on the defendant. Transfer is thus easier, quicker, and less costly. In addition, if the court dismisses the case, the statute of limitations may already have run or may expire before the plaintiff can refile the case in a proper venue. A transfer avoids this possibility because a transferred case is considered to have been filed on the date when it was filed in the original (transferor) court. For these reasons, a federal court will usually conclude that a transfer is in the interests of justice when a proper federal venue exists. *See Goldlawr, Inc. v. Heiman*, 369 U.S. 463, 466–67 (1962).

2. Limitations on intersystem transfers. A judge only has the authority to transfer cases within the same court system. For example, a state trial judge in Texas can transfer a case to another Texas state court, *see* TEX. CIV. PRAC. & REM. CODE ANN. § 15.002(b), but not to a state court in Arkansas or any other state's courts, because a Texas state court lacks the power to authorize an Arkansas state court to hear the case.

Moreover, a Texas state court has no power to "transfer" a case to a federal court—even one sitting in a district in Texas—because a federal court is in a different court system. State cases can be *removed* to federal court, but the state court itself does not have any control over that process. Rather, the defendant files a notice of removal in federal court, and the federal court decides whether to keep the case or remand it back to the state court. The state court, therefore, is in no position to "transfer" a case to federal court, so the federally controlled process is called "removal," not "transfer."

Within the federal court system, a federal district judge can transfer a case to another federal district court, even one in another state, because both courts are in the federal court system. For example, a federal district judge in Kansas can transfer a case to the federal District of Nebraska, but she has no authority to transfer a case to a *state* court in Kansas or to any other state court.

A federal judge can remand a case to state court when a party improperly removes a case to federal court, but a remand (like removal) is not a "transfer." It is simply a process of sending the case back to the court from which it came. In short, courts can transfer cases within their own court systems ("intrasystem" transfers), but not beyond them.

Q **3. Waiving objections to venue.** Recall that personal jurisdiction can be waived, but subject matter jurisdiction cannot. Is a motion to dismiss for improper venue more like personal jurisdiction, which is waivable under Rule 12, or more like subject matter jurisdiction, which is not? Why?

A Consider why each concept exists. Subject matter jurisdiction limits a court's power to hear a case. It is not a privilege or right that belongs to the parties, so the parties cannot waive it. In contrast, personal jurisdiction is a due process protection that belongs to the defendant. If the defendant decides not to take advantage of that protection, the defendant is free to do so.

Now consider venue. If a plaintiff files a case in an improper venue, that mistake does not implicate the court's constitutional authority to hear the matter (as subject matter jurisdiction does). Rather, the filing of a case in an improper venue means that the case was filed in a court that the legislature has determined to be inconvenient or inefficient for the parties or witnesses. In this sense, venue offers protection to the parties, making it more like personal jurisdiction. For this reason, a party is considered to waive a motion to dismiss for lack of proper venue unless the motion is made at an appropriate time, usually quite early in the case. *See* Fed. R. Civ. P. 12(g)–(h).

B. Section 1404 Transfers

Imagine that a plaintiff (like the plaintiff in the opening hypothetical) files a case in a *proper* federal venue, but another federal district is a more convenient place to conduct the litigation. A party, usually the defendant, can move to transfer the case to that other district under § 1404(a). Assuming the plaintiff does not consent to the transfer, the court will ask whether the case "might have been brought" in the other venue, and if so, whether transferring the case to that venue would promote the convenience of the parties and witnesses as well as the interests of justice.

READING *MacMUNN v. ELI LILLY CO.* The following case offers a straightforward analysis of a § 1404 transfer motion. The court methodically examines the "convenience of [the] parties and witnesses" and the "interest of justice" using various private and public interest factors.

- What are the private interest factors that the court considers?
- What are the public interest factors?
- Why do these public and private interest factors favor transfer?

MacMUNN v. ELI LILLY CO.

559 F. Supp. 2D 58 (D.D.C. 2008)

Ricardo M. Urbina, District Judge.

I. INTRODUCTION

Before the court is the defendant's motion to transfer this products liability case to Massachusetts. The defendant, Eli Lilly & Co. **[Eds.—a company with its principal place of business in Indiana]**, argues that both private and public interests favor transfer primarily because the case has little if any ties to this District. The plaintiffs, Judith MacMunn and her husband Michael MacMunn, oppose transfer citing numerous cases involving the same defendant and subject matter that have been resolved in this District. Because the contacts relevant to this dispute are overwhelmingly focused in Massachusetts and because this case is still in its nascent stages, the court grants the defendant's motion to transfer.

II. FACTUAL AND PROCEDURAL BACKGROUND

Plaintiff Judith MacMunn alleges that her mother ingested Diethylstilbestrol ("DES") while pregnant with her in 1962. The exposure to DES *in utero* purportedly resulted in uterine and cervical malformations, infertility, physical and mental pain and medical expenses and treatment. On September 14, 2007, the plaintiff and her husband, Michael MacMunn filed a 7-count complaint in D.C. Superior Court, claiming negligence, strict liability, breach of warranty, misrepresentation and loss of consortium. Collectively, the plaintiffs seek 3 million dollars in compensatory damages and 3 million dollars in punitive damages.

On November 2, 2007, the defendant removed the case to this court based on diversity of citizenship.... Four months after the initial status conference, the defendant filed a motion to transfer this case to the District of Massachusetts....

III. ANALYSIS

A. Legal Standard for Venue Under 28 U.S.C. § 1391(a) and Transfer Pursuant to 28 U.S.C. § 1404(a)*

When federal jurisdiction is premised solely on diversity, 28 U.S.C. § 1391(a) controls venue. . . .

In an action where venue is proper, 28 U.S.C. § 1404(a) nonetheless authorizes a court to transfer a civil action to any other district where it could have been brought "for the convenience of parties and witnesses, in the interest of justice[.]" 28 U.S.C. § 1404(a). Section 1404(a) vests "discretion in the district court to adjudicate motions to transfer according to [an] individualized, case-by-case consideration of convenience and fairness." *Stewart Org., Inc. v. Ricoh Corp.*, 487 U.S. 22, 27 (1988) (quoting *Van Dusen v. Barrack*, 376 U.S. 612, 622 (1964)). Under this statute, the moving party bears the burden of establishing that transfer is proper.

Accordingly, the defendant must make two showings to justify transfer. First, the defendant must establish that the plaintiff originally could have brought the action in the proposed transferee district. Second, the defendant must demonstrate that considerations of convenience and the interest of justice weigh in favor of transfer to that district. As to the second showing, the statute calls on the court to weigh a number of case-specific private and public-interest factors. The private-interest considerations include: (1) the plaintiff's choice of forum, unless the balance of convenience is strongly in favor of the defendants; (2) the defendant's choice of forum; (3) whether the claim arose elsewhere; (4) the convenience of the parties; (5) the convenience of the witnesses; and (6) the ease of access to sources of proof. The public-interest considerations include: (1) the transferee's familiarity with the governing laws; (2) the relative congestion of the calendars of the potential transferee and transferor courts; and (3) the local interest in deciding local controversies at home.

B. The Court Grants the Defendant's Motion to Transfer

1. The Private Interests Favor Transfer[1]

Surveying the private interest factors, the defendant concludes, based on the plaintiffs' responses to interrogatories, that "all of the potential witnesses and sources of proof concerning the injuries alleged in this case are located in the District of Massachusetts." Specifically, the defendant recounts that the plaintiff's

* **[Eds.—Section 1391 was amended in 2011. The provisions that previously appeared in § 1391(a) now appear in 1391(b).]**

1. For transfer to be proper, the defendant must first establish that the action could have been brought in the proposed transferee district. The plaintiffs do not contest the defendant's assertion that venue is proper in the District of Massachusetts. Because complete diversity exists, 28 U.S.C. § 1332; because Massachusetts's long-arm statute extends to torts allegedly committed in Massachusetts, Mass. Gen. Laws ch. 223A, § 3; and because a substantial part of the events occurred in Massachusetts, this case could have been brought in Massachusetts, 28 U.S.C. § 1391(a)(2).

mother (the principal witness for the issue of exposure) resides in Massachusetts; the medical records regarding the plaintiff's mother's pregnancy are likely in Massachusetts; any still-living physicians who prescribed the plaintiff's mother medicine during her pregnancy would likely reside in Massachusetts (outside the scope of the District of Columbia's subpoena power); the pharmacists and pharmacy records regarding the manufacturer of the DES that the plaintiff's mother allegedly ingested would be located in Massachusetts; and the physicians and medical records related to injuries allegedly caused by DES would all be in Massachusetts. The plaintiffs counter that the defendant has not met its burden to demonstrate that any of the witnesses will be unavailable for trial and, lacking that, the court should assume that the witnesses will voluntarily appear.

Although the plaintiffs are correct in stating that the defendant has not demonstrated, or even argued, that the nonparty witnesses would be unavailable at trial, the fact that almost all of the nonparty, nonexpert witnesses reside in Massachusetts clearly weighs in favor of transfer. 15 Wright, Miller & Cooper, Fed. Prac. & Proc. § 3851 (noting that "courts weigh more heavily the residence of important nonparty witnesses, who may be within the subpoena power of one district but not the other"). Furthermore, the plaintiffs do not dispute that all the sources of relevant medical records are located in Massachusetts. Accordingly, both the convenience of the witnesses and the ease of access to sources of proof both weigh in favor of transfer.[3]

This typically is not enough to overcome the plaintiffs' choice of forum, however. *See Piper Aircraft,* 454 U.S. at 255 (stating that "there is ordinarily a strong presumption in favor of the plaintiff's choice of forum, which may be overcome only when the private and public interest factors clearly point towards trial in the alternative forum"). It is enough in this case though because the District has no meaningful ties to the controversy and because the plaintiffs reside in Massachusetts. And the plaintiffs' suggestion that "an army of lobbyists and salespeople familiar with the marketing strategies and communications regarding DES" are located in the D.C. does not "tip the balance in favor of maintaining this case in the District of Columbia." Moreover, the operative facts giving rise to the plaintiffs' claim arose in Massachusetts. These circumstances coupled with the defendant's choice of forum, asserted before the parties have engaged in significant discovery, lead the court to conclude that the private interest factors favor transfer.

2. The Public Interests Favor Transfer

The defendant contends that Massachusetts has a strong interest "in seeing that the product liability claims of Massachusetts citizens are tried fairly and effectively." Furthermore, under D.C. choice of law provisions, Massachusetts law is likely to apply, and "there is no reason that the District of Massachusetts cannot

3. Although the parties set forth arguments regarding the relative convenience in continuing the suit in this District or transferring the suit to Massachusetts, the defendant has not demonstrated any hardship in continuing the suit in this District, and the plaintiffs have not demonstrated any hardship in resolving the matter in Massachusetts. Accordingly, this factor remains in equipoise.

adequately resolve this case." The plaintiffs do not dispute, and the court has little reason to doubt, the applicability of Massachusetts law in this case; rather, the plaintiffs contend that the District's law applies to the statute of limitations, which is an important issue in DES cases. In addition, the plaintiffs respond by noting that the history of DES litigation in the District is sufficient to prevent transfer. Although this District is familiar with DES litigation, "[t]here is an appropriateness . . . in having the trial of a diversity case in a forum that is at home with the state law that must govern the case." *Gulf Oil Corp. v. Gilbert,* 330 U.S. 501, 509 (1947). Familiarity with DES litigation does not counterbalance this interest; accordingly, this factor points toward Massachusetts.

The plaintiffs next contend that "there is nothing uniquely local about DES litigation." There are, however, local harms that one community may have a stronger interest in resolving over another. Here, plaintiff Judith MacMunn's mother allegedly ingested DES in Massachusetts; the plaintiffs allegedly suffered the ill-effects from this ingestion in Massachusetts; and these individuals all currently reside in Massachusetts. The District, while its contacts with the case are not "legally insignificant," does not derive as great an interest from those contacts as Massachusetts does from its interest in redressing the harms of its citizens. The fact that DES litigation involves nationwide marketing practices does not upend this local interest. Thus, this factor, too, favors transfer.

The court turns at last to the relative congestion of the courts. As the defendant notes, this District has a more congested docket than the District of Massachusetts. The plaintiffs do not dispute this fact but protest that Magistrate Judge Kay is experienced in settling DES cases, which would likely result in a speedy resolution to this case. The defendant responds that the District of Massachusetts has a similarly experienced magistrate judge whom both parties have requested to mediate other DES cases. While not striking definitively for or against transfer, the factor shades nearer to transfer. On balance then, both the private and the public interest factors support transferring the case to the District of Massachusetts, and the court, therefore, grants the defendant's motion.

IV. CONCLUSION

For the foregoing reasons the court grants the defendant's motion to transfer. An order consistent with this Memorandum Opinion is separately and contemporaneously issued this 19th day of June, 2008.

Notes and Questions: Transfers Under § 1404

1. More than meets the eye: The importance of case law when interpreting a statute. Courts weigh numerous private and public interest factors when considering a § 1404 transfer motion. These private and public interest factors are not explicitly mentioned in § 1404. As we saw in the subject matter jurisdiction context (e.g., the meaning of "citizen" under 28 U.S.C. § 1332), statutes frequently fail to specify all of the details necessary to apply them. Section 1404 is no exception; courts have had to look to the Supreme Court's decision in *Gulf Oil Corp. v. Gilbert,* 330 U.S. 501, 509 (1947), for guidance on how to apply the statute.

2. Balancing the factors. Drawing on *Gulf Oil*, the *MacMunn* court identifies the following private interest factors: "(1) the plaintiff's choice of forum, unless the balance of convenience is strongly in favor of the defendants; (2) the defendant's choice of forum; (3) whether the claim arose elsewhere; (4) the convenience of the parties; (5) the convenience of the witnesses; and (6) the ease of access to sources of proof." It then identifies the following public interest factors: "(1) the transferee's familiarity with the governing laws; (2) the relative congestion of the calendars of the potential transferee and transferor courts; and (3) the local interest in deciding local controversies at home."

The plaintiff's choice of forum is usually given great weight (especially if it is the plaintiff's home forum, which is presumptively convenient for the plaintiff and therefore not *just* a tactical choice). In this case, however, the court explains that the other factors strongly favor transfer. With regard to the private interest factors, most of the evidence and witnesses were located in Massachusetts, not the District of Columbia. Moreover, the defendant raised the issue relatively early in the case (i.e., before a substantial amount of discovery had been completed).

With regard to the public interest factors, the court notes that the District of Columbia's choice of law rules would probably result in Massachusetts law applying to the case. Because a Massachusetts federal court typically has more experience applying Massachusetts law, that factor also favored transfer. (It is important to note that this factor alone would not lead to a transfer. Courts frequently apply the law of other jurisdictions without any difficulty.)

Another factor favoring transfer was that the plaintiff's mother (the principal witness) resided in Massachusetts and the plaintiffs suffered harm from DES in Massachusetts. As a result, Massachusetts had a stronger interest in resolving this dispute than the District of Columbia. Finally, the court notes that the federal district for the District of Columbia was more congested than the District of Massachusetts, so the District of Massachusetts was more likely to resolve the case quickly.

No single factor is dispositive in this inquiry, but it is fair to say that a court will typically honor the plaintiff's choice of forum (i.e., not transfer the case) unless the factors clearly favor transfer.

Q **3. Chickens and eggs: Jurisdiction as a prerequisite?** Imagine that a defendant moves to dismiss a case on subject matter jurisdiction, personal jurisdiction, and venue grounds. Can a federal court grant a venue-related motion to dismiss without first addressing subject matter and personal jurisdiction?

A In general, the answer is "yes." The Supreme Court has held that a district court can dispose of a case without first determining whether the court has subject matter jurisdiction, but only if the dismissal does not involve a decision on the merits. For example, forum non conveniens dismissals and dismissals for lack of proper venue do not involve a decision on the merits of the case, so a court can grant those dismissals without first determining whether it has subject matter jurisdiction over the case. *Sinochem Int'l Co., Ltd. v. Malaysia Int'l Shipping Corp.*, 549 U.S. 422, 436 (2007). Similarly, the Supreme Court has held that a district court lacking personal jurisdiction has the authority to transfer the case to a district court that has personal jurisdiction over the defendant. *Goldlawr, Inc. v. Heiman*, 369 U.S. 463, 466 (1962).

4. Can plaintiffs move to transfer their own cases? The defendant is usually the party to raise an objection to venue, but a plaintiff can move to transfer as well. *See Ferens v. John Deere Co.*, 494 U.S. 516 (1990). For example, after filing the case in one forum, the plaintiff may discover that crucial evidence and witnesses are more closely connected to a different forum.

5. Pulling it all together. Consider the following multiple choice question.

Prinha (an Arizona citizen) sues Dirk (a New Mexico citizen) after the two are in a car accident in New Mexico. Prinha brings her suit in federal district court in Arizona. Assume that Dirk has never set foot in Arizona and has no contacts there. Also assume that Prinha's claim exceeds $75,000 and that Dirk immediately moves to dismiss the case, asserting that the court lacks personal jurisdiction and is an improper venue. (Arizona and New Mexico each have only one federal district.) A court would most likely

A. transfer the case to the federal district court of New Mexico pursuant to 28 U.S.C. §1404(a).
B. transfer the case to the federal district court of New Mexico pursuant to 28 U.S.C. § 1406(a).
C. dismiss the case pursuant to 28 U.S.C. § 1406(a), because the court lacks personal jurisdiction.
D. dismiss the case pursuant to 28 U.S.C. § 1406(a), because venue is improper in Arizona.
E. dismiss the case pursuant to 28 U.S.C. § 1404(a).

The first step is to determine whether the district of Arizona is a proper venue. If it is, the motion is pursuant to § 1404. If not, the motion falls under § 1406.

Here, venue is not proper in Arizona because the defendant does not reside there and none of the events giving rise to the suit occurred there. Dirk's motion, therefore, must be pursuant to 28 U.S.C. § 1406, which means that **A** and **E** are wrong. E is also wrong for a second reason—§ 1404 does not authorize a dismissal; it only authorizes a transfer.

In contrast, venue would be proper in New Mexico. Under § 1391(b)(1), New Mexico is a proper venue because all of the defendants (i.e., Dirk) are from the same state (i.e., New Mexico), and there is only one federal district in New Mexico. Thus, that district is one in which the case "could have been brought." Moreover, on the limited facts given, the only venue under § 1391(b)(2) where any part of the events giving rise to the claim occurred is New Mexico, because that is where the accident happened. In sum, the only proper federal venue in this case is the District of New Mexico.

The next question is whether the court will transfer the case to the federal District of New Mexico. As noted earlier, district courts have the authority to transfer a case even when they lack personal jurisdiction over the defendant, *Goldlawr, Inc. v. Heiman*, 369 U.S. 463, 466–67 (1962), so **C** is not the best answer.

The remaining question is whether the court will transfer the case under § 1406. Recall that § 1406 instructs a court to transfer a case rather than dismiss it when transfer is in the "interest of justice." As already explained, the interests of justice usually weigh in favor of a transfer because a transfer avoids the time and expense of having to refile the action in the alternative forum. This is true even if the moving party asks only for dismissal. Thus, transferring, as opposed to dismissing, is almost always in the interests of justice in this type of case. That makes **B** a better answer than **D**.

Cutting the Gordian Knot

Parties to a transaction frequently seek to avoid collateral litigation about forum choice by agreeing in advance that suits involving the transaction may or must be brought in a particular state or court. Such "forum selection clauses" are generally enforced if they select a forum that bears a reasonable relation to the parties or their contract. These clauses waive the parties' objections to both personal jurisdiction and venue in the chosen forum. For example, when you sign up for a Google service (e.g., Gmail), you agree to the provision that appears below.

> Google Privacy & Terms
>
> Google Terms of Service
>
> ...
>
> California law will govern all disputes arising out of or relating to these terms, service-specific additional terms, or any related services, regardless of conflict of laws rules. These disputes will be resolved exclusively in the federal or state courts of Santa Clara County, California, USA, and you and Google consent to personal jurisdiction in those courts.

6. Consenting to venue. As discussed earlier, parties can waive an objection to venue during litigation, such as by failing to raise the issue at an appropriate time. But parties can also *consent* to litigate in a particular venue before the dispute even arises. This consent is most commonly given when contracting parties agree to litigate in a particular state or court in the event of a dispute arising from the agreement. Federal courts will usually give these *forum selection clauses* great weight when deciding which court should hear a case as a matter of venue. *See Stewart Organization, Inc. v. Ricoh Corp.*, 487 U.S. 22, 29 (1988). In fact, the courts can enforce these clauses even if they specify a forum where personal jurisdiction would otherwise have been improper. *See Carnival Cruise Lines, Inc. v. Shute*, 499 U.S. 585, 589 (1991). These clauses, therefore, can constitute consent to both venue and personal jurisdiction.

7. Limitations on intrasystem transfers. Although federal district courts can transfer cases *within* the federal court system, there are some limits on this authority. Not only must the transferee court be a proper venue, but § 1404 specifies that the transferee court be one in which the case "might have been brought." The phrase "might have been brought" has been interpreted to mean that, if the case had originally been filed in the transferee court, that court would have been a proper venue and could have exercised both personal and subject matter jurisdiction.

At one time, defendants who wanted to transfer a case to a court that lacked personal jurisdiction or venue argued that they would have consented to personal jurisdiction or venue in the transferee court had it been brought there originally. Thus, they argued that the case "might have been brought" there. The Supreme Court has rejected that argument, concluding that such an expansive interpretation of the phrase would give defendants too much control over forum selection. The Court, therefore, held that the statute is satisfied only if the transferee court could have exercised personal and subject matter jurisdiction without the need for the defendant's consent to personal jurisdiction or venue in that district. *Hoffman v. Blaski*, 363 U.S. 335, 343–44 (1960). A recent amendment to § 1404(a) cuts back a bit on this holding in that it permits a district court to transfer a case to a district that otherwise would have been an improper venue, but only if "all parties" consent to it. In other words, if the plaintiff objects to the defendant's motion to transfer, *Hoffman* still bars the transfer to a district where the suit could not otherwise have been brought. But if the plaintiff does not object to the transfer, § 1404(a) now permits the transfer of the case to such a district.

III. Common Law Dismissals: Forum Non Conveniens

Section 1404 permits a federal court to transfer a case to a more convenient federal venue. The statute, however, does not authorize a court located in a proper venue to *dismiss* a case on venue grounds. Although the statute does not confer this authority, the courts have long recognized their common law power to dismiss such a case under the doctrine of forum non conveniens. The United States Supreme Court reaffirmed this authority in *Piper Aircraft Co. v. Reyno*, 454 U.S. 235 (1981), and clarified when a court should exercise it.

READING *PIPER AIRCRAFT CO. v. REYNO.* Keep in mind that this case moved through three trial level courts. The case was filed in a California state court, was removed to a federal district court in California, and was finally transferred to a federal district court in Pennsylvania. The Supreme Court's opinion focuses on the transferee (Pennsylvania) court's dismissal of the case on forum non conveniens grounds (and the reversal of that dismissal by the U.S. Court of Appeals).

The crux of the case is that the U.S. Court of Appeals for the Third Circuit reversed the forum non conveniens dismissal, relying heavily on the concern that the law of the alternative venue (in this case, Scotland) would be less favorable to the plaintiff than the applicable law in this country. As you read *Piper,* consider the following questions:

- Why have the courts retained the forum non conveniens doctrine, and under what circumstances should a court dismiss a case on forum non conveniens grounds?
- Should the substance of another country's law be a factor when considering a forum non conveniens dismissal? What reasons does the Court give in support of its conclusion?
- Under what circumstances might another country's court system be so inadequate that a forum non conveniens dismissal would be improper?

PIPER AIRCRAFT CO. v. REYNO

454 U.S. 235 (1981)

Justice MARSHALL delivered the opinion of the Court.

These cases arise out of an air crash that took place in Scotland. Respondent, acting as representative of the estates of several Scottish citizens killed in the accident, brought wrongful-death actions against petitioners that were ultimately transferred to the United States District Court for the Middle District of Pennsylvania. Petitioners moved to dismiss on the ground of *forum non conveniens.* After noting that an alternative forum existed in Scotland, the District Court granted their motions. The United States Court of Appeals for the Third Circuit reversed. The Court of Appeals based its decision, at least in part, on the ground that dismissal is automatically barred where the law of the alternative forum is less favorable to the plaintiff than the law of the forum chosen by the plaintiff. Because we conclude that the possibility of an unfavorable change in law should not, by itself, bar dismissal, and because we conclude that the District Court did not otherwise abuse its discretion, we reverse.

I

A

In July 1976, a small commercial aircraft crashed in the Scottish highlands during the course of a charter flight from Blackpool to Perth. The pilot and five passengers were killed instantly. The decedents were all Scottish subjects and residents, as are their heirs and next of kin. There were no eyewitnesses to the accident. At the time of the crash the plane was subject to Scottish air traffic control.

The aircraft, a twin-engine Piper Aztec, was manufactured in Pennsylvania by petitioner Piper Aircraft Co. (Piper). The propellers were manufactured in Ohio by petitioner Hartzell Propeller, Inc. (Hartzell). At the time of the crash the aircraft was registered in Great Britain and was owned and maintained by Air Navigation and Trading Co., Ltd. (Air Navigation). It was operated by McDonald Aviation, Ltd. (McDonald), a Scottish air taxi service. Both Air Navigation and McDonald were organized in the United Kingdom. The wreckage of the plane is now in a hangar in Farnsborough, England.

The British Department of Trade investigated the accident shortly after it occurred. A preliminary report found that the plane crashed after developing a spin, and suggested that mechanical failure in the plane or the propeller was responsible. At Hartzell's request, this report was reviewed by a three-member Review Board, which held a 9-day adversary hearing attended by all interested parties. The Review Board found no evidence of defective equipment and indicated that pilot error may have contributed to the accident. The pilot, who had obtained his commercial pilot's license only three months earlier, was flying over high ground at an altitude considerably lower than the minimum height required by his company's operations manual.

In July 1977, a California probate court appointed respondent Gaynell Reyno administratrix of the estates of the five passengers. Reyno is not related to and does not know any of the decedents or their survivors; she was a legal secretary to the attorney who filed this lawsuit. Several days after her appointment, Reyno commenced separate wrongful-death actions against Piper and Hartzell in the Superior Court of California, claiming negligence and strict liability. Air Navigation, McDonald, and the estate of the pilot are not parties to this litigation. The survivors of the five passengers whose estates are represented by Reyno filed a separate action in the United Kingdom against Air Navigation, McDonald, and the pilot's estate. Reyno candidly admits that the action against Piper and Hartzell was filed in the United States because its laws regarding liability, capacity to sue, and damages are more favorable to her position than are those of Scotland. Scottish law does not recognize strict liability in tort. Moreover, it permits wrongful-death actions only when brought by a decedent's relatives. The relatives may sue only for "loss of support and society."

On petitioners' motion, the suit was removed to the United States District Court for the Central District of California. Piper then moved for transfer to the United States District Court for the Middle District of Pennsylvania, pursuant to 28 U.S.C. § 1404(a). Hartzell moved to dismiss for lack of personal jurisdiction, or in the alternative, to transfer.[5] In December 1977, the District Court quashed

5. The District Court concluded that it could not assert personal jurisdiction over Hartzell consistent with due process. However, it decided not to dismiss Hartzell because the corporation would be amenable to process in Pennsylvania.

service on Hartzell and transferred the case to the Middle District of Pennsylvania. Respondent then properly served process on Hartzell.

B

In May 1978, after the suit had been transferred, both Hartzell and Piper moved to dismiss the action on the ground of *forum non conveniens.* The District Court granted these motions in October 1979. It relied on the balancing test set forth by this Court in *Gulf Oil Corp. v. Gilbert*, 330 U.S. 501 (1947), and its companion case, *Koster v. Lumbermens Mut. Cas. Co.*, 330 U.S. 518 (1947). In those decisions, the Court stated that a plaintiff's choice of forum should rarely be disturbed. However, when an alternative forum has jurisdiction to hear the case, and when trial in the chosen forum would "establish ... oppressiveness and vexation to a defendant ... out of all proportion to plaintiff's convenience," or when the "chosen forum [is] inappropriate because of considerations affecting the court's own administrative and legal problems," the court may, in the exercise of its sound discretion, dismiss the case. *Koster, supra,* at 524. To guide trial court discretion, the Court provided a list of "private interest factors" affecting the convenience of the litigants, and a list of "public interest factors" affecting the convenience of the forum. *Gilbert, supra,* at 330 U.S. at 508–509.[6]

After describing our decisions in *Gilbert* and *Koster*, the District Court analyzed the facts of these cases. It began by observing that an alternative forum existed in Scotland; Piper and Hartzell had agreed to submit to the jurisdiction of the Scottish courts and to waive any statute of limitations defense that might be available. It then stated that plaintiff's choice of forum was entitled to little weight. The court recognized that a plaintiff's choice ordinarily deserves substantial deference. It noted, however, that Reyno "is a representative of foreign citizens and residents seeking a forum in the United States because of the more liberal rules concerning products liability law," and that "the courts have been less solicitous when the plaintiff is not an American citizen or resident, and particularly when the foreign citizens seek to benefit from the more liberal tort rules provided for the protection of citizens and residents of the United States." 479 F. Supp., at 731.

The District Court next examined several factors relating to the private interests of the litigants, and determined that these factors strongly pointed towards Scotland as the appropriate forum. Although evidence concerning the design, manufacture, and testing of the plane and propeller is located in the United States, the connections with Scotland are otherwise "overwhelming." *Id.*, at 732. The real

6. The factors pertaining to the private interests of the litigants included the "relative ease of access to sources of proof; availability of compulsory process for attendance of unwilling, and the cost of obtaining attendance of willing, witnesses; possibility of view of premises, if view would be appropriate to the action; and all other practical problems that make trial of a case easy, expeditious and inexpensive." *Gilbert*. The public factors bearing on the question included the administrative difficulties flowing from court congestion; the "local interest in having localized controversies decided at home"; the interest in having the trial of a diversity case in a forum that is at home with the law that must govern the action; the avoidance of unnecessary problems in conflict of laws, or in the application of foreign law; and the unfairness of burdening citizens in an unrelated forum with jury duty.

parties in interest are citizens of Scotland, as were all the decedents. Witnesses who could testify regarding the maintenance of the aircraft, the training of the pilot, and the investigation of the accident—all essential to the defense—are in Great Britain.

Moreover, all witnesses to damages are located in Scotland. Trial would be aided by familiarity with Scottish topography, and by easy access to the wreckage.

The District Court reasoned that because crucial witnesses and evidence were beyond the reach of compulsory process, and because the defendants would not be able to implead potential Scottish third-party defendants, it would be "unfair to make Piper and Hartzell proceed to trial in this forum." *Id.* at 733. The survivors had brought separate actions in Scotland against the pilot, McDonald, and Air Navigation. "[I]t would be fairer to all parties and less costly if the entire case was presented to one jury with available testimony from all relevant witnesses." *Ibid.* Although the court recognized that if trial were held in the United States, Piper and Hartzell could file indemnity or contribution actions against the Scottish defendants, it believed that there was a significant risk of inconsistent verdicts.[7]

The District Court concluded that the relevant public interests also pointed strongly towards dismissal. The court determined that Pennsylvania law would apply to Piper and Scottish law to Hartzell if the case were tried in the Middle District of Pennsylvania.[8] As a result, "trial in this forum would be hopelessly complex and confusing for a jury." *Id.*, at 734. In addition, the court noted that it was unfamiliar with Scottish law and thus would have to rely upon experts from that country. The court also found that the trial would be enormously costly and time-consuming; that it would be unfair to burden citizens with jury duty when the Middle District of Pennsylvania has little connection with the controversy; and that Scotland has a substantial interest in the outcome of the litigation.

In opposing the motions to dismiss, respondent contended that dismissal would be unfair because Scottish law was less favorable. The District Court explicitly rejected this claim. It reasoned that the possibility that dismissal might lead to an unfavorable change in the law did not deserve significant weight; any deficiency in the foreign law was a "matter to be dealt with in the foreign forum." *Id.*, at 738.

---

7. The District Court explained that inconsistent verdicts might result if petitioners were held liable on the basis of strict liability here, and then required to prove negligence in an indemnity action in Scotland. Moreover, even if the same standard of liability applied, there was a danger that different juries would find different facts and produce inconsistent results.

8. Under *Klaxon v. Stentor Electric Mfg. Co.*, 313 U.S. 487 (1941), a court ordinarily must apply the choice-of-law rules of the State in which it sits. However, where a case is transferred pursuant to 28 U.S.C. § 1404(a), it must apply the choice-of-law rules of the State from which the case was transferred. *Van Dusen v. Barrack*, 376 U.S. 612 (1946). Relying on these two cases, the District Court concluded that California choice-of-law rules would apply to Piper, and Pennsylvania choice-of-law rules would apply to Hartzell. It further concluded that California applied a "governmental interests" analysis in resolving choice-of-law problems, and that Pennsylvania employed a "significant contacts" analysis. The court used the "governmental interests" analysis to determine that Pennsylvania liability rules would apply to Piper, and the "significant contacts" analysis to determine that Scottish liability rules would apply to Hartzell.

C

On appeal, the United States Court of Appeals for the Third Circuit reversed and remanded for trial. The decision to reverse appears to be based on two alternative grounds. First, the Court held that the District Court abused its discretion in conducting the *Gilbert* analysis. Second, the Court held that dismissal is never appropriate where the law of the alternative forum is less favorable to the plaintiff.

The Court of Appeals began its review of the District Court's *Gilbert* analysis by noting that the plaintiff's choice of forum deserved substantial weight, even though the real parties in interest are nonresidents. It then rejected the District Court's balancing of the private interests. It found that Piper and Hartzell had failed adequately to support their claim that key witnesses would be unavailable if trial were held in the United States: they had never specified the witnesses they would call and the testimony these witnesses would provide. The Court of Appeals gave little weight to the fact that Piper and Hartzell would not be able to implead potential Scottish third-party defendants, reasoning that this difficulty would be "burdensome" but not "unfair," 639 F.2d, at 162.[9] Finally, the court stated that resolution of the suit would not be significantly aided by familiarity with Scottish topography, or by viewing the wreckage.

The Court of Appeals also rejected the District Court's analysis of the public interest factors. It found that the District Court gave undue emphasis to the application of Scottish law: " 'the mere fact that the court is called upon to determine and apply foreign law does not present a legal problem of the sort which would justify the dismissal of a case otherwise properly before the court.' " *Id.*, at 163 (quoting *Hoffman v. Goberman*, 420 F.2d 427 (CA3 1970)). In any event, it believed that Scottish law need not be applied. After conducting its own choice-of-law analysis, the Court of Appeals determined that American law would govern the actions against both Piper and Hartzell. The same choice-of-law analysis apparently led it to conclude that Pennsylvania and Ohio, rather than Scotland, are the jurisdictions with the greatest policy interests in the dispute, and that all other public interest factors favored trial in the United States.

In any event, it appears that the Court of Appeals would have reversed even if the District Court had properly balanced the public and private interests. The court stated:

> "[I]t is apparent that the dismissal would work a change in the applicable law so that the plaintiff's strict liability claim would be eliminated from the case. But . . . a dismissal for forum non conveniens, like a statutory transfer, 'should not, despite its convenience, result in a change in the applicable law.' Only when American law is not applicable, or when the foreign jurisdiction would, as a matter of its own choice of law, give the plaintiff the benefit of the claim to which she is entitled here, would dismissal be justified."

---

9. The court claimed that the risk of inconsistent verdicts was slight because Pennsylvania and Scotland both adhere to principles of res judicata.

630 F.2d, at 163–164 (quoting *DeMateos v. Texaco, Inc.*, 562 F.2d 895, 899 (CA3 1977)). In other words, the court decided that dismissal is automatically barred if it would lead to a change in the applicable law unfavorable to the plaintiff.

We granted certiorari ... to consider ... [questions] concerning the proper application of the doctrine of *forum non conveniens.*

II

The Court of Appeals erred in holding that plaintiffs may defeat a motion to dismiss on the ground of *forum non conveniens* merely by showing that the substantive law that would be applied in the alternative forum is less favorable to the plaintiffs than that of the present forum. The possibility of a change in substantive law should ordinarily not be given conclusive or even substantial weight in the *forum non conveniens* inquiry.

We expressly rejected the position adopted by the Court of Appeals in our decision in *Canada Malting Co. v. Paterson Steamships, Ltd.*, 285 U.S. 413 (1932). That case arose out of a collision between two vessels in American waters. The Canadian owners of cargo lost in the accident sued the Canadian owners of one of the vessels in Federal District Court. The cargo owners chose an American court in large part because the relevant American liability rules were more favorable than the Canadian rules. The District Court dismissed on grounds of *forum non conveniens.* The plaintiffs argued that dismissal was inappropriate because Canadian laws were less favorable to them. This Court nonetheless affirmed:

> "We have no occasion to enquire by what law the rights of the parties are governed, as we are of the opinion that, under any view of that question, it lay within the discretion of the District Court to decline to assume jurisdiction over the controversy.... '[T]he court will not take cognizance of the case if justice would be as well done by remitting the parties to their home forum.' " *Id.*, at 419–420 (quoting *Charter Shipping Co., v. Bowring, Jones & Tidy,* 281 U.S. 515, 517 (1930))....

It is true that *Canada Malting* was decided before *Gilbert*, and that the doctrine of *forum non conveniens* was not fully crystallized until our decision in that case.[13] However, *Gilbert* in no way affects the validity of *Canada Malting.* Indeed, by holding that the central focus of the *forum non conveniens* inquiry is convenience, *Gilbert* implicitly recognized that dismissal may not be barred solely because of the possibility of an unfavorable change in law. Under *Gilbert,* dismissal will ordinarily be appropriate where trial in the plaintiff's chosen forum imposes a heavy

13. ... In previous forum non conveniens decisions, the Court has left unresolved the question whether under *Erie R. Co. v. Tompkins*, 304 U.S. 64 (1938), state or federal law of *forum non conveniens* applies in a diversity case. *Gilbert*, 330 U.S., at 509. The Court did not decide this issue because the same result would have been reached in each case under federal or state law. The lower courts in these cases reached the same conclusion: Pennsylvania and California law on *forum non conveniens* dismissals are virtually identical to federal law. See 630 F.2d, at 158. Thus, here also, we need not resolve the *Erie* question.

burden on the defendant or the court, and where the plaintiff is unable to offer any specific reasons of convenience supporting his choice.[15] If substantial weight were given to the possibility of an unfavorable change in law, however, dismissal might be barred even where trial in the chosen forum was plainly inconvenient.

The Court of Appeals' decision is inconsistent with this Court's earlier *forum non conveniens* decisions in another respect. Those decisions have repeatedly emphasized the need to retain flexibility. In *Gilbert*, the Court refused to identify specific circumstances "which will justify or require either grant or denial of remedy." 330 U.S., at 508. Similarly, in *Koster*, the Court rejected the contention that where a trial would involve inquiry into the internal affairs of a foreign corporation, dismissal was always appropriate. "That is one, but only one, factor which may show convenience." 330 U.S., at 527. And in *Williams v. Green Bay & Western R. Co.*, 326 U.S. 549, 557 (1946), we stated that we would not lay down a rigid rule to govern discretion, and that "[e]ach case turns on its facts." If central emphasis were placed on any one factor, the *forum non conveniens* doctrine would lose much of the very flexibility that makes it so valuable.

In fact, if conclusive or substantial weight were given to the possibility of a change in law, the *forum non conveniens* doctrine would become virtually useless. Jurisdiction and venue requirements are often easily satisfied. As a result, many plaintiffs are able to choose from among several forums. Ordinarily, these plaintiffs will select that forum whose choice-of-law rules are most advantageous. Thus, if the possibility of an unfavorable change in substantive law is given substantial weight in the *forum non conveniens* inquiry, dismissal would rarely be proper.

Except for the court below, every Federal Court of Appeals that has considered this question after *Gilbert* has held that dismissal on grounds of *forum non conveniens* may be granted even though the law applicable in the alternative forum is less favorable to the plaintiff's chance of recovery. [Numerous citations omitted.] Several courts have relied expressly on *Canada Malting* to hold that the possibility of an unfavorable change of law should not, by itself, bar dismissal.

The Court of Appeals' approach is not only inconsistent with the purpose of the *forum non conveniens* doctrine, but also poses substantial practical problems. If the possibility of a change in law were given substantial weight, deciding motions to dismiss on the ground of *forum non conveniens* would become quite difficult. Choice-of-law analysis would become extremely important, and the courts would frequently be required to interpret the law of foreign jurisdictions. First, the trial court would have to determine what law would apply if the case were tried in the chosen forum, and what law would apply if the case were tried in the alternative forum. It would then have to compare the rights, remedies, and procedures available under the law that would be applied in each forum. Dismissal would be appropriate only if the court concluded that the law applied by the alternative

15. In other words, *Gilbert* held that dismissal may be warranted where a plaintiff chooses a particular forum, not because it is convenient, but solely in order to harass the defendant or take advantage of favorable law. This is precisely the situation in which the Court of Appeals' rule would bar dismissal.

forum is as favorable to the plaintiff as that of the chosen forum. The doctrine of *forum non conveniens,* however, is designed in part to help courts avoid conducting complex exercises in comparative law. As we stated in *Gilbert,* the public interest factors point towards dismissal where the court would be required to "untangle problems in conflict of laws, and in law foreign to itself." 330 U.S., at 509.

Upholding the decision of the Court of Appeals would result in other practical problems. At least where the foreign plaintiff named an American manufacturer as defendant,[17] a court could not dismiss the case on grounds of *forum non conveniens* where dismissal might lead to an unfavorable change in law. The American courts, which are already extremely attractive to foreign plaintiffs,[18] would become even more attractive. The flow of litigation into the United States would increase and further congest already crowded courts.[19]

The Court of Appeals based its decision, at least in part, on an analogy between dismissals on grounds of *forum non conveniens* and transfers between federal courts pursuant to § 1404(a). In *Van Dusen v. Barrack,* 376 U.S. 612 (1964), this Court ruled that a § 1404(a) transfer should not result in a change in the applicable law. Relying on dictum in an earlier Third Circuit opinion interpreting *Van Dusen,* the court below held that that principle is also applicable to a dismissal on *forum non conveniens* grounds. However, § 1404(a) transfers are different than dismissals on the ground of *forum non conveniens.*

Congress enacted § 1404(a) to permit change of venue between federal courts. Although the statute was drafted in accordance with the doctrine of *forum non conveniens,* it was intended to be a revision rather than a codification

---

17. In fact, the defendant might not even have to be American. A foreign plaintiff seeking damages for an accident that occurred abroad might be able to obtain service of process on a foreign defendant who does business in the United States. Under the Court of Appeals' holding, dismissal would be barred if the law in the alternative forum were less favorable to the plaintiff—even though none of the parties are American, and even though there is absolutely no nexus between the subject matter of the litigation and the United States.

18. First, all but 6 of the 50 American States ... offer strict liability. Rules roughly equivalent to American strict liability are effective in France, Belgium, and Luxembourg. West Germany and Japan have a strict liability statute for pharmaceuticals. However, strict liability remains primarily an American innovation. Second, the tort plaintiff may choose, at least potentially, from among 50 jurisdictions if he decides to file suit in the United States. Each of these jurisdictions applies its own set of malleable choice-of-law rules. Third, jury trials are almost always available in the United States, while they are never provided in civil law jurisdictions. Even in the United Kingdom, most civil actions are not tried before a jury. Fourth, unlike most foreign jurisdictions, American courts allow contingent attorney's fees, and do not tax losing parties with their opponents' attorney's fees. Fifth, discovery is more extensive in American than in foreign courts.

19. In holding that the possibility of a change in law unfavorable to the plaintiff should not be given substantial weight, we also necessarily hold that the possibility of a change in law favorable to defendant should not be considered. Respondent suggests that Piper and Hartzell filed the motion to dismiss, not simply because trial in the United States would be inconvenient, but also because they believe the laws of Scotland are more favorable. She argues that this should be taken into account in the analysis of the private interests. We recognize, of course, that Piper and Hartzell may be engaged in reverse forum-shopping. However, this possibility ordinarily should not enter into a trial court's analysis of the private interests. If the defendant is able to overcome the presumption in favor of plaintiff by showing that trial in the chosen forum would be unnecessarily burdensome, dismissal is appropriate—regardless of the fact that defendant may also be motivated by a desire to obtain a more favorable forum.

of the common law. District courts were given more discretion to transfer under § 1404(a) than they had to dismiss on grounds of *forum non conveniens.*

The reasoning employed in *Van Dusen v. Barrack* is simply inapplicable to dismissals on grounds of *forum non conveniens.* That case did not discuss the common-law doctrine. Rather, it focused on "the construction and application" of § 1404(a). 376 U.S., at 613. Emphasizing the remedial purpose of the statute, *Barrack* concluded that Congress could not have intended a transfer to be accompanied by a change in law. The statute was designed as a "federal housekeeping measure," allowing easy change of venue within a unified federal system. *Id.* at 613. The Court feared that if a change in venue were accompanied by a change in law, forum-shopping parties would take unfair advantage of the relaxed standards for transfer. The rule was necessary to ensure the just and efficient operation of the statute.

We do not hold that the possibility of an unfavorable change in law should *never* be a relevant consideration in a *forum non conveniens* inquiry. Of course, if the remedy provided by the alternative forum is so clearly inadequate or unsatisfactory that it is no remedy at all, the unfavorable change in law may be given substantial weight; the district court may conclude that dismissal would not be in the interests of justice.[22] In these cases, however, the remedies that would be provided by the Scottish courts do not fall within this category. Although the relatives of the decedents may not be able to rely on a strict liability theory, and although their potential damages award may be smaller, there is no danger that they will be deprived of any remedy or treated unfairly.

III

The Court of Appeals also erred in rejecting the District Court's *Gilbert* analysis. The Court of Appeals stated that more weight should have been given to the plaintiff's choice of forum, and criticized the District Court's analysis of the private and public interests. However, the District Court's decision regarding the deference due plaintiff's choice of forum was appropriate. Furthermore, we do not believe that the District Court abused its discretion in weighing the private and public interests.

A

The District Court acknowledged that there is ordinarily a strong presumption in favor of the plaintiff's choice of forum, which may be overcome only when

22. At the outset of any *forum non conveniens* inquiry, the court must determine whether there exists an alternative forum. Ordinarily, this requirement will be satisfied when the defendant is "amenable to process" in the other jurisdiction. *Gilbert,* 330 U.S. at 506–507. In rare circumstances, however, where the remedy offered by the other forum is clearly unsatisfactory, the other forum may not be an adequate alternative, and the initial requirement may not be satisfied. Thus, for example, dismissal would not be appropriate where the alternative forum does not permit litigation of the subject matter of the dispute. Cf. *Phoenix Canada Oil Co. Ltd. v. Texaco, Inc.,* 78 F.R.D. 445 (Del. 1978) (court refuses to dismiss, where alternative forum is Ecuador, it is unclear whether Ecuadorean tribunal will hear the case, and there is no generally codified Ecuadorean legal remedy for the unjust enrichment and tort claims asserted).

the private and public interest factors clearly point towards trial in the alternative forum. It held, however, that the presumption applies with less force when the plaintiff or real parties in interest are foreign.

The District Court's distinction between resident or citizen plaintiffs and foreign plaintiffs is fully justified. In *Koster*, the Court indicated that a plaintiff's choice of forum is entitled to greater deference when the plaintiff has chosen the home forum.[23] When the home forum has been chosen, it is reasonable to assume that this choice is convenient. When the plaintiff is foreign, however, this assumption is much less reasonable. Because the central purpose of any *forum non conveniens* inquiry is to ensure that the trial is convenient, a foreign plaintiff's choice deserves less deference.

B

The *forum non conveniens* determination is committed to the sound discretion of the trial court. It may be reversed only when there has been a clear abuse of discretion; where the court has considered all relevant public and private interest factors, and where its balancing of these factors is reasonable, its decision deserves substantial deference. Here, the Court of Appeals expressly acknowledged that the standard of review was one of abuse of discretion. In examining the District Court's analysis of the public and private interests, however, the Court of Appeals seems to have lost sight of this rule, and substituted its own judgment for that of the District Court.

(1)

In analyzing the private interest factors, the District Court stated that the connections with Scotland are "overwhelming." 479 F. Supp., at 732. This characterization may be somewhat exaggerated. Particularly with respect to the question of relative ease of access to sources of proof, the private interests point in both directions. As respondent emphasizes, records concerning the design, manufacture, and testing of the propeller and plane are located in the United States. She would have greater access to sources of proof relevant to her strict liability and negligence theories if trial were held here. However, the District Court did not act unreasonably in concluding that fewer evidentiary problems would be posed if the trial were held in Scotland. A large proportion of the relevant evidence is located in Great Britain.

The Court of Appeals found that the problems of proof could not be given any weight because Piper and Hartzell failed to describe with specificity the evidence they would not be able to obtain if trial were held in the United States. It suggested that defendants seeking *forum non conveniens* dismissal must submit

---

23. ... Citizens or residents deserve somewhat more deference than foreign plaintiffs, but dismissal should not be automatically barred when a plaintiff has filed suit in his home forum. As always, if the balance of conveniences suggests that trial in the chosen forum would be unnecessarily burdensome for the defendant or the court, dismissal is proper.

affidavits identifying the witnesses they would call and the testimony these witnesses would provide if the trial were held in the alternative forum. Such detail is not necessary. Piper and Hartzell have moved for dismissal precisely because many crucial witnesses are located beyond the reach of compulsory process, and thus are difficult to identify or interview. Requiring extensive investigation would defeat the purpose of their motion. Of course, defendants must provide enough information to enable the District Court to balance the parties' interests. Our examination of the record convinces us that sufficient information was provided here. Both Piper and Hartzell submitted affidavits describing the evidentiary problems they would face if the trial were held in the United States.[27]

The District Court correctly concluded that the problems posed by the inability to implead potential third-party defendants clearly supported holding the trial in Scotland. Joinder of the pilot's estate, Air Navigation, and McDonald is crucial to the presentation of petitioners' defense. If Piper and Hartzell can show that the accident was caused not by a design defect, but rather by the negligence of the pilot, the plane's owners, or the charter company, they will be relieved of all liability. It is true, of course, that if Hartzell and Piper were found liable after a trial in the United States, they could institute an action for indemnity or contribution against these parties in Scotland. It would be far more convenient, however, to resolve all claims in one trial. The Court of Appeals rejected this argument. Forcing petitioners to rely on actions for indemnity or contributions would be "burdensome" but not "unfair." Finding that trial in the plaintiff's chosen forum would be burdensome, however, is sufficient to support dismissal on grounds of *forum non conveniens*.

(2)

The District Court's review of the factors relating to the public interest was also reasonable. On the basis of its choice-of-law analysis, it concluded that if the case were tried in the Middle District of Pennsylvania, Pennsylvania law would apply to Piper and Scottish law to Hartzell. It stated that a trial involving two sets of laws would be confusing to the jury. It also noted its own lack of familiarity with Scottish law. Consideration of these problems was clearly appropriate under *Gilbert*; in that case we explicitly held that the need to apply foreign law pointed towards dismissal.[29] The Court of Appeals found that the District Court's choice-of-law analysis was incorrect, and that American law would apply to both Hartzell and Piper. Thus, lack of familiarity with foreign law would not be a problem. Even

---

27. . . . The affidavit provided to the District Court by Piper states that it would call the following witnesses: the relatives of the decedents; the owners and employees of McDonald; the persons responsible for the training and licensing of the pilot; the persons responsible for servicing and maintaining the aircraft; and two or three of its own employees involved in the design and manufacture of the aircraft.

29. Many *forum non conveniens* decisions have held that the need to apply foreign law favors dismissal. Of course, this factor alone is not sufficient to warrant dismissal when a balancing of all relevant factors shows that the plaintiff's chosen forum is appropriate.

if the Court of Appeals' conclusion is correct, however, all other public interest factors favored trial in Scotland.

Scotland has a very strong interest in this litigation. The accident occurred in its airspace. All of the decedents were Scottish. Apart from Piper and Hartzell, all potential plaintiffs and defendants are either Scottish or English. As we stated in *Gilbert*, there is "a local interest in having localized controversies decided at home." 330 U.S., at 509. Respondent argues that American citizens have an interest in ensuring that American manufacturers are deterred from producing defective products, and that additional deterrence might be obtained if Piper and Hartzell were tried in the United States, where they could be sued on the basis of both negligence and strict liability. However, the incremental deterrence that would be gained if this trial were held in an American court is likely to be insignificant. The American interest in this accident is simply not sufficient to justify the enormous commitment of judicial time and resources that would inevitably be required if the case were to be tried here.

IV

The Court of Appeals erred in holding that the possibility of an unfavorable change in law bars dismissal on the ground of *forum non conveniens*. It also erred in rejecting the District Court's *Gilbert* analysis. The District Court properly decided that the presumption in favor of the respondent's forum choice applied with less than maximum force because the real parties in interest are foreign. It did not act unreasonably in deciding that the private interests pointed towards trial in Scotland. Nor did it act unreasonably in deciding that the public interests favored trial in Scotland. Thus, the judgment of the Court of Appeals is

Reversed.

Justice Powell took no part in the decision of these cases.

Justice O'Connor took no part in the consideration or decision of these cases.

Justice White, concurring in part and dissenting in part.

I join Parts I and II of the Court's opinion. However, like Justice Brennan and Justice Stevens, I would not proceed to deal with the issues addressed in Part III. To that extent, I am in dissent.

Justice Stevens, with whom Justice Brennan joins, dissenting....

Having decided that [a court can dismiss a case even though the other forum will apply law that is much less favorable to the plaintiff], I would simply remand the case to the Court of Appeals for further consideration of the question whether the District Court correctly decided that Pennsylvania was not a convenient forum....

Notes and Questions: Understanding Forum Non Conveniens

1. Rationale for the forum non conveniens doctrine. Why should courts have the authority to grant a forum non conveniens dismissal? Recall that judges lack the power to transfer cases outside of their own court systems, so if a federal court is a proper venue and concludes that a foreign court is a more convenient location for the suit, the judge's only option is to dismiss the case. Section 1404 does not give a district court the authority to dismiss such a case, so the forum non conveniens doctrine fills this statutory gap. Such a dismissal, however, would be unfair to the plaintiff unless the plaintiff can pursue the case in the alternative venue. Thus, a forum non conveniens dismissal is premised on the assumption that the plaintiff can, in fact, refile the case in the foreign venue.

Q **2. Coming to America.** The central holding in *Piper* is that a forum non conveniens dismissal is permissible even when the law of the foreign forum (in this case, Scotland) would likely give the plaintiff a less desirable remedy than the plaintiff could get in federal court. The Court reasoned that a contrary holding would effectively eliminate the forum non conveniens option in federal cases. How would such a holding have had this effect?

A American law tends to be procedurally and substantively more attractive for plaintiffs than the law found in most other countries. Well-known British jurist Lord Denning put it this way: "[A]s a moth is drawn to the light, so is a litigant drawn to the United States." *Smith Kline & French Labs. Ltd. v. Bloch*, 1 W.L.R. 730 (C.A. 1982). That is both colorful and largely accurate. If the Court had restricted forum non conveniens dismissals to cases where the applicable law of the foreign venue was at least as favorable to the plaintiff as American law, federal courts would rarely grant forum non conveniens dismissals.

The Court also explained that a contrary holding would require an American court to understand foreign law well enough to know how plaintiff-friendly foreign law is relative to American law. The Court believed that such a task was unnecessarily difficult and burdensome. Ultimately, the Court held that a federal court should not deny a forum non conveniens dismissal simply because a foreign court would apply law that is less favorable to the plaintiff.

This holding can have unfortunate consequences for plaintiffs. Consider *Gonzalez v. Chrysler Corp.*, 301 F.3d 377 (5th Cir. 2002), in which the court affirmed the dismissal of a wrongful death suit filed by a Mexican family whose three-year-old child was killed by an American car company's allegedly defective side air bag. The court concluded that a forum non conveniens dismissal was appropriate because the private and public interest factors strongly favored litigation in Mexico, where the car was purchased and where the accident happened. Citing *Piper,* the court concluded that the dismissal was warranted even though Mexican law rejected the strict liability claims that the family was alleging and capped damages in this type of case at a meager $2,500.

3. A narrow exception for a "clearly unsatisfactory remedy." The *Piper* Court emphasized that it did "not hold that the possibility of an unfavorable change in law should *never* be a relevant consideration in a *forum non conveniens* inquiry." A dismissal might be improper, for example, "if the remedy provided by the alternative forum is so clearly inadequate or unsatisfactory that it is no remedy at all. . . ."

For instance, in *Rasoulzadeh v. Associated Press*, 574 F. Supp. 854 (S.D.N.Y. 1983), a court denied a motion to dismiss on forum non conveniens grounds because the judge believed that, if the plaintiffs had to litigate their claims in the alternative foreign forum (Iran), they would probably be murdered. That certainly makes the other forum unsatisfactory.

In other cases, courts have denied a forum non conveniens motion if there is no available alternative forum. For example, one court refused to dismiss a claim that could not have been litigated in the other available venue (Canada). Canada only offered an administrative grievance procedure (not litigation) that would have been unlikely to yield any remedy. *National Hockey League Players' Ass'n v. Plymouth Whalers Hockey Club*, 166 F. Supp. 2d 1155 (E.D. Mich. 2001).

The *Piper* Court itself cited *Phoenix Canada Oil Co. Ltd. v. Texaco, Inc.*, 78 F.R.D. 445 (Del. 1978), in which the foreign tribunal might have decided not to hear the case, and there was no codified legal remedy for the contract and tort claims that the plaintiffs had asserted. Absent these kinds of unusual circumstances, however, federal courts will typically be unmoved by the argument that the foreign forum's law is less favorable for the plaintiff.

Q **4. Getting to Scotland.** The Court held that the district court's dismissal was reasonable and that Scotland was an appropriate alternative venue. Given that the federal district court lacks the power to transfer this case to Scotland, how would the case get there?

A After the federal court dismisses the case, the plaintiff would refile it in Scotland. Obviously, it must be legally possible for the plaintiff to bring the case in Scotland, so the defendant has the burden to show that a Scottish forum is, in fact, available.

Q **5. Conditioning forum non conveniens dismissals.** Suppose the *Piper* plaintiffs' claims would be time-barred in Scotland. Does this make the Scottish remedy inadequate and therefore require denial of the forum non conveniens motion?

A Not necessarily. Dismissal is typically granted if the court can avoid prejudice to the plaintiffs by placing conditions on the dismissal. For example, the federal court could grant the motion on the condition that the defendant waive any statute of limitations defense that might exist in the foreign forum. Dismissal, after all, is at the discretion of the trial court, so this sort of conditional dismissal is within the court's authority and is frequently employed. Indeed, the district court in the *Piper* case conditioned its dismissal on precisely these grounds. *Reyno v. Piper Aircraft Co.*, 479 F. Supp. 727, 728 (M.D. Pa. 1979). *See also Restatement (Second) Conflict of Laws* § 84 cmts. c & e (1971) (noting the power of courts to condition forum non conveniens dismissals on the defendant's waiver of statute of limitations defenses).

Although the federal court can condition a dismissal on the defendant's willingness to waive certain objections to suit in the foreign forum (e.g., agreeing to waive a statute of limitations defense), the federal court lacks the authority to order the foreign court to take any action in the case.

6. The familiar forum non conveniens factors. The *Piper* Court's balancing of private and public interest factors should look familiar. The *MacMunn* court employed a very similar analysis when considering a § 1404 transfer.

The similarity is not a coincidence. Prior to 1948, if a case was filed in a proper federal venue but the court believed that the case should be heard in a different federal district (i.e., a case that, today, would be transferred under § 1404), the federal district court had only one option: grant a forum non conveniens dismissal. *See, e.g., Gulf Oil Corp. v. Gilbert*, 330 U.S. 501 (1947). Because § 1404 had not yet been enacted, courts had no authority to transfer these cases.

Congress enacted § 1404(a) so that federal judges could transfer cases directly to another federal district and save the plaintiff the time and expense of refiling the case after a forum non conveniens dismissal. Congress intended for the § 1404 transfer analysis to be roughly the same as the analysis for forum non conveniens dismissals (a weighing of the various private and public interest factors). Congress simply wanted a federal district court to have a less drastic option than dismissal, that is, transfer. In short, Congress intended for § 1404 to give federal judges the option to transfer cases that had been filed in a proper venue, but Congress intended for the analysis (i.e., the use of the public and private interest factors) to be essentially the same as the forum non conveniens analysis that had preceded the statute.

Although courts now use very similar analyses when considering forum non conveniens dismissals and § 1404 transfers, the analyses are not identical. For example, the *Piper* Court observed that Congress intended for § 1404 transfers to occur more easily than forum non conveniens dismissals. Even though the factors are largely the same in both contexts, courts generally require the factors to weigh more heavily in favor of a forum non conveniens dismissal than a transfer before granting a motion. Moreover, when considering a forum non conveniens motion, a court must examine whether the foreign remedy is clearly unsatisfactory. In short, a court's analysis of § 1404 transfers and forum non conveniens dismissals is largely the same, but courts are generally more reluctant to grant a forum non conveniens dismissal.

Q **7. Piper picked a proper venue in Pennsylvania.** Which other proper venues can Piper properly pick?* Why was Piper's pick of Scotland supported by the various public and private interest factors?

A The Court observes that a plaintiff's forum choice is normally accorded great deference, but the choice is afforded less deference when the plaintiffs—such as the plaintiffs in this case—are not from the forum.

---

* Do you have a good nursery rhyme that you'd like to ruin for this book? Send it along to us. If we use it in the next edition, we'll drop a footnote in your honor.

Regarding the private interest factors, relevant evidence was in the United States, such as manufacturing data and designs for the plane and propeller in question. But more of the evidence, such as the physical evidence from the crash (e.g., the plane itself), was in Scotland. Moreover, many of the key witnesses were located outside of the United States and could not be compelled to appear in an American court. Finally, several potential third-party defendants, such as the charter company, could not be sued in the United States, so litigation in the federal court would have led to an incomplete or inefficient resolution of the controversy.

Regarding the public interest factors, there was a possibility that the district court would have had to apply Scottish law to some claims and Pennsylvania law to others. If so, the jury would have been confused, and the court would have struggled to figure out Scottish law. More importantly, the accident occurred in Scotland, and the plaintiffs were either Scottish or English; thus, Scotland had a much stronger interest in resolving this dispute than the United States. Accordingly, the Court concluded that the district court had not abused its discretion in concluding that the private and public interest factors favored dismissal.*

8. Tying it all together. Consider the following multiple choice question.

Dynamo Corp. is incorporated and has its principal place of business in France. Dynamo sells French wine to liquor stores in South Carolina, but the company has no contacts anywhere else in the United States. Perry, a South Carolina citizen, sues Dynamo in federal district court in South Carolina, alleging that he bought Dynamo wine at a South Carolina liquor store and got sick from it because it had been improperly bottled in France. (South Carolina has only one federal district.) Dynamo moves to dismiss the case and asserts that the case should be heard in France. The court would probably

A. dismiss the case under § 1406.
B. dismiss the case under § 1404.
C. transfer the case to France under § 1404.
D. transfer the case to France under § 1406.
E. dismiss the case on forum non conveniens grounds.
F. None of the above is correct.

South Carolina is a proper venue here under either 28 U.S.C. § 1391(b)(1) or (2). Under subsection (2), a substantial part of the events giving rise to this claim—the sale of the adulterated wine and the plaintiff's subsequent illness—occurred in South Carolina.

Under subsection (1), recall that, for venue purposes, a corporation resides in any district where it is subject to personal jurisdiction. In this case, Dynamo sold

* Because of the "abuse of discretion" standard of review, the only issue was whether the district court's analysis was reasonable, not whether the Court would have reached a different conclusion if it had considered the issue *de novo*, that is, anew.

wine in South Carolina, and this case arose directly out of that contact. (Students sometimes think that this case is like *Asahi*, but it's not. The foreign defendant in that case did not sell any goods directly into California, so the contact with the forum was much more attenuated. Dynamo is subject to personal jurisdiction in South Carolina under these facts, assuming, of course, that the South Carolina long arm provisions so provide.) Accordingly, Dynamo would be considered to reside in South Carolina under 28 U.S.C. §§ 1391(b)(1) and (c)(2).*

Given that venue is proper in the District of South Carolina, we can rule out any answer that invokes § 1406, which authorizes transfers of cases that were filed in an *improper* venue. Thus, **A** and **D** are incorrect. **D** is also wrong because a federal court does not have the authority to transfer a case to another country. **C** is wrong for this reason as well.

B is wrong because there is no such thing as a § 1404 dismissal. A federal court can *transfer* a case that is filed in a proper federal venue under § 1404, but if the court wants to *dismiss* such a case on the grounds that the case should be litigated somewhere else, the court must do so using the doctrine of forum non conveniens. That leaves **E** and **F**.

The question, then, is whether the court should dismiss this case on forum non conveniens grounds. It should not. In *Piper*, the plaintiffs were Scottish and English; the accident occurred in Scotland; some of the claims appeared to turn on Scottish law; key witnesses were in Scotland; and a lot of evidence was in Scotland. Scotland was clearly the more convenient location for that lawsuit. In contrast, the plaintiff in this case is from South Carolina, and for that reason alone, the venue choice deserves greater deference. Moreover, the incident occurred in South Carolina, and at least some of the evidence (the adulterated wine) is in South Carolina. This case has a much stronger connection to South Carolina than the *Piper* case did to Pennsylvania. Although some evidence about the bottling would be in France, Perry's medical treatment and diagnosis occurred in South Carolina. Moreover, evidence about Perry's illness and the handling of the wine is in South Carolina, and evidence regarding when and where the adulteration occurred is likely to be in South Carolina. A federal court, therefore, would likely conclude that the various public and private interest factors weigh against a forum non conveniens dismissal, making **F** the best answer.

IV. Transfers and Dismissals in State Court

State courts resolve venue-related transfers and dismissals in much the same way as federal courts. Many state statutes mirror § 1406 and authorize the dismissal of cases that are filed in the wrong venue or authorize the transfer of such cases to proper venues within the state. *See generally Freer* § 5.1. For example, most

* Although the corporation is foreign, it would not be considered an "alien" under § 1391(c)(1) because that provision applies only to "natural persons." Moreover, the corporation is not a "resident" of another country under § 1391(c)(3), because § 1391(c)(2) deems the corporation to be a resident of any district in which it could be subject to personal jurisdiction. In this case, the corporation is subject to personal jurisdiction in South Carolina, so it would appear to be a resident of South Carolina for purposes of § 1391(c)(2).

states allow a county or municipal trial court to dismiss a case that was filed in the wrong venue or to transfer it to another county or municipality in the same state. *Id.*

Similarly, most states have a provision that resembles § 1404, authorizing the transfer of a case filed in a proper venue to a more appropriate venue within the state's own court system. These provisions typically allow a trial court in one county to transfer a case to another proper venue in a different county within the state. *Id.*

Most states also permit forum non conveniens dismissals. *Id.* § 6.2.1. Remember that a state judge can only transfer a case within the state and not outside of it, so if a state judge concludes that a case was filed in a proper venue but should nevertheless be heard in another state or country, the judge's only option is to grant a forum non conveniens dismissal. Some states have codified this doctrine in a statute or rule, *see, e.g.,* CAL. CIV. PROC. CODE § 410.30(a); ILCS S. Ct. Rule 187(c)(2), while many other states continue to rely on the common law for this authority.

Notes and Questions: Understanding State Court Transfers and Dismissals

1. State court options. Consider the following multiple choice question.

> Paulie, a citizen of Illinois, sues Doron, a Minnesota citizen, in a state court in Minneapolis, Minnesota, alleging claims arising out of a business dispute that the two had in Minnesota and Illinois. Assume that venue would be proper in the following courts: the Minneapolis state court where the case was filed; a state court in Duluth, Minnesota; a state court in Chicago, Illinois; and the federal district court of Minnesota. Assuming Minnesota had a statute authorizing each of the options below, which of them would the Minnesota state judge have the power to order?
>
> A. A transfer to the state court in Duluth, Minnesota.
> B. A dismissal on forum non conveniens grounds.
> C. A transfer to the federal district of Minnesota.
> D. A transfer to the state court in Chicago, Illinois.
> E. None of the above.
> F. All of the above.
> G. A and B only.

A is certainly permissible. A state can authorize its trial courts to transfer cases to another court *within the same state.*

D, however, is impermissible. Even if Minnesota passes a statute that permits it, a state court does not have the power to transfer a case to a court in another state. Courts only have the power to transfer a case to another court in the same system.

C is also impermissible. A state court cannot "transfer" a case to the federal court. Although state cases can be removed to federal court, the state court does not initiate that process. Rather, a defendant initiates removal by filing a notice of removal directly with the federal court.

Finally, **B** is permissible. If a case is filed in a proper venue in state court, the court can grant a forum non conveniens dismissal if the judge believes that the case should be litigated in another state or in another country. Minneapolis is a proper venue, so if the judge believes that the case should be heard in Chicago (for example), the judge would have the authority to grant a forum non conveniens dismissal. Thus, **G** is the answer.

V. Challenges to Venue: Summary of Basic Principles

- Section 1406 applies to cases that are filed in an improper federal venue. The statute authorizes a federal court to dismiss such cases or, if it is in the interests of justice, transfer them to another federal district. Federal courts typically conclude that it is in the interests of justice to transfer a case when there is another federal venue where the case could have been brought.
- Section 1404 applies to cases that are filed in a proper venue and authorizes a federal court, after weighing a variety of private and public interest factors, to transfer a case to a more convenient federal district where it might have been brought.
- Federal district courts can transfer cases to other federal districts, but not to state courts or to courts in other countries.
- Parties can waive the issue of venue and usually can consent by a contractual forum selection clause to litigate in a particular venue in the event that a dispute arises.
- Federal courts use the common law doctrine of forum non conveniens to dismiss a case that was filed in a proper venue in favor of a foreign forum that can provide an adequate remedy to a plaintiff (i.e., a remedy that is consistent with basic notions of fairness). When deciding whether to grant a forum non conveniens dismissal, federal courts will apply the same private and public interest factors that they use to analyze a § 1404 transfer motion. In general, however, courts are more reluctant to grant a forum non conveniens dismissal than to grant a motion to transfer under § 1404.
- State courts typically have the power to dismiss a case that was filed in an improper venue or to transfer it to a proper venue in the same state, such as to a state court in another county. State courts also typically have the power to transfer a case that was filed in a proper venue to a more appropriate venue in the same state or to grant forum non conveniens dismissals when the most convenient venue is in another state or country. State courts, however, cannot transfer a case to a federal court or a court in another state or country.

PART V

Pleading

13

Basic Pleading

I. Introduction

Your new client, Paul Pollmer, was hit by a car in a crosswalk in Virginia, causing leg and back injuries that have required extended hospitalization and unpaid medical leave from his job. You know enough Virginia tort law to conclude that Paul has a claim for negligence against David Dupont, the car's driver. You could file such a claim in the local court of general subject matter jurisdiction, or in federal court, if Paul and David are citizens of different states and Paul's injuries, lost wages, and medical expenses exceed $75,000. You elect the federal court because you know the Federal Rules better than the Virginia state rules, and because you want to take advantage of the Federal Rules' generous provision for obtaining information from the defendants (called the "discovery rules"—see Chapters 22 and 23).

But *what* do you file? You would file a *pleading*—a paper containing factual assertions (*allegations*) that support jurisdiction and legal claims in a civil lawsuit. Fed. R. Civ. P. 8(a). The plaintiff's first pleading is called a *complaint*, stating grounds for federal subject matter jurisdiction, a short and plain statement of Paul's *claim* showing that he is entitled to relief, and a *demand for relief*. Rule 8(a).

The defendant's first pleading is called an *answer*, which responds to the factual allegations of the complaint and asserts defenses and sometimes claims by a defendant. Rule 8(b)–(c). If a defendant includes in his answer a claim against the plaintiff (a *counterclaim*) or against a codefendant (a *crossclaim*), then those parties may also file an answer. This normally completes the pleading process.* In most federal cases, therefore, the pleadings consist of a complaint and an answer.

Two parts of the complaint are straightforward. In federal court, Paul must state the grounds for subject matter jurisdiction. Rule 8(a)(1). He must also include a demand for relief, which is often somewhat desperately called a "prayer" for relief. Rule 8(a)(3).

The hardest part of drafting the complaint is stating Paul's claim for liability. The problem is not just finding a theory of liability in the applicable substantive law, but somehow translating it into a sufficient pleading. Historically, the purposes of pleading have been (1) giving notice of the nature of a claim or defense, (2) stating facts, (3) narrowing issues for litigation, and (4) helping the court throw out bogus claims and defenses without the burden of a trial. *See Wright & Miller* § 1202. How much a party has to plead depends substantially on the relative weight that a procedural system assigns to each of these functions.

A system that weighs the first function—notice—over the rest will tolerate fairly skimpy pleading ("Dupont negligently drove his car against me, breaking my leg"), while a system that weighs the second function—fact statement—more heavily will require detailed and specific pleading ("Dupont drove his car ten miles above the speed limit though a red light and hit me while I was crossing with the light inside the crosswalk," etc.). At least until quite recently, the central function of pleading under the Federal Rules of Civil Procedure was giving notice, which suggests that you could state a sufficient claim for Paul with a pretty bare bones statement like the first one above. Rule 8(a)(2) stresses that you need only make a "short and plain statement of a claim showing that the pleader is entitled to relief."

But, even if "short and plain" is easily understood, the rest sounds somewhat circular (you state a claim by stating a claim?) and gives no hint of what "showing" will suffice. Consequently, a defendant often challenges the sufficiency of the complaint to state a claim. An insufficient claim can be attacked in federal court by a defendant's *motion to dismiss the complaint for failure to state a claim*, Fed. R. Civ. P. 12(b)(6), which David is permitted to file before having to answer. (This motion is called a *demurrer* in some state courts.) Thus, most reported federal cases that discuss whether a claim has been sufficiently pleaded arise as rulings on a Rule 12(b)(6) motion to dismiss the complaint for failure to state a claim.

This chapter discusses how to state a claim, as well as how to plead special matters such as fraud or mistake. To understand the requirements for federal pleading, we will begin with a look at its ancestors—common law pleading, equity pleading, and code pleading. We will explore Rule 12 motion practice and answers in the next chapter. But first, consider this basic question.

* A court may allow one further pleading called a *reply* in rare cases when the answers present new facts to which a response would be useful. Rule 7(a)(7).

Q **Where in the rules of civil procedure are the elements of Paul's claim identified?**

A Nowhere. Rules of civil procedure are just that, rules of *procedure.* The elements of Paul's claim(s) are *substantive law,* not matters of procedure. In a diversity case, we would look to state substantive law for Paul's claim, here the Virginia common law of negligence. Federal Rules 8 through 10 regulate *how* you should plead Paul's claim in a complaint in federal court and even the style of the complaint, but Virginia law would determine the *elements* of Paul's tort claim: factual propositions that he must eventually prove to create liability under some applicable substantive law. Thus, for Paul's claim of negligence, Paul would probably have to prove that Dupont had a duty to look out for pedestrians in the crosswalk, that he failed to do so, and that his failure proximately caused Paul's injury.

Every pleading problem in real life therefore starts (after interviews with the client) with research into the substantive law. You cannot know how to state a claim, or whether your adversary has sufficiently stated a claim, without knowing the elements of the claim under the applicable law. Much of the first year of law school is spent teaching you the elements of tort, contract, and property claims and of defenses to those claims. But the substantive law guides human conduct in large part because of the threat that it can be enforced in court. And proper pleadings are the key to the courtroom. Ergo (all Civ Pro teachers agree), Civil Procedure is the most important first-year course.

II. Antecedents of Modern Pleading

No jurisdiction still follows the common law principles of pleading. Indeed, the majority of states now track the federal rules of pleading, and the rest follow rules that reflect many of the same principles as the Federal Rules. But these modern pleading principles cannot be understood without some understanding of their historical antecedents in common law, equity, and early codes of civil procedure.

A. Common Law Pleading

Pleading probably originated in oral exchanges between a complainant and a defendant before feudal or communal authorities. "Johnson stole my cow." "Did not. I paid for it." It must have been hard to keep track when such exchanges continued at great length and escalated in complexity. It is likely that the authorities therefore pressed for relatively short and simple exchanges, permitted to continue only long enough to reduce the dispute to a single issue like "Did Johnson pay for the cow?" *See generally* Henry John Stephen, A Treatise on the Principles of Pleading Civil Actions 37, 147–50 (Tyler ed. 1882). The primary function of this emerging pleading system was therefore to narrow the issues that had to be decided.

When written pleadings were introduced in the fourteenth century, this insistence on "pleading to the issue" was carried forward. At the same time, turf disputes among feudal, communal, and royal courts influenced the content of the pleadings. Plaintiffs in royal courts began their suits by getting a *writ* from the king—an order to the sheriff to compel the defendant to appear in court. For example, a plaintiff who wanted to assert a right to real property would seek a *writ of right.* At first, royal courts had jurisdiction only over some claims, and their writs were limited to such claims. If a plaintiff tried to use a writ for a claim beyond the court's limited jurisdiction, either the court would refuse to issue the writ, or the judge would dismiss the writ when it was challenged. But the royal courts gradually extended their jurisdiction by issuing new writs or simply pushing the envelope of existing writs. *See Shreve, Raven-Hansen & Geyh* § 8.02[1].

Over time, specific writs became associated with specific substantive legal theories of recovery and verbal formulas of pleading. A specific writ, court, and substantive law together would constitute a *form of action,* which came to include specific kinds of pleadings and procedures as well. The early forms of action included trespass, trespass on the case, and assumpsit, forerunners of the substantive legal theories in torts or contract. Some scholars have therefore suggested that procedure actually gave birth to substance rather than the other way around: " '[S]ubstantive law has at first the look of being gradually secreted in the interstices of procedure.' " F.W. Maitland, The Forms of Action at Common Law 1 (1909) (*internal quotation omitted*).

After a writ was issued, the plaintiff began pleading by filing a *declaration,* describing his case in formulaic terms corresponding to a particular form of action. The declaration had to elect a particular set of facts and legal theory of recovery from which any deviation in pleading (*departure*) or in the evidence at trial (*variance*) was fatal to the lawsuit. *See* Benjamin Johnson Shipman, Handbook of Common-Law Pleading §§ 82, 217–29 (H. Ballentine 3d ed. 1923). For example, a judgment for a plaintiff in assumpsit (an action on a promissory note) was reversed because he had pleaded a debt of $2,579.57 in his declaration, but proved a debt of $2,579.57½ at trial! (This makes no cents at all.) "It is a familiar rule of [common law] pleading that the contract must be stated correctly, and if the evidence differs from the statement, the whole foundation of the action fails, because the contract is entire and must be proved as laid," the court reasoned. *Spangler v. Pugh,* 21 Ill. 85 (1859).

Such insistence upon pleading to the issue also imposed a procedural straightjacket on the defendant. The defendant had several mutually exclusive choices. It could *demur* to the declaration, asserting that the plaintiff's allegations, even if true, stated no claim. The demurrer was the forerunner of the modern motion to dismiss for failure to state a claim (and of the motion for summary judgment). The defendant could file a *dilatory plea,* asserting some reason—incidental to the merits—why the court should not hear the case, such as a challenge to the court's jurisdiction. Such pleas, too, have their descendants in motions to dismiss for lack of jurisdiction. Or defendant could respond on the merits with a *plea in bar* denying the allegations in the plaintiff's declaration. One kind of plea in bar has evolved into what we now call a *denial* in the defendant's answer to a complaint. Finally, the defendant could admit (confess) the allegations of the declaration, but plead some new matter as an excuse from liability, by filing a *plea in confession and avoidance*, the forerunner of the *affirmative defense*.

Q **Avoiding a payment due under a contract.** Suppose the plaintiff's declaration states a claim for contract, based on the defendant's failure to pay for music lessons he had received. The defendant, however, was only fourteen when he agreed to pay for the lessons, and under the common law, minors are not liable by contract. How would defendant raise this defense? The defendant cannot in good faith deny that he agreed to pay for the lessons, which would, standing alone, make him liable for the money. Since the declaration does not state his age, he cannot just demur to it either. And the facts give no basis for delaying the suit.

A That leaves just one other alternative. He would "confess" (admit) that he made a bargain for music lessons, but plead "in avoidance" of liability that he was just a minor at the time that the contract was made. Other pleas of confession and avoidance might rest on duress (defendant was forced to do the wrongful act), fraud (defendant was fooled into doing it), license (defendant had a right to do it), or release (plaintiff released his claim in a settlement), depending on the common law. What these kinds of pleas have in common is that they do not dispute the plaintiff's claim; they just offer an excuse why defendant should not be held liable *despite the claim*.

Since a plea in confession and avoidance did not bring the case to a single issue, however, it was followed by a plaintiff's *replication*, essentially asserting one of the same set of responses to defendant's plea. Suppose, for example, plaintiff sued in "trespass" for a battery, and the defendant pleaded self-defense in confession and avoidance ("I did clobber the plaintiff, but he hit me first."). Now plaintiff could respond with a plea denying that he hit the defendant first. In fact, it was not unusual for pleading to proceed through rejoinder, sur-rejoinder, rebutter, and sur-rebutter before the case was brought to an issue—that is, reduced by the iterative process of pleading to a legal question that could be put to the judge or a fact dispute that could be put to the jury. "At the conclusion of this usually protracted and procedurally land-mined pleading process, trial with fact-finding by a jury was often 'something of an afterthought.' " *Shreve, Raven-Hansen & Geyh* § 8.02[1] (internal citation omitted). The system certainly showed what "turning on a technicality" really means, and why law professors and students alike are happy that the days of common law pleading are behind us.

B. Equity Pleading

Not only was the common law pleading system hypertechnical, but the common law was itself often rigid. Sometimes applying it strictly would not produce a just result. In such cases, a person might still turn to her king for justice or *equity*, asserting that she could not get an adequate remedy at common law. The king delegated these requests—called *bills of complaint*—to his chancellor, who handled them in what became known as a court of chancery. Provided that the complainant showed that she had no adequate remedy at law, the chancellor could "do equity" by issuing a decree ordering the defendant to do something or to refrain from doing something, typically an injunction or a decree of specific performance. *See generally* F.W. Maitland, Equity (2d rev. ed. 1936). Even today, one of the requirements a plaintiff must satisfy to obtain an injunction is to show that she has no adequate remedy at law.

The court of chancery developed its own equity procedures. For example, it permitted some discovery of facts by allowing a party to file a *bill of discovery* asking factual questions of the opposing party. It permitted the addition or *joinder* of parties who were needed to do equity, even when they could not be joined in a common law action. In addition, the chancellor tried an equity action by himself ("to the bench"—hence, *bench trial*), often on documentary evidence rather than oral testimony, instead of submitting factual disputes through witness testimony to a jury of citizens. Today, judges—not juries—still alone decide whether to grant equitable relief.

Both the requirement to show the special reasons why equity was needed for a particular series of events, and the availability of bills of discovery, made the equity system more fact-oriented than common law pleading. Equity procedures were important forerunners of modern discovery, joinder of claims and parties, and bench trials. Equity courts have been retained in a few states (Delaware, Mississippi, Tennessee) alongside common law courts.

But even equitable procedures gradually became complex and hypertechnical. Charles Dickens epitomized the worst of the equity system in his account of *Jarndyce v. Jarndyce*:

> *Jarndyce and Jarndyce* drones on. This scarecrow of a suit has, in course of time, become so complicated that no man alive knows what it means. The parties to it understand it least, but it has been observed that no two Chancery lawyers can talk about it for five minutes without coming to a total disagreement as to all the premises. Innumerable children have been born into the cause; innumerable young people have married into it; innumerable old people have died out of it.

Charles Dickens, Bleak House 4 (Bantam Books 1983) (1853).

C. Code Pleading

At first, the colonies and later the states borrowed the English legal system, including the complexities of its common law and equity pleading. But a clamor for reform led to the adoption of a written code of civil procedure in New York in 1848. The New York Code (called the "Field Code" after its principal author) spurred reform in more than half of the states, and codes of procedure are still retained at least in part in more than a dozen (including California, Connecticut, Delaware, Florida, Illinois, Maryland, New York, Oregon, and Texas).

The codes first wiped the slate clean by abolishing common law pleading and the old forms of action in favor of a single form of action, denominated "a civil action." N.Y. Code Civ. Proc. § 69 (1848). Their heart and hallmark was *fact pleading*: requiring the pleader simply to state "facts constituting a cause of action, in ordinary and concise language." Issue-narrowing was no longer the primary function of pleading. Instead, the complaints provided facts and a basis for judges to weed out legally insufficient claims and defenses. Without the emphasis on issue-narrowing, moreover, multiple rounds of pleading were unnecessary, so pleadings were now confined to the complaint, answer, and a reply.

But fact pleading generated two new questions. First, *what* facts had to be pleaded? Some spoke of just "dry, naked, actual facts," *Wright & Miller* § 1202 (internal quotation omitted), which seemed to preclude mere "conclusions of law." But most courts agreed that the pleader should not load up the pleading with evidence either. Instead, she had to skate the line between conclusory allegations (not specific enough) and evidence (too specific). That line proved hard to find. Is the allegation that "plaintiff and defendant mutually agreed" a mere conclusion of law or an ultimate fact? The line was blurred because the distinctions among conclusions, evidence, and ultimate facts are distinctions of context-sensitive degree rather than of kind. *See* Charles E. Clark, Handbook of the Law of Code Pleading § 38 (2d ed. 1947).

Q **The first question. What facts?** The plaintiff in a code pleading state alleges that

> [o]n or about May 5, 1959, and May 6, 1959, the defendants, without cause or just excuse and maliciously came upon and trespassed upon the premises occupied by the plaintiff as a residence, and by the use of harsh and threatening language and physical force directed against the plaintiff assaulted the plaintiff and placed her in great fear, and humiliated and embarrassed her by subjecting her to public scorn and ridicule, and caused her to be seized and exhibited to the public as a prisoner, and to be confined in a public jail.

Defendants file a *demurrer*, arguing that the complaint does not allege facts constituting a cause of action. How should the court rule?

A Even if you have not gotten very far into torts, you can discern that the plaintiff here complains of false arrest and false imprisonment and possibly of assault as well. Moreover, the allegations of "without cause or just excuse and maliciously" seem to be allegations of intent. Assume for the moment that these and the rest of the allegations correspond to the elements needed to state a cause of action (a claim) for false arrest and imprisonment.

Nevertheless, the court sustained (agreed with) the demurrer and dismissed the complaint. In affirming on appeal, the Supreme Court of North Carolina faulted the complaint for pleading "legal conclusions," which "do not disclose *what* occurred, *when* it occurred, *where* it occurred, *who* did *what*, the relationships between defendants and plaintiff or of defendants *inter se*, or any other factual data that might identify the occasion or describe the circumstances . . . ." *Gillespie v. Goodyear Service Stores*, 128 S.E.2d 762, 766 (N.C. 1963) (emphasis in original). But is "maliciously" a legal conclusion or a fact? How would plaintiff comply with these requirements without pleading evidence?

And, more fundamentally, what purpose would it serve? Defendant knows what we know from the complaint—that it has been sued for false arrest and false imprisonment on account of what happened on May 5–6,

1959. It could presumably find out more details by asking its own employees or asking the plaintiff in discovery. The court therefore seems to think that pleading serves not just to give notice, but to spell out the details of the case even before the parties have had a chance to collect evidence.

Les avocats et les plaideurs, by Honoré Daumier (1808–1879)

Scala/White Images/Art Resource, NY

This work bears the following inscription:

> L'avocat—L'affaire marche, l'affaire marche.
>
> Le plaideur—Vous me dites cela depuis quatre ans. Si elle marche encore longtemps comme ca, je finirai par n'avoir plus de bottes pour la suivre!

This is loosely translated as:

> Lawyer: The case is moving forward, moving along quickly.
>
> Client: You've been telling me that for four years. If it moves forward much longer, I won't have boots left to follow it.

The Federal Rules reflect the recurring efforts of reformers to simplify procedure, which too often leaves litigants feeling like the client in Daumier's print. Rule 1 proclaims that the Federal Rules "should be construed, administered, and employed by the court and the parties to secure the just, speedy, and inexpensive determination of every action and proceeding." Fed. R. Civ. P. 1.

Q **The second question under code pleading is what is the "cause of action"?** Under common law pleading, the forms of action sharply defined the contours of an action, but code pleading opened up the question. Was the cause of action only the legal theory specifically identified in the complaint, or did it also include other legal theories that might be supported by the facts alleged?

A Some courts held the pleader to her stated *theory of the pleadings*, denying recovery on any other legal theory even when the allegations or the evidence would support it. In *Jones v. Windsor*, 118 N.W. 716 (S.D. 1908), for example, the plaintiff sued for return of a fee paid to his lawyer, claiming *conversion*—that the lawyer had converted plaintiff's money to his own use. However, because the complaint failed to allege that plaintiff owned the money, the court found that it did not state a cause of action for conversion. On the other hand, if the plaintiff had styled his claim as a contract claim, the complaint would have been sufficient. It does not matter under contract law that the plaintiff did not own the money to begin with; he is entitled under the contract to get it back if the lawyer did not perform. Nevertheless, the court sustained a demurrer and dismissed the action. The plaintiff was thus stuck with his (deficient) theory of the pleadings, even though the same allegations would have supported the alternative—but not pled—theory of contract. Such rigid applications of the theory of the pleadings raised the ghost of common law pleading's insistence on forms of action and on ruthless consistency.

III. The Original Federal Baseline: "Notice Pleading"

The problems with code pleading called for more reform. In 1938, the Federal Rules of Civil Procedure were promulgated for federal courts, abandoning fact pleading in favor of something even more simple: pleading "a short and plain statement of the claim showing that the pleader is entitled to relief." Fed. R. Civ. P. 8(a)(2). By also providing for extensive discovery of facts after pleading, and by authorizing a device for judgment without trial when facts were shown to be undisputed (summary judgment), the Federal Rules made notice the primary function of pleading. Just how liberating these changes were—and how relaxed pleading could be under the new rules—is illustrated by the following complaint and an opinion written by one of the authors of the Federal Rules just six years after they were promulgated.

READING *DIOGUARDI v. DURNING*. Dioguardi was a gutsy, if not yet English-fluent, Italian immigrant who was aggrieved by the loss of "tonics" that he had imported. He filed a complaint *pro se*, meaning without the benefit of a lawyer. The following opinion quotes from Dioguardi's original complaint in part. The district court dismissed, with leave to amend (permission for Dioguardi to try again by refiling an amended complaint), which, as we shall see in Chapter 20, is customary after a court first grants a motion to dismiss. Undaunted, and still also unlawyered, Dioguardi filed the following amended complaint, which was dismissed again. He then appealed, resulting in the opinion that follows the amended complaint.

- Forget that you are a law student and cast aside legal terms of art for a minute. Ask yourself, what is Dioguardi complaining about? What's his gripe? Can you tell?
- Now think like a law student again. What legal theory or theories *does the amended complaint identify* that would entitle Dioguardi to relief on the facts he has alleged? What legal theories does the court of appeals identify that could entitle Dioguardi to relief? Where did the court find them?

UNITED STATES DISTRICT COURT
SOUTHERN DISTRICT OF NEW YORK

JOHN DIOGUARDI	)
Plaintiff,	)
	)
-against	)
	)
HARRY M. DURNING	)
Individually and as Collector of	)
Customs at the Port of New York	)
Defendant	)

Plaintiff, as and for his bill of amended complaint the defendant, respectfully alleges:

FIRST: I want justice done on the basis of my medicinal extracts which have disappeared saying that they had leaked, which could never be true in the manner they were bottled.

SECOND: Mr. E.G. Collord Clerk in Charge, promised to give me my merchandise as soon as I paid for it. Then all of a sudden payments were stopped.

THIRD: Then, he didn't want to sell me my merchandise at catalogue price with the 5% off, which was very important to me, after I had already paid $5,000 for them, beside a few other expenses.

FOURTH: Why was the medicinaly [sic] given to the Springdale Distilling Co. with my betting [sic] price of $110; and not their price of $120.

FIFTH: It isn't so easy to do away with two cases with 37 bottles of one quart. Being protected, they can take this chance.

SIXTH: No one can stop my rights upon my merchandise, because of both the duly [sic] and the entry.

WHEREFORE: Plaintiff demands judgment against the defendant, individually and as Collector of Customs at the Port of New York, in the sum of Five Thousand Dollars ($5,000) together with interest from the respective dates of payment as set forth herein, together with the costs and disbursements of this action.

Figure 13–1: **DIOGUARDI'S AMENDED COMPLAINT***

* This is Dioguardi's amended complaint, which is the subject of the court of appeals' opinion. (We have taken the liberty of showing its allegations in handwriting, although we are not sure whether, by describing it as "home drawn," the court of appeals meant not only that it was written by Dioguardi himself, but also that it was written by hand.)

DIOGUARDI v. DURNING

139 F.2d 774 (2d Cir. 1944)

CLARK, Circuit Judge.

In his [original] complaint, obviously home drawn, plaintiff attempts to assert a series of grievances against the Collector of Customs at the Port of New York growing out of his endeavors to import merchandise from Italy "of great value," consisting of bottles of "tonics."* We may pass certain of his claims as either inadequate or inadequately stated and consider only these two: (1) that on the auction day, October 9, 1940, when defendant sold the merchandise at "public custom," "he sold my merchandise to another bidder with my price of $110, and not of his price of $120," and (2) "that three weeks before the sale, two cases, of 19 bottles each case, disappeared." Plaintiff does not make wholly clear how these goods came into the collector's hands, since he alleges compliance with the revenue laws; but he does say he made a claim for "refund of merchandise which was two-third paid in Milano, Italy," and that the collector denied the claim. These and other circumstances alleged indicate (what, indeed, plaintiff's brief asserts) that his original dispute was with his consignor as to whether anything more was due upon the merchandise, and that the collector, having held it for a year (presumably as unclaimed merchandise under 19 U.S.C.A. § 1491), then sold it, or such part of it as was left, at public auction. For his asserted injuries plaintiff claimed $5,000 damages, together with interest and costs, against the defendant individually and as collector. This complaint was dismissed by the District Court, with leave, however, to plaintiff to amend, on motion of the United States Attorney, appearing for the defendant, on the ground that it "fails to state facts sufficient to constitute a cause of action."

Thereupon plaintiff filed an amended complaint, wherein, with an obviously heightened conviction that he was being unjustly treated, he vigorously reiterates his claims, including those quoted above and how stated as that his "medicinal extracts" were given to the Springdale Distilling Company "with my betting (bidding?) price of $110: and not their price of $120," and "It isnt so easy to do away with two cases with 37 bottles of one quart. Being protected, they can take this chance." An earlier paragraph suggests that defendant had explained the loss of the two cases by "saying that they had leaked, which could never be true in the manner they were bottled." On defendant's motion for dismissal on the same ground as before, the court made a final judgment dismissing the complaint, and plaintiff now comes to us with increased volubility, if not clarity.

It would seem, however, that he has stated enough to withstand a mere formal motion, directed only to the face of the complaint, and that here is another instance of judicial haste which in the long run makes waste. Under the new rules of civil procedure, there is no pleading requirement of stating "facts sufficient to

* [EDS.—We could not find a copy of Dioguardi's original complaint, which the Court of Appeals quotes in the opening paragraph of its opinion. The court then addressed and quoted the amended complaint (reproduced on p. 430) in the second paragraph of its opinion.]

constitute a cause of action," but only that there be "a short and plain statement of the claim showing that the pleader is entitled to relief," Federal Rules of Civil Procedure, rule 8(a), and the motion for dismissal under Rule 12(b) is for failure to state "a claim upon which relief can be granted." The District Court does not state why it concluded that the complaints showed no claim upon which relief could be granted; and the United States Attorney's brief before us does not help us, for it is limited to the prognostication—unfortunately ill founded so far as we are concerned—that "the most cursory examination" of them will show the correctness of the District Court's action.

We think that, however inartistically they may be stated, the plaintiff has disclosed his claims that the collector has converted or otherwise done away with two of his cases of medicinal tonics and has sold the rest in a manner incompatible with the public auction he had announced—and, indeed, required by 19 U.S.C.A. § 1491, above cited, and the Treasury Regulations promulgated under it, formerly 19 CFR 18.7–18.12, now 19 CFR 20.5, 8 Fed. Reg. 8407, 8408, June 19, 1943. As to this latter claim, it may be that the collector's only error is a failure to collect an additional ten dollars from the Springdale Distilling Company; but giving the plaintiff the benefit of reasonable intendments in his allegations (as we must on this motion), the claim appears to be in effect that he was actually the first bidder at the price for which they were sold, and hence was entitled to the merchandise. Of course, defendant did not need to move on the complaint alone; he could have disclosed the facts from his point of view, in advance of a trial if he chose, by asking for a pre-trial hearing or by moving for a summary judgment with supporting affidavits. But, as it stands, we do not see how the plaintiff may properly be deprived of his day in court to show what he obviously so firmly believes and what for present purposes defendant must be taken as admitting. It appears to be well settled that the collector may be held personally for a default or for negligence in the performance of his duties.

On remand, the District Court may find substance in other claims asserted by plaintiff, which include a failure properly to catalogue the items (as the cited Regulations provide), or to allow plaintiff to buy at a discount from the catalogue price just before the auction sale (a claim whose basis is not apparent), and a violation of an agreement to deliver the merchandise to the plaintiff as soon as he paid for it, by stopping the payments. In view of plaintiff's limited ability to write and speak English, it will be difficult for the District Court to arrive at justice unless he consents to receive legal assistance in the presentation of his case. The record indicates that he refused further help from a lawyer suggested by the court, and his brief (which was a recital of facts, rather than an argument of law) shows distrust of a lawyer of standing at this bar. It is the plaintiff's privilege to decline all legal help; but we fear that he will be indeed ill advised to attempt to meet a motion for summary judgment or other similar presentation of the merits without competent advice and assistance.

Judgment is reversed and the action is remanded for further proceedings not inconsistent with this opinion.

Notes and Questions: "Notice Pleading"

1. Dioguardi's "claim." It may take close reading, but you can tell roughly what Dioguardi was complaining about. He imports tonics from Italy. He claims that the Collector of Customs held up a shipment from which some bottles disappeared and the rest were auctioned off to another merchant for less than that merchant bid. Dioguardi is complaining that he should be paid the value of the imports that the Collector took or gave away to the lower bidder. Whether or not this is true, or legally actionable, we can surely figure out what is bothering Dioguardi from his complaint.

2. "Entitled to relief." But it is not enough to state a claim in the sense of a grievance; the Rules require a plaintiff to state "a claim showing that the pleader is entitled to relief." When does a claim entitle a pleader to relief?

A

A plaintiff is entitled to relief only if the substantive law would make the defendant liable on the facts alleged in the complaint. "Jimmy hurt me because he made a bad face" is a claim or grievance, but it does not entitle the claimant to relief under any known law, even if Jimmy did hurt the plaintiff's feelings. A court would therefore grant a motion to dismiss this grievance for failure to state a claim.

Now we immediately see a problem with Dioguardi's complaint: He doesn't identify any substantive law, likely because he didn't know any. He knows he has been injured and he thinks he has "rights upon my merchandise," but he nowhere identifies what those rights might be. In code pleading terms, you might say he has failed to identify *any* "theory of the pleadings."

Q

3. Entitled to relief under what law? Even though Dioguardi identified no law that would entitle him to relief, the court of appeals found two possible theories of liability: one for conversion (doing away with or "disappearing" some cases of tonics), and one for violating 19 U.S.C.A. § 1491 and Treasury regulations promulgated thereunder. How did the court identify these theories, when neither is identified in the complaint and, indeed, both are probably unknown to Dioguardi?

A

The court (most probably some hapless judicial clerk recently out of law school) found them by legal research. The clerk might even remember the theory of conversion from her first-year Property class. She would probably not know a thing about customs law, but the allegations against the Customs Collector would probably lead her to sections of the United States Code dealing with Customs to determine if the law there might entitle Dioguardi to relief. Of course, Dioguardi does not cite § 1491 and the odds are good that he has never seen it, let alone the regulations promulgated under it. But courts can take account of the law regardless of whether the parties know it or what the parties say it is. "Everyone is deemed to know the law" is a tough adage, but surely it is fair to apply it to federal judges.

In other words, in deciding whether the complaint states a claim showing that the pleader is entitled to relief, the court considers not just the law that the pleader specifically invokes, but also *any* applicable law that would entitle the plaintiff to relief. Of course, this doesn't mean that a good lawyer leaves the work of identifying applicable law to the judge and her clerks. In fact, the typical complaint not only separates its claims for relief, *see* Rule 10(b), but identifies and labels them: "Claim One for Conversion," and "Claim Two for Taking of Property by Violation of Public Auction Regulations," or words to that effect. It is primarily the pleader's responsibility to identify the law entitling her to relief, but if the court finds some law that the pleader has not identified that would entitle her to relief, it must still deny the motion to dismiss. By contrast, under traditional code pleading, the complaint had to state "facts constituting a cause of action," arguably placing a greater burden on the pleader to identify its legal theory.

Q **4. The truth of factual allegations.** But suppose that what really happened is different from what Dioguardi alleges in his complaint—perhaps that his actual bid was $100, for example, not $110 (making his the low bid), and no bottles were broken. If the facts are not what Dioguardi alleges, and the true facts would not entitle him to relief under the applicable law, why couldn't the court dismiss his complaint?

A The facts stated in the complaint are not necessarily true; that's why we call them "allegations." But for purposes of the motion to dismiss for failure to state a claim, a court usually *assumes* that the factual allegations of the complaint are true. For this reason, most judicial decisions you will read on motions to dismiss for failure to state a claim start by saying that the facts were drawn from the complaint and *taken as true* for purposes of the motion. These are not necessarily the true facts, nor even facts found by the court, and they may actually be false. But the issue is whether, *if they were true*, they would entitle the pleader to relief under the substantive law. Furthermore, the motion is decided "within the four corners of the complaint." The judge does not look outside the complaint, as she would need to do in order to take the foregoing counter-facts about Dioguardi's bid into account. This makes good sense because a court does not decide factual disputes (or usually, therefore, hold evidentiary hearings) in ruling on a motion to dismiss for failure to state a claim.

Does this mean that the plaintiff can simply allege anything that might state a claim, regardless of the truth? As you might imagine, that would take pleading generosity a step too far; we don't want to facilitate lying by parties in court. And sure enough, there is a rule that we will explore in Chapter 15 that requires a pleader to have "evidentiary support" for factual contentions or suffer a sanction. *See* Rule 11(b)–(c).

Q **5. Disputing factual allegations.** Does the prior question mean that if the Customs Collector disputes Dioguardi's allegations, the government will have to go to trial?

A

No, not necessarily. When the rules simplified pleading, they also authorized a way to challenge factually baseless claims short of trial. The lawyer for the government can have the Collector swear to the facts within his personal knowledge in a written statement called an *affidavit,* and then submit the affidavit in support of the motion to dismiss. (He might swear, "The only bid we received from Mr. Dioguardi was for $100, a true and accurate copy of which is attached hereto.")

Providing an affidavit in support of a motion to dismiss under Rule 12(b)(6) converts it into a motion for summary judgment under Rule 56, to which the court of appeals alludes. As we will see in Chapter 27, if the Customs Collector could show that there is no genuine dispute of material facts and that, on the undisputed facts, he is entitled to judgment as a matter of law, he could then obtain a judgment without need for a trial. Before the court could rule on a summary judgment motion, however, Dioguardi would be offered the opportunity to offer facts to show that there is a genuine factual dispute. (He might submit a counter-affidavit swearing, "I phoned the Collector with a bid of $110.")

This procedure, however, would only determine whether there is a real factual dispute, not decide it. *Any* dispute of material fact would preclude summary judgment and send the parties to trial to try that dispute. But that is as it should be. In our system, we resolve factual disputes by trying them to a fact-finder (either the judge or the jury). It is only when there is no genuine factual dispute that the court can decide the case as a matter of law on the undisputed facts without a trial.

6. "Notice pleading." Some would say that *Dioguardi* was the highwater mark of relaxed pleading, but it was defended on the theory that the chief purpose of federal pleading is to give notice of a claim and not to state facts or to screen factually bogus claims short of trial. His complaint met that purpose — the defendant could figure out what the claim was. Subsequently, the Supreme Court cited *Dioguardi* with approval for "the accepted rule that a complaint should not be dismissed for failure to state a claim unless it appears beyond doubt that the plaintiff can prove no set of facts in support of his claim which would entitle him to relief." *Conley v. Gibson*, 355 U.S. 41, 45–46 (1957). Though the *Conley* Court did not use the term "notice pleading," the courts soon accepted its premise that a bare statement of a claim sufficed under the rules and should be construed generously in favor of surviving a motion to dismiss.

7. Applying the *Conley* standard. Consider the following multiple choice question.

Reread the *Conley* "no-set-of-facts" standard quoted in the last note. Could it possibly mean what it literally says? Which of the following allegations is sufficient to state a claim under the notice pleading standard quoted from *Conley*? Which is best?

A. Plaintiff Paul Pollmer claims against Defendant David Dupont.
B. Plaintiff Paul Pollmer alleges that Defendant David Dupont negligently injured the plaintiff.

C. On August 5, 2010, at the intersection of Wilson Boulevard and Adams Street in Arlington, Virginia, defendant David Dupont negligently drove a car against the plaintiff Paul Pollmer. As a result, plaintiff was physically injured, lost wages, suffered physical and mental pain, and incurred medical expenses of $42,200.

D. Same as C, except that Pollmer now includes a description of the weather, the intersection, all identifiable witnesses to the accident, the license plate and color of Dupont's car, a description of Dupont and the clothes he wore, a list of all of Pollmer's doctors and the dates of visits to them for his injuries, and on and on.

E. Same as C, except that complaint omits the adverb "negligently."

We can eliminate **A** on the sophisticated legal theory that it's just plain silly. Logic says there has to be more than this. But can we say that Pollmer "can prove no set of facts in support of his claim that would entitle him to relief"? On the facts already supplied in this chapter about the intersection collision, he could possibly prove a claim for negligence. *But none of them is alleged in the complaint.* Whatever an overly literal reading of the *Conley* standard could justify, Rule 8(a)(2) itself seems to require more. **A** is as "short and plain" as you can get, but it does not begin to "show[] that the pleader is entitled to relief" or give notice of any facts underlying the claim.

In **B**, Pollmer has at least identified a legal theory, and there are facts under the law of negligence that would entitle him to relief for his injuries. Furthermore, Dupont has "notice" that he is being sued for negligence. Claim **B** omits any facts, but didn't notice pleading replace fact pleading?

Not so fast. When the Federal Rules were first promulgated, they included sample pleadings (called the *forms*), to "serve as guides in pleading." Fed. R. Civ. P. 84 advisory committee's note (1937).* One of those forms was a complaint for negligence that stated the claim as follows (the allegations of jurisdiction and the demand for relief are omitted):

> 2. On ____ *date, at* ____ place, *the defendant negligently drove a motor vehicle against the plaintiff.*
>
> 3. As a result, the plaintiff was physically injured, lost wages or income, suffered physical and mental pain, and incurred medical expenses of $____ [Form 11 (emphasis added) (since abrogated)].

Although "negligently" is completely conclusory, this statement of claim still included facts. It identified time and place and described the plaintiff's injuries. Claim **B** does not. Dupont has no idea from the allegation in **B** where or when he

* In 1948, Federal Rule 84 was added, stating that the forms were "sufficient under the rules and are intended to indicate the simplicity and brevity of statement which the rules contemplated." In 2015, this rule and the forms were abrogated on the rationale that its purpose "has been fulfilled" and therefore the forms were "no longer necessary," although "[t]he abrogation of Rule 84 does not alter existing pleading standards or otherwise change the requirements of Civil Rule 8." Fed. R. Civ. P. 84 advisory committee's note to 2015 amendment; *2015 Rules Transmittal Package*, U.S. Courts (Apr. 29, 2015).

was negligent. Form 11 suggested that "notice pleading" requires *some* pleading of facts. Arguably this is what Rule 8(a)(2) contemplates by requiring that a claim "show" that the pleader is entitled to relief—some facts that, in combination with more conclusory language, might establish liability under some theory of law. **B**, therefore, is insufficient.

C, on the other hand, includes both a theory of liability and a few facts. Sounds like we're there. How do we know? Before the federal forms were abrogated, we knew because this claim slavishly aped Form 11, and Rule 84 told us that the forms "suffice under these rules." Since the abrogation was not intended to alter existing pleading standards, this is presumably still true. And it makes sense: Dupont certainly has notice of what is being claimed, but now he also can trace it to a time and place, which should enable him to identify an event or occurrence.

And yet, Dupont still has no idea whether he hit Pollmer in a crosswalk, drove too fast, failed to keep a lookout, lost his brakes, or whacked Pollmer with a protruding ladder—"negligently" describes a conclusion about conduct, not the conduct itself. This is justifiable for two reasons. First, Dupont will be able to learn more details through the process of discovery. Second, it is possible that Pollmer is himself not sure, at this early stage of the lawsuit. He just knows that Dupont ran him over, not whether it was because Dupont was texting instead of watching the road or because his brakes failed. Requiring Pollmer to plead even more specifically could well prevent him from suing at all, especially when the facts are primarily within defendant's control. So **C** is sufficient.

If the claim in **C** was pleaded sufficiently, it is hard to see how adding more specificity in claim **D** would make it insufficient, but it sure could make it inefficient, transforming a one- or two-page complaint into a prolix fifteen-pager. Dupont learns more about the case, which may help him both with discovery and trial, but the haystack of allegations could also hide the needles; it certainly is harder for a court to sift the complaint's allegations on a motion to dismiss. Under code pleading, this kind of complaint risked dismissal for "pleading evidence." That risk is lower under federal pleading, where even overpleaded "pleadings must be construed so as to do justice," Fed. R. Civ. P. 8(e). But, as a tactical matter, why give Dupont more to work with than necessary?

The answer, in some cases, is that a plaintiff may want to show its hand in the hope of an early settlement or to impress the judge with the strength of the claim. It is hard to see how describing the color of Dupont's car or his clothes would accomplish that goal (or even how they are in any way material to the negligence claim), so although **D** might be sufficient, **C** is the better answer here, at least from a tactical perspective.

Finally, **E** is not as good as **C** because it gives less notice to Dupont. But does it give enough? Dupont doesn't know what theory of liability Pollmer is asserting, yet the factual allegations might support a theory of negligence. In other words, there is an applicable legal theory under which Pollmer would be entitled to relief, provided also that when he drove the car against Pollmer, Dupont did so negligently. Most courts would probably give the benefit of a doubt to Pollmer under the *Conley* standard and find **E** sufficient.

Q **8. Hindsight is 20/20.** On remand, Dioguardi ultimately went to trial and lost. The government established that "the goods destroyed were done so according to law when they showed signs of spoiling and that the bid accepted was actually the highest bid received." *Dioguardi v. Durning*, 151 F.2d 501, 502 (2d Cir. 1945). "It is clear," the court of appeals commented in affirming the judgment against Dioguardi, "that his lively sense of injustice is not properly directed against the customs officials, and that his grievance is against the vendor in Italy, whose charges against the goods he refused to pay at the outset, thereby precipitating the chain of events leading to the present futile suit." *Id.* Does the ultimate futility of the suit mean that the district court's original dismissal for failure to state a claim was correct after all?

A No. A Rule 12(b)(6) motion does not ask a court to rule on whether Dioguardi will ultimately win or lose; it asks only whether he has stated a claim sufficiently to go forward. The Rule 12(b)(6) motion is effectively a gatekeeper, but not a very strict one. It can let unmeritorious claims through as well as meritorious ones. The exception is a claim that is *so* unmeritorious that, assuming its factual allegations to be true, it would still not entitle the pleader to relief on *any* legal theory.

Dioguardi would have been entitled to relief if his claims (generously construed) were true. So he was properly permitted to go through the gates and given his chance to prove his case at trial. He just couldn't. The pleading rules, after all, are not just intended to give notice to the defendant, but also to give the plaintiff a fair chance to have his claim heard.

This answer highlights the fact that the federal pleading standard—at least under the generous *Conley* standard of notice pleading—no longer did much work screening frivolous cases (i.e., giving the courts a tool to dismiss them). Instead, other procedural devices under the Rules, such as summary judgment or, as we will see in Chapter 29, judgment as a matter of law, have been assigned that role. But it would be a mistake to conclude that a Rule 12(b)(6) motion is therefore a wasted motion. Recall that the district court in *Dioguardi* dismissed Dioguardi's original complaint, which led him to submit an amended complaint that gave better notice to the defendant. In other cases, a Rule 12(b)(6) motion succeeds in weeding out a few claims even if it does not knock out the whole lawsuit. And its *in terrorem* effect may well be to make plaintiffs plead more fully and specifically than the minimum that the rules require.

Q **9. May Dioguardi plead inconsistently?** One way to read Dioguardi's complaint is that he alleges both that the Customs Collector lost or destroyed the tonic, and that he auctioned it off. But it has to be one or the other, doesn't it? If the Collector lost or destroyed the tonic, how could he have auctioned it off? At common law, such arguably inconsistent pleading was disallowed, subjecting the plaintiff's declaration to a demurrer. Does inconsistent pleading also require dismissal for failure to state a claim under the Federal Rules?

A No, as long as a claim would entitle the plaintiff to relief under the applicable law, it should not be dismissed. Here, *either* claim could entitle Dioguardi to relief.

The real objection here is that both cannot be true, so one is false. We have seen that the Rule 12(b)(6) motion is not used to dispute the facts, but how can we assume that two mutually contradictory allegations are true?

A

We can if we treat them *alternatively. Either* the Customs Collectors lost the tonic *or* he had it, but auctioned it off. Dioguardi did not say this, but Rule 8(d)(2) expressly permits pleading alternatively or hypothetically and states that "[i]f a party makes alternative statements, the pleading is sufficient if any one of them is sufficient." And Rule 8(d)(3) expressly permits inconsistent claims, as long as the pleader reasonably and in good faith believes that either might have evidentiary support. *See* Fed. R. Civ. P. 11(b) (setting out care and candor requirements for pleading, which we will discuss in detail in a later chapter).

10. When are alternative theories impermissible?

Suppose plaintiff's spouse, Pierre, was killed in an automobile accident five minutes after he had the last of several drinks at a bar. Plaintiff sues both the other driver (for speeding) and the bar owner (for serving Pierre so many drinks that Pierre was drunk at the time of the accident). Plaintiff also pleads that Pierre was not negligent in causing the accident, because his contributory negligence would bar her recovery from the other driver. Under applicable law, a driver who is legally drunk at the time of an accident is contributorily negligent *per se*. Which of the following is correct, in light of Rule 8(d)?

A. The court may dismiss the complaint for factual inconsistency. *Either* Pierre was drunk at the time of the accident *or* he was not.
B. The complaint is sufficient, but the plaintiff should be sanctioned for lying.
C. The complaint is sufficient, but at trial, the plaintiff must pick which theory the jury is permitted to consider before the case is submitted to the jury.
D. The complaint is sufficient and both theories can be submitted to the jury, but if the jury returns a logically inconsistent verdict against *both* the other driver and the bar owner, the court must set it aside

The complaint *is* inconsistent, but in federal court (and most, if not all, state courts), that is not a basis for dismissal. Rule 8(d)(2) expressly permits pleading in the alternative, and Rule 8(d)(3) expressly permits inconsistent claims. At the *pleading* stage of this lawsuit, therefore, there is no error. **A** is incorrect.

B is more troubling, because your intuitive sense of ethics (we hope) should raise a red flag about lying to a court in any form. Yet, it is important to realize that the plaintiff often does not know at the pleading stage which alternative is correct. Pierre's widow wasn't in the accident or at the bar, so she has no personal knowledge of what happened (though she may have a well-founded suspicion that Pierre had one too many on the way home from work). Even if she has learned that he stopped at the bar for a drink, it is possible that he had one too many, and it is also possible that he left the bar in a sober state. The bartender would know more; and an autopsy might also shed light on the questions. She could truthfully and in good faith plead alternatively, in the hope that later discovery of the facts (by questioning the bartender or ordering the autopsy report) might settle the issue.

The same rationale allows the victim of a hunting accident to plead claims against two hunters alternatively in the same complaint, when she doesn't know which of them fired the shot that hit her. We'll see that Rule 11 requires a reasonable pre-filing inquiry into the facts by the pleader, which may settle these kinds of questions *before* the pleading is filed, but if the inquiry does not do so, neither ethics nor the Federal Rules of Civil Procedure preclude pleading alternatively. **B** is not correct.

Pierre's widow may develop evidence that Pierre had a few at the defendant's bar, but that evidence may not show how many or, more important, that the bartender knew how many. The evidence, in other words, is unclear as to whether the bartender served Pierre one too many, or whether Pierre was sufficiently in command of his senses to be free of contributory negligence in the crash. That is a fact issue for the jury. Pierre's spouse is entitled to have the dispute submitted to the jury as long as there is enough evidence from which they could find one or the other. So **C** is not correct either. Of course, whether Pierre's widow would *want* to submit inconsistent theories to the jury is a tactical question for her and her lawyer.

Once the jury deliberates, however, it cannot find *both* that Pierre had one too many *and* that he was sober enough to be free of contributory negligence. The jury is charged with *deciding* factual disputes. It must decide one way or the other. If it decides both, given that being legally drunk is negligence *per se* under the applicable law, then the verdict is internally inconsistent and can be set aside for a new trial. The technicalities of challenging jury verdicts are complicated and will be taken up in Chapter 31. The point here is that by this late stage of the lawsuit, we no longer tolerate keeping multiple balls in the air. **D** is the best answer, and a new trial should probably be ordered to allow a new jury to decide.

In short, pleading in the alternative is expressly permitted by the Rules and often practically necessary at the front of a lawsuit, before a plaintiff has had the chance to take discovery. On the other hand, alleging an alternative that you *know* is false is never permitted. Consider, for example, how the answer to **B** would change if Pierre survived the crash and told his lawyer that he got drunk at the bar.

Q **11. The form of pleadings.** Suppose Dioguardi's original "home drawn" complaint contained only one run-on paragraph and no identified claims. Does this make the complaint vulnerable to a 12(b)(6) motion?

A Rule 10(b) addresses the "form of pleadings" and requires numbered paragraphs, each limited as far as possible to a single set of circumstances. Though it does not require the identification of claims, it urges that each claim should be stated in a separate count when "doing so would promote clarity." Dioguardi's original complaint as described fails both requirements, although his amended complaint did number the paragraphs.

Yet dismissing a complaint that is comprehensible just because it does not number the paragraphs or separate claims would elevate form over substance, resurrecting the kind of technicality that eventually besmirched common law pleading. The drafters of the rules knew this and therefore took pains to stress that "[p]leadings must be construed so as to do justice." Fed. R. Civ. P. 8(e). Small errors of *form* are unlikely to be fatal; indeed, it could well be reversible error for a court to penalize the pleader for minor errors. That said, how hard is it to use the right form?

READING *DOE v. SMITH.* *Dioguardi* is instructive, but eccentric, *pro se*, and dated. The following complaint and decision provides a more modern example of "notice pleading" and a forgiving application of the *Conley* standard. A federal statute provides that:

> [A]ny person whose wire, oral, or electronic communication is intercepted, disclosed, or intentionally used in violation of this chapter may in a civil action recover from the person or entity, other than the United States, which engaged in that violation such relief as may be appropriate.

18 U.S.C. § 2520(a).

- What is the applicable law by which the court measures whether Doe's federal claim would entitle her to relief?
- Doe alleges neither "interception" nor that Smith's conduct was in "interstate commerce," which are the predicates for the federal claim. How, then, are these elements of her federal claim satisfied?

UNITED STATES DISTRICT COURT
CENTRAL DISTRICT OF ILLINOIS

Jane DOE, Plaintiff,	)	
	)	
v.	)	No. 04-3173
	)	
Jason SMITH, Defendant.	)	

COMPLAINT . . .

NOW COMES the Plaintiff, JANE DOE, by and through her attorneys, . . . and for her Complaint pursuant to 18 U.S.C. Section 2520 and [28] U.S.C. Section 1367 against Defendant, JASON SMITH, states as follows:

ALLEGATIONS COMMON TO ALL COUNTS

1. Plaintiff, Jane Doe, was born XX/XX/1985 and is presently 18 years of age. At the time of the occurrence set forth in said Complaint, Plaintiff, Jane Doe, was a minor 16 years old.

2. Upon knowledge and belief, the Defendant, Jason Smith, is 19 years of age and at the time of the occurrence set forth in said Complaint was a minor approximately 17 years old.

3. The Plaintiff, Jane Doe, is a resident of Springfield, County of Sangamon, State of Illinois.

4. The Defendant, Jason Smith, is a resident of Springfield, County of Sangamon, State of Illinois and at the time of the occurrence set forth herein Defendant was a student at Springfield High School, Springfield, Illinois.

5. During the school year of 2002–2003 Plaintiff and Defendant were engaged in a dating relationship.

6. During the months of 2002, Plaintiff and Defendant had occasion to go to Defendant, Jason Smith's, home and engaged in sexual intimacy in the privacy of Defendant's bedroom at said residence.

7. During the spring of 2002, Defendant, while engaging in sexual intimacy with the Plaintiff, covertly and surreptitiously recorded said acts with a video camera recorder.

8. Plaintiff did not consent to, authorize, ratify, give permission for or have knowledge of being videotaped.

9. Defendant never informed Plaintiff he was videotaping her during the parties' period of sexual intimacy.

10. Shortly after the occurrence, for unrelated reasons, the Plaintiff and Defendant ended their dating relationship.

11. That during the spring of 2002, Defendant, Jason Smith, without the consent, authority, permission or knowledge of Plaintiff, Jane Doe, published said video camera recording to fellow students of Springfield High School, in the City of Springfield, County of Sangamon, State of Illinois.

12. On May 2003, Plaintiff was notified of the existence of the videotape and that Defendant had published it to other persons.

13. In May 20, 2003, Plaintiff confronted Defendant regarding the existence of said video camera recording, whereupon Defendant admitted the existence of said recording and that he had published it to other persons without the consent, authority, permission or knowledge of Plaintiff.

14. Defendant claims he destroyed the video camera recording.

15. That pursuant to 13 U.S.C. § 1367, supplemental jurisdiction, plaintiffs Jane Doe's state law claims are properly before this Court.

COUNT I

18 U.S.C. SECTION 2520

WIRE AND ELECTRONIC COMMUNICATIONS INTERCEPTION AND INTERCEPTION OF ORAL COMMUNICATIONS

As and for her first cause of action against Defendant, Jason Smith, Plaintiff, Jane Doe, states as follows:

1–14. Plaintiff repeats and realleges paragraph 1 through 14 of the Allegations Common to all Counts as paragraphs 1 through 14 of Count I as though fully set forth herein.

15. That pursuant to 18 U.S.C. Section 2520, any person whose wire, oral or electronic communication is intercepted, disclosed or intentionally used in violation of this Chapter

may in a civil action recover from the person or entity other than the United States, which engaged in that violation such relief as may be appropriate.

16. That Defendant JASON SMITH'S covert video camera recording of the Plaintiff, JANE DOE, constitutes an intentional disclosure within the meeting of 18 U.S.C. S. [sic] Section 2520.

17. As a result of Defendant, JASON SMITH'S intentional disclosure of the video camera recording, Plaintiff, JANE DOE, has suffered and continues to suffer extreme emotional distress, embarrassment and humiliation. As a result of the aforementioned intentional acts, Plaintiff has retracted from her social and community relationships.

WHEREFORE, pursuant to 18 U.S.C. 2520, Plaintiff, JANE DOE, prays this Honorable Court grant the following relief:

(a) Pursuant to 18 U.S.C. Section 2520, enter a judgment in an amount in excess of $50,000.00 sufficient to compensate Plaintiff for her injuries.

(b) Enter a judgment for punitive damages in an amount adequate to punish and restrain further violation of the Act.

(c) Enter a judgment in an amount sufficient to pay Plaintiff's reasonable attorneys' fees and other litigation costs reasonable incurred.

COUNT II

720 ILCS 5/14-2

EAVESDROPPING ...

COUNT III

INTENTIONAL INFLICTION OF EMOTIONAL DISTRESS ...

COUNT IV

INVASION OF PRIVACY ...

COUNT V

720 ILCS 5/12–1

BATTERY ...

PLAINTIFF DEMANDS TRIAL BY JURY

Respectfully submitted,
[Signature and address of plaintiff's attorney]

DOE v. SMITH

429 F.3d 706 (7th Cir. 2005)

Easterbrook, Circuit Judge.

... Doe and Smith are citizens of Illinois, so the litigation is in federal court only because one of her claims is that the video recording is an unauthorized interception and its disclosure forbidden by the federal wiretapping statute, 18 U.S.C. §§ 2510–22. Yet the district court dismissed the suit under Fed. R. Civ. P. 12(b)(6), ruling that Doe's complaint is defective because it does not allege in so many words that the recording was an "interception" within the meaning of § 2510(4).

The complaint does not maintain that Smith "intercepted" anything. Yet pleadings in federal court need not allege facts corresponding to each "element" of a statute. It is enough to state a claim for relief—and Fed. R. Civ. P. 8 departs from the old code-pleading practice by enabling plaintiffs to dispense with the need to identify, and plead specifically to, each ingredient of a sound legal theory. *See, e.g., Swierkiewicz v. Sorema N.A.,* 534 U.S. 506 (2002). Plaintiffs need not plead facts; they need not plead law; they plead claims for relief. Usually they need do no more than narrate a grievance simply and directly, so that the defendant knows what he has been accused of. Doe has done that; it is easy to tell what she is complaining about. Any district judge (for that matter, any defendant) tempted to write "this complaint is deficient because it does not contain ..." should stop and think: What rule of law *requires* a complaint to contain that allegation? Rule 9(b) has a short list of things that plaintiffs must plead with particularity, but "interception" is not on that list.

Complaints initiate the litigation but need not cover everything necessary for the plaintiff to win; factual details and legal arguments come later. A complaint suffices if any facts consistent with its allegations, and showing entitlement to prevail, could be established by affidavit or testimony at a trial. *See, e.g., Conley v. Gibson,* 355 U.S. 41 (1957). The consistency proviso is why some complaints may be dismissed pronto: litigants may plead themselves out of court by alleging facts that defeat recovery. Complaints also may be dismissed when they show that the defendant did no wrong. For example, a complaint alleging that a sports team violated the antitrust laws by restricting peanut sales on the stadium's grounds is defective because the antitrust laws do not entitle one person to sell goods on someone else's property. Doe has not pleaded herself out of court; none of the complaint's allegations shows that Smith is sure to succeed. The complaint does not say, for example, that she consented to the recording. Doe will have to prove some facts that she did not plead, but that's common. Nor is her claim legally deficient. To see this one has only to step through the statute.

The prohibitions bearing on Doe's allegations are in § 2511(1):

> (1) Except as otherwise specifically provided in this chapter any person who—
>
> (a) intentionally intercepts, endeavors to intercept, or procures any other person to intercept or endeavor to intercept, any wire, oral, or electronic communication;
>
> ...

(c) intentionally discloses, or endeavors to disclose, to any other person the contents of any wire, oral, or electronic communication, knowing or having reason to know that the information was obtained through the interception of a wire, oral, or electronic communication in violation of this subsection; . . .

. . . shall be subject to suit as provided in subsection (5).

The first question is whether Doe could show, without contradicting any of the complaint's allegations, that Smith captured a "wire, oral, or electronic communication." The answer is yes. Doe may be able to establish that the recording had a sound track and that she had an expectation of privacy, the two ingredients of the statutory definition: " 'oral communication' means any oral communication uttered by a person exhibiting an expectation that such communication is not subject to interception under circumstances justifying such expectation, but such term does not include any electronic communication." 18 U.S.C. § 2510(2). A silent film would be outside this definition, but most video recorders capture sound as well.

Next comes the question whether Smith "intercepted" the oral communication. This defined term "means the aural or other acquisition of the contents of any wire, electronic, or oral communication through the use of any electronic, mechanical, or other device." 18 U.S.C. § 2510(4). If Doe and Smith engaged in "oral communication" in Smith's bedroom, then its acquisition by a video recorder—an "electronic . . . device"—is covered. And if the interception was forbidden by § 2511(1)(a), then its disclosure was forbidden by § 2511(1)(c).

Liability generally requires proof that the interception or disclosure occurred in or through the means of interstate commerce, such as the telephone network. A home taping followed by a viewing at the local high school does not seem connected to interstate or international commerce. But if as plaintiff suspects Smith dispatched copies by email, which uses the interstate communications network, then the problem is solved. Smith contends that, if a link to interstate commerce cannot be shown, or if Doe relies on a subsection under which it need not be shown, then the statute is unconstitutional. That gets ahead of the game; there is no need to reach constitutional questions before we know what Doe will be able to demonstrate. Moreover, if Smith wants to call the constitutionality of this statute into question, then he must alert the district court and arrange for notice to be given to the Attorney General, so that the federal government may intervene to defend the legislation. *See* 28 U.S.C. § 2403(a); Fed. R. Civ. P. 25(c). **[Eds.—The relevant rule is now Rule 24(b)(2).]** That has not been done.

The statute provides some defenses, such as consent. Any one private participant's consent usually suffices. 18 U.S.C. § 2511(2)(d). Smith obviously consented to the recording, but that does not justify dismissing the suit. Complaints need not anticipate or attempt to defuse potential defenses. What's more, the defense of single-party consent has limits. The full text of this subsection reads:

> It shall not be unlawful under this chapter for a person not acting under color of law to intercept a wire, oral, or electronic communication where such person is a party to the communication or where one of the parties to the communication has given prior consent to such interception unless such communication is

> intercepted for the purpose of committing any criminal or tortious act in violation of the Constitution or laws of the United States or of any State.

Doe may be able to show that Smith made the recording "for the purpose of committing any criminal or tortious act"—for example, the creation of child pornography, or the intentional infliction of emotional distress. Doe presented several claims under state law; the district court relinquished supplemental jurisdiction without deciding whether any of these theories is tenable. *See* 28 U.S.C. § 1367(c)(3).* Success on one of the state-law theories would prevent Smith from using the defense under § 2511(2)(d). Because the state and federal issues are intertwined, both should be resolved in federal court. . . .

The judgment is reversed, and the case is remanded for further proceedings consistent with this opinion.

Notes and Questions: *Doe v. Smith*

Q **1. Elements of the federal claim.** The elements of the federal claim are set out with uncommon clarity in the statute (except the requirement that the conduct be in interstate commerce, which is apparently a judicial gloss on the statute). The statutory elements thus provide a measuring rod for whether Doe has stated a claim (as well as a guidepost for her lawyer in framing the complaint). Some courts have gone so far as to require that "a complaint ... must contain either direct or inferential allegations respecting *all* the material elements necessary to sustain a recovery under *some* viable legal theory." *In re Plywood Antitrust Litig.*, 655 F.2d 627, 641 (5th Cir. 1981) (first emphasis supplied). This is certainly good practice, but do the rules *require* a pleader to plead allegations respecting each and every element (often called pleading a *prima facie* claim)?

A The court of appeals in *Doe* says no, ascribing any rigid elements-pleading requirement to the discarded rules of code pleading. The court cited *Swierkiewicz v. Sorema, N.A.*, 534 U.S. 506 (2002), in which the Supreme Court held that a plaintiff need not plead facts establishing a *prima facie* employment discrimination claim. Rule 8(a) requires Doe only to plead a "claim," as Dioguardi did, sufficient to let Smith know what she is complaining about. Her complaint leaves no doubt on that score.

Nevertheless, the court of appeals ends up searching the complaint for allegations respecting the statutory elements of Doe's claim. Even though it denies that a complaint *must* plead allegations respecting all the elements, its actual analysis certainly encourages elements-pleading.

---

* [Eds.—As we will see in Chapter 20, a federal court may hear state law claims even absent diversity, if they arise from the same transaction as a federal claim, but it does not have to.]

Q **2. Inferring the elements.** Did Doe plead the elements of the federal claim, a statutory tort? Consider the following questions to explore her complaint.

A. Suppose Doe pleads that Smith told his friends that Doe and he had had sexual relations. Would this complaint suffice?

A No, because it would not allege that Doe had "intercept[ed]" anything, or told anyone of information "obtained through the interception. . . ." 18 U.S.C. §§ 2511(1)(a) & (c). Indeed, the statutory provision is titled "*Interception* and disclosure of wire, oral, or electronic communications prohibited" (emphasis added). Telling people about your intimate sexual relations is indiscrete and unclassy, but it does not violate the statute. If that's all Doe pleaded, her § 2520 claim should be dismissed.

B. Suppose Doe pleads that Smith photographed their acts with a film camera. Would this complaint suffice?

A No. The statute requires the information that is obtained to be "the contents of *any wire, electronic, or oral* communication" (emphasis added). Doe has not alleged that any *communication* was obtained, just pictures, since an old film camera does not record sounds. This seems like an odd statutory omission, until you realize that the statute was aimed primarily at wiretaps and other eavesdropping, not hidden cameras.

C. Doe expressly pleaded neither "interception" as such, nor the capture of a "wire, electronic, or oral communication," and the district court dismissed for the former omission. Why did the court of appeals conclude that Doe had adequately pleaded interception?

A The court of appeals notes that paragraph 7 of the complaint alleges that Smith recorded their acts with a video camera recorder. It reasons that most video camera recorders capture sounds as well as pictures. Furthermore, "interception" is defined by the statute as the "aural or other acquisition of the contents of any . . . oral communication through the use of any electronic, mechanical, or other device." 18 U.S.C. § 2510(4). Clearly, a video camera recorder is at least an "other," if not an "electronic," device. Thus, though Doe never uses the word "interception" or alleges that Smith recorded their sounds, the court infers these elements from what she does plead.

To put it differently, Doe does not plead "interception" "in so many words," but Rule 8(a) does not require so many words, just enough to give notice of the claim and to hold out the possibility of liability under some law—here the statute. Under the *Conley* regime, even courts that have required elements-pleading have usually found that the elements could be stated directly *or* by implication.

D. Congress's regulatory authority in this case is limited to interstate commerce. Doe's complaint alleges only that Smith "published said video camera recording to fellow students of Springfield High School, in the City of Springfield, County of Sangamon, State of Illinois." Compl. ¶ 11. Why didn't this require dismissal of her complaint?

A

The court of appeals fills the gap by speculation—"*if* a plaintiff suspects Smith dispatched copies by email, which uses the interstate communications network, then the problem is solved" (emphasis added). But *does* this solve the problem? It is a hypothetical suspicion, not an allegation in the pleading. Doe never alleged that Smith dispatched copies by email, or even that she suspected this "on information and belief," a common pleading formula for, "I'm guessing, but I don't know for sure." This sounds like an especially heroic application of the literal *Conley* formula: "if on any state of facts. . . ."

Or is it? The complaint does not say that Smith distributed copies of the videotape; it says he "*published*" them. Another adage of Rule 12(b)(6) decision making is that reasonable doubts should be resolved in favor of the pleader. Here "published" can certainly be construed to mean "posted on the Internet," and so should be, if the adage is still right.

3. Pleading yourself out of court. We've suggested that even under the forgiving *Conley* regime of pleading, it is safest to plead all allegations respecting the elements of each claim. But a pleader can also plead too much. Had Doe tried to color her claim by asserting that Smith videotaped their private silent conduct, perhaps the court would not have inferred that Smith had intercepted "oral communications."

Q

4. Conceding consent? The statute states that any private participant's consent to the interception is a defense to liability. *See* 18 U.S.C. § 2511(2). By setting up the recording, Smith obviously himself consented. Has Doe therefore pled herself out of court by inferentially, at least, alleging his defense?

A

No, because the consent provision of the statute expressly includes the caveat "unless such communication is intercepted for the purpose of committing any criminal or tortious act. . . ." *Id.* Doe's supplemental state law claims allege that, by recording his activity with Doe, Smith committed several tortious acts.

Perhaps the most common instance of a plaintiff pleading herself out of court is the plaintiff who alleges dates in her complaint that show her claims to be time-barred by the statute of limitations. Although the statute of limitations is an affirmative defense that defendant usually pleads in his answer, Fed. R. Civ. P. 8(c)(1), the court can grant a motion to dismiss if the availability of this defense is apparent on the face of the complaint. *See Adams v. Rotkvich*, 325 Fed. Appx. 450, 453 n.1 (7th Cir. 2009) (permitting pre-answer dismissal when affirmative defense of limitations is "apparent and unmistakable from the face of a complaint"). Had Doe filed her action in 2010, for example, and had the applicable statute of limitations on her claims been two years, then her allegation in her complaint that the recording occurred in 2002 and that she was notified of it in 2003 would probably suffice to permit a pre-answer dismissal on limitations grounds.

IV. Heightened Pleading: Pleading "With Particularity"

Suppose what the court of appeals dryly described as Dioguardi's "lively sense of injustice" led him to plead that "the Collector of Customs took my bottles of tonic by fraud." If you were the defendant, your natural reaction would be, "Fraud? How?" Was the alleged fraud that the Collector misled Dioguardi about whether Customs had the tonic bottles? About their condition? Something about how the public auction was conducted? Or some other interaction with him?

At least in Dioguardi's case, the plaintiff and defendant appear to have had a single or discrete series of transactions. But suppose the plaintiff is a wealthy investor who has been investing regularly and frequently through the same broker for a decade. If the investor sues the broker and makes the unamplified claim that he lost hundreds of thousands of dollars because the broker defrauded him, does the broker have fair notice of the claim? Which of the dozens of their transactions over the decade were fraudulent? How? What misrepresentations or deceptive practices, among the multiple representations the broker is likely to have made over decades of their business relationship, constituted the fraud? Fraud comes in infinite varieties and, precisely because it involves deceit and deception, is not self-evident. Simply alleging fraud may damage the defendant's reputation, especially if defendant is a professional or a publicly traded corporation.

Fraud is therefore one kind of allegation that has been singled out for *heightened pleading* or *pleading with particularity*. Rules of civil procedure, statutes, and courts imposed heightened pleading requirements for such allegations and, at least before the following decision, a small set of others.

Federal Rule of Civil Procedure 9 imposes heightened pleading for allegations of fraud and mistake: "[A] party must state with particularity the circumstances constituting fraud or mistake." Dioguardi must therefore plead more than a naked claim of fraud; he must allege more specifically when, where, and how the fraud was committed. Countless federal decisions reject conclusory pleadings of fraud because the pleader fails to state with particularity the circumstances of the alleged fraud. *See, e.g., Wright & Miller* § 1300 (citing cases).

So common were allegations of fraud in securities fraud litigation that Congress even raised the heightened pleading standard of Rule 9(b). In the Private Securities Litigation Reform Act, Pub. L. No. 104-52, 109 Stat. 737 (codified in scattered sections of 15 U.S.C.A.), it required plaintiffs to "state with particularity facts giving rise to a strong inference that the defendant acted with the required state of mind." It also required specific pleading of false or misleading statements. While these statutorily heightened pleading requirements may not pose serious obstacles to most securities fraud plaintiffs, they at least motivate courts to take a closer look at the complaints on motions to dismiss.

Finally, courts have on their own initiative imposed heightened pleading requirements for certain allegations. For example, at one time, claims of civil rights violations or discrimination by government officials and entities were singled out by some circuits for heightened pleading. The district court in the following case had applied such a judicially created heightened pleading standard to dismiss a civil rights claim against a municipality for failing adequately to train narcotics officers about how to conduct a raid. On appeal, the Supreme Court addressed whether the court had authority to do so.

READING *LEATHERMAN v. TARRANT COUNTY NARCOTICS INTELLIGENCE & COORDINATION UNIT.* A special narcotics S.W.A.T. team had raided homes based on detection of odors associated with drug use. Plaintiffs alleged that in one case, members of the team killed her dogs, and that in another, they assaulted the plaintiffs and subjected them to abuse. Courts had previously held that municipal governments were not liable for civil rights violations on a *respondeat superior* theory (the principal is liable for the acts of its agent), but could be liable if a municipal custom or policy caused constitutional injuries. The plaintiffs therefore sued the municipality, among other defendants, on the theory that it had approved a "custom and policy" of inadequate training for its S.W.A.T. team. The district court summarized the allegations as follows:

> The allegations against [defendant] are that, at pertinent times, he, as director of TCNICU [the narcotics unit], was vested with official authority and responsibility for establishing policies for and supervising the day-to-day operations and practices of law enforcement personnel participating in and comprising TCNICU; that TCNICU acted by and through "its official policymaker" [defendant], in respect to policies and practices of TCNICU having to do with training of its officers; and, that a custom and policy of TCNICU of which plaintiffs complain was so persistent and widespread that [defendant], as the official policymaker of TCNICU, either knew or should have known of its existence.

755 F. Supp. 726, 728 (N.D. Tex. 1991).

The district court found that "the complaint does not suggest the kind of training that plaintiffs contend should have been, but was not, given; nor, is there any specificity or particularity as to other elements of the inadequate training theory." It then applied a heightened pleading standard devised by the Court of Appeals for the Fifth Circuit for civil rights claims against municipalities (though not expressly required by statute or rule) and dismissed the complaint for failure to state a claim. The court of appeals affirmed, summarizing its heightened pleading standard as follows: "Under the heightened pleading standard, a complaint must allege with particularity all material facts establishing a plaintiff's right of recovery, . . . and, in cases like this one, facts that support the requisite allegation that the municipality engaged in a policy or custom for which it can be held responsible." 954 F.2d 1054, 1055 (5th Cir. 1992) (citation omitted).

- Judging from the paraphrases of the complaint by the district court, did the complaint give fair and sufficient notice to defendants of the claim against them under the *Conley* standard?

- If the complaint did meet the *Conley* notice pleading standard, what reasons do you think led the Fifth Circuit to require more?
- Given that Rule 9 already requires pleading with particularity for certain types of allegations, is it error for the Fifth Circuit to require a heightened pleading standard in civil rights cases that are not singled out by the Rule?

LEATHERMAN v. TARRANT COUNTY NARCOTICS INTELLIGENCE & COORDINATION UNIT

507 U.S. 163 (1993)

Chief Justice REHNQUIST delivered the opinion of the Court.

We granted certiorari to decide whether a federal court may apply a "heightened pleading standard"—more stringent than the usual pleading requirements of Rule 8(a) of the Federal Rules of Civil Procedure—in civil rights cases alleging municipal liability under Rev. Stat. § 1979, 42 U.S.C. § 1983. We hold it may not.

We review here a decision granting a motion to dismiss, and therefore must accept as true all the factual allegations in the complaint. *See United States v. Gaubert,* [499 U.S. 315, 327 (1991)]. . . . The stated basis for municipal liability under *Monell v. New York City Dept. of Social Services*, 436 U.S. 658 (1978), was the failure of [County and the TCNICU] . . . to adequately train the police officers involved. . . .

[R]espondents contend that the Fifth Circuit's heightened pleading standard is not really that at all. According to respondents, the degree of factual specificity required of a complaint by the Federal Rules of Civil Procedure varies according to the complexity of the underlying substantive law. To establish municipal liability under § 1983, respondents argue, a plaintiff must do more than plead a single instance of misconduct. This requirement, respondents insist, is consistent with a plaintiff's Rule 11 obligation to make a reasonable prefiling inquiry into the facts.

But examination of the Fifth Circuit's decision in this case makes it quite evident that the "heightened pleading standard" is just what it purports to be: a more demanding rule for pleading a complaint under § 1983 than for pleading other kinds of claims for relief. This rule was adopted by the Fifth Circuit in *Elliott v. Perez,* 751 F.2d 1472 (1985), and described in this language:

> "In cases against governmental officials involving the likely defense of immunity we require of trial judges that they demand that the plaintiff's complaints state with factual detail and particularity the basis for the claim which necessarily includes why the defendant-official cannot successfully maintain the defense of immunity." *Id.,* at 1473.

In later cases, the Fifth Circuit extended this rule to complaints against municipal corporations asserting liability under § 1983. *See, e.g., Palmer v. San Antonio,* 810 F.2d 514 (1987).

We think that it is impossible to square the "heightened pleading standard" applied by the Fifth Circuit in this case with the liberal system of "notice pleading" set up by the Federal Rules. Rule 8(a)(2) requires that a complaint include only "a short and plain statement of the claim showing that the pleader is entitled to relief." In *Conley v. Gibson,* 355 U.S. 41 (1957), we said in effect that the Rule meant what it said:

> "[T]he Federal Rules of Civil Procedure do not require a claimant to set out in detail the facts upon which he bases his claim. To the contrary, all the Rules require is 'a short and plain statement of the claim' that will give the defendant fair notice of what the plaintiff's claim is and the grounds upon which it rests." *Id.,* at 47 (footnote omitted).

Rule 9(b) does impose a particularity requirement in two specific instances. It provides that "[i]n all averments of fraud or mistake, the circumstances constituting fraud or mistake shall be stated with particularity." Thus, the Federal Rules do address in Rule 9(b) the question of the need for greater particularity in pleading certain actions, but do not include among the enumerated actions any reference to complaints alleging municipal liability under § 1983. *Expressio unius est exclusio alterius.*

The phenomenon of litigation against municipal corporations based on claimed constitutional violations by their employees dates from our decision in *Monell, supra,* where we for the first time construed § 1983 to allow such municipal liability. Perhaps if Rules 8 and 9 were rewritten today, claims against municipalities under § 1983 might be subjected to the added specificity requirement of Rule 9(b). But that is a result which must be obtained by the process of amending the Federal Rules, and not by judicial interpretation. In the absence of such an amendment, federal courts and litigants must rely on summary judgment and control of discovery to weed out unmeritorious claims sooner rather than later.

The judgment of the Court of Appeals is reversed, and the case is remanded for further proceedings consistent with this opinion.

It is so ordered.

Notes and Questions: Heightened Pleading

Q **1. Reasons for heightened pleading.** Consider possible reasons for requiring heightened pleading.

A. *Fair notice.* One reason is presumably that because of the subject matter, general pleading under the *Conley* standard does not give fair and sufficient notice. A general claim of fraud may not help the defendant who has had a long course of dealing with a plaintiff know what particular acts constituted a fraud; a general claim of a municipal custom or policy that causes constitutional injuries may also leave a government defendant in the dark about what the custom or policy was and how it caused the injuries. Well, then, does the general claim that "defendant negligently drove a motor vehicle against the plaintiff" give fair notice?

A That's the problem with the "defendant-needs-better-notice" explanation for heightened pleading. This allegation was lifted straight out of the old Form 11's negligence complaint, which the rules deemed sufficient to meet the Rule 8(a)(2) pleading standard. It leaves the defendant in the dark about whether she drove too fast or drove inattentively or drove negligently in some other way, yet it suffices under the rules. How is a claim of municipal custom or policy different?

B. *Protecting reputation*. Presumably another reason that Rule 9(b) singles out "fraud" for pleading with particularity is the reputational damage that a pending fraud claim could cause. Heightened pleading here protects defendants' reputations by making it easier for them to ask courts to weed out weak fraud claims. Is this still a good reason for heightened pleading today?

A Maybe not. It smacks of long bygone sensibilities and civilities. In the modern litigious age, it is unclear how much more damaging fraud claims are than many other claims (such as claims of race discrimination), or, in fact, whether even fraud claims have much of a reputational effect any longer.

C. *The substance of procedure*. Government officials who are defendants to civil rights claims are entitled to the affirmative defense of qualified immunity to liability if they acted in actual and reasonable belief that their conduct was lawful. *See, e.g., Harlow v. Fitzgerald*, 457 U.S. 800, 818 (1982). (A succession of Supreme Court opinions has made it increasingly difficult for civil rights plaintiffs like Leatherman to get past this affirmative defense. We discuss the evolution of the defense *infra* p. 518.) The Court had held that municipal governments were not entitled to qualified immunity. But that left them exposed to potentially ruinous liability (many municipal governments self-insure). How might that concern justify a heightened pleading standard for claims against them?

A For government defendant-officials, heightened pleading might help flush out the facts pertinent to their immunity defense, facilitating summary judgment on the basis of the defense and thus avoiding a costly trial. For municipal government defendants, it would reduce the number of cases that reach discovery or trial. The costs to the municipal government (and the courts), after all, ultimately come back to the taxpayer. Should a court take into account policy concerns about drains on the public treasury when fashioning pleading rules? For this reason, defendants argue that a heightened pleading standard has a positive public policy effect.

On the other hand, a heightened pleading standard makes it more difficult for plaintiffs with meritorious claims against government officials. Specifically, a heightened pleading standard means that plaintiffs will need far more details about their cases to survive a motion to dismiss, details that are often hard to uncover without discovery. The point is that the decision to require a heightened pleading standard in this context has important substantive, policy consequences about who will win the case. Should the courts weigh them, or is this a task for legislatures?

D. *Suspect plaintiffs*. The *Leatherman* plaintiffs were the subjects of narcotics raids. Many civil rights complaints are filed by prisoners *pro se* (by themselves without a lawyer) with time on their hands. What difference might this make to the applicable pleading standards?

A None under the Rule. But perhaps the courts before *Leatherman* were showing some distrust of narcotics suspects and convicts when they fashioned the heightened pleading standard, although one could as easily conclude that it is precisely such plaintiffs who are most likely to suffer civil rights violations at the government's hands.

Q **2. Authority for heightened pleading.** Rule 9 authorizes heightened pleading for a small number of subjects. Civil rights claims are not among them. *"Expressio unius est exclusio alterius."* (How many of you looked this up?) "The express mention of one thing excludes all others." Why should it?

A If the drafters of the Rules meant to authorize more general heightened pleading, why bother to itemize at all? And if they itemize, shouldn't we assume that omitted items were intentionally omitted? In fact, how else can we reconcile Rule 8(a)(2)'s short and plain statement with Rule 9(b)'s "state with particularity" commands? The former governs generally; the latter is the exception for *just the itemized matters. Expressio unius* is a frequently used tool or *canon* of statutory construction, making it one of a small number of Latinisms worth committing to memory.

But there is more to this canon than logic and Latin. Rule 9(b) was promulgated under the authority of the Rules Enabling Act, 28 U.S.C. § 2072, pursuant to the multi-step rulemaking process we described in Chapter 2. If it is good policy to add allegations of municipal custom and policy to the items listed in the Rule, how should this be done?

A By that same rulemaking process and not by ad hoc judicial rulemaking. Ultimately, the Court asserts that the Fifth Circuit Court of Appeals lacked the authority to amend Rule 9(b) by tacking on its heightened pleading requirement for civil rights claims, irrespective of whether it would be a good idea. Justice Rehnquist admonishes the lower courts that this change should be made by rule amendment, not by "judicial interpretation."

3. Heightened pleading of "special damages." Rule 9(g) also requires that "special damages ... be specifically stated." General damages are those that would normally be anticipated from a particular event (pain and suffering from a broken leg; lost profits from a breach of contract). "Specials" are those that would not normally be anticipated, such as damages for a later miscarriage or higher blood pressure said to have resulted from an automobile accident. *See, e.g., Ziervogel v. Royal Packing Co.*, 225 S.W.2d 798 (Mo. Ct. App. 1949) (reversing judgment for plaintiff because defendant was not on "legal notice that plaintiff would claim damages [for increased blood pressure] ... unless and until plaintiff 'specifically' stated such injury in her ... [complaint] because the increased blood pressure was not shown to be the necessary or inevitable result of the injuries that were pleaded"). The Rules require that special damages be specifically stated in order to avoid surprise to the defendant. In addition, plaintiffs are required by substantive law to plead some kinds of special damages specifically, as when the common law of defamation requires a plaintiff to plead specifically his damages from reputational injury. *See, e.g., Fairyland Amusement Co. v. Metromedia*, 413 F. Supp. 1290 (W.D. Mo. 1976) (dismissing a defamation complaint for failure to plead loss of patronage from false publication).

4. Applying *Conley* and Rule 9.

Assuming a jurisdictionally sufficient complaint with a sufficient statement of proximately caused injuries and a prayer for relief, which of the following allegations *fails* under the *Conley* pleading standard or Rule 9?

A. After alleging a contract between plaintiff and defendant, an allegation that "Defendant breached said contract."
B. After alleging plaintiff's employment by defendant as a Deputy Sheriff and that plaintiff gave an interview to the press concerning cost overruns in the Sheriff's office, an allegation that "Defendant retaliated for plaintiff's exercise of his constitutional rights by adversely changing plaintiff's circumstances of employment."
C. An allegation that "Defendant knowingly made false reports to the financial press to defraud purchasers like plaintiff in reliance on which plaintiff purchased shares in defendant's company at inflated prices."
D. In a suit for defamation, which requires "publication"—communication of the defamatory matter to third parties—an allegation that "Defendant caused his security personnel to remove the plaintiff from defendant's restaurant, loudly telling them to 'throw that pimp out!' "

A is entirely conclusory and does not state how the defendant breached the contract. While Rule 8 seems to allow the pleading of some conclusions ("negligently"), old Form 11 conjoined the conclusory phrase with at least some particularizing facts. By comparison, this allegation arguably fails without similar specification of other particulars of the breach.

The allegation in **B** does not specify the plaintiff's constitutional rights and how plaintiff's conditions of employment were changed. This would probably fail under a heightened pleading standard, especially since some job changes could be justified or defendant could reasonably believe them justified, helping him establish qualified official immunity. But because *Leatherman* rejected judge-made heightened pleading in a civil rights case, *Conley* still seemed to control pleading in those cases. Here the defendant can infer from the allegation of the press interview that the constitutional right is a First Amendment right, and if he wants to know more about the alleged adverse job changes, he can ask in discovery. This allegation seems to pass muster under the lenient *Conley* notice pleading standard.

C is easy, once you identify the nature of the claim. Although it does not say "fraud," it alleges that defendant acted to "defraud" plaintiff. Rule 9(b) requires that fraud be stated with particularity. Here almost all courts will require the plaintiff to identify at least the time and place of the reports, as well as how they were false. Thus, **C** is insufficient.

D is sufficient, although the reasoning is more subtle. There is no allegation of a *written* publication, but "publication" means not just publishing in a written medium, but also "the act of bringing before the public; announcement." WEBSTER'S COLLEGE DICTIONARY 1091 (1991). By this definition, the allegation of public statements in the presence of third parties is sufficient (as, indeed, Judge Easterbrook found in the different context of *Doe v. Smith supra* at p. 441). Here the security personnel are third parties, and the adverb "loudly" may support an inference that others would have heard. *See Garcia v. Hilton Hotels Int'l, Inc.*, 97 F. Supp. 5 (D.P.R. 1951) (denying Rule 12(b)(6) motion on similar facts). Of course, you cannot answer this question definitively without knowing the applicable substantive law, *but that is generally true for pleading questions*, which is why we said above that it is important to start with the elements of possible legal theories (just like Judge Easterbrook does).

V. The (Still) Evolving Standard of Plausible Pleading

Conley ruled the federal pleading roost for fifty years. It was the standard invoked for most of the reported cases, and it is important to understand the *Conley* standard for that reason alone. But in 2007, the Supreme Court *seemed* to end its reign. In a sharply divided opinion in a complicated antitrust case that turned on allegations of an anti-competitive agreement among the defendants, the Supreme Court broke from the long line of *Conley* precedents in *Bell Atlantic Corporation v. Twombly*, 550 U.S. 544 (2007). At issue in *Twombly* was a federal law that prohibited restraints of trade resulting from agreements among competitors. While parallel business conduct is admissible as circumstantial evidence from which an illegal agreement could be inferred, it is not conclusive evidence or itself unlawful. Indeed, the courts have held that even "conscious parallelism" can be innocent if it reflects a common reaction of competitors to shared economic circumstances. *Id.* at 554–55. In light of this substantive law (here necessarily oversimplified), the Court stated in *Twombly*

> . . . that stating such a claim requires a complaint with enough factual matter (taken as true) to suggest that an [anti-competitive] agreement was made. Asking for plausible grounds to infer an agreement does not impose a probability requirement at the pleading stage; it simply calls for enough fact to raise a reasonable expectation that discovery will reveal evidence of illegal agreement. . . .
>
> The need at the pleading stage for allegations plausibly suggesting (not merely consistent with) agreement reflects the threshold requirement of Rule 8(a)(2) that the "plain statement" possess enough heft to "sho[w] that the pleader is entitled to relief." A statement of parallel conduct, even conduct consciously undertaken, needs some setting suggesting the agreement

> necessary to make out a § 1 claim; without that further circumstance pointing toward a meeting of the minds, an account of a defendant's commercial efforts stays in neutral territory. An allegation of parallel conduct is thus much like a naked assertion of conspiracy in a [Sherman Act] complaint: it gets the complaint close to stating a claim, but without some further factual enhancement it stops short of the line between possibility and plausibility of "entitle[ment] to relief."

Id. at 556–57 (internal citations omitted).

To the plaintiffs' invocation of the *Conley* "no set of facts" standard (on which the court of appeals had relied in reversing dismissal of their complaint), the Court responded:

> On such a focused and literal reading of *Conley's* "no set of facts," a wholly conclusory statement of claim would survive a motion to dismiss whenever the pleadings left open the possibility that a plaintiff might later establish some "set of [undisclosed] facts" to support recovery. [*For example,* allegation A *supra* at p. 455.] So here, the Court of Appeals specifically found the prospect of unearthing direct evidence of conspiracy sufficient to preclude dismissal, even though the complaint does not set forth a single fact in a context that suggests an agreement. It seems fair to say that this approach to pleading would dispense with any showing of a " 'reasonably founded hope' " that a plaintiff would be able to make a case; Mr. Micawber's optimism would be enough.

Id. at 561–62.

Consequently, the Court concluded that "this famous observation [from *Conley*] has earned its retirement. The phrase is best forgotten as an incomplete, negative gloss on an accepted pleading standard: once a claim has been stated adequately, it may be supported by showing any set of facts consistent with the allegations in the complaint." *Id.* at 563. Finally, the Court emphasized that "we do not require heightened fact pleading of specifics, but only enough facts to state a claim to relief that is plausible on its face. Because the plaintiffs here have not nudged their claims across the line from conceivable to plausible, their complaint must be dismissed." *Id.* at 570.

The dissenters clearly believed that the majority had not just decided a case of specialized antitrust law, but had effected a sea change in the rules of pleading. Thus, Justice Stevens wrote:

> This is a case in which the intentions of the drafters of three important sources of law—the Sherman Act, the Telecommunications Act of 1996, and the Federal Rules of Civil Procedure—all point unmistakably in the same direction, yet the Court marches resolutely the other way. Whether the Court's actions will benefit only defendants in antitrust treble-damages cases, or whether its test for the sufficiency of a complaint will inure to the benefit of all civil defendants, is a question that the future will answer. But that the Court has announced a significant new rule that does not even purport to respond to any congressional command is glaringly obvious.

> The transparent policy concern that drives the decision is the interest in protecting antitrust defendants—who in this case are some of the wealthiest corporations in our economy—from the burdens of pretrial discovery. Even if it were not apparent that the legal fees petitioners have incurred in arguing the merits of their Rule 12(b) motion have far exceeded the cost of limited discovery, or that those discovery costs would burden respondents as well as petitioners, that concern would not provide an adequate justification for this law-changing decision. For in the final analysis it is only a lack of confidence in the ability of trial judges to control discovery, buttressed by appellate judges' independent appraisal of the plausibility of profoundly serious factual allegations, that could account for this stark break from precedent.
>
> If the allegation of conspiracy happens to be true, today's decision obstructs the congressional policy favoring competition that undergirds both the Telecommunications Act of 1996 and the Sherman Act itself. More importantly, even if there is abundant evidence that the allegation is untrue, directing that the case be dismissed without even looking at any of that evidence marks a fundamental—and unjustified—change in the character of pretrial practice.

Id. at 596–97.

Twombly shocked plaintiffs' lawyers, delighted defense lawyers, and confused Civil Procedure teachers (and students). It seemed to resurrect the untenable code pleading distinction between conclusions and ultimate facts. It also raised the threshold of sufficient pleading from the possible (a statement of claim that *could* entitle the pleader to relief on some legal theory) to the plausible, if still short of the probable. Because the allegations of parallel conduct in *Twombly* were equally consistent with the existence of an unlawful agreement among defendants and with lawful, independent business decisions, they were no longer sufficient. The plaintiff had to plead something more to suggest that an illegal agreement was a more plausible explanation.

But had the Supreme Court really changed the pleading standard, or just applied it differently than the court of appeals on particular facts? If it changed the standard, had it changed it across the board, or had it only adopted a context-specific "flexible plausibility standard" for some factual allegations (like "agreement" or "conspiracy") in contexts where greater specificity is needed to render a claim plausible? In the following case, the Second Circuit Court of Appeals had adopted the narrower reading of *Twombly* and held that the civil rights claims asserted by Iqbal did not present a context in which greater specificity was needed. The Supreme Court then granted certiorari.

READING *ASHCROFT v. IQBAL*. Iqbal, a Muslim from Pakistan, was detained in the investigation that followed the 9/11 attacks. He sued Attorney General Ashcroft and FBI Director Mueller, among others, for illegal detention (and treatment in detention) based on his religion, race, and/or national origin. Because federal law creates no *respondeat superior* (vicarious) liability of such superiors for the acts of their subordinates, he needed to allege that Ashcroft and Mueller (yes, the Mueller of the later *Mueller Report*) were somehow directly responsible for his detention and conditions of confinement.

- The Supreme Court explains in Part IV.A that *Twombly* requires a two-part inquiry for deciding motions to dismiss a claim. In what respects do Iqbal's allegations fail the first part of the inquiry? Is this a departure from the *Conley* line of cases, or consistent with it?
- Why do Iqbal's remaining allegations fail the second part of the inquiry? By finding them "implausible," does the Supreme Court effectively take a sneak peek at the merits?
- The key allegations go to the intent of the Attorney General and the Director of the FBI. How is the Court's rejection of the sufficiency of these allegations of intent consistent with Rule 9(b)? With its analysis of the same Rule in *Leatherman*?

ASHCROFT v. IQBAL

556 U.S. 662 (2009)

Justice Kennedy delivered the opinion of the Court.

[Eds.—Javaid Iqbal (the plaintiff below and respondent on appeal) was a citizen of Pakistan and a Muslim who was arrested in the investigation in the wake of the September 11, 2001, terrorist attacks and detained by federal officials. He filed a complaint against various officials involved in his detention in a facility known as the Administrative Maximum Special Housing Unit, or ADMAX SHU, up to and including Attorney General Ashcroft and FBI Director Mueller (the defendants below and petitioners on appeal), alleging that his treatment while in detention violated his constitutional rights.] . . .

[Though he cites a litany of abuses against guards and other lower-ranking officials, his claims against Ashcroft and Mueller were that they] designated respondent a person of high interest on account of his race, religion, or national origin, in contravention of the First and Fifth Amendments to the Constitution. The complaint alleges that "the [FBI], under the direction of Defendant MUELLER, arrested and detained thousands of Arab Muslim men . . . as part of its investigation of the events of September 11." It further alleges that "[t]he policy of holding post-September-11th detainees in highly restrictive conditions of confinement until they were 'cleared' by the FBI was approved by Defendants ASHCROFT and MUELLER in discussions in the weeks after September 11, 2001." Lastly, the complaint posits that petitioners "each knew of, condoned, and willfully and maliciously agreed to subject" respondent to harsh conditions of confinement "as a matter of policy, solely on account of [his] religion, race, and/or national origin and for no legitimate penological interest." The pleading names Ashcroft as the "principal architect" of the policy, and identifies Mueller as "instrumental in [its] adoption, promulgation, and implementation."

[Eds.—The district court denied petitioners' motion to dismiss on the grounds that "it cannot be said that there [is] no set of facts on which [Iqbal] would be entitled to relief as against" them, relying on *Conley v. Gibson*, 355 U.S. 41 (1957). On appeal, the Second Circuit Court of Appeals held that *Twombly* adopted a "flexible plausibility standard" that did not apply to the context of Iqbal's complaint, and that his pleading was adequate to allege petitioners' personal involvement in discriminatory decisions that, if true, violated clearly established constitutional law. In other words, the Court of Appeals concluded that *Twombly* was not universally applicable, but instead, context-specific. It applied, that Court reasoned, only to cases in which the complexity of the facts and the availability of competing inferences requires additional facts for the court to decide whether the plaintiff's claim was plausible. It found that Iqbal's seemingly straightforward claim of race, religious, and national-origin discrimination against defendants did not present these problems and therefore was not subject to *Twombly*.] . . .

III

In *Twombly*, the Court found it necessary first to discuss the antitrust principles implicated by the complaint. Here too we begin by taking note of the elements a plaintiff must plead to state a claim of unconstitutional discrimination against officials entitled to assert the defense of qualified immunity.

In *Bivens*—proceeding on the theory that a right suggests a remedy—this Court "recognized for the first time an implied private action for damages against federal officers alleged to have violated a citizen's constitutional rights." *Correctional Services Corp. v. Malesko*, 534 U.S. 61, 66 (2001). . . .

Based on the rules our precedents establish, respondent correctly concedes that Government officials may not be held liable for the unconstitutional conduct of their subordinates under a theory of *respondeat superior*. Because vicarious liability is inapplicable to *Bivens* and § 1983 suits, a plaintiff must plead that each Government-official defendant, through the official's own individual actions, has violated the Constitution.

The factors necessary to establish a *Bivens* violation will vary with the constitutional provision at issue. Where the claim is invidious discrimination in contravention of the First and Fifth Amendments, our decisions make clear that the plaintiff must plead and prove that the defendant acted with discriminatory purpose. Under extant precedent purposeful discrimination requires more than "intent as volition or intent as awareness of consequences." *Personnel Administrator of Mass. v. Feeney*, 442 U.S. 256, 279 (1979). It instead involves a decisionmaker's undertaking a course of action " 'because of,' not merely 'in spite of,' [the action's] adverse effects upon an identifiable group." *Ibid.* It follows that, to state a claim based on a violation of a clearly established right, respondent must plead sufficient factual matter to show that petitioners adopted and implemented the detention policies at issue not for a neutral, investigative reason but for the purpose of discriminating on account of race, religion, or national origin. . . .

IV

A

We turn to respondent's complaint. . . .

Two working principles underlie our decision in *Twombly.* First, the tenet that a court must accept as true all of the allegations contained in a complaint is inapplicable to legal conclusions. Threadbare recitals of the elements of a cause of action, supported by mere conclusory statements, do not suffice. *Id.,* at 555 (Although for the purposes of a motion to dismiss we must take all of the factual allegations in the complaint as true, we "are not bound to accept as true a legal conclusion couched as a factual allegation" (internal quotation marks omitted)). Rule 8 marks a notable and generous departure from the hyper-technical, code-pleading regime of a prior era, but it does not unlock the doors of discovery for a plaintiff armed with nothing more than conclusions. Second, only a complaint that states a plausible claim for relief survives a motion to dismiss. Determining whether a complaint states a plausible claim for relief will, as the Court of Appeals observed, be a context-specific task that requires the reviewing court to draw on its judicial experience and common sense. But where the well-pleaded facts do not permit the court to infer more than the mere possibility of misconduct, the complaint has alleged—but it has not "show[n]"—"that the pleader is entitled to relief." Fed. Rule Civ. Proc. 8(a)(2).

In keeping with these principles a court considering a motion to dismiss can choose to begin by identifying pleadings that, because they are no more than conclusions, are not entitled to the assumption of truth. While legal conclusions can provide the framework of a complaint, they must be supported by factual allegations. When there are well-pleaded factual allegations, a court should assume their veracity and then determine whether they plausibly give rise to an entitlement to relief.

Our decision in *Twombly* illustrates the two-pronged approach. There, we considered the sufficiency of a complaint alleging that incumbent telecommunications providers had entered an agreement not to compete and to forestall competitive entry, in violation of the Sherman Act, 15 U.S.C. § 1. Recognizing that § 1 enjoins only anticompetitive conduct "effected by a contract, combination, or conspiracy," the plaintiffs in *Twombly* flatly pleaded that the defendants "ha[d] entered into a contract, combination or conspiracy to prevent competitive entry . . . and ha[d] agreed not to compete with one another." 550 U.S., at 551 (internal quotation marks omitted). The complaint also alleged that the defendants' "parallel course of conduct . . . to prevent competition" and inflate prices was indicative of the unlawful agreement alleged. *Ibid.* (internal quotation marks omitted).

The Court held the plaintiffs' complaint deficient under Rule 8. In doing so it first noted that the plaintiffs' assertion of an unlawful agreement was a " 'legal conclusion' " and, as such, was not entitled to the assumption of truth. *Id.,* at 555. Had the Court simply credited the allegation of a conspiracy, the plaintiffs would have stated a claim for relief and been entitled to proceed perforce. The Court next addressed the "nub" of the plaintiffs' complaint—the well-pleaded, nonconclusory factual allegation of parallel behavior—to determine whether it gave rise to a "plausible suggestion of conspiracy." *Id.*, at 565–566. Acknowledging that parallel conduct was consistent with an unlawful agreement, the Court nevertheless concluded that it did not plausibly suggest an illicit accord because it was not only compatible with, but indeed was more likely explained by, lawful, unchoreographed free-market behavior. *Id.*, at 567. Because the well-pleaded fact of parallel conduct, accepted as true, did not plausibly suggest an unlawful agreement, the Court held the plaintiffs' complaint must be dismissed. *Id.*, at 570.

B

Under *Twombly*'s construction of Rule 8, we conclude that respondent's complaint has not "nudged [his] claims" of invidious discrimination "across the line from conceivable to plausible." *Ibid.*

We begin our analysis by identifying the allegations in the complaint that are not entitled to the assumption of truth. Respondent pleads that petitioners "knew of, condoned, and willfully and maliciously agreed to subject [him]" to harsh conditions of confinement "as a matter of policy, solely on account of [his] religion, race, and/or national origin and for no legitimate penological interest." The complaint alleges that Ashcroft was the "principal architect" of this invidious policy, and that Mueller was "instrumental" in adopting and executing it. These bare assertions, much like the pleading of conspiracy in *Twombly*, amount to nothing more than a "formulaic recitation of the elements" of a constitutional discrimination claim, namely, that petitioners adopted a policy " 'because of,' not merely 'in spite of,' its adverse effects upon an identifiable group." *Feeney*, 442 U.S., at 279. As such, the allegations are conclusory and not entitled to be assumed true. To be clear, we do not reject these bald allegations on the ground that they are unrealistic or nonsensical. We do not so characterize them any more than the Court in *Twombly* rejected the plaintiffs' express allegation of a " 'contract, combination or conspiracy to prevent competitive entry,' " because it thought that claim too chimerical to be maintained. It is the conclusory nature of respondent's allegations, rather than their extravagantly fanciful nature, that disentitles them to the presumption of truth.

We next consider the factual allegations in respondent's complaint to determine if they plausibly suggest an entitlement to relief. The complaint alleges that "the [FBI], under the direction of Defendant MUELLER, arrested and detained thousands of Arab Muslim men ... as part of its investigation of the events of September 11." It further claims that "[t]he policy of holding post-September-11th detainees in highly restrictive conditions of confinement until they were 'cleared' by the FBI was approved by Defendants ASHCROFT and MUELLER in discussions in the weeks after September 11, 2001." Taken as true, these allegations are consistent with petitioners' purposefully designating detainees "of high interest" because of their race, religion, or national origin. But given more likely explanations, they do not plausibly establish this purpose.

The September 11 attacks were perpetrated by 19 Arab Muslim hijackers who counted themselves members in good standing of al Qaeda, an Islamic fundamentalist group. Al Qaeda was headed by another Arab Muslim—Osama bin

Laden—and composed in large part of his Arab Muslim disciples. It should come as no surprise that a legitimate policy directing law enforcement to arrest and detain individuals because of their suspected link to the attacks would produce a disparate, incidental impact on Arab Muslims, even though the purpose of the policy was to target neither Arabs nor Muslims. On the facts respondent alleges the arrests Mueller oversaw were likely lawful and justified by his nondiscriminatory intent to detain aliens who were illegally present in the United States and who had potential connections to those who committed terrorist acts. As between that "obvious alternative explanation" for the arrests, *Twombly, supra,* at 567, and the purposeful, invidious discrimination respondent asks us to infer, discrimination is not a plausible conclusion.

But even if the complaint's well-pleaded facts give rise to a plausible inference that respondent's arrest was the result of unconstitutional discrimination, that inference alone would not entitle respondent to relief. It is important to recall that respondent's complaint challenges neither the constitutionality of his arrest nor his initial detention in the [Metropolitan Detention Center in Brooklyn, New York]. Respondent's constitutional claims against petitioners rest solely on their ostensible "policy of holding post-September-11th detainees" in the ADMAX SHU once they were categorized as "of high interest." To prevail on that theory, the complaint must contain facts plausibly showing that petitioners purposefully adopted a policy of classifying post-September-11 detainees as "of high interest" because of their race, religion, or national origin.

This the complaint fails to do. Though respondent alleges that various other defendants, who are not before us, may have labeled him a person "of high interest" for impermissible reasons, his only factual allegation against petitioners accuses them of adopting a policy approving "restrictive conditions of confinement" for post-September-11 detainees until they were " 'cleared' by the FBI." Accepting the truth of that allegation, the complaint does not show, or even intimate, that petitioners purposefully housed detainees in the ADMAX SHU due to their race, religion, or national origin. All it plausibly suggests is that the Nation's top law enforcement officers, in the aftermath of a devastating terrorist attack, sought to keep suspected terrorists in the most secure conditions available until the suspects could be cleared of terrorist activity. Respondent does not argue, nor can he, that such a motive would violate petitioners' constitutional obligations. He would need to allege more by way of factual content to "nudg[e]" his claim of purposeful discrimination "across the line from conceivable to plausible." *Twombly,* 550 U.S., at 570. . . .

It is important to note, however, that we express no opinion concerning the sufficiency of respondent's complaint against the defendants who are not before us. Respondent's account of his prison ordeal alleges serious official misconduct that we need not address here. Our decision is limited to the determination that respondent's complaint does not entitle him to relief from petitioners.

C

Respondent offers three arguments that bear on our disposition of his case, but none is persuasive.

1

Respondent first says that our decision in *Twombly* should be limited to pleadings made in the context of an antitrust dispute. This argument is not supported by *Twombly* and is incompatible with the Federal Rules of Civil Procedure. Though *Twombly* determined the sufficiency of a complaint sounding in antitrust, the decision was based on our interpretation and application of Rule 8. That Rule in turn governs the pleading standard "in all civil actions and proceedings in the United States district courts." Fed. Rule Civ. Proc. 1. Our decision in *Twombly* expounded the pleading standard for "all civil actions," *ibid.*, and it applies to antitrust and discrimination suits alike.

2

Respondent next implies that our construction of Rule 8 should be tempered where, as here, the Court of Appeals has "instructed the district court to cabin discovery in such a way as to preserve" petitioners' defense of qualified immunity "as much as possible in anticipation of a summary judgment motion." We have held, however, that the question presented by a motion to dismiss a complaint for insufficient pleadings does not turn on the controls placed upon the discovery process. *Twombly, supra,* at 559 ("It is no answer to say that a claim just shy of a plausible entitlement to relief can, if groundless, be weeded out early in the discovery process through careful case management given the common lament that the success of judicial supervision in checking discovery abuse has been on the modest side" (internal quotation marks and citation omitted)). . . .

We decline respondent's invitation to relax the pleading requirements on the ground that the Court of Appeals promises petitioners minimally intrusive discovery. That promise provides especially cold comfort in this pleading context, where we are impelled to give real content to the concept of qualified immunity for high-level officials who must be neither deterred nor detracted from the vigorous performance of their duties. Because respondent's complaint is deficient under Rule 8, he is not entitled to discovery, cabined or otherwise. [Eds.—**The judicially created defense of "qualified immunity" protects public officials from personal liability for unlawful acts, as long as they did not violate "clearly established law."** ***See infra*** **pp. 518–19. The plaintiffs argued that the post-complaint procedural devices of discovery (fact-finding) and summary judgment (judgment as a matter of law on what the movant shows to be undisputed material facts) could head off trial and thus protect such officials from liability. But the Court responded that even "cabined" (limited) discovery and summary judgment motion practice may be so costly and burdensome that fear of being sued will deter and distract officials from doing their jobs.]**

3

Respondent finally maintains that the Federal Rules expressly allow him to allege petitioners' discriminatory intent "generally," which he equates with a conclusory allegation. Iqbal Brief 32 (citing Fed. Rule Civ. Proc. 9). It follows, respondent says, that his complaint is sufficiently well pleaded because it claims that petitioners discriminated against him "on account of [his] religion, race, and/or national origin and for no legitimate penological interest." Were we required to accept this allegation as true, respondent's complaint would survive petitioners' motion to dismiss. But the Federal Rules do not require courts to credit a complaint's conclusory statements without reference to its factual context.

It is true that Rule 9(b) requires particularity when pleading "fraud or mistake," while allowing "[m]alice, intent, knowledge, and other conditions of a person's mind [to] be alleged generally." But "generally" is a relative term. In the context of Rule 9, it is to be compared to the particularity requirement applicable to fraud or mistake. Rule 9 merely excuses a party from pleading discriminatory intent under an elevated pleading standard. It does not give him license to evade the less rigid—though still operative—strictures of Rule 8. And Rule 8 does not empower respondent to plead the bare elements of his cause of action, affix the label "general allegation," and expect his complaint to survive a motion to dismiss.

V

We hold that respondent's complaint fails to plead sufficient facts to state a claim for purposeful and unlawful discrimination against petitioners. The Court of Appeals should decide in the first instance whether to remand to the District Court so that respondent can seek leave to amend his deficient complaint.

The judgment of the Court of Appeals is reversed, and the case is remanded for further proceedings consistent with this opinion.

It is so ordered.

Justice SOUTER, with whom Justice STEVENS, Justice GINSBURG, and Justice BREYER join, dissenting.

This case is here on the uncontested assumption that *Bivens v. Six Unknown Fed. Narcotics Agents,* 403 U.S. 388 (1971), allows personal liability based on a federal officer's violation of an individual's rights under the First and Fifth Amendments, and it comes to us with the explicit concession of petitioners Ashcroft and Mueller that an officer may be subject to *Bivens* liability as a supervisor on grounds other than *respondeat superior*. . . .

II

Given petitioners' concession, the complaint satisfies Rule 8(a)(2). Ashcroft and Mueller admit they are liable for their subordinates' conduct if they "had actual knowledge of the assertedly discriminatory nature of the classification of suspects as being 'of high interest' and they were deliberately indifferent to that discrimination." . . . The complaint thus alleges, at a bare minimum, that Ashcroft and Mueller knew of and condoned the discriminatory policy their subordinates carried out. Actually, the complaint goes further in alleging that Ashcroft and Muller affirmatively acted to create the discriminatory detention policy. If these factual allegations are true, Ashcroft and Mueller were, at the very least, aware of the discriminatory policy being implemented and deliberately indifferent to it.

Ashcroft and Mueller argue that these allegations fail to satisfy the "plausibility standard" of *Twombly.* They contend that Iqbal's claims are implausible because such high-ranking officials "tend not to be personally involved in the specific actions of lower-level officers down the bureaucratic chain of command." But this response bespeaks a fundamental misunderstanding of the enquiry that *Twombly* demands. *Twombly* does not require a court at the motion-to-dismiss stage to consider whether the factual allegations are probably true. We made it clear, on the contrary, that a court must take the allegations as true, no matter how skeptical the court may be. *See Twombly,* 550 U.S., at 555 (a court must proceed "on the assumption that all the allegations in the complaint are true (even if doubtful in fact)"); *id.*, at 556 ("[A] well-pleaded complaint may proceed even if it strikes a savvy judge that actual proof of the facts alleged is improbable"); *see also Neitzke v. Williams,* 490 U.S. 319, 327 (1989) ("Rule 12(b)(6) does not countenance . . . dismissals based on a judge's disbelief of a complaint's factual allegations"). The sole exception to this rule lies with allegations that are sufficiently fantastic to defy reality as we know it: claims about little green men, or the plaintiff's recent trip to Pluto, or experiences in time travel. That is not what we have here.

Under *Twombly,* the relevant question is whether, assuming the factual allegations are true, the plaintiff has stated a ground for relief that is plausible. That is, in *Twombly*'s words, a plaintiff must "allege facts" that, taken as true, are "suggestive of illegal conduct." 550 U.S., at 564, n.8. In *Twombly,* we were faced with allegations of a conspiracy to violate § 1 of the Sherman Act through parallel conduct. The difficulty was that the conduct alleged was "consistent with conspiracy, but just as much in line with a wide swath of rational and competitive business strategy unilaterally prompted by common perceptions of the market." *Id.,* at 554. We held that in that sort of circumstance, "[a]n allegation of parallel conduct is . . . much like a naked assertion of conspiracy in a § 1 complaint: it gets the complaint close to stating a claim, but without some further factual enhancement it stops short of the line between possibility and plausibility of 'entitlement to relief.' " *Id.,* at 557 (brackets omitted). Here, by contrast, the allegations in the complaint are neither confined to naked legal conclusions nor consistent with legal conduct. The complaint alleges that FBI officials discriminated against Iqbal solely on account of his race, religion, and national origin, and it alleges the knowledge and deliberate indifference that, by Ashcroft and Mueller's own admission, are sufficient to make them liable for the illegal action. Iqbal's complaint therefore contains "enough facts to state a claim to relief that is plausible on its face." *Id.,* at 570 . . . .

The majority says that these are "bare assertions" that, "much like the pleading of conspiracy in *Twombly,* amount to nothing more than a 'formulaic recitation of the elements' of a constitutional discrimination claim" and therefore are "not entitled to be assumed true." The fallacy of the majority's position, however, lies in looking at the relevant assertions in isolation. The complaint contains specific allegations that, in the aftermath of the September 11 attacks, the Chief of the FBI's International Terrorism Operations Section and the Assistant Special Agent in Charge for the FBI's New York Field Office implemented a policy that discriminated against Arab Muslim men, including Iqbal, solely on account of their race, religion, or national origin. Viewed in light of these subsidiary allegations, the allegations singled out by the majority as "conclusory" are no such thing. Iqbal's claim is not that Ashcroft and Mueller "knew of, condoned, and willfully and maliciously agreed to subject" him to a discriminatory practice that is left undefined; his allegation is that "they knew of, condoned, and willfully and maliciously agreed to subject" him to a particular, discrete, discriminatory policy detailed in the complaint. Iqbal does not say merely that Ashcroft was the architect of some amorphous discrimination, or that Mueller was instrumental in an ill-defined constitutional violation; he alleges that they helped to create the discriminatory policy he has described. Taking the complaint as a whole, it gives Ashcroft and Mueller " 'fair notice of what the ... claim is and the grounds upon which it rests.' " *Twombly,* 550 U.S., at 555 (quoting *Conley v. Gibson,* 355 U.S. 41, 47 (omission in original)). . . .

I respectfully dissent.

[Dissenting opinion of Justice Breyer omitted.]

Notes and Questions: Plausible Pleading

1. The starting point: The elements of the claim. Recall that every pleading problem starts with the substantive law. *Iqbal,* too, "begin[s] by taking note of the elements a plaintiff must plead to state a claim of unconstitutional discrimination against officials entitled to assert the defense of qualified immunity."

Q **2. The "first" prong of the *Twombly-Iqbal* test: Are the allegations well pleaded?** In deciding whether a pleading states a claim showing that the pleader is entitled to relief, the court must still accept as true the factual allegations of the complaint. But the Supreme Court has added (or reminded us of) a caveat: The court should accept as true only the "*well-pleaded* allegations." Only after a court had found "that there are well-pleaded factual allegations," the Supreme Court explained, can it "assume their veracity. . . ."

An allegation is well pleaded when it is more than a "mere conclusory statement"—more than just a "threadbare recital of the elements of the cause of action." Thus, it was not enough to plead that the defendants reached an anticompetitive "agreement" in *Twombly.* Such an allegation is nothing more than a threadbare recital of an element of the antitrust claim made there. Plaintiffs had to supply facts consistent with an agreement. Similarly, it is not enough that Iqbal alleges that Ashcroft and Mueller "knew of, condoned, and willfully and maliciously agreed to subject" Iqbal to harsh confinement "solely on account of his religion, race, and/or national origin and for no legitimate penological interest." This is also merely a restatement of an element of the discrimination claim. One way to define a conclusory allegation, then, may be that it is an allegation so generic (usually reciting an element of the *prima facie* case) that it could be cut and pasted without modification into any number of diverse fact patterns.

Conversely, the fact that an allegation in the complaint is *not* just a restatement of the elements of the claim supports the conclusion that it is not conclusory. *See Williams v. Dart*, No. 19-2108, 2020 WL 4217764 (7th Cir. July 23, 2020) (allegation in support of equal protection claim that Sheriff targeted plaintiffs for pretrial detention on basis of "racist assumptions about the likelihood that people from primarily African American neighborhoods pose a public safety risk or are likely to reoffend" was not conclusory; "[b]ecause we can think of no cause of action that contains as an element proof of racist assumptions about neighborhoods in Chicago, plaintiffs' allegation cannot fairly be characterized as conclusory.").

Is the difference (if any) between this allegation and Iqbal's allegation that he was subjected to harsh conditions of confinement "solely on account of [his] religion, race, and/or national origin and for no legitimate penological interest" that the latter too closely echoes the "purpose" element of his equal protection claim? What more could Iqbal have pleaded at this stage of the litigation that would pass beyond "conclusory"?

A He could have alleged that the defendants wrote or told their subordinates that they should target Muslim immigrants to "send a message" to the immigrant community. Such an allegation is no longer a threadbare recitation of the elements; it would be a factual allegation supporting the elements. The Catch-22, however, is that these kinds of facts are typically in the exclusive control of the defendant and first found by discovery *after* pleading, not available *before*.

Q **3. The next prong of the *Twombly-Iqbal* test: Do the well-pleaded allegations plausibly state a claim for relief?** After the district court has identified and taken as true a complaint's well-pleaded allegations, it must "then determine whether they plausibly give rise to an entitlement to relief." This is, indeed, a "context-specific task," as the court of appeals had concluded in *Iqbal*, but it is not limited to antitrust claims. *Twombly*, the Court emphasizes, was based on the meaning of Rule 8, which governs pleading in *all* civil actions.

But don't the allegations in *Iqbal* plausibly state a claim for discrimination on the account of race, religion, or national origin in violation of Iqbal's First and Fifth Amendment rights?

A They are at least conceivable. However, they are also consistent with innocent explanations. The defendants may have targeted Arab Muslims not because they were Arabs or Muslims, but because the 9/11 terrorists were Arab Muslims, making it more likely that their co-conspirators and associates would be, too. Both the "guilty" (liability-creating) and the innocent explanations are possible, but the Court says that when both are possible, the plaintiffs must plead something "more by way of factual content to 'nudge' his claim ... 'across the line from conceivable to plausible.' " *But see* Shirin Sinnar, *The Lost Story of Iqbal*, 105 Geo. L.J. 379, 414–28 (2017) (concluding that "significant evidence supports the idea that the ethnicity and religion of individuals factored heavily into investigative and detention decisions," and that many public officials knew that "the factual basis linking detained individuals to suspicions of terrorism was often thin or absent").

The Court's view seems to break with the *Conley* regime of notice pleading in two ways. First, it does not seem to draw all reasonable inferences in favor of the pleader; dueling inferences appear to cancel each other out, unless one is *more* plausible than the other. Second, the Court insists on "more by way of factual content," while courts construing the *Conley* standard were fond of asserting, as did Judge Easterbrook in *Doe v. Smith*, that "[p]laintiffs need not plead facts."

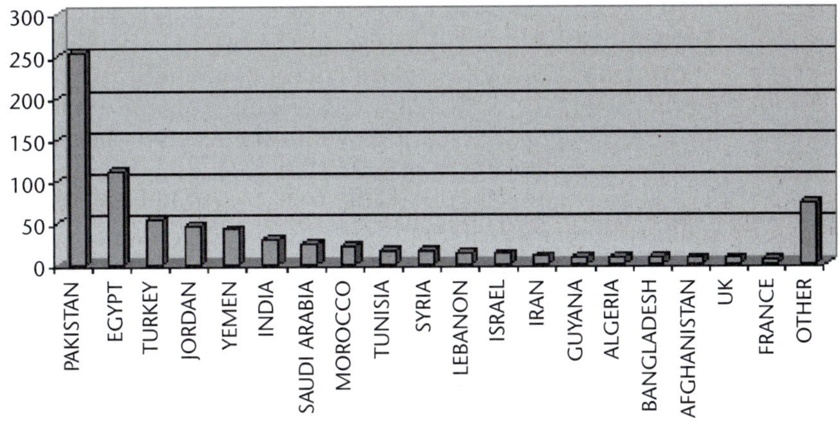

The Iqbal plaintiffs alleged that the arrests and detentions invidiously discriminated against them on account of religion or national origin. The Court found this implausible, when "the obvious alternative explanation for the arrests" was that they simply targeted persons like (and therefore possibly linked to) the 9/11 hijackers, who were "Arab Muslims." In fact, Iqbal was Pakistani, not Arab, and probably only half of the detainees came from Arab countries, as this graph shows. *See generally* Sinnar, 105 Geo. L.J. at 417. Did the Court know the difference?

Figure 13–2: **NATIONALITY OF SEPTEMBER 11 DETAINEES***

4. Critiques of plausible pleading. The *Twombly-Iqbal* plausible pleading standard has been sharply criticized for at least three reasons.

First, Iqbal may be unable to make non-conclusory plausible allegations about Ashcroft's and Mueller's state of mind—an essential element of his discrimination claim—without discovery of information that they control. But a motion to dismiss is typically made before much, if any, formal discovery is allowed. Thus, the plausible pleading standard may "deny access to court to plaintiffs and

* From Office of the Inspector General, Dep't of Justice, The September 11 Detainees: *A Review of the Treatment of Aliens Held on Immigration Charges in Connection with the Investigation of the September 11 Attacks* (June 2003) figure 2, http://www.justice.gov/oig/special/0306/chapter2.htm#IV.

prospective plaintiffs with meritorious claims who cannot satisfy those decisions' requirements either because they lack the resources to engage in extensive pre-filing investigation or because of informational asymmetries." *Hearing on Whether the Supreme Court Has Limited Americans' Access to Court Before the Senate Comm. on Judiciary*, 111th Cong., 1st Sess. 17 (2009) (prepared statement of Stephen B. Burbank).

Second, by relying on "judicial experience and common sense," rather than a factual record that had not yet been developed, the *Iqbal* majority arguably gave expression to its own belief that Ashcroft and Mueller didn't harbor any discriminatory intent. *See* Sinnar, *supra* p. 468, n.3, 105 Geo. L.J. at 414–28. *Iqbal* requires largely unconstrained comparative judgments by judges that "depend . . . on a judge's background knowledge and assumptions, which seem every bit as vulnerable to the biasing effect of that individual's cultural predispositions as are judgments about adjudicative facts [who did what, when, and how]." *Id.* at 14. As a civil rights litigator explained, "*Iqbal* and *Twombly* have brought more unpredictability to civil rights cases because judges are being asked to fill in information gaps from their own experience—one view may be that judges perceive less discrimination than I do." Iqbal, Twombly *Pleading Standards Hotly Debated by Conference Panelists,* 78 U.S.L.W. 2782 (June 29, 2010). Consider, for example, how such biasing effects might affect civil suits for police misconduct.

Third, these judgments come awfully close to deciding facts that plaintiffs would otherwise be entitled to try to a jury. From this perspective, *Twombly-Iqbal* not only overturns the generous pleading standard intended by the Federal Rules, but intrudes on plaintiffs' constitutional right to a jury trial.

5. Defenses of plausible pleading. Supporters of the *Twombly-Iqbal* plausible pleading standard make at least three arguments in its defense.

First, they argue that it was a corrective measure for a pleading system made too costly by the explosion in the amount and therefore cost of formal discovery. Indeed, the Court in *Twombly* stressed the high cost of discovery if the case was allowed to proceed:

> [I]t is one thing to be cautious before dismissing an antitrust complaint in advance of discovery, but quite another to forget that proceeding to antitrust discovery can be expensive. As we indicated over 20 years ago in *Associated Gen. Contractors of Cal., Inc. v. Carpenters*, 459 U.S. 519, 528, n.17 (1983), "a district court must retain the power to insist upon some specificity in pleading before allowing a potentially massive factual controversy to proceed." *See also Car Carriers, Inc. v. Ford Motor Co.*, 745 F.2d 1101, 1106 (C.A.7 1984) ("[T]he costs of modern federal antitrust litigation and the increasing caseload of the federal courts counsel against sending the parties into discovery when there is no reasonable likelihood that the plaintiffs can construct a claim from the events related in the complaint"). That potential expense is obvious enough in the present case: plaintiffs represent a putative class of at least 90 percent of all subscribers to local telephone or high-speed Internet service in

> the continental United States, in an action against America's largest telecommunications firms (with many thousands of employees generating reams and gigabytes of business records) for unspecified (if any) instances of antitrust violations that allegedly occurred over a period of seven years.

550 U.S. at 558–59. The Court suggested that overly generous pleading standards would permit overly expensive discovery, creating unfair settlement pressure on the defendant. Thus, *Twombly* noted the concern that "a plaintiff with 'a largely groundless claim' be allowed to 'take up the time of a number of other people, with the right to do so representing an *in terrorem* increment of the settlement value.' " 550 U.S. at 557–58 (quoting *Blue Chip Stamps v. Manor Drug Stores*, 421 U.S. 723, 741 (1975)). "Judicial scrutiny of the pleading provides an important counterbalance to the broad discovery authorized under the Federal Rules." Douglas G. Smith, *The* Twombly *Revolution?*, 36 PEPP. L. REV. 1063, 1094 (2009). Consider whether such concerns about overly expensive discovery might carry special weight in suits for damages against public officials.

Second, the plausibility standard is not a departure from the Federal Rules, but rather a return to them to make the foregoing practical correction. The plausibility standard simply expresses the traditional view that a defendant is entitled to notice of a "logically coherent" theory of liability. *Id.* at 1098.

Third, viewed in context of the Rules as a whole, "the *Twombly* decision merely reinforces the importance of the Rule 8(a) pleading standard as the gateway to further proceedings under the generous discovery provisions of the Federal Rules." *Id.* at 1099.

Q **6. Interpreting Rule 9(b).** In *Leatherman,* the Court cautioned the lower courts against expanding Rule 9(b), a process that should be left to formal amendment. The second part of Rule 9(b) states that "malice, intent, knowledge, and other conditions of a person's mind may be alleged generally." Isn't alleging generally just what Iqbal did when he alleged that defendants "knew of, condoned, and willfully and maliciously agreed..."? In other words, is *Iqbal* consistent with *Leatherman*?

A The Court arguably dodges the question by saying that " 'generally' is a relative term"—the kind of cute nitpicking that otherwise gives lawyers a bad name (don't try this on a family member). This part of Rule 9 excuses a pleader from pleading discriminatory intent "under an elevated pleading standard," says the Court, but not from "the less rigid—though still operative—strictures of Rule 8." That is, you may not need to plead state of mind with "particularity," but even general pleading must be well pleaded (that is, not entirely conclusory), as well as plausible.

Q **7. Plausible lawyering after *Twombly-Iqbal*.** Consider whether the following allegations meet the new pleading standard.

A. "Defendant negligently drove into plaintiff at a [time and place]."

A

Isn't this nothing more than a classic "threadbare recital of the elements" of negligence? (Actually it's worse. The relevant elements are that defendant had a duty of due care that he breached, as well as proximate causation and injury.) Even if this allegation is somehow found to be "well pleaded" because it is conjoined with time and place, knowing the time and place of the accident hardly helps a court decide whether the allegation of negligence is *plausible*. While this allegation would have sufficed before *Iqbal* because it is taken from old Form 11, it no longer seems to be justified under *Iqbal's* logic (and the forms have been abrogated).

B. Atherton alleges that defendant officials conspired to remove him from a grand jury because he was half Mexican. He alleges that he was the only semi-fluent Spanish-speaking grand juror, and that, after he openly thanked a witness in Spanish, defendants communicated with one another about his removal.

A

The allegation that the defendants communicated together is consistent with a discriminatory conspiracy, but they would also need to communicate to remove him for a non-discriminatory purpose. Calling their communication "conspiracy" is nothing more than a "threadbare recital of the elements of a cause of action" and is insufficient without more under *Iqbal. See Atherton v. District of Columbia Office of Mayor*, 576 F.3d 672 (D.C. Cir. 2009). Should it have mattered that what the officials said to each other and agreed upon is information uniquely within their control? *See Trustees of the Automobile Mechanics' Indus. Welfare & Pensions Fund Local 701 v. Elmhurst Lincoln Mercury*, 677 F. Supp. 2d 1053, 1056 (N.D. Ill. 2010) (answering yes, in rejecting defendant's claim that the complaint was too conclusory, and explaining that "[c]ourts typically afford plaintiffs greater latitude and require less specificity where such allegations are concerned").

C. In *Doe v. Smith, supra* p. 444, Doe alleges that Smith intercepted oral communications and published the intercepted communications to students at her high school.

A

Ironically, before *Iqbal*, the allegation of "interception" might have improved her position on the motion to dismiss (remember how the court of appeals in *Smith* strained to find an interception by video recording of sounds during the taping of intimate sexual relations). But after *Iqbal*, isn't this allegation a bare-bones recital (actually, a direct quote) of an element of the statutory tort? Or is it enough together with allegations of video recording? But isn't "video recording" equally consistent with capturing only images, not images and sounds? If so, is an allegation that sounds were also recorded necessary to make the complaint plausible?

And what are we now to make of the allegation that Smith "published" the intercepted communications in view of the requirement that his disclosure be made in interstate commerce? Isn't this allegation equally consistent with giving out copies of the videotapes to his friends? Is it more plausible that he put the images on the Internet? This allegation seems more vulnerable after *Iqbal*. It's not hard to see why plaintiffs might load up their complaints with factual allegations after *Iqbal*.

D. Plaintiffs, housekeepers at the Governor's mansion, allege they were fired because they had supported the losing party in the last election. In support of this claim, plaintiffs alleged that they were fired without explanation immediately after the election, and that defendants had overheard the plaintiffs speaking favorably about the losing party and its candidates.

A As always, we would need to know more about the elements of the legal theories on which plaintiffs assert this claim. The lower court decided that, although the allegations were consistent with plaintiffs' claims of political motivation, they did not, without more, make it plausible that the new Governor, his wife, and his staff would fire housekeepers wholesale because of their political affiliation. *Ocasio-Hernandez v. Fortuno-Burset*, 639 F. Supp. 2d 217 (D.P.R. 2009). It added:

> The court notes that its present ruling, although draconianly harsh to say the least, is mandated by the recent *Iqbal* decision construing Rules 8(a)(2) and 12(b)(6). The original complaint, filed before *Iqbal* was decided by the Supreme Court, as well as the Amended Complaint, clearly met the pre-*Iqbal* pleading standard under Rule 8. As a matter of fact, counsel for defendants, experienced beyond cavil in political discrimination litigation, did not file a 12(b)(6) motion to dismiss the original complaint because the same was properly pleaded under the then existing, pre-*Iqbal* standard. This case was, in fact, fast-tracked for a . . . trial date . . . and discovery had just commenced when *Iqbal* was decided.
>
> As evidenced by this opinion, even highly experienced counsel will henceforth find it extremely difficult, if not impossible, to plead a section 1983 political discrimination suit without "smoking gun" evidence. In the past, a plaintiff could file a complaint such as that in this case, and through discovery obtain the direct and/or circumstancial [sic] evidence needed to sustain the First Amendment allegations. If the evidence was lacking, a case would then be summarily disposed of. This no longer being the case, counsel in political discrimination cases will now be forced to file suit in Commonwealth [e.g., the local, not the federal] court, where *Iqbal* does not apply and post-complaint discovery is, thus, available. Counsel will also likely only raise local law claims to avoid removal to federal court where *Iqbal* will sound the death knell. Certainly, such a chilling effect was not intended by Congress when it enacted Section 1983 [creating a civil rights action against state officers for deprivation of civil rights].

Id. at 226 n.4.

The court of appeals reversed. 640 F.3d 1 (1st Cir. 2011).

> The district court erred by not affording the plaintiffs' allegations the presumption of truth to which they were entitled. First, as we explained above, the Supreme Court's concerns about conclusory allegations expressed in *Twombly* and *Iqbal* focused on allegations of ultimate legal conclusions and on unadorned recitations of a cause-of-action's elements couched as factual assertions. Allegations of discrete factual events such as the defendants questioning the plaintiffs and replacing the plaintiffs with new employees are not "conclusory" in the relevant sense. Second, factual allegations in a complaint do not need to contain the level of specificity sought by the district court. The plaintiffs' allegations were sufficiently detailed to provide the defendants "fair notice of what the . . . claim is and the grounds upon which it rests." Those allegations should not have been disregarded.

Id. at 14–15.

8. Emerging trends or themes after *Twombly-Iqbal*? As *Ocasio-Hernandez* shows, the application of the plausible pleading standard seems unpredictable. But, surveying the cases, a few trends or themes emerge:

A. *Defendants make more Rule 12(b)(6) motions.* Last time we looked, *Twombly-Iqbal* had been cited more than 125,000 times, ousting *International Shoe* from first place in the field of civil procedure, and studies report a significant increase in the rate of filings of Rule 12(b)(6) motions. *See* Joe S. Cecil et al., *Motions to Dismiss for Failure to State a Claim After Iqbal* (Federal Judicial Center March 2011). But the data on the rate of *granting* the motions is more mixed. This rate has reportedly increased for some kinds of cases (e.g., civil rights and employment discrimination cases), but not across the board. *Id. But see* Patricia Hatamyar Moore, *An Updated Quantitative Study of* Iqbal*'s Impact on 12(b)(6) Motions*, 45 U. Richmond L. Rev. 603 (2012) (reporting significant increase in rate of grants).

B. *Plaintiffs are pleading more specific facts.* This effort may explain why the rate of granting *Twombly-Iqbal* motions has not risen more across the board. But it also means that *Twombly-Iqbal* has increased the cost of litigation to plaintiffs, or "creat[ed] greater symmetry between the plaintiff's and the defendant's litigation costs, . . . reduc[ing] the scope for extortionate discovery," as one pro-*Twombly-Iqbal* judge put it. *Swanson v. Citibank, N.A.*, 614 F.3d 400, 412 (7th Cir. 2010) (Posner, J., dissenting from denial of Rule 12(b)(6) motion). Perversely, it also poses the risk of pleading *too much*! *See Wright & Miller* § 1216 ("Now that plaintiffs appear to be attempting to meet the factual pleading requirements of *Twombly-Iqbal* with longer, more detailed complaints, Rule 8's 'short and plain' statement appears to be the latest procedural vehicle to justify dismissing claims before trial.").

C. Twombly-Iqbal *is context-specific.* The more complex the claim, the higher the plausibility bar. The plaintiff who pleads a simple intersection collision can plead fewer facts than the plaintiff who alleges a complex business tort. On the other hand, as *Elmhurst Lincoln* showed above, some courts take into account the degree to which the necessary facts are in the defendant's knowledge or control. In such cases, they may either lower the plausibility bar or allow some pre-motion discovery.

D. *Some courts say that the plausibility standard should be applied to the pleadings as a whole and not to each discrete allegation.* In *Ocasio-Hernandez*, the court of appeals explained:

> [T]he district court erred when it failed to evaluate the cumulative effect of the factual allegations. The question confronting a court on a motion to dismiss is whether *all* the facts alleged, when viewed in the light most favorable to the plaintiffs, render the plaintiff's entitlement to relief plausible. No single allegation need "lead to the conclusion"—in the district court's words—of some necessary element, provided that, in sum, the allegations of the complaint make the claim as a whole at least plausible. Indeed, the Supreme Court has suggested that allegations that would individually lack the heft to make a claim plausible may suffice to state a claim in the context of the complaint's other factual allegations. *See Twombly,* 550 U.S. at 557 ("An allegation of parallel conduct . . . gets the complaint close to stating a claim, but without some further factual enhancement it stops short of the line between possibility and plausibility.").

Ocasio-Hernandez, 640 F.3d at 14–15. It is unclear how many courts follow the pleadings-as-a-whole approach.

E. *The cases are hopelessly unclear about what makes an allegation "conclusory."* Beyond agreeing that allegations that simply repeat the language of the statute are insufficient, the courts have not predictably applied the "conclusory statement" prong of the *Twombly-Iqbal* analysis. One judge's "factual allegation" is another's "conclusory statement." *See* Donald J. Kochan, *While Effusive, "Conclusory" Is Still Quite Elusive: The Story of a Word,* Iqbal*, and a Perplexing Lexical Inquiry of Supreme Importance*, 73 U. PITT. L. REV. 215 (2011) (summing up the case law guidance as, "You know it when you see it").

9. Confused? So are the judges. Unsettled law often leaves law students in a state of panic. First, at some level they doubt that the law really is confused (how can judges disagree?) and suspect that it is just them, or maybe their professors. Second, they cannot cope with ambiguity on the exam: There must be a black letter rule or all is lost.

But law is rarely made as a finished product. It evolves in application and is made as much by the process of judicial interpretation as by its original drafter. In the meantime, ambiguity is often inevitable. Some judges find that *Twombly-Iqbal* signaled a major change in the law of federal pleading. Others see a change in only certain contexts, although they do not agree about which ones. Finally, some are skeptical:

> [Y]ou don't have to be a nuclear physicist to recognize that *Twombly* and *Iqbal* don't operate as a kind of universal "get out of jail free" card. That seems to be the approach . . . of too many defense counsel, just as though these decisions had somehow blotted out what had been two unanimous Supreme Court decisions, the first written by that noted liberal, Chief Justice Rehnquist, in that Leatherman against Tarrant County, and then the latter one written by the even better known flaming liberal, you know, Justice Thomas, in Swierkiewicz against Sorema.

Transcript of Proceeding at 2–3, *Madison v. City of Chicago*, No. 09 C 3629 (N.D. Ill., Aug. 10, 2009) (sarcasm in original!).

The lessons to be taken from the cases so far and from *Iqbal* itself are for the plaintiff to err on the side of fact pleading, avoiding bare-bones recitations of the elements of the claims in favor of alleging specific facts underlying each element, facts that make your legal theories plausible instead of relying on the old saw that reasonable inferences are to be drawn in favor of the pleader. For defendants, the lesson is to move to dismiss for failure to state a claim in far more cases, liberally citing *Iqbal* and *Twombly* and targeting any allegation that is remotely "conclusory," as well as any liability-favoring inference if it is no more plausible than the liability-disfavoring inference. This is risk-averse and unspecific guidance to be sure, but perhaps the best that we can offer until the Supreme Court—or Congress—has more to say on the subject.

VI. Basic Pleading: Summary of Basic Principles

- A complaint in federal court must contain a statement of subject matter jurisdiction, a short and plain statement of a claim showing that the pleader is entitled to relief under *any* applicable law (whether or not she has identified it in the complaint), and a prayer for relief.
- Heightened pleading is required only for matters required by Rule 9(b) or by statute to be pled with more specific factual detail, and the courts lack the authority to require heightened pleading on their own initiative by judicial interpretation.
- The sufficiency of a complaint may be tested in federal court by a motion under Rule 12(b)(6) to dismiss for failure to state a claim.
- On a Rule 12(b)(6) motion, the court must take all well-pleaded allegations as true and will consider only those allegations within the four corners of the complaint (or incorporated therein by reference).
- An allegation is not "well pleaded" if it is merely conclusory—no more than a naked recital of an element of a cause of action.
- A court should grant a Rule 12(b)(6) motion if, assuming the truth of the *well-pleaded* factual allegations, it determines that they do not *plausibly* show an entitlement to relief under the applicable law. It is not enough that such allegations are equally consistent with an "innocent" explanation as with a liability-creating explanation.
- A plaintiff in federal court is not required to plead factual allegations respecting each and every element of a theory of liability under an applicable law ("elements-pleading"), but pleading allegations for each element is good practice.
- Although Rule 8 does not, in terms, require fact pleading, pleading specific facts in sufficient detail to suggest the plausibility of liability under applicable law is nevertheless a wise precaution, if not a necessity, after the Supreme Court decisions in *Twombly* and *Iqbal*.

14

Responding to the Complaint (or Not?)

I. Introduction

Suppose Macy has been downloading copyrighted music on her computer. One day her teenage son answers the door at her house, and a process server hands him a complaint and summons for Macy. The complaint, brought by Virgin Records, Motown Records, Sony BMG Music Entertainment, and BMG Music asserts a claim against her for copyright violations, seeking damages and an injunction (a court order) ordering her to stop illegally downloading copyrighted music and to destroy the music she has already downloaded. (Some of you may recognize the fact pattern; you know who you are.) How can Macy respond?

Actually, putting the question like that seems to presume that she *will* respond. But she could just ignore the complaint. That is her first option. The rules of civil procedure do not force a defendant to respond affirmatively in any way to a complaint. They spell out the consequences of *not responding*—a sequence of steps driven by the non-defaulting party that can lead to a *default judgment*. Although such judgments are disfavored by the courts, because they are not judgments on the merits and because of a fear that they may take unfair advantage of the defendant in some way, Rule 55 authorizes default judgments if the non-defaulting party and the court carefully follow the prescribed procedures. A substantial number of defendants every year suffer default judgments, many of them electing to default either because they are judgment-proof (i.e., they have no assets from which the judgment can be collected) or because they gamble that the default judgment winner will not track down their assets in order to enforce the judgment. In section II, we will explore the steps that lead to a default judgment.

More likely, Macy will want to defend. As we saw in prior chapters, depending on the circumstances, she could file a motion to dismiss the complaint for lack of subject matter jurisdiction, lack of personal jurisdiction, improper venue, insufficient process, or insufficient service of process (and one other defense that we have not yet discussed: failure to join a required party). As we saw in the last chapter, she could also move to dismiss the complaint for failure to state a claim. These defenses are listed in Rule 12, which also describes other objections that can be raised by Rule 12 motion and sets out rules for making such motions. In the last chapter, we considered Rule 12(b)(6) motions to dismiss for failure to state a claim. Section III explores other aspects of Rule 12 motion practice and the "waiver trap" it sets for the sloppy lawyer.

Finally, Macy could simply answer the complaint (and must, if the court does not dismiss the complaint on a pre-answer motion). An *answer* is a pleading that admits or denies factual allegations in the complaint, sets out defenses, and, if a defendant has some, asserts counterclaims by the defendant against the plaintiff or crossclaims against co-defendants. *See* Chapter 17. Rule 8 sets forth the fairly specific requirements for *admissions* and *denials* and provides an illustrative list of *affirmative defenses*—defenses setting forth new matter outside the original complaint, in the tradition of pleas of confession and avoidance at common law. Section IV discusses these and other issues in answering the complaint.

These responses are not necessarily mutually exclusive. As you may have surmised, the defendant who decides to respond to a complaint often leads with a Rule 12 motion to dismiss and then, if the motion does not succeed in getting the entire case dismissed, follows with an answer. Even if the motion does not succeed in disposing of the case permanently, it may delay the litigation by forcing the plaintiff to serve the complaint again or file the case in a different court. It may also narrow the claims by causing the court to dismiss one or several of them. At the very least, a motion to dismiss calls the plaintiff's bluff (some plaintiffs file complaints in the hopes of a quick settlement offer, but lack the resources or will to keep litigating if the defendant instead resists). Motions and answers are therefore more accurately seen as staged responses to a complaint than as mutually exclusive alternatives.

II. Doing Nothing—The Default Option

Why would Macy do nothing? After all, a summons warns a defendant that:

> Within 21 days after service of this summons on you (not counting the day you received it), you must serve on the plaintiff an answer to the attached complaint or a motion under Rule 12 of the Federal Rules of Civil Procedure.... If

> you fail to do so, judgment by default will be entered against you for the relief demanded in the complaint....

Fed. R. Civ. P. Form 3 (abrogated 2015).

For one thing, she might not know what this means (and, as it turns out, it is not entirely accurate either). "Judgment by default" is not an everyday phrase, and even law students who can guess at the meaning do not (yet) know the legal consequences of such a judgment. Macy's son may forget to tell her about the complaint and summons, or, if he is the one who was actually downloading the music to Mom's computer, hide the documents from her! Or Macy may think to herself, "Good luck to you, Virgin, Sony, and BMG, because I've been out of work for eleven weeks and have nothing left but debts." She may have no fear of a default judgment when she has nothing from which it can be collected.

If she brings the complaint and summons to a lawyer, the lawyer and Macy may make a more strategic, but often risky, decision. The lawyer may reason that her thirteen-year-old son does not qualify as a person of "suitable age and discretion" to accept service of process for Macy. *See* Fed. R. Civ. P. 4(e)(2)(B). Because it would be unfair to enter a default judgment against a defendant who was never informed of the suit against her, courts insist on proof of proper service in the record before they will entertain a motion for a default judgment (although proper service does not guarantee or require actual service, as we saw in *Mullane v. Central Hanover Bank & Trust Co.*, 339 U.S. 306 (1950)). On the other hand, the courts do not refuse to enter a default judgment just because a defendant may have defenses—including defenses on the merits (she did not download the music; the songs were not copyrighted; she is the wrong Macy). If the defendant has defenses, she should assert them by motion or answer. If she is "defaulted" for doing nothing, she usually has only herself to blame.

READING *VIRGIN RECORDS AMERICA, INC. v. LACEY.* The following case traces most of the steps to a default judgment. Make sure you can do the same. Distinguish the default itself, the entry of default, and the entry of a default judgment.

- What did Lacey do (or not do) to cause a default?
- What is an entry of default and how did it happen?
- What is the legal effect of a default?
- What is the predicate and standard for a judgment of default?
- Why doesn't a default establish damages?

VIRGIN RECORDS AMERICA, INC. v. LACEY

510 F. Supp. 2d 588 (S.D. Ala. 2007)

WILLIAM H. STEELE, District Judge.

This case is before the Court on plaintiffs' Motion for Entry of Default Judgment.

I. BACKGROUND

On October 10, 2006, plaintiffs Virgin Records America, Inc., Motown Record Company, L.P., UMG Recordings, Inc., Sony BMG Music Entertainment, and BMG Music filed a Complaint for Copyright Infringement against defendant, Bertha Lacey. In particular, plaintiffs maintained that Lacey had utilized an online media distribution system to download or distribute copyrighted music recordings belonging to plaintiffs, and/or to make such recordings available for distribution to others, thereby infringing on plaintiffs' copyrights and exclusive rights under copyright. On that basis, the Complaint requested the following relief: (1) statutory damages pursuant to 17 U.S.C. § 504(c); (2) attorney's fees and costs pursuant to 17 U.S.C. § 505; and (3) injunctive relief pursuant to 17 U.S.C. §§ 502 and 503, prohibiting Lacey from further infringing conduct and requiring her to destroy all copies of sound recordings made in violation of plaintiffs' exclusive rights.

On November 14, 2006, plaintiffs filed a Return of Service reflecting that defendant had been served with process by a private process server on October 26, 2006. According to the server's declaration, copies of the summons and complaint were left at Lacey's dwelling house or usual place of abode (6005 Howells Ferry Road, Mobile, AL 36618) and were given to Lacey's son, Brad Lacey.

Notwithstanding service of process in accordance with Rule 4(e), Fed. R. Civ. P., nearly three months ago, Lacey has never filed an answer or otherwise appeared in this action. Upon motion by plaintiffs, a Clerk's Entry of Default was entered against Lacey on December 13, 2006 for failure to plead or otherwise defend. The Clerk of Court mailed a copy of that Entry of Default to defendant at the same address at which process was served. Once again, Lacey failed to respond. No further activity occurring in this matter in the subsequent 30 days, plaintiffs now seek entry of default judgment.

II. ANALYSIS

A. Propriety of Default Judgment

In this Circuit, "there is a strong policy of determining cases on their merits and we therefore view defaults with disfavor." *In re Worldwide Web Systems, Inc.,* 328 F.3d 1291, 1295 (11th Cir. 2003); *see also Varnes v. Local 91, Glass Bottle Blowers Ass'n of U.S. and Canada,* 674 F.2d 1365, 1369 (11th Cir. 1982) ("Since this case involves a default judgment there must be strict compliance with the legal prerequisites establishing the court's power to render the judgment."). Nonetheless, it is well established that a "district court has the authority to enter default judgment for failure . . . to comply with its orders or rules of procedure." *Wahl v. McIver,* 773 F.2d 1169, 1174 (11th Cir. 1985).

Where, as here, a defendant has failed to appear or otherwise acknowledge the pendency of a lawsuit against her for some three months after being served, entry of default judgment may be appropriate. Indeed, Rule 55 itself provides for entry of default and default judgment where a defendant "has failed to plead or otherwise defend as provided by these rules." Rule 55(a), Fed. R. Civ. P. In a variety of contexts, courts have entered default judgments against defendants who have failed to defend the claims against them following proper service of process. *See, e.g., In re Knight,* 833 F.2d 1515, 1516 (11th Cir. 1987) ("Where a party offers no good reason for the late filing of its answer, entry of default judgment against that party is appropriate."); *Matter of Dierschke,* 975 F.2d 181, 184 (5th Cir. 1992) ("when the court finds an intentional failure of responsive pleadings there need be no other finding" to justify default judgment); *Kidd v. Andrews,* 340 F. Supp. 2d 333, 338 (W.D.N.Y. 2004) (entering default judgment against defendant who failed to answer or move against complaint for nearly three months); *Viveros v. Nationwide Janitorial Ass'n, Inc.,* 200 F.R.D. 681, 684 (N.D. Ga. 2000) (entering default judgment against counterclaim defendant who had failed to answer or otherwise respond to counterclaim within time provided by Rule 12(a)(2)). In short, then, "[w]hile modern courts do not favor default judgments, they are certainly appropriate when the adversary process has been halted because of an essentially unresponsive party." *Flynn v. Angelucci Bros. & Sons, Inc.,* 448 F. Supp. 2d 193, 195 (D.D.C. 2006) (citation omitted).[2]

The law is clear, however, that Lacey's failure to appear and the Clerk's subsequent entry of default against her do not automatically entitle plaintiffs to a default judgment. Indeed, a default is not "an absolute confession by the defendant of his liability and of the plaintiff's right to recover," but is instead merely "an admission of the facts cited in the Complaint, which by themselves may or may not be sufficient to establish a defendant's liability." *Pitts ex rel. Pitts v. Seneca Sports, Inc.,* 321 F. Supp. 2d 1353, 1357 (S.D. Ga. 2004); *see also Descent v. Kolitsidas,* 396 F. Supp. 2d 1315, 1316 (M.D. Fla. 2005) ("the defendants' default notwithstanding, the plaintiff is entitled to a default judgment only if the complaint states a claim for relief"). Stated differently, "a default judgment cannot stand on a complaint that fails to state a claim." *Chudasama v. Mazda Motor Corp.,* 123 F.3d 1353, 1370 n.41 (11th Cir. 1997).

Review of the Complaint confirms that it does indeed assert detailed facts against Lacey, including a recitation of eight specific copyrighted recordings that Lacey has used and continues to use an online media distribution system

2. To be sure, courts have generally required some notice to be given to a defendant between the time of service of process and entry of default judgment. *See, e.g., International Brands USA, Inc. v. Old St. Andrews Ltd.,* 349 F. Supp. 2d 256, 261 (D. Conn. 2004) ("Where a party fails to respond, *after notice* the court is ordinarily justified in entering a judgment against the defaulting party.") (emphasis added and citations omitted). For unknown reasons, plaintiffs elected not to give Lacey notice of their efforts to secure a default against her, as their Motion for Entry of Default was unaccompanied by a Certificate of Service or other indicia that plaintiffs had placed Lacey on notice that they were seeking entry of default. Nothing in the text of Rule 55 excuses the service requirement for requests for entry of default (as distinguished from motions for default judgment). Nonetheless, any harm arising from plaintiffs' omission is negated by the fact that the Clerk of Court mailed a copy of the Clerk's Entry of Default to Lacey at the address where service was perfected. As such, Lacey is on notice that plaintiffs have moved forward with default proceedings, yet she has elected not to defend herself. Given Lacey's failure to appear in this case, despite actual notice that this lawsuit was pending, that her responsive pleading was due by a date certain, and that a default had been entered against her, she is entitled to no further notice at this time. *See* Rule 55(b)(2) (defaulted defendant is entitled to notice of request for default judgment only if defendant has appeared in the action).

to download and/or distribute without plaintiffs' permission.[3] The Complaint further states that plaintiffs are the copyright owners for those specific recordings. These facts, which are deemed admitted by virtue of Lacey's default, are sufficiently detailed and specific to give rise to a cognizable claim for direct copyright infringement in violation of the copyright laws of the United States, as codified at 17 U.S.C. §§ 101 et seq. Accordingly, the Court finds that the Complaint states a claim for relief.

The legal effect of Lacey's default is that she has now admitted the facts recited in the Complaint, which are sufficient to establish her liability to plaintiffs on a theory of copyright infringement. Moreover, because she has made no attempt to defend this action in the three months since being served with process, despite notice that plaintiffs were moving forward with default proceedings against her, Lacey's course of conduct amounts to a deliberate and intentional failure to respond, which is just the sort of dilatory litigation tactic for which the default judgment mechanism was created. For these reasons, plaintiffs' Motion is **granted** as to entry of default judgment. Default judgment will be entered against Lacey, in accordance with Rule 55(b)(2), Fed. R. Civ. P. The Court will next consider which remedies will be awarded to plaintiffs.

B. Remedies

Plaintiffs seek three forms of relief, to-wit: minimum statutory damages, costs, and a permanent injunction. In considering these requests, the Court bears in mind that, notwithstanding the default against Lacey, "judgment may be granted only for such relief as may lawfully be granted upon the well-pleaded facts alleged in the complaint." *Pitts,* 321 F. Supp. 2d at 1358 (citation omitted).[5] Each form of relief sought will be considered in turn.

1. Statutory Damages

A copyright owner whose copyright has been infringed may recover, at his election, either actual damages or statutory damages for the infringing activity. 17 U.S.C. § 504(a)–(c). Where the copyright owner elects the latter option, a court may award, "instead of actual damages and profits, an award of statutory damages for all infringements involved in the action, with respect to any one work, for which any one infringer is liable individually . . . in a sum of not less than $750 or more than $30,000 as the court considers just." § 504(c)(1). Plaintiffs have elected statutory damages, in lieu of actual damages and profits, and seek entry of only the statutory minimum amount of $750 per work for each of the eight works that the Complaint charged Lacey with unlawfully downloading and/or distributing, for a total of $6,000 in statutory damages.

As mentioned above, the entry of default judgment against Lacey in no way obviates the need for determinations of the amount and character of damages.

3. Those recordings include Janet Jackson "This Time," Rick James "Fire and Desire," Dru Hill "5 Steps," Jennifer Lopez "If You Had My Love," Michael Jackson "Heal the World," Michael Jackson "You Rock My World," Tyrese "Lately," and Dru Hill "Beauty." The Complaint lists each of these recordings by reference to copyright owner (which in each instance is one of the named plaintiffs herein), album title, and SR#.

5. While well-pleaded facts in the complaint are deemed admitted, plaintiffs' allegations relating to the amount of damages are not admitted by virtue of default; rather, the court must determine both the amount and character of damages. . . .

Rule 55(b)(2) specifically provides that if "it is necessary to take an account or to determine the amount of damages or to establish the truth of any averment by evidence or to make an investigation of any other matter, the court may conduct such hearings or order such references as it deems necessary and proper." **[Eds.—This language has been slightly revised in the current Rule.]** That said, there is no requirement that a hearing be conducted in all default judgment proceedings to fix the appropriate level of damages. *See S.E.C. v. Smyth,* 420 F.3d 1225, 1232 n. 13 (11th Cir. 2005) (explaining that evidentiary hearing is not *per se* requirement for entry of default judgment, and may be omitted if all essential evidence is already of record). Where the amount of damages sought is a sum certain, or where an adequate record has been made via affidavits and documentary evidence to show statutory damages, no evidentiary hearing is required.

... Irrespective of the evidence presented, given the admitted facts as to liability, there is no scenario under which the Court could award less than $6,000 in statutory damages here. Plaintiffs have waived their right to request any more than that minimum amount, and § 504(c)(1) forbids a lesser award; therefore, the Court finds that no constructive purpose would be served by conducting an evidentiary hearing prior to awarding plaintiffs the minimum statutory damages of $6,000, or $750 for each of the eight copyrighted works that Lacey has admitted infringing.

2. Injunctive Relief

Plaintiffs also seek a permanent injunction to enjoin Lacey from infringing plaintiffs' rights in copyrighted recordings, including by using the Internet or online media distribution systems to reproduce or distribute any of plaintiffs' recordings, or to make any of plaintiffs' recordings available for distribution to the public, except pursuant to a license or with plaintiffs' consent. Plaintiffs also seek an injunction requiring Lacey to destroy all copies of plaintiffs' recordings that she has downloaded or transferred onto computer hard drives, servers or physical devices or media without plaintiffs' authorization.

This type of relief is specifically authorized by copyright law....

Here, plaintiffs have established Lacey's liability for infringing their copyrights as to eight copyrighted recordings. They have shown that Lacey is continuing her infringing conduct on an ongoing basis through her use of an online media distribution system to download and/or distribute such copyrighted recordings without plaintiffs' permission or consent. Despite service of process and notice of the default proceedings, Lacey has made no effort to defend against these charges of copyright infringement, suggesting that she does not take seriously the illegality of her infringing activity. Based on all of the foregoing, the Court concludes that plaintiffs have shown a strong likelihood that, unless enjoined, Lacey will pose a continuing threat to infringe their copyrighted recordings. As such, the permanent injunction sought by plaintiffs is reasonably necessary to protect plaintiffs from further infringement of their copyrights by Lacey. Plaintiffs' request for entry of permanent injunction as part of the default judgment in this case is **granted**.

3. Costs

[The court also awarded costs in accordance with the statute.]

III. CONCLUSION

holding

For all of the foregoing reasons, plaintiffs' Motion for Entry of Default Judgment is **granted** pursuant to Rule 55(b)(2), Fed. R. Civ. P. . . .

Notes and Questions: Getting a Default Judgment

Q **1. The default.** What did Lacey do (or not do) to cause a default?

A She "failed to plead or otherwise defend." Rule 55(a). In fact, she did nothing at all. Of course, that can't be all there is to it, because no one has pleaded or otherwise defended, for example, on the day after service, but that could hardly mean that the defendant has defaulted at that point. It must be that the defendant failed to plead or otherwise defend *within the time set by the Rules.* As noted above, a federal court summons presently advises a defendant to move or answer within twenty-one days after service of the summons and complaint, a deadline set by Rule 12(a).

Filing a motion is "otherwise defend[ing]," but this is peculiarly indirect wording if filing a motion were the only way to "otherwise defend." While the mere appearance by a defending party (an *appearance* is usually entered by filing a paper with the court listing the name and address of the party, or when the party is represented, of the lawyer) is not enough to prevent a default, some courts have said that an appearance coupled with some other indication of defendant's desire to contest the action can be enough. Note that the court finds that Lacey never even appeared in the action.

2. It's da fault of the defendant? Consider the following multiple choice question.

Which of the following responses by the defendant to service of the complaint and summons constitutes a default? (There is more than one.)

A. Defendant does not answer, but files a motion to dismiss for improper venue within twenty-one days. The motion is denied.
B. Defendant answers within twenty-one days and admits the allegations of the complaint.
C. Defendant's lawyer files an appearance within twenty-one days by submitting a paper to the clerk (called a *praecipe* in many courts) giving her name, address, and bar number, and stating that she is appearing for the defendant.
D. Defendant herself brings a paper to the clerk saying that she plans to defend, and then shows up in court on the twenty-first day saying she is ready to go to trial.
E. Defendant answers the complaint twenty-five days after service of the summons and complaint.

A is clearly not a default. Filing a motion is "otherwise defend[ing]" and, indeed, it is one response listed in the summons itself. That the motion is not granted is irrelevant; nothing says that your initial defense has to be successful. The important point is that you are actively defending in the manner and time set by the Rules. In fact, Rule 12 allows you to answer after a Rule 12 motion to dismiss is denied.

B is not right either, because by answering, the defendant has pled. But doesn't admitting the complaint set up a judgment? Well, maybe. We will see that a plaintiff may seek a judgment by motion under Rule 12(c) (for judgment as a matter of law based on undisputed facts in the complaint and the answer), but it is not a *default* judgment and therefore is not controlled by the procedures set out in Rule 55. Moreover, an answer may admit the allegations of the complaint but still contain defenses and claims, as we said in the introduction, so any talk of judgment may be premature.

The defendant in **C** has begun to respond to the complaint, but we just said that a mere appearance cannot stave off default; you must do something in addition to show a desire to defend. So the defendant in this case is in default (and should think about suing her lawyer).

By contrast, in **D**, defendant *has* done something more than appear, although she seems to be under the misapprehension that there is a trial on the twenty-first day. It is not clear whether her mistake coupled with her appearance is "otherwise defend[ing]," but the fact that she appears to be defending herself (*pro se*) may earn her the court's indulgence. The courts not only "view defaults with disfavor," as the *Lacey* court observes, but they are especially hesitant to find *pro se* litigants in default when the default results from their good faith misunderstanding of the rules.

Finally, **E** is a default. It is not enough to answer or move if you miss the deadline set by the Rules. One function of default is to encourage litigants to follow the Rules, including the timelines they set. Finding a default here certainly provides an incentive to meet the twenty-one-day deadline. On the other hand, how prejudicial could it be to the plaintiff or inconvenient for the court that the defendant missed the deadline by four days? Rule 55(c) gives a court the discretion to set aside an entry of default for "good cause," and the courts have been quite generous in finding such causes in clerical errors, communication lapses, attorney vacations, and sometimes nothing more than the press of business.

Q **3. The entry of default.** By what process was a default entered in Lacey's case?

A The plaintiffs made a motion for entry of default. "Entry" here refers to an actual notation in the *docket*—the clerk-kept list of filings, hearings, and orders in this particular action. It's thus a written indication that the defendant is in default. But the clerk does not note the default automatically. Rule 55(a) states that the clerk shall enter the default only if there has been a default *and* "that failure is shown by affidavit or otherwise." Ordinarily, then, entry of default requires some action by the plaintiff to bring the fact of default to the clerk's attention, such as filing an *affidavit*—a sworn written declaration of facts.

Once the clerk has entered a default, can the non-defaulting party enforce the entry to collect damages from the defaulting party?

> No. There is an important difference between a *default*—a failure to respond as the rules require—and *a default judgment*. The entry of default is simply a step toward obtaining a default judgment—an official notation that defendant has failed to respond—and not itself an enforceable judgment.

4. Standards for entering a default judgment. *Lacey* makes it clear that the entry of a default alone does not automatically entitle plaintiffs to a default judgment. By defaulting, Lacey admitted the *facts* alleged in the complaint, but whether the admitted facts establish her liability is a question of *law* for the court. It cannot enter a default judgment unless it finds, as a matter of law, that the complaint states a claim for relief. It made that finding in the paragraph beginning "Review of the Complaint," before finding that the "legal effect" of her admission of facts was "to establish her liability on a theory of copyright infringement." It is as if the defaulting party had filed a phantom motion to dismiss for failure to state a claim under Rule 12(b)(6), which the court must decide before entering a default judgment.

Rule 55(b) is not mandatory; courts have the discretion to enter a default judgment or to decline. Moreover, if the defendant has in some way appeared (even though it did not respond as required by the Rules), it is entitled to at least seven days' written notice of a hearing about entering a default judgment at which it can argue against entering a judgment and to set aside the entry of default. Courts have refused to enter default judgments and have let the defendant belatedly defend, for example, when very large sums of money are involved, the case involves issues of public importance, the default was largely technical or caused by a good faith mistake or excusable neglect by the defendant, or the delay occasioned by default caused little prejudice to the plaintiff. *See Wright & Miller* § 2685.

Finally, as noted above, damages must be fixed before a default judgment can be entered. If the claim is for a sum certain (e.g., for $83,411.22 on an account due), as shown by an affidavit by the plaintiff, the clerk can enter judgment for this amount.

The plaintiffs' claims against Lacey were for *unliquidated* damages (not for a predetermined "sum certain," Fed. R. Civ. P. 55(b), but for an indefinite amount to be determined by the court after weighing the evidence), and for injunctive relief as well. The statute did not prescribe a specific penalty either, but instead sets a range. In that case, which of the following statements is correct? *See* Fed. R. Civ. P. 55(b).

A. The clerk can calculate the damages and enter judgment for the calculated amount, leaving the question of injunctive relief to the judge.
B. The court must hold an evidentiary hearing to decide damages and injunctive relief.
C. The court can enter a default judgment without holding an evidentiary hearing.
D. The clerk can enter a judgment for damages and issue an injunction.
E. A default judgment must be entered for the relief sought in the complaint.

We can readily reject **E**, for, as *Lacey* says, the entry of the default judgment "in no way obviates the need for determinations of the amount and character of damages." Indeed, Rule 55(b) itself contemplates such a computation before entry of the default judgment. Interestingly, Rule 54(c) *does* tie a default judgment to the complaint, but only by using the amount or kind of relief set out in the complaint *as a ceiling*. This makes sense, because it allows the defendant to make a reasoned calculation of the risk of defaulting.

D also sounds wrong, because even if a clerk could enter a judgment for damages, it seems intuitively wrong to let the clerk decide whether to issue an injunction, which turns, in part, on the likelihood that Lacey poses a "continuing threat" of infringement. Deciding this question requires judging, not clerking. For this reason, the Rule states that in all cases other than claims for a sum certain, the non-defaulting party must apply to the court for a default judgment. Fed. R. Civ. P. 55(b)(2).

By this same rule, **A** is incorrect, because plaintiffs did not seek a "sum certain." They sought "statutory damages" (which are between $750 and $30,000 per work, "as the court considers just"). The theory of letting the clerk alone enter a default judgment for a sum certain is that the entry is no more than a ministerial act. But the calculation of damages "as the court considers just" is another act of judging.

B, therefore, sounds like the right answer and normally would be, as a court would need to decide what amount of damages in the wide statutory range would be just. As it happens, though, the plaintiffs in *Lacey* made it easy by electing to accept just the minimum statutory damages of $750 per downloaded work. The ease of that computation removed any necessity for an evidentiary hearing on damages. The Rule does not require one; it only states that a court *may* conduct a hearing if it thinks one is necessary to ascertain the amount of damages. Fed. R. Civ. P. 55(b)(2). The court also apparently found that it had enough evidence to issue the injunction without a further hearing. On *Lacey*'s facts, therefore, **C** is the best answer.

Q **5. The implied predicates: Service and personal jurisdiction.** Suppose the plaintiffs had never served Lacey. In that case, the reason she never responded to the complaint is simply that she never knew she had been sued. It would then be grossly unfair for the court to enter a default judgment against her. We have seen that due process entails, at a minimum, service that is reasonably calculated to provide notice in the circumstances (*not* that service resulted in actual notice). As a result, a court deciding a motion for a default judgment will typically require that the record show that proper service was made. As a practical matter, however, some courts go beyond what due process and the applicable service rules minimally require and deny the motion if the defendant makes a credible showing that it never received actual notice. In addition, a court will often look for evidence that it has personal jurisdiction over the defaulting party before entering a default judgment. How was personal jurisdiction shown in *Lacey*?

A The court, the United States District Court for the Southern District of Alabama, expressly noted that the plaintiffs had filed a valid return of service on defendant's son at her house in Alabama. She was therefore served in-state with claims for acts conducted in-state (and she was probably also domiciled in-state). Her in-state domicile is sufficient for minimum contacts per *Milliken v. Meyer*, 311 U.S. 457 (1940), and, in any case, her purposeful in-state tortious acts presumably also satisfy any applicable long arm statute and the minimum contacts test.

6. Setting aside a default or a default judgment. Default is disfavored. Accordingly, the Rule makes it easy to set aside entry of default "for good cause." Fed. R. Civ. P. 55(c). Once a default judgment has been entered, however, the standard is tightened. A default judgment is a final judgment on which the plaintiffs and others may have relied. Setting it aside may be prejudicial to such parties, especially when some time has passed since its entry. The defaulting party must therefore move for relief under Rule 60(b), which places time limits on the motion for certain causes, like mistake or excusable neglect. Fed. R. Civ. P. 60(c)(1).

When deciding to set aside a default judgment on grounds of mistake or neglect, the courts almost always consider whether the default was willful, whether setting it aside would prejudice the plaintiff, and whether the defendant has any meritorious defenses. By contrast, courts set aside judgments as "void" if they find that service was never made or that the court that entered the judgment lacked personal jurisdiction. *See Wright & Miller* § 2695.

III. Moving to Dismiss—Rule 12 Motion Practice

A. The Rule 12 Motions

Suppose, in our opening hypothetical case, Macy retains you as her attorney to respond to the complaint and defend the lawsuit. How should you proceed? One wise starting point is to ascertain as soon as possible when a response to the complaint is due—a date that is stated in the summons. (If your time is short, you may want to contact the plaintiffs' lawyer to ask for more.) Obviously, you'll want to interview Macy carefully, not only to learn her side of the events giving rise to the claim (the alleged downloading), but also about the opening events in the litigation—service of process. And, of course, you'll read the complaint to explore defenses and make an early evaluation of your client's liability exposure.

For this purpose, Rule 12(b) provides a handy checklist of the most common defenses that can be raised by a motion to dismiss. Running through the list, for example, may cause you to inquire about the age of Macy's son, in order to decide whether he is "someone of suitable age and discretion" who can accept process for Macy. *See* Rule 4(e)(2)(B). If not, the defense of "insufficient service of process" is available. Rule 12(b)(5). The list also includes "failure to state a claim," Rule 12(b)(6), which will probably require legal research into the theories of liability advanced in the complaint (unless you're already a copyright expert), in order to decide both whether the claims have been plausibly pleaded and whether your client has any substantive defenses. Finally, Rules 12(e) and 12(f) suggest two additional motions available to challenge a complaint, which are explained in the following case.

READING *MATOS v. NEXTRAN, INC.* After he is injured when his truck rolled over, Matos sues the truck manufacturer and seller, predictably stating counts for negligence, breach of warranty, and strict liability, and then, more unusually, independent "counts" for loss of consortium and punitive damages.

- Why do the defendants file motions under Rules 12(b)(6), 12(e), and 12(f) at the same time, instead of seriatim?
- Why does the court dismiss the express warranty count? Is that dismissal necessarily the end of the line for the plaintiff on this count?
- The court also dismisses the count for punitive damages. Why? Does this take punitive damages out of the case?

MATOS v. NEXTRAN, INC.

2009 WL 2477516 (D.V.I. 2009)

GÓMEZ, Chief Judge.

Before the Court is the motion of defendant Nextran, Inc. ("Nextran") to dismiss this matter, to strike certain allegations, and for a more definite statement.

I. FACTUAL AND PROCEDURAL BACKGROUND

On May 2, 2006, Eduardo Matos was driving a truck carrying concrete in an area known as Mahogany Run on St. Thomas, U.S. Virgin Islands.[1] He suffered injuries when the truck rolled over. The truck was allegedly manufactured and sold by Nextran and defendant Mack Truck Sales of South Florida ("Mack Truck").

Mr. Matos and his wife, Santa Matos (together, the "Plaintiffs"), subsequently commenced this action against Nextran and Mack Truck (together, the "Defendants"), asserting six causes of action: (1) negligence; (2) breach of the warranty of fitness for a particular purpose; (3) strict liability; (4) breach of the warranty of merchantability; (5) loss of consortium; and (6) punitive damages. . . .

Nextran now moves to dismiss the complaint pursuant to Federal Rule of Civil Procedure 12(b)(6). In the alternative, Nextran moves to strike certain allegations in the complaint pursuant to Federal Rule of Civil Procedure 12(f) or for a more definite statement pursuant to Federal Rule of Civil Procedure 12(e).

II. DISCUSSION

A. Rule 12(b)(6) Standard

"[W]hen ruling on a defendant's motion to dismiss, a judge must accept as true all of the factual allegations contained in the complaint." *Erickson v. Pardus,*

1. Because Nextran's motion is brought pursuant to Federal Rule of Civil Procedure 12(b)(6), all allegations in the complaint are taken as true.

551 U.S. 89, 93 (2007) (per curiam) (citing *Bell Atlantic Corp. v. Twombly,* 550 U.S. 544, 555 (2007)). All reasonable inferences are drawn in favor of the non-moving party. A court must ask whether the complaint "contain[s] either direct or inferential allegations respecting all the material elements necessary to sustain recovery under *some* viable legal theory." *Bell Atlantic Corp.,* 550 U.S. at 562 (emphasis in original) (quoting *Car Carriers, Inc. v. Ford Motor Co.,* 745 F.2d 1101, 1106 (7th Cir. 1984)). "While a complaint attacked by a Rule 12(b)(6) motion to dismiss does not need detailed factual allegations, a plaintiff's obligation to provide the 'grounds' of his 'entitlement to relief' requires more than labels and conclusions, and a formulaic recitation of a cause of action's elements will not do." *Id.* at 555 (internal citations omitted). Thus, "[t]o survive a motion to dismiss, a ... plaintiff must allege facts that 'raise a right to relief above the speculative level on the assumption that the allegations in the complaint are true (even if doubtful in fact).' " *Victaulic Co. v. Tieman,* 499 F.3d 227, 234 (3d Cir. 2007) (quoting *Bell Atlantic Corp.,* 550 U.S. at 555).

B. Rule 12(f)

Rule 12(f) provides that a district court "may strike from a pleading an insufficient defense or any redundant, immaterial, impertinent, or scandalous matter." Fed. R. Civ. P. 12(f). "[I]t is settled that [a Rule 12(f)] motion will be denied, unless it can be shown that no evidence in support of the allegation would be admissible." *Lipsky v. Commonwealth United Corp.,* 551 F.2d 887, 893 (2d Cir. 1976) (citations omitted). Allegations that are "repugnant" or that contain "superfluous descriptions and not substantive elements of the cause of action" also may be stricken. Indeed, a court has "considerable discretion" in striking an allegation. "Striking a party's pleading, however, is an extreme and disfavored measure." *BJC Health Sys.,* 478 F.3d at 917; *see also Waste Mgmt. Holdings v. Gilmore,* 252 F.3d 316, 347 (4th Cir. 2001) ("Rule 12(f) motions are generally viewed with disfavor because striking a portion of a pleading is a drastic remedy and because it is often sought by the movant simply as a dilatory tactic." (quotation marks and citation omitted)); *Lipsky,* 551 F.2d at 893 ("[T]he courts should not tamper with the pleadings unless there is a strong reason for so doing." (citations omitted)).

C. Rule 12(e)

Rule 12(e) allows a party to "move for a more definite statement of a pleading to which a responsive pleading is allowed but which is so vague or ambiguous that the party cannot reasonably prepare a response." Fed. R. Civ. P. 12(e). Such a motion "must point out the defects complained of and the details desired." *Id.* Such a motion may be granted, for instance, where "a shotgun complaint fails to adequately link a cause of action to its factual predicates." *Wagner v. First Horizon Pharm. Corp.,* 464 F.3d 1273, 1275 (11th Cir. 2006); *see also Beanal v. Freeport-McMoran, Inc.,* 197 F.3d 161, 164 (5th Cir. 1999) ("[A] complaint, which contains a bare bones allegation that a wrong occurred and which does not plead any of the facts giving rise to the injury, does not provide adequate notice." (internal quotation marks and citation omitted)).

III. ANALYSIS

A. Rule 12(b)(6)

1. Counts Two and Four

Nextran first argues that the [express breach of warranty claims] . . . asserted in Counts Two and Four should be dismissed.

. . . To state a claim for breach of an express warranty generally, a plaintiff must allege the following: "(1) plaintiff and defendant entered into a contract; (2) containing an express warranty by the defendant with respect to a material fact; (3) which warranty was part of the basis of the bargain; and (4) the express warranty was breached by defendant." . . .

Missing from either Count Two or Count Four is either an explicit or even oblique allegation that the express affirmation of fact that the Defendants made to Mr. Matos's employer "was part of the basis of the [parties'] bargain." Such an allegation is an essential element of a breach of an express warranty claim. Accordingly, the Court finds that the Plaintiffs have failed to state a breach of an express warranty claim. Notwithstanding that deficiency, in accordance with this circuit's precedent, the Court will give the Plaintiffs an opportunity to amend their complaint with respect to their express warranty claims in Counts Two and Four. *See Phillips v. County of Allegheny,* 515 F.3d 224, 228 (3d Cir. 2008) ("[I]n the event a complaint fails to state a claim, unless amendment would be futile, the District Court must give a plaintiff the opportunity to amend her complaint." (citing *Shane v. Fauver,* 213 F.3d 113, 116 (3d Cir. 2000)). . . .

claim

2. Count One

Nextran moves to dismiss Count One's negligence claim for failure to state a claim.

To state a claim for negligence in the Virgin Islands, a plaintiff must allege (1) a duty; (2) a breach of that duty; (3) causation; and (4) damages.

In the general allegations section of their complaint, which is incorporated by reference into the substantive allegations of each count, the Plaintiffs allege that the Defendants "designed, manufactured, assembled and/or sold" a truck "for [Mr. Matos] and other drivers . . . to operate in their daily work of transporting and pouring concrete." (Am. Compl. ¶ 10.) In Count One itself, the Plaintiffs allege that Nextran "caused a cement mixer to be mounted on [the] truck." (*Id.* ¶ 13.) They further allege that Nextran "was responsible for performing the final inspection on the truck before selling and shipping it to" Mr. Matos's employer and "to make sure that the truck worked properly, was in good order and condition, and was free of all defects." (*Id.* ¶ 15.) According to the complaint, Nextran failed to fulfill that responsibility. (*Id.*) The Plaintiffs further allege that they suffered injuries as a result of that failure. Specifically, Mr. Matos allegedly "suffered serious physical injuries to his body, including his legs, arm, back and head." (*Id.* ¶ 7.) Mrs. Matos allegedly "suffered a loss of consortium and was unable to enjoy the assistance, companionship and society of [Mr.] Matos and to engage in the customary joys of the marital relationship." (*Id.* ¶ 35.)

Although not stated explicitly, the allegations in the complaint make clear that the Defendants owed the Plaintiffs a duty to manufacture, design and/or sell a truck that was in good working condition. *See, e.g., Fisher v. Roberts,* 125 F.3d 974, 978 (6th Cir. 1997) ("Although the complaint does not allege explicitly that defendant owed plaintiff a duty of care and breached that duty, it contains enough information from which the material elements of plaintiff[']s claim can be inferred."). The Plaintiffs further allege that the Defendants' failure to do so caused Mr. Matos's accident and, by extension, the Plaintiffs' various injuries.

Because the Plaintiffs have specified negligent acts and characterized the duty whose breach caused their alleged injuries, the Court finds that the Plaintiffs' allegations are sufficient to defeat the Defendants' Rule 12(b)(6) challenge to Count One. The motion will thus be denied with respect to that count....

4. Count Six

In Count Six, the Plaintiffs allege that the Defendants are "liable for punitive damages for their reckless disregard and indifference to [the] Plaintiffs' safety." (Am. Compl. ¶ 37.) Nextran contends that Count Six, which asserts a punitive damages claim, must be dismissed because the Plaintiffs have not pled any basis for awarding such damages.

The Court need not reach Nextran's contention that the Plaintiffs' allegations falls [sic] short of warranting a punitive damages award. As this Court has recently explained, it is well-established law that a "punitive damages claim cannot stand alone." *McDonald v. Davis,* No. 2004-93, 2009 U.S. Dist. LEXIS 17309, at *56–57, 2009 WL 580456 (D.V.I. Mar. 5, 2009) (collecting cases); *see also Urgent v. Hovensa, LLC,* No. 2006-105, 2008 U.S. Dist. LEXIS 77455, at *31, 2008 WL 4526677 (D.V.I. Oct. 2, 2008) (dismissing a punitive damages count on the defendant's motion to dismiss because such a claim "is not a distinct cause of action and was improperly plead[ed] as a separate count").

Accordingly, the Court will grant Nextran's motion as it pertains to Count Six.[9] The Court's ruling in this vein is, of course, without prejudice to the Plaintiffs' request for punitive damages at the appropriate stage of these proceedings.

B. Rule 12(f)

Nextran asserts that the Court should strike certain allegations from the complaint. Nextran describes the following allegations, the relevant portions of which are italicized, as prejudicial:

> The *illegal conduct,* as stated herein, of Defendants enhanced the accident alleged and Plaintiffs' injuries and damages alleged herein.
>
> . . .

9. Nextran also seeks the "dismissal" of the Plaintiffs' request for attorney's fees and costs. To the extent that request is not asserted as an independent cause of action, Nextran's challenge warrants no ruling. To the extent Nextran seeks to strike the Plaintiffs' fee and cost request, the motion is denied. The Virgin Islands' fee-shifting statute, V.I. Code Ann. tit. 5, § 541, authorizes a court to award fees and expenses to the "prevailing party" in an action. As there is no prevailing party at this stage, Nextran's motion is premature.

> The aforementioned truck was unreasonably dangerous and Defendants are strictly liable for the incident and *all damages of every kind* suffered by Plaintiffs as a direct and proximate result.
>
> . . .
>
> Plaintiff Santa Matos is the wife of Plaintiff Eduardo Matos and, as a direct and proximate result of the negligence, breach of warranty and other *illegal acts* and/or omissions of Defendants, Plaintiff Santa Matos suffered a loss of consortium[.]

(Am. Compl. ¶¶ 16, 29, 35) (emphasis supplied).

According to Nextran, "[t]hese are extraneous statements, untrue and unnecessary for Plaintiffs to plead their cause(s) of action, and are irrelevant and prejudicial."

To the extent Nextran seeks to strike the Plaintiffs' request to recover "all damages of every kind," the Court is singularly unconvinced. That request appears in the Plaintiffs' strict liability claim. Damages are an element of such a claim and thus a request that they be awarded is hardly out of place. The Plaintiffs perhaps overreach when they ask for any and all damages, but such overreaching is certainly not inconsistent with the expansive prayers for relief that are drafted into many complaints. In any event, any damages the Plaintiffs seek to recover will have to be proven at trial, if need be. Simply asking for them now works no prejudice to the Defendants. In the absence of such prejudice, the Court will deny the motion to strike as it pertains to the Plaintiffs' damages request.

To the extent Nextran wants any references to the Defendants' alleged "illegal conduct" or "illegal acts" stricken, the Court is similarly unpersuaded. While illegality may not be an element per se of any of the Plaintiffs' substantive claims, it is at least conceivable that the Plaintiffs intend to show that the Defendants broke the law to prove their breach of warranty claims or their strict liability claim. *See Lilley v. Charren,* 936 F. Supp. 708, 713 (N.D. Cal. 1996) (holding that a motion to strike should not be granted unless it is absolutely clear that the matter to be stricken could have no possible bearing on the litigation). Furthermore, the Court fails to understand what prejudice might inure to Nextran by virtue of mere allegations of illegal conduct.[10] *Cf. Flanagan v. Wyndham Int'l, Inc.,* No. 2002-237, 2003 U.S. Dist. LEXIS 24211, at *4–5, 2003 WL 23198798 (D.V.I. Apr. 21, 2003) ("Scandalous matter does not merely offend someone's sensibilities; it must improperly cast a person or entity in a cruelly derogatory light." (citation omitted)). Indeed, Nextran has elected not to explain the nature of that alleged prejudice. Given the strong disfavor with which courts view motions to strike, the motion will be denied with respect to the complaint's fleeting allegations of illegality.

C. Rule 12(e)

Nextran argues that it is entitled to a more definite statement because the Plaintiffs have "improperly commingled allegations in separate causes of

---

10. Prejudice might arise, of course, if a jury is permitted to view the complaint. To forestall such a scenario, appropriate measures may be taken at a later time if need be.

action." Nextran spotlights the various sections of the complaint that incorporate by reference all preceding allegations. Nextran's argument in this vein is wholly deficient and betrays a surprising ignorance of pleading norms. Incorporating preceding allegations by reference is a time-honored tradition. There is certainly nothing novel about the way the complaint in this matter observes that tradition.

Nextran also claims that Count Four confusingly alleges a breach of the "express and/or implied warranty of merchantability." In Nextran's view, the Plaintiffs are required to allege a claim for either an express or an implied warranty of merchantability or to assert such claims as separate causes of action. The Court does not doubt that stating express and implied warranty claims in separate counts would achieve greater clarity. However, a complaint need not be a literary gem. Under the Federal Rules, a plaintiff must do no more than make "a short and plain statement" of his claim, Fed. R. Civ. P. 8(a)(2), so that the defendant can "reasonably prepare a response." Fed. R. Civ. P. 12(e). The Plaintiffs have adequately done so here. *See Government Guar. Fund v. Hyatt Corp.*, 166 F.R.D. 321, 324 (D.V.I. 1996) ("While the first amended complaint is hardly a paragon of pithiness, it is quite comprehensible and provides enough information to allow [the defendant] to frame a responsive pleading.").

Finally, Nextran contends that the Plaintiffs should specify which claims are asserted against which of the Defendants. That contention is unavailing. No authority of which the Court is aware—and Nextran has identified none—requires the Plaintiffs to refer to each defendant by name in each substantive count. And in fact the complaint does direct certain allegations at certain defendants by name. The Court does not find that the Plaintiffs' frequent references to the Defendants as a collective gives rise to any confusion or otherwise hampers Nextran's ability to defend itself.

IV. CONCLUSION

For the reasons given above, Nextran's motion will be denied in part and granted in part. The Plaintiffs will be afforded an opportunity to amend their complaint with respect to the breach of express warranty claims. An appropriate order follows.

Notes and Questions: The Rule 12 Motions

Q **1. Stating claims (again) and fixing claims.** The court's grant of Nextran's Rule 12(b)(6) motion to dismiss the express warranty claim, and its denial of the motion to dismiss the negligence claim, are unexceptional applications of the pleading standards we examined in Chapter 13, because Rule 8(a)(2) and Rule 12(b)(6) contain essentially reciprocal standards. The court, however, finds the omission of one element of the warranty claim fatal, while it is willing to infer elements of the negligence claim from the complaint. Why the difference?

A The court apparently construes express warranty claims under Virgin Islands law to require some sort of express representation, and the complaint gives the court nothing from which it can infer such a representation. By contrast, the court is willing to infer that defendant Nextran had a duty to manufacture, design, or sell a truck in good working condition from the allegation that it manufactured, designed, assembled, or sold the truck, that it mounted a cement mixer on it, and that it was responsible for checking it for defects. In essence, the complaint gives the court more to work with for this claim.

Another possible reason: Perhaps the court suspects that the reason Matos did not allege an express representation is that Nextran made none. If so, Matos's problem is not pleading, but the absence of any factual basis for this claim. By contrast, if Nextran manufactured, designed, or sold the truck, and the truck was defective, then a claim of negligence for breach of duty is plausible. Matos has simply pleaded it inartfully.

These distinctions may seem awfully arbitrary. But the court concludes by saying that "[t]he plaintiffs will be afforded an opportunity to amend their complaint with respect to the breach of express warranty claims," so no lasting harm is done. The plaintiffs will have the chance to allege an express representation in an amended complaint. As the court noted, leave to amend is routine on motions to dismiss for failure to state a claim when the complaint is merely missing a factual allegation corresponding to an element of the claim. The rationale is that the flaw may be a pleading oversight, which can be cured by amendment, rather than a reflection of the absence of those facts, which is incurable. In *Matos*, the court *sua sponte* (on its own initiative) gave leave to amend. In other circuits, the plaintiff must file a motion under Rule 15. Courts differ as to whether the plaintiff has an absolute right to amend *after* the court grants a motion to dismiss for failure to state a claim, *see Shreve, Raven-Hansen & Geyh* § 8.10[1] n.340, although the general rule seems to be to liberally allow amendment on motion. *Wright & Miller* § 1483.

The court in *Matos*, on the other hand, says nothing about leave to amend the "count" asserting a claim for punitive damages. That is because it reflects a more fundamental flaw—there is no such thing as an independent, free-standing *claim* for punitive damages. Punitive damages are simply an element of damages for a claim, typically a claim of intentional or grossly reckless conduct. As the court says, a " 'punitive damages claim cannot stand alone.' " Making this its own count is like pleading a count for $5,000 or for injunctive relief without pleading any basis for liability. No harm done, however, because should the plaintiffs prove any count that would entitle them to such damages, the dismissal is "without prejudice to the Plaintiffs' request for punitive damages at the appropriate stage of these proceedings." *See* Fed. R. Civ. P. 54(c) (a final judgment should grant a party the relief to which it is entitled).

2. Strike that. A motion to strike has a certain violent sound, because it *does* violence to the complaint—by cutting it up. Stricken matter is treated as if it was not there, and, in some instances, actually stricken from the record as well. *Wright & Miller* § 1382. But defendants' Rule 12(f) motions have a circumscribed role, targeting only "redundant, immaterial, impertinent, or scandalous matter" when the motion takes aim at a complaint. Consequently, "there appears to be general judicial agreement . . . that they should be denied unless the challenged allegations have no possible relation or logical connection to the subject matter of the controversy" and "cause some form of significant prejudice" to the moving party. *Id.*

Giving Rule 12(f) a common sense interpretation, which, if any, of the following allegations could be stricken?

A. In a claim for breach of contract in the sale of a car, that the car was a "death trap."
B. In a negligence claim, that defendant acted "illegally."
C. In a claim for conspiracy to commit fraud, that the conspirators were "racketeers."
D. In a breach of contract claim against a stock broker, that the brokerage house for which he worked had been sanctioned by the Securities and Exchange Commission for unrelated conduct two years ago.
E. In an action for missed child support payments, that defendant was consorting with a prostitute.

Welcome to the gentle world of litigation!

We can eliminate **B** off the bat—that's the same allegation that the *Matos* court refused to strike. Although illegality is not typically an element of a negligence claim, it could be, if the claim was negligence *per se* for violation of some traffic law. In any case, the unstated but self-evident premise of the 12(f) motion is that the offending matter may be prejudicial. It's hard to see how this assertion would cause any prejudice in today's jaded world. **A** is harsher but not necessarily irrelevant, if the claim is that the breach made the car unsafe or was a breach of warranty. **C** is harsher yet and arguably prejudicial by asserting criminal conduct and hinting at a criminal racket. Of course, the fraud may have criminal overtones (which is one reason that Rule 9(b) requires it to be pled with particularity). If not, this may be a candidate for striking. **D**, if true, is not "scandalous," but it sounds like it is immaterial. If so, it has only been stuck in the complaint for color and is therefore a good candidate for striking. Finally, **E** may suffer the same defect. Whatever the defendant's acts had to do with a previous divorce or separation, they don't seem to have anything to do with child support. The answer might change, however, if the action was for child custody.

The bottom line: **D** and **E** are probably the best candidates for striking, but whether material is "redundant, immaterial, impertinent, or scandalous" really depends on context and the specific nature of claims and issues. By now, though, you may be beginning to share the *Matos* court's skepticism of the Rule 12(f) motion in general. Sticks and stones may break your bones, but names will never—well, hardly ever—hurt you, especially in the heat of the adversary contest. To most judges, the Rule 12(f) motion to strike redundant, immaterial, impertinent, or scandalous matter is mainly a waste of time and even when granted, it rarely accomplishes anything but delay.

Q **3. More definite statements and "literary gems."** The Rule 12(e) motion is a descendant of an equity procedure to obtain a *bill of particulars*. But this procedure made more sense when the rules did not allow far-ranging discovery. The Rule 12(e) motion still has some limited role to play when the complaint is hopelessly garbled and confused. We say "hopelessly" advisedly, because the Rule itself says that the motion is available only when the pleading "is so vague or ambiguous that the party cannot reasonably prepare a response."

If that is true, why didn't Nextran effectively waive its Rule 12(e) motion by filing its Rule 12(b)(6) motion, which showed that it clearly could "reasonably prepare a response"?

A One reason is that it made its motions "in the alternative." *See* Fed. R. Civ. P. 8(d)(2). Rule 12(b) expressly states that no defense or objection is waived by joining it with one or more others in a motion. (Indeed, as we will see in the next case, some defenses and objections are waived by *not* joining them in a pre-answer motion.) Sometimes the defendant is arguing that he is entitled to a more definite statement, but if the court disagrees, he is also making his best effort to respond to the complaint by his other motions. In addition, a Rule 12(b)(6) motion may target only certain claims, while a Rule 12(e) may target others, without any logical inconsistency.

That said, incorporating prior allegations by reference and even failing to separate counts cleanly does not make a complaint subject to a Rule 12(e) motion, as the court states. Incorporation by reference is expressly authorized by Rule 10(c), although there is a good argument that it is a useless anachronism. See Antonio Gidi, *Incorporation by Reference: Requiem for A Useless Tradition*, 70 Hastings L.J. 989, 1044 (2019). Separation of claims by counts to promote clarity is urged by Rule 10(b), but a complaint "need not be a literary gem" as long as the defendant can figure it out.

To put it another way, pleading is not an end in itself under the Federal Rules, but just a starting point. If a complaint is a rock, the court will not make the pleader waste time polishing it into a gem. If the defendant can reasonably respond, the Rules make him do so and thus move the case along.

4. The "four corners of the complaint." In ruling on a Rule 12(b)(6) motion, the court will often say that it is confined to "the four corners of the complaint." What this means is that it takes the well-pleaded allegations of the complaint as true, and only those—not looking beyond the pleading to outside materials or the Internet for additional facts. Of course, it is free to look beyond them for the law, as the court can always take account of what the law is.

Q **5. Finding the law.** Plaintiff alleges various facts and then pleads that the Federal Turnstile Act gives him a right to sue for damages on those facts. Must the court assume that the Act gives the plaintiff a right to sue just because he alleges it?

A No. In the first place, we have seen that the Supreme Court in *Iqbal* held that the district court only has to take as true the non-conclusory allegations in the complaint. In the second place, it never has to take a legal conclusion as true. Whether the Federal Turnstile Act gives the plaintiff a claim for damages is a question of law that the court must decide for itself. In doing so, it not only can read the Turnstile Act, whether or not it is quoted in the complaint (usually parties do not quote the law in their pleadings), but it can also read its legislative history and the case law gloss on the Act (or send its clerk to do it). A judge can hardly be limited to the four corners of the complaint in deciding what the law is.

There are two exceptions to the "four corners" rule. First, after the defendant has answered, she may file a Rule 12(c) motion for judgment on the pleadings. In this case, the court can consider the well-pleaded factual allegations of all the pleadings, the answer (and reply, if any), as well as the complaint. Second, the parties may present matters outside the pleadings—facts outside the four corners—to support or oppose a Rule 12(b)(6) motion to dismiss for failure to state a claim. Unless the court excludes such materials, the inclusion of such matters converts the motion into a motion for summary judgment. *See* Rule 12(d). In that case, all of the parties must be given an opportunity to present all material pertinent to that motion. The motion will then be decided by the summary judgment standards in Rule 56. Under Rule 56, the court can grant summary judgment if it finds that the material facts are undisputed (either because the parties concede them or because the evidence outside the pleadings shows that there is no genuine dispute), and that on the undisputed facts, the moving party is entitled to judgment as a matter of law. By contrast, in deciding a Rule 12(b)(6) motion, the court simply takes the well-pleaded allegations as true.

B. The Rule 12 Waiver Trap

Although Rule 12 permits a defendant to assert several different defenses and objections to a complaint, he may not ordinarily assert them one at a time. Instead, the Rule mandates joinder of available defenses and objections in one omnibus pre-answer motion and imposes waiver as a penalty for leaving certain defenses out.

READING *HUNTER v. SERV-TECH, INC.* The motion practice in this case is extensive and confusing. Sort it out chronologically.

- What is the first motion that Offshore files?
- What defense does Offshore plead in its answer?
- An answer by itself requires the court to do nothing. How does Offshore get the court to act on the defense asserted in its answer?
- Which Rule did Offshore violate by making the motion to dismiss for lack of personal jurisdiction?
- Which Rules spell out the consequences of Offshore's violation?

HUNTER v. SERV-TECH, INC.

2009 WL 2858089 (E.D. La. 2009)

KURT D. ENGELHARDT, District Judge. . . .

I. BACKGROUND

[EDS.—Hunter sued Serv-Tech, Inc., Offshore Contractors, Dynamic Industries, and others on November 19, 2007. Offshore was a Dutch company that had negotiated in Angola and the United Kingdom to charter the vessel on which Hunter was injured in the waters off Angola. Offshore filed a motion to dismiss for insufficiency of service of process on June 19, 2008. This motion contained the following language in its second paragraph:

> **None of these Defendant Movants submits to the jurisdiction of this Court. Defendants expressly reserve all rights to challenge the subject matter and/or personal jurisdiction of this Court over Defendant Movants and/or raise other defenses to this claim.**

By leave of Court, Hunter filed an amended complaint on July 10, 2008. Offshore answered on September 11, 2008, raising lack of personal jurisdiction as its third affirmative defense.

After the original motion to dismiss was denied as moot when Offshore conceded that Hunter had perfected service, Offshore again moved to dismiss, this time for lack of personal jurisdiction on the grounds that it lacked minimum contacts with the Eastern District of Louisiana. Hunter and Dynamic opposed the motion, arguing that Offshore waived personal jurisdiction pursuant to Rules 12(g)(2) and 12(h)(1) by filing its original pre-answer motion to dismiss without including its personal jurisdiction defense in the motion. Offshore responded that the "reservation" language cited above in the original motion to dismiss was sufficient to put Hunter and other parties on notice that it challenged personal jurisdiction and that it had accordingly not waived the defense.]

II. ANALYSIS

The requirement that a court have personal jurisdiction over the parties is a due process right that may be waived either explicitly or implicitly. *See Insurance Corp. of Ireland v. Compagnie des Bauxites de Guinee,* 456 U.S. 694, 703–05 (1982). Rule 12(h)(1) of the Federal Rules of Civil Procedure requires that objections to personal jurisdiction, venue, and service of process be raised in a party's first responsive pleading. Under this rule, defendants wishing to raise any of these four [sic] defenses must do so in their first responsive pleading, either a Rule 12 motion to dismiss[1*] or an answer, or the omitted defense is waived.... Rule 12(g)(2) is specific about what a litigant must do to avoid waiving his 12(b)(2)–(5) defenses if he chooses to move for dismissal prior to answering: "a party that *makes a motion* under this rule must not *make another motion* under this rule raising a defense or objection that was available to the party but omitted from its earlier motion." Fed. R. Civ. P. 12(g)(2). (emphasis added). Accordingly, under Rule 12(g)(2), a party that makes a motion to dismiss under Rule 12(b) prior to answering must consolidate all its Rule 12 defenses into one motion. If it omits any of the defenses delineated in Rule 12(b)(2)–(5) in a pre-answer motion to dismiss, that defense is waived.

The language of these two rules, 12(g)(2) and 12(h)(1), with their use of phrases such as "make it by motion" and "makes a motion," suggests that to preserve its 12(b)(2)–(5) defenses prior to answering, a party cannot simply "assert" or "reserve" the defense, but must actually *argue* that defense in a motion that prays the Court to enter a ruling or order. A motion, after all, is "[a]n application made to a court or judge for the purpose of obtaining a rule or order directing some act to be done in favor of the applicant." *Black's Law Dictionary* 1013 (6th ed. 1990); *see also* Fed. R. Civ. P. 7(b)(1) ("A request for a court order must be made by motion."). To "make[ ] a motion" within the meaning of Rule 12(g)(2), therefore, is to request the Court to take some action—in the instant case, to dismiss the suit for insufficiency of service of process. By contrast, to "reserve" something (as Offshore purported to do in its earlier motion) is "[t]o keep back, to retain, to keep in store for future or special use, and to retain or hold over to a future time." *Black's Law Dictionary* 1473 (4th ed. 1968). To "reserve" an issue has no quality of present demand for some action by the Court. Under this interpretation of the Rules, informing a court that you "reserve" a personal jurisdiction defense for argument on a later motion is not sufficient to prevent waiver of the omitted defense. The defense must actually be raised by motion that requests the Court to dismiss the action on personal jurisdiction grounds, along with any other 12(b)(2)–(5) defenses a party may have.

This interpretation gains force when one considers the Advisory Notes to the Rule, which state:

> Subdivision (g) has forbidden a defendant who makes a preanswer motion under this rule from making a further motion presenting any defense or objection which was available to him at the time he made the first motion and which he could have included, but did not in fact include therein. Thus if the defendant moves before answer to dismiss the complaint for failure to state a claim, he is barred from making a further motion presenting the defense of improper venue, if that defense was available to him when he made his original motion.... *This required consolidation of defenses and objections in a Rule 12 motion is salutary in that it works against piecemeal consideration of a case.*

Fed. R. Civ. P. 12(g)(2) Advisory Notes to 1966 Amendment (emphasis added). Other commentators have noted the policy underlying the Rule, which is to

---

*** [Eds.—Here the court slips. Pleadings and motions are different. A "responsive pleading" to a complaint is an answer, Rule 7(a)(2). A motion is not a pleading; it is a request for a court order. Rule 7(b). The court presumably meant to say "first responsive pleading or motion," or simply, "first response to the complaint."]**

> eliminate unnecessary delay at the pleading stage. Subdivision (g) contemplates the presentation of an omnibus pre-answer motion in which the defendant advances every available Rule 12 defense and objection he may have that is assertable by motion. The defendant cannot delay the filing of a responsive pleading *by interposing these defenses and objections in piecemeal fashion.*

5C Wright & Miller, *Federal Practice and Procedure,* § 1384 (3d ed. 2004) (emphasis added); *see also Flory v. United States,* 79 F.3d 24, 25 (5th Cir. 1996) (noting that purpose of Rule is to "encourage the consolidation of motions and discourage the dilatory device of making them in a series"). The policy underlying the Rule, then, is *not* one of providing notice to other litigants. Rather, the policy is one of promoting judicial efficiency by avoiding piecemeal, pre-answer litigation of 12(b)(2)–(5) defenses. To allow a litigant to "reserve" a 12(b)(2)–(5) defense for later argument without actually making and arguing the motion cuts against both the plain language of the Rule and the policy that the Rule seeks to enact. This interpretation of the Rule, thus, is not hypertechnical, but squarely supports the policy choice that the Rule drafters made: forcing litigants to combine certain preliminary defenses in one motion in the interest of preventing delay. . . .

The Court is aware that the outcome it reaches today is a harsh one, especially in light of the fact that it appears that, absent waiver, this motion might well be granted.[5] But the Court is duty-bound to apply the law as it is written, and as written the Rules enact a policy of requiring all 12(b)(2)–(5) defenses to be made by motion, once, prior to filing an answer. Given this policy, Offshore's "reservation" language is not sufficient to preclude waiver pursuant to Rules 12(g)(2) and 12(h)(1). The Court concludes that Offshore's second 12(b) motion is barred by Rules 12(h)(1) and 12(g)(2) and that it has waived personal jurisdiction in this matter.

III. CONCLUSION

Considering the foregoing, Offshore Contractors' motion to dismiss for lack of personal jurisdiction is DENIED.

Notes and Questions: The Waiver Trap

Q **1. The waiver trap.** Offshore fell into the "waiver trap." How did it do so?

A First, it filed a pre-answer motion. When it did so, it triggered Rule 12(g)(2), which forbids it from making another motion under Rule 12 based on

5. In light of its determination that Offshore has waived personal jurisdiction, the Court declines to consider the parties' arguments regarding whether Offshore has minimum contacts with this forum sufficient to support the exercise of the Court's jurisdiction over it. However, though the Court does not hereby decide the issue, after reading the briefs it appears that defending the instant lawsuit constitutes Offshore's only contact with this forum.

a defense or objection that was available to it when it filed the pre-answer motion, with some exceptions discussed below.

Second, Rule 12(h)(1)(A) provides that omitting any of the Rule 12(b)(2)–(5) defenses of lack of personal jurisdiction, improper venue, insufficient process, or insufficient service of process from the pre-answer motion *waives that defense.* Thus, when Offshore omitted the defense of lack of personal jurisdiction from its pre-answer motion, it waived the defense and couldn't revive it by sticking it in the answer or filing a second motion.

Rule 12(g) is sometimes called the "omnibus motion rule," because it effectively requires a party to consolidate all of the Rule 12 defenses and objections then available to it in a single omnibus pre-answer motion, instead of presenting them serially. Omitting any of these defenses from the pre-answer motion not only prevents a party from raising it again by another pre-answer motion, but also from raising the Rule 12(b)(2)–(5) defenses again by *any means*. They are gone for good. Here Offshore's waiver resulted in the court asserting personal jurisdiction, even though Offshore seems to lack minimum contacts with the forum state. *See* footnote 5 ("it appears that defending the instant lawsuit constitutes Offshore's only contact with this forum"). In other words, Offshore waived a perfectly good personal jurisdiction defense!

Q **2. The waivable defenses.** Taking Rule 12(g)(2) and Rule 12(h)(1)(A) together, only the four defenses listed in Rule 12(b)(2)–(5) are waived by omitting them from a pre-answer motion or answer, whichever comes first. Why does the Rule single out these defenses for waiver? What do they have in common?

A One thing they have in common is that they should be evident to a defendant right at the start of a civil action. For example, Offshore should know from the start whether it has been served properly and whether its alleged conduct involves sufficient contact with the forum to satisfy due process and any applicable long arm statute. In addition, these defenses typically only delay a lawsuit (until the plaintiff picks the right court or perfects service) rather than end it. The waiver rule reflects a sense that these kinds of defenses ought to be decided up front, in time for a cure or a refiling in a proper court.

Q **3. The "unwaivable" defenses.** Rule 12(g)(2) excepts defenses addressed by Rule 12(h)(2)–(3). Rule 12(h)(2) does not permit a second *pre-answer* motion to dismiss for failure to state a claim or to join a party who is required to be joined by Rule 19, but it does permit a party to raise these defenses by a *post*-answer motion or pleading any time before the close of trial. Rule 12(h)(3) impliedly permits a motion to dismiss for lack of subject matter jurisdiction at any time. Why are these defenses excepted from the waiver rule?

A Congress vests subject matter jurisdiction in the federal courts, and the parties cannot enlarge their jurisdiction by their actions. Thus, lack of subject matter jurisdiction is not a personal defense that's up to the defendant to assert. Instead, the court must dismiss an action *any time* that the court finds it lacks subject matter jurisdiction, even if it first makes that finding on appeal!

The defense of failure to join a party required to be joined under Rule 19 requires an analysis of the merits for the court to ascertain who is "required."

See Chapter 18 for a fuller exploration of this defense. The same is self-evidently true for the defense of failure to state a claim. These two defenses are therefore singled out for "special treatment" in part because they "are more closely enmeshed with the substantive merits of the lawsuit." *Wright & Miller* § 1392. If a party could waive them by omitting them from its pre-answer motion, the action might continue without a required party or, anomalously, on a claim that has no support in applicable law.

As we said, you can't waive these other Rule 12(b) defenses by leaving them out of a pre-answer motion or even out of your answer. But we place quotation marks around "unwaivable," because the forgiveness of Rule 12(h)(2) is not unlimited. You *can* waive the defenses of failure to state a claim or failure to join a required party if you fail to assert them before the close of trial.

Q **4. When is a defense "unavailable"?** The omnibus motion rule only applies to the Rule 12 defenses that are "available" to the party when it files the pre-answer motion. When is a defense "unavailable"? The *Matos* case provides one answer. In an omitted part of the opinion, the court notes that Nextran first unsuccessfully moved to dismiss for lack of personal jurisdiction. Later it moved to dismiss for failure to state a claim (a defense) and, in the alternative, for a more definite statement and to strike parts of the complaint (objections) under Rule 12. Why, in light of the omnibus motion rule, was Nextran permitted to file the second pre-answer motion?

A This question requires some detective work, because the court does not explain the seeming violation of the omnibus motion rule. But if you read carefully, the court quotes from the complaint with citations to "Am. Compl." In other words, the plaintiffs amended their original complaint. If the amendment added new claims, then clearly the defense of failure to state a claim was not available to the new claims when Nextran filed its first motion; *they weren't even in the complaint at that time.* Even if the plaintiffs only changed their claims by amendment, the changes may raise new issues vulnerable to the Rule 12(b)(6) defense that were not present in the original pleading.

And suppose that the Matos complaint was so vague and ambiguous that Nextran did not know how to prepare a response. Then the defense of failure to state a claim would be "unavailable," as well as any other defense that turns, to a significant degree, on the content of the pleading. By contrast, a vague complaint would not make unavailable the defenses of insufficient process or insufficient service of process, which are not dependent on the contents of the complaint.

Q **5. Answering instead of moving.** Suppose Offshore had filed no pre-answer motion at all and instead filed an answer including the defense of lack of personal jurisdiction. Has Offshore waived this defense by waiting until the answer?

A Plainly, no. Or at least, not yet. Rule 12(g) does not *require* a party to file a pre-answer motion. It provides only that *if* a party files a pre-answer motion, it must consolidate available defenses in the motion. Nor does waiting until

A

the answer waive any defense. Rule 12(h)(1) only requires that the waivable defenses be asserted in Offshore's first response to the complaint, whether it is a motion *or* a responsive pleading. Of course, if Offshore waits until the answer and then omits its personal jurisdiction defense from the answer, it does waive the defense.

However, even asserting the defense in the answer does not preserve it in perpetuity. A defendant must still litigate it in timely fashion by filing a subsequent motion, as it can be lost "by failure to assert it seasonably, by formal submission in a cause, or by submission through conduct." *Neirbo Co. v. Bethlehem Shipbuilding Corp.*, 308 U.S. 165 (1939).

Easy, right? Actually, it is, if you just remember that you should assert the waivable defenses in a pre-answer motion or in your answer, whichever you do first, and then follow up in a timely fashion.

6. "Reserving" your right to violate the Rules, and other nonsense. As we saw in the last chapter, even the Supreme Court does not purport to have authority to change the Rules; "that is a result which must be obtained by the process of amending the Federal Rules and not by judicial interpretation." *Leatherman v. Tarrant County Narcotics Intelligence and Coordination Unit*, 507 U.S. 163, 168 (1993). Why a mere party therefore thinks it can "reserve" a defense that is subject to waiver under the Rules is a mystery. There are some Rules that, by their terms, can be changed by agreement of the parties, *see* Rule 29, and some that give the trial court discretion to authorize departures, *see* Rule 6(b), but Rule 12 is not one of these rules.

Q

7. A running review question. Hunter sues Offshore for breach of contract. Offshore moves to dismiss for insufficient *process* (meaning that it was served, but the papers were deficient in some respect, like omitting or using an outdated summons). The court denies the motion.

A. May Offshore now move to dismiss for failure to state a claim and insufficient *service of process* (which challenges the sufficiency of service, not of the papers served prior to filing an answer)?

A

No. Unless these defenses were somehow unavailable when Offshore filed its first pre-answer motion, the defenses should have been joined in that motion. No second pre-answer motion is permitted.

B. Has Offshore therefore waived these defenses?

A

Yes and no. The defense of insufficient service of process is waived by its omission from a pre-answer motion or answer, whichever comes first. But Rule 12(h)(2) still allows Offshore to assert failure to state a claim by answer or later motion, up until the close of trial.

C. But assume that Offshore argues that the defense of insufficient service of process was unavailable to it when it filed its first pre-answer motion. Is this a sound reason to allow a second pre-answer motion?

A Only if that argument is correct. Rule 12(g)(2) exempts unavailable defenses from its omnibus requirement, but how likely is it that the defense of insufficient *service* of process was unavailable when Offshore moved to dismiss for insufficient *process*? The latter motion presupposes that Offshore was served with process of some kind and therefore makes it very probable that it knew enough about *how* it was served to be able to challenge service of process as well.

D. Exasperated but still game, Offshore now files a motion to strike some scandalous matter from the complaint. How should the court rule?

A The court should deny this motion, too, because this objection was also subject to Rule 12(g)'s omnibus rule. Rule 12(g)(2) extends to any "motion under this rule raising a defense or objection that was available to the party but omitted from its earlier motion." Offshore had the complaint at the time it filed its pre-answer motion and therefore could have read the supposedly scandalous matter in it. Because this objection was then "available" to it, it is now waived.

IV. Answering the Complaint

If Offshore's pre-answer motion fails, it must file an answer within fourteen days after notice of the court's action on the motion. Rule 12(a)(4)(A). (Since a court may take months to rule on Rule 12 motions, such a motion can buy much more time than just the fourteen days even if it proves unsuccessful.) Offshore can assert four kinds of matter by answer.

First, as our discussion of Rule 12 motion practice suggested, it can assert the "leftover" Rule 12(b) defenses, that is, any defense the party has not waived by omitting it from a pre-answer motion.

Second, it must admit or deny the factual allegations of the complaint. Rule 8(b)(1)(B). After all, one purpose of pleading is to identify facts in dispute, and the denials will flush out many of these (though far fewer than you might expect). Of course, to deny one or more facts that are essential to a claim is itself a defense—the defense that the litigation-provoking transaction or event did not happen as plaintiff alleges (and therefore does not create liability). In other words, denial is a defense on the merits.

Third, even if Offshore admits the facts, it may have some reason why Hunter should not recover anyway. For example, Hunter might have filed suit too late under an applicable statute of limitations, or he might previously have released his claim against Offshore pursuant to some settlement agreement, or he might even have sued Offshore on the same claim before and now is precluded by the doctrine of claim preclusion (essentially, that a litigant gets only one bite at the apple) from suing for the same event again. These defenses are all descendants of the common law plea of confession and avoidance, now called an affirmative defense, that provides an excuse from liability on the basis of facts outside of the complaint. *See* Rule 8(c) (listing illustrative affirmative defenses).

Fourth, Offshore may have counterclaims against Hunter or crossclaims against fellow defendants Serv-Tech or Dynamic. Because Hunter, Serv-Tech, and Dynamic are already joined as parties to the lawsuit, they do not need to be summoned again by service of a summons or served with a separate complaint in accordance with the strict demands of Rule 4. Rule 5 permits service of answers and other papers in a civil action in accordance with its more lenient provisions, including sending the paper electronically to a registered user by filing it with the court's electronic filing system. It is therefore enough that Offshore included these claims in its answer and mailed the answer to these parties.

Finally, Offshore is not required to elect among these options (Rule 8(d)(2)); it may incorporate them all into its answer.

READING *REIS ROBOTICS USA, INC. v. CONCEPT INDUSTRIES, INC.* In the following case, defendant Concept Industries consolidated several of these alternatives in its answer to a breach of contract action brought by Reis Robotics.

- What motion does plaintiff Reis use to challenge the legal sufficiency of a defense in the answer?
- How does Concept's denial run afoul of the Rules? How should it have pleaded its denial?
- Why does the court strike the affirmative defenses of fraud, laches, waiver, estoppel, and unclean hands?

REIS ROBOTICS USA, INC. v. CONCEPT INDUSTRIES, INC.

462 F. Supp. 2d 897 (N.D. Ill. 2006)

Castillo, District Court.

This is a diversity action governed by Illinois law in which Plaintiff Reis Robotics USA, Inc. ("Reis") filed a complaint against Defendant Concept Industries, Inc. ("Concept"), seeking redress for breach of contract. Concept has answered the complaint, asserted six affirmative defenses, and brought seven counterclaims against Reis. Reis now moves to strike and dismiss Concept's affirmative defenses; strike portions of Concept's answer; and dismiss Concept's counterclaims. For the reasons set forth below, Reis's motions are granted in part and denied in part....

MOTION TO STRIKE AND DISMISS AFFIRMATIVE DEFENSES

We turn first to Reis's motion to strike and dismiss various portions of Concept's affirmative defenses.

I. Legal Standard

Federal Rule of Civil Procedure 12(f) permits the Court to strike "any insufficient defense or any redundant, immaterial, impertinent or scandalous matter." Fed. R. Civ. P. 12(f). Motions to strike are generally disfavored because of their potential to delay proceedings. *Heller Fin., Inc. v. Midwhey Powder Co., Inc.,* 883

F.2d 1286, 1294 (7th Cir. 1989). Nonetheless, a motion to strike can be a useful means of removing "unnecessary clutter" from a case, which will in effect expedite the proceedings. *Id.*

Affirmative defenses are pleadings and, as such, are subject to all the same pleading requirements applicable to complaints. Thus, affirmative defenses must set forth a "short and plain statement" of the basis for the defense. Fed. R. Civ. P. 8(a). Even under the liberal notice pleading standards of the Federal Rules, an affirmative defense must include either direct or inferential allegations as to all elements of the defense asserted. "[B]are bones conclusory allegations" are not sufficient. *Heller Fin.,* at 1295.

This Court applies a three-part test for examining the sufficiency of an affirmative defense. First, we determine whether the matter is appropriately pled as an affirmative defense. Second, we determine whether the defense is adequately pled under Federal Rules of Civil Procedure 8 and 9. Third, we evaluate the sufficiency of the defense pursuant to a standard identical to Federal Rule of Civil Procedure 12(b)(6). Before granting a motion to strike an affirmative defense, the Court must be convinced that there are no unresolved questions of fact, that any questions of law are clear, and that under no set of circumstances could the defense succeed. Additionally, in a case premised on diversity jurisdiction, "the legal and factual sufficiency of an affirmative defense is examined with reference to state law." *Williams v. Jader Fuel Co.,* 944 F.2d 1388, 1400 (7th Cir. 1991). With these principles in mind, we turn to the specific arguments raised in the motion.

II. Analysis . . .

As its second affirmative defense Concept states: "Reis breached the contract on which it purports to rely, and that contract may be void for fraud and/or failure of consideration." Breach of contract, fraud, and failure of consideration are all matters that may be pled as affirmative defenses. *See* Fed. R. Civ. P. 8(c). However, the Court agrees with Reis that Concept's defenses, as pled, do not satisfy the pleading requirements of Rule 8(a). The breach of contract defense fails to make reference to any of the elements of a breach of contract claim, and additionally, Concept fails to plead with heightened particularity the alleged circumstances constituting fraud as required by Rule 9(b). Again, although Concept has included detailed allegations in its counterclaim, it does not link these allegations in any way to the affirmative defenses, nor is it clear what particular paragraphs of the counterclaim allegations would apply to this affirmative defense. Accordingly, the Court strikes Concept's second affirmative defense without prejudice.

As its third affirmative defense, Concept alleges: "Reis's payment claims for the silencer fixture are barred because Concept never authorized Reis to begin manufacturing the fixture, as Reis itself has acknowledged." Reis argues that this affirmative defense is legally inadequate. The concept of an affirmative defense under Rule 8(c) "requires a responding party to *admit* a complaint's allegations but then permits the responding party to assert that for some legal reason it is nonetheless excused from liability (or perhaps from full liability)." *Menchaca v. Am. Med. Resp. of Ill.,* 6 F. Supp. 2d 971, 972 (N.D. Ill. 1998) (emphasis in original). Concept's third affirmative defense does not meet this criteria, but instead is merely a restatement of the denials contained in its answer. As such, the affirmative defense is not only unnecessary but also improper. However, to the extent Concept intended to raise some affirmative matter here, the Court will give Concept an opportunity to replead. Accordingly, the third affirmative defense is stricken without prejudice. . . .

Concept's fifth affirmative defense states: "Reis's claims are barred or limited by laches, waiver, estoppel, unclean hands, or similar legal or equitable doctrines." Laches, waiver, estoppel, and unclean hands are equitable defenses that must be pled with the specific elements required to establish the defense. Merely stringing together a long list of legal defenses is insufficient to satisfy Rule 8(a). "It is unacceptable for a party's attorney simply to mouth [affirmative defenses] in formula-like fashion ('laches,' 'estoppel,' 'statute of limitations' or what have you), for that does not do the job of apprising opposing counsel and this Court of the predicate for the claimed defense—which after all is the goal of notice pleading." [*State Farm Mut. Auto Ins. Co. v. Riley*, 199 F.R.D. 276, 279 (N.D. Ill. 2001).] *This* is precisely what Concept has done here. Indeed, in asserting "similar legal or equitable doctrines," Concept fails to put Reis on notice as to even the legal bases for its defenses. Thus, the Court strikes Concept's fifth affirmative defense without prejudice.

Concept's sixth affirmative defense states: "Concept reserves the right to add additional affirmative defenses as they become known through discovery." This is not a proper affirmative defense. If at some later point in the litigation Concept believes that the addition of another affirmative defense is warranted, it may seek leave to amend its pleadings pursuant to Rule 15(a); such a request will be judged by the appropriate standards, including the limitations set forth in Rule 12(b) and (h). Accordingly, Concept's sixth affirmative defense is stricken with prejudice.

MOTION TO STRIKE PORTIONS OF DEFENDANT'S ANSWER

Reis next moves to strike various portions of Concept's answer for failing to comply with Rule 8. Rule 8 provides in relevant part:

> A party shall state in short and plain terms the party's defenses to each claim asserted and shall admit or deny the averments upon which the adverse party relies. If a party is without knowledge or information sufficient to form a belief as to the truth of an averment, the party shall so state and this has the effect of a denial. Denials shall fairly meet the substance of the averments denied. When a pleader intends in good faith to deny only a part or a qualification of an averment, the pleader shall specify so much of it as is true and material and shall deny only the remainder.

Fed. R. Civ. P. 8(b) [now restyled as Rule 8(b)(1)–(4)]. Reis argues that Concept has violated Rule 8 by including improper qualifying language in Paragraphs 5, 6, and 7. Specifically, Reis objects to the following language, which is contained in each of the aforementioned Paragraphs: "To the extent the alleged 'contract' created by issuance of this purchase order failed to warrant the trim speed and cycle time that Concept required, it was procured by fraud and was of no validity; accordingly, the remaining allegations in this paragraph are denied as true." Upon review, the Court concludes that the above language does not constitute an admission or denial of Reis's allegations as required by Rule 8; instead the language is equivocal and serves to confuse the issues that are in dispute....

... Accordingly, Paragraphs 5, 6, 7, 15, 16, and 20 are stricken with leave to amend. In repleading, Concept shall follow Rule 8(b)'s directive that it admit, deny, or state that it is without sufficient knowledge to admit or deny. To the extent Concept must give a qualified answer, Concept must "specify so much of it as is true and material and shall deny only the remainder." See Fed. R. Civ. P. 8(b).

CONCLUSION

For the reasons set forth above, Reis's motion to strike affirmative defenses, motion to strike portions of Concept's answer, and motion to dismiss Concept's counterclaim are granted to the extent that:

1. Concept's first, second, third, fourth, and fifth affirmative defenses are stricken without prejudice;
2. Concept's sixth affirmative defense is stricken with prejudice;
3. Paragraphs 5, 6, 7, 15, 16, and 20 of Concept's answer are stricken without prejudice ...

Reis's motions are denied in all other respects. Concept shall file and serve an amended pleading that conforms to this order within 30 days of the date of this order.

Notes and Questions: Answers

Q **1. Challenging the legal sufficiency of a defense.** It stands to reason that a plaintiff must have the same opportunity to challenge the legal sufficiency of a defense as a defendant has to challenge a claim. The plaintiff, in other words, needs something like a motion to dismiss for failure to state a defense. Rule 12(f) calls it a motion to "strike ... an insufficient defense." By what standard is it decided?

A Unsurprisingly, given its equivalency to a Rule 12(b)(6) motion, *Reis* states that the "standard [is] identical to ... 12(b)(6)." Both test whether the supporting allegations state a claim or defense under any applicable law. The Rule 12(f) motion to strike an insufficient defense is thus a plaintiff's version of the Rule 12(b)(6) motion.

Suppose, for example, that Concept Industries had pleaded the affirmative defense of contributory negligence. On Reis's Rule 12(f) motion to strike this defense as insufficient, how should the court rule?

A

Reis is suing for breach of contract, not for negligence. Contributory negligence is not a defense to breach of contract. The court should grant the motion and strike the defense. Concept is not usually required to file a new answer omitting this defense; the court and the parties will simply treat the existing answer as if this defense is no longer in the case.

Q

2. Generally denying? Read Rule 8(b). At common law, a defendant could enter a general denial, a single plea that put the entire plaintiff's declaration at issue. Can a defendant still enter a general denial to a complaint in federal court?

A

Yes, because Rule 8(b)(3) expressly permits this. But the Rule is rightly skeptical of such denials. The general denial is only permitted when "[a] party . . . intends in good faith to deny *all* the allegations of a pleading. . . ." *Id.* (emphasis added). But *Reis* is a diversity case. The complaint therefore should contain allegations of defendant Concept's place of incorporation and principal place of business. It is possible that Reis got these wrong, but not likely. And there are probably other factual allegations that Concept could not "in good faith" deny. If so, it can't use a general denial. For these reasons, in the vast majority of federal cases, a defendant will have to admit at least some allegations of the complaint. In its common law one-line form, therefore, the general denial is essentially obsolete.

Q

3. Admitting *and* denying. Suppose Reis Robotics alleges that "plaintiff and defendant made a contract for the delivery of thirty-six widgets to plaintiff on or before June 1, 2005." If Concept Industries Inc. had made a contract for the delivery of widgets to Reis, but the delivery date was October 1, how should it answer?

A

It might deny, because the contract was *not* for delivery on June 1. But since Concept *had* made a contract for delivery of widgets, does this absolute denial "fairly respond to the substance of the allegation"? *See* Rule 8(b)(2). Or should Concept admit that the parties made a contract for delivery of widgets, but deny that the delivery date was June 1? Rule 8(b)(4) seems to suggest that this bifurcated response would be more appropriate. Admissions and denials, in other words, are discriminating and often word- or phrase-specific. The Rules require a defendant to admit part of an allegation and deny the rest, when its information so requires.

Q

4. Fudging is not an option. But isn't admitting in part and denying in part precisely what Concept did in paragraphs 5 through 7 discussed at the end of the *Reis* opinion?

A

Not really. It hedged its denial of some of the allegations in these paragraphs with the fudge language, "To the extent that the alleged 'contract' . . . failed to warrant the trim speed and cycle that Concept required, it was procured by fraud and was of no validity...." Does this mean that if the contract *did* warrant these things, the remaining allegations were true and admitted, or does the "to the extent" language hedge even this conditional admission, depending on how much the contract warranted? Who knows? But that is just the problem, according to the court. "[T]he language is equivocal and serves to confuse the issues that are in dispute." The Rule requires a defendant not only to admit or deny, but to admit or deny "specifically" in a way that "fairly respond[s] to the substance of the allegation."

Q **5. When you don't know.** Suppose a plaintiff who was injured in a car crash alleges that the defendant "owned and operated the car." The defendant knows that it owned the car, but it does not know who was driving it at the time of the accident. How should it answer?

A Clearly, it must admit ownership. The problem is the second part of the plaintiff's allegation, as to which the defendant does not have enough information to admit or deny. The Rule provides a way out: "A party that lacks knowledge or information sufficient to form a belief about the truth of an allegation must so state, and the statement has the effect of a denial." Rule 8(b)(5).

Would it therefore be sufficient for the defendant to admit ownership and plead that it "lacks knowledge of who operated the car"?

A Not if Rule 8(b)(5) is taken literally. What's missing in this answer is the phrase "information." But "information" is not just a lawyer's redundancy. It is perfectly plausible that a corporate defendant in these circumstances lacks knowledge and at the same time has information in its records, or could acquire information by reasonable inquiry of its employees, with which to admit or deny the "operated" part of the plaintiff's allegation. In fact, as we shall see in Chapter 15, Rule 11(b)(4) states that by presenting an answer to the court, an attorney certifies that to the best of her "knowledge, information, and belief, *formed after an inquiry reasonable under the circumstances,* ... the denials of factual contentions are warranted on the evidence, or, if specifically so identified, are reasonably based on belief or lack of information" (emphasis added).

Q **6. Pleading affirmative defenses.** The *Reis* court does not find the affirmative defenses of "fraud," "failure of consideration," "laches, waiver, and estoppel" to be legally insufficient, but it strikes them anyway. Why?

A These are all listed as affirmative defenses in Rule 8(c). What they have in common is that they afford an excuse to liability based on facts outside the complaint. It is therefore arguable that the defendant should plead some factual support for each, even if only in "short and plain terms" per Rule 8(b)(1)(A). Without some factual support for these affirmative defenses, Concept Industries' answer "fails to put Reis on notice as to even the legal bases for its defenses." In addition, fraud must also be pled with particularity according to Rule 9. Nothing excuses a defendant from having to comply with this heightened pleading requirement when the defendant asserts fraud as a defense.

Does this mean that the *Twombly-Iqbal* plausibility pleading standard applies to defenses in the answer as well as to claims in the complaint? The logic of *Reis*, a pre-*Twombly-Iqbal* decision, would point in that direction, but the courts are divided. *See GEOMC Co. v. Calmare Therapeutics Inc.*, 918 F.3d 92, 97 n.8 (2d Cir. 2019) (collecting cases). The Second Circuit Court of Appeals recently held that it does.

> We conclude that the plausibility standard of *Twombly* applies to determining the sufficiency of all pleadings, including the pleading of an affirmative defense, but with recognition that, as the Supreme Court explained in *Iqbal*, applying the plausibility standard to any pleading is a "context-specific" task. 556 U.S. at 679.
>
> The key aspect of the context relevant to the standard for pleading an affirmative defense is that an affirmative defense, rather than a complaint, is at issue. This is relevant to the degree of rigor appropriate for testing the pleading of an affirmative defense. The pleader of a complaint has the entire time of the relevant statute of limitations to gather facts necessary to satisfy the plausibility standard. By contrast, the pleader of an affirmative defense has only the 21-day interval to respond to an original complaint, *see* Fed. R. Civ. P. 12(a)(1)(A)(i), the 21-day interval to amend, without court permission, an answer that requires a responsive pleading, *see* Fed. R. Civ. P. 15(a)(1)(B), or the 14-day interval to file a required response to an amended pleading that makes a new claim, *see* Fed. R. Civ. P. 15(a)(3). That aspect of the context matters. In addition, the relevant context will be shaped by the nature of the affirmative defense. For example, the facts needed to plead a statute-of-limitations defense will usually be readily available; the facts needed to plead an ultra vires defense [e.g., that the contract on which plaintiff sues is unlawful], for example, may not be readily known to the defendant, a circumstance warranting a relaxed application of the plausibility standard.

Id. at 98.

Compare Rule 8's general pleading standard for claims, Rule 8(a)(2), with its general pleading standard for defenses, Rule 8(b)(1)(A). What is the textual difference between the standards? Can you make an argument from that difference for a "more relaxed application of the plausibility standard" for defenses?

READING *INGRAHAM v. UNITED STATES.* The latter questions suggest that it is important to know what makes a defense an affirmative defense. In *Ingraham*, the court tackles this question directly. Ingraham and Bonds were plaintiffs in medical malpractice lawsuits under the Federal Tort Claims Act (FTCA) who won million-dollar judgments against the United States. On appeal, the government challenged the amount of the judgments. It cited the Medical Liability and Insurance Improvement Act of Texas, which imposed a $500,000 limit on certain damages against a physician or health care provider, including damages arising out of FTCA claims. The problem was that the government had never filed any pleading asserting this limitation prior to the judgments.

- What is the effect of failing to plead an affirmative defense?
- Does the omission of medical malpractice damages caps from the listing of affirmative defenses in Rule 8(c) show that a statutory damages cap is not an affirmative defense?
- If inclusion in Rule 8(c)'s list is not dispositive, what factors determine whether a defense is an affirmative defense?

INGRAHAM v. UNITED STATES

808 F.2d 1075 (5th Cir. 1987)

Before CLARK, Chief Judge, RUBIN and POLITZ, Circuit Judges.
POLITZ, Circuit Judge:

...

In 1977, in response to what was perceived to be a medical malpractice crisis, the Legislature of Texas, like several other state legislatures, adopted certain limitations on damages to be awarded in actions against health care providers, for injuries caused by negligence in the rendering of medical care and treatment. Of particular significance to these appeals is the $500,000 cap placed on the *ex delicto* recovery,[1] not applicable to past and future medical expenses....

ANALYSIS

Appellees maintain that we should not consider the statutory limitation of liability invoked on appeal because it is an affirmative defense under Rule 8(c) of the Federal Rules of Civil Procedure, and the failure to raise it timely constitutes a waiver. We find this argument persuasive.

Rule 8(c) first lists 19 specific affirmative defenses, and concludes with the residuary clause "any other matter constituting an avoidance or affirmative defense." **[EDS.—This clause has been deleted from the restyled Rule.]** In the years since adoption of the rule, the residuary clause has provided the authority for a substantial number of additional defenses which must be timely and affirmatively pleaded. These include: exclusions from a policy of liability insurance; breach of warranty; concealment of an alleged prior undissolved marriage; voidable preference in bankruptcy; noncooperation of an insured; statutory limitation on liability; the claim that a written contract was incomplete; judgment against a defendant's joint tortfeasor; circuity of action; discharge of a contract obligation through novation or extension; recission or mutual abandonment of a contract; failure to mitigate damages; adhesion contract; statutory exemption; failure to exhaust state remedies; immunity from suit; good faith belief in lawfulness of action; the claim that a lender's sale of collateral was not commercially reasonable; a settlement agreement or release barring an action; and custom of trade or business.

Determining whether a given defense is "affirmative" within the ambit of Rule 8(c) is not without some difficulty. We find the salient comments of Judge Charles E. Clark, Dean of the Yale Law School, later Chief Judge of the United States Second Circuit Court of Appeals, and the principal author of the Federal Rules, to be instructive:

---

1. Tex. Rev. Civ. Stat. Ann. art. 4590i, § 11.02(a), provides:

> In an action on a health care liability claim where final judgment is rendered against a physician or health care provider, the limit of civil liability for damages of the physician or health care provider shall be limited to an amount not to exceed $500,000.

> [J]ust as certain disfavored allegations made by the plaintiff . . . must be set forth with the greatest particularity, so like disfavored defenses must be particularly alleged by the defendant. These may include such matters as fraud, statute of frauds . . . , statute of limitations, truth in slander and libel . . . and so on. In other cases the mere question of convenience may seem prominent, as in the case of payment, where the defendant can more easily show the affirmative payment at a certain time than the plaintiff can the negative of nonpayment over a period of time. Again it may be an issue which may be generally used for dilatory tactics, such as the question of the plaintiff's right to sue . . . a vital question, but one usually raised by the defendant on technical grounds. These have been thought of as issues "likely to take the opposite party by surprise," which perhaps conveys the general idea of fairness or the lack thereof, though there is little real surprise where the case is well prepared in advance.

Clark, *Code Pleading,* 2d ed. 1947, § 96 at 609–10, *quoted in* 5 C. Wright & A. Miller, *Federal Practice and Procedure: Civil,* § 1271, p. 313 (1969).

Also pertinent to the analysis is the logical relationship between the defense and the cause of action asserted by the plaintiff. This inquiry requires a determination (1) whether the matter at issue fairly may be said to constitute a necessary or extrinsic element in the plaintiff's cause of action; (2) which party, if either, has better access to relevant evidence; and (3) policy considerations: should the matter be indulged or disfavored?

Central to requiring the pleading of affirmative defenses is the prevention of unfair surprise. A defendant should not be permitted to "lie behind a log" and ambush a plaintiff with an unexpected defense. The instant cases illustrate this consideration. Plaintiffs submit that, had they known the statute would be applied, they would have made greater efforts to prove medical damages which were not subject to the statutory limit. In addition, plaintiffs maintain that they would have had an opportunity and the incentive to introduce evidence to support their constitutional attacks on the statute.

This distinction separates the present cases from our recent decision in *Lucas v. United States,* 807 F.2d 414 (5th Cir. 1986). In *Lucas,* although the limitation of recovery issue was not pleaded, it was raised at trial. We held that the trial court was within its discretion to permit the defendant to effectively amend its pleadings and advance the defense. The treatment we accorded this issue in *Lucas* is consistent with long-standing precedent of this and other circuits that " 'where [an affirmative defense] is raised in the trial court in a manner that does not result in unfair surprise, . . . technical failure to comply with Rule 8(c) is not fatal.' " *Bull's Corner Restaurant v. Director, Federal Emergency Management Agency,* 759 F.2d 500, 502 (5th Cir. 1985), *quoting Allied Chemical Corp. v. Mackay,* 695 F.2d 854, 855 (5th Cir. 1983).

We view the limitation on damages as an "avoidance" within the intendment of the residuary clause of 8(c). Black's Law Dictionary, 5th ed. 1979, defines an avoidance in pleadings as "the allegation or statement of new matter, in opposition to a former pleading, which, admitting the facts alleged in such former pleading, shows cause why they should not have their ordinary legal effect." Applied to the present discussion, a plaintiff pleads the traditional tort theory of malpractice and seeks full damages. The defendant responds that assuming recovery is in order under the ordinary tort principles, because of the new statutory limitation, the traditional precedents "should not have their ordinary legal effect."

Considering these factors, against the backdrop and with the illumination provided by other applications of Rule 8(c), we conclude that the Texas statutory limit on medical malpractice damages is an affirmative defense which must be pleaded timely and that in the cases at bar the defense has been waived....

The judgments in each of the consolidated cases is AFFIRMED.

Notes and Questions: Identifying Affirmative Defenses

Q **1. Omitting an affirmative defense.** What is the consequence of failing to plead an affirmative defense?

A Rule 8(c) is not explicit about the effects of omitting an affirmative defense from an answer, but the implication is dire: "A party *must* affirmatively state any avoidance or affirmative defense ..." (emphasis added). The *Ingraham* court therefore finds that failure to timely plead waives the defense. If a purpose of pleading is notice, this makes good sense after trial. As the Ingrahams argued, "had they known the statute would be applied, they would have made greater efforts to prove medical damages which were not subject to the statutory limit" and, indeed, they might have tried to offer evidence to support "constitutional attacks on the statute." Now, after judgment, it's too late.

But the omission of an affirmative defense does not always have such serious consequences. If a defendant omits an affirmative defense from its answer, it should ordinarily be permitted to amend the answer to add the defense, as long as the amended answer still gives the plaintiff sufficient notice to prepare for the defense. And even at trial, "where [an affirmative defense] is raised in the trial court in a manner that does not result in an unfair surprise," courts will allow it, as *Ingraham* says. Pleading an affirmative defense avoids surprise. But if there is no surprise anyway, for whatever reason, a court will often allow defendant to offer proof of the defense despite the omission, or to cure it by amendment of the answer.

2. Listing affirmative defenses. Damages caps are not listed in Rule 8(c). Under the Rule in effect when *Ingraham* was decided, this was not fatal to the Ingrahams' argument that the cap was an affirmative defense because a residuary clause added "any *other* matter constituting an avoidance or affirmative defense" (emphasis added). The deletion of this clause in the restyling of the Rule in 2008 probably has not changed this inclusiveness, because the Rule still encompasses "any avoidance or affirmative defense, *including* . . ." (emphasis added). Thus, the Rule's list of affirmative defenses is illustrative rather than exclusive.

Q **3. Explaining affirmative defenses.** The Ingrahams were free to argue that a cap was an affirmative defense, but how? Judge Clark offers several arguments: Some defenses are disfavored, so they must be identified more particularly; others involve facts more accessible to a defendant than to a plaintiff; and others are relatively unusual, and therefore are presumably inapplicable unless asserted by the defendant. But the reason most "[c]entral to requiring the pleading of affirmative defenses is prevention of unfair surprise." "A defendant should not be permitted to 'lie behind a log' and ambush a plaintiff with an unexpected defense," the court explains in *Ingraham*.

The surprise of an unpleaded affirmative defense is related to another characteristic that they share: that they are supported by new facts—facts outside the four corners of the complaint. Just as proving them will require evidence beyond what the plaintiff proffers in proof of her claims, so will disproving them. Without the notice afforded by pleading, the plaintiff may not have collected or prepared such evidence. (This characteristic suggests another possible consequence of omitting an affirmative defense: the exclusion on relevance grounds of evidence to prove it at trial.)

So why place the burden of pleading the damages cap in *Ingraham* on the defendant?

A Chiefly to avoid surprise, without which the plaintiffs might have structured their proof differently. The cap applied only to *ex delicto* damages, including pain and suffering, and not to past and future medical expenses, according to the court. Had plaintiffs known that the former—usually the largest item of damages—would be capped at $500,000, then they claim that "they would have made greater efforts to prove medical damages which were not subject to the statutory limit." Moreover, they also claim that they might have been better prepared to mount constitutional attacks on the statutory cap itself. The United States' failure to plead the cap thus lulled plaintiffs into a different, less effective, presentation of their case. Requiring a defendant to plead the cap as an affirmative defense avoids such surprise and resulting unfairness to plaintiffs.

Q **4. Differentiating affirmative defenses from denials.** Look back at *Reis Robotics* (p. 506). There the court strikes Concept's third "affirmative defense" that Concept never authorized Reis to begin making the fixture. What is wrong with this defense?

A Nothing, except that it is really a denial, not an affirmative defense. An affirmative defense is an excuse from liability, *even if the plaintiff proves its allegations.* Concept's third affirmative defense, however, effectively contests the allegations in the complaint; it does not say, "even if Concept authorized Reis to make the fixtures," there is a reason Reis cannot win.

5. Identifying affirmative defenses. Consider the following scenario.

Billy Builder is putting a huge garage right on his property line, and his excavation equipment crosses the line, leaving big ruts in Neil Neighbor's property and knocking down Neighbor's ornamental Japanese maple. Neighbor sues Builder, alleging that Neighbor owns the damaged property and that Builder entered the property and did serious damage to it. Builder answers. Which of the following should be pled as an affirmative defense?

A. Builder never went upon Neighbor's property.
B. Builder had permission from Neighbor to enter the property.
C. By adverse possession (open and notorious claim of ownership for a length of time), Builder had previously acquired the property that was damaged.
D. Neighbor negligently failed to prune his oak, as a result of which it fell on Builder's property, causing extensive damage to his garden, for which he is entitled to recover $1,500.

A is easily rejected. It's nothing more than a denial of an element of Neighbor's claim. This is a defense on the merits ("I didn't do it"), not an affirmative defense ("I did it, but I had an excuse").

B sounds like "license," which is listed in Rule 8(c), or "easement" (a property law term for something similar). In any case, it rests on facts outside the complaint and would likely take Neighbor by surprise if Builder first argued it at trial, so it should probably be pled as an affirmative defense.

C sounds the same, but it also, in effect, denies that Neighbor owns the property, an element of Neighbor's claim for property damage. Ordinarily, the failure to plead an affirmative defense results in exclusion of evidence of that defense on the grounds that it is not relevant to any issue formed by the pleadings. This makes sense when you consider that an affirmative defense, by definition, depends upon new facts beyond those relevant to establishing or refuting the plaintiff's claims. However, some courts have reasoned that because proof of an easement would tend to destroy or negate ownership, an essential element of the plaintiff's claim in trespass, it is relevant and admissible to support the *denial* of the plaintiff's claim even when the defendant did not plead the affirmative defense of easement. *See Denham v. Cuddeback*, 311 P.2d 1014, 1016 (Or. 1957). **C** is therefore best treated as a denial of Neighbor's ownership, not as an affirmative defense.

D does not defend against Neighbor's claims at all. He neither denies it, nor offers any reason why he had an excuse for coming on Neighbor's property and damaging it. Instead, he asserts that Neighbor damaged *his* property. But we don't award damages on defenses; we award them on claims. This is therefore a counterclaim masquerading as a defense (even though damages to Builder might conceivably be used to offset damages to Neighbor). No matter; Rule 8(c)(2) is uncommonly forgiving and lets the court "treat the pleading as though it were correctly designated. . . ."

Accordingly, only **B** is clearly an affirmative defense.

Qualified Immunity: Affirmative Defense or Barrier?

Immunity is a judicially created affirmative defense from personal liability for government officials sued for unlawful acts. *Gomez v. Toledo*, 446 U.S. 635 (1980). Most officials (including police officers) enjoy "qualified immunity," i.e., immunity from liability as long as "their conduct does not violate clearly established statutory or constitutional rights of which a reasonable person would have known." *Harlow v. Fitzgerald*, 457 U.S. 800, 818 (1982). As the Court suggested in *Iqbal* (*supra* p. 464) the qualified immunity defense is intended to address the concern that litigation (mainly civil rights litigation) could deter or distract public officials from carrying out their public duties. *Id.* at 814.

The courts have made it increasingly difficult for a plaintiff to overcome the defense. *See generally* Nathaniel Sobel, *What Is Qualified Immunity, and What Does It Have to Do With Police Reform?*, Lawfare, June 6, 2020. First, they have assumed that to find a right "clearly established," a court "must locate a controlling case that 'squarely governs the specific facts at issue,' except in the 'rare obvious case' in which a general legal principle makes the unlawfulness of the officer's conduct clear despite a lack of precedent addressing similar circumstances." *West v. City of Caldwell*, 931 F.3d 978, 983 (9th Cir. 2019) (alleging destruction by police SWAT team's excessive force in firing tear gas canisters into plaintiff's home), *cert. denied sub nom. West v. Winfield*, No. 19-899, 2020 WL 3146698 (U.S. June 15, 2020). As one federal judge explained, "Merely proving a constitutional deprivation doesn't cut it; plaintiffs must cite functionally identical precedent that places the legal question 'beyond debate' to 'every' reasonable officer. Put differently, it's immaterial that someone acts unconstitutionally if no prior case held such misconduct unlawful. This current 'yes harm, no foul' imbalance leaves victims violated but not vindicated." *Zadeh v. Robinson*, 928 F.3d 457, 479 (5th Cir. 2019) (J. Willett, concurring in part and dissenting in part), *cert. denied*, No. 19-676, 2020 WL 3146691 (U.S. June 15, 2020).

Dan Pelle/Credit SR

Second, the Supreme Court at first held that courts should consider whether misconduct broke the law before considering whether the law was clearly established. The Court, however, reversed course in *Pearson v. Callahan*, 555 U.S. 223 (2009). Now courts "grant qualified immunity based only on the clearly established prong—and without ever determining if there was a constitutional violation." Sobel, *supra*. The perverse result is that "[i]mportant constitutional questions go unanswered precisely because no one's answered them before. Courts then rely on that judicial silence to conclude there's no equivalent case on the books. No precedent = no clearly established law = no liability. . . . Heads government wins, tails plaintiff loses." *Zadeh*, 928 F.3d at 479–80.

As instances of police misconduct have become more widely known, the qualified immunity doctrine's role in limiting civil rights lawsuits is coming under increased scrutiny. *See, e.g., Jamison v. McClendon*, No. 3:16-CV-595-CWR-LRA, 2020 WL 4497723 (S.D. Miss. Aug. 4, 2020) (tracing the tortured history of the defense and sharply criticizing it, but acknowledging that the court is bound by stare decisis). As a result, a variety of reform proposals have emerged to change the doctrine. *See* Sobel, *supra*.

V. Further Pleading

You may recall that common law pleading often continued for many rounds, to the point that the common law was pressed for names for the later rounds (sur-reply, sur-sur-reply?). De-emphasizing pleading and narrowing the purposes of pleading, the Federal Rules tried to cut this process off at a much earlier stage. Thus, Rule 7(a) contemplates a complaint (or a third-party complaint) and an answer. When the answer contains a counterclaim or crossclaim, the Rule also requires an answer to these claims. In short, for every claim of any kind that is not dismissed, an answer is allowed.

Suppose the answer contains new factual allegations in support of defenses. Shouldn't they also be admitted or denied? Here the rule makers drew a hard line: generally *no*, adding that "[i]f a responsive pleading is not required, an allegation is considered denied or avoided." Rule 8(b)(6). It's a hard line, but not a fast line: "[I]f the court orders one, a reply to an answer [is allowed]." Rule 7(a)(7). For example, if Builder answered Neighbor's complaint in the last question by saying, "Defendant did not make ruts in Neighbor's property; Johnson Landscaping did," this allegation would require no response in a reply. It is simply deemed denied, according to Rule 8(b)(6). On rare occasions, the court may conclude that the litigation would be advanced by requiring a reply admitting or denying the additional factual allegations, perhaps to flush out some potentially dispositive defense that could be heard on a Rule 12(c) motion for judgment on the pleadings or a Rule 56 motion for summary judgment.

VI. A Concluding Exercise: What's Wrong with This Picture?

Lawyers often draft answers less attentively than they do complaints, perhaps because Rule 12(b)(6) motions testing complaints are more common than Rule 12(f) motions testing answers. As a result, answer drafting is often formulaic, in apparent derogation of Rule 8. Consider the following judge's impatient response, before considering a "what's wrong with this picture" question about our hypothetical answer to the complaint in *Doe v. Smith* (p. 444), the secret videotape case in the prior chapter.

STATE FARM MUTUAL AUTOMOBILE INSURANCE CO. v. RILEY

199 F.R.D. 276 (N.D. Ill. 2001)

Shadur, Senior District Judge.

Nancy DeMarco ("DeMarco"), one of the defendants in this interpleader action brought by State Farm Mutual Automobile Insurance Company ("State Farm"), has filed her Answer to Complaint of Interpleader. For the reasons stated in this sua sponte memorandum opinion and order, the Answer is stricken in its entirety—but with leave granted to DeMarco's counsel (an Assistant Attorney General) to replead promptly.

For too many years this Court has been required to treat with a battery of basic pleading errors committed by defendants' lawyers who have failed to conform to the clear directives—or to the basic thrust—of the Federal Rules of Civil Procedure. Both to simplify the process of correcting such deficiencies in the future and to save unwarranted wear and tear on its secretary, this Court has decided to issue the attached Appendix as a compendium of most of those frequently-encountered errors. In that way future flaws of the same types in later cases can be addressed by a simple reference to the Appendix rather than by a set of repeated substantive discussions from case to case.

In this instance DeMarco's counsel has been guilty of "only" two of the errors listed in the Appendix. But counsel has made up for that by the pervasiveness of those fundamental missteps—only the final Answer ¶ 21 is in proper form, each of the Answer's other 20 paragraphs having involved one or both of the repeated infractions. That pervasiveness alone should justify using this case as the poster child to which the Appendix is attached for future citation. . . .

As stated at the outset, the entire Answer is stricken, and DeMarco's counsel is ordered (1) to file a self-contained Amended Answer (see App. ¶ 7) in this Court's chambers on or before March 5, 2001, and to comply with App. ¶ 8 as well.

APPENDIX

After years of unsuccessful efforts to correct a gaggle of fundamental pleading errors that continue to crop up in responsive pleadings, this Court—perhaps as much out of consideration for its highly skilled and substantially overworked secretary as for any other reason—has decided on a different approach. This Appendix will cover those most common flaws, so that corrective orders required to be entered in future cases can simply incorporate the treatment here by reference.

1. Fed R. Civ. P. ("Rule") 8(b)

Even though the second sentence of Rule 8(b) marks out an unambiguous path for any party that seeks the benefit of a deemed denial when he, she or it can neither admit outright nor deny outright a plaintiff's allegation (or plaintiff's "averment," the word used in Rule 8(b)), too many lawyers feel a totally unwarranted need to attempt to be creative by straying from that clear path. Most frequently such lawyers will omit any reference to "belief," or they will sometimes omit any reference to "information," or they may be guilty of both those omissions—and they do so even though Rule 8(b)'s drafters deliberately chose those terms as elements of the Rule's necessary disclaimer in order to set a higher hurdle for the earning of a deemed denial.[1] And although the concept of "strict proof," whatever that may mean, is nowhere to be found in the Rules (or to this Court's knowledge in any other set of rules or in any treatise on the subject of pleading), some members of the same coterie of careless defense counsel will also often include an impermissible demand for such proof. . . .

2. Legal Conclusions

Another regular offender is the lawyer who takes it on himself or herself to decline to respond to an allegation because it "states a legal conclusion." That of course violates the express Rule 8(b) requirement that *all* allegations must be responded to. But perhaps even more importantly, it disregards established law from the highest authority on down that legal conclusions are an integral part of the federal notice pleading regime. Indeed, could anything be more of a legal conclusion than a plaintiff's allegation of subject matter jurisdiction, which must of course be answered? ...

3. "Speaks for Itself"

Another unacceptable device, used by lawyers who would prefer not to admit something that is alleged about a document in a complaint (or who may perhaps

1. "Information" is of course much easier to come by than "knowledge." And very often it doesn't require much in the way of information to form a belief about the truth or lack of truth in someone else's assertions.

be too lazy to craft an appropriate response to such an allegation), is to say instead that the document "speaks for itself." This Court has been attempting to listen to such written materials for years (in the forlorn hope that one will indeed give voice)—but until some such writing does break its silence, this Court will continue to require pleaders to employ one of the three alternatives that *are* permitted by Rule 8(b) in response to all allegations about the contents of documents (or statutes or regulations).

4. Other Failure to Answer

On occasion some defense counsel will fail or refuse to answer an allegation for some asserted reason other than those discussed above. Again such an omission is at odds with the plain mandate of Rule 8(b)'s first sentence, so that this Court regularly requires that every allegation in a complaint be responded to in conformity with Rule 8(b).

5. Rule 8(c)

Some defense counsel are inordinately fond of following the direct responses to a complaint's allegations with a set of purported affirmative defenses ("ADs") that don't really fit that concept. Though not identical in scope to the common law plea in confession and avoidance, the AD essentially takes the same approach of *admitting* all of the allegations of a complaint, but of then going on to explain other reasons that defendant is not liable to plaintiff anyway (or, as with comparative negligence or non-mitigation of damages, may be liable for less than plaintiff claims)—see the laundry list of ADs in Rule 8(c). This Court has made that point for many years in almost innumerable cases.... Accordingly:

(a) Where a claimed AD is inconsistent with a complaint's allegation, it will be stricken (nothing is lost by defendant in that situation, because the denial of that allegation in the answer has already put the matter at issue).*

(b) It is unacceptable for a party's attorney simply to mouth ADs in formula-like fashion ("laches," "estoppel," "statute of limitations" or what have you), for that does not do the job of apprising opposing counsel and this Court of the predicate for the claimed defense—which is after all the goal of notice pleading. Any such AD will also be stricken, but with leave often granted to advance a properly fleshed-out AD to the same effect the next time around.

---

* [Eds.—An affirmative defense that disputes factual allegations of the complaint is really a denial. If the answer already contains a denial, "nothing is lost" by striking the redundant defense. Recall that this was precisely the mistake the defendant made in *Reis Robotics* when it pled as an "affirmative defense" that it owed nothing because it had never authorized the work that the plaintiff alleged in its complaint. The court therefore held that this was not an affirmative defense at all, but "merely a restatement of the denials contained in the answer."]

6. District Court LR 10.1

For decades this District Court has imposed this obligation (now redesignated as LR [Local Rule] 10.1 as part of the court's required 1999 renumbering of its local rules to track the Federal Rules of Civil Procedure) on all defendants:

> Responsive pleadings shall be made in numbered paragraphs each corresponding to and stating a concise summary of the paragraph to which it is directed.

As a matter of practice, that requirement is most often complied with by a defendant's verbatim copying of the complaint's allegations in each paragraph, followed immediately by defendant's response to that paragraph. Its purpose is obvious: to provide a self-contained pleading, so that the judicial or adversary reader can avoid the inconvenience of having to flip back and forth between two pleadings to see just what is or is not being placed at issue. But even apart from that fostering of convenience, there is no justification for any lawyer's noncompliance with such a plain directive of long standing—something that should be known by everyone practicing in this district.

7. Compliance

For much the same reason that has occasioned the adoption of LR 10.1, it is most often preferable that a flawed responsive pleading—one that contains a number of errors of one or more of the types described above—be cured by filing a full-blown self-contained amended pleading, rather than just an amendment limited to correcting those errors. That practice also avoids a kind of patchwork pleading, in which more than one document must be examined to see the totality of the responding party's pleading. This Court frequently includes an order to that effect after having identified the violations involved.

8. Cost of Correction

Because all of the matters that have been addressed here are the product of some lawyer's deficient performance, there is no reason that the client should bear the cost of correction via a revised pleading (as stated in the preceding paragraph, that most frequently takes the form of a self-contained amended answer). Accordingly, no charge is to be made to the client by its counsel for the added work and expense incurred in correcting counsel's own errors. And counsel are ordered to apprise their client to that effect by letter, with a copy to be transmitted to this Court's chambers as an informational matter (not for filing).

What's wrong with this picture (answer)? Recall that in the last chapter we considered the complaint in *Doe v. Smith*, at p. 441. Assume that after the defendant filed a motion to dismiss for failure to state a claim, which was denied, it filed the following (fictitious) answer to that complaint. What is wrong with it?

UNITED STATES DISTRICT COURT
for the
CENTRAL DISTRICT OF ILLINOIS

Jane DOE, Plaintiff,	)	
	)	
v.	)	Civil Action No. 04-3173
	)	
Jason SMITH, Defendant.	)	

ANSWER

Responding to Allegations of Complaint

1. Defendant lacks knowledge to form a belief about the truth of the allegations in paragraphs 1, 3, and 17.

2. Defendant admits paragraphs 2, 4, 5, 10, 14.

3. Defendant admits that during the spring of 2002, he recorded with a video camera recorder, but denies the rest of paragraph 7.

4. Defendant admits that on May 20, 2003, Plaintiff confronted him regarding the existence of the video camera recording and that he admitted the existence of the recording, but Defendant neither admits nor denies the rest of the paragraph insofar as it states a legal conclusion.

5. Defendant neither admits nor denies paragraphs 8, 11, 12, (the first numbered) 15, (the second numbered) 15, and 16 insofar as each states a legal conclusion.

6. Defendant denies all the remaining paragraphs of the complaint.

Failure to State a Claim

7. The complaint fails to state a claim upon which relief can be granted.

Lack of Subject Matter jurisdiction

8. This court lacks subject matter jurisdiction.

Insufficient Service of Process

9. The service of process herein was insufficient.

Affirmative Defense: Consent or Permission

10. The Plaintiff consented to the video camera recording of which she complains.

Affirmative Defense: Assumption of the Risk

11. The Plaintiff assumed the risk that the acts which she described would be video camera recorded.

Respectfully submitted,
John Q. Attorney
John Q. Attorney
42 E. Main St., Springfield, Illinois 62701
jqattorney@gmail.com
217-812-3333
Illinois Bar # 21775

"A Gaggle of Fundamental Pleading Errors"?

1. All paragraphs. To understand this answer, one would have to read it side-by-side with the complaint, risking whiplash. This is why the Northern District of Illinois has adopted Local Rule 10.1, which requires the answer to incorporate or summarize each paragraph of the complaint to which an answer is directed. This rule is not typical (and thus a reminder that knowing the federal or state rules of civil procedure is not enough; you should always check the local rules, as well as any individual rules of the particular judge assigned to your case, before filing anything.) Whether or not a local rule requires such incorporation, it is good practice at least to align the numbering of responsive paragraphs in your answer with those in the complaint, in order to make the answer easier to follow.

2. Answer ¶ 1: Pleading lack of knowledge or information. As Judge Shadur points out, knowledge and information are two different things. The Rules do not allow empty-headed pleading ("I don't know"); they presume that the pleader conducted a reasonable inquiry (Rule 11(b)), which includes acquiring reasonably accessible information in order to admit or deny allegations in the complaint. It's unclear whether Defendant would have to obtain information about Plaintiff's birth date, but he can probably ascertain whether she is a resident of Springfield (compl. para. 3). Defendant could probably plead lack of knowledge or information sufficient to form a belief for ¶ 17, even though he has some inkling of her distress and embarrassment, as these are details in her complaint, but he should track the formula of Rule 8(b)(5), at least if he filed in Judge Shadur's court! But Rule 8(e) instructs that "Pleadings must be construed so as to do justice." Does a niggling insistance on the phrasing, "lacks knowledge or information," do justice?

3. Answer ¶ 3: Fairly responding. It is arguable whether the partial admission in answer ¶ 3 fairly responds to complaint ¶ 7. Does Defendant mean to deny that he recorded "said acts" (admittedly not the most specific allegation), that he did so "covertly and surreptitiously," *and* that he made the recording "while engaging in sexual intimacy with the Plaintiff"?

4. Answer ¶ 5: Legal conclusions. As we saw in the last chapter, the Supreme Court was critical of conclusory pleading in *Iqbal*. Whether or not "conclusions of law" would support a motion to dismiss for failure to state a claim after *Iqbal* and *Twombly*, they provide no safe harbor in which a defendant could avoid either admitting or denying under Judge Shadur's rules. Defendant here should have denied.

5. Answer ¶ 7: Failure to state a claim, again? When the defendant first made his Rule 12(b)(6) objection by motion, it was denied. It therefore seems redundant to include it again in the answer. But defendants commonly do, just to make the record completely clear. Including it, of course, does not put it before the judge again. Once the court denied the motion, that decision became what we call "law of the case," and the court will ordinarily not revisit it. Pleading this defense in the answer thus does nothing more than make it clear in the pleadings that it was raised.

6. Answer ¶¶ 8–9: Other Rule 12(b) defenses. This one is easy. The defense of subject matter jurisdiction can be asserted at any time. The defense of insufficient service of process was waived by its omission from the pre-answer Rule 12(b)(6) motion. *See* Rule 12(h)(1).

7. Answer ¶ 10: Mislabeled affirmative defenses. While "permission or consent" sounds like an affirmative defense, here it is really no more than a denial of ¶ 8 of the complaint and thus encompassed already in the answer's partial general denial in ¶ 6 *of the answer*. Under Judge Shadur's rules, it would be stricken. Recall that the court in *Reis Robotics* would agree; it also struck a denial masquerading as an affirmative defense.

8. Answer ¶ 11: Legally insufficient defense. If *Iqbal* applies to defenses, then this defense may require more factual detail. (How did the plaintiff assume a risk if she didn't know she was being videotaped?) Moreover, "Assumption of the Risk" is a defense in some jurisdictions only to negligence, not to an intentional tort, let alone one against a minor child. If so, on a proper motion by the plaintiff, the court should strike this defense as legally insufficient.

VII. Responding to the Complaint (or Not?): Summary of Basic Principles

- A defendant can respond to a complaint by doing nothing (and risking an entry of default and perhaps a default judgment), by moving to dismiss under Rule 12, or by answering. We use "defendant" and "plaintiff" in this summary for the sake of simplicity, but any party who has been sued, whether by complaint, counterclaim, crossclaim, third-party complaint, or interpleader, has the same options. After the answer, no reply is required unless the court orders one.

- A defendant who fails to respond to the complaint within the time limit set by the Rules is subject to an entry of default when that failure is shown by affidavit or otherwise.
- A default judgment admits the facts stated in the complaint, but a default judgment neither admits that the facts are sufficient to establish a defendant's liability nor the amount of damages or other remedies. After entry of default, on motion, the clerk may enter judgment when a plaintiff's claim is for a sum certain. Alternatively, if a plaintiff seeks a default judgment for an unliquidated sum, the court may enter judgment after finding that it has jurisdiction, that service was properly made, that the admitted facts establish liability, and that the relief sought has been established by evidentiary hearing, accounting, or other investigation.
- Obey the omnibus motion rule! A defendant is not required to file a pre-answer motion under Rule 12, but if she does, she must consolidate all the Rule 12 defenses and objections then available to her in a single omnibus motion, and she may not thereafter make a second pre-answer motion except to dismiss for lack of subject matter jurisdiction.
- Beware the waiver trap! If a defendant omits the Rule 12(b)(2)–(5) defenses from her pre-answer motion or from her answer, whichever she files first, she waives the omitted defense. If she omits the Rule 12(b)(6)–(7) defenses, she may still make them in any pleading or post-pleading motion until the close of trial.
- Rule 12(b)(6) motions assume as true the well-pleaded allegations of the complaint. If a defendant introduces supporting factual matter not alleged in the complaint, and the court accepts that matter, then the motion is converted under Rule 12(d) into a Rule 56 summary judgment motion.
- Answers can include admissions and denials, Rule 12(b) defenses, affirmative defenses (which provide excuses why a defendant is not liable even if the facts alleged in the complaint are established), and new claims such as counterclaims or crossclaims.
- A plaintiff can test the legal sufficiency of a defense by moving to strike it under Rule 12(f), which is decided under the same principles that the court uses to decide Rule 12(b)(6) motions to dismiss for failure to state a claim.

15

Care and Candor in Pleading

I. Introduction

Suppose Peters files a legally sufficient complaint alleging that Dupont "negligently drove his car against" Peters, breaking Peters's leg. (This allegation was made in now-abrogated Form 11, which then-Rule 84 declared as sufficient under the Rules.)

But what if Peters actually broke his leg playing basketball and simply lied in his complaint? Or what if neither he nor his lawyer bothered to investigate who was driving the car or to read the police report stating that it was Edmunds, and that Peters therefore sued passenger Dupont by mistake? Nothing in Rule 12(b)(6) or 12(f) protects against dishonest, sloppy, mistaken, or ill-motivated allegations. What does?

If your instinct is to say that there must be some rule intended to provide this kind of protection, you are partly right. If Peters broke his leg playing basketball, there is no basis in fact for Peters's allegation that Dupont's car broke his leg. Moreover, any basis-in-fact requirement logically presupposes some duty of research or inquiry before suing, or an "empty head" defense ("I wasn't pleading in bad faith; I just didn't know") could too easily defeat such a requirement. Even if Peters did not know that Dupont was not the driver of the car, he should have conducted some inquiry (reading the police report?) to ascertain whether his allegations had a basis in fact.

In federal courts, Rule 11 sets out both the standard for care and candor in pleading (and in the filing of other papers before the court) and the sanctions for violations of the standard. Rule 11 provides that by presenting a paper to the court, an attorney of record or, in some cases, a party certifies that

> to the best of the person's knowledge, information, and belief, formed after an inquiry reasonable under the circumstances:
>
> (1) it is not being presented for any improper purpose, such as to harass, cause unnecessary delay, or needlessly increase the cost of litigation;
>
> (2) the claims, defenses, and other legal contentions are warranted by existing law or by a nonfrivolous argument for extending, modifying, or reversing existing law or for establishing new law;
>
> (3) the factual contentions have evidentiary support or, if specifically so identified, will likely have evidentiary support after a reasonable opportunity for further investigation or discovery; and
>
> (4) the denials of factual contentions are warranted on the evidence or, if specifically so identified, are reasonably based on belief or a lack of information.

To put it more pithily, *presenting*—signing, filing, submitting, or later advocating—a paper to the court certifies that the presenter believes, after conducting a reasonable inquiry, that the paper has evidentiary support (or at least is likely to have support after an opportunity for further fact-gathering), a legal basis (either in existing law or in a good faith argument for its change), and a proper purpose.*

This chapter explores the required pre-filing inquiry, the scope of a "good faith argument" for changes in the law, the required evidentiary support for factual allegations, and the meaning of "proper purpose," before closing with an examination of the procedure for imposing sanctions under Rule 11.

II. Reasonable Inquiry

All of Rule 11's certifications to the court must be based on a pre-filing "inquiry reasonable under the circumstances." Even Rule 11(b)(3), which tolerates factual contentions that may lack evidentiary support at filing as long as they are specifically identified as "likely [to] have evidentiary support after a reasonable opportunity for *further* investigation or discovery," obviously presupposes *initial* investigation. What pre-filing inquiry is "reasonable under the circumstances" is clearly a fact-bound question.

* ABA Model Rules of Professional Conduct Rule 3.1, "Meritorious Claims and Contentions," also provides that "[a] lawyer shall not bring or defend a proceeding, or assert or controvert an issue therein, unless there is a basis in law and fact for doing so that is not frivolous, which includes a good faith argument for an extension, modification or reversal of existing law. . . ." Rules of professional conduct have been adopted in every jurisdiction, nearly all modeled closely on the ABA Model Rules. Thus, in egregious cases, a violation of Rule 11 can also lead to bar discipline, in addition to a court sanction.

The following case characterizes Rule 11 as a standard of malpractice and considers whether the plaintiffs' lawyer reasonably researched both the facts and the law before filing copyright claims that were seemingly beyond his general experience.

READING *HAYS v. SONY CORP. OF AMERICA.* The plaintiffs wrote a manual for operating their school's DEC word processors, and the school asked Sony to adapt that manual for use with the word processors. When Sony did so (without charging the school or using the adapted manual anywhere else), plaintiffs sued Sony for common law and statutory copyright infringement. The federal copyright statute, however, abolished common law copyright as of January 1, 1978, well before the events giving rise to plaintiffs' claims.

The plaintiffs sought damages and injunctive relief. For a statutory copyright violation, a plaintiff can recover her actual damages plus the infringer's profits. Or, instead, she can recover statutory damages (damages according to a statutory formula), which can be increased for willful infringement.

The district court granted Sony's motion to dismiss for failure to state a claim and then granted Sony's Rule 11 motion for sanctions. At the time of the decision, Rule 11 required that, after "reasonable inquiry," pleadings had to be "well grounded in fact" and warranted by existing law or a good faith argument for its change.

- What should a "reasonable inquiry" (under the current Rule, "an inquiry reasonable under the circumstances") have revealed about the legal basis for the common law copyright claim? Why wasn't the plaintiffs' lawyer's inexperience in copyright law an excuse for any deficiency in his legal research?
- What inquiry into the facts should the plaintiffs' lawyer have made?
- Did the plaintiffs' lawyer act in bad faith? If not, why sanction him?

HAYS v. SONY CORP. OF AMERICA

847 F.2d 412 (7th Cir. 1988)

POSNER, Circuit Judge.

The appeal in this copyright suit brings before us a medley of questions involving jurisdiction, copyright, and sanctions. The plaintiffs, Stephanie Hays and Gail MacDonald, teach business courses at a public high school in Des Plaines, Illinois. In 1982 or 1983 they prepared a manual for their students on how to operate the school's DEC word processors, and distributed copies to students and to other faculty members. In 1984 the school district, having bought word processors from Sony Corporation of America (the defendant in this suit), gave Sony the plaintiffs' manual and asked Sony to modify it so that it could be used with Sony's word processors. This Sony proceeded to do, resulting in a manual very similar to—in many places a verbatim copy of—the plaintiff's manual. Sony did not charge the school district anything for preparing the manual, which was delivered to the school district in December 1984 and, sometime afterward, distributed to the students. Nor is there any evidence that Sony has sold or disseminated the manual elsewhere.

In February 1985 the plaintiffs, presumably spurred by knowledge of Sony's manual, registered their own manual with the Copyright Office, and in July they filed this lawsuit in federal district court. Count I charges a violation of common law (i.e., state) copyright, Count II a violation of statutory (i.e., federal) copyright. The complaint alleges that Sony "has made large profits by reason of appropriating to its own use Plaintiffs' workbook," and demands compensatory and punitive damages, an accounting for profits, an injunction, attorney's fees, and other relief.

[Eds.—The district court dismissed for failure to state a claim and subsequently granted Sony's Rule 11 motion for sanctions. The court awarded Sony $14,895.46 in sanctions against the plaintiffs' counsel, Emmanuel F. Guyon, but not against the plaintiffs. This appeal followed.]

. . .

The suit is a mixture of the frivolous and the nonfrivolous. The claim of infringement of a common law copyright is frivolous. . . . Hays and MacDonald wrote their manual long after the abolition of common law copyright.

Guyon argues (for the first time on appeal, and in the face of his clients' contrary affidavits) that though not actually written until 1982, the manual incorporated materials created in the early 1970s, not published, and therefore covered by common law copyright. This argument is irrelevant, as well as untimely and factually unsupported. The [federal copyright] statute explicitly abolishes common law copyright as of January 1, 1978, whether the work was created before or after that date. . . . By the time Sony commenced the activities that are alleged to have infringed the plaintiffs' common law copyright, the plaintiffs no longer had any common law copyright.

Although, as we shall see, the plaintiffs' claim that their statutory copyright was infringed is not frivolous, most of their requests for relief against that alleged infringement are frivolous. The plaintiffs could not obtain statutory damages or attorney's fees, because they did not register their copyright within three months after first publishing the manual . . . and before Sony published its allegedly infringing manual. *See* 17 U.S.C. § 412(2). They could not obtain an accounting for profits, because, according to Sony's uncontradicted affidavit, Sony never obtained any profits from the sale or distribution of the manual—indeed, never sold it. Sony may have earned goodwill or repeat sales by complying with the school district's request to modify the plaintiffs' manual, but the plaintiffs did not seek profits on that theory.

The plaintiffs could not obtain actual damages either. Although in the sanctions hearing Guyon told the judge that the plaintiffs had put out some (unsuccessful) feelers to publishers, he had presented no evidence in the suit itself that his clients had any plans or prospects for publishing their manual or otherwise obtaining a monetary return on it. And of course there is no evidence that Sony killed their market by distributing its version of the manual. Finally, the plaintiffs could not obtain punitive damages. Although authority on the question is surprisingly sparse, it appears to be accepted that punitive damages are not recoverable in federal copyright suits. If there is any reason to doubt this conclusion, Guyon has not indicated to us what it might be. A willful infringer can be required to pay statutory damages of up to $50,000 instead of the usual maximum of $10,000, *see* 17 U.S.C. § 504(c)(2), but, as already pointed out, the plaintiffs in this case are not eligible for statutory damages. And they have never suggested that Sony was acting willfully. It appears that Sony either believed that the manual it was asked to modify was not copyrighted or believed that the school district owned the copyright. Either belief would have been reasonable; the manual contained no copyright notice or other attempted reservation of rights. . . .

Every request that the plaintiffs made for monetary relief thus was frivolous, yet they might have been entitled to an injunction, for they may have had a valid statutory copyright that was infringed. . . .

. . . The presence of a nonfrivolous claim would create a serious problem if the district judge had based his award of sanctions on a belief that the lawsuit was entirely frivolous, for while we have upheld sanctions against plaintiffs or their attorneys for bringing suits frivolous only in part . . . , an award of sanctions that was premised on a seriously exaggerated view of the frivolousness of the suit could not stand. But that was not the nature of Judge Mihm's award. Realizing that the claim of statutory infringement had not been negligible, he made clear in awarding sanctions that the problem was not that the complaint had been frivolous but that the suit had not been pursued effectively. . . . He therefore awarded Sony the following percentages of the attorney's fees that it had incurred in defending against the suit: 10 percent of the fees incurred between the filing of the suit in July 1985 and April 1, 1986, by which time it should have been obvious to Guyon, the district judge thought, that the suit was hopeless; 50 percent of the fees incurred after April 1; and 75 percent of the fees incurred in successfully moving to strike materials filed by Guyon in June 1986, after the close of the record on summary judgment, in a futile effort to stave off dismissal.

This method of calculation was lenient. The common law copyright claim and the requests for monetary relief showed that Guyon had not conducted the reasonable precomplaint inquiry into fact and law required by Rule 11, for that inquiry would have shown that he had no basis for these aspects of the suit. His argument that he didn't know how to find out whether Sony was selling its manual rings hollow, when he did not so much as write Sony (before suing it) to explain his clients' position and to inquire whether Sony was distributing the manual or planning to do so. Of course Sony might not have answered such a letter but at least Guyon would have discharged his duty of inquiring to the extent feasible to do. Copyright law makes it easy for the copyright holder to prove an entitlement to monetary relief (even if he is ineligible for statutory damages, which require no proof of injury), by allowing him to prove and recover either his actual damages or the infringer's profits, whichever is larger, and to presume profits from the gross revenues obtained by the infringer from the infringing work. It should not have been difficult for Guyon to obtain the minimal facts necessary to decide whether there was a basis for seeking monetary as well as injunctive relief; anyway Guyon didn't try. Certainly more than 10 percent of Sony's attorney's fees before April 1 were incurred in opposing the frivolous aspects of the suit, and by April 1 it should have been plain to Guyon that his clients' only hope was to obtain an injunction for infringement of a statutory copyright—but he continued to press his frivolous claims with undiminished enthusiasm.

In requiring reasonable inquiry before the filing of any pleading in a civil case in federal district court, Rule 11 demands "an objective determination of whether a sanctioned party's conduct was reasonable under the circumstances." *Brown v. Federation of State Medical Boards,* 830 F.2d 1429, 1435 (7th Cir. 1987). In effect it imposes a negligence standard, for negligence is a failure to use reasonable care. The equation between negligence and failure to conduct a reasonable pre-complaint inquiry is transparent in *Szabo Food Service, Inc. v. Canteen Corp.,* 823 F.2d 1073, 1083 (7th Cir. 1987), where we said that "the amount of investigation required by Rule 11 depends on both the time available to investigate and on the probability that more investigation will turn up important evidence; the Rule does not require steps that are not cost-justified."

Restating the standard in negligence terms helps one to see that Rule 11 defines a new form of legal malpractice, and there is thus no more reason for a competent attorney to fear being sanctioned under Rule 11 than to fear being punished for any other form of malpractice. The difference is merely in the victim. In the ordinary case of legal malpractice the victim is the lawyer's client, though there are exceptions . . . . In the Rule 11 setting the victims are the lawyer's adversary, other litigants in the court's queue, and the court itself. By asserting claims without first inquiring whether they have a plausible grounding in law and fact, a lawyer can impose on an adversary and on the judicial system substantial costs that would have been—and should have been—avoided by a reasonable pre-pleading inquiry.

From his papers in both the district court and this court it is apparent that Mr. Guyon is not a specialist either in copyright law or in federal litigation. As a solo practitioner in the town of Streator, Illinois—population 14,000—Mr. Guyon is not to be criticized for having failed to acquire expertness in an esoteric field of federal law and in the niceties of federal procedure. But the Rule 11 standard, like the negligence standard in tort law, is an objective standard, as we have said. It makes no allowance for the particular circumstances of particular practitioners. There is no "locality rule" in legal malpractice, and while a legal specialist may be held to an even higher standard of care than a generalist, the generalist acts at his peril if he brings a suit in a field or forum with which he is unacquainted. A lawyer who lacks relevant expertise must either associate with him a lawyer who has it, or must bone up on the relevant law at every step in the way in recognition that his lack of experience makes him prone to error. He must litigate very carefully, just as a new driver must drive very carefully. Mr. Guyon failed to heed this precept, booting what may have been a meritorious though modest claim by pressing frivolous claims. . . .

. . . The award of Rule 11 sanctions against Mr. Guyon is affirmed. Sony is directed to submit to the clerk of this court within 15 days a statement of its fees and expenses reasonably incurred in defending against so much of Guyon's appeal as sought to overturn the judgment on the merits. . . .

Notes and Questions: Pre-Filing Inquiries

Q **1. Guyon's legal research and the legal basis for the complaint.** It is obvious that before you file a claim for violation of common law copyright, you should familiarize yourself with the existing law of common law copyright. How else would you know whether it was warranted by existing law or a non-frivolous argument for its change? Even cursory research would presumably have found the federal copyright statute and therefore discovered that it explicitly abolished common law copyright as of January 1, 1978, at least *six years before* Sony did anything with the plaintiffs' manual.

But this is not self-evident to a non-specialist in the field. Why doesn't the reasonableness of the pre-filing inquiry required by Rule 11 depend on the expertise of the lawyer?

A Rule 11's standard of care is an objective standard that makes no express allowance for the particular circumstances of the individual lawyer. The question is whether *any* reasonable lawyer would familiarize herself with—that is, conduct research about—the copyright statute before filing a complaint alleging copyright violations. Moreover, unlike medical malpractice law, Rule 11 does not look to the standard of care in the particular lawyer's community of practice; "there is no 'locality rule' in legal malpractice," Judge Posner says. The standard is national (which seems particularly fitting for practice under the national Federal Rules of Civil Procedure, which apply to all federal district courts). Lacking copyright expertise, Guyon should either have consulted or associated with a lawyer who had it or have made up for his own lack of expertise by performing extra research.

Q **2. Guyon's factual inquiry and the evidentiary support for the complaint.** The court found that the plaintiffs' claim for damages was frivolous. Why?

A Recall that for a statutory copyright violation, the statute gives plaintiffs a choice of their actual damages plus the infringer's profits, or, instead, damages determined according to a statutory formula, which can be increased for willful infringement. But Sony's uncontradicted affidavit showed that it neither sold nor otherwise distributed the manual and therefore had neither revenues nor profits from it, and plaintiffs "never suggested that Sony was acting wilfully." Thus, the problem with plaintiffs' damage claims was not that such claims have no legal basis, but that *here* they lacked any evidentiary support. Moreover, Guyon undertook no pre-filing inquiry to determine whether they had evidentiary support. He apparently developed no evidence that the plaintiffs had lost any profits from Sony's acts (it was only at the sanctions hearing itself that he first suggested that the plaintiffs had put out some unsuccessful feelers to publishers). He never wrote Sony to ask whether it was distributing the manual or planning to do so and never made any other effort to ascertain whether Sony was making any revenue from the manual.

Does this mean that the reasonableness of a plaintiff's pre-filing inquiry depends on the defendant's willingness to cooperate? Hardly. The court notes that just asking "would have discharged his duty of inquiring *to the extent feasible to do*" (emphasis added). Reasonableness is always a question of balancing the cost in time and resources of the pre-filing inquiry against the likely benefits. Here, asking Sony would have been cheap even if unlikely to produce much. As the same court announced in *Szabo Food Service*, "the amount of investigation required by Rule 11 depends on both the time available to investigate and on the probability that more investigation will turn up important evidence; the Rule does not require steps that are not cost-justified." 823 F.2d at 1083. This cost-benefit principle applies with special force to the pre-filing inquiry into evidentiary support, which can be very costly when it entails interviews and field work, compared to relatively inexpensive legal research for which the benefits are usually clear. That said, Judge Posner's cost-benefit evaluation may have been a bit harsh on the plaintiffs. It is arguable that even the small costs of asking Sony were too much in light of the small likelihood that Sony's lawyer would have let it provide much, if any, information in reply.

Q **3. Bad faith?** There is nothing in the *Hays* opinion suggesting that the plaintiffs' lawyer acted in bad faith. In fact, there is every indication that, as a small-town solo practitioner who did not specialize in copyright law, he acted in good faith, but was simply ignorant of copyright law. Why was he punished for his good faith mistakes?

A There are at least two reasons. The first is that since 1983, Rule 11 has not required bad faith to find a violation. By positing a "*reasonable*" inquiry, it embraces a negligence standard of care. Judge Posner therefore accurately calls Rule 11 violations a "new form of malpractice," not a form of morally culpable conduct. Ignorance is no defense; a good heart will not excuse an empty head.

Second, Guyon was responsible for his own ignorance. Had he conducted even the most basic research into copyright law, he would have discovered that common law copyright was abolished long before Sony adapted the plaintiffs' manual. Had he written Sony to explain his clients' position and inquired about sales or distribution, Sony's lawyers might have told him both that he had no common law copyright claim, and that there was no sale or distribution (and therefore no revenue or profit for his clients to claim). Repeat after us: Ignorance is no defense.

Q **4. Snapshot or continuing duty?** Suppose Guyon had inquired of Sony, as the appellate court suggests, but it refused to answer his letter. That "would have discharged his duty of inquiring to the extent feasible to do," according to the court. What, then, if after he filed a complaint for a statutory violation (omitting any common law claim), he had learned that, in fact, Sony made no sales or distributions, and therefore earned no revenue from the manual? Has he violated Rule 11 by filing a complaint that proves later to lack evidentiary support?

A It would seem unfair to sanction him with the benefit of hindsight, if his pre-filing inquiry was sufficient, as the hypothetical posits. Rule 11, as amended in 1993, now reflects this intuition. It states that by "presenting [a paper] to the court," a lawyer or other presenter makes representations to the court. One "presents" the paper chiefly by "signing, filing, [or] submitting." Rule 11(b). The representations are made at the time of signing, filing, or submitting. To put it differently, it's what you know—or should know after reasonable inquiry—at the time of presenting that controls. Some courts have said that Rule 11 takes a "snapshot" of your state of mind at the time of presenting that serves as the basis for deciding whether your paper complied with the Rule. There is therefore no general obligation to withdraw the paper on the basis of later-acquired information. (Prior to the 1993 amendments, some courts had ruled that there was.)

However, "presenting" also includes "later advocating." If, *after* learning the information that showed that the complaint's claims for monetary relief lacked evidentiary support, Guyon defended these claims in oral argument, he would be "later advocating" the now-discredited claims and would thereby violate the Rule, even though, on this hypothetical, he had not violated it by filing. The Advisory Committee explained as follows:

> [The rule] does not cover matters arising for the first time during oral presentations to the court, when counsel may make statements that would not have been made if there had been time for study and reflection. However, a litigant's obligations with respect to the contents of papers are not measured solely as of the time they are filed with or submitted to the court, but include reaffirming to the court and advocating positions contained in those pleadings and motions after learning that they cease to have any merit.

Fed. R. Civ. P. 11 advisory committee's notes (1993).

5. Reasonableness factors. The *Hays* court acknowledged that the reasonableness of a pre-filing inquiry depends in part on the time available for an investigation. Thus, if the statute of limitations is expiring the next day, a quick inquiry by phone or on the Internet may be reasonable "under the circumstances," but it would be unreasonable had there been more time. (But be careful: If the statute is expiring tomorrow because the lawyer dawdled for three months before starting the inquiry, the self-created time bind will be of no avail.) What other factors affect reasonableness? One treatise lists, among many:

- the complexity of the factual and legal issues in question;
- the extent to which pertinent facts were under the control of opponents and third parties (recall that the *Hays* court only required Guyon to try to contact Sony and not that he necessarily get a response);
- the extent to which the lawyer relied on the client for the facts (if Guyon's clients told him that they had lost a sale to a publisher because of Sony's adaptation of their manual, that might have been enough, unless the cost of corroborating this statement—"give me a copy of your correspondence with the publisher"—was low);
- whether the case was accepted from another lawyer and the extent to which the receiving lawyer relied on the referring lawyer (but be careful: the duty of inquiry is non-delegable; reliance on the inquiry of other lawyers is just

a factor in assessing the receiving lawyer's discharge of her duty, not a substitute for it);

- the resources reasonably available to the lawyer to conduct an inquiry (in this respect, arguably less may be required of Guyon than of a large, multiperson law firm even though his lack of expertise is no defense);
- the extent to which the lawyer was on notice that further inquiry might be appropriate. (Suppose Guyon's clients told him that they had no intent to market their manual and they had heard nothing about Sony doing so. Shouldn't that have prompted further inquiry into the evidentiary basis for claims of monetary relief?)

Adapted from 1 *Sanc. Fed. Law of Lit. Abuse* § 8 (2019) ("*Sanc. Fed. Law*").

Q 6. **"Mixed" papers.** The court found that the plaintiffs' claim for statutory copyright infringement was *not* frivolous. Why didn't that immunize Guyon from Rule 11 sanctions?

A At one time, some circuits held that a single non-frivolous claim in the complaint *did* immunize the pleader. They reasoned that sanctions were unwarranted unless the paper "as a whole" was frivolous, partly on the theory that, "[b]y definition, every unsuccessful complaint, at some level of analysis, contains either a flawed argument or an unsupported allegation." *Burull v. First National Bank*, 831 F.2d 788, 789 (8th Cir. 1989). The 1993 Advisory Committee, however, disagreed. It therefore proposed making Rule 11 apply specifically to all "claims, defenses, and other legal contentions," as well as "factual contentions" and "denials of factual contentions," and not just to the filed paper as a whole. Fed. R. Civ. Proc. 11 advisory committee's notes (1993). The Rule now includes this language.

new rule

Does this mean that if you include a single unsupported allegation in an otherwise well-supported complaint, or a single unwarranted claim along with twelve well-supported claims, you will be sanctioned?

A Not necessarily. Not only did the 1993 Advisory Committee caution that "Rule 11 motions should not be made or threatened for minor, inconsequential violations . . . [,]" but it added that, in deciding on an appropriate sanction, a court should consider whether a violation "infected the entire pleading, or only one particular count or defense. . . ." *Id.* Thus, even the odd unsupported contention or claim violates the Rule, but it may not warrant a sanction.

7. Doing enough pre-filing homework?

Based on *Hays* and the preceding notes, which of the following pre-filing inquiries, without more, would most likely comply with Rule 11? Assume you are considering filing a complaint in a proper federal district court for negligence arising out of an accident in Massachusetts.

A. You interview the client, who tells you that the defendant backed into his car in a drug store parking lot last week, causing him whiplash and totaling his brand new Mercedes.
B. Same interview, but this time it occurs almost two years after the accident, just two days before the statute of limitations expires.
C. Same information, but you obtain it in a phone call one week after the accident from Dewey, a lawyer in New York who interviewed the client and is proposing to refer the case to you for filing in Connecticut. You don't know Dewey.
D. Same as C, but you know Dewey and have taken prior referrals from him.
E. Same as C, but you have Dewey fax you copies of the medical reports, if any, and the repair invoice indicating that the car was totaled.

A sounds good at first blush, because most pre-filing inquiries begin with the client, and some can properly end there if the client's story is persuasive (and, better yet, corroborated). But such reliance, like the inquiry itself, must be reasonable under the circumstances. Here the claim that a new car was "totaled" from another car backing into it in a parking lot seems questionable (how fast does a driver in a parking lot usually back up?), and if a client's story raises questions, you need to try to answer them before filing, if there is time. Since the accident occurred just a week ago, there is plenty of time to ask for documentation or names of other witnesses (including, maybe, the mechanic who examined the car).

B cuts the available time for inquiry to forty-eight hours. Obviously, you can do less in forty-eight hours—especially given the press of other existing cases—than in twenty-four months. Still, the client's claim that the car was "totaled" may seem so unlikely that you should at least ask for some corroborating evidence in the short time available, even if the time is insufficient for you to interview the mechanic or other witnesses.

Lawyers are entitled to rely, to some extent, on each other, but ultimately Rule 11's "stop-and-think" obligation is non-delegable. First, you should at least inquire of Dewey what inquiry *he* has made. Second, if the "totaled" claim is questionable, it remains questionable even after a referring lawyer passes it on. Third, you don't know Dewey. The reasonableness of reliance on referring lawyers, like the reasonableness of reliance on clients, may turn in part on how well you know them and your prior experience with their care and candor. Under these circumstances, **C** does not sound like a reasonable inquiry.

D is better, because you have a stronger case for relying on Dewey, having known him longer. But it still seems like you should ask him what he did to check the "totaled" claim. **D** is better, but perhaps not good enough.

As a result, **E** is probably the most reasonable pre-filing inquiry. Here you have tried to corroborate the claims. Of course, even after getting this documentation, there remains the question of who was at fault. On that, you could try to track down every witness to the accident and have an investigator interview them and measure and photograph the accident site. But "reasonableness" inherently implicates a cost-benefit analysis, and the cost of this much pre-filing inquiry may well exceed the benefit. Rule 11, after all, does not require that you develop evidence that will satisfy the preponderance standard of proof—evidence that proves your proposed claim. It only requires that your factual contentions have "evidentiary support" (or, if specifically so identified, "likely" will have evidentiary support after further investigation). Except when time precludes it, a lawyer can almost always inquire more before filing (and often will, not just to avoid any Rule 11 problems, but to make a start on building her case), but the Rule 11 question is just whether what she did was enough "under the circumstances."

III. Good Faith Arguments for Changes in the Law

It would be nice for lawyers if their clients' claims or defenses were always warranted by existing law, but sometimes the law is against them. When that is true for your client, you can't just throw up your hands. You might advise the client to settle. Or you might advise the client to keep fighting and search for the best argument you can find for distinguishing, extending, or changing the unfavorable law. Rule 11(b)(2) recognizes this possibility by tolerating "nonfrivolous argument for extending, modifying, or reversing existing law or for establishing new law." How far can you push in making such arguments before crossing the Rule 11 line?

Q **A question of lawyering.** In what practice area do you think plaintiffs' lawyers most often face Rule 11 motions for making arguments for changes in the law?

A Probably civil rights. When they advocate for new civil rights, or for the extension of existing civil rights to new classes of rights holders, they necessarily must make arguments for extending existing law or establishing new law. As long as the Rule 11 line on such arguments is unclear—that is, as long as "non-frivolous" has uncertain meaning—their arguments may attract motions for Rule 11 sanctions.

READING *HUNTER v. EARTHGRAINS CO. BAKERY* The civil rights lawyer in *Hunter* brought a class action on behalf of minority employees of a bakery that was eventually closed. The complaint included claims for employment discrimination against the bakery and for fraudulent misrepresentations in connection with its shutdown. The defendant denied that it had engaged in discrimination and argued that the lawsuit was precluded because the class discrimination claims were subject to binding arbitration under a collective bargaining agreement. The district court granted summary judgment to the defendant on both the merits and the arbitration defense.

Then, *sua sponte* (meaning, on its own initiative and not in response to a motion by a party), the court issued an order to the plaintiffs' lawyer to show cause why she should not be sanctioned under Rule 11. (When a court acts *sua sponte* under Rule 11, the lawyer charged with violating Rule 11 is not afforded a chance to withdraw the offending paper, as she would be before a party can file a motion for sanctions under Rule 11. *See* Rule 11(c)(2) (offending lawyer must be given twenty-one days to withdraw or correct the paper before the motion is filed).) The court ultimately imposed the draconian sanction of suspending her from practice in the federal district court for five years.

- Plaintiffs argued that a generally stated arbitration clause was inapplicable to statutory employment discrimination claims. Yet just two years before they filed the complaint, the Fourth Circuit Court of Appeals had rejected that theory in *Austin v. Owens-Brockway Glass Container, Inc.* Given that plaintiffs filed the case in a district court in the Fourth Circuit, was the complaint "warranted by existing law"?
- What was the plaintiffs' lawyer's argument for modifying or reversing *Austin*? How could she have made it better?
- The district court ultimately granted summary judgment for the defendant. Is that the basis for the Rule 11 sanctions?
- After the plaintiffs filed their complaint and opposition to summary judgment, but *before* the district court sanctioned the plaintiffs' counsel, the Supreme Court reached a decision in *Wright v. Universal Maritime Serv. Corp.* that validated the plaintiffs' theory on the applicability of arbitration clauses. Was that decision a necessary predicate for reversing the Rule 11 sanction?

HUNTER v. EARTHGRAINS CO. BAKERY

281 F.3d 144 (4th Cir. 2002)

King, Circuit Judge.

By Order of October 23, 2000, appellant Pamela A. Hunter, a practicing attorney in Charlotte, North Carolina, and an active member of the North Carolina State Bar, was suspended from practice in the Western District of North Carolina for five years. Ms. Hunter appeals this suspension, imposed upon her pursuant to Rule 11 of the Federal Rules of Civil Procedure. As explained below, we conclude that her appeal has merit, and we vacate her suspension from practice by the district court.

I. . . .

[Eds.—In 1997, Ms. Hunter and co-counsel filed a class action suit on behalf of former employees against Earthgrains for (among other claims) employment discrimination in violation of Title VII of the Civil Rights Act of 1964. After Earthgrains removed the action to the Western District of North Carolina, plaintiffs amended the complaint. Earthgrains denied the plaintiffs' allegations and moved for summary judgment, partly on the grounds

that the employees were bound to arbitrate their Title VII claims under their collective bargaining agreement (the "Earthgrains CBA"). In response, the plaintiffs consistently asserted that the Earthgrains CBA did not apply to the Title VII claims at issue.

The district court granted summary judgment for Earthgrains, concluding in part that the plaintiffs were obligated to arbitrate under the Earthgrains CBA. The court also ordered plaintiffs' lawyers to show cause why Rule 11 sanctions should not be imposed on them for their conduct in the lawsuit (the "Show Cause Order"). Ultimately, the district court found that plaintiffs' lawyers had violated Rule 11 and sanctioned them by barring Ms. Hunter from the practice of law in the Western District of North Carolina for a period of five years, and reprimanding and admonishing her co-counsel "to be conscious of and strictly abide by the provisions of Rule 11 in the future." The court based its Sanctions Order primarily on plaintiff counsel's "frivolous" challenge to a 1996 decision of the Fourth Circuit in *Austin v. Owens-Brockway Glass Container, Inc.*, 78 F.3d 875 (4th Cir. 1996), in which the court held that CBAs applied to Title VII claims. Ms. Hunter's appeal of the Sanctions Order followed.]

II.

A.

We review for abuse of discretion a district court's imposition of Rule 11 sanctions on a practicing lawyer. Advisory Committee Notes to the 1993 Amendments, Fed. R. Civ. P. 11 ("Note, FRCP 11"); *Cooter & Gell v. Hartmarx Corp.*, 496 U.S. 384 (1990). Of course, an error of law by a district court is by definition an abuse of discretion. . . .

B.

Although Rule 11 does not specify the sanction to be imposed for any particular violation of its provisions, the Advisory Committee Note to the Rule's 1993 amendments provides guidance with an illustrative list. A court may, for example, strike a document, admonish a lawyer, require the lawyer to undergo education, or refer an allegation to appropriate disciplinary authorities. While a reviewing court owes "substantial deference" to a district court's decision to suspend or disbar, *In re Evans*, 801 F.2d 703, 706 (4th Cir. 1986), it is axiomatic that asserting a *losing* legal position, even one that fails to survive summary judgment, is not of itself sanctionable conduct.

Under Rule 11, the primary purpose of sanctions against counsel is not to compensate the prevailing party, but to "deter future litigation abuse." *In re Kunstler*, 914 F.2d 505, 522 (4th Cir. 1990) (disallowing award of attorneys' fees which compensated defendants "rather than . . . deter[ring] improper litigation"). Importantly, a sua sponte show cause order deprives a lawyer against whom it is directed of the mandatory twenty-one day "safe harbor" provision provided by the 1993 amendments to Rule 11. In such circumstances, a court is obliged to use extra care in imposing sanctions on offending lawyers. The Advisory Committee contemplated that a sua sponte show cause order would only be used "in situations that are akin to a contempt of court," and thus it was unnecessary for Rule 11's "safe harbor" to apply to sua sponte sanctions. Note, FRCP 11. Furthermore, when imposing sanctions under Rule 11, a court must limit the penalty to "what is sufficient to deter repetition of such conduct," and "shall describe the conduct determined to constitute a violation of this rule and explain the basis for the sanction imposed." Fed. R. Civ. P. 11(c).

III. . . .

B.

The primary basis for the suspension of Ms. Hunter is that she advanced a frivolous legal position. . . . By presentation of a pleading to a court, an attorney is certifying, under Rule 11(b)(2), that the claims and legal contentions made therein "are warranted by existing law or by a nonfrivolous argument for the extension, modification, or reversal of existing law or the establishment of new law." In its Sanctions Order, the district court found the legal assertions of Ms. Hunter to be "utter nonsense" that were "paradigmatic of a frivolous legal contention." Sanctions Order at 7.

We have recognized that maintaining a legal position to a court is only sanctionable when, in "applying a standard of objective reasonableness, it can be said that a reasonable attorney in like circumstances could not have believed his actions to be legally justified." *In re Sargent,* 136 F.3d 349, 352 (4th Cir. 1998) (internal citations and quotations omitted). That is to say, as Judge Wilkins recently explained, the legal argument must have "absolutely no chance of success under the existing precedent." *Id.* Although a legal claim may be so inartfully pled that it cannot survive a motion to dismiss, such a flaw will not in itself support Rule 11 sanctions—only the lack of any legal or factual basis is sanctionable. We have aptly observed that "[t]he Rule does not seek to stifle the exuberant spirit of skilled advocacy or to require that a claim be proven before a complaint can be filed. The Rule attempts to discourage the needless filing of groundless lawsuits." *Cleveland Demolition Co. v. Azcon Scrap Corp.,* 827 F.2d 984, 988 (4th Cir. 1987). And we have recognized that "[c]reative claims, coupled even with ambiguous or inconsequential facts, may merit dismissal, but not punishment." *Brubaker v. City of Richmond,* 943 F.2d 1363, 1373 (4th Cir. 1991) (quoting *Davis v. Carl,* 906 F.2d 533, 536 (11th Cir. 1990)).

In its Sanctions Order, the court maintained, with respect to Ms. Hunter, that "[p]laintiffs' standing to file suit was challenged based on a binding arbitration clause in the [Earthgrains] CBA. Plaintiffs' response to this gateway issue rested on a tenuous, if not preposterous, reading of the CBA and applicable law." Sanctions Order at 5. The court was correct that the legal position it found frivolous—that a collective bargaining agreement ("CBA") arbitration clause must contain specific language to mandate arbitration of a federal discrimination claim—had been rejected by us four years earlier in *Austin v. Owens-Brockway Glass Container, Inc.,* 78 F.3d 875 (4th Cir. 1996). However, our reasoning in *Austin,* as of April 22, 1998 (when the Show Cause Order issued), stood alone on one side of a circuit split. Six of our sister circuits (the Second, Sixth, Seventh, Eighth, Tenth, and Eleventh) had taken the legal position contrary to *Austin* on whether a CBA could waive an individual employee's statutory cause of action. [Citations to those circuit court opinions omitted.] In point of fact, and consistent with the foregoing, none of our sister circuits, as of April 1998, had agreed with the position we took in *Austin.*

The circuit split evidenced by these decisions concerned whether collective bargaining agreements containing general language required arbitration of individuals' statutory claims, such as those arising under the ADEA and Title VII. The disagreement of the circuits on this issue resulted from varying interpretations of the Court's decisions in *Alexander v. Gardner-Denver Company,* 415 U.S. 36 (1974), and *Gilmer v. Interstate/Johnson Lane Corp.,* 500 U.S. 20 (1991). This Court, in *Austin,* had deemed *Gilmer* to be the controlling authority, while the other circuits chose the alternate route, finding the Court's decision in *Alexander* to control.

In opposition to Earthgrains' summary judgment motion, Ms. Hunter repeatedly relied upon the Supreme Court's decision in *Alexander* (failing, however, to rely on the decisions of the six circuits that had followed *Alexander*). She further sought to align her case against Earthgrains with *Alexander* by discussing the generality of the applicable clause of the Earthgrains CBA, which included the agreement not to "illegally discriminate." She contended that this provision was not sufficiently specific to require her clients to arbitrate. . . .

[Eds.—After plaintiffs filed the relevant papers, but before the district court actually issued its Sanctions Order the Supreme Court decided that, in order for a CBA to waive individuals' statutory claims, it must at least "contain a clear and unmistakable waiver of the covered employees' rights to a judicial forum for federal claims of employment discrimination." ***Wright v. Universal Mar. Serv. Corp.,*** **525 U.S. 70, 82 (1998). Thus,]** [w]hen the district court suspended Ms. Hunter for advancing a legal position that was "not the law of this circuit," *see* Sanctions Order at 7, it was itself propounding a legal proposition in conflict with the Supreme Court's *Wright* decision. . . .

In pursuing the . . . [lawsuit], Ms. Hunter, under Rule 11(b)(2), was plainly entitled (and probably obligated),[18] to maintain that *Austin* was incorrectly decided. While she could expect the district court to adhere to *Austin,* she was also entitled to contemplate seeking to have this court, en banc [that is, all the judges on the court of appeals together rehearing the decision of the panel] correct the error (perceived by her) of its earlier *Austin* decision. If unsuccessful, she might then have sought relief in the Supreme Court on the basis of the circuit split. Indeed, our good Chief Judge . . . [has] observed that if it were forbidden to argue a position contrary to precedent,

18. *See* North Carolina Rule of Professional Conduct 1.3 cmt. (2001) ("A lawyer should act with commitment and dedication to the interests of the client and with zeal in advocacy upon the client's behalf."); *McCoy v. Court of Appeals of Wisconsin,* 486 U.S. 429, 444 (1988) ("In searching for the strongest arguments available, the attorney must be zealous and must resolve all doubts and ambiguous legal questions in favor of his or her client.") (discussing criminal defense attorneys).

> the parties and counsel who in the early 1950s brought the case of *Brown v. Board of Ed.,* 347 U.S. 483 (1954), might have been thought by some district court to have engaged in sanctionable conduct for pursuing their claims in the face of the contrary precedent of *Plessy v. Ferguson,* 163 U.S. 537 (1896). The civil rights movement might have died aborning.

[*Blue v. United States Dep't of Army,* 914 F.2d 525, 534 (4th Cir. 1990).]

This astute observation of Judge Wilkinson is especially pertinent in the context of this case. The district court's erroneous view of the law in its suspension of Ms. Hunter necessarily constitutes an abuse of discretion. *Hartmarx,* 496 U.S. at 405. Although Ms. Hunter and the other lawyers (i.e., her co-counsel and the lawyers for Earthgrains) failed to provide the court with a thorough exposition on the circuit split and the Supreme Court's decision in *Wright,* their lack of thoroughness does not render her position frivolous. Because Ms. Hunter's legal contentions in the . . . [lawsuit] on the issue of arbitrability were not frivolous, her suspension from practice in the Western District of North Carolina on this basis does not withstand scrutiny.

IV.

Pursuant to the foregoing, we vacate the suspension of Ms. Hunter from practice in the Western District of North Carolina, as set forth in the Sanctions Order of October 23, 2000.

SUSPENSION FROM PRACTICE VACATED.

Notes and Questions: Arguments for Changes in the Law

Q **1. Warranted by existing law.** *Austin* was the law of the Fourth Circuit; all other circuits that had reached the issue had reached a different conclusion. Wasn't the plaintiffs' theory therefore "warranted by existing law"?

A No. While you could say in typical law schoolese that the "majority rule" was that general arbitration clauses did not apply to statutory discrimination claims, the search for the existing law is not an abstract law school exercise. Until the Supreme Court decides the issue (and its two cases on point seemed to be in conflict), the law in each circuit is what the circuit's court of appeals says it is, provided that the court has reached the issue. In fact, the North Carolina Rules of Professional Conduct (which the instant opinion cites in footnote 18 and which are replicated in almost every other state) make it unethical for a lawyer "knowingly to fail to disclose to the tribunal legal

Authority in the controlling jurisdiction known to the lawyer to be directly adverse to the position of the client and not disclosed by opposing counsel." N.C. Rule Prof. Conduct 3.3(a)(2). *Austin* was therefore the "existing law" in the Fourth Circuit, regardless of the majority rule, and plaintiffs' theory was not warranted by it. It appears that Ms. Hunter acknowledged this contrary authority, but argued against it on the basis of one of the prior conflicting Supreme Court decisions.

Q **2. Arguing for change.** How did Ms. Hunter argue for a change in the law?

A The court explains:

> Ms. Hunter repeatedly relied upon the Supreme Court's decision in *Alexander* (failing, however, to rely on the decisions of the six circuits that had followed *Alexander*). She further sought to align her case against Earthgrains with *Alexander* by discussing the generality of the applicable clause of the Earthgrains CBA, which included the agreement not to "illegally discriminate." She contended that this provision was not sufficiently specific to require her clients to arbitrate. . . .

Thus, it seems that she used the *Alexander* decision either to distinguish or discredit *Austin*, and argued that the language of the collective bargaining agreement was not specific enough to satisfy *Alexander*. Of course, Ms. Hunter could have made a stronger argument had she cited the six circuits that followed *Alexander*. Although the Fourth Circuit is not bound to follow "the majority rule," that rule could supply a persuasive reason for the circuit's court of appeals to revisit its own law.

Q **3. "Non-frivolous" arguments for change.** Why was Ms. Hunter's argument for changing the law "non-frivolous"?

A It was non-frivolous because it was based on a Supreme Court decision that arguably supported it (or, as lawyers sometimes say, "gave it color"). It also had a basis in decisions of all the other circuits that had reached the issue, although Ms. Hunter did not rely on them. As the court of appeals explained,

> In pursuing the . . . [lawsuit], Ms. Hunter, under Rule 11(b)(2), was plainly entitled (and probably obligated), to maintain that *Austin* was incorrectly decided. While she could expect the district court to adhere to *Austin,* she was also entitled to contemplate seeking to have this court, en banc, correct the error (perceived by her) of its earlier *Austin* decision. If unsuccessful, she might then have sought relief in the Supreme Court on the basis of the circuit split. . . .
>
> Although Ms. Hunter and the other lawyers (i.e., her co-counsel and the lawyers for Earthgrains) failed to provide the court with a thorough exposition on the circuit split and the Supreme Court's decision in *Wright,* their lack of thoroughness does not render her position frivolous.

In sum, Ms. Hunter could have done better, but what she did in reliance on identified Supreme Court authority was good enough.

While a split in the circuits thus supplies a strong reason for why an argument against existing law is non-frivolous, weaker arguments may also suffice. The 1993 Advisory Committee suggests that "the extent to which a litigant has researched the issues and found some support for its theories even in minority opinions, in law review articles, or through consultation with other lawyers should certainly be taken into account" in deciding whether the legal basis requirement of Rule 11(b)(2) has been violated. Fed. R. Civ. P. 11 advisory committee's note (1993).

4. Does losing violate Rule 11(b)? The district court gave summary judgment to the defendant partly on the basis of *Austin,* which was controlling law in the Fourth Circuit at the time of the judgment. Does it follow that the plaintiffs violated the Rule 11(b)(2) requirement that their claims have a legal basis? The court of appeals is crystal clear about this:

> [I]t is axiomatic that asserting a *losing* legal position, even one that fails to survive summary judgment, is not of itself sanctionable conduct.

Any time a court enters a judgment, at least one party loses. It is not losing that violates Rule 11; it's *why* you lose. If you lose because your claims were legally frivolous—without a basis in existing law or support by a non-frivolous argument for its change—then you have violated the Rule because your arguments were frivolous, not just because you were wrong.

It was therefore not a necessary predicate for reversing the sanctions against Ms. Hunter that the Supreme Court later endorsed her legal theory. In the first place, we measure a paper's compliance with Rule 11 as of the time of its filing—remember the "snapshot rule." When she filed her complaint, there were dueling Supreme Court decisions, a circuit split, and an adverse decision in the controlling circuit. Consider, in contrast, what the legal basis for her complaint would have been had the only Supreme Court decision rejected her theory and had there been no conflict in the circuits. In the second place, even if the Supreme Court had ultimately *rejected* her theory, the legal theory a litigant advances to change the law does not ultimately have to succeed for it to be non-frivolous and therefore compliant with Rule 11. Of course, the fact that the Supreme Court ultimately agreed with her (just two years after the complaint was filed and before the sanctions were imposed) certainly helps make the case that her argument was not frivolous.

IV. Proper Purpose

We have seen that a pleading or other paper must have evidentiary support and a legal basis to avoid Rule 11 sanctions. But the Rule also requires that it not be "presented for any improper purpose, such as to harass, cause unnecessary delay, or needlessly increase the cost of litigation." Rule 11(b)(1). Although the courts are divided about whether a non-frivolous paper can ever be found to have an improper purpose in violation of this rule, *see* 1 *Sanc. Fed. Law, supra,* § 13(C), the Rule's conjunctive statement of the requirements suggests that even a meritorious paper can have an improper purpose, as a majority of courts have held. *Id.*

A paper's purpose is determined by an objective standard. Some courts refuse to consider the presenter's subjective intent even just as one factor in the objective inquiry, out of concern that " 'inquiries into subjective bad faith . . . would invite a number of potentially harmful consequences, such as generating satellite litigation, inhibiting speech and chilling advocacy.' " *Sussman v. Bank of Israel,* 56 F.3d 450, 458 (2d Cir.) (citation omitted), *cert. denied,* 516 U.S. 916 (1995). In some cases, the only objective basis for any inference of improper purpose is the papers themselves. If they are non-frivolous, there is no inference of improper purpose. However, in other cases, there may be an objective basis for that inference beyond just the papers themselves. For example, courts have held improper:

- "Papering" your adversary through successive filings even though some are non-frivolous. *1 Sanc. Fed. Law, supra,* § 13(A)(1) (citing cases); *Sheets v. Yamaha Motors Corp., U.S.A.,* 891 F.2d 533, 538 (5th Cir. 1990). The frequency and timing of the filings supplies an objective basis for the inference of an improper basis.
- Filing papers containing "scandalous, libelous, and impertinent matters" to harass or embarrass an adversary, even if the paper is otherwise non-frivolous. *Coats v. Pierre,* 890 F.2d 728, 734 (5th Cir.) (post-trial briefs said that opposing counsel "acted like a little nasty dumb female Mexican pig in heat," and that she was "nothing but garbage"), *cert. denied,* 498 U.S. 821 (1990). Here the basis for the inference is the outrageous nature of these characterizations. (Of course, it's easier yet if the language is outrageous *and* the paper is frivolous: for example, alleging in your pro se complaint that your law school dean is " 'totally inept, totally incompetent, and is not even familiar with the Federal Rules of Civil Procedure . . . needs to go back to law school, . . . [and] is a complete and total moron.' " *See Katz v. Looney,* 733 F. Supp. 1284, 1287–88 (W.D. Ark. 1990).)
- Filing a non-frivolous motion to amend when the lawyer and client have agreed to drop the motion if the defendant makes any effort to resist. *See Cohen v. Virginia Elec. & Power Co.,* 788 F.2d 247 (4th Cir. 1986) ("Although Cohen's attorney did not act in bad faith in filing the pleading, because there was a legal basis for the claims he asserted, the evidence before the district court established that Cohen and his attorney decided in advance that if VEPCO indicated any opposition to their motion, they would withdraw it."). In other words, they had no intention to follow through if the defendant called their bluff.
- Orchestrating a "media event" in connection with filing a paper to embarrass the defendant and to get personal recognition. *See Whitehead v. Food Max of Mississippi, Inc.,* 332 F.3d 796, 806-07 (5th Cir. 2003). The basis for the inference is evidence of the planning and conduct of the media event.

Apart from the Rules, a court has some inherent power to supervise and control its own proceedings and to sanction counsel or a litigant for bad-faith conduct. Inherent power differs from Rule 11 authority chiefly in two ways. First, it is triggered by bad faith conduct, while Rule 11 extends to "good heart, empty head" conduct as well (recall Judge Posner's characterization in *Hays* of Rule 11 as "a new form of legal malpractice" imposing a negligence standard).

Second, inherent sanctioning power applies to all litigation conduct, including oral representations and behavior in the courtroom, while Rule 11 applies only to *papers* presented to the court. Inherent power and Rule 11 authority thus overlap, although in practice, most courts will follow Rule 11 procedures in cases to which it applies.

Third, a federal law also provides:

> Any attorney or other person admitted to conduct cases in any court of the United States or any Territory thereof who so multiplies the proceedings in any case unreasonably and vexatiously may be required by the court to satisfy personally the excess costs, expenses, and attorneys' fees reasonably incurred because of such conduct.

28 U.S.C. § 1927. Section 1927 is like Rule 11 in that it focuses on the purpose of the lawyer's conduct ("unreasonably *and* vexatiously") (emphasis added), but it is narrower than the Rule in that it applies only to conduct that "multiplies" proceedings.

V. Procedure for Rule 11 Sanctions

Sailing Rule 11 motions through safe harbors. Ordinarily, a party initiates proceedings for Rule 11 sanctions by filing a motion. A Rule 11 motion must be made separately from other motions (such as Rule 12(b)(6) or Rule 56 motions) and must be served on the offender twenty-one days before it is filed with the court. Fed. R. Civ. P. 11(c)(2). This gives the offender time to reconsider and withdraw or correct the offending paper. In theory, this "twenty-one-day safe harbor" reduces satellite litigation about Rule 11 sanctions and affords the merely negligent lawyer a chance to make things right without suffering the ignominy of being found in violation.

The rougher waters of *sua sponte* sanctions. A court need not wait for a Rule 11 motion to impose sanctions, and when it acts *sua sponte*—on its own initiative—there is no safe harbor either. But due process still requires notice and a chance for the offender to explain or defend. Rule 11(c)(3) therefore requires a court acting on its own initiative to order the offender "to show cause why conduct specifically described in the order has not violated Rule 11(b)," as the court did in *Hunter*. Since the lawyer or party who is ordered to show cause has no safe harbor, "a court is obliged to use extra care in imposing sanctions" and confine them to situations that are "akin to a contempt of court," as the court said in *Hays* (internal quotation omitted). After such an order, it is too late to withdraw the offending pleading, but at least you can try to talk your way out of sanctions or, less often, even a finding of a violation.

"Appropriate" sanctions. If the court finds that a lawyer or party has violated Rule 11, it "*may* impose an appropriate sanction" (emphasis added). Sanctions can be monetary (for costs, attorneys' fees, or a penalty paid to the court) or nonmonetary, which can include a tongue-lashing that may be preserved for posterity on Lexis or Westlaw, an apology or reprimand, required Continuing Legal Education courses, writing "I will not [repeat the violation]" on a courtroom blackboard, referrals for disciplinary action, and claim- or defense-related sanctions like dismissal. But the court's discretion to choose and impose a sanction is not unlimited: The sanction "must be limited to what suffices to deter repetition of the conduct or comparable conduct by others similarly situated." Rule 11(c)(4). In other words, the court is charged with imposing the least severe sanction that will deter repetition of the violation, and the objective is deterrence, not compensation or punishment *per se*. *See* 1 *Sanc. Fed. Law, supra*, § 16(C). "[T]he judge should take pains neither to use an elephant gun to slay a mouse nor to wield a cardboard sword if a dragon looms." *Anderson v. Beatrice Foods Co.*, 900 F.2d 388, 395 (1st Cir. 1990) (decided under 1983 Rule).

Yet, sanctioning a lay *client* is unlikely to deter legally insupportable arguments by her lawyer. How would the client know when arguments are warranted by existing law or a non-frivolous argument for its change? Rule 11(c)(5)(A) therefore prohibits monetary sanctions against a client for violations of the legal basis provision in Rule 11(b)(2). Of course, this does not give the lawyer a free pass to violate this rule—the lawyer can still be sanctioned. In *Hays,* recall that the court therefore imposed a sanction of $14,895.46 on the lawyer, not on the plaintiffs, for failing to inquire sufficiently into copyright law.

Plaintiff Peter Pint's complaint asserts a single claim against the defendant for violating a federal statute, although every circuit to have considered the statute has found that it does not apply to the fact pattern alleged in the complaint. Defendant moves to dismiss for failure to state a claim and the court grants the motion. In which of the following circumstances would Rule 11 sanctions be proper?

A. The court grants defendant's motion to dismiss Pint's complaint for failure to state a claim.
B. Defendant moves, without more, for Rule 11 sanctions.
C. The court issues an order to show cause why Pint and his lawyer should not be sanctioned. After Pint's lawyer files a brief in response, and the court holds a hearing, the court imposes a sanction on both.
D. Same facts as C, but in opposing defendant's motion to dismiss, Pint's lawyer argued that the circuit law against him is wrong, based on a law review article from the leading law school in the jurisdiction and two dissenting opinions.
E. Same facts as D, but before Pint's lawyer filed the complaint, she sent a copy to the defendant with a cover letter threatening to file, which she said would generate "reams of terrible publicity," unless defendant paid Pint a large sum of money for his alleged injuries. When defendant ignored the threat, Pint's lawyer filed the complaint.

Sanctions for **A** would be improper without more, because losing does not automatically violate Rule 11. It's *why* Pint lost that matters. If Pint lost because the complaint was frivolous, then he is vulnerable to a Rule 11 motion, properly made.

B is also not yet ripe for sanctions, because Rule 11(c)(2) requires a defendant to serve the motion for sanctions on Pint's lawyer twenty-one days before it files the motion with the court. The twenty-one-day safe harbor is intended to give Pint's lawyer a chance to withdraw or correct the complaint.

If the complaint violated the rule, it is because it was unwarranted by existing law (all circuits that had ruled on the statute had held it inapplicable to facts like those alleged in Pint's complaint) and there appears to be no non-frivolous argument for modifying it. *See* Rule 11(b)(2). But monetary sanctions cannot be imposed on a represented party for violations of the legal basis part of the Rule. Rule 11(c)(5)(A). The sanctions against Pint in **C** are therefore improper, although the sanctions against Pint's lawyer can stand if the complaint violated Rule 11(b)(2).

D now offers a possible argument for modifying the law. The Advisory Committee has said that the extent to which a lawyer finds support for her argument even in law review articles should be taken into account in deciding whether she has violated the legal basis requirement of the Rule. Moreover, the fact that two dissenting judges support the same argument suggests that it is not frivolous. After all, if reasonable judges disagree, how can her argument be unreasonable? It also helps that she openly acknowledged and discussed the contrary circuit court authority. None of this necessarily makes sanctioning Pint's lawyer wrong, but it gives serious pause; these authorities may be just enough to make her argument non-frivolous.

Even if the dissident authorities save her argument from violating Rule 11(b)(2), the facts added by **E** suggest an alternative basis for sanctions: violating the proper purpose requirement of Rule 11(b)(1). This sounds like extortion. But there are two problems with this basis for sanctions. First, if her arguments for rejecting the circuit court authority are non-frivolous, then some courts will presume a proper purpose. Second, even those circuits that hold that a non-frivolous complaint can have an improper purpose, and which would therefore consider the pre-filing letter as objective evidence of purpose, might not view the so-called extortion as an improper purpose. Pint's lawyer is only threatening a non-frivolous lawsuit for the purpose of obtaining a settlement of Pint's claims.

Finally, even if you conclude that the Rule was violated in **C** and **D**, we can't tell whether the sanction was "appropriate" without knowing exactly what it is, as well as facts indicating whether it is the least severe sanction to deter Pint's lawyer from repeating the violation. These facts, for example, might include whether she acted in bad faith or in empty-headed good faith, whether she is an experienced practitioner in the field or a novice, and other facts bearing on the likelihood of repetition. If she is unlikely to repeat her error because she acted in good faith and vows to consult with more experienced counsel in the future, a severe sanction would not be needed (or appropriate) to deter repetition. A mild oral reprimand might do the job.

VI. Care and Candor in Pleading: Summary of Basic Principles

- Care and candor in federal court litigation are policed by rules of professional conduct, Rule 11, statutes, the inherent power of the courts to control litigation conduct, and legal malpractice law.
- Rule 11 defines a form of legal malpractice based on an objective negligence standard. Bad faith is not required to violate the rule, and good faith is no defense against a violation.
- Before presenting any paper to a district court, the presenter must undertake an inquiry into the law and the evidence that is reasonable under the circumstances. What is reasonable involves balancing the costs and time available for investigation against the likelihood that more investigation will turn up relevant law and evidence. "The Rule does not require steps that are not cost-justified." *Szabo Food Service, Inc. v. Canteen Corp.*, 823 F.2d 1073, 1083 (7th Cir. 1987).
- Presenting a paper certifies that it has a proper purpose; that its claims, defenses, and other legal contentions have a legal basis; and that its factual contentions have evidentiary support under Rule 11(b) *as of the time the paper is presented.* While Rule 11 imposes no duty of correction based on after-acquired information, it does forbid "later advocating" a paper the presenter then knows to be legally or factually insupportable.
- Lawyers may be ethically bound to disclose to the court adverse authority in the controlling jurisdiction. *See ABA Model Rules of Professional Conduct* Rule 3.3(a)(2). But they are not prohibited from making non-frivolous arguments to change it, including arguments based on minority opinions, cases (and trends) in other jurisdictions, law review articles, and even the informed views of experts in the field.
- Presenting a paper certifies that it is not presented for an improper purpose. Although some circuits hold that a non-frivolous paper cannot have an improper purpose, the majority rule is that even a non-frivolous paper can have an improper purpose, when such a purpose can be inferred from objective facts.
- A party who plans to file a Rule 11 motion for sanctions must serve it on the offender twenty-one days before filing. The twenty-one-day safe harbor is not applicable when a court *sua sponte* considers Rule 11 sanctions by issuing an order to show cause why sanctions should not be imposed.
- A court that finds that Rule 11 has been violated may (but need not) issue sanctions, but if it does, it must choose the least severe sanction to deter repetition of the violation, and it may not impose a monetary sanction on a represented party for a violation of the legal basis requirement of Rule 11(b)(2).
- Courts can also use their inherent authority to punish bad faith litigation conduct and their statutory authority under 28 U.S.C. § 1927 to punish unreasonably and vexatiously "multiplied" litigation.

16

Amending Pleadings

I. Introduction

Surgeon Kevorkean performed a stomach tuck on Sam Suma. Afterwards Suma developed a continuous pain in his side. When Dr. Kevorkean dismissed it as a normal recovery symptom, Suma asked Dr. Booker for a second opinion. Booker ordered an x-ray, which showed that a small surgical clamp had been left in Suma, presumably causing the pain.

Suma promptly sued Kevorkean for negligence in leaving the clamp. After he brought suit, he had Dr. Booker remove the clamp. During that surgery, Booker finds that Kevorkean had also removed part of Suma's lower intestine. Suma would now like to add a claim for battery against Kevorkean for performing this additional surgery without his informed consent, as well as a claim for breach of contract.

Suma could perhaps bring a second lawsuit against Kevorkean, but this would obviously be inefficient and likely duplicative, in that much of the evidence for his claims would be the same. Can he instead amend his original complaint to add the new claims? Does it matter if Kevorkean has already responded to the original complaint? Or that discovery has been completed? Suppose that, instead of amending his complaint, Suma simply offers evidence at trial of the removal of part of his intestine and of his lack of consent? Does that place the unpleaded battery claim before the jury? And what if Suma discovers that Dr. Bumbly, rather than Kevorkean, actually conducted the surgery? Can Suma now add or substitute Bumbly as a defendant to his lawsuit? Would it matter if the statute of limitations (the statutory time limit for bringing claims) had run between the filing of his original complaint against Kevorkean and his attempted joinder or substitution of Bumbly as a defendant to the lawsuit?

The answer to most of these questions was usually *no* under the common law. Not only did the common law prohibit almost any *departure* from the original pleading, but it also frowned on *variances* between the pleading and the proof at trial.

The Federal Rules of Civil Procedure reject this restrictive approach as too formalistic and inefficient. A guiding principle of the Federal Rules is that procedure should be flexible enough to allow the parties to litigate the entire dispute between them, as long as any changes or enlargement of the lawsuit to achieve this objective do not prejudice opposing parties in their preparation of their case. "Rule 15 was promulgated to provide the maximum opportunity for each claim to be decided on its merits rather than on procedural niceties. While variances between the pleadings and the proof were not tolerated before the federal rules were enacted, such variances are now freely allowed under Rule 15." *Hardin v. Manitowoc-Forsythe Corp.*, 691 F.2d 449, 456 (10th Cir. 1982) (internal citation omitted). "Liberal amendment"—a change of an original pleading to reflect additional facts, parties, claims, or defenses or to conform to evidence produced at trial—is therefore the order of the day in federal court (and most state courts), usually dictating a *yes* to the questions above, instead of the *no* given by the common law. Typically, the amending party tries to file an amended pleading that supersedes the original pleading, and, if the party needs the court's permission, a motion for leave to amend.

Rule 15(a) addresses two types of amendments before trial: amendments allowed *as a matter of course*, that is, amendments that can be filed without the court's permission (*see* Fed. R. Civ. P. 15(a)(1)) and amendments by leave of court, which require such permission. Fed. R. Civ. P. 15(a)(2). Section II addresses amendments as of right. Section III addresses the liberal standard for amendments by leave of court, as well as the analytical framework that courts have developed for assessing amendments before trial.

After trial starts, changes in the pleadings are more likely to prejudice opposing parties in their preparation for the case simply because there is less time for preparation. Rule 15(b) therefore sets a somewhat less generous standard for amendment during or after trial than Rule 15(a) sets for amendments before trial, as discussed in section IV.

Finally, Rule 15(c) addresses the thorny problem of amendments attempted after a statute of limitations has run and whether they can *relate back*—in effect, be backdated—to the date of a timely original pleading that they amend. This problem is addressed in sections V and VI, which examine the relation back of amendments changing claims and parties, respectively.

Of course, a liberal policy of amendment is no reason not to try to get it right the first time. But last-minute filing of lawsuits (often because of the clients' tardiness in bringing the matter to a lawyer), broad discovery, and tactical developments at trial, as well as occasional errors and oversights by even the best lawyers, make amendments an important procedure in modern civil litigation.

II. Amending Without Leave of Court

Rule 15(a) authorizes amendment once as a matter of course—without leave—in three circumstances.

- First, a party may amend the original pleading once without leave of court within twenty-one days of serving that pleading. Fed. R. Civ. P. 15(a)(1)(A). Thus, if Suma serves Dr. Kevorkean with the complaint and summons, and then wants to amend his complaint, he can do so without leave of court if he files the amendment within twenty-one days of serving the complaint. Similarly, if Kevorkean answers the complaint admitting that he had removed part of the intestine, and then decides to change the admission to a denial, he can do so without leave of court by filing the amended answer within twenty-one days of serving the original answer.
- Second, if the original pleading is one to which a responsive pleading is required, a party may amend the original pleading within twenty-one days after the responsive pleading is served. Fed. R. Civ. P. 15(a)(1)(B).

Q **To what pleadings is a "responsive pleading" required?**

A Rule 7(a) describes the pleadings that require a responsive pleading. A defendant must file an answer to a complaint. A plaintiff must also serve an answer to a counterclaim, a co-defendant must serve an answer to a crossclaim, and a third-party defendant must serve an answer to a third-party complaint (these are part of impleader practice, described in the next chapter).

Because a complaint is a pleading to which a responsive pleading (an answer) is due, Suma could amend his complaint as a matter of course even after Dr. Kevorkean files his answer. If he served the answer on day six, Suma could still amend that complaint as a matter of course until day twenty-seven.

- Third, if a party files a motion under Rule 12(b) to dismiss a complaint, counterclaim, crossclaim, or third-party complaint; or files a motion under Rule 12(e) (for a more definite statement); or makes a motion under Rule 12(f) (to strike), then the pleader may amend within twenty-one days after the motion is served. Fed. R. Civ. P. 15(a)(1)(B). Thus, if Dr. Kevorkean had moved to dismiss Suma's complaint for failure to state a claim or to strike scandalous material, Suma could have amended his complaint, by adding a missing element or dropping the scandalous matter, within twenty-one days after service of Kevorkean's motion. Such an amendment "may avoid the need to decide the motion or reduce the number of issues to be decided. . . ." Fed. R. Civ. P. 15 advisory committee's note (2009).

But the amending party doesn't get two bites at the apple without leave of court. The twenty-one-day periods just described are not cumulative; "if . . . [an amended pleading] is served after one of the designated motions is served, for example, there is no new 21-day period." *Id.* Furthermore, amendment without leave is possible only once under any circumstance. The second time, the amending party must get leave unless the opposing party consents.

Why twenty-one days? Twenty-one days after service of the pleading or of a response to it (whether by responsive pleading or by Rule 12 motion) is such a short period that it makes it unlikely that the opposing party or the court has yet expended substantial resources in responding to the original pleading or that the party would be prejudiced in preparing to defend against the amended pleading. Of course, this will not always be true. But it will usually be true, at least often enough to justify adoption of this bright chronological line.

Q **Amending before trial.** In which of the following cases is amendment allowed?

A. Plaintiff amends her complaint one week after filing it.

A **A** is allowed. A pleader can amend once without leave within twenty-one days after serving the pleading.

B. Plaintiff amends her complaint four weeks after serving it and two weeks after defendant files a motion to dismiss for failure to state a claim.

A **B** is also allowed. She cannot amend under Rule 15(a)(1)(A), because more than twenty-one days have passed since she served her complaint. But she can still amend without leave under Rule 15(a)(1)(B), within twenty-one days after defendant's motion to dismiss. One reason for this generosity is that her amendment may either obviate the need to decide the motion or may make the court's decision on the motion easier.

C. Defendant amends his answer two weeks after serving it.

A **C** is also allowed for the same reason as **A**. Complaints, answers, and replies, when permitted, are all pleadings, and the Rule 15(a)(1)(A) twenty-one-day window for amendment without leave is open for all pleadings.

D. Defendant serves an answer to the complaint that includes various defenses and a counterclaim. Plaintiff serves a Rule 12(f) motion to strike one of the defenses. Twenty days later, defendant amends his answer.

A **D** is allowed as well. An answer that contains a counterclaim is a pleading to which a responsive pleading is required, *see* Fed. R. Civ. P. 7(a)(3), so Rule 15(a)(1)(B) gives the defendant twenty-one days to amend after being served with the Rule 12(f) motion. Again, this amendment may make it unnecessary for the court to rule on the motion.

E. Plaintiff serves a complaint on the defendant. The defendant requests and is granted a three-week extension of time to answer. Consequently, the answer is filed six weeks after service of the complaint on the defendant. Two weeks later, plaintiff amends her complaint.

A | **E** is timely as well under Rule 15(a)(1)(B), because the amended complaint is within twenty-one days after service of the answer.

III. Amending Before Trial with Leave of Court

Amendments by leave of court require a judge to consider a number of factors concerning the stage of the litigation, the reason for the amendment, the viability of the amended claim or defense, and the reason for *not* including the new allegations in the original pleading.

Q **Liberal amendments.** Suppose Suma files his negligence complaint against Dr. Kevorkean and the very next day tries to file an amended complaint adding a breach of contract claim arising out of the same ill-fated surgery. Postponing, for the moment, consideration of what Rule 15 provides, should Suma be allowed to make this amendment as a matter of common sense, fairness, and efficiency?

A | Why not? If it comes just a day later, it is most improbable that Dr. Kevorkean has taken any action or expended any resources yet to respond to the original pleading. It is equally unlikely he would have discarded any evidence essential to defending the contract claim or that such evidence has otherwise been destroyed—too little time has elapsed. He would therefore suffer no discernible prejudice in preparing to defend the new claim beyond the fact that it gives Suma another legal theory on which to recover. On the other hand, permitting the amendment would enable Suma and Kevorkean to litigate the dispute about the surgery on both legal theories. Since it would not prejudice Kervorkean and would let Suma litigate his entire dispute, the common sense approach is to allow the amendment—on a "no harm, no foul" rationale—instead of rigidly holding Suma to his original pleading.

Now consider the same amendment on the day before trial (but before the statute of limitations has run). How does the common sense answer change?

A | Given the lapse of time, it is now somewhat more likely that evidence essential to the contract claim has been lost. Furthermore, if the trial date holds, Kevorkean would have only twenty-four hours to prepare to defend against the new legal theory. In short, there is a greater risk of prejudice to Kevorkean in preparing his defense, which may give the court pause in allowing this late amendment. On the other hand, wouldn't the original negligence claim have caused Kevorkean to preserve all of his paperwork concerning the surgery, some of which would be evidence relating to the contract claim as well? And wouldn't his lawyer inevitably end up speaking to mostly the same witnesses—his nurses and office staff, in addition to other doctors involved in the surgery—whom he might need to interview in preparing a defense to the contract claim? If this is true, then perhaps he would not make many, or any, changes to prepare to defend the contract claim, and there is no great prejudice from allowing it even at this late hour.

READING *BEECK v. AQUASLIDE 'N' DIVE CORP.* The foregoing kind of common sense balancing informs Rule 15(a). But it is not always so easy. In the following case, the defendant manufacturer admitted, in its answer to the original complaint, that it had manufactured the water slide that the plaintiff alleged to have caused his severe injuries. Only much later in the lawsuit, after the statute of limitations had seemingly run on any new claims by the plaintiff arising out of the water slide accident, did the defendant realize that the water slide was not, in fact, *its* water slide. (Apparently, a pirate manufacturer used its name and logo.) Defendant then sought to amend its answer to change its admission of manufacturing the slide to a denial.

- Why did the defendant need leave of court to amend? Under what circumstances could it instead have amended its answer without leave, "as a matter of course"?
- What factors did the court consider in deciding whether to grant the defendant leave to amend?
- The case illustrates perfectly the effect that a dry procedural dispute may have on substantive claims. What was the effect of the amendment on Beeck? On the defendant?
- Why was the effect on Beeck not sufficiently prejudicial to warrant denying leave to amend?

Question of Identity?

Dreamstime.com

The item pictured here looks like an Aquaslide. Maybe it is one. Maybe not. A crucial question in the wrenching *Aquaslide* case, below, was whether the water slide on which Jerry Beeck suffered catastrophic injury was or was not an Aquaslide. More particularly, however, the opinion addresses whether the defendant, Aquaslide 'N' Dive Corporation, *would be allowed to deny* that it was an Aquaslide. The case poignantly illustrates the profound impact that procedure frequently has on substance.

BEECK v. AQUASLIDE 'N' DIVE CORP.

562 F.2d 537 (8th Cir. 1977)

Benson, District Judge [sitting by designation].* . . .

Jerry A. Beeck was severely injured on July 15, 1972, while using a water slide. He and his wife, Judy A. Beeck, sued Aquaslide 'N' Dive Corporation (Aquaslide), a Texas corporation, alleging it manufactured the slide involved in the accident, and sought to recover substantial damages on theories of negligence, strict liability and breach of implied warranty.

Aquaslide initially admitted manufacture of the slide, but later moved to amend its answer to deny manufacture; the motion was resisted. The district court granted leave to amend. On motion of the defendant, a separate trial was held on the issue of "whether the defendant designed, manufactured or sold the slide in question." This motion was also resisted by the plaintiffs. The issue was tried to a jury, which returned a verdict for the defendant, after which the trial court entered summary judgment of dismissal of the case. Plaintiffs took this appeal, and stated the issues presented for review to be:

1. Where the manufacturer of the product, a water slide, admitted in its Answer and later in its Answer to Interrogatories both filed prior to the running of the statute of limitations that it designed, manufactured and sold the water slide in question, was it an abuse of the trial court's discretion to grant leave to amend to the manufacturer in order to deny these admissions after the running of the statute of limitations? . . .

I. FACTS . . .

[Eds.—In 1971, Kimberly Village Home Association of Davenport, Iowa, ordered an Aquaslide product, which its employees installed, from a local distributor. On July 15, 1972, Jerry A. Beeck was injured while using the slide at a social gathering sponsored at Kimberly Village by his employer, Harker Wholesale Meats, Inc. On October 31, 1972, Aquaslide first learned of the accident through a letter sent by a representative of Kimberly Village's insurer to Aquaslide, advising that "one of your Queen Model #Q-3D slides" was involved in the accident. The complaint was filed October 15, 1973. Investigators for three different insurance companies, representing Harker, Kimberly Village, and the defendant, each concluded that the slide had been manufactured by Aquaslide, and the defendant, with no information to the contrary, answered the complaint on December 12, 1973, and admitted that it "designed, manufactured, assembled and sold" the slide in question.

The statute of limitations on plaintiff's personal injury claim expired on July 15, 1974. About six and one-half months later, Carl Meyer, president and owner

* **[Eds.—District judges are sometimes designated to sit on appeals with appellate judges due to the volume of appeals. Judge Benson thus served on a panel with two judges of the court of appeals.]**

of Aquaslide, visited the site of the accident at the plaintiff's request prior to the taking of his deposition by the plaintiff. From his on-site inspection of the slide, he determined it was not a product of the defendant. Thereafter, Aquaslide moved the court for leave to amend its answer to deny manufacture of the slide.]

II. LEAVE TO AMEND

Amendment of pleadings in civil actions is governed by Rule 15(a), F. R. Civ. P., which provides in part that once issue is joined in a lawsuit, a party may amend his pleading "only by leave of court or by written consent of the adverse party; and leave shall be freely given when justice so requires."

In *Foman v. Davis*, 371 U.S. 178 (1962), the Supreme Court had occasion to construe that portion of Rule 15(a) set out above:

> Rule 15(a) declares that leave to amend "shall be freely given when justice so requires," this mandate is to be heeded.... If the underlying facts or circumstances relied upon by a plaintiff may be a proper subject of relief, he ought to be afforded an opportunity to test his claim on the merits. In the absence of any apparent or declared reason such as undue delay, bad faith or dilatory motive on the part of the movant, repeated failure to cure deficiencies by amendments previously allowed, undue prejudice to the opposing party by virtue of allowance of the amendment, futility of amendment, etc. the leave sought should, as the rules require, be "freely given." Of course, the grant or denial of an opportunity to amend is within the discretion of the District Court....

371 U.S. at 182.

... The burden is on the party opposing the amendment to show such prejudice. In ruling on a motion for leave to amend, the trial court must inquire into the issue of prejudice to the opposing party, in light of the particular facts of the case. Certain principles apply to appellate review of a trial court's grant or denial of a motion to amend pleadings. First, as noted in *Foman v. Davis*, allowance or denial of leave to amend lies within the sound discretion of the trial court ..., and is reviewable only for an abuse of discretion....

It is evident from the order of the district court that in the exercise of its discretion in ruling on defendant's motion for leave to amend, it searched the record for evidence of bad faith, prejudice and undue delay which might be sufficient to overbalance the mandate of Rule 15(a), and *Foman v. Davis*, that leave to amend should be "freely given." Plaintiffs had not at any time conceded that the slide in question had not been manufactured by the defendant, and at the time the motion for leave to amend was at issue, the court had to decide whether the defendant should be permitted to litigate a material factual issue on its merits.

In inquiring into the issue of bad faith, the court noted the fact that the defendant, in initially concluding that it had manufactured the slide, relied upon the conclusions of three different insurance companies, each of which had conducted an investigation into the circumstances surrounding the accident. This reliance upon investigations of three insurance companies, and the fact that "no contention has been made by anyone that the defendant influenced this possibly erroneous conclusion," persuaded the court that "defendant has not acted in such bad faith as to be precluded from contesting the issue of manufacture at trial." The court further found "(t)o the extent that 'blame' is to be spread regarding the original identification, the record indicates that it should be shared equally."

In considering the issue of prejudice that might result to the plaintiffs from the granting of the motion for leave to amend, the trial court held that the facts presented to it did not support plaintiffs' assertion that, because of the running of the two year Iowa statute of limitations on personal injury claims, the allowance of the amendment would sound the "death knell" of the litigation. In order to accept plaintiffs' argument, the court would have had to assume that the defendant would prevail at trial on the factual issue of manufacture of the slide, and further that plaintiffs would be foreclosed, should the amendment be allowed, from proceeding against other parties if they were unsuccessful in pressing their claim against Aquaslide. On the state of the record before it, the trial court was unwilling to make such assumptions,[7] and concluded "(u)nder these circumstances, the Court deems that the possible prejudice to the plaintiffs is an insufficient basis on which to deny the proposed amendment." The court reasoned that the amendment would merely allow the defendant to contest a disputed factual issue at trial, and further that it would be prejudicial to the defendant to deny the amendment.

The court also held that defendant and its insurance carrier, in investigating the circumstances surrounding the accident, had not been so lacking in diligence as to dictate a denial of the right to litigate the factual issue of manufacture of the slide.

On this record we hold that the trial court did not abuse its discretion in allowing the defendant to amend its answer.

III. SEPARATE TRIALS

After Aquaslide was granted leave to amend its answer, it moved pursuant to Rule 42(b), F. R. Civ. P., for a separate trial on the issue of manufacture of the slide involved in the accident. The grounds upon which the motion was based were:

(1) a separate trial solely on the issue of whether the slide was manufactured by Aquaslide would save considerable trial time and unnecessary expense and preparation for all parties and the court, and

---

7. The district court noted in its order granting leave to amend that plaintiffs may be able to sue other parties as a result of the substituting of a "counterfeit" slide for the Aquaslide, if indeed this occurred. The court added:

> [a]gain, the Court is handicapped by an unclear record on this issue. If, in fact, the slide in question is not an Aquaslide, the replacement entered the picture somewhere along the . . . chain of distribution. Depending upon the circumstances of its entry, a cause of action sounding in fraud or contract might lie. If so, the applicable statute of limitations period would not have run. Further, as defendant points out, the doctrine of equitable estoppel might possibly preclude another defendant from asserting the two-year statute as a defense.

67 F.R.D. at 415.

(2) a separate trial solely on the issue of manufacture would protect Aquaslide from substantial prejudice.

The court granted the motion for a separate trial on the issue of manufacture, and this grant of a separate trial is challenged by appellants as being an abuse of discretion. . . .

After . . . [the inspection of the slide by Aquaslide's President] and Aquaslide's subsequent assertion that it was not an Aquaslide product, plaintiffs elected to stand on their contention that it was in fact an Aquaslide. This raised a substantial issue of material fact which, if resolved in defendant's favor, would exonerate defendant from liability.

Plaintiff Jerry A. Beeck had been severely injured, and he and his wife together were seeking damages arising out of those injuries in the sum of $2,225,000.00. Evidence of plaintiffs' injuries and damages would clearly have taken up several days of trial time, and because of the severity of the injuries, may have been prejudicial to the defendant's claim of non-manufacture. The jury, by special interrogatory [**Eds.—a written question to the jury that it answers in writing. See Rule 49**], found that the slide had not been manufactured by Aquaslide. That finding has not been questioned on appeal. Judicial economy, beneficial to all the parties, was obviously served by the trial court's grant of a separate trial. We hold the Rule 42(b) separation was not an abuse of discretion.

The judgment of the district court is affirmed.

Notes and Questions: Amendments Before Trial with Leave of Court

1. The factors in granting leave to amend. Because Rule 15(a)(1)'s window for amendment without leave had long since shut, Aquaslide could only amend with leave of court. It therefore filed a motion for leave, accompanied by a copy of the proposed amended answer, denying manufacture. As we noted above, the Rule is encouraging but unspecific: "The court should freely give leave when justice so requires." But the cases have filled in the blanks, starting with the Supreme Court's decision in *Foman v. Davis*, 371 U.S. 178 (1962). Courts weigh the reason for the amendment, the amending party's diligence, any prejudice that the amendment may cause the opposing party, whether the amendment would be futile as a matter of law, and the amending party's prior amendments, if any. Let's look at each of these factors in the following questions.

Q **2. Reasons for amendment.** What was Aquaslide's reason for amendment?

A The reason was its recent discovery that the water slide was not one it had manufactured. (And it probably only discovered it then because Aquaslide's president finally looked at the slide himself to prepare for his deposition.) The

A

discovery of new facts or, more rarely, new legal theories, is a common reason for amendment. This is a good reason insofar as the amendment will almost always advance litigation of the merits, but the court will also consider *why* the new matter was only recently discovered. If, for example, Aquaslide had not inspected or caused anyone else to inspect the water slide until late in the lawsuit and just dawdled until the deposition and after the statute of limitations ran to inspect the slide, a court might have disallowed the amendment for Aquaslide's lack of diligence. Here, however, not only had Aquaslide's own insurer previously inspected the slide and reported (erroneously, it turns out) that it was manufactured by Aquaslide, but so had Kimberly Village's insurer and Beeck's employer's insurer. The court therefore found that Aquaslide's error was neither in bad faith nor unreasonable.

In some cases, the reason for amendment is that the amending party's lawyer thought of a new legal theory for a claim or defense. This seems less forgivable than late discovery of new facts, inasmuch as the lawyer could have spent more time in the library before filing the original pleading. But this may be both a hard-hearted and unrealistic view of the lawyer's task; legal theories may be more appealing on a fuller view of the facts. Tactical considerations may change. Even the law may change during the pendency of litigation. Furthermore, it may be unfair to punish the client for the lawyer's late discovery of a new legal theory. Courts therefore quite routinely give leave to amend to add additional claims or defenses, even when the reason is not discovery of new facts supporting them.

Of course, if the amending party has deliberately delayed adding a new claim or defense until the eve of trial in order to deprive its opponent of the opportunity to prepare, that would be a sound reason for the court to deny leave to amend. Any evidence of bad faith may be equally fatal to the proposed amendment. The timing of the amendment in *Aquaslide* (after the statute of limitations had run) might have raised a question about Aquaslide's motive, but the fact that the parties all misidentified the slide helped to remove any whiff of bad faith.

Q

3. Prejudice from amendment in general. If, in the opening hypothetical, Suma is allowed to add a battery claim to his negligence claim, Kevorkean will have to defend against two claims, not just one. Allowing the amendment thus prejudices him. Is such prejudice "undue prejudice" that warrants denial of leave to amend?

A

Presumably, *every* amendment gives the amending party some litigation advantage and therefore hurts the opposing party. Otherwise, why would the amending party bother to amend? This kind of detriment or prejudice to the opposing party—what we might call *merits prejudice*—cannot be what the Supreme Court in *Foman* meant by "undue prejudice," or almost no amendments would be allowed. For example, where plaintiffs amended well before trial to add a claim for malicious prosecution to a complaint that was originally for false imprisonment, the court of appeals said:

> Defendants-appellants argue that they were prejudiced by this. There is invariably some practical prejudice resulting from an amendment, but this is not the test for refusal of an amendment. In this instance the amendment was authorized

> several months prior to trial. The defendants were not prejudiced in terms of preparing their defense to the amendment. There was practical prejudice also arising from the fact that damages were awarded on the amended count. Had there been no amendment the defendants might have prevailed. This is not the test. The inquiry again is whether the allowing of the amendment produced a grave injustice to the defendants.
>
> *Patton v. Guyer*, 443 F.2d 79, 86 (10th Cir. 1971).

Thus, "undue prejudice" consists of prejudice to preparing to defend—in collecting and presenting evidence—that flows from the lateness of the amendment, what we might call *preparation prejudice*. This kind of prejudice could be avoided or reduced if the matter that would be added by amendment had been included in the original pleading. The issue raised by Suma's amendment to add a battery claim is therefore whether Kevorkean is prejudiced in preparing to defend the new claim by the loss of evidence (death or relocation of witnesses, destruction of evidence, completion of discovery, etc.), not simply whether he would be worse off on the merits—that's a given unless Suma's lawyer is an idiot. Since the party opposing the amendment knows best whether allowing the amendment would prejudice it, the courts place the burden on that party to show preparation prejudice.

Q **4. Prejudice to Beeck.** So *was* Beeck prejudiced by Aquaslide's amendment of its answer from an admission of manufacturing the slide to a denial?

A Certainly he was prejudiced on the merits. Because of the amendment he had to prove that Aquaslide manufactured a slide that apparently wasn't Aquaslide's, and he failed. But did he also suffer preparation prejudice? This turns out to be a tough question. While there is nothing in the opinion to suggest that he was any worse off in proving the manufacture issue at the time of the amendment than he would have been at the time of the answer (i.e., no evidence had been lost), he had seemingly lost the opportunity to sue the real manufacturer, or someone with knowledge in the chain of distribution, because the statute of limitations on a negligence or strict liability claim had run. In this broader sense, he was prejudiced in preparing for the new matter—the denial—by the difficulty of suing someone else at that late date.

But the district court also concluded that he might yet have a crack at the true manufacturer or distributors:

> Depending upon the circumstances of its entry, a cause of action sounding in fraud or contract might lie. If so, the applicable statute of limitations period would not have run. **[Eds.—The statute of limitations for these claims might be longer, or the action might have accrued at a later date.]** Further, as defendant points out, the doctrine of equitable estoppel might possibly preclude another defendant from asserting the two-year statute as a defense. **[Eds.—That is, the real manufacturer or a distributor with knowledge of the substitution might be estopped from pleading the limitations defense by its connivance in falsely labeling the slide as an Aquaslide.]**

67 F.R.D. at 415 n.7. If so, Beeck *would* be prepared to meet the denial by substituting new defendants and therefore not as severely prejudiced by the amendment.

Another option was to sue Aquaslide again, but this time on the grounds that its erroneous answer resulted in a lost opportunity to sue (and collect damages from) the real manufacturer. Indeed, Beeck brought precisely such a suit and won a $3 million judgment on these grounds. He proved that Aquaslide's owner had known that distributors often claimed to be selling Aquaslides (which were a well-regarded brand), but then substituted cheaper slides before delivery. Beeck proved that Aquaslide's owner failed to tell his lawyers about this common practice, resulting in a negligent misrepresentation in the defendant's answer.

The Iowa Supreme Court, however, reversed in part and remanded the case, requiring Beeck to prove that such a judgment would have been collectible from the real manufacturer (i.e., to prove that the real manufacturer was not, in fact, judgment-proof). *Beeck v. Aquaslide*, 350 N.W.2d 149 (Iowa 1984). After remand, the plaintiffs were able to identify the real manufacturer of the slide (which still manufactures water slides today). It turned out that the real manufacturer had considerable insurance that could have been used to cover the judgment if the suit had been brought against it in the first place. (There is no evidence that it knew that its slide had been sold as an Aquaslide in this case.) In sum, because Beeck showed that the judgment was, in fact, collectible, Aquaslide settled the case on remand for $5 million (the original $3 million judgment, plus $2 million in interest).

Amazingly, the case did not end there. Beeck's children then sued the real manufacturer for loss of consortium. Although the case was filed more than a decade after Beeck's injury, the applicable statute of limitations had a savings clause that permitted the claims by the children. As a result, the children also recovered a judgment—this one from the real manufacturer. Beeck's lawyer told us that Beeck's was a "once in a lifetime" case, and it is easy to see why!

Q **5. Prejudice to Aquaslide.** The court does not expressly address the prejudice to Aquaslide from a denial of its motion to amend. What prejudice would Aquaslide suffer if it was not granted leave to amend?

A It would be stuck with its admission that it had manufactured the water slide. This, alone, would not establish its liability; it would still be free to argue at trial that the water slide was not negligently designed or manufactured. But this admission would certainly place Aquaslide in a peculiar position: how exactly would it show the jury that it did not negligently design a slide that it, in fact, did not design? Its initial admission was an apparently innocent counterfactual statement. Once this counter-fact is perpetuated at trial, it seems to threaten the integrity of much of what follows, to Aquaslide's detriment.

6. Another factor: Futility. Suppose the applicable substantive law in *Suma v. Kevorkean* forbids battery claims against doctors for good faith, even if mistaken or negligent, medical services. Under these circumstances, if the amendment were allowed, Kevorkean would be entitled to respond to the amended complaint. *See* Rule 15(a)(3). He would presumably file a motion to dismiss the battery claim for failure to state a claim, and the court would have to grant it under the substantive law as described. In short, such an amendment to add the battery claim would be futile—wasting both Kevorkean's and the court's time. The Supreme Court in *Foman* thus noted, uncontroversially, that a court need not grant leave to amend when an amendment would be futile. 371 U.S. at 182. In effect, under the futility prong of the analysis, "the court must analyze a proposed amendment as if it were before the court on a motion to dismiss pursuant to Fed. R. Civ. P. 12(b)(6)." *Acker v. Burlington N. & Santa Fe R.R. Co.*, 215 F.R.D. 645, 647 (D. Kan. 2003). An amendment can be futile because it fails to state a claim or a legally sufficient defense under the applicable law.

Q **7. Futile or disputed?** Suppose the court concludes that Suma would probably be unable to prove the battery claim by a preponderance of the evidence, given a factual dispute about the scope of his consent to the surgery. Can it deny leave on grounds of futility of the amendment?

A Neither the Rule nor the conclusory phrase "futile" supplies the answer to this question, but your understanding of the role of the court in reviewing pleadings should. That answer is no. The amendment is futile if the amended complaint fails to allege facts that plausibly support the battery claim (i.e., if it fails the *Twombly-Iqbal* standard), but the court should not make forecasts about how factual disputes will be decided at trial, any more than it should in deciding a motion to dismiss for failure to state a claim. If the amended pleading alleges sufficient facts to support the claim, it will survive a motion to dismiss and is not futile.

8. Amendment after dismissal. A common reason for amendment of a complaint is that the defendant has filed a Rule 12(b)(6) motion to dismiss that is likely to succeed. The amendment is intended to cure the deficiency (e.g., allege the missing element; restate the claim, etc.). If the amendment is made within twenty-one days after service of the motion, no leave is required (if it is the first amendment).

Suppose, however, that the court grants the motion before the amendment. Can the plaintiff then amend? If the dismissal comes more than twenty-one days after the motion to dismiss, the amending party can no longer amend without leave, according to the literal terms of the rule. But many district courts grant a motion to dismiss the complaint "with leave to amend" by a date certain if they believe that the plaintiff could cure the deficiency. *See Wright & Miller* § 1483. In such cases, the court enters a final judgment on the dismissal only if the plaintiff does not successfully amend by the stated date. If the court does not expressly dismiss with leave to amend, the safe course is to move for leave to amend promptly after a motion to dismiss is granted.

9. Responding to an amended pleading. Once a pleading has been amended, it is a new pleading, and the opposing party has the same right to respond to the amended pleading that it had to the original pleading. *See* Rule 15(a)(3) (setting response times). The district court in *Nelson v. Adams USA, Inc.*, 529 U.S. 460 (2000), denied this right by allowing a post-judgment amendment that had the effect of making a new party liable without any chance to respond. The Supreme Court reversed.

> When a court grants leave to amend to add an adverse party after the time for responding to the original pleadings has lapsed, the party so added is given "10 [now 14] days after service of the amended pleading" to plead in response. Fed. Rule Civ. Proc. 15(a) [now 15(a)(3)]. This opportunity to respond, fundamental to due process, is the echo of the opportunity to respond to original pleadings secured by Rule 12.

Id. at 466.

Q **10. The motion for separate trial in *Aquaslide*.** After Aquaslide was permitted to change its answer from an admission that it manufactured the slide to a denial, the plaintiff elected to go forward with a trial against Aquaslide. If the plaintiff could not locate the real manufacturer, then it was Aquaslide or nobody. And plaintiff reasoned that she might still be able to convince a jury that Aquaslide *did* manufacture the slide, notwithstanding, and maybe precisely because of, its suspiciously late denial.

But Aquaslide then successfully asked the court to order the jury to try the defense of non-manufacture separately—that is, before it tried the issues of fault and damages. The trial court agreed and directed the jury to answer a written question called a special interrogatory asking whether Aquaslide had manufactured the slide. Why did Aquaslide seek separate trial of that issue?

A Presumably it thought it could win. Trying just the defense of non-manufacture would also be simpler, shorter, and less costly than trying everything together. But most important, Aquaslide may have feared that trying everything together could prejudice it on the pivotal issue of manufacture. If Aquaslide really had not manufactured the slide, it would have been left in the awkward position of trying to prove that someone else's slide was properly designed and manufactured. Furthermore, as the court of appeals observes, the jury deciding these issues would also be exposed to the gut-wrenching evidence of Beeck's severe injuries. Better to cut off any possible resulting prejudice at the pass, by having the jury first hear and decide only the defense of non-manufacture.

IV. Amending During and After Trial with Leave of Court

We have seen that the later the amendment, the greater the risk of preparation prejudice. It follows that a party's chances of obtaining leave to amend should narrow after trial starts, absent consent to the amendment by the opposing party. Thus, if Suma tries to add his battery claim at trial, the court would be less generous in granting leave than it would have been earlier in the litigation. Even then, leave should be granted at trial if there is no preparation prejudice to Kevorkean, or if delaying ("continuing") the trial would mitigate that prejudice by giving him a chance to prepare a defense to the battery claim.

Even absent formal amendment, if an issue that is not raised by the pleadings—like battery in Suma's case—is nevertheless actually tried with Kevorkean's consent, there seems to be no reason not to treat it as part of the case. There has been, in effect, a de facto amendment to include the issue with the consent of the parties. Thus, if Suma put on evidence of battery and explained that it was for this purpose, and Kevorkean expressly consented to this de facto amendment, he could not complain later that it was outside the original pleadings.

But what if he does not expressly consent and instead simply fails to object? The following case addresses this tough question.

READING *HARDIN v. MANITOWOC-FORSYTHE CORP.* Under the tort theory of comparative negligence in some jurisdictions, the plaintiff and the tortfeasors are liable only according to their percentage of fault. If a plaintiff is 50 percent responsible and suffers $100,000 in damages, and the sole defendant is 50 percent liable, then the plaintiff will recover only $50,000. But sometimes there are additional tortfeasors who may also be at fault but have not been sued as defendants for some reason. If, for example, the defendant and an additional tortfeasor who was not sued were each 25 percent at fault, then the plaintiff in our hypothetical would recover only $25,000 from the defendant.

In *Hardin*, Hardin sued three defendants. After trial, however, the judge proposed to instruct the jury to include three additional possible tortfeasors—whom it called "phantom parties" to emphasize that they had not been named as defendants—in its allocation of fault. Hardin objected. The court found that Hardin had tried the phantom parties' fault by implied consent, and their fault should therefore be "treated in all respects as if raised in the pleadings" (*see* Rule 15(b)(2))—in effect, a de facto amendment.

- First things first. Be sure you understand why Hardin objected—the effect that considering the phantom parties' fault would have on his recovery and why.
- Hardin objected to the jury instruction. How could defendants then argue that Hardin had consented to the inclusion of the phantom parties?
- Why did the court of appeals permit inclusion of Manitowoc Engineering, but not Lummus Company?

HARDIN v. MANITOWOC-FORSYTHE CORP.

691 F.2d 449 (10th Cir. 1982)

McKay, Circuit Judge.

[Eds.—Plaintiff, Darel Hardin, brought a products liability suit, naming Manitowoc-Forsythe Corp. and Columbus-McKinnon Corp. as defendants, to recover for injuries he sustained in an on-the-job accident allegedly caused by a defectively designed push-pull jack. Plaintiff's employer, Combustion Engineering (who was immune from suit under the Kansas workmen's compensation law), leased a Manitowoc crane with an attached Columbus-McKinnon-made jack from a wholly-owned subsidiary corporation, Lummus Company. Defendant Manitowoc-Forsythe ordered the crane from its parent corporation, Manitowoc Company, Inc., and allegedly sold it to Lummus. Of these potential defendants, plaintiff chose to sue only Manitowoc-Forsythe and Columbus-McKinnon.

The applicable law adopted a comparative negligence standard by which the jury could allocate a percentage of fault among plaintiff, defendants, and "phantom parties"—persons who shared in potential liability but had not been sued as defendants. At the close of trial, the judge proposed to instruct the jury to assess the fault of Combustion Engineering, Manitowoc Engineering, and the Lummus Company as phantom parties, and the plaintiff objected. The court overruled the objection on the ground that the issue of the fault of Manitowoc Engineering and Lummus had been tried by consent and would thus be treated as if it had been raised by the pleadings under Fed. R. Civ. P. 15(b).

The jury then allocated fault as follows:

Columbus-McKinnon (defendant)	13.5%
Manitowoc-Forsythe (defendant)	0
Plaintiff	20.0
Combustion Engineering (phantom party)	45.0
Manitowoc Engineering (phantom party)	9.0
Lummus Company (phantom party)	12.5
	100.0%

It assessed damages of $150,000 and the court awarded plaintiff judgment against Columbus-McKinnon for 13.5 percent of $150,000, or $20,250. Judgment was not entered against Manitowoc-Forsythe because no fault was assessed to it.] . . .

II. PROCEDURAL PROPRIETY OF COMPARING FAULT OF PHANTOMS . . .

Rule 15 was promulgated to provide the maximum opportunity for each claim to be decided on its merits rather than on procedural niceties. While variances between the pleadings and the proof were not tolerated before the federal rules were enacted, such variances are now freely allowed under Rule 15. Thus, when evidence is presented on an issue beyond the scope of the pretrial order, Rule 15(b) may be invoked to effect an amendment of the pretrial order.[6]

This circuit permits a post-judgment amendment of a pretrial order to conform to the evidence if an issue has been tried with the express or implied consent of the parties and not over objection. The test of consent is whether the opposing party had a fair opportunity to defend and whether he could have presented additional evidence had he known sooner the substance of the amendment. Even where there is no consent, and objection is made at trial that evidence is outside the scope of the pretrial order, amendment may still be allowed unless the objecting party satisfies the court that he would be prejudiced by the amendment. Fed. R. Civ. P. 15(b). In the absence of a showing of prejudice, the objecting party's only remedy is a continuance to enable him to meet the new evidence.

Plaintiff argues that the addition of Manitowoc Engineering and Lummus came so late in the trial as to deprive him of a fair opportunity to defend against the theory of their liability. He argues that the evidence pertaining to the phantoms was not sufficient to make an "issue" of their comparative fault within the meaning of Rule 15(b). In essence, he argues that there was no consent.

Implied consent is found where the parties recognized that the issue entered the case at trial and acquiesced in the introduction of evidence on that issue without

6. Several courts have permitted de facto amendment of the pretrial order where the policy behind Rule 15(b) in favor of having every claim decided on its merits outweighs the policy behind Rule 16 of preventing unfair surprise at trial.

objection. Under the terms of Rule 15(b), the objection must be on the ground that the evidence is not within the issues raised by the pleadings. Since the purpose of Rule 15 is to bring the pleadings in line with the issues actually tried, it does not permit amendment to include collateral issues which may find incidental support in the record. When the evidence claimed to show that an issue was tried by consent is relevant to an issue already in the case, and there is no indication that the party presenting the evidence intended thereby to raise a new issue, amendment may be denied in the discretion of the trial court. Consent will, however, be found when the party opposing the amendment himself produces evidence on the new issue. Whether the issue was tried by consent is a matter within the sound discretion of the trial court whose judgment will only be reversed for an abuse of discretion.

A. Manitowoc Engineering

With respect to Manitowoc Engineering, we hold that there was no abuse of discretion in the trial court's finding that the issue of its fault was tried by consent. Plaintiff was put on notice that defendants intended to have the fault of nonparties compared, both from the pretrial order, ... and from the order granting defendant's motion to compare fault of nonparties. Our review of the record convinces us that plaintiff received information well in advance of trial which should have made him aware that the fault of Manitowoc Engineering was in issue. Plaintiff took the deposition of Malcolm Fell on April 25, 1978, more than a year before trial. The deposition revealed that Fell worked for Manitowoc Engineering, which ordered the jack. Manitowoc Engineering supplied Columbus-McKinnon with a few general specifications for the jack, but Columbus-McKinnon supplied most of the specifications and tested the jacks. Plaintiff discovered that Manitowoc Engineering was aware that the jack might be used apart from the crane, and that it did not specify safety stops as a precaution or place a warning on the jack. Thus plaintiff had discovered, more than a year before trial, all the elements of fault necessary for a products liability case against Manitowoc Engineering.

Even if Fell's deposition were not enough to put plaintiff on notice of the issue of Manitowoc Engineering's fault, the proceedings at trial suffice. Plaintiff himself called Mr. Fell to the stand and again pursued the issue of Manitowoc Engineering's fault under a products liability theory. Plaintiff also explored the issue on cross-examination. Plaintiff's claim of surprise is unreasonable. He had ample opportunity to defend against the strict liability theory that Manitowoc Engineering was partly at fault. Plaintiff has not pointed to any additional evidence he might have introduced were it not for the claim[ed] surprise. Finally, plaintiff failed to object to any evidence at trial as being beyond the scope of the pretrial order. We therefore hold that plaintiff did consent to the trial of the issue of Manitowoc Engineering's fault, thereby impliedly amending the pretrial order....

Even though the fault of phantom parties is in the nature of an affirmative defense, the policy behind Rule 15(b) can override the failure to plead it. If the issue was tried by consent without objection, the answer must be treated as if the defense had been raised. Fed. R. Civ. P. 15(b). But because the major purpose of Rule 8(c) is to provide particularized notice of certain matters, courts must be particularly careful to scrutinize the record to ensure that plaintiff had adequate notice and opportunity to rebut the tardily-raised Rule 8(c) defense before finding that it was tried by consent. After careful scrutiny of the record, we hold that plaintiff had sufficient notice and opportunity to rebut the defense that Manitowoc Engineering was at fault, and that the court did not abuse its discretion in finding that the issue of Manitowoc Engineering's fault was tried by consent under Rule 15(b)....

B. Lummus Company

With respect to Lummus, we know only that it is a wholly-owned subsidiary of Combustion Engineering, to which it rents tools and machinery. There is no evidence on the issue of the fault of Lummus. At most, the evidence shows that Lummus was a mere conduit in the chain of distribution. This was enough to satisfy the trial judge, but it does not satisfy this court. The evidence regarding Lummus was relevant to the issue of how the jack arrived at the worksite, and defendants gave no indication that they intended to make an issue of Lummus' fault. Plaintiff was denied a fair opportunity to defend against the theory that Lummus was at fault, and might have presented additional evidence had he known the theory earlier. In fact, the absence of evidence before or even during trial on at least one element of a possible case against Lummus (even standing by itself) leads us to the conclusion that plaintiff had inadequate notice that the fault of Lummus was at issue. The trial court abused its discretion in ruling that plaintiff consented to the trial of the issue of the fault of Lummus....

CONCLUSION

Since our judgment is that Lummus was improperly included as a phantom party, it is not necessary to reach the numerous other issues raised on appeal. Those issues will not necessarily arise in the retrial of this matter. While under some circumstances it might be possible to correct the erroneous inclusion of a phantom party by the retrial of the issue of apportionment only, after full consideration of the record we believe that all the issues are so intertwined that a retrial of the entire matter is the only proper way to correct the error....

As regrettable as it is to order a retrial of a matter of this magnitude, it illustrates the danger of leaving to the implications of the trial the formal introduction of phantom parties. Defendants intending to avoid liability by asserting phantom party fault delay raising the identity of those parties at their peril.

REVERSED with directions to grant a new trial.

Notes and Questions: *Hardin*

Q **1. Why did Hardin object?** Amendment is not an intellectual abstraction. A party usually seeks to amend to gain some advantage. Similarly, an opposing party objects to avoid prejudice, both from the relative change in the posture of the case on the merits due to the amendment and from any preparation prejudice. So why, specifically, did Hardin object? What was the prejudice he feared?

A

The jury would be instructed to allocate fault to both the parties before the court and the phantom tortfeasors—adding up to 100 percent. Including the phantom tortfeasors in the allocation—who together accounted for 66.5 percent of the fault in this case—reduced the percentage of fault allocated to the named defendants. If the jury had not been instructed to apportion fault to the phantom tortfeasors, they would have allocated all of the fault among the named defendants and Hardin, probably raising the defendants' share and thus increasing the amount of Hardin's judgment against them. It's all about the money!

Although fault was apportioned to Manitowoc Engineering and to Lummus, that does not make them liable to Hardin for his injury. They were not made defendants in the case and cannot therefore be ordered to pay damages even if the jury finds them at fault. The purpose of allocating fault to absent tortfeasors in such cases is to determine the percentage of fault of those who are parties in the case, not to impose liability on the absent tortfeasors.

Q

2. Consent and objection. Hardin objected to the jury instruction, but by that time, some evidence of the phantom parties' fault had already been presented during the trial. Since Hardin never expressly consented to their inclusion in the allocation of comparative fault, the only remaining argument for defendants was that Hardin had impliedly consented. What was the defendants' argument?

A

By not objecting when the evidence of the phantom parties' fault was offered, Hardin impliedly consented to trial of the phantom parties' fault even though it was not raised by the original pleadings.

Q

3. Finding implied consent. Why was Hardin deemed to have impliedly consented to the inclusion of one but not the other phantom party?

A

When evidence is offered at trial that is relevant only to an unpleaded issue, the proffer gives notice that the unpleaded issue is being injected into the lawsuit. "To demonstrate lack of consent, the objection should be on the ground that the contested matter is 'not within the issues made by the pleadings.' " *Matter of Prescott*, 805 F.2d 719, 725 (7th Cir. 1986). If a party does not object that the evidence is irrelevant, he has impliedly consented to interjection of the new issue by his silence. The presumption of implied consent is even stronger if the party opposing interjection of the new issue was himself the one who offered the evidence. Here Hardin called a Manitowoc Engineering employee as a witness "and pursued the issue of Manitowoc Engineering's fault under a products liability theory." He could hardly claim surprise that their fault was now in the case, or that he had no opportunity to defend against the theory that Manitowoc Engineering was partly at fault.

On the other hand, when evidence is offered that is relevant *both* to an issue raised by the pleadings and to a new issue outside the pleadings, the opposing party is not on notice that the new issue is in play. For all he knows, the evidence is offered only to prove or disprove an existing issue within the pleadings. He cannot therefore be said to have impliedly consented to de facto amendment of the pleadings to include the new issue. Here, evidence of Lummus's role was relevant to showing how the faulty jack arrived at the work-site, an issue subsumed in the original pleadings. There was no indication that this evidence was offered to show *Lummus's* fault, and Hardin therefore had no reason to try to defend against the theory that it was partly at fault.

In short, the theory of implied consent rests chiefly on notice to the opposing party that a new issue, not raised by the pleadings, has been interjected at trial, or to put it differently, that the pleadings have been amended de facto to include the new issue. Sometimes the proffer of evidence alone supplies that notice, but only when the evidence is relevant to the new issue alone, absent other, clearer indications in the record that the opposing party knew about the new issue and therefore had a chance to defend.

Q **4. Implied consent or not?** Suppose that Washington is injured using a chainsaw and sues the manufacturer, Lincoln Products, for negligence in designing it. Lincoln pleads the affirmative defense of contributory negligence (i.e., that Washington's own negligence contributed to his injuries, which bars recovery in some jurisdictions). Washington testifies that he read the safety instructions that accompanied the chain saw and offers them into evidence, without objection from Lincoln. At the conclusion of the trial, Washington seeks to amend to add a claim against Lincoln for failure to warn based on its inadequate safety instructions, arguing that by failing to object to his testimony about the safety instructions and his proffer of the instructions as evidence, Lincoln impliedly consented to trying this additional claim. Should the court permit the amendment?

A No. Washington will not be able to show that his failure-to-warn theory was tried by implied consent. The basis for allowing an amendment at trial under Rule 15(b)(2) is that all parties clearly understood that they were trying the unpleaded issue. That isn't true here. The evidence that Washington had read the instructions was relevant to an issue *that was already in the case*: Lincoln's affirmative defense that Washington was contributorily negligent. When Washington's counsel offered this evidence, Lincoln's counsel would not realize that Washington was injecting a new theory of liability—failure to warn—into the case. He would simply infer that Washington was offering additional evidence about whether Washington was negligent. To argue after the fact that the parties were trying a different issue to which the same evidence might also be relevant is to take Lincoln by surprise.

5. Why raise a new issue at or after trial? Ideally, a party should amend its pleadings well before trial, when leave is more freely granted. Theoretically, discovery should unearth the relevant facts and leave no surprises for trial. But theory must bow to reality; witnesses fudge, lie, or suddenly open up; key testimony is unexpectedly ruled inadmissible or unexpectedly admitted; things fall apart. Thus, a district court dryly notes:

> Occasionally, the evidence produced at trial may differ significantly from the theory of the case.... Consequently, it may become necessary to modify the pleadings to reflect the case presented in the courtroom....
>
> Locking parties into the strict language of their pleadings creates a "tyranny of formalism" inhibiting courts from adjudicating cases upon their merits. Thus, amendments under Rule 15(b) prevent the necessity of holding a new trial when evidence in court supports an unpleaded theory.

American Eagle Credit Corp. v. Select Holding, Inc., 865 F. Supp. 800, 809 (S.D. Fla. 1994).

Consider, for example, the plaintiff who sues defendant for fraud in making certain representations about its product. At trial, the evidence of fraudulent intent is too weak to support a finding of fraud. It may, however, support a finding of negligent misrepresentation. The plaintiff may therefore seek leave to amend the pleadings to add this claim. Even if this effort draws an objection, the court may grant leave if it finds that an amendment will advance the merits and the defendant cannot show undue prejudice. Or plaintiff may wait until the end of trial, and then argue that defendant somehow impliedly consented to de facto amendment to include this claim, by its failure to object to certain offers of evidence.

Of course, this tactic will not always succeed. As one court noted:

> The effect of the amendment they propose would be not to conform the pleadings to a judgment they have won, but to jeopardize and perhaps to overthrow a judgment they have lost. If [amendment under 15(b)] were permitted, a losing party, by motions to amend and rehear, could keep a case in court indefinitely, trying one theory of recovery or defense after another, in the hope of finally hitting upon a successful one. Courts draw a dividing line between this use of amendment and those uses aimed at conformity.

Hart v. Knox County, 79 F. Supp. 654, 658 (E.D. Tenn. 1948) (citations omitted). In other words, courts should not let a losing party use the claim of "implied consent" after trial to keep adding new theories of recovery until he finally finds one that wins. Still, you can't blame someone for trying, especially given the inherent ambiguity of implied consent.

6. Rule 16(e) vs. Rule 15(b). *Hardin* raises a further complication in cases in which the court has entered a final pretrial order. A final pretrial order is an order issued by the court on the eve of trial identifying the issues for trial and the evidence the parties will offer. Rule 16(e) provides that such an order at trial can only be modified "to prevent manifest injustice." Rule 15(b), on the other hand, suggests a seemingly more lenient standard keyed to presentation of the merits and prejudice to the opposing party. The Tenth Circuit's answer was to treat Rule 15(b)'s goal of "presenting the merits" as the trump card. In any case, the conflict in the Rules may be more apparent than real: If the objecting party fails to carry its burden to show undue prejudice and that amendment would aid in presenting the merits, it would seem a "manifest injustice" to deny amendment.

V. Amending Claims or Defenses After the Limitations Period

A statute of limitations provides a *period* (usually of years) within which a claim must be filed. The period runs from the point at which the claim *accrued* or came into existence, until the period is *tolled* by filing of a complaint, or, if the statute permits, by service of the complaint within some relatively short period of time after filing (the *service period*). Thus, in the typical auto accident, the claim accrues at the time of the accident, the period is often three years, and the plaintiff must file and/or serve his complaint within three years of the accident or he can be barred by the affirmative defense of limitations. The purpose of statutes of limitations is to protect parties against the loss of evidence and to give them respite after a fixed period from the emotional distress and financial uncertainty of possible litigation.

So suppose Suma filed and served his negligence complaint against Dr. Kevorkean on the last day of the limitations period. (This is surprisingly common, because clients dither and lawyers procrastinate, and because sometimes lawyers file prophylactically, to protect their client from the expiration of the statute of limitations while the client is deciding whether to sue.) Assume the statute of limitations for battery is the same as the statute for negligence and that five months after filing his negligence complaint, Suma files a new lawsuit for battery against Dr. Kevorkean. That new lawsuit would be too late. But is it also too late to amend his complaint to add the battery claim? And what if Beeck had tried to amend his negligence complaint to add the true manufacturer of the water slide, after Aquaslide had amended its answer to deny manufacture? The statute had run there, too, but could he have gotten around it by amending the original complaint rather than instituting a new lawsuit?

If the answer in either case is yes, it must be because the amendment is, in effect, backdated to the date of the pleading that it amends: the date of the original complaint. The amended pleading is said to *relate back* to the date of the original pleading, thus bringing it within the time set out in the statute of limitations.

READING *BONERB v. RICHARD J. CARON FOUNDATION.* Bonerb was injured playing basketball in a mandatory exercise program at a drug rehabilitation center. He sued for negligence. Almost a year later, after changing lawyers, he moved for leave to amend his complaint to add a claim for "counseling malpractice."

- Had Bonerb asserted the malpractice claim in a separate suit, what affirmative defense could the defendant have raised?
- How does the "relation back" doctrine avoid that defense?
- The court acknowledges that simple negligence (Bonerb's original claim) and professional malpractice (his new claim) are "entirely different" in several important respects. Why is permitting the late-filed malpractice claim fair to the defendant?

BONERB v. RICHARD J. CARON FOUNDATION

159 F.R.D. 16 (W.D.N.Y. 1994)

HECKMAN, United States Magistrate Judge.

The parties have consented pursuant to 28 U.S.C. § 636(c) to have the undersigned conduct all further proceedings in the case. Plaintiff has moved to amend his complaint pursuant to Rule 15 of the Federal Rules of Civil Procedure. For the following reasons, plaintiff's motion is granted.

BACKGROUND

In this diversity action, plaintiff seeks damages for personal injuries allegedly sustained when he slipped and fell while playing basketball on defendant's recreational basketball court on November 29, 1991. Defendant is a not-for-profit corporation licensed and doing business as a drug and alcohol rehabilitation facility in Westfield, Pennsylvania. Plaintiff is a resident of Western New York.

The original complaint, filed on October 1, 1993, alleges that plaintiff was injured while he was a rehabilitation patient at defendant's Westfield facility, and was participating in a mandatory exercise program. Plaintiff claims that the basketball court was negligently maintained by defendant.

On July 25, 1994, this court granted plaintiff's motion for substitution of new counsel. On September 1, 1994, plaintiff moved to amend his complaint to add a new cause of action for "counseling malpractice." According to plaintiff's counsel, investigation and discussions undertaken after his substitution as counsel indicated to him that a malpractice claim was warranted under the circumstances. Defendant objects to the amendment on the grounds that the counseling malpractice claim does not relate back to the original pleading and is therefore barred by Pennsylvania's two-year statute of limitations.

DISCUSSION

Rule 15 of the Federal Rules of Civil Procedure provides that once time for amending a pleading as of right has expired, a party may request leave of court to amend, which "shall be freely given when justice so requires." Fed. R. Civ. P. 15(a) [now numbered Rule 15(a)(2)]. This provision has been liberally construed, and leave to amend should be granted absent undue prejudice to the party opposing the amendment, undue delay on the part of the party seeking the amendment, or bad faith. However, an amendment which seeks to add a time-barred claim would be futile, and should not be allowed unless the otherwise untimely claim "relates back" to the date of the original pleading. Fed. R. Civ. P. 15(c) [now numbered Rule 15(c)(1)(B)]. . . .

. . . Pennsylvania's two-year statute of limitations for negligence actions . . . applies to plaintiff's professional malpractice claim. Thus, since plaintiff's claim for professional malpractice accrued at the time of the injury on November 29, 1991, it is time-barred unless it relates back to the October 1, 1993 filing date of the original complaint.

Rule 15(c)(2) provides that where a party seeks to amend its pleading to assert a claim that would otherwise be time-barred, the claim may be saved by "relation back" to the date of the original pleading when "the claim or defense asserted in the amended pleading arose out of the conduct, transaction, or occurrence set forth or attempted to be set forth in the original pleading. . . ." In determining whether a claim relates back, courts look to the "operational facts" set forth in the original complaint to determine whether the defendant was put on notice of the claim that the plaintiff later seeks to add. As stated in *Tri-Ex Enterprises, Inc. v. Morgan Guaranty Trust Co.*, 586 F. Supp. 930, 932 (S.D.N.Y. 1984):

> [T]he relation back doctrine is based upon the principle that one who has been given notice of litigation concerning a given transaction or occurrence has been provided with all the protection that statutes of limitation are designed to afford.

> Thus, if the litigant has been advised at the outset of the general facts from which the belatedly asserted claim arises, the amendment will relate back even though the statute of limitations may have run in the interim.

An amendment which changes the legal theory of the case is appropriate if the factual situation upon which the action depends remains the same and has been brought to the defendant's attention by the original pleading. Thus, an amendment "that changes only the legal theory of the action, or adds another claim arising out of the same transaction or occurrence, will relate back." *Koal Industries Corp. v. Asland, S.A.*, 808 F. Supp. 1143, 1158 (S.D.N.Y. 1992) (quoting 3 *Moore's Federal Practice*, ¶ 15.15 [3.–2], at 15–149, 15–150).

In this case, the original complaint alleges that plaintiff was injured when he slipped and fell on a wet, muddy basketball court "while participating in a mandatory exercise program ..." at defendant's rehabilitation facility. Plaintiff alleges several instances of defendant's negligent conduct, such as failure to maintain the premises safely, failure to warn, failure to inspect and failure to "properly supervise and/or instruct plaintiff...." The proposed amendment seeks to allege that plaintiff "was caused to fall while playing in an outdoor basketball court ... in an exercise program mandated as part of his treatment in the rehabilitation program ...," and that "the rehabilitation and counseling care rendered ... was negligently, carelessly and unskillfully performed."

The allegations in the original and amended complaints derive from the same nucleus of operative facts involving the injury suffered by plaintiff on November 29, 1991. It is true that a claim for professional malpractice invokes an entirely different duty and conduct on the part of the defendant than does a claim for negligent maintenance of the premises. However, the original complaint advised defendant of the same transaction or occurrence giving rise to these different theories of negligence. Indeed, the original complaint alleged that participation in the exercise program was mandatory, and that the injury was caused by defendant's failure to "properly supervise and/or instruct plaintiff...." These allegations not only gave defendant sufficient notice of the general facts surrounding the occurrence, but also alerted defendant to the possibility of a claim based on negligent performance of professional duties. This is all that is required for relation back under Rule 15(c).

Defendant contends that it will be unduly prejudiced by the amendment because it will have to return to the drawing board to prepare an entirely new defense. However, as plaintiff points out, the period for discovery has not yet expired, depositions of defendant's personnel have not yet been taken, and expert witness information has not been exchanged. In addition, the parties have consented to trial before the undersigned, thereby simplifying any further supervision of discovery and the conduct and review of pretrial matters and dispositive motions.

Finally, there has been no showing of undue delay or bad faith on the part of plaintiff.

CONCLUSION

For the reasons set forth above, plaintiff's motion for leave to amend the complaint (Item 16) is granted. The amended complaint . . . shall be deemed filed and served as of the date of this order, and defendant shall plead in response in accordance with Fed. R. Civ. P. 15(a) [now numbered Rule 15(a)(3)].

Notes and Questions: Relation Back of Claims

1. Defending the malpractice claim. Had Bonerb brought an independent claim for counseling malpractice against the Foundation on September 1, 1994, it would have been filed more than two years after his injury on November 29, 1991. The Foundation could then have pled the affirmative defense of statute of limitations (*see* Fed. R. Civ. P. 8(c)(1)) in its answer. By trying to amend the complaint in the pending lawsuit, Bonerb can defeat this defense, *if* his amendment is treated as if it had been part of the original complaint that was filed on October 1, 1993, just inside of the two-year limitations period. When we treat an amendment this way, we say that it "relates back" to the date that the amended pleading was filed.

2. The threshold issue: Leave to amend? Once the window for amending without leave has closed, or a party has already used it once, the party must obtain leave to amend before trial, absent consent from the opposing party under Rule 15(a)(2). As we have seen, the court may consider a variety of factors in deciding whether to allow amendment. Had Bonerb's amendment been made in bad faith, or so late that the Foundation would not have had time to prepare to defend the malpractice claim, or had Bonerb already amended three or four times, the district court could well have exercised its discretion to deny leave to amend without regard to the limitations problem.

But futility is also a factor in deciding leave to amend, and when an amended claim would be time-barred, it is futile. In this respect, the threshold issue overlaps with the relation-back issue in *Bonerb*. If the amendment does not relate back, leave should be denied on grounds of futility because the new claim is time-barred.

Q **3. Relation back for transactionally related claims or defenses.** Even if the applicable limitations law (in *Bonerb*, Pennsylvania's law) does not expressly allow relation back, Rule 15(c)(1)(B) allows it if the new claim or defense arose out of the conduct, transaction, or occurrence set out in the original pleading. The court in *Bonerb* asks "whether the defendant was put on notice of the claim that the plaintiff later seeks to add." How is the transactional nexus described in the Rule related to the issue of notice?

A The theory of this relation-back rule is that the original pleading gave the party notice of the conduct, transaction, or occurrence for which she was being sued, so she will not be unfairly surprised by the addition of a new claim or defense *based on the same events*. The Fifth Circuit Court of Appeals famously explained it this way:

> Limitation is suspended by the filing of a suit because the suit warns the defendant to collect and preserve his evidence in reference to it. When a suit is filed in a federal court under the Rules, the defendant knows that the whole transaction described in it will be fully sifted, by amendment if need be, and that the form of the action or the relief prayed or the law relied on will not be confined to their first statement.

Barthel v. Stamm, 145 F.2d 487, 491 (5th Cir. 1944), *cert. denied*, 324 U.S. 878 (1945).

This makes sense, doesn't it? We've seen that a motion to dismiss a claim must be denied if, *on any legal theory*, including ones not stated in the complaint, the complaint plausibly alleges facts that would entitle the plaintiff to relief. A defendant should therefore begin preparing to defend any legal theory that could be supported by the allegations of the complaint—that is, that could entitle the plaintiff to relief from the conduct, transaction, or occurrence it sets forth. Notice of the transaction, not of a particular theory of liability, is what counts.

Q **4. Some easy questions on relation back.** Which of the following amendments, filed after the applicable statute of limitations has run, relate back to the original pleading under Rule 15(c)(1)(B)?

A. The original complaint alleges that defendant breached a contract for sale by not delivering lumber as promised on June 1, 2008. The amendment adds the claim that defendant breached a different contract for sale by delivering defective concrete on July 15, 2009, a "joinder" of claims permitted by Rule 18. See *supra* pp. 602–05, *infra* Chapter 17.

A The original complaint is about a lumber contract, and the amendment is about an entirely different contract breached at a different time and in a different way. These contracts involve completely distinct transactions that share nothing more than the identities of the parties. Of course, this doesn't mean that they cannot be joined. Rule 18 allows joinder of unrelated claims; it does not require that they arise from the same transaction. But Rule 15(c) relation back does. Here, knowing that it has been sued for breach of the first contract would give defendant no notice that it would be sued for breach of the second. To allow the amendment to relate back in these stark circumstances would essentially strip the defendant of the protection of the statute of limitations for the second contract.

B. The original complaint alleges that the defendant lawyer committed malpractice when he gave bad legal advice. The amendment alleges that the advice breached the contract for representation between the client plaintiff and the lawyer, pursuant to which he gave the advice.

A The conduct that gave rise to the malpractice complaint was the provision of advice by the lawyer to the plaintiff client. The amendment asserts a contract claim that arises out of the same conduct. The lawyer was on notice from

A

the original complaint that he had to collect and preserve evidence about his legal advice (indeed, maybe his entire representation of the plaintiff). This is a classic case for relation back; all the plaintiff has done is add a new legal theory for defendant's liability for the same conduct.

C. The original complaint alleges that the defendant police officers falsely arrested the plaintiff when they forcibly halted a bar fight in which he was engaged. The amendment alleges that the officers violated his civil rights when they seized him during the bar fight.

A

This is also a strong case for relation back. The conduct or transaction is what the officers did at the bar fight. Here again, plaintiff merely switches legal theories by the amendment, now characterizing what was just unlawful arrest as a civil rights violation.

5. The relation between Rule 15(a) and Rule 15(c) relation back. In the last hypothetical arising out of the bar fight, suppose the amendment to add the civil rights claim came five years after the lawsuit started, on the eve of trial. It would still satisfy the test for relation back for the reasons stated, but now plaintiff has another problem: He would need leave to amend, and there seems to be no good reason for waiting five years until the eve of trial. If the elements of false arrest and a civil rights violation differ dramatically (if, for example, the latter requires proof of some intent to discriminate), and evidence uniquely relevant to the civil rights claim has been lost or destroyed, a court might well deny leave to amend, *even though the amendment, had it been allowed, would relate back and would therefore not be futile.* "Leave to amend under subsection (a) and relation back under subsection (c), while obviously related, are conceptually distinct." *Arthur v. Maersk, Inc.*, 434 F.3d 196, 202–03 (3d Cir. 2006) (holding that undue delay is a factor in deciding leave to amend, not in deciding relation back).

Q

6. Some harder questions on relation back. Which of the following amendments, filed after the applicable statute of limitations has run, relate back to the original pleading under Rule 15(c)(1)(B)?

A. The complaint alleges that the defendant police officers falsely arrested the plaintiff when they forcibly halted a bar fight in which he was engaged. The amendment alleges that the officers libeled the plaintiff five weeks after the bar fight arrest when they told a reporter that the plaintiff was drunk at the bar fight.

A

The libel claim arises out of the discussion with the reporter and not directly out of the officers' conduct at the bar fight. While it can be said that but for the arrest, the discussion with the reporter would not have happened, the critical issue for relation back is notice, according to *Bonerb*. It is not apparent that notice of the claim about the bar fight would cause the officers to collect and preserve evidence of discussions with reporters. On the other hand, insofar as the libel claim could turn, in part, on the truth of what they told the reporter about the bar fight, there is an overlap. **A** could go either way.

B. Same complaint as A. The amendment alleges that the officers violated plaintiff's right to privacy when they supplied a copy of the bar fight arrest record to a potential employer of the plaintiff two years after the arrest.

A This seems a stretch for relation back. While there is a "but for" relationship between the arrest and the dissemination of the arrest record, the latter takes place two whole years later. The conduct giving rise to the privacy claim is the dissemination, which will presumably raise fact issues about how it came about and law issues about privilege, public records, and privacy, none of them implicated in the original false arrest claim. We'd guess that most courts would not permit the amendment to relate back on these facts.

Q **7. Why did Bonerb's malpractice negligence claim relate back?** The original negligence claim posed the question whether the Foundation breached a duty of reasonable care in maintaining the basketball court. The malpractice claim poses a completely different question: whether Bonerb's counselors' breached their duty of professional care *in mandating the exercise program in which Bonerb was injured*, presumably measured by the community standard of counseling care. Clearly the former will turn on the defendant's care of the premises; the latter on the quality and skill of the counseling with respect to the exercise program. How could the Foundation have seen the latter claim coming?

A What they should have seen coming from the original, timely filed complaint was a claim of liability for Bonerb's injury playing basketball. Although the complaint identified negligent maintenance as the theory of liability, the Foundation was on notice from that complaint that Bonerb could be entitled to relief on *any legal theory* supported by the allegations of the complaint describing the "transaction or occurrence" of the basketball game. (Recall the standard for deciding a motion to dismiss for failure to state a claim.) Furthermore, the Foundation should (and probably would, if it was well represented) have started collecting and preserving all evidence about the injury and how it came about, including the design and supervision—and attendant counseling—of the mandatory exercise program in which it occurred. The key here is notice—notice of the transaction identified in the complaint. Once the Foundation knows about the transaction or occurrence, it must prepare to defend the transaction or occurrence, not just a particular legal theory of liability arising from it.

But if Bonerb's amendment is a broader challenge to the quality of the counseling and rehabilitation, and not just to the mandatory exercise program, then arguably the Foundation was less likely to see it coming. The complaint focused on the exercise program as it played out on the basketball court, not on the non-exercise parts of the counseling and rehabilitation, let alone counseling and rehabilitation *after* Bonerb's injury. That's a different story—that is, arguably a different transaction. The touchstone for deciding this is fair notice; did the original complaint fairly put the Foundation on notice that Bonerb was alleging malpractice in the entire counseling and rehabilitation program, of which the mandatory exercise program was just an example?

Q **Suppose Bonerb's late-filed amendment tried to add a claim for false imprisonment, on the theory that his required participation in the rehabilitation program was tantamount to imprisonment. Would it relate back?**

A Close call, but probably not. This claim seems to go to Bonerb's participation in the rehabilitation program in general, rather than just in the exercise program. It thus precedes the latter in time and would turn on the reasons for and terms of his rehabilitation program participation, and not the reasons for his injury. Arguably, the differences in time and origin of these claims, as well as differences in the evidence needed to prove them, would be sufficiently great to make them separate transactions or occurrences for purposes of relation back. But we say "close call" because it is also arguable that, but for his required participation in the rehabilitation program, he would not have been injured in the exercise program. The "logical relationship" between the required participation in one and the injury in the other might make them part of a single transaction or occurrence for relation back purposes, though that may be a stretch.

8. Reading the statute of limitations.

In July 2000, a week before the three-year statute of limitations passes, Carson sues Herrera in federal court for breach of a contract to design a computer system for his store in Calpurnia, Illinois. In July 2001, he moves to amend his complaint to add a claim for violation of the state Consumer Protection Act, based on the same dispute. The Consumer Protection Act has a two-year statute of limitations, which accrued at the same time as the three-year statute. Which of the following is correct?

A. The second claim would not be barred by the limitations period, as long as the judge grants the motion to amend.
B. The second claim would "relate back" to the date of the original filing of the case, and therefore would not be barred by the statute of limitations.
C. The second claim will be barred by the limitations period, because it will not "relate back" to the original filing under Rule 15.
D. The amendment will be barred, even if it relates back to the filing of the original complaint.

Technically, grant of leave to amend does not decide the limitations issue. Carson could amend and Herrera might then answer, pleading the affirmative defense of limitations, and then seek summary judgment on it. **A** is wrong.

B and **C** are red herrings. To be sure, the amendment arises from the same conduct, transaction, or occurrence set out in the original complaint and relates back. So **C** is wrong. But that just "backdates" the amended complaint to July 2000, two years and fifty-one weeks after the litigation-provoking conduct. Since the Consumer Protection Act limitations period is only two years, even the original filing date is fifty-one weeks too late for the new claim. Gotcha. Here is one case in which relation back is unavailing because it is not far enough back.

D is therefore the correct answer. Always pay close attention to the statute of limitations, because it is, after all, what causes the problem.

9. Relation back under the statute of limitations. Pennsylvania law supplied the statute of limitations in *Bonerb v. Baker.* Rule 15(c)(1)(A) provides that, if the law supplying the statute of limitations also provides for relation back, then the court must apply that law. Sometimes, this will provide a more liberal relation-back rule than Rule 15(c) provides. Under Massachusetts law, for example, an amendment to add a new party always relates back, if it seeks recovery for the same injury. *See Wadsworth v. Boston Gas Co.*, 532 Mass. 86, 88–89 (1967). Thus, as long as the plaintiff has sued *someone* before the limitations period runs, she may add other defendants later without regard to the limitations in Rule 15(c). Under Rule 15(c)(1)(A), such state law provisions will apply if state law governs the limitations period. "If the [controlling limitations] law affords a more forgiving principle of relation back than the one provided in this rule, it should be available to save the claim." Fed. R. Civ. P. 15 advisory committee's notes (1991).

VI. Amending Parties After the Limitations Period

In *Beeck*, the court rather cavalierly assumed that Beeck would be able to sue the real manufacturer of the water slide after the statute of limitations ran. Could Beeck have amended its complaint to add that manufacturer—let's call it "Pirate Manufacturing, Inc."—after that point? Rule 15(c)(1)(C), in fact, authorizes relation back of an amendment "chang[ing] the party . . . against whom a claim is asserted," if several requirements are met. Beeck would simply be suing Pirate for the same injury he alleged in the original complaint. Could he also satisfy the other two requirements? Read the following case, and then we will return to Beeck's dilemma.

READING *KRUPSKI v. COSTA CROCIERE S.P.A.* Wanda Krupski suffered an injury on the cruise ship *Costa Magica*. Her ticket required any lawsuit to be "filed within one year after the date of injury" and to be "served upon the carrier within 120 days after filing." Krupski sued and served "Costa Cruise" within this period. Four days after the one-year period allowed for filing claims as set forth in the cruise ticket, Costa Cruise answered, denying that it was the carrier. Soon thereafter it identified the cruise ship operator as, "Costa Crociere," for which Costa Cruise was just the booking agent. Almost four months after Costa Cruise's answer, Krupski dismissed Costa Cruise and was given leave to amend to add Costa Crociere as the defendant. But the new defendant, represented by the same counsel as Costa Cruise, then successfully moved to dismiss on the grounds that the amended complaint did not relate back.

- Did Costa Crociere receive such notice, within the period specified by Rule 15(c)(1)(C), that it would not be prejudiced in defending?
- Did Krupski make a "mistake concerning the proper party's identity" or a choice? What difference does it make?
- Why didn't Krupski's delay in amending, after she learned of her mistake, preclude relation back?

Sonia Sotomayor

Collection of the Supreme Court of the United States

Justice Sonia Sotomayor (1954–) was born in New York City. Although diagnosed with diabetes at the age of eight, Justice Sotomayor was the valedictorian of her grade school and high school classes. Accepted to Princeton, she arrived from the Bronx (in her words) like "a visitor landing in an alien country." She graduated summa cum laude and entered Yale Law School, where she served on the *Yale Law Journal*. When a law firm interviewer suggested that she was only at Yale due to affirmative action, she filed a formal complaint against the firm, leading to a campus-wide debate and a highly publicized apology by the firm.

After law school she served as an Assistant United States Attorney and then entered private practice. She was appointed by President George H.W. Bush to the Federal District Court for the Southern District of New York—becoming the New York federal court's first Latina judge—and later to the Second Circuit Court of Appeals by President Clinton. She was nominated to the Supreme Court by President Obama in 2009 and became the first Latina to serve on the Court.

In *Krupski*, below, Justice Sotomayor addresses an issue that has bedeviled the lower federal courts: When does an amendment adding a new party "relate back" under Rule 15?

KRUPSKI v. COSTA CROCIERE S.P.A.

560 U.S. 538 (2010)

Justice Sotomayor delivered the opinion of the Court. . . .

[Eds.—On February 21, 2007, while sailing on a cruise on the cruise ship *Costa Magica*, Krupski tripped over a camera cable in the ship's theater and fractured her femur. She filed a personal injury action against "Costa Cruise Lines N.V., L.L.C." on February 1, 2008 and properly served it on February 4, 2008. Costa Cruise answered on February 25, 2008, asserting that it did not have the requisite status of "carrier" and thus was not a proper defendant. It eventually filed a motion for summary judgment based on this defense. Before the court ruled, Krupski dismissed the claim against Costa Cruise without prejudice and moved for leave to add "Costa Crociere S.p.A." as a defendant on July 11, 2008, which the court granted.

Costa Crociere then moved to dismiss, asserting that a Passage Contract between Krupski and the carrier, Costa Crociere S.p.A., contained a one-year statute of limitations pursuant to 46 U.S.C. App. § 183-b, and that Krupski's amended complaint did not satisfy the relation back requirements of what is now Rule 15(c)(1)(C). The district court found that the first two conditions for relation back under Rule 15(c)(1)(C) were satisfied.] . . .

[T]he court explained: The claim against Costa Crociere clearly involved the same occurrence as the original claim against Costa Cruise, and Costa Crociere had constructive notice of the action and had not shown that any unfair prejudice would result from relation back. But the court found the third condition fatal to Krupski's attempt to relate back, concluding that Krupski had not made a mistake concerning the identity of the proper party. Relying on Eleventh Circuit precedent, the court explained that the word "mistake" should not be construed to encompass a deliberate decision not to sue a party whose identity the plaintiff knew before the statute of limitations had run. Because Costa Cruise informed Krupski that Costa Crociere was the proper defendant in its answer, corporate disclosure statement, and motion for summary judgment, and because it was listed as the carrier on Krupski's ticket, but Krupski delayed for months in moving to amend and then in filing an amended complaint, the court concluded that Krupski knew of the proper defendant and made no mistake.

The Eleventh Circuit affirmed in an unpublished *per curiam* opinion **[Eds.—on the grounds set out by the district court, as well as on the grounds that relation back was inappropriate because Krupski delayed seeking leave to amend]**. . . .

II

. . .

In our view, neither of the Court of Appeals' reasons for denying relation back under Rule 15(c)(1)(C)(ii) finds support in the text of the Rule. We consider each reason in turn.

A

The Court of Appeals first decided that Krupski either knew or should have known of the proper party's identity and thus determined that she had made a deliberate choice instead of a mistake in not naming Costa Crociere as a party in her original pleading. By focusing on Krupski's knowledge, the Court of Appeals chose the wrong starting point. The question under Rule 15(c)(1)(C)(ii) is not whether Krupski knew or should have known the identity of Costa Crociere as the proper defendant, but whether Costa Crociere knew or should have known that it would have been named as a defendant but for an error. Rule 15(c)(1)(C)(ii) asks what the prospective *defendant* knew or should have known during the Rule 4(m) period, not what the *plaintiff* knew or should have known at the time of filing her original complaint.[3]

Information in the plaintiff's possession is relevant only if it bears on the defendant's understanding of whether the plaintiff made a mistake regarding the

3. Rule 15(c)(1)(C) speaks generally of an amendment to a "pleading" that changes "the party against whom a claim is asserted," and it therefore is not limited to the circumstance of a plaintiff filing an amended complaint seeking to bring in a new defendant. Nevertheless, because the latter is the "typical case" of Rule 15(c)(1)(C)'s applicability, we use this circumstance as a shorthand throughout this opinion.

proper party's identity. For purposes of that inquiry, it would be error to conflate knowledge of a party's existence with the absence of mistake. A mistake is "[a]n error, misconception, or misunderstanding; an erroneous belief." Black's Law Dictionary 1092 (9th ed. 2009); see also Webster's Third New International Dictionary 1446 (2002) (defining "mistake" as "a misunderstanding of the meaning or implication of something"; "a wrong action or statement proceeding from faulty judgment, inadequate knowledge, or inattention"; "an erroneous belief"; or "a state of mind not in accordance with the facts"). That a plaintiff knows of a party's existence does not preclude her from making a mistake with respect to that party's identity. A plaintiff may know that a prospective defendant—call him party A—exists, while erroneously believing him to have the status of party B. Similarly, a plaintiff may know generally what party A does while misunderstanding the roles that party A and party B played in the "conduct, transaction, or occurrence" giving rise to her claim. If the plaintiff sues party B instead of party A under these circumstances, she has made a "mistake concerning the proper party's identity" notwithstanding her knowledge of the existence of both parties. The only question under Rule 15(c)(1)(C)(ii), then, is whether party A knew or should have known that, absent some mistake, the action would have been brought against him.

Respondent urges that the key issue under Rule 15(c)(1)(C)(ii) is whether the plaintiff made a deliberate choice to sue one party over another. We agree that making a deliberate choice to sue one party instead of another while fully understanding the factual and legal differences between the two parties is the antithesis of making a mistake concerning the proper party's identity. We disagree, however, with respondent's position that any time a plaintiff is aware of the existence of two parties and chooses to sue the wrong one, the proper defendant could reasonably believe that the plaintiff made no mistake. The reasonableness of the mistake is not itself at issue. As noted, a plaintiff might know that the prospective defendant exists but nonetheless harbor a misunderstanding about his status or role in the events giving rise to the claim at issue, and she may mistakenly choose to sue a different defendant based on that misimpression. That kind of deliberate but mistaken choice does not foreclose a finding that Rule 15(c)(1)(C)(ii) has been satisfied.

This reading is consistent with the purpose of relation back: to balance the interests of the defendant protected by the statute of limitations with the preference expressed in the Federal Rules of Civil Procedure in general, and Rule 15 in particular, for resolving disputes on their merits. A prospective defendant who legitimately believed that the limitations period had passed without any attempt to sue him has a strong interest in repose. But repose would be a windfall for a prospective defendant who understood, or who should have understood, that he escaped suit during the limitations period only because the plaintiff misunderstood a crucial fact about his identity. Because a plaintiff's knowledge of the existence of a party does not foreclose the possibility that she has made a mistake of identity about which that party should have been aware, such knowledge does not support that party's interest in repose.

Our reading is also consistent with the history of Rule 15(c)(1)(C). That provision was added in 1966 to respond to a recurring problem in suits against the Federal

Government, particularly in the Social Security context. Advisory Committee's 1966 Notes 122. Individuals who had filed timely lawsuits challenging the administrative denial of benefits often failed to name the party identified in the statute as the proper defendant—the current Secretary of what was then the Department of Health, Education, and Welfare—and named instead the United States; the Department of Health, Education, and Welfare itself; the nonexistent "Federal Security Administration"; or a Secretary who had recently retired from office. *Ibid.* By the time the plaintiffs discovered their mistakes, the statute of limitations in many cases had expired, and the district courts denied the plaintiffs leave to amend on the ground that the amended complaints would not relate back. Rule 15(c) was therefore "amplified to provide a general solution" to this problem. *Ibid.* It is conceivable that the Social Security litigants knew or reasonably should have known the identity of the proper defendant either because of documents in their administrative cases or by dint of the statute setting forth the filing requirements. Nonetheless, the Advisory Committee clearly meant their filings to qualify as mistakes under the Rule. . . .

B

The Court of Appeals offered a second reason why Krupski's amended complaint did not relate back: Krupski had unduly delayed in seeking to file, and in eventually filing, an amended complaint. The Court of Appeals offered no support for its view that a plaintiff's dilatory conduct can justify the denial of relation back under Rule 15(c)(1)(C), and we find none. The Rule plainly sets forth an exclusive list of requirements for relation back, and the amending party's diligence is not among them. Moreover, the Rule mandates relation back once the Rule's requirements are satisfied; it does not leave the decision whether to grant relation back to the district court's equitable discretion. See Rule 15(c)(1) ("An amendment . . . *relates back* . . . when" the three listed requirements are met (emphasis added)).

The mandatory nature of the inquiry for relation back under Rule 15(c) is particularly striking in contrast to the inquiry under Rule 15(a), which sets forth the circumstances in which a party may amend its pleading before trial. By its terms, Rule 15(a) gives discretion to the district court in deciding whether to grant a motion to amend a pleading to add a party or a claim. Following an initial period after filing a pleading during which a party may amend once "as a matter of course," "a party may amend its pleading only with the opposing party's written consent or the court's leave," which the court "should freely give . . . when justice so requires." Rules 15(a)(1)–(2). We have previously explained that a court may consider a movant's "undue delay" or "dilatory motive" in deciding whether to grant leave to amend under Rule 15(a). *Foman v. Davis*, 371 U.S. 178, 182 (1962). As the contrast between Rule 15(a) and Rule 15(c) makes clear, however, the speed with which a plaintiff moves to amend her complaint or files an amended complaint after obtaining leave to do so has no bearing on whether the amended complaint relates back.

Rule 15(c)(1)(C) does permit a court to examine a plaintiff's conduct during the Rule 4(m) period, but not in the way or for the purpose respondent or the Court of Appeals suggests. As we have explained, the question under Rule

15(c)(1)(C)(ii) is what the prospective defendant reasonably should have understood about the plaintiff's intent in filing the original complaint against the first defendant. To the extent the plaintiff's postfiling conduct informs the prospective defendant's understanding of whether the plaintiff initially made a "mistake concerning the proper party's identity," a court may consider the conduct. Cf. *Leonard v. Parry*, 219 F.3d 25, 29 (CA1 2000) ("[P]ost-filing events occasionally can shed light on the plaintiff's state of mind at an earlier time" and "can inform *a defendant's* reasonable beliefs concerning whether her omission from the original complaint represented a mistake (as opposed to a conscious choice)"). The plaintiff's postfiling conduct is otherwise immaterial to the question whether an amended complaint relates back.[5]

C

Applying these principles to the facts of this case, we think it clear that the courts below erred in denying relation back under Rule 15(c)(1)(C)(ii). The District Court held that Costa Crociere had "constructive notice" of Krupski's complaint within the Rule 4(m) period. Costa Crociere has not challenged this finding. Because the complaint made clear that Krupski meant to sue the company that "owned, operated, managed, supervised and controlled" the ship on which she was injured, and also indicated (mistakenly) that Costa Cruise performed those roles, Costa Crociere should have known, within the Rule 4(m) period, that it was not named as a defendant in that complaint only because of Krupski's misunderstanding about which "Costa" entity was in charge of the ship—clearly a "mistake concerning the proper party's identity."

Respondent contends that because the original complaint referred to the ticket's forum requirement and presuit claims notification procedure, Krupski was clearly aware of the contents of the ticket, and because the ticket identified Costa Crociere as the carrier and proper party for a lawsuit, respondent was entitled to think that she made a deliberate choice to sue Costa Cruise instead of Costa Crociere. As we have explained, however, that Krupski may have known the contents of the ticket does not foreclose the possibility that she nonetheless misunderstood crucial facts regarding the two companies' identities. Especially because the face of the complaint plainly indicated such a misunderstanding, respondent's contention is not persuasive. Moreover, respondent has articulated no strategy that it could reasonably have thought Krupski was pursuing in suing a defendant that was legally unable to provide relief.

Respondent also argues that Krupski's failure to move to amend her complaint during the Rule 4(m) period shows that she made no mistake in that period. But as discussed, any delay on Krupski's part is relevant only to the

5. Similarly, we reject respondent's suggestion that Rule 15(c) requires a plaintiff to move to amend her complaint or to file and serve an amended complaint within the Rule 4(m) period. Rule 15(c)(1)(C)(i) simply requires that the prospective defendant has received sufficient "notice of the action" within the Rule 4(m) period that he will not be prejudiced in defending the case on the merits. The Advisory Committee Notes to the 1966 Amendment clarify that "the notice need not be formal." Advisory Committee's 1966 Notes 122.

extent it may have informed Costa Crociere's understanding during the Rule 4(m) period of whether she made a mistake originally. Krupski's failure to add Costa Crociere during the Rule 4(m) period is not sufficient to make reasonable any belief that she had made a deliberate and informed decision not to sue Costa Crociere in the first instance.[6] Nothing in Krupski's conduct during the Rule 4(m) period suggests that she failed to name Costa Crociere because of anything other than a mistake.

It is also worth noting that Costa Cruise and Costa Crociere are related corporate entities with very similar names; "crociera" even means "cruise" in Italian. Cassell's Italian Dictionary 137, 670 (1967). This interrelationship and similarity heighten the expectation that Costa Crociere should suspect a mistake has been made when Costa Cruise is named in a complaint that actually describes Costa Crociere's activities. Cf. *Morel v. DaimlerChrysler AG*, 565 F.3d 20, 27 (C.A. 1 2009) (where complaint conveyed plaintiffs' attempt to sue automobile manufacturer and erroneously named the manufacturer as DaimlerChrysler Corporation instead of the actual manufacturer, a legally distinct but related entity named DaimlerChrysler AG, the latter should have realized it had not been named because of plaintiffs' mistake); *Goodman v. Praxair, Inc.*, 494 F.3d 458, 473–475 (C.A. 4 2007) (en banc) (where complaint named parent company Praxair, Inc., but described status of subsidiary company Praxair Services, Inc., subsidiary company knew or should have known it had not been named because of plaintiff's mistake). In addition, Costa Crociere's own actions contributed to passenger confusion over "the proper party" for a lawsuit. The front of the ticket advertises that "Costa Cruises" has achieved a certification of quality, without clarifying whether "Costa Cruises" is Costa Cruise Lines, Costa Crociere, or some other related "Costa" company. Indeed, Costa Crociere is evidently aware that the difference between Costa Cruise and Costa Crociere can be confusing for cruise ship passengers. See, *e.g., Suppa v. Costa Crociere, S.p.A.*, No. 07-60526-CIV, 2007 WL 4287508, *1, (S.D. Fla., Dec. 4, 2007) (denying Costa Crociere's motion to dismiss the amended complaint where the original complaint had named Costa Cruise as a defendant after "find[ing] it simply inconceivable that Defendant Costa Crociere was not on notice . . . that . . . but for the mistake in the original Complaint, Costa Crociere was the appropriate party to be named in the action").

Holding

In light of these facts, Costa Crociere should have known that Krupski's failure to name it as a defendant in her original complaint was due to a mistake concerning the proper party's identity. We therefore reverse the judgment of the Court of Appeals for the Eleventh Circuit and remand the case for further proceedings consistent with this opinion.

It is so ordered.

---

6. . . . It is not clear why Krupski should have been found dilatory for not accepting at face value the unproven allegations in Costa Cruise's answer and corporate disclosure form. In fact, Krupski moved to amend her complaint to add Costa Crociere within the time period prescribed by the District Court's scheduling order.

Justice Scalia, concurring in part and concurring in the judgment.

I join the Court's opinion except for its reliance on the Notes of the Advisory Committee as establishing the meaning of Federal Rule of Civil Procedure 15(c)(1)(C). The Advisory Committee's insights into the proper interpretation of a Rule's text are useful to the same extent as any scholarly commentary. But the Committee's intentions have no effect on the Rule's meaning. Even assuming that we and the Congress that allowed the Rule to take effect read and agreed with those intentions, it is the text of the Rule that controls.

Notes and Questions: *Krupski*

Q **1. The theory behind relation back of amendments that change parties.** We've seen that amendments between the same parties asserting claims or defenses relate back as long as the claims or defenses arose out of the same transaction as the original pleading. The theory of this relation back, as *Bonerb* teaches, is notice. The party against whom the amendment is made had notice from the original pleading filed within the limitations period that the litigation could involve other claims arising from the transaction alleged in the original pleading. How is an amendment changing parties different?

A The new party was *not* served with the original complaint within the limitations period for the simple reason that it was *not* an original party. The transactional nexus between the original pleading and the amendment does it no good, *unless it somehow gets wind of the original action within the limitations period (or soon after, during the period allowed for service of a complaint after it has been filed) and realizes that the complaint would have named it, but for the pleader's mistake.* Rule 15(c)(1)(C) therefore spells out these additional requirements in fine detail. Its theory of relation back is still notice, but it recognizes that timely notice for a new party is more problematic than for a party who was actually sued and served within the limitations period. It therefore requires that some kind of notice of "the [original] action"—and thereby of the transaction that gave rise to that action—be received by the new party during the limitations period or the period allowed for service of a timely filed complaint, including any extension of the service period permitted by the court under Rule 4(m).

Q **2. When?** The Rule says a new party must receive notice of the original action within "the period provided by Rule 4(m) for serving the summons and complaint," but this can be confusing. Assume that Dick and Jane are in a car that runs down pedestrian Palmer on New Year's Day, January 1, 2008. Palmer sues Jane, thinking that she was the driver. The applicable period of limitations is two years.

A. Palmer files her complaint on December 30, 2009, and properly serves Jane ten days later. Is Palmer's action barred by the statute of limitations?

A This gets in just under the wire if the statute requires *filing* rather than service of a complaint to toll the statute. It is also timely even if the statutory tolling provision requires filing within the limitations period *and* service no more than thirty days thereafter.

B. Same facts, but on February 1, 2010, Jane shows Dick a copy of the complaint. On June 1, 2010, Palmer discovers that Dick was really driving the car. She therefore immediately seeks leave to amend the complaint to name Dick as the defendant. Dick objects that amendment would be futile because it is barred by the statute of limitations. Would the amendment relate back to December 30, 2009?

A Although the statute of limitations expired on January 1, 2010, and amendment is being offered five months later, Dick, "the party to be brought in by the amendment," saw the complaint in February 2010. This is well within the ninety-day period provided by Rule 4(m) for service of the original complaint and summons. As Dick got this "notice" within the service period, the amended complaint relates back to the filing of the original complaint on December 30, 2009, provided that this notice meets the other requirements of Rule 15(c)(1)(C).

C. Assume that Palmer files her original complaint on January 1, 2009. On June 1, 2009, more than ninety days after the filing, but within the statute of limitations period, Jane shows the complaint to Dick. In July 2010, past the two-year limitations period, Palmer finds out that Dick was the driver instead of Jane. Palmer immediately moves for leave to file an amended complaint naming Dick as a defendant. Would the amendment relate back to January 1, 2009?

A No, on a literal reading of the rule. The original complaint was filed on January 1, 2009, and Rule 4(m) sets the time limit for service as "90 days after the complaint is filed," or April 1, 2009. But Jane did not show Dick the original complaint until two months later, on June 1, 2009. Thus, he did not receive notice (from Jane showing him the original complaint) "within the period provided by Rule 4(m) for serving the summons and complaint. . . ." Rule 15(c)(1)(C).

But Dick did receive that notice within the limitations period! A few courts have therefore found that "notice received within the limitations period continues to support relation back of an amendment changing a party. . . ." *Wright & Miller* § 1498.1. While that may seem consistent with the policy of limitations (after all, Dick has notice within the imitations period), it is arguably not consistent with the text of the rule.

Q **3. What notice?** Costa Crociere was not served with a summons and complaint within 120 days of filing of the original complaint (the period then provided by Rule 4(m)), so why did the courts find that it had received notice?

A The Rule doesn't say that a new party must be served with the original complaint. Indeed, it doesn't say anything at all about "service" of notice to the new party. It only requires that the party "received such notice of the action that it will not be prejudiced in defending on the merits; and knew or should have known" about the pleader's mistake. This formulation leaves open the possibility that "such notice" can be received informally or through an intermediary.

Q **4. Sufficient notice?** How would you assess the sufficiency of the following sources of notice, assuming that they were received at a proper time?

A. Krupski sends a courtesy copy of the original complaint and summons to Costa Crociere's CEO.

A The only thing missing here is formal service. Costa Crociere has actual notice and should realize that the action would have named it as defendant but for Krupski's mistake.

B. Krupski serves her original complaint and summons on a registered agent—a person hired by a company to accept service of process on its behalf—who represents both Costa Cruise and Costa Crociere. The registered agent forwards the complaint and summons to Costa Cruise's General Counsel, who is also General Counsel for Costa Crociere.

A This is what happened in *Krupski.* As long as the General Counsel should have known from the original complaint that Krupski would have sued Costa Crociere but for a mistake, she surely received "such notice" that her employer would not be prejudiced in defending an amended complaint arising out of the same event.

C. The managing agent for Costa Crociere reads an article in the *Miami Herald* reporting that Krupski was injured on a *Costa Magica* cruise and blames the cruise vessel.

A In the foregoing cases, the notice consists of the original complaint itself, which supplies enough details of the incident (the transaction) that Costa Crociere would "not be prejudiced in defending on the merits." The district court in *Krupski* held that given the identity of interest and the "virtually identical claims" in the original complaint and the amendment, Costa Crociere "would have no difficulty preparing a defense in this case if required to." 2008 WL 7423654, at *5 (S.D. Fla. 2008), *aff'd*, 330 Fed. Appx. 892 (11th Cir. 2009), *rev'd*, 560 U.S. 538 (2010). In **C**, however, the putative notice is from a newspaper article, not the original complaint. The problem is that we don't know whether the newspaper article also provides enough information to avoid prejudice to Costa Crociere in defending itself.

First, the rule speaks of "notice *of the action*." If this means what it says, even an article that describes the event giving rise to Krupski's claim might not give notice that she had filed an *action.* Second, though a good argument can be made that notice of the event or transaction should be enough, *see Wright & Miller* § 1498.1, the sufficiency of the newspaper article still depends on whether it supplies enough information so that Costa Crociere will not be prejudiced in defending itself and would know or should know that Krupski would have sued it but for her mistake in naming the wrong Costa.

D. Krupski tells her travel agent about the suit, and he mentions it to the local agent for Costa Crociere.

A

Here the "notice" is from an oral communication. Notice by the game of "telephone" sounds pretty unreliable, as described. What does Krupski tell her travel agent, and how much does the travel agent (accurately) pass on to the local agent? Even if a sufficiently detailed (and accurate) account is relayed, what relationship does the local agent have to Costa Crociere (how high up)?

Q

5. Krupski's mistake. What mistake did Krupski make?

A

Obviously, she sued the wrong party in light of the district court's grant of summary judgment to Costa Cruise. But it's worth examining that mistake more closely. Initially, it could have been no more than (1) a scrivener's error or *misnomer*—typing Costa Cruise Lines instead of Costa Crociere. (Heck, the cruise boat itself was the *Costa Magica*—it was hard keeping the Costas straight.) If she knew that Costa Cruise was different from Costa Crociere, on the other hand, then her "mistake" was either (2) her conscious decision not to sue Costa Crociere for some reason, or (3) her failure to realize that only Costa Crociere could be sued.

Let's consider each kind of mistake in order in the following notes.

6. Misnomer mistakes. Prior to the *Krupski* decision in the Supreme Court, all courts agreed that the Rule's "mistake concerning the proper party's identity" included the first kind of error—the misnomer or scrivener's error, "when a plaintiff misnames or misidentifies a party in its pleadings but correctly serves that party." 3-15 *Moore* § 15.19[3][d]. The Advisory Committee not only gave the example of the plaintiff who mistakenly names the non-existent "Federal Security Administration," but states that the Rule includes "an amendment to correct a misnomer or misdescription of a defendant." Fed. R. Civ. P. 15(c) advisory committee's note to 1966 amendment.

> **Example.** Suppose Krupski names "Costa *Corsere*" in her original complaint instead of "Costa Crociere." Her lawyer just misspelled the name of the defendant. A proper legal claim should not be dismissed just because of what is, in effect, a typo, unless the typo somehow prejudiced the defendant.

7. "Deliberate" mistakes. Most courts were also agreed that if a party, *knowing* of the new party and its amenability to suit, deliberately chose not to name it (perhaps because it elected a different theory of liability, or perhaps because it didn't want to have to defend against multiple defendants and their counsel), then it has not made a mistake within the meaning of the Rule.

> **Example.** Plaintiff decides to sue the owner instead of the driver of the car for her injuries in an auto accident, because she thinks the owner has deep pockets and the driver does not. After the statute of limitations runs, she discovers that the owner is not that rich either. She now amends her complaint to add the driver. This amendment would not relate back. Even though it clearly arises from the same accident and was made to correct a mistaken tactical decision, it is not the kind of mistake that the Rule was enacted to cover.

Krupski has not changed this law, as it expressly states, "We agree that making a deliberate choice to sue one party instead of another while fully understanding the factual and legal differences between the two parties is the antithesis of making a mistake concerning the proper party's identity." Relation back will not relieve such a party from the consequences of its own deliberate tactical decision.

Suing unknown police officers: the John Doe problem. As this is written, various protestors allege that they have been injured, seized, or otherwise mistreated during a protest by police officers or federal officials whose identity is unknown to them (because the protester did not see the officer's name tag or because the officer had none). Prisoners who allege abuse or neglect by prison guards sometimes face the same dilemma. The alleged victims have therefore sometimes sued "John Doe" or "Unnamed Police Officer" within the limitations period and served the police department, Attorney General, the prison warden, or other government authority. *See* Rule 4(j). If the plaintiffs then learn the identity of their assailants after that period, they try to amend their complaints to add the named assailants based on "mistake concerning the proper party's identity." Rule 15(c)(1)(C)(ii).

Most (but not all) courts have rejected that argument, reasoning that ignorance is not mistake, and that plaintiffs must exercise diligence in discovering the identity of defendants. *See Wright & Miller* § 1498.3. Is that fair?

> [Identity] information is in the possession of the defendants, and many plaintiffs cannot obtain this information until they have had a chance to undergo extensive discovery following institution of a civil action. If such plaintiffs are not allowed to relate back their amended "John Doe" complaints, then the statute of limitations period for these plaintiffs is effectively substantially shorter than it is for other plaintiffs who bring the exact same claim but who know the names of their assailants; the former group of plaintiffs would have to bring their lawsuits well before the end of the limitations period, immediately begin discovery, and hope that they can determine the assailants' names before the statute of limitations expires. There seems to be no good reason to disadvantage plaintiffs in this way simply because, for example, they were not able to see the name tag of the offending state actor.
>
> .... [F]airness to the defendants is accommodated in the other requirements of Rule 15(c)(3), namely the requirements that (1) the newly named defendants had received "such notice of the institution of the action" during the relevant time period "that the party will not be prejudiced in maintaining a defense on the merits"; and (2) the newly named defendants knew or should have known that the original complaint was really directed towards them ("the action would have been brought against the party"). These requirements generally take care of the "springing a claim on an unsuspecting defendant" problem.

Singletary v. Pennsylvania Dep't of Corr., 266 F.3d 186, 202 n.5 (3d Cir. 2001).

Singletary was a civil rights suit against prison officials by the mother of a prisoner who committed suicide in custody. But after recognizing the desirability of allowing amendment, the court reluctantly felt constrained by the "mistake" requirement of what is now Rule 15(c)(1)(C)(ii) to disallow relation back. Instead, it urged the Rules Advisory Committee to consider an amendment to Rule 15 that would allow such relation back. *See* Edward H. Cooper, *Rule 15(c)(3) Puzzles at 3–5* (November 1999) (unpublished manuscript, on file with the Administrative Office of the United States Courts, Rules Committee Support Office) (suggesting changing the Rule's language to read "but for a mistake *or lack of information* concerning the identity of the proper party") (manuscript at 8). The Rule has not yet been changed.

Q **8. Krupski and John Doe relation back.** Does *Krupski* clearly settle the debate about whether (and which) mistakes of ignorance qualify under the Rule, and thus whether amendments to John Doe complaints can relate back?

A Not necessarily, because the Court only held that the lower courts were incorrect in inferring that Krupski had made a deliberate choice not to sue, based on her knowledge of Costa Cruise's answer and the identification of Costa Crociere as the carrier on the back of her ticket. Still, the Court's embrace of the broadest dictionary definition of "mistake" (including "a wrong action or statement proceeding from . . . inadequate knowledge . . .") provides some support for the liberal approach to mistakes of ignorance. *See* Robert A. Lusardi, *Rule 15(c) Mistake: The Supreme Court in* Krupski *Seeks to Resolve a Judicial Thicket*, 49 U. Louisville L. Rev. 317, 336–37 (2011) (arguing that *Krupski* "expand[ed] the concept of mistake of identity to include those situations in which a plaintiff knows of a prospective defendant, but misperceives his status or role in the events giving rise to the claim, and those in which the plaintiff may not have known of the existence of the prospective party until after the statute had run").

Rule from case

Some courts read *Krupski* even more expansively. In *White v. City of Chicago*, No. 14 CV 3720, 2016 WL 4270152 (N.D. Ill. Aug. 15, 2016), plaintiff White sued John Does for injuries White suffered when an unknown police officer allegedly shoved him down a flight of concrete stairs while White was handcuffed. The court acknowledged the case law holding that ignorance is not mistake, but reasoned that *Krupski* had altered the legal landscape.

> Adherence to the principles articulated in *Krupski* requires a different analysis of the facts of this case then simply applying the "lack of knowledge is not a mistake" principle of the traditional John Doe rule. The Court looks to whether there is any basis in the record for saying that the Individual Defendants could have legitimately believed that the limitations period had passed without any attempt to sue them. The answer is no. White named the John Doe police officer as a defendant, and the Individual Defendants have not argued that they were unaware of White's complaint within the prescribed time. Moreover, there is no basis for saying that White made "a deliberate choice to sue one party instead of another while fully understanding the factual and legal differences between the two parties." *Krupski*, 560 U.S. at 549. In fact, White's

> naming of a John Doe police officer shows the opposite—a clear intent to sue the person who he believes caused him to fall down the stairs. It would appear, therefore, that the Individual Defendants have no legitimate interest in repose and denying relation back would be a windfall to them.

Id. at *18. Of course, it may have influenced the court's analysis that the City of Chicago took slightly less than fourteen months after the statute of limitations had passed to identify the officer who shoved White *at the police station*. The court noted other cases with comparable unexplained delays by public agencies in identifying their John Doe employees. *Id.* at *20.

Q **9. What about Krupski's delay?** The Court squarely rejected the lower court's invocation of Krupski's delay in filing the amended complaint as a basis for disallowing relation back. Simply said, Rule 15(c) says nothing about the timing of plaintiff's diligence in making such an amendment, and if its relation-back requirements are satisfied, relation back is mandatory. Does this mean that Krupski's delay in amending her pleading is irrelevant to amendment?

A No. It's only irrelevant to relation back under Rule 15(c). But it is still a factor that a court may consider in giving leave to amend in the first place under Rule 15(a). If the window for amendment once without leave has closed, the court must consider such factors as the amending party's reason for amendment and any delay, as well as prejudice and futility, the factors that overlap with the relation-back inquiry. But here the district court *granted* leave to amend; it could not then import the delay factor into the wrong part of the equation—the relation back inquiry. In fact, the grant was almost certainly a proper exercise of its discretion: Krupski filed her motion for leave to amend just three and a half months after Costa Cruise answered and barely a month after Costa Cruise's summary judgment motion. As the Supreme Court noted in footnote 6, "It is not clear why Krupski should have been found dilatory for not accepting at face value the unproven allegations in Costa Cruise's answer and corporate disclosure form."

Q **10. Back to *Aquaslide*.** Suppose, after the statute of limitations ran, Beeck amended his complaint to add Pirate Manufacturing, Inc., as the defendant in his product liability claim. Would this amendment relate back?

A It satisfies the transactional nexus requirements in Rule 15(c)(1)(B); he is only adding a different defendant to the same occurrence. But there are no facts suggesting that the phantom manufacturer got notice within the ninety-day period now set out in Rule 4(m).

Suppose, however, that the CEO of Pirate, within that time period, read a detailed newspaper account not just of Beeck's accident, but also of his original lawsuit, carrying a picture of the slide, which he recognized as one his company manufactured. Should he have known from the article that, but for a mistake, Beeck would have sued him? That depends on whether Beeck's "mistake" falls within the Rule. It was no misnomer. But it was also not a deliberate choice to sue Aquaslide instead of Pirate Manufacturing. Beeck was innocently ignorant of the "proper party's identity." We think he'd have a good argument for relation back on these facts.

Q **11. Review.** Palin sues businessman Jones for breach of a contract to fix a leak in her basement. She mistakenly fails to sue Jones's associate, Day, not realizing that they are jointly legally responsible for performance of the contract. Within the limitations period, however, Jones mentions the lawsuit to Day. After the statute of limitations runs, Palin obtains leave to amend her complaint to add a claim against Day for breach of another contract to build a barn on her property. Does her amendment relate back?

A We only get into the weeds of "such notice" and "mistake" under Rule 15(c)(1)(C), *"if Rule 15(c)(1)(B) is satisfied. . . ."* Fed. R. Civ. P. 15(c)(1)(C) (emphasis added). In other words, the amendment must arise out of the same transaction as the original pleading. This one does not. It involves a completely different contract, even though it is among the same parties. We've said that a mere transactional nexus between the original pleading and the amendment is not *sufficient* to give notice, when the new party was not originally in the lawsuit, but it *is necessary*. No relation back here.

VII. Amending Pleadings: Summary of Basic Principles

- A pleading can be changed by filing an amended pleading, which then replaces the original pleading.
- Under Rule 15, the amending party does not need leave of court to amend a pleading once, if the amendment is filed no more than twenty-one days after the original pleading was served, or after a responsive pleading or motion under Rule 12(b), (e), or (f) was served, whichever is earlier. An amendment without leave ("as a matter of course") is effective on filing.
- In all other cases, the amending party may amend only with consent of the parties or by leave of court. For the latter, the party must file a motion for leave to amend, accompanied by the proposed amendment. Leave is in the court's discretion, which turns on the amending party's reason for amendment, its diligence, the number of prior amendments by the same party, "preparation prejudice" to the opposing party (and not just the "merits prejudice" resulting from the change in litigating posture), and the futility of the amendment (for failure to state a claim or defense or bar by an affirmative defense). Preparation prejudice is the key factor, however, and the Rule instructs that courts "should freely give leave when justice so requires."
- The likelihood of preparation prejudice increases as the trial date approaches and is often near its maximum at trial. Nevertheless, pleadings can be amended even during and after trial by express consent or over objection, if the objecting party cannot show prejudice from the amendment. In addition, an issue tried by implied consent—which a court may infer from a party's failure to object to evidence relevant *only* to the new issue, outside

the pleadings—will be treated as if it had been raised by the pleadings (what we've called "de facto amendment").

- When an amendment presents a claim after the relevant statute of limitations has run, the amendment is time-barred (and therefore futile) unless it "relates back" to the date of a timely original pleading—that is, the amendment is treated as if it were backdated to the date of the pleading it amends.
- Amendments asserting claims or defenses among the parties to the original pleading relate back when the claim or defense arose out of the same conduct, transaction, or occurrence set out in the original pleading.
- Amendments changing a party or the naming of a party but seeking recovery for the same events as the original complaint relate back when the party to be brought in by the amendment

  (1) receives such notice that it would not be prejudiced in defending on the merits,

  (2) is or should be aware that the action would have been brought against it but for a mistake concerning the proper party's identity, and

  (3) received the notice within the limitations period or ninety days (or such additional time for service as the court allows) after the filing of the original complaint (the extra time allows for service as provided by Rule 4(m)).
- A "mistake concerning the proper party's identity" can be a misnomer or lack of knowledge of the party's amenability to suit, but does not include a deliberate, knowing decision not to name the party in the original pleading. The courts are divided as to whether mistake can include ignorance of the identity of the omitted party, as in John Doe civil rights complaints.

PART VI

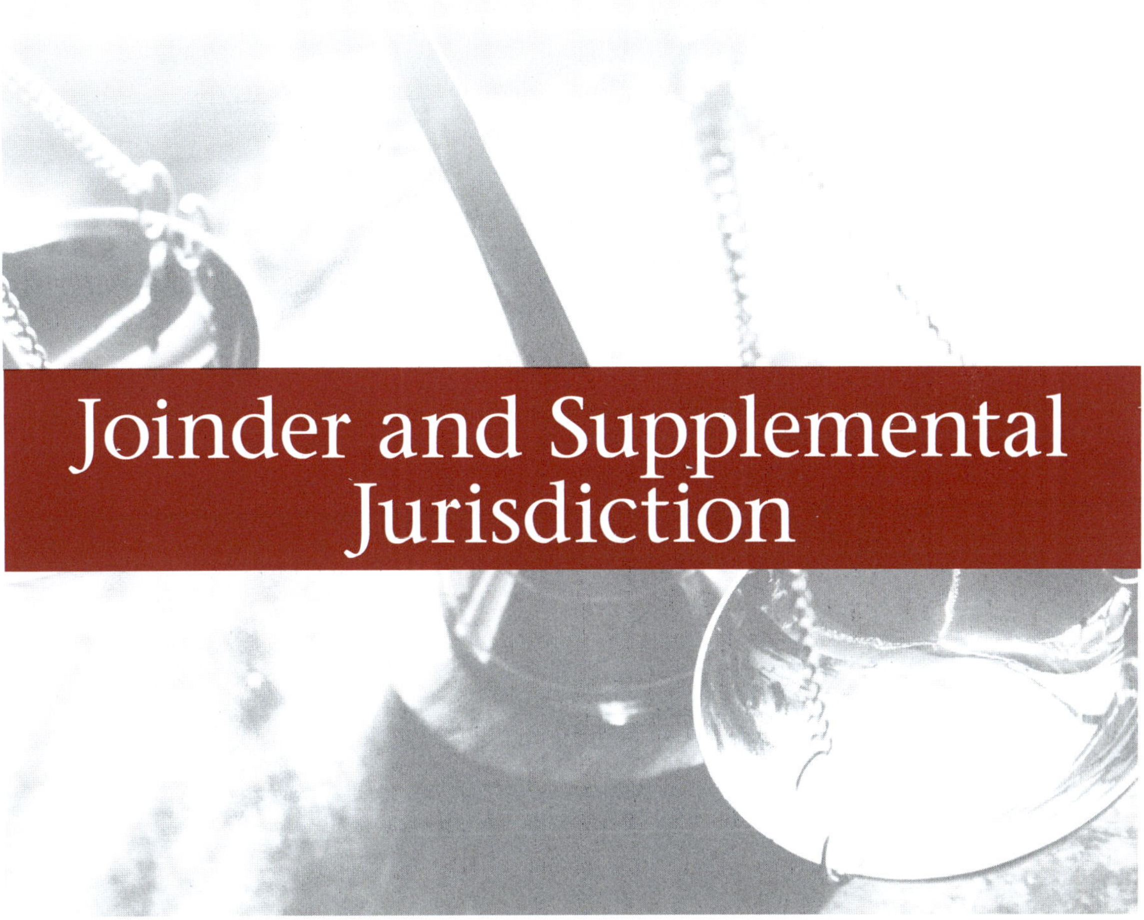

Joinder and Supplemental Jurisdiction

17

Joinder of Claims and Parties

I. Introduction

Once the plaintiff has decided where she is going to file her lawsuit, she has to make important decisions about the scope of the suit. She has to decide who the defendants are going to be, whether to sue alone or with other plaintiffs, and what claims to assert against the defendants. In civil procedure terms, she has to decide what *claims* and *parties* she is going to join in the action. This chapter addresses the basic rules that govern combining claims and parties in a single action in federal court. More complicated joinder devices such as intervention, interpleader, necessary parties, and class actions are addressed in the following two chapters.

Here's a simple example to illustrate the problem. Yee hires Protect Painting Company to paint her house in Virginia. During the course of the work, she is standing on the lawn talking with Pemberton, the owner of Protect, when Garza, a Protect employee, swings a ladder toward the house. The ladder contacts the Edison Electric service wire coming into the house, and brushes Yee at the same time, giving her a strong shock that injures her seriously and starts a fire that damages her house.

As a result of this accident, Yee may have a variety of claims against Protect Painting (and other defendants as well). She may have claims against Protect for negligence, for breach of contract, or under some state statute. She will need to decide which of these claims to assert, and whether the rules allow her to assert them all together or whether she must do so in separate lawsuits. She also needs to know whether she can seek different types of damages—for her personal injuries and for her property damage—in a single suit.

Yee might also want to sue Edison Electric. She might have negligence claims against Edison, breach of contract claims, and perhaps a strict liability claim as well. Again, she will have to know whether she can assert all of these claims against Edison in a single suit or whether she has to bring different actions on her different theories.

In addition to those questions of *joinder of claims*, Yee will also need to know whether she can sue various parties, such as Edison and Protect (and perhaps Garza and Pemberton) together in a single suit or whether she must file separate suits against each potential defendant. Similarly, she needs to know whether she can sue along with other possible plaintiffs. Perhaps Mr. Yee, her husband, wants to join as a coplaintiff to recover for loss of consortium or for damage to his possessions in the fire (or for both). Perhaps her neighbor, Worzek, wishes to join if the fire spread to his property as well. Yee's counsel needs to know the rules for joinder of defendants and for joinder of coplaintiffs in a single action.

All procedural systems have rules that determine the scope of joinder of claims and parties in a single action. For the federal courts, the rules of joinder are found in the Federal Rules of Civil Procedure. Each state adopts rules of procedure for its courts, either by statute or through rules adopted by the state's highest court. If you practice in Kansas, you will use the Federal Rules for cases in the federal court for the District of Kansas, but the Kansas rules of procedure for cases in the Kansas state courts. If you practice in New Hampshire, you will use the Federal Rules in the federal district court there, but New Hampshire's rules in the New Hampshire state courts.

II. Joinder of Multiple Claims Under the Federal Rules

Let's start with a fairly simple matter: the question of how many claims a plaintiff may assert in a single lawsuit. A system of procedural rules might take various approaches to the problem, including one or more of the following:

- The rules could confine the plaintiff to asserting a single claim. For example, if Yee decided to sue Protect for her injuries, the joinder rules might require her to sue Protect only for one claim, such as her negligence claim. If she wanted to assert a claim for her injuries on a breach of contract theory, she would have to bring a separate suit on that theory.
- The rules could allow Yee to bring any claims against Protect, so long as she seeks the same relief on those claims. For example, the joinder rules could authorize her to sue Protect for breach of contract and negligence

in a single suit, so long as she seeks only money damages for her personal injury.

- The joinder rules might allow Yee to sue Protect on any theory and for any relief, so long as the claims all arise out of the same events—such as Yee's accident with the ladder. Under this approach, she could sue Protect for her injuries on both a negligence and breach of contract theory in a single suit, and seek both damages and specific performance in that suit. But she couldn't assert a claim against Protect for poor work on an unrelated contract to paint her barn.
- The rules might take an even more liberal approach to joinder of claims, allowing Yee to sue Protect on any claims she has against it, even claims arising from unrelated events. Under this approach, Yee could sue Protect for injuries in the ladder accident and for unrelated work on another job in the same suit.

Q **The Federal Rules' approach.** Over the years, several of these approaches have been tried. Which does Rule 18(a) adopt?

A The Federal Rules take the most liberal of the four approaches described above. Rule 18(a) allows a plaintiff to assert *any claims she has* against an opponent, whether related or unrelated:

> A party asserting a claim, counterclaim, crossclaim, or third-party claim may join, as independent or alternative claims, as many claims as it has against an opposing party.

If Yee sues Pemberton, she could assert her claims for personal injury damages and for property damage together. She could also sue Pemberton for breach of contract if he did a poor paint job on the house. Or, if he had painted her summer cottage as well as her house, she could include a claim for that too, even though that claim arose out of completely unrelated events. She could even add an admiralty claim against Pemberton, if they had collided while racing their yachts the previous season.

Notes and Questions: Joinder of Claims

1. Rules as revolution. It is hard to appreciate how revolutionary this flexible approach to joinder is without knowing what pleading was like under the *ancien régime*. In the early days of English common law, the right to join claims was extremely limited. Claims were conceptualized in distinct categories and often handled by different courts. If a plaintiff brought an action at law for damages, it went to one court. If she had a claim against the same defendant—even one arising from the same events as the legal claim—that was classified as equitable, she had to bring that in an equity court. Admiralty and maritime claims went to an admiralty court.

Even actions at law could not always be joined together. Different types of actions at law were started with different writs, such as trespass, trespass on the case, assumpsit, and trover. A single set of events might give rise to claims that had to be brought in separate suits under different writs, even though they arose from the same events.

> Consider this situation: a deadbeat tenant fails to pay rent; when the lease ends he leaves the apartment in a mess, with finger painting all over the wallpaper, cigarette burns in the carpeting, an expensive lamp smashed into a million pieces, and an antique chair missing. The fuming landlord storms to his lawyer. . . . "Make that rascal pay," he demands.

Charles Alan Wright, *Modern Pleading and the Pennsylvania Rules*, 101 U. PA. L. REV. 909, 922 (1953). As Professor Wright points out, at common law, the lawyer would have had to bring two suits to recover this client's damages:

> Why? Because the claim for rent is a claim in assumpsit, the claim for damage to the wall and carpeting is a claim for breach of the covenant to restore the premises to good condition and thus a claim in assumpsit, but the claim for destruction of the lamp and taking of the chair is a claim in trespass.

Id. at 923. The Federal Rules are the culmination of a hundred-year trend to throw out such formalism in favor of a simple, flexible system allowing joinder of any claims the plaintiff wishes to bring—related or unrelated—in a single "civil action." Fed. R. Civ. P. 2.

2. How claims are actually "joined" in a complaint. Rule 18(a) authorizes "joining" claims in a single suit. This means that the claims may all be asserted as different counts or "claims for relief" in a single complaint, to be litigated together in a single lawsuit. *See* Fed. R. Civ. P. 8(d)(3) (a party may set forth as many claims as she has against an opposing party). The parties will litigate all of the claims together, unless the court orders otherwise. Testimony will be taken at depositions of witnesses about all claims, interrogatories and requests for documents will seek information relevant to all claims, and, quite likely, the various claims will be tried together in a single trial. Thus, joinder of related claims creates efficiency throughout the litigation.

Q **3. Joinder of unrelated claims under Rule 18(a).** It makes sense to allow related claims to be litigated together—but Rule 18(a) allows a party to assert unrelated claims as well. The efficiency rationale does not seem to support joinder of unrelated claims. Why does Rule 18(a) allow such broad joinder?

A One answer is, why not? The parties are already in court, represented by counsel, and poised to settle their differences, so why not settle them all without the bureaucratic hassle of filing two suits? In addition, the opportunity to resolve all their differences together may facilitate settlement. Perhaps one party has a stronger case on one of the claims, and the other party has a stronger case on the other claim. By litigating both together, the parties can put both disputes behind them and get on to other matters.

In addition, if the joinder rules only allowed joinder of related claims, parties would spend time and money litigating whether a particular claim was "related" to the others in the case. This is often a close question that is avoided by allowing broad joinder.

Q **4. Trial of unrelated claims joined under Rule 18(a).** Suppose that Yee joins completely unrelated claims under Rule 18(a). She sues Protect for her damages from the painting accident and for damages in an auto accident she had with a Protect employee the year before. How will these claims be tried?

A Although Rule 18 allows Yee to bring both claims together in a single lawsuit, it would not make sense to try Yee's unrelated motor vehicle claim with her claims for the house accident. The facts and legal issues raised by the two claims are different, and the evidence and witnesses needed to prove the claims will differ as well. Hearing these claims together would likely confuse the jury and waste time rather than save it. In such cases, Rule 42(b) authorizes the trial judge to order separate trials:

> For convenience, to avoid prejudice, or to expedite and economize, the court [i.e., the federal district judge] may order a separate trial of one or more separate issues, claims, crossclaims, counterclaims, or third-party claims.

Thus, the plaintiff determines the initial scope of the litigation by joining whatever claims she chooses to under Rule 18(a). But the district court judge retains control over the course of the litigation. She may sever unrelated claims completely (Fed. R. Civ. P. 21) or order separate trials of unrelated claims to avoid confusion or save time.

Q **5. Bringing suit later on claims that could have been joined in a prior action.** Suppose that Yee sues Protect for her injuries in the painting accident on a negligence theory and loses. Should she be allowed to bring a second action, for the same injuries, on a breach of contract theory?

A This question introduces the murky doctrine of *claim preclusion*, which generally bars a party who has sued a defendant once on a set of facts from doing so again. The doctrine (also called *res judicata*) avoids multiple suits about the same facts and prevents litigants from harassing adversaries by suing again for events they already litigated in a prior action.

Under claim preclusion principles, most courts would bar Yee from suing Protect a second time if she *could have joined her contract claim in her first suit*—as the contract claim could have been in this example. Because the contract claim is based on the same litigation facts and could have been asserted in the first suit, it seems fair to require the plaintiff to do so, to achieve efficiency and avoid inconsistent verdicts on the same facts.

If the joinder rules did not allow the contract claim to be joined in the first case, it would be unfair to bar Yee from bringing it in a second action. For example, if the system took the narrowest view of joinder, requiring Yee to sue on one theory only, it would be unduly rigid to bar a second action on a theory that could not have been joined in the first.

III. Joinder of the Parties to the Original Action

Let's turn now to the issue of initial *joinder of parties*, that is, who can be made proper plaintiffs and defendants in the case. In most cases, the plaintiff decides who the parties to the case will be by suing along with other plaintiffs if she chooses to and by naming one or more defendants in the action. But Rule 20(a) places some limits on the plaintiff's choices.

Rule 20(a)(1) allows plaintiffs to sue together if they assert claims that "aris[e] out of the same transaction, occurrence, or series of transactions or occurrences; and [if their claims involve] any question of law or fact common to all plaintiffs...." Under Rule 20(a)(2), defendants may be sued together if the same two criteria are met.

If Yee brings suit based on her injuries in the ladder accident, the two-part test for joinder in Rule 20(a)(1) allows her to sue with other plaintiffs who seek recovery from the same accident, as long as her claims and those of the other plaintiffs will involve (as they very likely will) some common question of law or fact. She may also sue multiple defendants under Rule 20(a)(2) if her claims against them satisfy the same test. Figure 17–1 illustrates some combinations of parties that Yee could properly join in her action under Rule 20(a):

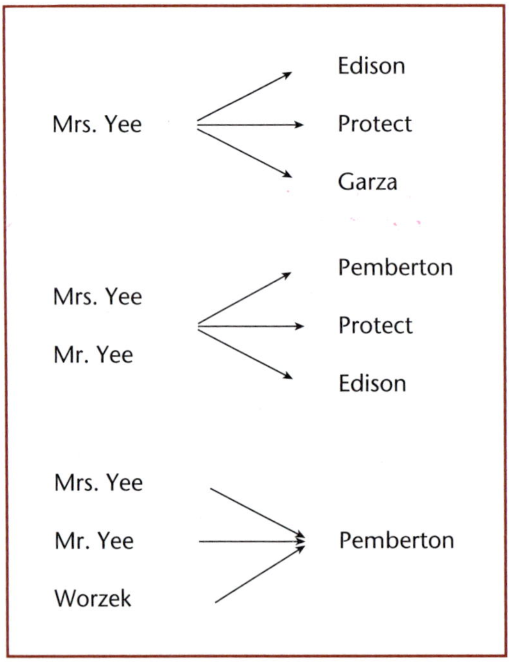

Figure 17–1: JOINDER POSSIBILITIES IN YEE'S CASE

Of course, other plaintiffs will only join in Yee's suit if they want to. Worzek might prefer to sue at a different time or in a different court. If so, he may simply decline to sue with Yee, and bring his own separate suit. But Yee will determine who the defendants will be by naming them as defendants in the suit.

Notes and Questions: Joinder of Parties

1. Applying Rule 20(a). Why would the requirements of Rule 20(a) be met in the second of the three suits illustrated above, by Mr. and Mrs. Yee against Pemberton, Protect, and Edison? b/c of consortium?

Q **2. Why not *require* parties who have claims based on a single transaction or occurrence to sue together?** Rule 20(a)(1) authorizes—but does not require—plaintiffs to sue together if they have claims arising from a single transaction or occurrence and there is a common issue of law or fact. Similarly, Rule 20(a)(2) authorizes but does not require the plaintiff to sue multiple defendants together in the same circumstances. Wouldn't it make sense to *require* plaintiffs to sue all defendants together for claims arising out of a single set of events? What problems would a compulsory joinder-of-parties rule create for plaintiffs?

A Requiring plaintiffs to sue all possible defendants together would increase efficiency, since the underlying events would only be litigated once. But it would often put plaintiffs in a very difficult position. Suppose, for example, that the defendants were not all subject to personal jurisdiction in one state. Or suppose they were all subject to jurisdiction in California, but the plaintiff wanted to sue in Oregon, where some were subject to jurisdiction but others were not. The plaintiff would be forced to sue in California if she had to sue them all together, though she would prefer to sue some defendants in Oregon.

Suppose that some of the defendants were diverse from the plaintiff but others were not. Forcing the plaintiff to sue all defendants together would prevent her from suing in federal court, though she could otherwise sue the diverse defendants alone in federal court. Thus, a compulsory joinder rule would greatly constrict plaintiffs' choices.

Similar problems would arise if plaintiffs were forced to sue together. Plaintiffs might prefer different courts, different lawyers, to sue different defendants, or to sue at different times. To avoid these kinds of complexities, Rule 20(a) allows, as procedural rules generally do, optional joinder of parties in most cases.*

Q **3. Suing alternative defendants in a single action.** Quinn was assaulted by a police officer. Based on his investigation, he concludes that it was either Officer Smith or Officer Radiola who committed the assault. Can he sue them both under Rule 20(a)(2)?

A Yes. Quinn seeks relief from both Smith and Radiola arising from the same assault. His claims also share a common question: Who assaulted him?

---

* The Federal Rules do require joinder of certain parties if a case cannot be fully adjudicated without their participation. *See* Fed. R. Civ. P. 19, discussed in Chapter 18.

Of course, Quinn will not recover from both defendants, since he was assaulted by only one. But he is suing the two of them for the same events, and the logic of the rule—efficiency in litigating the claims and consistency in outcomes—will be served by allowing Quinn to sue them together. And, if he could not sue them together, he might lose entirely, if each jury concluded that the other officer committed the assault.

Q **4. Suing defendants for different types of relief.** Quantum Chemical Company discharges chemicals into a stream over a period of time. Roberts wants to recover for damages to his farmland caused by the chemicals during flooding. Shukla wants to recover for an illness he claims resulted from drinking water polluted by Quantum. O'Leary, another owner, has not suffered any damage, but wants to avoid future damage by getting an injunction to prevent Quantum from continuing to release chemicals into the stream. May the three of them join as coplaintiffs under Rule 20(a)?

A These plaintiffs sue for different remedies but may still join under Rule 20(a)(1). All of these claims arise from the discharge of chemicals by the defendant. Presumably, all will involve some common question of fact or law, such as whether the chemicals came from Quantum's plant or whether the amount of the chemicals in the water exceeded permissible limits. Very likely, there will be some efficiency gained from litigating the issues common to all claims, even though other issues, such as Roberts's crop losses and the source of Shukla's illness, will be unique to each party's individual claims.

READING *HOHLBEIN v. HERITAGE MUTUAL INSURANCE CO.* The *Hohlbein* case below applies the Rule 20(a)(1) standard for joining plaintiffs. Although the issue seems rather dry, the joinder dispute was likely important to the litigants, as procedural issues frequently are. Consider the following questions in reading *Hohlbein*:

- How did the defendant raise the issue of "misjoinder" in *Hohlbein*?
- Why do you think the plaintiffs wanted to join as coplaintiffs, rather than bringing separate actions against the defendant?
- Conversely, why do you think the defendant preferred to defend four cases rather than one?
- The opinion quotes from the briefs of both parties. Note how nicely the briefs argue their side of the same-transaction-or-occurrence issue.

In 2007, the Federal Rules were amended to reflect "plain English" usage. No substantive change was intended. Before the 2007 amendments, there were no separate subsections for claims by multiple plaintiffs or against multiple defendants. So the *Hohlbein* opinion refers to Rule 20(a) but not to subsections (a)(1) and (a)(2), found in the current Rule.

HOHLBEIN v. HERITAGE MUTUAL INSURANCE CO.

106 F.R.D. 73 (E.D. Wis. 1985)

MEMORANDUM AND ORDER

WARREN, District Judge.

BACKGROUND

This action was initiated on January 31, 1985, when the plaintiffs, all individual residents of states other than Wisconsin, filed their complaint against the corporate defendant, which maintains its principal office in Sheboygan, Wisconsin. Invoking the Court's diversity jurisdiction as established under 28 U.S.C. § 1332(a)(1), the plaintiffs aver that the amount in controversy exceeds the sum or value of $10,000.00, exclusive of interest and costs, and is between citizens of different states.

Although the complaint is framed in twelve discrete counts, each of the four individual plaintiffs articulates three, independent causes of action under parallel theories of false or reckless misrepresentation, fraud, and breach of promise. The factual basis common to the claims of all four plaintiffs is that each was purportedly contacted and interviewed by the defendant's representatives in connection with executive employment positions; that the defendant made material misrepresentations of fact and failed to disclose other material information with respect to those executive positions during the course of the respective interviews; and, specifically, that the plaintiffs were not advised that their employment with the corporate defendant would be subject to a probationary period.

At the same time, the particular circumstances under which each of the four plaintiffs was allegedly misled to his damage are unmistakably different. Plaintiff Norbert Hohlbein was purportedly interviewed by the defendant's representatives on various occasions in February of 1982 for the position of Vice President of Sales. Despite its apparent initial decision not to fill that position, the defendant allegedly renewed negotiations with this plaintiff from October through December of 1982, during which it made material misrepresentations of fact with respect to, among other things, the present performance of the duties of the Vice President of Sales; the nature and scope of the authority vested in the individual hired to fill that position; its intention regarding the promotion of that employee to the President's post; and the financial assistance to be provided to the prospective employee to facilitate his relocation to the State of Wisconsin—all representations made knowingly or with reckless disregard for the truth, or so the complaint charges. This plaintiff further claims that the defendant failed to disclose that his employment would be subject to a period of probation during which he could presumably be terminated at will—a failure of disclosure purposely undertaken to induce the plaintiff to accept the job offer....

By his discrete claims in the complaint, plaintiff Winston Howell states that he, too, was interviewed by the defendant for the position of Vice President of Sales, although on various occasions in April of 1981. During the course of those negotiations, the defendant's representatives allegedly made material misrepresentations with respect to both the authority and responsibility attendant upon the sales position and the corporation's expectations for the promotion and future responsibilities of the individual selected to fill that spot. This plaintiff claims that, in reliance on the defendant's representations, he began his employment on or about June 1, 1981, only to terminate some two months later, on or about August 6, 1981, upon discovering that the duties and authority of the sales vice presidency were not as the defendant's representatives had stated. . . .

Plaintiff James R. Beckey alleges that he applied for the position of Regional Claims Manager for the defendant and was interviewed for that job on various occasions in August and September of 1983. The material misrepresentations purportedly made to him during the course of his discussions with the defendant's representatives included certain guarantees with respect to the manager's responsibilities for overall claims administration and a promise that he would be paid temporary living expenses during the period of his relocation to Wisconsin. Like the others, he also charges that he was not notified that the conditions of his employment included an initial, probationary period.

Relying on the defendant's material misrepresentations and omissions, this plaintiff purportedly accepted the employment offer on or about October 3, 1983, and was thereafter advised that he would not be provided with the temporary living and pre-employment interview expenses to the extent previously indicated. He also charges that he was not accorded the duties and responsibilities of the position as described to him during the course of employment negotiations.

Finally, it is the principal allegation of plaintiff Edward White that he, too, was materially misled during interviews with the defendant, in his case, for the position of Training and Educational Specialist, conducted in the month of March of 1982. Among other things, those material misrepresentations allegedly included a promise that he would be responsible for supervising all of the defendant corporation's training activities when it moved to a new home office. Paralleling the charges of his co-plaintiffs, this party avers that his reliance on the defendant's various promises and concomitant failure to disclose the probationary nature of the employment relationship led him to accept the offered position in June of 1982. However, upon his entry of service, he was purportedly not given the position of Training Manager but was instead terminated some three months later, in September of 1982. . . .

Presently before the Court is the motion of the defendant, pursuant to Rule 20(a) and Rule 21 of the Federal Rules of Civil Procedure, to sever this action into four discrete lawsuits, one by each party-plaintiff. In support of its petition, the defendant recites the factual averments upon which the complaint is premised and concludes that none of the four plaintiffs' claims arise "out of the same transaction, occurrence, or series of transactions or occurrences," as prescribed by Rule

20(a). It also suggests, in the language of Rule 20(a) that there is no "question of law or fact common to all of these persons," as follows:

> . . . [N]one of the Plaintiffs were concurrently employed by Defendant. Moreover, with the exception of the Plaintiffs Hohlbein and Howell, both of whom served as Vice President of Sales, the positions held by the Plaintiffs were highly dissimilar. Indeed, it is manifest from Plaintiffs' Complaint that the only common aspect of these four men's lives is that each was employed, albeit briefly, by the Defendant. . . . [T]hat commonality is not sufficient to allow these four individuals to ban [sic] together as plaintiffs in a single action against Defendant. . . . Plaintiffs have not alleged any common transactions or occurrences which touch upon their separate claims. Instead, the only commonalities of Plaintiffs' claims are the legal theories upon which they allege a right to recovery, and the fact that all are proceeding against the same defendant. These commonalities, however, are wholly insufficient to support joinder.

Invoking relevant authority on the circumstances under which joinder and severance are proper under Rule 20(a) and Rule 21, respectively, the movant also suggests that no legitimate interest in the promotion of judicial economy would be served if the action is prosecuted in its present form and, in fact, that the considerable likelihood of jury confusion strongly underscores the impropriety of trying the plaintiffs' discrete claims in one, consolidated proceeding.

Predictably, the plaintiffs take strong exception to the defendant's assertion that there does not exist sufficient commonality to permit consolidation of all of their claims in one action. The plaintiffs direct the Court's attention to these factual similarities between their discrete claims:

> Each of the plaintiffs are insurance executives. Each of the plaintiffs was contacted and interviewed by representatives of Defendant in connection with executive positions with the defendant company. Each of the plaintiffs allege that in connection with their interview and offers of employment representatives of the defendant made material misrepresentations of fact to each plaintiff and failed to disclose material facts to the plaintiffs; more specifically, each of the plaintiffs allege that notwithstanding the representations made by the representatives of defendant, the plaintiffs were not told that their employment with defendant company would be subject to a probationary period during which the defendant would determine whether the plaintiff was indeed the individual the defendant wished to employ.

Admitting to some factual dissimilarities between their discrete causes of action, the plaintiffs nonetheless maintain that the defendant-employer's treatment of each of them constitutes a "course of conduct" and an "on-going policy of material misrepresentations and fraud." In further support of this position, the plaintiffs discuss numerous cases, principally in the area of employment discrimination, in which federal trial courts have ruled that the joinder of claims is appropriate, notwithstanding certain individual peculiarities of the plaintiffs' factual averments. Where, as here, the discrete causes of action all spring from a consistent pattern or practice of employment behavior on the part of a single defendant, the action is properly prosecuted and defended in a consolidated format, or so the plaintiffs conclude.

. . . Although the Court opines that the question is a close one, it concludes, for the reasons set forth below, that the motion to sever the plaintiffs' claims should be denied.

RULE 20(a), RULE 21, AND THE DEFENDANT'S MOTION TO SEVER

As the parties to this action recognize, Rule 20(a) of the Federal Rules of Civil Procedure plainly establishes the right of all persons to "join in one action as plaintiffs if they assert any right to relief jointly, sever[al]ly, or in the alternative in respect of or arising out of the same transaction, occurrence, or series of transactions or occurrences and if any question of law or fact common to all these persons will arise in the action." The unmistakable purpose for the Rule is to promote trial convenience through the avoidance of multiple lawsuits, extra expense to the parties, and loss of time to the Court and the litigants appearing before it. Indeed, it is generally held that Rule 20(a) should be liberally interpreted and applied in practice when consistent with convenience in the disposition of litigation.

. . . At the same time, there are two fundamental prerequisites for joinder under Rule 20(a)—namely, that the right to relief be asserted by each plaintiff relating to or arising out of the same transaction or occurrence or series of transactions or occurrences and that some question of law or fact common to all of the parties arise in the action.

As the present movant accurately notes, the remedy for improper joinder is prescribed by Rule 21 of the Federal Rules of Civil Procedure, plainly establishing that "[a]ny claim against a party may be severed and proceeded with separately." Under this provision of the Rule, the determination of a motion to sever is committed to the broad discretion of the trial judge. In fact, the powers of the trial court to sever unrelated claims and afford them separate treatment when to do so would promote the legitimate interests of some of the parties is well established. The practical effect of severance of previously-joined claims is the creation of two or more separate actions.

Applying these general standards to the circumstances of the present lawsuit, the Court opines that resolution of the parties' various claims would best be promoted if the action is litigated as it is now fashioned. Admittedly, there are several, material dissimilarities between the substantive allegations of the four plaintiffs; most notably, each was employed by the defendant at a different time and—with the exception of plaintiffs Hohlbein and Howell—occupied different positions in its corporate structure. Moreover, each accepted the defendant's employment offer based on discrete application and interview processes; subsequently, each was terminated—either voluntarily or involuntarily—at a different time and for what appears to be a different reason.

Nonetheless, the Court finds persuasive the plaintiffs' characterization of the defendant's actions as demonstrative of a continuing pattern or practice with respect to its employment of admittedly unrelated individuals. All of the developments upon which this consolidated action is premised took place within a two and one-half year period. . . . The particular circumstances under which each of the four plaintiffs interviewed for, began, and ultimately terminated employment with the defendant are, in the Court's view, sufficiently similar to overcome the peculiar temporal and factual dissimilarities that might otherwise justify severance.

Furthermore, each plaintiff alleges that the defendant's representatives failed to disclose the employer's policy requiring any newly-hired executive to complete a probationary period. The Court also notes that all plaintiffs claim to have sustained similar damages, including, in at least three cases, those losses attendant upon relocation to the State of Wisconsin. All of these factors together convince the Court that the present complaint does, indeed, arise out of the same series of transactions or occurrences and implicates questions of law or fact common to each of the named plaintiffs. The Court finds some precedential support for this conclusion in the authority advanced by the plaintiffs in opposition to the pending severance request. *See, e.g., King v. Ralston Purina Company*, 97 F.R.D 477, 480–81 (W.D.N.C. 1983) (finding that, although the three plaintiffs worked in different places and in different divisions of the defendant company, their actions against that employer could be joined together in a single action where they each alleged a company-wide policy of age discrimination).

Finally, the Court feels strongly that any burden imposed upon the defendant in the consolidated trial of each of the plaintiffs' causes of action is far outweighed by the practical benefits likely to accrue to all players in the conservation of judicial, prosecutorial, and defensive resources. Likewise, the Court is unable to conclude, at this stage in the proceedings, that the specter of jury confusion is sufficiently ominous to justify wholesale severance of this matter into four, discrete lawsuits. As the case proceeds toward trial, the Court may find it appropriate to enter such pretrial orders as necessary to ensure that the several claims of the plaintiffs are presented to the jury in the clearest and most even-handed manner possible; to the extent that the Court shares with the parties this interest in developing an unobscure and transparent trial record, it will surely enlist the assistance of counsel in identifying the litigable issues and sharpening the presentations of their respective positions.

For the present, however, the Court simply cannot conclude that the interests of justice would be disserved if the action is permitted to proceed in its consolidated form. Rather, for the reasons stated above, the Court finds that severance of this matter into four, separate causes of action would, in the end, prove both unjustified and unwise. Accordingly, it will deny the defendant's motion for severance. . . .

Notes and Questions: *Hohlbein*

Q **1. Plaintiffs' tactical reasons for joining claims.** The defendant in *Hohlbein* filed a grim-sounding "motion to sever" the plaintiffs' claims into four separate cases. If the court granted the motion, it would break the case into four different lawsuits that would proceed independently. Why would the plaintiffs' counsel prefer a joint trial of the four plaintiffs' claims and why might defendant's counsel prefer to sever the claims into four separate suits?

A Plaintiffs would likely prefer the efficiency of one trial rather than four. In addition, plaintiffs' counsel may have concluded that trying these claims together would give the jury the impression that Heritage had a deliberate policy of misleading new employees. If the four claims were tried separately, evidence of the treatment of the other employees would probably not be admissible. If they are tried together, the jury will hear about repeated instances of this dubious conduct, which may bolster each plaintiff's case.

Defendant's counsel would likely prefer to take the cases one at a time, put each plaintiff to the expense of trial, and avoid the impact of repeated adverse testimony about Heritage's hiring practices.

Q **2. The efficiency rationale for joint litigation of claims.** One of the rationales for broad joinder under Rule 20(a) is that the claims can be processed more efficiently, both in the pretrial phase and at trial. Can you think of some ways in which litigating all four plaintiffs' claims together will lead to "conservation of judicial, prosecutorial and defensive resources" (*Hohlbein*, 106 F.R.D., at 79) during the pretrial phase of the *Hohlbein* case?

A If the cases are litigated together and handled by one attorney for the plaintiffs, the pleading and discovery phase of the case will be simpler. Only one complaint will be filed for the four claims. The defendant will be served with process once rather than four times, and will file one answer rather than four. Interrogatories will likely be sent jointly on behalf of all plaintiffs. Joint requests for production of documents to the defendant will likely be sent on behalf of all four plaintiffs. Depositions of parties and witnesses will happen once rather than four times. Motions common to all claims will be briefed and argued once, saving time for the parties and the court. In these and many other practical ways, much time and expense will be saved by litigating the claims jointly.

Hohlbein reflects a flexible approach to joinder of parties where litigation efficiency may be gained by processing claims together. As the court notes, joinder creates efficiency. And what harm is really done if loosely related claims are allowed to be joined? Even if trying the claims together might raise problems of jury confusion, the claims will probably *not* be tried, since well over 90 percent of cases are resolved without going to trial. If the claims are all litigated together, they will likely all settle together as well. Judge Warren's opinion reflects this "let's start with them together and see how it goes" approach to joint litigation of loosely related claims.

3. Severance and separate trial. As *Hohlbein* explains, Rule 21 empowers the court to sever claims that are improperly joined into separate cases. If claims are severed, they will proceed independently, just as though they had been filed as separate lawsuits. Suppose, however, that the court allows joinder of the claims in *Hohlbein* but later decides that the claims should be tried separately due to differences in the legal issues or evidence. If so, the court may order that the claims be tried in separate trials. Fed. R. Civ. P. 42(b). Even if it orders separate trials, efficiency is gained by litigating the claims together up until trial.

Q **4. The meaning of "transaction or occurrence."** Rule 20(a)'s "same transaction, occurrence, or series of transactions or occurrences" test is intended to allow litigation of related claims together where the overlap in the evidence on those claims will promote convenience and efficiency. Consider whether the same-transaction-or-occurrence test is satisfied in these cases.

A. *Hanes Dye & Finishing Co. v. Caisson Corp.*, 309 F. Supp. 237 (M.D.N.C. 1970). The plaintiff hired Blum, a general contractor, to construct a building. Blum subcontracted the pouring of concrete support pillars to Caisson. Seaboard Surety issued a surety bond for the proper performance of Caisson's work. Pittsburgh Testing tested the pillars for strength as they were poured.

The pillars failed, and Blum and Hands Dye & Finishing sued Caisson, Seaboard, and Pittsburgh for damages arising from the failure of the pillars.

A This case clearly satisfies the Rule 20(a) test. All of the claims arise from the construction of the pillars and involve the central question of why they failed. Frequently, plaintiffs will have claims against several defendants arising from a single accident, construction job, surgical procedure, or other event.

B. *Demboski v. CSX Transportation Inc.*, 157 F.R.D. 28 (S.D. Miss. 1994). Four individuals were injured in railroad crossing accidents involving the defendant's trains, at different times and in different cities. They joined as coplaintiffs to sue CSX.

A The court held that joinder was improper under Rule 20(a), because the claims involved four unrelated occurrences. The claims arose from accidents at different times in different parts of the state. The only relation among them was that they all arose from the defendant's railroading activity. If they were tried together, there would be little or no efficiency, because the evidence would not overlap, and it would be confusing to litigate the unrelated events together.

C. *Mosley v. General Motors Corporation*, 497 F.2d 1330 (8th Cir. 1974). Ten plaintiffs, all employed by General Motors but at two different divisions and factories, joined as plaintiffs alleging that the corporation discriminated against them on the basis of race and sex. The claimants alleged different acts of discrimination, such as failure to hire, failure to promote, retaliation for asserting their rights, and denial of break time.

A In *Mosley*, a much-cited decision, the court held that these plaintiffs could join under Rule 20(a), since they had alleged that they were "injured by the same general policy of discrimination on the part of General Motors and the Union." *Id.* at 1333.

Mosley offers an extremely expansive reading of the same-transaction-or-occurrence requirement. While there would be some overlap in the proof of the various plaintiffs' claims, a great deal of the evidence would be different for employees in different factories or claiming different types of discriminatory acts. Here the common-transaction-or-occurrence test is only met at the most general level: "GM discriminated in its employment policies based on race [or sex]." The *Hohlbein* court's conclusion that the same-transaction-or-occurrence test was met is less expansive: In *Hohlbein,* all plaintiffs alleged the same fraudulent misrepresentations and alleged that those representations induced them to accept employment with the defendant.

5. The "common question of law or fact" requirement. Rule 20(a) also requires a question of law or fact common to the claims. Where the same-transaction-or-occurrence test is met, it will be rare to find that there is no common question. In *Hohlbein,* the court suggests that the plaintiffs' "similar damages" meet this requirement, but that is doubtful. They each made different arrangements, came from different places, and left different positions to accept employment with Heritage. On the other hand, whether the company had a policy of fraudulently representing their status to new employees would likely qualify as a common question of fact.

Q **6. An important caveat: The right to join parties under the Rules does not confer subject matter or personal jurisdiction!** It is important to separate the concept of permission to join claims under the civil procedure rules from the concept of the court's jurisdiction to hear the claims. Consider whether the federal court can hear the cases below.

A. Vonn, from Oregon, sues Montega, from California and Calisher, from Oregon, for injuries suffered in an auto accident in Oregon. She brings the suit in the Federal District Court for the Eastern District of Oregon (the district in which the accident happened), seeking $200,000 in damages. Is joinder proper under Rule 20(a)(2)? May the court hear the case?

A Joinder is proper because Vonn is suing the defendants for the same occurrence, the accident, and there will be common questions of fact as to the cause of the accident and the damages suffered by Vonn. However, the court lacks subject matter jurisdiction over the case, since there is no federal claim asserted and the parties are not completely diverse. Even though Rule 20(a)(2) allows Vonn to join the two as codefendants, the court cannot hear the case.

B. Vonn, from Oregon, sues Montega, from California, and Trasker, from Idaho, seeking $200,000 in damages for injuries Vonn suffered in an accident in Oregon. She brings the action in a federal court in California. Is joinder proper under Rule 20(a)(2)? May the court hear the case?

Here, joinder is proper under Rule 20(a)(2), but the court lacks personal jurisdiction over Trasker for this claim, which arises from an Oregon accident. Trasker will be dismissed from the action.

To avoid problems like these, read the joinder rules as though they include the following parenthetical: "Assuming that the court has subject matter jurisdiction over the case and personal jurisdiction over the defendants, the parties may join...."

7. Rules in tandem: The confluence of Rules 20(a) and 18(a). Once a party has properly asserted a claim against a defendant, Rule 18(a) allows her to assert any other claims she has against the opposing party. Thus, if Yee and her neighbor Worzek sue Protect for damages arising out of the fire incident, either plaintiff could add additional unrelated claims against Protect as well. For example, Worzek could assert an unrelated claim for an auto accident with a Protect employee. Worzek could not join with Yee to sue on this claim alone, because their claims would not meet the Rule 20(a) test. However, once they join to sue on claims that do meet the test, Rule 18(a) allows either to add unrelated claims against Protect.

IV. Counterclaims Under the Federal Rules

Rules 18(a) and 20(a) of the Federal Rules define the plaintiff's choices in joining claims and parties in her initial complaint. Now we turn to several Rules that address joinder of claims and parties after the initial complaint. A counterclaim is a claim for relief by a defending party against the party who is claiming relief from her. Fed. R. Civ. P. 13. For example, if Yee sues Protect for her injuries in the ladder accident, Protect might assert a counterclaim against Yee for the amount due under its painting contract, in the same action.

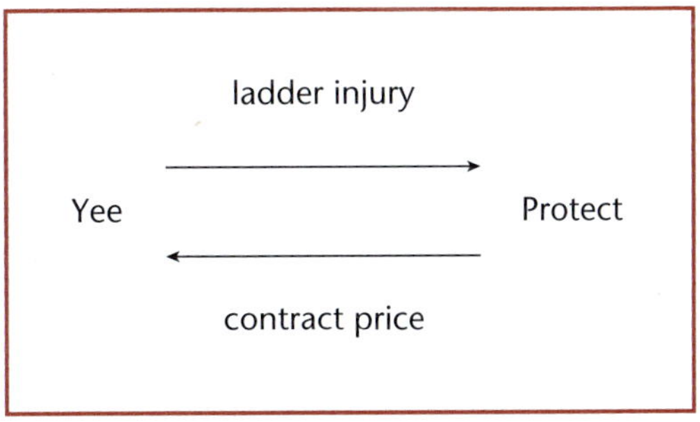

Figure 17–2: COUNTERCLAIM

For federal courts, Rule 13(a)(1)(A) provides that a counterclaim is compulsory (i.e., it must be asserted in the same action) if it "arises out of the transaction or occurrence that is the subject matter of the opposing party's claim." Protect's claim for the contract price for painting the house would probably be a Rule 13(a) compulsory counterclaim, because it arises from the same basic set of events—performance of the painting contract—as Yee's accident claim. Similarly, if Juno has an accident with Slovinsky and sues for her injuries, any claim Slovinsky has against Juno arising from the same accident would be a compulsory counterclaim.

Many states have rules identical or quite similar to Rule 13(a)(1)(A).

READING *KING v. BLANTON*. This case arose in North Carolina, which has a compulsory counterclaim rule almost identical to Federal Rule 13(a)(1). The parties had a motor vehicle accident, and one driver, Blanton, sued the other, King, for her injuries. Later, King sued Blanton for *her* injuries in the accident. Blanton argued that the second action was barred because the claim should have been asserted as a counterclaim in the first case.

- Why should King's second action on her claim for damages be barred? Does North Carolina's counterclaim rule say that it is?
- Who defended King in the first action? Does this suggest a reason why King's claim may have been omitted from the first case?
- What is the rationale for requiring claims like King's to be asserted in the initial action?

KING v. BLANTON

735 S.E.2d 451 (N.C. App. 2012)

McGee, Judge.

Sheila Denice Blanton (Blanton) filed a complaint on 14 July 2010 alleging that Ethel Myers King (King) ran a red light and struck Blanton's vehicle, damaging Blanton's vehicle and injuring Blanton. Blanton alleged that King was negligent, and that King's negligence "was the sole, direct and proximate cause of the accident, injuries and damages suffered by [Blanton] and her motor vehicle[.]"

King's insurance company, InsTrust Insurance Company (InsTrust), provided an attorney to defend King in the suit filed by Blanton. In May 2011, the parties reached an agreement, whereby Blanton agreed to voluntarily dismiss her claims with prejudice in exchange for a cash settlement. Blanton's action was voluntarily dismissed with prejudice on 3 May 2011. The record does not include any answer filed in response to Blanton's 14 July 2010 complaint, but Blanton and King agree that King did not file any counterclaim in response to Blanton's complaint.

King filed the present action on 30 June 2011. In her complaint, King alleged that it was Blanton who ran a red light and caused the 23 April 2010 collision, and that Blanton's negligence was the sole proximate cause of injury to King. Blanton filed an answer and motions to dismiss on 3 August 2011. Blanton alleged that King's action should have been filed as a compulsory counterclaim to Blanton's 14 July 2010 action and, therefore, King had lost her right to bring her negligence claim by failing to include it as a counterclaim to Blanton's 14 July 2010 action. The trial court heard Blanton's motions to dismiss on 19 September 2011. Because the trial court considered documents outside the pleadings, the trial court treated Blanton's motions to dismiss as motions for summary judgment, granted summary judgment in favor of Blanton, and dismissed King's action with prejudice. King appeals.

I.

The sole issue on appeal is whether the trial court erred in granting summary judgment in favor of Blanton. . . .

King argues that the trial court erred by granting summary judgment in favor of Blanton because King had not had the opportunity to prosecute her claim against Blanton. Blanton argued to the trial court, and argues on appeal, that King's action against Blanton was a compulsory counterclaim to Blanton's 14 July 2010 action and, because King failed to file this compulsory counterclaim, King is estopped from filing this claim now as a separate action.

N.C. Gen. Stat. § 1A-1, Rule 13(a) (2011) governs compulsory counterclaims, and states:

> Compulsory counterclaims.—A pleading shall state as a counterclaim any claim which at the time of serving the pleading the pleader has against any opposing party, if it arises out of the transaction or occurrence that is the subject matter of the opposing party's claim and does not require for its adjudication the presence of third parties of whom the court cannot acquire jurisdiction.

N.C.G.S. § 1A-1, Rule 13(a) (2011). . . . Our Court has explained Rule 13(a) as follows:

> "The purpose of Rule 13(a), making certain counterclaims compulsory, is to enable one court to resolve 'all related claims in one action, thereby avoiding a wasteful multiplicity of litigation.'" Determining whether a particular claim "arises out of the same transaction or occurrence" requires consideration of "(1) whether the issues of fact and law are largely the same; (2) whether substantially the same evidence is involved in each action; and (3) whether there is a logical relationship between the two actions." In addition, there must be "a logical relationship in the nature of the actions and the remedies sought."

Kemp v. Spivey, 602 S.E.2d 686, 688 (2004) (citations omitted). We hold that King's claim "arises out of the same transaction or occurrence[.]" *Id.* The same collision is at the heart of both actions; the only dispute is where the fault for the collision lay. King's claim was, therefore, a compulsory counterclaim to Blanton's 14 July 2010 action. The only remaining question is whether Rule 13(a) required dismissal of King's claim.

In *Kemp,* this Court addressed a similar situation. *Kemp* involved an automobile accident where one of the parties who had failed to file a compulsory counterclaim attempted to institute an action after the initial matter had been resolved by a settlement. This Court acknowledged that different considerations might come into play when an action is settled than when an action is determined on the merits. This Court looked to the following two federal opinions for guidance. In *Dindo v. Whitney,* the First Circuit reasoned:

> The bar arising out of Rule 13(a) has been characterized variously. Some courts have said that a judgment is res judicata of whatever could have been pleaded in a compulsory counterclaim. Other courts have viewed the rule not in terms of res judicata, but as creating an estoppel or waiver. The latter approach seems more appropriate, at least when the case is settled rather than tried. The purposes of the rule are "to prevent multiplicity of actions and to achieve resolution in a single lawsuit of all disputes arising out of common matters." If a case has been tried, protection both of the court and of the parties dictates that there should be no further directly related litigation. But if the case is settled, normally the court has not been greatly burdened, and the parties can protect themselves by demanding cross-releases. In such circumstances, absent a release, better-tailored justice seems obtainable by applying principles of equitable estoppel.
>
> If [the current plaintiff], clearly having opportunity to assert it, ... knew of the existence of a right to counterclaim, the fact that there was no final judgment on the merits should be immaterial, and a Rule 13(a) bar would be appropriate. His conscious inaction ... created the very additional litigation the rule was designed to prevent[.]

Dindo v. Whitney, 451 F.2d 1, 3 (1st Cir. 1971) (citations omitted). This Court then cited *LaFollette v. Herron,* 211 F. Supp. 919, 920–21 (E.D. Tenn. 1962), for the proposition that we should examine the actions of the party filing the subsequent action in determining whether Rule 13(a) should bar that subsequent action. The dispositive question in *LaFollette* seemed to be whether the settlement of the original action occurred in a manner which deprived the relevant party of a reasonable opportunity to file the compulsory counterclaim. *Id.*

This Court, in *Kemp,* adopted the waiver/estoppel approach for situations where the original action had been settled by the parties. We then determined that the plaintiff in *Kemp* had been aware of the relevant events and circumstances surrounding the claims, had an opportunity to present her counterclaim prior to settlement, and was represented by attorneys. *Kemp,* 602 S.E.2d at 689. This Court, in *Kemp,* suggested that this could be enough to find that the plaintiff was estopped from prosecuting the action because she had not filed it as a compulsory counterclaim.

However, this Court remanded because the trial court had dismissed the matter pursuant to a 12(b)(6) motion and, therefore, had not afforded the parties "full opportunity to present evidence on the issue of estoppel." *Id.* The trial court in *Kemp* had considered evidence outside the pleadings, so the motion to dismiss had been converted into a motion for summary judgment. However, because of this conversion, "the parties were not afforded a 'reasonable opportunity to present all material made pertinent to such a motion by Rule 56.' N.C.G.S. § 1A-1, Rule 12(b)." *Id.* at 602 S.E.2d at 690. The matter was remanded for a hearing. *Id.*

Unlike in *Kemp,* the trial court in this matter recognized that the motion to dismiss pursuant to N.C.G.S. § 1 A-1, Rule 12(b)(6) had been converted into a motion for summary judgment. The trial court held a hearing, and the attorneys for the parties argued the *Kemp* opinion and estoppel. King had her opportunity to present all pertinent material on estoppel.

King and Blanton were the two drivers involved in the 23 April 2010 collision. Blanton initiated a negligence action against King on 14 July 2010. King's insurance company, InsTrust, provided King with an attorney for her defense. When an attorney is hired by an insurer to defend an insured, "the attorney's primary allegiance must remain with the insured," even though the attorney may be representing the insurer as well. *Nationwide Mut. Fire Ins. Co. v. Bourlon,* 617 S.E.2d 40, 45 (2005) (citation omitted).

King had more than nine months between the time Blanton filed the 14 July 2010 action and the time of the settlement and voluntary dismissal of that action on 3 May 2011. King makes no argument, and the record includes nothing indicating that King was unaware of her right to file a counterclaim, or that she was not advised that she would forfeit her right to file a claim if she did not file the compulsory counterclaim. We hold that, on these facts, King's failure to file her compulsory counterclaim constituted a waiver and estops her from bringing a new action for negligence based upon the same events that were at the heart of Blanton's 14 July 2010 action. King's argument is without merit.

Affirmed.

Judges Bryant and Thigpen concur.

Notes and Questions on Counterclaims

1. What is a counterclaim? It is easy to confuse a counterclaim with defenses that a party might raise to avoid liability. If Blanton sues King, alleging that King was negligent, King might respond, "No, I wasn't negligent, so I'm not liable to you." This would simply be a denial that Blanton can prove her claim. Or King might plead, "Even if I was negligent, you were too, and under negligence law in this state a negligent plaintiff cannot recover damages." This would raise an affirmative defense, asserting additional facts that avoid liability even if Blanton proves her basic negligence claim. Or King might plead, "No, I wasn't negligent; it was your negligence that caused the accident and it caused injuries to *me* so I want damages from you." This, unlike the first two responses, is a counterclaim, because here King is asserting her own claim for relief back against Blanton—she wants the court to order King to pay damages to her.

2. The rationale for making some counterclaims compulsory. Requiring a defending party to assert counterclaims that arise from the same events as the opposing party's claim promotes efficiency and consistency of judgments. If, when Blanton sues King, the issues arising from the accident are going to be litigated, it makes sense to litigate them only once, rather than doing it again if King brings a second action against Blanton arising out of the same events. Litigating the issues once will obviously be more efficient and it will avoid the possibility that two juries, considering issues like whose negligence caused the accident, might reach opposite conclusions, a result that doesn't reflect well on the judicial system. So the rule sensibly requires the defending party to assert her claim in the original action.

Q **3. What happens if a defending party fails to assert a compulsory counterclaim?** In *King*, the defending party left out a counterclaim later held to be compulsory. What was the consequence of her failure to assert the claim?

A The counterclaim rule required King to assert her counterclaim, which clearly satisfied the transaction-or-occurrence test. But it doesn't explicitly say that it is lost if she fails to do so. When King later sues for her own damages, the court holds that she waived the claim by failing to include it as a counterclaim in the prior action. It is lost; King cannot recover on it. It is this waiver doctrine that puts teeth in the compulsory counterclaim rule.

4. Why did King leave the counterclaim out? We don't know why King failed to assert the counterclaim in the original action. There is little doubt that it was a compulsory counterclaim, since it arose from the same accident. She should have pleaded it. But it may be relevant that King did not hire her own attorney to defend Blanton's case—her insurer hired a lawyer to represent King. Liability insurance contracts generally require the insurer to provide a defense for the insured, so the insurer will choose the lawyer to defend its insured. Still, as the court notes, the lawyer represents King, not the insurer, and should assert King's counterclaim if there is a basis for doing so. The realities of settlement practice may explain why it didn't happen. Perhaps King assumed that her lawyer was there to fend off liability to Blanton, not to assert affirmative claims on King's behalf, and therefore failed to ask King about a possible counterclaim. In addition, the settlement of Blanton's claim came relatively early in the case, before an answer was filed, and perhaps with little development of the facts. Thus, counsel may have had little information about injuries to King that would support a counterclaim. The court concludes, however, that counsel had ample opportunity to plead the counterclaim, and therefore that counsel's failure to do so waived the claim.

Partly because insurers commonly provide the defense in most tort cases, some states do not make tort claims compulsory counterclaims. *See, e.g.*, Minn. R. 13.01, which makes a counterclaim compulsory if it "arises out of the transaction that is the subject of the opposing party's claim," but not if it arose out of the same "occurrence." This language was intended to avoid making tort counterclaims compulsory (as they are under the "transaction or occurrence" language of Federal Rule 13(a)(1)). *Leiendecker v. Asian Women United of Minnesota*, 731 N.W.2d 836, 840 (Minn. App. 2007).

5. Another important consequence of the compulsory/permissive distinction: Supplemental jurisdiction. Suppose that Perkins sues Johnston in federal court for breach of contract, seeking $200,000. If Perkins and Johnston are from different states, the federal court will have diversity jurisdiction over Perkins's claim. But suppose that Johnston asserts a counterclaim arising from the same facts for $40,000? That claim could not be brought in federal court as an original claim since it does not meet the amount-in-controversy requirement in 28 U.S.C. §1332(a). So, Rule 13(a)(1) requires it to be brought (because it is a compulsory counterclaim, arising from the same facts as the main claim), but the court does not have original jurisdiction over it.

Congress addressed this problem in 28 U.S.C. § 1367, the "supplemental jurisdiction" statute. (We analyze supplemental jurisdiction in detail in Chapter 20.) Section 1367(a) provides that if a federal court has subject matter jurisdiction over a case, it may also hear other claims in the action that arise out of the same nucleus of facts. A compulsory counterclaim will meet this test. Permissive counterclaims, however, are not related to the main claim and usually must have their own basis for subject matter jurisdiction.

6. Same transaction or occurrence: Some purported tests. The Federal Rules do not define "transaction or occurrence," even though the test is used in Rule 20(a), Rule 13(a), and Rule 13(g) (dealing with crossclaims). The concept of a single transaction or occurrence is often obvious but very hard to define at the margins—where a clear definition is needed most. As the *King* court notes, four tests are often invoked for determining whether claims arise from the same transaction or occurrence:

(a) Are the issues of fact and law raised in the claim and the counterclaim largely the same?
(b) Would res judicata bar a subsequent suit on the party's counterclaim, absent the compulsory counterclaim rule?
(c) Will substantially the same evidence support or refute the claim as well as the counterclaim?
(d) Is there a logical relationship between the claim and the counterclaim?

Unfortunately, these tests do not answer the question in any mechanical way; they are merely suggestive. Consider proposed test (c)—whether the evidence used to establish the claims is "substantially the same." In *Mosley*, for example (the case described at p. 615)—which involved a company-wide policy of racial discrimination—a great deal of evidence would be unique to each plaintiff's case, such as the particular discriminatory acts each experienced, and the damages that resulted. Yet the court there approved joinder under the same-transaction-or-occurrence test.

The "logical relationship" test is the broadest test. It allows joinder of claims when some factual relationship between them will make it efficient to hear the claims together. Yet courts sometimes deny joinder when the logical relation test appears to be met. For example, in *Pena v. McArthur*, 889 F. Supp. 403 (E.D. Cal. 1994), Pena sued McArthur for injuries in an accident and also sued the insurer, which she claimed had fraudulently induced her to settle her claim arising from the accident for a pittance. The court denied joinder under Rule 20(a), although intuitively there appears to be logical relationship between the claims.

> In this case, there were two occurrences or transactions—the automobile accident between plaintiff and McArthur and the alleged breach of fiduciary duty by State Farm in handling plaintiff's claims. There are two distinct torts (negligence and bad faith claim) committed by different defendants at different times, and they resulted in the invasion of separate legal interests.

889 F. Supp. at 406. Compare *Lucas v. City of Juneau*, 127 F. Supp. 730 (D.C. Alaska 1955), in which the plaintiff suffered a back injury in a Sears Roebuck store. He was hospitalized for eighteen days and then taken by ambulance to the airport, to be transferred to another hospital. En route, the driver had an epileptic fit, the ambulance crashed, and Lucas's injury was aggravated. He sued Sears and the City, which ran the ambulance service. The court held that the two claims could be joined under Rule 20(a), since Sears could be liable for the aggravation of the injury caused by the later accident as well as for the initial injury. Thus, the proof about that would be relevant to both claims.

There is no magic formula for applying the transaction-or-occurrence test or for reconciling the results in all cases. Fundamentally, the rule makers had in mind a set of related historical facts that make a logical grouping for efficient litigation. The more overlap there is in the legal and factual issues, the more likely the court is to allow joinder. The test focuses on the *underlying events giving rise to the litigation*, not on the party's legal theory or the type of relief she seeks. A counterclaim can be compulsory even though it is based on a different legal theory than the plaintiff's claim or is based on state law while the original claim invokes federal law.

7. Exceptions to the compulsory counterclaim rule. Both North Carolina's counterclaim rule and Federal Rule 13(a)(1) provide that a counterclaim that would otherwise be compulsory need not be asserted if it is the subject of another pending action or if jurisdiction over the main claim is based on attachment rather than on full personal jurisdiction over the defendant. In addition, counterclaims that arise after the defendant files an answer need not be asserted under either rule, because the defendant did not have the claim "at the time of service" (Rule 13(a)(1)) of the answer.

Rule 13 (both the federal and North Carolina versions) states that "a pleading" shall state compulsory counterclaims. At least in theory, if King defaulted in Blanton's suit or settled it without filing a pleading (her answer), King would not have violated the compulsory counterclaim rule. Some cases have allowed a later action on the counterclaim in this situation. *Wright & Miller* § 1417. Careful counsel may be able to avoid this risk by obtaining a stipulation or a court order in the first case that the judgment will not bar a separate action on the counterclaim.

8. Permissive counterclaims. If a counterclaim is not compulsory, it may still be brought as a permissive counterclaim. Fed R. Civ. P. 13(b). If Protect has a claim against Yee for the contract price for painting his summer home at another time, Protect could assert a counterclaim to collect on that contract in Yee's personal injury action. But omitting it from the other suit would not waive this unrelated claim; Protect would be free to bring it in a separate action.

A defendant's option to join unrelated counterclaims under Rule 13(b) mirrors a plaintiff's right under Rule 18(a) to assert unrelated claims together. Presumably, the rule makers authorized permissive counterclaims so parties can achieve "global peace" by settling all their differences in a single action. Permissive counterclaims may be litigated jointly up until trial, but will likely be separated for trial under Rule 42(b). Trying the unrelated claims together would not save time, since the evidence and issues are different, and sorting out the legal rules applicable to the different claims would be likely to confuse the jury.

9. State rules modeled on the Federal Rules. Well over half of the states have adopted procedural rules for their trial courts that are closely modeled on the Federal Rules. Usually, the state rules are adopted as a procedural code by the state's highest court rather than enacted as statutes. In North Carolina, however, the "rules," though referred to as the "Rules of Civil Procedure," are actually statutes that were adopted by the legislature in 1967. N.C. Laws, 1967, c. 954. They were the product of a twelve-year effort, spearheaded by the North Carolina Bar Association, to modernize North Carolina procedure by adopting rules modeled on the Federal Rules. *See* J. Sizemore, *General Scope and Philosophy of the New Rules*, 5 Wake Forest Intramural L. Rev. 1, 3–4 (1969).

10. More than one way to skin a cat: States without compulsory counterclaim rules. Not all states have compulsory counterclaim rules. *See, e.g.*, N.Y. C.P.L.R. 3019; *see also* Md. Rule 2-302, which provides that "[t]here may be a counterclaim. . . ." These states give priority to the defendant's autonomy in choosing when and where to assert her claim, rather than to forcing efficiency on the parties by requiring the defendant to assert the counterclaim in the original action.

V. Crossclaims Against Coparties

Under Rule 20(a), a suit may involve more than one—indeed, many more than one—plaintiff and defendant. In such cases, plaintiffs or defendants may choose to assert claims against each other. Such crossclaims against "coparties" are authorized by Rule 13(g):

> A pleading may state as a crossclaim any claim by one party against a coparty if the claim arises out of the transaction or occurrence that is the subject matter of the original action or of a counterclaim, or if the claim relates to any property that is the subject matter of the original action. . . .

Crossclaims are different from counterclaims. A counterclaim is a claim against an *opposing party*, for example, a claim by a defendant against a plaintiff. A crossclaim is a claim against a *coparty*, someone on the same side of the "v." For example, if Yee sues Protect for her injury claim, and Protect asserts a claim back against Yee to collect the balance on the painting contract, that's a counterclaim. If Yee sues Protect and Garza, the employee who caused the accident, and Protect asserts a claim against Garza for indemnification on Yee's claim, that would be a crossclaim—a claim by one party against a coparty.

Rule 13(g) establishes a familiar test for crossclaims: They must "arise[] out of the transaction or occurrence that is the subject matter of the original action or of a counterclaim." Here again, the Rules encourage joinder of claims arising from a common core of historical facts, since they will involve overlap in evidence, witnesses, and issues. Unlike Rule 13(a) and (b), however, which allow a defendant to assert *either* related or unrelated counterclaims against a plaintiff, Rule 13(g) limits crossclaims to those that arise out of a transaction or occurrence that is the subject matter of the main claim.

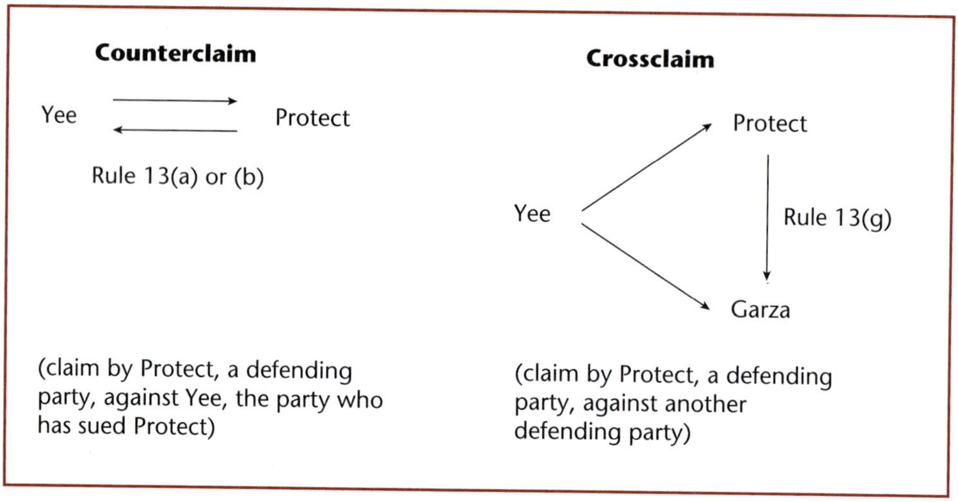

Figure 17–3: COUNTERCLAIMS AND CROSSCLAIMS

Notes and Questions: Crossclaims

Q **1. Crossclaim limits.** Yee sues Protect, Pemberton, and Garza for her injuries. May Garza assert a crossclaim against Protect for wages due on three other paint jobs completed the month before?

A No. The Rule only allows crossclaims that arise out of the events that give rise to the main claim. While Garza and Protect are codefendants, the claim for wages on other jobs does not satisfy that test, since it arises out of unrelated events.

Q **2. A contrasting case.** Yee sues Protect, Pemberton, and Garza as codefendants. Pemberton was also injured in the accident. If Pemberton believes that Garza's negligence caused the accident, may he assert a crossclaim against Garza for his own injuries?

A Yes. Pemberton's claim for his own injuries arises out of the accident that is the subject of the main claim and is against a codefendant, so it is a proper crossclaim under Rule 13(g).

Q **3. Is it may or must?** On the facts of question 2, *must* Pemberton assert his claim against Garza in Yee's suit?

A Because Rule 13(g) is permissive ("a pleading may state as a crossclaim . . .") Pemberton may choose to sue on this claim separately without fear of waiving the claim.

Q **4. Why not a compulsory crossclaim rule?** Rule 13(a) makes certain counterclaims compulsory, but Rule 13(g) does not compel assertion of crossclaims. Why not change "may" in Rule 13(g) to "must," so that parties would be required to assert related crossclaims against coparties?

A

There is much to be said for a compulsory crossclaim rule. If Yee sues Protect, Pemberton, and Garza together for her injuries, the issue of whose negligence caused the accident will be relevant to her claims, but also to any claims Protect might assert against Garza for indemnification. It would also be relevant if Pemberton were injured in the accident and had a claim against Garza for his injuries. These parties are already before the court litigating the same accident; why not resolve those claims together, instead of allowing Pemberton or Protect to multiply litigation by bringing a separate action against Garza?

Most of the problems that would arise from forcing plaintiffs to join claims don't arise with crossclaims, because the parties are already in the suit and personal and subject matter jurisdiction are not problematic. And we *do* force defendants to assert claims against plaintiffs if they arise from the same underlying facts. Fed. R. Civ. P. 13(a)(1).

While a mandatory crossclaim rule would make sense, the common law has traditionally allowed each party to choose when and where to assert claims. Here, the rule makers gave priority to litigant choice rather than forcing efficiency by making crossclaims compulsory.

Q

5. Additional parties to a crossclaim. Suppose that Yee sues Protect, Pemberton, and Garza for her injuries. Pemberton asserts a crossclaim against Garza for his own injuries in the accident and also alleges that Lopez, a passerby, had contributed to the accident by bumping into Garza while he was carrying the ladder. Can Pemberton make Lopez a party to his crossclaim?

A

Rule 13(h) authorizes the addition of new parties to a counterclaim or crossclaim if the claim against the added party satisfies the standard for joinder in Rule 19 or Rule 20. Thus, Pemberton may make Lopez an additional defendant on the crossclaim against Garza as long as the claim against Lopez arises from the same transaction or occurrence as the claim against Garza, and will share a common question of law or fact (i.e., the standard for joinder under Rule 20). The case now looks like this:

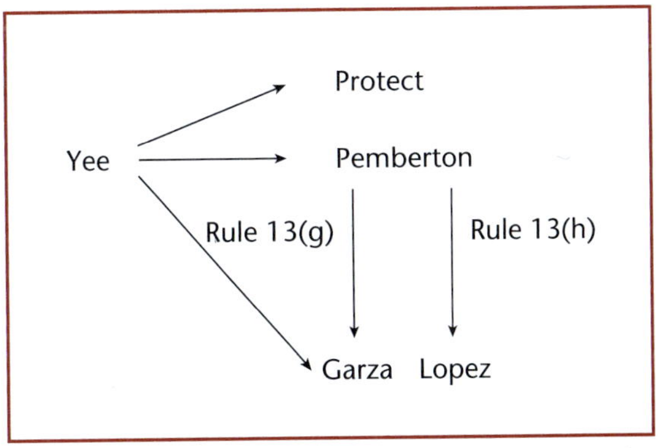

Figure 17–4: ADDING A PARTY TO A CROSSCLAIM

After Pemberton asserts the crossclaim, Lopez becomes a party to that claim. However, he is not a defendant on the main claim, nor is he an opposing party to Protect.

Q **6. Additional parties without a crossclaim?** Rule 13(h) allows a defending party to bring a stranger into the lawsuit—someone whom the plaintiff did not choose to sue. Could he do it without asserting a crossclaim against an *existing party?* For example, could Pemberton assert his claim for his injuries against Lopez without asserting a crossclaim against Garza?

A In some situations he could, but not under Rule 13(h). If he brought Lopez into the action without adding him to a crossclaim or counterclaim, he would have to do so by "impleading" Lopez under Fed. R. Civ. P. 14(a)(1). That Rule, which is discussed in the next section of this chapter, sets a more restrictive standard for adding a new party to the case.

Q **7. Crossclaims between coplaintiffs.** Plaintiffs can also assert crossclaims under Rule 13(g). Suppose that Yee sues Protect and Garza for her injuries and for property damage to her house. Ryan, who co-owns the house with Yee, joins as coplaintiff, seeking recovery for the property damage. Protect counterclaims against Yee (who signed the contract for painting the house) for the price of the paint job. Now, Yee asserts a claim against Ryan claiming that if Protect recovers on its counterclaim, Ryan should pay half the cost of the paint job. Visually, the case looks like this:

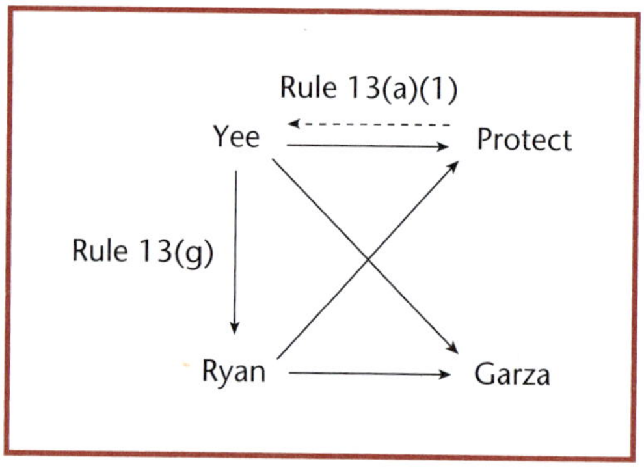

Figure 17–5: CROSSCLAIMS BETWEEN PLAINTIFFS

VI. Joinder by Defending Parties: Impleader Under Rule 14

Under narrow circumstances, Rule 14 allows a defendant to expand a lawsuit by asserting a claim of its own against a person who was not made a party by the plaintiff. When a defendant "impleads" a stranger to the case, the impleaded party becomes a "third-party defendant," and must defend the defendant's claim against it. The standard for impleading a third-party defendant, however, is narrower than the "transaction or occurrence" test used in the other basic joinder rules:

> A defending party may, as third-party plaintiff, serve a summons and complaint upon a nonparty who is or may be liable to it for all or part of the claim against it.

Fed. R. Civ. P. 14(a)(1). Impleader addresses the situation in which a plaintiff's claim against the defendant triggers a right of the defendant to be *reimbursed* by someone else if it pays the plaintiff's claim (or part of it). In such cases, it makes sense to litigate the reimbursement claim at the same time as the primary claim by the plaintiff. To implead a third party, the defendant must allege that the new party is or may be liable to the *defendant* for all or part of any judgment the plaintiff recovers from the defendant. It is a claim to *pass on liability* the defendant incurs, not for an independent loss the defendant has sustained. The party asserting an impleader claim under Rule 14(a) is called a "third-party plaintiff"; the party brought in is referred to as a "third-party defendant"; and the impleader complaint is called a third-party complaint.

READING *ERKINS v. CASE POWER & EQUIPMENT CO.* The case below illustrates the requirements for impleading a third party into a case. In *Erkins*, the court addresses the standard for bringing in a third party under Rule 14(a) and then applies that standard to the facts of the case. In reading *Erkins*, be sure to sort out the parties and the claims. Note that Rule 14(a)(1) is referred to as Rule 14(a) in the opinion, because the case predates the 2007 stylistic amendments. The language of the Rule is slightly different, but not in a way that affects its meaning.

- Who was the original defendant? On what theory was it sued?
- Who did the original defendant bring in as third-party defendants?
- Why did the claims against the impleaded third parties satisfy the standard in Rule 14(a)?
- What does the court decide in the last paragraph of the opinion?

ERKINS v. CASE POWER & EQUIPMENT CO.

164 F.R.D. 31 (D.N.J. 1995)

PISANO, United States Magistrate Judge:

. . .

BACKGROUND

This action arises out of a construction accident that occurred on May 1, 1992, during the removal of underground fuel tanks at the Tenacre Foundation Nursing Home in Princeton, New Jersey. The Tenacre Foundation had solicited and accepted a bid from T.A. Fitzpatrick Associates, Inc. ("Fitzpatrick") for the removal of seventeen underground tanks. Fitzpatrick later accepted a bid from ECRACOM . . . for certain work on the project, and ECRACOM then subcontracted a portion of its contracted work to Thomas J. O'Beirne & Company, the decedent's employer.

While riding in the bucket of a backhoe on the construction site, plaintiff's decedent fell out of the bucket and under the wheels of the machine, suffering fatal injuries. Two years later plaintiff [as representative of the decedent's estate] brought this products liability action against Case Power Equipment Corporation ("Case"), which manufactured the backhoe in question. Plaintiff's suit seeks to hold Case strictly liable for failing to provide adequate warnings regarding the dangers associated with riding in the bucket of the backhoe. Plaintiff has not named Fitzpatrick or ECRACOM as defendants in this action. . . .

Case maintains the position that the accident was solely the result of plaintiff's carelessness. In the event that the issue of its responsibility for the accident is submitted to a jury, however, Case seeks contribution from Fitzpatrick and ECRACOM based on their alleged negligence for failing to conduct safety meetings at the construction site. The essence of the proposed third-party complaint is that Fitzpatrick's and ECRACOM's alleged negligence was a contributing factor in the accident, and therefore any recovery by the plaintiff should be apportioned according to the relative faults of Case, Fitzpatrick, and ECRACOM. Through this motion, Case seeks leave to file a third-party complaint against Fitzpatrick and ECRACOM in order to permit this apportionment of responsibility in a single proceeding.

DISCUSSION

A motion for leave to file a third-party complaint impleading new parties is governed by Federal Rule of Civil Procedure 14(a) which provides in pertinent part:

> At any time after commencement of the action a defendant party, as a third-party plaintiff, may cause a summons and complaint to be served upon a person not a party to the action who is or may be liable to the third-party plaintiff.* The third-party plaintiff need not obtain leave to make the service if the third-party plaintiff files the third-party complaint not later than 10 days after serving the original answer.** Otherwise, the third-party plaintiff must obtain leave on motion upon notice to all parties to the action.

Fed. R. Civ. P. 14(a). A primary purpose of Rule 14 is to avoid circuity of action and multiplicity of litigation. In pursuit of this goal, many courts consider the following factors when deciding a motion under Rule 14: 1) the timeliness of the motion, 2) the potential for complication of issues at trial, 3) the probability of trial delay, and 4) whether the plaintiff may be prejudiced by the addition of parties.

While courts construe Rule 14(a) liberally in the interest of judicial economy, there are limits to the types of claims for which impleader is permissible. A defendant may only use Rule 14 to implead a third-party defendant where the third-party defendant is or may be liable to the defendant "derivatively or secondarily, and not to join a person who is or may be liable solely to the plaintiff." Accordingly, the basis for third-party liability is generally either contribution or indemnity.

Procedurally, Rule 14(a) clearly allows a defendant to file an action to join a third-party in an attempt to avoid duplicative proceedings. The issue then becomes

---

* **[EDS.—Ironically, this quotation omits the crucial language, "for all or part of the plaintiff's claim against the third-party plaintiff."]**

** **[EDS.—Rule 14(a)(1) now allows fourteen days to file an impleader claim without leave of court.]**

whether, from a substantive standpoint, New Jersey law permits a defendant in a strict products liability action to seek contribution from a third-party under a negligence theory.

Plaintiff has asserted strict products liability claims against Case for failure to warn. The putative third-party defendants argue that Case may not maintain negligence claims against them because those claims do not comprise "all or part" of plaintiff's original claim against Case as required by Federal Rule 14. Fitzpatrick and ECRACOM argue that impleader is inappropriate in this case because the third-party negligence claims are independent from and unrelated to the potential strict liability of the original defendant.

The Court finds the logic of this argument to be directly contrary to the purpose of Rule 14 and the law of contribution in New Jersey. Under the New Jersey Joint Tortfeasors Contribution Act, a right of contribution arises when the "injury or damage is suffered by any person as a result of the wrongful act, neglect or default of joint tortfeasors." N.J.S.A. 2A:53A-3. In such cases a joint tortfeasor may recover contribution from another tortfeasor for any excess paid in satisfaction of a judgment "over his pro rata share." *Id.*

The statute defines joint tortfeasors to mean "two or more persons jointly or severally liable in tort for the same injury to person or property." N.J.S.A. 2A:53A-1. Thus, the parties must either act together in committing the wrong, or their acts, if independent of each other, must unite in a single injury. If found to be liable for the decedent's accident, Case, Fitzpatrick, and ECRACOM satisfy this definition. Each party would be held liable in tort for plaintiff's injury: Case because of its failure to warn of the dangers of its product and Fitzpatrick and ECRACOM because of their negligence in failing to conduct safety meetings. That the plaintiff has not commenced its own suit against Fitzpatrick and ECRACOM does not prevent those parties from being joint tortfeasors under the Act.

Contrary to the arguments presented by Fitzpatrick and ECRACOM, the statute contains no requirement that joint tortfeasors be liable in tort under the same theories of liability. Further, New Jersey case law consistently holds that joint tortfeasors may be held liable under different theories of recovery.

. . .

Thus under New Jersey law, Case, Fitzpatrick, and ECRACOM may be joint tortfeasors, and each may be held liable to plaintiff under different theories of recovery. This result achieves the goal of the New Jersey Act to prevent plaintiffs from choosing which of multiple tortfeasors to sue and therefore electing unilaterally on whom to place the burden of a common fault. Clearly, New Jersey's contribution scheme permits Case, if found to be strictly liable to plaintiff, to institute a separate action for contribution against Fitzpatrick and ECRACOM based on their alleged negligence.

Federal Rule 14 provides the vehicle through which Case may seek contribution in a single proceeding rather than commencing a second action for contribution after the imposition of liability in the original plaintiff's suit. That the joint tortfeasors' conduct gives rise to liability under two entirely different theories does not foreclose a third-party claim for contribution, nor does the fact that plaintiff has failed to sue either of the putative third-party defendants under any theory of recovery.

An examination of the previously enumerated equitable principles guiding a decision to allow impleader under Rule 14 also compels the conclusion that the Court grant Case leave to file third-party complaints against Fitzpatrick and ECRACOM. First, the Court finds that defendant's motion is timely. Second, the Court finds that joinder of the proposed third-parties will facilitate resolution of the liability issues without creating unnecessary complications. Third, the Court finds that while impleader may delay trial, the delay will not be significant. Further, the third-party claims involve related issues that should be settled in a single lawsuit, and there is no indication that the additional claims will unduly complicate the case. Instead, joinder will promote justice and judicial economy by litigating several claims in a single proceeding. Finally, the Court finds that joinder of Fitzpatrick and ECRACOM presents no potential for prejudice to plaintiff. Accordingly, defendant Case's motion for leave to file a third-party complaint against Fitzpatrick and ECRACOM will be granted....

Notes and Questions: Impleader

1. The requirement for impleader. A party is entitled to "implead a third party" under Rule 14 if the third-party defendant may be liable to the defendant "for all or part of the [plaintiff's] claim against [the defendant]." Fed. R. Civ. P. 14(a)(1). This requirement is met if the impleaded third party may have to reimburse the defendant, partially or fully, if the defendant loses on the main claim. The defendant asserts that "I may be found liable to the plaintiff on her claim; if so, I want to pass on all or part of that liability to you [the third-party defendant]."

2. Typical impleader claims: Contribution. Many impleader claims under Rule 14(a) are brought for *contribution*. *Erkins* is an example. An injured party brings a tort claim against one defendant (Case) for damages. Under New Jersey law, the plaintiff can recover her full damages from Case, even if the negligence of others contributed to the accident. Case claims that, if Erkins recovers against Case, and Case pays the judgment, it should be able to make Fitzpatrick and ECRACOM reimburse it for a share of the judgment, since their negligence also contributed to the accident.

If Case did not bring the other contractors into the original case, it could sue them in an "action for contribution," after paying Erkins, to get partial reimbursement. Rule 14 allows Case to do this more efficiently (to avoid "circuity of actions") by bringing the alleged joint tortfeasors into the original action.

However, Case can only implead the other contractors if Case has a right to contribution from them. If the *Erkins* case arose in a state that does not allow contribution among tortfeasors, Case would not be able to implead the other contractors, since it would have no right to pass on part of its liability to Erkins.

3. Typical impleader claims: Indemnification. The second common type of impleader claim is for *indemnification*, that is, full reimbursement for any judgment the defendant incurs to the plaintiff. Suppose, on the facts of *Erkins*, that Fitzpatrick, the general contractor, was sued for wrongful death, based on the negligence of its subcontractor, ECRACOM, but that the contract between Fitzpatrick and ECRACOM required ECRACOM to indemnify Fitzpatrick for any judgments Fitzpatrick incurs due to ECRACOM's negligence. If Erkins sued Fitzpatrick, it could implead ECRACOM for indemnification, claiming that if it is held liable to Erkins for the negligence of ECRACOM, that subcontractor "is or may be liable" to it for *all* of the judgment it incurs.

Here again, Rule 14(a) provides a mechanism for resolving both the plaintiff's claim and the indemnification claim in the original suit. If Fitzpatrick is ordered to pay Erkins damages for ECRACOM's negligence, and the court determines that ECRACOM has agreed to indemnify Fitzpatrick, it will enter an order holding Fitzpatrick liable to Erkins and holding ECRACOM liable to Fitzpatrick for the damages Fitzpatrick must pay to Erkins.

4. Impleading a party directly liable to the plaintiff. A defendant cannot use Rule 14(a) to bring in a party who would only be liable directly to the plaintiff, but who would not be liable to the defendant. If New Jersey did not allow contribution between tortfeasors, Case would not have been able to implead the other contractors, even though Erkins could have sued them directly on a negligence theory. The defendant must have a claim for reimbursement from the third party, not simply an argument that the plaintiff could have sued the third party.

Here's a nice case to illustrate the point. Quinn is arrested by a red-headed police officer, and sues Jones, a red-headed police officer who was on duty at the time, claiming that Jones battered him during the arrest. Jones, believing that it was Smith who arrested Quinn rather than him, impleads Smith. Impleader is improper. If Jones made the arrest, he is liable to Quinn; if Smith did it, he is liable to Quinn. But there is no theory on which Smith would be liable to Jones. Jones is just offering a different target for Quinn. "Hey, Quinn, it wasn't me, it was Smith—so have at him!" That is not the role of impleader under Rule 14(a). Jones, rather than impleading Smith, should deny in his answer that he arrested Quinn. Quinn could then move to amend to add Smith as an additional defendant under Rule 20(a)(2) if he is unsure which officer made the arrest.

5. A confusing related example: Impleading a party who may be liable directly to the plaintiff. The last note suggests that a defending party cannot implead a party who may be liable directly to the plaintiff. Actually, Rule 14 does allow a defending party to implead someone who may be liable to directly to the plaintiff, as long as *the impleaded party may also be liable to the defending party for all or part of the plaintiff's claim.*

Here's an example. Masters is injured in an accident due to the negligence of two other drivers, Grainger and Ribeiro. He sues Grainger for his injuries, and Grainger impleads Ribeiro under Rule 14 for contribution. Here, Ribeiro would be liable directly to Masters for his injuries: Masters could have sued him alone or sued him with Grainger as a joint tortfeasor. But if Masters chooses to sue Grainger alone and recovers his damages from Grainger, Ribeiro would be liable to

Grainger for contribution if Grainger paid the full judgment and joint and several liability applies, as it did in *Erkins*. Grainger has paid a liability that they share, and has a right to get part of it back from Ribeiro. So a party can be impleaded if he is liable directly to the plaintiff, as long as he may be liable to the main defendant for contribution or indemnification as well.

The example in the previous note is different because there liability was an either/or proposition. Either Jones would be liable to the plaintiff, or Smith would, but there was no theory on which the officer who caused the injury could satisfy the judgment and seek contribution from the other.

Q **6. Impleader for the defendant's own injuries.** Suppose that Yee sues Protect for her injuries in the ladder accident, claiming that Protect's employee, Garza, negligently caused the accident and resulting fire. Suppose further that Protect's truck was destroyed in the fire. Could Protect implead its insurance company, claiming that the insurer agreed to reimburse Protect for property damage it suffers in the course of its business?

A This is not a proper impleader claim. Protect is not trying to pass on its liability for Yee's injury; it is trying to collect for a separate loss it incurred in the same accident. Rule 14(a) does not allow the defendant to expand the parties to a suit based on a claim for its own losses.

Q **7. Why is the Rule so restrictive on impleading other parties?** If one goal of the Rules is to adjudicate related claims together, why not allow the defendant to offer alternative targets to the plaintiff (e.g., in the red-headed police officer case) even if the defendant would not have a claim against that party?

A At one time Rule 14 *did* allow defendants to implead third parties who might be liable directly to the plaintiff, whether or not they might be liable to the defendant:

> In its original form the rule permitted a third party to be impleaded "who is or may be liable to him [the original defendant] or to the plaintiff for all or part of plaintiff's claim" against defendant. Thus, a defendant could implead any third party who might be liable on plaintiff's claim. But in some cases a plaintiff declined to press a claim against the third-party defendant and the plaintiff could not be compelled to amend the complaint in order to do so. When that occurred, the third-party action would have to be dropped since no one had alleged a claim against the third-party defendant.

Wright & Miller § 1441. To avoid this anomaly, the Rule was amended in 1948 to eliminate a defendant's right to implead alternative targets for the plaintiff.

8. The process of impleader. When a party impleads a third-party defendant, the new party must be served with the summons and complaint under Rule 4 just as an original defendant would be. The contents of the third-party complaint are governed by Rules 8 through 11 and the answer is governed by the same pleading rules as an original answer. Once impleaded, the third-party defendant may (or must) assert counterclaims under Rules 13(a) and (b) and crossclaims against coparties under Rules 13(g) and (h). The third-party defendant may also bring in additional parties who may be liable to reimburse her for all or part of the defendant's claim against her, under Rule 14(a)(5) (called a "fourth-party claim").

Q **9. Why does the third-party defendant get to "defend the defendant"?** Rule 14(a)(2)(C) authorizes the third-party defendant to "assert against the plaintiff any defense that the third-party plaintiff has to the plaintiff's claim." In *Erkins*, for example, the impleaded contractors could argue that Case had no duty to warn of the risk that caused the accident or that the warnings provided were adequate. Why does the Rule allow this?

A The third-party claim seeks to pass on liability that the defendant incurs to the plaintiff. If the defendant does *not* incur liability to the plaintiff, the third-party defendant wins too since there will be no liability to pass on. So the Rule allows the third-party defendant to assert defenses that may defeat the main claim as well as defenses to the third-party claim.

Q **10. Personal jurisdiction over impleaded third parties.** Suppose that the defendant meets the standard for impleading a third party but that third party would not be subject to personal jurisdiction in the state where the action is pending. Can the absentee be impleaded?

A No! Third-party defendants, like all other defendants, have a due process right not to be sued in a court that lacks jurisdiction over them. Would an out-of-state party feel any better about being dragged into Virginia to defend this case if it is dragged in as a third-party defendant rather than as an original defendant? Certainly not. Whether it is made a defendant under Rule 20 or a third-party defendant under Rule 14(a), it may raise any objection it has to personal jurisdiction.

11. Judicial discretion to deny impleader. Rule 14(a)(1) provides that a third party may be impleaded without leave of court within fourteen days of service of the answer to the complaint. After that period, impleader requires a motion and approval by the judge. Although this implies that the court must allow the third-party claim if it is filed within the fourteen-day period, case law holds that the court always has discretion to refuse to allow impleader if litigating the impleader claim with the main claim would unduly complicate matters, introduce unrelated issues, or delay resolution of the main claim. *See Wright & Miller* § 1443. In most cases, the court will allow the third-party claim to be joined (as the court did in *Erkins*) due to the efficiency and consistency to be gained from hearing the claims together.

VII. Asserting Additional Claims Under Rule 14

Once a party has been impleaded under Rule 14(a), the Rule allows other related claims to be asserted. The third-party defendant may assert any claims she has against the plaintiff arising from the transaction or occurrence that gave rise to the main claim. Fed. R. Civ. P. 14(a)(2)(D). The plaintiff may assert claims against the third-party defendant that meet the transaction-or-occurrence test. Fed. R. Civ. P. 14(a)(3). If either of these parties asserts a claim against the other, they become "opposing parties," triggering the counterclaim provisions of Rules 13(a) and (b) as well. The third-party defendant must assert counterclaims it has against the third-party plaintiff (Rule 13(a)(1)), and may assert other counterclaims under Rule 13(b). If several third-party defendants are brought in, they become "coparties" who may assert crossclaims against each other.

The question below allows you to test your understanding of the various joinder rules covered in this chapter.

Yee sues Protect Painting and Edison Electric Company for her injuries in the accident on her lawn. After it receives the complaint, Protect asserts a claim against Edison for damages to its truck in the accident. Edison asserts a claim for indemnification against Preferred Wire, claiming that Preferred's electrical wire caused the problem, and that Preferred had agreed to indemnify it for any damages it incurred from defects in the wire. Edison also asserts a claim against Garza, the employee who swung the ladder into the wire, seeking indemnification from him for any damages it must pay to Yee. Edison also seeks recovery from both Preferred and Garza for damages to its power lines caused by the fire.

Garza asserts a claim against Preferred for contribution as a joint tortfeasor and a claim against Yee for injuries Garza suffered, claiming that Yee had bumped him, causing the ladder to contact the wire. Yee, after receiving Garza's pleading, asserts a direct claim against Garza for her burn injuries. Last, Preferred asserts a claim against Edison for the price of the wire it had supplied to Edison. Here is a diagram of this avalanche of claims:

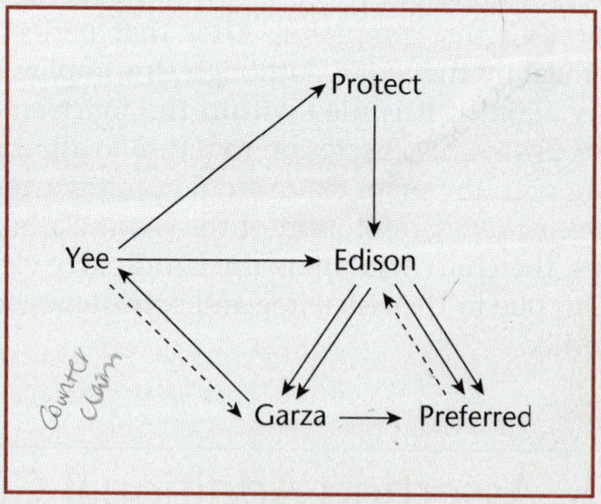

Figure 17–6: AVALANCHE OF CLAIMS

Label each of the added claims with the Rule number that allows the claim, and consider which of the following statements is correct.

A. Garza's claim against Yee is a crossclaim.
B. Garza's claim against Preferred is an impleader claim.
C. Protect's claim against Edison is a counterclaim.
D. Preferred's claim against Edison is a crossclaim.
E. Yee's claim against Garza is joined under Rule 20(a).
F. Yee's claim against Garza is a counterclaim.
G. Edison's claim against Garza and Preferred for damages to its lines is not properly joined, because it does not seek to pass on liability for its liability to Yee.
H. Garza's claim against Preferred is compulsory.
I. None of the above is true.

This is a morass, but you can wade across if you focus on each claim in turn. Yee has joined Protect and Edison as codefendants under Rule 20(a)(2). Edison then impleaded Garza and Preferred under Rule 14(a)(1), claiming that they are liable to reimburse it (Edison) for Yee's damages if it is held liable. Edison has added the second claim, for damage to its lines, under Rule 18(a). That Rule allows a party, once it has properly made another party an adversary, to add on any other claims it has against that party.

Let's march through the options in order. **A** is wrong. Garza, after being impleaded as a third-party defendant, asserts a claim against Yee. This is authorized (you Rules aficionados) by Rule 14(a)(2)(D), but it is not a crossclaim. Rule 13(g) defines a crossclaim as a claim against a coparty. Garza and Yee are not coparties, even though they are embroiled in the same lawsuit, because no one has claimed relief against them as codefendants.

B is also wrong; Garza's claim is not an impleader claim. Garza did not bring Preferred into the suit for contribution; Preferred was already a codefendant on Edison's claim against Garza and Preferred, so Garza's claim against it is a crossclaim. **C** fails as well, because Protect's claim against Edison, a codefendant, is also a crossclaim.

Preferred's claim against Edison is not a crossclaim. Edison brought a claim against Preferred, so Preferred is an opposing party. Therefore, Preferred's claim back against Edison is a counterclaim—**D** falls by the wayside. And **E** also comes up short. Yee sued Edison and Preferred as codefendants, but did not make Garza an original defendant under Rule 20(a) (though he could have if he'd wanted to).

After Garza was brought in as a third-party defendant, he asserted a claim against Yee, the plaintiff. This makes Yee and Garza opposing parties, though they weren't until Garza asserted this claim. Because they are now opposing parties, Yee's claim against Garza is a counterclaim. **F** takes the prize.

G is wrong. Edison has impleaded Garza and Preferred for indemnification under Rule 14(a)(1), seeking to recover the damages it must pay to Yee if found liable to Yee. It then adds a claim for its own damages to its power lines. This is an additional claim added under Rule 18(a). Edison could not have impleaded Garza and Preferred on this claim alone, because it is an independent claim for Edison's own damages. But once it asserts proper impleader claims against each of them under Rule 14, Rule 18 kicks in, allowing Edison to assert these additional claims. **H** fails, because Garza's claim against Preferred is a crossclaim, and they are not compulsory. And **I** is wrong because **F** is right!

By contrast: Pennsylvania's rule on joining additional parties. It is not writ in stone that impleader must be limited as it is in Federal Rule 14(a). Pennsylvania's rule governing joinder of additional parties by defendants is considerably broader. Under Pa. R. C. P. No. 2252(a), a defendant may join an additional defendant who may be

> (1) solely liable on the underlying cause of action against the joining party, or (2) liable to or with the joining party on any cause of action arising out of the transaction or occurrence or series of transactions or occurrences upon which the underlying cause of action against the joining party is based.

Subsection 1 of this rule, unlike Rule 14(a), allows a defendant to bring in a party who may be liable directly to the plaintiff on the claim, but not liable to the defendant. Subsection 2 allows the defendant to bring in a party who may be liable to the defendant for *completely different damages* arising out of the underlying transaction or occurrence. For example, if Chauncey is sued by Duchnowski for injuries in an auto accident, under Pa. Rule 2252(a), Chauncey could implead a third driver, Rivera, asserting a claim for his own injuries in the accident. Or he could bring in the third driver, claiming that the third driver was the sole cause of Duchnowski's injuries.

VIII. Joinder of Claims and Parties: Summary of Basic Principles

- The initial party structure of a federal case is generally governed by Rule 20(a). Rule 20(a)(1) allows plaintiffs to join as coplaintiffs in a single action if their claims arise out of the same transaction or occurrence (or series of them) and involve a common question of law or fact. Rule 20(a)(2) allows defendants to be sued together if the claims against them meet the same two criteria.
- Rule 18(a), governing joinder of claims, allows a plaintiff suing a defendant to join any claims she has against the defendant. The Rule also allows any other party, once she has properly made another party an adversary under some other joinder rule, to add unrelated claims.
- A counterclaim is a claim for relief by a defending party against an opposing party. Defending parties *must* assert counterclaims that arise out of the same transaction or occurrence as the claim against them or waive the claim. Rule 13(a)(1). They may also assert unrelated counterclaims against an opposing party under Rule 13(b).

- A crossclaim is a claim against a coparty—a codefendant or a coplaintiff. Crossclaims may be asserted if they arise from the same transaction or occurrence as the main claim in the action.
- The scope of a single transaction or occurrence is difficult to define. The court will consider the overlap in the evidence, witnesses, and issues involved in the various claims, the logical relationship between the claims, and the efficiency to be gained from litigating them together. The test is one of historically related events. It can be met even if the claims are based on different legal theories or different sources of law (e.g., one claim under state law and another under federal law).
- Rule 14(a) allows a defendant to implead a further party to a suit if applicable substantive law gives the impleading defendant a right to reimbursement for all or part of the claim the plaintiff has asserted against the impleading defendant. Rule 14(a) does not allow the defendant to implead an alternative target for the plaintiff or to seek damages the defendant herself may have suffered from the underlying litigation events.
- The Federal Rules govern actions in federal court. Every state has its own joinder rules that govern joinder of claims and parties in the courts of that state. Many state joinder rules closely follow the Federal Rules, but others do not. They may use different names for similar types of joinder or different standards for joining claims.
- The joinder rules do not confer subject matter jurisdiction or personal jurisdiction on a court. Fed. R. Civ. P. 82. Even if joinder of a claim or party is authorized by one of the joinder rules, the court must have a basis for exercising subject matter jurisdiction over the claim and personal jurisdiction over the defendant for that claim.

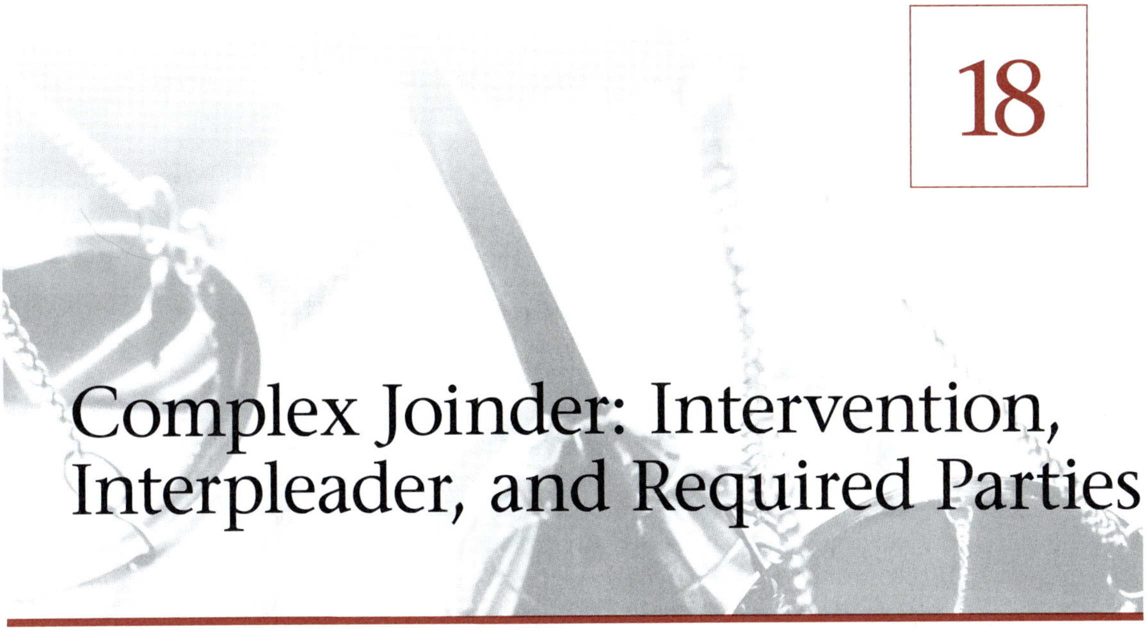

18

Complex Joinder: Intervention, Interpleader, and Required Parties

I. Introduction

As the last chapter explains, the plaintiff is generally "master of her claim." She decides who to sue and whether to sue alone or join with other plaintiffs under Fed. R. Civ. P. 20(a)(1). We also saw, however, that the plaintiff does not have absolute control over the parties and claims in a federal case. The defendant can assert counterclaims under Fed. R. Civ. P. 13(a) and (b). Parties can add crossclaims against coparties under Fed. R. Civ. P. 13(g). They can also add additional parties to a counterclaim or crossclaim under Fed. R. Civ. P. 13(h). And defendants may redesign the litigation by bringing in third-party defendants under Rule 14(a).

In this chapter, we address several Rules that involve joinder of persons who were not made parties to the original case but whose interests may be affected by it. Rule 19 addresses situations in which a person has not been made a party to the action, but ought to participate in the litigation for the court to fairly and adequately resolve the dispute. The Rule describes when such parties should be joined and how a court should proceed if the absentee ought to be made a party but cannot be. Rule 24 addresses a different situation in which an absentee's interests might be affected by litigation. It authorizes non-parties to *intervene*, that is, to become a party to the litigation at their own initiative, even though they were not sued in the original action. Under Rules 19 and 24, the lawsuit may end up including additional parties whom the plaintiff did not choose to sue. Many state civil procedure codes have rules similar to these two joinder devices.

Finally, this chapter also analyzes interpleader, a device by which a person faced with conflicting claims to property may also join all claimants in a single action to obtain a judgment resolving those claims.

II. Joinder of Parties Under Rule 19

The concept of necessary parties to a lawsuit has a long and complex history. Early equity practice took the approach that the court, if it were to enter an equity decree, should completely resolve the dispute among all those whose interests might be affected by it. Often, a suit could affect the interests of persons who had not been made parties to the action as well as the parties themselves. Frequently, this led the court to require joinder of such absentees in the action. If the equity court concluded that one or more absent persons were "indispensable" to the complete resolution of the dispute but could not be brought in, the court would dismiss the case. *See generally* Geoffrey Hazard, *Indispensable Party: The Historical Origin of a Procedural Phantom*, 61 Colum. L. Rev. 1254 (1961).

This concept, that all parties affected by a dispute should be brought before the court, could lead to grotesque scenarios and protracted delays in resolving cases. For example, *Hicks v. Southwestern Settlement & Development Corp.*, 188 S.W.2d 915 (Tex. Civ. App. 1945), was an action in trespass to try title to real estate brought by 104 heirs. Allegedly, 574 other heirs existed but were not joined. Bringing all the heirs before the court might be impossible, given the problems in identifying them, locating them, and subjecting them to the jurisdiction of the Texas court. Parties might acquire interests in the property, or die leaving their interest to others, more quickly than they could be joined in the case. If the absentees were deemed "indispensable," perhaps the case could not be resolved at all. Such scenarios evoke Charles Dickens's famous description of the unfortunate parties in *Jarndyce v. Jarndyce*, who "deliriously found themselves made parties in Jarndyce and Jarndyce, without knowing how or why."*

Although the equity courts may have taken the concept to extremes, the basic principle that persons who may be affected by litigation should take part in it makes sense. Here are a few examples of situations in which it may be important to include a non-party to deal effectively with the dispute.

A. Wu buys a building lot from Caudel and Polansky. He later learns that the water table is too high to build a septic system on it, and consequently no building can be constructed there. Claiming misrepresentation, he sues Caudel to rescind the sale.

> In this case, it makes sense to require Wu to sue Polansky as well as Caudel. The court cannot rescind the sale without having Polansky before it—it cannot order Polansky to return his part of the purchase price or rescind the sale

* Charles Dickens, Bleak House 3 (1956).

as to him unless he is before the court. Thus, the court cannot provide Wu the relief she seeks without making Polansky a party to the action.

B. City Realty Corporation rents the twentieth floor of a skyscraper to Stellar Corporation, which then sublets it to Taylor Publishing. The lease and the sublease both include a requirement that reasonable access to utilities will be provided to the lessee. After moving in, Taylor refuses to pay rent to Stellar, because the power supply is inadequate. Stellar claims that City Realty has caused the problem by refusing to upgrade the power supply to accommodate Taylor's needs. Stellar sues to collect the rent, but Taylor claims it doesn't owe rent because of the owner's unreasonable refusal to accommodate its electrical needs.

Here, it is difficult to determine whether there has been a breach of the sublease without the participation of the owner. If City Realty is made a party, the court will be able to decide whether it has a duty to upgrade the power supply, or whether Stellar agreed to a provision it couldn't fulfill. To resolve the controversy fully, City Realty should be made a party. In addition, affording relief to the parties may require an order to City Realty, the absentee, to comply with its duty to supply Taylor's electrical requirements.

C. Moreno sues Merrill for damages arising from a business transaction that Merrill entered into on behalf of his wife and himself. Moreno discovers that all of Merrill's assets are held as "community property" with his wife. Thus, it will be impossible to collect a judgment without getting a joint judgment against Merrill and his wife.

Although the court could adjudicate this case without making Mrs. Merrill a party, the resulting relief might not be adequate for the parties before the court. If Moreno recovers damages, the court cannot order execution on Mr. Merrill's community property assets without entry of a judgment against Mrs. Merrill as well.

These examples illustrate situations in which it may be appropriate to require an absentee to be made a party to the case. Rule 19 provides a three-step framework for analyzing such cases. First, Rule 19(a) addresses *whether* the absentee is a person who should be joined if feasible. Second, if the absentee should be joined, the court must determine if she can be. Third, if the absentee *should* be joined but cannot be (for example, because she is not subject to personal jurisdiction), Rule 19(b) provides guidance to the court in deciding how to proceed.

Step One: Deciding whether the absentee is a required party

The first question in these cases is *whether* the absentee should have been made a party to the suit. Rule 19(a) provides that a person should be joined "if feasible," if one of several conditions is met:

- "in that person's absence, the court cannot accord complete relief among existing parties." Fed. R. Civ. P. 19(a)(1)(A).

- "that person [the absentee] claims an interest relating to the subject of the action and is so situated that disposing of the action in the person's absence may:

  (i) as a practical matter impair or impede the person's ability to protect that interest; [Fed. R. Civ. P. 19(a)(1)(B)(i)] or
  (ii) leave an existing party subject to a substantial risk of incurring double, multiple, or otherwise inconsistent obligations because of the interest." Fed. R. Civ. P. 19(a)(1)(B)(ii).

The community property case above illustrates a Rule 19(a)(1)(A) situation: If the wife is not included, any damages awarded to the plaintiff will not be collectible, because the judgment cannot be satisfied out of community property. Thus, the court cannot afford complete relief to Moreno unless Mrs. Merrill is made a party. This provision might also be satisfied in the sublease example. If the court determines that the sublease includes an obligation to provide increased electrical service, it will be unable to order that relief if the owner of the building is not made a party, since the owner, not the lessee, would have the authority to make improvements to the building.

Andean v. Secretary of the U.S. Army, 840 F. Supp. 1414 (D. Kan. 1993), illustrates a situation in which an absentee should be joined under Rule 19(a)(1)(B)(i). The plaintiff sought an order to the Secretary of the Army to pay her a share of her ex-husband's military pension as provided in her divorce decree. The district court held that her ex-husband was a necessary party to the action, since if the court ordered a share paid to the ex-wife, it would impair his ability to protect his interest in the pension. *Id.* at 1423 n.8.

Here are several cases in which the court concluded that an absentee should be joined under subsection (a)(1)(B)(ii) to avoid a risk of multiple or inconsistent obligations to the original parties. In *O'Leary v. Moyer's Landfill, Inc.*, 677 F. Supp. 807 (E.D. Pa. 1988), an action by citizens seeking clean-up of a landfill, the court held that the federal Environmental Protection Agency (EPA) was a person to be joined if feasible. If the case went forward without the EPA's participation, the EPA might, pursuant to its regulatory authority, impose different requirements for remediation than those imposed by a court decree, leaving the defendant, the receiver of the landfill, subject to inconsistent obligations.

Similarly, in *Haas v. Jefferson National Bank of Miami Beach*, 442 F.2d 394 (5th Cir. 1971), Haas sued the bank, claiming that he actually had a half interest in certain stock in the bank, issued to Glueck in Glueck's name alone. The court held Glueck a necessary party to the action. If Haas's claim were adjudicated without Glueck in the suit, and the Bank was ordered to reissue half the shares in Haas's name, it might later be sued by Glueck, alleging that he owned all of the shares. Because the Bank was subject to this risk of inconsistent obligations in separate actions, Glueck was deemed a person to be joined if feasible under Rule 19(a).

Q **Applying Rule 19(a).** The Window Glass Cutters Union sues the employer of its members, claiming that the employer violated the collective bargaining agreement by failing to assign certain work to its members. The employer's position is that the employees actually perform work covered by a different collective bargaining agreement, with the United Glass and Ceramic Workers. The employer moves to join the United Glass and Ceramic Workers under Rule 19(a). Should the second union be joined under Rule 19(a), and, if so, under which subsection of the Rule?

A Rule 19(a)(1)(B)(ii) covers this case. If the action proceeds, and the court holds that the work must be assigned to workers covered by the Window Glass Cutters Union, it will order the employer to do so. Very likely, the employer will then be sued by the United Glass and Ceramic Workers, claiming the work should have been assigned to its members instead. The United Glass union would not be bound by that decision (since it was not a party to the first action), so it could litigate the question again in a later action. In that second action, the court might find United Glass workers entitled to the work, so that the employer would be whipsawed between two inconsistent judgments. On these facts, the court ordered joinder of the second union. *Window Glass Cutters League of America, AFL-CIO v. American St. Gobain Corp.*, 47 F.R.D. 255 (W.D. Pa. 1969).

Step Two: Determining whether joinder is feasible

If the court determines that an absentee falls into one of the categories in Rule 19(a), the court should consider whether it is "feasible" (Fed. R. Civ. P. 19(a)) to make the absentee a party. If so, it will order the person made a party and the case will proceed. However, it may not be possible to bring the absentee into the suit for several reasons. First, the party may not be subject to personal jurisdiction in the court where the plaintiff has brought suit. Even if the Rules call for the joinder of a party, she cannot be ordered to appear in the court if she is not subject to personal jurisdiction in the state where the court sits.

Second, in a diversity case, joinder of the absentee will destroy complete diversity if the absentee is from the same state as an opposing party, negating subject matter jurisdiction. Third, joining an absentee as a defendant may make venue improper because the absentee is from a different state than other defendants. *See* 28 U.S.C. § 1391(b)(1) (authorizing venue in certain districts if all defendants reside in the state where the district court is located). There may also be more exotic reasons why the absentee cannot be brought in. For example, in several cases involving tribal rights, the court concluded that an Indian tribe could not be made a party because it was immune from suit without its consent. *See, e.g., Makah Indian Tribe v. Verity*, 910 F.2d 555 (10th Cir. 1990).

Step Three: Deciding whether to dismiss or continue

If it is not feasible to join the absentee for one of the reasons just described, the court has to decide whether to proceed without the absentee, despite the potential problems that call for joinder under Rule 19(a), or to dismiss the case. Rule 19(b) lists four factors for the court to consider in deciding whether "in equity and good conscience, the action should proceed among the existing parties or should be dismissed." The court must consider the risk of prejudice to the absentee or the existing parties if the case goes forward, ways to lessen such prejudice by fashioning the judgment, whether a judgment rendered in the person's absence will be adequate, and whether the plaintiff will have an adequate remedy if the action is dismissed for nonjoinder.

In an earlier day, courts tried to solve such cases by putting parties in cubbyholes, labeling parties "necessary" or, if they should be joined but couldn't be, "indispensable." Rule 19 now mandates a series of practical judgments about the impact of the litigation. First, the court must determine, under Rule 19(a), whether proceeding without the absentee could have adverse consequences on the absentee or the parties. If it would, the person will be made a party if possible. If she cannot be brought in, the court has to make a discretionary judgment, under Rule 19(b), whether it can fairly adjudicate the case without the absentee.

READING *TORRINGTON CO. v. YOST.* Here is a straightforward case that applies Rule 19. As you read it, keep in mind the structure of the analysis dictated by the Rule.

- Why did the court conclude that INA, Yost's new employer, should be joined under Rule 19(a)?
- Why couldn't it be made a party?
- As a matter of litigation strategy, why do you think Yost—the defendant—made the motion to dismiss for failure to join INA in the case? What's in it for him?
- Since the court found that INA should be joined under Rule 19(a) but couldn't be, it went on to apply Rule 19(b). Why does it conclude, under Rule 19(b), that the case should be dismissed?

The 2007 "restyling amendments" to the Federal Rules led to changes in numbering of the subsections in Rule 19. The references in *Torrington* are to the old subsection numbers. Here's a quick conversion chart to help you read the case.

OLD RULE		NEW RULE
Rule 19(a)(1)	is now	Rule 19(a)(1)(A)
Rule 19(a)(2)(i)	is now	Rule 19(a)(1)(B)(i)
Rule 19(a)(2)(ii)	is now	Rule 19(a)(1)(B)(ii)

TORRINGTON CO. v. YOST

139 F.R.D. 91 (D.S.C. 1991)

HERLONG, District Judge.

This is a trade secrets case. From 1982 to 1990, the defendant, Mark Yost ("Yost"), worked for the plaintiff, The Torrington Company ("Torrington"), manufacturing various types of bearings. While at Torrington, Yost signed an agreement not to divulge any secret or confidential information of Torrington. After leaving Torrington, Yost went to work for INA Bearing Company, Inc. ("INA") which produces the same type of bearings as Torrington. On June 4, 1991, Torrington filed suit against Yost seeking, among other things, an injunction limiting Yost's employment at INA for eighteen (18) months, and actual damages from the alleged use of Torrington's trade secrets. Yost moved to dismiss under Rule 19 of the Federal Rules of Civil Procedure for failure to join Yost's new employer, INA, as an indispensable party. Yost contends that INA's absence will prejudice him and impair INA's interests.

The issue before this court is whether INA is an indispensable party to this action under Rule 19. For the reasons set forth below, the court concludes that INA, Yost's new employer, is an indispensable party whose joinder would deny the court of diversity jurisdiction. Therefore, this case must be dismissed.

Fed. R. Civ. P. 19 requires a two-step analysis. The first part of the rule, subdivision (a), identifies the persons who should be joined if feasible. If joinder is not feasible, then subdivision (b) is applied to decide whether the case should be dismissed.

Under subdivision (a), a person should be joined when feasible[1] if nonjoinder would under (a)(1) deny complete relief to the parties present, or under (a)(2), impair the absent person's interest or prejudice the persons already parties by subjecting them to a risk of multiple or inconsistent obligations.

In the matter *sub judice,* 19(a)(2) is the pertinent subsection. Clearly subsection (a)(2) [now, Rule 19(a)(1)(B)] applies, and INA should be joined if feasible. INA has an employment contract with Yost, and its interest in his fulfilling that contract would be adversely affected if Torrington were granted an injunction preventing Yost from continuing to work for INA in his current position. In addition, there is a real possibility that if INA were not joined, Yost may be subject to inconsistent obligations. In order to obey a court order enjoining him from working for INA (or enjoining him from working on certain projects at INA), Yost may have to breach his employment contract with INA. Because Yost may be prejudiced if INA is not joined and INA has an interest which may be impaired in its absence, under Rule 19(a) the court is required to join INA as a party if feasible.

The sole basis for federal court jurisdiction in this action is diversity of citizenship. Both INA and Torrington are Delaware corporations. Joinder of INA would destroy diversity jurisdiction. Therefore, it is not feasible to join INA, and the court must consider Rule 19(b) to determine whether the action should proceed with the parties before it, or should be dismissed.

Rule 19(b) contains four factors which must be considered when deciding whether to dismiss the action: (1) to what extent a judgment rendered in the person's absence may be prejudicial to the person or those already parties; (2) the extent to which, by protective provisions in the judgment, the prejudice can be lessened or avoided; (3) whether a judgment rendered in the person's absence will be adequate; and (4) whether the plaintiff will have an adequate remedy if the action is dismissed for nonjoinder.

1. Joinder is feasible when "A person . . . is subject to service of process and whose joinder will not deprive the court of jurisdiction over the subject matter of the action. . . ." Fed. R. Civ. P. 19(a).

The first factor weighs heavily in favor of dismissal. Torrington contends that INA is not an indispensable party and is at most a joint tortfeasor who would not be prejudiced by not being joined. In support of this position, Torrington points to *General Transistor Corp. v. Prawdzik,* 21 F.R.D. 1 (S.D.N.Y. 1957), as a similar case involving trade secrets in which the new employer was not joined, and was held not to be an indispensable party. In *General Transistor,* however, the plaintiff was merely seeking a temporary injunction preventing the individual defendant from "continuing to disclose any secret matter. . . ." 21 F.R.D. at 2. In the case at bar, Torrington is seeking to enjoin Yost from "working or consulting for INA for a period of eighteen (18) months, at any plant which makes thrust bearings or any supplier or subcontractor or tool designer involved with thrust bearings." Torrington is also asking the court to compel Yost "and those in privity with him, and those who became aware of any such injunction: . . . To return to Torrington, all documents, computerized and non-verbal disclosures, and physical embodiments of Torrington's trade secrets and confidential information." The potential impact upon the new employer is significantly greater in the case here than in *General Transistor.* In addition, the risk that Yost would be subjected to inconsistent obligations is significant. As already discussed, if the court limits the type of work Yost may do for INA, Yost may have inconsistent obligations to an order of the court and to INA.

The second factor requires the court to consider the feasibility of protective provisions. The drastic remedy of dismissal need not be invoked if the court can fashion relief so that neither the parties nor the person not joined is prejudiced. Torrington contends that if the court merely enjoins Yost from working at INA plants which manufacture the bearings in question, Yost could still work for INA. There is no evidence before the court, however, that such a protective provision would protect Yost from breaching his employment contract. Even if such a provision protects Yost, it would not protect INA. INA would be limited in the manner in which it could use its employee. There is no reasonable means of protecting Yost and INA from the prejudice they would suffer if INA were not a party.

Third, it is doubtful that any judgment Torrington receives would be adequate if INA were not made a party. Torrington's complaint is replete with references to INA. If Yost has revealed trade secrets to INA as Torrington fears, INA will be able to continue profiting from them if INA is not a party in this action. Even if Torrington is completely successful in this suit, if INA is not a party, INA cannot be prevented from using Torrington's trade secrets information.

Finally, another forum exists for the plaintiff. Torrington will not be left without a remedy if this action is dismissed. Torrington can sue both Yost and INA in state court.

The grounds for dismissal in this case are overwhelming. INA is clearly an indispensable party. Each of the four factors of Rule 19(b) indicates that dismissal is appropriate. If Torrington wishes to continue with this suit, it must do so in state court and join INA. For the foregoing reasons, this case is dismissed pursuant to Rule 19, Fed. R. Civ. P.

Notes and Questions: *Torrington* and Rule 19

1. Raising the Rule 19 joinder issue. Rule 19 deals with two fundamental questions: who will be parties to the action and whether the case should proceed in its present form. Sometimes, the court will conclude, as in *Torrington*, that the case should be dismissed entirely. The Federal Rules encourage the parties to focus on the issue early by allowing a defendant to raise the failure to join a party even before answering the complaint. Fed. R. Civ. P. 12(b)(7). However, because proceeding without the absentee risks impairment of substantive rights, a party does not waive the objection by failing to raise it at the outset; the objection may still be made later in the suit. Fed. R. Civ. P. 12(h)(2).

Q **2. *Torrington's* Rule 19(a) analysis.** The court starts by asking, under Rule 19(a), whether INA should be joined because of the potential impact if the case proceeds without it. Why does it conclude that INA ought to be a party to the case between Torrington and Yost?

A If INA, Yost's new employer, were not made a party, and the court enjoined Yost from working for INA, INA would be deprived of Yost's services without having had a chance to oppose the injunction. In addition, if Yost were barred from working for INA, it might sue him for breach of contract, and the court in that action might find that Yost breached by complying with the injunction. Thus, the two judgments might subject Yost to inconsistent obligations. Fed. R. Civ. P. 19(a)(1)(B)(ii). The resolution of this dispute will be tidier if INA becomes a party to the first suit, because its interests and arguments will be considered in the action, and any order entered by the court will bind INA as well as Yost. Thus, INA should be joined "if feasible."

Q **3. Why not join INA?** Since INA is a party to be joined under Rule 19(a), why didn't the court order it joined as a party to the case?

A If INA were made a party to the case, the question would arise whether the court would have subject matter jurisdiction over the case after its joinder. Torrington was a citizen of Delaware based on its state of incorporation. So was INA. If the court aligned INA as a plaintiff along with Torrington, the fact that both were citizens of Delaware would not defeat diversity, as long as Yost was not a Delaware citizen. If INA were aligned as a defendant, however, there would be Delaware citizens on both sides of the case, and diversity jurisdiction would fail. (For an analysis of this alignment problem, *see Wright & Miller* § 1605.)

Although the court does not explain its reasoning, it clearly concluded that INA, if made a party, should be aligned as a defendant. Its interest was the same as Yost's, to defeat Torrington's claim to enjoin Yost from working for INA. Thus, since joining INA would defeat diversity, the court had to decide whether to hear the case between the original parties, despite its potential effect on INA, or to dismiss it.

4. *Torrington's* Rule 19(b) analysis. Because INA could not be joined, the court turns to the Rule 19(b) analysis and concludes that dismissal is the better option.

Deciding the claim without INA would not really resolve the dispute, since INA might still use trade secret information it got from Yost. Yost could end up whipsawed, subject to inconsistent obligations to his former and current employers. And Torrington would not get all the relief it wanted, since the judgment would not bind INA. Perhaps the court would have chosen to proceed anyway if there were no alternative, but the fourth factor—whether the plaintiff will have an adequate remedy if the case is dismissed—also supported dismissal: Torrington can sue Yost and INA together in state court, where diversity is unnecessary and the parties can adjudicate the entire dispute in a single action.

Q **5. Lawyering strategy: Rule 19 as a forum-shopping tool.** In litigation, the *reasons* parties offer in support of a motion may differ from their *motives* for making those arguments. Why might Yost make his motion to dismiss even if he was not particularly concerned about incurring an inconsistent obligation to INA?

A Yost's lawyers may have used Rule 19 as a forum-shopping tool. INA may have known about Yost's agreement when it hired him. Perhaps it even provided Yost's defense in the federal case. Yost may have made his motion because he (and INA) preferred to litigate the case in state court. By convincing the court that INA is indispensable, Yost got the case dismissed from federal court for lack of jurisdiction, leaving Torrington to sue in state court instead.

After the federal case is dismissed, Torrington may have to sue Yost and INA in a Georgia state court instead of in South Carolina. Yost worked for Torrington in South Carolina, but for INA in Georgia. If INA must be made a defendant, it may not be subject to personal jurisdiction in South Carolina.

So, while Yost frames the argument for dismissal under the standards of Rule 19, everyone, including the judge, may understand that the parties are jockeying for a procedural advantage independent of the factors in Rule 19.

Q **6. Applying Rule 19.** Cardena, from Michigan, hires Kelleher Plumbing Company to do the plumbing work on his new house and Nashoba Electric Company to do the wiring. He is unhappy with both jobs and sues Nashoba (from Wisconsin) in federal court. Nashoba moves to join Kelleher (from Michigan) in the federal action under Rule 19. How should the court rule?

A The court should deny the motion. Nothing in Rule 19 makes Kelleher a person to be joined if feasible. Rule 19(a)(1)(A) does not require joinder, because Cardena can recover fully from Nashoba for any defects in its work without litigating his claim against Kelleher in the federal suit. Rule 19(a)(1)(B) is not implicated because Kelleher won't be affected in any way by this suit between Cardena and Nashoba about Nashoba's unrelated work. Cardena here has two claims based on separate disputes with different contractors on a single job.

7. A twist on the last question.

Assume the same facts, except that the house burned down while Kelleher and Nashoba were both working on it. Cardena sues Nashoba in federal court for the damage to the house, claiming that its negligence caused the fire. Nashoba moves to dismiss for failure to join Kelleher, arguing that negligence of Kelleher's plumbers may have caused the fire instead, or the plumbers' negligence may have contributed to the fire along with Nashoba's, so it must also be made a defendant.

A. The court should order Kelleher joined as a defendant under Rule 20(a)(2).
B. The court should order Kelleher joined if feasible under Rule 19(a)(1)(A).
C. The court should order Kelleher joined if feasible under Rule 19(a)(1)(B).
D. The court should not order Kelleher joined under either Rule 19 or Rule 20.

A is wrong. Rule 20(a) addresses when parties may be made parties at the *plaintiff's option*, not when they should be ordered joined by the court. Nashoba is a defendant claiming that an absentee should be made a party. Its motion should be analyzed instead under Rule 19(a).

B is wrong as well. Rule 19(a)(1)(A) does not apply, because complete relief can be given to Cardena without Kelleher's presence in the action. If Cardena proves that Nashoba's negligence caused the fire, Nashoba will be held liable for the full damages. Of course, if the jury finds that Nashoba was not negligent, Cardena will lose his suit against Nashoba. But he will still get the full relief he is entitled to *from Nashoba* (which would be nothing in that case). Rule 19(a)(1)(A) does not require any party who might be liable to the plaintiff *instead of the defendant* to be made a party.

C also fails; Rule 19(a)(1)(B) does not apply to these facts. The judgment in Cardena's suit will not have any effect on Kelleher. Suppose that the jury finds Nashoba not liable because Kelleher's employees caused the fire. That finding in the suit against Nashoba would not bind Kelleher, since it was not a party to the case. Nor would Nashoba (the original defendant) be subject to any "inconsistent obligations" if Kelleher is not joined. If it is found negligent in Cardena's suit, it will be held liable to him. If not, it won't be.

D is the best choice. Courts uniformly hold that Rule 19 does not require joinder of other tortfeasors in cases like this. *See, e.g., Temple v. Synthes Corp.*, 498 U.S. 5 (1990). The plaintiff has chosen her defendant. If she proves its liability, she will recover. If not, she will lose. But nothing requires that another potentially liable person be joined to effectively litigate the claim against the first tortfeasor.

8. Rule 19(b): The third step. Early cases treated the problem of joining absent parties in a formalistic way: A party was labeled necessary or indispensable. If necessary, she had to be brought in. If she couldn't be, she would be labeled "indispensable" and dismissal was generally ordered.

Rule 19 as revised in 1966 now treats the problem as a series of discretionary decisions to be made in the administration of justice. First—under Rule 19(a)—the court asks whether the absentee ought to be brought into the case. This question has no mechanical answer; it involves a discretionary evaluation of the parties' interests on which judges may differ. Such Rule 19(a) decisions will be reviewed under an abuse of discretion standard.

If a party should be brought in but cannot be, Rule 19(b) guides the judge in making a second discretionary decision: whether the case should proceed without the absentee, proceed on the basis of limited relief that will not prejudice the interests of the absentee, or be dismissed because the absentee cannot be made a party. Rule 19(b) describes four factors to guide the trial judge in choosing among those options. If the judge proceeds to hear the case, the Rule suggests several means of lessening any adverse effect on the absentee and those already parties. The judge is also to consider whether she can order appropriate relief without the absentee before the court and what will happen if she dismisses the case, such as whether there is another court in which the parties can obtain complete or more efficient relief.

9. Rule 19(b): Crafting the relief to avoid prejudice to absentees. Rule 19(b) also recognizes that if an absentee should be joined but cannot be, the judge may be able to hear the case but limit the relief to avoid adverse effects due to the absence of an interested party. Here are some examples in which a court might fairly choose to limit the scope of its judgment rather than dismiss the case.

A. Plaintiff sues A for rescission of a contract and for damages. However, B, a co-obligor under the contract with A, is not joined. The court cannot order rescission, since an order rescinding the contract would affect B's rights under the contract, but could grant damages for breach instead.

B. After Jones dies, Corea, who would inherit Jones's estate if he died without a will, sues to invalidate a will executed by Jones that leaves $2,000 to Danzig and the rest of the estate, worth $5 million, to Pressman. Pressman is made a party to the action, but Danzig is not subject to the court's jurisdiction. Very likely, Corea doesn't care much about the $2,000; her eyes are on the $5 million. The court could adjudicate the claim, and, if it holds the will invalid, order the $5 million paid to Corea but hold back $2,000 in the estate in case Danzig files a claim.

C. Defendant causes a motor vehicle accident in which Lopez, Pacheco, and Yu are seriously injured. Pacheco brings suit for his injuries. Defendant's insurance policy provides $100,000 coverage per accident. Defendant argues that Lopez and Yu should be joined as plaintiffs, since Pacheco's damages might exhaust the $100,000 in coverage, leaving Lopez and Yu with judgments that could not be satisfied if they sued in separate actions. The court might adjudicate the claim but suspend execution of the judgment (collection by Pacheco) until suits by Lopez and Yu are decided or until the statute of limitations passes.

As these examples demonstrate, a little creativity may alleviate the risk of prejudice to the interests of absentees. A court might not be able to do everything the parties want, but it may still be able to do a great deal to resolve the dispute.

III. Intervention Under Rule 24

It may seem unlikely that a person not named as a party in litigation would ever seek to get involved in it. Surprisingly, non-parties frequently seek to participate in cases in which they have not been made a party by moving to *intervene* in the case. A few examples illustrate why strangers to litigation might seek to participate in it.

A. In *Ford Motor Company v. Bisanz Brothers, Inc.*, 249 F.2d 22 (8th Cir. 1957), property owners sued a railroad to force it to close down certain storage tracks in

St. Paul, Minnesota. Ford Motor Company moved to intervene as a defendant. It alleged that those tracks were essential to the operation of its auto assembly plant and the plant would have to be closed down if the tracks were ordered closed.

B. In *Stuyvesant Town Corp. v. Impelletteri*, 113 N.Y.S.2d 593 (N.Y. App. Div. 1952), the owner of a rent-controlled housing development applied to the city for an increase in rents. In the court proceeding between the owner and the city, a tenant and several tenant organizations moved to intervene. They wanted to challenge the owner's evidence and arguments in favor of a rent increase.

C. *Dodd v. Reese*, 24 N.E.2d 995 (Ind. 1940), involved a probate action by nephews of a decedent. They sought to set aside the adoption of Wise, who, due to the adoption, became a beneficiary of the decedent's estate. The nephews claimed that the adoption was obtained through the fraudulent conduct of Dodd, an attorney. Dodd moved to intervene as a defendant to contest these allegations. He claimed he would suffer serious damage to his professional reputation if the court held that he had committed fraud in handling the adoption.

In each of these cases, the non-party is "a stranger to the suit" who was not named as a party. In each, however, the resolution of the case will likely have a significant practical effect on the non-party's interests. In each, the non-party would like to participate in deciding the issues that might affect those interests.

Intervention is frequently sought in large cases involving important public issues, sometimes referred to as "public law litigation." Consider these examples:

A. In *Sierra Club v. Espy*, 18 F.3d 1202 (5th Cir. 1994), the Sierra Club brought suit against the United States Forest Service, challenging certain logging practices implemented by the Service. The Texas Forestry Association and the Southern Timber Purchasers Council, two groups representing the lumbering industry, sought to intervene to argue in support of the Forest Service practices.

B. In *Natural Resources Defense Council v. United States Nuclear Regulatory Commission*, 578 F.2d 1341 (10th Cir. 1978), an environmental organization sued the federal agency that licenses uranium mills, seeking a declaratory judgment that federal law required the mills to file an environmental impact statement before the mills could be licensed. The American Mining Congress, representing mill operators, and Kerr-McGee, a company that operated a uranium mill, sought to intervene to argue that impact statements are not required under federal law.

Again, the intervenors in each of these cases were not named as original parties but foresaw that the case would have a practical impact on their interests. Unsurprisingly, they sought to have their interests considered by taking part in the litigation.

In many cases—including those described above—this is a reasonable request and should be granted. But adding additional parties to a case comes with a price, making litigation more expensive and time consuming. Instead of two lawyers at every deposition, there may be five. Instead of one lawyer cross-examining the plaintiff's witnesses at trial, there may be several. More claims may be added to the case if intervenors assert crossclaims or counterclaims in the action. Motions and notices must be served on more parties, and the court will have to read more briefs and hear from more lawyers at oral arguments. Thus, applications to intervene pose a dilemma for the court. The court wants to allow those with an interest to be heard, but it also wants to resolve cases quickly and efficiently.

Certainly, allowing everyone with an interest in a case to become a litigant could be unworkable. Consider a case brought by a natural gas pipe line company seeking a license to build a pipe line across property in a town. Which of the following interested spectators should be allowed to intervene in the litigation?*

A. Homeowners whose land is likely to be taken by eminent domain for construction of the pipe line.

B. A local public utility that will purchase gas transported through the pipe line.

C. A local oil company whose business will be hurt if a new pipe line creates competition from the gas company.

D. Homeowners a mile from the proposed pipe line who believe it will lower property values in the town.

E. An environmental organization that seeks to lessen global warming by encouraging use of alternative fuels.

F. A citizen of a nearby town who fears that escaping gas could pose a hazard to motorists driving nearby.

Manifestly, the interests of some of these bystanders are more immediate than others. (Who do you think has the strongest case for being allowed in? The weakest?) In drafting Rule 24, the drafters tried to define a standard that will allow the most significantly affected bystanders to intervene without making litigation unwieldy for those already parties to it.

The provisions of Rule 24. Rule 24 defines two categories of intervenors—intervenors of right under Rule 24(a) and permissive intervenors under Rule 24(b). An intervenor has a right to participate under Rule 24(a) if a federal statute authorizes intervention (Fed. R. Civ. P. 24(a)(1)) or if she

> (2) claims an interest relating to the property or transaction that is the subject of the action, and is so situated that disposing of the action may as a practical matter impair or impede the movant's ability to protect its interest, unless existing parties adequately represent that interest.

Fed. R. Civ. P. 24(a)(2). This subsection contains three requirements, or more accurately, two requirements and an exception. First, the intervenor must have an interest relating to the property or transaction at issue in the case. Second, there must be a risk that her ability to protect that interest will be impaired if the case is decided without her participation. Third, *even if the first two requirements are met*, the applicant will not be allowed to intervene if her interest is adequately protected by those who are already parties to the case.

Rule 24(b)(1)(B) provides an alternative route to intervention if an applicant does not satisfy the standard for intervention as of right under Rule 24(a). The court may grant permission if the applicant "has a claim or defense that shares with the main action a common question of law or fact." This standard is extremely broad, even broader than the standard in Rule 20(a) for joining original parties to the

*This example is based on one in David Shapiro, *Some Thoughts on Intervention Before Courts, Agencies, and Arbitrators*, 51 HARV. L. REV. 721, 724 (1968).

action (a common question of law or fact *and* that the claims arise out of a common transaction or occurrence). Under Rule 24(b)(1)(B), if Chung sued Ace Power Tool Company for an injury allegedly caused by a defectively designed saw manufactured by Ace, Noriega might be allowed to intervene to recover for an injury he suffered at a different time and place using the same model. These two claims do not arise out of the same occurrence, but would share a common question of fact—whether the saw was defectively designed.

While the Rule 24(b) standard is broad, the judge should only allow permissive intervention if she determines that the person's interest merits participation and that allowing her to participate will not "unduly delay or prejudice the adjudication of the original parties' rights." Fed. R. Civ. P. 24(b)(3).

READING *GRUTTER v. BOLLINGER.* The *Grutter* case below focuses on intervention as of right. It involves two "reverse discrimination" cases, one against the University of Michigan Law School (the *Grutter* litigation) and one against the undergraduate College of Literature, Science, and the Arts (the *Gratz* case). A "reverse discrimination" case challenges affirmative action programs on the ground that preferences to minority applicants discriminate against non-minority applicants (such as the plaintiff). Because the two cases posed the same issues against the same defendant (Bollinger was the President of the University), they were consolidated and litigated together in the federal district court. In reviewing the trial judge's decision to allow intervention in both cases, the court of appeals addresses each step in the Rule 24(a)(2) analysis.

- Identify what relief the plaintiffs in the two cases wanted from the court.
- Who moved to intervene in the case? Did they seek to intervene as plaintiffs or defendants?
- What was the applicants' interest in being heard in the case, and what did they fear might happen if the case was decided without their participation?
- Articulate the court's reasons for concluding that the applicants were not adequately represented by the original parties to the case.

GRUTTER v. BOLLINGER

188 F.3d 394 (6th Cir. 1999)

DAUGHTREY, Circuit Judge.

Before us are two cases in which proposed defendant-intervenors were denied intervention under Federal Rule of Civil Procedure 24(a) and (b), in actions brought against the University of Michigan contesting the use of an applicant's race as a factor in determining admission. The appeals come from separate district courts but present similar, and in some instances the same, issues for our consideration. We have therefore consolidated the two cases for purposes of this opinion, and we find in both instances that the district courts erred in denying intervention under Rule 24(a).

PROCEDURAL AND FACTUAL BACKGROUND

In each of the cases before the court, a group of students and one or more coalitions appeal the denial of their motion to intervene in a lawsuit brought to challenge a race-conscious admissions policy at the University of Michigan. The named plaintiffs in *Gratz v. Bollinger* are two white applicants who were denied admission to the College of Literature, Arts and Science. They allege that the College's admissions policy violates the Equal Protection Clause of the Fourteenth Amendment, 42 U.S.C. § 1981 and § 1983, and 42 U.S.C. §§ 2000d *et seq.* The plaintiffs seek compensatory and punitive damages, injunctive relief forbidding continuation of the alleged discriminatory admissions process, and admission to the College. The intervenors are 17 African-American and Latino/a individuals who have applied or intend to apply to the University, and the Citizens for Affirmative Action's Preservation (CAAP), a nonprofit organization whose stated mission is to preserve opportunities in higher education for African-American and Latino/a students in Michigan. The intervenors claim that the resolution of this case directly threatens the access of qualified African-American and Latino/a students to public higher education and that the University will not adequately represent their interest in educational opportunity. The district court denied their motion for intervention as of right, holding that the plaintiffs did not have a substantial interest in the litigation and that the University could adequately represent the proposed intervenors' interests. The district court also denied the proposed intervenors' alternative motion for permissive intervention.

The named plaintiff in *Grutter v. Bollinger* is a white woman challenging the admissions policy of the University of Michigan Law School. Like the plaintiffs in *Gratz*, she alleges that the race-conscious admissions policy utilized by the law school violates the Equal Protection Clause of the Fourteenth Amendment, 42 U.S.C. § 1981 and § 1983, and 42 U.S.C. §§ 2000d *et seq.* Grutter seeks compensatory and punitive damages, injunctive relief forbidding continuation of the alleged discriminatory admissions process, and admission to the law school. The proposed intervenors are 41 students and three pro-affirmative action coalitions. As described by the district court:

> [The] individual proposed intervenors include 21 undergraduate students of various races who currently attend [various undergraduate institutions], all of whom plan to apply to the law school for admission; five black students who currently attend [local high schools] and who also plan to apply to the law school for admission; 12 students of various races who currently attend the law school; a paralegal and a Latino graduate student at the University of Texas at Austin who intend to apply to the law school for admission; and a black graduate student at the University of Michigan who is a member of the Defend Affirmative Action Party.

The plaintiff opposed the motion to intervene, but the defendants, various officials of the Law School and the University, did not oppose the motion. The district court denied the motion to intervene as of right on the basis that the intervenors failed to show that their interests would not be adequately represented by the University. The district court also denied the proposed intervenors' alternative motion for permissive intervention.

DISCUSSION

The proposed intervenors in each of these cases contend principally that the district court erred by denying their motion to intervene as of right. . . . In this circuit, proposed intervenors must establish four elements in order to be entitled to intervene as a matter of right: (1) that the motion to intervene was timely; (2) that they have a substantial legal interest in the subject matter of the case; (3) that their ability to protect that interest may be impaired in the absence of intervention; and (4) that the parties already before the court may not adequately represent their interest. A district court's denial of intervention as of right is reviewed *de novo,* except for the timeliness element, which is reviewed for an abuse of discretion. The district court held in each of these cases that the motion for intervention was timely, and the plaintiffs do not contest this finding on appeal. We will therefore consider the motions timely and need address only the three remaining elements.

Substantial Legal Interest

The proposed intervenors must show that they have a substantial interest in the subject matter of this litigation. However, in this circuit we subscribe to a "rather expansive notion of the interest sufficient to invoke intervention of right." *Michigan State AFL-CIO v. Miller*, 103 F.3d 1240, 1245 (6th Cir. 1997). For example, an intervenor need not have the same standing necessary to initiate a lawsuit. We have also "cited with approval decisions of other courts 'reject[ing] the notion that Rule 24(a)(2) requires a specific legal or equitable interest.'" *Miller*, 103 F.3d at 1245 (quoting *Purnell* [*v. City of Akron,* 925 F.2d 941 (6th Cir. 1991)], at 948). "The inquiry into the substantiality of the claimed interest is necessarily fact-specific." *Id.*

The proposed intervenors argue that their interest in maintaining the use of race as a factor in the University's admissions program is a sufficient substantial legal interest to support intervention as of right. Specifically, they argue that they have a substantial legal interest in educational opportunity, which requires preserving access to the University for African-American and Latino/a students and preventing a decline in the enrollment of African-American and Latino/a students. The district court in *Grutter* "assumed without deciding" that the proposed intervenors do have a significant legal interest in this case and that their ability to protect that interest may be impaired by an adverse ruling in the underlying case. The district court in *Gratz*, however, determined that the proposed intervenors did *not* have a direct and substantial interest which is "legally protectable" and that they therefore failed to establish this required element. We conclude that Sixth Circuit precedent requires a finding to the contrary.

In *Jansen* [*v. City of Cincinatti*, 904 F.2d 336 (6th Cir. 1990)], black applicants and employees of the city's fire department sought to intervene in a reverse discrimination lawsuit challenging the department's use of a quota system. We noted that the proposed intervenors were parties to an earlier consent decree [an agreed judgment entered in the litigation] setting goals for minority hiring and found that the proposed intervenors did have a significantly protectable interest in the affirmative action challenged in the lawsuit. The district court in *Gratz* distinguished *Jansen*, . . . on the basis that the proposed intervenors . . . had a legally protected interest only by virtue of their status as parties to a consent decree. As the proposed intervenors point out, however, neither *Jansen* nor [a second case cited by the court] stands for the proposition that an interest must be protected by means of a consent decree or by any other particular means in order for the proposed intervenors to be able to establish that they have a substantial legal interest.

The *Gratz* district court's opinion relies heavily on the premise that the proposed intervenors do not have a significant legal interest unless they have a "legally enforceable right to have the existing admissions policy construed." We conclude that this interpretation results from a misreading of this circuit's approach to the issue. As noted earlier, we have repeatedly "cited with approval decisions of other courts 'reject[ing] the notion that Rule 24(a)(2) requires a specific legal or equitable interest.'" *Miller*, 103 F.3d at 1245. For example, in *Miller*, the Michigan Chamber of Commerce sought to intervene in a suit by labor unions challenging an amendment to Michigan's Campaign Finance Act, which extended the application of statutory restrictions on corporate political expenditures so that they applied to unions as well as to corporations. The majority found that the Chamber of Commerce did have a substantial legal interest by virtue of its role in the political process that resulted in the adoption of the contested amendments. The Chamber of Commerce was therefore allowed to intervene as of right, although the Chamber had no legal "right" to the enactment of the challenged legislation. We believe that the district court's attempt to distinguish *Miller*, as well as [other similar cases] . . . , on the sole basis that those cases involved challenges to legislation, was misguided. The case law of this circuit does not limit the finding of a substantial interest to cases involving the legislative context, any more than it limits such a finding to cases involving a consent decree. Neither a legislative context nor the existence of a consent decree is dispositive as to whether proposed intervenors have shown that they have a significant interest in the subject matter of the underlying case. We find that the interest implicated in the case now before us is even more direct, substantial, and compelling than the general interest of an organization in vindicating legislation that it had previously supported. This case is, if anything, a significantly stronger case for intervention than *Miller* and many of the cases on which *Miller* relied.

Even if it could be said that the question raised is a close one, "close cases should be resolved in favor of recognizing an interest under Rule 24(a)." *Miller*, 103 F.3d at 1247. The proposed intervenors have enunciated a specific interest in the subject matter of this case, namely their interest in gaining admission to the University, which is considerably more direct and substantial than the interest of the Chamber of Commerce in *Miller*—a much more general interest. We therefore hold that the district court erred in *Gratz* in failing to rule that the proposed intervenors have established that they have a substantial legal interest in the subject matter of this case.

Impairment

"To satisfy this element of the intervention test, a would-be intervenor must show only that impairment of its substantial legal interest is possible if intervention is denied. This burden is minimal." *Miller*, 103 F.3d at 1247. As noted above, the district court in *Grutter* "assumed without deciding" that the proposed intervenors met this element. The district court in *Gratz*, however, determined that because "the proposed intervenors [ ] failed to articulate the existence of a substantial legal interest in the subject matter of the instant litigation, it necessarily follows that the proposed intervenors cannot demonstrate an impairment of any interest." The proposed intervenors in *Gratz* continue to argue on appeal that a decision in favor of the plaintiff will adversely affect their interest in educational opportunity by diminishing their likelihood of obtaining admission to the University and by reducing the number of African-American and Latino/a students at the University.

As we have now decided, the district court erred in determining that the proposed intervenors did not have a substantial interest in the subject matter of this case. Consequently, we must likewise conclude that the district court erred in its analysis of the impairment element as well. There is little room for doubt that access to the University for African-American and Latino/a students will be impaired to some extent and that a substantial decline in the enrollment of these students may well result if the University is precluded from considering race as a factor in admissions. Recent experiences in California and Texas suggest such an outcome. The probability of similar effects in Michigan is more than sufficient to meet the minimal requirements of the impairment element.

Inadequate Representation

Finally, the prospective intervenors must show that the existing defendant, the University, may not adequately represent their interests. However, the proposed intervenors are "not required to show that the representation will in fact be inadequate." *Miller*, 103 F.3d at 1247. Indeed, "[i]t may be enough to show that the existing party who purports to seek the same outcome will not make all of the prospective intervenor's arguments." *Id.* . . .

The proposed intervenors insist that there is indeed a possibility that the University will inadequately represent their interests, because the University is subject to internal and external institutional pressures that may prevent it from articulating some of the defenses of affirmative action that the proposed intervenors intend to present. They also argue that the University is at less risk of harm than the applicants if it loses this case and, thus, that the University may not defend the case as vigorously as will the proposed intervenors. The district court in *Gratz*, however, found that the proposed intervenors did not identify any specific separate or additional defenses that they will present that the University will not present. The district court in *Grutter* also found that the proposed intervenors failed to show that the University would not adequately represent their interests.

We conclude that the district court erred in each of these cases. The Supreme Court has held, and we have reiterated, that the proposed intervenors' burden in showing inadequacy is "minimal." *See Trbovich v. United Mine Workers*, 404 U.S. 528, 538 n.10 (1972). The proposed intervenors need show only that there is a *potential* for inadequate representation. The proposed intervenors in these two cases have presented legitimate and reasonable concerns about whether the University will present particular defenses of the contested race-conscious admissions policies. We find persuasive their argument that the University is unlikely to present evidence of past discrimination by the University itself or of the disparate impact of some current admissions criteria, and that these may be important and relevant factors in determining the legality of a race-conscious admissions policy. We must therefore conclude that the proposed intervenors have articulated specific relevant defenses that the University may not present and, as a consequence, have established the possibility of inadequate representation.

CONCLUSION

For the reasons set out above, we find that the proposed intervenors have shown that they have a substantial legal interest in the subject matter of this matter, that this interest will be impaired by an adverse determination, and that the existing defendant, the University, may not adequately represent their interest. Hence, the proposed intervenors are entitled to intervene as of right and the district court's decision in each of these cases denying the motion for intervention as of right cannot be sustained....

The order of the district court in each case denying intervention is REVERSED and the cases are REMANDED for entry of an order permitting intervention by the proposed defendant-intervenors under Rule 24(a)....

STAFFORD, District Judge, dissenting.

I cannot agree that the proposed intervenors in these cases have established their right to intervene as of right. I do not believe, nor do I think *Michigan State AFL-CIO v. Miller*, 103 F.3d 1240 (6th Cir. 1997), compels us to find, that the proposed intervenors' subjective fears are sufficient to satisfy their burden, however minimal, of showing that the University of Michigan will not adequately represent the proposed intervenors' interests in these two lawsuits. Unlike the State of Michigan in *Miller*, the University of Michigan here has in no way "demonstrated that it will not adequately represent and protect the interests held by the [proposed intervenors]." *Miller*, 103 F.3d at 1248. There is nothing in the record of either case to suggest that the University of Michigan will not zealously defend its voluntarily-adopted admissions policies, will not present all relevant evidence in support of its admissions policies, will not resist unspecified pressures that could temper its ability to defend its admissions policies, or will not raise all defenses or make all arguments that the prospective intervenors may raise or make. Because I do not think that we should substitute our judgment for the informed judgment of the two respective trial judges who determined that, based on the record before them, intervention was not merited, I must respectfully dissent.

Notes and Questions: *Grutter v. Bollinger*

1. Further proceedings in *Grutter*. This case ultimately reached the United States Supreme Court, not on the intervention issue, but on the validity of the University's affirmative action policy. The Court upheld the policy in *Grutter* (*see* 539 U.S. 306 (2003)), but held that the University policy at issue in the companion case, *Gratz v. Bollinger*, was invalid under the Equal Protection Clause. *See* 539 U.S. 244 (2003).

2. Putting it through the Rule 24(a) hoops. The *Grutter* court adddresses each of the three requirements in Rule 24(a)(2): The applicant's interest, the likely impairment of that interest if the action goes forward without them, and the adequacy of representation of their views by the original parties. To support intervention, the court must find that the applicant has a significant interest and that her interest may be impaired if the action goes forward without her. Even if both requirements are met, intervention will still be denied if the applicant's interest is adequately represented by the existing parties.

3. The nature of the interest required under Rule 24(a). To intervene as of right the applicant must have "an interest relating to the property or transaction that is the subject of the action." Fed. R. Civ. P. 24(a)(2). Courts have struggled to define what the nature of the applicant's interest must be. Non-parties may have varying levels of interest in someone else's lawsuit, from general curiosity to an immediate stake in the dispute. The applicant's interest must be "more than a mere 'betting' interest." *Reich v. ABC/York-Estes Corp.*, 64 F.3d 316, 322 (7th Cir. 1995). It must implicate some "significantly protectable interest" in the subject matter of the action. *Donaldson v. United States*, 400 U.S. 517, 531 (1971).

> The range of possible interests may defy adequate classification, spreading over a spectrum that is extremely hard to chart. Whether a sufficient interest exists to make intervention appropriate calls for considerable and careful judgment, and perhaps a little faith as well, with attention to such factors as the legal and practical availability of other remedies, the contribution that the prospective intervener can make to the litigation, the immediacy and degree of the harm threatened, and the advantages of avoiding multiplicity of actions.

David Shapiro, *Some Thoughts on Intervention Before Courts, Agencies, and Arbitrators*, 81 Harv. L. Rev. 721, 740 (1968).

The applicant may have a right to intervene even if she would not be bound by a decision rendered without her participation. In *Grutter*, if the intervenors had not been allowed in, and the court had overturned the University's affirmative action programs, the minority applicants would not have been barred from bringing their own actions against the University, since they had not been parties to the original case. Indeed, it seems likely that, if they had not been allowed to intervene, and the affirmative action programs had been found unconstitutional, they would have brought suit to compel the University to continue its affirmative action programs. This probability is a good reason to let them into the first suit, which will then resolve the issues and bind both the original parties and the intervenors.

4. Some examples of the interest requirement. Here are several illustrative cases in which applicants have claimed a sufficient interest to support intervention as of right under Rule 24(a)(2).

A. A utility sued its gas supplier claiming that the supplier was overcharging under the contract. Customers of the utility moved to intervene, claiming an interest in the case because their rates would rise if the supplier won, leading to increased cost to the utility for gas.

> The court held that the customers could not intervene as of right. Although the customers might suffer an indirect economic impact from the case, they had no direct interest in the contract at issue in the case. *New Orleans Public Service Inc. v. United Gas Pipe Line Co.*, 732 F.2d 452 (5th Cir. 1984). Certainly, ratepayers have an interest in the cost of the gas they buy. Very likely, at least some of them would be entitled to intervene in a proceeding to set the gas company's rates. But it is more attenuated to claim that their interest supports intervention in a dispute between the gas company and a third party that might indirectly lead to an increase in rates.

B. The Sierra Club sued the Secretary of Agriculture, claiming that clear-cutting in national forests in Texas violated federal laws. Two trade associations, representing most of the purchasers of timber from the Texas national forests, sought to intervene as defendants, to argue that clear-cutting was authorized by federal law.

> The court held that the timber associations had "legally protectable property interests" in the dispute, since their members' current and future contracts to harvest timber in the forests would be affected. *Sierra Club v. Espy*, 18 F.3d 1202, 1207 (5th Cir. 1994).

C. The United States sued Alisal Water Corporation, a water supply company. The United States sought damages for violation of environmental regulations and the appointment of a receiver to manage the company and perhaps arrange for its sale. Silverwood Estates, a housing development that had obtained a judgment against Alisal, sought to intervene. It claimed that a large award of damages to the United States or a judicial sale of Alisal could impair its ability to collect its unrelated judgment.

> The court held that Silverwood did not have an interest in the underlying subject of the litigation—Alisal's violation of environmental regulations. Its interest was in collecting its unrelated judgment. "This interest is several degrees removed from the overriding public health and environmental policies that are the backbone of this litigation." *United States v. Alisal Water Corp.*, 370 F.3d 915, 920 (9th Cir. 2004). This makes sense; otherwise creditors of a defendant could jump into any litigation that might reduce the defendant's assets. Silverwood had an interest in the defendant's solvency, but not in the underlying transaction in the case.

5. The *Grutter* court's finding on adequacy of representation. After concluding that the intervenors had a significant interest in the two suits, and that their interests might be impaired if the suits were litigated in their absence, the *Grutter* court considered whether the University, the defendant in the two suits, adequately represented the intervenors' interests. The court's discussion suggests that the burden here is minimal, that the intervenors need only show a possibility that the original defendant will not adequately defend the action. Despite such language, intervention is frequently denied if the intervenor has the same interest in the dispute as a party and is likely to make the same arguments.

Under Rule 24(c), an applicant for intervention must attach a pleading to its motion "that sets out the claim or defense for which intervention is sought." The applicant's pleading may assist the court in assessing whether the applicant simply wants to reiterate an original party's arguments or add a truly different perspective to the case.

Supporters frequently argue that affirmative action programs serve to remedy past discrimination by an institution. After they were allowed to intervene in *Grutter*, the intervenors made this argument to support the University's challenged programs.

> [The] Defendant-Intervenors contend that the University's race-conscious admissions policies serve to "remedy the present effects of discrimination that it has caused or tolerated; remedy the negative racial climate that it has sustained or that has been caused by others on the campus; and, remedy or offset the effects of any current discrimination in which it is engaged."

Gratz v. Bollinger, 135 F. Supp. 2d 790, 792 (E.D. Mich. 2001) (quoting from intervenors' brief). As the court notes in the opinion reproduced above, the University was unlikely to make this argument in defense of its programs—very few defendants in reverse discrimination cases defend their programs by condemning their own past conduct. Instead, the educational institution is more likely to "proudly declare the importance of its academic freedom without admitting its own prior discrimination." Emma Coleman Jones, *Problems and Prospects of Participation in Affirmative Action Litigation: A Role for Intervenors*, 13 U.C. Davis L. Rev. 221, 228 (1980). Thus, the intervenors did bring a different perspective and offer different arguments in defense of the suits.*

6. Government intervenors. Rule 24(a)(1) authorizes intervention whenever a statute provides a right to intervene. An example of such a statute is 28 U.S.C. § 2403(a), which authorizes the United States to intervene in any action "wherein the constitutionality of any Act of Congress affecting the public interest is drawn in question." Some states have similar statutes authorizing their attorneys general to intervene in actions that challenge state statutes. *See, e.g.*, N.Y. C.P.L.R. § 1012(b)(1).

---

* It is not clear that arguments based on remedying past discrimination are still permissible, however. *See Fisher v. University of Texas at Austin*, 570 U.S. 297, 307–08 (2013) (arguments based on remedying past discrimination cannot constitute a compelling governmental interest sufficient to support racial preferences).

7. The relation of the Rule 19(a) standard to the Rule 24(a) standard. Rules 19 and 24 were both substantially revised in 1966. Note the similarity in the standard for joining a party under Rule 19(a)(1)(B)(i) and for intervening under Rule 24(a)(2). Both Rules refer to a person who claims an interest relating to the subject of the action and is so situated "that disposing of the action in the person's absence may . . . as a practical matter impair or impede the person's ability to protect the interest." This suggests that if a person is a required party under Rule 19(a)(1)(B)(i), he is also entitled to intervene under Rule 24(a)(2). One difference between joinder under the two Rules is who seeks joinder: Typically, defendants move for joinder of a party under Rule 19, while the absentee moves to intervene under Rule 24.

As a practical matter, there is some difference in the way these concepts are applied under the two Rules.

> The phrasing of Rule 24(a)(2) as amended parallels that of Rule 19(a)(2) [now Rule 19(a)(1)(B)] concerning joinder. But the fact that the two rules are entwined does not imply that an "interest" for the purpose of one is precisely the same as for the other. The occasions upon which a petitioner should be allowed to intervene under Rule 24 are not necessarily limited to those situations when the trial court should compel him to become a party under Rule 19.

Smuck v. Hobson, 408 F.2d 175, 178 (D.C. Cir. 1969). In *Grutter*, for example, the applicants were allowed to intervene under Rule 24 but would probably not be considered required parties under Rule 19. If the University had moved to dismiss the action, claiming that all potential applicants as well as an array of affirmative action advocacy groups should be joined under Rule 19, it is inconceivable that the court would order all such bystanders into the case. After all, if some potential applicants are necessary parties, aren't they all? It would be unworkable to order all possible applicants and interest groups into the case.

Where some of those bystanders move to intervene, however, the same court may *allow* them in as intervenors, though it would not *order* them in under Rule 19. Under Rule 19 "it is the court or one of the existing parties that suggests the propriety of protecting the absentee's interests; in intervention, the *absentee* has shown sufficient concern to take the initiative in becoming a party, and his or her 'vote' should count for something." Fleming James, Geoffrey Hazard & John Leubsdorf, Civil Procedure 300 (6th ed. 2011). In practice, there is a certain amount of discretion under Rule 19(a) and Rule 24(a).

8. Multiple applications to intervene. Problems can arise, particularly in public interest cases, if multiple applications to intervene are filed. Consider the following question.

Suppose that, a year after the suits in *Grutter* were filed, the individuals and advocacy groups who originally intervened in *Grutter* were granted the right to intervene. Twenty-three more potential applicants to the University, living in New York, learn of the action from an article about the intervention decision published in the *New York Times*. They quickly file applications to intervene as defendants under Rule 24, to argue in support of the University's affirmative action programs. The second application should be

A. denied, since the second group of applicants does not have an interest in the subject matter of the action.

B. denied, since their application is not timely.
C. denied, since their interests are adequately represented by those already parties to the action.
D. allowed, since they satisfy the standards for intervention under Rule 24(a)(2).

A is not correct; these further potential applicants have the same interest in preserving the University's affirmative action programs that the first group of intervenors has. If the first groups meet the standard, presumably the later applicants do too.

B seems like a possibility. Rule 24(a) specifies that an application to intervene must be "timely," and here the application to intervene was filed a year after the action was commenced. But timeliness is not measured rigidly from commencement of the action; it will be judged practically based on whether the intervenors acted promptly after becoming aware of the action. Here it appears that the second group applied to intervene shortly after learning of the case.

C seems like it shouldn't be right—after all, the court in the *Grutter* opinion held that the intervenors' interests were not adequately represented by the original parties. But now, those "already parties to the action" *includes the first group of intervenors*. Unless this other group of applicants are somehow distinguishable from the first group, in terms of their interests and arguments in support of the University's programs, the court is likely to avoid hydra-like expansion of the case by denying intervention on the ground that the later applicants' interests are adequately represented by the original intervenors. Thus **C**, not **D**, is the best answer.

9. Levels of participation in litigation: Conditions on intervention. Intervention is not necessarily an all-or-nothing proposition. A party might be allowed to intervene for limited purposes or only on certain claims in the case. *See* Advisory Committee Note to 1966 Amendment to Rule 24(a). In *Stringfellow v. Concerned Neighbors in Action*, 480 U.S. 370 (1987), for example, a case involving hazardous waste clean-up, the Supreme Court allowed a neighborhood group to intervene on certain claims but not others. The Court held that the group would not be allowed to assert any additional claims for relief not raised by the original plaintiffs. It also placed conditions on the intervenors' right to file motions or to seek discovery. Alternatively, an intervenor might be limited to filing briefs and arguing motions made by the original parties, thus limiting its ability to disrupt the underlying litigation by raising new issues or scheduling additional discovery.

Intervention may also be granted for a limited purpose. A common example involves efforts by news organizations to obtain information filed in court under a confidentiality order. In *Pansy v. Borough of Stroudsburg*, 23 F.3d 772 (3d Cir. 1994), for example, a group of newspapers moved to intervene in a civil rights action to challenge a protective order that prevented public access to a settlement agreement that had been filed in the case. Similarly, in *Public Citizen v. Liggett Group, Inc.*, 858 F.2d 775 (1st Cir. 1988), a citizen's group intervened solely to seek access to discovery documents that had been produced in the litigation.

Even if intervention is denied, an interested non-party may have other means to be heard. Courts often allow groups with an interest to file amicus briefs—"friend of the court" briefs—in support of a party's position. (Westlaw lists over fifty amicus briefs filed in the appellate courts in *Grutter*!) In appropriate cases, an amicus party may even be allowed to examine witnesses or introduce evidence. Jack Weinstein, *Litigation Seeking Changes in Public Behavior and Institutions—Some Views on Participation*, 13 U.C. Davis L. Rev. 231, 237 (1980).

Participation . . . Without Joinder

- **2003 WL 554403 (Appellate Brief) Brief Amicus Curiae of the New York State Black and Puerto Rican Legislative Caucus (Feb. 19, 2003)**
- **2003 WL 398292 (Appellate Brief) Brief of the American Educational Research Association, the Association of American Colleges and Universities, and the American Association for Higher Education as Amici Curiae in Support of Respondents (Feb. 18, 2003)**
- **2003 WL 398313 (Appellate Brief) Brief of the American Sociological Association, et al., as Amici Curiae in Support of Respondents (Feb. 18, 2003)**
- **2003 WL 398328 (Appellate Brief) Brief for the Arizona State University College of Law Supporting Respondents (Feb. 18, 2003)**
- **2003 WL 398358 (Appellate Brief) Brief Amici Curiae of the Coalition for Economic Equity, The Santa Clara University School of Law Center for Social Justice and Public Service, The Justice Collective, The Charles Houston Bar Association, and The California Association of Black Lawyers in Support of Respondents (Feb. 18, 2003)**
- **2003 WL 398384 (Appellate Brief) Brief Amici Curiae of The Hispanic National Bar Association and the Hispanic Association of Colleges and Universities in Support of Respondents (Feb. 18, 2003)**
- **2003 WL 398388 (Appellate Brief) Brief of King County Bar Association as Amicus Curiae in Support of Respondents (Feb. 18, 2003)**
- **2003 WL 399207 (Appellate Brief) Brief of the Harvard Black Law Students Association, Stanford Black Law Students Association and Yale Black Law Students Association as Amici Curiae Supporting Respondents (Feb. 18, 2003)**
- **2003 WL 399229 (Appellate Brief) Brief of the Law School Admission Council as Amicus Curiae in Support of Respondents (Feb. 18, 2003)**
- **2003 WL 402236 (Appellate Brief) (Brief for Respondents (Feb. 18, 2003) [Eds.—not an amicus]**
- **2003 WL 536754 (Appellate Brief) Brief of the Clinical Legal Education Association as Amicus Curiae Supporting Respondents (Feb. 18, 2003)**

If a party is not allowed to intervene in an action, it may still be able to be heard on the issues in the case by seeking leave to file an amicus brief in support of one party or another. This allows it to be heard on legal issues without becoming a party to the action. This snippet from Westlaw lists *some* of the amicus briefs filed in *Grutter v. Bollinger*. The excerpt reflects the range of groups that wished to be heard on the affirmative action issues in the case.

10. Appeals from denial of an application to intervene. Ordinarily, appeals may only be taken from "final decisions of the district courts." 28 U.S.C. § 1291. A party who believes that a trial judge's ruling is wrong has to wait until the end of the case to seek appellate review of that ruling. (For example, if the judge denied access to certain information in discovery early in the litigation, the party seeking that information would have to wait to appeal that decision until after the case went to final judgment in the federal district court.) If this general rule applied to intervenors, however, it would effectively insulate intervention decisions from appellate review. The motion to intervene seeks the opportunity to *participate in the litigation*. If § 1291 barred immediate appeal of intervention decisions, an applicant who was denied intervention would have to sit out the case, and then appeal claiming that she *should have been allowed* to participate. If the appellate court concluded that the applicant should have been allowed to intervene, it would have to undo the entire subsequent course of the case and order it relitigated with the applicant's participation. You can imagine how reluctant an appellate court would be to order such a monumentally inefficient procedure.

Consequently, federal courts hold that denial of an application to intervene as of right is a final decision that is immediately appealable. *See Dickinson v. Petroleum Conversion Corp.*, 338 U.S. 507, 513 (1950); *see generally Moore* § 24.24.* The intervenor may appeal right away, arguing that she should be allowed to participate. If the appellate court holds that intervention should have been granted, it can order it granted, and the case can proceed with the applicant's participation. This is why the applicants' appeal in *Grutter* reached the Sixth Circuit while the case was still proceeding below.

This solution isn't entirely satisfactory either. The applicant's appeal is going to take time—a year might be a rough average. If the underlying case proceeds in the trial court while the appeal is pending, the applicant is not participating. If the case is stayed (suspended) in the trial court pending the appeal, everyone loses time.

An order *granting* intervention, however, is generally held to be an interlocutory decision not immediately appealable. *See, e.g., Stringfellow v. Concerned Neighbors in Action*, 480 U.S. 370 (1987). So, a party who objects to the intervenor's presence must wait until the end of the case to appeal the grant of intervention. What should the appellate court do if intervention should have been denied? Can you imagine a court saying, "well, the intervenor shouldn't have participated, so we order the parties to go back and do it all over without the intervenor"? Very likely, a court would find that the intervenor's participation had not prejudiced the losing parties' rights and affirm based on the concept of "harmless error." As a practical matter, then, if intervention is *granted*, it is effectively unreviewable; if you are to win this battle at all, you must win it in front of the trial judge.

IV. An Introduction to Interpleader

Federal procedure provides another method for joining parties in certain circumstances. The device of interpleader allows a party facing conflicting claims to the same property or fund to *interplead* the various claimants to obtain a judgment of ownership that will bind all claimants. Interpleader "allows someone in

---

* Some courts have held that the denial of intervention may *only* be appealed at the time of denial. An appeal after final judgment in the case will be dismissed as untimely. *See, e.g., B.H. by Pierce v. Murphy*, 984 F.2d 196, 199 (7th Cir. 1993). At least one state—New Jersey—rejects the federal approach and bars appeal of the denial of intervention until a final judgment is entered. *See Huny & BH Associates Inc. v. Silverberg*, 149 A.3d 857 (2016).

possession of property or money to force all adverse claimants to that property to litigate the ownership of that property in a single proceeding." *Freer* § 13.2.1.

Here are some situations in which a party might invoke interpleader to settle conflicting claims to the same property:

A. In *Mark E. Mitchell, Inc. v. Charleston Library Society*, 114 F. Supp. 2d 259 (S.D.N.Y. 2000), a corporation consigned a rare 1776 edition of a newspaper, containing one of the earliest copies of the Declaration of Independence, to Christie's auction house to be sold at auction. The document was sold to a gallery, but before it was delivered, the Charleston Library Society asserted a claim that it owned the document. Christie's, which asserted no claim to ownership itself, sought to interplead the various claimants to the document to obtain a ruling as to who was entitled to receive it.

B. National Assurance Company issued a life insurance policy to Zobel. Zobel designated "my wife" as the beneficiary of the policy. At the time of the designation, he was married to Belle. He later divorced Belle and married Marina. After his death, Belle and Marina both claimed to be the "wife" entitled to the proceeds of the policy. The insurer brought an action in interpleader to determine who should receive the proceeds of the policy.

C. A bank foreclosed a mortgage on Carter's home and sold it at a foreclosure sale. The property brought more than the amount due on the mortgage, leaving the bank with the excess proceeds of the sale. The homeowner, a second mortgagee, and creditors of the owner all claimed that these funds should be paid to them. The bank made no claim to the excess but wanted to know who it should pay. It filed an action in interpleader naming the various claimants as defendants and seeking a ruling as to how it should distribute the excess.

Without interpleader, "stakeholders" in cases like these face a dilemma. In *Charlestown Library Society*, for example, suppose that Christie's concluded that the Society really owned the document and delivered it to the Society. It would probably be sued by the consigning corporation based on its claim of ownership. Similarly, in the foreclosure case, if the bank turns the excess over to the homeowner, it might be sued by the second mortgagee and others, claiming that the extra funds should have been paid to them. After litigation, the bank might end up paying twice. And in the life insurance case, if the insurer pays the proceeds to Belle, it will likely face a suit from Marina demanding payment to her. In all three cases, interpleader allows the holder of the property to tender the property or money to the court, and leave the various claimants to litigate ownership before a court that can bind all the parties by its resulting judgment.

Notes and Questions on Interpleader

1. The federal interpleader statute. The joinder devices covered so far in this chapter are found in the Federal Rules of Civil Procedure. Interestingly, Congress has provided a statutory procedure for litigating interpleader cases in the federal courts:

> **28 U.S.C. § 1335(a).** The district courts shall have original jurisdiction of any civil action of interpleader or in the nature of interpleader filed by any person,

> firm, or corporation, association, or society having in his or its custody or possession money or property of the value of $500 or more, or having issued a note, bond, certificate, policy of insurance, or other instrument of value or amount of $500 or more, or providing for the delivery or payment or the loan of money or property of such amount or value, or being under any obligation written or unwritten to the amount of $500 or more, if
>
> (1) Two or more adverse claimants, of diverse citizenship as defined in subsection (a) or (d) of section 1332 of this title, are claiming or may claim to be entitled to such money or property, or to any one or more of the benefits arising by virtue of any note, bond, certificate, policy or other instrument, or arising by virtue of any such obligation; and if
>
> (2) the plaintiff has deposited such money or property or has paid the amount of or the loan or other value of such instrument or the amount due under such obligation into the registry of the court, there to abide the judgment of the court, or has given bond payable to the clerk of the court in such amount and with such surety as the court or judge may deem proper, conditioned upon the compliance by the plaintiff with the future order or judgment of the court with respect to the subject matter of the controversy.

Under § 1335, a party may file a federal interpleader action if (1) it has possession of money or property worth more than $500; (2) there are two or more diverse claimants to the money or property; and (3) the plaintiff has deposited the money or property in the court or given a bond for compliance with the court's eventual order for payment of the money or property.

2. Statutory interpleader: Congress authorizes jurisdiction based on "minimal diversity." Section 1335 authorizes a stakeholder—the party holding the property or funds—to file an interpleader action in federal court as long as at least two claimants are from different states. If the stakeholder is from Minnesota, one claimant is from New York, and four claimants are from Minnesota, the court has jurisdiction, since there are two adverse claimants of diverse citizenship. Even though other claimants are from the same state, and the stakeholder is from the same state as some claimants, jurisdiction is proper based on "minimal diversity."

3. But can Congress do that? Yes, it can. Jurisdiction in interpleader cases is based on minimal diversity rather than "complete diversity" as required by *Strawbridge v. Curtiss*, 7 U.S. 267 (1806). However, *Strawbridge* interpreted 28 U.S.C. § 1332, not § 1335. In *State Farm Fire & Cas. Co. v. Tashire*, 386 U.S. 523 (1967), the Supreme Court held that a case is "between citizens of different states" within the *constitutional* grant in Article III, Section 2 as long as minimal diversity exists.

> In a variety of contexts this Court and the lower courts have concluded that Article III poses no obstacle to the legislative extension of federal jurisdiction, founded on diversity, so long as any two adverse parties are not co-citizens.

Id. at 531. In other words, a case satisfies the constitutional definition of a case "between citizens of different states" as long as there is diversity between any two adverse parties. In the interpleader statute, Congress granted diversity jurisdiction based on such minimal diversity. But Congress has never amended 28 U.S.C. § 1332(a), the basic diversity statute, to allow jurisdiction based on minimal diversity, so Chief Justice Marshall's complete diversity rule still applies to cases under § 1332(a).

4. Advantages of statutory interpleader. The Federal Rules also contain a provision authorizing interpleader, separate from the statutory procedure in 28 U.S.C. § 1335. *See* Fed. R. Civ. P. 22. However, statutory interpleader provides several advantages over rule interpleader (discussed further in note 6). First, as just explained, it authorizes subject matter jurisdiction based on minimal diversity. Second, the statute authorizes nationwide personal jurisdiction over the claimants. 28 U.S.C. § 2361. For a judgment to bind all claimants to the property, the court in which the action is filed must be able to bring all the claimants before the same court. Where the claimants are spread among several states, this would frequently not be possible under state long arm statutes.

For example, suppose that Jaworski buys a life insurance policy from General Life in Kentucky. He moves to Vermont and dies, leaving four claimants to the proceeds of the policy, residing in Texas, Utah, Vermont, and Michigan. The claimants from Texas, Utah, and Michigan might not be subject to personal jurisdiction in Vermont for a suit to determine the right to the proceeds. If suit were brought in Texas, that court might not have personal jurisdiction over the Utah, Vermont, and Michigan claimants, and so forth.

The interpleader statute addresses this difficulty by providing that claimants from anywhere in the country may be brought before the court through "nationwide service of process." "[A] district court may issue its process for all claimants..." wherever they are found. 28 U.S.C. § 2361. In Jaworski's case, the court in which the interpleader action is filed could exercise jurisdiction over all four claimants, even if they had no contacts in the state where the district court sat.

For an example of the efficacy of statutory interpleader, consider *Noble Energy Inc. v. Perkins*, No. 03CV1014, 2003 WL 24840163 (E.D. Tex. Oct. 1, 2003). In *Noble*, energy companies sought to distribute royalties to those with an interest in a tract of land from which they had extracted gas and other minerals. The complaint lists 152 claimants who might have a property interest in the tract, and thus be entitled to a share of the royalties. Nationwide jurisdiction under 28 U.S.C. § 1335 allowed the producers to get all potential claimants into one court, which could render a binding judgment that would determine the rights of all claimants.

5. Can Congress do that? It probably can. Recall that the constitutional limit on the exercise of personal jurisdiction by a federal court is found in the Fifth Amendment to the United States Constitution, not the Fourteenth, which constrains state court exercises of personal jurisdiction. This Fifth Amendment limit has been construed to allow a federal court to exercise jurisdiction over defendants as long as they have minimum contacts with the United States rather than with a particular state. *See, e.g., In re Federal Foundation, Inc.*, 165 F.3d 600, 602 (8th Cir. 1999).* All four of the

---

* Not all courts accept this view without qualification. *See, e.g., Peay v. BellSouth Med. Assistance Plan*, 205 F.3d 1206, 1211–13 (10th Cir. 2000) (even where federal statute authorizes nationwide service, forum must be fair and reasonable to the defendant). Even in courts that take this view, however, the fact that interpleader can only be effective if all parties are brought into a single forum is likely to influence the court's analysis of what is fair.

claimants in Jaworski's case have such contacts, since they are domiciled within the United States. Thus, all four would be subject to personal jurisdiction in the statutory interpleader action, so the court could resolve all claims to the proceeds of the policy.

6. "Rule interpleader" as an alternative. Confusingly, Rule 22 of the Federal Rules of Civil Procedure provides a separate mechanism for filing interpleader cases. The requirements of "Rule interpleader" are different from those under 28 U.S.C. § 1335, the federal interpleader statute:

- The nationwide service provision in 28 U.S.C. § 2361 does not apply to Rule interpleader. Thus, the claimants must be subject to personal jurisdiction under traditional analysis. Usually, this means that the federal court may exercise personal jurisdiction to the same extent as the courts of the state in which the federal court sits. Fed. R. Civ. P. 4(k)(1)(A).
- Subject matter jurisdiction in a Rule 22 interpleader case must be based on one of the usual bases of federal court jurisdiction, most commonly, diversity under 28 U.S.C. § 1332(a) or federal question jurisdiction under 28 U.S.C. § 1331. Thus, jurisdiction may not be based on minimal diversity, as it may be in a statutory interpleader case. In addition, diversity is measured by comparing the citizenship of the *stakeholder* to that of the claimants, not comparing the citizenship of the claimants to each other. In addition, the amount in controversy must exceed $75,000, rather than the $500 amount specified in § 1335.
- A special venue statute applies to statutory interpleader cases. 28 U.S.C. § 1397. The general federal venue statute governs Rule interpleader cases.

Q **7. Comparing statutory and Rule interpleader.** Which of following cases could be brought as an interpleader case under Fed. R. Civ. P. 22? Under 28 U.S.C. § 1335?

- A Nevada insurer holds $100,000 in proceeds of a policy, claimed by four claimants, three from Iowa and one from Nevada.
- A Kentucky county holds a $50,000 reward offered for apprehension of an armed robber. Four Arkansas citizens claim that their information led to the arrest.
- An art gallery, incorporated in Illinois with its principal place of business there, holds a painting, valued at $125,000, that is claimed by four heirs of the decedent. All four heirs live in Oklahoma.

A This question illustrates the differing requirements for subject matter jurisdiction in Rule interpleader and statutory interpleader cases. The first case could be brought as a statutory interpleader case because there is minimal diversity between the claimants and more than $500 is in controversy. But it could not be brought under Fed. R. Civ. P. 22 because there is not complete diversity between the stakeholder and the claimants.

The second case cannot be brought as an interpleader case. Section 1335(a) is not met, since there is not even minimal diversity among the claimants. And it cannot be brought as a Rule interpleader case because the $75,000 amount-in-controversy requirement for diversity cases is not met.

Given the flexibility of statutory interpleader, students often ask why a stakeholder would ever use Rule interpleader. The last case illustrates a situation in which Rule 22 interpleader is proper but statutory interpleader is not. There is diversity between all claimants and the stakeholder in this case and the $75,000 amount-in-controversy requirement is met. But there is not minimal diversity among the claimants, so statutory interpleader is not proper.

Note that interpleader, like Rules 19 and 24, serves the policy of bringing parties before the court who share an interest in the subject of the litigation.

8. Enjoining other actions. One of the purposes of interpleader is to avoid a multiplicity of actions, that is, to protect the stakeholder from being sued by different claimants in different courts. The interpleader statute expressly authorizes injunctions against other actions:

> a district court may . . . enter its order restraining [the claimants] from instituting or prosecuting any proceeding in any State or United States court affecting the property, instrument or obligation involved in the interpleader action until further order of the court.

28 U.S.C. § 2361. There's lots more to know about interpleader—one of the major federal procedure treatises, *Wright & Miller*, goes on about it quite learnedly for 180 pages. State rules provide for interpleader in their courts as well. But most of you will never litigate an interpleader case, so this should suffice for an introduction.

V. Complex Joinder: Summary of Basic Principles

- Rule 19 addresses situations in which a person who has not been made a party should participate in the litigation to assure a just resolution of the dispute. Rule 19(a) provides that absentees should be made parties to the action if their rights might be adversely affected or if the dispute between the original parties cannot be fully resolved without their participation.
- Rule 19(b) provides guidance to courts in deciding what to do if an absentee should be joined under Rule 19(a) but cannot be made a party due to jurisdictional or venue problems. Rule 19(b) lists discretionary factors a court should consider in deciding whether to allow the action to proceed or to dismiss it due to the absence of the person "needed for just adjudication."
- Rule 24 authorizes persons not joined in a suit to move to intervene. If the motion is granted, the intervenor becomes a party to the litigation. Rule 24(a) provides that a non-party has a right to intervene if she has an interest in the transaction and that interest may be impaired unless she is allowed to become a party.
- Even if a party has such an interest under Rule 24(a), intervention may be denied if that party's interest is adequately represented in the action by one of the existing parties.

- Rule 24(b) authorizes permissive intervention if the applicant's claim or defense involves a question of law or fact that is also raised by the main action. However, judges have wide discretion to deny permissive intervention even if this standard is met.
- Interpleader is a proceeding that brings all claimants to particular funds or property before the court in a single suit in order to avoid multiple suits and possible inconsistent judgments. An action in interpleader is brought by the stakeholder, the party holding the disputed property or fund, naming the contending claimants to the property or fund as defendants.
- Federal procedure provides two types of interpleader actions, statutory interpleader under 28 U.S.C. § 1335 and Rule interpleader under Fed. R. Civ. P. 22. Statutory interpleader has several advantages, including the right to file based on minimal diversity, a low amount-in-controversy requirement, and the authority to exercise jurisdiction over claimants found anywhere in the United States.

19

Class Actions

I. Introduction

Haynes purchased a washing machine with what was described as a stainless steel drum. When some of his best clothes are ruined by rust stains from the machine, he discovers that the drum is actually made of ceramic-coated "mild" steel, which is not regarded as stainless because it does not contain chromium. He thinks that the manufacturer, Fears Rawbuck, misled him by calling its product "stainless steel," and he would like to recover his purchase price for the washing machine ($525), plus $150 for the clothes that were ruined.

Consider Haynes's options for a lawsuit. If Haynes sues Fears and wins, Haynes will get $675 plus court costs (such as costs of service and filing of the complaint), but he will have to pay his lawyer and any costs that are not reimbursed as court costs. Under a one-third contingent fee arrangement (by which the lawyer gets one-third of any judgment that Haynes recovers, but nothing if Haynes loses), Haynes's lawyer would receive $225. Few lawyers would want to take this type of case for such a small fee. Alternatively, if Haynes has to pay the lawyer by the hour, Haynes would not want to sue because the lawyer's fee would almost certainly be higher than any recovery that Haynes might get. This type of lawsuit is known as a "negative value suit"—the cost of the lawsuit is likely to exceed any possible recovery. In sum, a lawsuit is not financially viable for Haynes and his lawyer no matter what fee arrangement they have.

But suppose that Fears Rawbuck *had* misrepresented its product, and the product was defective and caused rust stains. Should we let the economics of litigation permit Fears to go scot-free and continue its false marketing at buyers' expense? One answer is that this is a false dichotomy. Litigation is not the only response to such business misconduct: A regulatory agency could also act, if it has jurisdiction. For example, in many states, the state attorney general has statutory authority to go after unfair trade practices of this sort. Or, we could just let the market sort it out, assuming that consumers learn of the defect and refuse to buy Fears Rawbuck machines.

The problem is that government resources are limited, as is the jurisdiction of regulatory agencies and attorneys general, and consumers may lack reliable information (especially given the deceptive ads). For this reason, litigation by parties like Haynes is considered to be an important supplement to public enforcement. These "private attorneys general," however, confront the economic disincentives described above.

Class actions evolved, in part, to overcome these problems. In a class action, one or more "class representatives" litigate the action on behalf of a class of persons with similar interests,* thus allowing the parties to reduce the cost of litigating each claim and making a lawsuit more financially viable. Together, the class members' claims have a larger settlement value, and any contingent fee for the class lawyers is based on a percentage of the aggregate recovery, making class action suits more attractive to plaintiffs' lawyers. Furthermore, even when individual claims are economically viable and could be litigated separately, combining them offers possible efficiency gains to the judicial system and, sometimes, the parties. Instead of separately litigating many claims with common issues, the class action provides a vehicle for presenting the common issues in a single lawsuit for common disposition. A class action judgment is binding—has preclusive effect—not just on the class representatives, but also on the rest of the class that they represented. Thus, it prevents class members from suing for the same transaction again.

Q **Why isn't joining coplaintiffs under Rule 20 an effective substitute for suing as a class?**

A Sometimes it is. Rule 20 allows joinder of plaintiffs when their claims arise out of the same transaction and present some common question of law or fact. Haynes might therefore join with ten other buyers of Fears Rawbuck washers in a single action for damages, since their claims would arise out of the deceptive advertising of the washer and present the common question of whether the ads were deceptive, if they all bought the washers in reliance on the ads.

But suppose that there were one thousand other buyers with the same claim. "Additional parties take additional time. Even if they have no witnesses of their own, they are a source of additional questions, objections,

* We speak of representative plaintiffs because most class actions are plaintiffs' class actions. But nothing about this joinder device, or the rules regulating it, limits it to plaintiffs' class actions or prevents a plaintiff from asking the court to "certify"—approve—a class of defendants.

> briefs, arguments, motions and the like which tend to make the proceeding a Donnybrook Fair."* *Crosby Steam Gage & Valve Co. v. Manning, Maxwell & Moore, Inc.*, 51 F. Supp. 972, 973 (D. Mass. 1943). In addition, the defendant would have the right to take discovery from each plaintiff, making the litigation more expensive and time consuming.
>
> A class action is simply another kind of joinder for cases in which persons with similar interests are so numerous that it is more efficient for a few class representatives to litigate on behalf of the rest of the class, who do not participate in the day-to-day conduct of the lawsuit. The rest of the class members are not made active parties and are usually not individually involved in discovery. Having only the representative plaintiffs before the court makes the case easier to manage, yet assures that the interests they share with the class members will be heard and fairly litigated.

But class action litigation has several problems that becloud this rosy account. First, if a judgment in a class action is binding on absent class members who are not actually present and litigating and may not even know about the lawsuit, the device raises serious due process concerns. We address this problem in section II. In section III, we discuss how class actions are "certified" under Federal Rules 23(a) and 23(b). Finally, in section IV, we outline a few of the many additional complexities typically associated with class action litigation.

II. The Due Process Requirements for Class Actions

Suppose Haynes sues Fears Rawbuck for misleading ads and defective washers, purporting to represent a class of 400,000 buyers in thirty-two states. If his action qualifies as a class action, and he wins, each class member will share in the judgment. But if he loses, each member will also be bound. Under the law of claim and issue preclusion, see Chapters 33 and 34, *infra*, this means that no class member can sue Fears for the same claim again or relitigate the same facts that were actually litigated and necessarily decided in the class action. Each member will have had her "day in court."

Yet, only Haynes actually was in court! How is the binding effect of class action judgments on absent class members consistent with due process principles? Ordinarily, one cannot be bound by a judgment unless she has been made a party by proper service and has been afforded the opportunity to be heard in the court that rendered the judgment. Haynes, as class representative and a formal party to the class action, obviously had his day in court and can hardly complain when he is bound by the result. But how can all purchasers of the Fears Rawbuck washer have their claims decided (*i.e.*, have their legal rights to recovery adjudicated) without participating in the lawsuit or (in some cases) without even receiving notice of the lawsuit? The following case addresses this important question.

* The first Donnybrook Fair was held in Dublin, Ireland, and was famous for drunken brawls.

READING *HANSBERRY v. LEE.* In the 1920s, housing segregation in Chicago was enforced by white homeowners' adoption of racially restrictive covenants, which prohibited homeowners and their successors in title (including purchasers of their property) from selling to a Black buyer or leasing to a Black tenant.

The Hansberry Covenant

1.... [N]o part of said premises shall in any manner be used or occupied directly or indirectly by any negro or negroes, provided that this restriction shall not prevent the occupation, during the period of their employment, of janitors' or chauffeurs' quarters in the basement or in a barn or garage in the rear, or of servants' quarters by negro janitors, chauffeurs or house servants, respectively, actually employed as such for service in and about the premises by the rightful owner or occupant of said premises.

2.... [N]o part of said premises shall be sold, given, conveyed or leased to any negro or negroes, and no permission or license to use or occupy any part thereof shall be given to any negro except house servants or janitors or chauffeurs employed thereon as aforesaid.

Under Illinois law, for a covenant to be effective and "run with the land" (to pass from seller to buyer), 95 percent of the owners of a subdivision had to agree to it.

In 1934, Olive Ida Burke, a white homeowner in the Washington Park subdivision of Chicago, sued Issac Kleiman, another white homeowner, to enforce the covenant by stopping him from leasing land to a Black tenant. Kleiman stipulated (e.g., agreed to accept as true) that 95 percent of the relevant homeowners agreed to the covenant, and he did not challenge its constitutionality. Based in part on this stipulation, the *Burke* court found the covenant valid and enforceable, giving judgment to Burke.

Three years later, Olive Burke's husband, James J. Burke, had a change of heart and tried to sell land in the same subdivision (through middlemen) to Carl A. Hansberry, a Black businessman who worked with the NAACP to fight racially restrictive covenants.*

The adjacent white homeowner (Lee) joined several other individuals who sued Hansberry, Burke, and others involved in the sale to enforce the covenant and evict the Hansberrys. In their defense, Burke and the Hansberrys argued

* The Hansberrys' daughter, Lorraine Hansberry, wrote a famous play about her family's experiences, *Raisin in the Sun*. The background of their case is set out in Allen R. Kamp, *The History Behind Hansberry v. Lee*, 20 U.C. Davis L. Rev. 481 (1987), and in Jay Tidmarsh, "The Story of *Hansberry*: The Foundation for Modern Class Actions," in Civil Procedure Stories 233–93 (2d ed. 2008).

that the covenant was invalid because it had been approved by only 54 percent of the homeowners, notwithstanding the stipulation to the contrary in *Burke.*

The trial court agreed, finding that the stipulation was part of a fraud conducted by white homeowners. But it also found that the issue of approval decided in *Burke v. Kleiman* could not be relitigated. The Illinois Supreme Court agreed, concluding that *Burke* was "a class or representative suit" binding on all of the class members that Olive Burke had represented, including her husband James. The defendants were therefore precluded from relitigating the 95 percent finding in *Burke* by a branch of the law of *res judicata,* now called *issue preclusion.* "The mere fact that it later appears that the finding is untrue does not render the decree any less binding. The principle of *res judicata* [issue preclusion] covers wrong as well as right decisions, for the fundamental reason that there must be an end of litigation." *Lee v. Hansberry,* 372 Ill. 369, 372 (1939).

As we will see when we study issue preclusion, the Illinois courts erred in their application of issue preclusion, and more fundamentally, the United States Supreme Court struck down racially restrictive covenants on equal protection grounds many years later in *Shelley v. Kraemer,* 334 U.S. 1 (1948). But in *Hansberry,* the Supreme Court reached neither of these issues. Instead, it decided whether *Burke* really qualified for class action treatment given the due process concerns it raised.

- Did the Supreme Court rule that strangers to the first lawsuit, like James Burke, could *never* be precluded by the first judgment? If not, under what circumstances did the Court say that they could be precluded?
- What "class" did Olive Burke purport to represent? What interests did this class share?
- Why weren't the defendants (including James Burke and the Hansberrys, called the "petitioners" by the Court) bound under "the doctrine of representation of absent members in a class suit"?
- Rule 23 was promulgated after *Hansberry.* What due process protections described by *Hansberry* (see especially its last paragraph) were codified by Rule 23(a)?

HANSBERRY v. LEE

311 U.S. 32 (1940)

Mr. Justice Stone delivered the opinion of the Court.

The question is whether the Supreme Court of Illinois, by its adjudication that petitioners in this case are bound by a judgment rendered in an earlier litigation [*Burke v. Kleiman*] to which they were not parties, has deprived them of the due process of law guaranteed by the Fourteenth Amendment. . . .

. . . [T]he Supreme Court of Illinois concluded in the present case that *Burke v. Kleiman* was a class or representative suit and that in such a suit where the remedy is pursued by a plaintiff who has the right to represent the class to which he belongs, other members of the class are bound by the results in the case unless it is reversed or set aside on direct proceedings; that petitioners in the present suit were members of the class represented by the plaintiffs in the earlier suit and consequently were bound by its decree which had rendered the issue of performance of the condition precedent to the restrictive agreement *res judicata*, so far as petitioners are concerned. The court thought that the circumstance that the stipulation in the earlier suit that owners of 95 per cent of the frontage had signed the agreement was contrary to the fact as found [by the trial court in the instant case, *Hansberry v. Lee*] . . . did not militate against this conclusion since the court in the earlier suit had jurisdiction to determine the fact as between the parties before it and that its determination, because of the representative character of the suit, even though erroneous, was binding on petitioners until set aside by a direct attack on the first judgment. . . .

It is a principle of general application in Anglo-American jurisprudence that one is not bound by a judgment in personam in a litigation in which he is not designated as a party or to which he has not been made a party by service of process. *Pennoyer v. Neff*, 95 U.S. 714. A judgment rendered in such circumstances is not entitled to the full faith and credit which the Constitution and statute of the United States prescribe, *Pennoyer v. Neff, supra*; and judicial action enforcing it against the person or property of the absent party is not that due process which the Fifth and Fourteenth Amendments requires.

To these general rules there is a recognized exception that, to an extent not precisely defined by judicial opinion, the judgment in a class or representative suit, to which some members of the class are parties, may bind members of the class or those represented who were not made parties to it.

The class suit was an invention of equity to enable it to proceed to a decree in suits where the number of those interested in the subject of the litigation is so great that their joinder as parties in conformity to the usual rules of procedure is impracticable. Courts are not infrequently called upon to proceed with causes in which the number of those interested in the litigation is so great as to make difficult or impossible the joinder of all because some are not within the jurisdiction or because their whereabouts is unknown or where if all were made parties to the suit its continued abatement by the death of some would prevent or unduly delay a decree. In such cases where the interests of those not joined are of the same class as the interests of those who are, and where it is considered that the latter fairly represent the former in the prosecution of the litigation of the issues in which all have a common interest, the court will proceed to a decree.

. . . [T]here is scope within the framework of the Constitution for holding in appropriate cases that a judgment rendered in a class suit is *res judicata* as to members of the class who are not formal parties to the suit. Here, as elsewhere, the Fourteenth Amendment does not compel state courts or legislatures to adopt any particular rule for establishing the conclusiveness of judgments in class suits, nor does it compel the adoption of the particular rules thought by this court to be appropriate for the federal courts. With a proper regard for divergent local institutions and interests, this Court is justified in saying that there has been a failure of due process only in those cases where it cannot be said that the procedure adopted, fairly insures the protection of the interests of absent parties who are to be bound by it.

It is familiar doctrine of the federal courts that members of a class not present as parties to the litigation may be bound by the judgment where they are in fact adequately represented by parties who are present, or where they actually participate in the conduct of the litigation in which members of the class are present as parties, or where the interest of the members of the class, some of whom are present as parties, is joint, or where for any other reason the relationship between the parties present and those who are absent is such as legally to entitle the former to stand in judgment for the latter.

In all such cases, so far as it can be said that the members of the class who are present are, by generally recognized rules of law, entitled to stand in judgment for those who are not, we may assume for present purposes that such procedure affords a protection to the parties who are represented though absent, which would satisfy the requirements of due process and full faith and credit. Nor do we find it necessary for the decision of this case to say that, when the only circumstance defining the class is that the determination of the rights of its members turns upon a single issue of fact or law, a state could not constitutionally adopt a procedure whereby some of the members of the class could stand in judgment for all, provided that the procedure were so devised and applied as to insure that those present are of the same class as those absent and that the litigation is so conducted as to insure the full and fair consideration of the common issue. We decide only that the procedure and the course of litigation sustained here by the plea of *res judicata* do not satisfy these requirements.

The restrictive agreement did not purport to create a joint obligation or liability. **[Eds.—For example, the *Burke* plaintiffs did not sue to enforce some right to a single piece of property that they held in common.]** If valid and effective[,] its promises were the several obligations of the signers and those claiming under them. The promises ran severally to every other signer. It is plain that in such circumstances all those alleged to be bound by the agreement would not constitute a single class in any litigation brought to enforce it. Those who sought to secure its benefits by enforcing it could not be said to be in the same class with or represent those whose interest was in resisting performance, for the agreement by its terms imposes obligations and confers rights on the owner of each plot of land who signs it. If those who thus seek to secure the benefits of the agreement were rightly regarded by the state Supreme Court as constituting a class, it is evident that those signers or their successors who are interested in challenging the validity of the agreement and resisting its performance are not of the same class in the sense that their interests are identical so that any group who had elected to enforce rights conferred by the agreement could be said to be acting in the interest of any others who were free to deny its obligation.

Because of the dual and potentially conflicting interests of those who are putative parties to the agreement in compelling or resisting its performance, it is impossible to say, solely because they are parties to it, that any two of them are of the same class. Nor without more, and with the due regard for the protection of the rights of absent parties which due process exacts, can some be permitted to stand in judgment for all.

It is one thing to say that some members of a class may represent other members in a litigation where the sole and common interest of the class in the litigation, is either to assert a common right or to challenge an asserted obligation. It is quite another to hold that all those who are free alternatively either to assert rights or to challenge them are of a single class, so that any group merely because it is of the class so constituted, may be deemed adequately to represent any others of the class in litigating their interests in either alternative. Such a selection of representatives for purposes of litigation, whose substantial interests are not necessarily or even probably the same as those whom they are deemed to represent, does not afford that protection to absent parties which due process requires. The doctrine of representation of absent parties in a class suit has not hitherto been thought to go so far. Apart from the opportunities it would afford for the fraudulent and collusive sacrifice of the rights of absent parties, we think that the representation in this case no more satisfies the requirements of due process than a trial by a judicial officer who is in such situation that he may have an interest in the outcome of the litigation in conflict with that of the litigants.

The plaintiffs in the *Burke* case sought to compel performance of the agreement in behalf of themselves and all others similarly situated. They did not designate the defendants in the suit as a class or seek any injunction or other relief against others than the named defendants, and the decree which was entered did not purport to bind others. In seeking to enforce the agreement the plaintiffs in that suit were not representing the petitioners here whose substantial interest is in resisting performance. The defendants in the first suit were not treated by the pleadings or decree as representing others or as foreclosing by their defense the rights of others, and even though nominal defendants, it does not appear that their interest in defeating the contract outweighed their interest in establishing its validity. For a court in this situation to ascribe to either the plaintiffs or defendants the performance of such functions on behalf of petitioners here, is to attribute to them a power that it cannot be said that they had assumed to exercise, and a responsibility which, in view of their dual interests it does not appear that they could rightly discharge.

Reversed.

Mr. Justice McReynolds, Mr. Justice Roberts and Mr. Justice Reed concur in the result.

Notes and Questions: The Constitutionality of Class Actions

1. Who is bound by a judgment in an ordinary lawsuit? The Court answers this question by citing a familiar case.

> It is a principle of general application in Anglo-American jurisprudence that one is not bound by a judgment in personam in a litigation in which he is not designated as a party or to which he has not been made a party by service of process. *Pennoyer v. Neff*, 95 U.S. 714.

Of course, in studying *Pennoyer*, we focused on the binding effect on *defendants*, on whom process is served. But the Court in *Hansberry* reminds us that the principle it draws from *Pennoyer* is broader: A judgment is binding on all—*whether defendants or plaintiffs*—who were made parties to the lawsuit. Defendants become parties when they are served with the complaint and process, while plaintiffs voluntarily become parties by filing the suit. Party status is the key to due process because a party receives notice of the lawsuit and the opportunity to participate.

The due process problem of plaintiffs' class actions is that only the representative parties actually participate as formal parties, while the absent class members may not even know about the suit, and even if they know, do not participate in it. The Court therefore has to reconcile the "principle of general application"—that only parties can be bound—with this reality of class actions: that absentee class members do not participate as parties.

2. Why did the Illinois Supreme Court find that *Burke v. Kleiman* judgment was binding on James Burke and the other defendants in *Hansberry*? It viewed the *Burke* suit as a "class" or "representative" suit by which all of the members of the class "are bound by the results in the case unless it is reversed. . . ." The court then treated James Burke, who sold the property to the Hansberrys, as a member of the homeowner "class" bound by *Burke*. He was therefore precluded from relitigating the finding in *Burke* that the required 95 percent of the homeowners had approved the covenant. Because he was bound by the racially restrictive covenant, his attempted sale of property in the subdivision to the Hansberrys violated the covenant and was unlawful.

Q **3. Can a class action ever bind absent class members?** The United States Supreme Court expressly recognized that class or representative lawsuits as an exception to the general due process principle that one cannot be bound by a judgment in a lawsuit to which one is not a party. "[T]here is scope within the framework of the Constitution for holding in appropriate cases that a judgment rendered in a class suit is *res judicata* [preclusive] as to members of the class who are not formal parties to the suit." Why make such an exception to the general due process principle?

A For the sake of efficiency. Sometimes there are so many similarly situated persons that their joinder by the usual rules (such as Rule 20) "is impracticable," either because some are outside the jurisdiction, some are unknown, or there are just too many.

But the Supreme Court did not find that efficiency or "impracticality" was alone sufficient to justify the exception. In addition to efficiency, what other requirements must a class action satisfy in order to bind absent class members?

A The Court identified two and implied a third. First, "the interests of those not joined"—the absent class members not before the court—must be "of the same class as the interests of those who are" joined—the class representatives. That is, they must share common interests. Second, the absentees' interests must "in fact [be] adequately represented by parties who are present." Third (by implication), courts must adopt and employ procedures so "as to insure" that the common-interest and adequate-representation requirements are satisfied and that the litigation is "so conducted as to insure the full and fair consideration of the common issue."

(Hansberry Plat) Members of the Class?

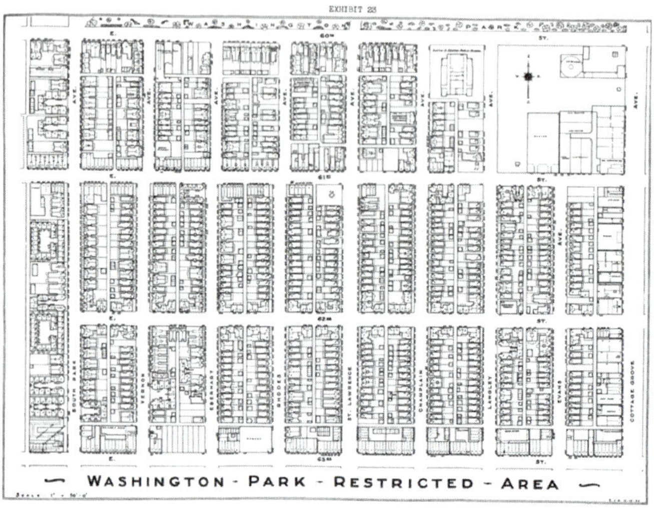

The covenant in *Hansberry v. Lee* excluded "negroes" from the entire Washington Park neighborhood of Chicago. As shown, the tract included some 540 properties and 8,100 residents. Property owners had brought an earlier suit to enforce the covenant. Later, in *Hansberry*, owners claimed that the earlier judgment enforcing the covenant barred new minority buyers and their sellers from challenging its validity, since they were represented by the defendants in the prior case.

Q **4. Applying the requirements.** Which of the requirements identified in the previous question did *Burke v. Kleiman* fail to satisfy?

A It failed three requirements. First, and most important, its "class" of some five hundred homeowners did not have common interests. The homeowners who sought to enforce the covenant could hardly "be said to be in the same class with or represent those whose interest was in resisting performance . . . ," but the Illinois Supreme Court lumped them together. When there are such "dual and potentially conflicting interests" in the "class," it would not be fair or accurate to conclude that the class representatives were surrogates for absent parties with conflicting interests. Olive Burke did not stand in for her husband (if they disagreed at the time of her lawsuit), let alone for the Hansberrys. In a true class action, the absentee class members have a surrogate in the class representative who litigates their *shared* interests.

Second, the absentee class members who were opposed to the covenant were not adequately represented in *Burke*. How do we know? Well, one tip-off is that it looked like the defendants in *Burke* falsely "stipulated"—agreed—that 95 percent of the homeowners approved the covenant. If this stipulation was false,* this could suggest that Olive Burke and the defendants in that action were in cahoots and that the purpose of the lawsuit *for both sides* was simply to obtain a judicial declaration of the validity of the covenant. Indeed, the trial court in *Hansberry* found that the stipulation was untrue and fraudulent, and two dissenting justices on the Illinois Supreme Court emphatically agreed. Nevertheless, the majority of that court ruled that any such finding was precluded by the *Burke* judgment. While the United States Supreme Court never explicitly says that *Burke* was a fraud, it surely hints at that conclusion by its deadpan observation that "it does not appear that [the *Burke* defendants'] interest in defeating the contract outweighed their interest in establishing its validity."

Third, the trial court in *Burke* apparently neither followed any procedures for treating the lawsuit as a class action nor issued a decree (the equity equivalent of a judgment) addressed to any class. Although Olive Burke did plead in *Burke* that she was suing "on behalf of herself and on behalf of all other property owners," she "did not designate the defendants in the suit as a class," and "the decree which was entered did not purport to bind others." Nor were the defendants there "treated by the pleadings or decree as representing others . . . ," although it was not altogether clear what treatment Illinois courts required at the time. Instead, the Illinois Supreme Court just eyeballed the case after the fact and said, in effect, "It looks like a class action to us."

Actually, the United States Supreme Court's characterization of what happened in *Hansberry* was pretty milquetoast. A dissenting justice in the Illinois Supreme Court was more harsh:

> The undisputed fact is that by means of fraud and collusion between total strangers an agreement which is void on its face has been imposed upon some ten million dollars worth of the property of five hundred other parties who were never in court, who never had notice of any law suit, who were never by name or as unknown owners made parties to any law suit, and who have never been accorded any process whatever, either due or otherwise. And it is said that this is binding upon them; that they constituted a class because one man fraudulently said they did and another man collusively, and with equal fraud, admitted the allegation, because this second man signed a stipulation saying they had signed an agreement which they had never signed.

Lee v. Hansberry, 372 Ill. 369, 377 (1939) (Shaw, J., dissenting).

Q **5. Rule 23(a)'s answer to *Hansberry*.** In criticizing the *Burke* case, the United States Supreme Court emphasized that it was not laying down any specific

* It might not have been. Research suggests that the number of true signatures at least approached the 95 percent target. *See* Tidmarsh, *supra* p. 678, n.*, at 680.

procedures. But its brief catalog of deficiencies, as explained in the previous question, certainly points to a few necessary procedures: designation as a class, express identification of the class in the pleadings and the ultimate judgment, and (perhaps) approval of the designation by a court.

Rule 23 was the rule makers' answer to the Court's reference to class action procedures. To what extent does Rule 23(a) reflect the constitutional analysis of *Hansberry*?

A Rule 23(a)(1) requires the court to "certify" the lawsuit as a class action, provided that the party seeking class action certification shows that joinder of all members is "impracticable." Rule 23(a)(2)–(3) requires that the representative parties share the interests of the absent class members (i.e., they present common questions and claims or defenses that are "typical" of those of the class). And Rule 23(a)(4) requires that the representatives fairly and adequately represent the class. Rule 23(b) describes additional requirements for some kinds of classes, which go primarily to the efficiency of the class action.

6. Re-thinking *Burke* under Rule 23(a). Rule 23 substantially addresses the deficiencies of a case like *Burke*. If *Burke* had been brought in federal court under the Rule, the complaint would have had to identify the class on whose behalf the plaintiffs sued. The class representatives would have been required to convince the court on a motion to certify the class that their claims presented common questions of law or fact with the class members' claims, and that their claims were typical of the claims of the class, as well as that they could adequately represent the class. On the facts given in *Burke*, the court would have denied the motion to certify a class because Olive Burke, a white homeowner with an interest in enforcing the racially restrictive covenant, would not have adequately represented homeowners who wanted to sell or lease to Black people, like Olive's contrarian husband, James (let alone Black persons who wanted to buy). That might not sound the death knell of Olive Burke's lawsuit, but if she pressed on, any judgment that resulted would bind only her and not the other homeowners.

7. Personal jurisdiction. *Hansberry* addressed one set of due process requirements for class actions—the requirements for the class to have common interests and to be adequately represented—but ignored another. Obviously, a court must have personal jurisdiction over the defendant in a class action. Just as obviously, it has personal jurisdiction over the class representatives who voluntarily chose the forum. But does it also have personal jurisdiction over absent class members who did not necessarily choose to sue in that forum? In a nationwide class action, many of these absentees may have no contact with the forum other than the class representative's selection of it.

The Supreme Court ruled, in *Phillips Petroleum Co. v. Shutts*, 472 U.S. 797 (1985), that out-of-state class members are entitled to due process protections. But it also found that the protections are different from those accorded defendants under the law of personal jurisdiction:

> In sharp contrast to the predicament of a defendant haled into an out-of-state forum, the [class member] plaintiffs in this suit were not haled anywhere to defend themselves upon pain of a default judgment. . . .

> A plaintiff class ... in numerous ... jurisdictions cannot first be certified unless the judge, with the aid of the named plaintiffs and defendant, conducts an inquiry into the common nature of the named plaintiffs' and the absent plaintiffs' claims, the adequacy of representation, the jurisdiction possessed over the class, and any other matters that will bear upon proper representation of the absent plaintiffs' interest. Unlike a defendant in a civil suit, a class-action plaintiff is not required to fend for himself. The court and named plaintiffs protect his interests....
>
> The concern of the typical class-action rules for the absent plaintiffs is manifested in other ways. Most jurisdictions ... require that a class action, once certified, may not be dismissed or compromised without the approval of the court. In many jurisdictions ... the court may amend the pleadings to ensure that all sections of the class are represented adequately.
>
> Besides this continuing solicitude for their rights, absent plaintiff class members are not subject to other burdens imposed upon defendants. They need not hire counsel or appear. They are almost never subject to counterclaims or cross-claims, or liability for fees or costs. Absent plaintiff class members are not subject to coercive or punitive remedies. Nor will an adverse judgment typically bind an absent plaintiff for any damages, although a valid adverse judgment may extinguish any of the plaintiff's claims which were litigated.
>
> Unlike a defendant in a normal civil suit, an absent class-action plaintiff is not required to do anything. He may sit back and allow the litigation to run its course, content in knowing that there are safeguards provided for his protection. In most class actions an absent plaintiff is provided at least with an opportunity to "opt out" of the class, and if he takes advantage of that opportunity he is removed from the litigation entirely....
>
> ... In this case we hold that a forum State may exercise jurisdiction over the claim of an absent class-action plaintiff, even though that plaintiff may not possess the minimum contacts with the forum which would support personal jurisdiction over a defendant.

Id. at 809–10. The class action in *Phillips*, however, was a Rule 23(b)(3) damages class action, in which each class member received notice with an opportunity to opt out of the class. See Rule 23(c)(2)(B). The Court emphasized that this notice with an opt-out option was part of the process that such class members were due. The Court has not since clarified whether due process is also satisfied for Rule 23(b)(1) or 23(b)(2) classes, which afford no such opt-out opportunity and are thus "mandatory" classes. *See Wright & Miller* § 1789.1.

III. Certifying a Class Action

Hansberry laid down constitutional requirements for a class action in order for a judgment to bind the class members. Rule 23 codified these requirements by establishing a certification procedure controlled by the court. The following case is one of hundreds of reported cases that illustrate the factors that a federal court considers in deciding whether to certify a class action. (Although states that authorize class actions may follow different procedures from those described in Rule 23, state class action procedures are permissible as long as they meet the baseline constitutional requirements.)

Rule 23 divides the analysis for certifying a class action into two parts. In the first part, the court must decide whether the party moving for class certification has proposed a class that meets the general requirements for any class, set out expressly and by implication in Rule 23(a). In the second part of the analysis, the court must decide which type of class to certify under Rule 23(b), which sets out specific requirements for three different types of classes.

READING *FLOYD v. CITY OF NEW YORK*. In *Terry v. Ohio*, 392 U.S. 1 (1968), the Supreme Court held that a police officer did not violate the Fourth Amendment when he stopped and frisked a person without probable cause to believe that a crime had been committed, if the officer "reasonably . . . conclude[d] in light of his experience that criminal activity may be afoot and that the persons with whom he is dealing may be armed and presently dangerous . . . ." *Id.* at 30. The decision opened the door to "*Terry* stops" by police. In the late 1990s, the New York City Police Department (NYPD) took *Terry* stops a step further by adopting a proactive department-wide *policy* of stop-and-frisk to deal with what was widely depicted as a rise in crime. In 2011 alone, New York police conducted over 685,000 stop-and-frisk stops, more than 85% of which did not result in an arrest.

In *Floyd*, four Black men brought a class action against the City and various officers seeking a declaration that the stop-and-frisk policy as executed violated the class members' Fourth and Fourteenth Amendment rights and requesting an injunction mandating significant changes to the police policy. They moved for class certification.

- What class did the plaintiffs seek to represent?
- Was that class "ascertainable"? Why must a class be ascertainable?
- How did the class satisfy the requirements of Rule 23(a)?
- The plaintiffs sought certification of their class as a Rule 23(b)(2) "injunctive relief" class, but any one of them could have sued for injunctive relief on the same legal theories. Why then was a class action needed or appropriate?
- Defendants asserted that, if an injunction could guarantee that the police will follow the Fourth Amendment in every encounter, the legislature would already have passed a law to that effect. They concluded, therefore, that an injunction would be a "judicial intrusion into a social institution that is disfavored." Assuming that you can follow this argument, how does the court respond?

FLOYD v. CITY OF NEW YORK

283 F.R.D. 153 (S.D.N.Y. 2012)

Shira A. Scheindlin, District Judge:

I. INTRODUCTION

Police officers are permitted to briefly stop any individual, but only upon reasonable suspicion that he is committing a crime. The source of that limitation is the Fourth Amendment to the United States Constitution, which guarantees that "the right of the people to be secure in their persons, houses, papers, and effects, against unreasonable searches and seizures, shall not be violated." The Supreme Court has explained that this "inestimable right of personal security belongs as much to the citizen on the streets of our cities as to the homeowner closeted in his study to dispose of his secret affairs."

The right to physical liberty has long been at the core of our nation's commitment to respecting the autonomy and dignity of each person: "No right is held more sacred, or is more carefully guarded, by the common law, than the right of every individual to the possession and control of his own person, free from all restraint or interference of others, unless by clear and unquestionable authority of law." Safeguarding this right is quintessentially the role of the judicial branch.

No less central to the courts' role is ensuring that the administration of law comports with the Fourteenth Amendment, which "undoubtedly intended not only that there should be no arbitrary deprivation of life or liberty, or arbitrary spoliation of property, but that equal protection and security should be given to all under like circumstances in the enjoyment of their personal and civil rights."

On over 2.8 million occasions between 2004 and 2009, New York City police officers stopped residents and visitors, restraining their freedom, even if only briefly. Over fifty percent of those stops were of Black people and thirty percent were of Latinos, while only ten percent were of Whites. The question presented by this lawsuit is whether the New York City Police Department ("NYPD") has complied with the laws and Constitutions of the United States and the State of New York. Specifically, the four named plaintiffs allege, on behalf of themselves and a putative class, that defendants have engaged in a policy and/or practice of unlawfully stopping and frisking people in violation of their Fourth Amendment right to be free from unlawful searches and seizures and their Fourteenth Amendment right to freedom from discrimination on the basis of race.

Plaintiffs David Floyd, Lalit Clarkson, Deon Dennis, and David Ourlicht are Black men who seek to represent a class of similarly situated people in this lawsuit against the City of New York, Police Commissioner Raymond Kelly, Mayor Michael Bloomberg, and named and unnamed police officers. On behalf of the putative class, plaintiffs seek equitable relief in the form of (1) a declaration that defendants' policies, practices, and/or customs violate the Fourth and Fourteenth Amendments, and (2) a class-wide injunction mandating significant changes in those policies, practices, and/or customs. . . .

Plaintiffs now move for certification of the following class:

> All persons who since January 31, 2005 have been, or in the future will be, subjected to the New York Police Department's policies and/or widespread customs or practices of stopping, or stopping and frisking, persons in the absence of a reasonable, articulable suspicion that criminal activity has taken, is taking, or is about to take place in violation of the Fourth Amendment, including persons stopped or stopped and frisked on the basis of being Black or Latino in violation of the Equal Protection Clause of the Fourteenth Amendment.

Because plaintiffs satisfy the legal standard for class certification, their motion is granted.

II. LEGAL STANDARD

A. Rule 23(a)*

Rule 23 of the Federal Rules of Civil Procedure permits individuals to sue as representatives of an aggrieved class. To be certified, a putative class must first meet all four prerequisites set forth in Rule 23(a), generally referred to as numerosity, commonality, typicality, and adequacy. "[C]ertification is proper only if the trial court is satisfied, after rigorous analysis, that the prerequisites of Rule 23(a) have been satisfied." This rigorous analysis requires examining the facts of the dispute, not merely the pleadings, and it will frequently "entail some overlap with the merits of the plaintiff's underlying claim."

. . . The court's "determination as to a Rule 23 requirement is made only for purposes of class certification and is not binding on the trier of facts, even if that trier is the class certification judge."

"The numerosity requirement in Rule 23(a)(1) does not mandate that joinder of all parties be impossible—only that the difficulty or inconvenience of joining all members of the class make use of the class action appropriate." Sufficient numerosity can be presumed at a level of forty members or more, and courts do not require "evidence of exact class size or identity of class members to satisfy the numerosity requirement."

Commonality requires plaintiffs "to demonstrate that the class members 'have suffered the same injury,' " and the claims "must depend upon a common contention . . . of such a nature that it is capable of classwide resolution—which means that determination of its truth or falsity will resolve an issue that is central to the validity of each one of the claims in one stroke."

In this context, "the commonality and typicality requirements of Rule 23(a) tend to merge." "Typicality 'requires that the claims of the class representatives be typical of those of the class, and is satisfied when each class member's claim arises from the same course of events[ ] and each class member makes similar

* [Eds.—Although we usually include internal citations for quotations, here, to save space we have omitted the court's numerous citations for the propositions it quotes in this part of the opinion concerning Rule 24(a) requirements. *See* 283 F.R.D. at 160 nn.13–33.]

legal arguments to prove the defendant's liability.' " Rather than focusing on the precise nature of plaintiffs' injuries, the typicality requirement may be satisfied where "injuries derive from a unitary course of conduct by a single system." A lack of typicality may be found in cases where the named plaintiff "was not harmed by the [conduct] he alleges to have injured the class" or the named plaintiff's claim is subject to "specific factual defenses" atypical of the class.

The question of adequacy "entails inquiry as to whether: 1) plaintiff's interests are antagonistic to the interest of other members of the class and 2) plaintiff's attorneys are qualified, experienced and able to conduct the litigation."

Some courts have added an "implied requirement of ascertainability" to the express requirements of Rule 23(a) and have refused to certify a class "unless the class description is sufficiently definite so that it is administratively feasible for the court to determine whether a particular individual is a member." . . .

B. Rule 23(b)(2)

If the requirements of Rule 23(a) are met, the court "must next determine whether the class can be maintained under any one of the three subdivisions of Rule 23(b)." Plaintiffs seek certification under Rule 23(b)(2), which applies where "the party opposing the class has acted or refused to act on grounds that apply generally to the class, so that final injunctive relief or corresponding declaratory relief is appropriate respecting the class as a whole."

III. FACTS . . . .

A. The NYPD's Stop and Frisk Program

It is indisputable that the NYPD has an enormous stop and frisk program. There were 2.8 million documented stops between 2004 and 2009. . . .

[T]he overwhelming and indisputable evidence shows that the NYPD has a department-wide stop and frisk program; the program has been designed and revised at the highest levels of the department; the implementation of the program is conducted according to uniform and centralized rules; and monitoring of compliance with the program is hierarchical. . . .

C. Statistical Evidence of Unlawful Stops . . . .

I find that the following factual determinations provide strong evidence regarding the existence of a Fourth Amendment class, and a Fourteenth Amendment subclass, which satisfy the requirements of Rule 23:

1. Fourth Amendment Class

- In at least six percent of all documented stops, police officers' stated reasons for conducting the stop were facially insufficient to establish reasonable suspicion. That is to say, according to their own explanations for their actions, NYPD officers conducted at least 170,000 unlawful stops between 2004 and 2009.
- In over 62,000 of those cases, police officers gave no reason other than "furtive movement" to justify the stop. . . .

- In over four thousand stops, police officers gave no reason other than "high crime area" to justify the stop. These facially unlawful stops also occurred in every precinct in the City. . . .
- The percentage of documented stops for which police officers failed to list an interpretable "suspected crime" has grown dramatically, from 1.1 percent in 2004 to 35.9 percent in 2009. Overall, in more than half a million documented stops—18.4 percent of the total—officers listed no coherent suspected crime.
- "High crime area" is listed as a justification for a stop in approximately fifty-five percent of all recorded stops, regardless of whether the stop takes place in a precinct or census tract with average, high, or low crime.
- 5.37 percent of all stops result in an arrest; 6.26 percent of stops result in a summons. In the remaining eighty-eight percent of cases, although they were required by law to have objective reasonable suspicion that crime was afoot when they made the stop, police officers ultimately concluded that there was no probable cause to believe that crime was afoot. That is to say, according to their own records and judgment, officers' "suspicion" was wrong nearly nine times out of ten.
- Guns were seized in 0.15 percent of all stops. This is despite the fact that "suspicious bulge" was cited as a reason for 10.4 percent of all stops. Thus, for every sixty-nine stops that police officers justified specifically on the basis of a suspicious bulge, they found one gun.

2. Fourteenth Amendment Subclass

- "The racial composition of a precinct, neighborhood, and census tract is a statistically significant, strong and robust predictor of NYPD stop-and-frisk patterns even after controlling for the simultaneous influences of crime, social conditions, and allocation of police resources."
- Based on [Eds.—**an expert's analysis of forms that officers must complete for stops**], "the search for weapons is (a) unrelated to crime, (b) takes place primarily where weapons offenses are less frequent than other crimes, and (c) is targeted at places where the Black and Hispanic populations are highest.... [T]he search for drug offenders is (a) negatively related to rates of crime or drug offenses specifically, and is (b) concentrated in neighborhoods with high proportions of Black and Hispanic residents."
- "NYPD stops-and-frisks are significantly more frequent for Black and Hispanic residents than they are for White residents, even after adjusting for local crime rates, racial composition of the local population, police patrol strength, and other social and economic factors predictive of police enforcement activity."
- "Black and Hispanic individuals are treated more harshly during stop-and-frisk encounters with NYPD officers than Whites who are stopped on suspicion of the same or similar crimes."
- Police officers are more likely to list no suspected crime category (or an incoherent one) when stopping Blacks and Latinos than when stopping Whites.

- Police officers are more likely to list the stop justification "furtive movement," which is a highly nebulous and not particularly probative of crime, when stopping Blacks and Latinos than when stopping Whites.

IV. DISCUSSION . . . .

B. Plaintiffs Satisfy the Four Prerequisites of Rule 23(a)

1. Ascertainability

Defendants argue that the "description of the class must be 'sufficiently definite so that it is administratively feasible for the court to determine whether a particular individual is a member.' " Defendants believe that plaintiffs' proposed class definition—all persons who have been or in the future will be unlawfully stopped in violation of the Fourth Amendment, including all persons stopped on the basis of being Black or Latino in violation of the Fourteenth Amendment—is impermissibly indefinite because "an individualized inquiry must be made into the facts and circumstances surrounding [each] stop" and the "analysis is highly specific and unique in every case." . . . .

Rule 23 does not demand ascertainability. The requirement is a judicial creation meant to ensure that class definitions are workable when members of the class will be entitled to damages or require notice for another reason. . . .

It would be illogical to require precise ascertainability in a suit that seeks no class damages. The general demarcations of the proposed class are clear—those people unlawfully stopped or who may be stopped by the NYPD—and that definition makes the class sufficiently ascertainable for the purpose of Rule 23(b)(2).

2. Numerosity . . . .

[T]he size of the class is likely to be well over one hundred thousand.

3. Commonality

Rule 23(a)(2) requires that there be "questions of law or fact common to the class." This requires plaintiffs "to demonstrate that the class members 'have suffered the same injury.' " In *Wal-Mart* [*Stores, Inc. v. Duke*, 564 U.S. 338 (2011)], plaintiffs sought to certify a class of approximately 1.5 million female employees of the retail giant, alleging that "the discretion exercised by their local supervisors over pay and promotion violates Title VII by discriminating against women." The Supreme Court found that the plaintiffs had failed to satisfy commonality because the putative class members were subjected to an enormous array of *different* employment practices:

> [P]ay and promotion decisions at Wal-Mart are generally committed to the local managers' broad discretion . . . [who may make employment decisions] with only limited corporate oversight . . . . Wal-Mart has no testing procedure or other companywide evaluation method that can be charged with bias. The whole point of permitting discretionary decisionmaking is to avoid evaluating employees under

> a common standard. . . . Other than the bare existence of delegated discretion, respondents have identified no "specific employment practice"—much less one that ties all their 1.5 million claims together.

Judge Richard Posner recently applied the *Wal-Mart* decision to the claims of Black Merrill Lynch brokers alleging racial discrimination. This was his summary of the *Wal-Mart* holding:

> *Wal-Mart* holds that if employment discrimination is practiced by the employing company's local managers, exercising discretion granted them by top management . . . rather than implementing a uniform policy established by top management to govern the local managers, a class action by more than a million current and former employees is unmanageable. . . .

[*McReynolds v. Merrill Lynch, Pierce, Fenner & Smith, Inc.*, 672 F.3d 482, 488 (7th Cir. 2012)]. [But Judge Posner went on to conclude that] even after *Wal-Mart*, Rule 23(b)(2) suits remain appropriate mechanisms for obtaining injunctive relief in cases where a centralized policy is alleged to impact a large class of plaintiffs, even when the magnitude (and existence) of the impact may vary by class member. . . .

As documented above, there can be no dispute that the NYPD has a single stop and frisk program. . . . The stop and frisk program is far more centralized and hierarchical than even the employment policies in [*McReynolds*]. Precinct commanders are not given leeway to conduct stops and frisks if, when, and how they choose; instead, they are required to use the tactic as a central part of the Department's pro-active policing strategy. They are required to monitor, document, and report their stop and frisk activity to headquarters using a uniform system; all officers are subject to centralized stop and frisk training; performance standards are obligatory and a recognized part of productivity evaluations in all precincts. . . . [D]efendants confuse the exercise of judgment in implementing a centralized *policy* with the exercise of discretion in formulating a local store policy or practice.

Plaintiffs allege that their Fourth and Fourteenth Amendment rights are violated as a result of the NYPD's policies and practices. As they argue, these claims raise "central and core questions of fact and law that, when answered, will resolve all class members' . . . claims against the City."[138] In the terminology of Wal-Mart, a classwide proceeding here will "generate common answers" to these questions that are "apt to drive the resolution of the litigation."

138. Plaintiffs list four such questions: (1) Whether New York City has a Policy and/or Practice of conducting stops and frisks without reasonable suspicion? (2) Whether the City has a Policy and/or Practice of stopping and frisking Black and Latino persons on the basis of race rather than reasonable suspicion? (3) Whether the NYPD's department-wide auditing and command self-inspection protocols and procedures demonstrate a deliberate indifference to the need to monitor officers adequately to prevent a widespread pattern of suspicionless and race-based stops? (4) Whether the NYPD's Policy and/or Practice of imposing productivity standards and/or quotas on the stop-and-frisk, summons, and other enforcement activity of officers is a moving force behind widespread suspicionless stops by NYPD officers?

4. Typicality and Adequacy

Defendants make overlapping objections on the basis of typicality and adequacy, and so I address these two Rule 23(a) prerequisites in tandem. "Typicality 'requires that the claims of the class representatives be typical of those of the class, and is satisfied when each class member's claim arises from the same course of events[ ] and each class member makes similar legal arguments to prove the defendant's liability.' " Rather than focusing on the precise nature of plaintiffs' injuries, the typicality requirement may be satisfied where "injuries derive from a unitary course of conduct by a single system."

The purpose of typicality is to ensure that class representatives "have the incentive to prove all the elements of the cause of action which would be presented by the individual members of the class were they initiating individualized actions." Similarly, "[a]dequacy is twofold: the proposed class representative must have an interest in vigorously pursuing the claims of the class, and must have no interests antagonistic to the interests of other class members." As defendants acknowledge, in order to defeat a motion for certification, any such conflicts must be "fundamental."

Here, the four named plaintiffs' stops arise from the same course of conduct—*i.e.*, the NYPD's centralized program of stops and frisks—and their legal arguments are precisely the typical ones that are made by others who bring or could bring claims for Fourth and Fourteenth Amendment violations by defendants. The named plaintiffs are vigorously pursuing their claims and defendants have failed to identify any ways in which plaintiffs' interests are antagonistic to those of other class members.

Defendants' argument is twofold: *First*, "the Court would be required to assess any unique defenses of the defendants before determining liability, which could include a fact-intensive qualified immunity defense"* and "the claims of putative class members who cannot identify an NYPD officer involved in the stop will be subject to unique defenses" that threaten to engulf the litigation. *Second*, because none of the named representatives are Latino, "they cannot represent the alleged Latino class members who make race-based claims." Neither argument is persuasive.

First, courts and juries must *always* consider defendants' individual defenses before determining liability. That is no bar at the certification stage. "In practice, courts in this Circuit . . . [refuse] certification only when confronted with a sufficiently clear showing" that a defense unique to the representative plaintiff's claims will in fact defeat those claims.

It is true that the parties have not been able to identify the police officers involved in five of the plaintiffs' eight alleged stops. At trial, defendants will argue that plaintiffs cannot establish liability for those stops; the jury may or may not agree. But defendants already moved [previously] for summary judgment on the claims of two of the four plaintiffs, including those of David Ourlicht, who was unable to identify the police officers who stopped him. Summary judgment was

* [Eds.—*See* pp. 518–19, *supra*.]

denied because I found that if a juror were to credit Ourlicht's testimony, she could find that he was stopped in the absence of objective reasonable suspicion that crime was afoot. That is to say, defendants failed to show that the John Doe defense will defeat plaintiffs' claims. **[Eds.—The John Doe defense is that plaintiff Ourlicht (and possibly other plaintiffs) will be unable to show that "the individuals who stopped [them during some stops] were actually from the NYPD."** ***See Floyd v. City of New York*, 813 F. Supp. 2d 417, 445 (S.D.N.Y.), *on reconsideration*, 813 F. Supp. 2d 457 (S.D.N.Y. 2011).]**

This issue does not create a "fundamental" conflict between named plaintiffs and unnamed class members: Indeed, it may be that officers often fail to complete [a required form] when they conduct a quick stop and frisk. In addition, three of the named plaintiffs allege stops involving identified police officers and at least two of those stops came from precincts in which commanding officers have acknowledged the use of performance standards or quotas. The issues involved in these stops go to the core of plaintiffs' claims.

The doctrine of unique defenses is intended to protect absent members of the plaintiff class by ensuring the presence of a typical plaintiff. The doctrine is not meant to protect defendants by permitting them to defeat certification because the facts raised by the claims of the representative plaintiffs are not *identical* to the facts raised by the claims of all putative class members. Because the named plaintiffs' claims arise from the same policy or practice and the same general set of facts as do the claims of the putative class members, the typicality prong is satisfied.

Defendants' contention regarding qualified immunity is similarly unavailing: the NYPD routinely argues that its officers are protected by qualified immunity. That defense is common to innumerable *Terry* stops and frisks; it cannot defeat typicality at the class certification stage.

Second, defendants' claim that the named plaintiffs cannot represent Latinos is likewise unconvincing. The cases that defendants cite denied certification because the named plaintiffs fell outside the subclass that they sought to represent. Plaintiffs seek certification of a Fourteenth Amendment subclass of Blacks and Latinos stopped because of their race; plaintiffs clearly fall inside that definition.

Plaintiffs' complaints are typical of those of the class and they will fairly and adequately protect the interests of the class. All four prerequisites of Rule 23(a) are met.

C. Class Certification Is Proper Under Rule 23(b)(2)

To certify a class under Rule 23(b)(2), plaintiffs must show that defendants "acted or refused to act on grounds that apply generally to the class, so that final injunctive relief or corresponding declaratory relief is appropriate respecting the class as a whole." As the Supreme Court explained in *Wal-Mart*, Rule 23(b)(2) is intended to cover cases such as this one:

> When a class seeks an indivisible injunction benefitting all its members at once, there is no reason to undertake a case-specific inquiry into whether class issues predominate or whether class action is a superior method of adjudicating the dispute [as would be required for a Rule 23(b)(3) class].

.... Defendants argue that certification under (b)(2) is inappropriate because they have not "acted or refused to act on grounds generally applicable to the class" and because plaintiffs "fail to identify an official policy, or its equivalent, and seek a broad-based structural injunction." Again, these arguments do not withstand the overwhelming evidence that there in fact exists a centralized stop and frisk program that has led to thousands of unlawful stops. The vast majority of New Yorkers who are unlawfully stopped will never bring suit to vindicate their rights. It is precisely for cases such as this that Rule 23(b)(2) was designed.

Defendants close their argument regarding the applicability of Rule 23 with this disturbing statement:

> [E]ven if [plaintiffs] prove a widespread practice of suspicionless stops [pursuant to a city policy], it is not at all clear that an injunction would be a useful remedy. Certainly, no injunction could guarantee that suspicionless stops would never occur or would only occur in a certain percentage of encounters.... Here, plaintiffs essentially seek an injunction guaranteeing that the Fourth Amendment will not be violated when NYPD investigates crime. If a court could fashion an injunction that would have this effect, then it is likely that lawmakers would have already passed laws to the same effect.... An injunction here is exactly the kind of judicial intrusion into a social institution that is disfavored . . .

Three points must be made in response. *First,* suspicionless stops should never occur. Defendants' cavalier attitude towards the prospect of a "widespread practice of suspicionless stops" displays a deeply troubling apathy towards New Yorkers' most fundamental constitutional rights.

Second, it is not readily apparent that if an injunction preventing such widespread practices could be fashioned, it would already have been passed by lawmakers.... It is rather audacious of the NYPD to argue that if it were possible to protect "the right of the people to be secure in their persons" from unlawful searches and seizures *by the NYPD,* then the legislature would already have done so and judicial intervention would therefore be futile. Indeed, it is precisely when the political branches violate the individual rights of minorities that "more searching judicial enquiry" is appropriate.[164]

Third, if the NYPD is engaging in a widespread practice of unlawful stops, then an injunction seeking to curb that practice is not a "judicial intrusion into a social institution" but a vindication of the Constitution and an exercise of the courts' most important function: protecting individual rights in the face of the government's malfeasance.

---

164. *United States v. Carolene Prods. Co.,* 304 U.S. 144, 153 n.4 (1938). "If we were to accept the State's argument, we would be enshrining the rather perverse notion that traditional rights are not to be protected in precisely those instances when protection is essential, *i.e.,* when a dominant group has succeeded in temporarily frustrating exercise of those rights. We prefer a view more compatible with the theory of this nation's founding: rights do not cease to exist because a government fails to secure them. *See The Declaration of Independence* (1776)." *Mescalero Apache Tribe v. New Mexico,* 630 F.2d 724, 730 (10th Cir. 1980), *vacated,* 450 U.S. 1036 (1981), *aff'd,* 462 U.S. 324 (1983).

V. CONCLUSION

Because plaintiffs have satisfied the requirements of Rule 23, their motion for class certification is granted....

SO ORDERED

Notes and Questions:

A. Rule 23(a) Class Certification

Q **1. Initiating the class action process.** Consistent with the implied requirements of *Hansberry*, the plaintiffs had to file and serve a complaint styled as a class action. Moreover, the complaint had to identify the class in some fashion. That is not enough, however, to make it a class action. What more did the plaintiffs have to do?

A They had to file a motion for a *class certification order* from the court. *See* Rule 23(c)(1). As the moving parties, plaintiffs had the burden of showing that certification was proper because their "putative class action" ("putative" because it is not a class action until the court certifies it as such) met the general prerequisites for class actions set out in Rule 23(a), and the specific requirements for one or more of the types of classes set out in Rule 23(b).

The court must then decide the motion to certify the class "at an early practicable time"—sometimes after limited discovery of facts pertinent to certification, but usually before substantial merits discovery gets underway.

2. Applying the "ascertainability" and "membership" requirements. Because a certification order "must define the class and the class claims, issues, or defenses," the first hurdle that the plaintiffs had to overcome was to define the class for the court. Courts have also added the "implied" requirements that the class be "ascertainable" (that we can determine who is in the class and who isn't), and that the representative plaintiffs be members of the class, according to their own definition. In *Floyd*, all the plaintiffs were Black, none Latino. How did they satisfy these requirements?

3. Numerosity. If, as *Hansberry* suggests, efficiency justifies the class action exception to the usual due process requirements, it should matter how many class members there are. If you have five, it can hardly be "impracticable" from an efficiency perspective for them to sue individually or join as coplaintiffs. If there are five thousand, the efficiency of treating their common issues and interests together is compelling, and the burden to the system of hearing five thousand separate lawsuits on many of the same issues is high. The Rule picks no bright line as to how many class members will satisfy the numerosity requirement, but some cases suggest that the line falls somewhere between twenty and forty members. *See, e.g., Cox v. Am. Cast Iron Pipe Co.*, 784 F.2d 1546, 1553 (11th Cir. 1986), *cert. denied*, 479 U.S. 883 (1986).

Geography can matter, too: It may be more "impracticable" for twenty members to join together as coplaintiffs under Rule 20(a)(1) if they are located in fifteen different states than for 200 class members from the same city to do the same thing.

4. Commonality. Lawyers typically seek class certification only if there are common questions of fact. Rule 23(a), however, does not require *all* or even most questions to be in common. Because the Floyd plaintiffs challenged a department-wide policy, it was easy for them to satisfy the commonality requirement. *See* n.138 (listing questions).

In *Wal-Mart Stores, Inc. v. Dukes*, 564 U.S. 338 (2011), the Supreme Court put teeth into the commonality requirement. Dukes brought a Frankenstein class action for employment discrimination on behalf of 1.5 million female employees of 3,500 Wal-Mart stores in all fifty states, seeking injunctive relief, backpay, and punitive damages. The plaintiffs argued that Wal-Mart's refusal to cabin the discretion of local store managers (almost all of them male) over pay and promotions had an unlawful disparate impact on female employees.

In an opinion by Justice Scalia, the Court said that to meet the commonality requirement of Rule 23(a)(2) it is not enough to allege that the class members all suffered a violation of the same law. "Their claims must depend upon a common contention . . . of such a nature that it is capable of classwide resolution, which means that determination of its truth or falsity will resolve an issue that is central to the validity of each one of the claims in one stroke." *Id.* at 350. What matters is not raising common questions, in other words, but "the capacity of a classwide proceeding to generate common *answers*. . . ." *Id.* (quoting Nagareda, *Class Certification in the Age of Aggregate Proof*, 84 N.Y.U. L. Rev. 97, 132 (2009)). Furthermore (and here the teeth showed not just for the commonality prong of the Rule 23(a) inquiry, but arguably for the entire Rule 23(a) inquiry), the Court said that Rule 23 is no "mere pleading standard." The party seeking class certification "must be prepared to prove that there are *in fact* sufficiently numerous parties, common questions of law or fact, etc." *Id.* at 351.

The Court then found that plaintiffs failed to show that there were in fact any common answers "to the crucial question *why was I disfavored*." *Id.* at 352. The store managers' exercise of discretion varied from store to store and from employee to employee, generating numerous uncommon (individualized) answers to that question. "Because respondents provide no convincing proof of a companywide discriminatory pay and promotion policy, we have concluded that they have not established the existence of any common question." *Id.* at 359.

The dissenters protested that, by emphasizing how many individualized questions permeated the putative class action, the majority had conflated Rule 23(a)(2)'s requirements for some "questions of law or fact common to the class" with Rule 23(b)(3)'s requirement "that the questions of law or fact common to class members *predominate* over any questions affecting only individual members." *See id.* at 375 (emphasis added).

Q **Look again at the questions listed in n.138.** Will the class action generate common answers to those questions?

A Yes, because each of these questions concerns a department-wide policy or practice. Either there is a policy or practice as described, or there isn't. On the other hand, none of the answers to these questions will answer, "Why was I

> stopped?" But unlike the *Wal-Mart* plaintiffs, the *Floyd* plaintiffs aren't asking for individualized backpay or damages, or even an individualized injunction against stopping and frisking any one of them. They are seeking injunctive relief against department-wide policies and practices, for which the common answers to these questions will be crucial.

5. Typicality. Commonality addresses issues of fact or law. Typicality addresses the class representatives' claims. Vastly dissimilar claims can have a common question of law or fact. By requiring class representatives to assert claims that are typical of the class, Rule 23 assures that the class representatives will "feel the pain" of the class members. *Freer* § 13.3. As *Floyd* points out, however, the claims need not be identical to satisfy the "typicality" requirement. After all, *Hansberry* merely insisted on similarity, *not identity*, of interests.

Q **6. Adequate representation.** The class members need to be adequately represented in two different respects. First, the class must be represented by adequate counsel. Rule 23(c)(1)(B) requires the court in its certification order to appoint class counsel under Rule 23(g) (usually by selecting counsel before the court, or if there are multiple counsel, from among them), which directs the court to consider the lawyers' preparation, experience, knowledge of the law, and resources.

Second, Rule 23(a)(4) refers to the adequacy of representation by the class representatives. This often overlaps with the typicality requirement, which is why *Floyd* treats them together. But not always. Suppose that Floyd is terminally ill with cancer. Can he adequately represent the class?

A

> He qualifies as a member of the class, and his claims of Fourth and Fourteenth Amendment violations are typical of the claims of the class. But he may not outlast the lawsuit, and his illness may also make it difficult for him to participate fully in discovery. For these reasons, it is doubtful that he could adequately represent the class. Similarly, if he was bankrupt, or his brother worked for the NYPD, these attributes might compromise his ability or desire to represent the class vigorously. Class representatives owe the class both a duty of loyalty and a duty of vigorous representation. Unique conflicts of interest, amenability to unique defenses, or restrictive personal circumstances can all interfere with that duty.

B. Rule 23(b) Class Certification

1. Rule 23(b)(2): The "injunctive relief class." The Rule 23(b)(2) class is frequently invoked for civil rights or employment discrimination claims.

But who needs it? Presumably, if Floyd successfully brought the case on his own behalf, and not for a class, he could still obtain an injunction ordering significant changes in the police policy. So why certify a Rule 23(b)(3) class, creating a much larger and potentially unwieldy action? The Second Circuit Court of Appeals has stated that certification of a Rule 23(b)(2) class is unnecessary when " 'prospective relief will benefit all members of a proposed class to such an extent that the certification of a class would not further the implementation of the judgment.' " *Galvan v. Levine*, 490 F.2d 1255, 1261 (2d Cir. 1973) (internal citation omitted). Hoping to thwart class certification by invoking the *Galvan* doctrine, the defendants in *Floyd* cleverly agreed that any injunction would apply to all "similarly situated" persons without conceding who they were.

The court was not fooled. It found that offer inconsistent with the defendants' Rule 23(a) arguments and the *Galvan* doctrine to be distinguishable:

> [T]he doctrine is only applicable when a defendant affirmatively states that it will apply any remedy across the board. Here, defendants have offered to apply any remedy to "all persons similarly situated to the named plaintiffs" but simultaneously argue that the alleged class members are not similarly situated to the named plaintiffs. "It is plainly inconsistent for Defendants to argue that any relief granted in connection with this action will be applied to benefit every member of the class, while at the same time they contest the existence of commonality and typicality." *Bishop v. New York City Dep't of Hous. Pres. and Dev.*, 141 F.R.D. 229, 241 (S.D.N.Y. 1992).

Floyd, 283 F.R.D. at 177, n.162.

2. Rule 23(b)(1): The "prejudice class." Rule 23(b)(1) reads like the flipside of Rule 19(a)(1), which defines a "required party" who should be joined if feasible. Rule 19 requires joinder of such persons because, if the person were left out of the lawsuit, either that person would be prejudiced in protecting her interest in the matter, or an existing party (usually the defendant) would be prejudiced by being put at risk of multiple or inconsistent obligations to the existing party-opponent and absentee. Rule 19 recognizes that these kinds of prejudice may be avoided or mitigated by requiring joinder of the absent person. Rule 23(b)(1)(B) recognizes that these kinds of prejudice can be avoided or mitigated by using a different, more ambitious joinder device: a class action treating the missing persons as members of the class. Hence, the shorthand phrase, "prejudice class" for both of the Rule 23(b)(1) types of classes. Some examples should help:

> A. Twelve hundred persons have been seriously injured, many permanently, by MegaPharm's combination sleep and cold medication, "Stone Coldeeze." If each sues for an average of $3 million, however, only the first one hundred will collect, because MegaPharm's net worth is only $300 million, and it is self-insured. In this case, there is a risk that "adjudications with respect to individual class members [the first hundred to win the average judgment] ... would substantially impair or impede the ability ... to protect [the] interests" of "other members not parties to the individual adjudications" (the other eleven hundred persons injured by the same product). The first one hundred judgments would drive MegaPharm into bankruptcy, leaving nothing for the last eleven hundred victims to recover. The interests of these absent parties in recovering damages for their personal injuries are thus impeded or nullified.
>
> The solution is a "limited fund" class under Rule 23(b)(1)(B), in which a class action judgment for the twelve hundred class members is shared pro rata. If the class action proceeded in this way, no one would recover all of her damages, but everyone could get something.
>
> B. OneBank is sued for making insufficient disclosures in its credit card application forms. If Jones successfully sues for an injunction ordering the

disclosures, and Day successfully sues for an injunction ordering different disclosures, OneBank will be unable to determine what disclosures it must make in its application materials. There is thus a risk of "inconsistent or varying adjudications with respect to individual class members [like Jones and Day] that would establish incompatible standards of conduct [here, of disclosure] for the party opposing the class [the Bank]." Rule 23(b)(1)(A).

The solution is a class under Rule 23(b)(1)(A) of all persons who applied for (or obtained) credit cards from OneBank, because the class relief—whether it ordered disclosure or not—would ensure that OneBank is not subject to inconsistent obligations.

C. Suppose a Patchwork Airlines plane goes down in an ice storm, killing all aboard, and the accident occurred due to improper de-icing by the Patchwork ground crew. Family members of the passengers bring separate lawsuits against Patchwork, and some win and some lose. Does the risk of these varying outcomes in individual litigation make this a case for class certification of the families under Rule 23(b)(1)(A)?

No, because even though the outcomes might be "inconsistent," the inconsistency does not establish incompatible standards of conduct for Patchwork. That is, the judgments would not result in conflicting orders to Patchwork. It must simply pay some plaintiffs, but not others.

3. Rule 23(b)(3): The "damages class." Most putative class actions seeking damages are certified under Rule 23(b)(3). Suppose, for example, that in the MegaPharm hypothetical above, MegaPharm could easily withstand twelve hundred individual lawsuits given its net worth and insurance coverage. A putative class would not qualify as a prejudice class because there is no limited fund. Moreover, although the individual suits would share common questions about whether Stone Coldeeze was hazardous to health, was insufficiently tested, or was misleadingly marketed, they would also pose sharply *different* questions of damages and, possibly, causation. (For example, did an individual plaintiff's heart problem result from the medication, her lifestyle, or both? Did she follow the dosage recommendations on the label?) Finally, with an expectation of an average judgment of $3 million, each individual action is economically viable: The individual plaintiff has a sufficient monetary incentive to bring the action, and a lawyer has a corresponding incentive to take it on a contingent fee basis.

For these reasons, Rule 23(b)(3) authorizes certification of a damages class action only if, despite the variability of many questions of fact and law among class members, a class action is more efficient than individual actions, the common questions predominate over the individualized questions, and the putative class members are given the chance to skip the class—to "opt out" from the class, leaving them free to pursue their own action (but also excluding them from the benefit of any class judgment).

Q **4. The Rule 23(b)(3) efficiency calculus: Predominance.** How does Rule 23(b)(3) suggest that a court should make the efficiency judgment? First, it has to assure that the questions common to class members "predominate" over the individualized questions. For example, in the MegaPharm product liability hypothetical, the court would have to find that the common liability questions of design, testing, production, and marketing predominate over individualized questions of injury causation and damages. If there is such predominance, then class action treatment of the common questions will produce efficiencies, even though the non-common questions will still need to be resolved individually, often by individual hearings or damages trials after the common liability questions are tried together.

But wait, didn't the court already do this in deciding whether the class met the general prerequisites under Rule 23(a)? How is this inquiry under Rule 23(b)(3) different from the Rule 23(a) analysis?

> The Rule 23(a) inquiry is only whether "there are questions of law or fact common to the class"—*some* questions, not all or most. Most monetary damages actions are likely to have many individualized—non-common—questions, like the amount (and sometimes cause) of each plaintiff's damages, and in some cases, whether a plaintiff relied on something the defendant did, contributed to her own injury, or assumed the risk. Having *some* common questions is enough for Rule 23(a), but having them "predominate" is an added requirement for designation under Rule 23(b)(3), to help identify the relatively small number of monetary damages actions for which class action treatment will nevertheless be efficient.
>
> In *Comcast Corp. v. Behrend*, 569 U.S. 27 (2013), however, the Court perhaps cast some doubt on this difference between the analyses under Rule 23(b)(3) and 23(a). Asserting that "[t]he same analytical principles [that apply under Rule 23(a)] govern Rule 23(b)," the Court reversed a predominance determination because plaintiffs had not provided "evidentiary proof" that antitrust damages were capable of measurement on a classwide basis. *Id.* at 33. Although the majority characterized the holding as "a straightforward application of class-certification principles" under Rule 23(b)(3), the dissent asserted that "predominance" "scarcely demands commonality as to all questions" and can be satisfied "even if damages are not provable in the aggregate." *Id.* at 41.

Whether *Behrend* is case-specific or more broadly applicable, a trial court ruling on certification of a Rule 23(b)(3) class must still decide whether common issues predominate. How? It surely can't be by counting them, because depending on who is doing the counting, one question can often be subdivided into two, and two combined into one. There is also no scale on which to weigh them. It follows that predominance is necessarily a pragmatic, not a quantifiable or mechanical, inquiry. In deciding predominance, courts have considered a number of factors, including whether:

- the substantive elements of class members' claims require the same proof for each class member;
- the proposed class is bound together by a mutual interest in resolving common questions more than it is divided by individual interests;
- the resolution of an issue common to the class would significantly advance the litigation;
- one or more common issues constitute significant parts of each class member's individual case;

- the common questions are central to all of the members' claims;
- the same theory of liability is asserted by or against all class members, and all defendants raise the same basic defenses.

5 *Moore* § 23.45[1].

Q **5. The Rule 23(b)(3) efficiency calculus: Superiority.** The second part of Rule 23(b)(3)'s efficiency calculus requires a finding that the class action is "superior to other available methods for fairly and efficiently adjudicating the controversy." Here the Rule does not leave the court at sea; it lists pertinent factors that balance the prospects and existence of individualized actions against the desirability and manageability of class actions. But the superiority inquiry is ultimately a comparison. A comparison with what? What are "other available methods" of adjudication?

> One obvious answer is actions by individual class members. Their interest in pursuing their own claims individually is a function partly of the likely value of their claims and partly of the extent to which they have already initiated their own claims at the time that class certification is sought. A variant on this is singling out one of the individual actions for an early trial as a "test case," providing information to the defendant and other plaintiffs that may facilitate the settlement calculus. If trying a test case has this effect, it is more efficient than trying a large class action.
>
> Another alternative is joinder of plaintiffs under Rule 20. The practicality of this alternative turns on where the plaintiffs are located geographically, the prospects for finding a local lawyer, and, of course, how many potential coplaintiffs there are.
>
> Individual pending actions can also be consolidated in a single court under 28 U.S.C. § 1407, which authorizes transfers of multidistrict litigation into a single venue for consolidated pretrial proceedings.
>
> Finally, remember where we started. Private litigation is not the only response to misconduct. Plaintiffs may complain to government authorities, and some authorities may even have jurisdiction to hold administrative trials and impose fines or obtain other kinds of remedies.

6. Which Rule 23(b) class? Who cares? It matters which Rule 23(b) class is designated, partly because Rule 23(b)(3) imposes additional procedural requirements for designation beyond Rule 23(a).

But there are two additional factors that make an even greater difference. First, Rule 23(c)(2)(B) requires that Rule 23(b)(3) class members each be given individual notice where practicable. For a large class, this can be expensive, and, as we shall see below, it is usually an expense carried by the party who seeks class certification. Second, the notice must afford each Rule 23(b)(3) class member an opportunity to request exclusion from the class—to "opt out"—in the class action vernacular. A class member who has already started her own lawsuit, or who thinks the stakes are high enough to warrant doing so, may choose to opt out and go it alone.

IV. Class Action Jurisdiction and Conduct

You may already be starting to appreciate that class actions are a special breed of civil action that is a litigation subspecialty. Their complexities and problems are the stuff of upper-level Advanced Civil Procedure, Complex Litigation, and Mass Tort Law courses, well beyond the basic Civil Procedure course. Still, it is important even in an introduction to class actions to appreciate two principles.

First, as different as they are, they remain civil actions that are subject to the baseline requirements of subject matter jurisdiction, personal jurisdiction, and venue in federal courts. Even if an action qualifies for certification, it cannot proceed in federal court unless it satisfies these requirements.

Second, to protect the rights and interests of absent class members, the trial court plays a more active role in conducting the class action than it typically plays in ordinary, non-class civil litigation. Rule 23 elaborates on that role by *permitting* the trial court to issue orders that relate to attorneys' fees, Fed. R. Civ. P. 23(d), (h), and by *requiring* the court to select and appoint class counsel and to approve any settlement, voluntary dismissal, or compromise of claims, issues, or defenses in a certified class action. Fed. R. Civ. P. 23(e), (g). The following discussion outlines some recurring issues of jurisdiction and conduct that arise in class actions.

Subject matter jurisdiction. If, unlike the *Floyd* plaintiffs, a class action plaintiff like Haynes in our opening hypothetical relies only on state statutory and common law remedies, rather than federal law, he cannot invoke federal question jurisdiction. He would then have to establish diversity jurisdiction.

Citizenship would not be a problem if Haynes proposed a class whose members were citizens of a state different from that of the defendant. But suppose he proposed a nationwide class, including members who are citizens of the same state(s) as the defendant (or any one of the defendants, if he sued several)? The Supreme Court held in a similar case that only the representative party's citizenship needs to be diverse from that of the defendant. *Supreme Tribe of Ben-Hur v. Cauble*, 255 U.S. 356 (1921). Because the class's lawyer can often pick and choose (and substitute, if necessary) the class representative, *Ben-Hur* allows easy satisfaction of the citizenship requirement for diversity-based class actions in federal court.

But what about the other half of the diversity equation—amount in controversy? The historical rule is that class members, like coplaintiffs with distinct claims, cannot aggregate their claims to reach the amount in controversy. See *supra* pp. 81–84. Thus, if Haynes and his one thousand class members had each shelled out $525 for the washing machine, the amount in controversy would still be $525, *not* $525,000. Suppose, however, that Haynes's machine had damaged $80,000 worth of designer clothes (say, two pairs of those really cool pre-faded, pre-shredded jeans). Even if the rest of the class members had less than $75,000 in damages, would the fact that the class representative alone pleaded an amount in controversy of more than $75,000 enable the class action to satisfy the amount-in-controversy requirement for diversity jurisdiction?

The Court said no in *Zahn v. International Paper Co.*, 414 U.S. 291 (1973), and required each class member to meet the amount individually. But in *Exxon Mobil Corp. v. Allapattah Servs., Inc.*, 545 U.S. 546 (2005), the Court changed direction, holding that a later-enacted statute, 28 U.S.C. § 1367, overruled *Zahn*. This statute gives a federal court *supplemental jurisdiction* over claims that arise out of the same transaction as a claim over which the court has original subject matter jurisdiction, as we will explore more thoroughly in Chapter 20. Thus, as long as Haynes's (or any other class representative's) claim meets the amount-in-controversy requirement, his claim can serve as the anchor claim for supplemental jurisdiction over the other class members' below-amount claims, inasmuch as they all arise from the same transaction—here the misleading marketing of the washing machine.

Subject matter jurisdiction and the Class Action Fairness Act of 2005. To get our washing machine hypothetical into federal court on diversity grounds, however, we had to clothe Haynes in credulity-straining designer jeans. In the more plausible case, no class member could meet the $75,000 amount-in-controversy requirement. In fact, this will often be the case in consumer class actions. Such cases were therefore often filed in state courts. Such courts also proved attractive to plaintiffs' class action lawyers because some state courts were more hospitable to massive punitive damage awards than federal courts. In addition, most state courts do not allow interlocutory appeals of class action certification orders. Thus, if the class is certified, the defendant must wait until a final judgment before it can challenge the certification, enhancing the bargaining power of the class action lawyers to "extort" (from defendants' perspectives) settlements generating large attorneys' fees. Finally, some state courts did not police class action settlements very carefully, raising the risk of sweetheart deals between the class lawyers and defendants to the detriment of the class members. *See Freer* § 13.3.9.

Business interests therefore lobbied for a change in the laws that would channel more class actions into federal courts, thought to be less hospitable to plaintiffs. These efforts led to the Class Action Fairness Act of 2005 (CAFA), Pub. L. No. 109-2, 119 Stat. 4 (codified in sections of 28 U.S.C.). It amended the subject matter jurisdiction requirements for certain class actions in several ways that enabled federal courts to exercise diversity jurisdiction in cases that were previously brought in state courts.

First, CAFA gives federal courts original subject matter jurisdiction over class actions in which the *aggregated* amount in controversy exceeds $5 million, if any plaintiff class member is a citizen of a state different from any defendant, or if any plaintiff class member is a foreign state or subject and the defendant is a citizen of a state, or the reverse. In other words, the Act requires only "minimal diversity" for qualifying class actions and apparently overrules the common law rule against aggregating individual plaintiffs' claims. 28 U.S.C. § 1332(d)(2).

Second, CAFA permits removal from state to federal court of actions that satisfy this amended diversity requirement, even by citizens of the forum state and even more than a year after the action was filed in state court. It thus eliminated the "forum defendant" bar to removal and relaxed the time limits for removal of class actions and mass torts. 28 U.S.C. § 1453(b).

At the same time, however, CAFA gives a federal court the discretion to decline jurisdiction if it finds that one-third to two-thirds of the plaintiff class members are from the same state as the primary defendants and the action has various attributes identifying it with a particular state. 28 U.S.C. § 1332(d)(3). Furthermore, in some circumstances, it requires the court to decline jurisdiction. The details are complex and beyond the scope of a first-year course, but they are clearly intended to "localize"—keep in state courts—certain kinds of plaintiff class actions that are primarily of interest to a particular state.

Notice. Unlike members of the other Rule 23(b) classes, members of a Rule 23(b)(3) damages action are entitled by rule to "the best notice practicable under the circumstances, including individual notice to all members who can be identified through reasonable effort." Fed. R. Civ. P. 23(c)(2)(B). Where does this requirement come from? You may recognize the "best notice practicable under the circumstances" as a close paraphrase of the principle of *Mullane v. Central Hanover Bank*, 339 U.S. 306 (1950), the leading constitutional case on notice. That's no coincidence, because *Mullane* involved classes of beneficiaries of the trust fund that was the subject of the lawsuit. Rule 23(c)(2) simply implements the *Mullane* principle in the context of Rule 23(b)(3) damages class actions.

But the Rule *mandates* notice only for Rule 23(b)(3) damages classes and not for Rule 23(b)(1) or Rule 23(b)(2) classes. Why the difference?

> The difference is that many Rule 23(b)(3) damages actions are viable as individual actions, while the other kinds of class actions are not, as a practical matter. They are "mandatory" in the sense that they are all or nothing—no class member can really (or would want to) act independently of the class. A court *may* order that notice be given in one of the other classes in some cases, but *must* do so only for a Rule 23(b)(3) damages class in order for putative class members to make the practical decision whether to go it alone.

If the damages class has 100,000 or 1 million class members, notice can be expensive (multiply this figure by the cost of postage and of the paper, assuming that notice by electronic means is not permitted or that email addresses are unavailable). Therefore, who pays for notice can itself make or break the plaintiffs' class action, if the class representatives or their lawyers can't ante up $50,000 or $500,000 for the mailing.

Class Action Notice

Notice of Pendency of Class Action

Superior Court of California, County of Alameda
Department 22, 1221 Oak Street, Oakland, CA 94612

IF YOU ARE OR WERE A SUBSCRIBER OF VERIZON WIRELESS AND YOU PAID, WERE CHARGED OR WERE SUBJECT TO AN EARLY TERMINATION FEE, YOUR RIGHTS MAY BE AFFECTED

- Customers of Verizon Wireless have sued that company alleging that Verizon Wireless violated their rights under California law and under the laws of other states, as well as federal law.
- The Court has allowed the lawsuits to be a class action on behalf of all subscribers to Verizon Wireless with personal accounts who paid or were charged a flat Early Termination Fee ("ETF") (generally $175) from July 23, 1999 to August 10, 2008.
- The Court has not decided whether the plaintiffs' claims have any merit. However, your legal rights are affected, and you have a choice to make now:

YOUR LEGAL RIGHTS AND OPTIONS IN THIS LAWSUIT	
SUBMIT A CLAIM FORM BY October 14, 2008	**Stay in this lawsuit. Submit a claim form. Await the outcome. If the settlement is approved by the Court you may be eligible for a payment of money under the settlement. Be bound by the result.** By submitting a claim form you keep the possibility of getting money or benefits that may come from the settlement. But you give up any rights to sue Verizon Wireless separately about the same legal claims in this lawsuit. If you do not file a claim form before October 14, 2008, you give up your right to get money from the settlement if it is approved by the Court.
SUBMIT AN OBJECTION BY October 7, 2008	**Object to the Settlement.** Stay in the lawsuit, but submit an objection. By objecting to the settlement you give up your right to be excluded from the settlement and your right to file your own action. If you object to the settlement, you may ask a lawyer to represent you at your own cost.
ASK TO BE EXCLUDED BY September 30, 2008	**Get out of this lawsuit. Get no benefits from it. Keep rights.** If you ask to be excluded and money or benefits are later awarded, you won't share in those. But you keep your right to sue Verizon Wireless separately about the same legal claims in this lawsuit.

After the court certifies a class under Rule 23(b)(3), Rule 23(c)(2)(B) requires individual notice to identifiable class members describing the action and the class and explaining a class member's right to "opt out" of the class. But some Rule 23(b)(3) class actions settle even before this notice can be mailed. In such cases, the required Rule 23(c)(2)(B) notice is often combined with the notice of the settlement that is required by Rule 23(e)(1). This notice in the Verizon Wireless litigation serves both functions.

Text Message Notice

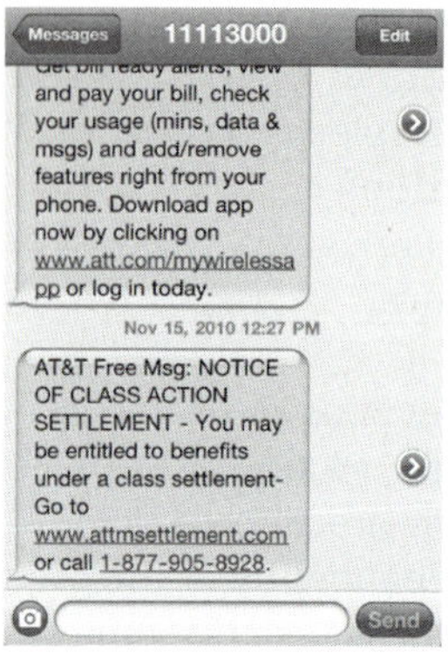

"Reasonable" notice under Rule 23 has usually been by first-class mail. But many class members never open the envelope, discarding it as junk mail, and many who do open it can't understand it. Here's a novel alternative. Notice by text message. Would you follow the hyperlink?

Some lawyers and commentators believe that the Supreme Court's decision in *Eisen v. Carlisle & Jacquelin*, 417 U.S. 156 (1974), which held that this burden falls on the class representatives, illustrates the federal courts' hostility to class actions.

Discovery. As the Supreme Court noted in *Phillips* in the excerpt quoted above, discovery in class actions is ordinarily directed at the class representatives. While limited discovery about the class is sometimes permitted in anticipation of the class certification decision, absent class members are not parties who must respond to discovery by interrogatories (written questions), requests for production of documents, or requests for admissions under the Federal Rules. Routinely permitting discovery of the entire class would significantly reduce the efficiency of the class action and increase the burden on the class members. Some courts, however, have allowed discovery of absent class members when the information sought is relevant to the resolution of common questions, the requests are made in good faith and are not unduly burdensome, and the information is not available from class representatives. *See, e.g., Transamerican Refining Corp. v. Dravo Corp.*, 139 F.R.D. 619 (S.D. Tex. 1991).

Settlement. Because of the financial risks of a class judgment, the defendant may have a greater incentive to settle a class action than many ordinary actions. At the same time, the prospect of a large contingent fee may provide a similar incentive to class counsel to settle. The result is a serious risk of a devil's bargain or sweetheart settlement, by which a defendant bargains to have the class release its claims (thus removing the risk of a class judgment and of future lawsuits by class members) in return for enriching the class lawyers and possibly the class representatives. Absent class members, by contrast, could get only marginal or even illusory benefits. For example, they may receive a coupon providing a trivial discount on some future purchase that the members probably won't make anyway. Or they may get, as one of us received, notice of the "right" to ask *and pay* for additional maintenance at the next automobile maintenance interval. Lawyers disagree about how widespread such abusive settlements are, but in passing the Class Action Fairness Act of 2005, Congress found that "[c]lass members often receive little or no benefit from class actions, and are sometimes harmed, such as where ... unjustified awards are made to certain plaintiffs at the expense of other class members." Pub. L. No. 109-2, § 2(a)(3), 119 Stat. 4.

Rule 23(e) deals with this problem by requiring that notice of the proposed settlement be sent to all class members who would be bound by the settlement. Unlike Rule 23(c)(2), this notice requirement applies to every type of class. (Sometimes, when the class action is settled before the notice required by Rule 23(c)(2)(B) for damages actions has been mailed, the two notices are combined into a single notice.) Second, it requires that the court hold a "fairness hearing" on the proposed settlement, at which objections from class members can be heard. Third, it requires the court to approve the settlement only if it finds it to be "fair, reasonable, and adequate." Fourth, the Rule allows a court to require a second opt-out opportunity in Rule 23(b)(3) damages class actions. Finally, the court also controls the award of attorneys' fees under Rule 23(h). These provisions provide the court with a kitbag of tools to police class action settlements and, thereby, protect the class.

VI. Class Actions: Summary of Basic Principles

- A class action is a civil action in which a party acts as a representative for similarly situated non-parties who are bound by any resulting judgment. The chief justification for class actions is efficiency, in that they facilitate the litigation of common issues and interests in a single, binding lawsuit instead of multiple individual lawsuits.

- The binding effect of a class action judgment on absent class members is consistent with due process because the class representative litigates as a surrogate for the class members. This surrogacy-based exception to the usual due process requirement of individual notice and an opportunity to be heard is premised on the substantial identity of interests between the class representatives and the class members, the adequacy of representation of those interests by the class representative, and the application of transparent judicial procedures for the designation and conduct of the class litigation.

- To certify an action as a class action, a court must find that the putative class meets the judicially implied requirements of "ascertainability" and plaintiffs' membership in the class, as well as the Rule 23(a) requirements of numerosity, commonality, typicality, and adequacy of representation.

- The class must also qualify as one or more of the Rule 23(b) classes. Because Rule 23(b)(3) damages classes are most likely to present individual issues and claims that could be viable as individual actions, Rule 23(b)(3) requires that, in addition to meeting the foregoing requirements, the class representative(s) must show that common issues predominate and that a class action would be superior to alternative methods of adjudication. Members of a Rule 23(b)(3) class must be given individual notice, where practicable, of the class action and of their right to exclude themselves from—opt out of—the class.

- Federal courts that conduct class actions, like all civil actions, must have subject matter jurisdiction. In diversity-based class actions, only the class representatives' citizenship must be diverse from that of opposing parties and only a single class representative needs to satisfy the amount in controversy.
- To protect the interests of absent class members, courts play a more active role in the conduct of class actions than in the conduct of other civil actions. For example, courts must certify the class, appoint class counsel, approve any settlement or dismissal of claims, issues, or defenses, and direct that notice of a proposed settlement be provided in a reasonable manner to all class members.

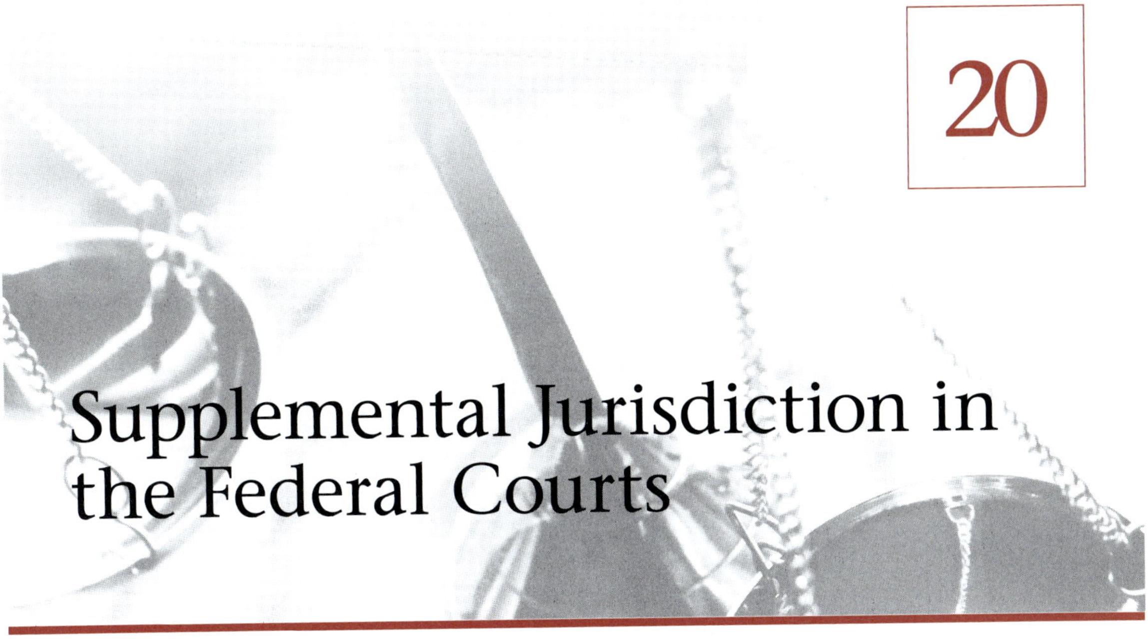

20

Supplemental Jurisdiction in the Federal Courts

I. Introduction: Related State Law Claims in Federal Court

The federal joinder rules provide a flexible vehicle for broad joinder of related claims in federal court. However, the fact that the Federal Rules authorize the joinder of a claim does not mean that a federal court has *subject matter jurisdiction* to hear that claim. As Rule 82 reminds us, "[t]hese rules do not extend or limit the jurisdiction of the [federal] district courts. . . ." Thus, there is an inherent tension between the rule makers' preference for joinder of all related claims in a single action and the need for subject matter jurisdiction over each claim in that action.

Consider this example. Caprera is arrested by Epstein and Ruiz, two police officers. He claims that the officers assaulted him during the arrest. Caprera sues the officers under 42 U.S.C. § 1983, alleging that they violated his federal constitutional right to be free of unreasonable seizures. He also asserts a state law claim for battery against each defendant. Thus, his complaint asserts four claims:

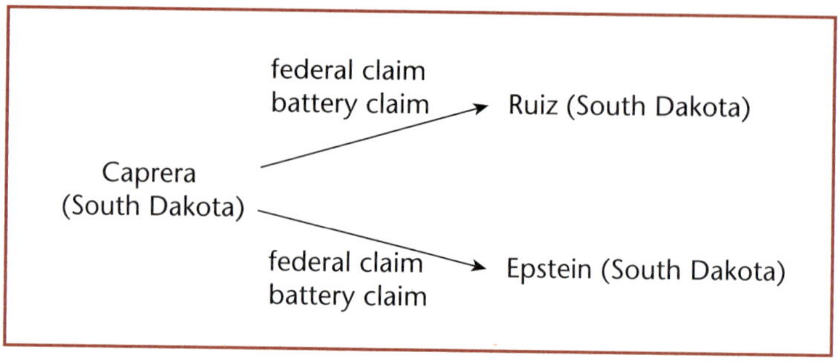

Figure 20–1: PENDENT STATE LAW CLAIMS

Caprera has properly joined the officers as codefendants under Rule 20(a)(2), because he seeks relief against them arising from the same arrest, and there will be a common question as to who assaulted Caprera. In addition, Rule 18(a) allows him to assert multiple claims against each defendant.

The federal court has subject matter jurisdiction over Caprera's federal civil rights claims against Ruiz and Epstein because they arise under federal law. However, Ruiz's battery claims are state law claims against parties from his own state. There is no independent basis for subject matter jurisdiction over these claims. If Caprera had sued on the battery claims alone, the federal court would have dismissed them for lack of subject matter jurisdiction.

But Caprera did not sue on the battery claims alone; he sued each officer on a proper federal claim and wants to *add* the state law claims. If the federal court is going to hear the federal claims, it makes sense for it to hear the battery claims as well, since they arise from the same underlying facts. Caprera's right to add such related claims in federal litigation is governed by the doctrine of *supplemental jurisdiction.*

II. The Constitutional Framework for Supplemental Jurisdiction: *United Mine Workers v. Gibbs*

One of the axioms of civil procedure is that a federal court cannot hear a claim unless the Framers authorized federal courts to do so in Article III, Section 2 of the United States Constitution. Certainly, nothing in that section *explicitly* authorizes jurisdiction over related state law claims in federal cases such as the battery claims in Caprera's case. In *United Mine Workers v. Gibbs,* however, the United States Supreme Court held that Article III, Section 2 implicitly authorizes jurisdiction over such related claims. The case creates an analytical framework that continues to govern the assertion of such additional claims today.

READING *UNITED MINE WORKERS v. GIBBS.* In *Gibbs*, the United Mine Workers, a national union, picketed a new mine to prevent its operation by miners from a rival union. As a result, Gibbs lost his contract to manage the mine and to haul ore from the mine. He sued the union in federal court, claiming that it had violated the Federal Labor Management Relations Act (LMRA) by engaging in a "secondary boycott"—that is, boycotting one party (Gibbs) to affect the outcome of a labor dispute with a different party, the mine owner. Gibbs also alleged that the same conduct constituted the state law tort of interference with his contract with the operator. Since he was not diverse from the union,* there was no independent basis for federal jurisdiction over this claim.

In *Gibbs*, the Court discusses the doctrine of "pendent" jurisdiction. Prior to enactment of the supplemental jurisdiction statute in 1990, state law claims such as Caprera's battery claims that were added by the plaintiff to a federal question case were labeled *pendent* claims, presumably because the party was trying to append them to the federal claim. When defendants or other parties sought to add state law claims to a case, such as counterclaims, crossclaims, and third-party claims, these were referred to as *ancillary*. (As we will see, both types of claims are now referred to as *supplemental* claims.)

In reading *Gibbs*, consider the following questions:

- The Court analyzes jurisdiction over the related state law claim in two parts. First, the Court asks whether the district court had the *power*—that is, subject matter jurisdiction—to hear the interference-with-contract claim. What standard does the Court establish for this first part of the "*Gibbs* test"?
- The Court then considers—one might even say, announces—a second part to the test for jurisdiction over the related state law claim. What is the second step?
- Justice Brennan suggests four reasons why a federal court, having concluded that it has power to entertain the related state law claims in a federal case, might decline to do so. What are they?

UNITED MINE WORKERS v. GIBBS

383 U.S. 715 (1966)

Mr. Justice Brennan delivered the opinion of the Court.

Respondent Paul Gibbs was awarded compensatory and punitive damages in this action against petitioner United Mine Workers of America (UMW) for alleged violations of § 303 of the Labor Management Relations Act and of the common law of Tennessee. The case grew out of the rivalry between the United Mine Workers and the Southern Labor Union over representation of workers in the southern Appalachian coal fields. Tennessee Consolidated Coal Company, not a party here, laid off 100 miners of the UMW's Local 5881 when it closed one of its mines in southern Tennessee during the spring of 1960. Late that summer,

* A union, like other unincorporated associations, is deemed a citizen of the state of each of its members for purposes of diversity. Presumably, many members of the UMW were from Tennessee, as was Gibbs.

Grundy Company, a wholly owned subsidiary of Consolidated, hired respondent as mine superintendent to attempt to open a new mine on Consolidated's property at nearby Gray's Creek through use of members of the Southern Labor Union. As part of the arrangement, Grundy also gave respondent a contract to haul the mine's coal to the nearest railroad loading point.

On August 15 and 16, 1960, armed members of Local 5881 forcibly prevented the opening of the mine, threatening respondent and beating an organizer for the rival union. The members of the local believed Consolidated had promised them the jobs at the new mine; they insisted that if anyone would do the work, they would. At this time, no representative of the UMW, their international union, was present. George Gilbert, the UMW's field representative for the area... [was away but] returned with explicit instructions from his international union superiors to establish a limited picket line, to prevent any further violence, and to see to it that the strike did not spread to neighboring mines. There was no further violence at the mine site; a picket line was maintained there for nine months; and no further attempts were made to open the mine during that period.

Respondent lost his job as superintendent, and never entered into performance of his haulage contract. He testified that he soon began to lose other trucking contracts and mine leases he held in nearby areas. Claiming these effects to be the result of a concerted union plan against him, he sought recovery not against Local 5881 or its members, but only against petitioner, the international union. The suit was brought in the United States District Court for the Eastern District of Tennessee, and jurisdiction was premised on allegations of secondary boycotts under § 303 [of the LMRA]. The state law claim, for which jurisdiction was based upon the doctrine of pendent jurisdiction, asserted "an unlawful conspiracy and an unlawful boycott aimed at him and [Grundy] to maliciously, wantonly and willfully interfere with his contract of employment and with his contract of haulage."

The trial judge refused to submit to the jury the claims of pressure intended to cause mining firms other than Grundy to cease doing business with Gibbs; he found those claims unsupported by the evidence. The jury's verdict was that the UMW had violated both § 303 and state law. Gibbs was awarded $60,000 as damages under the employment contract and $14,500 under the haulage contract; he was also awarded $100,000 punitive damages. On motion, the trial court set aside the award of damages with respect to the haulage contract on the ground that damage was unproved. It also held that union pressure on Grundy to discharge respondent as supervisor would constitute only a primary dispute with Grundy, as respondent's employer, and hence was not cognizable as a claim under § 303. Interference with the employment relationship was cognizable as a state claim, however, and a remitted award was sustained on the state law claim.... We granted certiorari. We reverse.

I.

A threshold question is whether the District Court properly entertained jurisdiction of the claim based on Tennessee law.... The fact that state remedies were not entirely pre-empted does not, however, answer the question whether the state claim was properly adjudicated in the District Court absent diversity jurisdiction. The Court held in *Hurn v. Oursler*, 289 U.S. 238 (1933), that state law claims are appropriate for federal court determination if they form a separate but parallel ground for relief also sought in a substantial claim based on federal law. The Court distinguished permissible from non-permissible exercises of federal judicial power over state law claims by contrasting "a case where two distinct grounds in support of a single cause of action are alleged, one only of which presents a federal question, and a case where two separate and distinct causes of action are alleged, one only of which is federal in character. In the former, where the federal question averred is not plainly wanting in substance, the federal court, even though the federal ground be not established, may nevertheless retain and dispose of the case upon the nonfederal *ground*; in the latter it may not do so upon the nonfederal *cause of action*." 289 U.S., at 246. The question is into which category the present action fell.

Hurn was decided in 1933, before the unification of law and equity by the Federal Rules of Civil Procedure. At the time, the meaning of "cause of action" was a subject of serious dispute; the phrase might "mean one thing for one purpose and something different for another." *United States v. Memphis Cotton Oil Co.*, 288 U.S. 62, 67–68 (1933). . . .

With the adoption of the Federal Rules of Civil Procedure and the unified form of action, Fed. Rule Civ. Proc. 2, much of the controversy over "cause of action" abated. The phrase remained as the keystone of the *Hurn* test, however, and, as commentators have noted, has been the source of considerable confusion. Under the Rules, the impulse is toward entertaining the broadest possible scope of action consistent with fairness to the parties; joinder of claims, parties and remedies is strongly encouraged.[10] Yet because the *Hurn* question involves issues of jurisdiction as well as convenience, there has been some tendency to limit its application to cases in which the state and federal claims are, as in *Hurn*, "little more than the equivalent of different epithets to characterize the same group of circumstances." 289 U.S., at 246.

This limited approach is unnecessarily grudging. Pendent jurisdiction, in the sense of judicial *power*, exists whenever there is a claim "arising under [the] Constitution, the Laws of the United States, and Treaties made, or which shall be made, under their Authority . . . ," U.S. Const., Art. III, § 2, and the relationship between that claim and the state claim permits the conclusion that the entire action before the court comprises but one constitutional "case." The federal claim must have substance sufficient to confer subject matter jurisdiction on the court. The state and federal claims must derive from a common nucleus of operative fact. But if, considered without regard to their federal or state character, a plaintiff's claims are such that he would ordinarily be expected to try them all in one judicial proceeding, then, assuming substantiality of the federal issues, there is *power* in federal courts to hear the whole.[13]

10. See, e.g., Fed. Rules Civ. Proc. 2, 18–20, 42.

13. While it is commonplace that the Federal Rules of Civil Procedure do not expand the jurisdiction of federal courts, they do embody "the whole tendency of our decisions . . . to require a plaintiff to try his . . . whole case at one time, and to that extent emphasize the basis of pendent jurisdiction." [(quoting from *Baltimore S.S. Co. v. Phillips*, 274 U.S. 316, 320 (1927)].

That power need not be exercised in every case in which it is found to exist. It has consistently been recognized that pendent jurisdiction is a doctrine of discretion, not of plaintiff's right. Its justification lies in considerations of judicial economy, convenience and fairness to litigants; if these are not present a federal court should hesitate to exercise jurisdiction over state claims, even though bound to apply state law to them, *Erie R. Co. v. Tompkins*. Needless decisions of state law should be avoided both as a matter of comity and to promote justice between the parties, by procuring for them a surer-footed reading of applicable law. Certainly, if the federal claims are dismissed before trial, even though not insubstantial in a jurisdictional sense, the state claims should be dismissed as well. Similarly, if it appears that the state issues substantially predominate, whether in terms of proof, of the scope of the issues raised, or of the comprehensiveness of the remedy sought, the state claims may be dismissed without prejudice and left for resolution to state tribunals. There may, on the other hand, be situations in which the state claim is so closely tied to questions of federal policy that the argument for exercise of pendent jurisdiction is particularly strong. In the present case, for example, the allowable scope of the state claim implicates the federal doctrine of pre-emption; while this interrelationship does not create statutory federal question jurisdiction, *Louisville & N.R. Co. v. Mottley*, its existence is relevant to the exercise of discretion. Finally, there may be reasons independent of jurisdictional considerations, such as the likelihood of jury confusion in treating divergent legal theories of relief, that would justify separating state and federal claims for trial, Fed. Rule Civ. Proc. 42(b). If so, jurisdiction should ordinarily be refused.

The question of power will ordinarily be resolved on the pleadings. But the issue whether pendent jurisdiction has been properly assumed is one which remains open throughout the litigation. Pretrial procedures or even the trial itself may reveal a substantial hegemony of state law claims, or likelihood of jury confusion, which could not have been anticipated at the pleading stage. Although it will of course be appropriate to take account in this circumstance of the already completed course of the litigation, dismissal of the state claim might even then be merited. For example, it may appear that the plaintiff was well aware of the nature of his proofs and the relative importance of his claims; recognition of a federal court's wide latitude to decide ancillary questions of state law does not imply that it must tolerate a litigant's effort to impose upon it what is in effect only a state law case. Once it appears that a state claim constitutes the real body of a case, to which the federal claim is only an appendage, the state claim may fairly be dismissed.

We are not prepared to say that in the present case the District Court exceeded its discretion in proceeding to judgment on the state claim. We may assume for purposes of decision that the District Court was correct in its holding that the claim of pressure on Grundy to terminate the employment contract was outside the purview of § 303. Even so, the § 303 claims based on secondary pressures on Grundy relative to the haulage contract and on other coal operators generally were substantial. Although § 303 limited recovery to compensatory damages based on secondary pressures, and state law allowed both compensatory and punitive damages, and allowed such damages as to both secondary and primary activity, the state and federal claims arose from the same nucleus of operative fact and reflected alternative remedies. Indeed, the verdict sheet sent in to the jury authorized only one award of damages, so that recovery could not be given separately on the federal and state claims.

It is true that the § 303 claims ultimately failed and that the only recovery allowed respondent was on the state claim. We cannot confidently say, however, that the federal issues were so remote or played such a minor role at the trial that in effect the state claim only was tried. Although the District Court dismissed as unproved the § 303 claims that petitioner's secondary activities included attempts to induce coal operators other than Grundy to cease doing business with respondent, the court submitted the § 303 claims relating to Grundy to the jury. The jury returned verdicts against petitioner on those § 303 claims, and it was only on petitioner's motion for a directed verdict and a judgment n.o.v. that the verdicts on those claims were set aside. The District Judge considered the claim as to the haulage contract proved as to liability, and held it failed only for lack of proof of damages. Although there was some risk of confusing the jury in joining the state and federal claims—especially since, as will be developed, differing standards of proof of UMW involvement applied—the possibility of confusion could be lessened by employing a special verdict form, as the District Court did. Moreover, the question whether the permissible scope of the state claim was limited by the doctrine of pre-emption afforded a special reason for the exercise of pendent jurisdiction; the federal courts are particularly appropriate bodies for the application of pre-emption principles. We thus conclude that although it may be that the District Court might, in its sound discretion, have dismissed the state claim, the circumstances show no error in refusing to do so.

. . .

REVERSED [on other grounds].

[Concurring opinion of Justice Harlan omitted.]

Notes and Questions: *United Mine Workers v. Gibbs*

1. The problem restated. *Gibbs* provides a straightforward example of the problem this chapter addresses. Gibbs sued the union on two claims, as he was authorized to do under Fed. R. Civ. P. 18(a). The federal district court had jurisdiction over the federal labor law claim, but no original jurisdiction over the state law interference with contract claim. Hearing both claims together would promote efficiency and consistency of outcomes, but cannot be done if the court lacks a basis for subject matter jurisdiction over the related state law claim.

2. Rewriting constitutional history. Let's suppose for a minute that the Supreme Court had written a very different opinion in *United Mine Workers v.*

Gibbs, one that refused to read the grant of jurisdiction in Article III, Section 2 expansively. A strict constructionist court might have written the *Gibbs* opinion like this:

> The federal district judge properly exercised jurisdiction over the LMRA claim in this case, because it arises under federal law. 28 U.S.C. § 1331. However, the plaintiff's second claim, for interference with contract, arises under state tort law. Nothing in Article III, Section 2 of the Constitution authorizes federal courts to hear state law claims in the absence of diversity between the parties.
>
> We recognize that hearing these related claims together would promote judicial efficiency and avoid inconsistent decisions by separate juries. However, whatever the practical benefits of approving jurisdiction in such circumstances, we resist the temptation to expand federal jurisdiction beyond the boundaries the Founding Fathers established in Article III, Section 2. Nothing in their grant of federal court jurisdiction includes the state law claim in this case.

Such a narrow reading of the scope of federal jurisdiction would seem logically defensible, but it certainly would have undermined the ability of federal courts, in cases like *Gibbs* or the Caprera hypothetical, to resolve all claims in a dispute together in a single forum.

Q **3. Tactical choices.** Suppose that you represented the plaintiff in a case like *Gibbs* and wanted to assert a claim under federal law and another under state law. Suppose further that the Supreme Court in *Gibbs* had written the narrow opinion quoted in note 2, rejecting the concept of pendent jurisdiction over such related claims. If you wanted to assert both claims, what would your options be for obtaining complete relief?

A If pendent jurisdiction did not exist, you could file in federal court on the federal claim and in state court on the state claim. This would require litigation in two courts to resolve a single dispute. This might lead to battles over which case would proceed first and to potential preclusion problems once one of the cases went to judgment.

Alternatively, you could file in federal court and give up the state claim. This is not a satisfactory choice, since you would waive any additional relief you could get under state law—and you might lose on the federal claim.

Very likely, your best strategy would be to file suit in state court on both the state and federal claims. Because state courts usually have concurrent jurisdiction over claims arising under federal law, you would be able to litigate the claims together in state court. Thus, if *Gibbs* had not recognized the doctrine of pendent jurisdiction, plaintiffs would frequently have chosen to file cases like this in state court, depriving federal courts of the opportunity to adjudicate federal claims for which they have particular experience and expertise.

Q **4. *UMW v. Gibbs* (part I):** Justice Brennan's central problem in *Gibbs* is to overcome the seemingly ineluctable logic of the imaginary opinion in note 2. There is no explicit authority in Article III, Section 2 for federal courts to hear related state law claims like those asserted in *Gibbs*. So how can the court do so?

A

Gibbs holds that when a federal court has jurisdiction over a case, because the plaintiff asserts a claim arising under federal law, it obtains jurisdiction not just over the *federal claim*, but over the entire *case*, that is, over the dispute that includes that federal claim. If the plaintiff asserts one substantial claim under federal law, the court acquires *power* to hear that claim and all other claims that arise from the same factual dispute—the same "nucleus of operative fact." The state law claims, jurisdictionally insufficient in themselves, may hang from the federal law hook.

Justice Brennan's opinion does not explain in detail where he finds this power in Article III, Section 2. He does note, however, that it refers to "cases," not to "claims." The Framers, many of them lawyers, understood that cases seldom come tidily confined to a single legal theory. A dispute will usually involve multiple claims based on different legal theories. Though Article III does not expressly authorize federal courts to hear all of the claims in such a case, it is a fair inference that the Framers (who after all wrote a constitution, not a legal treatise on the details) would have expected the federal court to hear the entire dispute, not just a single strand in a tangled skein of legal theories. Any other reading of Article III would severely hamstring federal courts in hearing complex cases.

Appalachia Mining Wars and Civil Procedure

AP Photo

The 1960s witnessed bitter and sometimes violent labor struggles at the coal mines of Appalachia. (The photo is evocative of that era—it was taken in Tennessee in 1963, though it does not depict the dispute involved in *United Mine Workers v. Gibbs*.) In *Gibbs*, the plaintiff, a mining superintendent, sued the United Mine Workers union under the federal labor laws. He also sought to assert state law claims against the union in the same federal action. The *Gibbs* Court's sensible approach to such combined actions provides the foundation for the modern doctrine of supplemental jurisdiction in federal courts.

5. A single "constitutional case." If the plaintiff asserts one proper federal claim, *Gibbs* holds that the court may hear related state law claims if they arise out of the same "common nucleus of operative fact." This standard focuses on the facts involved in the dispute, not on legal theories. In *Gibbs*, the federal and state claims both were based on the same underlying event, the union's reaction to the opening of the new mine.

The Court suggests that pendent jurisdiction will apply to the state law claims if "considered without regard to their federal or state character, a plaintiff's claims are such that he would ordinarily be expected to try them all in one judicial proceeding. . . ." One gauge of what would "ordinarily" be tried together is federal claim preclusion doctrine, which bars a party from suing on a claim if she has already litigated the underlying "transaction" before.

> What factual groupings constitutes a "transaction" . . . are to be determined pragmatically, giving weight to such considerations as whether the facts are related in time, space, origin, or motivation, whether they form a convenient trial unit, and whether their treatment as a unit conforms to the parties' expectations or business understanding or usage.

Restatement (Second) of Judgments § 24(2). If a party sues a defendant for one claim and has other claims against that defendant that arise from the same events, she would "ordinarily be expected to try them all" together and be barred by claim preclusion if she does not. *Gibbs* suggests that if a state law claim fits this (admittedly ambiguous) single-transaction test, it may be litigated with the federal claim under pendent jurisdiction.

6. *UMV v. Gibbs* (part II): Discretion to decline pendent jurisdiction. *Gibbs* holds that the federal court should decide whether it has the *power* to exercise pendent jurisdiction over the state law claims at the outset of the case (court's power should "be resolved on the pleadings"), as with other jurisdictional questions. However, *Gibbs* concludes that federal courts need not always exercise pendent jurisdiction even if they have the power to do so. The trial court may, in its discretion, decline jurisdiction over pendent claims based on "considerations of judicial economy, convenience and fairness to litigants."

Justice Brennan suggests several reasons why a court might decline jurisdiction over related state law claims, even though it has the power (under the first part of the *Gibbs* test) to hear them.

- **Federal claim drops out early.** The court might choose not to hear the related state claims if the federal claim in the case is dismissed relatively early in the litigation. Suppose that the federal claim in *Gibbs* had been dismissed three months after filing, leaving the state law interference with contract claim only. At that point, a Tennessee plaintiff would be left suing a non-diverse defendant on a state law claim in federal court. There would no longer be efficiency gained from litigating the related claims together, since the parties are no longer litigating the federal law claim. If they are just going to litigate a state claim, they might as well do so in state court.

  Although *Gibbs* suggests that the state law claims should "certainly" be dismissed in this situation, the Court later held that the federal court may retain jurisdiction of pendent claims after the federal claim drops out if the case has been through substantial pretrial litigation. *Rosado v. Wyman*, 397 U.S. 397, 403–05 (1970). In those circumstances, the judge is thoroughly familiar with the case and much of the preparation for trial has been done. It will be more efficient for the federal court to see the case through—even though no federal claim remains—than to dismiss the state law claim, which would force the plaintiff to commence a new action in state court on that claim.

- **State issues predominate.** If the federal judge can see that the plaintiff's case is fundamentally a state law case, to which a minor or dubious federal claim has been appended, she might decline jurisdiction over the predominant state law claims. "[R]ecognition of a federal court's wide latitude to decide ancillary questions of state law does not imply that it must tolerate a litigant's effort to impose upon it what is in effect only a state law case." 383 U.S. at 77.* In *Bostic v. AT&T of the Virgin Islands*, 166 F. Supp. 2d 350 (D.V.I. 2001), for example, the "vast majority" of the evidence was relevant to the state law claims only. Much of the evidence on the state claims would be inadmissible on the federal claim, complicating the presentation of evidence. In addition, the damages evidence would also differ, because recovery was sought for different harms on the state and federal claims, and the state claims presented several unsettled issues of state law. "The [state law] claims seek a remedy that is both distinct from the federal claims and in all likelihood, considerably more substantial." *Id.* at 365. The court dismissed the state law claims.

- **Surer footed readings of state law.** Under *Gibbs*, the federal court may also decline to exercise jurisdiction if the state law claims present novel or complex issues of state law. Justice Brennan noted that the parties could obtain a "surer footed reading" of state law from a state court. Why is this true?

  > Under the *Erie* doctrine, discussed in Chapters 24 and 25, the federal court cannot make state law; it must apply state law as it believes the state court would. This applies to a federal court hearing pendent state law claims in a federal question case just as it applies in diversity cases. If the parties litigate a complex, unsettled issue of state law in federal court, the federal judge's ruling will not establish state law, since she can only predict how the issue would be resolved by the state's highest court.

- **Likelihood of jury confusion.** If it would be confusing to try the state and federal claims together, it may make sense to dismiss the state law claims. As the Court notes, in *Gibbs* the elements of liability for the LMRA claim and the interference with contract claim were subtly different, different enough that a judge might decide to try them separately to avoid jury confusion in evaluating the claims. If the judge anticipates that the two claims would have to be tried separately, she might decline pendent jurisdiction over the state claim. If the state claim is going to be tried separately, it might as well be litigated in state court.

Justice Brennan did not say that these were the only reasons a court might decline jurisdiction over the related claims. Rather, he offered them as illustrations of the reasons why a court might choose to decline pendent jurisdiction, even though it had the power to hear the pendent claim.

---

* If the federal law claim really is peripheral, and the state claims are dismissed, the plaintiff will likely dismiss the federal suit entirely and litigate all her claims in state court.

William J. Brennan

Collection of the Supreme Court of the United States

President Dwight D. Eisenhower once said, "I made two mistakes [during my presidency], and both of them are sitting on the Supreme Court." One justice he referred to was Justice William Brennan (1906–1997). (The other was Chief Justice Earl Warren.) Eisenhower anticipated that Brennan, the son of Irish Catholic immigrants, would lean to the conservative side on the Court, but he became one of the most liberal justices of the twentieth century, and (according to Justice Scalia) that century's most influential. Professor Larry Tribe wrote: "If Chief Justice John Marshall was the chief architect of a powerful national government, then Justice William Brennan was the principal architect of the nation's system for protecting individual rights."

In *United Mine Workers v. Gibbs*, Brennan addresses an arcane issue of federal procedure. The sensible framework he crafted in *Gibbs* for jurisdiction over state law claims in federal cases has had a profound impact on the role of federal courts—and remains essentially intact today.

7. Exercises of discretion. The question below considers the federal district judge's options in addressing a case with state law claims.

Arch Technologies, Inc. is incorporated in Oregon, with its principal place of business in California. It sues Sullivan Castings Corporation (incorporated in Delaware with its principal place of business in Oregon) in federal court under a federal statute barring deceptive commercial practices in interstate commerce. It claims losses of $500,000. It also claims that Sullivan's conduct constitutes an unfair business practice under an Oregon statute and seeks punitive damages on the state law claim. Oregon courts have never decided whether punitive damages may be awarded under its business practices statute.

The federal judge wants to decline jurisdiction over the unfair business practices claim, since the governing law is unclear and the Oregon courts can provide a "surer footed" reading of the statute. The judge should

A. dismiss the state law claim.
B. remand the state law claim to the Oregon state courts.
C. dismiss the entire case.
D. remand the entire case to the Oregon state courts.

The issue posed here is what the federal court should do about the *federal claim* if it decides, in its discretion, not to hear the related state law claim. **B** fails; the court cannot remand the state claim to state court, because it did not come from the state court. That would, in essence, be imposing a case on the state court that the parties had not brought there. (A removed case is different, because in those cases, the plaintiff had filed in state court. If the federal court declines jurisdiction over a supplemental claim in a removed case, it can remand it to the state court.)

D fails for the same reason. Remand to a state court is not an option in a case filed originally in federal court. Nor can the judge dismiss the entire case, as **C** suggests. Even if it would be more efficient to dismiss the entire case, forcing the plaintiff to litigate all of her claims in state court, the federal court has jurisdiction over the federal claim and generally must hear it. So **A** is right: The judge should dismiss the state law claim, retaining jurisdiction over the federal claim.

If the judge does dismiss the state law claim, the plaintiff may decide to voluntarily dismiss the federal suit and bring the federal statutory claim and the state law claim together in state court. (Remember, state courts can hear most claims arising under federal law.) Presumably, it will be more efficient for her to litigate once rather than twice. But if she wants a federal forum on her federal claim, she is entitled to it, even if that court refuses to hear the related state law claim.

III. A Further Problem: The Need for Statutory Authority

The same problem that arose in *Gibbs* frequently arises when *defending parties* add claims in a case as well. Suppose that Epstein, one of the police officer defendants in our example case, asserts a state law counterclaim for battery in Caprera's lawsuit against him.

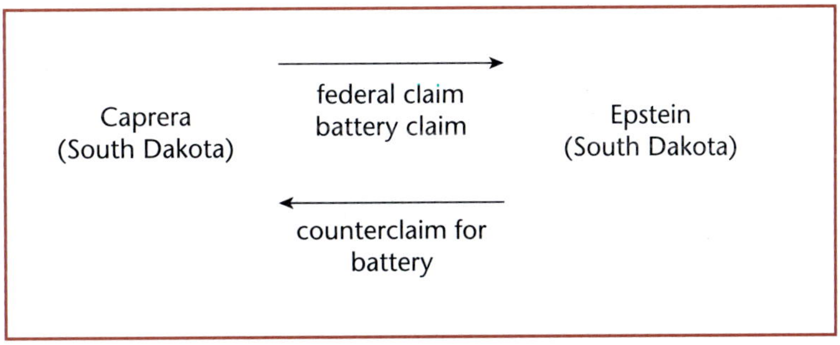

Figure 20–2: STATE LAW COUNTERCLAIM

The counterclaim here is a state law claim between non-diverse parties. There is no independent basis for subject matter jurisdiction over it, yet Rule 13(a)(1) *requires* Epstein to assert it if it arises from the same arrest as Caprera's federal claim.

Or, suppose that Ruiz asserts a crossclaim against Epstein for contribution on Caprera's battery claim (i.e., for Epstein to reimburse him for part of the judgment if Caprera recovers and Ruiz pays the judgment).

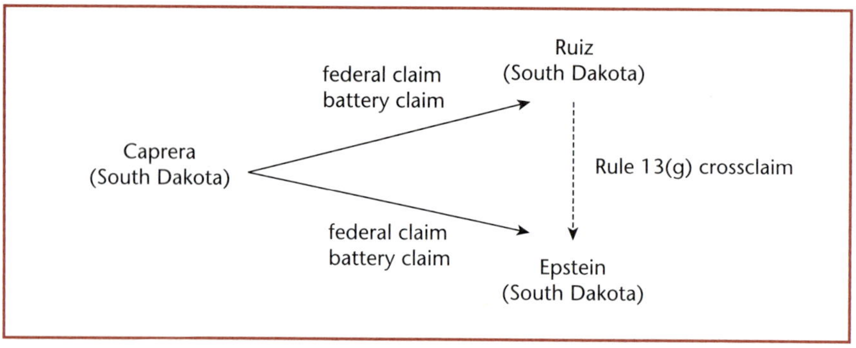

Figure 20-3: STATE LAW CROSSCLAIM

Here too, the Rules allow this, but there is no independent basis for federal subject matter jurisdiction over the added claim.

And one more: Suppose that Epstein impleads the City of Rapid City, his employer, in Caprera's suit, seeking indemnification under his contract of employment for any liability he incurs to Caprera. Here again, Rule 14(a) allows the claim, but the court has no independent basis for jurisdiction over it.

As noted at the begining of the chapter, cases in which an original plaintiff asserted a federal claim and added a related state law claim were analyzed as *pendent jurisdiction* cases. The same concept—that a federal court that had subject matter jurisdiction based on one claim could hear other claims that arise from the same set of facts—was extended to claims by defending parties (such as counterclaims, crossclaims, and third-party claims) under the rubric of *ancillary jurisdiction*. Ancillary jurisdiction over claims "logically related" to the main case was recognized in diversity cases as well as in federal question cases.

So things stood when *Owen Equipment & Erection Co. v. Kroger*, the case below, was decided. Federal courts routinely heard related state law claims in both federal question and diversity cases, either as pendent claims (if asserted by the original plaintiff) or as ancillary claims if added by defending parties.

In *Kroger*, however, the Supreme Court focused on a basic principle emphasized in the chapters on federal subject matter jurisdiction: Whenever a federal court exercises jurisdiction over a claim, the case must not only be within the Article III, Section 2 grant. The court must *also* have authority under a federal statute to hear the claim. In the peculiar posture of the claim in *Kroger*, that posed a significant problem.

READING *OWEN EQUIPMENT & ERECTION CO. v. KROGER*. As you read *Kroger*, diagram the case to make sure you understand the procedural posture of the disputed claim. Note that the court uses the term "ancillary jurisdiction" to refer to the disputed claim, even though it is asserted by Mrs. Kroger, the original plaintiff in the case. Consider the following questions in reading the case:

- Did the Court determine whether there was a *constitutional basis* for the federal court to hear the disputed claim? (Footnote 10 addresses this!)
- Why did the Court conclude that the lower court did not have jurisdiction to hear Mrs. Kroger's claim against Owen?

■ Does the Court approve or disapprove jurisdiction over claims added by defending parties, such as the Power District's third-party claim against Owen?

OWEN EQUIPMENT & ERECTION CO. v. KROGER

437 U.S. 365 (1978)

Mr. Justice STEWART delivered the opinion of the Court.

In an action in which federal jurisdiction is based on diversity of citizenship, may the plaintiff assert a claim against a third-party defendant when there is no independent basis for federal jurisdiction over that claim? The Court of Appeals for the Eighth Circuit held in this case that such a claim is within the ancillary jurisdiction of the federal courts. We granted certiorari because this decision conflicts with several recent decisions of other Courts of Appeals.

I

On January 18, 1972, James Kroger was electrocuted when the boom of a steel crane next to which he was walking came too close to a high-tension electric power line. The respondent (his widow, who is the administratrix of his estate) filed a wrongful-death action in the United States District Court for the District of Nebraska against the Omaha Public Power District (OPPD). Her complaint alleged that OPPD's negligent construction, maintenance, and operation of the power line had caused Kroger's death. Federal jurisdiction was based on diversity of citizenship, since the respondent was a citizen of Iowa and OPPD was a Nebraska corporation.

OPPD then filed a third-party complaint pursuant to Fed. Rule Civ. Proc. 14(a) against the petitioner, Owen Equipment and Erection Co. (Owen), alleging that the crane was owned and operated by Owen, and that Owen's negligence had been the proximate cause of Kroger's death.[3] OPPD later moved for summary judgment on the respondent's complaint against it. While this motion was pending, the respondent was granted leave to file an amended complaint naming Owen as an additional defendant. Thereafter, the District Court granted OPPD's motion for summary judgment in an unreported opinion. The case thus went to trial between the respondent and the petitioner alone.

The respondent's amended complaint alleged that Owen was "a Nebraska corporation with its principal place of business in Nebraska." Owen's answer admitted

3. Under Rule 14(a), a third-party defendant may not be impleaded merely because he may be liable to the *plaintiff.* While the third-party complaint in this case alleged merely that Owen's negligence caused Kroger's death, and the basis of Owen's alleged liability *to OPPD* is nowhere spelled out, OPPD evidently relied upon the state common-law right of contribution among joint tortfeasors....

that it was "a corporation organized and existing under the laws of the State of Nebraska," and denied every other allegation of the complaint. On the third day of trial, however, it was disclosed that the petitioner's principal place of business was in Iowa, not Nebraska,[5] and that the petitioner and the respondent were thus both citizens of Iowa. The petitioner then moved to dismiss the complaint for lack of jurisdiction. The District Court reserved decision on the motion, and the jury thereafter returned a verdict in favor of the respondent. In an unreported opinion issued after the trial, the District Court denied the petitioner's motion to dismiss the complaint.

The judgment was affirmed on appeal. The Court of Appeals held that under this Court's decision in *Mine Workers v. Gibbs*, the District Court had jurisdictional power, in its discretion, to adjudicate the respondent's claim against the petitioner because that claim arose from the "core of 'operative facts' giving rise to both [respondent's] claim against OPPD and OPPD's claim against Owen." It further held that the District Court had properly exercised its discretion in proceeding to decide the case even after summary judgment had been granted to OPPD, because the petitioner had concealed its Iowa citizenship from the respondent. . . .

II

It is undisputed that there was no independent basis of federal jurisdiction over the respondent's state-law tort action against the petitioner, since both are citizens of Iowa. And although Fed. Rule Civ. Proc. 14(a) permits a plaintiff to assert a claim against a third-party defendant, it does not purport to say whether or not such a claim requires an independent basis of federal jurisdiction. Indeed, it could not determine that question, since it is axiomatic that the Federal Rules of Civil Procedure do not create or withdraw federal jurisdiction.

In affirming the District Court's judgment, the Court of Appeals relied upon the doctrine of ancillary jurisdiction, whose contours it believed were defined by this Court's holding in *Mine Workers v. Gibbs.* The *Gibbs* case differed from this one in that it involved pendent jurisdiction, which concerns the resolution of a plaintiff's federal- and state-law claims against a single defendant in one action. By contrast, in this case there was no claim based upon substantive federal law, but rather state-law tort claims against two different defendants. Nonetheless, the Court of Appeals was correct in perceiving that *Gibbs* and this case are two species of the same generic problem: Under what circumstances may a federal court hear and decide a state-law claim arising between citizens of the same State?[8] But we believe that the Court of Appeals failed to understand the scope of the doctrine of the *Gibbs* case.

---

5. The problem apparently was one of geography. Although the Missouri River generally marks the boundary between Iowa and Nebraska, Carter Lake, Iowa, where the accident occurred and where Owen had its main office, lies west of the river, adjacent to Omaha, Neb. Apparently the river once avulsed at one of its bends, cutting Carter Lake off from the rest of Iowa.

8. No more than in *Aldinger v. Howard*, 427 U.S. 1, is it necessary to determine here "whether there are any 'principled' differences between pendent and ancillary jurisdiction; or, if there are, what effect *Gibbs* had on such differences." *Id.*, at 13.

The plaintiff in *Gibbs* alleged that the defendant union had violated the common law of Tennessee as well as the federal prohibition of secondary boycotts. This Court held that, although the parties were not of diverse citizenship, the District Court properly entertained the state-law claim as pendent to the federal claim. The crucial holding was stated as follows:

> "Pendent jurisdiction, in the sense of judicial *power*, exists whenever there is a claim 'arising under [the] Constitution, the Laws of the United States, and Treaties made, or which shall be made, under their Authority . . . ,' U.S. Const., Art. III, § 2, and the relationship between that claim and the state claim permits the conclusion that the entire action before the court comprises but one constitutional 'case.' . . . The state and federal claims must derive from a common nucleus of operative fact. But if, considered without regard to their federal or state character, a plaintiff's claims are such that he would ordinarily be expected to try them all in one judicial proceeding, then, assuming substantiality of the federal issues, there is *power* in federal courts to hear the whole." (emphasis in original).[9]

It is apparent that *Gibbs* delineated the constitutional limits of federal judicial power. But even if it be assumed that the District Court in the present case had constitutional power to decide the respondent's lawsuit against the petitioner,[10] it does not follow that the decision of the Court of Appeals was correct. Constitutional power is merely the first hurdle that must be overcome in determining that a federal court has jurisdiction over a particular controversy. For the jurisdiction of the federal courts is limited not only by the provisions of Art. III of the Constitution, but also by Acts of Congress.

That statutory law as well as the Constitution may limit a federal court's jurisdiction over nonfederal claims is well illustrated by two recent decisions of this Court, *Aldinger v. Howard*, and *Zahn v. International Paper Co.* In *Aldinger* the Court held that a Federal District Court lacked jurisdiction over a state-law claim against a county, even if that claim was alleged to be pendent to one against county officials under 42 U.S.C. § 1983. In *Zahn* the Court held that in a diversity class action under Fed. Rule Civ. Proc. 23(b)(3), the claim of each member of the plaintiff class must independently satisfy the minimum jurisdictional amount set by 28 U.S.C. § 1332(a), and rejected the argument that jurisdiction existed over those claims that involved $10,000 or less as ancillary to those that involved more. In each case, despite the fact that federal and nonfederal claims arose from a "common nucleus of operative fact," the Court held that the statute conferring jurisdiction over the federal claim did not allow the exercise of jurisdiction over the nonfederal claim.

9. The Court further noted that even when such power exists, its exercise remains a matter of discretion based upon "considerations of judicial economy, convenience and fairness to litigants," and held that the District Court had not abused its discretion in retaining jurisdiction of the state-law claim.

10. Federal jurisdiction in *Gibbs* was based upon the existence of a question of federal law. The Court of Appeals in the present case believed that the "common nucleus of operative fact" test also determines the outer boundaries of constitutionally permissible federal jurisdiction when that jurisdiction is based upon diversity of citizenship. We may assume without deciding that the Court of Appeals was correct in this regard. . . .

The *Aldinger* and *Zahn* cases thus make clear that a finding that federal and nonfederal claims arise from a "common nucleus of operative fact," the test of *Gibbs*, does not end the inquiry into whether a federal court has power to hear the nonfederal claims along with the federal ones. Beyond this constitutional minimum, there must be an examination of the posture in which the nonfederal claim is asserted and of the specific statute that confers jurisdiction over the federal claim, in order to determine whether "Congress in [that statute] has . . . expressly or by implication negated" the exercise of jurisdiction over the particular nonfederal claim.

III

The relevant statute in this case, 28 U.S.C. § 1332(a)(1), confers upon federal courts jurisdiction over "civil actions where the matter in controversy exceeds the sum or value of $10,000 . . . and is between . . . citizens of different States." This statute and its predecessors have consistently been held to require complete diversity of citizenship.[13] That is, diversity jurisdiction does not exist unless *each* defendant is a citizen of a different State from *each* plaintiff. Over the years Congress has repeatedly re-enacted or amended the statute conferring diversity jurisdiction, leaving intact this rule of complete diversity. . . . Whatever may have been the original purposes of diversity-of-citizenship jurisdiction, . . . this subsequent history clearly demonstrates a congressional mandate that diversity jurisdiction is not to be available when any plaintiff is a citizen of the same State as any defendant. . . .[16]

Thus it is clear that the respondent could not originally have brought suit in federal court naming Owen and OPPD as codefendants, since citizens of Iowa would have been on both sides of the litigation. Yet the identical lawsuit resulted when she amended her complaint. Complete diversity was destroyed just as surely as if she had sued Owen initially. In either situation, in the plain language of the statute, the "matter in controversy" could not be "between . . . citizens of different States."

It is a fundamental precept that federal courts are courts of limited jurisdiction. The limits upon federal jurisdiction, whether imposed by the Constitution or by Congress, must be neither disregarded nor evaded. Yet under the reasoning of the Court of Appeals in this case, a plaintiff could defeat the statutory requirement of complete diversity by the simple expedient of suing only those defendants who were of diverse citizenship and waiting for them to implead nondiverse

13. *E.g., Strawbridge v. Curtiss.* It is settled that complete diversity is not a constitutional requirement. *State Farm Fire & Cas. Co. v. Tashire.*

16. Notably, Congress enacted § 1332 as part of the Judicial Code of 1948, 62 Stat. 930, shortly after Rule 14 was amended in 1946. When the Rule was amended, the Advisory Committee noted that "in any case where the plaintiff could not have joined the third party originally because of jurisdictional limitations such as lack of diversity of citizenship, the majority view is that any attempt by the plaintiff to amend his complaint and assert a claim against the impleaded third party would be unavailing." 28 U.S.C. App., p. 7752. The subsequent re-enactment without relevant change of the diversity statute may thus be seen as evidence of congressional approval of that "majority view."

defendants.[17] If, as the Court of Appeals thought, a "common nucleus of operative fact" were the only requirement for ancillary jurisdiction in a diversity case, there would be no principled reason why the respondent in this case could not have joined her cause of action against Owen in her original complaint as ancillary to her claim against OPPD. Congress' requirement of complete diversity would thus have been evaded completely.

It is true, as the Court of Appeals noted, that the exercise of ancillary jurisdiction over nonfederal claims has often been upheld in situations involving impleader, cross-claims or counterclaims. But in determining whether jurisdiction over a nonfederal claim exists, the context in which the nonfederal claim is asserted is crucial. And the claim here arises in a setting quite different from the kinds of nonfederal claims that have been viewed in other cases as falling within the ancillary jurisdiction of the federal courts.

First, the nonfederal claim in this case was simply not ancillary to the federal one in the same sense that, for example, the impleader by a defendant of a third-party defendant always is. A third-party complaint depends at least in part upon the resolution of the primary lawsuit. See n.3, *supra*. Its relation to the original complaint is thus not mere factual similarity but logical dependence. The respondent's claim against the petitioner, however, was entirely separate from her original claim against OPPD, since the petitioner's liability to her depended not at all upon whether or not OPPD was also liable. Far from being an ancillary and dependent claim, it was a new and independent one.

Second, the nonfederal claim here was asserted by the plaintiff, who voluntarily chose to bring suit upon a state-law claim in a federal court. By contrast, ancillary jurisdiction typically involves claims by a defending party haled into court against his will, or by another person whose rights might be irretrievably lost unless he could assert them in an ongoing action in a federal court. A plaintiff cannot complain if ancillary jurisdiction does not encompass all of his possible claims in a case such as this one, since it is he who has chosen the federal rather than the state forum and must thus accept its limitations. "[T]he efficiency plaintiff seeks so avidly is available without question in the state courts." *Kenrose Mfg. Co. v. Fred Whitaker Co.*, 512 F.2d 890, 894 (CA4).

It is not unreasonable to assume that, in generally requiring complete diversity, Congress did not intend to confine the jurisdiction of federal courts so inflexibly that they are unable to protect legal rights or effectively to resolve an entire, logically entwined lawsuit. Those practical needs are the basis of the doctrine of ancillary jurisdiction. But neither the convenience of litigants nor considerations of judicial economy can suffice to justify extension of the doctrine of ancillary jurisdiction to a plaintiff's cause of action against a citizen of the same State in a diversity case. Congress has established the basic rule that diversity jurisdiction exists under 28 U.S.C. § 1332 only when there is complete diversity of citizenship. "The

17. This is not an unlikely hypothesis, since a defendant in a tort suit such as this one would surely try to limit his liability by impleading any joint tortfeasors for indemnity or contribution. . . . Nonetheless, the requirement of complete diversity would be eviscerated by such a course of events.

limit

policy of the statute calls for its strict construction." *Healy v. Ratta*, 292 U.S. 263, 270 (1934). To allow the requirement of complete diversity to be circumvented as it was in this case would simply flout the congressional command.

Accordingly, the judgment of the Court of Appeals is reversed.

[Dissenting opinion of Justice White omitted.]

Notes and Questions: *Owen Equipment & Erection Co. v. Kroger*

1. Sorting out the procedural complexities of *Kroger*. After Mrs. Kroger sued the Power District (OPPD), it impleaded Owen Erection Company as a third-party defendant under Rule 14(a). Mrs. Kroger then amended her complaint to assert a claim directly against Owen. The case looked like this:

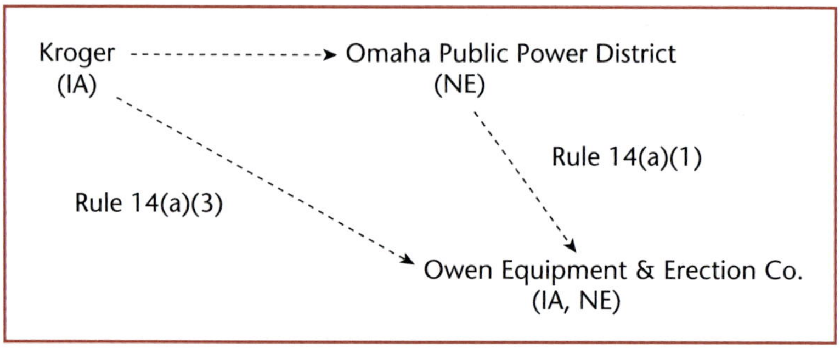

Figure 20–4: **MRS. KROGER'S ADDED CLAIM**

Later, the court concluded as a matter of law that OPPD was not liable to Mrs. Kroger and granted summary judgment in favor of OPPD. Once that happened, the only claim left was a state law claim between two Iowans.

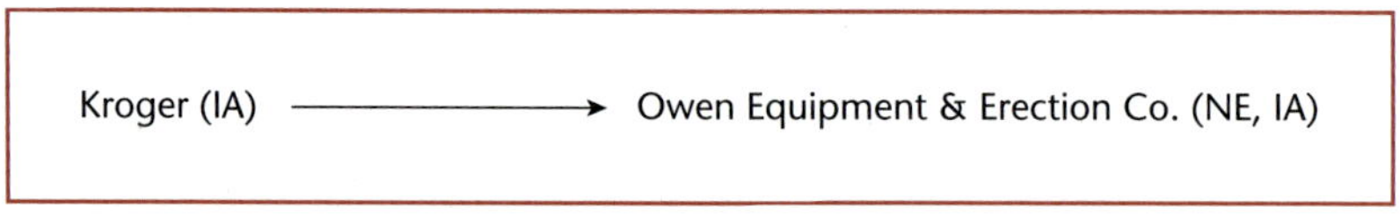

Figure 20–5: **THE REMAINING CLAIM IN *KROGER***

The court of appeals held that there was ancillary jurisdiction over this claim, relying partly on the "common nucleus of operative fact" analysis of *Gibbs*.

2. The source of the confusion about Owen's state citizenship. It appears unlikely that Owen's lawyers intended to deceive the plaintiffs when they answered Mrs. Kroger's complaint. Surely, they knew that Owen's principal place of business was in Iowa; it only had one place of business, in Carter Lake, Iowa. *See* Kevin Clermont,

Civil Procedure Stories 117 (2d ed. 2008). Very likely, the lawyers did not focus on the diversity allegations because they assumed that there was jurisdiction over the added claim against Owen. After all, the case was already in federal court, and Mrs. Kroger was just adding a claim against someone who was already a party.

Where Is Carter Lake?

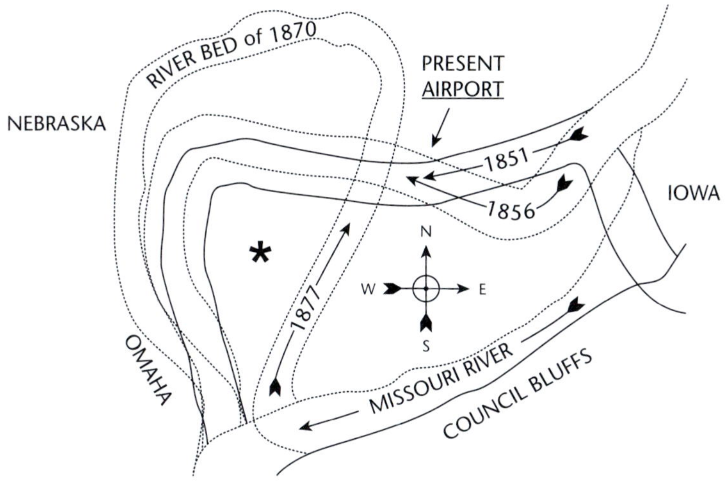

Provided by Mayor Russ Kramer

The illustration explains how Carter Lake (see the asterisk) got misplaced as the Missouri River changed its course. When a river changes course gradually, by erosion, the state border moves with it. When a sudden surge cuts off a bend (the river "avulses"), the boundary remains where it was. Because the Missouri avulsed at the bottom left point in the diagram, Carter Lake remains in Iowa although it is now on the west (Nebraska) side of the river. See footnote 5 in the *Kroger* opinion.

3. Pendent or ancillary? It is hard to characterize Mrs. Kroger's claim as either pendent or ancillary. It was a bit of a hybrid, since it was asserted by a plaintiff but arose after Owen was added as a third-party defendant. The court notes that, regardless of the label, these two concepts represent "two species of the same generic problem: Under what circumstances may a federal court hear and decide a state-law claim arising between citizens of the same State?" 437 U.S. at 370.

Since the adoption of 28 U.S.C. § 1367, the terms "pendent" and "ancillary" are no longer used. Jurisdiction over all related state-law claims is now governed by the supplemental jurisdiction statute, analyzed in the next section of this chapter.

Q **4. Constitutional authority to hear Mrs. Kroger's claim against Owen.** The *Kroger* Court concluded that exercising jurisdiction over Mrs. Kroger's claim against Owen, whether dubbed "ancillary" or "pendent," was inconsistent with the diversity statute. But would it be *constitutionally permissible* for the court to hear the claim?

A

This is an important question. If the federal courts have constitutional authority to hear claims like Mrs. Kroger's, Congress can amend the diversity statute to allow jurisdiction over them. If hearing the claim would be unconstitutional, however, the federal courts could never entertain such claims absent a constitutional amendment.

Kroger notes that "[i]t is apparent that *Gibbs* delineated the constitutional limits of federal judicial power." 437 U.S. at 371. Since *Gibbs* held that a federal court with original jurisdiction may hear all other claims in the case that arise from the same nucleus of operative facts, it seems clear that the federal court would have the *constitutional* power to hear Mrs. Kroger's claim against Owen. *See also* 437 U.S. at 371 n.10.

5. The Court rediscovers the need for a statutory grant of jurisdiction. In *UMW v. Gibbs*, the Supreme Court held that it was constitutionally permissible for a federal court to hear the related state law claim and provided federal trial judges guidance in deciding whether to do so. It did not discuss whether the district court had *statutory* authority to exercise jurisdiction over the pendent state law claim. In *Kroger*, however, the Court confronted the obvious contradiction between Mrs. Kroger's claim against Owen and the complete diversity rule. *Kroger* reemphasized that federal courts derive their jurisdictional authority not only from the Constitution but also from Congress.

> Beyond this constitutional minimum, there must be an examination of the posture in which the nonfederal claim is asserted and of the specific statute that confers jurisdiction over the federal claim, in order to determine whether "Congress in [that statute] has ... expressly or by implication negated" the exercise of jurisdiction over the particular nonfederal claim.

437 U.S. at 373. Even if it would be constitutional for the court to exercise jurisdiction over related state law claims, Congress must authorize the federal district courts to do so.

Consequently, the Court turned to 28 U.S.C. § 1332, the statute that authorizes jurisdiction over diversity cases. Section 1332 has long been interpreted to require complete diversity between the plaintiff and all defendants. Mrs. Kroger could not have sued OPPD and Owen Equipment & Erection Co. together as original defendants, since (it turned out) Owen was also a citizen of Iowa. Since she could not have sued them together as original defendants, the Court concluded that it would be inconsistent with the diversity statute to allow her to assert the claim against Owen after it was brought in as a third-party defendant.

Q

6. How about OPPD's claim against Owen? The Supreme Court rejects jurisdiction over Mrs. Kroger's claim against Owen for lack of diversity. Yet, OPPD's claim against Owen is *also* a state law claim between two citizens of the same state. Did the court have ancillary jurisdiction over that claim?

A

The analysis in *Kroger* clearly implies that it did. Justice Stewart distinguished OPPD's claim on two grounds, each somewhat dubious.

First, Justice Stewart argued that an impleader claim is dependent on the main claim in a way that Mrs. Kroger's was not. Rule 14(a)(1) only allows a defendant to implead a third-party defendant if she is trying to pass on liability that she may incur to the plaintiff. Thus, the main claim triggers the impleader claim, and the outcome on the impleader claim depends on the outcome of the main claim.

However, this is not true of crossclaims and counterclaims. A crossclaim, for example, need only meet the "same transaction or occurrence" test and might be for the crossclaimant's own damages, not to pass on liability on the main claim. Yet, Justice Stewart appears to approve ancillary jurisdiction over crossclaims as well.

Second, Justice Stewart argues that crossclaims, counterclaims, and third-party claims are asserted by a defending party, "haled into court against his will. . . ." 437 U.S. at 376. It seems fair to allow such parties, who did not choose the forum or their opponents in the action, to resolve related claims in the same suit, but it doesn't change the fact that such claims may still be inconsistent with the diversity statute. For example, if OPPD counterclaims against Mrs. Kroger for $20,000 based on the same accident, the claim would be inconsistent with the diversity statute, since it does not satisfy the amount-in-controversy requirement. Justice Stewart's analysis suggests that the claim would be within the court's ancillary jurisdiction. Similarly, if Mrs. Kroger had sued two Nebraska defendants for her husband's death, and one asserted a crossclaim against the other, that claim would be inconsistent with the complete diversity requirement, yet Justice Stewart would approve that one too.

While it may be appropriate to allow defending parties to add additional claims, the Court parses the diversity statute rather closely when it makes such fine distinctions between different types of claims based on the "posture" of the claims. As a practical matter, however, the line the *Kroger* Court drew, while not intellectually tidy, preserves the effectiveness of the broad federal joinder rules in most cases, while rejecting claims like Mrs. Kroger's that clearly contradict the complete diversity rule.

Q **7. What next?** The Court concludes that the trial court lacked supplemental jurisdiction over Mrs. Kroger's claim against Owen. How can she recover on this claim? Or does she lose it?

A Mrs. Kroger will have to refile it in state court. Claim preclusion would not bar her from doing so: Courts generally hold that a party will not be barred from asserting a claim in a second action if it could not have been joined in the prior action, and the Supreme Court had held that this one could not.

Mrs. Kroger's lawyers did refile in the Iowa courts, which held the claim timely under an Iowa statute that extends the statute of limitations in certain circumstances. The case settled for $234,756, the exact amount of the federal court judgment. See the excellent analysis of the case by John Oakley, in Kevin Clermont, Civil Procedure Stories 117 (2d ed. 2008).

IV. Congress Steps In: Supplemental Jurisdiction Under 28 U.S.C. § 1367

The *Kroger* decision raised serious doubts about when federal courts had statutory authority to hear related state law claims. Those doubts were multiplied by *Finley v. United States*, 490 U.S. 545 (1989), which held that the federal district court could not exercise pendent jurisdiction over a related state law claim against a private party in a case against the United States under the Federal Tort Claims Act (FTCA). The Court found no evidence in the FTCA that Congress intended to authorize jurisdiction over such additional claims. The analysis suggested that the Court would take a restrictive approach to pendent and ancillary jurisdiction, requiring evidence that the relevant statute granted jurisdiction over such related claims—evidence that is rarely found in jurisdictional statutes.

This uncertainty led Congress to enact 28 U.S.C. § 1367, the supplemental jurisdiction statute. The first subsection of 28 U.S.C. § 1367 provides broad authority for a federal court that has original jurisdiction over a case to hear related state law claims as well.

> (a) Except as provided in subsections (b) and (c) or as expressly provided otherwise by Federal statute, in any civil action of which the district courts have original jurisdiction, the district courts shall have supplemental jurisdiction over all other claims that are so related to claims in the action within such original jurisdiction that they form part of the same case or controversy under Article III of the United States Constitution. Such supplemental jurisdiction shall include claims that involve the joinder or intervention of additional parties.

Section 1367(b), however, makes exceptions to this broad grant of jurisdiction for certain claims in diversity cases. And § 1367(c) recasts the discretionary factors from *Gibbs*, authorizing the court to decline supplemental jurisdiction in several circumstances.

Notes and Questions: The Supplemental Jurisdiction Statute

1. New terminology: Supplemental jurisdiction. The drafters of the supplemental jurisdiction statute (three eminent Civil Procedure professors) adopted the term *supplemental* jurisdiction to refer to added state law claims, whether they would have been dubbed *pendent* or *ancillary* under prior case law. This unified terminology reflects the fact that, however the claim is added, the jurisdictional question is the same: whether the federal court has jurisdiction to hear the state law claim because of its relation to the main claim that supports federal jurisdiction. *Gibbs* and *Kroger* provide the essential background to understanding the supplemental jurisdiction statute, but their terminology is superseded by the statute.

Q **2. What is the meaning of the term "case or controversy" in § 1367(a)?**

A Both the structure of the statute and its legislative history affirm that the drafters intended this term to have the same meaning that it has in *UMW v. Gibbs*. *See Moore* § 106.21[1]. It authorizes the court to hear all other claims in the action that arise out of the same nucleus of operative facts as the original claim that confers original jurisdiction on the federal court.

Q **3. Applying § 1367(a).** Consider these straightforward applications of § 1367(a) to claims in *Gibbs* and *Kroger.*

A. Would § 1367(a) authorize jurisdiction over Gibbs's interference with contract claim against UMW in *UMW v. Gibbs*?

A Yes, it would. The federal LMRA claim gives the federal court original jurisdiction, because it arises under federal law. Under § 1367(a), the court may then hear all related claims that are part of the same "case." Since the interference with contract claim is based on the same underlying events as the LMRA claim, it is within the court's supplemental jurisdiction.

B. Would § 1367(a) grant supplemental jurisdiction over a counterclaim by OPPD against the plaintiff in *Kroger,* alleging that her husband had negligently damaged the power lines by causing the crane to approach it? (Assume that the counterclaim demands less than $75,000, so there is no independent basis for jurisdiction over it.)

A Yes, it would. The federal court has original jurisdiction over the action based on Mrs. Kroger's diversity case against OPPD. Under § 1367(a), the court can hear additional claims that arise from the same nucleus of operative facts. (The statute does not limit the added claims to those asserted by plaintiffs.) Since the counterclaim arises from the same accident, § 1367(a) applies.

4. The exceptions: § 1367(b). The grant of supplemental jurisdiction in § 1367(a) extends to any claim that arises from the same underlying events as the claim on which original jurisdiction is based. However, in § 1367(b), the drafters provided that supplemental jurisdiction shall not extend to certain categories of claims, even though they are within the grant of supplemental jurisdiction in subsection (a):

> (b) In any civil action of which the district courts have original jurisdiction founded solely on section 1332 of this title, the district courts shall not have supplemental jurisdiction under subsection (a) over claims by plaintiffs against persons made parties under Rule 14, 19, 20 or 24 of the Federal Rules of Civil Procedure, or over claims by persons proposed to be joined as plaintiffs under Rule 19 of such rules, or seeking to intervene as plaintiffs under Rule 24 of such rules, when exercising supplemental jurisdiction over such claims would be inconsistent with the jurisdictional requirements of section 1332.

Q **5. Applying § 1367 to *Kroger.*** First, does 28 U.S.C. § 1367(a) authorize jurisdiction over OPPD's impleader claim against Owen Equipment & Erection Co.?

A Yes, because the claim arises from the same events as the main claim. Although this claim involves an added party, the last sentence of § 1367(a) authorizes jurisdiction over claims against later-added parties: "Such supplemental jurisdiction shall include claims that involve the joinder or intervention of additional parties."

Second, is jurisdiction over OPPD's impleader claim taken away by the exceptions in § 1367(b)?

A No. Although this is a diversity case—and § 1367(b) bars certain claims in diversity cases—OPPD's claim is not asserted by a plaintiff, so subsection (b) does not apply. (The word "plaintiff" in § 1367(b) refers to the *original* plaintiff, not to a third-party plaintiff like defendant OPPD in this example.) Because subsection (a) grants jurisdiction over the claim and subsection (b) does not take it away, the court may hear the claim.

Q **6. Two more questions applying § 1367 to *Kroger*.** First, would a federal district court have jurisdiction over Mrs. Kroger's claim against Owen in the *Kroger* case, looking only at 28 U.S.C. § 1367(a)?

A Yes, it would. The court has original jurisdiction over the case between Kroger and OPPD, and this claim arises out of the same accident. Thus, it is part of the same "case or controversy" as the main claim, and the broad grant of supplemental jurisdiction in § 1367(a) applies.

Second, is jurisdiction barred by the exceptions in § 1367(b)?

A Subsection (b) bars jurisdiction over this claim. Because original jurisdiction over the case is based on diversity, subsection (b) must be considered. It bars supplemental jurisdiction over certain claims by plaintiffs, and Mrs. Kroger's claim is a claim by a plaintiff. And, her claim is "against a person [Owen] made a party under Rule 14," because Owen was impleaded by OPPD under Rule 14(a).

The primary purpose of § 1367 was not to *expand* jurisdiction over related claims, but to codify the state of the law at the time it was enacted. Subsection (b), like *Kroger*, bars jurisdiction over claims by plaintiffs against non-diverse third-party defendants in diversity cases.

Q **7. A pendent party case.** Adair, from California, sues the United States for injuries suffered in a plane crash at a California airport. Her suit is brought under the Federal Tort Claims Act, which authorizes federal courts to hear tort claims against the United States. She claims that negligence of a federal air traffic controller led to the crash. She also sues Vasquez, from California, for the same injuries, claiming that Vasquez, flying a private plane, got in the way as he was landing. The case (loosely based on *Finley v. United States)* looks like this:

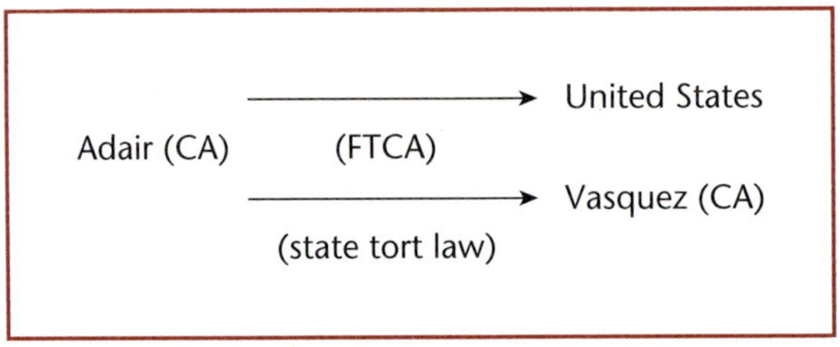

Figure 20–6: A PENDENT PARTY CASE

Considering both subsections (a) and (b), would a federal district court have jurisdiction over Adair's claim against Vasquez?

A Yes. The court has original jurisdiction over the claim against the United States under § 1346(b)(1), which authorizes jurisdiction of tort claims against the United States. Under § 1367(a), the court has jurisdiction over Adair's claim against Vasquez, which arises from the same airplane crash. (The last sentence of § 1367(a) expressly authorizes the court to hear supplemental claims against additional parties.) The exceptions in § 1367(b) do not apply to this claim, because the federal court's original jurisdiction is not based on § 1332.

8. Statutory discretion. In 28 U.S.C. § 1367(c), Congress provided authority for federal judges to decline jurisdiction over supplemental claims. The reasons in subsections (1), (2), and (3) echo reasons Justice Brennan described in *Gibbs* for declining supplemental jurisdiction. Subsection (4) is a "catchall" provision that authorizes the court to decline supplemental jurisdiction "in exceptional circumstances, [if] there are other compelling reasons for declining jurisdiction." Federal courts have disagreed as to whether the court's discretion under subsection (c) is more restrictive than under *Gibbs*. Justice Brennan described the reasons he listed in *Gibbs* as illustrative, but some courts have read § 1367(c) as narrower because of the restrictive language ("other compelling reasons") in § 1367(c)(4). *See, e.g., Itar-Tass Russian News Agency v. Russian Kurier,* 140 F.3d 442, 445–48 (2d Cir. 1998). *See generally Moore* § 106.60.

Q **Practice makes perfect.** The examples below should help you to understand how to apply the supplemental jurisdiction statute. In analyzing them, assume that all cases are brought in federal court.

A. Crowley (CO) sues Picard (IA) for $200,000, claiming that Picard, the broker in a real estate sale, misrepresented septic problems with the property, inducing Crowley to buy it. Picard impleads Banchevsky, the seller, for indemnification, arguing that if she misrepresented the septic problems to Crowley, it was because Banchevsky had given her the wrong information about them. Banchevsky is from Colorado. Does the court have jurisdiction over Picard's claim against Banchevsky?

A Yes, it does. Supplemental jurisdiction is unnecessary, because it is a claim between an Iowa citizen and a Colorado citizen for more than $75,000. Picard seeks reimbursement of the entire amount Crowley seeks from her; that's what indemnification means. So long as Crowley's claim is arguably worth more than $75,000, Picard's claim against Banchevsky satisfies the standards for *original jurisdiction* in federal court. Thus, there's no need to consider whether supplemental jurisdiction would apply to it.

Think of it this way: Picard could have sued Banchevsky for this claim separately, and the federal court would have had jurisdiction over it. If that is true, it also has jurisdiction over it when it is asserted as an impleader claim, without regard to supplemental jurisdiction.

B. Assume, on the facts of example A, that Banchevsky is from Iowa. Would the court have jurisdiction over Picard's impleader claim against her?

A If Banchevsky is from Iowa, there is no diversity between her and Picard, so we must look for another basis for jurisdiction over Picard's impleader claim. The main suit is based on diversity, not federal question, but supplemental jurisdiction applies in diversity cases as well as federal question cases. The court has original jurisdiction over the case between Crowley and Picard based on diversity. The court has supplemental jurisdiction over the impleader claim if it arises out of the same case or controversy as the main case. 28 U.S.C. § 1367(a). It does, since Picard's indemnification claim against Banchevsky arises from the same sale of property as the main claim.

Because original jurisdiction is based on diversity, we need to consider whether § 1367(b) excepts this claim from the grant of supplemental jurisdiction in § 1367(a). It does not, because this is not a claim asserted by a plaintiff. The word "plaintiff" in the statute means the original plaintiff, not a defendant acting as a third-party plaintiff.

C. On the facts of example A, Crowley, the plaintiff, asserts a claim directly against Banchevsky, the third-party defendant, for the misrepresentation, claiming the same damages, after Banchevsky is brought in by Picard. This is authorized by Fed. R. Civ. P. 14(a)(3). Assume that Banchevsky is from Iowa.

A If Banchevsky is from Iowa, there is original jurisdiction over Crowley's claim against her. It's a claim by a Colorado citizen against an Iowa citizen for more than $75,000. Crowley could have sued her on this claim in a separate action in federal court (or as a codefendant with Picard). So this claim is fine, without regard to supplemental jurisdiction. Remember, supplemental jurisdiction is a "gap filler," authorizing jurisdiction over a claim that the court otherwise lacks authority to hear. Where there is an independent basis for the court to hear the claim, there is no need for supplemental jurisdiction.

D. On the facts of example A, Crowley asserts a claim directly against Banchevsky for the misrepresentation, after she is brought in by Picard. Assume that Banchevsky is from Colorado.

A If Banchevsky is from Colorado, the court cannot hear Crowley's claim against Banchevsky based on diversity, so we need to assess whether supplemental jurisdiction applies. Certainly, § 1367(a) authorizes jurisdiction, since the claim arises from the same litigation events as the main claim. However, § 1367(b) bars jurisdiction over this claim, because it is a claim by a plaintiff against a person made a party under Rule 14. This is the same type of claim that the Supreme Court rejected in *Kroger.*

E. On the facts of example A, Crowley asserts a claim directly against Banchevsky (from Colorado) after she is brought in by Picard. Crowley claims that Banchevsky violated the Federal Truth-in-Real-Estate-Sales Act when she deliberately misrepresented the septic conditions on the property.

A | No problem here. Crowley asserts a claim against Banchevsky arising under federal law. She could have sued Banchevsky on this claim in a stand-alone federal suit, so she may add it to the original case as well. The court has original jurisdiction over it.

F. On the facts of example A, Banchevsky, after being brought in as a third-party defendant by Picard, asserts a claim for $25,000 against Picard (the original defendant) under Rule 14(a)(2)(B), for the balance of the purchase price for the property, which Picard had collected but not paid over to Banchevsky. Assume that Banchevsky is from Colorado.

A | There is no independent jurisdiction over this compulsory counterclaim by Banchevsky against Picard, because it does not meet the amount-in-controversy requirement. However, the court will have supplemental jurisdiction over it. It arises from the same dispute as the main claim, so § 1367(a) authorizes the court to hear it. And § 1367(b) does not apply, because the claim is asserted by the third-party defendant, not the plaintiff.

G. On the facts of example A, Banchevsky counterclaims against Picard, claiming that Picard did not pay her $60,000 that she collected on the sale of another property Picard sold for Banchevsky.

A | In this example, the third-party defendant asserts a permissive counterclaim against Picard arising out of unrelated events. Probably, the court lacks jurisdiction over it, since it fails the same-case-or-controversy requirement of § 1367(a).*

V. Complex Applications: *Exxon Mobil Corp. v. Allapattah Services*

In Chapter 3, we considered the rules governing aggregation of claims in diversity cases. The traditional rules, established by case law, allowed a plaintiff to add any claims she had against a single defendant to get over the $75,000 threshold. But if two plaintiffs sued one defendant, they each had to sue for more than $75,000. *Clark v. Paul Gray, Inc.*, 306 U.S. 583 (1939). The court would not add the plaintiffs' claims together to reach the required number. Nor would it aggregate claims against different defendants. If Ruffo sued Wang for $100,000 and Watts for $60,000, she met the amount requirement against Wang, but the court would lack jurisdiction over the claim against Watts.

Class actions also raise problems in applying the diversity rules. In *Supreme Tribe of Ben-Hur v. Cauble*, 255 U.S. 356 (1921), the Supreme Court held that

---

* There is some authority suggesting that a defendant asserting a "set-off" claim, to reduce recovery on the claim against her by setting off a debt the plaintiff owes to her, may invoke supplemental jurisdiction. *See, e.g., Jones v. Ford Motor Credit Co.*, 358 F.3d 205 (2d Cir. 2004).

diversity in a class action is determined by comparing the citizenship of the class representatives to that of the defendants—other class members need not be diverse from the defendants. However, the Court later held that each member of the class must meet the amount-in-controversy requirement. *Zahn v. International Paper Co.*, 414 U.S. 292 (1973). Even if the class representative sued for more than $75,000 in damages, class members who sued for less would not meet the amount requirement, even if the total damages sought in the class action were millions of dollars.

It was not clear, however, whether enactment of the supplemental jurisdiction statute changed these rules. Consider this example:

Example. Jericho, from Kansas, brings a diversity action against Morosky, from Texas, for $125,000 in damages. Torino, from Kansas, was injured in the same accident and joins as a coplaintiff with Jericho, seeking $40,000 in damages.

Under the traditional approach to aggregation of claims, the court has jurisdiction over Jericho's claim but not over Torino's.

However, the language of the supplemental jurisdiction statute raised a complex question as to whether a diversity court would have jurisdiction over a claim like Torino's, who sued for less than the $75,0000.01 amount-in-controversy requirement.

A. Did the Supplemental Jurisdiction Statute Change the Aggregation Rules?

After enactment of the supplemental jurisdiction statute, courts split dramatically on this question. On the one hand, the legislative history of the statute strongly suggested that it was not meant to change the long-standing aggregation rules in *Clark* and *Zahn*, which required each plaintiff to meet the amount-in-controversy requirement. If that were true, the federal court would not have subject matter jurisdiction over Torino's claim in the example above.

On the other hand, the language of 28 U.S.C. § 1367(a) appears to convey jurisdiction over Torino's claim. There is a claim that gives the federal court original jurisdiction—Jericho's $125,000 claim—and Torino's claim arises out of the same case or controversy—the accident that caused both of their injuries. Thus, the court has supplemental jurisdiction to hear it . . . unless it is within one of the exceptions in 28 U.S.C. § 1367(b). Careful scrutiny of § 1367(b), however, does not reveal any exception for an added plaintiff who fails to meet the amount-in-controversy requirement. There is an exception for claims *against* parties joined under Fed. R. Civ. P 20(a) that don't meet the amount requirement, but not for claims *brought by* parties (like Jericho and Torino) joined under Rule 20(a).

The same issue arose in class action cases. Prior to enactment of § 1367, the Supreme Court had held in *Zahn* that each member of a class had to meet the amount-in-controversy requirement. If the class representative sought $200,000 in damages, but other members of the class sought less than $75,000.01, the court lacked jurisdiction over those class members. Yet again, such class members' claims appear to be within the broad grant of supplemental jurisdiction in 28 U.S.C. § 1367(a). And there is no explicit exception in 28 U.S.C. § 1367(b) for such claims.

B. The *Allapattah* Decision

This issue actually reached the Supreme Court twice. In the first case, *Free v. Abbott Labs, Inc.*, 529 U.S 333 (2000), the court split four to four on the question, leaving everyone as bewildered as before. Parties continued to joust in the lower courts until 2005, when the Supreme Court again took certiorari in *Exxon Mobil Corp. v. Allapattah Services*, 545 U.S. 546 (2005). In *Allapattah*, the Court concluded that the plain language of 28 U.S.C. § 1367(a) of the supplemental jurisdiction statute authorizes jurisdiction over claims by additional plaintiffs that do not meet the amount-in-controversy requirement:

> Section 1367(a) is a broad grant of supplemental jurisdiction over other claims within the same case or controversy, as long as the action is one in which the district courts would have original jurisdiction. The last sentence of § 1367(a) makes it clear that the grant of supplemental jurisdiction extends to claims involving joinder or intervention of additional parties. The single question before us, therefore, is whether a diversity case in which the claims of some plaintiffs satisfy the amount-in-controversy requirement, but the claims of other plaintiffs do not, presents a "civil action of which the district courts have original jurisdiction." If the answer is yes, § 1367(a) confers supplemental jurisdiction over all claims, including those that do not independently satisfy the amount-in-controversy requirement, if the claims are part of the same Article III case or controversy. If the answer is no, § 1367(a) is inapplicable and, in light of our holdings in *Clark* and *Zahn*, the district court has no statutory basis for exercising supplemental jurisdiction over the additional claims.
>
> We now conclude the answer must be yes. When the well-pleaded complaint contains at least one claim that satisfies the amount-in-controversy requirement, and there are no other relevant jurisdictional defects, the district court, beyond all question, has original jurisdiction over that claim. The presence of other claims in the complaint, over which the district court may lack original jurisdiction, is of no moment. If the court has original jurisdiction over a single claim in the complaint, it has original jurisdiction over a "civil action" within the meaning of § 1367(a), even if the civil action over which it has jurisdiction comprises fewer claims than were included in the complaint.

545 U.S. at 558–59.

The Court further concluded that § 1367(b) did not exclude such claims, either in cases involving joinder of individual plaintiffs or in class actions:

> If § 1367(a) were the sum total of the relevant statutory language, our holding would rest on that language alone. The statute, of course, instructs us to examine § 1367(b) to determine if any of its exceptions apply, so we proceed to that section. While § 1367(b) qualifies the broad rule of § 1367(a), it does not withdraw supplemental jurisdiction over the claims of the additional parties at issue here. The specific exceptions to § 1367(a) contained in § 1367(b), moreover, provide additional support for our conclusion that § 1367(a) confers

> supplemental jurisdiction over these claims. Section 1367(b), which applies only to diversity cases, withholds supplemental jurisdiction over the claims of plaintiffs proposed to be joined as indispensable parties under Federal Rule of Civil Procedure 19, or who seek to intervene pursuant to Rule 24. Nothing in the text of § 1367(b), however, withholds supplemental jurisdiction over the claims of plaintiffs permissively joined under Rule 20 . . . or certified as class-action members pursuant to Rule 23 . . . . The natural, indeed the necessary, inference is that § 1367 confers supplemental jurisdiction over claims by Rule 20 and Rule 23 plaintiffs. This inference, at least with respect to Rule 20 plaintiffs, is strengthened by the fact that § 1367(b) explicitly excludes supplemental jurisdiction over claims against defendants joined under Rule 20.

545 U.S. at 559–60.

Notes and Questions on the *Allapattah* Decision

1. The role of legislative history. The contentious debate on this issue in the federal courts reflects a larger jurisprudential controversy about the role of legislative history in the interpretation of statutes. On one side is the argument that the primary source of meaning of a statute is found in its text; where the text is clear judges should not reach back to the process of enactment, committee reports, or statements of legislators to alter the meaning of the text enacted by the legislature. (This approach is often called "textualism.") On the other side are judges and scholars who argue that most language is ambiguous and that the intent of the legislature that enacted a statute should be sought in the context of its enactment.

Justice Kennedy's *Allapattah* majority opinion offered an interesting critique of the role of legislative history in interpreting statutes.

> As we have repeatedly held, the authoritative statement is the statutory text, not the legislative history or any other extrinsic material. Extrinsic materials have a role in statutory interpretation only to the extent they shed a reliable light on the enacting Legislature's understanding of otherwise ambiguous terms. Not all extrinsic materials are reliable sources of insight into legislative understandings, however, and legislative history in particular is vulnerable to two serious criticisms. First, legislative history is itself often murky, ambiguous, and contradictory. Judicial investigation of legislative history has a tendency to become, to borrow Judge Leventhal's memorable phrase, an exercise in " 'looking over a crowd and picking out your friends.' " . . . Second, judicial reliance on legislative materials like committee reports, which are not themselves subject to the requirements of Article I, may give unrepresentative committee members—or, worse yet, unelected staffers and lobbyists—both the power and the incentive to attempt strategic manipulations of legislative history to secure results they were unable to achieve through the statutory text.

545 U.S. at 568.

2. Does the supplemental jurisdiction statute overrule *Strawbridge v. Curtiss?* If § 1367 has changed the requirement that each plaintiff meet the amount requirement, has it also eliminated the need for complete diversity?

Consider this argument: Suppose that Gomez, a Nebraskan, sues Polito, from Iowa, seeking $200,000 in damages. Higgins, from Nebraska, joins as a coplaintiff with Gomez, seeking $20,000 in damages for injuries in the same collision. Under *Allapattah,* the federal court has original jurisdiction over Gomez v. Polito and supplemental jurisdiction over Higgins v. Polito. Can't a similar argument be made if Higgins is from Iowa? The court has original jurisdiction over Gomez v. Polito, based on diversity. And Higgins's claim against Polito arises from the same events, so there is supplemental jurisdiction over her claim. If this argument flies, *Strawbridge v. Curtiss* has been overruled by the supplemental jurisdiction statute.

In *Allapattah,* Justice Kennedy rejected this argument on the ground that, in a diversity case, there is not jurisdiction over *any* claim if there is not complete diversity.

> [We] have consistently interpreted § 1332 as requiring complete diversity: In a case with multiple plaintiffs and multiple defendants, the presence in the action of a single plaintiff from the same State as a single defendant deprives the district court of original diversity jurisdiction over the entire action. *Strawbridge v. Curtiss.*... The complete diversity requirement is not mandated by the Constitution, ... or by the plain text of § 1332(a). The Court, nonetheless, has adhered to the complete diversity rule in light of the purpose of the diversity requirement, which is to provide a federal forum for important disputes where state courts might favor, or be perceived as favoring, home-state litigants. The presence of parties from the same State on both sides of a case dispels this concern, eliminating a principal reason for conferring § 1332 jurisdiction over any of the claims in the action.... The specific purpose of the complete diversity rule explains both why we have not adopted *Gibbs'* expansive interpretive approach to this aspect of the jurisdictional statute and why *Gibbs* does not undermine the complete diversity rule. In order for a federal court to invoke supplemental jurisdiction under *Gibbs,* it must first have original jurisdiction over at least one claim in the action. Incomplete diversity destroys original jurisdiction with respect to all claims, so there is nothing to which supplemental jurisdiction can adhere.

545 U.S. at 568–69.

3. An alternative analysis. An interesting dissent by Justice Ginsburg, joined by three other justices, argued as follows:

> § 1367(a) addresses "civil action[s] of which the district courts have original jurisdiction," a formulation that, in diversity cases, is sensibly read to incorporate the rules on joinder and aggregation tightly tied to § 1332 at the time of § 1367's enactment. On this reading, a complaint must first meet that "original jurisdiction" measurement. If it does not, no supplemental jurisdiction is authorized. If it does, § 1367(a) authorizes "supplemental jurisdiction" over related claims. In other words, § 1367(a) would preserve undiminished,

> as part and parcel of § 1332 "original jurisdiction" determinations, both the "complete diversity" rule and the decisions restricting aggregation to arrive at the amount in controversy.

545 U.S. at 589. In other words, while the majority says there is no "original jurisdiction" in a diversity case unless there is complete diversity, Justice Ginsburg would conclude that there is no original jurisdiction unless there is complete diversity *and* the statutory amount-in-controversy requirement (as interpreted in *Clark* and *Zahn*) is met as well. This reading would explain the lack of a reference in § 1367(b) to plaintiffs' claims under Rules 20 and 23. An exception for these would not be necessary if the court lacked original jurisdiction when the amount requirement was not met by each plaintiff.

4. Credit where credit is due. The supplemental jurisdiction statute has been criticized because of ambiguities and inconsistencies like those addressed in *Allapattah*. However, we should not lose sight of the statute's virtues. It authorizes the federal courts to settle entire disputes by taking supplemental jurisdiction over most state law claims added to proper federal cases. It expressly extends jurisdiction to claims by and against added parties. It enacts standards for discretionary dismissal of supplemental claims and extends the statute of limitations for supplemental claims that are dismissed. The controversy over the exclusions for certain claims in diversity cases should not blind us to the considerable stability the statute has brought to supplemental jurisdiction practice.

VI. Supplemental Jurisdiction: Summary of Basic Principles

- Parties in federal cases often assert multiple claims, some that support original federal jurisdiction, and others that do not. For example, a plaintiff may sue a non-diverse defendant on a federal claim and a state claim. In a diversity case, a defendant may counterclaim for less than the jurisdictional amount, bring in a third-party defendant from the same state, or assert a state law crossclaim against a codefendant from the same state.
- Before enactment of 28 U.S.C. § 1367, the supplemental jurisdiction statute, such claims were analyzed as either pendent claims or ancillary claims, depending on their posture in the case. Today, both types of added claims are referred to as supplemental claims.
- In *United Mine Workers v. Gibbs*, the Supreme Court held that a federal court that has jurisdiction over one of the plaintiff's claims may hear others (in themselves jurisdictionally insufficient) that arise out of the same nucleus of operative fact. *Gibbs* further held that the federal court may decline to exercise that jurisdiction if it is more appropriate to have the state law claim decided in state court.

- The federal court cannot hear supplemental claims unless those claims satisfy the constitutional standard articulated in *Gibbs* and the court has statutory authority to hear them as well.
- Congress enacted the supplemental jurisdiction statute to clarify the federal courts' authority to hear such related claims. Section 1367(a) authorizes a federal court that has "original jurisdiction" over one claim in the original case to hear all other claims that are part of the same case or controversy.
- This grant of jurisdiction extends to claims by or against additional parties, even if no claim by or against that party confers original jurisdiction on the federal court.
- Section 1367(b) bars jurisdiction over certain claims *by plaintiffs* (even though they are within the broad grant of jurisdiction in § 1367(a)) in cases *based on diversity jurisdiction.*
- If the court has supplemental jurisdiction over a claim, it may still decline to hear it for the reasons listed in 28 U.S.C. § 1367(c).
- Supplemental jurisdiction provides a basis for jurisdiction over claims that cannot be asserted in federal court on their own. Where a party joins a claim in an action that could have been brought in federal court on its own, there is no need for supplemental jurisdiction.

PART VII

Discovery

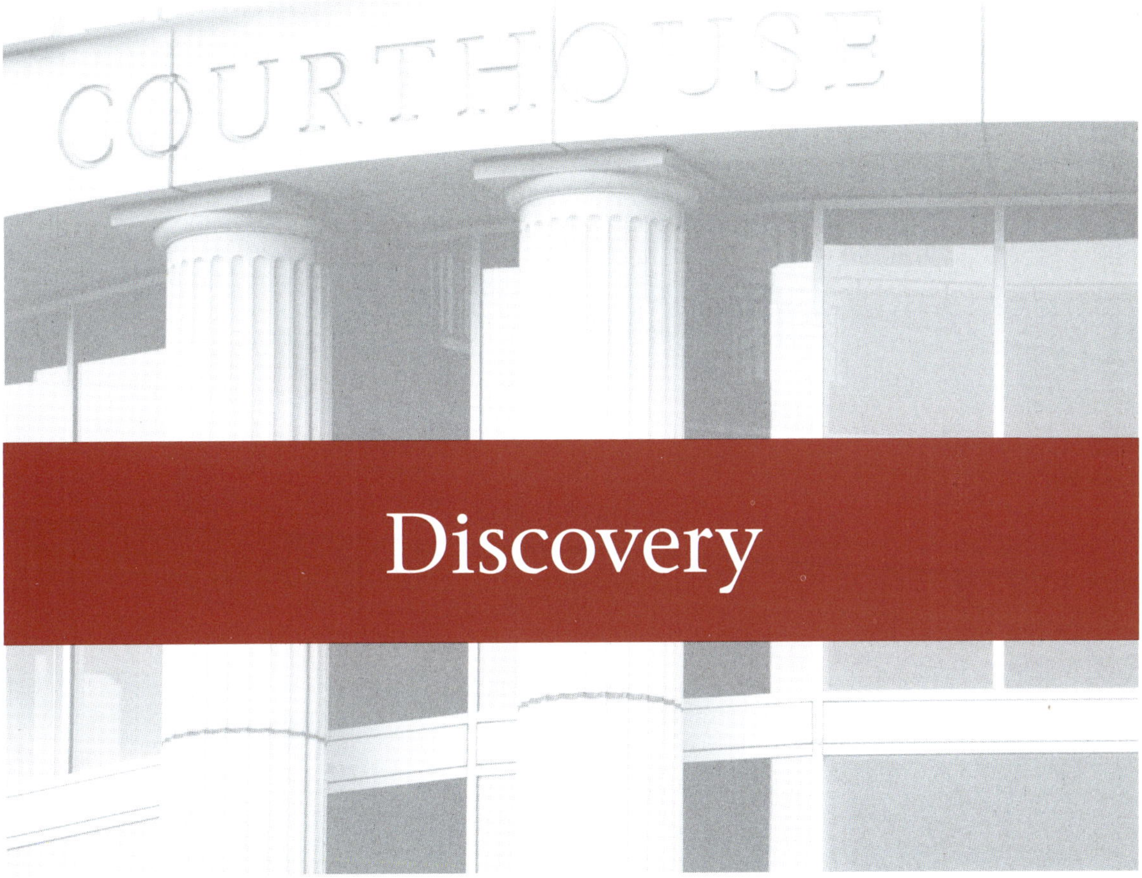

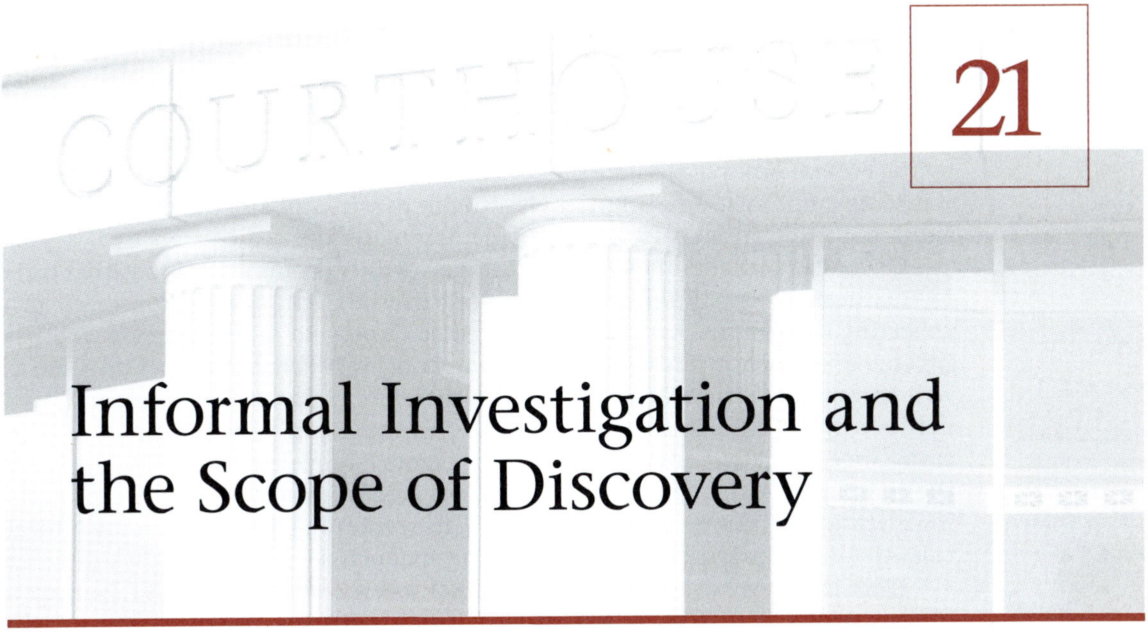

21

Informal Investigation and the Scope of Discovery

I. Introduction

Your client, the Toyota Car Company, has been served with a bare-bones complaint by Peter Painter. The complaint provides little more than minimal notice that Toyota has been sued for a product design defect in a Camry sedan resulting in an automobile accident that injured Painter. Because you believe that the claim is adequately (if not very fully) stated, it is not susceptible to a motion to dismiss for failure to state a claim. To your knowledge there are no other Rule 12 defenses available either. What should you do next?

The intuitive answer is easy: Find out more about the accident and what lies behind Painter's claims against Toyota. *Discovery* is the gathering of facts and evidence under the Federal Rules of Civil Procedure to help flesh out generally pleaded claims and defenses, to test them by motions for summary judgment, to make informed judgments about settlement, and to try the lawsuit should such motions or settlement efforts fail. Federal Rules 26 to 37 establish the scope of the information that is subject to discovery and govern methods by which parties can require disclosure of information. In fact, one of the reasons we let Painter get away with serving Toyota nothing more than a short plausible pleading is that Toyota can collect the facts it needs to evaluate Painter's claims and to prepare for trial by "taking discovery"—using the discovery rules to collect information—after it is served. Without discovery, parties would go to trial on their wits and with whatever facts they could learn on their own, with a high risk of surprise and an edge to the party with the most control of the facts, frequently a large corporate or other institutional defendant. The essential genius of the procedural reform made by the Federal Rules of Civil Procedure in 1938 (some might say the "evil genius") was to de-emphasize and simplify pleading in part by shifting the burden of fact-gathering and trial preparation from pleading to discovery.

Of course, you don't have to wait until a lawsuit is commenced to gather facts by "taking discovery." Painter's lawyer necessarily did some *informal investigation*—collecting facts on his own, outside the Federal Rules—in order to decide whether his client had a claim and to frame his complaint. Toyota will probably do some as well to respond to it. In fact, we have seen that Rule 11 presumes that, before signing the complaint, Painter's lawyer made "an inquiry reasonable under the circumstances" and that Toyota did the same before it moved to dismiss or answered the complaint. Although the discovery rules are not applicable to such informal investigation, it is not without limitations. In section II, we consider some ethical rules that limit how such discovery may be conducted.

Once litigation has commenced, the parties will conduct most of their fact-finding pursuant to the Federal Rules of Civil Procedure. What can they then discover? Rule 26(b)(1) is generous: It authorizes discovery of "any nonprivileged matter that is relevant to "any party's claim or defense and proportional to the needs of the case," even if it would not be "admissible in evidence." Toyota is therefore surely entitled to discover facts about Painter's medical condition, what Painter knows or asserts about the accident, and perhaps even his prior driving record, whether or not it would be admissible at trial. He, in turn, is entitled to discover information about Toyota's design and manufacture of the car in which he was injured, other accidents involving the same model, and probably subsequent redesign of the car to correct accident-causing defects, even though evidence of such "subsequent repairs" will ordinarily be inadmissible at trial to prove liability. *See* Fed. R. Evid. 407. On the other hand, Toyota will not be entitled to discover communications made in confidence by Painter's lawyer to him during and in furtherance of the lawyer-client relationship, because these are privileged. Nor would it be entitled, at least without a special showing, to discover memoranda prepared by Painter's lawyer in preparation for litigation, like an associate's memorandum about the applicable tort law or a summary of the lawyer's interview with a prospective witness. In section III, we consider these and other aspects of *what* may be discovered—the *scope* of formal discovery.

II. Informal Investigation

Prior to filing suit, Painter's lawyer has to conduct a reasonable inquiry into the facts on which he will rely in drafting the complaint. How would he do this? Obviously, he would start by asking Painter all he knows. He might also interview Painter's wife, if she was a passenger in the car. Perhaps he would collect information about the particular model of Camry in *Consumer Reports* or by googling "Camry accidents." He might also use computer-aided legal research to identify reported cases involving the same model and then contact the plaintiffs' lawyers who handled the cases.

Should he also talk to engineers at Toyota about their design of the car? What about an employee on the assembly line or a shift foreman? They appear to be promising, if not primary, sources of information about problems in the car. But they are on the payroll of the prospective defendant. Intuitively, this poses some problems—not just whether they will cooperate, but also whether it is fair and proper to talk to them before Toyota knows that it is a target of Painter's lawsuit. Must Painter's lawyer disclose the fact that he represents Painter? Once the complaint is filed, may he continue to collect information in this fashion? And the same kinds of questions run the other way: Can Toyota's lawyer call Painter to collect information? In either case, can the lawyer secretly tape-record telephone conversations with prospective witnesses or parties? The Federal Rules of Civil Procedure do not address these problems, but state law and state ethics rules often do.

READING *GAYLARD v. HOMEMAKERS OF MONTGOMERY, INC.* In the following case, an elderly woman was badly scalded in a bath given her by a home health care worker, Ms. Taylor. Mr. Dean, the woman's lawyer, then telephoned Ms. Taylor for details about the incident without the permission of her employer and prospective defendant, Homemakers of Montgomery (doing business as Oxford Health Care). The trial court refused to admit evidence from this telephone interview, finding that the lawyer's (Dean's) communication with Ms. Taylor violated Alabama's rules of professional conduct. The Alabama Supreme Court disagreed. While most states have adopted a broader ethical rule than Alabama, and many state courts would not follow the reasoning of this case, it still raises red flags for informal discovery.

- Ms. Taylor was not just an employee whose job could have been on the line if she talked too freely, but also a prospective defendant herself. Given this fact, why did she speak to Dean?
- What difference does it make whether the plaintiff had sued Homemakers before Dean contacted Ms. Taylor?
- If plaintiff had sued, and you represented her, what assumptions, if any, would you make about whether Homemakers had counsel?

GAYLARD v. HOMEMAKERS OF MONTGOMERY, INC.

675 So. 2d 363 (Ala. 1996)

ALMON, Justice.

The plaintiff appeals from a judgment entered on a jury verdict for the defendant. Alice Gaylard brought an action against Homemakers of Montgomery, Inc., d/b/a Oxford Health Care ("Oxford"), alleging negligence, wantonness, and breach of contract. . . . The circuit court ruled that Ms. Gaylard could not use a statement taken by her attorney from a witness who was an employee of Oxford to cross-examine that witness. The court based its ruling on its holding that the attorney, in taking the statement, had violated Rule 4.2 of the Alabama Rules of

Professional Conduct. The issue, therefore, is whether the circuit court erred in limiting cross-examination by prohibiting use of the witness's earlier statement.

Ms. Gaylard contracted with Oxford for Oxford to provide home health care services, including the periodic bathing of Ms. Gaylard. On December 16, 1992, an employee of Oxford, Dorothy Taylor, who was not named as a defendant in the action Ms. Gaylard later filed, was giving Ms. Gaylard a bath and allegedly caused Ms. Gaylard to be burned with hot water. Ms. Gaylard was subsequently hospitalized, and she alleges that the burns she says she sustained on December 16 required the hospitalization and caused her to suffer pain, discomfort, mental anguish, and emotional distress.

Before Ms. Gaylard filed this action against Oxford, Ms. Gaylard's attorney telephoned Ms. Taylor and recorded the ensuing conversation, without informing Ms. Taylor that it was being recorded. Initially, Ms. Taylor refused to discuss the bath and the burns, but, after the attorney persisted, Ms. Taylor began answering questions:

"Q. Do you remember what happened? Can you just tell me in your own words what you remember?

"A. I have to talk to my supervisor before I can talk to you. I can't discuss this.

"Q. Okay. Who is your supervisor? I don't mind giving her a call or him, whoever it is.

"A. Have you talked with anybody at Oxford?

"Q. No ma'am. Ms. Gaylard gave me your home number. I think she said you had given it to her back when you were working there.

"A. Um, hum.

"Q. And she gave me the home number. I was just trying to get you at home thinking maybe you'd talk to me about it.

"A. Well, I don't think I should talk to you.

"Q. Well, can you just tell me what happened?

"A. It was an incident report made. You can go to Oxford and get any information that you want.

"Q. But that would have come from your own statement or what you reported to them, wouldn't it? Nobody was there besides you and Ms. Gaylard, right?

"A. That's right.

". . . .

"Q. Well, can you tell me right quick what happened?

"A. I cannot discuss it with you. I'm not going to discuss it with you. Unless you talk to my supervisor, or you can contact Oxford.

". . . .

"Q. Can you tell me anybody to ask for when I call the company?

"A. No. You call Oxford and you can get all that information. They'll tell you who to talk to, who you should talk to and everything.

"Q. Okay. Thank you. You don't want to say anything about it all?

"A. No, I don't.

"Q. Will you admit or deny that the lady was ever burned? Either way?

"A. I'm not, no, I don't know. I can't say. All I can say, I wasn't aware that she was burned when I was there. I was, the only thing I knew was a couple of days after the incident, she said she was burned.

"Q. She didn't explain to you as soon as the hot water was poured on her leg that it hurt her and it burned her and she was being burned?

"A. No she didn't. Not when it happened. A couple of days later she said, 'Dot, I believe that water was too hot the other day when we bathed.' I bathed her like every other day, you know. It was on a Monday and this supposed to have happened on a Wednesday. When it happened she didn't say that it burned or anything.

"Q. Did you report it to Oxford as soon as it happened?

"A. No. I reported it when she told me she believed it was burned. That's when I reported it. I couldn't report anything that I wasn't aware of.

"Q. And you're saying that was a few days after it happened?

"A. Right.

"Q. You remember what day of the week it was that she told you she was burned?

"A. Oh, I don't know. It was on a Friday when I went back and she didn't get in the tub that day I don't think and she said cause she believed that water was too hot and her leg, something was wrong with her leg and she couldn't get in the tub anyway. On a Monday is when she said that she believed she was burned. . . ."

[Eds.—The lawyer continued pressing Ms. Taylor in the same vein, eliciting numerous additional answers about the incident and her role in it.]

Oxford filed a motion in limine to prevent Ms. Gaylard from introducing the recorded statement into evidence, citing Rule 4.2, Ala. R. Prof. Conduct:

> In representing a client, a lawyer shall not communicate about the subject of the representation with a party the lawyer knows to be represented by another lawyer in the matter, unless the lawyer has the consent of the other lawyer or is authorized by law to do so.

The comment to Rule 4.2 elaborates:

> In the case of an organization, this Rule prohibits communications by a lawyer for one party concerning the matter in representation [sic] with persons . . . whose act or omission in connection with that matter may be imputed to the organization for purposes of civil or criminal liability or whose statement may constitute an admission on the part of the organization. . . .
>
> This rule also covers any person, whether or not a party to a formal proceeding, who is represented by counsel concerning the matter in question. . . .

We begin our analysis by first determining if the attorney violated Rule 4.2. That rule applies only to communications with a party, and then only when the attorney knows that the party is represented by an attorney. Although the committee comments to Rule 4.2 indicate that the rule should reach an agent or an employee of a corporate party when the corporation's liability will be predicated on the agent's actions, Oxford itself was not a "party" at the time of the communication, because Ms. Gaylard had not yet filed an action against it. The rules do not require an attorney to immediately file an action at law before communicating with the person with whom the attorney's client has a dispute.

Aside from the question whether Oxford was a party, there is no evidence that Ms. Gaylard's attorney knew, or even had reason to think, that Oxford had retained counsel in regard to the matter of Ms. Gaylard's alleged injury. Notwithstanding the fact that Ms. Taylor initially objected and said that she should not talk to the attorney without talking to her supervisor first, she did not say or imply that her employer had retained counsel. Thus, Ms. Gaylard's attorney could not have violated Rule 4.2. Because this was the only basis on which the circuit court sustained the objection, it was error to sustain the objection, made during cross-examination of Ms. Taylor, to the use of her statement as a prior inconsistent statement.

Even if this communication had occurred after Ms. Taylor had been contacted by attorneys for Oxford, and even if Ms. Gaylard's attorney had known that Ms. Taylor was a "party," it would still have been error for the circuit court to sustain the objection and bar admission of the evidence. The Rules of Professional Conduct are "self-imposed internal regulations" and do not play a role in determining the admissibility of evidence. *Stringer v. State*, 372 So. 2d 378, 382–83 (Ala. Crim. App.), *cert. denied*, 372 So. 2d 384 (Ala. 1979); cf. *Terry Cove North, Inc. v. Marr & Friedlander, P.C.*, 521 So. 2d 22, 23–24 (Ala. 1988) ("The sole remedy is the imposition of disciplinary measures."). . . .

Consequently, the judgment is hereby reversed and the cause is remanded for a new trial.

Hooper, Chief Justice (dissenting):

. . . The record is unclear as to whether Attorney Richard C. Dean, Jr., knew, when he telephoned Ms. Taylor, who would be one of those persons mentioned in the comment to the rule, whether she was represented by counsel. Dean contends that he spoke with Taylor before he filed the lawsuit, but Taylor was unsure when she spoke with Dean. The record does not affirmatively state that Ms. Taylor was represented by counsel when Dean contacted her. Also, the record does not indicate whether Homemakers of Montgomery, Inc., had attorneys on its staff or on retainer. However, a reasonably prudent attorney should know that corporations routinely have in-house counsel or have retained counsel.

The following things are clear. First, Attorney Dean was procured by Ms. Gaylard for the purpose of filing a lawsuit against Homemakers based on the alleged acts or omissions of Taylor. Second, Dean contacted Taylor by telephone, knowing that her acts or omissions could be imputed to Homemakers, and knowing that her statements could constitute admissions on the part of Homemakers.

Third, Dean recorded the telephone conversation without Taylor's consent. Fourth, at the outset of the telephone conversation, Taylor told Dean repeatedly and in plain language that she did not want to speak with him because she believed that her employer would not want her to do so. Fifth, Dean repeatedly violated Taylor's requests to be excused from speaking with him, and he continued to pressure her until she spoke with him. Based upon the facts of this case, it is not clear whether Attorney Dean violated the letter of Rule 4.2. However, it is clear that Dean violated the spirit of Rule 4.2. . . .

The lawyer has an advantage over the layman. The lawyer, being more knowledgeable of the law and perhaps more cunning than the layman, can use knowledge and experience to lay a trap for the other. The purpose of cross-examining a witness is often to lay a trap for the witness. I would hope that with both parties' attorneys present and with the judge overseeing the proceeding, such a trap will lead to the truth. The layman being interviewed by an opponent's attorney or a potential opponent's attorney is not on a level playing field.

The spirit of our present Rule 4.2 is to level the legal playing field. In this case, Attorney Dean, knowing that he planned to sue Homemakers and knowing that Ms. Taylor had no attorney to assist her, manipulated Ms. Taylor. Dean felt free to use whatever artifice and coercion was necessary to interrogate Ms. Taylor because he knew that she had no attorney to object to his repeated and uninvited questions. The record shows that Taylor told Dean repeatedly and in certain terms that she did not want to talk with him, could not talk with him, and would not talk with him. Nevertheless, Attorney Dean persisted and coerced her into saying what he wanted her to say. There is little doubt that if Dean had contacted Taylor in the presence of an attorney for Homemakers or Taylor, or by writing only, as Hoffman suggests, this issue would not be before this Court.

Lawyers who find themselves in Attorney Dean's situation should do three things: (1) identify themselves to the prospective defendant; (2) advise the prospective defendant that they represent the prospective plaintiff; and (3) communicate with the prospective defendant in writing only, with no oral response being received. Attorneys who adhere to this three-pronged approach in communicating with unrepresented prospective defendants will not only bring honor to the legal profession, but will preserve the administration of justice, consistent with the Alabama Rules of Professional Conduct. . . .

Even though Dean may not have violated the letter of Rule 4.2, and therefore may not be subject to discipline, the trial judge in this case recognized the egregiousness of Dean's conduct. In granting the motion in limine, he sought to prevent Dean's client from profiting from such an unfair method of obtaining evidence. In addition, his granting the motion acted as a deterrence [sic] to other attorneys contemplating use of the same unfair tactic in future cases. I commend the trial judge for his discernment and the careful balancing he used in remedying for this manipulation of the justice system and its rules.

Therefore, I must respectfully dissent.

[Dissenting opinion by Justice Houston omitted.]

Notes and Questions: Ethical Limits on Informal Investigation

Q **1. Talking to lawyers.** What risks, if any, did Ms. Taylor run by speaking with lawyer Dean?

A The biggest risk she ran is that by telling him what happened, she exposed herself to liability, although she was likely to be too "shallow pocket" for that to be a real risk. (But note that some plaintiffs' lawyers might sue her anyway for leverage in obtaining her testimony against her employer.) She also risked exposing her employer to liability, and, if so, placing her own continued employment in jeopardy. If she was made a party, her statements will likely be admissible against her. (If she made them in the scope of her employment, they may also be admissible against Homemakers.)

Q **2. Lay ignorance.** If she ran any risks, why did she do it?

A She didn't, at first. Many, perhaps most, people are leery of speaking with lawyers, especially after an incident in which someone was hurt, lost money, or had property damaged. In a litigation-prone society, many people expect that such incidents are "blood in the water," the sharks being lawyers, of course. But not all people. Moreover, even those who are leery—as Ms. Taylor was at the start—may also want to cooperate, to correct what they perceive to be misapprehensions, to tell their stories, or even just to be polite. An effective lawyer can take advantage of such sentiments to get past the initial hesitation and obtain a statement, sometimes by leading the witness as if on cross-examination.

Q **3. The value of advice by counsel.** Would Ms. Taylor have made the same statements if she had been advised by counsel for Homemakers before speaking with Dean?

A Almost certainly not. In the first place, many lawyers in this situation would advise her against speaking with Dean at all. If suit is filed, Dean could question Ms. Taylor by taking her deposition under the formal discovery rules. But then the questions and answers would be recorded and transcribed by a court reporter, all parties would have notice of the deposition and an opportunity to attend and participate, and she could be represented either by the lawyer for Homemakers or by her own lawyer. The lawyer could help her prepare for the deposition, object to improper questions, and, if necessary, clarify the deposition record by asking her questions.

Second, if her lawyer did permit her to speak with Dean, her lawyer would usually want to be on the call and might try to limit the areas of inquiry or block unfair or ambiguous questions. The lawyer might even try to bargain with Dean for her testimony ("my client will talk to you only if we can get an agreement that she will not be sued personally for this incident," or something to that effect). And, the lawyer could coach her before the call to answer narrowly and volunteer nothing.

Q **4. Communicating with unrepresented parties.** Concern about the disparity in knowledge between a lawyer and an unrepresented person led the Alabama Bar to adopt the following rule, which, in relevant part, tracks the ABA Model Rules of Professional Conduct, adopted in most states:

> In dealing on behalf of a client with a person who is not represented by counsel, a lawyer shall not state or imply that the lawyer is disinterested. When the lawyer knows or reasonably should know that the unrepresented person misunderstands the lawyer's role in the matter, the lawyer shall make reasonable efforts to correct the misunderstanding.

Ala. R. Prof. Conduct 4.3. Should the court have considered this rule? Did Dean comply with it?

A It's unclear from this excerpt, but surely debatable. While he made no misrepresentations in the excerpted transcript, it is arguable that Ms. Taylor would not have kept talking with him had she understood his true role: to collect evidence for filing a suit against her employer, if not her, presumably based on her negligence in letting the water get too hot. And did his "role" include secret tape-recording? If so, she surely did not understand it.

The comment to the Alabama version of this rule adds that "the lawyer should not give advice to an unrepresented person other than the advice to obtain counsel." Can you see how easily a lawyer's interview with an unrepresented lay person can transmute into advice-asking and advice-taking? "Do you think I should keep talking to you?" or "Am I gonna need a lawyer?"—as naive as they may seem to first-year law students—are not surprising lay questions in a conversation such as that between Dean and Ms. Taylor, but any answer that he might give would risk running afoul of Alabama Rule 4.3.

Q **5. Communicating with represented parties.** Once a person is represented, the disparity in knowledge underlying Alabama Rule 4.3 is presumably eliminated because the witness can seek help from his own lawyer. But this is true only if that lawyer knows about the communication and consents to it. Alabama Rule 4.2 therefore prohibits communications with "a *party* the lawyer knows to be represented by another lawyer in the matter" unless such consent is obtained or the law otherwise authorizes the communication (emphasis added). This formulation of the restriction, however, poses its own problems, as *Gaylard* shows.

The Alabama rule is an exception. Most state rules are now modeled on the ABA Model Rules, which substitute "person" for "party." But this still leaves the issue of whether "person" then includes employees of organizational parties such as corporations and associations. If all Homemakers' employees are deemed persons within the rule's prohibition, and the plaintiff does not recall what happened to her, then she and her lawyer are effectively prohibited from obtaining information about Homemakers without the consent of its lawyer. By comparison,

Homemakers' lawyer does not suffer the same impediment; until she knows that Gaylard has retained a lawyer, Homemakers' lawyer would be free to call Gaylard and her family and friends who have heard about the incident, subject, of course, to Alabama Rule 4.3. Even after she knows, she could still call Gaylard's family and friends, while Gaylard and her lawyer would be prohibited from contacting certain Homemaker employees, including (probably) Ms. Taylor, without Homemakers' lawyer's permission.

How does this impact Dean's duty of "reasonable inquiry" under a state pleading rule like Rule 11, assuming that Alabama has one?

A It seems to put him and his client at a serious disadvantage. On one hand, he is obliged by the Rule to undertake a reasonable inquiry into the facts of the scalding incident before filing a complaint alleging that Ms. Taylor scalded his client and that her employer is responsible. On the other hand, if he knows that Homemakers has in-house or retained counsel, he can't call Ms. Taylor or any of its employees without its lawyer's permission. Maybe his inquiry is sufficient if he does everything *else* he can to learn the facts before filing, since he cannot "reasonably" call Taylor because of the ethics rule.

Viewing this dilemma, one court has asserted that "the rigid application of ABA Rule 4.2 to organizational contacts can frustrate the inquiry necessary to meet Rule 11 . . . standards," and that, so applied, ABA Rule 4.2 would not be "a matter of ethics but becomes, in reality, a rule of political and economic power that shelters organizations, corporations and other business enterprises from the legitimate less costly inquiry and fact gathering process sometimes necessary to make a legitimate assessment of whether a valid claim for relief exists." *Weider Sports Equipment Co. v. Fitness First, Inc.*, 912 F. Supp. 502, 508 (D. Utah 1996). That court therefore would only apply the Rule after litigation commences and then only to managerial employees or others sufficiently high in the organizational hierarchy to speak for the organization. *See also* D.C. Bar Legal Ethics Comm., *Op. 287* (Jan. 19, 1999) (construing D.C.'s version of ABA Rule 4.2 to apply only to those non-party employees who have the authority to bind their party-employer). Other courts take a much broader view of the ban, forbidding contact with practically all employees. *See, e.g., In re Air Crash Disaster near Roselawn, Ind.*, 909 F. Supp. 1116, 1121–22 (N.D. Ill. 1995). Still other courts occupy the middle ground by forbidding contact only with certain categories of employees. *See, e.g., Messing, Rudavsky & Weliky, P.C. v. President & Fellows of Harvard College*, 436 Mass. 347, 357 (2002).

In other words, "don't try this at home." Before you go off interviewing employees of a prospective institutional party, check the applicable rules of professional conduct and the judicial gloss on them.

6. Other ethical restrictions on informal investigation. Most courts have held that Rule 4.2 does not prohibit interviews with *former* employees. Because disgruntled ex-employees are often a fruitful source of information against their erstwhile employer, this is an important caveat to the Rule. We assume that Ms. Taylor was still employed by Homemakers at the time of her telephone interview in *Gaylard* (though possibly in a different location). Otherwise, her conversation would have been admissible for a different reason than the one given by the court: She'd be a former employee.

But some of these courts have found yet another ethical limitation on such interviews. "[A] lawyer may not solicit information when communicating with former employees of a party-opponent that is reasonably known or which reasonably should be known to the lawyer to be protected from disclosure by statute or by an established evidentiary privilege." D.C. Bar Legal Ethics Comm., *Op. 287* (Jan. 19, 1999). Information that the employer communicated in confidence to the employee (or vice versa) during a lawyer-client relationship to obtain or render legal advice may be subject to the lawyer-client privilege. A lawyer who knowingly asks about such information in an informal interview with a former employee, and certainly with a current employee, may violate ABA Model Rule 4.4, forbidding a lawyer from using "methods of obtaining evidence that violate the legal rights of a [third] person." The "third person" is the employer, to whom the lawyer-client privilege "belongs" in this context.

And you thought that informal investigation was wide open!

7. Tape-recording, wiretapping, and other means of taking statements. Should the court in *Gaylard* have considered Alabama Rule 4.4, which, like the ABA Model Rule, provides that "[i]n representing a client, a lawyer shall not use . . . methods of obtaining evidence that violate the legal rights of such a person"? Some states criminalize unconsented tape-recording of telephone conversations without prior court order. *See, e.g.*, MD. COURTS & JUD. PROC. CODE ANN. 10-402. Evidently, Alabama is not one of them.

The ethics committee of the Association of the Bar of the City of New York Bar observes, however, that:

> [t]he fact that a practice is legal does not necessarily render it ethical. Moreover, the fact that the practice at issue remains illegal in a significant number of jurisdictions is a powerful indication that the practice is not one in which an attorney should readily engage. Similarly, the fact that there are times when a valid reason exists to engage in undisclosed taping does not mean that it should be permitted when there is no valid reason for it. No societal good is furthered by allowing attorneys to engage in a routine practice of secretly recording their conversations with others, and there is considerable potential for societal harm.
>
> Accordingly, while this Committee concludes that there are circumstances other than those addressed in our prior opinions in which an attorney may tape a conversation without disclosure to all participants, we adhere to the view that undisclosed taping as a routine practice is ethically impermissible. We further believe that attorneys should be extremely reluctant to engage in undisclosed taping and that, in assessing the need for it, attorneys should carefully consider whether their conduct, if it became known, would be considered by the general public to be fair and honorable.

Association of the Bar of the City of New York, Comm. on Jud. & Prof. Ethics, *Formal Opin.* 2003-02: "Undisclosed Taping of Conversations by Lawyers" (2003).

Alabama (like most states) has also adopted a rule generally proscribing conduct involving "dishonesty, fraud, deceit, or misrepresentation" by an attorney.

Ala. R. Prof. Conduct 8.4(c). Did Dean violate this rule? The dissenting judge in *Gaylard* obviously thought so.

III. The Scope of Discovery

The scope of formal discovery established by Federal Rule of Civil Procedure 26(b)(1) is sweeping, virtually creating a presumption of discoverability:

> Unless otherwise limited by court order, the scope of discovery is as follows: Parties may obtain discovery regarding any nonprivileged matter that is relevant to any party's claim or defense and proportional to the needs of the case, considering the importance of the issues at stake in the action, the amount in controversy, the parties' relative access to relevant information, the parties' resources, the importance of the discovery in resolving the issues, and whether the burden or expense of the proposed discovery outweighs its likely benefit. Information within this scope of discovery need not be admissible in evidence to be discoverable.

A party can therefore use the discovery rules to obtain documents, electronic information (including e-mails), access to property, pictures, audiotapes, medical records, inspections, and the testimony of parties and non-party witnesses, whether or not the information would be admissible at trial, as long as it is not protected by one of a relatively few evidentiary privileges, it is relevant to any party's claim or defense, and it is proportional (in terms of the listed factors, including importance and burden or expense) to the needs of the case, whether or not it is admissible in evidence. Consider the effect of this Rule on what the parties may discover in *Painter v. Toyota.*

A. Discoverable "Matter"

Toyota undoubtedly has thousands of nonprivileged written documents about the model of Camry in which Painter was injured. But it also has thousands of electronically stored files that have never been produced in hard copies, as well as e-mails and maybe even instant messages (if used by its employees on the job) about the Camry. Or maybe it *had* such electronic information, but it has since been deleted, or backed up automatically for storage off the employees' hard drives and *then* deleted, except that, in the computer world, "deleted" often just means that the file remains on the hard drive until and unless it is overwritten by other data.

Q **Are these electronic data discoverable?**

A Why not? The scope-of-discovery rule reaches "matter," not just written documents or tangible things. Matter—information—is discoverable whatever its form, if it is also nonprivileged and relevant. The form of the matter only impacts the discovery tool that is appropriate to demand it, the method of production, and whether (and how) the court will take into account the costs of compliance in deciding to limit discovery or allocating the costs between the respondent and the discovering party. (Typically, each party pays for its own costs in taking or providing discovery, unless the court otherwise orders.)

B. ... That Is Not Privileged

Suppose, during discovery, Toyota's lawyer asks Painter what he told his psychiatrist about his mental state, even though Painter seeks no damages for mental injuries or pain and suffering. Or Painter's lawyer asks Toyota what legal advice its General Counsel has offered, if any, for handling litigation about the Camry accelerator. These questions would ordinarily be objectionable at trial because they call for "privileged information." They are also beyond the scope of permitted discovery for the same reason: Rule 26(b)(1) targets only information that is "nonprivileged."

Privileged information is usually a communication made in confidence during the course and in furtherance of a relationship—lawyer-client, doctor-patient, priest-penitent—that society has chosen to promote and protect. Such communications, "which by usual evidentiary standards may be highly probative as well as trustworthy, are excluded [from admission as evidence] because their disclosure is inimical to a principle or relationship (predominantly nonevidentiary in nature) that society deems worthy of preserving and fostering." Graham C. Lilly, Law of Evidence § 9.1, at 437–38 (3d ed. 1996). Thus, the privilege against self-incrimination reflects the principle codified in the Fifth Amendment ("No person . . . shall be compelled in any criminal case to be a witness against himself"), while the lawyer-client, spousal, and priest-penitent privileges all protect the confidentiality of communications in these socially encouraged relationships. These privileges are established by common law, constitutional law, or statute, and you will study them in detail in Evidence.

Q **A good strategy?** But can't Painter just be made to testify during discovery about his conversations with his psychiatrist and then simply object later if Toyota tries to offer that testimony at trial? Can't Toyota use the same strategy respecting the legal advice from its General Counsel?

A The answer is no, if they care about the confidentiality of their communications and not just about what is offered against them at trial. Even disclosure during pretrial discovery might deter Painter from speaking candidly with his psychiatrist, or Toyota from getting candid advice from its General Counsel, to the detriment of relationships that society otherwise promotes. A privilege therefore protects not only against admission at trial, but also against discovery.

This protection is not self-executing, however. When a party wishes to resist discovery by invoking a privilege, Rule 26(b)(5) requires that it make the claim expressly and "describe the nature of the documents, communications, or tangible things not produced or disclosed—and do so in a manner that, without revealing information itself privileged or protected, will enable other parties to assess the claim." Thus, Toyota may object to production of a document on the grounds of lawyer-client privilege by asserting in writing that "Toyota objects to the production of Document 112, from [its General Counsel] to Henry Toyota, President of Toyota, dated Oct. 12, 2020, on the grounds that it is a confidential communication from lawyer to client prepared during and in furtherance of the lawyer-client relationship."

C. . . . That Is Relevant to Any Party's Claim or Defense

Painter thinks it would be useful to know whether Toyota has experienced accelerator problems in the Sienna and the Corolla similar to those he had in his Camry, and he therefore requests that Toyota produce all accelerator repair records for these cars during discovery. Toyota believes that it might be embarrassing to Painter to inquire in discovery about his premarital sexual liaisons. Are these inquiries within the scope of permitted discovery?

Before 2000, discovery was permitted on matters relevant to the "subject matter involved in the pending action." Rule 26(b)(1). This generous relevancy standard did little to curtail discovery. Under the old standard, Painter could discover

> any matter that bears on, or that reasonably could lead to other matter involved that could bear on, any issue that is or may be in the case. Consistently with the notice pleading system established by the Rule, discovery is not limited to issues raised by the pleadings, for discovery itself is designed to help define and clarify the issues. Nor is discovery limited to the merits of the case, for a variety of fact-oriented issues may arise during litigation that aren't related to the merits.

Oppenheimer Fund, Inc. v. Sanders, 437 U.S. 340, 351 & n.12 (1978) (citations omitted). Painter alleges that an accelerator problem or design defect (among others) caused his accident. If Toyota's other models use the same accelerator as the Camry, or even a similar one, his discovery request would appear "relevant to the subject matter." By contrast, Toyota's request concerning Painter's liaisons clearly is not, unless Painter has complained of a loss of sexual function or possibly loss of consortium, in which case Toyota's inquiry might, conceivably, be relevant to the subject matter of his injuries.

In 2000, Rule 26(b)(1) was amended to permit discovery only of matter "relevant to any party's claim or defense." The new standard was intended to narrow the scope of discovery. But because the policy of notice pleading is to allow minimal pleading to initiate suit, with liberal amendment thereafter, most jurisdictions that have adopted such a policy will be equally liberal in construing the scope of permissible discovery, however it is phrased in their rules. On the other hand, there is a point at which the material sought is so remote from the existing or probable issues in the litigation, or the chain from inadmissible but relevant information to admissible evidence is so attenuated, that the burden of such discovery will substantially exceed the benefit. Painter's request for all repair records on other models may be approaching that point; Toyota's inquiry into his private life probably exceeds it. In such cases, some courts may try to restrict discovery by taking a narrow view of relevancy, possibly invoking the new standard of relevancy for discovery. But other Rules provide more direct relief by limiting discovery to what is proportional to the needs of the case (see below) and by authorizing the court to enter a protective order against relevant, but unduly burdensome discovery. Rule 26(c) (discussed in Chapter 23).

D. ... That Is Proportional to the Needs of the Case

Assume that Painter makes a discovery request for the accelerator repair records for all Toyota cars with the same or similar accelerator, including employee e-mails concerning accelerator problems. Such evidence is relevant to his claim, in that it might help him prove both that there was a defect and that Toyota knew but failed to undertake a timely fix. Defect and knowledge may both be elements of a product liability claim, and such evidence may make existence of the elements more likely. On the other hand, Toyota may have thousands of such records, and its e-mail traffic may be stored on forms of electronic media that are expensive to search. If Painter's claim is just for property damage (the car costs $30,000), he has other less expensive sources of similar evidence (for example, just the repair records and e-mails concerning his car), and it would cost Toyota $1,000,000 to comply with his request, is allowing the discovery "proportional to the needs of the case"? Rule 26(b)(1)'s list of multiple factors in the proportionality calculus necessarily makes answers to questions like this fact-dependent and case-specific. Consider how the court performed that calculus in the following case.

READING *OXBOW CARBON & MINERALS LLC v. UNION PACIFIC RAILROAD CO.*
In this antitrust suit by Oxbow against defendants for conspiring in anticompetitive conduct, the defendants sought discovery of what were apparently electronically stored records from Oxbow's founder, CEO, and principal owner, William I. Koch. (Koch is the billionaire brother of Frederick and Charles Koch and twin of David Koch. Oxbow has recently been ranked the 226th largest company in the United States with $2 billion in revenues.) Oxbow resisted on grounds of undue burden and cost.

- Assuming that Koch's records are business records relating to the Oxbow conglomerate, are they relevant to Oxbow's antitrust claim? If so, and if Oxbow makes no claim of privilege, why isn't that enough to require production?
- Do the defendants have the burden to show that their request is "proportional to the needs of the case," or does Oxbow have the burden to show the opposite? Why?
- Rule 26(b)(1) directs the court to consider "the importance of the issues at stake in the action"? "Importance" to whom?
- What is "information asymmetry," and how does it apply to this case?

OXBOW CARBON & MINERALS LLC v. UNION PACIFIC RAILROAD CO.

322 F.R.D. 1 (D.D.C. 2017)

G. Michael Harvey, United States Magistrate Judge . . . .

[Eds.—Five related companies (collectively, "Oxbow") that mine and sell coal and petroleum coke ("petcoke") sued Union Pacific and BNSF Railway Company (railroad companies with which Oxbow contracts to ship coal and petcoke) for conspiring to engage in anticompetitive conduct from 2004 to 2012. During the ensuing discovery, defendants filed a motion asking the court to compel Oxbow to add William I. Koch ("Koch") (Oxbow's founder, CEO, and principal owner) as a document custodian whose records would be searched for material responsive to defendants' discovery requests. Defendants believed that Koch's records contained information that would, among other things, reveal that market forces—as opposed to defendants' alleged collusion—contributed to the increasing rail freight costs and Oxbow's lost profits.

After opposing the defendants' request on grounds of undue burden and excessive cost, Oxbow agreed to analyze a random sample of Koch's digital records using agreed-upon search terms to provide concrete numbers regarding the responsiveness of Koch's documents to the terms and a basis for negotiating new search terms, if necessary. From the sampling (which cost $57,198), Oxbow determined that 11.67 percent of the "hits" in the sampled documents were actually responsive to the search terms and produced them to defendants. Based on that experience, Oxbow estimated that it would cost approximately $85,000 to process, review, and produce the remainder of Koch's documents to the defendants, bringing the total cost of the effort to approximately $142,000. When, citing this cost, Oxbow declined to produce the remainder of those documents, defendants renewed their motion to compel. The Magistrate Judge then conducted the following proportionality analysis of the discovery request.] . . .

LEGAL STANDARD. . . .

> "[N]o single factor is designed to outweigh the other factors in determining whether the discovery sought is proportional," and all proportionality determinations must be made on a case-by-case basis. *Williams [v. BASF Catalysts, LLC,* Civ. Action No. 11-1754, 2017 WL 3317295, at *4 (D.N.J. Aug. 3, 2017)]. To be sure, however, "the amendments to Rule 26(b) do not alter the basic allocation of the burden on the party resisting discovery to—in order to successfully resist a motion to compel—specifically object and show that . . . a discovery request would impose an undue burden or expense or is otherwise objectionable."

Mir v. L-3 Commc'ns Integrated Sys., L.P., 319 F.R.D. 220, 226 (N.D. Tex. 2016).

DISCUSSION

A. The Proportionality of Defendants' Discovery Request

1. The Importance of the Issues at Stake

This first Rule 26 factor calls for the Court to "examine[ ] 'the significance of the substantive issues [at stake in the litigation], as measured in philosophic, social, or institutional terms.' " [*Arrow Enter. Computing Solutions, Inc. v. BlueAlly, LLC*, No. 5:15-CV-37-FL, 2017 WL 876266, at *4 (E.D.N.C. Mar. 3, 2017)] (quoting Fed. R. Civ. P. 26 advisory committee's note). For example, courts should carefully scrutinize discovery requests in "cases in public policy spheres, such as employment practices, free speech, and other matters," which often "seek[ ] to vindicate vitally important personal and public values" and "may have importance far beyond the monetary amount involved." Fed. R. Civ. P. 26 advisory committee's note. By Oxbow's own suggestion, the instant case involves important issues and has the potential to broadly impact a wide range of third-parties not involved in the litigation. Oxbow has stated that a favorable ruling from this Court "could benefit all of America's shippers and consumers, saving billions of dollars a year in reduced rail freight charges in the United States." What is more, Koch himself has publicly accused Defendants of long relying on "overreaching and abusive behavior" to "shortchange[ ] the American consumer," and of "using aggressive tactics to prevent competition and intimidate customers," including "American farmers, miners[,] and shippers[.]"

Defendants, for their part, do not disagree with Oxbow's estimation of the significance of this case, noting that Oxbow has made serious allegations against Defendants that have the potential to impact many people. Accordingly, the undersigned finds that the importance of the issues at stake here weighs in favor of granting Defendants' discovery request, which Oxbow concedes will produce documents that are relevant to the resolution of this case's claims. *See BlueAlly*, 2017 WL 876266, at *4 (finding that this factor weighs against allowing discovery where the issues at stake in the case would not "have an impact beyond the parties involved").

2. The Amount in Controversy

Under the second proportionality factor, courts should "compare[ ] the cost of discovery to the amount in controversy to determine [the proposed discovery's] proportionality." *Id.* Here, Oxbow seeks to recover the more than $50,000,000 in illegal fuel surcharges it alleges were the result of the Defendants' collusion. It also seeks recovery of its "lost business and profits," and a trebling of its damages under 15 U.S.C. § 15. While Oxbow does not specifically quantify these damages in its Amended Complaint, Defendants have suggested that Oxbow seeks to recover over $150 million—a figure that Defendants do not appear to dispute. Meanwhile, Oxbow's estimated cost of complying with Defendants' proposed discovery is approximately $140,000, including the $57,197.95 that Oxbow has already spent on sampling Koch's documents. Given the very substantial amount of damages that Oxbow seeks to recover in this case, its cost of complying with the discovery request to produce information relevant to Defendants' defense of Oxbow's claims does not strike the undersigned as excessive. Accordingly, the Court finds that this factor, too, favors granting Defendants' discovery request.

3. The Parties' Relative Access to the Relevant Information

In considering this factor, courts look for "information asymmetry"—a circumstance in which one party has very little discoverable information while the other party has vast amounts of discoverable information. *See* Fed. R. Civ. P. 26 advisory committee's notes. In such a case, "the burden of responding to discovery lies heavier on the party who has more information, and properly so." *Id.* To the extent this factor is applicable here, any informational asymmetry favors Oxbow. **[Eds.—Meaning, as explained in the next sentence, that Oxbow is sitting on information to which the defendants have no other access.]** Indeed, neither party disputes that Koch is in possession of relevant, unique information, and there appears to be no other way for Defendants to obtain this information than moving to compel Oxbow to produce it. Accordingly, the Court finds that this factor militates in favor of granting Defendants' request.

4. The Parties' Resources

Taking into account the parties' resources, the Court again concludes that this factor weighs in favor of granting Defendants' request. While discovery should not be used to "wage a war of attrition or as a device to coerce a party," regardless of whether the party is "financially weak or affluent," *see* Fed. R. Civ. P. 26 advisory committee's notes, Oxbow represented at the hearing in this matter that it does not object to Defendants' request based on an inability to pay for it. Accordingly, the undersigned sees no reason to deny Defendants' request on this basis.

5. The Importance of the Discovery in Resolving the Issues

This fifth factor requires courts to determine whether "[t]he issues at stake are at the very heart of [the] litigation." *Labrier v. State Farm Fire and Casualty Co.*, 314 F.R.D. 637, 643 (W.D. Mo. 2016). Though Oxbow initially objected to the relevance of any documents in Koch's possession, it has since acknowledged that Koch's records contain relevant and unique documents, although not in the same ratio as other Oxbow custodians' records, and has produced a portion of these documents to Defendants. The Court appreciates that Koch's files do not appear to contain as a high a proportion of responsive documents as the files of custodians who dealt exclusively with Oxbow's coal and petcoke business, but it strains reason to suggest that the principal owner and CEO of a company, who has publicly commented on the importance and magnitude of litigation to which his company is a party and in which the financial health of his company is at issue would have no unique information relevant to that litigation in his possession. While it may be too early in the production process to determine exactly how significant Koch's records are, the categories of relevant documents identified by Defendants after reviewing the approximately 1,300 documents produced from Koch's files indicates to the Court that Defendants' discovery request has merit and is not intended to be the first strike in a war of attrition or a coercion tactic. Accordingly, the Court concludes that this factor favors granting Defendants' proposed discovery.

6. Whether the Burden or Expense of the Proposed Discovery Outweighs Its Likely Benefit

Oxbow rests its argument entirely on this final factor, asserting that it is the most important of the Rule 26 proportionality factors and counsels against granting Defendants' proposed discovery. In support of its argument, Oxbow contends that its random sampling analysis suggests that approximately half of the agreed-upon search terms' hits on Koch's documents are false positives with no or only marginal relevance to the litigation. To be sure, Oxbow also concedes that the cost of processing Koch's records for discovery is far less than it originally estimated and that the search terms narrowed the scope of Koch's responsive documents far more than it originally anticipated. Nevertheless, it asserts that the $85,000 that it estimates it will take to review and produce the remaining responsive documents from Koch's files is prohibitively burdensome.

The Court disagrees. The cost of reviewing and producing Koch's documents does not strike the undersigned as unduly burdensome or disproportionate, especially given the discovery conducted to date and the damages that Oxbow seeks in this action. Plaintiffs' counsel explained at the second hearing in this matter that Oxbow has spent $1.391 million to date on reviewing and producing approximately 584,000 documents from its nineteen other custodians and Oxbow's email archive. And again, Oxbow seeks tens of millions of dollars from Defendants. Through that lens, the estimated cost of reviewing and producing Koch's responsive documents—even considering the total approximate cost of $142,000 for that effort, which includes the expense of the sampling effort—while certainly high, is not so unreasonably high as to warrant rejecting Defendants' request out of hand. *See Zubulake v. UBS Warburg, LLC*, 217 F.R.D. 309, 321 (S.D.N.Y. 2003) (explaining, in the context of a cost-shifting request, that "[a] response to a discovery request costing $100,000 sounds (and is) costly, but in a case potentially worth millions of dollars, the cost of responding may not be unduly burdensome"); *Xpedior Creditor Trust v. Credit Suisse First Boston (USA), Inc.*, 309 F. Supp. 2d 459, 466 (S.D.N.Y. 2003) (finding no "undue burden or expense" to justify cost-shifting where the requested discovery cost approximately $400,000 but the litigation involved at least $68.7 million in damages)....

In light of the above analysis—including the undersigned's assessment of each of the Rule 26 proportionality factors, all of which weigh in favor of granting Defendants' motion—the Court is unwilling to find that the burden of reviewing the remaining 65,000 responsive documents for a fraction of the cost of discovery to date should preclude Defendants' proposed request. *See BlueAlly*, 2017 WL 876266, at *5 ("This [last Rule 26] factor may combine all the previous factors into a final analysis of burdens versus benefits." (citing Fed. R. Civ. P. 26 advisory committee's notes)). For all of the reasons stated above, and absent any evidence establishing that Defendants are using the discovery of Koch's records to wage a war of attrition or as a device to coerce Oxbow, the Court finds that Defendants' motion must be granted....

B. Oxbow's Request to Shift Discovery Costs to Defendants

In the event that the Court grants Defendants' motion, Oxbow asks in the alternative that the Court direct Defendants to bear the costs of the production, either in whole or in part. The Court denies that request. "The presumption under the Federal Rules of Civil Procedure is that the producing party bears the costs of complying with a discovery request," but "the Court may shift a portion of the costs to the requesting party in the event that the discovery request would unduly burden the producing party." *D'Onofrio v. SFX Sports Group, Inc.*, 254 F.R.D. 129, 134 (D.D.C. 2008) (citing *Peskoff v. Faber*, 251 F.R.D. 59, 61 (D.D.C. 2008)). . . .

Oxbow has failed to rebut the presumption imposed by the Federal Rules of Civil Procedure that it should bear the cost of complying with Defendants' proposed discovery. . . .*

Notes and Questions: Proportional Discovery

1. Isn't it relevant? This is obviously hard to answer definitively without knowing more about the claims and defense. Even then, it may not be easy. *See Wright & Miller* § 2008 ("[T]he boundaries defining information that is relevant to the subject matter involved in the action are necessarily vague and it is practically impossible to state a general rule by which they can be drawn.").

But we know that defendants will try to defend partly on the theory that market forces, rather than their alleged collusion, contributed to Oxbow's lost profits, and we can reasonably guess that Koch's records relating to Oxbow might address market forces. Such records are therefore likely relevant to the defendants' "market forces" defense. And, of course, the sampling arguably confirms that guess, by identifying some records that are responsive to the agreed-upon search terms, which were presumably themselves relevant. No wonder then that the court finds "it strains reason to suggest that the principal owner and CEO of a company, who has publicly commented on the importance and magnitude of litigation to which his company is a party and in which the financial health of his company is at issue would have no unique information relevant to that litigation in his possession."

But the relevancy of requested discovery is rarely the main issue. The real issue is far more often its breadth and burdensomeness. That is why it is not enough that the matter sought is relevant and nonprivileged; it must also be "proportional to the needs of the case."

2. The burden to show proportionality. The party seeking discovery has the burden of demonstrating relevancy, but Rule 26(b)(1) does not place a burden on that party to address "all proportionality considerations." Fed. R. Civ. P. 26(b)(1) advisory committee's notes to 2015 amendment. Most courts, like the *Oxbow*

* [Eds.—We explore "cost-shifting" for electronic discovery in the next chapter, p. 827.]

court, have placed the burden of showing disproportion on the party resisting discovery. That makes good sense. A key factor in the disproportionality analysis is the burden or expense of production, which are issues that the party resisting discovery is in the best position to determine.

3. Important to whom? If a plaintiff goes to the trouble of filing and serving the complaint, and the defendant defends, and they both fight hard enough to bring a discovery dispute before the court, then presumably they deem the issues at stake to be important. So, the "importance of the issues" must usually mean something more—issues that impact "personal and public values," according to the advisory committee. One way to read this is that any "issues [that] have an impact beyond the parties involved" support a presumption of discovery.

Don't confuse this with the other "importance" factor—"importance of the discovery in resolving the issues." That seems like a no-brainer in the proportionality calculus; the less useful the requested discovery for resolving the issues, the less proportional it will be to the needs of the case.

4. Information asymmetry. This refers to an imbalance in the parties' relative access to information. Often, for example, consumers like Painter who are injured by defective products have little or no information about how the product was designed or manufactured; the manufacturer like Toyota holds all the cards. This asymmetry is a factor that favors the consumer's discovery request. In *Oxbow*, it is defendants who have little or no access to information concerning Koch's take on market forces (say, Koch's e-mails lamenting the market forces (wind power?) that are eating into Oxbow's profits); Oxbow holds all the cards.

It may be hard to feel sorry for large corporate defendants like Union Pacific or BNSF, but consideration of the asymmetry and "parties' resources" factors together can also help level the discovery playing field for small and often resource-strapped parties like individual consumers or employees, tort victims, or victims of civil rights violations when they are up against institutional parties like corporations or governments. Of course, considering such factors does not close the frequent gap in lawyer resources.

5. Moving the proportionality standard. At first glance, it may seem odd that the standard was relocated from one part of the Rule to another without any change in its language. But the effect of the change is to reassign proportionality from being a mere discretionary "limitation" on discovery, Rule 26(b)(2)(C), to being an attribute of the "scope [of discovery] *in general*." Rule 26(b)(1) (emphasis added). Consequently, proportionality is now baked into every discovery request.

The increased emphasis on the proportionality inquiry may make sense when you consider the original purpose of the proportionality exception. That purpose was "to deal with 'the problem of overdiscovery,'" a problem now "exacerbated by the advent of e-discovery [discovery of electronically stored information like Koch's], and the rule makers moved the standard to reinforce its availability to curtail discovery." Fed. R. Civ. P. 26 advisory committee's notes to 2015 amendment (quoting the 1983 committee note). *See Black v. Buffalo Meat Serv., Inc.*, No. 15 CV 49S, 2016 WL 4363506 (W.D.N.Y. Aug. 16, 2016) (with this change, " 'the universe of discoverable information is smaller than before' ") (internal citation omitted).

The relocation of the language generated considerable controversy in light of the expected reduction in the "universe of discoverable information." In general, well-resourced defendants favored the change because they are usually the ones having to incur the often considerable cost of discovery that plaintiffs request. In contrast, plaintiffs' lawyers (especially lawyers who represent individuals against large entities) opposed the changes. These lawyers were concerned that corporate and institutional defendants (like governments) would find it easier to avoid disclosing damaging information that proves to be decisive in a plaintiff's case.

E. ... That Need Not Be Admissible

Painter wants to ask a Toyota mechanic during pretrial discovery what he has heard about the alleged defect in the Camry. His answer may well constitute inadmissible "hearsay" under the rules of evidence—an out-of-court statement that in many cases is not admissible *at trial* to prove the truth of the matter stated. (The rules of evidence are concerned about the reliability of such statements because they were not subjected, when made, to the rigors of cross-examination.) Or Painter may demand in discovery that Toyota produce documents showing changes in the design of the Camry that were made *after* his accident. This information, too, would ordinarily be inadmissible *at trial* to prove Toyota's liability. (The rules of evidence are concerned that making such evidence admissible might discourage parties from making necessary repairs after an accident.)

Q **Can either party refuse discovery on the grounds that the evidence sought in these examples would be inadmissible at trial?**

A No. Rule 26(b)(1) does not limit the scope of discovery to admissible evidence. Information otherwise within the scope of discovery (that is, nonprivileged, relevant, and proportional to the needs of the case) "need not be admissible in evidence to be discoverable." It may, for example, only form a link in a chain of discovery that could lead to admissible evidence. For example, Painter may be able to locate witnesses from the mechanic's hearsay testimony who could testify at trial from their own personal knowledge. Painter may learn of the existence of other admissible documents or witnesses from the inadmissible post-accident design documents he demanded, or he may try to offer them into evidence at trial for a purpose other than to establish liability.

Of course, in the unlikely event that Painter and Toyota actually go to trial, the Rules of Evidence will apply and the evidence offered must be admissible. Painter will ordinarily not be permitted to offer hearsay evidence (unless it qualifies for an exception to the evidentiary rule against hearsay) or to use evidence of Toyota's subsequent design modifications to establish their liability, because the Rules of Evidence exclude such evidence. Producing information in response to a valid discovery request ordinarily does not waive any objection the producer has to admission of such evidence at trial (unless the information is privileged, as we discuss below).

Notes and Questions: The Scope of Discovery

1. The lawyer-client privilege. The general scope of the modern attorney-client privilege is set out in the *Restatement (3d) of the Law Governing Lawyers* §§ 68, 70:

> Except as otherwise provided in this *Restatement*, the attorney-client privilege may be invoked as provided in § 86 with respect to:
>
> (1) a communication
> (2) made between privileged persons
> (3) in confidence
> (4) for the purpose of obtaining or providing legal assistance for the client. . . .
>
> Privileged persons within the meaning of § 68 are the client (including a prospective client), the client's lawyer, agents of either who facilitate communications between them, and agents of the lawyer who facilitate the representation. . . .

The privilege applies only to the communications between lawyer and client and not to the facts that are communicated. Thus, although Painter is not required to disclose his communication to his lawyer regarding his awareness of defects in his car, he can be asked directly what he knows about such defects. Similarly, if a client discloses to his lawyer that he ran a red light, the communication is privileged, but the client must still admit the fact that he ran the light if he is asked in a written interrogatory or in a question during his testimony at a deposition or at trial. A client cannot protect facts from discovery just by telling them to his lawyer, even when he tells the lawyer for the bona fide purpose of obtaining legal advice.

2. The corporate lawyer-client privilege. Suppose Toyota's lawyer communicated with Toyota's own employees about the design of the Camry and Painter's claims of defects. Would those communications be subject to the lawyer-client privilege? If so, does this mean that *all* communications between corporate employees at every level and the corporate counsel are protected by the lawyer-client privilege if they otherwise meet the requirements for the privilege? The result would be that corporations would enjoy a broad lawyer-client privilege that could insulate them from much discovery to which individuals are still subject. (Note that we encountered a similar problem in construing the ethical limitations on informal discovery against corporate parties in section II of this chapter.)

For this reason, some courts limited the corporate lawyer-client privilege to communications made by and to a "control group" of employees in a position to control or take a substantial part in deciding corporate action in response to legal advice. *See, e.g., City of Philadelphia v. Westinghouse Electric Corp.*, 210 F. Supp. 483, 485 (E.D. Pa. 1963). In *Upjohn Co. v. United States*, 449 U.S. 383 (1981), the United States Supreme Court rejected the control group test for applying the corporate lawyer-client privilege under federal law. It reasoned that the privilege exists to protect not only giving legal advice, but also giving information to help the corporate lawyer formulate that advice. The control group test was too narrow to protect necessary information-gathering from employees below the control group and therefore might hinder the rendering of legal advice. Instead of expressly stating a new test for the corporate privilege, however, the Court only impliedly applied one to the facts:

> The communications at issue were made by Upjohn employees to counsel for Upjohn acting as such, at the direction of corporate superiors in order to secure legal advice from counsel. As the Magistrate found, "Mr. Thomas consulted with the Chairman of the Board and outside counsel and thereafter conducted a factual investigation to determine the nature and extent of the questionable payments and to be in a position to give legal advice to the company with respect to the payments." Information, not available from upper-echelon management, was needed to supply a basis for legal advice concerning compliance with securities and tax laws, foreign laws, currency regulations, duties to shareholders, and potential litigation in each of these areas. The communications concerned matters within the scope of the employees' corporate duties, and the employees themselves were sufficiently aware that they were being questioned in order that the corporation could obtain legal advice. The questionnaire identified Thomas as "the company's General Counsel" and referred in its opening sentence to the possible illegality of payments such as the ones on which information was sought. A statement of policy accompanying the questionnaire clearly indicated the legal implications of the investigation. . . . Pursuant to explicit instructions from the Chairman of the Board, the communications were considered "highly confidential" when made, and have been kept confidential by the company. Consistent with the underlying purposes of the attorney-client privilege, these communications must be protected against compelled disclosure.

449 U.S. at 394–95.

3. Issue analysis: Applying the attorney-client privilege to a communication. You will learn more about this privilege in Evidence, but consider the following issue for now.

The issue. Lawyer Dickens is a business partner with Harris in a hedge fund called Leverage Plus. After the fund loses a lot of money, a disappointed investor sues the fund for mismanagement and seeks discovery of e-mails between Dickens and Harris discussing the fund's declining financial prospects and Dickens's ideas about better investments. The e-mails are marked "PRIVILEGED AND CONFIDENTIAL." Leverage objects to this discovery, invoking the lawyer-client privilege. Assuming that Leverage has the burden of establishing the privilege, are these e-mails privileged and protected from discovery for that reason?

The suggested analysis. Leverage is invoking the privilege and is presumably the client, but the e-mails are to Harris. Yet, Harris, as a business partner in Leverage Plus, may qualify as its agent and therefore be a "privileged person." Dickens is a lawyer, but it is not clear whether he was acting as a lawyer to Leverage when he sent the e-mails.

Assuming, for sake of argument, that Dickens and Harris qualify as "privileged persons," we can't tell whether Dickens's e-mails were sent in confidence. Courts don't draw such an assumption just because the sender says so by affixing the label "PRIVILEGED AND CONFIDENTIAL." You'll soon learn that virtually *all* e-mails sent by lawyers and by many corporate officers at work contain some similar or more draconian label. Calling it so does not make it so. The burden rests with the party invoking the privilege to establish a "foundation" for it. A label may be one factor that helps, but it is neither sufficient nor necessary.

Assuming that the sparse facts are consistent with an expectation of confidentiality, the real problem here is the purpose of the e-mails. The e-mails are certainly a communication, but do they meet the other standard of *Restatement* § 68? The *Restatement* formula requires that the communication be made in confidence for the purpose of obtaining or providing *legal* assistance for Leverage Plus. We protect attorney-client communications only to promote this purpose. Here the subject of the e-mails was the fund's declining business prospects and "ideas about better investments," not legal advice.

The privilege does not apply to Harris's e-mails on these facts and assumptions. But the multi-factor *Restatement* test is highly sensitive to the facts. Even small factual variations may make a difference to the analysis.

Q **4. A lawyer's communications with witnesses.** Suppose Toyota's lawyer communicated with witnesses to Painter's accident, promising to keep their statements in confidence and made notes of his communications. Are those notes subject to the lawyer-client privilege?

A This one you can answer without more facts. It is not sufficient that the communication was made in confidence, if it is not between "privileged parties," or if it was in the presence of strangers. Toyota's lawyer is certainly talking to witnesses to assist in a legal proceeding—the lawsuit—but they are strangers to the lawyer-client relationship, and the facts they relay are not facts from a privileged party, like the client. These notes are not protected by the lawyer-client privilege. (This does not mean that they are necessarily discoverable, however. As we will see, they may enjoy some qualified protection as the lawyer's "work product.")

To put it another way, the law of evidentiary privilege does not protect *all* communications made in confidence, let alone all private conversations, but only confidential communications that are essential to a relationship that society favors—like the lawyer-client, physician-patient, or priest-penitent relationships. An expectation of confidentiality is a necessary element of most privileges, but it is not sufficient. You may expect confidentiality when you tell your best friend a secret, but your expectation does not protect your secret from discovery.

F. Work Product

The work product of a lawyer can include her notes of an interview with a witness, an index of documents or deposition, an abstract of a document or deposition, a photograph or diagram, a research memo, or even something as crude as her yellow highlighting on a copy of a judicial opinion. Some cases and commentators speak of *work product* protection from discovery as a "privilege." Because this protection is not aimed at the protection of confidential communications, however, it is more accurate to speak simply of a *work product protection* or *qualified immunity* from discovery.

An Example of Work Product

MEMORANDUM

TO: Carla Moskowitz, Partner
FROM: Al Paretti, Office Investigator
RE: Robinson witness interview in Reynolds v. Tulsa, Our File #2009-117
DATE: August 17, 2020

As requested I interviewed Jonas Benson on August 16, 2020. Jonas was a witness to the arrest of our client, Willie Reynolds, by Tulsa police officers on September 28, 2019. You asked me to get Benson's story, to give you my assessment of whether he will make a favorable witness, and to try to feel out whether he will cooperate with us in our suit arising out of Reynolds's arrest.

First, let me say that while Benson's description of the incident certainly was favorable to our position that the police used excessive force, I have several reasons to doubt his credibility. First, his version of the facts varies from all others (including our client's) on several obvious factual points. It seems likely that he did not actually see the events at all, or his view was blocked, or he was too inebriated to really take it in. Second, I had the definite impression that he was trying to tell a story that we wanted to hear, and that he might be angling for some kind of payment or something to testify in our favor. Third, when I came back later in the interview to several points he had described earlier, his testimony was inconsistent with what he had said before. I conclude that he is unlikely to provide credible testimony and might seriously hurt our case if the jury concludes that he is trying to protect a friend. (Benson is a friend and frequent drinking buddy of Reynolds.)

At any rate, here is a description of Benson's testimony.

On the evening of September 28, 2019, I went to Carson's Bar & Grill with Willie Reynolds to drink beer and see a baseball game on the big screen TV. Willie and I were there for a few hours. We each had a couple of . . . .

In preparing for litigation and for trial, lawyers, clients, and their agents and employees produce many documents reflecting their work. These documents often include not only statements of fact, but also legal or strategic assessments of what evidence to present at trial, the credibility of witnesses, the strength of legal positions, settlement prospects, and discovery planning. Naturally, lawyers consider such documents confidential and resist their disclosure in discovery even though they are "relevant to the claims and defenses in the action" under Federal Rule 26(b)(1). The Federal Rules did not originally address such "work product" issues, but the problem emerged early and soon reached the Supreme Court in *Hickman v. Taylor*.

1. The Seminal Case: *Hickman v. Taylor*

READING HICKMAN v. TAYLOR. The tugboat *J.M. Taylor* sank with loss of life. The tugboat owners, expecting to be sued by survivors and next of kin, retained lawyer Fortenbaugh to help them prepare for suit. He interviewed witnesses to the accident. When suit was eventually filed against his client, the plaintiffs sought to discover Fortenbaugh's notes of the interviews. Fortenbaugh objected, but the lower court overruled his objections.

- As you read *Hickman*, visualize lawyer Fortenbaugh's work product. We mean that literally: What did Fortenbaugh's work product look like?
- What are three principle(s) this protection advances? (You'll have to look at Justice Jackson's concurring opinion as well as the majority opinion.)
- Under what circumstances would the protection from discovery be overcome and discovery of work product allowed?
- Why didn't the Supreme Court find those circumstances present in *Hickman*?

Note that when this case was decided, the Federal Rules were silent about work product; Fed. R. Civ. P. 26(b) was subsequently amended to codify the principles declared in the case.

HICKMAN v. TAYLOR

329 U.S. 495 (1947)

Mr. Justice Murphy delivered the opinion of the Court.

This case presents an important problem under the Federal Rules of Civil Procedure as to the extent to which a party may inquire into oral and written statements of witnesses, or other information, secured by an adverse party's counsel in the course of preparation for possible litigation after a claim has arisen. Examination into a person's files and records, including those resulting from the professional activities of an attorney, must be judged with care. It is not without reason that various safeguards have been established to preclude unwarranted excursions into the privacy of a man's work. At the same time, public policy supports reasonable and necessary inquiries. Properly to balance these competing interests is a delicate and difficult task.

On February 7, 1943, the tug "J. M. Taylor" sank while engaged in helping to tow a car float of the Baltimore & Ohio Railroad across the Delaware River at Philadelphia. The accident was apparently unusual in nature, the cause of it still being unknown. Five of the nine crew members were drowned. Three days later the tug owners and the underwriters employed a law firm, of which respondent Fortenbaugh is a member, to defend them against potential suits by representatives of the deceased crew members and to sue the railroad for damages to the tug.

A public hearing was held on March 4, 1943, before the United States Steamboat Inspectors, at which the four survivors were examined. This testimony was recorded and made available to all interested parties. Shortly thereafter, Fortenbaugh privately interviewed the survivors and took statements from them with an eye toward the anticipated litigation; the survivors signed these statements on March 29. Fortenbaugh also interviewed other persons believed to have some information relating to the accident and in some cases he made memoranda of what they told him. At the time when Fortenbaugh secured the statements of the survivors, representatives of two of the deceased crew members had been in communication with him. Ultimately claims were presented by representatives of all five of the deceased; four of the claims, however, were settled without litigation. The fifth claimant, petitioner herein, brought suit in a federal court under the Jones Act on November 26, 1943, naming as defendants the two tug owners, individually and as partners, and the railroad.

One year later, petitioner filed 39 interrogatories directed to the tug owners. The 38th interrogatory read:

> State whether any statements of the members of the crews of the Tugs "J. M. Taylor" and "Philadelphia" or of any other vessel were taken in connection with the towing of the car float and the sinking of the Tug "John M. Taylor." Attach hereto exact copies of all such statements if in writing, and if oral, set forth in detail the exact provisions of any such oral statements or reports.

Supplemental interrogatories asked whether any oral or written statements, records, reports or other memoranda had been made concerning any matter relative to the towing operation, the sinking of the tug, the salvaging and repair of the tug, and the death of the deceased. If the answer was in the affirmative, the tug owners were then requested to set forth the nature of all such records, reports, statements or other memoranda.

The tug owners, through Fortenbaugh, answered all of the interrogatories except No. 38 and the supplemental ones just described. While admitting that statements of the survivors had been taken, they declined to summarize or set forth the contents. They did so on the ground that such requests called "for privileged matter obtained in preparation for litigation" and constituted "an attempt to obtain indirectly counsel's private files." It was claimed that answering these requests "would involve practically turning over not only the complete files, but also the telephone records and, almost, the thoughts of counsel."

In connection with the hearing on these objections, Fortenbaugh made a written statement and gave an informal oral deposition explaining the circumstances under which he had taken the statements. But he was not expressly asked in the deposition to produce the statements. The District Court for the Eastern District of Pennsylvania, sitting en banc, held that the requested matters were not privileged. The court then decreed that the tug owners and Fortenbaugh, as counsel and agent for the tug owners forthwith "Answer Plaintiff's 38th interrogatory and supplemental interrogatories; produce all written statements of witnesses obtained by Mr. Fortenbaugh, as counsel and agent for Defendants; state in substance any fact concerning this case which Defendants learned through oral statements made by witnesses to Mr. Fortenbaugh whether or not included in his private memoranda and produce Mr. Fortenbaugh's memoranda containing statements of fact by witnesses or to submit these memoranda to the Court for determination of those portions which should be revealed to Plaintiff." Upon their refusal, the court adjudged them in contempt and ordered them imprisoned until they complied.

The Third Circuit Court of Appeals, also sitting en banc, reversed the judgment of the District Court. It held that the information here sought was part of the "work product of the lawyer" and hence privileged from discovery under the Federal Rules of Civil Procedure. The importance of the problem, which has engendered a great divergence of views among district courts, led us to grant certiorari.

The pre-trial deposition-discovery mechanism established by Rules 26 to 37 is one of the most significant innovations of the Federal Rules of Civil Procedure. Under the prior federal practice, the pre-trial functions of notice-giving, issue-formulation and fact-revelation were performed primarily and inadequately by the pleadings. Inquiry into the issues and the facts before trial was narrowly confined and was often cumbersome in method. The new rules, however, restrict the pleadings to the task of general notice-giving and invest the deposition-discovery process with a vital role in the preparation for trial. The various instruments of discovery now serve (1) as a device, along with the pre-trial hearing under Rule 16, to narrow and clarify the basic issues between the parties, and (2) as a device for ascertaining the facts, or information as to the existence or whereabouts of facts, relative to those issues. Thus civil trials in the federal courts no longer need be carried on in the dark. The way is now clear, consistent with recognized privileges, for the parties to obtain the fullest possible knowledge of the issues and facts before trial.

There is an initial question as to which of the deposition-discovery rules is involved in this case. Petitioner, in filing his interrogatories, thought that he was proceeding under Rule 33. . . . **[Eds.—The Court noted that interrogatories and document production requests can be served only on parties, not on Fortenbaugh, and that he could not therefore be sanctioned for failing to comply with the production demand. In addition, his client could not be held in contempt for *his* failure to comply with a subpoena. After noting the "procedural irregularity," however, the Court chose to overlook it and reach the merits of the parties' discovery claims.]**

In urging that he has a right to inquire into the materials secured and prepared by Fortenbaugh, petitioner emphasizes that the deposition-discovery portions of the Federal Rules of Civil Procedure are designed to enable the parties to discover the true facts and to compel their disclosure wherever they may be found. It is said that inquiry may be made under these rules, epitomized by Rule 26, as to any relevant matter which is not privileged; and since the discovery provisions are to be applied as broadly and liberally as possible, the privilege limitation must be restricted to its narrowest bounds. On the premise that the attorney-client privilege is the one involved in this case, petitioner argues that it must be strictly confined to confidential communications made by a client to his attorney. And since the materials here in issue were secured by Fortenbaugh from third persons rather than from his clients, the tug owners, the conclusion is reached that these materials are proper subjects for discovery under Rule 26.

As additional support for this result, petitioner claims that to prohibit discovery under these circumstances would give a corporate defendant a tremendous advantage in a suit by an individual plaintiff. Thus in a suit by an injured employee against a railroad or in a suit by an insured person against an insurance company the corporate defendant could pull a dark veil of secrecy over all the pertinent facts it can collect after the claim arises merely on the assertion that such facts were gathered by its large staff of attorneys and claim agents. At the same time, the individual plaintiff, who often has direct knowledge of the matter in issue and has no counsel until some time after his claim arises could be compelled to disclose all the intimate details of his case. By endowing with immunity from disclosure all that a lawyer discovers in the course of his duties, it is said, the rights of individual litigants in such cases are drained of vitality and the lawsuit becomes more of a battle of deception than a search for truth.

But framing the problem in terms of assisting individual plaintiffs in their suits against corporate defendants is unsatisfactory. Discovery concededly may work to the disadvantage as well as to the advantage of individual plaintiffs. Discovery, in other words, is not a one-way proposition. It is available in all types of cases at the behest of any party, individual or corporate, plaintiff or defendant. The problem thus far transcends the situation confronting this petitioner. And we must view that problem in light of the limitless situations where the particular kind of discovery sought by petitioner might be used.

We agree, of course, that the deposition-discovery rules are to be accorded a broad and liberal treatment. No longer can the time-honored cry of "fishing expedition" serve to preclude a party from inquiring into the facts underlying his opponent's case. Mutual knowledge of all the relevant facts gathered by both parties is essential to proper litigation. To that end, either party may compel the other to disgorge whatever facts he has in his possession. The deposition-discovery procedure simply advances the stage at which the disclosure can be compelled from the time of trial to the period preceding it, thus reducing the possibility of surprise. But discovery, like all matters of procedure, has ultimate and necessary boundaries. As indicated by Rules 30(b) and (d) and 31(d), limitations inevitably arise when it can be shown that the examination is being conducted in bad faith or in such a manner as to annoy, embarrass or oppress the person subject to the inquiry. And as Rule 26(b) provides, further limitations come into existence when the inquiry touches upon the irrelevant or encroaches upon the recognized domains of privilege.

We also agree that the memoranda, statements and mental impressions in issue in this case fall outside the scope of the attorney-client privilege and hence are not protected from discovery on that basis. It is unnecessary here to delineate the content and scope of that privilege as recognized in the federal courts. For present purposes, it suffices to note that the protective cloak of this privilege does not extend to information which an attorney secures from a witness while acting for his client in anticipation of litigation. Nor does this privilege concern the memoranda, briefs, communications and other writings prepared by counsel for his own use in prosecuting his client's case; and it is equally unrelated to writings which reflect an attorney's mental impressions, conclusions, opinions or legal theories.

But the impropriety of invoking that privilege does not provide an answer to the problem before us. Petitioner has made more than an ordinary request for relevant, non-privileged facts in the possession of his adversaries or their counsel. He has sought discovery as of right of oral and written statements of witnesses whose identity is well known and whose availability to petitioner appears unimpaired. He has sought production of these matters after making the most searching inquiries of his opponents as to the circumstances surrounding the fatal accident, which inquiries were sworn to have been answered to the best of their information and belief. Interrogatories were directed toward all the events prior to, during and subsequent to the sinking of the tug. Full and honest answers to such broad inquiries would necessarily have included all pertinent information gleaned by Fortenbaugh through his interviews with the witnesses. Petitioner makes no suggestion, and we cannot assume, that the tug owners or Fortenbaugh were incomplete or dishonest in the framing of their answers. In addition, petitioner was free to examine the public testimony of the witnesses taken before the United States Steamboat Inspectors. We are thus dealing with an attempt to secure the production of written statements and mental impressions contained in the files and the mind of the attorney Fortenbaugh without any showing of necessity or any indication or claim that denial of such production would unduly prejudice the preparation of petitioner's case or cause him any hardship or injustice. For aught that appears, the essence of what petitioner seeks either has been revealed to him already through the interrogatories or is readily available to him direct from the witnesses for the asking.

The District Court, after hearing objections to petitioner's request, commanded Fortenbaugh to produce all written statements of witnesses and to state in substance any facts learned through oral statements of witnesses to him. Fortenbaugh was to submit any memoranda he had made of the oral statements so that the court might determine what portions should be revealed to petitioner. All of this was ordered without any showing by petitioner, or any requirement that he make a proper showing, of the necessity for the production of any of this material or any demonstration that denial of production would cause hardship or injustice. The court simply ordered production on the theory that the facts sought were material and were not privileged as constituting attorney-client communications.

In our opinion, neither Rule 26 nor any other rule dealing with discovery contemplates production under such circumstances. That is not because the subject matter is privileged or irrelevant, as those concepts are used in these rules. Here is simply an attempt, without purported necessity or justification, to secure written statements, private memoranda and personal recollections prepared or formed by an adverse party's counsel in the course of his legal duties. As such, it falls outside the arena of discovery and contravenes the public policy underlying the orderly prosecution and defense of legal claims. Not even the most liberal of discovery theories can justify unwarranted inquiries into the files and the mental impressions of an attorney.

Historically, a lawyer is an officer of the court and is bound to work for the advancement of justice while faithfully protecting the rightful interests of his clients. In performing his various duties, however, it is essential that a lawyer work with a certain degree of privacy, free from unnecessary intrusion by opposing parties and their counsel. Proper preparation of a client's case demands that he assemble information, sift what he considers to be the relevant from the irrelevant facts, prepare his legal theories and plan his strategy without undue and needless interference. That is the historical and the necessary way in which lawyers act within the framework of our system of jurisprudence to promote justice and to protect their clients' interests. This work is reflected, of course, in interviews, statements, memoranda, correspondence, briefs, mental impressions, personal beliefs, and countless other tangible and intangible ways—aptly though roughly termed by the Circuit Court of Appeals in this case as the "Work product of the lawyer." Were such materials open to opposing counsel on mere demand, much of what is now put down in writing would remain unwritten. An attorney's thoughts, heretofore inviolate, would not be his own. Inefficiency, unfairness and sharp practices would inevitably develop in the giving of legal advice and in the preparation of cases for trial. The effect on the legal profession would be demoralizing. And the interests of the clients and the cause of justice would be poorly served.

We do not mean to say that all written materials obtained or prepared by an adversary's counsel with an eye toward litigation are necessarily free from discovery in all cases. Where relevant and non-privileged facts remain hidden in an attorney's file and where production of those facts is essential to the preparation of one's case, discovery may properly be had. Such written statements and documents might, under certain circumstances, be admissible in evidence or give clues as to the existence or location of relevant facts. Or they might be useful for purposes of impeachment or corroboration. And production might be justified where the witnesses are no longer available or can be reached only with difficulty. Were production of written statements and documents to be precluded under such circumstances, the liberal ideals of the deposition-discovery portions of the Federal Rules of Civil Procedure would be stripped of much of their meaning. But the general policy against invading the privacy of an attorney's course of preparation is so well recognized and so essential to an orderly working of our system of legal procedure that a burden rests on the one who would invade that privacy to establish adequate reasons to justify production through a subpoena or court order. That burden, we believe, is necessarily implicit in the rules as now constituted.

Rule 30(b), as presently written, gives the trial judge the requisite discretion to make a judgment as to whether discovery should be allowed as to written statements secured from witnesses. But in the instant case there was no room for that discretion to operate in favor of the petitioner. No attempt was made to establish any reason why Fortenbaugh should be forced to produce the written statements. There was only a naked, general demand for these materials as of right and a finding by the District Court that no recognizable privilege was involved. That was insufficient to justify discovery under these circumstances and the court should have sustained the refusal of the tug owners and Fortenbaugh to produce.

But as to oral statements made by witnesses to Fortenbaugh, whether presently in the form of his mental impressions or memoranda, we do not believe that any showing of necessity can be made under the circumstances of this case so as to justify production. Under ordinary conditions, forcing an attorney to repeat or write out all that witnesses have told him and to deliver the account to his adversary gives rise to grave dangers of inaccuracy and untrustworthiness. No legitimate purpose is served by such production. The practice forces the attorney to testify as to what he remembers or what he saw fit to write down regarding witnesses' remarks. Such testimony could not qualify as evidence; and to use it for impeachment or corroborative purposes would make the attorney much less an officer of the court and much more an ordinary witness. The standards of the profession would thereby suffer.

Denial of production of this nature does not mean that any material, non-privileged facts can be hidden from the petitioner in this case. He need not be unduly hindered in the preparation of his case, in the discovery of facts or in his anticipation of his opponents' position. Searching interrogatories directed to Fortenbaugh and the tug owners, production of written documents and statements upon a proper showing and direct interviews with the witnesses themselves all serve to reveal the facts in Fortenbaugh's possession to the fullest possible extent consistent with public policy. Petitioner's counsel frankly admits that he wants the oral statements only to help prepare himself to examine witnesses and to make sure that he has overlooked nothing. That is insufficient under the circumstances to permit him an exception to the policy underlying the privacy of Fortenbaugh's professional activities. If there should be a rare situation justifying production of these matters, petitioner's case is not of that type.

We fully appreciate the wide-spread controversy among the members of the legal profession over the problem raised by this case. It is a problem that rests on what has been one of the most hazy frontiers of the discovery process. But until some rule or statute definitely prescribes otherwise, we are not justified in permitting discovery in a situation of this nature as a matter of unqualified right. When Rule 26 and the other discovery rules were adopted, this Court and the members of the bar in general certainly did not believe or contemplate that all the files and mental processes of lawyers were thereby opened to the free scrutiny of their adversaries. And we refuse to interpret the rules at this time so as to reach so harsh and unwarranted a result.

We therefore affirm the judgment of the Circuit Court of Appeals.

Affirmed.

Mr. Justice Jackson, concurring.

. . . The primary effect of the practice advocated here would be on the legal profession itself. But it too often is overlooked that the lawyer and the law office are indispensable parts of our administration of justice. Law-abiding people can go nowhere else to learn the ever changing and constantly multiplying rules by which they must behave and to obtain redress for their wrongs. The welfare and tone of the legal profession is therefore of prime consequence to society, which would feel the consequences of such a practice as petitioner urges secondarily but certainly. . . .

It seems clear and long has been recognized that discovery should provide a party access to anything that is evidence in his case. It seems equally clear that discovery should not nullify the privilege of confidential communication between attorney and client. But those principles give us no real assistance here because what is being sought is neither evidence nor is it a privileged communication between attorney and client.

To consider first the most extreme aspect of the requirement in litigation here, we find it calls upon counsel, if he has had any conversations with any of the crews of the vessels in question or of any other, to "set forth in detail the exact provision of any such oral statements or reports." Thus the demand is not for the production of a transcript in existence but calls for the creation of a written statement not in being. But the statement by counsel of what a witness told him is not evidence when written. Plaintiff could not introduce it to prove his case. What, then, is the purpose sought to be served by demanding this of adverse counsel?

Counsel for the petitioner candidly said on argument that he wanted this information to help prepare himself to examine witnesses, to make sure he overlooked nothing. He bases his claim to it in his brief on the view that the Rules were to do away with the old situation where a law suit developed into "a battle of wits between counsel." But a common law trial is and always should be an adversary proceeding. Discovery was hardly intended to enable a learned profession to perform its functions either without wits or on wits borrowed from the adversary.

The real purpose and the probable effect of the practice ordered by the district court would be to put trials on a level even lower than a "battle of wits." I can conceive of no practice more demoralizing to the Bar than to require a lawyer to write out and deliver to his adversary an account of what witnesses have told him. Even if his recollection were perfect, the statement would be his language permeated with his inferences. Everyone who has tried it knows that it is almost impossible so fairly to record the expressions and emphasis of a witness that when he testifies in the environment of the court and under the influence of the leading question there will not be departures in some respects. Whenever the testimony of the witness would differ from the "exact" statement the lawyer had delivered, the lawyer's statement would be whipped out to impeach the witness. Counsel producing his adversary's "inexact" statement could lose nothing by saying, "Here is a contradiction, gentlemen of the jury. I do not know whether it is my adversary or his witness who is not telling the truth, but one is not." Of course, if this practice were adopted, that scene would be repeated over and over again. The lawyer who delivers such statements often would find himself branded a deceiver afraid to take the stand to support his own version of the witness's conversation with him, or else he will have to go on the stand to defend his own credibility—perhaps against that of his chief witness, or possibly even his client.

Every lawyer dislikes to take the witness stand and will do so only for grave reasons. This is partly because it is not his role; he is almost invariably a poor witness. But he steps out of professional character to do it. He regrets it; the profession discourages it. But the practice advocated here is one which would force him to be a witness, not as to what he has seen or done but as to other witnesses' stories, and not because he wants to do so but in self-defense.

And what is the lawyer to do who has interviewed one whom he believes to be a biased, lying or hostile witness to get his unfavorable statements and know what to meet? He must record and deliver such statements even though he would not vouch for the credibility of the witness by calling him. Perhaps the other side would not want to call him either, but the attorney is open to the charge of suppressing evidence at the trial if he fails to call such a hostile witness even though he never regarded him as reliable or truthful. . . .

I agree to the affirmance of the judgment of the Circuit Court of Appeals which reversed the district court.

Mr. Justice FRANKFURTER joins in this opinion.

Notes and Questions: *Hickman*

Q **1. What if you had to disclose your own work product?** Why, as a practical matter, might you object to disclosing to opposing lawyers or their clients memoranda or other products you had prepared or collected to prepare for litigation? In that regard, consider how, if at all, you would prepare such memoranda differently if you thought that they might be discoverable.

A Obviously, you would write with a different level of candor if you thought that your memos and e-mails would be seen only by other lawyers in your firm, than if you thought the opposing counsel or world at large would read them. In memos that might be seen by opposing counsel or their clients, you would surely hold back and temper your conclusions. Indeed, you might even withhold sensitive conclusions altogether in favor of oral briefings of your co-counsel and your own client, if work product was routinely discoverable. But then the quality—and certainly the efficiency—of trial preparation would surely suffer.

Q **2. The reasons for work product protection.** The Court and Justice Jackson offered at least three policy reasons in *Hickman* for protecting such work product. What were they?

A First, the Court was concerned about the *chilling effect* of requiring disclosure. Disclosure of work product prepared "with a certain degree of privacy" might discourage lawyers from candidly memorializing their views. This would not just "demoralize" the profession. It would make lawyers less effective in representing clients. Writing presupposes thinking. If you don't write it out for fear of later disclosure, you may not think it out as well, either.

Second, the Court was concerned about giving the requesting party a *free ride*. Generally, we make parties litigate on their own nickel. It cost the tugboat owners money to have Fortenbaugh interview witnesses. Letting the plaintiffs get Fortenbaugh's work product for free is, well, un-American.

Finally, the Court was concerned about the *lawyer-as-witness*. Justice Jackson emphasizes that ethics rules generally forbid a lawyer from acting as an advocate at trial in which she is likely to be a witness. The exceptions are for testimony that relates to an uncontested issue or to the nature and value of legal services rendered in the case, if they are contested; or when the disqualification of the lawyer would work substantial hardship on the client. *See ABA Model Rule of Professional Conduct* 3.7. The comments to the ABA Rule explain that combining the roles of advocate and witness can create a conflict of interest and prejudice the opposing party by confusing the fact-finder, because a witness is expected to testify on personal knowledge, while an advocate is expected to explain and comment on the evidence. "It may not be clear whether a statement by an advocate-witness should be taken as proof or as an analysis of the proof." *Id.* Rule 3.7 comment.

Q **3. Learning the facts without the adversary lawyer's work product.** If Fortenbaugh was entitled to withhold his work product from discovery, how else might opposing lawyers and their client learn the facts of the tugboat sinking?

A They could themselves ask the witnesses (but recall the ethical traps in informal discovery). Or they could look at the public testimony taken by the Steamboat Inspectors. They could also just ask Fortenbaugh's client through interrogatories (written questions he must answer under oath) or by deposition. "Full and honest answers to such broad inquiries would necessarily have included all pertinent information gleaned by Fortenbaugh through his interviews with the witnesses," the Court explains.

But wait a minute! If they could just ask Fortenbaugh's client what facts Fortenbaugh learned from the witnesses, how is that different from asking Fortenbaugh or just getting his accounts of the witness interviews?

A Sounds like the same stuff, and it is the same facts. But not in the same *form*. It is the *compilation and selection* of work product information that is protected, not the underlying facts themselves, as Rule 26(b)(3) now reflects by targeting just "documents and tangible things" prepared in anticipation of litigation. These include diagrams, drawings, photographs, and models, as well as memoranda, audio and video tapes, and correspondence. The difference between the facts themselves, and Fortenbaugh's compilation and selection of the facts, is Fortenbaugh's value added. His memos ineluctably reflect his mental filtering and sorting of the facts. The work product rule is intended to protect that value added (because the plaintiffs' lawyers can add their own value), but not the facts themselves.

4. Codifying *Hickman*. After *Hickman* was decided, the Federal Rules were amended to reflect the work product protection that *Hickman* recognized. Rule 26(b)(3) now provides:

> **(3) Trial Preparation: Materials.**
>
> **(A) Documents and Tangible Things.** Ordinarily, a party may not discover documents and tangible things that are prepared in anticipation of litigation or for trial by or for another party or its representative (including the other party's attorney, consultant, surety, indemnitor, insurer, or agent). But, subject to Rule 26(b)(4), those materials may be discovered if:
>
> (i) they are otherwise discoverable under Rule 26(b)(1); and
>
> (ii) the party shows that it has substantial need for the materials to prepare its case and cannot, without undue hardship, obtain their substantial equivalent by other means.
>
> **(B) Protection Against Disclosure.** If the court orders discovery of those materials, it must protect against disclosure of the mental impressions, conclusions, opinions, or legal theories of a party's attorney or other representative concerning the litigation. . . .

In one respect, the Rule seems narrower than *Hickman*, insofar as it speaks only of "documents and tangible things." The common law protection that *Hickman* recognized is broader than the literal protection afforded by Rule 26(b)(3)(A), and most authorities still apply it to intangible work product. *See Wright & Miller* § 2024 (common law protection includes intangible work product).

5. Prepared by whom? In *Hickman*, it was lawyer Fortenbaugh who had prepared the work product. But at least two of the policy concerns raised there would apply equally to any agent of the client, or to the client himself, who prepares documents or tangible things in anticipation of litigation. The rule of *Hickman* ought to be no different had Fortenbaugh employed a paralegal or private investigator to conduct the interviews; in either case, free discovery of the work product might discourage Fortenbaugh from undertaking such preparation in the future (or, just as inefficiently, discourage him from using such personnel to help him prepare), and would give his adversaries a free ride. As a result, the Rule protects work product prepared "by or for another party or its representative (including the other party's attorney, consultant, surety, indemnitor, insurer, or agent)." Fed. R. Civ. P. 26(b)(3).

Thus, if Painter's lawyer asks him to prepare a written chronology of all the events leading up to his accident, for example, in order to help the lawyer prepare for trial of Painter's claim against Toyota, then that chronology would be protected work product (even though the facts that went into the chronology would themselves still be discoverable from Painter). In short, calling it "attorney work product" is misleading. Even the client can prepare work product if it is in anticipation of litigation.

2. Anticipation of Litigation

Rule 26(b)(3) extends work product protection only to matter that is "prepared in anticipation of litigation or for trial." This condition is the key to identifying work product.

What is "litigation"? "Litigation" has not proven hard to define; it includes any adversary court or administrative proceeding, including a civil action, criminal case, grand jury proceeding, and administrative hearing.

Must litigation have commenced? *Hickman* itself supplies the answer because there Fortenbaugh began interviewing witnesses before any complaint had been filed. The Rule reflects this circumstance by speaking to "anticipation of litigation."

What is "anticipation of litigation"? Any time a substantial personal injury or property loss is incurred in the United States today, a realist must anticipate litigation. If this general cautionary anticipation is enough, almost all documents prepared after the event that caused the injury or loss would qualify as work product.

The specific claim approach. Some courts require that the person invoking work product show that "the documents must have been prepared with a specific claim supported by concrete facts which would likely lead to litigation in mind." *Coastal States Gas Corp. v. Dep't of Energy*, 617 F.2d 854, 865 (D.C. Cir. 1980). If Peter Painter's lawyer had written Toyota before filing suit, demanding that it compensate Painter for his injuries and threatening suit if it did not, this demand letter would presumably constitute a "specific claim" for purposes of characterizing subsequently generated materials as work product. Other formulae include "articulable claim," *Coastal States*, 617 F.2d at 865, "an identifiable resolve to litigate," *Janicker v. George Washington University*, 94 F.R.D. 648, 650 (D.D.C. 1982), or even "a substantial probability that litigation will occur and that commencement of such litigation is imminent." *Homes Insurance Co. v. Ballenger Corp.*, 74 F.R.D. 93, 101 (N.D. Ga. 1977).

The ad hoc approach. Other courts have rejected the "specific claim" requirement as too narrow, reasoning that

> [i]t is often prior to the emergence of specific claims that lawyers are best equipped either to help clients avoid litigation or to strengthen available defenses should litigation occur. For instance, lawyers routinely meet with potential grand jury targets to discuss possible charges, consider whether business decisions might result in antitrust or securities lawsuits, analyze copyright and patent implications of new technologies or works of art, and assess the possibility that new products might give rise to tort actions. If lawyers had to wait for specific claims to arise before their writings could enjoy work-product protection, they would not likely risk taking notes about such matters or communicating in writing with colleagues, thus severely limiting their ability to advise clients effectively. A lawyer advising a potential grand jury target, for example, might be reluctant to write something like "the critical facts which could harm my client are . . ." even though it would help the lawyer organize complex thoughts, because in the government's hands, such a note could become a powerful weapon against the client. Likewise, asked by a client to evaluate the antitrust implications of a proposed merger and advised that no specific claim had yet surfaced, a lawyer knowing that work product is unprotected would not likely risk preparing an internal legal memorandum assessing the merger's weaknesses, jotting down on a yellow legal pad possible areas of vulnerability, or sending a note to a partner—"After reviewing the proposed merger, I think it's O.K., although I'm a little worried about . . . What are your views?" Nor would the partner respond in writing, "I disagree. This merger is vulnerable because . . . ." Discouraging lawyers from engaging in the writing, note-taking, and communications so critical to effective legal thinking would, in *Hickman*'s

words, not only "demoralize" the legal profession, but also "the interests of the clients and the cause of justice would be poorly served." . . .

Of course, not all work undertaken by lawyers finds protection in the work-product privilege. In some cases, the absence of a specific claim will suggest that the lawyer had not prepared the materials "in anticipation of litigation." . . . We hold only that where, as here, lawyers claim they advised clients regarding the risks of potential litigation, the absence of a specific claim represents just one factor that courts should consider in determining whether the work-product privilege applies.

In re Sealed Case, 146 F.3d 881, 886–87 (D.C. Cir. 1998).

The primary purpose approach. By this approach, the primary motivation for preparing the putative work product must be to assist in preparing for possible litigation. This motive is shown circumstantially by how the document is labeled (although this is not conclusive), whether a lawyer participated in the preparation (thus, not all client agents are created equal), whether the document comments on litigation, and whether it has an ordinary business purpose. Documents prepared for an ordinary business purpose or to fulfill regulatory requirements therefore do not usually qualify as work product.

Q **Testing your understanding of "prepared in anticipation of litigation or trial."** Applying the foregoing principles, how would you decide claims of work product protection for the following documents?

A. At his lawyer's request, Painter prepares a chronology of events leading to his accident and labels it "WORK PRODUCT—NOT FOR DISCLOSURE." He would not have prepared it but for the possibility that he might file a lawsuit arising out of the accident.

A This one is easy. Although Painter is not a lawyer, he is acting at his lawyer's request in anticipation of filing a lawsuit. There is no apparent other reason for his preparing the chronology. And he characterizes it as "work product." An interested party's contemporaneous characterization, of course, cannot be dispositive, but it may be taken as circumstantial evidence of "anticipation-of-litigation" motivation for preparing the document. The chronology should qualify as work product under any test.

B. Toyota's design division routinely prepares a statistical summary of dealer repair invoices to identify design defects for the purpose of correcting such defects in future models. Such a summary might well be helpful to Toyota's lawyer in preparing to resist Painter's suit and others like it.

A The fact that it might help in preparing for litigation, even after suit has commenced, is not enough to qualify it for work product protection. By definition, anything that might qualify as evidence would also be helpful in preparing for litigation. The touchstone of the protection in many courts is the primary purpose for which the document was prepared. Because this summary is routinely prepared for the *business* purpose of correcting defects, it should not qualify as work product, even in jurisdictions that do not apply the specific-claim test. In a circuit following the primary purpose approach, the same result would probably obtain even if *another* purpose of preparing the summary was to help Toyota's general counsel prepare for litigation, as long as the *primary* purpose of preparing the summary was still the business purpose.

C. An insurance claims adjuster prepares a report deciding whether to pay out on a claim. Would it affect your answer if the report was prepared *after* the insurer had denied coverage on a claim?

A It is the business of insurance companies to adjust—decide whether and how much to pay—claims made under their policies. Hence, many courts have denied work product protection to initial insurance claims adjuster's reports because they are prepared primarily to carry out the ordinary business of insurance. But after coverage has been denied, litigation is more clearly imminent because the disappointed claimant has no other recourse against the insurer. A second claims adjuster's report, prepared after denial of coverage, is therefore likely to have been prepared primarily in anticipation of that litigation, and some courts have correspondingly held it to be protected work product under the ad hoc approach or primary purpose approach to defining work product.

D. What about a locomotive engineer's report of an accident at a railroad crossing?

A Most courts have denied work product protection to routine accident reports on the theory that they, too, are prepared primarily for ordinary business purposes of accident prevention, insurance planning, and employee monitoring. *See, e.g., Wainwright v. Washington Metropolitan Transit Authority*, 163 F.R.D. 391, 395 (D.D.C. 1995) (compelling disclosure of defendant escalator company's accident report and defendant transit authority's escalator testing report because each report "was a routine business report not work product"). Conceding that any aircraft accident presents the contingency of litigation, for example, one court nevertheless concluded that "given the equally reasonable desire of Defendant to improve its aircraft products, to protect future pilots and passengers of its aircraft, to guard against adverse publicity in connection with such aircraft crashes, and to promote its own economic interests by improving its prospect for future contracts for production of such aircraft, it can hardly be said that defendant's 'in-house' report is not prepared in the ordinary course of business." *Soeder v. General Dynamics Corp.*, 90 F.R.D. 253, 255 (D. Nev. 1980). Of course, litigation is a contingency from the time of an accident, and the reports in question *could* help in preparing for litigation, but that is not the standard.

Remember, however, that just because an accident report will not ordinarily qualify for protection from discovery, it does not follow that it will be admissible as evidence at trial. *See* Fed. R. Evid. 407 (excluding evidence of "subsequent remedial measures" to prove negligence or design defect). Discoverability and admissibility are different.

E. A publicly traded stock corporation is required to file an annual trading report with the Securities and Exchange Commission. Its General Counsel prepares the report, which contains information that may be relevant to shareholder litigation. Is this report discoverable?

Another easy one. When a party is required by regulatory law to prepare a document, the document cannot be said to have been prepared primarily in anticipation of litigation. It was prepared to conduct business in compliance with regulatory law. Absent some claim of privilege, the party should produce it.

3. Overcoming Work Product Protection

The general showing required. In *Hickman*, the Court stressed that the plaintiff had not made a sufficient showing to overcome the work product protection for Fortenbaugh's files. Rule 26(b)(3) drew on this discussion in setting out the showing necessary to overcome the work product protection. Normally, the discoverer would need to make that showing by filing an affidavit in support of a motion to compel discovery.

Q What showing does the Rule require?

A First, the discoverer must show "substantial need for the materials to prepare its case." Fed. R. Civ. P. 26(b)(3)(A)(ii). Obviously, mere relevancy of the material is not enough, because the rule presupposes that *all* discoverable material is relevant to a claim or defense. Nor is it sufficient that the discoverer wants to make sure he hasn't overlooked anything, because that is the showing that the plaintiff in *Hickman* made unsuccessfully. On the other hand, certainly a showing that the materials were needed to establish or defeat an essential element of a claim or defense should suffice. What does *Hickman* say about the intermediate need for the materials to impeach or corroborate other evidence? In any case, specificity helps; a motion to compel discovery that is backed by an affidavit that merely alleges a need for the materials "to help prepare . . . to examine witnesses" is doomed to failure. *See, e.g., Delco Wire & Cable, Inc. v. Weinberger*, 109 F.R.D. 680, 689–90 (E.D. Pa. 1986).

Second, the discoverer must show that he "cannot, without undue hardship, obtain [the] substantial equivalent [of the work product] by other means." Fed. R. Civ. P. 26(b)(3)(A)(ii). What hardships does *Hickman* identify as sufficient? How did the plaintiff there fall short? Where the work product consists of statements of witnesses, the "other means" are interviewing the witnesses directly. Thus, if the discoverer can show that the witness is now dead, beyond the court's reach, hostile, or memory-impaired, courts have often held that he has made the requisite showing of undue hardship.

Overcoming the protection. Suppose that the work product consisted of statistical summaries compiled by Toyota from over 750,000 dealer repair invoices. Peter Painter could obtain the "substantial equivalent" by the "other means" of discovering and collating the 750,000 dealer invoices themselves, which, as ordinary business documents, would not qualify as work product. What argument would you make on Painter's behalf to make the requisite undue hardship showing on these facts?

A

Obviously, the burden of reviewing and then summarizing 750,000 invoices would be substantial, especially for an individual, non-corporate plaintiff like Painter. Of course, all discovery imposes a hardship in the form of the routine costs of searching, reviewing, and often photocopying. Courts are unlikely to find such routine costs to impose an "undue" hardship. But the numbers in this hypothetical suggest a greater than routine cost, and therefore possibly an undue hardship on Painter, especially compared to the relatively low cost of the alternative—accessing Toyota's summaries. *See* Rule 26(b)(1) (proportionality requirement).

Special protection for opinion work product? Even as it conceded that some showing of necessity and hardship might have overcome the work product protection for written witness statements in *Hickman*, the Court sharply distinguished Fortenbaugh's "mental impressions" of those witnesses. The former could be called *ordinary or factual work product*, consisting chiefly of unexpurgated facts or written statements by witnesses, to distinguish it from the latter *opinion work product*. With respect to disclosure of opinion work product, the Court was adamant: "[W]e do not believe that any showing of necessity can be made under the circumstances of this case to justify production." 329 U.S. at 512. Why not?

A

Recall your reconstruction of Fortenbaugh's work product and the probable consequences for his future trial preparation of forcing him to disclose it on request. Although he might not reduce the facts—such as witnesses' names or dates and times—to writing if he thought that they would be disclosed to the other side, such facts are ultimately available to the other side anyway in most cases. His chief reason for wanting to withhold them is not their confidentiality or sensitivity, but his unwillingness to let his opponents have a "free ride" on his work effort.

But his opinions and mental impressions are distinguishable from the facts he has collected. He is more likely to feel that *they are* confidential—for him, and his client, alone—and is therefore less likely to record them in any fashion if he thinks that he might be forced to disclose them. It is arguable, therefore, that the policy concerns animating the work product protection apply with special force to opinion work product, materials that go to the heart of uninhibited trial preparation.

Rule 26(b)(3) thus follows *Hickman* by providing that even when the required showing of substantial need and undue hardship has been made, "the court shall protect against disclosure of the mental impressions, conclusions, opinions, or legal theories of any attorney or other representative of a party concerning the litigation." Some courts have construed this language to confer absolute protection on opinion work product. *See, e.g., Duplan Corp. v. Moulinage et Retorderie de Chavanoz*, 509 F.2d 730, 734 (4th Cir. 1974).

How should a court therefore rule on Toyota's objection to producing a memorandum by its lawyer evaluating the strengths and weaknesses of prospective trial witnesses? Many courts would rule that the lawyer's mental impressions and opinions reflected in that memorandum would not be subject to discovery on "any showing," in the language of the *Hickman* court. If the memorandum also contained verbatim statements of witnesses, then a court interpreting the Rule in this fashion might "protect against disclosure of mental impressions, conclusions, opinions, or legal theories" by allowing Toyota to excise or *redact* such impressions from the memorandum before disclosing the remainder upon a showing of need and hardship. Or it might not even require redacted disclosure, on the theory that the lawyer's very selection of verbatim statements to include in his memorandum would itself reflect his mental impressions or legal theories.

But the *Hickman* Court was perhaps not so absolute, after all. It doubted only that "any showing of necessity can be made *under the circumstances of this case*. . . ." 329 U.S. at 512 (emphasis added). Since then, the Court has suggested that at least "a far stronger showing of necessity and unavailability by other means" than is usually sufficient to overcome the work product protection for ordinary or factual work product is needed to force disclosure of opinion work product. *Upjohn Co. v. United States*, 449 U.S. 383, 402 (1981). Some lower federal courts have suggested that the "plus factor" is a demonstration that the "mental impressions are the pivotal issue in the current litigation and the need for the material is compelling." *Holmgren v. State Farm Mutual Automobile Insurance Co.*, 976 F.2d 573, 577 (9th Cir. 1992). In *Holmgren*, for example, in a lawsuit against an insurer for settling an insurance claim in bad faith, the insurer withheld a claims adjuster's report that evaluated the insurer's potential liability on the plaintiff's claims. Although the court found the report to be opinion work product, it also found that the adjuster's thought processes and opinions were directly at issue, necessary to establish bad faith, and unavailable by any other means than discovery of the report.

4. Putting It All Together

Harris's car is struck by a train at a poorly marked railroad crossing, and he is seriously injured. He sues the railroad for negligence and seeks discovery of all documents of any kind concerning the crossing accident. The railroad requires the engineer of any train involved in an accident to file an immediate report of the incident, providing details not only on the accident, but on the speed of the train, observed condition of the crossing, health of the engineer, reasons why the engineer thought the accident happened, and what he thinks could be done, if anything, to avoid such accidents in the future. The reports are prepared on a form designed by the railroad's lawyers, and copies go to the chief of the railroad operating division (usually a senior engineer), its insurance department, and its general counsel. Lawsuits about accidents at railroad crossings are common, and the railroad expects to be sued whenever there are serious injuries.

The railroad objects to discovery of the accident report on grounds that it is work product. Which of the following is true?

A. The report is not work product because it was not prepared by a lawyer, claims adjuster, or other representative of the client.
B. The report is not work product because it was prepared before any lawsuit from the accident was filed.
C. The report is work product because it was prepared in anticipation of litigation, as the railroad expects to be sued when there are serious injuries and it commonly *is* sued.
D. The report is discoverable because it is relevant to plaintiff's claim for negligence, he could use it to prepare his case, and it is nonprivileged.
E. The report is not work product because it was prepared for the ordinary business purpose of running the trains more safely.

A takes far too narrow a view of who can prepare work product. While Fortenbaugh was a lawyer, and many courts speak of "attorney work product," the Rule itself speaks of a slew of party "representative[s]," as well as a party himself. Eligibility as a preparer should turn on the function of the Rule—whether he is someone who works on behalf of a party in anticipation of litigation, such that discovery of his work might have the same deleterious consequences as discovery of lawyer work product. Thus, the fact that the railroad's employee (who could be viewed as an "agent" of the party for this purpose) prepared the report does not disqualify it from consideration as work product.

B is obviously wrong. The timeline is "anticipation of litigation or trial," not that either has actually started.

C is appealing, and there are some cases that rule this way. The railroad gets sued so often after such crossing accidents that it anticipates a suit, as a practical matter. Certainly, sending the report to counsel is partly to help her prepare for the probable (inevitable?) suit, or its sometime antecedent, the demand letter (a letter from the plaintiff's lawyer demanding compensation on threat of a civil lawsuit). But in a litigation-prone society, any accident is a possible (probable?) personal injury suit, so this contingency could protect a large number of corporate communications. Some circuits therefore take a narrower view of the protection by protecting just those communications prepared *primarily* in anticipation of litigation. This report seems to have been prepared *both* in anticipation of litigation *and* for a business purpose of fixing bad crossings or identifying negligent engineers, as it is also sent to the senior engineer. There is little to suggest that it was prepared primarily in anticipation of litigation.

D sounds right as far as it goes, but all it tells us is that the report meets the basic presumption of discoverability. If it wasn't relevant, it would not be discoverable, whether or not it was work product. Plaintiff might find it useful, but that falls well short of any showing that he has "substantial need" to prove his claim; there are many other sources of evidence, including witnesses, police reports, photographs, diagrams of the scene prepared by plaintiff's agents, and his own testimony. Finally, just because the report is nonprivileged does not resolve the question of whether it is work product. As *Hickman* carefully noted, Fortenbaugh's witness statements were not privileged either, but they were still protected as work product.

Actually, it is not altogether clear that the report *is* nonprivileged. The *Upjohn* analysis raises at least a possibility that the report is a communication of fact by an employee at the direction of corporate superiors to the general counsel for the purpose of obtaining legal advice to the railroad. The distribution of the report to the operating division and maybe its distribution to the insurance division, however, cuts the other way.

E sounds like the flipside of **C**, but as we suggested, both are partly true. The report was prepared for both purposes. But if one important purpose was conducting the ordinary business of railroads, then the report was probably not prepared "primarily" in anticipation. Furthermore, if the report was prepared in part to satisfy some regulatory requirement, that would further undercut the claim of work product. Thus, if the jurisdiction endorses the primary purpose test, **E** is a better answer than **C**.

G. Expert Work Product

Suppose Painter's lawyer retained a mechanical engineer to help him prepare for trial against Toyota. He asked the engineer for a report on how a defect in the accelerator mechanism might have caused Painter's accident. An expert is someone qualified by knowledge, skill, experience, training, or education to give an opinion or offer an explanation that we would not normally permit from a lay person. *See* Fed. R. Evid. 701 (restricting opinion testimony by lay witnesses) and 702 (authorizing expert testimony). The mechanical engineer probably qualifies as an expert, therefore, at least with respect to questions of mechanical engineering, which he is specially trained and experienced to answer. If Toyota seeks discovery of the name of any expert Painter has consulted, production of a copy of the expert's report, or a deposition of the expert, how must Painter respond under the Federal Rules?

Rules 26(a)(2) and 26(b)(4) deal with these issues and distinguish between experts who will testify at trial and those who will not. Experts who are expected to testify at trial (testifying experts) must produce reports and then are subject to pretrial discovery by deposition. Non-testifying experts are not "ordinarily" subject to discovery, but can be discovered on a special showing, somewhat similar to that required to overcome ordinary work product.

Notes and Questions: Discovery of Experts

1. Categorizing experts for discovery purposes. Rule 26(b)(4) distinguishes between experts who may testify at trial and those who are employed only to help a party prepare for trial and not to testify at trial. So far, so good. But a party could also consult with an expert whom it decides *not to* employ, a "consulted but not employed expert," for want of a better term. A fourth kind of expert is one who is also a *fact witness*—someone who has personal knowledge of the events giving rise to the lawsuit (often called a *percipient witness* because he would testify to litigation-related events that he directly perceived). Finally, consider yet another kind of expert witness—one who neither perceived facts giving rise to a lawsuit nor was retained or even consulted by any party. Let's consider each of these experts in turn.

2. Cross-examining testifying experts. Rule 26 distinguishes between experts who will testify at trial and those who will consult on the case but not testify. To explore why, ask yourself how you would cross-examine an opposing party's expert at trial if you had no prior discovery from her. In this regard, heed the advice of the Advisory Committee, which states in the notes to the original Rule 26(b)(4) that

> [e]ffective cross-examination of an expert witness requires advance preparation. The lawyer even with the help of his own experts frequently cannot anticipate the particular approach his adversary's expert will take or the data on which he will base his judgment on the stand. . . . Similarly, effective rebuttal requires advance knowledge of the line of testimony by the other side.

Of course, it is always nice to know in advance what any witness will say at trial, but it may be essential when the witness is an expert in the subject and may offer complicated and influential opinions that would be difficult for a non-expert lawyer to cross-examine without detailed advance knowledge. The disadvantage is worse when the testifying expert is a professional witness who has been in court as often or more often than the lawyer who has to cross-examine her. In short, the rule makes special provision for discovery of testifying experts to level the playing field between them and their cross-examiners.

Q **3. Discovery from non-testifying experts.** On the other hand, if the defendant's expert had merely been retained to consult about the case and had no better opportunity to view the scene of the accident giving rise to the claim than other available experts of the same kind, what need would the plaintiff have for discovery of the defendant's expert? If the plaintiff were granted discovery from such a non-testifying expert, how, if at all, might this be unfair to the defendant?

A *If* there were other experts with comparable expertise, the plaintiff wouldn't need the defendant's non-testifying expert. He could just hire his own similar expert at his own expense. Getting discovery from defendant's expert would give the plaintiff a free ride at the defendant's expense, especially if the plaintiff was not required to pay that expert a fee.

4. The rule makers' compromise about testifying and non-testifying expert witnesses. Balancing the frequent difficulty of cold cross-examination of a testifying expert at trial against the unfairness of "free rides" on an opponent's expert and trial preparation budget, the rule makers struck a compromise. The Rule permits discovery of the testifying expert, while conditionally denying discovery of the non-testifying expert who is retained or specially employed in anticipation of litigation.

The Rule now, in fact, requires parties to disclose the identity of each testifying expert and to provide her written report of her opinions and their basis, her qualifications, and a listing of other cases in which she has testified during the preceding four years, without the need for opposing parties to request the report. Fed. R. Civ. P. 26(a)(2)(B). On the other hand, it "ordinarily" prohibits discovery of a non-testifying expert on the assumption that a party can find facts or opinions on the subject "by other means." Fed. R. Civ. P. 26(b)(4)(B). Chiefly, of course, those means are hiring an expert of the same kind.

5. When "other means" of obtaining facts and opinions held by non-testifying experts are unavailable. The Rule 26(b)(4) prohibition on discovery of non-testifying experts rests on the assumption that a party can hire its own expert. But suppose there are no other experts of the same kind; your opponent's retained or specially employed non-testifying expert is the only one in the world? Then the expert's uniqueness is surely an "exceptional circumstance[] under which it is impracticable" for you to get the needed information by other means.

Q **6. The unretained non-testifying expert witness.** Suppose that a defendant's lawyer called several experts before finally retaining one. The lawyer may have decided against retaining these experts because they were unable or unwilling to give him the opinion he needed, making them especially attractive discovery targets for the plaintiff. May the plaintiff discover the names of the experts who were not retained or specially employed, but merely consulted in the search for an expert?

A The Rule does not expressly discuss such experts. You could argue that the omission is intentional and that the Rule exhausts the categories of experts whose work product may be discovered under any circumstances, which is the view expressed by the Advisory Committee. Fed. R. Civ. P. 26(b), advisory committee's notes to the 1970 amendment (Rule "precludes discovery against experts who were informally consulted in preparation for trial, but not retained or specially employed"). Some have read the omission differently, concluding that the Rule exclusively identifies those experts whose facts and opinions are protected, leaving the rest vulnerable to discovery.

7. The fact witness who also happens to be an expert. Someone who is an expert can also learn facts or form opinions from her direct involvement or perception of events giving rise to the claim without anticipating litigation. She's still an expert, of course, *but, by this argument, she came by the facts like any other witness*. She must therefore testify like any other witness, without any special protection. It is thus worth emphasizing that it is not all facts known or opinions held by experts that are protected, but only those learned or held in anticipation of litigation—what we might call *expert work product*, by analogy to the general work product that was the subject of *Hickman*.

Q **8. Deposing the fact witness who is also an expert.** Suppose Gene Gressman is an automotive engineer employed by Toyota who originally designed the Camry's accelerator system. Assume that by education, training, and experience, Mr. Gressman would qualify as an expert. May Painter take his deposition over Toyota's expert work product objection?

A Yes. Mr. Gressman did not acquire facts and opinions about the accelerator in anticipation of litigation, but as an ordinary fact witness who participated in the events giving rise to Painter's product liability claim. That Gressman is also an expert is irrelevant; he must testify about those events like any other witness. Note, incidentally, that we did not answer yes just because Gressman was an employee of Toyota. Corporate parties may often look inside for a testifying expert. As long as such an inside expert testifies to facts known or opinions that she acquires in anticipation of litigation, her employment status does not divest her of the expert work product protection (although it may affect her credibility).

9. Picking the independent expert's brain (and pocket?). There is still another possible expert. Suppose an automotive design expert who works for the Auto Safety Institute has not been retained, consulted, or employed by any party in *Painter v. Toyota*. May either party subpoena this expert for a deposition in order to tap her expertise without retaining her? Ordinarily, a party is not obliged to pay a deponent more than a standard and modest witness fee for attending a deposition. And the expert cannot be said to have learned facts or acquired opinions in anticipation of litigation; learning facts and acquiring opinions in her area of expertise is, instead, her business as technical staff for a non-governmental organization. In short, can we use discovery to obtain free expertise from someone who has nothing to do with the lawsuit?

Unretained and unconsulted experts have the same duty to give evidence as the rest of us, but forcing them to testify to their expertise without paying them for it is tantamount to "a 'taking' of their intellectual property." *See* Fed. R. Civ. P. 45(c) advisory committee's notes. Rule 45(d)(3)(B)(ii) therefore provides that a subpoena that requires "disclosing an unretained expert's opinion or information that does not describe specific occurrences in dispute and results from the expert's study that was not requested by a party" may be quashed or modified unless the discoverer "shows a substantial need for the testimony or material that cannot be otherwise met without undue hardship; and ensures that the subpoenaed person will be reasonably compensated." So, you *can* pick the independent expert's brain, but not her pocket, if you make the showing required by the Rule.

In short, not all experts are created equal. The Rules expressly or impliedly distinguish among testifying experts, non-testifying but retained or specially employed experts, unretained but consulted experts, fact witnesses who are also experts, and independent experts who are not fact witnesses. Permitted discovery varies accordingly. Obviously, it takes an expert to know one.

IV. Informal Investigation and the Scope of Discovery: Summary of Basic Principles

- Rule 11 requires a lawyer to make a "reasonable inquiry" before filing a complaint or other paper and therefore presumes that the lawyer will conduct an informal investigation before he files a complaint.

- Ethics rules in most jurisdictions prohibit lawyers from speaking to represented persons—including in some cases agents or employees of corporate entities—without the consent of the person's or entity's lawyer.

- Even when a person is unrepresented, ethics rules may require lawyers to identify themselves clearly, avoid and correct misunderstandings about the lawyer's role, and refrain from deceitful or unfair conduct, including, in many jurisdictions, secret recording of conversations.

- Once litigation has started, parties may discover any nonprivileged matter relevant to a claim or defense and proportional to the needs of the case, whether or not it is itself admissible. This means that substantive evidentiary objections other than privilege are generally unavailable to resist discovery. But the multi-factor "proportionality" calculus may sometimes result in discovery limitations when the party resisting discovery meets its burden of showing that a request is disproportionate to the needs of the case.

- Matter is privileged when it is protected from discovery (and from admissibility as evidence at trial as well) by an evidentiary privilege. Such privileges have usually been established by the common law, a statute, or a rule of evidence to protect the confidentiality of certain communications made in furtherance of relationships that society favors, such as the lawyer-client, physician-patient, or priest-penitent relationships. Civil procedure rules do not create privileges; Rule 26(b)(1) simply recognizes evidentiary privilege as a ground for protection from discovery.

- Chiefly to facilitate effective preparation of cases for trial, work product—documents and tangible things prepared on behalf of a client in anticipation of litigation or trial—enjoy a qualified protection from discovery under Rule 26(b)(3). But it is the lawyer's (or her agent's) value added that is protected, not the facts themselves. The work product protection can be overcome if the discovering party shows substantial need of the work product to prove its case or defense in chief, and undue hardship—beyond the ordinary costs of discovery—in obtaining the equivalent by other means.
- For work product to have been prepared in anticipation of litigation or trial, the litigation need not yet have begun. Instead, depending on the law of the circuit, it is enough if the product was primarily prepared with some specific claim in mind, to provide legal advice about possible claims, or prepared for the primary purpose of litigation.
- The opinions held and the facts known by a testifying expert (those acquired in her capacity as an expert) are discoverable. The opinions and facts known by a non-testifying but retained expert are discoverable only on a showing that it is impracticable for the discovering party to obtain facts and opinions on the same subject by other means, such as hiring its own expert.
- Take care to identify an expert precisely when deciding on the availability of discovery! If the expert is neither employed nor testifying, but was just consulted, the Rules impliedly—by omission—permit no discovery at all. When the expert was a percipient witness—fancy lawyer talk for "eyeball" or fact witness—then discovery is available as it would be from any such witness.

22

Discovery Tools

I. Introduction

In Chapter 21, we explored *what* a party may discover. The next logical question is *how* a party may discover. After commencement of Painter's action against Toyota for an alleged defect in his Camry, discovery would usually proceed in two stages. Under Rule 26(a), Painter and Toyota will be required, without awaiting any formal discovery requests, to exchange information that they may use to support their claims or defenses, including names, addresses, and telephone numbers of fact witnesses, copies or descriptions of documents, and materials underlying computations of damages. These *required disclosures* are intended to arm the parties as early as possible with the basic information they need to prepare for trial and to make informed decisions about settlement.

After required disclosures, the parties may also take *discretionary discovery* using *depositions* (oral or written examinations of live witnesses under oath before a court reporter), *interrogatories* (written questions that must be answered in writing under oath), *document production requests, physical and mental examinations*, and *requests for admissions*. For example, because Painter seeks damages for his personal injuries, Toyota will almost certainly wish to have a physician of its choice conduct a physical examination of Painter to ascertain the extent of those injuries. Painter, in turn, may well wish to "depose"—ask questions in a deposition of—the Toyota engineer who designed the Camry. In this chapter, we survey these discovery tools generally and explore a few specific issues in more depth.

II. Mandatory Discovery Procedures

After Painter's lawyer files his complaint against Toyota, what happens next? The parties are now required to make initial disclosures of the core information in a lawsuit, as well as additional disclosures on the eve of trial, in all but a small set of relatively simple actions exempted by rule. *See* Fed. R. Civ. P. 26(a)(1). These requirements for mandatory discovery are intended to accelerate and, to some degree, defang discovery, in the hope of encouraging settlements and making discovery less adversarial and less costly.

Painter's lawyer would therefore be obliged initially, without awaiting a discovery request or an answer to the complaint, to identify witnesses and produce or describe documents Painter would use to support his claims, and to disclose materials on which his computation of damages was based. Toyota would have comparable obligations regarding its defenses.

Suppose, for example, Painter's complaint alleges that the Toyota in which he was injured "had one or more manufacturing or design defects in the braking, steering, and/or suspension systems," which proximately caused the accident in which he was injured. Toyota denies that there were any such defects. Which witnesses must Toyota list and which documents must it produce or identify in light of this denial? Often hundreds—even thousands—of employees are involved in the design and manufacture of a car. Must Toyota, pursuant to Rule 26(a)(1)(A), identify *all* who are likely to have discoverable information? Sometimes a car manufacturer uses the same or a similar "platform" or similar mechanical systems for several models of its cars. If Painter was injured in a Camry, must Toyota produce or identify documents it might use to support its defense pertinent not just to the Camry, but also to the Corolla, or even the Prius or Venza as well, if these models share some of the same systems? It is partly to answer such questions that the Rules require the parties to meet and confer to prepare a discovery plan. *See* Fed. R. Civ. P. 26(f)(2).

READING *FLORES v. SOUTHERN PERU COPPER CORP.* The Rule sets a schedule for initial disclosures. But in *Flores*, the defendant filed a "dispositive motion"—presumably a Rule 12(b)(6) motion. Should the defendant still have to make its initial disclosures when the motion could dispose of the case? Consider the following questions as you read the case:

- Why don't the parties have to make the initial disclosures required by what is now Rule 26(a)(1)(A)(i)–(iii) before the court rules?
- Just how burdensome would it be for the defendant to make the remaining required disclosure of insurance policies?
- The court relies on the advisory committee notes and a civil procedure treatise in its reasoning. Had the parties held a discovery conference (it is unclear from the case whether they had), is there a more direct authority for the result in this case? *See* Fed. R. Civ. P. 26(a)(1)(C).

FLORES v. SOUTHERN PERU COPPER CORP.

203 F.R.D. 92 (S.D.N.Y. 2001)

HAIGHT, Senior District Judge:

The Court has examined the parties' joint Report and Proposed Discovery Plan ("the Plan"), submitted in obedience to Rule 26(f), Fed. R. Civ. P. The Plan reveals one present and one potential dispute. This opinion resolves the former . . . .

Rule 26(a)(1) deals with "initial disclosures." It provides that, "without waiting for a discovery request" and unless "otherwise stipulated or directed by order," the parties must provide to each other four categories of information. Rule 26(a)(1)(A)–(D) **[EDS.—now 26(a)(1)(A)(i)–(iv)]**. The parties have stipulated to adjourn the making of the initial disclosures required by subsections (A)–(C) until the Court has ruled on a dispositive motion defendant filed and served on March 5, 2001.[12] They dispute whether the disclosure called for by Rule 26(a)(1)(D) **[EDS.—now 26(a)(1)(A)(iv)]** should be similarly adjourned. Defendant says it should. Plaintiffs say it should not.

Rule 26(a)(1)(D) **[EDS.—now 26(a)(1)(A)(iv)]** requires the production "for inspection and copying as under Rule 34 any insurance agreement under which any person carrying on an insurance business may be liable to satisfy part or all of a judgment which may be entered in the action or to indemnify or reimburse for payments made to satisfy the judgment." Defendant argues that since the Amended Complaint complains "of the alleged effects on the environment of activities undertaken by defendant over more than 40 years, it is likely that more than one insurance policy potentially provides coverage." Counsel's carefully chosen phrases suggest that they have not actually looked to see if that is so, but the natural instincts of underwriters to review, reissue, and revise the policies they write and to reinsure the risks they cover lend plausibility to the notion

12. The motion has not yet been fully briefed, and so cannot be regarded as sub judice.

that more than one liability policy applies to 40 years of a company's mining operations.

Defendant argues further that its pending dispositive motion raises no issue "to which the question of defendant's insurance coverage, if any, is relevant," *id.*, so that the efforts involved in searching for the policy or policies and drafting a confidentiality agreement to protect them, as well as the risk of an unwarranted disclosure even in the presence of such an agreement, may all be avoided if the motion succeeds.

Plaintiffs respond that disclosure of any insurance policies must be made now because Rule 26(a)(1)(D) **[EDS.—now 26(a)(1)(A)(iv)]** "requires" it, and plaintiffs have not agreed to waive that specific provision of the Rule....

[P]laintiffs' argument that in the absence of their consent to a delay, Rule 26(a)(1) "requires" defendant to **[EDS.—now says "a party must"]** disclose any pertinent insurance policies overlooks the provision in the Rule that the designated disclosures must be made "except ... to the extent otherwise stipulated or *directed by order*." The drafters of the Rule built in two delay buttons to these initial disclosures: stipulation by the parties if they agree, and an order by the district court if they do not. The parties pushed the first delay button in respect of three disclosure categories; defendant asks the Court to push the second button in respect of the fourth category.

... [T]he Advisory Committee's Notes to the 2000 amendments ... expressly recognizes the continuing authority of the district courts to make "case-specific orders" deferring initial disclosures under the Rule. That authority has always existed; a leading treatise recognizes a district court's discretionary power to stay all Rule 26(a)(1) initial disclosure "pending resolution of [a] motion to dismiss, if the defendant makes a strong showing that the plaintiff's claim is unmeritorious." 6 *Moore's Federal Practice* § 26.22[3][b] at 26–64 (3d ed. 1997).

The necessity for the showing suggested by *Moore* does not arise in the case at bar, where plaintiffs have agreed to adjourn three of the four initial disclosures until defendant's dispositive motion has been decided; nor have I made even a cursory examination of defendant's motion, which is not yet fully briefed. The decisive factor is that plaintiffs offer no reasoned analysis why they are willing to defer the identifying of individuals with discoverable information, the production or description of pertinent documents and tangible things in the parties' possession, and a computation of plaintiffs' damages, the categories of information covered by Rule 26(a)(1)(A), (B), and (C) **[EDS.—now 26(a)(1)(A)(i)–(iii)]** respectively, and yet insist upon the defendant's immediate production of any insurance policies.

Plaintiffs do not suggest any way in which their response to defendant's motion would be enhanced or aided by that information. Plaintiffs say only that "the expense of producing the insurance policy is obviously minimal," (note plaintiffs' assumption that there is only one policy), and that "the expense of negotiation and drafting a protective order is also minimal," *id.* Maybe so, but maybe not so. No useful purpose will be served by putting defendant to the effort in order to find out.

The defendant's objection to disclosure under Rule 26(a)(1)(D) [Eds.—now 26(a)(1)(A)(iv)] at this time is sustained. Disclosure under this category will be made at the same time as the other information embraced by Rule 26(a)(1) if defendant's dispositive motion is denied....

Notes and Questions: Required Initial Disclosures

Q **1. Scheduling initial disclosures.** When must required initial disclosures be made?

A Even from a strictly mechanical perspective, this proves to be no easy question. Rule 26(f) requires the parties to meet and confer (imaginatively called a "meet-and-confer") to discuss a discovery plan at least twenty-one days before a scheduling conference is held or a scheduling order is due under Rule 16(b). That order is due within ninety days after any defendant has been served with the complaint or sixty days after any defendant has appeared. Fed. R. Civ. P. 16(b). The disclosures are due within fourteen days *after* the meet-and-confer by the parties under Rule 26(f), unless a party asserts that required initial disclosures are inappropriate in the circumstances of the case.

The contemplated sequence of initial discovery events thus looks like this:

filing → service → 26(f) meet-and-confer → 26(a)(1) required disclosures & 26(f) proposed plan → 16(b) scheduling conference and order

Figure 22–1: TIMELINE FOR INITIAL DISCOVERY

Q **2. The complication of Rule 12 motions.** The foregoing is just the arithmetic computation. The timing can be complicated by motion practice. In *Flores*, the defendant had filed a "dispositive motion" (probably a Rule 12(b)(6) motion) and did not want to disclose its insurance agreements before the court ruled on the motion. Why not?

A It seems unlikely that the defendant was troubled by the burden of disclosing the insurance agreements. Even forty years of insurance coverage was unlikely to involve more than a few policies. But the reference to a "confidentiality agreement to protect them" suggests that the defendant was anxious to avoid producing them, if it could. One reason might be the very reason that they are ordinarily subject to required initial disclosure: They reveal coverage limits that suggest a settlement range to plaintiffs. They may also be evidence of ownership or control of environmentally sensitive lands (the defendant is a copper company). If the court grants the "dispositive motion" and dismisses the case, the defendant avoids the risk of disclosing that information.

3. Defendant's options to avoid required initial disclosures.

Which, if any, of the following options are available to a party who, like the defendant in *Flores*, wants to hold back insurance agreements from its initial disclosures?

A. It could simply withhold the insurance agreements until the court ruled.
B. It could ask the plaintiffs to stipulate to delay the required disclosure of the insurance agreements until after the court ruled.
C. It has no option: "Required" disclosure means just what it says; the obligation is absolute.
D. It could object to the disclosure during a discovery conference with plaintiffs and then state that objection in the resulting proposed discovery plan.
E. It could move for a court order postponing this disclosure until after the court ruled on the dispositive motion.

A is not an authorized option under the Rules. Rule 26(a)(1)(C) states that a party "must make the initial disclosures" within the time it provides, "unless" one of the delay buttons it lists is pushed. This seems to foreclose self-help by flat-out non-disclosure.

B is an authorized delay button: obtaining a stipulation from the other party. *See* Rule 26(a)(1)(C). In fact, the parties in *Flores* had stipulated to delay the first three categories of initial disclosure. They just could not agree on delaying the fourth category—insurance agreements. In other words, the defendant tried this option, but the plaintiffs refused. It takes two to tango—or stipulate.

C is obviously incorrect because of Rule 26(a)(1)(C)'s "unless" clause: the delay buttons. Pushing those buttons delays required disclosures. But Rule 26(a)(1)(A) seems to qualify the required disclosure even apart from delay, by providing an exception if "otherwise . . . ordered by the court." So "required" doesn't mean just what it says; it has unstated exceptions plus delay buttons for timing.

D is expressly authorized by Rule 26(a)(1)(C). The parties in *Flores* may have had a discovery conference; they can be, and usually are, held by telephone. Very likely, in such a telephone conference, the parties stipulated to delay disclosures of the first three categories of initial disclosures, but the plaintiff refused to stipulate to delay the defendant's disclosure of the insurance agreements. However, the Rule requires not just an objection; the objection must be stated in the proposed discovery plan. When it is, the court will then rule on the objection and "must set the time for disclosure." Apparently, the parties had not yet proposed a discovery plan in *Flores*.

E is also correct, because Rule 26(a)(1)(C) makes "a court order" an alternative to a ruling on an objection in the discovery plan described in answer **D**. This alternative seems to be the one eventually pursued in the case.

In short, the Rules suggest three, not just two, "delay buttons." Answers **B**, **D**, and **E** are all correct.

4. What must be initially disclosed? The Rule does not require disclosure of all evidence relevant to any party's claim or defense, which is the general standard of relevancy for discovery. *See* Rule 26(b)(1). The scope of required initial disclosures is narrower: just "information that the disclosing party may use to support *its* claims or defenses" (emphasis added). Although Toyota may have hundreds, if not thousands, of employees, agents, and individual contractors with information relevant to Painter's allegations of defective design and manufacture, it only initially has to disclose the names of witnesses and documents it intends to use to support its defenses. This is likely to be a far smaller universe.

Consider, then, this scenario. DiMento sues Bashad for injuries in a motor vehicle accident. The parties exchange required initial disclosures under Fed. R. Civ. P. 26(a)(1). Bashad's disclosure of witnesses under Rule 26(a)(1)(A) does not include Patrick, who was present at the time of the accident. Patrick told Bashad's lawyer that Bashad ran a red light before he hit DiMento.

Later DiMento's lawyer learns from her own investigation that Patrick witnessed the accident. Which, if any, of the following is correct?

A. DiMento should seek to interview or depose Patrick.
B. DiMento should seek sanctions for Bashad's violation of Rule 26(a)(1)(A).
C. Bashad must now send a supplementary disclosure to DiMento, providing Patrick's name and address as required by Rule 26(a)(1)(A).
D. Bashad is not subject to sanctions, because, while he violated his disclosure obligations under Rule 26(a)(1)(A), DiMento learned about Patrick before trial.
E. After required initial disclosures, DiMento's lawyer should send Bashad an interrogatory asking for the names of all witnesses to the accident.

A is correct. In her haste to punish Bashad, DiMento's lawyer must not lose sight of the main object: collecting the information she needs to win the case for her client. Now that she has identified this witness, she should try for an informal interview and/or a deposition of Patrick.

B is wrong because Bashad did not violate the Rule. He is required only to make initial disclosures of witnesses with information that *he* may use to support *his defense*. Patrick's testimony would damage Bashad's case, so Bashad would not use Patrick as a witness to support his defense.

Because Bashad did not violate the rules, both **C** and **D** are also wrong. Unless he has been subject to discretionary discovery demands, Bashad only has to supplement or correct disclosures he was required to make under Rule 26(a). He was not required to disclose Patrick's name under Rule 26(a)(1)(A), and he still is not. He is protected from sanctions because he did not violate the required initial disclosure rule, not because DiMento's lawyer learned about Patrick before trial.

All of these answers suggest that even after required initial disclosures by Bashad, DiMento's lawyer should *still* serve interrogatories asking for the names of witnesses, because then Bashad would be required to disclose the names of those with information DiMento could use to support *her* claims, and not just names of those with information Bashad would use to support *his* defense. So **A** and **E** are both correct as a matter of good practice.

5. Other required disclosures. Rule 26(a)(2) also requires timely disclosure of expert trial witnesses and their reports at least ninety days before trial. Rule 26(a)(3) adds the requirement that at least thirty days before trial, parties make mutual "pretrial disclosures" by exchanging lists of witnesses they expect to call and exhibits they intend to introduce at trial. These disclosure requirements were already widely imposed *ad hoc* by pretrial orders in many cases, and they have therefore been mainly uncontroversial.

6. The sanction for failure to give required disclosure. Rule 37(c)(1) provides a self-executing sanction, without the need for a motion, against a party who fails to make a required disclosure without substantial justification. The party is precluded from using the undisclosed evidence or witness. Fed. R. Civ. P. 37(c)(1). The court may also, on motion, impose additional sanctions.

III. Discovery Sequencing and Interrogatories

If you represented Painter against Toyota in our hypothetical product liability case, what discovery would you conduct first? It might be very productive to depose the engineer who developed the Camry and fish for an admission about flaws or weaknesses in the design, or to depose some officer in Toyota who collects and evaluates information about defects in cars that are already being sold. But even if you could identify these witnesses, or ask Toyota to do so, you could be at a substantial disadvantage asking them questions without advance preparation. How would you prepare for their depositions? How would you decide what to ask?

It takes little thought to realize that you ordinarily want to obtain other information from Toyota before deposing such potentially important witnesses. Ideally, you would like to have copies of the design documents and summaries of defect reports that come to Toyota to prepare deposition questions and to nail down answers. In Evidence, you will also learn that you might want the witnesses to identify some documents during their depositions to help you later establish the documents' authenticity should you want to offer them into evidence at trial.

Considerations such as these often—though not always—suggest that depositions of key witnesses should come last, not first, in a well-planned course of discretionary discovery. One common sequence is (1) to use interrogatories first to locate and identify evidence, (2) to use requests for document production to collect the identified written evidence or electronically stored information, and then, (3) armed with that evidence, to use depositions to collect spontaneous evidence from witnesses and parties, often leaving the key witnesses until last.

One discovery handbook suggests the following slightly different sequence:

1. [Required disclosures]
2. Depose secondary witnesses
3. Issue follow-up requests for production and interrogatories
4. Depose key witnesses
5. Depose the adverse party
6. Issue follow-up requests to admit
7. Depose expert witnesses
8. Issue contention interrogatories
9. Issue final, "clean up" discovery requests

Lawrence J. Zweifach, *Deposition Strategy in the Framework of an Overall Discovery Plan* 26 (PLI 1992). In a case in which physical or mental conditions are in controversy, it is also common for the parties to stipulate to appropriate medical examinations. Finally, when other discovery is concluded, a party may use requests for admissions to authenticate documents it plans to offer into evidence at trial and to narrow issues.

Although the sequence of discovery is thus not set in stone, it is common in many cases for the parties to initiate discretionary discovery with an exchange of interrogatories. *See* Rules 33 and 26(g). In the following example, we have skipped Painter's First Set of Interrogatories to Toyota, because the interrogatories are incorporated verbatim into Toyota's answers, excerpts of which are set forth below. (In real life, the answers would be longer.)

In addition, the interrogatories included the following preamble:

> The following definitions apply to these interrogatories:
>
> Document: "Document" means any writing, drawing, graph, chart, photograph, electronically stored information, or other data compilation from which information can be obtained, translated, if necessary, by the person answering these interrogatories through detection devices into reasonably usable form. A draft or non-identical copy is a separate document within the meaning of this term.
>
> Identify (with respect to persons): When referring to persons, "identify" means to give, to the extent known, the person's full name, present or last known address, home telephone, present or last known place of employment, and business telephone. Once a person has been identified in accordance with this subparagraph, only the name of the person need be listed in response to subsequent discovery requesting the identification of that person....
>
> These interrogatories are intended as continuing interrogatories, requiring you to answer by supplemental answer, setting forth any information within the scope of your interrogatories as may be acquired by you, your agents, attorneys, or representatives following your original answers....

UNITED STATES DISTRICT COURT
DISTRICT OF OLD JERSEY

PETER PAINTER, Plaintiff	)	CIVIL ACTION NO. 09-2114
v.	)	DEFENDANT TOYOTA CO.'S ANSWERS TO PLAINTIFF'S FIRST SET OF INTERROGATORIES
TOYOTA CO., INC., Defendant	)	

Defendant Toyota Co., Inc., responds to the plaintiff's first set of interrogatories as follows. Defendant will supplement these answers if and to the extent required by the Federal Rule of Civil Procedure 26(e).

1. Identify the person signing the verification to these interrogatory responses, and identify such person's job title and/or capacity with Defendant.

> Answer: Mildred Chevron, 11 Ermine Place, Torrance, California 34512; Toyota Co., 3rd St. NW, Torrance, California 34511; 313-511-3600 x76; Assistant Vice President for Automotive Division. . . .

6. Identify the persons presently or formerly in your employ who were involved in the development and manufacture or design of the Camry.

> Answer: Defendant objects to Interrogatory No. 6 on the grounds that it is ambiguous, overbroad, and burdensome, and that, insofar as it asks for the identification of employees who were employed after the date on which the plaintiff's car was manufactured, it asks for information that is irrelevant.

7. Identify each person who was a member of the Camry Design Team at any time between May 1, 2010, and the present date, and for each person identified, state the dates during which they were members and their titles.

> Answer: William Conrad, 215 Erskine Ave., Torrance, California 34511, 313-299-7454; Toyota Co., 3rd St. NW, Torrance, California 34511, 313-511-3600 x211, May 1, 2005–June 1, 2015, Project Engineer; ... [This would presumably be a lengthy answer.]

29. Identify each standard, code, regulation, or manual which was consulted in the development and manufacture or design of the Camry.

> Answer: The answer to Interrogatory No. 29 may be derived or ascertained from the business records of the defendant located at Reference Library, Rm. 311, Toyota Co.,

3rd St. NW, Torrance, California 34511, and the burden of deriving or ascertaining the answer is substantially the same for the plaintiff as for the defendant. These records may be examined and copied at a reasonable time at this location.

37. Describe in complete detail all changes, modifications, or alterations made to the design of the Camry since it was first sold or available to the public, including the change, alteration, and/or modifications in any warnings, instructions, and/or directions provided with the Camry, up to the present date.

Answer ... [This could obviously be a monster answer.]

114. Is assumption of the risk a defense in Old Jersey?

Answer: Defendant objects to Interrogatory No. 114 on the grounds that it calls for a conclusion or opinion on the law unrelated to the facts of this case or an application of the law to those facts.

115. Do you contend that the plaintiff assumed the risk of the accident described in his complaint ¶¶ 12–14?

Answer: Yes.

116. If the answer to Interrogatory No. 115 is yes, state the basis for your answer.

Answer: Knowing that the instrument panel had indicated a potential brake failure, plaintiff drove the Camry on May 11, 2019 ...

SIGNED UNDER THE PAINS AND PENALTIES OF PERJURY THIS 20TH DAY OF November 2019.

/S/
Mildred Chevron for Toyota Co., Inc.

SIGNED AS TO OBJECTIONS:
/S/
Baker Farley Fish, Attorney for the Defendant
Erstwhile & Fish
117 Main Street
Oldark, Old Jersey 30221

Notes and Questions: Interrogatories

Q **1. Procedure for interrogatories.** The procedure is simple. The lawyer seeking discovery prepares and serves a party with up to twenty-five written questions. (Interrogatories are not available against non-parties.) Although any good set of interrogatories should be tailored to the case, the lawyer may adapt so-called pattern interrogatories that are tailored to particular kinds of claims and that are published in form books. Interrogatories No. 29 and 37, for example, were drawn from 8A *Am. Jur. Pleading & Prac. Forms Annot.* § 433 (database updated 2016). The responding party must then answer or object within thirty days. Answers are made in writing under oath by the party, who signs them; objections are made in writing by the party's lawyer. But the lawyer must also sign a discovery response pursuant to Rule 26(g) (discovery's analog to Rule 11), certifying that she has made a "reasonable inquiry" before submitting the response. (The same is true for discovery requests.) In practice, it is usually the party's lawyer who prepares the answers to interrogatories.

What does this procedure, especially the lawyer's preparation of answers, suggest about the pros and cons of discovery by interrogatory?

A It makes interrogatories a relatively inexpensive tool for discovery compared to depositions, but it also makes them less effective because answers drafted by a lawyer are usually as bare and unhelpful as the lawyer can make them without running afoul of Rule 26(g)'s certification requirement.

Q **2. The scope of the answering party's obligation.** Will Mildred Chevron be able to answer Interrogatory No. 29 from her personal knowledge? If not, can she answer, truthfully, that she doesn't know?

A Ms. Chevron—who is signing the answers for Toyota Co.—probably has no personal knowledge of all of the information sought by this interrogatory, especially if the Camry was designed before she joined Toyota. Indeed, there may be no present employee of Toyota who can answer all the interrogatories from personal knowledge. No matter. The duty imposed on Toyota, as a corporation, by Rule 33(b)(1)(B) is to "furnish such information *as is available to the party*" (emphasis added). Toyota has available to it not only the information known to its employees, but also to its agents, including its lawyers.

This is one reason why the discoverer can access facts contained in work product documents by directing interrogatories to the corporate party on whose behalf those documents were prepared (e.g., to Fortenbaugh's client in *Hickman*). That party must answer on the basis of all information available to it, including any available to it from the work effort of its lawyer. Toyota must therefore conduct a reasonable inquiry to answer the interrogatories, which may include interviewing employees and reviewing documents. And then it must certify that it has done so, by signing the answers. *See* Fed. R. Civ. P. 26(g)(1).

Q **3. The option to produce business records.** Planning and conducting the inquiry needed to answer interrogatories for a major corporation is no small task. But the Rule offers at least one problematic form of relief. If the answers to Interrogatory No. 29 can be found in Toyota's business records, and the burden of searching them is no greater for Painter than for Toyota, then it may make them available to Painter in lieu of answering. Fed. R. Civ. P. 33(d). Why is this option problematic?

A

Practically speaking, Toyota would not want Painter's lawyer rummaging through its files. For one thing, it could be concerned that privileged materials or trade secrets may be found among them. If they were not identified and withheld under objection beforehand, the opposing party may see them. *See* Rule 26(b)(5) (restricting their use, however). Toyota is therefore unlikely to make its actual design or customer complaint files available to Painter instead of assuming the burden of deriving the answers itself after searching and inventorying those files. Of course, if Toyota knows that they contain no privileged communications or trade secrets, it might exercise this option to shift the search costs to Painter.

Q

4. Particular objections.

A

A. "General objections." Many sets of answers to interrogatories begin with a set of "general objections" like these:

> Plaintiff hereby submits these answers to Defendant's First Set of Interrogatories, subject to and without waiving the following general objections:
>
> 1. Plaintiff objects to each instruction, definition, document request, and interrogatory to the extent that it purports to impose any requirement or discovery obligation greater than or different from those under the Federal Rules of Civil Procedure and the applicable Rules and Orders of the Court.
>
> 2. Plaintiff objects to each document request and interrogatory that is overly broad, unduly burdensome, or not reasonably calculated to lead to the discovery of admissible evidence.
>
> 3. Plaintiff objects to each instruction, definition, document request, and interrogatory to the extent that it seeks documents protected from disclosure by the attorney-client privilege, deliberative process privilege, attorney work product doctrine, or any other applicable privilege. Should any such disclosure by Plaintiff occur, it is inadvertent and shall not constitute a waiver of any privilege. . . .

While such boilerplate "general objections" are still common (perhaps made "at least in part, out of 'lawyer paranoia' not to waive inadvertently any objections that might protect" the clients, *Liguria Foods, Inc. v. Griffith Labs., Inc.*, 320 F.R.D. 168, 181 (N.D. Iowa 2017)), they have come under increasing fire from the courts. Citing, *inter alia*, Rules 26(b)(1) (imposing proportionality standard), 26(b)(5) (requiring that assertions of privilege or work product immunity be made "expressly," with a description of the nature of withheld information), and 33(b)(4) (requiring that objections to interrogatories be stated "with specificity"), courts have sometimes stricken such "general objections" or even sanctioned the party who made them.

> When, as here, an objecting party makes no attempt to "show specifically how . . . each interrogatory [or request for production] is not relevant or how each question is overly broad, burdensome or oppressive," and no attempt to "articulat[e]

> the particular harm that would accrue if [the responding party] were required to respond to [the proponent's] discovery requests," but relies, instead, on "the mere statement . . . that the interrogatory [or request for production] was overly broad, burdensome, oppressive and irrelevant," the response "is not adequate to voice a successful objection"; instead, the response is an unacceptable "boilerplate" objection. *St. Paul Reins. Co., Ltd.*, 198 F.R.D. at 511–12 (internal quotation marks and citations omitted). Moreover, simply stating that a response is "subject to" one or more general objections does not satisfy the "specificity" requirement, because, for example, it leaves the propounding party unclear about which of the numerous general objections is purportedly applicable as well as whether the documents or answers provided are complete, or whether responsive documents are being withheld.

Liguria, 320 F.R.D. at 186–87. Toyota's answers therefore omit such general objections.

B. *The interrogatories as a whole.* Still, interrogatories as a whole can be "burdensome and oppressive" when they are copied mindlessly and at great length from "pattern interrogatories": sets of suggested interrogatories from a commercial form book organized by type of claim or defense. For this reason, the 1993 Federal Rule revision imposed a numerical limit (twenty-five), following the lead of many states. Painter's first set of interrogatories clearly exceeds the twenty-five-interrogatory limit, especially if one counts against this limit each subpart required by the definitions (e.g., name, address, telephone, etc.). But a party wanting more can seek the agreement of the other parties or leave of court.

C. *Interrogatory No. 6.* Interrogatory No. 6 may require Toyota to identify numerous employees, even though few, if any, production-line employees would have information useful to the case and even though many of these employees first became involved long after the model year involved in Painter's accident. Toyota has asserted a relevancy objection, but such persons *are* arguably "relevant to the claim" in Painter's complaint. The real objection is simply to the burden of such unrestricted discovery. This interrogatory evidences that individual interrogatories, like the collective set, can be burdensome and oppressive. How can a court respond to this objection if it agrees that the interrogatory, as written, is burdensome and oppressive?

A The qualifier, "as written," suggests the answer. While the Rules do not expressly make burden an objection, they do make undue burden or expense a basis for an order limiting such discovery (Fed. R. Civ. P. 26(b)(2)(C)(i)) & 26(c)(1)) and it is widely recognized as a valid objection to discovery requests. In this case, if Painter moves to compel answers from Toyota in response to its objection, the court could deal with the objection by exempting production-line employees or limiting the relevant time period for the identification, effectively rewriting the interrogatory by narrowing it. Of course, ideally, the parties should do this themselves in the "meet-and-confer" required by Rule 26(f).

D. *Interrogatories Nos. 114 and 115.* What is wrong with these interrogatories, if anything? Hint: What would you need to do in order to answer Interrogatory No. 114?

A

Rule 33(a)(2) states that an interrogatory is not objectionable just because it asks for "an opinion or contention that relates to fact or the application of law to fact." Such "contention interrogatories" are needed to ascertain how a party will contend that the law applies to the facts come trial. Of course, a party may not know what it contends until it has taken appropriate discovery. The Rule therefore allows the court to postpone the time for answering contention interrogatories until such discovery has been completed. Fed. R. Civ. P. 33(a)(2). By negative implication, on the other hand, an interrogatory that calls for a pure legal conclusion or opinion, not applied to the facts of the case, is objectionable. The asking party can answer it as readily as the responding party, by looking in the library.

Interrogatory No. 114 is therefore objectionable for seeking a pure legal conclusion. You would have to go to the law library to prepare a response and it "would necessarily amount to [a] free-form legal essay[] . . . [bearing] no necessary relation to the facts of [the] case." *Kendrick v. Sullivan*, 125 F.R.D. 1, 3 (D.D.C. 1989). Interrogatory No. 115, on the other hand, is not objectionable; the subtle difference is that it asks for a contention regarding the application of the assumption of risk defense to this case. You don't have to hit the library to answer this one; you have to decide how you are contending that the law applies to the facts of your particular case. A negative answer will help narrow the issues for trial.

Q

5. The duty to supplement. Painter attempts to impose a duty of supplementation on Toyota by his preamble. Has Painter accurately described the duty of supplementation imposed by Rule 26(e)?

A

No. He overstates it. Rule 26(e) does require Toyota to supplement its answers, but only with information that makes its answer materially incomplete or incorrect, if that information has not already otherwise been made known to the other parties. If the information comes out during a deposition of which all parties have notice, the Rule does not literally require any further supplementation. And the discovering party's instructions cannot impose obligations inconsistent with the Rules.

Of course, in this as in so many other discovery matters, what the Rules require at a minimum, and what is best practice, may be two different things. Many lawyers will therefore supplement answers that have been rendered incomplete or incorrect by such testimony, if for no other reason than to preclude any colorable claim that they or their client tried to mislead the other parties.

IV. Requests for Production of Documents and Things

Read Fed. R. Civ. P. 34. Consider Painter's first request for production of documents and how Toyota should respond.

UNITED STATES DISTRICT COURT
DISTRICT OF OLD JERSEY

PETER PAINTER, Plaintiff v. TOYOTA CO., INC., Defendant	))))))))	CIVIL ACTION NO. 09-2114 PLAINTIFF'S FIRST REQUEST FOR PRODUCTION OF DOCUMENTS

Plaintiff Peter Painter requests defendant Toyota Co. to respond within 30 days to the following requests.

Definitions: . . .

1. That defendant produce at Law Offices of Marjorie Runnels, 62 Lawyers Row, Oldark, Old Jersey, and permit plaintiff to inspect and copy each of the following documents:

(a) patents granted to the defendant for the Toyota Camry or any of its components;
(b) warnings, restrictions, or advertisements, if any, included with, placed upon, and/or distributed with the Toyota Camry;
(c) any writings identified in answer to Interrogatory 51 in Plaintiff's First Set of Interrogatories . . .
(f) reports, memoranda, documents, or other writings pertaining to any investigation conducted by defendant or any person or entity on its behalf, of any defects or alleged defects in the Toyota Camry or any of its components;
(g) blueprints, schematics, drawings, and/or photographs pertaining to the design specifications, manufacturing requirements, and safety features, if any, of the Toyota Camry; . . .

2. That defendant produce at the location where it is kept and permit plaintiff to inspect and photograph any mock-up, sample, or test model of the Toyota Camry. . . .

Jan. 20, 2020

/S/
Marjorie Runnels
Attorney for the Plaintiff
62 Lawyers Row
Oldark, Old Jersey 30221
201-878-6755

Notes and Questions: Requests for Production of Documents

1. Procedure for requests for documents. Ask and ye shall receive. Note first, however, that you should already have received copies or descriptions of some of the documents you most want in the opposing party's required initial disclosures. If that first phase of discovery worked as intended, there should be less need for extensive document requests in the subsequent, discretionary phase of discovery because each side should at least have disclosed or identified evidence it would use to support its claims or defenses.

If you choose to ask anyway, you have simply to describe "with reasonable particularity" the document or category of documents or things you seek and then serve the request on a party, with copies to all other parties. That party must then comply or object in writing within thirty days, unless the parties stipulate to a longer time, as is often the case. This production is often made at the requesting party's office, but in some cases the sheer bulk of the materials may require that production be at the producing party's location. Of course, when the requester seeks to inspect land or a large, immobile object, that inspection will usually be where the land lies or the object is kept.

2. The scope of the producing party's obligation.

Suppose Toyota has made an extensive study of the precise defect that it believed caused Painter's accident, in which its accountants concluded that it was less costly to pay occasional damages for resulting accidents than to fix it.

This is obviously a smoking gun. (Or what amounts to the same thing—it can be made to look that way to a jury.) Toyota would hope never to have to produce it. Which, if any, of the following options is open to it?

A. Hiding the study from discovery by giving it to its lawyer.
B. Shredding the study, as long as Painter has not yet asked for it.
C. Placing the study in a thick folder marked "Ashtray Specifications" in the middle of twenty-two file cabinets of Camry files and then making those files available to Painter's lawyer.
D. Silently withholding the study, if Toyota's lawyer concludes that it qualifies as work product.
E. Silently withholding the study, if Painter has asked *only* for all documents "related to design or manufacture of this product," on the theory that the study does not directly relate to the original design or manufacture of the car.

The short answer is that none of these are proper options.

A won't work, because the Rule gives a clear answer: It targets documents and things "in the responding party's possession, custody, *or control*." Fed. R. Civ. P. 34(a)(1) (emphasis added). Any document held for Toyota by its lawyer is in its control; agents like lawyers, accountants, and banks must follow the instructions of their principals regarding documents entrusted to them. Thus, Toyota still controls the disposition of documents given to its lawyers. Furthermore, by signing its response to the document request, through a representative, Toyota certifies that it made "reasonable inquiry." Fed. R. Civ. P. 26(g)(1). It must conduct a search of its employees and agents, including its lawyers, for responsive documents. Merely handing off a discoverable document to your lawyer will not shield it from discovery.

Intuitively, you know that Toyota cannot destroy the smoking gun either, so **B** must be wrong. In the first place, it would violate the spirit, if not the letter, of the Rule 26(g) certification. In addition, it would run afoul of the rule that a lawyer shall not "unlawfully alter, destroy or conceal a document or material having potential evidentiary value" or "assist another person to do any such act." *ABA Rules of Professional Conduct* 3.4(a). Furthermore, evidentiary rules against *spoliation* (a fancy way of describing the intentional or sometimes grossly negligent destruction of discoverable information) may lead to sanctions against Toyota, and under some circumstances, document destruction could even be a crime.

C is also wrong. A bar committee dryly noted in 1977 that "[i]t is apparently not rare for parties deliberately to mix critical documents with others in hopes of obscuring significance." *Report of the Special Committee for the Study of Discovery Abuse, Section of Litigation of the American Bar Association* 22 (1977). The Rule was therefore amended to require the producing party to produce documents "as they are kept in the usual course of business" or to "organize and label them to correspond to the categories in the request." Fed. R. Civ. P. 34(b). ("Ashtray Specifications," indeed! Why not stick it in the "naugahyde trim" folder? Give us a break.)

D sounds more plausible at first glance, but poses two problems. First, *is* the study work product? Recall from Chapter 21 that in some circuits, work product must have been prepared primarily in anticipation of litigation and not just for an ordinary business purpose. We need more facts to ascertain whether the study meets this standard. Second, even if it does, work product is an objection that you must "expressly" make, describing the study in a manner that, without revealing the protected information, will enable your adversaries to assess the claim. Fed. R. Civ. P. 26(b)(5). If Toyota only makes a "silent objection," Painter would erroneously assume that Toyota had no documents responsive to his request and would therefore never test Toyota's "objection" by a *motion to compel discovery*, which is the device by which Painter would put the issue to the trial judge or magistrate. Only by *expressly* making an objection does a party afford opposing parties and, ultimately, the court the chance to assess the objection. *There is no "silent objection" under the federal discovery rules.* Toyota's duty under the Rules is reinforced by the ethics prohibition against "knowingly disobey[ing] an obligation under the rules of a tribunal except for an *open refusal* based on an assertion that no valid obligation exists." *ABA Model Rules of Professional Conduct* 3.4(c) (emphasis added).

This leaves **E**. Except for required disclosures and supplemental information pursuant to Rule 26(e), no party is obliged to give information to other parties if they have not asked for it. The trick is to fairly construe their discovery requests. For example, because this study was prepared after the design or manufacture of the Camry, some lawyers might read it as falling outside the scope of a request for documents "related to the design and manufacture of this product." On the other hand, the request does not specify any time frame, and a study that considered the costs of fixing a manufacturing defect arguably relates to manufacturing of the car and thus falls within the scope of Painter's request. This, ultimately, is more a question of lawyering than of the rules, and sometimes of ethics. There is a substantial risk that the study will surface anyway (companies often make multiple copies that are distributed to many employees). If the cost study does surface,

Painter's lawyer will argue to the jury that Toyota tried to hide the study, which may hurt Toyota more than the study itself. Thus, the safe thing to do may well be to construe the request to include the study, quite apart from Rule 26(g)(1)'s certification requirement that a disclosure is "complete and correct as of the time it is made." An alternative that some lawyers might choose would be to hold on to the study, but explain in response to the discovery request that the defendant is producing nonprivileged documents generated by the "original" design and manufacture of the car, or generated before a specified date, so as to disclose (or suggest?) the narrow construction that they have put on the request.

In short, this multiple choice question seems to be an instance of the old discovery adage, "If all else fails, do the right thing." If the study is responsive to the discovery request, relevant to the claim or defense of any party, nonprivileged, and in Toyota's possession, custody, or control, you must produce it.

V. Electronic Discovery ("E-discovery")

Until December 1, 2006, the discovery rules reflected the unstated premise that most information was stored in documents. While the Rules did authorize discovery of "data compilations," they were not crafted to deal clearly and effectively with electronically stored information ("ESI"). Yet, already by 1999, 93 percent of all information generated was generated in digital form on computers. *See In re Bristol-Myers Squibb Securities Litigation*, 205 F.R.D. 437, 440 n.2 (D.N.J. 2002). Although some of the ESI concerning business information is eventually printed, it is estimated that 30 percent never appears in printed form. *See* Michael R. Arkfeld, Electronic Discovery and Evidence § 1.1A (2020). Most e-mail messages are never printed, and, indeed, most are probably generated without the parties ever intending, or perhaps even knowing, that they will be preserved electronically.

"Doc Review"—Then and Now

Jim Pickerell / Fotosearch

Many cases turn on documentary evidence. This tends to be especially true in large-scale commercial litigation. Requests for production of documents are therefore important parts of initial discovery in such cases. But they place huge burdens on both the producing party and the requesting party, burdens which disproportionately fall on junior associates assigned to perform document review. The producing party may have to review boxes of documents like those in the picture to determine which documents are within the scope of the request and then to identify any that may be protected by a privilege or work product immunity, or eligible for protection as trade secrets or other "confidential research, development, or commercial information" under Rule 26(e)'s provision for a protective order.

The requesting party will want to review every document that is produced in an inevitably tedious search for occasional needles in the haystack. The advent of ESI has significantly changed the form and, in most cases, increased the quantity of discovery. The warehouse of documents may now have been replaced by backup tapes or other storage media, and the "doc review" may now be performed on a computer using "predictive coding" — search protocols that a lawyer helps improve by an iterative process.

The transformation in the way people and entities generate and keep information inevitably affected discovery. On one hand, it opened up new vistas for discovery (think smoking gun e-mails); on the other, it increased the burden both for the discovering party and the responding party of retrieving and translating often relatively inaccessible electronic data. The following decision was a pioneer in electronic discovery—or "e-discovery"—helping to lay the groundwork for subsequent revisions to the Rules addressing problems of "e-discovery."

READING *ZUBULAKE v. UBS WARBURG LLC.* Ms. Zubulake sued her former employer for gender discrimination and illegal retaliation. Having herself produced 450 relevant e-mails apparently generated at or in communication with her workplace, she reasonably believed that the employer would have more, and she made a production request for them. When the employer balked, arguing that it would cost $175,000 to restore e-mails (not counting attorney time to review them!), Zubulake moved for an order compelling production. The motion raised a classic cost-benefit question under what is now renumbered as Rule 26(b)(1). (Rule 26(b)(2)(B)—specifically dealing with e-discovery—was first added in 2006 after this opinion.)

- Does the defendant object that the ESI is irrelevant or privileged? If not, what precisely is its objection?
- What would be wrong with ordering the defendant simply to produce all of the relevant e-mails on its backup tapes at its own expense? Alternatively, what would be wrong with making Zubulake pay the costs of producing all of the backup tapes? What is the default principle of cost allocation in discovery under the Federal Rules?
- By what authority can a court overrule this default principle? Does the seeming compromise struck by the court put the e-discovery dispute to rest for this litigation?

ZUBULAKE v. UBS WARBURG LLC [ZUBULAKE I]

217 F.R.D. 309 (S.D.N.Y. 2003)

Scheindlin, District Judge.

The world was a far different place in 1849, when Henry David Thoreau opined (in an admittedly broader context) that "[t]he process of discovery is very simple."

That hopeful maxim has given way to rapid technological advances, requiring new solutions to old problems. The issue presented here is one such problem, recast in light of current technology: To what extent is inaccessible electronic data discoverable, and who should pay for its production?

I. INTRODUCTION . . .

The Rules contemplate a minimal burden to bringing a claim; that claim is then fleshed out through vigorous and expansive discovery.

In one context, however, the reliance on broad discovery has hit a roadblock. As individuals and corporations increasingly do business electronically—using computers to create and store documents, make deals, and exchange e-mails—the universe of discoverable material has expanded exponentially. The more information there is to discover, the more expensive it is to discover all the relevant information until, in the end, "discovery is not just about uncovering the truth, but also about how much of the truth the parties can afford to disinter."

This case provides a textbook example of the difficulty of balancing the competing needs of broad discovery and manageable costs. Laura Zubulake is suing UBS Warburg LLC, UBS Warburg, and UBS AG (collectively, "UBS" or the "Firm") under Federal, State and City law for gender discrimination and illegal retaliation. Zubulake's case is certainly not frivolous[8] and if she prevails, her damages may be substantial. She contends that key evidence is located in various e-mails exchanged among UBS employees that now exist only on backup tapes and perhaps other archived media. According to UBS, restoring those e-mails would cost approximately $175,000.00, exclusive of attorney time in reviewing the e-mails. Zubulake now moves for an order compelling UBS to produce those e-mails at its expense.

II. BACKGROUND . . .

C. UBS's E-Mail Backup System

In the first instance, the parties agree that e-mail was an important means of communication at UBS during the relevant time period. Each salesperson, including the salespeople on the Desk, received approximately 200 e-mails each day. Given this volume, and because Securities and Exchange Commission regulations require it, UBS implemented extensive e-mail backup and preservation protocols. In particular, e-mails were backed up in two distinct ways: on backup tapes and on optical disks.

1. Backup Tape Storage

UBS employees used a program called HP OpenMail, manufactured by Hewlett-Packard, for all work-related e-mail communications. With limited exceptions, *all*

8. Indeed, Zubulake has already produced a sort of "smoking gun": an e-mail suggesting that she be fired "ASAP" after her EEOC charge was filed, in part so that she would not be eligible for year-end bonuses.

e-mails sent or received by *any* UBS employee are stored onto backup tapes. To do so, UBS employs a program called Veritas NetBackup, which creates a "snapshot" of all e-mails that exist on a given server at the time the backup is taken. Except for scheduling the backups and physically inserting the tapes into the machines, the backup process is entirely automated.

UBS used the same backup protocol during the entire relevant time period, from 1999 through 2001. Using NetBackup, UBS backed up its e-mails at three intervals: (1) daily, at the end of each day, (2) weekly, on Friday nights, and (3) monthly, on the last business day of the month. Nightly backup tapes were kept for twenty working days, weekly tapes for one year, and monthly tapes for three years. After the relevant time period elapsed, the tapes were recycled.

Once e-mails have been stored onto backup tapes, the restoration process is lengthy. Each backup tape routinely takes approximately five days to restore, although resort to an outside vendor would speed up the process (at greatly enhanced costs, of course). Because each tape represents a snapshot of one server's hard drive in a given month, each server/month must be restored separately onto a hard drive. Then, a program called Double Mail is used to extract a particular individual's e-mail file. That mail file is then exported into a Microsoft Outlook data file, which in turn can be opened in Microsoft Outlook, a common e-mail application. A user could then browse through the mail file and sort the mail by recipient, date or subject, or search for key words in the body of the e-mail.

Fortunately, NetBackup also created indexes of each backup tape. Thus, Behny was able to search through the tapes from the relevant time period and determine that the e-mail files responsive to Zubulake's requests are contained on a total of ninety-four backup tapes.

2. Optical Disk Storage

In addition to the e-mail backup tapes, UBS also stored certain e-mails on optical disks. . . .

. . . Thus, UBS has *every* e-mail sent or received by registered traders (except internal e-mails) during the period of Zubulake's employment, even if the e-mail was deleted instantaneously on that trader's system.

The optical disks are easily searchable using a program called Tumbleweed. . . . For example, UBS personnel could easily run a search for e-mails containing the words "Laura" or "Zubulake" that were sent or received by Chapin, Datta, Clarke, or Hardisty. . . .

IV. DISCUSSION

A. Should Discovery of UBS's Electronic Data Be Permitted?

Under Rule 34, a party may request discovery of any document, "including writings, drawings, graphs, charts, photographs, phonorecords, and other data compilations. . . ." The "inclusive description" of the term document "accord[s] with changing technology." "It makes clear that Rule 34 applies to *electronics* [sic] data compilations."* Thus, "[e]lectronic documents are no less subject to disclosure than paper records." This is true not only of electronic documents that are currently in use, but also of documents that may have been deleted and now reside only on backup disks.

That being so, Zubulake is entitled to discovery of the requested e-mails so long as they are relevant to her claims, which they clearly are. As noted, e-mail constituted a substantial means of communication among UBS employees. To that end, UBS has already produced approximately 100 pages of e-mails, the contents of which are unquestionably relevant.

Nonetheless, UBS argues that Zubulake is not entitled to any further discovery because it already produced all responsive documents, to wit, the 100 pages of e-mails. This argument is unpersuasive for two reasons. *First*, because of the way that UBS backs up its e-mail files, it clearly could not have searched all of its e-mails without restoring the ninety-four backup tapes (which UBS admits that it has not done). UBS therefore cannot represent that it has produced all responsive e-mails. *Second*, Zubulake herself has produced over 450 pages of relevant e-mails, including e-mails that would have been responsive to her discovery requests but were never produced by UBS. These two facts strongly suggest that there are e-mails that Zubulake has not received that reside on UBS's backup media.

B. Should Cost-Shifting Be Considered?

Because it apparently recognizes that Zubulake is entitled to the requested discovery, UBS expends most of its efforts urging the court to shift the cost of production to "protect [it] . . . from undue burden or expense." Faced with similar applications, courts generally engage in some sort of cost-shifting analysis, whether the refined eight-factor *Rowe [Entm't, Inc. v. William Morris Agency, Inc.*, 205 F.R.D. 421 (S.D.N.Y. 2002)] test or a cruder application of Rule 34's proportionality test, or something in between.

The first question, however, is whether cost-shifting must be considered in every case involving the discovery of electronic data, which—in today's world—includes virtually all cases. In light of the accepted principle, stated above, that electronic evidence is no less discoverable than paper evidence, the answer is, "No." The Supreme Court has instructed that "the presumption is that the responding party must bear the expense of complying with discovery requests. . . ." Any principled approach to electronic evidence must respect this presumption.

Courts must remember that cost-shifting may effectively end discovery, especially when private parties are engaged in litigation with large corporations. As large companies increasingly move to entirely paper-free environments, the frequent use of cost-shifting will have the effect of crippling discovery in discrimination and retaliation cases. This will both undermine the "strong public policy favor[ing] resolving disputes on their merits," and may ultimately deter the filing of potentially meritorious claims.

*** [Eds.—Rule 34 was amended in 2006 to include an express reference to "electronically stored information," as well as provisions for responding to and producing requested for such information.]**

Thus, cost-shifting should be considered *only* when electronic discovery imposes an "undue burden or expense" on the responding party. The burden or expense of discovery is, in turn, "undue" when it "outweighs its likely benefit, taking into account the needs of the case, the amount in controversy, the parties' resources, the importance of the issues at stake in the litigation, and the importance of the proposed discovery in resolving the issues." **[Eds.—now Rule 26(b)(1).]**

Many courts have automatically assumed that an undue burden or expense may arise simply because electronic evidence is involved. This makes no sense. Electronic evidence is frequently cheaper and easier to produce than paper evidence because it can be searched automatically, key words can be run for privilege checks, and the production can be made in electronic form obviating the need for mass photocopying.

In fact, whether production of documents is unduly burdensome or expensive turns primarily on whether it is kept in an *accessible or inaccessible* format (a distinction that corresponds closely to the expense of production). In the world of paper documents, for example, a document is accessible if it is readily available in a usable format and reasonably indexed. Examples of inaccessible paper documents could include (a) documents in storage in a difficult to reach place; (b) documents converted to microfiche and not easily readable; or (c) documents kept haphazardly, with no indexing system, in quantities that make page-by-page searches impracticable. But in the world of electronic data, thanks to search engines, any data that is retained in a machine readable format is typically accessible.

Whether electronic data is accessible or inaccessible turns largely on the media on which it is stored. Five categories of data, listed in order from most accessible to least accessible, are described in the literature on electronic data storage:

1. Active, online data: "On-line storage is generally provided by magnetic disk. It is used in the very active stages of an electronic records [sic] life—when it is being created or received and processed, as well as when the access frequency is high and the required speed of access is very fast, i.e., milliseconds." Examples of online data include hard drives.
2. Near-line data: "This typically consists of a robotic storage device (robotic library) that houses removable media, uses robotic arms to access the media, and uses multiple read/write devices to store and retrieve records. Access speeds can range from as low as milliseconds if the media is already in a read device, up to 10–30 seconds for optical disk technology, and between 20–120 seconds for sequentially searched media, such as magnetic tape." Examples include optical disks.
3. Offline storage/archives: "This is removable optical disk or magnetic tape media, which can be labeled and stored in a shelf or rack. Off-line storage of electronic records is traditionally used for making disaster copies of records and also for records considered 'archival' in that their likelihood of retrieval is minimal. Accessibility to off-line media involves manual intervention and is much slower than on-line or near-line storage. Access speed may be minutes, hours, or even days, depending on the access-effectiveness of the

storage facility." The principled [sic] difference between nearline data and offline data is that offline data lacks "the coordinated control of an intelligent disk subsystem," and is, in the lingo, JBOD ("Just a Bunch Of Disks").

4. Backup tapes: "A device, like a tape recorder, that reads data from and writes it onto a tape. Tape drives have data capacities of anywhere from a few hundred kilobytes to several gigabytes. Their transfer speeds also vary considerably.... The disadvantage of tape drives is that they are sequential-access devices, which means that to read any particular block of data, you need to read all the preceding blocks." As a result, "[t]he data on a backup tape are not organized for retrieval of individual documents or files [because] ... the organization of the data mirrors the computer's structure, not the human records management structure." Backup tapes also typically employ some sort of data compression, permitting more data to be stored on each tape, but also making restoration more time-consuming and expensive, especially given the lack of uniform standard governing data compression.
5. Erased, fragmented or damaged data: "When a file is first created and saved, it is laid down on the [storage media] in contiguous clusters.... As files are erased, their clusters are made available again as free space. Eventually, some newly created files become larger than the remaining contiguous free space. These files are then broken up and randomly placed throughout the disk." Such broken-up files are said to be "fragmented," and along with damaged and erased data can only be accessed after significant processing.

Of these, the first three categories are typically identified as accessible, and the latter two as inaccessible. The difference between the two classes is easy to appreciate. Information deemed "accessible" is stored in a readily usable format. Although the time it takes to actually access the data ranges from milliseconds to days, the data does not need to be restored or otherwise manipulated to be usable. "Inaccessible" data, on the other hand, is not readily usable. Backup tapes must be restored using a process similar to that previously described, fragmented data must be de-fragmented, and erased data must be reconstructed, all before the data is usable. That makes such data inaccessible.

The case at bar is a perfect illustration of the range of accessibility of electronic data. As explained above, UBS maintains e-mail files in three forms: (1) active user e-mail files; (2) archived e-mails on optical disks; and (3) backup data stored on tapes. The active (HP OpenMail) data is obviously the most accessible: it is online data that resides on an active server, and can be accessed immediately. The optical disk (Tumbleweed) data is only slightly less accessible, and falls into either the second or third category. The e-mails are on optical disks that need to be located and read with the correct hardware, but the system is configured to make searching the optical disks simple and automated once they are located. For these sources of e-mails—active mail files and e-mails stored on optical disks—it would be wholly inappropriate to even consider cost-shifting. UBS maintains the data in an accessible and usable format, and can respond to Zubulake's request cheaply and quickly. Like most typical discovery requests, therefore, the producing party should bear the cost of production.

E-mails stored on backup tapes (via NetBackup), however, are an entirely different matter. Although UBS has already identified the ninety-four potentially responsive backup tapes, those tapes are not currently accessible. In order to search the tapes for responsive e-mails, UBS would have to engage in the costly and time-consuming process detailed above. It is therefore appropriate to *consider* cost shifting.

C. What Is the Proper Cost-Shifting Analysis?

In the year since *Rowe* was decided, its eight factor test has unquestionably become the gold standard for courts resolving electronic discovery disputes. But there is little doubt that the *Rowe* factors will generally favor cost-shifting. Indeed, of the handful of reported opinions that apply *Rowe* or some modification thereof, *all of them* have ordered the cost of discovery to be shifted to the requesting party.

In order to maintain the presumption that the responding party pays, the cost-shifting analysis must be neutral; close calls should be resolved in favor of the presumption. The *Rowe* factors, as applied, undercut that presumption for three reasons. *First*, the Rowe test is incomplete. *Second*, courts have given equal weight to all of the factors, when certain factors should predominate. *Third*, courts applying the *Rowe* test have not always developed a full factual record. . . .

a. A Modification of Rowe: Additional Factors

Certain factors specifically identified in the Rules are omitted from *Rowe*'s eight factors. In particular, Rule 26 requires consideration of "the amount in controversy, the parties' resources, the importance of the issues at stake in the litigation, and the importance of the proposed discovery in resolving the issues." Yet *Rowe* makes no mention of either the amount in controversy or the importance of the issues at stake in the litigation. These factors should be added. Doing so would balance the *Rowe* factor that typically weighs most heavily in favor of cost-shifting, "the total cost associated with production." The cost of production is almost always an objectively large number in cases where litigating cost-shifting is worthwhile. But the cost of production when compared to "the amount in controversy" may tell a different story. A response to a discovery request costing $100,000 sounds (and is) costly, but in a case potentially worth millions of dollars, the cost of responding may not be unduly burdensome.

Rowe also contemplates "the resources available to each party." But here too—although this consideration may be implicit in the *Rowe* test—the absolute wealth of the parties is not the relevant factor. More important than comparing the relative ability of a party to pay for discovery, the focus should be on the total cost of production as compared to the resources available to each party. Thus, discovery that would be too expensive for one defendant to bear would be a drop in the bucket for another.

Last, "the importance of the issues at stake in the litigation" is a critical consideration, even if it is one that will rarely be invoked. For example, if a case has the potential for broad public impact, then public policy weighs heavily in favor of permitting extensive discovery. Cases of this ilk might include toxic tort class actions, environmental actions, so-called "impact" or social reform litigation, cases involving criminal conduct, or cases implicating important legal or constitutional questions....

2. The Seven Factors Should Not Be Weighed Equally

... The first two factors—comprising the marginal utility test—are the most important. These factors include: (1) The extent to which the request is specifically tailored to discover relevant information and (2) the availability of such information from other sources. The substance of the marginal utility test was well described in *McPeek v. Ashcroft,* [202 F.R.D 31, 34 (D.D.C. 2001)]:

> The more likely it is that the backup tape contains information that is relevant to a claim or defense, the fairer it is that the [responding party] search at its own expense. The less likely it is, the more unjust it would be to make the [responding party] search at its own expense. The difference is "at the margin." ...

D. A Factual Basis Is Required to Support the Analysis ...

[Eds.—The court notes that requiring the party seeking e-discovery to prove that there is a high probability that it will contain relevant information—that such discovery will have significant marginal utility—is contrary to Rule 26(b)(1)'s allowance of discovery of "any matter" that "is relevant to [a] claim or defense."]

The best solution to this problem is found in *McPeek*:

> Given the complicated questions presented [and] the clash of policies ... I have decided to take small steps and perform, as it were, a test run. Accordingly, I will order DOJ to perform a backup restoration of the e-mails attributable to Diegelman's computer during the period of July 1, 1998 to July 1, 1999.... The DOJ will have to carefully document the time and money spent in doing the search. It will then have to search in the restored e-mails for any document responsive to any of the plaintiff's requests for production of documents. Upon the completion of this search, the DOJ will then file a comprehensive, sworn certification of the time and money spent and the results of the search. Once it does, I will permit the parties an opportunity to argue why the results and the expense do or do not justify any further search.

Requiring the responding party to restore and produce responsive documents from a small sample of backup tapes will inform the cost-shifting analysis laid out above. When based on an actual sample, the marginal utility test will not be an exercise in speculation—there will be tangible evidence of what the backup tapes may have to offer. There will also be tangible evidence of the time and cost required to restore the backup tapes, which in turn will inform the second group of cost-shifting factors. Thus, by requiring a sample restoration of backup tapes, the entire cost-shifting analysis can be grounded in fact rather than guesswork.

IV. CONCLUSION AND ORDER

In summary, deciding disputes regarding the scope and cost of discovery of electronic data requires a three-step analysis:

First, it is necessary to thoroughly understand the responding party's computer system, both with respect to active and stored data. For data that is kept in an accessible format, the usual rules of discovery apply: the responding party should pay the costs of producing responsive data. A court should consider cost-shifting *only* when electronic data is relatively inaccessible, such as in backup tapes.

Second, because the cost-shifting analysis is so fact-intensive, it is necessary to determine what data may be found on the inaccessible media. Requiring the responding party to restore and produce responsive documents from a small sample of the requested backup tapes is a sensible approach in most cases.

Third, and finally, in conducting the cost-shifting analysis, the following factors should be considered, weighted more-or-less in the following order:

1. The extent to which the request is specifically tailored to discover relevant information;
2. The availability of such information from other sources;
3. The total cost of production, compared to the amount in controversy;
4. The total cost of production, compared to the resources available to each party;
5. The relative ability of each party to control costs and its incentive to do so;
6. The importance of the issues at stake in the litigation; and
7. The relative benefits to the parties of obtaining the information.

Accordingly, UBS is ordered to produce *all* responsive e-mails that exist on its optical disks or on its active servers (*i.e.*, in HP OpenMail files) at its own expense. UBS is also ordered to produce, at its expense, responsive e-mails from any *five* backups tapes selected *by Zubulake.* UBS should then prepare an affidavit detailing the results of its search, as well as the time and money spent. After reviewing the contents of the backup tapes and UBS's certification, the Court will conduct the appropriate cost-shifting analysis. . . .

Notes and Questions: E-discovery

1. The problem of relevance. UBS Warburg did not argue that electronic data is outside the scope of Rule 34. Even the old Rule 34(a) in effect at the time of the *Zubulake I* decision included "data compilations from which information can be obtained." The later 2006 amendments removed any possible doubt. UBS Warburg's objection, instead, was in part that there was no way of knowing whether the backup tapes contained relevant data and thus met the threshold requirement for discovery under Rule 26(b)(1).

2. The problem of accessibility. UBS Warburg's other objection was that it would be unduly costly to perform a search of the 94 backup tapes because their contents could only be accessed—"restored" or made readable—by extracting them to a disk or hard drive, importing them into a different data file, opening that file, and then browsing and sorting it by various selectors, a procedure that would take five days for each tape.

This cost varies with the form of the data. The optical disks, for example, could easily be searched with a software program. In fact, such accessible e-data may be easier to search than paper documents, which need to be searched by hand (actually the ink-stained, paper-cut hands of newly minted young associates on "doc duty").

Q **3. Who pays?** As we saw in *Oxbow* (*supra* p. 764), the presumption is that the responding party pays for its own costs of production. But not only is this principle nowhere stated as such in the rules, it is not ironclad either. Even the costs of responding to a paper document request could be so enormous as to justify a departure from the principle by shifting all or part of the cost to the discovering party, or simply limiting the discovery to reduce the cost. What rule gave the *Zubulake I* court the authority to allocate costs in this fashion?

A Even before the 2006 amendments, Rule 26(b) (now Rule 26(b)(1)]) set out a cost-benefit formula that the court could use for these purposes. The *Zubulake I* court, like the *Rowe* court before it (which it cites), took this formula as a point of departure for considering cost shifting in e-discovery disputes. It places a burden both on the discovering party to show why it needs the discovery in light of issues in and needs of the case, and on the responding party to show the likely expense.

Q **4. A Catch-22?** But this seems to put plaintiffs in a Catch-22: They have to show the likely importance of costly e-discovery in order to get the e-discovery. How did the court deal with this dilemma?

A It found that requiring Zubulake to prove that the e-discovery she sought would hit paydirt was inconsistent with the lenient federal presumption of discovery and the relevancy standard. Instead, it limited the discovery that UBS Warburg had to provide *in the first instance* to a sample of just five tapes, which would then supply the parties and the court with a basis for deciding whether more e-discovery (and more cost) would be likely to turn up relevant evidence. Of course, its decision was made easier here by the fact that Zubulake had already found one smoking gun e-mail, urging that she be fired "ASAP" after her EEOC complaint in order to deprive her of year-end bonuses! See footnote 8 in the opinion. Where there's smoke, there's fire. She also had retained 450 relevant e-mails from work suggesting strongly that there would be more such e-mails on the backup tapes.

Q **5. Accessibility under Rule 26(b)(2)(B).** Rule 26(b)(2)(B) now provides express authority for limitations on electronic data. How would it have applied to the discovery dispute in *Zubulake I*?

A The Rule was practically written for this case. It excuses a party from providing e-discovery "from sources that the party identifies as not reasonably accessible because of undue burden or cost." UBS Warburg would therefore have the burden to show the undue cost of accessing the backup tapes. Even if it made that showing, Zubulake could still try to show good cause for going forward anyway, and the court is authorized to use a cost-benefit analysis to "specify conditions for the discovery." Rule 26(c)(1)(B) also now expressly authorizes the court to order the allocation of expenses. In sum, *Zubulake I* would likely come out the same way today.

Ideally, however, the parties should avoid burdening the court with this dispute. At the mandatory discovery conference, they must generate a proposed discovery plan that must address, *inter alia*, "any issues about disclosure, discovery, or preservation of electronically stored information, including the form or forms in which it should be produced." Fed. R. Civ. P. 26(f)(3)(C). As parties gain experience with e-discovery, and as more parties on both sides of the "v" find that possibly relevant data is stored electronically, it is more and more common for them to stipulate to mutually agreed limitations on discovery of the less readily accessible forms of such data (such as sampling the data by providing discovery only of randomly selected parts).

Zubulake I was ahead of its time in crafting such a solution. In fact, Judge Scheindlin has taken the lead in forging e-discovery law, much of it in her successive discovery opinions in this litigation, which are widely cited in other e-discovery decisions.

6. Handling an e-discovery request. Although we fear that our e-mails are stored somewhere forever, in fact e-data is often ephemeral. For example, *Zubulake I* tells us that UBS Warburg kept its backup tapes only for limited periods, then recycled them. Moreover, UBS's periodic "snapshot" backups necessarily also involved loss of certain e-mails that were deleted between backups. They would be only recoverable until the computer writes over the "deleted" data. *See Zubulake I*, 217 F.R.D. at 313. What obligation does a party (or prospective party) have to retain such data for litigation purposes, and what is the corresponding duty of its lawyer?

In *Zubulake IV*, 220 F.R.D. 212, 218 (S.D.N.Y. 2003), Judge Scheindlin answered by asserting that:

> Once a party reasonably anticipates litigation, it must suspend its routine document retention/destruction policy and put in place a "litigation hold" to ensure the preservation of relevant documents. As a general rule, that litigation hold does not apply to inaccessible backup tapes (*e.g.*, those typically maintained solely for the purpose of disaster recovery), which may continue to be recycled on the schedule set forth in the company's policy. On the other hand, if backup tapes are accessible (*i.e.*, actively used for information retrieval), then such tapes *would* likely be subject to the litigation hold.

In *Zubulake V*, 229 F.R.D. 422, 432 (S.D.N.Y. 2004), she added that:

> A party's discovery obligations do not end with the implementation of a "litigation hold"—to the contrary, that's only the beginning. Counsel must oversee compliance with the litigation hold, monitoring the party's efforts to retain and produce the relevant documents.... A lawyer cannot be obliged to monitor her client like a parent watching a child. At some point, the client must bear responsibility for a failure to preserve. At the same time, counsel is more conscious of the contours of the preservation obligation; a party cannot reasonably be trusted to receive the "litigation hold" instruction once and to fully comply with it without the active supervision of counsel.

In short, e-discovery may impose a continuing duty on the client and her lawyer alike to locate and preserve e-data.

7. Predictive coding in e-discovery. The figure on p. 817 shows an associate lugging boxes through a giant warehouse and raises the question whether today, he wouldn't instead be sitting at a computer reviewing documents. But maybe even that scenario is obsolete: Can computers simply take the associate out of the picture altogether?

Happily for the law students who aspire to become associates, the answer is still no. But *predictive coding* will significantly change the associate's (or partner's) role in discovery in cases involving very large numbers of documents or large amounts of electronically stored information. Such coding

> use[s] sophisticated algorithms to enable the computer to determine relevance, based on interaction with (i.e., training by) a human reviewer.
>
> Unlike manual review, where the review is done by the most junior staff, computer-assisted coding involves a senior partner (or [small] team) who review and code a "seed set" of documents. The computer identifies properties of those documents that it uses to code other documents. As the senior reviewer continues to code more sample documents, the computer predicts the reviewer's coding. (Or, the computer codes some documents and asks the senior reviewer for feedback.)
>
> When the system's predictions and the reviewer's coding sufficiently coincide, the system has learned enough to make confident predictions for the remaining documents. Typically, the senior lawyer (or team) needs to review only a few thousand documents to train the computer.
>
> Some systems produce a simple yes/no as to relevance, while others give a relevance score (say, on a 0 to 100 basis) that counsel can use to prioritize review. For example, a score above 50 may produce 97% of the relevant documents, but constitutes only 20% of the entire document set.
>
> Counsel may decide, after sampling and quality control tests, that documents with a score of below 15 are so highly likely to be irrelevant that no further human review is necessary. Counsel can also decide the cost-benefit of manual review of the documents with scores of 15–50.

Moore v. Publicis Groupe, 287 F.R.D. 182, 183–84 (S.D.N.Y. 2012) (citation omitted). Predictive coding is sometimes described as "keyword-agnostic": It does not rely simply on keyword searches. Nor does "coding" mean placing any code into a document. Instead, it involves interactions between humans and computer that identify "seed documents" by an iterative process.

Although traditionalists may still consider manual review the gold standard for document review, statistics show that this is a myth: Technology-assisted searches have been found to be at least as accurate as manual review, yet " 'require, on average, human review of only 1.9% of the documents, a fifty-fold savings over exhaustive manual review.' " *Id.* at 190 (citations omitted). Associates or their partners, in other words, are still needed to "train" the computer, to develop the "seed set" of documents, and to review the final "recall"—the relevant documents ultimately identified by the computer-assisted search—but they can be deployed more efficiently (and in lesser numbers) than in traditional document review.

Today, predictive coding is "widely accepted for limiting e-discovery of ESI without an undue burden," and it is "black letter law that where the producing party wants to utilize TAR [technology-assisted review] for document review, courts will permit it." *Rio Tinto PLC v. Vale S.A.*, 306 F.R.D. 125, 127 (S.D.N.Y. 2015). The remaining issues concern the parties' obligations to cooperate and to share information concerning seed sets and training sets. *Id.* at 128.

Of course, the unfamiliar terminology in this note and the rapid evolution of TAR alone sound a caution: *Don't try this at home. See, e.g., Lawson v. Spirit AeroSystems, Inc.*, No. 18-1100-EFM-ADM, 2020 WL 1813395 (D. Kan. Apr. 9, 2020) (discussing party disputes about "recall rates" and "precision" standards for TAR). Indeed, there is an emerging ethical obligation of lawyers to develop competency in e-discovery and TAR. Thus, an ethics opinion from a state bar committee concluded that attorneys handling e-discovery should be able to perform (either by themselves or in association with experts) the following tasks:

> (i) initially assess e-discovery needs and issues, if any;
>
> (ii) implement/cause to implement appropriate ESI preservation procedures;
>
> (iii) analyze and understand the client's ESI systems and storage;
>
> (iv) advise the client on available options for collection and preservation of ESI;
>
> (v) identify custodians of potentially relevant ESI;
>
> (vi) engage in competent and meaningful [meet-and-confer] with opposing counsel concerning an e-discovery plan;
>
> (vii) perform data searches;
>
> (viii) collect responsive ESI in a manner that preserves the integrity of that ESI; and
>
> (ix) produce responsive non-privileged ESI in a recognized and appropriate manner.

State Bar of Cal. Standing Comm. on Prof. Resp. and Conduct, Formal Op. 2015-193, at 3–4. *See generally* Andrew Perlman, *The Twenty-First Century Lawyer's Evolving Ethical Duty of Competence*, 22 PROF. LAW. 1 (2014).

VI. Depositions

Interrogatories and document requests are ubiquitous and important, but, as one court noted,

> [d]epositions are the factual battleground where the vast majority of litigation actually takes place. It may safely be said that Rule 30 has spawned a veritable cottage industry. The significance of depositions has grown geometrically over the years to the point where their pervasiveness now dwarfs both the time spent and the facts learned at the actual trial—assuming there is a trial, where there usually is not. The pretrial tail now wags the trial dog.

Hall v. Clifton Precision, 150 F.R.D. 525, 531 (E.D. Pa. 1993). Let's therefore take a close look at a deposition in Painter's case.

One of the witnesses identified by Toyota Co. in its required initial disclosures is Harvey Gannick, a retired automotive engineer who was on the team that designed the original Toyota Camry. Peter Painter's lawyer decides to take Gannick's deposition and to obtain any documents that Gannick may still have regarding the Camry. What procedures must he follow? *See* Fed. R. Civ. P. 30 and 45.

UNITED STATES DISTRICT COURT
DISTRICT OF OLD JERSEY

PETER PAINTER, Plaintiff	)	CIVIL ACTION NO. 09-2114
v.	)	NOTICE OF DEPOSITION
TOYOTA CO., INC., Defendant	)	

TO: Baker Farley Fish, Attorney for the Defendant
Erstwhile & Fish
117 Main Street
Oldark, Old Jersey 30221

Please take notice that, pursuant to Rules 26 and 30 of the Federal Rules of Civil Procedure, the Defendant in the above-entitled action will conduct a deposition of Harvey Gannick, commencing at 10:00 A.M. on November 14, 2020, and continuing from that time until complete, at the law offices of Marjorie Runnels, 62 Lawyers Row, Oldark, Old Jersey.

The deposition will be by oral examination, with a written record made thereof, before a notary public or some other officer authorized by law to administer oaths. A copy of the designation of materials to be produced by the witness at the deposition is attached.

Date: October 1, 2020

/S/
Marjorie Runnels
Attorney for the Plaintiff
62 Lawyers Row
Oldark, Old Jersey 30221
201-878-6755

UNITED STATES DISTRICT COURT
DISTRICT OF OLD JERSEY

PETER PAINTER, Plaintiff	)	CIVIL ACTION NO. 09-2114
v.	)	SUBPOENA TO TESTIFY AND PRODUCE DOCUMENTS
TOYOTA CO., INC., Defendant	)	

TO: Harvey Gannick
Last Leisure Retreat
Apt. 211
Sunset Hills, Old Jersey 30111

You are hereby commanded to appear at the law offices of Marjorie Runnels, 62 Lawyers Row, Oldark, Old Jersey, at 10:00 A.M. on November 14, 2020, to testify at the taking of a deposition in the above-entitled action pending in the District of Old Jersey, and to bring with you for inspection and copying the documents (and things) described in the attachment to this subpoena entitled "Attachment to Subpoena Duces Tecum." [Here the subpoena should set forth the full text of Fed. R. Civ. P. 45(c) and (d).]

Date: October 1, 2020

/S/
Clerk of Court

ATTACHMENT TO SUBPOENA DUCES TECUM

1. Any writing, drawing, graph, chart, photograph, computer file, or other data compilations from which information can be obtained (translated, if necessary, by you through detection devices into reasonably usable form) used in, or referring to, the design, manufacture, assembly, or repair of the Toyota Camry or Corolla. . . .

Notes and Questions: Depositions

Q **1. Procedure for obtaining a deposition.** Serving a notice of the time and place of a deposition on a non-institutional party-deponent, with copies to the other parties to the action, is normally sufficient to secure that party's deposition. This is often called "noticing" a deposition. The notice must specify the method of recording the deposition; although most depositions are still recorded stenographically, audio and video taping are expressly permitted under the Rules and are gaining in popularity. *See* Fed. R. Civ. P. 30(b)(3). Usually, the deposition of a party-deponent is held in the discoverer's offices within the district where the civil action is pending or at a place agreed to by the parties. *See* Fed. R. Civ. P. 29 (authorizing party stipulations regarding discovery procedure).

Why isn't a simple notice of deposition sufficient to compel a non-party like Harvey Gannick to attend?

A Unlike a party who was served with a summons at the outset of the case, a non-party is not within the personal jurisdiction of a court or subject to its discovery rules until and unless that non-party is served with process. Painter's lawyer therefore had Gannick served with a *subpoena*, and, because he also wanted Gannick to bring documents with him to the deposition, a *subpoena duces tecum*. This is a document that orders the deponent to bring documents with him (think of it as a subpoena "take 'em with you"). Rule 45 authorizes the court where the action is pending to issue a subpoena and permits nationwide service. Fed. R. Civ. P. 45(a)(2) & (b)(2). But the subpoena can only command compliance within 100 miles of where (or, if the person is a party or party's officer, in the state where) the deponent resides, is employed, or regularly transacts business in person. *Id.* 45(c). A person objecting to a subpoena can seek relief in the court for the district where compliance is sought. *Id.* 45(d). In state court actions, depositions of non-resident non-parties must often be taken under the rules of the deponent's home state and then used by rule or reciprocity agreement in the state where the action is pending.

Taking Testimony at a Deposition

Photo by John Gillooly

Note several things about this picture of lawyers taking a deposition. (The man to the reporter's right is the deponent, accompanied by his lawyer at his side.) First, the setting is a lawyer's conference room, not a courtroom. Still, the atmosphere is formal and often intimidating to witnesses. The testimony is being recorded verbatim by a court reporter (in the foreground) hired by the party calling the deposition.

The reporter has the legal authority to administer oaths, so the testimony given is subject to penalties for perjury, as it would be if given at trial. Note also that there is no judge present; a lawyer calls ("notices") the deposition, and the lawyers conduct the examination without judicial supervision. Objections to questions may be made by opposing counsel, but "the examination still proceeds; the testimony is taken subject to any objection." Fed R. Civ. P. 30(c)(2). If the deposition is used later at trial, the judge will have to rule on all objections before the testimony is admitted in evidence.

Q **2. Deposing the corporate or institutional witness.** Suppose you did not know who, within Toyota, to depose. Could you just depose Toyota Co.? How?

A Institutional parties can be deposed. You should send a notice to Toyota Co.'s lawyer describing the matters on which examination is requested. Toyota must then designate a deponent knowledgeable about those matters to testify on its behalf. *See* Fed. R. Civ. P. 30(b)(6).*

UNITED STATES DISTRICT COURT
DISTRICT OF OLD JERSEY

PETER PAINTER, Plaintiff	)	CIVIL ACTION NO. 09-2114
v.	)	DEPOSITION OF HARVEY GANNICK
TOYOTA CO., INC., Defendant	)	

Deposition of Harvey Gannick, taken on the 14th day of November, 2020, at 10:00 A.M., in the law offices of Marjorie Runnels, 62 Lawyers Row, Oldark, Old Jersey, before William McElroy, a notary public in and for the County of Mercer, State of Old Jersey, with all objections to be reserved until the time of trial.

HARVEY GANNICK, was called as a witness by the defendants, and, having been first duly sworn, testified as follows:

. . .

Q1. Did you read the attachment to the subpoena duces tecum that was served upon you?
A. Yes.

* [Eds.—At this writing, a proposed amendment to Rule 30(b)(6) would require the parties "to confer in good faith about the number and description of the matters for examination and the identity of each person who will testify. A subpoena must advise a nonparty organization of its duty to make this designation and to confer with the serving party."]

Q2. Did you make or cause a search to be made for any writings or other things that would be responsive to the attachment?

A. Yup.

Q3. And what were the results of your search?

A. Well, I brought it all with me....

Q4. When you received this subpoena, did you call your lawyer?

A. [Gannick's lawyer, Thomas Bobbin] Now wait a minute. I'm not going to let Mr. Gannick testify to what we said.

Q5. I am not asking him about any conversation. I am entitled to know whether and when he communicated with you.

A. [Bobbin] Alright, Harvey, you can answer that, but only that.

A. I did call Tom when I got this.

Q6. "This" being the subpoena duces tecum?

A. Yes.

Q7. And did Mr. Bobbin tell you what questions to expect at this deposition?

A. [Bobbin] I object. That question calls for communications which are subject to the attorney-client privilege. I instruct the witness not to answer.

Q8. Will you answer?

A. I guess not. No....

Q9. Turning your attention to the final meeting with the Camry Design Team, did they reach a consensus on the thickness of the brake lining and did you join in it?

A. Objection. Compound.

Q10. I'll rephrase it. Did the Design Team reach a consensus?

A. Yup.

Q11. Did you join in that consensus?

A. If you mean, did I agree, the answer is yes....

Q12. Did any member of the Design Team, either at the meeting or later, in private, tell you of any concern he may have had about this decision?

A. Well, Gurney [an automotive engineer] said he'd make the lining thicker or we'd get sued some day. Guess he was right.

Q13. Do you have any idea why he said he'd make the lining thicker?

A. [Bobbin, counsel for Gannick] Objection. How would he know what's going on in someone else's mind? Go on to your next question.

Q14. You may answer.

A. How would I know what's going on in someone's mind?

Q15. Well, did he explain his concern to you at any point?

A. [Bobbin, counsel for Gannick]. Asked and answered. Let's get on with it.

Q16. Well, Tom, I'm entitled—

A. Don't "Tom" me, asshole. You can ask some questions, but get off of that. I'm tired of you. You could gag a maggot off a meat wagon.

Q17. Let's just take it easy.

A. No, we're not going to take it easy. Get done with this. This deposition is going to be over with. Obviously someone wrote out a long outline of stuff for you to ask. You have no concept of what you're doing....

Q18. Directing your attention to the last meeting again, was anyone present who was not on the Design Team?

A. [Bobbin, counsel for Gannick] You mean other than the secretary?

Q19. I'm deposing Mr. Gannick, not you. I am going to seek a court order unless you stop disrupting this deposition and coaching the witness....

Notes and Questions: Conduct of Depositions

1. Taking the deposition. Taking a deposition is an art that goes beyond the coverage of a Civil Procedure course. But the admittedly contrived excerpt from Gannick's deposition helps to explain a few of the rules and principles that govern the taking.

The oral deposition is simply the live examination of a witness under oath outside the presence of the judge. The deposition on written questions differs only in that the questions are served on the deponent in advance and then read to him by the court reporter at the deposition; the answers are live and under oath. *See* Fed. R. Civ. P. 31.

Question 12. All objections made at the time of the examination are noted on the record and the testimony is still taken, subject to the objection Fed. R. Civ. P. 30(c)(2). Even inadmissible evidence is discoverable, as long as it is relevant and not privileged. In addition, most discovery by deposition will never be offered as evidence at trial, rendering any evidentiary objections moot. If and when selected deposition testimony *is* offered as evidence at trial, the evidentiary objections can be raised then. Furthermore, the judge is not present at a deposition to rule on objections, in any case. It would interrupt discovery continuously if a deposition had to be stopped to go to the judge every time someone made an evidentiary objection (although this option remains in isolated cases).

For all of these reasons, most evidentiary objections other than privilege are preserved until trial and need not be made at the deposition. *See* Fed. R. Civ. P. 32(d)(3)(A) ("An objection to a deponent's competency—or to the competency, relevance, or materiality of testimony—is not waived by a failure to make the objection before or during the deposition, unless the ground for it might have been corrected at that time"). Thus, Q12 arguably calls for hearsay, asking Gannick to relate an out-of-court statement that was not subject to cross-examination when made, but Toyota's lawyer can make this objection in court if and when the question and answer are offered into evidence there.

Question 14. Alternatively, even if he does object, the objection is simply noted by the reporter, and the witness answers anyway, subject to the objection. *See* Fed. R. Civ. P. 30(c)(2). This is why Ms. Runnels says "You may answer" in Q14, after Bobbin objects.

Questions 4–8. If a deponent answers after an objection that the question calls for privileged communications, he effectively loses the protection; a later court ruling that sustains the privilege may keep the communications out of evidence but cannot restore their confidentiality. A party may therefore refuse to answer on grounds of privilege, or his lawyer, after making the objection, may instruct his client not to answer. Bobbin interjects as soon as the deposition heads in the direction of his privileged communications with his client and carefully instructs Gannick on what he may testify to in the colloquy at Q4. When Runnels persists in Q7, Bobbin instructs his client not to answer, and Gannick follows that instruction. If Runnels now wants an answer, she will need to obtain a court ruling on the privilege by filing a motion to compel discovery.

Questions 9–11. There are, in addition, a small class of evidentiary objections that are waived unless made at the deposition. These are objections made on grounds that can be corrected then and there by simply reforming the question.

See Fed. R. Civ. P. 32(d)(3)(B). Thus, Gannick's attorney properly objects to Q9 as compound—mixing two questions together so as to invite an ambiguous answer—but the cure is simply to separate the questions, as Runnels does in Q11 and Q12.

Questions 13–16. What about Bobbin's objection to Q13? This is not just a weak objection. (Runnels is entitled to Gannick's speculation, even if it may not be admissible at trial.) It's really a cover for coaching the client and succeeding, as the answer to Q14 shows. Well-prepared clients are told to listen to their lawyers' objections and interjections and to educate themselves accordingly. But clearly, this kind of coaching can disrupt a deposition and may interfere with the discoverer's efforts to obtain unvarnished and spontaneous answers from the deponent. The purpose of a deposition, after all, is to obtain the deponent's answers, not the lawyer's. Bobbin's subsequent conduct goes well beyond even coaching and looks like outright and obnoxious obstruction. Unfortunately, this conduct is neither hypothetical (we took it straight out of *Paramount Communications Inc. v. QVC Network Inc.*, 637 A.2d 34 (Del. 1994)), nor rare.

The Rules refer obliquely to such conduct. Rule 30(d)(1) cautions that objections "must be stated concisely in a nonargumentative and nonsuggestive manner" and limits the circumstances in which a party may instruct a deponent not to answer. The Model Rules of Professional Conduct also proscribe "unlawfully obstruct[ing] another party's access to evidence" or "fail[ing] to make reasonably diligent effort to comply with a legally proper discovery request by an opposing party." *ABA Model Rules of Professional Conduct* 3.4(a) & (d). But it is doubtful that this kind of deposition conduct is "unlawful," and because it sometimes results in tit-for-tat allegations of misconduct, parties are often not in a position to press ethics objections. Characterizing the problem as one of etiquette more than ethics, an increasing number of jurisdictions have adopted voluntary standards for "civility" in professional conduct. Thus, for example, the D.C. standards provide in relevant part that

> [w]e will not engage in any conduct during a deposition that would not be appropriate if a judge were present. Accordingly, we will not obstruct questioning during a deposition or object to deposition questions, unless permitted by the applicable rules to preserve an objection or privilege. . . .

D.C. Bar Voluntary Standards for Civility in Professional Conduct ¶ 16 (1997). The Delaware court in *Paramount Communications* took another approach. It ordered the offending out-of-state lawyer who gave the answer at Question 16 to show cause why his "extraordinarily rude, uncivil, . . . vulgar, . . . unprofessional, . . . outrageous and unacceptable" behavior should not be considered as a bar to any future *pro hac vice* (permitted only for the purposes of the case) appearance in a Delaware proceeding. 637 A.2d at 53, 56–57.

2. Using the deposition. The use to which a deposition is put depends on the purpose for which it was taken. Some depositions are taken strictly for discovery purposes (discovery deposition); the witness is expected to offer live testimony at trial, and the deposition only provides a preview of what the witness may say, as well as possible impeachment material. Other depositions are taken as a substitute for live testimony (*"de bene esse"* deposition) because the witness will be unavailable for trial. While discovery depositions are often characterized by relatively open-ended questioning, *de bene esse* depositions are typically more guarded and directed, as examination would ordinarily be at trial. In either case, the number of cases that actually reach trial is so small that "[t]he reality is that what is learned at depositions becomes the factual basis upon which most cases are disposed of—not by trial, but by settlement." *Hall,* 150 F.R.D. at 531.

If the deposition is used at trial or a hearing, however, it poses a two-layered evidentiary problem. A deposition is hearsay: an out-of-court statement offered in court for its truth. Rule 32(a) therefore only permits a deposition to be used under limited circumstances. Moreover, even if the Rule is satisfied, the part of the deposition that its proponent seeks to offer into evidence is itself subject to the rules of evidence. As a state court has explained it,

> [s]peaking metaphorically, a deposition is like a box that contains certain evidence. The court must make two determinations. The first is a procedural one: whether to admit the box itself into the trial.... Once the court has decided that the deposition meets these procedural requirements [of the state's counterpart to Fed. R. Civ. P. 32(a)], the court then must address the ancillary evidentiary issues such as whether the contents of the box qualifies as admissible evidence. This is akin to opening the box, assessing its content and then ruling on its admissibility.

Shives v. Furst, 521 A.2d 332, 334 (Md. Ct. Spec. App. 1987).

Rule 32 provides that the box gets in against any party who was represented at the deposition or had reasonable notice of it, for impeaching the deponent as a witness at trial or hearing; as an admission by a party-deponent or the institutional party for whom the deponent was an officer, director, managing agent, or designated deponent; or when the deponent is unavailable by reason of death, illness, infirmity, or location beyond the range of trial subpoena.

Q *Question 12.* Apply the box-and-contents metaphor to decide whether Painter can offer question 12 and the answer to it into evidence at trial against Toyota.

A First, consider whether the "box" gets in: whether, under Rule 32, the deposition can be used at all. Recall that Gannick is a retired employee of Toyota who apparently lives in the district where the action is pending. So maybe he *is* available for trial, in which case his deposition cannot be used in lieu of his testimony (though it can still be used to impeach his testimony).

Second, consider whether the contents get in: whether Q12 or the corresponding answer is objectionable under the Federal Rules of Evidence. Since this isn't Evidence, we will help. Although this appears to call for hearsay, Federal Rule of Evidence 801(d) provides, in relevant part, that a statement is admissible against a party if it was made by a person authorized by the party to make a statement on the subject or by the party's agent or servant concerning a matter within the scope of the agency or employment, made during the existence of the relationship. Because Gannick is retired and was not designated as a deponent for Toyota, we doubt that his answer to Q12 would be admissible under this Rule. *These* contents of the box are not admissible at trial; this is not to say that other contents of the box—other parts of the same deposition—would also be inadmissible under the Federal Rules of Evidence.

VII. Physical and Mental Examinations

Painter is seeking damages for personal injuries suffered from an alleged product defect. Toyota would surely want to have him examined by its own or a neutral physician to ascertain the true extent of his injuries. Rule 35 authorizes such an examination, but because of the invasive nature of such an examination, the Rule also requires a court order absent agreement of the parties. In most personal injury cases, however, the plaintiff, conceding the inevitable, will stipulate to an examination. *See* Fed. R. Civ. P. 29.

Rule 35 establishes several predicates for a court-ordered physical or mental examination. How would Toyota obtain a physical examination of Painter? Could it obtain a mental examination (perhaps on the theory that he must be nuts to sue)? Reconsider these questions after reading the following case.

READING *SACRAMONA v. BRIDGESTONE/FIRESTONE, INC.* Sacramona sued a tire company for injuries suffered from an exploding tire, and the defendant then sought an order requiring him to take a blood test to determine if he was HIV positive.

- Identify Sacramona's claim and requested relief on that claim.
- Rule 35 allows a physical examination of a party if his "mental or physical condition—including blood group—is in controversy. . . ." Are the conditions "in controversy" limited to those that a party alleges in its complaint?
- Even if Sacramona's physical condition *was* in controversy, does it necessarily follow that the defendant will be entitled to get his physical examination?
- Do you think that the defendant was chiefly interested in the results of a blood test for HIV? What other motive could it have had for seeking such a test?

SACRAMONA v. BRIDGESTONE/FIRESTONE, INC.

152 F.R.D. 428 (D. Mass. 1993)

Bowler, United States Magistrate Judge.

On July 23, 1993, defendant The Budd Company ("Budd") filed a motion to compel plaintiff Robert J. Sacramona ("plaintiff") to submit to a blood test. Defendant Bridgestone/Firestone, Inc. ("Bridgestone") filed a memorandum in support of Budd's motion to compel. . . .

BACKGROUND

This personal injury action arises out of an accident occurring on May 4, 1988, while plaintiff was mounting a tire on a rim at Economy Mobil in Pawtucket, Rhode

Island. Plaintiff allegedly sustained serious and permanent injuries from an explosion resulting from the mismatching of the tire, manufactured by Bridgestone, on the rim, manufactured by Budd.

Plaintiff seeks damages from Budd and Bridgestone (collectively: "defendants") for his future lost wages, medical expenses and disability. Defendants contend that since plaintiff makes claims for future damages, plaintiff placed his life expectancy in issue.

During discovery defendants learned that plaintiff was a former drug abuser, having injected drugs intravenously and shared hypodermic needles. In addition, plaintiff admits to being bisexual and engaging in unprotected homosexual activity. Plaintiff's treating physician, Dr. Patrick Cimino, encouraged plaintiff to submit to a test for HIV[2] due to high risk factors which make plaintiff substantially more likely to acquire AIDS.[3] Plaintiff, however, has never taken a blood test to determine his HIV status.

Defendants argue that information obtained from plaintiff's blood test is essential to their ability to defend against plaintiff's alleged future damages. Defendants further contend that if plaintiff is HIV positive, plaintiff's life expectancy will be dramatically lower than the life expectancy a person not infected with the virus. Thus, defendants contend, plaintiff's HIV status bears on his life expectancy and is relevant to determining future damages.

Defendants further argue that since plaintiff placed his life expectancy in issue, it would not be prejudicial or burdensome to require plaintiff to take a blood test for HIV. Plaintiff refuses to submit voluntarily to a blood test citing his statutory and constitutional right to privacy. Plaintiff asserts that taking such a test will cause him to suffer unjust oppression, embarrassment and annoyance. In lieu of compelling plaintiff to submit to a blood test to determine his HIV status, defendants alternatively request to preclude plaintiff from introducing evidence at trial of his life expectancy or future damages.

DISCUSSION

... Rule 26(b)(1), Fed. Rule Civ. P. ("Rule 26(b)(1)"), provides that "[p]arties may obtain discovery regarding any matter, not privileged, which is relevant to the subject matter involved in the pending action." **[Eds.—Rule 26(b)(1) now defines the scope of discovery to reach only "nonprivileged matter that is relevant to any party's claim or defense and proportional to the needs of the case. . . ."]** Discovery is therefore relevant "if there is any possibility that the information sought may be relevant to the subject matter of the action." *Gagne v. Reddy*, 104 F.R.D. 454, 456 (D. Mass. 1984). Moreover, this court has substantial leeway in managing pretrial matters, particularly decisions pertaining to the scope of discovery.

2. HIV is defined as "human immunodeficiency virus" which is associated with AIDS. See Random House Dictionary of the English Language 908 (2d ed. 1987).

3. AIDS is defined as "[a]cquired immune deficiency syndrome, a breakdown of the immune system that renders individuals vulnerable to a variety of serious opportunistic diseases." Melloni's Illustrated Medical Dictionary 11 (2d ed. 1985).

Notwithstanding, a party "ought not to be permitted to use broadswords where scalpels will suffice, nor to undertake wholly exploratory operations in the vague hope that something helpful will turn up." *Mack v. Great Atlantic & Pacific Tea Co.*, 871 F.2d 179, 187 (1st Cir. 1989) (recognizing that 1983 amendments to the Federal Rules of Civil Procedure greatly increased court's ability to curb excesses). Under Rule 26(b)(1)(iii) **[Eds.—now 26(b)(1)]**, this court may limit the scope of relevant discovery if such discovery is "disproportionate to the individual lawsuit as measured by such matters as its nature and complexity" and the importance of the issues at stake. Notes of Advisory Committee, 1983 Amendment, Fed. R. Civ. P. 26. . . .

In accordance with Rule 35(a), the court may order a physical examination when the physical condition of a party is "in controversy" and "good cause" is shown. *Schlagenhauf v. Holder*, 379 U.S. 104, 111 (1964). The moving party must make an affirmative showing that the condition is genuinely in controversy and that good cause exists for ordering a particular examination. *Schlagenhauf*, 379 U.S. at 118. Although the Federal Rules of Civil Procedure are liberally construed, physical examinations should be ordered only upon a discriminating application of the limitations of the Rule. *Schlagenhauf*, 379 U.S. at 121. "[S]weeping examinations of a party who has not affirmatively put into issue his own mental or physical condition are not to be automatically ordered merely because the person has been involved in an accident. . . ." *Schlagenhauf*, 379 U.S. at 121.

Defendants assert that by seeking future damages, plaintiff placed his life expectancy directly in controversy. Defendants also argue that because plaintiff engaged in activities that place him in a higher risk category than the average person for contracting AIDS, defendants have shown good cause for compelling plaintiff to submit to a blood test during a medical examination.

This court acknowledges defendants' position that if plaintiff has AIDS, plaintiff's life expectancy will likely be shorter than for a person who does not have AIDS. Nevertheless, the relevance of the results from a compelled blood test to plaintiff's cause of action is too attenuated. In essence, defendants are asking this court to take extraordinary measures because plaintiff's admitted lifestyle is relevant to the possibility that plaintiff might be infected with AIDS, which is relevant to plaintiff's life expectancy, which is relevant to future damages in plaintiff's underlying cause of action. Defendants essentially seek to engage in "wholly exploratory operations in the vague hope that something helpful will turn up." See *Mack v. Great Atlantic & Pacific Tea Co.*, 871 F.2d 179, 187 (1st Cir. 1989). As such, the information defendants seek, which is not yet in existence, is not relevant under Rule 26 and this court exercises its discretion to limit defendants' discovery.

Alternatively, this court disagrees with defendants' contention that plaintiff placed his life expectancy "in controversy" as required by Rule 35(a).

Bridgestone cites several actions filed against G.D. Searle & Co. ("Searle") in which the court required the plaintiff to submit to a blood test. In each case, the plaintiff sued Searle, the manufacturer of an intrauterine device ("IUD"), alleging that the IUD manufactured by Searle caused the plaintiff to contract pelvic inflammatory disease ("PID").

The blood tests in the Searle cases, however, were required in order to determine the exact cause of PID. Thus, the results of the blood tests were relative to causation which the plaintiffs placed in controversy by virtue of bringing the lawsuits. In contrast, in the instant action defendants seek the blood test to determine future damages, not liability. The Searle cases cited by defendants are distinguishable inasmuch as plaintiff is not claiming that the accident caused him to acquire HIV. Therefore, by seeking future damages, plaintiff has not placed his HIV status in controversy for purposes of Rule 35(a).

In order to comply with Rule 35(a), defendants must also show good cause for requesting a medical examination. Defendants assert that the information obtained from discovery, regarding the high risk factors pertaining to plaintiff's possible HIV status, prompted them to seek a blood test.

In support of establishing good cause, defendants refer to several cases where the court either compelled the production of documents containing plaintiffs' HIV status despite the plaintiffs' privacy interests or ordered the disclosure of the identity of an HIV positive individual so that the defendants could depose that individual. None of these cases are particularly relevant to the issue now before this court because each case deals with HIV information and/or documents already in existence. These cases do not establish "good cause" for purposes of Rule 35(a). In the instant action, defendants seek to compel plaintiff to create HIV information so that defendants may then discover it. While this court sympathizes with defendants' efforts to prepare a comprehensive defense to plaintiff's future damage claims, the extraordinary relief defendants seek stretches beyond the parameters of Rule 35(a).[4]

CONCLUSION

In accordance with the foregoing discussion, Budd's motion to compel is DENIED.

Notes and Questions: Physical and Mental Examinations

Q **1. Method for obtaining.** How did defendants go about seeking a blood test of the plaintiff?

A Absent his consent, this method of discretionary discovery requires a motion asking the court to order the examination. The movant must show that the

4. Since defendants do not meet their burden relative to Rules 26 and 35, there is no need for this court to address the legitimacy of plaintiff's statutory and constitutional privacy arguments.

condition of the plaintiff is in controversy and that good cause exists for the requested examination. The court may then enter an order specifying the scope of the examination. Usually, at least when the plaintiff sues to recover for physical injuries, the parties will enter into a stipulation for the necessary examination without going to court. Sacramona, however, balked.

Q

2. Condition in controversy.

A. What physical or mental conditions are in controversy in *Sacramona*?

A

In exploding tire cases, eye injuries are common, but it is also possible that the plaintiff sustained other injuries to his upper body. Whether they are in controversy depends upon whether he pleaded them in his complaint or whether the movant has shown them to be in controversy. The Supreme Court has said that the merely conclusory allegations of the Rule 35 movant's pleadings are not necessarily sufficient. *Schlagenhauf v. Holder*, 379 U.S. 104, 118 (1964). It added that this does not mean that the movant has to prove its case to obtain the order, but it may need to show by affidavit or other materials that the condition is in controversy when the party to be examined has not already admitted it in its pleadings.

B. Since Sacramona is suing for future damages, has he not placed his life expectancy in controversy? After all, the fact-finder will need to factor in the number of years Sacramona is expected to live in calculating future damages, whether these damages are for future pain and suffering, physical impairment, or lost earning capacity.

A

It is true that any claim for future damages in the form of lost wages implicates the claimant's life expectancy. Obviously, the longer he will live, the greater the number of wage-earning years, the greater the likelihood of wage increases, and therefore the greater the damages. But if this is enough to warrant compulsory blood tests in a search for life-threatening ailments, every claimant who seeks future damages would be subject to such testing.

In fact, why stop there? Why not order a complete physical—a battery of tests, including genetic testing—to see if there are any other ailments, physical defects, or health risks that might affect life expectancy? Or even a mental test, on the possibility that if the claimant goes nuts, his earning capacity will be reduced? It would be the proverbial "fishing expedition," but in *Hickman v. Taylor* the Supreme Court celebrated the federal discovery rules by stating that "[n]o longer can the time-honored cry of 'fishing expedition' serve to preclude a party from inquiring into facts underlying his opponent's case." 329 U.S. 495, 507 (1949). The answer is presumably that this particular form of discovery is "extraordinary," as the court says in *Sacramona*, because it is more invasive and destructive of personal privacy than all the others. This is why it is the only form of discovery that requires a court order. It is also a reason for the court to read "condition in controversy" narrowly to mean only a condition for which plaintiff seeks a recovery. In fact, Rule 35's condition-in-controversy requirement is really nothing more than a narrower substitute for Rule 26(b)(1)'s general relevant-to-the-claim-or-defense scope of discovery.

C. Suppose the court had found Sacramona's condition in controversy for purposes of the requested examination. Must it then order the requested examination?

A No. The defendants still must show "good cause." Neither the Rule nor the court explains how this requirement is much different from the "in-controversy" requirement, but it gives this court another basis for denying the examinations. In the cases where the courts found good cause for disclosure of blood tests, the tests had already been performed; there was no need for a further blood test. Arguably, the invasion of privacy—and hence the need for "cause"—is greater when the data would first be created by a court-imposed blood test.

Furthermore, even with good cause, defendant faces a final hurdle. Sacramona has kicked up enough of a fuss about the privacy burden of the requested test to invoke the proportionality calculus of what is now Rule 26(b)(1). Here the court finds that this burden outweighs the likely benefit (speculative as it is), given the needs of the case (defendant can still go after other damages data, such as employability and promotability), the importance of the issues (just an element of damages and not part of liability), and the importance of the test in resolving the issues (it disposes neither of liability nor even of damages, but goes only to their size, in some degree).

All of which may raise some question about defendant's motivation in seeking a blood test. Might it have been *precisely* for the purpose of invading Sacramona's privacy, so he would drop his suit rather than comply?

Note that both the appropriate discovery tool and the balancing of interests might be different if Sacramona had already had his blood tested for HIV and had control of the resulting test records. Then the discovery tool would be a request for production of documents, and the balance *might* swing in favor of disclosure, because ordering him to turn over existing records invades his privacy less than ordering him to undergo a new invasive test.

D. Go back to *Painter v. Toyota Co.* Could Toyota obtain a mental examination of Painter?

A Presumably not, if his complaint only seeks damages for his physical injuries. On the other hand, if he includes a claim for emotional distress, he arguably places his mental condition in controversy.

Q **3. Who may be examined?** Suppose Painter seeks to recover for his loss of consortium (loss of the benefits of a family relationship, including affection, companionship, and sexual relations) in his complaint against Toyota. May Toyota obtain an order for a physical examination of his wife, on these facts?

A Probably not. In the first place, it is doubtful that his pleading puts his wife's condition in controversy. It's *Painter's* physical or emotional loss that his claim puts at issue, not his wife's. In addition, it is arguable that she is not a party or "a person in the custody or legal control of a party," although this is unclear. *See Wright & Miller* § 2233 (stating that "it would seem" that wife is under legal control of husband when he sues to recover for *her* injuries). That said, the defendant could still depose Painter's wife and inquire about intimate matters, including the couple's sexual history after the incident. This uncomfortable line of questioning could sometimes cause a plaintiff to reconsider asserting his claims. And, of course, if the wife joined in the suit seeking recovery for her *own* loss of consortium or pain and suffering, then her claim could well place her condition in controversy.

Rule 35 examinations are not available against mere witnesses outside the custody or control of parties. Minor children may qualify as persons in the custody of their parents when their parents are parties and the condition, or blood type, of the child is in controversy, as it might be, for example, in a paternity suit.

4. Scope of examination. In *Schlagenhauf v. Holder,* 379 U.S. 104 (1964), the movants had requested some half dozen physical and mental examinations in the alternative, and the trial court had thoughtlessly and indiscriminately approved them *all* instead of choosing among them. The Supreme Court held this to be a clear abuse by the trial court, emphasizing that a court's Rule 35 order must fit the scope of the ordered examination to the condition in controversy. 379 U.S. at 121.

VIII. Requests for Admission

One of the purposes of discovery is to narrow the issues for trial, especially now that pleading no longer serves that function as well as it did under the common law. In theory, perhaps the ultimate discovery tool for achieving this purpose is the *request for admission*. *See* Fed. R. Civ. P. 36 and Form 51. A party may request that an opposing party admit or deny the truth of statements in the request or the authenticity of documents attached to it. Usually, the request is made after other discovery, which is needed to frame the statement or locate the document. This timing suggests that the request for admission is less a discovery tool than a pretrial tool used to simplify the case on the eve of trial.

An admission conclusively establishes the matter admitted, for the purposes of the particular case. Fed. R. Civ. P. 36(b). This means that the fact-finder takes it as a given, unlike other fruits of discovery, which are not conclusive, but merely evidence on which the fact-finder can draw in reaching its own decision.

The theory of requests for admission, however, does not match reality. Toyota is hardly likely to admit the truth of the statement that "a defect in the design of the brakes, known to defendant, caused the accident described in the complaint." Even though Rule 26(g)'s certification requirement applies to responses to requests for admission no less than to other discovery responses, ambiguities in the evidence usually enable the responding party to deny the truth of such ultimate contentions in the case without offending the Rule.

There is usually less ambiguity about whether a document is authentic—whether it is what it purports to be. *See* Fed. R. Evid. 901 (noting, *inter alia*, that testimony by a witness with knowledge that the document is what it appears to be—"I wrote this document on or about the date it bears"—will authenticate it). Rule 36 is therefore still useful for the more modest task of authenticating documents that the requester expects to offer into evidence. If the responding party admits the authenticity of the document, the requester is spared the burden and expense of authenticating it at trial.

IX. Discovery Tools: Summary of Basic Principles

- The parties must meet early in a case to discuss discovery issues and propose a discovery plan to the court.
- In all but a small number of cases, a party must make initial disclosures of information that it may use to support its claim or defenses, but not information that the other parties will use to make their cases or information it plans to use solely to impeach adverse witnesses.
- Apart from required initial disclosures, disclosures of information about testifying experts, and certain pretrial disclosures, all other discovery is discretionary and party-driven. Parties may take discovery from parties by interrogatories and requests for production of documents and ESI, and from parties and non-parties alike by depositions. The fruits of such discovery may be admissible, and in some instances constitute admissions against the responding party, but it is not conclusive. Admissions made in response to requests for admission, however, are conclusive in the action in which they are made.
- There is no mandated sequence of discovery, but parties often use interrogatories to identify documents and witnesses, then request document production, and conclude with depositions.
- Interrogatories must be answered with all the information *available to the party.* An "empty head" answer is rarely proper, especially from a corporate or other institutional party that must collect information from its employees and agents (including its lawyers) to answer interrogatories.
- Document production requests target information "in the responding party's possession, custody, *or control.*" Thus, a request cannot be avoided by transferring the information to an agent (including the party's lawyer).
- E-discovery may often pose unique issues of proportionality, because of the volume of ESI, its variable accessibility (depending upon the storage medium), the use of predictive coding and other technology or software for accessing and analyzing it, and the resulting expenses for all parties. Special rules have therefore been promulgated for limiting e-discovery, responding to requests for ESI, and producing ESI.
- Claims of privilege or work product are proper objections to interrogatories and production requests, but they must be expressly stated with a proper foundation. There is no such thing as a "silent objection" under the Rules.
- Both parties and non-parties can be deposed, but a deposition of a non-party can only be compelled if it is served with a subpoena to bring the non-party within the court's jurisdiction. A corporation or other institution can also be deposed by a Rule 30(b)(6) notice, requiring it to designate a person to testify on its behalf. The deposition testimony of such a designate is admissible against the designating institution.

- Depositions can be used in court against any party who had notice of the deposition for impeaching the deponent, as an admission by the deponent, or for any purpose when the deponent is unavailable, as defined by Rule 32(a)(4). Evidentiary objections, except as to form of the question and as to other objections that could have been corrected at the time of the deposition, are automatically preserved until the deposition is offered in court, when they can be asserted.
- A court order is required for a physical or mental examination because of concerns for privacy. Such an order is available only as to conditions in controversy and on a showing of good cause.

23

Discovery Control and Abuse

I. Introduction

The prior chapter showed that discovery is mainly party-driven. That is, the lawyers for Painter and Toyota should ordinarily make the required disclosures and respond to discretionary discovery requests without a court order or any judicial intervention. But leaving discovery to the parties in an adversarial contest risks—some would say assures—that discovery will become contentious. The Supreme Court has complained that to the extent that discovery

> permits a plaintiff with a largely groundless claim to simply take up the time of a number of other people, with the right to do so representing an *in terrorem* increment of settlement value, rather than a reasonably founded hope that the process will reveal relevant evidence, it is a social cost rather than a benefit.

Blue Chip Stamps v. Manor Drug Stores, 421 U.S. 723, 741 (1975). The defendant can also make it a social cost by foot-dragging and obstructionism to wear the plaintiff down, to conceal damaging evidence, and thus to reduce settlement value. As a result, discovery often takes longer and costs more than any other part of a civil lawsuit.

For example, Painter may ask for *all* records from every Toyota dealer evidencing a problem in the suspension, accelerator, or braking system of the Camry, even though this request might involve thousands or even tens of thousands of invoices from hundreds of Toyota dealers across the country. Indeed, Painter's lawyer may hope that the cost of compliance will itself figure in Toyota's settlement calculus. In response, Toyota might try to read Painter's request as narrowly as possible to avoid having to disclose some documents, or it may ask the court to enter an order narrowing the request to records generated within the six months prior to Painter's accident or records indicating particular kinds of problems, or even just a sampling of records. Their dispute about Painter's request could well divert litigation energy and resources from the real dispute on the merits, in part because one party or the other *wants* to divert them. This chapter considers the devices that the parties and the courts use to control discovery and punish discovery abuse.

II. Tools for Controlling Discovery

Discovery can be extremely burdensome and expensive, not to mention time-consuming. But you may not yet appreciate how the adversarial dynamics can aggravate the burden and tempt the parties to abuse discovery. The following case is perhaps extraordinary for the trial court's lethargy and the willingness of the court of appeals to intervene, but we doubt that either the discovery initiatives by the parties, taken individually, or the perverse way in which they affect each other, are uncommon.

READING *CHUDASAMA v. MAZDA MOTOR CORP.* In the following case, Mazda was subjected to sweeping and burdensome discovery requests and tried a variety of responses. In reading this opinion, consider the following questions:

- Which of the parties is abusing the discovery process and how?
- How did the plaintiffs' inclusion of a claim for fraud affect the discovery burden on Mazda?
- What options does Mazda have for responding to or controlling the plaintiff's discovery? You should be able to identify at least five, most of them laid out by Rules 26(b) (the proportionality standard was moved from Rule 26(b)(2) to Rule 26(b)(1) after this opinion was written), 26(c), and 26(g)(3).
- How did the trial court respond to Mazda's choices and by what authority?
- By what standard did the appeals court review the trial court's order?
- What was wrong with the trial court's sanction order, according to the court of appeals? Was it that no sanction was warranted at all?

CHUDASAMA v. MAZDA MOTOR CORP.

123 F.3d 1353 (11th Cir. 1997)

Before TJOFLAT and ANDERSON, Circuit Judges, and NANGLE, Senior Circuit Judge.

TJOFLAT, Circuit Judge:

[EDS.—Chudasama and his wife sued Mazda for injuries arising out of an accident in their used 1989 Mazda MPV minivan (the "MPV minivan").] The complaint pointed to two alleged defects in the MPV minivan as the cause of the Chudasamas' accident and resulting injuries: (1) the brakes were likely to cause "the driver's unexpected loss of control ... in the highway environment of its expected use," and (2) the "doors, side panels and supporting members [were] inadequately designed and constructed, and fail[ed] to provide a reasonable degree of occupant safety so that they [were] unreasonably likely to crush and deform into the passenger compartment." Their complaint contained four counts: three standard products liability counts—strict liability, breach of implied warranty, and negligent design and manufacture—and one count of fraud....

Over the next two years, the parties engaged in protracted discovery disputes. As has become typical in recent years, both sides initially adopted extreme and unreasonable positions; the plaintiffs asked for almost every tangible piece of information or property possessed by the defendants, and the defendants offered next to nothing and took several steps to delay discovery. In this case, however, the district court never attempted to resolve the parties' disputes and force the parties to meet somewhere in the middle of their respective extreme positions. As a result, what began as a relatively common discovery dispute quickly deteriorated into unbridled legal warfare.

We see no useful purpose in describing the drawn-out discovery battle in detail;[1] a relatively brief summary will suffice. On July 28, 1993, the Chudasamas served Mazda with their first interrogatories and requests for production. Both documents were models of vague and overly broad discovery requests. The production requests, for example, contained 20 "special instructions," 29 definitions, and 121 numbered requests (some containing as many as 11 subparts). Similarly, the interrogatories contained 18 "special instructions," 29 definitions, and 31 numbered interrogatories. "One" interrogatory included five separate questions that applied to each of the 121 numbered requests for production, arguably expanding the number of interrogatories to 635.

The production requests all but asked for every document Mazda ever had in its possession and then some. For example, the Chudasamas sought detailed information about practically all of Mazda's employees worldwide. They requested production of

> all documents relating to organizational charts, books or manuals of Mazda ... which will or may assist in identifying an [sic] locating those operating divisions,

1. The district court's docket sheet contains no fewer than ninety-five entries of discovery-related pleadings. The parties have further supplemented the record with hundreds of pages of additional unfiled correspondence between counsel for both sides and the court.

> committees, groups, departments, employees, and personnel ... involved in the conception, market analysis, development, testing, design safety engineering and marketing of the product for all years during which the product has been developed, designed, manufactured and marketed.

They also sought "all documents relating to any organizational chart or structure for each of Mazda['s] ... committees, sub-committees, boards, task forces, and technical groups which took any part in overseeing the design, market analysis, cost/benefits analysis, economic feasibility analysis, development, testing and safety engineering of the product."

The scope of these requests becomes apparent only after reading the Chudasamas' definition of the term "product":

> This word means the Mazda MPV Minivan involved in the incident and all vehicles similar, though not necessarily identical, to that Minivan. The word includes all variations of 1989 Mazda MPV Minivan vehicles, as well as all variations of the MPV Minivan vehicles produced by Mazda ... in all years before and after the incident. The term should be construed to include each and every component part of the vehicle and more specifically the related components of the assemblies and subassemblies of the vehicle's chassis, wheelbase, steering system, suspension system, braking system, side and side supporting system.

The Chudasamas thus asked for production of nearly every document ever made that would list or assist in finding every person that ever had anything to do with any component of any year model of the MPV minivan "and all vehicles similar." ...

In addition to being broad, several requests were so vague as to be all but unintelligible. For example, the Chudasamas requested "all documents reflecting the conditions and circumstances of the environment of use of the product." "Environment of use" is defined by the Chudasamas as "real-world conditions to which motor vehicles are actually exposed in their use by members of the public including, but not limited to, the occurrence of collisions and/or side-impacts."

Other requests simply asked Mazda to research the Chudasamas' case. They requested "copies of any and all governmental statutes, regulations, or standards, industry standards, corporate standards, authoritative articles or treatises, which Mazda ... contends or admits are applicable to the design, development, testing, safety engineering or distribution of the product," and "all documents in [Mazda's] libraries ... which address the design, engineering, and manufacturing of cars and trucks that address brake failures and/or side-impact accidents, injuries, integrity, and/or crush[.]" Neither request was limited to documents prepared by or for Mazda or to documents relating to the "product." Again, we emphasize that the above examples are only a few representative samples.

In response to the Chudasamas' excessively broad discovery requests, Mazda adopted four different strategies. First, it objected to almost every production request and interrogatory on almost every imaginable ground. While some of its objections were clearly boilerplate and bordered on being frivolous, many were directly on point and raised bona fide questions of law. . . . The district court never directly ruled on any of these objections or requests for rulings; nor did it ever give any indication that it had considered them in even the most cursory fashion. Accordingly, the Chudasamas continued their broad demands, unchecked by the district court.

On October 21, 1993, Mazda began pursuing a second strategy for countering the Chudasamas' vague and overbroad discovery requests. It filed a motion to dismiss their fraud count for failure to plead fraud with particularity, pursuant to Fed. R. Civ. P. 9(b). Mazda contended that the Chudasamas had failed to point to any specific misrepresentation made by Mazda. The Chudasamas' fraud claim is based on the Federal Motor Vehicle Safety Standards, promulgated by the National Highway and Traffic Safety Administration.[2]. . .

Mazda recognized that the fraud count substantially widened the scope of discovery. Absent the fraud count, the only information that the Chudasamas would be entitled to discover would be information related to the 1989 MPV minivan's brakes and side structure. The fraud count, however, arguably widened the scope of discovery to include information relating to Mazda's intentions in designing and marketing the MPV minivans, and possibly other "vehicles similar." Therefore, if Mazda could convince the district court to dismiss the fraud count, discovery would become substantially more manageable.

In its motion to dismiss the fraud count, Mazda contended that the Chudasamas failed to allege the "time, place and content of the alleged misrepresentations." . . .

Despite the fact that both parties fully briefed Mazda's motion to dismiss, the district court never ruled on it. . . .

Mazda's third strategy was to seek a protective order. Much of the information requested by the Chudasamas involved confidential documents that went to the heart of Mazda's business. They sought, inter alia, marketing studies, internal memoranda, and documentation on the history of the development and design of the MPV minivan and other vehicles. Fearing disclosure of this information to its competitors or to other potential plaintiffs, Mazda sought a "non-sharing" protective order that would keep the information under seal and prohibit the Chudasamas from sharing Mazda's proprietary information with anyone. They filed a motion for such a protective order on August 16, 1994. The Chudasamas objected, but indicated that they would accept a "sharing" protective order that would allow them to share the information with similarly situated plaintiffs, but not with anyone else.

At a hearing in September 1994, Mazda offered to stipulate to a sharing protective order if the Chudasamas would narrow their proposed definition of similarly

2. The Chudasamas' complaint is an all-too-typical shotgun pleading. The four counts it presents follow forty-three numbered paragraphs of factual allegations, many of which are vague. Each count has two numbered paragraphs, the first of which incorporates by reference all forty-three paragraphs of factual allegations. Many of the factual allegations appear to relate to only one or two counts, or to none of the counts at all. Thus, a reader of the complaint must speculate as to which factual allegations pertain to which count.

vague

situated plaintiffs. The Chudasamas declined this invitation, and on September 15, 1994, the district court began an alarming trend by adopting nearly verbatim the proposed sharing protective order drafted by counsel for the Chudasamas. . . .

Perhaps because it realized that the district court had no intention of ruling on its motion to dismiss the fraud count or its various objections, Mazda adopted a fourth strategy; it withheld a substantial amount of information that it later conceded was properly discoverable. . . .

On November 12, 1993, the Chudasamas filed a motion to compel Mazda to respond "fully and completely" to a laundry list of their interrogatories and requests for production. . . .

The district court held a hearing on January 21, 1994, to address the discovery disputes. Counsel for the Chudasamas and counsel for Mazda discussed the various disputed issues at the hearing, and Mazda repeatedly asked the court to rule on its objections. The district court remained silent throughout most of the hearing, and at the end of the hearing made it clear that it did not want to rule on any objections or motions relating to discovery and warned that, if forced to rule, it would be inclined to issue sanctions "on somebody." Instead of managing the disputes itself, the court wanted the parties to confer and settle the disputes on their own. The hearing thus ended without any rulings from the bench. . . .

[Eds.—The court of appeals describes much ensuing motion practice, during which the trial court continually failed to rule on Mazda's motions. Finally, after the trial court granted the Chudasamas' motion to compel and issued an order, Mazda tried to comply. On the very same day it filed its responses, the Chudasamas moved for sanctions.]

On June 26, 1995, the court issued an opinion and order granting the Chudasamas' motion for sanctions (the "sanctions order"). The seventy-page order was largely identical to the proposed order drafted by counsel for the Chudasamas, except that sixteen pages of material had been deleted. In its order, the court struck Mazda's answers and affirmative defenses and directed the clerk to enter a "default judgment" in favor of the Chudasamas. The order noted that a jury trial would be required to determine the amount of damages. The order also directed Mazda to pay the Chudasamas' expenses, including attorneys' fees [based in part on Rule 26(g)(3)]. Finally, the order vacated the previously entered protective order. . . .

III.

A.

We find that the district court's decision to compel discovery in this case was an abuse of discretion. We draw this conclusion based on the district court's failure adequately to manage this case. District courts must take an active role in managing cases on their docket. . . .

1.

Failure to consider and rule on significant pretrial motions before issuing dispositive orders can be an abuse of discretion. Resolution of a pretrial motion that turns on findings of fact—for example, a motion to dismiss for lack of personal jurisdiction pursuant to Fed. R. Civ. P. 12(b)(2)—may require some limited discovery before a meaningful ruling can be made. Facial challenges to the legal sufficiency of a claim or defense, such as a motion to dismiss based on failure to state a claim for relief, should, however, be resolved before discovery begins. Such a dispute always presents a purely legal question; there are no issues of fact because the allegations contained in the pleading are presumed to be true. Therefore, neither the parties nor the court have any need for discovery before the court rules on the motion. *See Kaylor v. Fields*, 661 F.2d 1177, 1184 (8th Cir. 1981) ("Discovery should follow the filing of a well-pleaded complaint. It is not a device to enable a plaintiff to make a case when his complaint has failed to state a claim.").

Although mechanisms for effective discovery are essential to the fairness of our system of litigation, they also carry significant costs, *see generally* Maurice Rosenberg, *Federal Rules of Civil Procedure in Action: Assessing Their Impact*, 137 U. Pa. L. Rev. 2197, 2204–05 (1989) (discussing costs and noting that in survey of 1000 judges, "abusive discovery was rated highest among the reasons for the high cost of litigation"). Discovery imposes several costs on the litigant from whom discovery is sought. These burdens include the time spent searching for and compiling relevant documents; the time, expense, and aggravation of preparing for and attending depositions; the costs of copying and shipping documents; and the attorneys' fees generated in interpreting discovery requests, drafting responses to interrogatories and coordinating responses to production requests, advising the client as to which documents should be disclosed and which ones withheld, and determining whether certain information is privileged. The party seeking discovery also bears costs, including attorneys' fees generated in drafting discovery requests and reviewing the opponent's objections and responses. Both parties incur costs related to the delay discovery imposes on reaching the merits of the case. Finally, discovery imposes burdens on the judicial system; scarce judicial resources must be diverted from other cases to resolve discovery disputes. . . .

In sum, as the burdens of allowing a dubious claim to remain in the lawsuit increase, so too does the duty of the district court finally to determine the validity of the claim. Thus, when faced with a motion to dismiss a claim for relief that significantly enlarges the scope of discovery, the district court should rule on the motion before entering discovery orders, if possible. The court's duty in this regard becomes all the more imperative when the contested claim is especially dubious.

Turning to the facts of the instant case, we note that even the most cursory review of the Chudasamas' shotgun complaint reveals that it contains a fraud count that is novel and of questionable validity. Upon reading the complaint, the district court should have noted that the fraud count dramatically enlarged the scope of the Chudasamas' case. . . . The presence of the fraud count accordingly contributed greatly to the discovery disputes. Furthermore, as long as the fraud claim remained in the case without a dispositive ruling from the bench, any analysis of "the needs of the case," as required of the court by Rule 26(b)(2) **[Eds.—now 26(b)(1)]** and of the litigants by Rule 26(g)(2)(C) **[Eds.—now 26(g)(1)(B)(iii)]**, would be hindered. As a result, Mazda faced significant uncertainty in certifying that any of its responses were "complete, proper, and non-evasive." ...

The dubious nature of the fraud count made the need for a ruling even more imperative. While the question of whether the Chudasamas' allegations of fraud state a claim for relief is not directly before us, we find it hard to believe that Georgia law would recognize such a claim. At any rate, we conclude that this claim was dubious enough to require the district court to rule on Mazda's motion to dismiss prior to entering the compel order. When the court refused to do so and, instead, allowed the case to proceed through discovery without an analysis of the fraud claim, it abused its discretion.

2.

By and large, the Federal Rules of Civil Procedure are designed to minimize the need for judicial intervention into discovery matters. They do not eliminate that need, however. When the parties to a case inform the court that there are objections to discovery requests that they cannot resolve, the court should provide rulings on the objections. When a party moves the court to compel discovery, the court should consider and rule on the objections filed by the resisting party. While it has discretion to grant or deny the motion, it should not grant the motion in the face of well-developed, bona fide objections without a meaningful explanation of its decision....

Our review of the record in this case convinces us that Mazda filed and argued numerous good-faith objections based on persuasive grounds. Although we express no opinion as to whether the objections should have been sustained, we are deeply concerned by the district court's failure either to explain why it granted the compel order over Mazda's objections or otherwise to indicate that it had taken the objections into consideration. As with the court's refusal to rule on the motion to dismiss, we find that this mismanagement by the court strongly suggests that the court abused its discretion in issuing the compel order. When both instances of the court's mismanagement are viewed together, any doubt that the court abused its discretion in issuing the compel order disappears. That order must be vacated.

B.

Having determined that the district court abused its discretion in ordering Mazda to respond to the Chudasamas' requests, we turn to the subsequent sanctions order to determine whether it fell within the district court's broad discretion. The answer is fairly clear: the district court would have been hard pressed to fashion sanctions more severe than those included in its order. Mazda lost nearly everything that was at stake in the litigation and more. In addition to granting costs and attorneys' fees to the Chudasamas, the court struck Mazda's answer and ordered that a default be entered on all claims, reserving damages as the only issue to be tried on the merits. Moreover, it vacated its previously entered protective order. This may have been as prejudicial a sanction as it could adopt. Not only could Mazda's commercial competitors gain access to the design documents, marketing materials, and other proprietary information which Mazda had already disclosed, the order made it clear that Mazda had to disclose even more sensitive information to assist the Chudasamas in the looming trial on damages. These sanctions were so unduly severe under the circumstances as to constitute a clear abuse of discretion.

The severity of these sanctions required the court to find that Mazda's "non-compliance" with the compel order was intentional or in bad faith. "Violation of a discovery order caused by simple negligence, misunderstanding, or inability to comply will not justify a Rule 37 default...." *Malautea* [*v. Suzuki*], 987 F.2d [1536,] 1542 [(11th Cir.), *cert. denied*, 510 U.S. 863 (1993)]. Moreover, a district court abuses its discretion under Rule 37(b)(2) if it enters a default when "less draconian but equally effective sanctions were available." *Adolph Coors Co. v. Movement Against Racism & the Klan*, 777 F.2d 1538, 1543 (11th Cir. 1985).

In its sanctions order, the district court found that Mazda acted in bad faith when it failed to comply with the compel order. This finding has little support in the record and is erroneous. The district court's compel order required Mazda to "make complete, proper, non-evasive responses" to a list of the Chudasamas' discovery requests. The order itself and the record in general are completely devoid of any guidance from the court as to how Mazda was to respond. As we have illustrated above, many of these requests were extremely broad, vague, or both. Literal compliance with several of the requests was simply not possible. Thus, Mazda's assumption that literal compliance was not required is at least understandable....

IV.

As noted, the district court also based its sanctions order on Rule 26(g). This rule requires that discovery-related filings bear the signature of an attorney of record....

The decision whether to impose sanctions under Rule 26(g)(3) is not discretionary. Once the court makes the factual determination that a discovery filing was signed in violation of the rule, it must impose "an appropriate sanction." *See Malautea*, 987 F.2d at 1545. The decision of what sanction is appropriate, however, is committed to the district court's discretion. Fed. R. Civ. P. 26(g) advisory committee's note (1983 amend.) ("The nature of the sanction is a matter of judicial discretion to be exercised in light of the particular circumstances.")....

The record does contain some evidence that Mazda abused the discovery procedures, withheld admittedly relevant information, and engaged in dilatory tactics. Accordingly, the court's determination that Mazda certified its discovery responses and objections in violation of Rule 26(g) is not clearly erroneous. Contrary to the Chudasamas' assertions, however, this evidence is not enough to support the severe sanctions order. First, the majority of Mazda's misconduct was due to the court's utter failure to exercise its discretion in managing the case. While we do not condone self-help, under the circumstances here, we find the entry of a default and the vacatur of the protective order to be undue punishment.

Second, the imposition of such severe sanctions "is appropriate only as a last resort." *Malautea*, 987 F.2d at 1542. Had the court taken the time to examine Mazda's motion to dismiss or its discovery objections and then issued a meaningful ruling, we believe that Mazda's compliance with the Chudasamas' requests would have been satisfactory.

Finally and most importantly, in exercising its discretion under Rule 26(g)(3) for determining an appropriate sanction, the district court must analyze the needs of the case. *See* Fed. R. Civ. P. 26(g)(2)(C) **[Eds.—now 26(g)(1)(B)(iii)]**. As our earlier analysis demonstrates, the court clearly failed to do this. It never ruled on Mazda's motion to dismiss or offered any indication that it had given the motion serious consideration. The court's failure to rule on the motion to dismiss or to address Mazda's discovery objections demonstrates that it did not analyze the needs of the case. Although sanctions may have been appropriate, the severe sanctions imposed were clearly excessive, and the court's determination of the "appropriate sanction" under Rule 26(g)(2)(C) **[Eds.—now 26(g)(3)]** was therefore an abuse of discretion....

VI.

For the foregoing reasons, we VACATE both the district court's order compelling discovery and its order granting the appellee's amended motion for sanctions and REMAND this case with the instruction that the Chief Judge of the Middle District of Georgia reassign the case to a different district judge for further proceedings consistent with this opinion.

Notes and Questions: *Chudasama*

A. Requesting, Responding, Objecting, and Compelling

1. Certifying discovery papers. The initial control on discovery abuse is the Rule 26(g) certification requirement. Read Rule 26(g)(1) carefully, and compare it with the other certification requirement, Rule 11. While a Rule 26(g) certification sounds like a Rule 11 certification, in that it certifies that the papers are warranted by law and have a proper purpose, Rule 26(g) certifications also warrant that disclosures are complete and correct as of the time they are made and neither burdensome nor unduly burdensome or expensive (echoing the proportionality standard of Rule 26(b)(1)). Rule 26(g) thus focuses partly on the integrity of the discovery *process*; the advisory committee notes speak of a "duty to engage in pretrial discovery in a responsible manner...." Rule 26(g), advisory committee notes to 1983 amendment. Theoretically, therefore, Rule 26(g) supplies a basis for controlling that process, as the court of appeals noted in *Chudasama*.

Q **2. Who was the bad guy?**

A Especially in retrospect, it seems that the Chudasamas' lawyer started it. The Chudasamas' sweeping discovery demands were "models of vague and overly broad discovery requests" and "all but unintelligible" to boot. Of course, this could simply have been incompetence, rote reproduction of pattern discovery forms from commercial form books, or tactical, and you might therefore say: "So what? Isn't it up to the responding party to carve them back?"

But the answer to that is, technically, "No, it isn't." Rule 26(g), after all, required the Chudasamas' lawyer (who signed the discovery requests) to certify both that they were not interposed to harass, delay, or run up Mazda's bill, and that they were not "unreasonable or unduly burdensome or expensive" in all the circumstances. It is hard to see how the lawyer could sign the discovery requests pursuant to Rule 26(g) if the court of appeals was right in characterizing them as models of overbreadth.

Once the Chudasamas started down this road, however, Mazda did not respond with model correctness either. First, it made objections "on almost every imaginable ground," including many that were "clearly boilerplate and bordered on the frivolous." Such responses seemingly violated *its* Rule 26(g) certification that objections had a basis in law and were not unreasonable. Moreover, Mazda then withheld "a substantial amount of information that it later conceded was properly discoverable." The Rules never authorize such self-help.

3. Did Mazda have any choice? Given the trial court's inaction, this turns out to be a tougher question than one would think. Because the trial court ruled on nothing, there was no trial court ruling from which to seek even an interlocutory appeal—that is, an appeal before final judgment. And even if the trial court had made a ruling, interlocutory appeal of a discovery ruling is rare. Mazda could have sought a special kind of interlocutory appeal by petitioning for a *writ of mandamus* from the appeals court, directing the trial court to do its duty, but these are also rare. This tactic is also like shooting at the king; you don't want to miss. Instead, Mazda's conduct did produce an appealable final judgment (the default judgment), which finally brought the matter to appellate attention.

Fortunately, in our experience, very few federal district courts would be so unresponsive to the party's motions. Moreover, in many cases, discovery management is given to a federal magistrate judge. *See* Fed. R. Civ. P. 72. Because discovery is a major part of their docket, magistrate judges are even less likely, we think, to neglect their responsibilities as the district court did in *Chudasama*.

Q **4. Objections?** Mazda's first strategy in responding to the Chudasamas' overly broad discovery requests was to object. What objections would you have made on its behalf under Rule 26(b)(1)? How?

A Three kinds spring to mind. "Disproportional" leaps to mind, although at that level of generality, it is essentially boilerplate. Rule 26(b)(1) lists the factors of proportionality, and both Rules 33 and 34 require an objecting party to be specific, so Mazda would at least need to spell out how the Chudasamas'

> requests were disproportional. It might, for example, file an affidavit by its lawyer attesting to how many documents were involved and estimating the costs of producing them. Another objection would be relevance. The objection would likely have failed in 1997, when the standard was relevance to the subject matter. After 2000, it might have fared better, when the standard became relevance to a claim or defense. Finally, given the breadth of the requests, the discovery requests may well have encompassed materials protected by the lawyer-client privilege. Any assertion of privilege would have to meet the foundational standard of Rule 26(b)(5).

5. Motions to compel. Objections in discovery responses do not automatically go before the court. First, the requesting party must try to resolve the dispute informally. This effort may bear fruit without having to involve the court. Second, if informal discussions fail, the requesting party can file a motion for a court order compelling discovery pursuant to Rule 37(a) (a "motion to compel"). In ruling on the motion, the court will then determine the validity of the responding party's objections. If it finds them invalid, it will issue an order compelling discovery. Third, should the objecting party defy such an order, the requesting party can go back to court with a motion for sanctions. Fed. R. Civ. P. 37(b). The intermediate step of seeking a motion to compel is excused, however, if the recalcitrant party has stonewalled discovery by failing to respond to discovery requests or to attend its deposition, instead of making particular objections. The requesting party can then go straight for sanctions. Rule 37(d).

Finally, instead of waiting for the requesting party to file a motion to compel, the responding party can raise its objections by a motion for a protective order, discussed below in the next part (B. Using Protective Orders) of this Notes and Questions. Fed. R. Civ. P. 26(c).

Q **6. Mazda's objections in *Chudasama*.** The trial court's almost complete inertia in *Chudasama* denied Mazda any judicial determination of the validity of its objections to the Chudasamas' discovery requests. If the court had considered the objections, either on a motion to compel or on a motion for a protective order, how should it have ruled?

A

> Judging from the court of appeals' characterizations of the discovery requests, the trial court should have upheld some of the objections and ordered that the requests be narrowed, either by time period, car model, car component, or all of these. Rule 26(b)(2)(C). If it granted the Rule 12(b)(6) motion to dismiss the fraud claim, this would also have justified narrowing the requests, as the fraud claim would then drop out of the case.

Q **7. Discovery sanctions.** Rule 37 gives the court the discretion to impose a discovery sanction that is "just" in the circumstances. In addition to holding a party in contempt, the sanctions can include orders deeming specified facts to be established for purposes of the action, precluding the violator from introducing certain evidence, striking or dismissing claims or defenses, or even entering a default judgment against the violator. Fed. R. Civ. P. 37(b). What does the court of appeals say in *Chudasama* about a trial court's discretion to determine the appropriate sanction?

A It states that the trial court had "broad discretion" to decide the sanction. But it also finds that the trial court should have reserved the most severe sanctions—entry of default judgment—for bad faith discovery misconduct, and that a court abuses its discretion if it enters a default when lesser, but equally effective, sanctions are available.

Q **8. Rule 26(g) carries its own sanctions for violations of the certification requirement. How are they different from Rule 37 sanctions?**

A Except for failure to participate in a discovery planning meeting, Rule 37 sanctions are triggered by motion of a party, while Rule 26(g) sanctions may be imposed by the court on its own initiative. In addition, while Rule 26(g)(3) authorizes "an appropriate sanction," the only one it identifies is making the violator pay the opposing party's reasonable expenses, including attorneys' fees. In practice, most courts ignore Rule 26(g) and punish discovery abuse within the framework of Rule 37, probably because most requests for sanctions are presented by motions made under Rule 37(b).

Q **9. The Rule 26(g) sanction against Mazda.** Since the court of appeals holds that the trial court's finding that Mazda violated Rule 26(g) was not clearly erroneous, what was wrong with the sanction the trial court imposed for this violation?

A It was wildly excessive—and therefore not "appropriate"—given the Chudasamas' overbroad discovery requests and the trial court's inaction. To issue an appropriate 26(g) sanction, a court must take into account the "needs of the case," Fed. R. Civ. P. 26(g)(1)(B)(iii), which the trial court here totally ignored. The sanction was also excessive in light of Mazda's many valid objections to discovery.

10. Spoliation. Suppose that instead of withholding evidence from discovery, Mazda simply destroyed it? Or, after litigation had commenced, it permitted its usual document housekeeping system to purge old e-data, some of which was relevant to the claims in the lawsuit? Or that it did the same thing *before* litigation commenced, but when, from an accident report and a demand letter from the Chudasamas' lawyer, it should have seen the lawsuit coming?

The common law called such document destruction *spoliation*. The lengthy saga of the *Zubulake* litigation (see Chapter 22, *supra*) provides this explanation:

> Spoliation is "the destruction or significant alteration of evidence, or the failure to preserve property for another's use as evidence in pending or reasonably foreseeable litigation." "The determination of an appropriate sanction for spoliation, if any, is confined to the sound discretion of the trial judge, and is assessed on a case-by-case basis." The authority to sanction litigants for spoliation arises jointly under the Federal Rules of Civil Procedure and the court's inherent powers.
>
> The spoliation of evidence germane "to proof of an issue at trial can support an inference that the evidence would have been unfavorable to the party

> responsible for its destruction." A party seeking an adverse inference instruction (or other sanctions) based on the spoliation of evidence must establish the following three elements: (1) that the party having control over the evidence had an obligation to preserve it at the time it was destroyed; (2) that the records were destroyed with a "culpable state of mind"; and (3) that the destroyed evidence was "relevant" to the party's claim or defense such that a reasonable trier of fact could find that it would support that claim or defense.
>
> In this circuit, a "culpable state of mind" for purposes of a spoliation inference includes ordinary negligence. When evidence is destroyed in bad faith (*i.e.*, intentionally or willfully), that fact alone is sufficient to demonstrate relevance. By contrast, when the destruction is negligent, relevance must be proven by the party seeking the sanctions.

Zubulake v. UBS Warburg LLC (*Zubulake V*), 229 F.R.D. 422, 430–31 (S.D.N.Y. 2004). In that case, the court found that the defendant had willfully continued deleting e-mails even after a "litigation hold," violating its duty to preserve possibly relevant e-mails. The court therefore imposed the sanction of instructing the jury that it could infer that the deleted e-mails would have been unfavorable to the defendant from the defendant's failure to produce the deleted e-mails. Other sanctions for spoliation include precluding the spoliator from using certain evidence, deeming facts adverse to the spoliator established, striking a claim or defense of the spoliator, or entering a default judgment against the spoliator, although the latter are usually reserved for bad faith spoliation.

After *Zubulake V*, however, the rule makers took a more forgiving view of failure to produce electronically stored information (ESI). When it is lost because a party failed to take reasonable steps to preserve it, the court can order measures no greater than necessary to cure the resulting prejudice and can only order the most severe sanctions for intentional destruction. Rule 37(e). ESI, after all, is stored in multiple, often decentralized locations, and is therefore hard to locate, let alone preserve. The new Rule is therefore lenient with merely negligent spoliation of ESI.

B. Using Protective Orders

Q **1. The predicates for protective orders.** Mazda's third strategy for dealing with the Chudasamas' overbroad discovery requests was to seek a protective order under Rule 26(c).

A. What is the predicate for moving for a protective order?

A The movant must certify that it has made a good faith effort to resolve the dispute without court action, and then show that the protective order is necessary to protect it from "annoyance, embarrassment, oppression, or undue burden and expense. . . ." Rule 26(c).

B. Mazda argued the need to protect "confidential" documents like market studies, internal memoranda, and design and development documents. Why did it not simply object to their disclosure on privilege grounds?

A

Most of these documents are *not* privileged. That is, they are not confidential communications made in furtherance of some protected relationship, like confidential communications from client to lawyer for the purpose of obtaining legal advice. They clearly *are* sensitive, however, for Mazda, who understandably wishes to keep them from its competitors. Rule 26(c) therefore expressly provides for protection of trade secrets and "confidential research, development, or commercial information," though this rarely justifies their non-disclosure, as is required for privileged communications. Instead, a protective order usually provides for guarded disclosure to a limited number of persons who are required to protect against further disclosures, and sometimes, for the return of the protected material once the case is over.

2. Deciding motions for protective orders. How should a court decide a motion for a protective order when the information sought is discoverable, but the party resisting discovery makes a good faith showing that it is highly sensitive or burdensome to produce? The very dialectic posed by the question suggests that balancing is the answer. A Rule 26(c) motion

> requires the district judge to compare the hardship to the party against whom discovery is sought, if discovery is allowed, with the hardship to the party seeking discovery if discovery is denied. He must consider the nature of the hardship as well as its magnitude and thus give more weight to interests that have a distinctively social value than to purely private interests; and he must consider the possibility of reconciling the competing interests through a carefully crafted protective order.

Marrese v. American Academy of Orthopaedic Surgeons, 726 F.2d 1150, 1159 (7th Cir. 1984) (en banc), *rev'd on other grounds*, 470 U.S. 373 (1985).

Q

3. Special issues presented by protective orders. Defendants in product liability suits have a particularly strong interest in preventing disclosure of possibly damaging information to other existing or prospective plaintiffs. How did Mazda pursue this interest?

A

Mazda sought a "non-sharing" protective order forbidding the plaintiffs from sharing Mazda's proprietary information with other plaintiffs. An even more extreme protective order that is sometimes sought by commercial litigants is an *umbrella protective order*, which forbids the requesting party from disclosing to others any information that the producing party designates as "confidential." Of course, either kind of protective order could be violated by plaintiffs' lawyers over drinks, but that is true of all orders and rules. The system assumes, probably reasonably, that most lawyers will abide by such orders.

Should courts enter non-sharing or umbrella protective orders if the protected information concerns a potentially dangerous product defect that would otherwise be kept from the general public? This question suggests that protective orders for sensitive product information can pose a trade-off between the interests of the parties and the interests of the public at large. Consequently, some states regulate the scope of protective orders in cases involving health or safety hazards, *see, e.g.*, FLA. STAT. § 69.081 (Sunshine in Litigation Act), and similar proposals have been made to amend Rule 26(c). Even absent such legislative interventions, a court may consider the public's interests when balancing the hardships and crafting the protective order. On the other hand, the Supreme Court has held that rules authorizing protective orders do not, without more, occasion "heightened First Amendment scrutiny," in part because discovery materials are "not public components of a civil trial," and because the public has no First Amendment right of access to information made available only for purposes of trying a lawsuit. *See Seattle Times Co. v. Rinehart*, 467 U.S. 20, 32–33, 36 (1984).

If courts grant protective orders to protect trade secrets, should they grant them also to protect privacy interests or First Amendment rights of free association? Some courts have said yes, ordering in camera production of membership lists or redaction of personal identifying matter, or placing other protective restrictions on the use of information that might chill associational rights. *See, e.g., Marrese*, 726 F.2d at 1160 (suggesting in camera inspection of membership lists in antitrust action against professional association); *EEOC v. University of Notre Dame Du Lac*, 715 F.2d 331, 338–39 (7th Cir. 1983) (ordering redaction of tenure files in employment discrimination action against university).

C. Other Controls on Discovery

Q **1. Sequence and timing controls on discovery.** When sensitive privacy, commercial, or First Amendment interests are implicated by discovery requests, an alternative control on discovery may be to delay the sensitive discovery until less sensitive discovery has been taken, or legal challenges to the complaint have been heard, because the need for the sensitive discovery may thus be mooted. *See* Fed. R. Civ. P. 26(d).

Suppose Toyota had counterclaimed against Painter for libel, seeking $5 million in punitive damages. His tax returns and other private financial information would be relevant to such a counterclaim, because they could indicate how large the punitive damages would need to be to deter similar conduct in the future. But Painter might be very reluctant to share private information about his finances with Toyota unless he absolutely had to. How might you, as Painter's lawyer, postpone or avoid disclosure of this confidential financial data?

A You would want to delay discovery of his financial information until you had tested Toyota's punitive damage claim by summary judgment, or possibly even until Toyota came forward at trial with sufficient proof of liability to warrant punitive damages. Under the applicable tort law, if Toyota can't show malice or recklessness, for example, then it can't collect punitive damages, and there is no need for the disclosure. The best tool for delaying and possibly avoiding this discovery altogether would be a motion for a protective order under Rule 26(c).

More commonly, a plaintiff has pleaded multiple claims, only one or a few of which permit punitive damages. If the defendant can get these out of the case, either by motion to dismiss for failure to state a claim or motion for summary judgment, the plaintiff's need to discover the defendant's net worth in order to ascertain how big the punitive damages would have to be to really deter the defendant is eliminated as well.

Q 2. **Cost-benefit controls on discovery.** Mazda apparently overlooked a fifth strategy for responding to the Chudasamas' burdensome discovery requests. *See* Fed. R. Civ. P. 26(b)(1). The Advisory Committee explained that the 1983 version of the proportionality standard was intended "to deal with the problem of over-discovery . . . by giving the court authority to reduce the amount of discovery that may be directed to matters that are otherwise proper subjects of inquiry." How could Mazda have used this rule in *Chudasama*, assuming, of course, that the trial court had been less lethargic?

A This seems like just the tool for controlling discovery in this case, had the trial court been more active. It expressly allows the court to consider the burden or expense of the discovery, in light of its benefit, taking into account the needs of the case (narrower if the fraud claim were struck), the amount in controversy (possibly large, if the Chudasamas' injuries in the minivan rollover were extensive), the parties' relative access to information (Mazda controls almost all the relevant information about the design and manufacture of the car), the parties' resources (Mazda has big bucks), the importance of the issues at stake (this, again, depends on the continued viability of the fraud claim and, perhaps, on what discovery gradually shows about the relative importance of particular defects), and the importance of discovery in resolving the issues. The proportionality calculus gives a judge enormous discretion to head off runaway discovery like that in *Chudasama*.

3. Review of discovery control.

Plaintiff has filed an unduly broad and burdensome production request, targeting, *inter alia*, thousands of documents, vast electronic databases (including some that cannot be accessed without great expense), and some ostensibly privileged communications between defendant and its lawyer. When defendant fails to produce *any* documents in response, and a telephone conference with defendant's lawyer makes no progress, plaintiff files a motion for sanctions along with a certification that it made a good faith effort to resolve the discovery dispute with defendant. Defendant opposes the motion, filing a brief arguing that the request is overbroad and the requested e-discovery would be too costly and invoking the lawyer-client privilege. The only supporting document defendant files is a "privilege log" supporting the invocation of the lawyer-client privilege as required by Rule 26(b)(5)(A).

Which of the following actions should the court take?

A. Deny the motion because the production request is improper in scope.
B. Grant the motion because defendant failed to respond.
C. Grant the motion in part: ordering a partial sample of electronic data to be produced and upholding the objections as to privilege.
D. Deny the motion because it is premature, in that plaintiff must first file a motion to compel discovery.
E. Order the parties to propose a compromise discovery plan.

Working backwards, **E** sounds like a judicial cop-out. But, in real life (where many such disputes are heard, in the first instance, by a magistrate judge—see Rule 72(a)), judges will often defer action by badgering the parties to thrash it out themselves. This makes good sense, because the parties have interests they can trade in reaching a deal, and their deals are binding on them, while a court decision could possibly be cited as reversible error on appeal of a final judgment. This is one reason that the Rules require discovery conferences and that Rule 37(a)(1) requires a moving party to certify that it has in good faith conferred or attempted to confer with the opposing party to resolve the dispute.* Here, however, the plaintiff made that effort and filed the required certification. It seems unlikely that ordering the parties back to the conference table will resolve this dispute.

A is tempting because the production request *is* improper in scope. It is arguably overbroad because it seeks electronic data that is not reasonably accessible owing to excessive cost. *See* Fed. R. Civ. P. 26(b)(2)(B). Moreover, it also seeks privileged information for which a proper foundation has been laid in the privilege log. But **C** reminds us that the burden of showing that electronic data is not reasonably accessible because of undue cost lies on the responding party—the defendant here. *See* Fed. R. Civ. P. 26(b)(2)(B). Defendant has supplied no documents to meet this burden by supporting this naked claim, yet the Rule requires the responding party to "show" the burden or cost. If the required showing is made, moreover, a court may nonetheless order e-discovery if the requesting party shows good cause. *Id.* It must do a cost-benefit analysis, which may suggest placing cost-saving or cost-sharing conditions on such discovery. Ordering a sampling could be one such condition. *Cf. Zubulake I*, p. 818, *supra*. **C**, therefore, sounds better than **A**. Moreover, **C** also takes the claims of privilege into account. When such claims are properly asserted, the court should not order discovery of the privileged matters.

But **D** suggests that neither of the foregoing answers is correct, because plaintiff has not sought to compel discovery, but only to obtain sanctions against defendant for non-discovery. A prior motion to compel would place discovery objections before the court and lay the ground for the kind of reasonable discovery orders we have just discussed. It is therefore tempting to conclude that the court should deny plaintiff's motion for sanctions, without prejudice to its filing a motion to compel, or else leniently treat the instant motion as a motion to compel.

However, when the requesting party is not claiming that an opposing party's discovery response was incomplete or evasive or that its objections are unsound, but rather that the opposing party has *completely stonewalled* the discovery request, then the requesting party can bypass the motion to compel and go directly to the motion for sanctions. *See* Fed. R. Civ. P. 37(d). In such a case, the opposing party cannot defend against sanctions by making objections to the discovery request. It's too late. The Rule expressly provides that a stonewall "is not excused on the ground that the discovery sought is objectionable," absent a pending motion for a protective order. Fed. R. Civ. P. 37(d)(2). In this question, the defendant failed to respond at all to the production request and waited until the motion for sanctions to raise its objections. Since the defendant filed no written objections before, it is now out of luck. Its objections come too late, and the court can order sanctions. So **B** is the best answer.

---

* This is one reason for the proposed amendment to Rule 30(b)(6) that also requires such an effort when scheduling a Rule 30(b)(6) deposition.

III. Discovery Control and Abuse: Summary of Basic Principles

- The parties themselves are the first control on discovery, as the Rules presuppose that they confer and negotiate about discovery demands, responses, and disputes. Not only are they required to produce a discovery plan and to consult when disputes arise, but Rule 29(b) authorizes them to stipulate to changes in most of the discovery rules. So talk first, move later.
- When the responding party thinks a discovery request is improper, it can try to negotiate a narrowing or other limitation of the request with the requesting party, make express objections in the time provided by the Rules, or seek court-ordered limitations by a motion for limitations under Rule 26(b)(2) (authorizing a cost-benefit analysis by the court), and/or a motion for a protective order under Rule 26(c). If the responding party believes that the requesting party violated the certification requirement of Rule 26(g), it may also seek sanctions under that Rule.
- "Silent objections" or self-help by non-production are never proper options under the Rules. Rule 26(b)(5) requires an objecting party to "expressly make the claim" with a proper foundation. If you object, do it in writing.
- Ordinarily, discovery sanctions involve a two-step process. When the responding party expressly makes objections to a discovery request, the requesting party may move for an order compelling discovery under Rule 37(a). That motion places the objections before the court to resolve by issuing an appropriate order. If the responding party violates such an order, then the requesting party may seek sanctions.
- If, on the other hand, the party from which discovery is requested "stonewalls"—that is, fails to make any response (or fails to attend its own deposition)—the requesting party may bypass the motion to compel (the first step in the usual "two-step") and go straight for sanctions under Rule 37(d). The two-step becomes a one-step. In such a case, it is no excuse for the lack of response that the discovery sought was objectionable. The objections come too late.

PART VIII

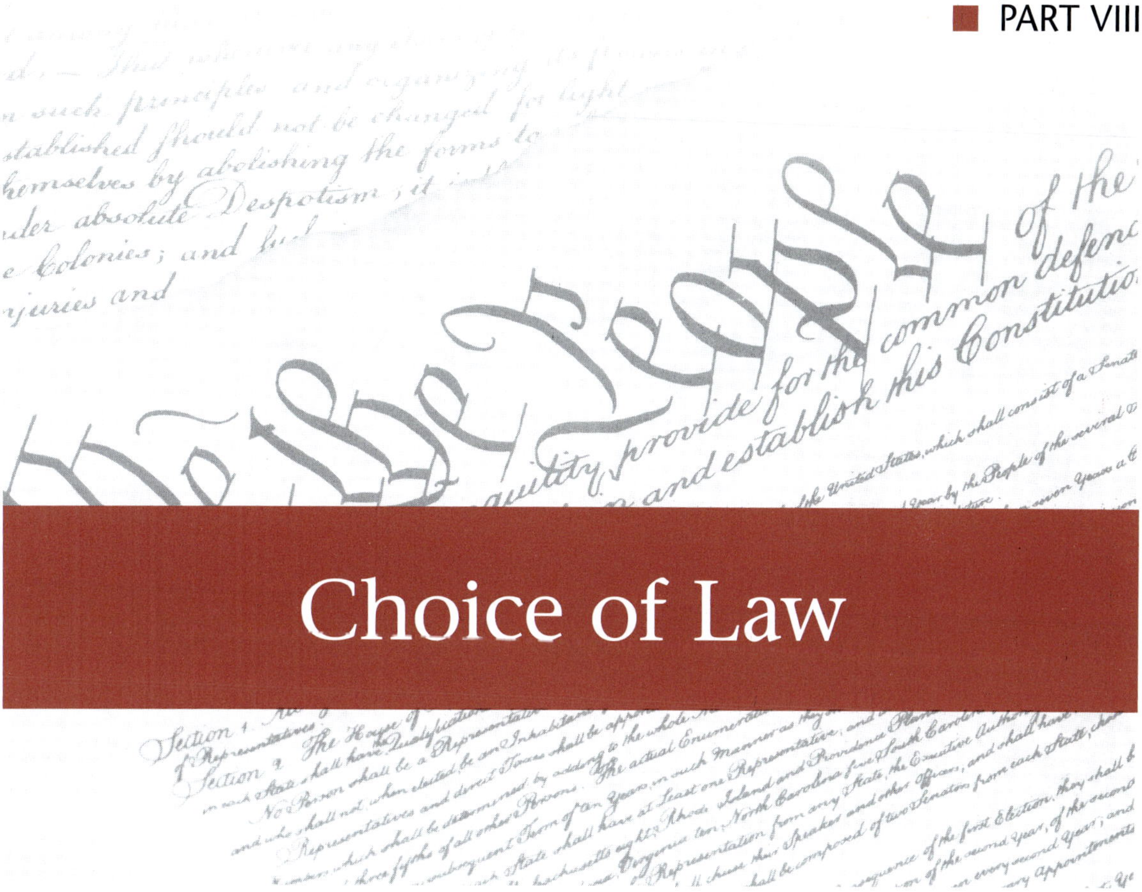

Choice of Law

24

State Law in Federal Courts: The *Erie* Doctrine

I. Introduction: The Era of *Swift v. Tyson*

One of the basic premises of our federal system is that the federal government has limited power to make law. The subjects upon which Congress has the authority to legislate are enumerated in Article I, Section 8 of the Constitution. These subjects, not surprisingly, involve matters of national interest, like defense, customs duties, naturalization, coinage, and interstate commerce. Congress has pushed the envelope a good deal, aggressively invoking the Commerce Clause and the spending power to regulate other areas of the national life. But still, federal law-making power is limited under our constitutional structure, and large areas of activity are predominantly or exclusively regulated by the states.

Consequently, many disputes arise in which the legal issues involve state law rather than federal law. Contracts, torts, and property cases provide straightforward examples. Nothing in the United States Constitution gives Congress the power to make a general law of contracts, so the law applied in a contract case will usually be state law. The same is true in a tort case, a property case, and many others.

However, cases that involve state law are not always litigated in a state court because Article III, Section 2 authorizes federal courts to hear cases between citizens of different states. Thus, if Rivera, from California, brings a federal diversity action against Palfrey, from Oregon, for breach of contract, the law that governs the dispute will be state contract law, although the case is being heard in a federal court.

This is an interesting anomaly. The federal court hears the case, but federal law does not apply. So what law does apply? Well, state law, of course. That seems obvious. In fact, the first Congress provided in Section 34 of the Judiciary Act of 1789 that the federal courts should apply state law in cases that did not involve federal law. This famous statute, the Rules of Decision Act (RDA), has been in the United States Code ever since. The RDA, codified at 28 U.S.C. § 1652, reads today nearly as it did in 1789:

> The laws of the several states, except where the Constitution or treaties of the United States or Acts of Congress otherwise require or provide, shall be regarded as the rules of decision in civil actions in the courts of the United States, in cases where they apply.

Basically, the RDA instructs a federal court to apply federal law to the case if federal law governs the issue, but otherwise to decide the case under applicable principles of state substantive law.

This seems straightforward, but early Supreme Court interpretations of the RDA placed an important gloss on the statute. In *Swift v. Tyson,* 41 U.S. 1 (1842), Justice Story concluded that the RDA required federal courts to apply relevant state *statutes* to a case, but that they were not bound to follow the *common law rulings* of state judges:

> the true interpretation of the 34th section limited its application to state laws, strictly local, that is to say, to the positive statutes of the state, and the construction thereof adopted by the local tribunals, and to rights and titles to things having a permanent locality, such as the rights and titles to real estate, and other matters immovable and intra-territorial in their nature and character.

41 U.S. at 18.

The term *common law* refers to rules of law established by judges in deciding individual cases, as opposed to rules enacted by statute. Judges regularly create common law rules because cases present issues that are not addressed by any statute. In such cases, the judge, in order to decide the case, must pronounce a governing rule (e.g., "a plaintiff may not recover if her negligence contributed to the accident"—the rule of contributory negligence). The judge writes an opinion explaining her reasons for ruling as she does, and these opinions establish common law precedents that apply in later cases unless overruled or supplanted by statute. Much of the law of contracts, torts, and property, for example, consists of such judge-made rules. For example, the meaning of offer and acceptance in contract or the meaning of a duty of care in a negligence case have been developed largely through rulings in individual cases.

At the time of *Swift v. Tyson,* such common law rules were thought of as a single body of rules, developed by the English courts and adopted by the American states, rather than as the law of any individual state. Justice Story, proceeding from this premise about common law precedents, concluded that the RDA did not require a federal court in a diversity case to apply *any one state's* common law, but to look at all common law cases to divine the "true" common law rule on the issue before it.

READING *BLACK & WHITE TAXICAB & TRANSFER CO. v. BROWN & YELLOW TAXICAB & TRANSFER CO.* The *Swift* regime is hard to grasp without an example. The *Black & White Taxicab* case, below, will help you to understand how federal courts applied "general common law" under *Swift*. In reading the case, consider the following questions:

- Why did Brown & Yellow *not* want to sue Black & White in a state court in Kentucky?
- What did Brown & Yellow do to create federal jurisdiction, so that it could sue in federal court instead?
- In *which* federal court did Brown & Yellow sue Black & White?
- Why did the federal court apply different contract law to the case than the Kentucky courts would have applied?
- Articulate the difference between the majority's conception of the sources of "law" and that of Justice Holmes, the "Great Dissenter."

While not clear from the opinion, Brown & Yellow Taxicab was the original plaintiff, the company that had the contract for exclusive access to the railroad's premises. Black & White is listed first in the case title because it lost below and sought review in the Supreme Court.

BLACK & WHITE TAXICAB & TRANSFER CO. v. BROWN & YELLOW TAXICAB & TRANSFER CO.

276 U.S. 518 (1928)

Mr. Justice Butler delivered the opinion of the Court.

Respondent [Brown & Yellow Taxicab] sued petitioner and the Louisville & Nashville Railroad Company in the United States court for the Western District of Kentucky to prevent interference with the carrying out of a contract between the railroad company and the respondent. The District Court entered a decree in favor of respondent. The railroad company declining to join, petitioner [Black & White Taxicab] alone appealed. The Circuit Court of Appeals affirmed and this court granted a writ of certiorari.

Respondent is a Tennessee corporation carrying on a transfer business at Bowling Green, Ky. The petitioner is a Kentucky corporation in competition with respondent. The railroad company is a Kentucky corporation. In 1925 it made a contract with respondent whereby it granted the exclusive privilege of going upon its trains, into its depot, and on the surrounding premises to solicit transportation of baggage and passengers. And it assigned a plot of ground belonging to it for the use of respondent's taxicabs while awaiting the arrival of trains. In consideration of the privileges granted, respondent agreed to render certain service and to make monthly payments to the railroad company. The term of the contract was fixed at one year to continue for consecutive yearly periods until terminated by either party on 30 days' notice.

Jurisdiction of the District Court was invoked on the ground that the controversy was one between citizens of different states. The complaint alleges that the railroad company failed to carry out the contract in that it allowed others to enter upon its property to solicit transportation of baggage and passengers and to park on its property vehicles used for that purpose. It alleges that petitioner entered, solicited business and parked its vehicles in the places assigned to respondent, and also on an adjoining street so as to obstruct the operation of respondent's taxicabs. Petitioner's answer alleges that respondent was incorporated in Tennessee for the fraudulent purpose of giving the District Court jurisdiction and to evade the laws of Kentucky. It asserts that the contract is contrary to the public policy and laws of Kentucky as declared by its highest court, and that it is monopolistic in excess of the railroad company's charter power and violates section 214 of the Constitution of the state.

The record shows that, in September, 1925, respondent was organized in Tennessee by the shareholders of a Kentucky corporation of the same name then carrying on a transfer business at Bowling Green and having a contract with the railroad company like the one here involved; that the business and property of the Kentucky corporation were transferred to respondent, and the former was dissolved. Respondent's incorporators and railroad representatives, preferring to have this controversy determined in the courts of the United States, arranged to have respondent organized in Tennessee to succeed to the business of the Kentucky corporation and to enter into this contract in order to create a diversity of citizenship. The District Court found there was no fraud upon its jurisdiction, held the contract valid, and found, substantially as alleged in the complaint, that petitioner violated respondent's rights under it. The decree enjoins petitioner from continuing such interference.

. . .

The Court of Appeals of Kentucky held such contracts [like the one at issue in the case] invalid in *McConnell v. Pedigo,* [92 Ky. 465,] and *Palmer Transfer Co. v. Anderson*, 131 Ky. 217. Invalidity of a similar contract was assumed arguendo in *Commonwealth v. Louisville Transfer Co.*, 181 Ky. 305. As reasons for its conclusion, that court suggests that the grant of such privileges prevents competition, makes such discrimination as is unreasonable and detrimental to the public and constitutes such a preference over other transfer men as to give grantee a practical monopoly of the business. It has not held them repugnant to any provision of the statutes or Constitution of the state. The question there decided is one of general law. This court **[Eds.—i.e., the Supreme Court]** holds such contracts valid. And these decisions show that, without its consent, the property of a railroad company may not be used by taxicabmen or others to solicit or carry on their business, and that it is beyond the power of the state in the public interest to require the railroad company without compensation to allow its property so to be used.

And state courts quite generally construe the common law as this court has applied it . . . [citing seventeen cases from various states].

In harmony with the Kentucky decisions, the highest courts of Indiana and Mississippi hold such contracts invalid. . . .

Arrangements similar in principle to that before us are sustained in English courts. . . .

The cases cited show that the decisions of the Kentucky Court of Appeals holding such arrangements invalid are contrary to the common law as generally understood and applied. And we are of opinion that petitioner here has failed to show any valid ground for disregarding this contract and that its interference cannot be justified. Care is to be observed lest the doctrine that a contract is void as against public policy be unreasonably extended. Detriment to the public interest is not to be presumed in the absence of showing that something improper is done or contemplated. And it is to be remembered . . . that public policy requires that competent persons "shall have the utmost liberty of contracting, and that their contracts, when entered into fairly and voluntarily, shall be held sacred, and shall be enforced by courts of justice." [*Printing Company v. Sampson*, L.R. 19 Eq. 462, 465.] The station grounds belong to the railroad company, and it lawfully may put them to any use that does not interfere with its duties as a common carrier. The privilege granted to respondent does not impair the railroad company's service to the public or infringe any right of other taxicabmen to transport passengers to and from the station. While it gives the respondent advantage in getting business, passengers are free to engage any one who may be ready to serve them. . . . It would be unwarranted and arbitrary to assume that this contract is contrary to public interest. . . .

The decree below should be affirmed unless federal courts are bound by Kentucky decisions which are directly opposed to this court's determination of the principles of common law properly to be applied in such cases. Petitioner argues that the Kentucky decisions are persuasive and establish the invalidity of such contracts, and that the Circuit Court of Appeals erred in refusing to follow them. But, as we understand the brief, it does not contend that, by reason of the rule of decision declared by section 34 of the Judiciary Act of 1789 [the Rules of Decision Act], this court is required to adopt the Kentucky decisions. But, granting that this point is before us, it cannot be sustained. The contract gives respondent, subject to termination on short notice, license or privilege to solicit patronage and park its vehicles on railroad property at train time. There is no question concerning title to land. No provision of state statute or Constitution and no ancient or fixed local usage is involved. For the discovery of common-law principles applicable in any case, investigation is not limited to the decisions of the courts of the state in which the controversy arises. State and federal courts go to the same sources for evidence of the existing applicable rule. The effort of both is to ascertain that rule. Kentucky has adopted the common law, and her courts recognize that its principles are not local but are included in the body of law constituting the general jurisprudence prevailing wherever the common law is recognized. As respects the rule of decision to be followed by federal courts, distinction has always been made between statutes of a state and the decisions of its courts on questions of general law. The applicable rule sustained by many decisions of this court is that, in determining questions of general law, the federal courts, while inclining to follow the decisions of the courts of the state in which the controversy arises, are free to exercise their own independent judgment. That this case depends on such a question is clearly shown by many decisions of this court. *Swift v. Tyson* was an action on a bill of exchange. Mr. Justice Story, writing for the court, fully expounded section 34 of the Judiciary Act....

The lower courts followed the well-established rule, and rightly held the contract valid. The facts shown warrant the injunction granted.

Decree affirmed.

Mr. Justice Holmes.

This is a suit brought by the respondent, the Brown and Yellow Taxicab and Transfer Company, as plaintiff, to prevent the petitioner, the Black and White Taxicab and Transfer Company, from interfering with the carrying out of a contract between the plaintiff and the other defendant, the Louisville and Nashville Railroad Company. The plaintiff is a corporation of Tennessee. It had a predecessor of the same name which was a corporation of Kentucky. Knowing that the Courts of Kentucky held contracts of the kind in question invalid and that the Courts of the United States maintained them as valid, a family that owned the Kentucky corporation procured the incorporation of the plaintiff and caused the other to be dissolved after conveying all the corporate property to the plaintiff. The new Tennessee corporation then proceeded to make with the Louisville and Nashville Railroad Company the contract above mentioned, by which the Railroad Company gave to it exclusive privileges in the station grounds, and two months later the Tennessee corporation brought this suit. The Circuit Court of Appeals, affirming a decree of the District Court, granted an injunction and upheld this contract. It expressly recognized that the decisions of the Kentucky Courts held that in Kentucky a railroad company could not grant such rights, but this being a "question of general law" it went its own way regardless of the Courts of this State.

The Circuit Court of Appeals had so considerable a tradition behind it in deciding as it did that if I did not regard the case as exceptional I should not feel warranted in presenting my own convictions again after having stated them in *Kuhn v. Fairmont Coal Co.,* 215 U.S. 349 (1910). But the question is important and in my opinion the prevailing doctrine has been accepted upon a subtle fallacy that never has been analyzed. If I am right the fallacy has resulted in an unconstitutional assumption of powers by the Courts of the United States which no lapse of time or respectable array of opinion should make us hesitate to correct. Therefore I think it proper to state what I think the fallacy is. The often repeated proposition of this and the lower Courts is that the parties are entitled to an independent judgment on matters of general law. By that phrase is meant matters that are not governed by any law of the United States or by any statute of the State—matters that in States other than Louisiana are governed in most respects by what is called the common law. It is through this phrase that what I think the fallacy comes in.

Books written about any branch of the common law treat it as a unit, cite cases from this Court, from the Circuit Courts of Appeal, from the State Courts, from England and the Colonies of England indiscriminately, and criticise them as right or wrong according to the writer's notions of a single theory. It is very hard to resist the impression that there is one august corpus, to understand which clearly is the only task of any Court concerned. If there were such a transcendental body of law outside of any particular State but obligatory within it unless and until changed by statute, the Courts of the United States might be right in using their independent judgment as to what it was. But there is no such body of law. The fallacy and illusion that I think exist consist in supposing that there is this outside thing to be found. Law is a word used with different meanings, but law in the sense in which courts speak of it today does not exist without some definite authority behind it. The common law so far as it is enforced in a State, whether called common law or not, is not the common law generally but the law of that State existing by the authority of that State without regard to what it may have been in England or anywhere else. It may be adopted by statute in place of another system previously in force. But a general adoption of it does not prevent the State Courts from refusing to follow the English decisions upon a matter where the local conditions are different. It may be changed by statute, as is done every day. It may be departed from deliberately by judicial decisions, as with regard to water rights, in States where the common law generally prevails. Louisiana is a living proof that it need not be adopted at all. (I do not know whether under the prevailing doctrine we should regard ourselves as authorities upon the general law of Louisiana superior to those trained in the system.) Whether and how far and in what sense a rule shall be adopted whether called common law or Kentucky law is for the State alone to decide.

If within the limits of the Constitution a State should declare one of the disputed rules of general law by statute there would be no doubt of the duty of all Courts to bow, whatever their private opinions might be. I see no reason why it should have less effect when it speaks by its other voice. If a State Constitution should declare that on all matters of general law the decisions of the highest Court should establish the law until modified by statute or by a later decision of the same Court, I do not perceive how it would be possible for a Court of the United States to refuse to follow what the State Court decided in that domain. But when the Constitution of a State establishes a Supreme Court it by implication does make that declaration as clearly as if it had said it in express words, so far as it is not interfered with by the superior power of the United States. The Supreme Court of a State does something more than make a scientific inquiry into a fact outside of and independent of it. It says with an authority that no one denies except when a citizen of another State is able to invoke an exceptional jurisdiction that thus the law is and shall be. Whether it be said to make or to declare the law, it deals with the law of the State with equal authority however its function may be described.

Mr. Justice Story in *Swift v. Tyson*, evidently under the tacit domination of the fallacy to which I have referred, devotes some energy to showing that section 34 of the Judiciary Act of 1789 refers only to statutes when it provides that except as excepted the laws of the several States shall be regarded as rules of decision in trials at common law in Courts of the United States. An examination of the original document by a most competent hand has shown that Mr. Justice Story probably was wrong if anyone is interested to inquire what the framers of the instrument meant. 37 Harvard Law Review, 49, at pages 81–88. But this question is deeper than that; it is a question of the authority by which certain particular acts, here the grant of exclusive privileges in a railroad station, are governed. In my opinion the authority and only authority is the State, and if that be so, the voice adopted by the State as its own should utter the last word. I should leave *Swift v. Tyson* undisturbed, as I indicated in *Kuhn v. Fairmont Coal Co.*, but I would not allow it to spread the assumed dominion into new fields.

. . .

Mr. Justice Brandeis and Mr. Justice Stone concur in this opinion.

Notes and Questions: Deciding the Applicable Law Under *Swift*

1. The dramatic impact of *Swift v. Tyson*. Isn't this an amazing case? The plaintiff, because it had the choice to sue in federal court based on diversity, obtained a different result—indeed, the *opposite* result—on the merits from the result it would have gotten in state court. By choosing federal court, it could choose a different contracts regime. The following excerpt from the majority opinion in *Black & White* (edited out of the case report reprinted above) illustrates the wide variety of contexts in which the principle of *Swift v. Tyson* allowed such schizophrenic administration of justice within a single state.

> *Lane v. Vick* involved the construction of a will. It was said (page 476):
>
> > "This court do not [sic] follow the state courts in the construction of a will or any other instrument, as they do in the construction of statutes."
>
> *Foxcroft v. Mallett* held that the decision of a state court construing a deed is not conclusive on this court. *Chicago City v. Robbins* declined to follow the determination of the state court as to what constitutes negligence. *Yates v. Milwaukee* held that the determination of what constitutes a dedication of land to public use is one of general law. *Olcott v. Fond du Lac County* held that the determination of what is a public purpose to warrant municipal taxation involves a question of general law. *New York Cent. R. Co. v. Lockwood* declined to follow the state rule as to liability of common carriers for injury of passengers. *Liverpool & G.W. & Co. v. Phenix Ins. Co.*, held a question concerning the validity of a contract for carriage of goods is one of general law. *Baltimore & Ohio Railroad v. Baugh* so held as to the responsibility of a railroad company to its employees for personal injuries. *Beutler v. Grand Trunk Railway* decides who are fellow servants as a question of general law.

276 U.S. at 530–31. In these and many other cases, the federal courts made their own judgments about what the proper rule should be, as a question of "general law," without regard to the rule applied in the state courts.

The *Swift* regime deprecated the authority of the states, particularly of state courts. *Swift* recognized that state statutes must be applied by federal courts in diversity cases. However, the law pronounced by the state's "other voice"—its courts—were dispositive in state courts but could be ignored by federal courts. This does not seem like a very good way to run a railroad, or a taxi service.

Q **2. Advising clients in the *Swift* era.** Suppose that you were a Kentucky lawyer representing taxi companies during the reign of *Swift v. Tyson*. One of your clients, a Kentucky corporation, which is considering an exclusive contract like the one at issue in *Black & White Taxicab*, comes to you for advice about whether such a contract would be enforced by the courts. What would you advise her? (Remember that, at the time, a corporation was only a citizen of its state of incorporation.)

A You would have to advise her that you are not sure whether the contract would be enforced or not. If the other company was a citizen of Kentucky, and suit was brought in Kentucky, the Kentucky courts would not enforce it. But, if there was diversity, and you could sue to enforce the contract in federal court, it would be enforced. "The answer to your question, Client, is either 'yes' or 'no,' depending on whether we can get into federal court."

Q **3. Consider the converse case.** Assume (contrary to the situation in *Black & White*) that the federal courts generally denied enforcement of exclusive contracts, on the theory that they are against public policy. However, the Kentucky courts generally enforced them. If *Swift v. Tyson* were still the law, in what court would Brown & Yellow, the plaintiff, want to litigate the claim? What would Black & White want to do in order to forum shop for more favorable contract law? Why wouldn't Black & White be able to do it?

A On these assumptions, Brown & Yellow would sue in state court to enjoin interference with the contract. Black & White would want to remove to federal court, since those courts, under *Swift*, could apply a different rule under "general common law." However, as an in-state defendant, Black & White would be barred from removing. 28 U.S.C. § 1441(b). It would be stuck with the Kentucky rule. Here again, one party gets to choose a more favorable rule of contract law because it has a choice of state or federal court.

4. Fraud in creating federal jurisdiction. The defendant argued that Brown & Yellow had fraudulently created jurisdiction by reincorporating in Tennessee to create diversity of citizenship. This seems like a good argument; clearly, Brown & Yellow reincorporated solely to get the case before a federal court that would enforce the contract. So Black & White invoked 28 U.S.C. § 1359, which bars collusively joining parties to create federal jurisdiction:

> A [federal] district court shall not have jurisdiction of a civil action in which any party, by assignment or otherwise, has been improperly or collusively made or joined to invoke the jurisdiction of such court.

The Court in *Black & White* concluded that Brown & Yellow had not "improperly or collusively" created diversity jurisdiction. It had actually become a Tennessee citizen, by reincorporating, so that diversity existed between the parties. The Court refused to get into motives; where there was actual diversity, it was unwilling to interpret the statute to bar a party from moving in order to create diversity and use the federal courts. *See also Baker v. Keck*, 13 F. Supp. 486 (E.D. Ill. 1936), in which the plaintiff changed his domicile in order to create diversity jurisdiction and sue in federal court. Jurisdiction was upheld in *Baker* as well.*

So Brown & Yellow's strategy allowed it to create diversity and bring the action in federal court. It would not work today, however. Under 28 U.S.C. § 1332(c)(1), if Bowling Green remained its principal place of business, Brown & Yellow would be a citizen of Kentucky *as well as* Tennessee.

The Great Dissenter

Library of Congress

Oliver Wendell Holmes Jr. (1841–1935) was raised in Massachusetts and graduated from Harvard at the beginning of the Civil War. He enlisted in the Union army and was seriously wounded three times. After the war, he somewhat reluctantly studied law, then practiced for fifteen years. His brilliant and original lectures, later published as *The Common Law*, led to appointment as a professor at Harvard Law School, which he soon left to join the bench. He served for twenty years as a justice of the Massachusetts Supreme Judicial Court, and subsequently for thirty years as a justice of the United States Supreme Court, retiring at the age of ninety-one.

Holmes rejected the formalistic legal analysis of his day in favor of legal realism. "The life of the law," he famously declared, "has not been logic; it has been experience." He rejected the premise that law was "a brooding omnipresence in the sky," a set of eternal "true" principles independent of those who make and apply law to people's lives. Rather, Holmes argues, law is a human construct crafted to serve the purposes of a particular time and place. Holmes became known as the Great Dissenter for his frequent dissents from opinions that refused to reconsider outmoded precedents. His powerful dissent in *Black & White Taxicab* eloquently challenges the philosophical underpinnings of the oft-repeated "doctrine of *Swift v. Tyson*."

5. The work of the law: Discovery . . . or creation? It is interesting to note how the majority's and dissent's different conceptions of law in *Black & White Taxicab* are reflected in the language they use. The majority, proceeding from the natural law premise that a "true rule" of monopoly contracts exists independent of any particular judge's views (the "outside thing to be found," as Holmes puts it), speaks of "the discovery of common-law principles," 276 U.S. at 529, going to "the same

---

* Section 1359 has been applied where a party tries to create diversity by assigning a claim to a party from another state, but retains the right to the ultimate recovery. *See, e.g., Kramer v. Caribbean Mills, Inc.*, 394 U.S. 823 (1969).

sources for evidence of the existing applicable rule" *id.* at 530, and of the effort to "ascertain" the proper rule. *Id.* Holmes, proceeding from the premise that law is created by those who have been delegated the authority to make it, speaks of "adopt[ing]" a rule, *id.* at 534, and of "mak[ing] or…declar[ing] the law." *Id.* at 535. He rejects the notion that courts "make a scientific inquiry into a fact outside of and independent of" their individual legal judgment. *Id.*

II. The *Erie* Decision

A decade after *Black & White Taxicab,* Civil Procedure's most famous case, *Erie Railroad Co. v. Tompkins,* reached the Court. Justice Holmes was no longer on the Court, so Justice Brandeis, who had joined Holmes's dissent in *Black & White Taxicab,* delivered the death blow to *Swift v. Tyson.* His decision in *Erie Railroad Co. v. Tompkins* fundamentally altered the relationship between the state and federal courts. It also created, as we will see, some very sophisticated problems that have bedeviled students and courts ever since. But the *Erie* decision itself is fairly straightforward.

Unforeseen Consequences

Collection of the Supreme Court of the United States

In 1934 this stretch of the Erie Railroad's tracks in rural Pennsylvania was the scene of an ordinary accident with unexpected and momentous consequences. Harry Tompkins was hit by a train while walking along the tracks, fell under the train, and lost an arm. Fortuitously, he hired a New York lawyer, who sued the Erie Railroad for damages in a New York federal court based on diversity jurisdiction. Relying on *Swift v. Tyson,* Tompkins' lawyer argued that the federal court did not have to apply Pennsylvania tort law to Tompkins' case. That argument spawned an appeal that fundamentally changed the relationship between the state and federal courts.

READING *ERIE RAILROAD CO. v. TOMPKINS.* *Erie* was a personal injury case brought against the Erie Railroad in federal court based on diversity jurisdiction. The trial court, invoking *Swift v. Tyson,* had refused to apply Pennsylvania's restrictive duty of care to a trespasser, instructing the jury that the railroad should be held to a standard of ordinary care instead. The railroad lost below and appealed to the United States Supreme Court. However, it did not directly challenge *Swift.* Rather, it argued that Tompkins's case came within a narrow category of "local usages," as to which federal courts applied state common law even under *Swift.*

In reading *Erie*, consider the following questions:

- How did Tompkins's lawyers, under the rule of *Swift v. Tyson*, obtain a crucial advantage by suing in federal court?
- What categories of litigants did the rule of *Swift v. Tyson* discriminate against?
- Why was "the course pursued" by the federal courts under *Swift* unconstitutional?

ERIE RAILROAD CO. v. TOMPKINS

304 U.S. 64 (1938)

Mr. Justice Brandeis delivered the opinion of the Court.

The question for decision is whether the oft-challenged doctrine of *Swift v. Tyson* shall now be disapproved.

Tompkins, a citizen of Pennsylvania, was injured on a dark night by a passing freight train of the Erie Railroad Company while walking along its right of way at Hughestown in that state. He claimed that the accident occurred through negligence in the operation, or maintenance, of the train; that he was rightfully on the premises as licensee because on a commonly used beaten footpath which ran for a short distance alongside the tracks; and that he was struck by something which looked like a door projecting from one of the moving cars. To enforce that claim he brought an action in the federal court for Southern New York, which had jurisdiction because the company is a corporation of that state. It denied liability; and the case was tried by a jury.

The Erie insisted that its duty to Tompkins was no greater than that owed to a trespasser. It contended, among other things, that its duty to Tompkins, and hence its liability, should be determined in accordance with the Pennsylvania law; that under the law of Pennsylvania, as declared by its highest court, persons who use pathways along the railroad right of way—that is, a longitudinal pathway as distinguished from a crossing—are to be deemed trespassers; and that the railroad is not liable for injuries to undiscovered trespassers resulting from its negligence, unless it be wanton or willful. Tompkins denied that any such rule had been established by the decisions of the Pennsylvania courts; and contended that, since there was no statute of the state on the subject, the railroad's duty and liability is to be determined in federal courts as a matter of general law.

The trial judge refused to rule that the applicable law precluded recovery. The jury brought in a verdict of $30,000; and the judgment entered thereon was affirmed by the Circuit Court of Appeals, which held, (2 Cir., 90 F.2d 603, 604), that it was unnecessary to consider whether the law of Pennsylvania was as contended, because the question was one not of local, but of general, law, and that "upon questions of general law the federal courts are free, in absence of a local statute, to exercise their independent judgment as to what the law is; and it is well settled that the question of the responsibility of a railroad for injuries caused by its servants is one of general law. . . . Where the public has made open and notorious use of a railroad right of way for a long period of time and without objection, the company owes to persons on such permissive pathway a duty of care in the operation of its trains. . . . It is likewise generally recognized law that a jury may find that negligence exists toward a pedestrian using a permissive path on the railroad right of way if he is hit by some object projecting from the side of the train."

The Erie had contended that application of the Pennsylvania rule was required, among other things, by section 34 of the Federal Judiciary Act of September 24, 1789, which provides: "The laws of the several States, except where the Constitution, treaties, or statutes of the United States otherwise require or provide, shall be regarded as rules of decision in trials at common law, in the courts of the United States, in cases where they apply."

Because of the importance of the question whether the federal court was free to disregard the alleged rule of the Pennsylvania common law, we granted certiorari.

First. *Swift v. Tyson* held that federal courts exercising jurisdiction on the ground of diversity of citizenship need not, in matters of general jurisprudence, apply the unwritten law of the state as declared by its highest court; that they are free to exercise an independent judgment as to what the common law of the state is—or should be; and that, as there stated by Mr. Justice Story, "the true interpretation of the 34th section limited its application to state laws, strictly local, that is to say, to the positive statutes of the state, and the construction thereof adopted by the local tribunals, and to rights and titles to things having a permanent locality, such as the rights and titles to real estate, and other matters immovable and intra-territorial in their nature and character. It never has been supposed by us, that the section did apply, or was designed to apply, to questions of a more general nature, not at all dependent upon local statutes or local usages of a fixed and permanent operation, as, for example, to the construction of ordinary contracts or other written instruments, and especially to questions of general commercial law, where the state tribunals are called upon to perform the like functions as ourselves, that is, to ascertain, upon general reasoning and legal analogies, what is the true exposition of the contract or instrument, or what is the just rule furnished by the principles of commercial law to govern the case."

The Court in applying the rule of section 34 to equity cases, in *Mason v. United States*, 260 U.S. 545, 559, said: "The statute, however, is merely declarative of the rule which would exist in the absence of the statute." The federal courts assumed, in the broad field of "general law," the power to declare rules of decision which Congress was confessedly without power to enact as statutes. Doubt was repeatedly expressed as to the correctness of the construction given section 34, and as to the soundness of the rule which it introduced. But it was the more recent research of a competent scholar, who examined the original document, which established that the construction given to it by the Court was erroneous; and that the purpose of the section was merely to make certain that, in all matters except those in which some federal law is controlling, the federal courts exercising jurisdiction in diversity of citizenship cases would apply as their rules of decision the law of the state, unwritten as well as written.[5]

Criticism of the doctrine became widespread after the decision of *Black & White Taxicab & Transfer Co. v. Brown & Yellow Taxicab & Transfer Co.*, 276 U.S. 518. There, Brown & Yellow, a Kentucky corporation owned by Kentuckians, and the Louisville & Nashville Railroad, also a Kentucky corporation, wished that the former should have the exclusive privilege of soliciting passenger and baggage transportation at the Bowling Green, Ky., railroad station; and that the Black & White, a competing Kentucky corporation, should be prevented from interfering with that privilege. Knowing that such a contract would be void under the common law of Kentucky, it was arranged that the Brown & Yellow reincorporate under the law of Tennessee, and that the contract with the railroad should be executed there. The suit was then brought by the Tennessee corporation in the federal court for Western Kentucky to enjoin competition by the Black & White; an injunction issued by the District Court was sustained by the Court of Appeals; and this Court, citing many decisions in which the doctrine of *Swift & Tyson* had been applied, affirmed the decree.

Second. Experience in applying the doctrine of *Swift v. Tyson*, had revealed its defects, political and social; and the benefits expected to flow from the rule did not accrue. Persistence of state courts in their own opinions on questions of common law prevented uniformity; and the impossibility of discovering a satisfactory line of demarcation between the province of general law and that of local law developed a new well of uncertainties.[8]

On the other hand, the mischievous results of the doctrine had become apparent. Diversity of citizenship jurisdiction was conferred in order to prevent apprehended discrimination in state courts against those not citizens of the state. *Swift v. Tyson* introduced grave discrimination by noncitizens against citizens. It made rights enjoyed under the unwritten "general law" vary according to whether enforcement was sought in the state or in the federal court; and the privilege of selecting the court in which the right should be determined was conferred upon the noncitizen. Thus, the doctrine rendered impossible equal protection of the law. In attempting to promote uniformity of law throughout the United States, the doctrine had prevented uniformity in the administration of the law of the state.

The discrimination resulting became in practice far-reaching. This resulted in part from the broad province accorded to the so-called "general law" as to which federal courts exercised an independent judgment. In addition to questions of purely commercial law, "general law" was held to include the obligations under contracts entered into and to be performed within the state, the extent to which

5. Charles Warren, *New Light on the History of the Federal Judiciary Act of 1789* (1923) 37 Harv. L. Rev. 49, 51–52, 81–88, 108.

8. Compare 2 Warren, The Supreme Court in United States History, Rev. Ed. 1935, 89: "Probably no decision of the Court has ever given rise to more uncertainty as to legal rights; and though doubtless intended to promote uniformity in the operation of business transactions, its chief effect has been to render it difficult for business men to know in advance to what particular topic the Court would apply the doctrine. . . ." The *Federal Digest* through the 1937 volume, lists nearly 1,000 decisions involving the distinction between questions of general and of local law.

a carrier operating within a state may stipulate for exemption from liability for his own negligence or that of his employee; the liability for torts committed within the state upon persons resident or property located there, even where the question of liability depended upon the scope of a property right conferred by the state; and the right to exemplary or punitive damages. Furthermore, state decisions construing local deeds, mineral conveyances, and even devises of real estate, were disregarded.

In part the discrimination resulted from the wide range of persons held entitled to avail themselves of the federal rule by resort to the diversity of citizenship jurisdiction. Through this jurisdiction individual citizens willing to remove from their own state and become citizens of another might avail themselves of the federal rule. And, without even change of residence, a corporate citizen of the state could avail itself of the federal rule by reincorporating under the laws of another state, as was done in the Taxicab Case.

The injustice and confusion incident to the doctrine of *Swift v. Tyson* have been repeatedly urged as reasons for abolishing or limiting diversity of citizenship jurisdiction. Other legislative relief has been proposed. If only a question of statutory construction were involved, we should not be prepared to abandon a doctrine so widely applied throughout nearly a century. But the unconstitutionality of the course pursued has now been made clear, and compels us to do so.

Third. Except in matters governed by the Federal Constitution or by acts of Congress, the law to be applied in any case is the law of the state. And whether the law of the state shall be declared by its Legislature in a statute or by its highest court in a decision is not a matter of federal concern. There is no federal general common law. Congress has no power to declare substantive rules of common law applicable in a state whether they be local in their nature or "general," be they commercial law or a part of the law of torts. And no clause in the Constitution purports to confer such a power upon the federal courts. As stated by Mr. Justice Field when protesting in *Baltimore & Ohio R.R. Co. v. Baugh,* 149 U.S. 368, 401, against ignoring the Ohio common law of fellow-servant liability: "I am aware that what has been termed the general law of the country—which is often little less than what the judge advancing the doctrine thinks at the time should be the general law on a particular subject—has been often advanced in judicial opinions of this court to control a conflicting law of a state. I admit that learned judges have fallen into the habit of repeating this doctrine as a convenient mode of brushing aside the law of a state in conflict with their views. And I confess that, moved and governed by the authority of the great names of those judges, I have, myself, in many instances, unhesitatingly and confidently, but I think now erroneously, repeated the same doctrine. But, notwithstanding the great names which may be cited in favor of the doctrine, and notwithstanding the frequency with which the doctrine has been reiterated, there stands, as a perpetual protest against its repetition, the constitution of the United States, which recognizes and preserves the autonomy and independence of the states,—independence in their legislative and independence in their judicial departments. Supervision over either the legislative or the judicial action of the states is in no case permissible except as to matters by the constitution specifically authorized or delegated to the United States. Any interference with either, except as thus permitted, is an invasion of the authority of the state, and, to that extent, a denial of its independence."

The fallacy underlying the rule declared in *Swift v. Tyson* is made clear by Mr. Justice Holmes. The doctrine rests upon the assumption that there is "a transcendental body of law outside of any particular State but obligatory within it unless and until changed by statute," that federal courts have the power to use their judgment as to what the rules of common law are; and that in the federal courts "the parties are entitled to an independent judgment on matters of general law":

"But law in the sense in which courts speak of it today does not exist without some definite authority behind it. The common law so far as it is enforced in a State, whether called common law or not, is not the common law generally but the law of that State existing by the authority of that State without regard to what it may have been in England or anywhere else. . . .

"The authority and only authority is the State, and if that be so, the voice adopted by the State as its own whether it be of its Legislature or of its Supreme Court should utter the last word."

Thus the doctrine of *Swift v. Tyson* is, as Mr. Justice Holmes said, "an unconstitutional assumption of powers by the Courts of the United States which no lapse of time or respectable array of opinion should make us hesitate to correct." In disapproving that doctrine we do not hold unconstitutional section 34 of the Federal Judiciary Act of 1789 or any other act of Congress. We merely declare that in applying the doctrine this Court and the lower courts have invaded rights which in our opinion are reserved by the Constitution to the several states.

Fourth. The defendant contended that by the common law of Pennsylvania as declared by its highest court . . . the only duty owed to the plaintiff was to refrain from willful or wanton injury. The plaintiff denied that such is the Pennsylvania law. In support of their respective contentions the parties discussed and cited many decisions of the Supreme Court of the state. The Circuit Court of Appeals ruled that the question of liability is one of general law; and on that ground declined to decide the issue of state law. As we hold this was error, the judgment is reversed and the case remanded to it for further proceedings in conformity with our opinion.

Reversed.

Mr. Justice Reed (concurring in part).

I concur in the conclusion reached in this case, in the disapproval of the doctrine of *Swift v. Tyson*, and in the reasoning of the majority opinion, except in so far as it relies upon the unconstitutionality of the "course pursued" by the federal courts.

The "doctrine of *Swift v. Tyson*," as I understand it, is that the words "the laws," as used in section 34, line 1, of the Federal Judiciary Act of September 24, 1789, do not included in their meaning "the decisions of the local tribunals." Mr. Justice Story, in deciding that point, said,

> Undoubtedly, the decisions of the local tribunals upon such subjects are entitled to, and will receive, the most deliberate attention and respect of this court; but

they cannot furnish positive rules, or conclusive authority, by which our own judgments are to be bound up and governed.

To decide the case now before us and to "disapprove" the doctrine of *Swift v. Tyson* requires only that we say that the words "the laws" include in their meaning the decisions of the local tribunals. As the majority opinion shows, by its reference to Mr. Warren's researches and the first quotation from Mr. Justice Holmes, that this Court is now of the view that "laws" includes "decisions," it is unnecessary to go further and declare that the "course pursued" was "unconstitutional," instead of merely erroneous.

The "unconstitutional" course referred to in the majority opinion is apparently the ruling in *Swift v. Tyson* that the supposed omission of Congress to legislate as to the effect of decisions leaves federal courts free to interpret general law for themselves. I am not at all sure whether, in the absence of federal statutory direction, federal courts would be compelled to follow state decisions. There was sufficient doubt about the matter in 1789 to induce the first Congress to legislate. No former opinions of this Court have passed upon it. Mr. Justice Holmes evidently saw nothing "unconstitutional" which required the overruling of *Swift v. Tyson*, for he said in the very opinion quoted by the majority, "I should leave *Swift v. Tyson* undisturbed, as I indicated in *Kuhn v. Fairmont Coal Co.*, but I would not allow it to spread the assumed dominion into new fields." If the opinion commits this Court to the position that the Congress is without power to declare what rules of substantive law shall govern the federal courts, that conclusion also seems questionable. The line between procedural and substantive law is hazy, but no one doubts federal power over procedure. The Judiciary Article, 3, and the "necessary and proper" clause of article 1, § 8, may fully authorize legislation, such as this section of the Judiciary Act.

In this Court, stare decisis, in statutory construction, is a useful rule, not an inexorable command. It seems preferable to overturn an established construction of an act of Congress, rather than, in the circumstances of this case, to interpret the Constitution.

. . .

Notes and Questions: Riding the *Erie* Railroad

1. The illusion of uniformity. One of the rationales for the *Swift* doctrine was that over time federal interpretations of common law issues would tend to converge, and that state judges would eventually fall into line with their eminent colleagues on the federal bench. As the *Erie* opinion points out, however, it did not happen. State judges, believing themselves as well qualified as the federal judges to perceive the "true rule" in a common law case, often refused to follow the federal decisions. Consequently, the likelihood of getting one rule of law in the state court and another in the federal court across the street persisted or even increased.

Q **2. What discrimination?** Justice Brandeis's opinion suggests that *Swift* led to discrimination against some litigants in diversity cases. Who obtained an advantage from this discrimination, and who was discriminated against?

A Out-of-state defendants usually had an advantage, but this wasn't always true. Suppose that a Kentucky taxi company wanted to sue an out-of-state competitor to enforce an exclusive contract with the railroad. If it knew that the federal courts would enforce the contract but the state courts would not, it could sue in federal court to obtain the more favorable contract rule. Thus, it had the same chance to choose between different contract rules that the plaintiff had in *Black & White Taxicab.*

But an in-state *defendant* would not have such a choice if sued by an out-of-state plaintiff. If sued in federal court, it would be stuck there, subject to whatever rule the court chose under *Swift*, since there is no right to "remove" from federal to state court. If the defendant were sued in state court, it would be stuck in *that* court, since the removal statute bars removal by an in-state defendant. 28 U.S.C. § 1441(b). If an in-state plaintiff brought suit in state court, the out-of-state defendant could leave it there if state law was favorable to it or remove to federal court if it was not. Thus, under *Swift*, the out-of-state litigant frequently had crucial tactical choices denied to the in-state litigant. As Justice Brandeis notes, diversity jurisdiction was created to avoid bias against out-of-state parties, but under *Swift* the federal courts administered diversity in a manner that clearly favored them.

3. "The unconstitutionality of the course pursued." Justice Brandeis condemns the unconstitutionality of the *Swift* doctrine, but nowhere cites any provision of the Constitution that it transgresses. Yet, it seems clear that the Court viewed as unconstitutional the federal judges' practice under *Swift* of pronouncing substantive rules of law—like the duty owed to a trespasser or the enforceability of a monopoly contract—in areas where the federal Constitution gives no law-making authority to either Congress or the federal courts. The most obviously applicable provision is the Tenth Amendment:

> The powers not delegated to the United States by the Constitution, nor prohibited by it to the States, are reserved to the States respectively, or to the people.

Justice Reed's concurrence suggests that a delegation of power to make the substantive law for diversity cases may be inherent in Article III itself, which authorizes the creation of federal courts and confers the diversity jurisdiction, together with the Necessary and Proper Clause in Article I. Consequently, he would decide the case on the narrower ground that Justice Story's view of the Rules of Decision Act was simply wrong as a matter of statutory interpretation.

4. Did *Erie* hold the RDA unconstitutional? No. The Court concluded that interpreting the RDA to apply only to state statutes and local usages, but not judicial decisions, was unconstitutional. The RDA now mandates federal courts to apply state law in diversity cases, whether that law is made by the state legislature or by the state's "other voice," its courts.

5. An idea whose time had come. Interestingly, the railroad did not base its appeal on the argument that *Swift v. Tyson* should be overruled. See the wonderful historical article about *Erie* by Irving Younger, *What Happened in* Erie, 56 Tex. L. Rev. 1011, 1025–26 (1978), and the equally fine analysis of the case by Edward Purcell in Kevin Clermont, Civil Procedure Stories 21–77 (2d ed. 2008). Overruling *Swift* would mean a sea change in the role of the federal courts in cases that turn on state law—a change distinctly unfavorable to corporate clients like the Erie Railroad. Federal courts were viewed as favorable to business interests, and the *Swift* doctrine allowed them to bypass unfavorable local law.

Instead, the Erie Railroad tried to distinguish *Swift*, arguing that the case fell within a narrow exception to the *Swift* doctrine for "local usages" with regard to land use. But the Court went swiftly (excuse the pun) for the jugular, pronouncing somewhat inaccurately in the opening sentence of the opinion that "[t]he question for decision is whether the oft-challenged doctrine of *Swift v. Tyson* shall now be disapproved." Although Justice Butler's dissent (omitted here—*see* 304 U.S. at 82–90) criticizes the majority for deciding the case without briefing or reargument from the parties on the broader issue of overruling *Swift*, the Court proceeded remorselessly to inter it.

6. A contrary view. Not all scholars agree that *Erie* was rightly decided. For an emphatic professorial dissent, see Suzanna Sherry, *Wrong, Out of Step and Pernicious:* Erie *as the Worst Decision of All Time*, 33 Pep. L. Rev. 129 (2011). Professor Sherry argues that *Erie* was wrong as an interpretation of the Rules of Decision Act, wrong as an interpretation of the limits of federal legislative and judicial authority, and wrong as a matter of policy.

III. *Erie* Guesses: Federal Judges Applying State Law

While *Erie* has had a profound impact on federal practice, the basic command of *Erie* is straightforward: In cases that are not governed by federal law, the federal court must apply state law rather than taking its own view of what the applicable rule should be. This mandate is carried out by the federal courts every day, usually with little trouble. If the case is a contracts case, the court applies the contract law of the relevant state. If it's a torts case, it uses state tort law, and so on.

The federal judge's *Erie* task can be difficult, however, if the content of state law is unclear. For example, a novel question of state law may arise on which there is no precedent from the courts of the state. How is the federal judge to carry out her mission to apply rather than to make state law? Suppose, for example, that the question of duty of care to a trespasser arises in a diversity case involving North Carolina law. The federal judge researches the North Carolina precedents and finds no cases involving the question. The judge's job is still to *apply* North Carolina law, rather than "make up" federal common law, but it is hard to apply a principle that hasn't yet been proclaimed.

Q **If you were the federal judge facing this dilemma, what would you do?**

A If you think about it, it seems fairly clear what you would do. You would look at North Carolina law in related areas and try to extrapolate from analogous principles how the North Carolina courts would decide the trespasser issue. Perhaps, for example, North Carolina cases have consistently refused to abolish the traditional distinction between licensees and invitees. This persistence in the common law approach to landowner liability suggests that North Carolina courts would be unlikely to expand the duty owed to a trespasser.

If you didn't find useful cases involving landowner liability, you would look at North Carolina's general approach to negligence issues. Perhaps you could discern a trend in the cases, on issues like product liability, contributory negligence, and contribution rights, that suggests that North Carolina courts would abandon—or reaffirm—traditional tort limitations on recovery in landowner cases. You would also look for dicta in related North Carolina decisions. If these avenues bore no fruit, you would likely look at the trend of the law in other states on the issue, and consider, based on the general orientation of the North Carolina courts, whether they would follow or buck the trend.

(Another option in some cases is to "certify" a question of state law to the state's highest court—to ask it to decide the issue of law so the federal case can proceed. This option is discussed below in note 5.)

In looking at all this, however, you would keep your basic goal in mind: not to decide the case "right," or according to the "modern" trend, but to decide it as a North Carolina court would.

The state supreme court predictive approach. Suppose that the federal judge in a diversity case finds a case from the North Carolina Court of Appeals (the intermediate appellate court of North Carolina) holding that a trespasser on a railroad right of way is owed a duty of due care. This is persuasive evidence of what North Carolina law "is." Would the federal judge be bound to follow that case?

Early decisions from the Supreme Court held that the federal judge would have to follow *any* state court precedent on the point. *See West v. American Tel. & Tel. Co.*, 311 U.S. 223, 238 (1940) (court should follow decision of the intermediate appellate court "even though it may think that the state Supreme Court may establish a different rule in some future litigation"); *Fidelity Trust Co. v. Field*, 311 U.S. 169 (1940) (federal court must follow decisions of a state trial court, though those decisions would not bind any other trial or appellate judge in the state).

The Supreme Court subsequently adopted a more flexible view of the federal trial judge's role in making "*Erie* guesses." *Cf. Commissioner v. Bosch*, 387 U.S. 456 (1967) (federal court, in determining law of the state, should follow intermediate state court precedents, unless convinced that the state's highest court would rule otherwise). Under this "state supreme court predictive approach," the federal judge would consider decisions on point from the intermediate appellate court of the state or from trial courts. However, her job is to determine how the case would come out *if it were decided today by the state supreme court*. That court might not follow the intermediate court's decision. If the federal judge, after reviewing decisions from the state supreme court in related areas, dicta, scholarly commentaries, and other sources of North Carolina authority, concludes that the North Carolina Supreme Court would not uphold the lower court's ruling, she could decide that it is not "North Carolina law" under the predictive approach. *See McKenna v. Ortho Pharm. Corp.*, 622 F.2d 657, 661–63 (3d Cir. 1980) (describing in detail district court judge's task in ascertaining applicable state law).

Notes and Questions: Ascertaining State Law

Q **1. The state trial court's role in applying precedent.** Suppose that the North Carolina Supreme Court had held, in *Hugo v. Decker*, in 1920, that a trespasser on a railroad right of way could not recover from the railroad unless she established that the conduct of the railroad in causing her injury was willful or wanton. Assume that McDermott is injured in a similar accident in 2020, and sues in a North Carolina *state* court, alleging negligence—but not willful or wanton conduct—by the railroad. What should the trial court do?

A It will dismiss the case, because North Carolina trial courts are bound to follow the state supreme court's *Hugo* decision unless it had been so eviscerated by later decisions as to be "impliedly overruled." The state trial court has no authority to ignore a precedent directly on point, even if it predicts that the state supreme court would overrule that case.

Of course, McDermott could appeal the dismissal. If the North Carolina Supreme Court chooses to hear his case, he can try to convince that court to change its rule.

Q **2. The federal court's role in applying state law precedent in a diversity case.** Suppose that McDermott is injured on the railroad right of way in 2020 and sues in federal district court, based on diversity jurisdiction. The court researches North Carolina law and discovers *Hugo v. Decker*, the 1920 decision establishing the willful/wanton rule. It also finds dicta in recent North Carolina Supreme Court cases suggesting that the willful/wanton rule is outdated, and other cases in related areas that have established a due care standard in related situations. The federal judge is convinced from these recent precedents that if the North Carolina Supreme Court were to decide the issue today, it would hold that the railroad owes trespassers a duty of due care. What rule should the federal judge apply to McDermott's case?

A If truly convinced that the North Carolina Supreme Court would apply a due care rule, the federal judge would apply the due care standard. Of course, in doing so, she is making a prediction about what the North Carolina Supreme Court would do and is likely to be reluctant to conclude that what has been the law will not be in the future. But if firmly convinced that the state court would change the rule today, under the "supreme court predictive approach," the federal judge should apply the due care standard. If she does, the law applied to the issue will differ in the state and federal courts—at least at the trial court level.

3. Multiple possibilities: The precedential effect of an "*Erie* guess."

Suppose, on the facts above, that McDermott sues in federal court. The federal trial judge, applying the state supreme court predictive approach, concludes that the North Carolina Supreme Court would overrule *Hugo v. Decker* and adopt a due care standard. Consequently, she applies the due care standard to McDermott's case. Six months later, a new plaintiff, Gretsky, sues the railroad on a similar claim in a North Carolina state trial court. What law should the North Carolina state trial court judge apply?

A. The North Carolina trial court judge should apply the due care standard to Gretsky's case, because the most recent case (the federal case) held that the due care standard is now the law of North Carolina.
B. The North Carolina trial court judge should apply the due care standard to Gretsky's case, if it agrees that the North Carolina Supreme Court would adopt that rule today.
C. The North Carolina trial court judge should apply the willful/wanton standard to Gretsky's case, because it is bound by the decision in *Hugo v. Decker.*
D. The North Carolina trial court judge should apply the willful/wanton standard to Gretsky's case, unless the federal district court's decision to apply the due care rule has been affirmed by the federal court of appeals.

The key to this question is that the North Carolina trial court judges are not bound by a federal court's "*Erie* guess." Instead, they are bound by North Carolina Supreme Court decisions until those decisions are overruled. *Hugo v. Decker* never has been overruled, though a federal judge has predicted that it will be. Thus, the state trial court judge in Gretsky's case should follow *Hugo v. Decker* and apply the willful/wanton rule. Even if the federal court of appeals reviewed McDermott's case and agreed with the federal trial judge that *Hugo* would be overruled, the state trial judge cannot use that as a reason to ignore a decision on point from the North Carolina Supreme Court. **C** is the right answer.

4. Charting new paths in cases governed by state law. The question above suggests that sometimes, under the "state supreme court predictive approach," the federal court will apply a different rule than the state trial court would—the very disparity condemned in *Erie*.

In a very clear case, the federal judge may go out on a limb and apply a rule that flies in the face of established state precedent—after all, that's what the predictive approach requires. *See, e.g., Mason v. American Emery Wheel Works*, 241 F.2d 906 (1st Cir. 1957) (federal court predicted that the Supreme Court of Mississippi would reject privity requirement in products liability case, though existing Mississippi case law imposed a privity requirement). But federal courts will be extremely cautious about making such predictions and ignoring state case law that would bind a state trial judge. As one federal court put it, "[w]e have warned, time and time again, that litigants who reject a state forum in order to bring suit in federal court under diversity jurisdiction cannot expect that new [state-law] trails will be blazed." *Carleton v. Worcester*, 923 F.2d 1, 3 (1st Cir. 1991) (quoting *Ryan v. Royal Ins. Co.*, 916 F.2d 731, 744 (1st Cir. 1990)); *see also Anderson v. Marathon Petroleum Co.*, 801 F.2d 936, 942 (7th Cir. 1986) (litigants "who seek adventurous departures in state common law are advised to sue in state rather than federal court"). Despite this reticence, a recent article states that "diversity courts can and frequently do depart from standing precedent of the highest state court." Doris D. Brogan, *Less Mischief, Not None: Respecting Federalism, Respecting States and Respecting Judges in Diversity Jurisdiction Cases*, 51 Tulsa L. Rev. 39, 82 (2015). Professor Brogan's article recounts case law from the Third Circuit, which, under the state supreme court predictive approach, concluded that the Pennsylvania

Supreme Court would adopt the *Third Restatement of Torts'* approach to design defect products liability claims. Based on this prediction, the federal court applied the Third Restatement rule over a period of five years, while the Pennsylvania courts continued to apply a narrower rule under the Second Restatement. Five years later, the Pennsylvania Supreme Court finally addressed the issue . . . and refused to adopt the Third Restatement approach.

Q **5. If the court needs to know state law, why not ask?** Since federal courts cannot "make" state law, but are called upon to apply it, it would be helpful if they could ask a state court what the law of that state is. Many states have statutes or court rules authorizing federal courts (or the courts of another state) to "certify" questions of state law to the state supreme court for decision. The Massachusetts court rule below is typical of state certification provisions.

RULES OF THE MASSACHUSETTS SUPREME JUDICIAL COURT

RULE 1:03. UNIFORM CERTIFICATION OF QUESTIONS OF LAW

Section 1. **Authority to Answer Certain Questions of Law.** This court may answer questions of law certified to it by the Supreme Court of the United States, a Court of Appeals of the United States, or of the District of Columbia, or a United States District Court, or the highest appellate court of any other state when requested by the certifying court if there are involved in any proceeding before it questions of law of this state which may be determinative of the cause then pending in the certifying court and as to which it appears to the certifying court there is no controlling precedent in the decisions of this court.

Section 2. **Method of Invoking.** This rule may be invoked by an order of any of the courts referred to in Section 1 upon that court's own motion or upon the motion of any party to the cause.

Section 3. **Contents of Certification Order.** A certification order shall set forth

(1) the question of law to be answered; and

(2) a statement of all facts relevant to the questions certified and showing fully the nature of the controversy in which the questions arose. . . .

Under such provisions, a federal court may certify a question of that state's law to the state's highest court. The state court has discretion to accept or decline the certification. If it accepts and decides the issue, the federal court will receive a definitive answer on the state law issue.

Why would certification probably *not* be an option, under the Massachusetts certification rule, for the federal district court in McDermott's case in Note 1?

A Read literally, section 1 of the certification rule does not authorize certification of the case because there *is* controlling precedent on point. The federal judge's problem is that she isn't sure whether that "controlling precedent" would be followed today. One wonders if some courts may read this requirement flexibly: Often, there is a question as to whether the older case would still "control" the outcome today. *But see In re Air Crash at Lexington, Kentucky, August 27, 2006*, 556 F. Supp. 2d 665, 669 (E.D. Ky. 2008) (certification not appropriate where there is state precedent on point).

Although certification provides a clear answer as to the meaning of state law, it is not routinely used. Federal judges decide a great many cases each year that turn on state law. If all debatable state law issues in such cases were certified to a state court, such proceedings would monopolize the docket of the state supreme courts. Second, certification is expensive and may delay the federal case. A case certified to a state supreme court will be placed on its docket, much like a regular appeal. It will be briefed by the parties to the federal case and argued before the state court, which will render its decision in a written opinion. This process could take a year or more and will generate additional attorneys' fees.* Since most cases settle, the case can probably be resolved without a definitive ruling on the question. (One frustrating aspect of law practice is that so many interesting legal questions arise that never get answered by a court.) Thus, certification is the exception rather than the rule in resolving unclear issues of state law.

Q **6. State law as of when?** Suppose that Marden brings a negligence action in federal court. The federal judge dismisses the case, concluding that her contributory negligence is a complete bar to recovery under East Dakota law (which governs under *Erie*). Marden appeals to the federal court of appeals, claiming that the East Dakota Supreme Court would apply comparative negligence today, allowing her to recover part of her damages. While the appeal is pending, the East Dakota Supreme Court takes a state case on review and adopts comparative negligence, overruling the contributory negligence rule. What law should the federal court of appeals apply to Marden's case?

A The appeal should be decided under East Dakota law as it stands at the time of the appeal. Marden is entitled to the federal appeals court's best judgment about what East Dakota law is at that time rather than affirming the federal trial judge's ruling because she made her best guess about East Dakota law based on earlier evidence: "[W]e are of the view that, until such time as a case is no longer sub judice [in the process of decision], the duty rests upon federal courts to apply state law under the Rules of Decision statute in accordance with the then controlling decision of the highest state court. Any other conclusion would but perpetuate the confusion and injustices arising from inconsistent federal and state interpretations of state law." *Vandenbark v. Owens-Illinois Glass Co.*, 311 U.S. 538, 543 (1941). Thus, though the federal district judge conscientiously did her job, the case will be reversed for retrial if the state law has changed or been clarified after the federal district judge's prediction.**

---

* "Certification burdens litigants, who foot the bill while their lawyers reargue the controversy in a different forum. The parties will now file briefs in the California Supreme Court, explaining why it should or should not accept the certification request. Cal. Rules of Court 29.5(e)(1). Next, they will reply to each other's briefs. *Id.* 29.5(e)(4). If the court accepts the request, the parties will file more briefs and replies, arguing the case on the merits. *Id.* 29.5(h)(1). Once the state supreme court sends the case back to us, the parties will no doubt want to argue some more over how we should interpret its response. These are the sorts of things that make lawyers rich but litigants understandably frustrated." *Kremen v. Cohen*, 325 F.3d 1035, 1052–53 (9th Cir. 2003) (Kozinski, J., dissenting).

** "'When we write to a state law issue, we write in faint and disappearing ink,' and 'once the state supreme court speaks the effect of anything we have written vanishes like a proverbial bat in daylight, only faster.'" *LeFrere v. Quezada*, 582 F.3d 1260, 1262 (11th Cir. 2009) (quoting from *Sultenfuss v. Snow*, 35 F.3d 1494, 1504 (11th Cir. 1947)) (Carnes J., dissenting).

Note that **B** is close, but wrong. The federal court, under *Klaxon*, does not apply the law of the state in which it sits. It applies the law that *the state in which it sits would apply* to the case.

3. Spinning out the implications of *Erie* and *Klaxon*. Under *Klaxon*, a federal district court sitting in New York must ask, "What body of tort law would a New York state court apply if the plaintiff had sued there?" A federal district court sitting in Pennsylvania must ask, "What body of tort law would a Pennsylvania court apply if the plaintiff had sued in the state courts there?" Because the federal judge chooses the same body of law that the local state courts would, the case will be decided under the same law whether it is in a New York state court or a New York federal court.

> The conflict of laws rules to be applied by the federal court in Delaware must conform to those prevailing in Delaware's state courts. Otherwise the accident of diversity of citizenship would constantly disturb equal administration of justice in coordinate state and federal courts sitting side by side. *See Erie Railroad v. Tompkins, supra.*

Klaxon, 313 U.S. at 496.

Q **4. Vertical uniformity and horizontal chaos.** Consider the implications of *Klaxon* for a party choosing whether to bring suit in state or federal court in a particular state. Assume that New York's choice of law rule for torts cases requires New York courts to use its own tort law, as long as the case or the parties have some connection to New York. Assume also that Pennsylvania's choice of law rule is the place-of-the-accident rule. Finally, assume that New York tort law holds that a railroad owes a duty of due care to a trespasser, while Pennsylvania's tort rule only holds a railroad liable to a trespasser if its conduct is willful/wanton.

A. Tompkins sues for his Pennsylvania accident in a New York state court. What state's law would the court apply?

A A New York state court judge will apply New York's choice of law rule to choose which state's tort law to apply. New York's choice of law rule for torts (the question assumes) is to apply New York law to the case if it has a meaningful connection to New York. This case does have such a connection, because the defendant is a New York corporation. Thus, the court will apply New York tort law, which allows recovery if the defendant failed to use due care.

B. Tompkins sues in a New York federal court. What state's law would the court apply?

A The federal court will apply New York law, because *Klaxon* tells it to apply the same body of tort law that the New York state court would choose. The due care rule applies.

C. Tompkins sues in a Pennsylvania state court. What state's law would the court apply?

A The Pennsylvania state court judge will apply Pennsylvania's choice of law rule for torts to decide which state's tort law to apply. Pennsylvania's choice of law rule is to apply the law of the place of the accident. Since the accident occurred in Pennsylvania, the Pennsylvania state court judge will apply Pennsylvania law to the case. Tompkins is stuck with its willful/wanton rule in this example.

D. Tompkins sues in a Pennsylvania federal court. What state's law would the court apply?

A The federal court in Pennsylvania will apply Pennsylvania law, because *Klaxon* tells it to apply the same law that would be applied by the Pennsylvania courts. Again, the willful/wanton rule applies.

These variations illustrate that just as the state courts in the two states will apply different tort rules, so will the federal courts in those two states. *Klaxon* mandates "vertical uniformity" between the state and federal courts in the same state—the state and the federal court in New York will apply the same tort rule to the case. But it leads to the application of different legal rules in the federal courts in New York and Pennsylvania—the federal court in New York would apply a simple negligence standard, while the Pennsylvania federal court would apply the willful or wanton conduct rule. (So who says forum shopping is dead?) The *Klaxon* Court recognized this consequence of its decision:

> Whatever lack of uniformity this may produce between federal courts in different states is attributable to our federal system, which leaves to a state, within the limits permitted by the Constitution, the right to pursue local policies diverging from those of its neighbors.

313 U.S. at 496. Perhaps the Court should have noted the freedom of the states to choose "local policies" *and* local choice of law rules different from those of their neighbors.

5. The scholarly attack on *Klaxon*. While almost everyone accepts the wisdom of *Erie*'s command to federal courts to apply state law in diversity cases, some scholars have panned *Klaxon*'s extension of *Erie* to state choice of law rules. The choice of law rules that states adopt may tend to favor local litigants. Forcing the federal courts to echo parochial state choice of law rules exacerbates the problem. Might not the Framers have created diversity jurisdiction in part to allow a neutral federal court to choose the appropriate body of state substantive law in a diversity case?

> The federal courts are in a peculiarly disinterested position to make a just determination as to which state's laws ought to apply.... By disabling them from doing this, the Supreme Court [in *Klaxon*] has not only impeded the development of a sound body of private interstate law but has placed it within the power of a plaintiff who can find the defendant in a state where he wants him to make the choice of law for himself. Justice is not ordinarily served by putting it in the hands of one of the litigants.

Henry M. Hart, Jr., *The Relations Between State and Federal Law*, 54 COLUM. L. REV. 489, 515 (1954) (footnote omitted). The grant of diversity jurisdiction in Article III probably includes the implied authority for federal courts to adopt independent choice of law rules for diversity cases. Such independent choice of law rules would reduce forum shopping based on favorable choice of law rules in the local courts. Notwithstanding this critique, the Supreme Court reaffirmed *Klaxon* in *Day & Zimmerman Inc. v. Challoner*, 423 U.S. 3 (1975).

V. Federal Common Law: Federal Judges Making Federal Law

In *Erie*, Justice Brandeis declared that "there is no federal general common law." 304 U.S. 64, 78 (1938). That would seem to settle that.

Not so fast. There are some areas in which the law must be federal, yet Congress has never enacted a governing statute. Suppose, for example, that Wyoming and Colorado both claim the right to withdraw unlimited amounts of water from an interstate stream. What law should govern a dispute like that? Surely neither Colorado nor Wyoming law. The matter is uniquely interstate, of national interest, and requires a neutral, federal rule of decision, whether Congress has enacted a federal statute to apportion the water or not. Consequently, if Colorado sues Wyoming on this water rights claim, the court will have to apply a federal apportionment rule to the case, and, if Congress hasn't provided one, the court will create a federal common law rule, one created by judicial decision rather than by statute.

Ironically, the Supreme Court affirmed this principle on *the very day* that it decided *Erie*—in a decision written by Justice Brandeis! In *Hinderlider v. La Plata River & Cherry Creek Ditch Co.*, 304 U.S. 92, 110 (1938), the Court announced that "whether the water of an interstate stream must be apportioned between the two States is a question of 'federal common law' upon which neither the statutes nor the decisions of either State can be conclusive." There may not be "federal general common law," but in some narrow areas there is still federal specific common law.

Here is another example in which a federal court applied a federal common law rule. In *Illinois v. City of Milwaukee*, 406 U.S. 91 (1972), the State of Illinois brought suit in federal court to abate the pollution of Lake Michigan by four Wisconsin cities. No federal statute directly governed the issue in the case. The Supreme Court held that Illinois' claim for interstate pollution gave rise to an action under federal common law.

In the case below the Supreme Court discusses the circumstances in which it should—or must—create a federal common law rule to address an issue that by its nature cannot be resolved under state law.

READING *UNITED STATES v. STANDARD OIL CO. OF CALIFORNIA*. In *United States v. Standard Oil Co.*, the Supreme Court considers whether an issue should be governed by federal common law, and if so, what the content of that law should be. In reading the case, consider the following questions:

- For what damages did the United States seek compensation in the case?
- Why would it be problematic to apply state law to the issue in the case?
- If the Court did not apply state law, what law would it apply? Where would it look for the applicable rule?
- Why did the Court decide not to create the right to damages asserted by the plaintiff?

Because *Standard Oil* is a difficult case, we have inserted some editorial guideposts, in brackets, in the opinion.

UNITED STATES v. STANDARD OIL CO. OF CALIFORNIA

332 U.S. 301 (1947)

Mr. Justice Rutledge delivered the opinion of the Court.

Not often since the decision in *Erie R. Co. v. Tompkins*, is this Court asked to create a new substantive legal liability without legislative aid and as at the common law. This case of first impression here seeks such a result. It arises from the following circumstances.

Early one morning in February, 1944, John Etzel, a soldier, was hit and injured by a truck of the Standard Oil Company of California at a street intersection in Los Angeles. The vehicle was driven by Boone, an employee of the company. At the Government's expense of $123.45 Etzel was hospitalized, and his soldier's pay of $69.31 was continued during his disability. Upon the payment of $300 Etzel released the company and Boone "from any and all claims which I now have or may hereafter have on account of or arising out of" the accident.

From these facts the novel question springs whether the Government is entitled to recover from the respondents as tort-feasors the amounts expended for hospitalization and soldier's pay, as for loss of Etzel's services. . . . [W]e granted certiorari because of the novelty and importance of the principal question.

As the case reaches us, a number of issues contested in the District Court and the Circuit Court of Appeals have been eliminated. Remaining is the basic question of respondents' liability for interference with the government-soldier relation and consequent loss to the United States, together with questions whether this issue is to be determined by federal or state law.[4] . . . [W]e have reached the conclusion that respondents are not liable for the injuries inflicted upon the Government.

[Eds.—The Court discusses here why the claimed right of indemnification must be determined by federal law, not state law.]

We agree with the Government's view that the creation or negation of such a liability is not a matter to be determined by state law. The case in this aspect is governed by the rule of *Clearfield Trust Co. v. United States*, 318 U.S. 363 . . . , rather than that of *Erie R. Co. v. Tompkins*. In the *Clearfield* case, involving liabilities arising out of a forged indorsement of a check issued by the United States, the Court said: "The authority to issue the check had its origin in the Constitution and the statutes of the United States and was in no way dependent on the laws of Pennsylvania or of any other state. The duties imposed upon the United States and the rights acquired by it as a result of the issuance find their roots in the same federal sources. In the absence of an applicable Act of Congress it is for the federal courts to fashion the governing rule of law according to their own standards." 318 U.S. at pages 366, 367.

4. The Circuit Court of Appeals, considering that at the outset it was "'confronted with the problem of what law should apply,'" said: "'Aside from any federal legislation conferring a right of subrogation or indemnification upon the United States, it would seem that the state rules of substantive common law would govern an action brought by the United States in the role of a private litigant." *Erie R. Co. v. Tompkins*. . . .

Although the *Clearfield* case applied these principles to a situation involving contractual relations of the Government, they are equally applicable in the facts of this case where the relations affected are non-contractual or tortious in character.

Perhaps no relation between the Government and a citizen is more distinctively federal in character than that between it and members of its armed forces. To whatever extent state law may apply to govern the relations between soldiers or others in the armed forces and persons outside them or nonfederal governmental agencies, the scope, nature, legal incidents and consequences of the relation between persons in service and the Government are fundamentally derived from federal sources and governed by federal authority. So also we think are interferences with that relationship such as the facts of this case involve. For, as the Federal Government has the exclusive power to establish and define the relationship by virtue of its military and other powers,[7] equally clearly it has power in execution of the same functions to protect the relation once formed from harms inflicted by others.

Since also the Government's purse is affected, as well as its power to protect the relationship, its fiscal powers, to the extent that they are available to protect it against financial injury, add their weight to the military basis for excluding state intrusion. Indeed, in this aspect the case is not greatly different from the *Clearfield* case or from one involving the Government's paramount power of control over its own property, both to prevent its unauthorized use or destruction and to secure indemnity for those injuries.

As in the *Clearfield* case, moreover, quite apart from any positive action by Congress, the matter in issue is neither primarily one of state interest nor exclusively for determination by state law within the spirit and purpose of the *Erie* decision. The great object of the *Erie* case was to secure in the federal courts, in diversity cases, the application of the same substantive law as would control if the suit were brought in the courts of the state where the federal court sits. It was the so-called "federal common law" utilized as a substitute for state power, to create and enforce legal relationships in the area set apart in our scheme for state rather than for federal control, that the *Erie* decision threw out. Its object and effect were thus to bring federal judicial power under subjection to state authority in matters essentially of local interest and state control.

Conversely there was no purpose or effect for broadening state power over matters essentially of federal character or for determining whether issues are of that nature. The diversity jurisdiction had not created special problems of that sort. Accordingly the *Erie* decision, which related only to the law to be applied in exercise of that jurisdiction, had no effect, and was intended to have none, to bring within the governance of state law matters exclusively federal, because made so by constitutional or valid congressional command, or others so vitally affecting interests, powers and relations of the Federal Government as to require uniform national disposition rather than diversified state rulings. Hence, although federal judicial power to deal with common-law problems was cut down in the realm of liability or its absence governable by state law, that power remained

---

7. Including the powers of Congress to "provide for the common Defense," "raise and support Armies," and "make Rules for the Government and Regulation of the land and naval Forces," U.S. Const. Art. 1, § 8, as well as "To declare War" and "To make all Laws which shall be necessary and proper for carrying into Execution the foregoing Powers. . . ." *Ibid.*

unimpaired for dealing independently, wherever necessary or appropriate, with essentially federal matters, even though Congress has not acted affirmatively about the specific question.

In this sense therefore there remains what may be termed, for want of a better label, an area of "federal common law" or perhaps more accurately "law of independent federal judicial decision," outside the constitutional realm, untouched by the *Erie* decision....

Whether or not, therefore, state law is to control in such a case as this is not at all a matter to be decided by application of the *Erie* rule. For, except where the Government has simply substituted itself for others as successor to rights governed by state law, the question is one of federal policy, affecting not merely the federal judicial establishment and the groundings of its action, but also the Government's legal interests and relations, a factor not controlling in the types of cases producing and governed by the *Erie* ruling. And the answer to be given necessarily is dependent upon a variety of considerations always relevant to the nature of the specific governmental interests and to the effects upon them of applying state law. These include not only considerations of federal supremacy in the performance of federal functions, but of the need for uniformity and, in some instances, inferences properly to be drawn from the fact that Congress, though cognizant of the particular problem, has taken no action to change long-settled ways of handling it.

Leaving out of account, therefore, any supposed effect of the *Erie* decision, we nevertheless are of opinion that state law should not be selected as the federal rule for governing the matter in issue. Not only is the government-soldier relation distinctively and exclusively a creation of federal law, but we know of no good reason why the Government's right to be indemnified in these circumstances, or the lack of such a right, should vary in accordance with the different rulings of the several states, simply because the soldier marches or today perhaps as often flies across state lines.

Furthermore, the liability sought is not essential or even relevant to protection of the state's citizens against tortious harms, nor indeed for the soldier's personal indemnity or security, except in the remotest sense, since his personal rights against the wrongdoer may be fully protected without reference to any indemnity for the Government's loss. It is rather a liability the principal, if not the only, effect of which would be to make whole the federal treasury for financial losses sustained, flowing from the injuries inflicted and the Government's obligations to the soldier. The question, therefore, is chiefly one of federal fiscal policy, not of special or peculiar concern to the states or their citizens. And because those matters ordinarily are appropriate for uniform national treatment rather than diversified local disposition, as well where Congress has not acted affirmatively as where it has, they are more fittingly determinable by independent federal judicial decision than by reference to varying state policies.

[Eds.—Because federal law must govern the federal government's right to indemnification, the Court next considers whether it should create such a "federal common law" right.]

We turn, finally, to consideration of the policy properly to be applied concerning the wrongdoer, whether of liability or of continued immunity as in the past. Here the Government puts forward interesting views to support its claim of responsibility. It appeals first to the great principle that the law can never be wholly static. Growth, it urges, is the life of the law as it is of all living things. And in this expansive and creative living process, we are further reminded, the judicial institution has had and must continue to have a large and pliant, if also a restrained and steady, hand. Moreover, the special problem here has roots in the ancient soil of tort law, wherein the chief plowman has been the judge, notwithstanding his furrow may be covered up or widened by legislation.

. . .

[Eds.—The Court here reviews the Government's arguments based on the analogy to common law tort claims such as claims for loss of services of an employee or child.]

Starting with these long-established instances, illustrating the creative powers and functions of courts, the argument leads on in an effort to show that the government-soldier relation is, if not identical, still strongly analogous; . . . and that an exertion of creative judicial power to bring the government-soldier relation under the same legal protection against tortious interferences by strangers would be only a further and a proper exemplification of the law's capacity to catch up with the times. . . .

. . .

We would not deny the Government's basic premise of the law's capacity for growth, or that it must include the creative work of judges. Soon all law would become antiquated strait jacket and then dead letter, if that power were lacking. And the judicial hand would stiffen in mortmain if it had no part in the work of creation. But in the federal scheme our part in that work, and the part of the other federal courts, outside the constitutional area is more modest than that of state courts, particularly in the freedom to create new common-law liabilities, as *Erie R. Co. v. Tompkins* itself witnesses.

Moreover, . . . we have not here simply a question of creating a new liability in the nature of a tort. For grounded though the argument is in analogies drawn from that field, the issue comes down in final consequence to a question of federal fiscal policy, coupled with considerations concerning the need for and the appropriateness of means to be used in executing the policy sought to be established. The tort law analogy is brought forth, indeed, not to secure a new step forward in expanding the recognized area for applying settled principles of that law as such, or for creating new ones. It is advanced rather as the instrument for determining and establishing the federal fiscal and regulatory policies which the Government's executive arm thinks should prevail in a situation not covered by traditionally established liabilities.

Whatever the merits of the policy, its conversion into law is a proper subject for congressional action, not for any creative power of ours. Congress, not this Court or the other federal courts, is the custodian of the national purse. By the same token it is the primary and most often the exclusive arbiter of federal fiscal affairs. And these comprehend, as we have said, securing the treasury or the government against financial losses however inflicted, including requiring reimbursement for injuries creating them, as well as filling the treasury itself.

Moreover Congress without doubt has been conscious throughout most of its history that the Government constantly sustains losses through the tortious or even criminal conduct of persons interfering with federal funds, property and relationships. We cannot assume that it has been ignorant that losses long have arisen from injuries inflicted on soldiers such as occurred here. The case therefore is not one in which, as the Government argues, all that is involved is application of "a well-settled concept of legal liability to a new situation, where that new situation is in every respect similar to the old situation that originally gave rise to the concept. . . ." Among others, one trouble with this is that the situation is not new, at any rate not so new that Congress can be presumed not to have known of it or to have acted in the light of that knowledge.

When Congress has thought it necessary to take steps to prevent interference with federal funds, property or relations, it has taken positive action to that end. We think it would have done so here, if that had been its desire. This it still may do, if or when it so wishes.

In view of these considerations, exercise of judicial power to establish the new liability not only would be intruding within a field properly within Congress' control and as to a matter concerning which it has seen fit to take no action. To accept the challenge, making the liability effective in this case, also would involve a possible element of surprise, in view of the settled contrary practice, which action by Congress would avoid, not only here but in the many other cases we are told may be governed by the decision.

Finally, if the common-law precedents relied on were more pertinent than they are to the total problem, particularly in view of its federal and especially its fiscal aspects, in none of the situations to which they apply was the question of liability or no liability within the power of one of the parties to the litigation to determine. In them the courts stood as arbiters between citizens, neither of whom could determine the outcome or the policy properly to be followed. Here the United States is the party plaintiff to the suit. And the United States has power at any time to create the liability. The only question is which organ of the Government is to make the determination that liability exists. That decision, for the reasons we have stated, is in this instance for the Congress, not for the courts. Until it acts to establish the liability, this Court and others should withhold creative touch.

The judgment is affirmed.

Notes and Questions: Federal Common Law

1. Federal common law, but not "federal general common law." The exercise of federal common law power in cases like *Standard Oil* is not inconsistent with *Erie*. Before applying a federal common rule to the case, the court must find that a federal interest requires application of federal law. Once it determines that federal law must govern the issue, it proceeds (in the absence of a federal statute) to create it.

Q **2. The federal interest.** What federal interest in *Standard Oil* led the Court to conclude that federal law had to supply the governing rule of decision?

A The federal government has a significant interest in determining the right to indemnification in this case. Soldiers in the armed forces receive their medical care from the federal government, so federal funds had paid for the medical care caused by Etzel's injury. In addition, the army lost Etzel's services until his recovery. It sought recovery from a private tortfeasor for causing these consequences to the efficiency of the armed forces and the federal government's revenues.

Q **3. Why should the issue be governed by federal law?** This accident took place in California. California has tort law that could be applied to resolve the issue in *Standard Oil*. Why did the Court hold that the rule of decision must be federal?

A If the federal government's right to recover in such cases were governed by state law, the right would vary from state to state. Why should the rights—and the resulting impact on the federal treasury—be at the whim of state governments, which might even pass legislation barring all recovery in such circumstances? The issue involves the rights of the federal government, triggered by injury to a member of the United States armed forces, and impacting national policy. It is best addressed by a uniform rule applicable throughout the nation. Congress had not enacted one, so if a federal rule was to apply, it would have to be adopted by the federal court as a matter of federal common law.

Q **4. Why did the Court decide not to create a right to indemnification in such cases?**

A Although the *Standard Oil* Court concluded that federal law should control the government's right to indemnification for Etzel's treatment and lost services, it also noted that the issue posed in the case arises frequently, yet Congress had never created a right to indemnification by statute. Adopting a federal common law right to indemnification would upset settled expectations. While the Court did not doubt its authority to create a right to indemnification, it expressed reluctance to create such a right under the circumstances. On balance, it seemed wiser to defer to Congress.

Q **5. Creating a federal common law rule.** If a federal interest requires a federal rule of decision, what sources should the court look to for guidance in formulating one? How should it decide what the federal common law rule should be?

A If the court must establish a new federal common rule to decide the case, it is in the same position as a state court creating common law. It must consider the policies relevant to the field of law, basic principles of equity, rules of law established in analogous fields, scholarly writings, and other considerations. The resulting rule is a creative enterprise, but not an unguided or arbitrary one.

There is another possibility. The federal court may decide that the governing rule must be federal, but choose to borrow local state law as the rule of decision, where state law would serve the relevant purpose and would not frustrate the objectives of federal law. *See, e.g., Kamen v. Kemper Financial Services, Inc.,* 500 U.S. 90 (1991) (incorporating state law as the federal rule of decision in federal shareholder derivative action). This is appropriate where a federal rule is needed but the rule need not be uniform in all federal cases. *See also Semtek Int'l Inc. v. Lockheed Martin Corp.,* 531 U.S. 497, 503 (2001) (applying state claim preclusion principles as the federal rule of preclusion in diversity cases).

This third category, in which the federal court adopts state law as the federal rule of decision, is a little confusing. How can state law be federal law? Consider this example of a federal statute incorporating state law: Suppose that Congress wants to limit the interest that a national bank can charge but does not want to place it at an advantage or disadvantage compared to local state banks. It might enact a statute limiting the interest a national bank may charge to the rate allowed by state law in the state where it does business. That statute would be federal law, but the substantive limit would be the same as the local state limit. If a plaintiff sued a national bank for exceeding the limit, she could do so in federal court; her case would arise under the federal statute.

Similarly, federal courts sometimes incorporate local state law as federal common law. In *United States v. Kimbell Foods,* 440 U.S. 715 (1979), the Court concluded that the priority of a federal agency as a creditor in reaching a debtor's assets must be determined by federal law. However, the Court chose to incorporate local state law on the issue instead of adopting a uniform federal rule. That way, the agency would have the same priority as a private creditor in that state, enhancing predictability. The *Kimbell Foods* Court created a federal common law rule that *incorporates state law by reference.*

6. Action and reaction. In *Standard Oil,* the Court did create a federal common law rule: It held that there is no federal right to indemnification in such cases. Fifteen years after *Standard Oil,* Congress enacted the Federal Medical Care Recovery Act, 42 U.S.C. § 2651, which creates a statutory right for the federal government to recover medical costs for treatment of members of the armed forces injured due to private negligence. This statute supersedes the *Standard Oil* Court's federal common law no-indemnification rule.

In *Illinois v. City of Milwaukee, Wis.,* 406 U.S. 91 (1972), the Court created a federal common law cause of action for nuisance to address interstate pollution. The court noted that "new federal laws and new federal regulations may in time pre-empt the field of federal common law of nuisance. But until that comes to pass, federal courts will be empowered to appraise the equities of the suits alleging creation of a public nuisance by water pollution." 406 U.S. at 107. The Court's speculation was prescient: In 1972, Congress amended the Federal Pollution Control Act to regulate pollution of interstate waters. In a later proceeding in the *City of Milwaukee* case, the Supreme Court concluded that, since Congress had legislated in the area, its regulatory scheme superseded the federal common law nuisance remedy that the Court had earlier endorsed. *City of Milwaukee v. Illinois and Michigan,* 451 U.S. 304 (1981). *See also American Electric Power Co. v. Connecticut,*

564 U.S. 410 (2011) (refusing to recognize federal common law claim for public nuisance arising from interstate air emissions, in light of federal statutory and agency regulation of those emissions).

VI. The *Erie* Doctrine: Summary of Basic Principles

- Under *Swift v. Tyson*, federal courts did not always apply state law to the substantive issues in diversity cases. Instead, they often applied "federal general common law" to issues of property law, torts, contracts, and other areas of the common law.
- In *Erie Railroad Co. v. Tompkins*, the Supreme Court held that the federal court may not apply federal general common law to determine the applicable legal principles in diversity cases, as they did under *Swift v. Tyson*. The Rules of Decision Act, properly (and constitutionally) construed, requires federal courts to apply state substantive law in diversity cases and on other issues not governed by federal law.
- Where the meaning of applicable state law is unclear, a federal court should apply the "state supreme court predictive approach" to determine what the law of the state is. Under this approach, the federal court asks what rule the state's highest court would apply today, even if older cases have applied a different rule. However, federal judges are likely to require strong evidence before disregarding a state supreme court decision based on a prediction that it would be overruled today.
- State courts use choice of law rules to determine which state's substantive law to apply to a claim. In *Klaxon Co. v. Stentor Manufacturing Co.*, the Supreme Court held that a federal diversity court, to implement *Erie*'s policy of uniform outcomes, must apply the choice of law rules of the state in which it sits to determine which state's substantive law to apply to a diversity case.
- While *Erie* decreed that "there is no federal general common law," there still is federal specific common law. In some cases, because of the national character of a question or the federal interests at stake, the law applied must be federal. In such situations, if no federal statute provides a rule of decision, a federal court must create a federal rule of decision.
- In some such cases, where national uniformity is not needed, the federal court may incorporate local state law as the federal rule of decision, rather than creating a uniform federal common law rule.

25

Substance and Procedure Under the *Erie* Doctrine

I. Introduction: The Problem Emerges

The *Erie* decision represented a dramatic change in federal court practice. Instead of creating federal general common law, the federal courts after *Erie* are bound to use state common law as their rules of decision if federal law is inapplicable. The federal courts no longer pronounce the applicable law in a diversity case (or on a supplemental state law claim); they follow and apply state law.

However, *Erie* left a difficult problem for another day. Must a federal court in a diversity case apply state *procedural* law as well as state substantive law? *Erie* itself involved an obviously substantive issue, the tort duty of care owed to a trespasser, but many procedural issues will arise in a diversity case as well. For example, the federal court will have to decide what rules of discovery to apply to the case, what privileges may bar introduction of evidence, who has the burden of proof on an issue at trial, and many other issues. Some of these issues could arguably be classified as either "substantive" or "procedural." It is hardly self-evident, for example, whether the proper statute of limitations to apply to a claim is a matter of court process or a substantive limit on the underlying right—very probably, it is both.

While *Erie* undeniably required federal diversity courts to apply state law on purely substantive matters, it did not address whether they had to use state law in diversity cases on matters that might be classified as procedural rather than substantive. This chapter analyzes a series of cases decided after *Erie* that seeks to distinguish "substantive" issues (on which a diversity court must defer to state law) from "procedural" issues (on which the federal court will apply its own practice or rules).

Whether or not Justice Brandeis anticipated this difficult problem, it did not take long for it to surface after *Erie* was decided. The following year, in *Cities Service Oil Co. v. Dunlap*, 308 U.S. 208 (1939), the Court considered whether *Erie* required a federal diversity court to apply the state rule on the issue of who bore the burden of proof on a question of title to land. The burden of proof is a matter that relates to court process, not directly to underlying substantive rights that exist outside of litigation. But the Supreme Court held that the issue "relates to a substantial right" and required the federal court to apply the state burden of proof rule.

Cities Service Oil suggested that the federal court in a diversity case would be required to defer to state law on at least some procedural issues, in order to implement the *Erie* principle of consistent results in state and federal court, even though it would apply a different rule in a federal question case. *Erie*, it seemed, had not only altered the relationship between the state and federal courts. It had opened a jurisprudential can of worms.

II. The Court Gropes for a Test: *Guaranty Trust Co. of New York v. York*

In *Guaranty Trust Co. of New York v. York*, the Supreme Court attempted to clarify when lower federal courts should defer to state law in a diversity case. To understand *Guaranty Trust*, it helps to have a sense of the ancient distinction between law and equity. In English practice, from which American court practice—both state and federal—evolved, there were separate law and equity courts. The law courts administered causes of action for damages, such as actions in tort, property, or contract. Equity courts provided a more flexible panoply of remedies, such as an accounting of funds, specific performance of a contract, creation of a constructive trust of assets, and the power to enjoin parties from engaging in certain conduct. Its decrees constituted personal orders to the defendant, which could be enforced through contempt proceedings. An equity court could also exercise continuing jurisdiction over a dispute to assure compliance with its orders, while an action at law yielded only a judgment that the defendant owed a certain sum to the plaintiff.

Although early practice in American courts was largely based on the English system, procedure varied from state to state. Some did not create separate law and equity courts, using instead a single court system that administered both legal and equitable remedies in separate "sessions." When federal courts were established, they also were granted both legal and equitable jurisdiction. *See* Art. III, § 2, "The judicial Power shall extend to all Cases, in Law and Equity [within the delegated categories]. . . ." Thus, federal courts have exercised both legal and equitable jurisdiction since they were established.

issue

READING *GUARANTY TRUST CO. OF NEW YORK v. YORK.* The issue in *Guaranty Trust Co. v. York* was whether the plaintiff's claim was barred by the state statute of limitations. The case was a diversity case, brought "on the equity side" of the federal court. Traditionally, federal courts applied the doctrine of *laches* to equitable claims, rather than the statute of limitations that applied to actions at law. The laches doctrine is like a limitations period, but more flexible; in deciding whether the plaintiff is allowed to proceed with her case, the court considers whether the plaintiff has "slept on her rights," whether the defendant has been prejudiced by delay, and other factors.

In *Guaranty Trust,* the plaintiff's action might go forward if the federal court applied the laches doctrine but was barred if it must apply the state statute of limitations—which the state court certainly would. So the case posed the issue of whether *Erie* required a federal diversity court to use the state statute of limitations, an arguably procedural defense, or could apply the laches doctrine instead. The broader question was whether the independent system of equitable remedies administered in the federal courts would have to give way in diversity cases to the procedures used by the local state courts. In reading *Guaranty Trust,* consider the following questions:

- What test does *Guaranty Trust* establish to determine when a federal diversity court should apply state law on matters that might be classified as either "procedural" or "substantive"?
- What is the rationale for adopting that test?
- Does the opinion suggest that a diversity court is constitutionally bound to apply state limitations law or that it *should* do so for reasons of policy?

GUARANTY TRUST CO. OF NEW YORK v. YORK

326 U.S. 99 (1945)

Mr. Justice Frankfurter delivered the opinion of the Court.

. . .

[Eds.—York, the plaintiff in the case, was the owner of certain notes issued by the Van Sweringen Corporation. She brought a class action suit against Guaranty Trust Company, which had held the notes as a trustee for the noteholders. The suit was based on diversity jurisdiction, but, as a class action, it sought a remedy available on the "equity side" of the federal court. York alleged that Guaranty had failed to protect the interests of the noteholders in a transaction involving the notes. One of Guaranty's defenses was that York's suit was barred by the New York statute of limitations. The Second Circuit Court of Appeals had held that the federal court was not bound to apply the state statute of limitations. Instead, it could decide whether the action was barred by the passage of time under the more flexible laches doctrine.]

Appellate court

The suit, instituted as a class action on behalf of non-accepting noteholders and brought in a federal court solely because of diversity of citizenship, is based on an alleged breach of trust by Guaranty in that it failed to protect the interests of the noteholders in assenting to the exchange offer and failed to disclose its self-interest when sponsoring the offer. . . . On appeal, the Circuit Court of Appeals, one Judge dissenting, . . . held that in a suit brought on the equity side of a federal district court that court is not required to apply the State statute of limitations that would govern like suits in the courts of a State where the federal court is sitting even though the exclusive basis of federal jurisdiction is diversity of citizenship. The importance of the question for the disposition of litigation in the federal courts led us to bring the case here.

. . .

We put to one side the considerations relevant in disposing of questions that arise when a federal court is adjudicating a claim based on a federal law. Our problem only touches transactions for which rights and obligations are created by one of the States, and for the assertion of which, in case of diversity of the citizenship of the parties, Congress has made a federal court another available forum.

Our starting point must be the policy of federal jurisdiction which *Erie R. Co. v. Tompkins* embodies. In overruling *Swift v. Tyson, Erie R. Co. v. Tompkins* did not merely overrule a venerable case. It overruled a particular way of looking at law which dominated the judicial process long after its inadequacies had been laid bare. Law was conceived as a "brooding omnipresence" of Reason, of which decisions were merely evidence and not themselves the controlling formulations. Accordingly, federal courts deemed themselves free to ascertain what Reason, and therefore Law, required wholly independent of authoritatively declared State law, even in cases where a legal right as the basis for relief was created by State authority and could not be created by federal authority and the case got into a federal court merely because it was "between Citizens of different States" under Art. III, § 2 of the Constitution of the United States.

This impulse to freedom from the rules that controlled State courts regarding State-created rights was so strongly rooted in the prevailing views concerning the nature of law, that the federal courts almost imperceptibly were led to mutilating construction even of the explicit command given to them by Congress to apply State law in cases purporting to enforce the law of a State. *See* § 34 of the Judiciary Act of 1789. . . .

In relation to the problem now here, the real significance of *Swift v. Tyson* lies in the fact that it did not enunciate novel doctrine. Nor was it restricted to its particular situation. It summed up prior attitudes and expressions in cases that had come before this Court and lower federal courts for at least thirty years, at law as well as in equity. The short of it is that the doctrine was congenial to the jurisprudential climate of the time. Once established, judicial momentum kept it going. Since it was conceived that there was "a transcendental body of law outside of any particular State but obligatory within it unless and until changed by statute," State court decisions were not "the law" but merely someone's opinion—to be sure an opinion to be respected—concerning the content of this all-pervading law. Not unnaturally, the federal courts assumed power to find for themselves the content of such a body of law. The notion was stimulated by the attractive vision of a uniform body of federal law. To such sentiments for uniformity of decision and freedom from diversity in State law the federal courts gave currency, particularly in cases where equitable remedies were sought, because equitable doctrines are so often cast in terms of universal applicability when close analysis of the source of legal enforceability is not demanded.

In exercising their jurisdiction on the ground of diversity of citizenship, the federal courts, in the long course of their history, have not differentiated in their regard for State law between actions at law and suits in equity. Although § 34 of the Judiciary Act of 1789, directed that the "laws of the several States . . . shall be regarded as rules of decision in trials of common law . . . ," this was deemed, consistently for over a hundred years, to be merely declaratory of what would in any event have governed the federal courts and therefore was equally applicable to equity suits. Indeed, it may fairly be said that the federal courts gave greater respect to State-created "substantive rights," in equity than they gave them on the law side, because rights at law were usually declared by State courts and as such increasingly flouted by extension of the doctrine of *Swift v. Tyson*, while rights in equity were frequently defined by legislative enactment and as such known and respected by the federal courts.

Partly because the States in the early days varied greatly in the manner in which equitable relief was afforded and in the extent to which it was available, Congress provided that "the forms and modes of proceeding in suits . . . of equity" would conform to the settled uses of courts of equity. Section 2, 1 Stat. 275, 276, 28 U.S.C. § 723, 28 U.S.C.A. § 723. From the beginning there has been a good deal of talk in the cases that federal equity is a separate legal system. And so it is, properly understood. The suits in equity of which the federal courts have had "cognizance" ever since 1789 constituted the body of law which had been transplanted to this country from the English Court of Chancery. But this system of equity "derived its doctrines, as well as its powers, from its mode of giving relief." Langdell, *Summary of Equity Pleading* (1877) xxvii. In giving federal courts "cognizance" of equity suits in cases of diversity jurisdiction, Congress never gave, nor did the federal courts ever claim, the power to deny substantive rights created by State law or to create substantive rights denied by State law.

This does not mean that whatever equitable remedy is available in a State court must be available in a diversity suit in a federal court, or conversely, that a federal court may not afford an equitable remedy not available in a State court. Equitable relief in a federal court is of course subject to restrictions: the suit must be within the traditional scope of equity as historically evolved in the English Court of Chancery; a plain, adequate and complete remedy at law must be wanting, explicit Congressional curtailment of equity powers must be respected, the constitutional right to trial by jury cannot be evaded. That a State may authorize its courts to give equitable relief unhampered by any or all such restrictions cannot remove these fetters from the federal courts. State law cannot define the remedies which a federal court must give simply because a federal court in diversity jurisdiction is available as an alternative tribunal to the State's courts. Contrariwise, a federal court may afford an equitable remedy for a substantive right recognized by a State even though a State court cannot give it. Whatever contradiction or confusion may be produced by a medley of judicial phrases severed from their environment, the body of adjudications concerning equitable relief in diversity cases leaves no doubt that the federal courts enforced State-created substantive rights if the mode of proceeding and remedy were consonant with the traditional body of equitable remedies, practice and procedure, and in so doing they were enforcing rights created by the States and not arising under any inherent or statutory federal law.

. . .

And so this case reduces itself to the narrow question whether, when no recovery could be had in a State court because the action is barred by the statute of limitations, a federal court in equity can take cognizance of the suit because there is diversity of citizenship between the parties. Is the outlawry, **[Eds.—that is, unenforceability due to passage of the state limitations period]**, according to State law, of a claim created by the States a matter of "substantive rights" to be respected by a federal court of equity when that court's jurisdiction is dependent on the fact that there is a State-created right, or is such statute of "a mere remedial character," which a federal court may disregard?

Matters of "substance" and matters of "procedure" are much talked about in the books as though they defined a great divide cutting across the whole domain of law. But, of course, "substance" and "procedure" are the same key-words to very different problems. Neither "substance" nor "procedure" represents the same invariants. Each implies different variables depending upon the particular problem for which it is used. And the different problems are only distantly related at best, for the terms are in common use in connection with situations turning on such different considerations as those that are relevant to questions pertaining to ex post facto legislation, the impairment of the obligations of contract, the enforcement of federal rights in the State courts and the multitudinous phases of the conflict of laws.

Here we are dealing with a right to recover derived not from the United States but from one of the States. When, because the plaintiff happens to be a nonresident, such a right is enforceable in a federal as well as in a State court, the forms and mode of enforcing the right may at times, naturally enough, vary because the two judicial systems are not identic. But since a federal court adjudicating a state-created right solely because of the diversity of citizenship of the parties is for that purpose, in effect, only another court of the State, it cannot afford recovery if the right to recover is made unavailable by the State nor can it substantially affect the enforcement of the right as given by the State.

And so the question is not whether a statute of limitations is deemed a matter of "procedure" in some sense. The question is whether such a statute concerns merely the manner and the means by which a right to recover, as recognized by the State, is enforced, or whether such statutory limitation is a matter of substance in the aspect that alone is relevant to our problem, namely, does it significantly affect the result of a litigation for a federal court to disregard a law of a State that would be controlling in an action upon the same claim by the same parties in a State court?

It is therefore immaterial whether statutes of limitation are characterized either as "substantive" or "procedural" in State court opinions in any use of those terms unrelated to the specific issue before us. *Erie R. Co. v. Tompkins* was not an endeavor to formulate scientific legal terminology. It expressed a policy that touches vitally the proper distribution of judicial power between State and federal courts. In essence, the intent of that decision was to insure that, in all cases where a federal court is exercising jurisdiction solely because of the diversity of citizenship of the parties, the outcome of the litigation in the federal court should be substantially the same, so far as legal rules determine the outcome of a litigation, as it would be if tried in a State court. The nub of the policy that underlies *Erie R. Co. v. Tompkins* is that for the same transaction the accident of a suit by a non-resident litigant in a federal court instead of in a State court a block away, should not lead to a substantially different result. And so, putting to one side abstractions regarding "substance" and "procedure," we have held that in diversity cases the federal courts must follow the law of the State as to burden of proof, *Cities Service Oil Co. v. Dunlop,* 308 U.S. 208, as to conflict of laws, *Klaxon Co. v. Stentor Co.,* 313 U.S. 487, as to contributory negligence, *Palmer v. Hoffman,* 318 U.S. 109. *Erie R. Co. v. Tompkins* has been applied with an eye alert to essentials in avoiding disregard of State law in diversity cases in the federal courts. A policy so important to our federalism must be kept free from entanglements with analytical or terminological niceties.

Plainly enough, a statute that would completely bar recovery in a suit if brought in a State court bears on a State created right vitally and not merely formally or negligibly. As to consequences that so intimately affect recovery or non-recovery a federal court in a diversity case should follow State law. The fact that under New York law a statute of limitations might be lengthened or shortened, that a security may be foreclosed though the debt be barred, that a barred debt may be used as a set-off, are all matters of local law properly to be respected by federal courts sitting in New York when their incidence comes into play there. Such particular rules of local law, however, do not in the slightest change the crucial consideration that if a plea of the statute of limitations would bar recovery in a State court, a federal court ought not to afford recovery.

. . .

To make an exception to *Erie R. Co. v. Tompkins* on the equity side of a federal court is to reject the considerations of policy which, after long travail, led to that decision. Judge Augustus N. Hand thus summarized below the fatal objection to such inroad upon *Erie R. Co. v. Tompkins*: "In my opinion it would be a mischievous practice to disregard state statutes of limitation whenever federal courts think that the result of adopting them may be inequitable. Such procedure would promote the choice of United States rather than of state courts in order to gain the advantage of different laws. The main foundation for the criticism of *Swift v. Tyson* was that a litigant in cases where federal jurisdiction is based only on diverse citizenship may obtain a more favorable decision by suing in the United States courts." 2 Cir., 143 F.2d 503, 529, 531.

Diversity jurisdiction is founded on assurance to non-resident litigants of courts free from susceptibility to potential local bias. The Framers of the Constitution, according to Marshall, entertained "apprehensions" lest distant suitors be subjected to local bias in State courts, or, at least, viewed with "indulgence the possible fears and apprehensions" of such suitors. And so Congress afforded out-of-State litigants another tribunal, not another body of law. The operation of a double system of conflicting laws in the same State is plainly hostile to the reign of law. Certainly, the fortuitous circumstance of residence out of a State of one of the parties to a litigation ought not to give rise to a discrimination against others equally concerned but locally resident. The source of substantive rights enforced by a federal court under diversity jurisdiction, it cannot be said too often, is the law of the States. Whenever that law is authoritatively declared by a State, whether its voice be the legislature or its highest court, such law ought to govern in litigation founded on that law, whether the forum of application is a State or a federal court and whether the remedies be sought at law or may be had in equity.

. . .

The judgment is reversed and the case is remanded for proceedings not inconsistent with this opinion.

So ordered.

Notes and Questions: *Guaranty Trust Co. of New York v. York*

1. The Court's dilemma. Try to appreciate the Court's dilemma here. The federal courts had a well-developed doctrine for dealing with the timeliness of an equitable claim—the laches doctrine. The local state court would apply the statute of limitations and dismiss the claim. If the *Guaranty Trust* case arose under federal law, the federal court would have used the laches doctrine to decide whether it could proceed. But the case did not arise under federal law; it was in federal court based on diversity. And *Erie* reflected a concern that parties ought to get the same law in a diversity case whether they filed suit in state court or federal court. Was the court to abandon its long-accepted equity procedure or ignore a state statute that would govern the case in state court? Clearly, the *Guaranty Trust* Court, by requiring the federal court to apply the state statute of limitations, chose to give priority to *Erie*'s policy of assuring uniform outcomes in state and federal diversity cases.

Q **2. Equity procedure in a federal question case.** Suppose, after *Guaranty Trust* was decided, that a plaintiff brings a similar case against Guaranty Trust Company but asserts a claim under federal law. She seeks equitable relief from the federal court, and Guaranty Trust asserts the local statute of limitations as a defense. Should the federal court apply the local limitations statute or the laches doctrine?

A *Erie* and *Guaranty Trust* mandated use of state law in *diversity* cases. In a *federal question* case, however, the proper time limit for bringing the claim is a matter of federal law. So the laches doctrine would apply in a case arising under federal law. Thus, the federal court would apply one rule in diversity cases and another in cases based on other categories of federal jurisdiction. *See Holmberg v. Armbrecht*, 327 U.S. 392 (1946) (applying laches doctrine to determine timeliness in a federal question case).

Q **3. Articulating a test for when state law should apply.** In *Guaranty Trust,* the court of appeals had concluded that the *Erie* doctrine should not affect the separate administration of equitable "remedial rights" in the federal courts. 143 F.2d at 521–22. Justice Frankfurter, however, refused to make application of the *Erie* doctrine turn on whether the issue might be labeled one of substance or procedure. What standard does he establish for deciding whether the federal court should adopt state practice in a diversity case?

A Instead of relying on "substance/procedure" labels to resolve the issue, Frankfurter looks to the rationale underlying *Erie*: Would allowing the federal court to ignore state law lead to a different outcome in federal court than the plaintiff would receive in the state court "a block away"?

> In essence, the intent of ... [*Erie*] was to insure that, in all cases where a federal court is exercising jurisdiction solely because of the diversity of citizenship of the parties, the outcome of the litigation in the federal court should be substantially the same, so far as legal rules determine the outcome of a litigation, as it would be if tried in a State court. The nub of the policy that underlies *Erie R. Co. v. Tompkins* is that for the same transaction the accident of a suit by a non-resident litigant in a federal court instead of in a State court a block away, should not lead to a substantially different result.

326 U.S. at 109. This logic suggests that, if applying a federal procedural rule instead of a state rule would affect the outcome, the federal court should use the state rule. This came to be referred to as the *outcome-determinative* test.

4. An "unchecked engine of destruction"? Although Justice Frankfurter predicted that this approach would not undermine equity practice in the federal courts, federal district judges may not have been reassured. The logic of the opinion suggests that if there is a difference in practice that could affect the result of the case, the federal court should adopt the state's approach. The test "was an unchecked engine of destruction for all conceivable federal procedural rules. . . ." Dan Crump, *The Twilight Zone of the* Erie *Doctrine: Is There Really a Different Choice of Equitable Remedies in the "Court a Block Away"?,* 1991 Wis. L. Rev. 1233, 1239 (1991).

Even the most trivial difference—the number of days to file an answer, the time the courthouse closes, or the method of serving process on the defendant—could be "outcome determinative." If federal procedure requires an answer to be filed within twenty days but state procedure requires one within fifteen, that could lead to a different outcome if the answer is filed on the seventeenth day. Arguably, *Guaranty Trust*'s outcome-determinative test would require the federal court to substitute state procedure for its own practice in every such case. This would be particularly ironic, since the Federal Rules of Civil Procedure were adopted in 1938—the year *Erie* was decided—to introduce uniform rules of procedure in the federal courts!

5. Looking at outcome determination prospectively or retrospectively. Suppose that state practice requires that the summons and complaint be *served on the defendant* within the limitations period, while federal practice only requires that the papers be *filed in the court* within that period to satisfy the statute of limitations. Is this difference "outcome determinative"?

A difference in state and federal practice may be outcome determinative if we look at it retrospectively (after the fact), but not if we look at it prospectively. On the day the claim arises, this difference between the state and federal limitations rules does not seem to affect the outcome: Either requirement (service or filing) can easily be met. However, if we assess this difference in procedures *retrospectively,* it may make all the difference. If the plaintiff filed suit within the limitations period but served process after it had run, the difference between the state rule (requiring actual service within the period) and the federal rule (requiring only filing) is now outcome determinative, because the plaintiff can no longer comply with the state service requirement.

In *Guaranty Trust,* the state limitations period had run before suit was filed. At that point, the state rule barred the claim, while the more flexible laches doctrine might allow it to go forward. Justice Frankfurter assessed the outcome-determinative effect of the two rules retrospectively. When the limitations defense was raised, it was clear that ignoring the state rule would make a dramatic difference, although at the time the claim arose, it would likely have made none at all.

6. The constitutional and policy dimensions of *Erie*. One rationale of *Erie* is that federal courts cannot ignore state substantive law on matters as to which there is no federal power to make the governing law. Under the Constitution, many matters (like the standard of care in *Erie* and the enforceability of monopoly contracts in *Black & White Taxicab*) are generally left for the states to regulate. Thus, *Erie* reflects a constitutional limit on the power of federal courts to establish separate substantive legal rules in diversity cases.

However, there *is* a constitutional basis for Congress and the federal courts to regulate *procedure* in the federal courts. As Justice Reed stated in his *Erie* concurrence, "[t]he line between procedural and substantive law is hazy, but no one doubts federal power over procedure." 304 U.S. at 92. Article III and the Necessary and Proper Clause (art. I, § 8, par. 18) provide constitutional authority for federal courts to make and apply their own rules for processing cases in their courts, including diversity cases. Thus, it is hard to argue that a federal court is *constitutionally prohibited* from applying the laches doctrine in a diversity case or deciding for itself which party will bear the burden of proof on an issue.

Read closely, Justice Frankfurter's opinion does not argue that it would be unconstitutional for the federal court to apply the laches doctrine to York's case. Instead, the opinion reiterates that it is the *policy of uniformity* reflected in *Erie* that supports the *Guaranty Trust* holding. . . .

> *Erie R. Co. v. Tompkins* . . . expressed a *policy* that touches vitally the proper distribution of judicial power between State and federal courts. . . . The nub of the *policy* that underlies *Erie R. Co. v. Tompkins* is that for the same transaction the accident of a suit by a non-resident litigant in a federal court instead of in a State court a block away, should not lead to a substantially different result. . . . A *policy* so important to our federalism must be kept free from entanglements with analytical or terminological niceties. . . .
>
> To make an exception to *Erie R. Co. v. Tompkins* on the equity side of a federal court is to reject the considerations of *policy* which, after long travail, led to that decision.

326 U.S. at 101, 110–11 (italics added).

Thus, *Guaranty Trust* suggests that a federal court should sometimes choose to follow state practice to further *Erie*'s policy of uniform outcomes in diversity cases—*even if there is constitutional authority for the federal court to go its own way.* In this sense, *Guaranty Trust* extended the *Erie* principle beyond the area in which it was constitutionally mandated.

7. Troubling cases decided after *Guaranty Trust*. The Supreme Court's decisions following *Guaranty Trust* appeared to reinforce the concern that *Erie* would require federal courts to abandon their own procedures in diversity cases and apply state procedure instead. In *Ragan v. Merchants Transfer & Warehouse Co.*, 337 U.S. 530 (1949), for example, the Court considered whether a plaintiff satisfies the statute of limitations by filing the complaint within the statutory period or serving it on the defendant within that period. Although Federal Rule 3 provides that an action is commenced by filing the complaint in court, local state practice required that the papers be served on the defendant within two years to satisfy the limitations period. The Court held that the federal diversity court had to follow state practice on the point.

And in *Cohen v. Beneficial Industrial Loan Corp.*, 337 U.S. 541 (1949), the Court held that a state statute requiring the plaintiff to post a bond for costs in a stockholder's derivative action must be applied in a derivative action brought in federal court based on diversity, even though federal practice did not require a bond. This statute dealt with a requirement that applied to the processing of a lawsuit, not a right independent of and prior to litigation. Yet, the Court still held that the federal court must apply the state statute. "Rules which lawyers call procedural do not always exhaust their effect by regulating procedure." 337 U.S. at 555.

8. *Byrd v. Blue Ridge*: A counterbalance to the outcome-determinative test. The *Ragan* and *Cohen* cases suggested that *Guaranty Trust*'s outcome-determinative test would frequently require federal courts to apply state procedural law in diversity cases even though they would ordinarily apply a different approach under federal procedure or under the Federal Rules. This seeming threat to uniform federal procedure was muted somewhat by the decision in *Byrd v. Blue Ridge Rural Electric Cooperative, Inc.*, 356 U.S. 525 (1958). *Byrd v. Blue Ridge* considered whether the judge or the jury should decide, in a state-law workers' compensation case, whether or not the plaintiff was a covered "employee" under the compensation statute. Under South Carolina practice, that issue was decided by the judge, while federal practice assigned the issue to the jury. Because the case was in federal court based on diversity, the defendant argued that *Erie* and *Guaranty Trust* required the federal court to apply South Carolina practice on this arguably outcome-determinative issue.

The *Byrd* Court recognized that *Erie* requires federal diversity courts to apply state law on matters of substantive law—"the definition of state-created rights and obligations." 356 U.S. at 535. The Court further reaffirmed that even on arguably procedural matters ("matters of form and mode" of enforcing state substantive rights), a diversity court should often defer to state practice if the difference between state and federal procedure is likely to be outcome-determinative. *Id.* at 536–37. However, the *Byrd* Court suggested that when the issue before a federal diversity court is one of procedure, the decision to defer to state law is a policy choice — a choice to apply the state rule to assure the same outcome in federal court that the parties would get in federal court — and not a constitutional command. (Compare the decision to defer to state substantive law, which *Erie* held is required by the Constitution.) In these procedural conflicts, *Guaranty Trust*'s policy of assuring uniform outcomes in state and federal court may sometimes have to yield to "affirmative countervailing considerations" — a different, strong federal policy. *Id.* at 537. In *Byrd*, the Court concluded that given the importance of the right to jury trial in the federal system, and the apparently happenstance South Carolina policy of having judges decide whether the plaintiff was a covered employee, the trial court should follow federal practice and have the jury decide this question, even if that might be outcome determinative.

This holding did not overrule *Guaranty Trust*. Federal courts sitting in diversity cases still must follow state substantive law under *Erie*'s constitutional command. But where a difference between state and federal practice involves matters of procedure, so that the federal courts have authority to establish their own practices and rules, federal courts are not constitutionally compelled to follow state procedure. They may choose to do so after balancing the state interest in the procedure against any countervailing federal interests. *Byrd* recognizes that state practice should frequently be followed to assure uniform outcomes, but that in some circumstances, that policy must yield if applying state law would interfere with other policies important to the administration of the federal courts.

III. Two Tracks of the *Erie* Doctrine: *Hanna v. Plumer*

Guaranty Trust and *Byrd* both involved conflicts between a federal judicial practice (i.e., a practice not required by federal statute or Federal Rule, but adopted by the federal judge to facilitate processing of cases) and state law. They did not address the question whether a federal diversity court should follow a state practice that conflicted with one of the Federal Rules of Civil Procedure.

Several cases after *Erie* involved conflicts in which federal practice was arguably controlled by one of the Federal Rules of Civil Procedure. *See, e.g.*, *Ragan v. Merchants Transfer & Warehouse Co.*, 337 U.S. 530 (1949) (Rule 3); *Cohen v. Beneficial Industrial Loan Corp.*, 337 U.S. 541 (1949) (Rule 23). In both of those cases, the Court required deference to state law, without considering whether the analysis should differ when the federal approach is embodied in one of the Federal Rules. In *Hanna v. Plumer*, below, the Court develops a separate analysis for conflicts between state law and a Federal Rule.

READING *HANNA v. PLUMER*. In *Hanna*, Chief Justice Warren analyzes the conflict between the state and federal approaches in *Hanna* twice. First, he considers how it should be decided if the conflict is between state law and a judge-made federal practice, adopted by federal judges but not mandated by a federal statute or by a Federal Rule of Civil Procedure. (The conflicts in *Guaranty Trust* and in *Byrd* were of this type; in those cases there was no Federal Rule or statute governing the federal approach to the issue.)

- What test does Chief Justice Warren offer for resolving conflicts between federal judicial practice (not mandated by a Federal Rule or statute) and state law?
- How does the test relate to *Guaranty Trust*'s outcome-determinative test?

The first analysis in *Hanna* is dicta, because the case involved a conflict between Federal Rule of Civil Procedure Rule 4(d)(1) [*see* now Rule 4(e)(2)] and state law. In the second part of *Hanna* (beginning with the sentence, "[t]here is, however, a more fundamental flaw in respondent's syllogism..."), Chief Justice Warren offers a distinct analysis for such conflicts. He concludes that because Congress delegated to the Supreme Court the authority to adopt the Federal Rules in the Rules Enabling Act (REA), the Rules apply unless they exceed the authority granted in the REA to write the Rules.

- What questions should the court ask in analyzing a conflict between a Federal Rule and state practice?
- Does the Federal Rule always win under this second *Hanna* analysis?
- If a Federal Rule directly contradicts a state rule or practice, what would a party have to show to convince the court to follow the state approach?

HANNA v. PLUMER

380 U.S. 460 (1965)

Mr. Chief Justice Warren delivered the opinion of the Court.

The question to be decided is whether, in a civil action where the jurisdiction of the United States district court is based upon diversity of citizenship between the parties, service of process shall be made in the manner prescribed by state law or that set forth in Rule 4(d)(1) of the Federal Rules of Civil Procedure.

On February 6, 1963, petitioner, a citizen of Ohio, filed her complaint in the District Court for the District of Massachusetts, claiming damages in excess of $10,000 for personal injuries resulting from an automobile accident in South Carolina, allegedly caused by the negligence of one Louise Plumer Osgood, a Massachusetts citizen deceased at the time of the filing of the complaint. Respondent, Mrs. Osgood's executor and also a Massachusetts citizen, was named as defendant. On February 8, service was made by leaving copies of the summons and the complaint with respondent's wife at his residence, concededly in compliance with Rule 4(d)(1), which provides:

> "The summons and complaint shall be served together. The plaintiff shall furnish the person making service with such copies as are necessary. Service shall be made as follows:
>
> (1) Upon an individual other than an infant or an incompetent person, by delivering a copy of the summons and of the complaint to him personally or by

leaving copies thereof at his dwelling house or usual place of abode with some person of suitable age and discretion then residing therein...."*

Respondent filed his answer on February 26, alleging, *inter alia*, that the action could not be maintained because it had been brought "contrary to and in violation of the provisions of Massachusetts General Laws (Ter. Ed.) Chapter 197, Section 9." That section provides:

> "Except as provided in this chapter, an executor or administrator shall not be held to answer to an action by a creditor of the deceased which is not commenced within one year from the time of his giving bond for the performance of his trust, or to such an action which is commenced within said year unless before the expiration thereof the writ in such action has been served by delivery in hand upon such executor or administrator or service thereof accepted by him or a notice stating the name of the estate, the name and address of the creditor, the amount of the claim and the court in which the action has been brought has been filed in the proper registry of probate...." Mass. Gen. Laws Ann., c. 197, § 9 (1958).

[T]he District Court granted respondent's motion for summary judgment, citing *Ragan v. Merchants Transfer & Warehouse Co.*, 337 U.S. 530, and *Guaranty Trust Co. of New York v. York*, 326 U.S. 99, in support of its conclusion that the adequacy of the service was to be measured by § 9.... On appeal, petitioner admitted noncompliance with § 9, but argued that Rule 4(d)(1) defines the method by which service of process is to be effected in diversity actions. The Court of Appeals for the First Circuit, finding that "[r]elatively recent amendments [to § 9] evince a clear legislative purpose to require personal notification within the year," concluded that the conflict of state and federal rules was over "a substantive rather than a procedural matter," and unanimously affirmed. Because of the threat to the goal of uniformity of federal procedure posed by the decision below, we granted certiorari.

We conclude that the adoption of Rule 4(d)(1), designed to control service of process in diversity actions, neither exceeded the congressional mandate embodied in the Rules Enabling Act nor transgressed constitutional bounds, and that the Rule is therefore the standard against which the District Court should have measured the adequacy of the service. Accordingly, we reverse the decision of the Court of Appeals.

The Rules Enabling Act, 28 U.S.C. § 2072 (1958 ed.), provides, in pertinent part:

> "The Supreme Court shall have the power to prescribe, by general rules, the forms of process, writs, pleadings, and motions, and the practice and procedure of the district courts of the United States in civil actions.
>
> "Such rules shall not abridge, enlarge or modify any substantive right and shall preserve the right of trial by jury...."

* [Eds.—*See* Fed. R. Civ. P. 4(e)(2)(B) for the current version.]

Under the cases construing the scope of the Enabling Act, Rule 4(d)(1) clearly passes muster. Prescribing the manner in which a defendant is to be notified that a suit has been instituted against him, it relates to the "practice and procedure of the district courts."

> "The test must be whether a rule really regulates procedure,—the judicial process for enforcing rights and duties recognized by substantive law and for justly administering remedy and redress for disregard or infraction of them." *Sibbach v. Wilson & Co.*, 312 U.S. 1, 14.

In *Mississippi Pub. Corp. v. Murphree*, 326 U.S. 438, this Court upheld Rule 4(f), which permits service of a summons anywhere within the State (and not merely the district) in which a district court sits:

> "We think that Rule 4(f) is in harmony with the Enabling Act.... Undoubtedly most alterations of the rules of practice and procedure may and often do affect the rights of litigants. Congress' prohibition of any alteration of substantive rights of litigants was obviously not addressed to such incidental effects as necessarily attend the adoption of the prescribed new rules of procedure upon the rights of litigants who, agreeably to rules of practice and procedure, have been brought before a court authorized to determine their rights. *Sibbach v. Wilson & Co.*, 312 U.S. 1, 11–14. The fact that the application of Rule 4(f) will operate to subject petitioner's rights to adjudication by the district court for northern Mississippi will undoubtedly affect those rights. But it does not operate to abridge, enlarge or modify the rules of decision by which that court will adjudicate its rights." *Id.*, at 445–46.

Thus were there no conflicting state procedure, Rule 4(d)(1) would clearly control. However, respondent, focusing on the contrary Massachusetts rule, calls to the Court's attention another line of cases, a line which—like the Federal Rules—had its birth in 1938. *Erie R. Co. v. Tompkins*, overruling *Swift v. Tyson*, held that federal courts sitting in diversity cases, when deciding questions of "substantive" law, are bound by state court decisions as well as state statutes. The broad command of *Erie* was therefore identical to that of the Enabling Act: federal courts are to apply state substantive law and federal procedural law. However, as subsequent cases sharpened the distinction between substance and procedure, the line of cases following *Erie* diverged markedly from the line construing the Enabling Act. *Guaranty Trust Co. of New York v. York* made it clear that *Erie*-type problems were not to be solved by reference to any traditional or common-sense substance-procedure distinction:

> "And so the question is not whether a statute of limitations is deemed a matter of 'procedure' in some sense. The question is... does it significantly affect the result of a litigation for a federal court to disregard a law of a State that would be controlling in an action upon the same claim by the same parties in a State court?"

326 U.S., at 109.

Respondent, by placing primary reliance on *York* and *Ragan*, suggests that the *Erie* doctrine acts as a check on the Federal Rules of Civil Procedure, that despite the clear command of Rule 4(d)(1), *Erie* and its progeny demand the application of the Massachusetts rule. Reduced to essentials, the argument is: (1) *Erie*, as refined in *York*, demands that federal courts apply state law whenever application of federal law in its stead will alter the outcome of the case. (2) In this case, a determination that the Massachusetts service requirements obtain will result in immediate victory for respondent. If, on the other hand, it should be held that Rule 4(d)(1) is applicable, the litigation will continue, with possible victory for petitioner. (3) Therefore, *Erie* demands application of the Massachusetts rule. The syllogism possesses an appealing simplicity, but is for several reasons invalid.

[Eds.— Here, in what we refer to as "*Hanna* Part I," the Court considers the proper analysis of a conflict between state practice and a federal judicial practice (not governed by any Federal Rule of Civil Procedure).]

In the first place, it is doubtful that, even if there were no Federal Rule making it clear that in-hand service is not required in diversity actions, the *Erie* rule would have obligated the District Court to follow the Massachusetts procedure. "Outcome-determination" analysis was never intended to serve as a talisman. *Byrd v. Blue Ridge Rural Elec. Cooperative*. Indeed, the message of *York* itself is that choices between state and federal law are to be made not by application of any automatic, "litmus paper" criterion, but rather by reference to the policies underlying the *Erie* rule. *Guaranty Trust Co. of New York v. York*.

The *Erie* rule is rooted in part in a realization that it would be unfair for the character of result of a litigation materially to differ because the suit had been brought in a federal court.

> "Diversity of citizenship jurisdiction was conferred in order to prevent apprehended discrimination in state courts against those not citizens of the state. *Swift v. Tyson* introduced grave discrimination by noncitizens against citizens. It made rights enjoyed under the unwritten 'general law' vary according to whether enforcement was sought in the state or in the federal court; and the privilege of selecting the court in which the right should be determined was conferred upon the noncitizen. Thus, the doctrine rendered impossible equal protection of the law." *Erie R. Co. v. Tompkins*, 304 U.S. at 74–75.

The decision was also in part a reaction to the practice of "forum-shopping" which had grown up in response to the rule of *Swift v. Tyson*. That the *York* test was an attempt to effectuate these policies is demonstrated by the fact that the opinion framed the inquiry in terms of "substantial" variations between state and federal litigation. Not only are nonsubstantial, or trivial, variations not likely to raise the sort of equal protection problems which troubled the Court in *Erie*; they are also unlikely to influence the choice of a forum. The "outcome-determination" test therefore cannot be read without reference to the twin aims of the *Erie* rule: discouragement of forum-shopping and avoidance of inequitable administration of the laws.

The difference between the conclusion that the Massachusetts rule is applicable, and the conclusion that it is not, is of course at this point "outcome-determinative" in the sense that if we hold the state rule to apply, respondent prevails, whereas if we hold that Rule 4(d)(1) governs, the litigation will continue. But in this sense *every* procedural variation is "outcome-determinative." For example, having brought suit in a federal court, a plaintiff cannot then insist on the right to file subsequent pleadings in accord with the time limits applicable in state courts, even though enforcement of the federal timetable will, if he continues to insist that he must meet only the state time limit, result in determination of the controversy against him. So it is here. Though choice of the federal or state rule will at this point have a marked effect upon the outcome of the litigation, the difference between the two rules would be of scant, if any, relevance to the choice of a forum. Petitioner, in choosing her forum, was not presented with a situation where application of the state rule would wholly bar recovery; rather, adherence to the state rule would have resulted only in altering the way in which process was served. Moreover, it is difficult to argue that permitting service of defendant's wife to take the place of in-hand service of defendant himself alters the mode of enforcement of state-created rights in a fashion sufficiently "substantial" to raise the sort of equal protection problems to which the *Erie* opinion alluded.

[Eds.—Here, in what we refer to as "*Hanna* Part II," the Court switches gears, analyzing the conflict as one between a formal Federal Rule of Civil Procedure and state practice.]

There is, however, a more fundamental flaw in respondent's syllogism: the incorrect assumption that the rule of *Erie R. Co. v. Tompkins* constitutes the appropriate test of the validity and therefore the applicability of a Federal Rule of Civil Procedure. The *Erie* rule has never been invoked to void a Federal Rule. It is true that there have been cases where this Court has held applicable a state rule in the face of an argument that the situation was governed by one of the Federal Rules. But the holding of each such case was not that *Erie* commanded displacement of a Federal Rule by an inconsistent state rule, but rather that the scope of the Federal Rule was not as broad as the losing party urged, and therefore, there being no Federal Rule which covered the point in dispute, *Erie* commanded the enforcement of state law.

. . .

(Here, of course, the clash is unavoidable; Rule 4(d)(1) says—implicitly, but with unmistakable clarity—that inhand service is not required in federal courts.) At the same time, in cases adjudicating the validity of Federal Rules, we have not applied the *York* rule or other refinements of *Erie*, but have to this day continued to decide questions concerning the scope of the Enabling Act and the constitutionality of specific Federal Rules in light of the distinction set forth in *Sibbach*.

Nor has the development of two separate lines of cases been inadvertent. The line between "substance" and "procedure" shifts as the legal context changes. "Each implies different variables depending upon the particular problem for which it is used." *Guaranty Trust Co. of New York v. York*, 326 U.S. at 108. It is true that both the Enabling Act and the *Erie* rule say, roughly, that federal courts are to apply state "substantive" law and federal "procedural" law, but from that it need not follow that the tests are identical. For they were designed to control very different sorts of decisions. When a situation is covered by one of the Federal Rules, the question facing the court is a far cry from the typical, relatively unguided *Erie* Choice: the court has been instructed to apply the Federal Rule, and can refuse to do so only if the Advisory Committee, this Court, and Congress erred in their prima facie judgment that the Rule in question transgresses neither the terms of the Enabling Act nor constitutional restrictions.

We are reminded by the *Erie* opinion that neither Congress nor the federal courts can, under the guise of formulating rules of decision for federal courts, fashion rules which are not supported by a grant of federal authority contained in Article I or some other section of the Constitution; in such areas state law must govern because there can be no other law. But the opinion in *Erie*, which involved no Federal Rule and dealt with a question which was "substantive" in every traditional sense (whether the railroad owed a duty of care to Tompkins as a trespasser or a licensee), surely neither said nor implied that measures like Rule 4(d)(1) are unconstitutional. For the constitutional provision for a federal court system (augmented by the Necessary and Proper Clause) carries with it congressional power to make rules governing the practice and pleading in those courts, which in turn includes a power to regulate matters which, though falling within the uncertain area between substance and procedure, are rationally capable of classification as either. Neither *York* nor the cases following it ever suggested that the rule there laid down for coping with situations where no Federal Rule applies is coextensive with the limitation on Congress to which *Erie* had adverted. Although this Court has never before been confronted with a case where the applicable Federal Rule is in direct collision with the law of the relevant State, courts of appeals faced with such clashes have rightly discerned the implications of our decisions.

> "One of the shaping purposes of the Federal Rules is to bring about uniformity in the federal courts by getting away from local rules. This is especially true of matters which relate to the administration of legal proceedings, an area in which federal courts have traditionally exerted strong inherent power, completely aside from the powers Congress expressly conferred in the Rules. The purpose of the *Erie* doctrine, even as extended in *York* and *Ragan*, was never to bottle up federal courts with 'outcome-determinative' and 'integral-relations' stoppers—when there are 'affirmative countervailing [federal] considerations' and when there is a Congressional mandate (the Rules) supported by constitutional authority." *Lumbermen's Mutual Casualty Co. v. Wright*, 322 F.2d 759, 764 (C.A.5th Cir. 1963).

Erie and its offspring cast no doubt on the long-recognized power of Congress to prescribe housekeeping rules for federal courts even though some of those rules will inevitably differ from comparable state rules. "When, because the plaintiff happens to be a non-resident, such a right is enforceable in a federal as well as in a State court, the forms and mode of enforcing the right may at times, naturally enough, vary because the two judicial systems are not identic." *Guaranty Trust Co. of New York v. York*, 326 U.S. at 108. Thus, though a court, in measuring a Federal Rule against the standards contained in the Enabling Act and the Constitution, need not wholly blind itself to the degree to which the Rule makes the character and result of the federal litigation stray from the course it would follow in state courts, it cannot be forgotten that the *Erie* rule, and the guidelines suggested in *York*, were created to serve another purpose altogether. To hold that a Federal Rule of Civil Procedure must cease to function whenever it alters the mode of enforcing state-created rights would be to disembowel either the Constitution's grant of power over federal procedure or Congress' attempt to exercise that power in the Enabling Act. Rule 4(d)(1) is valid and controls the instant case.

Reversed.

Mr. Justice HARLAN, concurring.

It is unquestionably true that up to now *Erie* and the cases following it have not succeeded in articulating a workable doctrine governing choice of law in diversity actions. I respect the Court's effort to clarify the situation in today's opinion. However, in doing so I think it has misconceived the constitutional premises of *Erie* and has failed to deal adequately with those past decisions upon which the courts below relied.

Erie was something more than an opinion which worried about "forum-shopping and avoidance of inequitable administration of the laws," although to be sure these were important elements of the decision. I have always regarded that decision as one of the modern cornerstones of our federalism, expressing policies that profoundly touch the allocation of judicial power between the state and federal systems. *Erie* recognized that there should not be two conflicting systems of law controlling the primary activity of citizens, for such alternative governing authority must necessarily give rise to a debilitating uncertainty in the planning of everyday affairs. And it recognized that the scheme of our Constitution envisions an allocation of law-making functions between state and federal legislative processes which is undercut if the federal judiciary can make substantive law affecting state affairs beyond the bounds of congressional legislative powers in this regard. Thus, in diversity cases *Erie* commands that it be the state law governing primary private activity which prevails.

The shorthand formulations which have appeared in some past decisions are prone to carry untoward results that frequently arise from oversimplification. The Court is quite right in stating that the "outcome-determinative" test of *Guaranty Trust Co. of New York v. York* if taken literally, proves too much, for any rule, no matter how clearly "procedural," can affect the outcome of litigation if it is not obeyed. In turning from the "outcome" test of *York* back to the unadorned forum-shopping rationale of *Erie*, however, the Court falls prey to like oversimplification, for a simple forum-shopping rule also proves too much; litigants often choose a federal forum merely to obtain what they consider the advantages of the Federal Rules of Civil Procedure or to try their cases before a supposedly more favorable judge. To my mind the proper line of approach in determining whether to apply a state or a federal rule, whether "substantive" or "procedural," is to stay close to basic principles by inquiring if the choice of rule would substantially affect those primary decisions respecting human conduct which our constitutional system leaves to state regulation. If so, *Erie* and the

Constitution require that the state rule prevail, even in the face of a conflicting federal rule.

The Court weakens, if indeed it does not submerge, this basic principle by finding, in effect, a grant of substantive legislative power in the constitutional provision for a federal court system and through it, setting up the Federal Rules as a body of law inviolate.

> "[T]he constitutional provision for a federal court system...carries with it congressional power...to regulate matters which, though falling within the uncertain area between substance and procedure, *are rationally capable of classification as either.*" (Emphasis supplied.)

So long as a reasonable man could characterize any duly adopted federal rule as "procedural," the Court, unless I misapprehend what is said, would have it apply no matter how seriously it frustrated a State's substantive regulation of the primary conduct and affairs of its citizens. Since the members of the Advisory Committee, the Judicial Conference, and this Court who formulated the Federal Rules are presumably reasonable men, it follows that the integrity of the Federal Rules is absolute. Whereas the unadulterated outcome and forum-shopping tests may err too far toward honoring state rules, I submit that the Court's "arguably procedural, *ergo* constitutional" test moves too fast and far in the other direction.

...

It remains to apply what has been said to the present case. The Massachusetts rule provides that an executor need not answer suits unless in-hand service was made upon him or notice of the action was filed in the proper registry of probate within one year of his giving bond. The evident intent of this statute is to permit an executor to distribute the estate which he is administering without fear that further liabilities may be outstanding for which he could be held personally liable. If the Federal District Court in Massachusetts applies Rule 4(d)(1) of the Federal Rules of Civil Procedure instead of the Massachusetts service rule, what effect would that have on the speed and assurance with which estates are distributed? As I see it, the effect would not be substantial. It would mean simply that an executor would have to check at his own house or the federal courthouse as well as the registry of probate before he could distribute the estate with impunity. As this does not seem enough to give rise to any real impingement on the vitality of the state policy which the Massachusetts rule is intended to serve, I concur in the judgment of the Court.

Notes and Questions: The *Erie* Tracks Diverge

1. From the profound to the trivial. Consider how far we have come from the issue in *Erie* to the issue in *Hanna*. *Erie* involved a clearly substantive question of tort law, the duty of care owed to a trespasser. *Hanna* involved the method of delivering the initial papers in the lawsuit to the defendant: service in hand under the state statute or leaving the papers at his home with a person residing therein under Federal Rule 4. If the federal court were required to imitate state practice on this relatively tepid service issue, there would not be many issues, no matter how clearly "procedural," on which it could go its own way in a case governed by state law. Somehow, it seems very doubtful that this is what Justice Holmes or Justice Brandeis had in mind in rejecting *Swift*.

Q **2. Revisiting *Guaranty Trust*.** How would *Hanna v. Plumer* come out under Justice Frankfurter's original outcome-determinative test in *Guaranty Trust*?

A *Guaranty Trust*'s outcome-determinative test would likely mandate use of state law. The defendant in *Hanna* laid out a seemingly airtight "syllogism" to support his motion to dismiss: *Guaranty Trust* requires use of state law if ignoring it might affect the outcome; the case would proceed if the plaintiff was entitled to serve process under the Federal Rules, but would be barred if the state in-hand-service rule must be used; that's a dramatic difference. Therefore, state law must be used. Not a bad argument, if the Court adheres to *Guaranty Trust's* outcome-determinative test and applies it retrospectively, as the Court did in *Guaranty Trust*. In *Hanna,* however, Chief Justice Warren refined the *Guaranty Trust* test in light of the "twin aims" of the *Erie* doctrine.

Q **3. Assessment under the "relatively unguided" *Hanna* Part I test.** Suppose that the federal service method—leaving the papers at the defendant's home with a person of suitable age and discretion—was not specified by a Federal Rule. Instead, it was simply accepted practice in federal court to allow service in that manner. Under *Hanna*, could the federal court use that method, even though state law required in-hand service?

A Chief Justice Warren concludes in *Hanna* Part I that it could. Although state and federal practice differ, the difference is not substantial enough to lead a plaintiff to choose federal court over state court nor does it provide a significant litigation advantage that makes it "inequitable" to ignore state practice. 380 U.S. at 468–69.

Note that Warren looks at the difference in rules *prospectively*. He asks whether the difference between Federal Rule 4 and state practice would lead a lawyer to choose one court system over the other. It probably would not. But if a lawyer has failed to comply with state law (as the plaintiff's lawyer had in *Hanna*), the difference between the two approaches will later become "outcome determinative," because it is too late to comply with the state service rule. Thus, Warren seems to adopt a prospective approach to outcome determination, while *Guaranty Trust* takes a retrospective approach.

4. The Rules Enabling Act: The statutory authority for promulgating the Federal Rules. The Rules Enabling Act (REA) was enacted in 1934. It authorizes the Supreme Court to adopt rules of practice and procedure for the federal district courts:

> The Supreme Court shall have the power to prescribe general rules of practice and procedure and rules of evidence for cases in the United States district courts (including proceedings before magistrate judges thereof) and courts of appeals. [28 U.S.C. § 2072(a).]
>
> Such rules shall not abridge, enlarge or modify any substantive right. All laws in conflict with such rules shall be of no further force or effect after such rules have taken effect. [28 U.S.C. § 2072(b).]

After the REA was enacted, the Supreme Court appointed an Advisory Committee to draft the Rules and submit them to the Court for approval. The Court approved the new Rules and transmitted them to Congress. Under the REA, rules approved by the Court take effect seven months after transmittal to Congress, unless Congress acts to intercept them. 28 U.S.C. § 2074. The original Federal Rules took effect under this procedure in 1938. (The Advisory Committee continues to review the Rules and submits recommended amendments of the Rules to the Court. If adopted by the Court, amendments take effect under the same procedure.)

The figure below illustrates the current procedure for the adoption and amendment of the Federal Rules.

5. Why should a conflict between a Federal Rule and state law be analyzed differently from other conflicts? Chief Justice Warren holds that a conflict between one of the Federal Rules of Civil Procedure and state law requires a distinct analysis from the "typical, relatively unguided *Erie* Choice." 380 U.S. at 471. In Federal Rules conflicts, the Court has adopted a federal rule under a delegation of power from Congress to govern in federal courts. If Congress enacts federal law (or the Supreme Court does under the REA's delegation of authority), the resulting law is the "supreme Law of the Land" (the Supremacy Clause of the United States Constitution, Art. VI, para. 2), as long as Congress had the power to enact it. Because Congress delegated its power to govern federal procedure to the Supreme Court in the REA, the validity of a Federal Rule turns on whether Congress had the constitutional power to regulate the issue covered by the Federal Rule itself, and if so, whether the Supreme

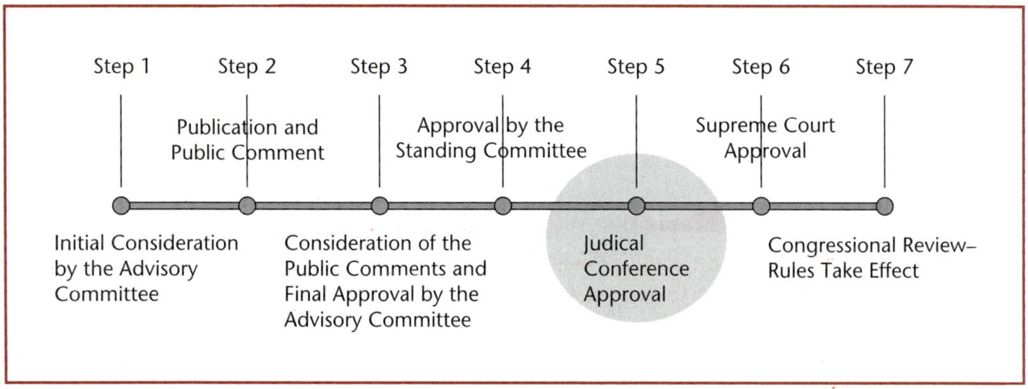

Figure 25–1: THE RULEMAKING PROCESS

Court, in adopting the Rule, acted in accordance with the congressional delegation. If so, the Rule is valid and applies in the face of contrary state law.

6. Assessing the validity of a Federal Rule under *Hanna* Part II. The second part of the *Hanna* opinion provides standards for answering both of the questions stated in the previous note.

- *First*, did Congress have the authority to enact (and hence, to delegate to the Supreme Court the power to adopt) the Federal Rule in question? Here, Chief Justice Warren asks whether *Congress itself* could have written the Rule in question. Presumably, if Congress could have written a Federal Rule like Rule 4(d)(1) itself, it may delegate that authority to the Supreme Court. Congress has very broad power, Warren concludes, to regulate practice in the federal courts:

  > For the constitutional provision for a federal court system [Article III] (augmented by the Necessary and Proper Clause) carries with it congressional power to make rules governing the practice and pleading in those courts, which in turn includes a power to regulate matters which, though falling within the uncertain area between substance and procedure, are rationally capable of classification as either.

  380 U.S 472.

  Justice Harlan characterizes this as "the Court's 'arguably procedural, *ergo* constitutional'" test. 380 U.S. at 476. That is probably a fair characterization; certainly, *Hanna* concluded that Congress has very broad authority to regulate (and therefore, to delegate to the Court authority to regulate) issues that relate to the processing of cases in the federal courts.

- *Second,* in determining whether Federal Rule 4 must be applied, we must ask whether Congress has delegated the power to write the Rule to the Supreme Court in the REA. Here, Chief Justice Warren concludes that a Rule is within the delegation in the REA if it satisfies a similarly broad test.

  > "The test must be whether a rule really regulates procedure,—the judicial process for enforcing rights and duties recognized by substantive law and for justly administering remedy and redress for disregard or infraction of them."

  380 U.S. at 464 (quoting *Sibbach v. Wilson & Co.*, 312 U.S. 1, 14 (1941)). This arguably circular standard also establishes a test broad enough to drive a truck through. Almost any rule relating to the administration of cases is likely to satisfy this generous standard.

Thus, the bottom line is that if Congress has authorized the Court to write the Rule and the Rule is "arguably procedural," it is valid federal law that applies under the Supremacy Clause, even if it contradicts state practice. However, there is an additional limit on Congress's delegation in the REA: A Rule (even if it passes the test of "procedurality" quoted above) may not "abridge, enlarge, or modify any substantive right." 28 U.S.C. § 2072(b). (This perplexing proviso is discussed further below.)

7. Revisiting *Guaranty Trust* after *Hanna*. Consider the following question.

> Assume that one year after *Hanna v. Plumer* was decided a case arises (we'll call it *York v. Guaranty Trust II)*, presenting the same conflict between state procedure (limitations period bars the claim) and the federal practice (applying the laches doctrine) that the Court addressed in *Guaranty Trust*. The defendant argues that the statute of limitations bars the claim. The federal court should
>
> A. apply the state statute of limitations, because no Federal Rule governs the conflict.
> B. apply the laches doctrine, as long as it is arguably procedural.
> C. apply the state statute of limitations, under the *Hanna* Part I analysis.
> D. apply the laches doctrine, because there is a direct conflict between it and the state statute of limitations.

A does not reflect a clear understanding of the *Hanna* opinion. *Hanna* did not hold that a federal court applies state law whenever there is no Federal Rule on point. It held that different analyses are required for conflicts between a Federal Rule and state law and for conflicts between a federal judicial practice and state law. Since this case involves a conflict between a federal judicial practice and state law, it must be analyzed under *Hanna* Part I. The court must consider whether ignoring the state statute would lead to forum shopping or inequitable administration of the laws.

B also misconstrues the difference between *Hanna* Part I and *Hanna* Part II. In Part II of the *Hanna* opinion, the Court held that Congress has the power to enact procedural statutes that are arguably procedural ("matters which, though falling within the uncertain area between substance and procedure, are rationally capable of classification as either"). 380 U.S. at 472. But the conflict in *Guaranty Trust* did not involve a federal procedural statute or rule; it involved a conflict between the federal judicial practice of applying the laches doctrine, not mandated by Federal Rule or statute, and the state limitations statute. Thus, the proper analysis (under *Hanna* Part I) is to ask whether applying the laches doctrine instead of the state limitations statute would lead to forum shopping or inequitable administration of the laws.

Nor is **D** correct. It implies that any time there is a direct conflict between federal practice and state law, the court must use the federal practice. That would certainly solve this difficult substance/procedure problem, but it is not the solution provided in *Hanna*. Instead, because this case involves a conflict between federal judicial practice and state law, it should be analyzed under the dicta in *Hanna* Part I. And since many plaintiffs would choose federal court if it applied a longer limitations period, the *Hanna* Part I analysis should lead the federal court to apply the state limitations period, just as it did in *Guaranty Trust*. **C** is the correct answer. *See Walker v. Armco Steel Co.*, 446 U.S. 740 (1980).

Q **8. More than one way to skin a cat.** Suppose that Congress were to enact a statute setting a two-year limitations period for bringing diversity actions in federal court. Rodriguez brings a diversity action against Pollard for negligence, two years and four months after the accident that caused his injury. The relevant state statute of limitations is four years. Should the federal court allow the case to proceed or dismiss it under the federal limitations statute?

A Under the Supremacy Clause, federal statutes apply, even in the face of contrary state law, if they are valid. This statute is valid, *Hanna* tells us, if it "regulate[s] matters which, though falling within the uncertain area between substance and procedure, are rationally capable of classification as either." 380 U.S. at 472. The period within which to bring a claim in the court has a procedural purpose, to protect the court from having to litigate stale claims. Thus, a federal statutory limitations period for diversity cases would very likely be upheld under congressional authority to regulate procedure in federal court and would preempt the state limitations period.

Note the difference between the analysis here and in the previous question. There, the decision involved the "typical, relatively unguided *Erie* Choice" under *Hanna* Part I. This example, however, involves a conflict between positive federal law—the federal statute—and state law. When that is true, the federal statute prevails under the Supremacy Clause if Congress had the authority to enact it.

9. The "substantive rights" proviso in the REA. While the REA, as interpreted in *Hanna,* grants broad authority to adopt Federal Rules, even if they differ from state practice, the REA itself contains a limiting proviso. "Such rules shall not abridge, enlarge or modify any substantive right. . . ." 28 U.S.C. § 2072(b). This suggests that a Rule that complies with the delegation in § 2072(a) will not be within Congress's delegation of rulemaking power to the Court if the Rule infringes on state substantive rights. This is one of the agonizingly hard aspects of the *Erie* doctrine: A Rule may be within *Congress's* power to enact (because it is "arguably procedural") but not within its delegation of rulemaking authority to the *Supreme Court* in the REA (because it affects substantive rights). The Court has never clarified exactly when a Rule impermissibly infringes on substantive rights—perhaps it never will be able to definitively do so. (More on this below.) But you should recognize that the substantive rights proviso in § 2072(b) opens up a narrow avenue to challenge the validity of a Federal Rule even though it governs a procedural matter.

IV. Track Selection After *Hanna*: Assessing Direct Conflicts with a Federal Rule

After *Hanna*, the analysis of a conflict between state and federal practice in diversity cases depends on the nature of the conflict. Conflicts between federal judicial practice and state law depend on a "modified outcome-determinative" analysis under *Hanna* Part I. Conflicts between the Federal Rules of Civil Procedure and state law require analysis under *Hanna* Part II. So, the first question the federal court must ask is which track to pursue. The case below, *Walker v. Armco Steel Company*, addresses this problem.

READING *WALKER v. ARMCO STEEL CO.* In *Walker*, the plaintiff brought a tort case against the defendant in an Oklahoma federal court, based on diversity jurisdiction. An Oklahoma statute required that the summons be served on the defendant within sixty days after the expiration of the limitations period. The plaintiff failed to do so. However, he had filed the complaint in federal court within the limitations period, and claimed that his suit was timely under Federal Rule 3, which provides that "[a] civil action is commenced by filing a complaint with the court."

- Why did the plaintiff argue that he had satisfied the statute of limitations?
- Is this a *Hanna* Part I conflict or a *Hanna* Part II conflict?
- Once the Court chose the appropriate conflict, how did the Court resolve it?

WALKER v. ARMCO STEEL CO.

446 U.S. 740 (1980)

Mr. Justice Marshall delivered the opinion of the Court.

This case presents the issue whether in a diversity action the federal court should follow state law or, alternatively, Rule 3 of the Federal Rules of Civil Procedure in determining when an action is commenced for the purpose of tolling the state statute of limitations.

I

. . .

The District Court dismissed the complaint as barred by the Oklahoma statute of limitations. The court concluded that Okla. Stat., Tit. 12, § 97 (1971) was "an integral part of the Oklahoma statute of limitations," and therefore, under *Ragan v. Merchants Transfer & Warehouse Co.*, 337 U.S. 530 (1949), state law applied. The court rejected the argument that *Ragan* had been implicitly overruled in *Hanna v. Plumer*.

The United States Court of Appeals for the Tenth Circuit affirmed. The court concluded that Okla. Stat., Tit. 12, § 97 (1971), was in "direct conflict" with Rule 3. However, the Oklahoma statute was "indistinguishable" from the statute involved in *Ragan*, and the court felt itself "constrained" to follow *Ragan*.

We granted certiorari because of a conflict among the Courts of Appeals. We now affirm.

II

The question whether state or federal law should apply on various issues arising in an action based on state law which has been brought in federal court under diversity of citizenship jurisdiction has troubled this Court for many years. In the landmark decision of *Erie R. Co. v. Tompkins*, we overturned the rule expressed in *Swift v. Tyson* that federal courts exercising diversity jurisdiction need not, in matters of "general jurisprudence," apply the nonstatutory law of the State. The Court noted that "[d]iversity of citizenship jurisdiction was conferred in order to prevent apprehended discrimination in state courts against those not citizens of the State." The doctrine of *Swift v. Tyson* had led to the undesirable results of discrimination in favor of noncitizens, prevention of uniformity in the administration of state law, and forum shopping. In response, we established the rule that "[e]xcept in matters governed by the Federal Constitution or by Acts of Congress, the law to be applied in any [diversity] case is the law of the State."

In *Guaranty Trust Co. v. York* . . . [w]e concluded that the state statute of limitations should be applied. "Plainly enough, a statute that would completely bar recovery in a suit if brought in a State court bears on a State-created right vitally and not merely formally or negligibly. As to consequences that so intimately affect recovery or non-recovery a federal court in a diversity case should follow State law." [326 U.S.] at 110.

The decision in *York* led logically to our holding in *Ragan v. Merchants Transfer & Warehouse Co.* In *Ragan*, . . . [t]he defendant moved for summary judgment on the ground that the Kansas statute of limitations barred the action since service had not been made within either the 2-year period or the 60-day period. It was conceded that had the case been brought in Kansas state court it would have been barred. Nonetheless, the District Court held that the statute had been tolled by the filing of the complaint. The Court of Appeals reversed because "the requirement of service of summons within the statutory period was an integral part of that state's statute of limitations." *Ragan*, 337 U.S. at 532.

We affirmed, relying on *Erie* and *York*. "We cannot give [the cause of action] longer life in the federal court than it would have had in the state court without adding something to the cause of action. We may not do that consistently with *Erie R. Co. v. Tompkins*." 337 U.S. at 533–534. We rejected the argument that Rule 3 of the Federal Rules of Civil Procedure governed the manner in which an action was commenced in federal court for purposes of tolling the state statute of limitations. Instead, we held that the service of summons statute controlled because it was an integral part of the state statute of limitations, and under *York* that statute of limitations was part of the state-law cause of action.

Ragan was not our last pronouncement in this difficult area, however. In 1965 we decided *Hanna v. Plumer*, holding that in a civil action where federal jurisdiction was based upon diversity of citizenship, Rule 4(d)(1) of the Federal Rules of Civil Procedure, rather than state law, governed the manner in which process was served. Massachusetts law required in-hand service on an executor or administrator of an estate, whereas Rule 4 permits service by leaving copies of the summons and complaint at the defendant's home with some person "of suitable age and discretion." The Court noted that in the absence of a conflicting state procedure, the Federal Rule would plainly control. We stated that the "outcome-determination" test of *Erie* and *York* had to be read with reference to the "twin aims" of *Erie*: "discouragement of forum-shopping and avoidance of inequitable administration of the laws." 380 U.S., at 468. We determined that the choice between the state in-hand service rule and the Federal Rule "would be of scant, if any, relevance to the choice of a forum," for the plaintiff "was not presented with a situation where application of the state rule would wholly bar recovery; rather, adherence to the state rule would have resulted only in altering the way in which process was served." *Id.*, at 469 (footnote omitted). This factor served to distinguish that case from *York* and *Ragan*.

The Court in *Hanna*, however, pointed out "a more fundamental flaw" in the defendant's argument in that case. *Id.*, at 469. The Court concluded that the *Erie* doctrine was simply not the appropriate test of the validity and applicability of one of the Federal Rules of Civil Procedure:

> "The *Erie* rule has never been invoked to void a Federal Rule. It is true that there have been cases where this Court had held applicable a state rule in the face of an argument that the situation was governed by one of the Federal Rules. But the holding of each such case was not that *Erie* commanded displacement of a Federal Rule by an inconsistent state rule, but rather that the scope of the Federal Rule was not as broad as the losing party urged, and therefore, there being no Federal Rule which covered the point in dispute, *Erie* commanded the enforcement of state law." 380 U.S., at 470.

The Court cited *Ragan* as one of the examples of this proposition.[7] The Court explained that where the Federal Rule was clearly applicable, as in *Hanna*, the test was whether the Rule was within the scope of the Rules Enabling Act, and if so, within a constitutional grant of power such as the Necessary and Proper Clause of Art. I.

III

The present case is indistinguishable from *Ragan*. The statutes in both cases require service of process to toll the statute of limitations, and in fact the predecessor to the Oklahoma statute in this case was derived from the predecessor to the Kansas statute in *Ragan*. . . . Accordingly, as the Court of Appeals held below, the instant action is barred by the statute of limitations unless *Ragan* is no longer good law.

Petitioner argues that the analysis and holding of *Ragan* did not survive our decision in *Hanna*. Petitioner's position is that Okla. Stat., Tit. 12, § 97 (1971), is in direct conflict with the Federal Rule. Under *Hanna*, petitioner contends, the appropriate question is whether Rule 3 is within the scope of the Rules Enabling Act and, if so, within the constitutional power of Congress. In petitioner's view, the Federal Rule is to be applied unless it violates one of those two restrictions. This argument ignores both the force of *stare decisis* and the specific limitations that we carefully placed on the *Hanna* analysis.

We note at the outset that the doctrine of *stare decisis* weighs heavily against petitioner in this case. Petitioner seeks to have us overrule our decision in *Ragan*. *Stare decisis* does not mandate that earlier decisions be enshrined forever, of course, but it does counsel that we use caution in rejecting established law. In this case, the reasons petitioner asserts for overruling *Ragan* are the same factors which we concluded

7. The Court in *Hanna* noted that "this Court has never before been confronted with a case where the applicable Federal Rule is in direct collision with the law of the relevant State." 380 U.S., at 472.

in *Hanna* did not undermine the validity of *Ragan*. A litigant who in effect asks us to reconsider not one but two prior decisions bears a heavy burden of supporting such a change in our jurisprudence. Petitioner here has not met that burden.

This Court in *Hanna* distinguished *Ragan* rather than overruled it, and for good reason. Application of the *Hanna* analysis is premised on a "direct collision" between the Federal Rule and the state law. In *Hanna* itself the "clash" between Rule 4(d)(1) and the state in-hand service requirement was "unavoidable." 380 U.S., at 470. The first question must therefore be whether the scope of the Federal Rule in fact is sufficiently broad to control the issue before the Court. It is only if that question is answered affirmatively that the *Hanna* analysis applies.[9]

As has already been noted, we recognized in *Hanna* that the present case is an instance where "the scope of the Federal Rule [is] not as broad as the losing party urge[s], and therefore, there being no Federal Rule which cover[s] the point in dispute, *Erie* command[s] the enforcement of state law." *Ibid.* Rule 3 simply states that "[a] civil action is commenced by filing a complaint with the court." There is no indication that the Rule was intended to toll a state statute of limitations, much less that it purported to displace state tolling rules for purposes of state statutes of limitations. In our view, in diversity actions[11] Rule 3 governs the date from which various timing requirements of the Federal Rules begin to run, but does not affect state statutes of limitations.

In contrast to Rule 3, the Oklahoma statute is a statement of a substantive decision by that State that actual service on, and accordingly actual notice by, the defendant is an integral part of the several policies served by the statute of limitations. The statute of limitations establishes a deadline after which the defendant may legitimately have peace of mind; it also recognizes that after a certain period of time it is unfair to require the defendant to attempt to piece together his defense to an old claim. A requirement of actual service promotes both of those functions of the statute. It is these policy aspects which make the service requirement an "integral" part of the statute of limitations both in this case and in *Ragan*. As such, the service rule must be considered part and parcel of the statute of limitations. Rule 3 does not replace such policy determinations found in state law. Rule 3 and Okla. Stat., Tit. 12, § 97 (1971), can exist side by side, therefore, each controlling its own intended sphere of coverage without conflict.

Since there is no direct conflict between the Federal Rule and the state law, the *Hanna* analysis does not apply. Instead, the policies behind *Erie* and *Ragan* control the issue whether, in the absence of a federal rule directly on point, state service requirements which are an integral part of the state statute of limitations should control in an action based on state law which is filed in federal

9. This is not to suggest that the Federal Rules of Civil Procedure are to be narrowly construed in order to avoid a "direct collision" with state law. The Federal Rules should be given their plain meaning. If a direct collision with state law arises from that plain meaning, then the analysis developed in *Hanna v. Plumer* applies.

11. The Court suggested in *Ragan* that in suits to enforce rights under a federal statute, Rule 3 means that filing of the complaint tolls the applicable statute of limitations. . . . We do not here address the role of Rule 3 as a tolling provision for a statute of limitations . . . if the cause of action is based on federal law.

court under diversity jurisdiction. The reasons for the application of such a state service requirement in a diversity action in the absence of a conflicting federal rule are well explained in *Erie* and *Ragan*, and need not be repeated here. It is sufficient to note that although in this case failure to apply the state service law might not create any problem of forum shopping, the result would be an "inequitable administration" of the law. *Hanna v. Plumer*. There is simply no reason why, in the absence of a controlling federal rule, an action based on state law which concededly would be barred in the state courts by the state statute of limitations should proceed through litigation to judgment in federal court solely because of the fortuity that there is diversity of citizenship between the litigants. The policies underlying diversity jurisdiction do not support such a distinction between state and federal plaintiffs, and *Erie* and its progeny do not permit it.

The judgment of the Court of Appeals is *Affirmed*.

Notes and Questions: *Walker v. Armco Steel*

1. Finding—and avoiding—direct conflicts. In *Walker*, the Court begins by asking whether there is a direct conflict between the state service rule and Federal Rule 3. If there is, the analysis must be under the second part of *Hanna*. The Court concludes, however, that there is no direct conflict between the Rule and the state statute, because Federal Rule 3 does not address what act satisfies the statute of limitations; it only defines "commencement of an action" for purposes of measuring various time periods under the Federal Rules themselves.

This is a narrow—one might even say cramped—interpretation of Rule 3. (Ironically, the Court has held that filing, not service, satisfies the limitations period in *a federal question* case. *West v. Conrail*, 481 U.S. 35, 38–40 (1987).) The *Walker* Court, however, construed Rule 3 narrowly to avoid a direct collision with the state statute. As the Court notes, no similar narrowing construction could avoid a direct collision between Federal Rule 4(d)(1) and state law in *Hanna v. Plumer*, since the Federal Rule in that case authorized service in one manner while the state rule required another.

2. Assessing the service conflict under *Hanna* Part I. Once the Court concluded that Rule 3 did not apply, it faced a conflict between the state statute and the federal judicial practice of deeming the limitations period met by filing within the two-year period. Such a "relatively unguided" *Erie* conflict is analyzed under *Hanna* Part I, which asks whether ignoring the state rule would lead to forum shopping or inequitable administration of the laws. Justice Marshall recognized that using a different tolling rule in federal court probably would not lead to forum shopping—after all, a plaintiff who recognizes the difference could presumably comply with either rule fairly easily. However, the difference would lead to an inequitable difference in treatment of litigants in the state and federal courts.

> There is simply no reason why, in the absence of a controlling federal rule, an action based on state law which concededly would be barred in the state courts by the state statute of limitations should proceed through litigation to judgment in federal court solely because of the fortuity that there is diversity of citizenship between the litigants.

446 U.S. at 753.

Curiously, the Court here reverts to a retrospective analysis of the distinction. *Hanna* suggested that differences between state and federal practice should be assessed prospectively, as to whether they would make a difference to the litigants at the outset of litigation. The conflict in *Walker* would not, because at the time of filing suit, either procedure could easily be met. But the Court requires use of state law anyway, based on the fact that, *at the time the defendant moved to dismiss the case*, the difference between the federal and state approaches would provide a significant litigation advantage in federal court. This inconsistency has never been resolved by the Court.

Substance and Procedure Under the Rules Enabling Act

Because the Court in *Walker* categorized the conflict as a *Hanna* Part I problem and resolved it under the "twin aims" test, it deftly avoided a tough question: If a Federal Rule is arguably procedural—and therefore authorized under 28 U.S.C. § 2072(a), the first section of the REA—when will it be invalid under the second section of the REA because it "abridge[s], enlarge[s] or modif[ies]" a substantive right? The REA authorizes the Court to adopt rules of procedure, but bars those rules from altering substantive rights. Congress must have contemplated that a rule could be "procedural" (and thus authorized by 28 U.S.C. § 2072(a)) yet still "abridge, enlarge or modify a substantive right." So a Federal Rule is not necessarily valid as long as it addresses a procedural matter. However, the Court has yet to provide a clear test for when a Federal Rule that is "procedural" under 28 U.S.C. § 2072(a) abridges, enlarges, or modifies a substantive right.

1. Suggested standards for "abridging, enlarging or modifying a substantive right." Here are a few tests that have been suggested for making the distinction.

- Professor John Hart Ely suggested that a Federal Rule, though it regulates procedure (and therefore satisfies the first subsection of the REA), affects substantive rights if it affects a state right "granted for one or more non-procedural reasons, for some purpose or purposes not having to do with the fairness or efficiency of the litigation process." John H. Ely, *The Irrepressible Myth of* Erie, 87 HARV. L. REV. 693, 725 (1974).
- An interesting student note suggests that a right is substantive if the parties, in stating their claims and defenses to each other on the eve of suit, would refer to the right in making the strongest case for their position on the merits of the case. If they would, the right should be viewed as substantive under the second subsection of the REA. Note, *The Law Applied in Diversity Cases: The Rules of Decision Act and the* Erie *Doctrine*, 85 YALE L.J. 679, 696–97 (1976).

- A congressional committee report suggests that a Rule would abridge substantive rights if it:

> would have the effect of altering existing remedial rights conferred as an integral part of the applicable substantive law scheme . . . such as an arrangement for attorney's fees. . . . [S]ection 2072 is intended to allocate to Congress, as opposed to the Supreme Court exercising delegated legislative power, lawmaking choices that necessarily and obviously require consideration of policies extrinsic to the business of the courts, such as the recognition or non-recognition of a testimonial privilege.

H.R. Rep. No. 99-422, at 21–22 (1985).

- Justice Harlan, concurring in *Hanna*, argues that the thrust of *Erie* is that state law should govern "primary private activity" that occurs before and independent of litigation. 380 U.S. at 475. He distinguishes such "primary decisions respecting human conduct," *id.*, from litigation-related matters such as the method of service of process at issue in *Hanna*. This test would certainly lead to application of state law in *Erie*. Arguably, it would lead to application of the laches doctrine in *Guaranty Trust* rather than the state limitations period.

No Supreme Court case has held a Federal Rule invalid under the substantive rights proviso in § 2072(b). In *Semtek Int'l Inc. v. Lockheed Martin Corp.*, 531 U.S. 497, 503–04 (2001), the Court suggested that Fed. R. Civ. P. 41(b) might run afoul of the proviso if it were interpreted to establish a rule of claim preclusion different from that under applicable state law. In *Semtek*, however, the Court avoided that risk by interpreting the Rule as inapplicable. The Court has also held that "incidental" effects on a substantive right do not render a Federal Rule invalid. *Burlington Northern R. Co. v. Woods*, 480 U.S. 1, 5 (1987). Thus, we know that the Rules must be tested against § 2072(b), but we still do not know exactly how to do so.

2. The substantive rights proviso: protecting separation of powers. Much of the analysis of the substantive rights proviso has focused on its role in protecting *state* substantive rights from incursion by the Federal Rules. Ironically, the legislative history of the Rules Enabling Act suggests that Congress enacted the proviso to protect *its own* prerogatives from incursion by Court rulemaking, not to protect state substantive rights. Concern was repeatedly expressed, during the twenty years that the REA was debated, that the Court might adopt rules that would interfere with Congress's authority to determine matters, such as the limitations period for federal claims, that affect the substance of federal regulations.

> Nothing could be clearer from the pre-1934 history of the Rules Enabling Act than that the procedure/substance dichotomy in the first two sentences was intended to allocate lawmaking power between the Supreme Court as rule-maker and Congress.

Steven B. Burbank, *The Rules Enabling Act of 1934*, 130 U. Pa. L. Rev. 1015, 1106 (1982). The Rules apply in federal question cases too, so the same line must be drawn in such cases between the substance of the claim being adjudicated—reserved to Congress by the substantive rights proviso—and the procedural methods of processing the case, which are subject to Court rulemaking under the first subsection of the REA.

Q **3. Some examples to test the tests.** Consider, in the three cases below, what analytical framework the court should apply to resolve the conflict and how you think it would be resolved.

A. Assume that federal judges, as a matter of general practice in the District of Arcadia, read the jury instructions to the jury, but do not provide them in writing. Assume that the court rules of Arcadia require the jury instructions to be given both orally and in writing to the jury. What should the federal judge do in a diversity case?

A This is a conflict between federal judicial practice and contrary state law. The analysis should ask whether allowing federal courts to use their own approach in state law cases would lead to forum shopping or inequitable differences in litigation opportunities in state and federal court. That seems very unlikely. The difference is modest, and any additional clarity provided by having the instructions given in writing can probably be provided by emphasizing important instructions in closing argument. This seems unlikely to influence forum choice at the outset or to create unfair litigation advantages for one side or the other. Use of the federal approach would very likely be upheld under *Hanna* Part I, even though it differs from local state practice.

B. Federal Rule 54(c) provides that "[e]very . . . final judgment should grant the relief to which each party is entitled, even if the party has not demanded that relief in its pleading." Case law in the state of West Dakota holds that no punitive damages may be recovered in a negligence case. The plaintiff in a diversity case argues that the conduct proved at trial merits punitive damages and asks the judge to instruct the jurors that they may award such damages. What should the federal judge do?

A There is no "direct conflict" between Rule 54 and state law here. Rule 54 simply states that a party should be awarded relief to which the party is "entitled," whether she demanded it in a pleading or not. In a diversity case, a party is only entitled to relief that is available under relevant state law. Here, punitive damages are not available, so nothing in Rule 54 suggests that the plaintiff can recover them.

Since Federal Rule 54 does not contradict state law, *Hanna*'s REA analysis is irrelevant. The basic command of *Erie* applies: The right to punitive damages (or to be free of them, in this case) is about as "substantive" as a right can be, a basic rule of the state's tort law. *Erie* commands application of state substantive law in a diversity case, because, as *Hanna* stated, "there can be no other law." The judge should not allow the jury to consider awarding punitive damages.

C. The plaintiff recovers punitive damages at trial in a federal diversity case in California. The defendant moves for judgment as a matter of law in his favor, arguing that there was insufficient evidence of malicious conduct to support a punitive damages recovery. Federal Rule 50(b) provides that a party may only seek judgment as a matter of law after verdict if she sought the same relief on the same ground *before* the verdict under Fed. R. Civ. P. 50(a). The plaintiff had failed to move for judgment under Rule 50(a) on this ground. However, under California law, the objection that punitive damages are unwarranted is never waived. It can be raised after a verdict or on appeal, even if the objection was not asserted earlier. Should the federal judge apply Rule 50(b) or the state approach?

A This is the toughest of the three. Rule 50(b) bars the court from considering the argument that the proof was too weak to support a finding of malice, because the plaintiff never sought judgment on that ground before the case went to the jury. But state law is to the contrary. The two seem inevitably inconsistent, in "direct conflict." The question, then, is whether Rule 50(b) is valid under the REA. There is no question that it governs procedure, since it deals with the preservation of objections at a trial. The only possible ground for disregarding it is that it "abridges or modifies" substantive rights.

In *Freund v. Nycomed Amersham*, 347 F.3d 752 (9th Cir. 2003), the court held that Federal Rule 50 should apply on these facts, since the Rule "affects only the process of enforcing litigants' rights and not the rights themselves." 347 F.3d at 762 (quoting *Burlington N. R.R. Co. v. Woods,* 480 U.S. 1, 8 (1987)). While acknowledging that the state rule "has its roots in the State's public policy," the court noted that many procedural rules are rooted in policy concerns. *Id.* "[T]he mere fact that California's no-waiver rule concerning punitive damages is rooted in public policy does not render it substantive for purposes of our analysis." *Id.*

The *Freund* court may be right, but there is certainly a strong argument that California has crafted a policy intimately associated with limits on recovery for punitive damages, so that Rule 50(b) contradicts a policy with a significant non-procedural purpose. This one is close to the line under 28 U.S.C. § 2072(b).

4. *Guaranty Trust* redux.

Consider the following twist on *Guaranty Trust.* Assume that the Supreme Court, on the recommendation of the Rules Advisory Committee, adopts a new Federal Rule 3.1, which provides that no federal diversity action shall be brought more than two years after the claim arises. York brings an action in federal court against the Guaranty Trust Company two years and four months after the claim arises. He bases jurisdiction on diversity. The relevant state limitations period is three years. Guaranty Trust moves to dismiss the case based on Rule 3.1. The court should

A. hear the case. Rule 3.1 is invalid under 28 U.S.C. § 2072(a) because it does not regulate procedure.

B. hear the case. Rule 3.1 is invalid under 28 U.S.C. § 2072(b) because it modifies the parties' substantive rights.

C. hear the case because applying a different statute of limitations in federal court would lead to forum shopping and inequitable administration of the laws.
D. dismiss the case, since Rule 3.1 is valid and is in direct conflict with the state limitations period.

This question asks whether a Federal Rule of Civil Procedure that established a limitations period for diversity cases would be valid. Because the limitation period is provided in a Federal Rule, **C** is wrong here. That answer suggests that the conflict should be analyzed under *Hanna* Part I. However, where a Federal Rule conflicts with state practice, the *Hanna* Part II analysis applies.

A takes the position that 28 U.S.C. § 2072(a) does not authorize the adoption of this Rule, because it does not regulate procedure. However, it probably does. The Court held in *Hanna* that a federal rule is "procedural" if it "really regulates procedure—the judicial process for enforcing rights and duties recognized by substantive law and for justly administering remedy and redress for disregard or infraction of them." *Hanna,* 380 U.S. at 464 (quoting from *Sibbach v. Wilson & Co.,* 312 U.S. 1, 14 (1941)). Under this broad definition, Rule 3.1 probably passes muster, since it governs the time within which a case may be filed, which certainly relates to the judicial process.

However, even if this Rule is "procedural" under 28 U.S.C. § 2072(a), it probably modifies substantive rights under § 2072(b). The time available to bring an action is closely tied to the existence of the right itself. In Ely's analysis, it serves a "non-procedural purpose" to provide defendants peace of mind after a certain date that a lawsuit will not be filed. Ely, *supra,* 87 Harv. L. Rev. at 726–27. Very likely, this Rule would run afoul of the substantive rights proviso, leading the Court to invalidate the Rule. Thus, **B** is the best answer.

D is wrong. While the Rule would be in direct conflict with the state limitations period, it would not be valid if it abridged a substantive right. Indeed, during the debates over the enactment of the REA, limitations periods were repeatedly cited as examples of substantive rights that should not be subject to Court rulemaking.

If you review the two questions based on *Guaranty Trust* in this chapter (pp. 934, n.7, and 944, n.4), you will see that a separate limitations period for diversity cases would probably not pass muster if it were a matter of judicial practice, since it would fail the "modified outcome-determinative" analysis of *Hanna* Part I. It would probably also fail if enacted as a Federal Rule, since it would run afoul of the "substantive rights" provision in § 2072(b). However, such a provision would likely be valid and preempt state law if Congress enacted it, since (while it does affect state rights) it has a procedural purpose. Wisely, Congress has not chosen to interfere with state rights by adopting a limitations period for state law claims adjudicated in federal court.

5. Substance or procedure? ***Shady Grove Orthopedic Associates, P.A. v. Allstate Ins. Co.*, 559 U.S. 393 (2010).** This case illustrates how difficult it can be to apply the Rules Enabling Act analysis of *Hanna* and *Walker* to a close case.

The facts of *Shady Grove*. The plaintiff in *Shady Grove*, a health care provider, brought a class action lawsuit in federal court against Allstate Insurance Company, claiming that Allstate had delayed paying claims and failed to pay statutory interest due on such late payments under New York law. (The statute set the interest rate on delayed payments at 2 percent per month. Doubtless, this high rate was intended to encourage prompt payment of claims.) Shady Grove's individual claim was small—perhaps about $500. A provider would not be likely to sue for that individually—the cost of litigating the claim would exceed the recovery. However, a class action on behalf of all similarly situated providers would be worth litigating: The total recovery on behalf of the class of providers might reach $5 million. Many lawyers would gladly pursue a class action for a percentage of that recovery.

Federal Rule 23 authorizes class actions in federal court if certain criteria are met. New York law also authorizes class actions, but the New York class action statute bars class actions to enforce a penalty—and the statutory interest at issue in *Shady Grove* was viewed as a penalty. The apparent purpose of New York's ban on class actions to collect penalties is that a class action in which the penalty is collected for all members of the class can lead to "excessively harsh results" for the defendant. 559 U.S. at 444 (Ginsburg, J., dissenting). Federal Rule 23 has no similar restriction on class actions that seek penalty damages. Thus, Federal Rule 23 authorizes the case to proceed as a class action but New York law would not. Hence the *Erie* problem, or, more accurately, the *Hanna* problem. Did applying Federal Rule 23 "abridge, enlarge or modify" a substantive right under New York law?

The plurality opinion. Justice Scalia's plurality opinion addressed the three key questions that determine the applicability of a Federal Rule of Civil Procedure under *Hanna* and *Walker*.

First. Is there a direct conflict between Rule 23 and New York law? Justice Scalia's plurality opinion starts by asking whether Rule 23 applies to the case: the "direct conflict" question analyzed in *Walker v. Armco*. He concludes that it does apply—it authorizes class action litigation in all kinds of cases including Shady Grove's claim. Justice Scalia also concludes that Rule 23 conflicts with New York's rule barring class actions for penalties. Federal Rule 23 says you can bring a class action if certain criteria are satisfied, while N.Y. Civ. Prac. Ann. § 901(b) says you cannot bring a class action to recover a penalty.

> The central difficulty is that even artificial narrowing cannot render § 901(b) compatible with Rule 23. Whatever the policies they pursue, they flatly contradict each other. Allstate asserts (and the dissent implies), that we can (and must) interpret Rule 23 in a manner that avoids overstepping its authorizing statute. If the Rule were susceptible of two meanings—one that would violate § 2072(b) and another that would not—we would agree. But it is not. Rule 23 unambiguously authorizes any plaintiff, in any federal civil proceeding, to maintain a class action if the Rule's prerequisites are met. We cannot contort its text, even to avert a collision with state law that might render it invalid. What the dissent's approach achieves is not the avoiding of a "conflict between Rule 23 and § 901(b)," but rather the invalidation of Rule 23

> (pursuant to § 2072(b) of the Rules Enabling Act) to the extent that it conflicts with the substantive policies of § 901. There is no other way to reach the dissent's destination. We must therefore confront head on whether Rule 23 falls within the statutory authorization.

559 U.S. at 405–06.

This seems clear, but it isn't to Justice Ginsburg and her co-dissenters. Her opinion argues that the scope of Rule 23 must be construed with sensitivity to state interests. She argues that New York sought to achieve a substantive purpose in § 901(b)—to avoid excessive imposition of penalties. Justice Ginsburg argues that Rule 23 can be construed to avoid a conflict (as Rule 3 was in *Walker*) if it is read to establish criteria for a class action where one is allowed, but not to create a blanket right to use the class action device even if state law would bar it for a particular claim. *Id.* at 1445. In view of the purpose of New York's ban on penalty class actions, and the impact that allowing a class action under Rule 23 will have on the parties' substantive rights, she would avoid the conflict by interpreting Rule 23 more narrowly. Since she finds Federal Rule 23 inapplicable, she turns in her dissent to *Hanna* Part I's modified outcome-determinative test and finds that ignoring New York's limit would be improper under both prongs of that analysis. 559 U.S. at 456–58.

Second. Is Rule 23 valid under the first subsection of the REA? Justice Scalia then addresses the validity of Rule 23 under 28 U.S.C. § 2072(a), the first subsection of the Rules Enabling Act. Applying *Hanna's* test, he concludes that it does:

> We have long held that this limitation means that the Rule must "really regulat[e] procedure,—the judicial process for enforcing rights and duties recognized by substantive law and for justly administering remedy and redress for disregard or infraction of them," *Sibbach,* 312 U.S., at 14. The test is not whether the rule affects a litigant's substantive rights; most procedural rules do. What matters is what the rule itself *regulates*: If it governs only "the manner and the means" by which the litigants' rights are "enforced," it is valid; if it alters "the rules of decision by which [the] court will adjudicate [those] rights," it is not.
>
> ....
>
> Applying that criterion, we think it obvious that rules allowing multiple claims (and claims by or against multiple parties) to be litigated together are also valid. *See, e.g.,* Fed. Rules Civ. Proc. 18 (joinder of claims), 20 (joinder of parties), 42(a) (consolidation of actions). Such rules neither change plaintiffs' separate entitlements to relief nor abridge defendants' rights; they alter only how the claims are processed. For the same reason, Rule 23—at least insofar as it allows willing plaintiffs to join their separate claims against the same defendants in a class action—falls within § 2072(b)'s authorization. A class action, no less than traditional joinder (of which it is a species), merely enables a federal court to adjudicate claims of multiple parties at once, instead of in separate suits. And like traditional joinder, it leaves the parties' legal rights and duties intact and the rules of decision unchanged.

559 U.S. at 408.

Third. Does Rule 23 "abridge, enlarge or modify" a substantive right under New York law? This would seem to be the toughest issue in *Shady Grove*. However, Justice Scalia's opinion disposes of the question almost as an afterthought:

> The fundamental difficulty with both these arguments is that the substantive nature of New York's law, or its substantive purpose, *makes no difference.* A Federal Rule of Procedure is not valid in some jurisdictions and invalid in others—or valid in some cases and invalid in others—depending upon whether its effect is to frustrate a state substantive law (or a state procedural law enacted for substantive purposes). . . . *Hanna* unmistakably expressed the same understanding that compliance of a Federal Rule with the Enabling Act is to be assessed by consulting the Rule itself, and not its effects in individual applications:
>
>> "[T]he court has been instructed to apply the Federal Rule, and can refuse to do so only if the Advisory Committee, this Court, and Congress erred in their prima facie judgment that the Rule in question transgresses neither the terms of the Enabling Act nor constitutional restrictions."
>
> 380 U.S., at 471. In sum, it is not the substantive or procedural nature or purpose of the affected state law that matters, but the substantive or procedural nature of the Federal Rule. We have held since *Sibbach,* and reaffirmed repeatedly, that the validity of a Federal Rule depends entirely upon whether it regulates procedure. If it does, it is authorized by § 2072 and is valid in all jurisdictions, with respect to all claims, regardless of its incidental effect upon state-created rights.

559 U.S. at 409–10.

Here, Justice Scalia's analysis is less convincing. He suggests that Rule 23 is valid as long as it regulates procedure. But that is the § 2072(a) analysis. Section 2072(b) requires a second step: Does the Rule (if authorized under § 2072(a) because it regulates procedure) unduly affect substantive rights? Here, Scalia's reasoning appears to fall back on the conclusory pronouncement that Rule 23 "leaves the parties' legal rights and duties intact and the rules of decision unchanged." 559 U.S. at 408.

This analysis skirts the key question. As Justice Ginsburg argues in dissent, "New York's decision to block class-action proceedings for statutory damages makes scant sense, except as a means to a manifestly substantive end: Limiting a defendant's liability in a single lawsuit in order to prevent the exorbitant inflation of penalties—remedies the New York Legislature created with individual suits in mind." 559 U.S. at 445 (Ginsburg, J., dissenting). Why does allowing the class action to proceed in federal court not modify that substantive right?

Ultimately both Justices' positions have problems. Justice Scalia's approach can be criticized as interfering with New York's policy to avoid excessive penalty judgments. Justice Ginsburg's must deal with the fact that Rule 23 directly addresses the certification question, clearly a procedural issue, and the fact that the New York statute bars penalty class actions even if the underlying claims in those cases are not based on New York law. (It hardly seems that New York can define the "substance" of rights under federal law or other states' law.)

6. Justice Stevens's concurrence? Justice Stevens, concurring in the judgment, takes issue with both the plurality and the dissent. He criticizes Scalia's opinion for focusing solely on the § 2072(a) analysis (whether the Federal Rule "really regulates procedure") without adequately considering the § 2072(b) issue (whether the Rule abridges, enlarges or modifies a substantive right). He criticizes Ginsburg's dissent for avoiding the hard part of the Rules Enabling Act analysis by denying the existence of a conflict between the Federal Rule and state law whenever a conflict would pose a tough choice. "The dissent would apply the Rules of Decision Act inquiry under *Erie* [and *Hanna* Part I] even to cases in which there is a governing federal rule, and thus the [Rules of Decision] Act, by its own terms, does not apply." 559 U.S. at 431.

Because Justice Stevens concludes that Rule 23 "squarely governed" the question of class certification, he goes on to consider whether applying Rule 23 will abridge or modify a substantive right. He concludes that "the bar for finding an Enabling Act problem is a high one" and finds little evidence that § 901(b) was enacted to restrict substantive rights. *Id.* at 432. "The mere possibility that a federal rule would alter a state-created right is not sufficient. There must be little doubt." *Id.* After assessing both prongs of the REA analysis, he casts his vote with the plurality, upholding application of Rule 23.

V. Substance and Procedure: Summary of Basic Principles

- The *Erie* doctrine reflects the constitutional division of powers between the states and the federal government. *Erie* held that federal courts may not make substantive law in areas not delegated to the federal government. None of the post-*Erie* decisions reviewed in this chapter retreats from this fundamental position.
- Thus, federal courts must apply state rules of substantive law in cases not governed by federal law. In many cases, the courts have little trouble applying this principle, because the issues involved are clearly substantive, such as the existence of duty in a tort case, the adequacy of consideration for a contract, or the validity of a mortgage.
- Other rules used in litigation, such as statutes of limitations, cannot be definitively classified as "substantive" or "procedural" because they serve both substantive and procedural purposes. In determining whether state law must be applied in these borderline situations, the Supreme Court has developed an analysis that starts by asking whether the federal practice that is challenged is established by the Constitution, federal statute, Federal Rule, or judicial practice.
- If the rule applied in federal court is mandated by a federal statute, the Supremacy Clause requires the court to apply that statute, unless it is beyond Congress's power to enact. *Hanna* holds that Congress has power to enact legislation governing federal court practice that "regulate matters

which, though falling within the uncertain area between substance and procedure, are rationally capable of classification as either." This suggests that any federal statute with a procedural purpose will apply in the face of contrary state procedure.

- If a federal practice found in a Federal Rule of Civil Procedure directly conflicts with state law, the analysis is under the Rules Enabling Act. That Act delegates Congress's power to regulate federal court procedure to the Supreme Court in very broad terms. Virtually any Rule that deals with the administration of litigation will satisfy the broad test of 28 U.S.C. § 2072(a), as a rule governing practice and procedure.
- Under the enigmatic proviso in § 2072(b), the Rules must not "abridge, enlarge or modify any substantive right." A Rule that addresses a procedural issue is presumptively valid, but may be challenged if it interferes significantly with state or federal substantive rights. The Court has not established a clear test for when such interference will be found.
- If the approach taken in federal court is a matter of judicial practice (not a federal statute or Federal Rule), *Hanna v. Plumer* requires the court to consider the impact that ignoring state law will have on the case. If using a different rule in federal court would lead to forum shopping or significantly different litigation opportunity, the federal court should apply the state rule to further the policy of uniform outcomes in diversity cases in state and federal court.

PART IX

Trial and Pretrial

26

Pretrial Case Management

I. Introduction

David sues Goliath for assault. Goliath files a timely answer. What happens next? David serves interrogatories on Goliath. Goliath answers a few, but objects to most of them. What happens next? Discovery enters its third year. Goliath takes a deposition. What happens next?

The answers to these questions are the same: *nothing*. The American adversary process was historically party-driven and self-regulating; the judge's role was passive until one of the parties asked her to do something by filing a motion. Judges and their clerks have enough to do without searching the docket for more (although they will dismiss a case on their own initiative if the plaintiff is inactive for too long). *See* Fed. R. Civ. P. 41(b) (providing for involuntary dismissal "[i]f the plaintiff fails to prosecute").

But heavy dockets and the costs of litigation have created pressure for judges to play a more active role in managing civil litigation. We saw in the chapter on discovery tools that in most federal cases, the court is required to enter a scheduling order after receiving the parties' report or consulting with them at a scheduling conference. Fed. R. Civ. P. 16(b)(1). Such an order may itself schedule subsequent pretrial conferences. Many courts have adopted local rules and individual judges have issued "standing orders" requiring such conferences and addressing other aspects of case management. Moreover, before a case goes to trial, the court will commonly hold a pretrial conference to identify the issues for trial, make pretrial rulings on the admissibility of evidence, discuss the order of trial, and, sometimes, explore settlement.

The authority in federal court for such case management by pretrial conference and pretrial orders is chiefly Rule 16, which we explore in section II. Under that Rule, the final pretrial order typically controls the course of trial. It may list the claims or defenses that will be litigated there or identify the witnesses each side will call. If a witness is not listed in the final pretrial order, the court may exclude that witness from testifying at trial. Section III discusses final pretrial orders and their exclusionary effect.

II. General Pretrial Authority

A federal judge has the authority to issue scheduling orders. But what else can she do to manage civil cases? Rule 16(c)(2) identifies "matters for consideration" at pretrial conferences, but how far can the judge go to order the parties to attend, "consider," and, even more, resolve or agree on such matters?

STANDING ORDER ON PRE-TRIAL CONFERENCES IN NORTHERN DIVISION CIVIL [S.D. Ill.]

. . .

III. A FINAL pre-trial conference will be scheduled by the Court as soon as feasible after the date set for completion of discovery.

A. Notice of such final pre-trial conference will be given to all counsel in sufficient time, customarily not less than ten days, so that they may, AND THEY ARE HEREBY DIRECTED TO CONFER IN ADVANCE of much [sic] pre-trial conference for the following purposes:

1. Explore carefully the prospects of settlement.
2. Enter into a written stipulation or statement of all uncontested facts....

B. AT SUCH FINAL PRE-TRIAL CONFERENCE, which shall be attended by attorneys, representing all parties who are authorized into [sic] enter into such agreements as may be appropriate, presumably the counsel who are to try the case, counsel SHALL SUBMIT to the Court the following:

1. The written stipulation or statement of the uncontested facts signed on behalf of all parties....

D. IMMEDIATELY FOLLOWING SUCH FINAL PRE-TRIAL CONFERENCE, an appropriate order will be prepared by an attorney for a plaintiff, unless otherwise agreed at the conference, reflecting the action taken and agreements made at such conference, in the general form attached hereto. Approval of such proposed order shall be obtained from counsel for all other parties by signature thereon, and such approved order will be entered by the Court upon submission, which should not be more than two weeks after the conference, unless otherwise agreed at the conference. The case will then be added to the Court's trial calendar. FAILURE OF COUNSEL TO APPEAR AT ANY SCHEDULED PRE-TRIAL CONFERENCE OR OTHERWISE TO COMPLY WITH THE PROVISIONS OF THIS ORDER MAY RESULT IN DISMISSAL OR DEFAULT AS MAY BE APPROPRIATE.

IV. The Court finds that strict compliance with this procedure, generally followed in this Division since September, 1967, is important to the prompt, orderly, and fair disposition of cases; and counsel will be expected to comply therewith in the interest of sound administration of justice. THE COURT HENCEFORTH WILL NOT HESITATE TO IMPOSE THE SANCTIONS MENTIONED FOR WILLFUL OR CARELESS FAILURE OF STRICT COMPLIANCE BY COUNSEL....

[*J.F. Edwards Constr. Co. v. Anderson Safeway Guard Rail Corp.*, 542 F.2d 1318, 1326–28 (7th Cir. 1976).]

Figure 26–1: EXCERPT FROM A STANDING PRETRIAL ORDER IN *EDWARDS CONSTR. CO.*

READING J.F. EDWARDS CONSTRUCTION CO. v. ANDERSON SAFEWAY GUARD RAIL CORP. Rule 83(b) provides that "[a] judge may regulate practice in any manner consistent with federal law, [the Federal Rules of Civil Procedure and Federal Rules of Evidence], and the district's local rules." In the following case, the trial judge used that authority to issue a "Standing Order on Pre-Trial Conferences" governing pretrial conferences in his court, the relevant parts of which are shown in Figure 26-1. A "standing order" applies to all cases in that court (while a specific order would be directed just to a particular case).

The trial judge held a pretrial conference. At the conference, he ordered the parties to file a stipulation of facts pursuant to the Standing Order. By stipulating, a party agrees to treat the matter stipulated as an undisputed fact for purposes of the action. When defendant Anderson refused to agree to the other parties' proposed stipulations, the court struck its pleadings, dismissed its claims, and entered judgment against it.

- Why did the court order the parties to confer about stipulations?
- Does Rule 16 require parties to confer, if the court so orders at a pretrial conference?
- Does Rule 16 require the parties to stipulate?
- Did the Standing Order require the parties to stipulate? If it had, would such an order be authorized under the Federal Rules?

J.F. EDWARDS CONSTRUCTION CO. v. ANDERSON SAFEWAY GUARD RAIL CORP.

542 F.2d 1318 (7th Cir. 1976)

Before CASTLE, Senior Circuit Judge, CUMMINGS and PELL, Circuit Judges.

PER CURIAM.

[EDS.—J.F. Edwards Construction Company sued Anderson Safeway Guard Rail Corporation for damages arising out of a construction project, and Anderson separately sued Westinghouse for damages arising out of the same project. The two federal actions were consolidated. In the consolidated action, Anderson asserted various claims and claims were made against it. At this conference, pursuant to the district court's Standing Order on Pre-Trial Conferences (see Figure 26-1) the parties were directed to file a stipulation of facts by July 1, 1975, and a pretrial order by August 1, 1975, each to be signed by the respective parties. Edwards and Westinghouse agreed to a stipulation, but, after much give and take, including Edwards's deletion of some proposed stipulated facts by Anderson, Anderson balked.]

On January 29, Anderson's counsel wrote the trial judge amplifying Anderson's reasons for refusing to sign the stipulation. Anderson's counsel maintained that Edwards' counsel had deleted 19 specified matters from the stipulation of facts supposedly agreed upon December 22, thus causing Anderson's counsel to refuse to execute the stipulation of facts. However, he stated that he would be amenable *"once again* to resolve these matters in a reasonable, prudent, and professional manner."

On January 28, Edwards and Westinghouse filed a motion requesting the district court to enter an order striking Anderson's pleadings and for other relief....

On February 9, 1976, Judge Morgan also took the following actions:

1. All Anderson's pleadings were stricken.
2. Judgment was entered for Edwards on Anderson's counter-claim.
3. Anderson's complaint against Westinghouse was dismissed.
4. Judgment was entered against Anderson on Edwards' complaint "subject to jury verdict on the dollar amount of damages proven in *ex parte* proceedings."
5. Westinghouse's cross-complaint against Anderson was dismissed as moot.

... On the next day, the district court permitted a jury to render an ex parte verdict against Anderson in the sum of $89,018.66 after hearing the testimony of John F. Edwards, Sr., the chairman of the board of Edwards. Anderson's motion to vacate judgments, for a new trial and other relief was denied on February 24 and its notice of appeal was filed on March 11....

In supporting the district judge's draconian orders against Anderson, Edwards and Westinghouse rely primarily on Rule 16 of the Federal Rules of Civil Procedure, Rule 10 of the Rules of the United States District Court for the Southern District of Illinois (Local Rule 10), and the trial court's Standing Order on Pre-Trial Conferences in Northern Division Civil Cases (Standing Order). Rule 16 permits a trial court to direct attorneys for the parties to appear before it for a pre-trial conference to consider five prescribed matters and "(s)uch other matters as may aid in the disposition of the action." Under this catch-all clause and paragraph 3 of Rule 16 **[Eds.—now Rule 16(c)(2)(C)]**, Judge Morgan was clearly within his rights in asking counsel for the three parties to try to stipulate all possible facts. By all means, such stipulations should be encouraged. Yet, on the other hand, nothing in Rule 16 empowers a court to compel the parties to stipulate facts. Similarly, Local Rule 10 does not make it mandatory to stipulate facts.

... Two sections of the Standing Order deal with stipulations of facts in the context of a pre-trial conference. Section III(A)(2), in pertinent part, directs counsel to confer in advance of the pre-trial conference for the purpose of entering into a written stipulation or statement of all uncontested facts. Counsel for the parties complied with this provision by attempting to arrive at a mutually acceptable stipulation. Anderson's counsel submitted its stipulation of facts to Westinghouse and Edwards, whose counsel refused to agree thereto. Earlier, Edwards had submitted a stipulation of facts to which Westinghouse agreed but Anderson did not. It is most unfortunate that counsel for the three parties could not at least agree to stipulate to some facts, but Section III(A)(2) only requires the parties to confer for the purpose of generating stipulations and this the parties clearly did.

Section III(B)(1) of the Standing Order, however, does require counsel to submit "(t)he written statement ... of the uncontested facts signed on behalf of all parties" at the final pre-trial conference. To the extent that this language can be read to mandate that stipulations of facts must be made, it may not stand. On its face, Rule 16 of the Federal Rules of Civil Procedure does not authorize a court to force parties to stipulate facts to which they will not voluntarily agree. Under Rule 83 of the Federal Rules, the district court's Local Rule 10 and its Standing Order must be consistent with the Federal Rules of Civil Procedure. As noted in this case, the parties could not agree on a final stipulation of uncontested facts. Of course, counsel should have been more tractable and stipulated all possible facts to shorten the trial instead of being so intransigent in their respective positions. Yet even in this posture, the Standing Order cannot authorize sanctions which are not explicitly authorized by the Federal Rules. As Moore's Treatise notes, a pre-trial conference may save time and expense "perhaps by leading the parties to stipulate that certain documents will be produced or desired information furnished" (3 Moore's *Federal Practice*, ¶ 16.16, at 1126 (2d ed. 1974)), but we have been cited to no authorities showing that a district court has the power to force parties to stipulate facts unless they can agree on the same....

Behind the face of Rule 16, a narrowly circumscribed area of power has developed which the judge may employ to compel obedience to his requests and demands relating to the pre-trial conference. This power may be founded either upon Rule 41(b) or upon the inherent power of courts to manage their calendars to have an orderly and expeditious disposition of their cases. *Link v. Wabash R.R. Co.*, [370 U.S. 626, 629–32 (1962)]. Whatever the exact genesis of this power to compel obedience, the key is a failure to prosecute, whether styled as a failure to appear at a pre-trial conference, failure to file a pre-trial statement, failure to prepare for the conference or failure to comply with the pre-trial order. Therefore Rule 41(b), dealing with involuntary dismissals, and the inherent power of district courts[,] do not support the sanctions imposed.

Obstreperous as the parties' refusal to reduce at least some facts to a stipulation might be, Anderson cannot be characterized as dilatory to the point of manifesting a failure to prosecute....

While we sympathize with the district court's distress at having to face a trial where the parties had not agreed upon any stipulation of facts, Edwards and Westinghouse have not convinced us that the sanctions imposed upon Anderson were permissible. Although Anderson did not agree to the Edwards-Westinghouse stipulation of facts, it did propose its own stipulation of facts and pre-trial order, and on December 22 agreed upon a stipulation of facts, which Edwards' counsel later revised in terms unacceptable to Anderson. On October 3, all parties signed a pre-trial order prepared by Anderson and then submitted it to the court. In view of the continuing contretemps between counsel, the famous Shakespearean stricture, "A plague on both your houses"[11] seems singularly apt....

---

11. Shakespeare, *Romeo and Juliet*, Act III, Scene i.

To recapitulate, Rule 16 of the Federal Rules of Civil Procedure does not compel a stipulation of facts, so that sanctions for failure to file one are not available. Of course a trial court must have the power to make effective a pre-trial order within the four corners of Rule 16, but an order forcing parties to stipulate facts is not authorized by that rule. As the reporter of the Supreme Court's Advisory Committee on the Rules of Civil Procedure has written,

> "So the proper function of pre-trial is not to club the parties or one of them into submission. Rather the function is to see that the parties and the court are fully acquainted with the case, leaving no room for the tactic of surprise attack or defense, and to uncover and record the points of agreement between the parties all to the end of shortening and simplifying the eventual trial. Note the emphasis of Rule 16 upon 'the agreements made by the parties as to any of the matters considered'; there is here no basis for forcing the parties to replead or restate their legal propositions in terms more limited than the issues framed by the pleadings. Pre-trial, in purpose and in its most successful use, is informational and factual, rather than legal and coercive. It may well lead to settlement as the parties come to know their case better, but that must remain an uncoerced by-product."

Clark, *To an Understanding Use of Pre-Trial*, 29 F.R.D. 454, 456 (1961)....

While we applaud Judge Morgan's assiduous efforts to produce an agreed-upon stipulation of facts, under the Federal Rules of Civil Procedure judicial compulsion is not allowable in this area. Since we must hold that Anderson's failure to agree to the Edwards-Westinghouse stipulation of facts did not justify dismissal of its complaint against Westinghouse, it follows that it was improper to enter judgment for Edwards on Anderson's counterclaim and against Anderson on Edwards' amended complaint. Anderson's pleadings having been improperly stricken, it was also erroneous to dismiss Westinghouse's cross-complaint against Anderson as moot....

... The order on the motion to strike pleadings and the judgments of February 9 and 10, 1976, are vacated, and the cause is remanded for trial pursuant to Circuit Rule 18.[14]

Notes and Questions: Pretrial Purposes and Authority

1. Why stipulations? The answer is suggested by the Standing Order. It directs the parties to confer in advance of a final pretrial conference for the purpose of entering into written stipulations of "all uncontested facts." The purpose of trial

14. If further discovery or other pre-trial matters remain to be completed, the next trial judge should attempt to control any undue rigidity of counsel for any of the parties. Sanctions are often available to counter pre-trial recalcitrance, even though not authorized for failure to agree on a stipulation of facts.

is to try disputed facts. If the parties can agree—"stipulate"—to undisputed facts, it leaves less to be tried and may shorten the trial. Similarly, if they can agree to the conditions for the admission of some evidence—such as the qualification of an expert to testify or the authenticity of a document—that would also shorten the trial. A good part of the final pretrial conference is directed toward streamlining trial and making it more efficient. Stipulations are one streamlining device; identification of the issues and of expected trial witnesses is another.

2. Other purposes of pretrial conferences. While *Edwards* is concerned with those provisions of the Standing Order that applied to the final pretrial conference, Rule 16 is more expansive. After stating five broad purposes of pretrial conferences, primarily aimed at what Rule 1 calls "speedy, and inexpensive determination" of an action, the Rule lists no less than sixteen "matters for consideration," which provide a pretty thorough survey of what pretrial management may involve. *See* Fed. R. Civ. P. 16(c)(2).

Q **3. Requiring parties to confer (or attend).** Could the court require the parties or their lawyers in *Edwards* to attend a pretrial conference?

A The Standing Order certainly assumes so, for it shouts that "FAILURE OF COUNSEL TO APPEAR AT ANY SCHEDULED PRE-TRIAL CONFERENCE . . . MAY RESULT IN DISMISSAL OR DEFAULT AS MAY BE APPROPRIATE." Rule 16 originally stated that "the court may in its discretion direct the attorneys for the parties to appear before it for a conference. . . ." Now Rule 16(f) not only authorizes sanctions "if a party or its attorney fails to appear at a scheduling or other pretrial conference," but also if the party appears but is "substantially unprepared to participate—or does not participate in good faith—at the conference." Rule 16(f)(1)(A)–(B).

Q **4. Requiring stipulations?** If a lawyer can be ordered to attend a pretrial conference and to confer in advance about stipulations, why can't she be ordered to stipulate?

A First, the Standing Order did not go so far. While it said that the lawyers "SHALL SUBMIT . . . [t]he written stipulation" of the parties, this arguably only requires submission *if there is a stipulation.* Second, had the Order required a stipulation, it would have gone too far, well beyond Rule 16. The version of Rule 16 then in effect referred just to "the *possibility of obtaining admissions of fact and of documents* which will avoid unnecessary proof." Rule 16(c)(3) (emphasis added). Even the more ambitious amended Rule that has since been adopted lists "stipulations about facts and documents to avoid unnecessary proof" simply as a "matter[] for consideration" and not as a binding requirement. Rule 16(c)(2)(C). Because a Standing Order that mandates stipulations would be inconsistent with Rule 16 itself, it would be invalid. Just as local rules must be consistent with the Federal Rules, so must standing orders or specific orders regulating practice before a particular judge, according to Rule 83. See the discussion of hierarchy of authorities in Chapter 2.

The reason that Rule 16 does not require stipulations was well stated by Judge Clark, the father of the Federal Rules. The purpose of pretrial is to acquaint the parties and the court with the issues, to uncover points of agreement, and thus to shorten and simplify an eventual trial, not "to club the parties . . . into submission." Clark, *supra*, 29 F.R.D. at 456. If pretrial management is handled diplomatically and creatively by the judge or magistrate, a by-product can be a streamlined trial, or even settlement, but that by-product must remain "uncoerced." To put it differently, Anderson had a right to try the facts it disputed and could not be forced to stipulate to them.

5. Requiring settlement? The same reasoning—that Anderson has a right to try disputes of fact—supports the conclusion that a court cannot use the pretrial process as a club to force a party to settle its case. To be sure, the Rule clearly identifies "facilitating settlement" as a purpose of pretrial and even makes consideration of alternative dispute resolution ("ADR") procedures proper in some cases. But it does no more; no party can be forced to settle rather than try its dispute.

6. Management by magistrate. So far we have assumed that the case is managed by the trial judge. Federal district court judges are appointed under Article III for life. A life appointment gives the litigants before a federal judge some assurance of her independence, though of course no guarantee.

In practice, however, federal district court judges often assign pretrial case management—primarily the management of discovery—to magistrate judges. Magistrate judges are also federal judges, but they are appointed only for eight-year terms. Although every magistrate judge also tries to make independent decisions, a term appointment does not provide the same assurance of independence that a life appointment provides. Theoretically, then, if magistrate judges were allowed to make the same decisions in civil actions as Article III judges, parties to the actions could be denied a measure of the independence that the Article III life appointment was intended to promote.

As a result, Congress has tried to limit the kinds of decisions that can be assigned to magistrate judges. First, it forbid magistrate judges from trying cases unless all the parties consent. *See* 28 U.S.C. § 636(c); Fed. R. Civ. P. 73. Second, it provided that

> (A) [a federal] judge may designate a magistrate judge to hear and determine any pretrial matter pending before the court, except a motion for injunctive relief, for judgment on the pleadings, for summary judgment, . . . to dismiss or to permit maintenance of a class action, to dismiss for failure to state a claim upon which relief can be granted, and to involuntarily dismiss an action. A judge of the court may reconsider any pretrial matter under this subparagraph (A) where it has been shown that the magistrate judge's order is clearly erroneous or contrary to law.

28 U.S.C. § 636(b)(1)(A). The trial judge, however, can assign the excepted motions to the magistrate for the magistrate's *recommendations*, which the trial judge can accept or reject. *Id.* § 636(b)(1)(B)–(C). Thus, the statute distinguishes between ordinary pretrial matters, which a magistrate can decide subject only to review (on objection by a party) by the district court judge for clear error or mistake of

law, and certain motions for which a magistrate judge may only *recommend* a decision, and the district court judge is free to accept or reject. Federal Rule 72 therefore also distinguishes between the former, which it calls "nondispositive matters," and the latter, which it calls "dispositive motions."

III. The Effect of the Pretrial Order

As the final pretrial conference approaches, the court may require the parties to exchange final pretrial briefs, identifying their claims and defenses, identifying issues to be tried, listing proposed witnesses and exhibits, and objecting to the opposing parties' witnesses and exhibits. The court will often craft a final pretrial order on the basis of these briefs and the final pretrial conference, constituting "a trial plan, including a plan to facilitate the admission of evidence." Fed. R. Civ. P. 16(e). The final pretrial order supersedes the pleadings (which may well have contained claims or defenses that the parties have decided to drop after discovery) and can be modified "only to prevent manifest injustice." *Id.*

READING *DAVEY v. LOCKHEED MARTIN CORP.* In the following employment discrimination case, the defendant sought to modify the final pretrial order to add an affirmative defense of "good faith compliance" on the Friday before a Monday trial.

- Why did the trial court refuse to modify the pretrial order?
- What was the effect of the trial court's refusal?
- How could the trial court have addressed its concern about the eleventh-hour addition of the affirmative defense without excluding the defense?

DAVEY v. LOCKHEED MARTIN CORP.

301 F.3d 1204 (10th Cir. 2002)

Briscoe, Circuit Judge.

Susan Davey brought this employment discrimination action against her former employer, Lockheed Martin Corporation (LMC), alleging LMC discriminated against her on the basis of gender and retaliated against her for complaining about the discrimination when LMC selected her for layoff during a reduction in force.... **[Eds.—A jury trial resulted in a verdict in favor of Davey on one of her retaliation claims]**. In accordance with the jury's verdict, the district court awarded Davey compensatory damages of $50,000 and punitive damages of $200,000, and further entered judgment in favor of Davey for back pay of $112,800, front pay of $36,000, and attorney fees of $65,610, plus pre-judgment and post-judgment interest.

LMC appeals the verdict in favor of Davey on the ... retaliation claim, contending ... the district court erroneously denied it the opportunity to present a material aspect of its case to the jury, which led to an unfair award of punitive damages....

II.

As regards the punitive damages award, LMC contends the district court erred in not allowing LMC to present a material aspect of its case to the jury—good faith compliance with Title VII. On Friday, August 20, 1999, the parties filed an amended pretrial order to reflect several additions, but were unable to agree on one addition—whether LMC could assert the affirmative defense that it could not be liable for punitive damages because it made a good faith effort to comply with Title VII. According to LMC, the newly-proposed affirmative defense was based on the recent decision in *Kolstad v. American Dental Assoc.*, 527 U.S. 526 (1999). The amended pretrial order was filed with a space for the trial court to mark whether it granted or denied LMC's request to add the affirmative defense. At the beginning of trial on Monday, August 23, 1999, prior to selection of the jury, the court stated it would not allow LMC to assert that it made a good faith effort to comply with Title VII as a defense to punitive damages because allowing the defense would be "fundamentally unfair to the plaintiff." The court noted that the defense was factually intensive and "the plaintiff did not have an opportunity during the discovery phase of the case to take discovery as to whether or not there's a response to that defense."

A pretrial order, which measures the dimensions of the lawsuit, both in the trial court and on appeal, may be modified "only to prevent manifest injustice." Fed. R. Civ. P. 16(e). The party moving to amend the order bears the burden to prove the manifest injustice that would otherwise occur. *See Koch v. Koch Indus., Inc.*, 203 F.3d 1202, 1222 (10th Cir. 2000). The purpose of the pretrial order is to "insure the economical and efficient trial of every case on its merits without chance or surprise." *See Hull v. Chevron U.S.A., Inc.*, 812 F.2d 584, 588 (10th Cir. 1987). Because the issues and defenses of the lawsuit are defined by the terms of the order, "total inflexibility is undesirable." *Id.*

We review the denial of a motion to amend a pretrial order for an abuse of discretion. A district court can abuse its discretion when it "bases its ruling on an erroneous conclusion of law," *Kiowa Indian Tribe v. Hoover*, 150 F.3d 1163, 1165 (10th Cir. 1998), or "fails to consider the applicable legal standard," *Ohlander v. Larson*, 114 F.3d 1531, 1537 (10th Cir. 1997)....

... *Kolstad* was decided two months prior to commencement of this trial. The original pretrial order was filed a year and a half prior to the *Kolstad* decision. As stated, the district court did not allow LMC the benefit of the *Kolstad* defense because Davey had not had the opportunity to conduct discovery on the issue and, therefore, allowing the defense would be "fundamentally unfair" to plaintiff. We consider the following factors in a challenge to a district court's denial of a motion to amend the pretrial order and resulting exclusion of an issue:

"(1) prejudice or surprise to the party opposing trial of the issue; (2) the ability of that party to cure any prejudice; (3) disruption by inclusion of the new issue; and (4) bad faith by the party seeking to modify the order." *Koch*, 203 F.3d at 1222. We also take into consideration the timeliness of the movant's motion to amend the order. *See id.* at 1223.

Prejudice/Surprise/Timeliness

The district court's denial of LMC's proposed amendment rested entirely on prejudice to Davey. Davey argues the district court's decision was correct because the request was contained in the amendments to the pretrial order filed on the Friday before trial was to begin the following Monday and she could not have conducted any meaningful discovery over the weekend while also preparing for the trial. LMC responds that Davey could have moved to continue the trial.

In *Moss v. Feldmeyer*, 979 F.2d 1454 (10th Cir. 1992), this court affirmed the district court's admission of testimony from two expert witnesses either not listed or not fully described in the initial pretrial order. The district court permitted defendant to amend the pretrial order to add Dr. DeJong as an expert witness and to expand the scope of Dr. Evans' testimony on the morning of trial. The court reasoned that the opposing party, the plaintiff, was not prejudiced or surprised by the additions because

> both doctors were designated as witnesses in the [amended] pretrial order; Dr. DeJong was designated as an expert more than two weeks before the trial; [the plaintiff] received a summary of both doctors' reports prior to their trial testimony; both doctors were available for discovery prior to testifying; and [the plaintiff], at her option, deposed Dr. DeJong but did not depose Dr. Evans.

Id. at 1459. The court contrasted the facts in *Moss* with the facts in *Smith v. Ford Motor Co.*, 626 F.2d 784 (10th Cir. 1980), where the prejudice factor was found to weigh in favor of the opposing party. In *Smith*, the "surprise" testimony was presented *during* the trial. One of the plaintiff's witnesses, Dr. Freston, was listed in the pretrial order as a treating physician. However, to the defendant's surprise, Dr. Freston was allowed to give an expert opinion on the cause of the plaintiff's injury. Counsel for the defendant was granted only a ten-minute recess to prepare a cross-examination. Thus, we found that defendant was prejudiced by the new expert testimony. The court noted, however, that "[i]f Ford had been apprised in advance of Dr. Freston's testimony, it could have taken his deposition, discovered the article, and been well prepared at trial to cross-examine him." *Id.* at 798.

In *Summers v. Missouri Pacific R.R. System*, 132 F.3d 599, 604 (10th Cir. 1997), this court reversed the denial of a motion to amend a pretrial order to add an expert witness, relying on the fact that the motion was filed *prior* to trial and therefore, trial would not be disrupted. *See id.* at 605. Thus, the timing of the motion in relation to commencement of trial is an important element in analyzing whether the amendment would cause prejudice or surprise. Here, the amended pretrial order was filed on Friday, August 20, and trial was to begin the following Monday, August 23. Trial had not started and therefore could not have been disrupted. However, LMC's motion to amend was untimely given the two-month period that had elapsed between the filing of the *Kolstad* decision and the filing of LMC's motion to amend the pretrial order.

Ability to Cure

Closely related to the prejudice and surprise factor is whether the opposing party had the ability to cure any prejudice or surprise caused by the amendment. For example, in *Smith*, we found this factor weighed in favor of the defendant because after the witness gave "surprise" expert testimony, the defendant's counsel had only ten minutes to prepare for cross-examination and to review the witness' use of an empirical study not disclosed during discovery. *See Smith*, 626 F.2d at 798–99. If, however, the motion to amend is made *prior* to trial, it is more easily found that the opposing party could cure any prejudice. *See, e.g., Summers*, 132 F.3d at 605 (finding second factor weighed in favor of granting the plaintiff's motion to amend to add two expert witnesses because motion was filed eighty days prior to trial, giving the defendant time to conduct discovery). *See also, Moss*, 979 F.2d at 1459 (holding "whereas Ford had only [ten] minutes to prepare for cross-examination, Moss had over two weeks to prepare for Dr. DeJong's cross-examination and eight days to prepare for Dr. Evans' cross-examination, during which time, in each instance, Moss had their respective reports. Under these circumstances, we hold that Moss' ability to cure was not significantly impaired.").

LMC argues Davey easily could have cured any prejudice or surprise by moving to continue the trial. *See Hull v. Chevron U.S.A., Inc.*, 812 F.2d 584, 588 (10th Cir. 1987) (stating that if opposing party was surprised by new theory of recovery first discussed in plaintiff's opening statement, "it should have moved for a continuance of the trial with sufficient support to satisfy the trial court that additional time was needed to meet the change in theory"). Davey responds that a continuance would have prejudiced her because of the availability and fading memories of the witnesses. She reasons that she would "have been forced to choose between having the ability to obtain discovery on [the] new affirmative defense and having her case tried within three years of the date that she filed her complaint." . . .

Disruption

The third factor to be considered is whether the amendment to the pretrial order would "disrupt the orderly and efficient trial of the case or other cases in court." *Smith*, 626 F.2d at 797. In *Smith*, we concluded this factor did not weigh in favor of amending the pretrial order because the challenged testimony first was revealed in the midst of the trial. Adjournment of the trial for depositions would have resulted in significant disruption. However, if the motion to amend is made *prior* to trial, no disruption of an ongoing trial is threatened. *See, e.g., Moss*, 979 F.2d at 1459 (stating no disruption of trial threatened because additional expert witnesses and their respective reports were made available to plaintiff prior to their testimony). In this case, a continuance might have been necessary so Davey could conduct discovery on the *Kolstad* defense, but because the trial had not started when the motion to amend was made, disruption to the trial process would have been minimal. In its reply brief, LMC states that Davey had already deposed most of the witnesses who would have testified regarding LMC's good faith compliance with Title VII. Therefore, re-deposing these witnesses on the limited issue of good faith compliance would not have been a lengthy process. We acknowledge a continuance may have caused disruption of other cases scheduled for trial on the court's docket.

Bad Faith

Finally, the court must consider the "bad faith or willfulness in failing to comply with the court's order." *Smith*, 626 F.2d at 797. In this case, the district court, at the time of denying LMC's motion, stated "I'm not criticizing the defense because [*Kolstad*] wasn't issued until June [22], 1999." There is no evidence LMC acted with any bad faith or willful disregard of the order. Instead, it merely wanted to amend a pretrial order to reflect a defense recently set forth in a Supreme Court opinion.

While the untimeliness of LMC's motion weighs against LMC, the other factors weigh in favor of allowing LMC to amend the pretrial order to assert its defense to punitive damages. We conclude the district court abused its discretion in not allowing LMC to assert its defense and vacate the jury's punitive damage award and remand for new trial limited to the issue of punitive damages....

Notes and Questions: Final Pretrial Orders

Q **1. Reliance interests in final pretrial orders.** The trial court denied the defendant's request to modify the final pretrial order because it would be "fundamentally unfair to the plaintiff." Why?

A The purpose of the final pretrial order is to formulate a trial plan that permits an efficient trial of the merits "without chance or surprise." *Davey v. Lockheed Martin Corp.*, 301 F.3d at 1208 (quoting *Hull v. Chevron U.S.A., Inc.*, 812 F.2d 584, 588 (10th Cir. 1987)). Knowing the issues and evidence beforehand reduces the influence of chance or surprise. Of course, the pleadings are the initial device for giving notice of issues. Discovery helps uncover the evidence. But the final pretrial order supplants both, in taking the last pretrial cut at the issues, claims, and defenses, and often in identifying the witnesses and exhibits. Therefore, a party can ordinarily rely on the final pretrial order as it makes its game plan for trial. Davey had banked on this order in preparing her case, and the last-minute addition of a brand new, fact-intensive defense about which she had no prior opportunity for discovery would upset that reliance interest and therefore be "fundamentally unfair," reasoned the trial court.

Q **2. Rule 16(e)'s unspoken exclusionary rule.** Rule 16(e) is silent about the effects of a final pretrial order on attempts to litigate claims or defenses or to introduce witnesses or exhibits that were omitted from the order. But because

Rule 16(d) states that any pretrial order "controls the course of the action unless the court modifies it," and Rule 16(e) permits modification of the final pretrial order only to prevent manifest injustice, the effect of such omissions is that the omitted matter or witness can be excluded from the trial. The final order "controls" the claims, defenses, witnesses, and exhibits that can be offered at trial, and those omitted are waived. There are hundreds of cases like *Davey, Moss*, and *Smith* (discussed in the opinion) in which a party attempts at trial to offer matter outside the final pretrial order. Why so many?

A We can think of several possible reasons. One is that the lawyers were simply negligent and either overlooked or just forgot the omitted matter. "The preparation of a pretrial order requires careful attention and review by the parties and their attorneys." *Wilson v. Muckala*, 303 F.3d 1207, 1215 (10th Cir. 2002). As a trial date approaches, the frenzy of preparation spikes, and even good lawyers may overlook something.

Another reason is that, when the trial goes badly and a party's claim or defense fails, its lawyer may try to salvage the outcome by trying to substitute an omitted claim or defense that the trial record might support.

Last, the lawyer may be *trying* to win by chance or surprise. A witness may have been omitted on purpose, in order to avoid pretrial discovery of the witness and to ambush the opponent at trial. Of course, this is unfair and violates the spirit of the Rules,* which accounts for the controlling effect usually given the final order. The ambusher is gambling that the court will allow the witness to testify to avoid manifest injustice.

Q **3. Satisfying the "manifest injustice" test.** It may be that suspicion of ambush evidence contributed to Rule 16(e)'s demanding test for modification. Understandably, it focuses primarily on prejudice and surprise to the opposing party, who, after all, is entitled to rely on the final pretrial order, but the extent of prejudice depends on whether there is time for that party to meet the new matter. Timing affects the "ability to cure": A motion to modify an order to add a defense that is made several months before trial may permit re-opening of discovery to depose the new witness or collect more evidence to meet the new defense. On the other hand, final pretrial orders come "as close to the start of trial as is reasonable," Rule 16(e) (referring to time of final pretrial conference), so sometimes the only "cure" is a continuance. Why wasn't a continuance a sufficient cure in *Davey*, according to the plaintiff?

A Postponement of the trial could affect the availability and memory of witnesses and would certainly postpone even further the remedy to which she claims she is entitled. It would also have an impact beyond the parties, in that it could disrupt the court's trial calendar. Here the court of appeals seems to us a bit sanguine in concluding that a modification would not disrupt a trial scheduled to start three days later, though it did "acknowledge [that] a

* "We are shocked, shocked, to think that litigation by ambush is going on here." *Cf.* Claude Raines in *Casablanca*.

continuance may have caused disruption of other cases scheduled for trial on the court's docket." Of course, it is logically impossible to disrupt a trial when it hasn't yet started, but it is more than likely that any delay of the trial to allow plaintiff additional time to meet the late-added affirmative defense will wreak havoc on the judge's schedule.

Still, the trial court must also consider why a party seeks modification of the order and the prejudice to the opposing party if modification is denied. Here the reason for modification was a Supreme Court decision that recognized the affirmative defense a year and a half after the final pretrial order. Clearly, the employer was not acting in bad faith in raising this new matter, although it strangely waited two months after the decision to do so.

Q **4. Modifying a final pretrial order vs. amending the pleadings at trial.** Suppose an objection is made at trial to the proffer of matter outside the pleadings and outside the pretrial order. Rule 15(b) permits amendment of the pleadings "when doing so will aid in presenting the merits and the objecting party fails to satisfy the court that the evidence will prejudice the party's action or defense on the merits." Should the court apply this standard or the "manifest injustice" standard of Rule 16(e)?

A Although the "manifest injustice" standard sounds stiffer, some courts have held that Rule 15(b) controls—as it applies later in time than the final pretrial order. *See, e.g., Wallin v. Fuller*, 476 F.2d 1204, 1209 (5th Cir. 1973) (asserting that unbending adherence to Rule 16's stiff standard would frustrate policy favoring liberal amendment; "it is unlikely that the pretrial order under Rule 16 was intended to make the pleadings, and therefore Rule 15, obsolete"); *Wright & Miller* § 1527.1. Yet, since both Rules consider prejudice to the opposing party, it may make little practical difference which test the trial judge uses in many cases. Several circuits require trial judges who are asked to modify a final pretrial order to consider prejudice to the opposing party, the ability of the moving party to cure the prejudice, the effect of modification on the orderly and efficient trial of the case, and the movant's bad faith and willfulness in failing to comply with the pretrial order. 3 *Moore* § 16.78[4][a]. These factors do not seem materially different from those the courts consider in allowing amendment under Rule 15(a)(2) or 15(b).

IV. Pretrial Case Management: Summary of Basic Principles

- Rule 16 provides broad authority to district court judges (and magistrates acting on assignment from judges) to manage civil cases by holding pretrial conferences and issuing scheduling orders and other pretrial orders.
- Federal judges have authority to require the attendance and good faith participation of parties and lawyers at pretrial conferences. But they lack

authority to require parties to stipulate to facts or to settle claims. Parties are entitled to try the issues and cannot be coerced by pretrial orders to forgo trial.

- A pretrial order controls the matters to which it applies unless the court modifies the order, but a final pretrial order governing the plan of trial can be modified only to prevent manifest injustice. Thus, witnesses, exhibits, claims, or defenses that are omitted from a final pretrial order will typically be excluded from trial, unless the proponent of the omitted matter carries its burden of showing that it will be substantially prejudiced from the exclusion, that any prejudice to the opposing party from allowing modification (and inclusion of the omitted matter) can be cured or alleviated, that modification of the order will not disrupt the court calendar, and that it has acted in good faith.

27

Dispositions Without Trial

I. Introduction

Suppose plaintiff Gary Groman has filed a creative complaint against Mark Magoff, alleging fraud and conspiracy, seeking damages for an investment gone bad. Magoff responds by filing a timely Rule 12(b)(6) motion to dismiss for failure to state a claim, asserting that the complaint does not plausibly allege key elements of the fraud and conspiracy claims. As Groman's lawyer, you file a brief in opposition and then argue against the motion at a hearing. Your arguments are not well received, however; the judge gives you a hard time, making no secret of her disdain for your complaint and legal theories and signaling quite clearly that she intends to grant Magoff's motion. You leave the hearing wishing fervently that you had another judge.

Is it too late to get one? Not necessarily. Rule 41(a) authorizes a party to voluntarily dismiss a complaint *without prejudice* to suing on the same claim or claims at another time or in another court under some circumstances.* Plaintiffs

* "Without prejudice" and "with prejudice" are terms of art that refer to the effect of a dismissal on the claimant's ability to sue on the claim again. In general, a claim that is dismissed "without prejudice" by a federal court can be sued on again without running afoul of the law of claim preclusion—also called *res judicata*—whereby a claim that is dismissed with prejudice cannot be brought again in federal court. We leave the complicated law of claim preclusion to Chapter 33.

voluntarily dismiss for many practical reasons, including forum or judge shopping in circumstances like yours. Section II discusses voluntary dismissals and their effect.

Of course, you could also stick it out to see how the judge rules. (Litigators will tell you that it is often difficult to guess how a judge will rule from reading the tea leaves of oral argument.) If you guess wrong, however, and the judge grants the motion, she will dismiss the case (though probably with leave to amend). Since you resisted dismissal, this would be an *involuntary dismissal*. A party can also suffer an involuntary dismissal for failure to prosecute its action or as a sanction for failure to comply with a discovery order. Section III discusses involuntary dismissals and their effect.

Finally, suppose that Magoff waits until after discovery and then files a motion for summary judgment under Rule 56. If he can show by his supporting materials that the undisputed evidence shows that he acted without fraudulent intent (an essential element of Groman's claim), and that he is entitled on those undisputed facts to judgment as a matter of law, the court can grant judgment. We call it *summary judgment* because it is typically based on written evidence and decided without live testimony or a trial. Section IV discusses summary judgment.

All three devices can end a lawsuit without a trial. In fact, far more cases are disposed of by voluntary or involuntary dismissal, or by summary judgment, than by trial itself.

II. Voluntary Dismissal

Recall that as the lawyer for Gary Groman, in our opening hypothetical, you had a bad feeling about how the judge was going to rule on defendant Magoff's motion to dismiss for failure to state a claim. You would like to dismiss your case and start over, in the hope of finding a more favorable judge. But what if Magoff's motion is supported by a sixty-five-page brief, reflecting substantial legal research and many hours of lawyer time? What if the motion has been pending for seven months, during which Magoff also spent substantial resources making required disclosures and responding to some discovery requests?

READING *IN RE BATH AND KITCHEN FIXTURES ANTITRUST LITIGATION.* The following case suggests some answers to these questions. As in the hypothetical, the defendant filed a Rule 12(b)(6) motion. But here, without granting the motion, the court issued an opinion inviting plaintiffs to supplement their argument, if they could, and perhaps hinting that if they couldn't, the court would dismiss.

- Procedurally, how does a plaintiff obtain a voluntary dismissal without court order?
- Why does Rule 41(a)(1)(A) permit voluntary dismissal without a court order at certain points in the litigation time line?
- If a defendant has labored mightily on its motion, why should the plaintiff still be permitted to dismiss voluntarily without conditions or court order?

IN RE BATH AND KITCHEN FIXTURES ANTITRUST LITIGATION

535 F.3d 161 (3d Cir. 2008)

Scirica, Chief Judge.

Plaintiffs appeal the District Court's order striking as untimely their notice of voluntary dismissal filed under Fed. R. Civ. P. 41(a)(1)(A)(i). We will vacate and remand with instructions to enter an order dismissing the complaint without prejudice.

I.

Purchasers of bath and kitchen plumbing fixtures filed putative class action complaints against manufacturers, alleging a price-fixing conspiracy in violation of Section 1 of the Sherman Act, 15 U.S.C. § 1. . . . Instead of filing an answer, defendants moved to dismiss the consolidated and amended complaint for failure to state a claim under Fed. R. Civ. P. 12(b)(6).

On July 19, 2006, the District Court issued a memorandum opinion finding plaintiffs needed to plead more facts to meet the notice standard of Fed. R. Civ. P. 8(a)(2). The memorandum stated in relevant part:

> [T]he Court will not dismiss the consolidated and amended complaint with prejudice at this time as the defendants request. At oral argument, the Court asked counsel for the plaintiffs if there were any supplemental facts that could be pled to address the defendants' arguments that the consolidated and amended complaint did not provide sufficient notice of the grounds upon which the conspiracy claim was based. Counsel implied that they might possess more information than was alleged in the pleadings, but did not supplement the complaint. . . . The Court, nevertheless, will allow the plaintiffs an opportunity to amend their pleadings. . . . An appropriate Order follows.

. . . [I]nstead of amending the complaint, plaintiffs filed a notice under Fed. R. Civ. P. 41(a)(1)(A)(i), voluntarily dismissing the action (the "Notice"). With one exception, not applicable here, a timely notice of voluntary dismissal is without prejudice. Fed. R. Civ. P. 41(a)(1)(B). Defendants, seeking instead a dismissal with prejudice, filed a "Motion for Entry of Judgment in Accordance with the Court's Memorandum and Order of July 19, 2006," contending plaintiffs could no longer voluntarily dismiss by notice because the District Court already had granted defendants' motion to dismiss on July 19, 2006. Defendants asked the District Court to strike the Notice and enter an order of dismissal with prejudice. Plaintiffs opposed the motion. On January 24, 2007, the District Court struck the Notice as untimely filed and entered an order dismissing the complaint.[2] This appeal followed.

2. Although the January 24, 2007, order does not state the complaint is dismissed "with prejudice," defendants do not dispute the finality of that order. *See Shane v. Fauver,* 213 F.3d 113, 115 (3d Cir. 2000) ("Because the order did not specify that the dismissal was without prejudice, under Fed. R. Civ. P. 41(b) the dismissal 'operates as an adjudication upon the merits.' "). . . .

II.

Fed. R. Civ. P. 41(a)(1) provides:

> (A) *Without a Court Order.* Subject to Rules 23(e), 23.1(c), 23.2, and 66 and any applicable federal statute, the plaintiff may dismiss an action without a court order by filing: (i) a notice of dismissal before the opposing party serves either an answer or a motion for summary judgment; or (ii) a stipulation of dismissal signed by all parties who have appeared. (B) *Effect.* Unless the notice or stipulation states otherwise, the dismissal is without prejudice. But if the plaintiff previously dismissed any federal—or state—court action based on or including the same claim, a notice of dismissal operates as an adjudication on the merits.

Three key aspects of Rule 41(a)(1)(A)(i) control our analysis. First, a filing under the Rule is a notice, not a motion. Its effect is automatic: the defendant does not file a response, and no order of the district court is needed to end the action.[7] Second, the notice results in a dismissal without prejudice (unless it states otherwise), as long as the plaintiff has never dismissed an action based on or including the same claim in a prior case. Third, the defendant has only two options for cutting off the plaintiff's right to end the case by notice: serving on the plaintiff an answer or a motion for summary judgment.

Here, it is undisputed that on the date plaintiffs filed the Notice: (1) plaintiffs had never before dismissed an action based on or including the same claim; and (2) defendants had not served an answer or a motion for summary judgment. Accordingly, the parties agree a timely Notice would have resulted in automatic dismissal without prejudice. The timeliness of the Notice depends on whether the "action" to which the Rule refers remained pending when the Notice was filed.

The Rule "affixes a bright-line test to limit the right of dismissal to the early stages of litigation," *Manze* [*v. State Farm Ins. Co.*, 817 F.2d 1062, 1065 (3d Cir. 1987)], which "simplifies the court's task by telling it whether a suit has reached the point of no return. If the defendant has served either an answer or a summary judgment motion it has; if the defendant has served neither, it has not." *Id.* (quoting *Winterland Concessions Co. v. Smith*, 706 F.2d 793, 795 (7th Cir. 1983)). Up to the "point of no return," dismissal is automatic and immediate—the right of a plaintiff is "unfettered," *Carter v. United States*, 547 F.2d 258, 259 (5th Cir. 1977). A timely notice of voluntary dismissal invites no response from the district court and permits no interference by it. *See Am. Cyanamid Co. v. McGhee*, 317 F.2d 295, 297 (5th Cir. 1963) ("[The notice] itself closes the file. There is nothing the defendant can do to fan the ashes of that action into life and the court has no role to play. This is a matter of right running to the plaintiff and may not be extinguished or circumscribed by adversary or court."). A proper notice deprives the district

---

7. When the notice is filed, the Clerk makes an appropriate entry on the docket noting the termination of the action.

court of jurisdiction to decide the merits of the case.[8] *See* 9 Charles Alan Wright & Arthur R. Miller, Federal Practice & Procedure: Civ. 3d § 2367, at 559–61 (3d ed. 2008) ("After the dismissal, the action no longer is pending in the district court and no further proceedings in the action are proper.").

Because a motion to dismiss under Fed. R. Civ. P. 12(b)(6) is neither an answer nor a motion for summary judgment, its filing generally does not cut off a plaintiff's right to dismiss by notice. *Manze,* 817 F.2d at 1066. Only when a motion filed under Fed. R. Civ. P. 12(b)(6) is converted by the district court into a motion for summary judgment does it bar voluntary dismissal.[9] *Id.* Here, defendants do not contend their motion was converted to a motion for summary judgment, or that it should be treated as an answer.

In *Manze,* we rejected the defendant's argument that its motion to dismiss under Fed. R. Civ. P. 12(b)(6) was "equivalent" to a motion for summary judgment that should have barred the plaintiff's dismissal by notice. *Id.* We acknowledged the defendant's preferred approach had some "theoretical appeal" because motions to dismiss may impose much labor and expense on parties and judges—sometimes they are as time-consuming as motions for summary judgment. Moreover, Rule 41 may permit a strategic advantage for a plaintiff: if prospects for prevailing on the merits appear dim, the plaintiff can obtain a dismissal without prejudice after imposing high costs on defendants and judges. But the drafters of Rule 41 provided for only two responses—answer and motion for summary judgment—as "point[s] of no return." *Id.* (quoting *Winterland Concessions,* 706 F.2d at 795). It would be improper to graft a new category onto the literal text of the Rule. *Id.*

As in *Manze,* we apply the literal terms of Rule 41. Furthermore, we reject defendants' contention that the District Court's granting plaintiffs the right to amend, and an extension of time within which to do so, limited or nullified the option of dismissing available to plaintiffs under the Rule. Here, the Notice was timely because defendants had filed neither an answer nor a motion for summary judgment as of the date of the Notice, and because the District Court's July 19, 2006, order had not clearly put an end to the "action" to which Rule 41 refers.

III.

For the foregoing reasons, we will vacate the January 24, 2007, order of the District Court and remand with instructions to enter an order dismissing the complaint without prejudice.

---

8. A district court retains jurisdiction to decide "collateral" issues—such as sanctions, costs, and attorneys' fees—after a plaintiff dismisses an action by notice. *See Cooter & Gell v. Hartmarx Corp.,* 496 U.S. 384, 396–98 (1990).

9. *See* Fed. R. Civ. P. 12(d) ("If, on a motion under Rule 12(b)(6) or 12(c), matters outside the pleadings are presented to and not excluded by the court, the motion must be treated as one for summary judgment under Rule 56. All parties must be given a reasonable opportunity to present all the material that is pertinent to the motion.").

Notes and Questions: Voluntary Dismissal

1. Procedure for voluntary dismissal without court order (a/k/a "notice dismissal"). The plaintiffs in *Bath and Kitchen Fixtures* did not *move* for a voluntary dismissal because they didn't have to—they had a right to dismiss without a court order. Thus, they simply filed a "Notice of Voluntary Dismissal"—they "noticed" a voluntary dismissal, as it is sometimes put. When a notice is timely, it "invites no response from the district court and permits no interference by it," as the Third Circuit states. The notice "itself closes the file"; it deprives the court of jurisdiction and the action is no longer pending. Thus, when such a notice is timely filed, the court cannot even rule on the pending motion to dismiss (though, as the Third Circuit notes, it retains jurisdiction to decide the collateral questions of sanctions or attorneys' fees).

Q **2. Reasons for voluntary dismissal.** Why did the plaintiffs notice a voluntary dismissal in *Bath and Kitchen Fixtures*?

A We're guessing, but the district court's opinion suggests that the plaintiffs did not *have* more facts. A voluntary dismissal would head off a dismissal for failure to state a claim, but it would be "without prejudice" to the plaintiffs suing the same defendants again. Maybe the plaintiffs hoped either to get more facts at a subsequent time or to get another judge who might not require more facts.

Thus, the reasons for seeking a voluntary dismissal without prejudice are sometimes tactical—to give the plaintiff an advantage. Reported reasons for voluntary dismissal include:

— to marshal new evidence needed to state or support a claim;
— to correct or redraft pleadings;
— to facilitate consolidation with another action;
— to preserve diversity jurisdiction by dismissing non-diverse parties;
— to defeat diversity jurisdiction by refiling in state court and joining non-diverse parties;
— to avoid unfavorable state law by refiling in a different jurisdiction with better law or a longer statute of limitations;
— to delay or avoid an anticipated adverse determination on the merits;
— to delay or avoid discovery; and even
— to draw a different judge by refiling in a state court.

See Moore § 41.11.

Another common reason for voluntary dismissal is that the parties have settled the case. In that circumstance, the notice of dismissal usually states that dismissal is "with prejudice."

Q **3. The point of no return for notice dismissals.** The Third Circuit states that a timely notice of voluntary dismissal is one filed "before the opposing party serves either an answer or a motion for summary judgment." Why these "points of no return"?

A Before these points in the normal time line of civil litigation, defendants have usually not spent enough resources in their defense to suffer much prejudice from the voluntary dismissal. However, to prepare an answer, a defendant will need to make the reasonable inquiry required by Rule 11(b). For the defendant manufacturers in the *Bath and Kitchen Fixtures* price-fixing class action, this could well entail substantial time and expense, for which they would receive no reimbursement on a voluntary dismissal without court order. A motion for summary judgment "may require even more research and preparation than the answer itself." Fed. R. Civ. P. 41 advisory committee's notes (1946). Thus, service of an answer or motion for summary judgment roughly "fix[es] the point at which the resources of the court and the defendant are so committed that dismissal without preclusive consequences [precluding suing again] can no longer be had as of right." *In re Piper Aircraft Distribution Sys. Antitrust Litig.*, 551 F.2d 213, 220 (8th Cir. 1997).

We say "roughly" because it is entirely conceivable that a defendant would also commit substantial resources to a motion to dismiss for failure to state a claim. For this reason, the Second Circuit held in *Harvey Aluminum, Inc. v. Am. Cyanamid Co.*, 203 F.2d 105 (2d Cir. 1953), that when the parties and the court had already expended substantial resources (on briefing, arguing, hearing, and deciding a motion for a preliminary injunction), it would be unfair to permit plaintiff to dismiss as of right. But other circuits have been sharply critical of *Harvey* for blurring Rule 41's bright line. A reason for the answer/summary judgment points of no return is simply that they provide "bright lines" that "simplif[y] the court's task by telling it" when a notice is no longer sufficient to obtain voluntary dismissal, instead of complicating the court's task by requiring a case-by-case inquiry into how much effort defendants have expended. These points of no return may not always accurately reflect the effort by—and therefore possible prejudice to—defendants, but their clarity makes up for the unfairness in particular cases.

Q **4. The summary judgment point of no return.** We said Rule 41(a)(1)(A)(i) provides a bright line test for voluntary dismissal without court order, but suppose the defendants in *Bath and Kitchen Fixtures* had supported their Rule 12(b)(6) motion to dismiss for failure to state a claim with materials outside the complaint, such as economic data about price disparities in their markets that seemed to rebut plaintiffs' allegations of price-fixing? Is voluntary dismissal without a court order still permitted?

A Rule 12(d) provides that when "materials outside the pleadings are presented to and not excluded by the court, the [12(b)(6)] motion must be treated as one for summary judgment." Courts must take the well-pleaded allegations of the complaint as true on a Rule 12(b)(6) motion, but when the movant offers materials beyond these allegations, the court no longer takes the allegations as true. Instead, when such materials "are . . . not excluded by the court," it considers whether they show that material facts are genuinely undisputed—the standard applied by the summary judgment rule. But then the Rule 41(a) point of no return has been reached, *because now the motion is treated as a motion for summary judgment even though it was not styled as one.*

5. Timing dismissal.

Plaintiff sues defendants Abbott and Costello. Assuming that only the events listed in each answer have occurred in the lawsuit, in which of the following instances may the plaintiff voluntarily dismiss without order of the court? Reread Rule 41(a)(1)(A) first.

A. Abbott has filed and served a motion to dismiss for lack of personal jurisdiction.
B. Defendants filed and served a motion to dismiss for failure to state a claim, attacking the complaint without providing any matters outside the complaint.
C. Defendants filed and served a motion to dismiss for failure to state a claim, attaching materials outside the complaint.
D. Defendants filed and served a motion to dismiss for failure to state a claim, attaching materials outside the complaint, which the court said it would accept in deciding the motion.
E. Abbott has filed and served a motion to dismiss for lack of personal jurisdiction, attaching materials (about his contacts with the forum) in support of the motion, on which the court said it will rely in deciding the motion.
F. Abbott filed and served an answer to the complaint.
G. After defendants filed and served their answers, Defendant Costello stipulated to dismissal of the action by plaintiff.

This question requires a straightforward reading and application of the Rule. Recall that a motion is not a pleading, per Rule 7, and a motion is therefore not an answer.

No answer or motion for summary judgment has been served in **A** or **B**, so the points of no return have not been reached. This bright line applies even if the filed motion is a "merits motion" to dismiss for failure to state a claim.

By attaching supporting materials outside the complaint, defendants in **C** afford the court the opportunity to convert their motion to dismiss for failure to state a claim into a summary judgment motion, as provided by Rule 12(d), but the case has still not yet reached the point of no return for two reasons. First, defendants did not characterize their motion as a motion for summary judgment under Rule 56. Second, the court has not yet seized this opportunity by accepting ("not exclud[ing]") the materials outside the complaint. Thus, defendants' motion remains what they called it—a motion to dismiss for failure to state a claim—which is not the point of no return set out in the Rule.

In **D**, by contrast, the court has taken this step, thus converting the motion into one for summary judgment. If plaintiffs have not filed the notice of dismissal before this conversion, it marks the point of no return and they cannot now dismiss without a court order.

E sounds suspiciously like **D**, but with a critical difference. Rule 12(d)'s conversion applies only to Rule 12(b)(6) motions to dismiss for failure to state a claim or Rule 12(c) motions for judgment on the pleadings. A court can consider materials outside the complaint in ruling on motions to dismiss for lack of personal jurisdiction, improper venue, insufficient service of process, or insufficient process, but none of these motions with or without materials outside the complaint converts into a summary judgment motion that cuts off the right to voluntary dismissal. And probably none should, on the general effort theory of voluntary dismissal, since they are threshold procedural defenses requiring no effort on the merits.

F reflects the other point of no return: serving an answer. The Rule presumes that filing an answer required enough effort by the defendant to justify a measure of judicial control on voluntary dismissal.

G is a reminder of an alternative way to dismiss without court order, even after an answer or motion for summary judgment has been filed—by agreement of the parties. But it is defective as framed. Rule 41(a)(1)(A)(ii) requires a stipulation "to be signed by *all* parties who have appeared" (emphasis supplied). Abbott did not sign, so **G** is not correct.

Q **6. Voluntary dismissal by court order.** Answers **D** and **G** to the last multiple choice question are situations in which the plaintiff can no longer dismiss absent a court order or a stipulation signed by all the parties who have appeared. However, it does not follow that the plaintiff is stuck. Rule 41(a)(2) provides for voluntary dismissal "at the plaintiff's request . . . by court order." Though he can no longer simply *notice* a voluntary dismissal, he can still *move* for a voluntary dismissal under Rule 41(a)(2). But voluntary dismissal is then discretionary with the judge and may be granted conditionally, "on terms that the court considers proper."

The primary purpose of giving the judge this discretion is to prevent a dismissal that unfairly causes "plain legal prejudice" to the opposing party. *Wright & Miller* § 2364; *Moore* § 41.40[6]. *See, e.g., Harris v. Devon Energy Prod. Co., L.P.*, 500 F. App. 267, 268 (5th Cir. 2012) ("Plain legal prejudice may occur when the plaintiff moves to dismiss a suit at a late stage of the proceedings or seeks to avoid an imminent adverse ruling in the case, or where a subsequent refiling of the suit would deprive the defendant of a limitations defense.")* Is having to defend the lawsuit if the plaintiff brings it again after dismissal that kind of prejudice?

A No. The prospect of having to defend a second lawsuit cannot ordinarily be enough, without more, to constitute prejudice that would justify denying the motion for voluntary dismissal, *because otherwise almost every motion for voluntary dismissal by court order would have to be denied.* By similar reasoning, such prejudice is not established just because the plaintiff may gain some tactical advantage in a future lawsuit. *Of course, the plaintiff is getting some tactical advantage; otherwise, why, in most cases, would the plaintiff seek voluntary dismissal?* If some legal advantage to the plaintiff by itself constituted

* Dismissals "with prejudice" and "without prejudice" are terms from the law of *res judicata* that refer to prejudice from suing again. *See supra* p. 969, note *. The judge-made term "plain legal prejudice" on a motion for a voluntary dismissal has a more prosaic meaning, relating to how much effort by the defendant will be wasted if the motion is granted. That's why we believe that our term, "preparation prejudice," comes closer to the mark for most cases.

sufficient prejudice to the defendant to disallow voluntary dismissal, the Rule would effectively be a dead letter. Instead, it was intended to allow plaintiffs a do-over, at least early in the lawsuit.

The courts have found the requisite prejudice where a defendant has spent significant time, effort, and expense in preparing its defense of the suit, or what we called "preparation prejudice" in Chapter 16 in the context of amended pleadings. For example, one circuit looks to whether: (1) the suit is still in pretrial status or further along, (2) the parties have filed numerous papers and memoranda, (3) the parties have attended many pretrial conferences, (4) there are prior court rulings adverse to plaintiff's position, (5) hearings have been held, and (6) the parties have undertaken substantial discovery. *Id.* (citing decisions of the Fifth Circuit Court of Appeals). Though the plaintiff's reason for seeking dismissal is usually not a factor, it may become more important as the litigation progresses. *See Zagano v. Fordham Univ.*, 900 F.2d 12, 14 (2d Cir.) (considering the plaintiff's diligence in bringing the motion, the adequacy of plaintiff's explanation for dismissal, and any "undue vexatiousness" on plaintiff's part, in addition to costs and burdens of defendant), *cert. denied*, 494 U.S. 899 (1990).

7. "Terms that the court considers proper." Preparation prejudice is the touchstone of Rule 41(a)(2) discretion. At the same time, it is something that a court can mitigate by imposing "terms" on the dismissal. For example, where the litigation is advanced, so that defendant has incurred heavy costs in filing papers, attending hearings and conferences, and conducting discovery (all factors pointing in the direction of denying the motion under the plain legal prejudice standard), the court might condition dismissal on plaintiff's payment of some or all of those costs to the defendant. In fact, even where the plaintiff moved for voluntary dismissal because an important witness was absent when the jury was about to be called to the box, a court granted the motion for dismissal without prejudice on the condition that plaintiff pay defendant's expenses and reasonable attorneys' fees. *See American Cyanamid Co. v. McGhee*, 317 F.2d 295 (5th Cir. 1963).

Primary concern

8. Effect of voluntary dismissal. The chief concern all parties have with a voluntary dismissal is whether it will permit or preclude the dismissing party from suing again on the same claim.

The first voluntary dismissal without court order—that is, one noticed before the points of no return—is by rule "without prejudice" to the commencement of another action on the same claim. Rule 41(a)(1)(B). Of course, this does not mean that the dismissing party will win or avoid some of the same defenses that he faced or would have faced in the dismissed lawsuit. It only means that the party can ordinarily file the claim again (assuming that the party refiles within the period set by the relevant statute of limitations).

After the first voluntary dismissal without court order, should the dismissing party sue on the same claim again and then notice another voluntary dismissal without court order, the second voluntary dismissal "operates as an adjudication on the merits." Rule 41(a)(1)(B). Under the law of claim preclusion, this generally means that the second voluntary dismissal precludes the dismissing party from filing a third time in the same court. This part of the Rule is sometimes called "the two-dismissal rule," intended to protect the defendant from the harassment of repeated plaintiffs' dismissals. It applies only when the second dismissal is by notice—without court order or stipulation. *See Wright & Miller* § 2368.

Finally, a voluntary dismissal by court order is "without prejudice" to commencing a new action on the same claim unless the court states otherwise. But part of the court's discretion in ruling on a motion for voluntary dismissal is to order it "with prejudice," based on the same factors that enter into the court's decision whether to allow the dismissal at all. *See Moore* § 41.40[6].

9. Revisiting voluntary dismissal.

Which of the following voluntary dismissals (with the indicated effect or conditions) is authorized by Rule 41(a)?

A. Defendant files a notice of voluntary dismissal of plaintiff's claim without order of court.
B. After having voluntarily dismissed and refiled the action, plaintiff files another notice of voluntary dismissal without prejudice and without order of court.
C. When plaintiff notices a first voluntary dismissal before defendant answers or moves for summary judgment, the court dismisses on condition that plaintiff pay defendant's incurred costs.
D. After having voluntarily dismissed, plaintiff brings the same claim again and then files a stipulation of dismissal without prejudice signed by all the parties.

A is not authorized because voluntary dismissal is a plaintiff's remedy. A defendant *can* move to dismiss the case, under Rule 12, for example, but unless the plaintiff then voluntarily dismisses, any resulting dismissal is *involuntary*, as we discuss below.

In **B**, the second dismissal is by notice—without order of the court. The two-dismissal rule therefore applies, and the second dismissal is *with prejudice*. So **B**, seeking dismissal *without prejudice*, is wrong.

If plaintiff has filed the notice before the points of no return, the court has no role to play, as *Bath and Kitchen Fixtures* teaches. The court has no authority to condition the first such dismissal on payment of costs. So **C** is not authorized by the Rule.

D may also look wrong at first glance because plaintiff is again trying to voluntarily dismiss a second time *without prejudice*. This looks like a violation of the two-dismissal rule. But careful reading of the Rule shows that a second voluntary dismissal must be with prejudice only when the dismissal is by notice, not when it is by stipulation or order of the court. So **D** is correct, after all.

III. Involuntary Dismissal

Although involuntary dismissal sounds like the next logical topic, we have already discussed it. When a court grants a defendant's Rule 12(b) motion to dismiss, the dismissal is involuntary and does not require the plaintiff's consent and, in fact, is usually hotly contested by the plaintiff. In addition, Rule 41(b) describes two other grounds for involuntary dismissal: plaintiff's failure to prosecute and a party's failure to comply with the Rules. A federal court "is not a parking lot for stagnant cases." *Lopez-Gonzalez v. Municipality of Comerio*, 404 F.3d 548, 550 (1st Cir. 2005) (quoting the trial court). At some point, the plaintiff's inaction justifies involuntary dismissal of the action, the precise point often being set by rule or statute (e.g., a year), and the actual decision of dismissal depending on plaintiff's excuses for inaction, prejudice to the defendant, and other ad hoc factors. Involuntary dismissal for failure to comply with the Rules depends on the specific Rules that were violated and the specific litigation history of the case, with dismissal typically being reserved chiefly for serial violators who have abused the litigation process.

Rule 41(b) provides that an involuntary dismissal "operates as an adjudication on the merits," which means that an action based on the same claims cannot be brought again in the same court. The Rule excepts involuntary dismissals for lack of jurisdiction, improper venue, or failure to join a required party, because these are all defects that prevent adjudication of the merits. We will return to this topic in more detail in the chapter on claim preclusion.

IV. Summary Judgment

A. Introduction to Summary Judgment

Suppose Harold Spinoza died from asbestosis after working for thirty years for a heating, cooling, and insulation contractor. His wife Sophie concludes that he contracted asbestosis from his exposure on the job to asbestos-containing insulating foam and panels. She files an action for damages in a federal district court with jurisdiction against United Fibreboard, which manufactures insulating foam and panels, alleging that her husband's exposure to United's products caused his asbestosis and resulting death and asserting various tort theories, including wrongful death and strict product liability.

If her complaint survives a motion to dismiss for failure to state a claim, and United answers denying that any of its products were the ones used by Spinoza, the parties would normally proceed to collect evidence by pretrial discovery. When Sophie and United had completed fact-gathering (if they did not settle the dispute), they would probably go to trial. At trial, Sophie would present evidence of the facts necessary to establish the elements of her claim(s), and United would cross-examine and offer rebuttal evidence to disprove them and/or offer direct evidence to prove any affirmative defenses that it had timely pleaded in its answer. The fact-finder—whether the judge or a jury—would decide disputed issues of fact by a preponderance of the evidence, and the court would enter judgment accordingly.

But what if even prior to trial there is no dispute about the facts? Then there is no need for a trial. When the facts are undisputed, all that remains is to apply the relevant law. If all the facts that the judge needs to apply the law are undisputed, she can go ahead and apply the law without waiting for trial. The purpose of trial, after all, is for the parties to "try" factual disputes. There is nothing to try if the facts are undisputed, and, indeed, trial would be a waste of time and resources.

For example, if the record showed without dispute that no product manufactured by United was ever used in any workplace in which Spinoza had worked, the judge could, without trial, apply the relevant tort law to give judgment for

United on the ground that Sophie could not prove that Harold was ever exposed to United's product. This would be true even if that tort law was itself contested. A dispute about the applicable law is not tried by fact-finders; it is decided by a judge.

How, then, could the judge decide before trial that the facts are undisputed? One way would be for Sophie and United to agree or stipulate that the facts are undisputed. In fact, we have seen this already, because this is, in effect, what the parties do on defendant's motion to dismiss for failure to state a claim. By this motion, the defendant agrees, *for purposes of the motion only*, that the well-pleaded factual allegations in the plaintiff's complaint are true, and asks the judge to decide, as a matter of law, whether it states a claim based on those taken-as-true allegations.

Alternatively, a party might try to show in advance of trial that the evidence is so one-sided that no reasonable fact-finder could dispute the existence or non-existence of certain facts. Of course, the party could try to do this by putting on live witnesses at a hearing in court. But then the showing would hardly be different from a full-blown trial—there would be nothing "summary" about it. Instead, therefore, the Rules afford the option of making a more summary showing in advance of trial by mainly documentary evidence, including sworn witness statements called *affidavits*. A motion for summary judgment effectively previews, usually in documentary form, the evidence that parties would put on at trial in order to determine if it would establish any dispute that requires trial. As Judge Posner has said about motions for summary judgment in jury cases, the court must decide "whether the state of the evidence is such that, if the case were tried tomorrow, the [non-moving party] would have a fair chance of obtaining a verdict." *Palucki v. Sears, Roebuck & Co.*, 879 F.2d 1568 (7th Cir. 1989).

For example, United might obtain all of the supply invoices from Spinoza's employer to establish that the employer had never purchased its products, or an affidavit by its salesman swearing that he had never sold any of its products to the employer, or a deposition by Spinoza's co-worker, also under oath, asserting that the only insulating foam or panels ever used at Spinoza's workplace were manufactured exclusively by a company other than United. Armed with this evidence, it could file a motion for summary judgment any time up until thirty days after the close of discovery. *See* Fed. R. Civ. P. 56(b). If United's motion is properly made and supported—that is, "if the movant shows that there is no genuine dispute as to any material fact and the movant is entitled to a judgment as a matter of law" (*id.* Rule 56(a))—then Sophie would have to identify evidence showing that there is a genuine dispute of material fact. In other words, Sophie would have to offer affidavits or other comparable evidence setting out specific facts from which a fact-finder could reasonably find that Spinoza *had* been exposed to some of United's products. If the evidence provided on summary judgment did not include such facts, the judge should, as a matter of the applicable tort law, grant summary judgment for United on this record, without trial.

Q **Offering evidence for summary judgment.** What if United's evidence consisted of its sales manager's statement that he "heard" one of Spinoza's co-workers, whose name he had forgotten, "guess" that they had not used United products? Would this "evidence" support summary judgment?

A If, as we have said, a motion for summary judgment previews the evidence the parties would put on at trial, this offer would not suffice. United's "evidence" would be inadmissible on objection at trial because it is hearsay (an out-of-court statement that is offered as evidence to prove the truth of the matter stated), and because it is not based on the personal knowledge of the anonymous co-worker. *See* Rule 56(c)(2) & (4). If it could not be considered at trial, it should not be considered at summary judgment either (on timely objection), as long as summary judgment is to function as an accurate preview of trial.

Q **What if Sophie had opposed United's summary judgment motion by *promising* in her lawyer's memorandum of law to produce evidence at trial that would establish that her husband had used United's products at his workplace ("I'm sure we'll come up with something.")?** Would her promise stave off summary judgment?

A Sophie's "promise" of evidence creates no present factual dispute and defeats the purpose of previewing the evidence at trial. In fact, Sophie's factual allegations in the complaint are already really nothing more than promises of what she hopes to prove at trial. Summary judgment, it is often said, is intended to "pierce" the allegations of the pleadings and flush out the evidence, if any, that could be introduced at trial to prove them. If the motion is properly made and supported, promises are not enough to defeat it. *See* Rule 56(c)(1)(B) & (2). Admissible evidence is required setting forth specific facts to create a genuine dispute to defeat the motion.

B. The Fundamental Purpose of Summary Judgment: Flushing Out the Absence of a Genuine Dispute of Material Fact

The basic purpose of summary judgment is to determine from the record whether there is a genuine dispute of material fact, and if not, whether the moving party is entitled to judgment as a matter of law on the undisputed facts. Because summary judgment is "a matter of law," however, the starting point is always identifying the applicable substantive law. Doing so also helps identify which facts are material. Having performed these tasks, a court in ruling on a motion for summary judgment can then examine whether the evidence in the record offered by the moving party shows that there is no genuine dispute of material fact and that it is entitled to judgment as a matter of law. If the moving party meets this burden, the burden shifts to the non-moving party, and the court would then consider whether the non-moving party has identified specific facts in the record that create a genuine dispute, notwithstanding the movant's showing. *See Wright & Miller* § 2727.2. The court would grant or deny the motion, in whole or in part.

But the described sequencing of this analysis is more theoretical than real. In practice, a court usually considers the briefs of the moving and nonmoving parties and their supporting materials together* (including in some cases, by local

* The practice is facilitated in some courts by the judge's adoption of a "bundle rule," by which the movant cannot file motion papers "until the motion has been fully briefed [by all parties]." *See* Individual Motion Practice and Rules of Judge Dora L. Irizarry (E.D.N.Y.), Rule IV-D. Under a bundle rule, the movant is responsible for filing a complete set of all the parties' briefs and supporting materials at the same time.

rule, the movant's statement of undisputed material facts and the nonmovant's responses, with citations to the record) in deciding whether there is any genuine dispute of material fact.

READING *SLAVEN v. CITY OF SALEM*. In the following case, a prisoner in the custody of the Salem police department hanged himself in his cell. His sister then sued Salem, asserting that it was liable for her brother's death. After some discovery, Salem moved for summary judgment, arguing that the undisputed material facts disproved an essential element of the plaintiff's claim. Use the following summary judgment checklist to analyze the court's decision.

- What is the rule of substantive law applicable to the motion?
- Which facts matter—are "material"—to applying that rule of law?
- What is the proper record for summary judgment? That is, what evidence may the court consider in ruling on such a motion?
- Has the moving party met its burden of showing that there is no genuine dispute of material fact in that record and that it is entitled to judgment under the applicable rule of law?
- If the movant has met its burden, has the non-moving party met its burden of showing specific facts in that record that create a genuine dispute of material fact under the applicable rule of law?
- What is the proper disposition of the motion?

The Massachusetts summary judgment rule discussed in the case is slightly different from the federal rule, as noted in the opinion.

SLAVEN v. CITY OF SALEM

438 N.E.2d 348 (Mass. 1982)

Before Wilkins, Liacos, Nolan and Lynch, JJ.

Liacos, Justice.

The plaintiff, as administratrix of her brother's estate, commenced an action against the defendant (city) pursuant to G.L. c. 258, the Massachusetts Tort Claims Act. The plaintiff appeals and challenges the correctness of an order by a Superior Court judge granting the defendant's motion for summary judgment. Mass. R. Civ. P. 56, 365 Mass. 824 (1974). We transferred the appeal here on our own motion and we now affirm.

facts

The tragic facts underlying this appeal are shown in the plaintiff's complaint, deposition testimony, and the city's affidavits. Joseph Fitzgibbons, a prisoner in the custody of the city's police department, committed suicide by hanging himself in his cell on May 19, 1979. A police officer, James M. Driscoll, had arrested Fitzgibbons for open and gross lewdness at approximately 1:15 p.m. on the same afternoon, took him to the police station, and informed him of his rights. The prisoner made two telephone calls; one to his sister, the plaintiff administratrix, and the other to his employer. Officer Driscoll then asked Fitzgibbons to empty his pockets, recorded the charges against him, and placed him alone in a cell. The prisoner was wearing a red shirt which was not tucked into his trousers.

At approximately 4:30 P.M. that afternoon, the plaintiff and her husband, accompanied by a police officer, Nelson Dionne, visited the prisoner in his cell for a short period of time. The plaintiff agreed to assist her brother in raising bail and to return later with some sandwiches and another visitor. The plaintiff saw that he was wearing a belt.

While inspecting the cell area at approximately 5:30 P.M., another police officer, Charles Bergman, saw Fitzgibbons hanging from a bar in the cell door. A belt was tied to the upper bar of the cell door and looped around his neck. Officer Bergman cut the belt and called to other police officers for assistance. Efforts to resuscitate him failed, and he was pronounced dead on arrival at Salem Hospital.

The plaintiff argues that the judge erred in granting the city's motion for summary judgment because a genuine issue of material fact was raised and the city was not entitled to judgment as a matter of law. See Mass. R. Civ. P. 56(c), 365 Mass. 824 (1974). The plaintiff's other claims of error are stated in the text of the opinion.

. . . [In prior cases], this court addressed the issue of the defendant's liability for another's suicide in terms of proximate cause. The court, in both cases, had first concluded that the defendants' actions were negligent. The court reached the issue of the circumstances in which a tortfeasor is liable for a resulting suicide only because it first found a duty to the plaintiff and then found a breach of that duty. Thus, before the issue of proximate causation is reached in the instant case, the plaintiff, in order to survive the motion for summary judgment, must show that there were material facts in issue relating to the city's duty and the breach thereof.

This court has never specifically addressed the issue of the duty, if any, owed by prison officials to a person within their custody and control. The Restatement (Second) of Torts recognizes the duty of a jailor as being similar to the duty of common carriers or innkeepers. One who is required by law to take or voluntarily takes the custody of another under circumstances such as to deprive the other of his normal opportunities for protection is under a duty (1) to protect them against unreasonable risk of physical harm, and (2) to give them first aid after it knows or has reason to know that they are ill or injured, and to care for them until they can be cared for by others. Restatement (Second) of Torts § 314A (1965). The comments to § 314A state that a "defendant is not liable where he neither knows nor should know of the unreasonable risk, or of the illness or injury," Restatement, supra at Comment e, and that a "defendant is not required to take any action until he knows or has reason to know that the plaintiff is endangered, or is ill or injured," Restatement, supra at Comment f. We assume, without deciding, that the Restatement would be followed in this Commonwealth.

We note, also, that the case law from other jurisdictions generally follows the *Restatement* view. In cases that have addressed the issue of the liability of a jailor for the suicide of one in his custody, most have required that there be evidence that the defendant knew, or had reason to know, of the plaintiff's suicidal tendency.

The plaintiff, in her complaint, did allege that the defendant "knew or had reason to know from observations of the prisoner that he was a suicidal risk." The city, through the above named police officers, submitted affidavits accompanying its motion for summary judgment. Each officer averred to facts within his personal knowledge which evidenced that none of them knew, or should have known, that the prisoner was suicidal. To avoid entry of summary judgment against her, the plaintiff was then required to allege specific facts which established that there is a genuine, triable issue. "[A]n adverse party may not rest upon the mere allegations or denials of his pleading, but his response, by affidavits or as otherwise provided in this rule, must set forth specific facts showing that there is a genuine issue for trial. If he does not so respond, summary judgment, if appropriate, shall be entered against him." Mass. R. Civ. P. 56(e) **[Eds.—The federal equivalent is Rule 56(c)(1)(A)]**, 365 Mass. 824 (1974). "The party failing to file an opposing affidavit in such a situation cannot rely on the hope that the judge may draw 'contradictory inferences' in his favor from the apparently undisputed facts alleged in the affidavit of the moving party." *Farley v. Sprague*, 374 Mass. 419, 425 (1978), citing *Community Nat'l Bank v. Dawes*, supra. Specifically, the plaintiff was required to proffer facts which supported her assertion that the police knew, or had reason to know, that the prisoner was suicidal.

The plaintiff, however, further contends that the judge erred in granting the city's motion for summary judgment because the city's affidavits raised an issue of credibility. In the city's affidavits, the arresting officer avers that he did not know that the prisoner was wearing a belt. Officer Dionne's and Officer Bergman's affidavits are silent on this issue. The plaintiff, in her deposition, stated that her brother was wearing a belt. Although that fact appears to be in dispute, the fact is not material because the fact could not aid in establishing negligence without at least a preliminary finding that the city knew, or should have known, that the deceased was a suicidal risk. Compare *Dezort v. Village of Hinsdale*, supra (police regulations required jailor to take belt away from prisoner before confinement).[3] Until the city's duty is established, by the facts or otherwise, whether the prisoner was wearing a belt at the time of his arrest is immaterial.

The plaintiff further contends that the judge erred in granting summary judgment for the city because the affidavits were based on facts known only to the police officers who were interested parties. If, however, the plaintiff is unable to "present by affidavit facts essential to justify [her] opposition" to summary judgment, the plaintiff must file an affidavit and state the reasons for that inability. Mass. R. Civ. P. 56(f), 365 Mass. 824 (1974). "A party must resort to [Rule 56(f)] **[Eds.—The federal equivalent is Rule 56(d)]** when it is opposing summary judgment and is unable to present a sufficient affidavit because the necessary facts or evidence are possessed or controlled by the moving party." *A. John Cohen Ins. Agency, Inc. v. Middlesex Ins. Co.*, 8 Mass. App. Ct. 178, 183 (1979). The plaintiff in the instant case failed to allege any facts that contested the affiants' assertions of facts; nor does the plaintiff argue that conflicting inferences could be drawn from the city's affidavits. The plaintiff, to prevail, must indicate that she can produce the requisite quantum of evidence to enable her to reach the jury with her claim. We firmly reject the plaintiff's contention that she could prove that the city knew, or should have known, of her brother's alleged suicidal tendencies by

3. There is nothing in the record to show any duty to remove a belt from all prisoners as a matter of due care, or as a matter of regulation, or standard practice.

cross-examining the police officers, and, on the officers' denial of this matter, thereby establish the affirmative.

Finding no error, we affirm the judgment of the Superior Court.

SO ORDERED.

Notes and Questions: Moving for Summary Judgment

Q **1. The substantive law.** What is the tort law applicable to the City's motion? (Hint: Salem is trying to disprove an essential element of the plaintiff's tort claim, so look to the tort law governing that claim.)

A This is simple, but vital. If you can't figure out the applicable substantive law, then you can't figure out summary judgment. Not only does summary judgment involve the application of substantive law to undisputed facts, but the substantive law also identifies the facts that are material.

Slaven argues that the City negligently caused her brother's death. Negligence traditionally requires breach of a duty of reasonable care proximately causing injury. Under the *Restatement (Second) of Torts* § 314A, a jailor has a duty to protect prisoners from an unreasonable risk of which it knows or should have known. Here the risk is that the prisoner will commit suicide. Hence, the essential elements of the applicable tort law (the court assumes) are that (1) Salem knew, or should have known, of the brother's suicidal tendencies, (2) it breached its duty to protect him against this known risk, and (3) its breach proximately caused his suicide.

Q **2. The material facts.** Slaven testified at her deposition, under oath, that her brother was wearing a belt when she visited him in his cell. The arresting officer's affidavit (a sworn written statement averring admissible facts personally known to the officer) avers that he did not know whether her brother was wearing a belt, and two other officers' affidavits are silent on this issue. From these averments, a fact-finder might reasonably infer that the prisoner was wearing a belt. Surely they pose a genuine dispute about the officer's prior knowledge of the very means of the suicide. Why is this dispute not enough to defeat Salem's motion?

A Whether or not he was wearing a belt is immaterial absent evidence that his jailors knew or should have known of his suicidal tendency. The Supreme Court has said that "substantive law will identify which facts are material. Only disputes which might affect the outcome of the suit under the governing law will properly preclude the entry of summary judgment." *Anderson v. Liberty Lobby*, 477 U.S. 242, 248 (1986). If Salem neither knew nor should have known of the brother's suicidal tendencies, it would have no duty to remove his belt. Thus, a dispute about whether he was wearing a belt will not affect the outcome; Salem will win either way.

Q **3. Does the truth matter?** Pelkey sues Dilbert for assault, after Dilbert hit him because of an article he wrote about Dilbert. The elements of assault are presumably (this is Civil Procedure, after all, not Torts) that defendant intentionally caused reasonable apprehension of immediate harmful or offensive contact. The parties dispute whether the article was true. Is the truth of the article a material fact?

A The applicable tort law looks to *what* Dilbert did and its effect on Pelkey, not *why* Dilbert did it, at least until and unless he pleads a defense that hinges on his state of mind, like self-defense. Hence, it doesn't matter whether the article was true or false. Either way, Dilbert can't haul off and whack Pelkey. When a fact doesn't matter to the disposition of the claim (or defense), it's immaterial.

4. What is a proper record for summary judgment? Rule 56(c)(1)(A) lists materials that may be considered in deciding summary judgment. But all discovery materials do not automatically qualify for consideration on summary judgment; they must be admissible under the rules of evidence before they are properly considered as part of the record for summary judgment. *See* Rule 56(c)(2) ("A party may object that material cited to support or dispute a fact cannot be presented in a form that would be admissible in evidence"). Why should supporting materials have to be admissible?

> Applying the admissibility tests to all evidence on a summary judgment motion serves the purposes of summary judgment. Rule 56 is designed to avoid a trial that would be unnecessary. The motion could not serve that function if, in deciding whether issues exist for trial, courts were to consider evidence that could not subsequently be admitted at trial.

Edward J. Brunet et al., Summary Judgment § 8.6 (Nov. 2019). Thus, a statement at a deposition that the deponent George "heard Bill say that Joe told him that Larry did it" would be inadmissible as unreliable hearsay, even though George testified under oath.

However, Rule 56(c)(4) makes a narrow exception for affidavits and declarations—certain written statements by witness. Ordinarily, these would not be admissible at trial; instead, the witness (*declarant* or *affiant*) would be required to testify in person subject to cross-examination. But insisting on live witness testimony for a summary judgment would take the "summary" out of summary judgment, because the parties would then need to hold a deposition or the court would need to hold a hearing. Rule 56 therefore expressly permits the presentation of such evidence by affidavit or declaration, even though it would not be admissible *in that form* at trial. Yet this exception is really narrow, because the Rule still requires that the affidavit or declaration "must be made on personal knowledge, [and] set out facts that would be admissible in evidence. . . ." Fed. R. Civ. P. 56(c)(4).

Q **5. Relying on pleadings for summary judgment.** Plaintiff alleged in her complaint that defendants "knew or had reason to know from observations of the prisoner that he was a suicidal risk." Why wasn't this enough to create a genuine dispute of material fact? Mass. Rule 56(e) itself expressly prohibits the non-moving party from "rely[ing] merely on allegations or denials in its own pleading" to defeat a properly supported motion for summary judgment. But *why* does the Massachusetts Rule prohibit the plaintiff from resting on her complaint?

A

Recall that the typical pleading is unsworn and often contains allegations that are not made on the personal knowledge of the pleader. It is therefore not usually evidence that would be admissible at trial. The whole purpose of the summary judgment motion is to "pierce" or go beyond the pleadings to the admissible evidence that the pleader expects to offer to prove them. "Summary judgment effectively distinguishes the merely formal existence of a dispute as framed in the pleadings from the actual substantive existence of a controversy requiring trial," *Moore* § 56.02, and distinguishes the allegations of the pleadings from evidence of the allegations.

Unlike the Massachusetts rule, Federal Rule 56(c)(1)(A) does not expressly exclude a movant from relying on her own pleadings to support summary judgment. But Federal Rule 56(c)(2) provides that the opposing party may object that material "cannot be presented in a form that would be admissible in evidence" at trial. The movant's own unsworn pleadings are not in such form and could not be offered as evidence by that party at trial. In contrast, an *opposing* party's pleadings could be admitted at trial as "admissions" by the pleader. On rare occasions, a party may also rely on its *own* pleading, but only *if* the party swore to the truth of the pleading allegations, made them from personal knowledge, and those allegations would be admissible at trial—in other words, if the pleading is the equivalent of an affidavit. *See* Rule 56(e)(1).

6. Admissible materials. Which, if any, of the following materials could the court properly consider as part of the record for deciding summary judgment in *Slaven,* if Federal Rule 56 applied?

A. An affidavit by Slaven's lawyer describing what happened when the deceased was left alone in his cell.
B. A newspaper article about the suicide written by a journalist who collected her facts by telephone interviews with Slaven and several anonymous policemen.
C. Pages of the log maintained at the jail in which the jailor inventories the possessions and clothing of a prisoner when he is first received for confinement.
D. A security videotape of the cellblock where the deceased was confined, bearing the date and time at which he was led to his jail cell.
E. Deposition testimony by the jailor who found the deceased after he hanged himself, asserting that "I have heard around town that [the deceased] was really happy and got drunk celebrating his upcoming marriage."

A almost certainly cannot be considered. An affidavit must be "made on personal knowledge." Fed. R. Civ. P. 56(c)(4). That is, the affiant must personally know the facts she avers, having learned them as an "eyeball witness" or what lawyers call a *percipient witness*—one who personally perceived the facts to which she attests. Not only could Slaven's lawyer not know what went on in the cell when the deceased was alone, but if he did, he will likely find himself having to testify as a witness at trial, placing him in conflict with his role as advocate. *See Hickman v. Taylor*, 329 U.S. 495, 516 (1974) (Jackson, J., concurring).

You haven't taken Evidence yet, but fact-gathering from "anonymous" policemen suggests the problem with **B**. How do we know whether the journalist's secondhand information is correct without speaking directly to the sources? Roughly speaking (Evidence teachers, please avert your eyes), secondhand information is *hearsay* (the journalist heard these sources say . . .), and unreliable because we cannot test the journalist's sources by cross-examination. But if Evidence law would exclude it, then it should not be considered for summary judgment either. **B** is not correct.

Intuitively, **C** sounds more reliable. (In fact, these pages are probably also hearsay, but as records regularly maintained by the jail to conduct its everyday business, the log pages are generally a reliable and admissible form of hearsay under the business records exception to the rule against hearsay.) If they are what they appear to be—that is, if these are *authentic* pages from the actual log (in Evidence, we say, if they can be "authenticated")—then they should be considered on the summary judgment motion. (Documents like this could probably be authenticated pretty easily by the desk sergeant testifying, "Yep, that's the log.")

D, too, sounds reliable if, in fact, it was made at or about the date and time it bears, and if it has not been altered. In other words, if it also can be authenticated, it may also be considered.

Finally, **E**, at first glance, sounds good, too. Depositions are expressly listed as materials in the record that a party may cite on summary judgment, *see* Fed. R. Civ. P. 56(c)(1)(A), and the jailor testified under oath. But remember that depositions are boxes with contents. *See* pp. 837–38, *supra*. Even if the box can be used under Rule 32, the particular contents have themselves to pass evidentiary muster. Thus, if the jailor had testified to what he saw, his testimony would be admissible. But here he testified to what he "heard around town"—classic hearsay that will almost certainly be ruled inadmissible. **E** cannot be considered on summary judgment. Whether deposition testimony can be used for summary judgment depends on which part of the deposition is offered and for what purpose.

7. Summary judgment and the standard of proof. In the typical civil action, the standard of proof is *preponderance of the evidence*. That is, the plaintiff carries the burden of convincing the finder of fact at trial that the evidence on each element of his claim preponderates in his favor—that it is more likely than not that facts exist that establish each element. In *Anderson v. Liberty Lobby, Inc.*, 477 U.S. 242 (1986), the Court said that the trial judge's inquiry on a summary judgment motion is therefore, properly speaking, whether the evidence presented is such that a reasonable jury could not find by a preponderance of the evidence for the non-moving party.

In *Anderson* itself, however, the libel plaintiff had the burden of proving actual malice by *clear and convincing evidence*, a higher standard of proof than the usual preponderance standard. Therefore, the Court found, "the appropriate summary judgment question will be whether the evidence in the record could support a reasonable jury finding either that the plaintiff has shown actual malice by clear and convincing evidence or that the plaintiff has not." *Id.* at 255. In other words, the determination whether there is a genuine dispute must be guided by the standard of proof applicable to the issue in the case.

Notes and Questions: Responding to Summary Judgment

Q **1. A preliminary question: Dispute of law?** The court in *Slaven* admits that it "has never specifically addressed the issue of duty, if any, owed by prison officials to a person within their custody and control." Suppose lower courts have split on this question of law, some adopting the *Restatement* (as the *Slaven* court ultimately does), and others opting for a theory of strict custodial liability—that jailors are absolutely liable for suicides by inmates in their custody. Would a genuine dispute about the applicable legal standard preclude summary judgment?

A No. Rule 56 expressly looks to genuine disputes of "material *fact*," not of law. As we noted in the introduction, the difficulty of a legal issue is not ordinarily a reason to insist on trial. Judges just have to bite the bullet when the record is adequate (the material facts are undisputed) and decide the hard questions of law. That's why we pay them. When all that stands in the way of summary judgment is a difficult dispute of law, "a denial merely postpones coming to grips with the problem at the cost of engaging in a full-dress trial that is unnecessary for a just adjudication of the dispute." *Wright & Miller* § 2725.

Occasionally, however, a judge will deny summary judgment and make the parties go to trial because a fuller record may clarify the correct legal analysis. The Supreme Court has approved the deferral of decision in such circumstances, reasoning that it is "good judicial administration to withhold decision of the ultimate questions involved in this case until this or another record shall present a more solid basis of findings based on litigation or on a comprehensive statement of agreed facts. While we might be able, on the present record, to reach a conclusion that would decide the case, it might well be found later to be lacking in the thoroughness that should precede judgment of this importance and which it is the purpose of the judicial process to provide." *Kennedy v. Silas Mason Co.*, 334 U.S. 249, 256 (1948).

Q **2. Needing time to respond.** Isn't it unfair to Slaven to base summary judgment on factual assertions known only to the defendant's employees, the jailors?

A Slaven *is* at an initial disadvantage, since Salem has access, obviously, to its own employees, and they are unlikely to be willing to speak candidly and unguardedly with Slaven after she files her lawsuit. But the discovery rules, we have seen, allow Slaven to require them to testify under oath in depositions or answers to interrogatories, and Mass. Rule 56(f) (Fed. Rule 56(d)) expressly lets her file an affidavit to obtain a continuance (a delay before having to respond to the motion) in order to complete any discovery that she needs to respond to the city's motion. Thus, "I don't yet know whether the facts are disputed" is not a sufficient response to defeat summary judgment, although it can buy an opposing party time in which to find out, by taking discovery.

3. Disputing your adversary's state of mind. If the jailors deny knowing that Slaven's brother was suicidal, how would Slaven ever be able to prove it? If she could prove it at trial, what should she do now to survive summary judgment?

The key to answering these questions is the applicable substantive law. Recall that it required plaintiff to show that the jailors knew, *or had reason to know*, of the prisoner's suicidal tendency. They deny knowing. Slaven may be able to break them down at trial on cross-examination, but the hope of doing this is not enough to stave off summary judgment, as we saw above. But could she show that (or at least create a genuine dispute about whether) the jailors *should have* known? The following question explores her options.

Which, if any, of the following showings would defeat defendants' summary judgment motion?

A. The prisoner told them that he hated being confined.
B. The prisoner cried and ranted when they led him to the cell.
C. The prisoner kept repeating, "I can't stay the night here. I won't make it to morning."
D. The prisoner's arrest record showed that he had threatened suicide during a prior incarceration, though he had not actually attempted suicide.
E. The Massachusetts Department of Corrections had published a report drawing a profile of prison suicides, which matched Slaven's brother in several respects.

A is not enough. Most prisoners probably hate being confined, but that doesn't make them suicidal, or, more to the point, appear suicidal.

B is closer. Crying and ranting may be sufficiently abnormal as to raise questions about the prisoner's mental state, though whether an observer should infer that he is suicidal may be a stretch. Still, the burden is on Salem as the movant to show the absence of a genuine dispute, and reasonable inferences must be drawn against the movant. One inference is that the crying and raving prisoner is so distraught as to require special observation—a suicide watch. **B** might be enough to defeat summary judgment.

C is also close. "I can't make it to morning" could be a red flag of suicidal tendencies. It could also mean that the prisoner is physically ill or dependent on some medication. While the latter would not raise an inference of suicidal tendencies, does it matter? Doesn't the alternative inference of illness still raise an unreasonable risk of harm if he is left alone? Probably this, even more than **B**, should be enough to defeat the city's summary judgment motion.

D sounds easy by comparison. If he threatened suicide once, he's still a risk. Or is he? Suppose it was seventeen years ago that he was last arrested. Maybe we need more information for this one.

The Massachusetts Special Commission Suicide Report

Check List

Signs and Symptoms	Yes	No	Describe any Yes
Abnormal Feelings			
Abnormal Thoughts			
Abnormal Behavior			
Alcohol or Drugs			
Mental Illness			
Medications			
Physical Illness			
Accidents			
Background			
prior mental illness			
prior physical illness			
vomiting or breathing difficulty			
overreaction to crime			
crime of passion			
family not available			
suicide of family/friend			
death of family/friend			
unemployed			
Suicide			
thinking of suicide			
prior thought of suicide			
tried to hurt self			
details of plan			

This checklist appeared as an appendix to the Massachusetts Special Commission to Investigate Suicide in Municipal Detention Centers, *Suicide in Massachusetts Lockups, 1973–1984 Final Report*, Appendix 16 (1984).

If the report had been distributed to the Salem jail keepers and they had read it before the brother's suicide, would this checklist have created a genuine dispute about whether they knew or should have known of a risk of his suicide in detention?

E is easier yet, *if* the jail authorities were aware of the above report and if its profile was sufficiently specific to present a close match. But if it is a general profile—white males between twenty-one and twenty-three, intoxicated at time of arrest, with two or more prior arrests for public drunkenness and/or drunk driving—then it may be over-predictive, in that it applies to a much larger part of the jail population than are actually suicidal. On the other hand, aren't these the kind of judgments that we normally leave to the jury? If so, this, too, could defeat summary judgment.

In a subsequent tort action based on a prison suicide, the court denied summary judgment after comparing the profile in such a report with the characteristics of the deceased prisoner, including his intoxication at the time of arrest, his age, his prior arrest record, the arresting officers' awareness of that prior record, his place of residence, his method and means of suicide, and the time of his arrest and suicide. While it did "not vouch for any of the . . . [report's] statistics or conclusions," the court concluded that "enough appears to compel the conclusion that the plaintiff is entitled to a jury trial on the question whether the . . . police knew or should have known that . . . [the prisoner] was a suicide risk, as well as on all the other issues raised by the pleadings." *White v. Town of Seekonk*, 499 N.E.2d 842, 843–44 (Mass. App. Ct. 1986). Of course, any match between such a profile and Slaven's brother might be entirely coincidental, but, again, on summary judgment the court must draw any reasonable inferences against the movant.

Q **4. The lying affiant and the slightest doubt standard.** Slaven argued that the police officers were "interested parties" who might therefore slant their testimony in their employer's favor (or even lie to protect their jobs). Even if she had filed nothing in response, why wouldn't it be sufficient for her to argue that there is a genuine dispute about the police officers' veracity, given their self-interest? After all, if an officer testified live at trial and Slaven's lawyer cross-examined him, the jury *might* find that he had lied. Doesn't this raise at least the "slightest doubt" as to his veracity?

A After some early indecision, the cases have generally rejected the "disbelief of denial" and "slightest doubt" theories for denying summary judgment. *See Brunet, supra,* § 6.3. As the father of the Federal Rules asserted, the "slightest doubt" standard would eviscerate summary judgment because "at least a slight doubt can be developed as to practically all things human." Charles Clark, *Special Problems in Drafting and Interpreting Procedural Codes and Rules,* 3 VAND. L. REV. 493, 503–04 (1950). The Supreme Court has also apparently rejected the slightest doubt standard: "The mere existence of a scintilla of evidence in support of the plaintiff's position will be insufficient; there must be evidence on which a jury could reasonably find for the [non-moving party]." *Anderson,* 477 U.S. at 252. Of course, had one of the officers lied on the stand before, evidence of that fact might be sufficient to create a credibility dispute. *Wright & Miller* § 2726 ("The general rule is that specific facts must be produced in order to put credibility in issue so as to preclude summary judgment. Unsupported allegations that credibility is in issue will not suffice.").

Notes and Questions: More About Genuine Disputes

Q **1. Genuine dispute of material fact for summary judgment purposes.** The Supreme Court has said that a dispute is genuine "if the evidence is such that a reasonable jury could return a verdict for the nonmoving party." *Anderson,* 477 U.S. at 248. To put it slightly differently, whether a dispute is "genuine" depends on whether any reasonable fact-finder could decide an issue of material fact for the non-moving party. The summary judgment standard is not whether a reasonable jury *would* find for her, but whether it *could.* It is commonly said that courts deciding summary judgment motions cannot "weigh" the evidence or decide credibility, but there is some point at which the evidence for one side so outweighs all other evidence that a fact-finder could reasonably reach but one conclusion.

So suppose plaintiff Robinson sues police officer Pezzat for killing her dog Wrinkles during a search pursuant to a search warrant. Robinson's uncorroborated deposition testimony is that after she locked Wrinkles in a bathroom at the officers' request, officer Pezzat opened the bathroom door, saw the recumbent Wrinkles, and shot Wrinkles as the dog got up. Officer Pezzat's deposition testimony is that the dog attacked her, a version of events corroborated by other officers. Summary judgment for the officer?

A No. While Robinson's uncorroborated testimony may raise credibility issues, "it [is] quite obvious that the uncorroborated nature of Robinson's testimony had nothing at all to do with the question before the district court: did Robinson present a genuine dispute of material fact as to whether Wrinkles posed an imminent threat to Pezzat's safety? Corroboration goes to credibility, a question for the jury, not the district court. Perhaps a jury will disbelieve Robinson because her testimony was uncorroborated, but at this stage of the litigation, the district court must 'believe[ ]' her testimony and must not make '[c]redibility determinations.' " *Robinson v. Pezzat*, 818 F.3d 1, 9 (D.C. Cir. 2016) (quoting *Anderson*, 477 U.S. at 255).

Q **2. Judicial fact-finding.** A judge decides many motions, some of which may require her to resolve disputes of fact. A motion to dismiss for lack of diversity jurisdiction may require the court to resolve factual disputes about the parties' citizenship. A motion to dismiss for lack of personal jurisdiction may require the court to resolve factual disputes about the defendant's contacts with the forum. Judges are empowered—indeed, the timing of such motions generally requires them—to decide such factual disputes before trial and without a jury. Rule 43(c) offers them a procedural device to assist them in such fact-finding.

How is Rule 56 different? Look again carefully at the standard it establishes for summary judgment. Does it expressly or by implication require or even allow the court to decide a genuine dispute of material fact? Or does it require the court only to decide *whether* such a dispute exists?

A Clearly, the Rule authorizes summary judgment only if the record "show[s] that there is no genuine dispute. . . ." If there is such a dispute, summary judgment must be denied. In other words, it is the *existence* of the genuine dispute, not its resolution, that is key to summary judgment.

READING *TOLAN v. COTTON*. Police officer Cotton shot Tolan after Tolan had been detained on a mistaken report of driving a stolen vehicle. Tolan suffered a life-altering injury and sued Cotton under 42 U.S.C. § 1983 for, *inter alia*,

using excessive force in violation of the Fourth Amendment. Cotton pleaded the affirmative defense of qualified immunity (see *supra* p. 518), arguing that the shooting was reasonable under the circumstances.

The district court agreed and granted summary judgment for Cotton. The court of appeals affirmed on the basis that the use of force under the circumstances did not violate a "clearly established right." But both lower court opinions rested on the conclusion that the material circumstances were not genuinely disputed.

- What is the rule of substantive law applicable to Cotton's motion?
- What facts matter—are "material"—to applying that rule of law?
- The Supreme Court unanimously finds that there was a genuine dispute precluding summary judgment. How, then, could the four lower court federal judges have found that there wasn't?

TOLAN v. COTTON

572 U.S. 650 (2014)

PER CURIAM.

During the early morning hours of New Year's Eve, 2008, police sergeant Jeffrey Cotton fired three bullets at Robert Tolan; one of those bullets hit its target and punctured Tolan's right lung. At the time of the shooting, Tolan was unarmed on his parents' front porch about 15 to 20 feet away from Cotton. . . . In articulating the factual context of the case, the Fifth Circuit failed to adhere to the axiom that in ruling on a motion for summary judgment, "[t]he evidence of the nonmovant is to be believed, and all justifiable inferences are to be drawn in his favor." *Anderson v. Liberty Lobby, Inc.*, 477 U.S. 242, 255 (1986). For that reason, we vacate its decision and remand the case for further proceedings consistent with this opinion.

I

A

[EDS.—At 2:00 AM police officer Edwards observed a vehicle turning quickly into a residential street in Bellaire, Texas, and parking in front of a house. Edwards entered the license plate of the vehicle into his computer, but keyed one incorrect digit, causing an incorrect match with a stolen vehicle of the same color and make. Edwards exited his cruiser, drew his service pistol, and ordered Tolan and Cooper, who had just exited their vehicle, to the ground. When Edwards accused them of stealing the car, Cooper denied it and said, "That's my car." Tolan then complied with the officer's demand to lie facedown on the home's front porch.

As it turned out, Tolan and Cooper were at the home where Tolan lived with his parents, who came out in their pajamas on hearing the commotion. Tolan's father told him to stay facedown and, with his hands in the

air, explained, "[T]his is my nephew. This is my son. We live here. This is my house." His mother agreed, saying, "[S]ir this is a big mistake. This car is not stolen.... That's our car."

Soon police officer Cotton arrived on the scene, drew his weapon, and ordered Tolan's mother to stand against the family's garage door. She responded, "[A]re you kidding me? We've lived her[e] 15 years. We've never had anything like this happen before." The parties disagree as to what happened next. Tolan, his mother, and Cooper say that Cotton grabbed her and slammed her against the garage door, causing her to fall. Photographic evidence showed bruises on her arms and back. Cotton, on the other hand, said that when he was escorting the mother to the garage, she flipped her arm up and told him to get his hands off her. Tolan testified that upon seeing his mother being pushed, he rose to his knees. The police officers said he rose to his feet.

Both parties agree that Tolan then exclaimed, from roughly 15 to 20 feet away, "[G]et your fucking hands off my mom." Cotton then drew his pistol and fired three shots at Tolan, hitting his chest, collapsing his right lung and piercing his liver.]

B....

... [In affirming the summary judgment for Cotton,] [t]he Court of Appeals reasoned that Tolan failed to overcome the qualified-immunity bar because "an objectively-reasonable officer in Sergeant Cotton's position could have ... believed" that Tolan "presented an 'immediate threat to the safety of the officers.'" In support of this conclusion, the court relied on the following facts: the front porch had been "dimly-lit"; Tolan's mother had "refus[ed] orders to remain quiet and calm"; and Tolan's words had amounted to a "verba[l] threa[t]." Most critically, the court also relied on the purported fact that Tolan was "moving to intervene in" Cotton's handling of his mother, and that Cotton therefore could reasonably have feared for his life. Accordingly, the court held, Cotton did not violate clearly established law in shooting Tolan....

II

A

In resolving questions of qualified immunity at summary judgment, courts engage in a two-pronged inquiry. The first asks whether the facts, "[t]aken in the light most favorable to the party asserting the injury, ... show the officer's conduct violated a [federal] right[.]" *Saucier v. Katz,* 533 U.S. 194, 201 (2001). When a plaintiff alleges excessive force during an investigation or arrest, the federal right at issue is the Fourth Amendment right against unreasonable seizures. *Graham v. Connor,* 490 U.S. 386, 394 (1989). The inquiry into whether this right was violated requires a balancing of " 'the nature and quality of the intrusion on the individual's Fourth Amendment interests against the importance of the governmental interests alleged to justify the intrusion.' " *Tennessee v. Garner,* 471 U.S. 1, 8 1 (1985).

The second prong of the qualified-immunity analysis asks whether the right in question was "clearly established" at the time of the violation. *Hope v. Pelzer*, 536 U.S. 730, 739 (2002). Governmental actors are "shielded from liability for civil damages if their actions did not violate 'clearly established statutory or constitutional rights of which a reasonable person would have known.' " *Ibid.* "[T]he salient question ... is whether the state of the law" at the time of an incident provided "fair warning" to the defendants "that their alleged [conduct] was unconstitutional." *Id.*, at 741.

Courts have discretion to decide the order in which to engage these two prongs. But under either prong, courts may not resolve genuine disputes of fact in favor of the party seeking summary judgment. This is not a rule specific to qualified immunity; it is simply an application of the more general rule that a "judge's function" at summary judgment is not "to weigh the evidence and determine the truth of the matter but to determine whether there is a genuine issue for trial." *Anderson*, 477 U.S., at 249. Summary judgment is appropriate only if "the movant shows that there is no genuine issue as to any material fact and the movant is entitled to judgment as a matter of law." Fed. Rule Civ. Proc. 56(a). In making that determination, a court must view the evidence "in the light most favorable to the opposing party." *Adickes v. S.H. Kress & Co.*, 398 U.S. 144, 157 (1970).

Our qualified-immunity cases illustrate the importance of drawing inferences in favor of the nonmovant, even when, as here, a court decides only the clearly-established prong of the standard. In cases alleging unreasonable searches or seizures, we have instructed that courts should define the "clearly established" right at issue on the basis of the "specific context of the case." Accordingly, courts must take care not to define a case's "context" in a manner that imports genuinely disputed factual propositions.

B

In holding that Cotton's actions did not violate clearly established law, the Fifth Circuit failed to view the evidence at summary judgment in the light most favorable to Tolan with respect to the central facts of this case. By failing to credit evidence that contradicted some of its key factual conclusions, the court improperly "weigh[ed] the evidence" and resolved disputed issues in favor of the moving party, *Anderson*, 477 U.S., at 249.

First, the court relied on its view that at the time of the shooting, the Tolans' front porch was "dimly-lit." The court appears to have drawn this assessment from Cotton's statements in a deposition that when he fired at Tolan, the porch was "'fairly dark,'" and lit by a gas lamp that was "'decorative.'" In his own deposition, however, Tolan's father was asked whether the gas lamp was in fact "more decorative than illuminating." He said that it was not. Moreover, Tolan stated in his deposition that two floodlights shone on the driveway during the incident, and Cotton acknowledged that there were two motion-activated lights in front of the house. And Tolan confirmed that at the time of the shooting, he was "not in darkness."

Second, the Fifth Circuit stated that Tolan's mother "refus[ed] orders to remain quiet and calm," thereby "compound[ing]" Cotton's belief that Tolan "presented an immediate threat to the safety of the officers." But here, too, the court did not credit directly contradictory evidence. Although the parties agree that Tolan's mother repeatedly informed officers that Tolan was her son, that she lived in the home in front of which he had parked, and that the vehicle he had been driving belonged to her and her husband, there is a dispute as to how calmly she provided this information. Cotton stated during his deposition that Tolan's mother was "very agitated" when she spoke to the officers. By contrast, Tolan's mother testified at Cotton's criminal trial* that she was neither "aggravated" nor "agitated."

Third, the Court concluded that Tolan was "shouting," and "verbally threatening" the officer, in the moments before the shooting. The court noted, and the parties agree, that while Cotton was grabbing the arm of his mother, Tolan told Cotton, "[G]et your fucking hands off my mom." But Tolan testified that he "was not screaming." And a jury could reasonably infer that his words, in context, did not amount to a statement of intent to inflict harm. Tolan's mother testified in Cotton's criminal trial that he slammed her against a garage door with enough force to cause bruising that lasted for days. A jury could well have concluded that a reasonable officer would have heard Tolan's words not as a threat, but as a son's plea not to continue any assault of his mother.

Fourth, the Fifth Circuit inferred that at the time of the shooting, Tolan was "moving to intervene in Sergeant Cotton's" interaction with his mother. [S]ee [713 F.3d] at 308 (characterizing Tolan's behavior as "abruptly attempting to approach Sergeant Cotton," thereby "inflam[ing] an already tense situation"). The court appears to have credited Edwards' account that at the time of the shooting, Tolan was on both feet "[i]n a crouch" or a "charging position" looking as if he was going to move forward. Tolan testified at trial, however, that he was on his knees when Cotton shot him, a fact corroborated by his mother. Tolan also testified in his deposition that he "wasn't going anywhere," and emphasized that he did not "jump up."

Considered together, these facts lead to the inescapable conclusion that the court below credited the evidence of the party seeking summary judgment and failed properly to acknowledge key evidence offered by the party opposing motion. And while "this Court is not equipped to correct every perceived error coming from the lower federal courts," *Boag v. MacDougall* 454 U.S. 364, 366 (1982) (O'Connor, J., concurring), we intervene here because the opinion below reflects a clear misapprehension of summary judgment standards in light of our precedents.

The witnesses on both sides come to this case with their own perceptions, recollections, and even potential biases. It is in part for that reason that genuine disputes are generally resolved by juries in our adversarial system. By weighing the evidence and reaching factual inferences contrary to Tolan's competent evidence, the court below neglected to adhere to the fundamental principle that at the summary judgment stage, reasonable inferences should be drawn in favor of the nonmoving party.

Applying that principle here, the court should have acknowledged and credited Tolan's evidence with regard to the lighting, his mother's demeanor, whether he shouted words that were an overt threat, and his positioning during the shooting. This is not to say, of course, that these are the only facts that the Fifth Circuit

*** [Eds.—Officer Cotton was criminally tried for aggravated assault by a public servant and acquitted after a jury trial. 713 F.3d 299, 303 (5th Cir. 2013).]**

should consider, or that no other facts might contribute to the reasonableness of the officer's actions as a matter of law. Nor do we express a view as to whether Cotton's actions violated clearly established law. We instead vacate the Fifth Circuit's judgment so that the court can determine whether, when Tolan's evidence is properly credited and factual inferences are reasonably drawn in his favor, Cotton's actions violated clearly established law.

* * *

The petition for certiorari and the NAACP Legal Defense and Educational Fund's motion to file an *amicus curiae* brief are granted. The judgment of the United States Court of Appeals for the Fifth Circuit is vacated, and the case is remanded for further proceedings consistent with this opinion.

It is so ordered.

Justice ALITO, with whom Justice SCALIA joins, concurring in the judgment. . . . In my experience, a substantial percentage of the civil appeals heard each year by the courts of appeals present the question whether the evidence in the summary judgment record is just enough or not quite enough to support a grant of summary judgment. The present case falls into that very large category. There is no confusion in the courts of appeals about the standard to be applied in ruling on a summary judgment motion, and the Court of Appeals invoked the correct standard here. Thus, the only issue is whether the relevant evidence, viewed in the light most favorable to the nonmoving party, is sufficient to support a judgment for that party. In the courts of appeals, cases presenting this question are utterly routine. There is no question that this case is important for the parties, but the same is true for a great many other cases that fall into the same category.

On the merits of the case, while I do not necessarily agree in all respects with the Court's characterization of the evidence, I agree that there are genuine issues of material fact and that this is a case in which summary judgment should not have been granted.

I therefore concur in the judgment.

Notes and Questions

1. The applicable law. As we noted *supra* p. 518, the two-pronged law of qualified immunity is complicated. The first prong asks whether the officer violated a federal right: in *Tolan*, the Fourth Amendment right against unreasonable seizures. (The use of force to stop or restrain a subject is viewed as a seizure.) The second prong asks whether that right was "clearly established" at the time of the violation, which the courts have construed quite strictly by looking for a case precedent specifically on point. As the Court notes, courts have the discretion to skip the first prong and to go straight to the second.

2. The common factual question. Both prongs of qualified immunity pose questions of law, but "the resolution of these legal issues will entail consideration of the factual allegations that make up the plaintiff's claim for relief . . . ." *Mitchell v.*

Forsyth, 472 U.S. 511, 528 (1985). That is, they depend on what the police officer did. Thus, the Supreme Court states that even when the lower court is considering the purely legal question whether the relevant law was "clearly established" at the time, it must consider the "specific context of the case." Cotton's motion for summary judgment therefore depends in part on whether the material facts about what he did and his use of force "in the circumstances" are genuinely undisputed.

3. The record. The excerpt from *Tolan* indicates that the record included the sworn deposition (and criminal trial) testimony of the parties about the circumstances of the shooting, as well as the photographic evidence of the mother's bruises. Admissibility of the evidence is not an issue here.

4. Video evidence. Would the four lower court federal judges have found the circumstances undisputed had the scene been recorded by a body camera, dashboard camera, or smartphone? The increasing availability of such video evidence (think of the video of George Floyd's death) may make it harder for defendants to obtain summary judgment on the grounds of qualified immunity.

Or maybe not? In *Scott v. Harris*, 550 U.S. 372 (2007), a motorist was severely injured when a police officer rammed the fleeing motorist's car to end a high-speed chase. Like Tolan, the motorist brought a § 1983 claim against the officer, who pleaded qualified immunity and moved for summary judgment. The district court denied the motion, and the court of appeals affirmed. All four lower court judges concluded that a reasonable jury could find that the defendant used excessive force in ramming the plaintiff's vehicle (the record showed that the officer's superiors had approved an alternative way to stop the vehicle).

The Supreme Court reversed 8-1. Relying on the dashboard camera's video of the high-speed chase (see for yourselves at https://www.supremecourt.gov/media/video/mp4files/scott_v_harris.mp4), the Court concluded:

> Far from being the cautious and controlled driver the lower court depicts, what we see on the video more closely resembles a Hollywood-style car chase of the most frightening sort, placing police officers and innocent bystanders alike at great risk of serious injury....
>
> When opposing parties tell two different stories, one of which is blatantly contradicted by the record, so that no reasonable jury could believe it, a court should not adopt that version of the facts for purposes of ruling on a motion for summary judgment.
>
> That was the case here with regard to the factual issue whether respondent was driving in such fashion as to endanger human life. Respondent's version of events is so utterly discredited by the record that no reasonable jury could have believed him. The Court of Appeals should not have relied on such visible fiction; it should have viewed the facts in the light depicted by the videotape.

550 U.S. at 380–81.

How then could *five* federal judges (including dissenting Justice Stevens) find a genuine dispute even after viewing the video evidence? Accepting Justice Scalia's offer "to allow the videotape to speak for itself," 550 U.S. at 878 n.5, researchers subsequently showed it to a randomly selected panel of 1,350 diverse Americans. *See* Dan M. Kahan, David A. Hoffman, Donald Braman, *Whose Eyes Are You Going to Believe?* Scott v. Harris *and the Perils of Cognitive Illiberalism*, 122 HARV. L. REV. 837 (2009). While most viewers interpreted the facts as did the Supreme Court majority, "members of various subcommunities did not. African Americans, low-income workers, and residents of the Northeast, for example, tended to form more pro-plaintiff views of the facts than did the Court." *Id.* at 841. The study concluded:

> Although an admitted minority of American society, citizens disposed to see the facts differently from the *Scott* majority share a perspective founded on common experiences and values. By insisting that a case like *Scott* be decided summarily, the Court not only denied those citizens an opportunity, in the context of jury deliberations, to inform and possibly change the view of citizens endowed with a different perspective. It also needlessly bound the result in the case to a process of decisionmaking that deprived the decision of any prospect of legitimacy in the eyes of that subcommunity whose members saw the facts differently. Told that the law must be made in a fashion that rigorously excludes their understanding—which the opinion in *Scott* stigmatizes as being one only "unreasonable" people could hold—those who disagree with the outcome cannot divorce their assent to it from acceptance of their status as defeated outsiders.

Id. at 841–42.

The question cases like *Scott* and *Tolan* pose is not so much whether the Court's view of the facts is correct, but "who decides"? "Thus," the study concludes, "the question posed by the data is not . . . whether to believe one's eyes, but rather whose eyes the law should believe when identifiable groups of citizens form competing factual perceptions." *Id.* at 841.

5. The Settlement. After the Supreme Court ruling in *Tolan*, the case was reportedly settled by the city and Cotton for $110,000. *Settlement Reached in Police Shooting of Former MLB Player's Son*, Legal Reader, Sept. 18, 2015, available at https://www.legalreader.com/settlement-reached-in-police-shooting-of-former-mlb-players-son/.

> The settlement comes as a bit of a surprise given the lengthy process to keep the case alive. Harmon [the federal District Court judge who first granted summary judgment for Cotton] had already shown a weak reception to the case considering her prior ruling, and during Friday's pretrial hearing she indicated her desire to dismiss the case against Cotton. Harmon denied the motion for summary judgment, writing "I am very tempted to grant it, but I'm not going to right now. I think the Supreme Court sent it back to the circuit so that they could reanalyze my case. The Fifth Circuit didn't want to do that, so they punted it to me. And I don't think . . . they would ever be satisfied if we didn't take this case to trial." Harmon added, "I thought I was right the first time." Harmon also denied the Tolans' motion to remove herself from the case on Monday in light of her sentiment. Harmon however, responded to the motion saying that she "has never expressed a personal bias or prejudice against Robert R. Tolan or in favor of Jeffrey Cotton." Tolan's family agreed to the settlement after realizing the case would continue under Harmon's jurisdiction, despite her less than enthusiastic comments.

Id. It seems likely that the city indemnified officer Cotton. *See* Joanna C. Schwartz, *Police Indemnification*, 89 N.Y.U. L. Rev. 886 (2014) ("[P]olice officers are virtually always indemnified: During the study period, governments paid approximately 99.98% of the dollars that plaintiffs recovered in lawsuits alleging civil rights violations by law enforcement").

C. Relationship to Other Motions: Summary Judgment's Cousins

The motion for summary judgment is not the only motion seeking judgment as a matter of law. The Rule 12(b)(6) motion to dismiss for failure to state a claim shares that honor, because it, like the summary judgment motion, asks the court to make a decision as a matter of law on (presumptively) undisputed facts.

Q So how is the Rule 12(b)(6) motion different?

A The record for decision is different. The Rule 12(b)(6) motion is decided strictly on the factual allegations contained in the complaint, which are presumed to be true for purposes of the motion. The summary judgment motion is decided on the record of facts contained in all the supporting materials, and any opposing materials, that would be admissible at trial.

The Rule 12(c) motion for judgment on the pleadings is another cousin. *See supra* p. 485. The record for decision under this motion is the complaint and the answer, as well as the reply, if any.

Furthermore, either of these motions can be converted into a motion for summary judgment by the movant's presentation of material outside the complaint in support of the motion. If the court does not exclude such materials, it must treat the motion as one for summary judgment. *See* Rule 12(d).

Finally, a motion for judgment as a matter of law, as its name indicates, is a third cousin to summary judgment. It can be filed when "a party has been fully heard on an issue during a jury trial and the court finds that a reasonable jury would not have a legally sufficient evidentiary basis for the party on that issue," which can be at various points during trial. Rule 50(a). Indeed, the Supreme Court has equated the standard for summary judgment with the standard for a directed verdict at trial (now called a motion for judgment as a matter of law) under Rule 50(a). "In essence, ... the inquiry under each [Rule] is the same: whether the evidence presents a sufficient disagreement to require submission to a jury or whether it is so one-sided that one party must prevail as a matter of law." *Anderson*, 477 U.S. at 251–52.

Q What, then, is the difference between a motion for summary judgment and a motion for directed verdict or judgment as a matter of law?

A Primarily, timing and the record for decision. "[S]ummary judgment motions are usually made before trial and decided on documentary evidence, while directed verdict motions are made at trial and decided on the evidence that has been admitted." *Id.* at 251 (internal citation omitted).

In short, there are four different motions that can dispose of a case as a matter of law on what we might call "established" facts. *See Shreve, Raven-Hansen & Geyh* § 12.09[3][c]. They differ primarily in their timing and therefore in how the facts are "established" to furnish the record for decision. The following time line of a civil action from pleading to trial illustrates this point:

Motion Seeking Decision as a Matter of Law

12(b)(6)	12(c)	56	50(a)(1) after P's case	50(a)(1) after P's & D's case
facts alleged in complaint	facts alleged in complaint and answer	facts in movant's and non-movant's materials	facts in trial record after P's case	facts in full trial record

Factual Record for Decision

D. The Relationship Between the Movant's Burden and the Burden of Proof at Trial

We have seen that the party who moves for summary judgment has the burden of showing that there is no genuine dispute of material fact and that she is entitled to judgment as a matter of law.

If the moving party would have the burden of proof (also sometimes called the *burden of persuasion* in this context) on a claim or defense at trial, then he must present undisputed facts supporting each and every element of the claim or defense in order to obtain summary judgment. We might call this a *proof-of-the-elements* motion for summary judgment. It will sometimes be made by the plaintiff, who has the burden of proof on his claims at trial. But it may also be made by a defendant on an affirmative defense, as to which he ordinarily has the burden of proof at trial.

If the moving party would not have the burden of proof at trial, then she—typically a defendant—has two alternatives. She could present undisputed facts negating—proving the non-existence of—an essential element of the non-moving party's claim. We will call this a *disproof-of-an-element* motion for summary judgment. Or she could demonstrate that there is no evidence whatsoever in the record by which the non-moving party could establish the existence of an essential element of his claim. We will call this an *absence-of-evidence* motion for summary judgment.

Proof-of-the-Elements Summary Judgment

If the moving party would have the burden of proof on a claim or defense at trial, then her burden on summary judgment is to show that there is no genuine dispute of material facts about each and every element of her claim or defense. Thus, in our hypothetical tort case between Sophie and United Fibreboard, were

Sophie to move for summary judgment on her strict product liability claims, she would need to establish the material facts supporting each element of the claim (including United's manufacture of the product to which the deceased was exposed, proximate causation, product defect, and damages) in order to obtain summary judgment.

1. Defendant's proof-of-the-elements motion for summary judgment. It is not just the plaintiff who may have a burden of proof at trial. When a defendant pleads an affirmative defense, it usually has the burden of proving that defense at trial. Suppose, for example, that in *Slaven*, the city had pled the affirmative defense that Slaven's action was barred by the statute of limitations. To prove this defense at trial, the city would have the burden of showing when Slaven knew (or should have known) of the facts giving her a claim against the city, the period of limitations, and the date the complaint was filed (or served, depending on how the particular statute of limitations is tolled). It would therefore have the same burden on a proof-of-the-elements motion for summary judgment based on this affirmative defense.

Q **2. "Partial" summary judgment.** Rule 56(a) authorizes summary judgment on a "part of . . . [a] claim or defense." A court may therefore grant summary judgment as to one or fewer than all claims (or parties) or even as to part of a claim, leaving the rest for trial. Such a *partial summary judgment* does not decide the entire case.

Another kind of partial summary judgment is possible for plaintiffs' claims. Suppose, for example, that Slaven moved for summary judgment, supported by an affidavit from a remorseful jailor who admits, "the brother was saying, 'I'll kill myself before I spend another night in jail,' and I thought he meant it, so I kept telling [the other jailors], 'we've got to watch him or medicate him, or he'll do something awful to himself.' But we didn't do anything." She supports her motion with three more affidavits from other prisoners, which are consistent with the jailor's affidavit. Salem offers no counter-affidavits. Should the court grant full summary judgment for Slaven?

A The answer is tipped off by the adjective "full." The undisputed facts at best establish just Salem's *liability*. But the extent of Slaven's *damages*, especially if they include compensation for pain and suffering and emotional distress, or punitive damages, are almost always genuinely disputed and must therefore be ascertained by trial. While, on these facts, Slaven may obtain a partial summary judgment as to the city's liability, she still has to prove her damages.

Disproof-of-an-Element Motion for Summary Judgment

Although any party may file a motion for summary judgment, it is most often the defendant who does so. If he does not file a proof-of-the-elements motion to obtain summary judgment on an affirmative defense, then he is most likely to seek summary judgment by disproving an element of the claim against him. Thus, in our hypothetical product liability claim by Sophie against United Fibreboard, United might seek summary judgment on the basis of undisputed facts establishing that it did not manufacture any product containing asbestos, or that the deceased had never been exposed to any United product. On such undisputed facts, Sophie would necessarily lose at trial because she would be unable to prove an essential element of her claim: that United manufactured an asbestos-containing product to which the deceased had been exposed.

Slaven v. City of Salem, 438 N.E.2d 348 (Mass. 1982) (p. 1017, *supra*) is another example. In *Slaven*, an essential element of the plaintiff's tort claim was that Salem knew or should have known that the plaintiff's brother was a suicide risk. Salem moved for summary judgment, seeking to disprove the required knowledge by submitting the affidavits of the jailors denying knowledge. When the plaintiff could not point to specific facts creating a genuine dispute about the defendant's knowledge, the court granted the defendant's motion. You can see how it is usually easier for a defendant to obtain summary judgment than for the plaintiff. Salem only had to disprove one element of the plaintiff's claim, while the plaintiff would have to prove—to establish that there is no genuine dispute about—all of the elements of liability in order to obtain partial summary judgment on liability.

Some courts and commentators, including the Supreme Court, have referred to the burden that Salem assumed as the burden of "negating the opponent's claim." *See, e.g., Celotex Corp. v. Catrett*, 477 U.S. 317, 323 (1986). This means that the movant must produce real evidence to prove the nonexistence of the element, to prove that it is not true, or, in our terminology, to "disprove" it.

The Absence-of-Proof Motion for Summary Judgment

In *Slaven*, the defendants sought summary judgment by providing affirmative evidence (the officers' affidavits) showing that none of the arresting police officers or guards knew that the deceased was suicidal. But proving a negative is rarely so easy. And if the burden of proof of an element at trial would rest on the plaintiff, why should a defendant have to shoulder the burden of disproof of that element to obtain summary judgment?

READING *CELOTEX CORP. v. CATRETT.* In *Celotex*, plaintiff Catrett claimed that her husband's death from asbestosis resulted from exposure to the products of numerous defendants, including Celotex's. Celotex moved for summary judgment, arguing that, after an opportunity for discovery, Catrett had not produced any evidence that her husband had been exposed to Celotex's products. Catrett responded by identifying three pieces of evidence that she claimed would support her husband's exposure to Celotex's products. A divided court of appeals agreed with her, but a divided Supreme Court reversed.

- Which party had the burden of proving at trial that Mr. Catrett had been exposed to Celotex's products?

- The opinions assert that Celotex could have tried to obtain summary judgment by "negating" the allegation that Mr. Catrett had been exposed to its products. How would it have done this? Why didn't it try?
- The opinions offered Celotex an alternative way to meet its burden on summary judgment. Why couldn't Celotex meet this burden with a brief assertion that Mrs. Catrett had produced no evidence showing that her husband had been exposed to Celotex's products?
- Mrs. Catrett identified three pieces of evidence in opposition to Celotex's motion. Even without a course in Evidence, do you think that any of these pieces of evidence, in the form in which she offered them in opposition to summary judgment, could have been admitted at trial?
- What should Celotex have done to meet its burden on its motion for summary judgment?

CELOTEX CORP. v. CATRETT

477 U.S. 317 (1986)

Justice Rehnquist delivered the opinion of the Court. . . .

Respondent commenced this lawsuit in September 1980, alleging that the death in 1979 of her husband, Louis H. Catrett, resulted from his exposure to products containing asbestos manufactured or distributed by 15 named corporations. Respondent's complaint sounded in negligence, breach of warranty, and strict liability. [Celotex filed a first motion for summary judgment arguing] . . . that summary judgment was proper because respondent had "failed to produce evidence that any [Celotex] product . . . was the proximate cause of the injuries alleged within the jurisdictional limits of [the District] Court." In particular, petitioner noted that respondent had failed to identify, in answering interrogatories specifically requesting such information, any witnesses who could testify about the decedent's exposure to petitioner's asbestos products. In response to petitioner's summary judgment motion, respondent then produced three documents which she claimed "demonstrate that there is a genuine material factual dispute" as to whether the decedent had ever been exposed to petitioner's asbestos products. The three documents included a transcript of a deposition of the decedent, a letter from an official of one of the decedent's former employers whom petitioner planned to call as a trial witness, and a letter from an insurance company to respondent's attorney, all tending to establish that the decedent had been exposed to petitioner's asbestos products in Chicago during 1970–1971. Petitioner, in turn, argued that the three documents were inadmissible hearsay and thus could not be considered in opposition to the summary judgment motion.

[Eds.—**Celotex withdrew its first motion for summary judgment, but filed another, making the same argument. Catrett responded by incorporating her prior response. The district court granted the motion. A divided court**

appeals reversed, holding that Celotex's failure to support its motion with evidence tending to negate such exposure precluded the entry of summary judgment in its favor. The Supreme Court granted certiorari to resolve an inter-circuit conflict.] . . .

We think that the position taken by the majority of the Court of Appeals is inconsistent with the standard for summary judgment set forth in Rule 56(c) of the Federal Rules of Civil Procedure. Under Rule 56(c), summary judgment is proper "if the pleadings, depositions, answers to interrogatories, and admissions on file, together with the affidavits, if any, show that there is no genuine issue as to any material fact and that the moving party is entitled to a judgment as a matter of law." **[Eds.—Fed. R. Civ. P. 56 was revised after *Celotex* to reflect the Court's decision. The summary judgment standard is now stated in Rule 56(a), while the record for deciding summary judgment is now described in Rule 56(c).]** In our view, the plain language of Rule 56(c) mandates the entry of summary judgment, after adequate time for discovery and upon motion, against a party who fails to make a showing sufficient to establish the existence of an element essential to that party's case, and on which that party will bear the burden of proof at trial. In such a situation, there can be "no genuine issue as to any material fact," since a complete failure of proof concerning an essential element of the nonmoving party's case necessarily renders all other facts immaterial. The moving party is "entitled to a judgment as a matter of law" because the nonmoving party has failed to make a sufficient showing on an essential element of her case with respect to which she has the burden of proof. "[T]h[e] standard [for granting summary judgment] mirrors the standard for a directed verdict under Federal Rule of Civil Procedure 50(a). . . ." *Anderson v. Liberty Lobby, Inc.*, 477 U.S. 242, 250 (1986).

Of course, a party seeking summary judgment always bears the initial responsibility of informing the district court of the basis for its motion, and identifying those portions of "the pleadings, depositions, answers to interrogatories, and admissions on file, together with the affidavits, if any," which it believes demonstrate the absence of a genuine issue of material fact. But unlike the Court of Appeals, we find no express or implied requirement in Rule 56 that the moving party support its motion with affidavits or other similar materials *negating* the opponent's claim. On the contrary, Rule 56(c), which refers to "the affidavits, *if any*" (emphasis added), suggests the absence of such a requirement. And if there were any doubt about the meaning of Rule 56(c) in this regard, such doubt is clearly removed by Rules 56(a) and (b), which provide that claimants and defendants, respectively, may move for summary judgment "*with or without supporting affidavits*" (emphasis added). The import of these subsections is that, regardless of whether the moving party accompanies its summary judgment motion with affidavits, the motion may, and should, be granted so long as whatever is before the district court demonstrates that the standard for the entry of summary judgment, as set forth in Rule 56(c), is satisfied. One of the principal purposes of the summary judgment rule is to isolate and dispose of factually unsupported claims or defenses, and we think it should be interpreted in a way that allows it to accomplish this purpose.

Respondent argues, however, that Rule 56(e) [Eds.— **not fully retained in the amended Rule, although parts are now found in Rule 56(c) and 56(d)**], by its terms, places on the nonmoving party the burden of coming forward with rebuttal affidavits, or other specified kinds of materials, only in response to a motion for summary judgment "made and supported as provided in this rule." According to respondent's argument, since petitioner did not "support" its motion with affidavits, summary judgment was improper in this case. But as we have already explained, a motion for summary judgment may be made pursuant to Rule 56 "with or without supporting affidavits." In cases like the instant one, where the nonmoving party will bear the burden of proof at trial on a dispositive issue, a summary judgment motion may properly be made in reliance solely on the "pleadings, depositions, answers to interrogatories, and admissions on file." Such a motion, whether or not accompanied by affidavits, will be "made and supported as provided in this rule," and Rule 56(e) therefore requires the nonmoving party to go beyond the pleadings and by her own affidavits, or by the "depositions, answers to interrogatories, and admissions on file," designate "specific facts showing that there is a genuine issue for trial."

We do not mean that the nonmoving party must produce evidence in a form that would be admissible at trial in order to avoid summary judgment. Obviously, Rule 56 does not require the nonmoving party to depose her own witnesses. Rule 56(e) permits a proper summary judgment motion to be opposed by any of the kinds of evidentiary materials listed in Rule 56(c), except the mere pleadings themselves, and it is from this list that one would normally expect the nonmoving party to make the showing to which we have referred....

Respondent commenced this action in September 1980, and petitioner's motion was filed in September 1981. The parties had conducted discovery, and no serious claim can be made that respondent was in any sense "railroaded" by a premature motion for summary judgment. Any potential problem with such premature motions can be adequately dealt with under Rule 56(f) [Eds.—**now Rule 56(d)**], which allows a summary judgment motion to be denied, or the hearing on the motion to be continued, if the nonmoving party has not had an opportunity to make full discovery.

In this Court, respondent's brief and oral argument have been devoted as much to the proposition that an adequate showing of exposure to petitioner's asbestos products was made as to the proposition that no such showing should have been required. But the Court of Appeals declined to address either the adequacy of the showing made by respondent in opposition to petitioner's motion for summary judgment, or the question whether such a showing, if reduced to admissible evidence, would be sufficient to carry respondent's burden of proof at trial. We think the Court of Appeals with its superior knowledge of local law is better suited than we are to make these determinations in the first instance.

The Federal Rules of Civil Procedure have for almost 50 years authorized motions for summary judgment upon proper showings of the lack of a genuine, triable issue of material fact. Summary judgment procedure is properly regarded not as a disfavored procedural shortcut, but rather as an integral part of the Federal Rules as a whole, which are designed "to secure the just, speedy and inexpensive determination of every action." Fed. Rule Civ. Proc. 1. Before the shift to "notice pleading" accomplished by the Federal Rules, motions to dismiss a complaint or to strike a defense were the principal tools by which factually insufficient claims or defenses could be isolated and prevented from going to trial with the attendant unwarranted consumption of public and private resources. But with the advent of "notice pleading," the motion to dismiss seldom fulfills this function any more, and its place has been taken by the motion for summary judgment. Rule 56 must be construed with due regard not only for the rights of persons asserting claims and defenses that are adequately based in fact to have those claims and defenses tried to a jury, but also for the rights of persons opposing such claims and defenses to demonstrate in the manner provided by the Rule, prior to trial, that the claims and defenses have no factual basis.

The judgment of the Court of Appeals is accordingly reversed, and the case is remanded for further proceedings consistent with this opinion.

It is so ordered.

Justice White, concurring.

... It is not enough to move for summary judgment without supporting the motion in any way or with a conclusory assertion that the plaintiff has no evidence to prove his case.

A plaintiff need not initiate any discovery or reveal his witnesses or evidence unless required to do so under the discovery Rules or by court order. Of course, he must respond if required to do so; but he need not also depose his witnesses or obtain their affidavits to defeat a summary judgment motion asserting only that he has failed to produce any support for his case. It is the defendant's task to negate, if he can, the claimed basis for the suit.

Petitioner Celotex does not dispute that if respondent has named a witness to support her claim, summary judgment should not be granted without Celotex somehow showing that the named witness' possible testimony raises no genuine issue of material fact. It asserts, however, that respondent has failed on request to produce any basis for her case. Respondent, on the other hand, does not contend that she was not obligated to reveal her witnesses and evidence but insists that she has revealed enough to defeat the motion for summary judgment. Because the Court of Appeals found it unnecessary to address this aspect of the case, I agree that the case should be remanded for further proceedings.

Justice Brennan, with whom The Chief Justice and Justice Blackmun join, dissenting.

... [B]ecause I believe that Celotex did not meet its burden of production under Federal Rule of Civil Procedure 56, I respectfully dissent from the Court's judgment.

I

... The burden of establishing the nonexistence of a "genuine issue" is on the party moving for summary judgment. This burden has two distinct components:

an initial burden of production, which shifts to the nonmoving party if satisfied by the moving party; and an ultimate burden of persuasion, which always remains on the moving party. The court need not decide whether the moving party has satisfied its ultimate burden of persuasion unless and until the Court finds that the moving party has discharged its initial burden of production.

The burden of production imposed by Rule 56 requires the moving party to make a prima facie showing that it is entitled to summary judgment. The manner in which this showing can be made depends upon which party will bear the burden of persuasion on the challenged claim at trial. If the *moving* party will bear the burden of persuasion at trial, that party must support its motion with credible evidence—using any of the materials specified in Rule 56(c)—that would entitle it to a directed verdict if not controverted at trial. Such an affirmative showing shifts the burden of production to the party opposing the motion and requires that party either to produce evidentiary materials that demonstrate the existence of a "genuine issue" for trial or to submit an affidavit requesting additional time for discovery. Fed. Rules Civ. Proc. 56(e), (f).

If the burden of persuasion at trial would be on the *nonmoving* party, the party moving for summary judgment may satisfy Rule 56's burden of production in either of two ways. First, the moving party may submit affirmative evidence that negates an essential element of the nonmoving party's claim. Second, the moving party may demonstrate to the Court that the nonmoving party's evidence is insufficient to establish an essential element of the nonmoving party's claim. If the nonmoving party cannot muster sufficient evidence to make out its claim, a trial would be useless and the moving party is entitled to summary judgment as a matter of law.

Where the moving party adopts this second option and seeks summary judgment on the ground that the nonmoving party—who will bear the burden of persuasion at trial—has no evidence, the mechanics of discharging Rule 56's burden of production are somewhat trickier. Plainly, a conclusory assertion that the nonmoving party has no evidence is insufficient. Such a "burden" of production is no burden at all and would simply permit summary judgment procedure to be converted into a tool for harassment. Rather, as the Court confirms, a party who moves for summary judgment on the ground that the nonmoving party has no evidence must affirmatively show the absence of evidence in the record. This may require the moving party to depose the nonmoving party's witnesses or to establish the inadequacy of documentary evidence. If there is literally no evidence in the record, the moving party may demonstrate this by reviewing for the court the admissions, interrogatories, and other exchanges between the parties that are in the record. Either way, however, the moving party must affirmatively demonstrate that there is no evidence in the record to support a judgment for the nonmoving party.

If the moving party has not fully discharged this initial burden of production, its motion for summary judgment must be denied, and the Court need not consider whether the moving party has met its ultimate burden of persuasion. Accordingly, the nonmoving party may defeat a motion for summary judgment that asserts that the nonmoving party has no evidence by calling the Court's attention to supporting evidence already in the record that was overlooked or ignored by the moving party. In that event, the moving party must respond by making an attempt to demonstrate the inadequacy of this evidence, for it is only by attacking all the record evidence allegedly supporting the nonmoving party that a party seeking summary judgment satisfies Rule 56's burden of production.[2] Thus, if the record disclosed that the moving party had overlooked a witness who would provide relevant testimony for the nonmoving party at trial, the Court could not find that the moving party had discharged its initial burden of production unless the moving party sought to demonstrate the inadequacy of this witness' testimony. Absent such a demonstration, summary judgment would have to be denied on the ground that the moving party had failed to meet its burden of production under Rule 56. . . .

II

I do not read the Court's opinion to say anything inconsistent with or different than the preceding discussion. My disagreement with the Court concerns the application of these principles to the facts of this case. . . .

[W]hen Celotex filed its second summary judgment motion, the record *did* contain evidence—including at least one witness—supporting plaintiff's claim. Indeed, counsel for Celotex admitted to this Court at oral argument that Celotex was aware of this evidence and of plaintiff's intention to call Mr. Hoff as a witness at trial when the second summary judgment motion was filed. Moreover, plaintiff's response to Celotex' second motion pointed to this evidence—noting that it had already been provided to counsel for Celotex in connection with the first motion—and argued that Celotex had failed to "meet its burden of proving that there is no genuine factual dispute for trial."

On these facts, there is simply no question that Celotex failed to discharge its initial burden of production. Having chosen to base its motion on the argument that there was no evidence in the record to support plaintiff's claim, Celotex was not free to ignore supporting evidence that the record clearly contained. Rather, Celotex was required, as an initial matter, to attack the adequacy of this evidence. Celotex' failure to fulfill this simple requirement constituted a failure to discharge its initial burden of production under Rule 56, and thereby rendered summary judgment improper.

[Dissenting opinion of Justice Stevens omitted.]

---

2. Once the moving party has attacked whatever record evidence—if any—the nonmoving party purports to rely upon, the burden of production shifts to the nonmoving party, who must either (1) rehabilitate the evidence attacked in the moving party's papers, (2) produce additional evidence showing the existence of a genuine issue for trial as provided in Rule 56(e), or (3) submit an affidavit explaining why further discovery is necessary as provided in Rule 56(f). Summary judgment should be granted if the nonmoving party fails to respond in one or more of these ways, or if, after the nonmoving party responds, the court determines that the moving party has met its ultimate burden of persuading the court that there is no genuine issue of material fact for trial.

Notes and Questions: The Absence-of-Proof Motion for Summary Judgment

Q **1. The elements of Catrett's claims.** Once again, you can't decide a summary judgment question without starting with the applicable substantive law. Mrs. Catrett sued for wrongful death based on negligence, breach of warranty, and strict liability. What factual element do these claims share, apart from the injury?

A Each requires some proof that Celotex's product proximately caused Mr. Catrett's death, which presupposes proof that he was exposed to that product. If he was never exposed to any product made by Celotex, then the product can't have caused his death.* In other words, Mrs. Catrett will have the burden at trial to prove that Mr. Catrett was exposed to Celotex's product.

Q **2. "Negating" an essential element of the nonmovant's case.** The majority and dissenters agree that one option for Celotex was to try to "negate"—what we have called "disprove"—Mrs. Catrett's claim that her husband was exposed to its product. How could it have done that?

A It might have tried to prove that another of the other fifteen manufacturers that Catrett sued made all of the products to which Mr. Catrett was exposed. But under this approach, Celotex would assume on summary judgment a burden that otherwise would clearly rest on *Mrs. Catrett* at trial. That is, it would have had to prove beyond a genuine dispute that Acme Corporation made all of the products to which Mr. Catrett was exposed (foreclosing the possibility that Celotex made any), whereas at trial it would be Mrs. Catrett who would have to prove that Celotex—and not some other company—manufactured the products to which Mr. Catrett was exposed. This might well have been a difficult, if not impossible, burden for Celotex to carry. Moreover, even if Celotex could prove that Mr. Catrett had been exposed to the product of another defendant, that does not mean that Mr. Catrett wasn't also exposed to Celotex's product.

Of course, it could be a good deal easier if Celotex could prove that it never sold its products that were used in any workplace in which Mr. Catrett worked during his career. The problem is that Mr. Catrett may have worked on hundreds of jobs over many years, making such a demonstration exceedingly difficult. This kind of disproof or "negating" ultimately requires what Justice Brennan calls "affirmative evidence," and such evidence may be unavailable or too costly for the movant to obtain and present in admissible form for summary judgment.

---

* Actually, it's not that simple. Some jurisdictions have imposed "enterprise liability" by market share when multiple manufacturers have made an essentially fungible product (usually a drug) and it is impossible to show which manufacturer's product was the one ingested by the victim. It doesn't appear that Mrs. Catrett relied upon the enterprise liability theory.

Q **3. The "show me" or "naked" summary judgment motion.** For the reasons stated in note 2, it is often easier for a defendant to argue that the plaintiff has no evidence to prove an essential element of the plaintiff's case than it is to disprove that element. So why not let Celotex support its motion with nothing more than a one-sentence brief alleging that Mrs. Catrett has no evidence showing that her husband was exposed to a Celotex product?

A Because it would be altogether too easy and nearly cost-free for a defendant to force the plaintiff to show its hand by this device. Justice White and the dissenters therefore agree that it is plainly insufficient for the movant to support the motion with nothing more than a "conclusory assertion that the plaintiff has no evidence to prove his case." As Justice Brennan points out, "[s]uch a 'burden' of production is no burden at all and would simply permit summary judgment procedure to be converted into a tool for harassment." *Celotex*, 477 U.S. at 332. The trick is deciding how much more the movant has to do to support an absence-of-proof motion.

4. "Showing" that Ms. Catrett has no evidence to establish exposure. The old rule suggested an answer to the last question, because it described materials by which a movant could "*show* that there is no genuine issue . . ." (emphasis added). The *Celotex* majority concludes that this wording meant that the movant "has the initial responsibility of . . . identifying those portions of 'the pleadings, depositions, answers to interrogatories, and admissions on file, together with affidavits, if any,' which it believes demonstrate the absence of a genuine issue of material facts." *Id.* at 323. Justice Brennan adds, "If there is literally no evidence in the record, the moving party may demonstrate this by reviewing for the court the admissions, interrogatories, and other exchanges between the parties that are in the record." *Id.* at 332. In short, Celotex can't just say that Mrs. Catrett doesn't have any evidence; Celotex must review and identify relevant parts of the discovery record—including answers to interrogatories or depositions, for example—to *show* that there is no evidence. This burden on summary judgment also points the way to discovery in anticipation of an eventual motion for summary judgment: Ask Mrs. Catrett in interrogatories what witnesses and documentary evidence she has that her husband was exposed to Celotex's products.

The Court in *Celotex* had to cobble together support for the absence-of-proof approach to summary judgment by implication from general language in the old summary judgment rule. The amended rule is now explicit: A party can assert that a fact cannot be genuinely disputed by "showing that the materials cited do not establish the absence or presence of a genuine dispute, *or that an adverse party cannot produce admissible evidence to support the fact*." Fed. R. Civ. P. 56(c)(1)(B) (emphasis added).

Q **5. How did Celotex fall short?** Celotex did seemingly *show* that Mrs. Catrett had no evidence, because "it noted that [Mrs. Catrett] had failed to identify, in answering interrogatories specifically requesting such information, any witnesses who could testify about the decedent's exposure to [Celotex's] asbestos products." *Celotex*, 477 U.S. at 321. In other words, it did not rely merely on a conclusory assertion, but reviewed the record for the court to support its motion. Why wasn't this enough?

A It apparently *was* enough on Celotex's first summary judgment motion to shift the burden of production to Mrs. Catrett. But she then produced three pieces of additional evidence, including her husband's own deposition from a workmen's compensation proceeding and two letters from witnesses describing products to which her husband has been exposed. On Celotex's second motion for summary judgment, these pieces of evidence were part of the record that Celotex had to address.

Q **6. What should Celotex have done?**

A Once the record contained three pieces of evidence that seemed to create a dispute about Mr. Catrett's exposure to Celotex's products, Celotex should have attacked that evidence. It could have tried to show that the evidence would not be admissible at trial. The majority thought that the court of appeals would be better equipped to decide the admissibility of Mrs. Catrett's evidence and remanded for it to make that assessment in re-deciding summary judgment. See the next note. Or Celotex could have tracked down Mrs. Catrett's witnesses and shown by their affidavits or depositions that they actually had no admissible evidence of exposure. The dissenters emphasized that once Mrs. Catrett had identified the three pieces of evidence, "Celotex was not free to ignore supporting evidence that the record clearly contained." *Id.* at 332. By this view, summary judgment should be denied and the case below could proceed to trial.

7. What evidence is admissible on summary judgment? *Celotex* clarified the summary judgment standard, but the case does not clearly explain when a court applying the summary judgment standard is permitted to consider a particular piece of evidence. In other words, when is a piece of evidence sufficiently trustworthy that a court can consider it as part of the summary judgment process?

Consider the evidence in *Celotex*: Mrs. Catrett offered her husband's deposition and two documents. His deposition passed the first hurdle of admissibility, given his unavailability by reason of death (Fed. R. Civ. P. 32(a)(4)(A)), but the particular answers he gave could present their own evidentiary problems. For example, if he testified only that he "guessed" that Celotex products were used at a job on which he worked, that testimony would be inadmissible as speculation not made on personal knowledge. Or if he testified that he "heard" the same thing, that testimony would probably be inadmissible as hearsay. In either case, it would therefore not be admissible to create a genuine dispute.

Mrs. Catrett also provided a letter from Mr. Hoff, her husband's former supervisor, describing asbestos products to which her husband had been exposed. *In that form*, this evidence also would be inadmissible as hearsay (and possibly also because it was not authenticated). But if Mrs. Catrett called Hoff as her witness at trial, then he could presumably so testify from personal knowledge and overcome both objections.

The Court reasoned that to exclude evidence in this form from consideration in Mrs. Catrett's opposition to summary judgment would force her to depose her own witness (when she might otherwise just interview him informally and then present him at trial). But Justice White (concurring) said:

> A plaintiff need not initiate any discovery or reveal his witness or evidence unless required to do so under the discovery Rules or by court order. Of course, he must respond if required to do so, but he need not also depose his witnesses or obtain their affidavits to defeat a summary judgment motion asserting only that he has failed to produce any support for his case. It is the defendant's task to negate, if he can, the claimed basis for the suit.

477 U.S. at 328. Justice Brennan, too, asserted that the movant on an absence-of-proof summary judgment motion may have "to depose the nonmoving party's witnesses or to establish the inadequacy of documentary evidence," as part of his burden to "affirmatively demonstrate that there is no evidence in the record to support a judgment for the nonmoving party." *Id.* at 332. In short, once Mrs. Catrett identified Mr. Hoff as a witness who would testify to exposure, Celotex was obliged to attack this evidence by taking his deposition or obtaining his affidavit to show the inadequacy of the evidence.

The majority summarized this analysis by asserting, "We do not mean that the nonmoving party must produce evidence in a form that would be admissible at trial in order to avoid summary judgment." *Id.* at 324. As some scholars have explained, "As long as it is clear at the time the summary judgment motion is made that the evidence can be put into admissible form at trial, there is little benefit from requiring the nonmovant to take the time and effort to restructure the evidence at summary judgment." Brunet § 8.6. Instead, the Rule gives the party opposing such evidence the right to "object that the material cited to support or dispute a fact cannot be presented in a form that would be admissible in evidence." Fed. R. Civ. P. 56(c)(2). The advisory committee notes explain that "[t]he objection functions much as an objection at trial, adjusted for the pretrial setting. The burden is on the proponent to show that the material is admissible as presented or to explain the admissible form that is anticipated." Fed. R. Civ. P. 56 advisory committee's note (2010). If the proponent cannot, the court will not consider its evidence.

Accordingly, even though Mr. Hoff's letter would presumably not be admissible at trial, his testimony at trial *would* be "in a form that would be admissible in evidence." In other words, the test is not whether the evidence itself would be admissible at trial, but whether the evidence suggests that the party would be able to offer admissible evidence at trial. On the other hand, had his letter itself revealed his lack of personal knowledge, then arguably even his testimony at trial could not overcome this deficiency and Celotex would have had a good objection to the letter at summary judgment. Neither *Celotex* nor the amended rule tells us much about what kinds of evidence at summary judgment meet or fail the "form that would be admissible" standard; the trial judge must make a prediction informed by the rules of evidence.

Interestingly, on remand of *Celotex*, a divided court of appeals again affirmed denial of summary judgment for Celotex, finding that Celotex had failed to object to the admissibility of the Hoff letter, and that, "even if the Hoff letter itself would not be admissible at trial, Mrs. Catrett has gone on to indicate that the substance of the letter is reducible to admissible evidence in the form of trial testimony." *Catrett v. Johns-Manville Sales Corp.*, 826 F.2d 33, 38 (D.C. Cir. 1987), *cert. denied*, 484 U.S. 1066 (1988).

V. Dispositions Without Trial: Summary of Basic Principles

- A plaintiff may voluntarily dismiss without court order simply by filing a notice of dismissal before the opposing party serves either an answer or a motion for summary judgment—or by stipulation of all the parties.
- The first such voluntary dismissal by notice—notice dismissal—is without prejudice to commencing a new action for the same claim. But under the two-dismissal rule, the second notice dismissal operates as an adjudication on the merits that precludes suing on the dismissed claims again in federal court.
- A plaintiff may also still move for voluntary dismissal by court order. The court considers whether dismissal will cause plain legal prejudice to the defendant, beyond simply the tactical advantage that presumably any plaintiff is seeking by dismissal, and may take into account the plaintiff's reasons for dismissal. The court can condition dismissal on plaintiff's payment of defendant's costs and such other terms as will mitigate the legal prejudice to defendant from dismissal. A voluntary dismissal by court order is without prejudice to commencing a new action for the same claims, unless the court states otherwise.
- Dismissals for failure of prosecution, violation of the Rules, and all other dismissals under the Rules (except for lack of jurisdiction, improper venue, and failure to join a required party) operate as adjudications on the merits, which usually preclude the dismissed party from commencing a new action in a federal court based on the same claims.
- Summary judgment is a device to dispose of a claim or defense on the merits without trial. But parties are entitled to try factual disputes whether or not they have asked for a jury. Therefore, summary judgment is only available when there is no genuine dispute of material fact, and the movant shows that on the undisputed facts, he is entitled to judgment as a matter of law. The court must ascertain whether there is a genuine dispute of material fact, but does not decide any disputes. The court does not weigh the evidence or assess credibility and must resolve doubts in favor of the non-moving party.
- Rule 12(b)(6) motions to dismiss for failure to state a claim, Rule 12(c) motions for judgment on the pleadings, and Rule 50(a) motions for judgment as a matter of law are also devices that ask a court to dispose of a claim on the merits as a matter of law. Rule 12(b)(6) motions are decided on the allegations of the complaint; Rule 12(c) motions on the allegations of the complaint, answer, and reply, if any; and Rule 50(a) motions on the trial record at the time the motion is made.
- The substantive law determines which facts are material. A dispute about the law does not preclude summary judgment.

- The movant's burden on summary judgment depends on whether it would have the burden of proof at trial on a claim or defense. If the movant would have the burden at trial, then its burden on summary judgment is to show that the facts necessary for each element of its claim or defense are not genuinely disputed. If it would not have the burden of proof at trial, then it has two choices: to disprove an element of the opposing party's claim, or to show that there is an absence of proof by which the opposing party could prove an element of its claim.
- A movant for summary judgment may support its motion with evidence that is admissible, or could be presented in a form at trial that would be admissible, from the non-moving party's pleadings, from the discovery materials on file, as well as from affidavits and declarations made on personal knowledge by competent witnesses setting out facts that would be admissible.

28

The Right to Jury Trial

I. Introduction: The Seventh Amendment Conundrum

One often hears that the Constitution grants litigants "the right to a trial by jury." In some cases that is true, but in many it is not. The original Constitution did not address trial by jury in civil cases, but the Bill of Rights, adopted in 1791, added the Seventh Amendment to the Constitution. The Seventh Amendment provides:

> In Suits at common law, where the value in controversy shall exceed twenty dollars, the right of trial by jury shall be preserved, and no fact tried by a jury, shall be otherwise re-examined in any Court of the United States, than according to the rules of the common law.

Note some limitations on the right created by this Amendment. First, it says nothing about criminal cases—it is the Sixth Amendment that guarantees jury trial in criminal prosecutions. Second, it only applies to "Suits at common law." At the time the Amendment was adopted, there was a well-understood difference between suits at common law and actions brought in the courts of equity or admiralty. In equity and admiralty actions, the facts were found by a judge; there was no right to a jury. And the Seventh Amendment, since it only preserves the right in suits at common law, does not create a right to a jury in equity or admiralty cases.

Third, although the Amendment is not clear on the point, the Supreme Court has held that it only applies to the federal courts. It does not guarantee jury trial in any cases in state courts. States are free to create a right to jury trial in their own courts—or not—either in their constitutions or by statute. *See Walker v. Sauvinet*, 92 U.S. 90, 92 (1875) (Seventh Amendment "relates only to trials in the courts of the United States. The States, so far as this amendment is concerned, are left to regulate trials in their own courts in their own way."). Most states have created such guarantees, often mirroring closely the guarantee in the Seventh Amendment.

Fourth, parties are not required to try their cases to juries even if they have a right to a jury trial. If neither party requests a jury trial in a case to which the Seventh Amendment guarantee applies, the case will be tried to the judge instead.

Fifth, the Amendment "preserves" the right to trial by jury in common law actions. This little word has created myriad interpretive problems concerning the scope of the jury trial right. There were thirteen colonies when the Constitution was adopted, with widely differing adaptations of the English court system. The extent of the right to jury trial varied significantly from colony to colony. Perhaps because of these differences, and because local loyalties were fierce at the time, the Framers of the Amendment did not specify *which* state's jury trial practice was preserved by the Amendment. (As good politicians, they probably did not want to open a can of worms by choosing among the states.) So just what does the Amendment "preserve"?

The Supreme Court resolved this perplexity by holding that the Amendment preserves the right to jury trial as it existed, not in any of the colonies, but in the courts of England! "The right of trial by jury thus preserved is the right which existed under the English common law when the amendment was adopted." *Baltimore & Carolina Line v. Redman*, 295 U.S. 654, 657 (1935). This "historical test," which may or may not reflect the Framers's actual intent,* continues to be used by the Court. Under the test, the court considers practice in the courts of law and equity in England in 1791 to determine whether a claim goes to a jury today. As we will see, this search for an historical analogue becomes increasingly awkward as federal court procedure evolves.

* "[T]here is not a single shred of evidence indicating that anyone in the First Congress, or any ratifier, thought that the parameters of the right to jury trial preserved by the Clause had been fixed by the English Courts in 1791." Stanton D. Krauss, *The Original Understanding of the Seventh Amendment Right to Jury Trial*, 33 U. Rich. L. Rev. 407, 456 (1999).

II. A Short History of Law and Equity

A little background on law and equity practice in the English courts will help you to understand the challenge a federal court faces in determining whether the Seventh Amendment guarantees a jury on a particular type of claim. We described the distinction between the law and equity courts at the beginning of the chapter on pleading, but do so again here with particular emphasis on the implications for jury trial.

A. Actions at Law

Two systems of courts evolved over five or six centuries of English legal history: the common law courts and the court of Chancery or equity court. In the early history of English law, an aggrieved party would go to the King's officers for justice, and the King's minister would issue a "writ," ordering the defendant to appear and respond to the plaintiff's claim. Over time, the writs became specific to particular types of claims. A litigant who had a claim for breach of contract, for example, would seek a writ of *assumpsit*. A plaintiff who had a claim for battery would seek a writ of *trespass*. If the claim was for negligence, the proper writ was a writ of *trespass on the case*. To recover possession of real property, the proper action was *ejectment*, which allowed the court to try title to the land. While we might expect substantive rights to exist independent of procedures to protect them, under the writ system, the writ defined the substantive rights that could be enforced. "[T]he Right of Action at Common Law was dependent upon whether the litigants' facts fell within the scope of a limited and arbitrary list of Writs." Joseph H. Koffler & Alison Reppy, Common Law Pleading 47–48 (1969).

Over time, these writs multiplied and became increasingly specialized and formal. A plaintiff had to properly recite the allegations required under a particular writ in order to state a recognized claim. If she had two claims against the defendant arising from the same facts, she could not join those claims in a single suit if they required different writs. For example, if a plaintiff wanted to sue for negligence and breach of contract arising from the construction of a house, the negligence claim fell under the writ of trespass on the case, while the contract claim was covered by the writ of assumpsit. "The Character of the Writ definitely defined and limited the Character of the Action." *Id.* at 51. To pursue both claims, she would have to bring separate actions pursuant to the two separate writs.

The remedies available were also set by the writ. If the plaintiff pleaded assumpsit in the case arising from building a house, the court could award damages, but it could not order the defendant to complete the building. The common law courts didn't do that. The writ authorized damages, period.* In an action in ejectment—to

* Usually, the remedy in actions at law was damages. However, some writs authorized other remedies, such as ejectment (to recover possession of real property) and replevin (to recover possession of personal property).

recover real property—the court could declare that the plaintiff had good title and award damages for profits from the land earned by the trespasser. But it could not enter an order enjoining trespasses. For reasons of history, an injuction wasn't one of the remedies the law court could order under that writ.

Once a writ issued, the plaintiff would file a declaration setting forth her claim in compliance with the writ she had sought. As the writs became more rigid and formal, it became essential to draft the declaration with exceeding care, to be sure it contained the exact allegations required under that writ. Lawyers needed to be highly skilled pleaders; if the declaration failed to trace the stylized requirements of the writ, the plaintiff could lose for sloppy pleading, without any consideration of the merits of her claim.

The defendant was similarly constrained by the pleading process. Defendants could respond with a demurrer, challenging the legal sufficiency of the case. Alternatively, they could "traverse the allegations"—deny their truth. Or a defendant could "confess and avoid," that is, admit the truth of the allegations of the declaration, but assert additional facts to avoid liability—such as a release or statute of limitations defense. But they could not take multiple positions at the same time. For example, to raise an affirmative defense, the defendant had to admit the truth of the declaration, and she would lose if the affirmative defense was not established. A defendant could not deny the facts and raise affirmative defenses at the same time, or challenge the legal validity of the complaint and deny the facts as well.

The writs became so complex, and pleading became such an arcane art, that one English judge—clearly an ardent procedurist—is said to have bragged that he never saw a case that he couldn't dispose of without reaching the merits. That hardly seems like something to boast about, but it does reflect the almost absurd level of complexity that the legal writs achieved in their heyday.

B. The Equity Courts

The rigidity of the common law forms of action under the writs and the limited remedies available in an action at law left plaintiffs without a practical remedy in unusual cases. Plaintiffs who could not get an appropriate remedy at law began to appeal to the Chancellor, the King's minister, to "do equity," to grant extraordinary relief they could not recover at law. Over time, the Chancellor delegated his power to grant such relief to assistants, and this office evolved into a second court, the Chancery court (court of equity). To bring a bill in equity, the plaintiff had to assert that she had "no adequate remedy at law" (i.e., under the established common law writs) and had to request special relief from the equity court. In such cases, the equity court developed a panoply of remedies not available at law, tailored to reach a fair result in cases where the rigid causes of action available at law would not.

For example, the equity court could enter direct orders to a defendant, requiring her to do certain acts or refrain from doing them, unlike the law court, which could only award damages or declare ownership of property. The equity court could enter an injunction ordering a defendant not to trespass on property. It could enter an order for specific performance, that is, order the defendant to perform her obligations under a contract. It could order an accounting of the affairs of a partnership—the unraveling of complex transactions to settle the respective rights of each partner. It could order a fiduciary, such as a trustee, to fulfill the obligations she had assumed. It could reform a contract to read as the parties intended it to read. It could rescind a contract if it was procured by fraud. In each of these cases, the court could tailor an order responsive to the individual circumstances of the case, which imposed a personal obligation on the defendant to comply. The equity court could enforce its orders by holding the defendant in contempt of court if she did not comply.* The law courts, by contrast, awarded damages and declared rights, but did not enter orders to the defendant to engage in or refrain from engaging in a course of conduct.

Q **Suppose that the plaintiff sought relief available from the law court as well as other relief only available in equity.** For example, a plaintiff might seek damages for breach of contract (an action at law under the writ of assumpsit) and also seek specific performance of remaining obligations under the contract (a remedy given by the court of equity). What would she have to do to obtain these remedies under the classical English system?

A Under traditional practice, the plaintiff would have to bring two actions, one at law for damages and the other in equity for specific performance. In later times (perhaps even by 1791, when the Seventh Amendment was adopted), she could go to equity for specific performance and the court might award incidental, "clean-up" damages for the breach as well. The remedies available from the two courts evolved over time, so any statement about what each court could or could not do has to be qualified. But under the strict law/equity distinction, this plaintiff would have had to bring two actions in two courts to obtain complete relief.

C. Court Procedure in Law and Equity

Because the law courts and the Chancery courts evolved separately, procedure in the two courts systems also diverged. In actions at law, cases were tried to juries, while the facts were tried to the judge in equity. In the law courts, pleading was extremely rigid, and parties could only be joined if they sought recovery on a joint interest. (For example, two plaintiffs both injured in the same accident could not sue together, since their rights were "several" rather than joint.) Pleading required defending parties to stake their claim on one position, challenging either the legal sufficiency of the complaint or its factual truth.** Under traditional practice

* "[A]t Common Law, a Judgment merely determined the matter of right between the Parties; it did not order the defendant to do anything...whereas, in Equity, the Decree not only determined the matter of right between the Parties, but it actually ordered the defendant to do something in recognition of that established right on peril of being punished for contempt for failure so to do." Joseph H. Koeffler & Alison Reppy, Common Law Pleading 34 (1969).

** "[T]he Pleadings at Common Law were required to reduce the controversy to a single, clear-cut, well-defined Issue of Fact or of Law, whereas in Equity, there could be as many Issues of Law or of Fact as the Pleader desired." Koeffler & Reppy, Common Law Pleading 33–34 (1969).

in the law courts, there was no discovery; the case went from pleading to trial. At trial (believe it or not), the parties were not allowed to testify, evidently on the premise that their testimony would merely be self-serving.* Because the law courts tried cases to a jury, the law of evidence—intended to protect the jury from unreliable evidence—evolved primarily in the law courts.

Procedure in the equity court was more flexible. In equity, an effort was made to join all parties with an interest, so as to resolve the entire controversy. Parties were freer to join multiple claims. Pleading was much less rigidly prescribed. Evidence was presented in writing rather than through oral testimony. The equity court developed some methods of pretrial discovery, including interrogatories to parties and depositions, though these were strictly controlled by the court, not freely available as they are under modern American procedure. And, as already mentioned, equity courts were not confined to a single remedy prescribed by a writ; they could fashion the remedy to fit the case and exert continuing jurisdiction over a defendant to assure compliance after judgment, rather than simply declaring a judgment for damages, as the law courts usually did.

Because of these differences, a litigant who filed in one court or the other chose not just a remedy, but a complete procedural system. An action at law (a "lawsuit") brought with it jury trial, oral presentation of evidence at a continuous trial, very limited discovery, and strict limits on remedies and joinder. Proceeding in the equity court brought a more flexible procedure, a broader right to join claims and parties, some pretrial discovery, and a broader range of remedies. But equity courts did not offer jury trial, and a plaintiff could not obtain relief in the equity court if an adequate remedy was available in an action at law.

Determining the right to jury trial under traditional procedure. Consider whether the following cases would have been tried to a judge or to a jury under traditional procedure in 1791.

A. Gardner sues Miranda for damages for breach of contract. She seeks $120,000 in damages.

> This is a traditional suit for damages for breach of contract. If it had been brought in 1791, it would have been brought in the law court under the writ of assumpsit and would have been triable to the jury.

B. Gardner sues Miranda for breach of contract. She seeks an order from the court that Miranda complete the work yet to be done under the contract.

> This action is based in contract, but seeks specific performance, a remedy available only in equity under classic English procedure. So, the case would have been tried to the judge under traditional procedure. Note that the issue of whether Miranda breached the contract will likely be central to this claim, just as it was to the damages claim in the first example.

* Kenneth S. Abraham, *The Common Law Prohibition on Party Testimony and the Development of Tort Liability*, 95 Va. L. Rev. 489, 490 (2009).

C. Gardner brings the same action against Miranda, but seeks both damages for breach of contract and specific performance of Miranda's obligations under the contract.

> Under traditional English procedure, the plaintiff would probably have had to seek damages in the law court and specific performance in the equity court. Both actions would involve the common question ("Did Miranda breach the contract?"), and either one might have been tried first. If the equity case was decided first, the judge would decide whether the contract was breached, and that finding would bind the law court in the damages action (i.e., the law court would take as established that the contract was breached [or that it wasn't]). If the action at law went to trial first, the jury would decide the issue of breach, and that finding would bind the equity court in deciding the equitable claim.

III. Determining the Right to Jury Trial After the Merger of Law and Equity

Most of the practice described above has been dramatically altered over the last one hundred and fifty years, both in England and in the United States. Beginning with the Field Code in New York in 1848, most American jurisdictions have gradually merged law and equity courts into a single system of judicial administration. The federal courts had separate rules for actions at law and equity cases until the adoption of the Federal Rules of Civil Procedure in 1938. *Wright & Kane* § 61. One of the dramatic effects of the Rules was to "merge law and equity" into a single set of court procedures under the new Rules.

Thus Federal Rule 2, which seems tepid on first acquaintance ("There is one form of action—the civil action"), reflects the culmination of a centuries-long march from separate court systems to a unified court that administers all available remedies, whether formerly legal or equitable, under a single set of procedural rules. No longer are federal courts constrained by the separate limitations on the power of the chancellor or the law court. No longer must litigants choose between the courts of equity or the courts of law in framing an action or bounce from one system to the other to obtain complete relief on a set of facts. Whatever relief either system could provide before, the federal court can provide under the Rules in a unified "civil action."

So actions brought in the federal courts today often assert some claims that would have been classified as "legal" before merger and others that seek equitable remedies. In adjudicating such "mixed actions," the federal courts must decide whether, under the Seventh Amendment, the common issues in the case will be tried to a judge or to a jury.

Under merged procedure, Gardner will not have to file separate actions to obtain complete relief in his action against Miranda. Gardner's claims for breach of contract and specific performance will be litigated together in a single civil action and the federal court will hear and determine both claims. Fed. R. Civ. P. 2. However, the specific performance claim is still an equitable claim and the breach of contract claim is still a legal claim. What should be done about jury trial? Will the judge or the jury decide the issue that is common to the equitable and legal claims—whether the contract was breached? That is the basic problem addressed in *Dairy Queen, Inc. v. Wood*, the case below.

The Dairy Queen Trademark

Courtesy of American Dairy Queen Corporation

The case below concerns the right to use Dairy Queen's iconic trademark. The case arose in the 1950s, a time of dramatic expansion for the Dairy Queen franchise. The company went from 10 stores in 1941 to 2600 in 1955. The *Dairy Queen* Court addresses how to apply the Seventh Amendment's jury trial mandate in mixed actions that involve both legal and equitable claims.

READING *DAIRY QUEEN, INC. v. WOOD.* This case involved a suit brought by a partnership (the McCullough partnership), which owned the famous Dairy Queen trademark. McCullough had licensed the mark to other parties, who then sub-licensed the mark to Dairy Queen, Inc., the defendant in the case. McCullough claimed that Dairy Queen, Inc. had failed to make contractual payments for the right to use the mark. McCullough and its licensees sued Dairy Queen, Inc., seeking an injunction against further use of the mark, an accounting for profits Dairy Queen had made through licensing the mark to other vendors, and an injunction barring Dairy Queen, Inc. from continuing to collect licensee fees for use of the mark. At the heart of each of these claims was the question of what the contract required and whether Dairy Queen, Inc. had breached it.

Who, then, was Wood? He was the federal district judge who denied Dairy Queen, Inc.'s request for a jury trial. Dairy Queen, Inc. sought a writ of mandamus from the court of appeals (and then from the Supreme Court) ordering Wood to grant a jury trial. Because it sought an order to Judge Wood, he is named in the case caption, but it was Dairy Queen, Inc. that had requested a jury trial in the trial court, that petitioned for the writ, and that is referred to as the petitioner in the Supreme Court opinion. McCullough is referred to as the respondent (though not by name) because it is responding to (opposing) the petition for mandamus, even though it was the plaintiff below.

Consider these questions in reading *Dairy Queen*:

- Under traditional practice, which court—law or equity—could render an accounting to unravel the details of the parties' business relationship and determine the amount due to the partnership?

- Under traditional practice, which court would have heard the action for damages for trademark infringement?
- How did the Court rule on whether the judge or the jury should resolve the question common to all claims (breach of the contract)? What is the Court's rationale?

DAIRY QUEEN, INC. v. WOOD

369 U.S. 469 (1962)

Mr. Justice Black delivered the opinion of the Court.

The United States District Court for the Eastern District of Pennsylvania granted a motion to strike petitioner's demand for a trial by jury in an action now pending before it on the alternative grounds that either the action was "purely equitable" or, if not purely equitable, whatever legal issues that were raised were "incidental" to equitable issues, and, in either case, no right to trial by jury existed. The petitioner then sought mandamus in the Court of Appeals for the Third Circuit to compel the district judge to vacate this order. When that court denied this request without opinion, we granted certiorari because the action of the Court of Appeals seemed inconsistent with protections already clearly recognized for the important constitutional right to trial by jury in our previous decisions.

At the outset, we may dispose of one of the grounds upon which the trial court acted in striking the demand for trial by jury—that based upon the view that the right to trial by jury may be lost as to legal issues where those issues are characterized as "incidental" to equitable issues—for our previous decisions make it plain that no such rule may be applied in the federal courts. In *Scott v. Neely*, decided in 1891, this Court held that a court of equity could not even take jurisdiction of a suit "in which a claim properly cognizable only at law is united in the same pleadings with a claim for equitable relief." [140 U.S. 106, 117 (1891).] That holding, which was based upon both the historical separation between law and equity and the duty of the Court to insure "that the right to a trial by a jury in the legal action may be preserved intact," created considerable inconvenience in that it necessitated two separate trials in the same case whenever that case contained both legal and equitable claims. Consequently, when the procedure in the federal courts was modernized by the adoption of the Federal Rules of Civil Procedure in 1938, it was deemed advisable to abandon that part of the holding of *Scott v. Neely* which rested upon the separation of law and equity and to permit the joinder of legal and equitable claims in a single action. Thus Rule 18(a) provides that a plaintiff "may join either as independent or as alternate claims as many claims either legal or equitable or both as he may have against an opposing party." . . .

The Federal Rules did not, however, purport to change the basic holding of *Scott v. Neely* that the right to trial by jury of legal claims must be preserved. Quite the contrary, Rule 38(a) expressly reaffirms that constitutional principle, declaring: "The right of trial by jury as declared by the Seventh Amendment to the Constitution or as given by a statute of the United States shall be preserved to the parties inviolate." Nonetheless, after the adoption of the Federal Rules, attempts were made indirectly to undercut that right by having federal courts in which cases involving both legal and equitable claims were filed decide the equitable claim first. The result of this procedure in those cases in which it was followed was that any issue common to both the legal and equitable claims was finally determined by the court and the party seeking trial by jury on the legal claim was deprived of that right as to these common issues. This procedure finally came before us in *Beacon Theatres, Inc. v. Westover*,[6] a case which, like this one, arose from the denial of a petition for mandamus to compel a district judge to vacate his order striking a demand for trial by jury.

. . . The holding in *Beacon Theatres* was that where both legal and equitable issues are presented in a single case, "only under the most imperative circumstances, circumstances which in view of the flexible procedures of the Federal Rules we cannot now anticipate, can the right to a jury trial of legal issues be lost through prior determination of equitable claims." [359 U.S. 500, 510–11 (1959).] That holding, of course, applies whether the trial judge chooses to characterize the legal issues presented as "incidental" to equitable issues or not.[8] Consequently, in a case such as this where there cannot even be a contention of such "imperative circumstances," *Beacon Theatres* requires that any legal issues for which a trial by jury is timely and properly demanded be submitted to a jury. There being no question of the timeliness or correctness of the demand involved here, the sole question which we must decide is whether the action now pending before the District Court contains legal issues.

The District Court proceeding arises out of a controversy between petitioner and the respondent owners of the trademark "DAIRY QUEEN" with regard to a written licensing contract made by them in December 1949, under which petitioner agreed to pay some $150,000 for the exclusive right to use that trademark in certain portions of Pennsylvania. . . . In August 1960, the respondents wrote petitioner a letter in which they claimed that petitioner had committed "a material breach of that contract" by defaulting on the contract's payment provisions and notified petitioner of the termination of the contract and the cancellation of petitioner's right to use the trademark unless this claimed default was remedied immediately. When petitioner continued to deal with the trademark despite the notice of termination, the respondents brought an action based upon their view that a material breach of contract had occurred.

The complaint filed in the District Court alleged, among other things, that petitioner had "ceased paying . . . as required in the contract"; that the default "under the said contract . . . [was] in excess of $60,000.00"; that this default constituted a "material breach" of that contract; that petitioner had been notified by letter that its failure to pay as alleged made it guilty of a material breach of contract which if not "cured" would result in an immediate cancellation of the

6. 359 U.S. 500.

8. "It is therefore immaterial that the case at bar contains a stronger basis for equitable relief than was present in *Beacon Theatres*. It would make no difference if the equitable cause clearly outweighed the legal cause so that the basic issue of the case taken as a whole is equitable. As long as any legal cause is involved the jury rights it creates control. This is the teaching of *Beacon Theatres*, as we construe it." *Thermo-Stitch, Inc. v. Chemi-Cord Processing Corp.*, 5 Cir. 294 F.2d 486, 491.

contract; that the breach had not been cured but that petitioner was contesting the cancellation and continuing to conduct business as an authorized dealer; that to continue such business after the cancellation of the contract constituted an infringement of the respondents' trademark; that petitioner's financial condition was unstable; and that because of the foregoing allegations, respondents were threatened with irreparable injury for which they had no adequate remedy at law. The complaint then prayed for both temporary and permanent relief, including: (1) temporary and permanent injunctions to restrain petitioner from any future use of or dealing in the franchise and the trademark; (2) an accounting to determine the exact amount of money owing by petitioner and a judgment for that amount; and (3) an injunction pending accounting to prevent petitioner from collecting any money from "Dairy Queen" stores in the territory.

In its answer to this complaint, petitioner raised a number of defenses, including: (1) a denial that there had been any breach of contract...; (2) laches and estoppel arising from respondents' failure to assert their claim promptly ...; and (3) alleged violations of the antitrust laws by respondents in connection with their dealings with the trademark. Petitioner indorsed upon this answer a demand for trial by jury in accordance with Rule 38(b) of the Federal Rules of Civil Procedure.

Petitioner's contention... is that insofar as the complaint requests a money judgment it presents a claim which is unquestionably legal. We agree with that contention. The most natural construction of the respondents' claim for a money judgment would seem to be that it is a claim that they are entitled to recover whatever was owed them under the contract as of the date of its purported termination plus damages for infringement of their trademark since that date. Alternatively, the complaint could be construed to set forth a full claim based upon both of these theories—that is, a claim that the respondents were entitled to recover both the debt due under the contract and damages for trademark infringement for the entire period of the alleged breach including that before the termination of the contract. Or it might possibly be construed to set forth a claim for recovery based completely on either one of these two theories—that is, a claim based solely upon the contract for the entire period both before and after the attempted termination on the theory that the termination, having been ignored, was of no consequence, or a claim based solely upon the charge of infringement on the theory that the contract, having been breached, could not be used as a defense to an infringement action even for the period prior to its termination.[13] We find it unnecessary to resolve this ambiguity in the respondents' complaint because we think it plain that their claim for a money judgment is a claim wholly legal in its nature however the complaint is construed. As an action on a debt allegedly due under a contract, it would be difficult to conceive of an action of

13. This last possible construction of the complaint, though accepted as the correct one in the concurring opinion, actually seems the least likely of all. For it seems plain that irrespective of whatever else the complaint sought, it did seek a judgment for the some $60,000 allegedly owing under the contract. Certainly, the district judge had no doubt that this was the case: "'Incidental to this relief, the complaint also demands the $60,000 now allegedly due and owing plaintiffs under the aforesaid contract.'" 194 F. Supp., at 687.

a more traditionally legal character. And as an action for damages based upon a charge of trademark infringement, it would be no less subject to cognizance by a court of law.

The respondents' contention that this money claim is "purely equitable" is based primarily upon the fact that their complaint is cast in terms of an "accounting," rather than in terms of an action for "debt" or "damages." But the constitutional right to trial by jury cannot be made to depend upon the choice of words used in the pleadings. The necessary prerequisite to the right to maintain a suit for an equitable accounting, like all other equitable remedies, is, as we pointed out in Beacon Theatres, the absence of an adequate remedy at law. Consequently, in order to maintain such a suit on a cause of action cognizable at law, as this one is, the plaintiff must be able to show that the "accounts between the parties" are of such a "complicated nature" that only a court of equity can satisfactorily unravel them. In view of the powers given to District Courts by Federal Rule of Civil Procedure 53(b) to appoint masters to assist the jury in those exceptional cases where the legal issues are too complicated for the jury adequately to handle alone,[18] the burden of such a showing is considerably increased and it will indeed be a rare case in which it can be met.[19] But be that as it may, this is certainly not such a case. A jury, under proper instructions from the court, could readily determine the recovery, if any, to be had here, whether the theory finally settled upon is that of breach of contract, that of trademark infringement, or any combination of the two. The legal remedy cannot be characterized as inadequate merely because the measure of damages may necessitate a look into petitioner's business records.

Nor is the legal claim here rendered "purely equitable" by the nature of the defenses interposed by petitioner. Petitioner's primary defense to the charge of breach of contract—that is, that the contract was modified by a subsequent oral agreement—presents a purely legal question having nothing whatever to do either with novation, as the district judge suggested, or reformation, as suggested by the respondents here. Such a defense goes to the question of just what, under the law, the contract between the respondents and petitioner is and, in an action to collect a debt for breach of a contract between these parties, petitioner has a right to have the jury determine not only whether the contract has been breached and the extent of the damages if any but also just what the contract is.

We conclude therefore that the district judge erred in refusing to grant petitioner's demand for a trial by jury on the factual issues related to the question of whether there has been a breach of contract. Since these issues are common with those upon which respondents' claim to equitable relief is based, the legal claims involved in the action must be determined prior to any final court determination of respondents' equitable claims. The Court of Appeals should have corrected the

18. Even this limited inroad upon the right to trial by jury "'should seldom be made, and if at all only when unusual circumstances exist.'" *La Buy v. Howes Leather Co.*, 352 U.S. 249, 258.

19. It was settled in *Beacon Theatres* that procedural changes which remove the inadequacy of a remedy at law may sharply diminish the scope of traditional equitable remedies by making them unnecessary in many cases. "'Thus, the justification for equity's deciding legal issues once it obtains jurisdiction, and refusing to dismiss a case, merely because subsequently a legal remedy becomes available, must be re-evaluated in the light of the liberal joinder provisions of the Federal Rules which allow legal and equitable causes to be brought and resolved in one civil action. . . .'" 359 U.S., at 509.

error of the district judge by granting the petition for mandamus. The judgment is therefore reversed and the cause remanded for further proceedings consistent with this opinion.

Reversed and remanded.

[The concurring opinion of Justice Harlan is omitted.]

Notes and Questions: *Dairy Queen, Inc. v. Wood*

1. Making arguments under the historical test. Both sides in *Dairy Queen* frame their arguments under the historical test of the Seventh Amendment, which preserves the right to jury trial if it would have been available in the English courts in 1791. The plaintiffs (McCullough) argue that this is an action for an accounting. The law courts didn't provide that remedy in 1791; you had to go to equity if it was necessary to unravel a complex set of transactions like this. They also argue that they are seeking injunctive relief, which was also granted only in equity. So, plaintiffs argue, this is an easy case—to be faithful to historical practice, Dairy Queen, Inc.'s request for jury trial should be denied.

Dairy Queen, Inc.'s counsel argues that the plaintiffs are seeking damages for breach of contract and for trademark infringement. Such actions were unquestionably tried to a jury in 1791. If assessing the damages is complex, Dairy Queen argues that the court may use a master to help to assess them. Both parties are right. In the good (?) old days, parts of the case would probably have been litigated in both the law court and the equity court. But now we don't do that; the federal court can hear both legal and equitable claims and grant both equitable remedies (such as the preliminary and permanent injunctions sought in *Dairy Queen*) and damages for trademark infringement in a single action. Times have changed but the mandate of the Seventh Amendment looks back to prior practice. The Court must reconcile the resulting tension between the historical test and modern procedural flexibility.

Q **2. What's so hard about this?** What's the big problem? Why not have the judge decide the equitable claims and have the jury decide the contract and trademark infringement claims?

A This is exactly what will happen. But the problem (the same one posed by Gardner's case, described before the *Dairy Queen* opinion) is, who goes first? Whichever fact-finder decides its part of the case first will decide the common issue of breach of the agreement, which is central to both the equitable and legal claims. If plaintiffs' claims for an accounting and an injunction in *Dairy Queen* are tried first, to the judge, his finding on breach of the contract would bind the jury in the trial of the infringement action. The jury would not be allowed to decide anew whether Dairy Queen, Inc. had breached the contract. Once an issue of fact has been decided in pending litigation, that finding will settle the issue between the parties to the case. Economy and common sense both suggest that the parties should not litigate an issue twice—perhaps leading to opposite conclusions by the judge and jury—just because it is relevant to two claims in a case. So the first decision on the issue of breach will be deemed "the law of the case," and the fact-finder in the second part of the case will be bound by it. Thus, while it is possible to have the jury decide the legal claim and the judge decide the equitable claims, the parties are really fighting about which fact-finder will go first and decide the common issue of breach.

Q **3. The Supreme Court's solution.** The Supreme Court opts for a solution that favors jury trial in actions that assert legal and equitable claims together. Because the plaintiffs' claims for breach of contract and trademark infringement were traditional "legal" claims, either party would be entitled to a jury trial on those claims. However, because their action also sought injunctive relief and an accounting, it also had aspects of an equitable action. Under traditional practice, the common issue of breach might have been decided by the equity court, depending on where the first suit was filed. But under merged procedure they will be filed together, and the federal court can honor the right to a jury by trying the legal claims in the case first. That way the jury will decide the common issue of whether Dairy Queen, Inc. breached the contract and infringed the trademark. The judge can then apply that finding in deciding the equitable claims as well.

A. Suppose that the jury finds that Dairy Queen, Inc. did not breach the contract, was lawfully using the mark, and did not infringe on the plaintiffs' trademark rights. How should the judge rule on the plaintiffs' claim for an injunction against Dairy Queen, Inc.'s continuing to use the mark?

A Because the jury has found that Dairy Queen, Inc. had (and presumably still has) the right to use the mark, the judge must accept that finding on the common issue. Thus, the judge should deny the plaintiffs' request for an injunction against Dairy Queen's use of the mark.

B. Suppose instead that the jury finds that Dairy Queen, Inc. did breach the contract and awards damages for trademark infringement. How should the judge rule on the plaintiffs' claim for a permanent injunction?

A The judge will take as established that Dairy Queen, Inc. breached the contract and consider whether, in light of the breach, an injunction is an appropriate remedy under the circumstances. Back in the 1700s, a similar sequence might have taken place in two courts. If the plaintiffs had sued first at law for damages, the law court would have decided the issue of breach. If they won, they would then have sought an injunction in equity, and the equity court would have accepted the finding from the action at law that the contract had been breached.

C. How would Gardner's case against Miranda, seeking both damages for breach of contract and specific performance of Miranda's obligations under the contract, be decided after *Dairy Queen*?

A Gardner's right to jury trial on the damages claim will be "preserved" by trying the case to a jury, which will decide whether the contract was breached.

The judge will accept the jury's finding that there was a breach—or that there wasn't—in deciding whether Gardner is entitled to specific performance.

4. An "historical test"? The approach suggested in *Dairy Queen* is frequently referred to as an "historical test" for jury trial, since it considers how various issues would have been resolved under prior English practice. But *Dairy Queen* clearly does not command blind fidelity to historical practice. Even if parts of this case might have been decided first in equity, the Court notes that the claim for damages is a traditional legal claim. Under modern procedure, due to merger and the availability of masters to assist with complex fact-finding, a jury trial on that claim is feasible and should be provided. Under this logic, issues that might have been decided in equity and then applied by estoppel (taken as established) in related legal proceedings will now be tried to the jury, a modest expansion of jury trial as a result of the merger of law and equity.

Q **5. Equitable claims and legal counterclaims.** Assume that the plaintiffs in *Dairy Queen* sue to enjoin Dairy Queen, Inc. from using the trademark and that Dairy Queen, Inc. counterclaims against them for damages, claiming that they had violated the contract by denying its right to use of the mark. How would the case have been tried under traditional English procedure?

A The plaintiffs, as holders of the mark, would have gone to the equity court seeking the injunction, which would have decided whether Dairy Queen, Inc. had breached the contract. If it decided that Dairy Queen, Inc. had not breached, it would have denied the plaintiffs' request for an injunction and dismissed the case. Dairy Queen, Inc. would then have sued at law for damages and invoked the equity court's finding that it had not breached the contract to establish that issue in the law court. Although this reflects the classic roles of law and equity, actual practice was less clear; by the late 1700s equity courts sometimes retained jurisdiction to grant "incidental" or "clean-up" damages after making findings in an equitable action. *See* Fleming James, Jr., *Right to a Jury Trial in Civil Actions*, 72 Yale L.J. 655, 659 (1963).

Q **6. Implementing *Dairy Queen's* ruling.** How should the case posited in the previous question be tried after the Supreme Court's decision in *Dairy Queen, Inc. v. Wood*?

A Even if an equity court might have heard the entire case in 1791, the *Dairy Queen* opinion compels a different result today. In the example just above, Dairy Queen, Inc. asserted a legal claim to damages for breach of contract, so the judge would order a jury trial of that claim first and decide the right to an injunction afterward. Thus, the jury would decide the common issue of breach and the judge would use the jury finding to consider the right to the injunction requested by the plaintiffs. As stated in note 4, this reflects an *expansion* of the right to jury trial, since it calls for the jury to decide issues that might have been decided in equity under earlier practice.

7. *Beacon Theatres, Inc. v. Westover*: Another example of the scope of jury trial under merged procedure. *Beacon Theatres, Inc. v. Westover*, 359 U.S. 500 (1959), decided three years before *Dairy Queen*, involved a dispute between two movie companies, Fox and Beacon. Fox had an agreement with certain movie distributors for exclusive rights to show first-run pictures, which Beacon claimed violated the antitrust laws. Beacon threatened to sue if Fox continued the practice. So Fox took the offensive: It brought an action for declaratory judgment against Beacon, seeking a ruling that its contract did not violate the antitrust laws and an injunction preventing Beacon from threatening suit under the antitrust laws.

An action for a declaratory judgment allows a party involved in a controversy to bring suit to obtain a judicial determination of its rights. In *Beacon Theatres*, for example, Fox could have waited to be sued by Beacon and defended on the ground that its contract was legal. But the declaratory judgment statute (28 U.S.C. § 2201) allowed it to bring suit itself for a declaration that its contract was legal, rather than wait to be sued and risk liability for damages. Thus, Fox, which would have been the defendant in a traditional action under the antitrust laws, became the plaintiff in the declaratory judgment suit.

When Fox brought the declaratory judgment action, Beacon counterclaimed for damages under the antitrust laws. Beacon's counterclaim was a legal claim that would ordinarily be triable to a jury, and Beacon claimed a jury trial. But Fox argued that declaratory judgments were traditionally available only in equity, so historically, the judge would have decided whether it had violated the antitrust laws.

The Supreme Court held that Beacon was entitled to a jury trial on its antitrust claim, even though its counterclaim would have been decided by the judge in 1791 in an equitable proceeding under the "cleanup" doctrine. The antitrust claim is a legal claim, and under merged procedure, the court is able to provide a jury trial, and must do so. If the jury finds that Fox violated the antitrust laws, the judge would take that finding as established in ruling on Fox's equitable claim for an injunction. The judge would decide the right to equitable remedies traditionally available only in equity, but the issue common to both remedies—violation of the antitrust laws—would be decided by the jury. Thus, both *Beacon Theatres* and *Dairy Queen* require the court to structure the trial so as to provide jury trial on claims that, if litigated separately, could be tried to a jury.

Lest this arcana prove traumatic, keep your eye on the basics. Today, as in 1791, a party who brings a traditional legal claim alone has a right to jury trial. A party who sues for traditional equitable relief alone does not. These paradigms are clear. In the "mixed" cases like *Dairy Queen* and *Beacon*, the Court has held that the trial court should structure the trial so that the legal claims will be tried to a jury if either party requests one.

8. A state court goes its own way. The Seventh Amendment does not apply to state courts. However, most states have their own constitutional guarantees of jury trial, many fairly closely echoing the law/equity distinction in the Seventh Amendment. *See, e.g.*, Alaska Constitution Art. I, Section 16 ("In civil cases where the amount in controversy exceeds two hundred and fifty dollars, the right of trial by a jury of twelve is preserved to the same extent as it existed at common law."). But states don't always interpret their jury trial guarantees the same way as the Supreme Court interprets the Seventh Amendment. *See, e.g., Pelfrey v. Bank of Greer*, 244 S.E.2d 315 (S.C. 1978), in which the South Carolina court interpreted the jury trial guarantee in the South Carolina Constitution differently than the United States Supreme Court interpreted the Seventh Amendment in *Ross v. Bernhard*, 396 U.S. 531 (1970).

IV. Applying the Seventh Amendment to New Statutory Rights

Congress frequently enacts statutes that create new rights and remedies. For example, it has enacted federal statutes that authorize damages for age discrimination in employment and authorize injunctive relief and damages for violations of new environmental statutes. Because the Seventh Amendment "preserves" the right to jury trial, one might argue that there is no constitutional right to jury trial for such claims, which did not exist in 1791. Although this is a reasonable argument, the Supreme Court has taken a different approach to such cases, analogizing new causes of action to those that existed in 1791 to determine whether the Seventh Amendment assures a right to jury trial for newly created remedies.

READING *CURTIS v. LOETHER*. In *Curtis,* the Supreme Court considers whether there is a right to jury trial on a new statutory cause of action for violation of the fair housing act provisions of the 1968 Civil Rights Act (Title VIII). The Court must decide whether the right to jury trial applies to a claim that looks partly like a traditional equitable claim and partly like an action at law. In reading *Curtis,* consider the analytic framework the Court uses to assess whether the Seventh Amendment applies to a new legal remedy.

- The defendants argued that the Civil Rights Act itself creates a right to jury trial in cases under Title VIII. How did the Court rule on this argument?
- What are the two tests the Court considers in analogizing the Title VIII claim to traditional types of claims?

CURTIS v. LOETHER

415 U.S. 189 (1974)

Mr. Justice Marshall delivered the opinion of the Court.

Section 812 of the Civil Rights Act of 1968, 42 U.S.C. § 3612, authorizes private plaintiffs to bring civil actions to redress violations of Title VIII, the fair housing provisions of the Act, and provides that "[t]he court may grant as relief, as it deems appropriate, any permanent or temporary injunction, temporary restraining order, or other order, and may award to the plaintiff actual damages and not more than $1,000 punitive damages, together with court costs and reasonable attorney fees. . . ." The question presented in this case is whether the Civil Rights Act or the Seventh Amendment requires a jury trial upon demand by one of the parties in an action for damages and injunctive relief under this section.

Petitioner, a Negro woman, brought this action under § 812, claiming that respondents, who are white, had refused to rent an apartment to her because of her race, in violation of § 804(a) of the Act, 42 U.S.C. § 3604(a). In her complaint she sought only injunctive relief and punitive damages; a claim for compensatory damages was later added.[1] After an evidentiary hearing, the District Court granted preliminary injunctive relief, enjoining the respondents from renting the apartment in question to anyone else pending the trial on the merits. This injunction was dissolved some five months later with the petitioner's consent, after she had finally obtained other housing, and the case went to trial on the issues of actual and punitive damages.

Respondents made a timely demand for jury trial in their answer. The District Court, however, held that jury trial was neither authorized by Title VIII nor required by the Seventh Amendment, and denied the jury request. After trial on the merits, the District Judge found that respondents had in fact discriminated against petitioner on account of her race. Although he found no actual damages, see n. 1, *supra*, he awarded $250 in punitive damages, denying petitioner's request for attorney's fees and court costs.

The Court of Appeals reversed on the jury trial issue.... In view of the importance of the jury trial issue in the administration and enforcement of Title VIII and the diversity of views in the lower courts on the question, we granted certiorari.

The legislative history on the jury trial question is sparse, and what little is available is ambiguous. There seems to be some indication that supporters of Title VIII were concerned that the possibility of racial prejudice on juries might reduce the effectiveness of civil rights damages actions. On the other hand, one bit of testimony during committee hearings indicates an awareness that jury trials would have to be afforded in damages actions under Title VIII. Both petitioner and respondents have presented plausible arguments from the wording and construction of § 812. We see no point to giving extended consideration to these arguments, however, for we think it is clear that the Seventh Amendment entitles either party to demand a jury trial in an action for damages in the federal courts under § 812.

The Seventh Amendment provides that "[i]n suits at common law, where the value in controversy shall exceed twenty dollars, the right of trial by jury shall be preserved." Although the thrust of the Amendment was to preserve the right to jury trial as it existed in 1791, it has long been settled that the right extends beyond the common-law forms of action recognized at that time. Mr. Justice Story established the basic principle in 1830:

> "The phrase 'common law,' found in this clause, is used in contradistinction to equity, and admiralty, and maritime jurisprudence.... By *common law*, [the Framers of the Amendment] meant...not merely suits, which the *common* law recognized among its old and settled proceedings, but suits in which *legal* rights were to be ascertained and determined, in contradistinction to those where equitable rights

---

1. Although the lower courts treated the action as one for compensatory and punitive damages, petitioner has emphasized in this Court that her complaint sought only punitive damages. It is apparent, however, that petitioner later sought to recover actual damages as well....

alone were recognized, and equitable remedies were administered. . . . In a just sense, the amendment then may well be construed to embrace all suits which are not of equity and admiralty jurisdiction, whatever might be the peculiar form which they may assume to settle legal rights." *Parsons v. Bedford*, 7 L. Ed. 732 (1830) (emphasis in original).

Petitioner nevertheless argues that the Amendment is inapplicable to new causes of action created by congressional enactment. As the Court of Appeals observed, however, we have considered the applicability of the constitutional right to jury trial in actions enforcing statutory rights "as a matter too obvious to be doubted." 467 F.2d, at 1114. Although the Court has apparently never discussed the issue at any length, we have often found the Seventh Amendment applicable to causes of action based on statutes. *See, e.g., Dairy Queen, Inc. v. Wood*, (trademark laws). Whatever doubt may have existed should now be dispelled. The Seventh Amendment does apply to actions enforcing statutory rights, and requires a jury trial upon demand, if the statute creates legal rights and remedies, enforceable in an action for damages in the ordinary courts of law.

NLRB v. Jones & Laughlin Steel Corp., 301 U.S. 1 (1937), relied on by petitioner, lends no support to her statutory-rights argument. The Court there upheld the award of back pay without jury trial in an NLRB unfair labor practice proceeding, rejecting a Seventh Amendment claim on the ground that the case involved a "statutory proceeding" and "not a suit at common law or in the nature of such a suit." *Id.*, at 48. *Jones & Laughlin* merely stands for the proposition that the Seventh Amendment is generally inapplicable in administrative proceedings, where jury trials would be incompatible with the whole concept of administrative adjudication[8] and would substantially interfere with the NLRB's role in the statutory scheme. *Katchen v. Landy*, 382 U.S. 323 (1966), also relied upon by petitioner, is to like effect. There the Court upheld, over a Seventh Amendment challenge, the Bankruptcy Act's grant of summary jurisdiction to the bankrutpcy court over the trustee's action to compel a claimant to surrender a voidable preference; the Court recognized that a bankruptcy court has been traditionally viewed as a court of equity, and that jury trials would "dismember" the statutory scheme of the Bankruptcy Act. *Id.*, at 339. These cases uphold congressional power to entrust enforcement of statutory rights to an administrative process or specialized court of equity free from the strictures of the Seventh Amendment. But when Congress provides for enforcement of statutory rights in an ordinary civil action in the district courts, where there is obviously no functional justification for denying the jury trial right, a jury trial must be available if the action involves rights and remedies of the sort typically enforced in an action at law.

We think it is clear that a damages action under § 812 is an action to enforce "legal rights" within the meaning of our Seventh Amendment decisions. *See, e.g., Ross v. Bernhard; Dairy Queen, Inc. v. Wood.* A damages action under the statute

8. "[T]he concept of expertise on which the administrative agency rests is not consistent with the use by it of a jury as fact finder." L. Jaffe, *Judicial Control of Administrative Action* 90 (1965).

sounds basically in tort—the statute merely defines a new legal duty, and authorizes the courts to compensate a plaintiff for the injury caused by the defendant's wrongful breach. As the Court of Appeals noted, this cause of action is analogous to a number of tort actions recognized at common law.[10] More important, the relief sought here—actual and punitive damages—is the traditional form of relief offered in the courts of law.[11]

We need not, and do not, go so far as to say that any award of monetary relief must necessarily be "legal" relief. A comparison of Title VIII with Title VII of the Civil Rights Act of 1964, where the courts of appeals have held that jury trial is not required in an action for reinstatement and back pay, is instructive, although we of course express no view on the jury trial issue in that context. In Title VII cases the courts of appeals have characterized back pay as an integral part of an equitable remedy, a form of restitution. But the statutory language on which this characterization is based—

> "[T]he court may enjoin the respondent from engaging in such unlawful employment practice, and order such affirmative action as may be appropriate, which may include, but is not limited to, reinstatement or hiring of employees, with or without back pay . . . , or any other equitable relief as the court deems appropriate," 42 U.S.C. § 2000e–5(g) (1970 ed., Supp. II)—

contrasts sharply with § 812's simple authorization of an action for actual and punitive damages. In Title VII cases, also, the courts have relied on the fact that the decision whether to award back pay is committed to the discretion of the trial judge. There is no comparable discretion here: if a plaintiff proves unlawful discrimination and actual damages, he is entitled to judgment for that amount. Nor is there any sense in which the award here can be viewed as requiring the defendant to disgorge funds wrongfully withheld from the plaintiff. Whatever may be the merit of the "equitable" characterization in Title VII cases, there is surely no basis for characterizing the award of compensatory and punitive damages here as equitable relief.

10. For example, the Court of Appeals recognized that Title VIII could be viewed as an extension of the common-law duty of innkeepers not to refuse temporary lodging to a traveler without justification, a duty enforceable in a damages action triable to a jury, to those who rent apartments on a long-term basis. *See* 467 F.2d at 1117. An action to redress racial discrimination may also be likened to an action for defamation or intentional infliction of mental distress. Indeed, the contours of the latter tort are still developing, and it has been suggested that under the logic of the common law development of a law of insult and indignity, racial discrimination might be treated as a dignitary tort. C. Gregory & H. Kalven, *Cases and Materials on Torts* 961 (2d ed. 1969).

11. The procedural history of this case generated some question in the courts below as to whether the action should be viewed as one for damages and injunctive relief, or as one for damages alone, for purposes of analyzing the jury trial issue. The Court of Appeals concluded that the right to jury trial was properly tested by the relief sought in the complaint and not by the claims remaining at the time of trial. 467 F.2d, at 1118–1119. We need express no view on this question. If the action is properly viewed as one for damages only, our conclusion that this is a legal claim obviously requires a jury trial on demand. And if this legal claim is joined with an equitable claim, the right to jury trial on the legal claim, including all issues common to both claims, remains intact. The right cannot be abridged by characterizing the legal claim as incidental to the equitable relief sought. *Beacon Theatres, Inc. v. Westover*; *Dairy Queen, Inc. v. Wood.*

We are not oblivious to the force of petitioner's policy arguments. Jury trials may delay to some extent the disposition of Title VIII damages actions. But Title VIII actions seeking only equitable relief will be unaffected, and preliminary injunctive relief remains available without a jury trial even in damages actions[.] *Dairy Queen, Inc. v. Wood,* 369 U.S., at 479 n.20. . . . We recognize, too, the possibility that jury prejudice may deprive a victim of discrimination of the verdict to which he or she is entitled. Of course, the trial judge's power to direct a verdict, to grant judgment notwithstanding the verdict, or to grant a new trial provides substantial protection against this risk, and respondents' suggestion that jury trials will expose a broader segment of the populace to the example of the federal civil rights laws in operation has some force. More fundamentally, however, these considerations are insufficient to overcome the clear command of the Seventh Amendment. The decision of the Court of Appeals must be affirmed.

Affirmed.

Notes and Comments: *Curtis v. Loether*

1. Cutting both ways. The general presumption is that plaintiffs prefer to try cases to juries and defendants prefer to avoid them. In *Curtis,* however, the defendant landlord asked for a jury and Curtis, the plaintiff, argued that the Seventh Amendment did not guarantee the right to jury trial in actions under the fair housing statute. The NAACP Legal Defense Fund (LDF), a civil rights advocacy group, took the case to the Supreme Court, where Jack Greenberg, chief counsel for the LDF, argued that the Seventh Amendment jury trial guarantee did not extend to actions under Title VIII.

2. The two branches of the Seventh Amendment test. The Court has consistently rejected the argument that the Seventh Amendment does not apply to newly created legal claims. Instead, to determine whether there is a right to jury trial for a newly created statutory claim, the Court has focused on two issues: First, is the claim analogous to one that would have been brought in equity or at law under traditional practice? And second, does the plaintiff seek relief that was traditionally available at law or in equity? In *Curtis*, the Court concludes that the best analogies to a Title VIII claim are various tort claims for damages, which are legal claims. In addition, the Court notes that the relief the plaintiff seeks under Title VIII—compensatory and punitive damages—was available at law under traditional practice. Since the remedy seems most analogous to an action at law and seeks damages, the Court concludes that the Seventh Amendment right to jury trial applies.

3. Analogous analogies? For a more adventurous search by the Court for the proper historical analogy to a new statutory remedy, consider *Chauffeurs, Teamsters and Helpers, Local No. 391 v. Terry*, 494 U.S. 558 (1990). In that case, union members

Jack Greenberg

Courtesy of Columbia Law School

Jack Greenberg (1924–2016) served as co-counsel with Thurgood Marshall in the landmark civil rights case, *Brown v. Board of Education*. He succeeded Marshall as Director-Counsel of the NAACP Legal Defense Fund. A life-long civil rights advocate, he argued a number of important civil rights cases in the Supreme Court. He taught at Columbia Law School for many years and served as Dean of Columbia College. Evidently a Renaissance person, he authored a cookbook—*Dean Cuisine*—with the Dean of Harvard Law School, as well as a book on Franz Kafka.

In light of his background, it may seem odd that Greenberg argued in *Curtis v. Loether* against the right to jury trial in housing discrimination cases under Title VIII. Evidently, civil rights advocates feared that juries would share the racial prejudices of local landlords and refuse to find them liable for discrimination. "[T]he expansion of individual civil rights frequently took place against the backdrop of hostile local juries. . . ." William Young, *Vanishing Trials, Vanishing Juries, Vanishing Constitution*, 40 Suffolk U. L. Rev. 67, 76 (2006).

Ironically, Greenberg's former colleague, Thurgood Marshall, was on the Supreme Court when *Curtis* was decided—and wrote the opinion unanimously upholding the right to jury trial.

sued their union for breach of the duty to fairly represent them in dealing with their employer. (A union has a duty to fairly represent the interests of all members in dealing with the employer.) The members sought injunctive relief, restoration of benefits, and damages. Because this type of claim "was unknown in 18th-century England" (*id.* at 565), the Court applied its two-part test to determine whether the claim was more analogous to a legal or equitable claim under traditional practice. The Court considered analogies to an action to vacate an arbitration award, an action against a trustee for breach of fiduciary duty, and an action against an attorney for malpractice. The Court then considered the nature of the remedy sought. Under the two-part test, the Court concluded that the right to jury trial attached.

In his concurring opinion, Justice Brennan argued that the Court should jettison the first part of its Seventh Amendment test, the effort to analogize the claim to eighteenth-century practice.

> Requiring judges, with neither the training nor time necessary for reputable historical scholarship, to root through the tangle of primary and secondary sources to determine which of a hundred or so writs is analogous to the right at issue has embroiled courts in recondite controversies better left to legal historians. . . . I have grappled with this kind of inquiry for three decades on this Court and have come to the realization that engaging in such inquiries is impracticable and unilluminating.

494 U.S. at 576, 578. Since the Court already treated the nature of the remedy sought as the more important factor, Justice Brennan argued that the Seventh Amendment right to jury trial should be based solely on that factor. As Justice Brennan noted, the line between law and equity was fluid and unsettled under English practice. Even after herculean efforts in "rattling through dusty attics of ancient writs," *id.* at 575, he argues, the Court is unlikely to find a perfect analogy to new statutory claims.

4. Money damages and "incidental" relief. One problem with grounding the law/equity distinction (at least in part) on whether a party seeks monetary damages is that a party seeking to avoid jury trial might characterize damages as "restitution," or as an "incidental" remedy in an equitable proceeding. Eighteenth-century English equity courts would at times award damages as an incidental remedy, so there is some ground for the argument. Thus, the power to grant damages (or something that looks very much like damages) does not automatically mean that the court will find a right to jury trial. As *Curtis* notes, the right to back pay under Title VII has been characterized as an element of an equitable remedy, while the *Curtis* Court holds that the right to damages under Title VIII supports jury trial. There is no tidy answer to this conundrum, especially since actual practice in the English courts two hundred years ago is somewhat obscure.

5. If the Seventh Amendment does not authorize jury trial, may Congress do so? In *Curtis*, the defendant landlord argued that Title VIII itself guarantees jury trial in housing discrimination cases and alternatively that the Seventh Amendment does. When a case raises both statutory and constitutional issues, a court will usually decide the statutory question first to avoid unnecessary decisions of constitutional law. In *Curtis*, however, the Court viewed the constitutional issue as so "clearly settled" that it decided the case on constitutional grounds. Thus, the Court did not decide whether Congress had created a statutory right to jury trial in Title VIII cases.

Where the Seventh Amendment jury trial right does not apply, Congress may still authorize jury trial by statute. *The Propeller Genesee Chief v. Fitzhugh*, 53 U.S. 443, 459–60 (1851); *Moore* § 38.44(3).

6. Special administrative tribunals. Although the Court has endorsed and even expanded the right to jury trial in cases like *Beacon Theatres* and *Dairy Queen*, it has sometimes held that the Seventh Amendment guarantee does not apply to claims otherwise legal in nature. In *N.L.R.B. v. Jones & Laughlin Steel Corp.*, 301 U.S. 1 (1937), for example, the Court held that the Seventh Amendment does not apply in an unfair labor practices proceeding before the National Labor Relations Board, a federal administrative agency.

> The instant case is not a suit at common law or in the nature of such a suit. The proceeding is one unknown to the common law. It is a statutory proceeding. Reinstatement of the employee and payment for time lost are requirements imposed for violation of the statute and are remedies appropriate to its enforcement. The contention under the Seventh Amendment is without merit.

Id. at 48–49. In *Atlas Roofing Co. v. Occupational Safety and Health Review Commission*, 430 U.S. 442, 450 (1977), the Court held that the Constitution does not require jury trials in a federal administrative proceeding even if a party seeks damages.

> At least in cases in which "public rights" are being litigated—*e.g.*, cases in which the Government sues in its sovereign capacity to enforce public rights created by statutes within the power of Congress to enact—the Seventh Amendment does not prohibit Congress from assigning the fact finding function and initial adjudication to an administrative forum with which the jury would be incompatible.

Under this rationale, if Congress had provided for adjudication of housing discrimination claims by administrative law judges within an administrative agency, that procedure would likely have been upheld, even though it barred jury trial. *Cf. Pernell v. Southall Realty*, 416 U.S. 363, 383 (1974) (suggesting that Congress could, without abridging the Seventh Amendment, consign landlord-tenant disputes to administrative agency adjudication).

V. The Evolving Nature of the Right to Jury Trial

Procedure in the federal courts has changed radically over the centuries since the adoption of the Seventh Amendment. These changes have altered the way that juries are empaneled, their size, and the role of the judge in administering jury trials. Such changes have frequently been challenged as an abridgement of the right to jury trial. The following notes discuss how the Supreme Court has ruled on Seventh Amendment challenges to various changes in federal procedure.

A. Control of the Jury by Directed Verdict

In *Galloway v. United States*, 319 U.S. 372 (1943), the trial judge granted a directed verdict for the defendant (the United States). The plaintiff argued that this deprived him of his Seventh Amendment right to jury trial, because courts did not order directed verdicts in 1791. A "demurrer to the evidence" was recognized back then, as well as the motion for a new trial, but not the authority to "direct a verdict," that is, to order entry of judgment for the defendant based on the insufficiency of the plaintiff's proof—thus taking the case away from the jury entirely. The plaintiff in *Galloway* conceded that the judge controlled jury verdicts under traditional practice, but argued that, under the Seventh Amendment, she was confined to the procedures for doing so recognized in 1791. The Court was not persuaded:

> The Amendment did not bind the federal courts to the exact procedural incidents or details of jury trial according to the common law in 1791, any more than it tied them to the common-law system of pleading or the specific rules of evidence then prevailing. Nor were "the rules of the common law" then prevalent, including those relating to the procedure by which the judge regulated the jury's role on questions of fact, crystalized in a fixed and immutable system. On the contrary, they were constantly changing and developing during the late eighteenth and early nineteenth centuries. In 1791 this process already had

> resulted in widely divergent common-law rules on procedural matters among the states, and between them and England. And none of the contemporaneous rules regarding judicial control of the evidence going to juries or its sufficiency to support a verdict had reached any precise, much less final, form....
>
> ...The more logical conclusion, we think, and the one which both history and the previous decisions here support, is that the Amendment was designed to preserve the basic institution of jury trial in only its most fundamental elements, not the great mass of procedural forms and details, varying even then so widely among common-law jurisdictions.

319 U.S. at 390–92.

B. The Size of the Jury

In the second half of the twentieth century, federal district courts began adopting local rules authorizing six-person juries in civil cases instead of the traditional jury of twelve. In *Colgrove v. Battin*, 413 U.S. 149 (1973), the petitioner argued that the Seventh Amendment requires juries of twelve in civil cases. The Supreme Court held that to use juries of as few as six members is permissible under the Seventh Amendment. The Court held that it is "'the substance of the common-law right of trial by jury, as distinguished from mere matters of form or procedure,'" that must be preserved. 413 U.S. at 156 (quoting from *Baltimore & Carolina Line, Inc. v. Redman*, 295 U.S. 654, 657 (1935)).

> The Amendment, therefore, does not "bind the federal courts to the exact procedural incidents or details of jury trial according to the common law in 1791," and "[n]ew devices may be used to adapt the ancient institution to present needs and to make of it an efficient instrument in the administration of justice...."

413 U.S. at 156–57 (quoting from *Galloway v. United States*, 319 U.S. 372, 390 (1943)).

It is not clear whether the Seventh Amendment requires jury verdicts to be unanimous in civil cases. The Court upheld use of non-unanimous juries in a state criminal case in *Johnson v. Louisiana*, 406 U.S. 356 (1972). Because Rule 48(b) of the Federal Rules of Civil Procedure requires unanimous verdicts, the Court has not had occasion to decide whether the Seventh Amendment requires jury unanimity.

C. Partial New Trial

In *Gasoline Products Co. v. Champlin Refining Co.*, 283 U.S. 494 (1931), the defendant prevailed on a counterclaim for damages. The court of appeals concluded that the defendant had proved liability on the counterclaim but remanded the case for a new trial limited to the issue of damages. Under traditional practice, judges who found part of a verdict unsupported by the evidence would grant a full new trial. The plaintiff (who had lost on the counterclaim) argued that the Seventh Amendment barred the court from ordering a partial retrial. The Supreme Court affirmed the grant of a partial new trial:

> It is the Constitution which we are to interpret; and the Constitution is concerned, not with form, but with substance.... [T]he Seventh Amendment does not exact the retention of old forms of procedure. It does not prohibit the introduction of new methods for ascertaining what facts are in issue, or require that an issue once correctly determined... be tried a second time, even though justice demands that another distinct issue, because erroneously determined, must again be passed on by a jury.

283 U.S. at 498.

D. Questions of Law and Fact

Even in jury cases, not all of the issues are decided by the jury. For example, in a negligence case, the judge decides whether the defendant owed a duty of care to the plaintiff. Similarly, the judge decides whether a plaintiff's negligence is a complete bar to recovery. Such issues are matters of law, not questions of fact for the jury.

Interestingly, it appears that when the Seventh Amendment was adopted, juries in some states had the authority to determine both the facts and the law. However, during the nineteenth century, courts (acting through judges, of course!) gradually reinterpreted jury trial guarantees to confine the jury to finding the facts under instructions from the court as to the law. The issue was settled for the federal courts by *Sparf v. United States*, 156 U.S. 51 (1895), which held that it is the judge's role to declare the law and the jury's role to apply it.

Frequently, however, cases present "mixed questions of law and fact." For example, whether a defendant was negligent in particular circumstances involves the application of a legal standard to facts the jury must decide. To determine whether a party breached a contract, a jury may need to decide the meaning the parties attached to a particular term in their contract. Such mixed issues, involving application of agreed principles of law to particular facts, may be allocated to judges in some situations or to juries in others, frequently based on ad hoc policy concerns unique to the particular issue.

In *Markman v. Westview Instruments, Inc.*, 517 U.S. 370 (1996), the Supreme Court considered whether the judge or the jury should decide the meaning of terms used in a patent. *Markman* recognized that patent claims have historically been tried to juries and reaffirmed that whether the defendant has infringed a patent is a jury question under the Seventh Amendment. However, the Court held that interpreting the meaning of the claims covered by a patent is an issue of law for the judge.

The Court offered several reasons for this conclusion. First, judges generally construed written documents in lawsuits under traditional practice (although there was no clear practice with regard to construction of patent claims). Since historical practice did not clearly answer the question, Justice Souter turned to "functional considerations" in delineating the roles of judge and jury. He noted that judges are better trained to construe legal documents than juries and that national uniformity in the construction of patents was an important value. Congress has created a specialized court, the Court of Appeals for the Federal Circuit, to hear all patent appeals. If patent construction decisions are treated as legal conclusions, the Federal Circuit's construction of a patent will create governing legal precedent, while a jury's construction of those terms would not.

In summary, the Supreme Court's flexible approach to "preserving" jury trial has led to some expansion of the right, when legal claims and equitable claims are both present. But it has also recognized that changes in court administration may limit the right in some respects without abridging the fundamental Seventh Amendment guarantee.

VI. Administering Jury Trial

When there is a right to a jury trial, various issues arise in administering the right. Several of them are described below.

A. Claiming Jury Trial

Where the right to a jury trial applies, either party may demand it. Federal Rule 38(b) provides that a party demanding jury trial must file a demand with the court and serve it on all parties no later than fourteen days after service of the last pleading directed to the issue on which a jury is sought. Fed. R. Civ. P. 38(b). It is permissible—and wise—to place the demand for jury trial in your complaint or answer. Otherwise, you may forget to make the demand within the short period for making a jury claim, inadvertently waiving the right by omission.

If one party wants a jury trial but others do not, the case will be tried to a jury. If no party to the action wants a jury, the parties will waive jury trial by not requesting it, and the case will be tried to the judge.

Q Suppose that counsel mistakenly lets the period for claiming jury trial go by without making a demand under Rule 38(b). What should she do when she discovers this and believes a jury would be advantageous?

A Litigators should always check the Rules to see if they offer any cure for a procedural miscue. Here they do. Rule 39(b) allows the judge to order a jury trial anyway, on "any issue for which a jury might have been demanded." The Rule provides that the judge "may" grant a jury trial and sets no standard. Evidently, some courts are quite grudging in granting such motions, but others are more flexible, considering such factors as how late in the litigation the motion is made and possible prejudice to other parties if the motion is granted. *See generally Wright & Miller* § 2334.

B. Advance Waivers of Jury Trial

Parties may waive jury trial before a dispute arises—by contract. Parties drafting commercial or employment agreements often include either arbitration clauses—which require the parties, in the event of a dispute, to go to arbitration rather than to court—or clauses waiving the right to jury trial, that is, agreeing that a dispute arising from the agreement will be tried to the judge. For example, an employer may insert such a clause in an employment agreement. When a dispute arises, the employee may be surprised to learn that a clause in her contract (virtually always drafted by the employer) bars her from claiming a jury trial. Courts purport to look with skepticism at such waivers, but usually enforce them, even if the employee did not read the clause. *See, e.g., Brown v. Cushman & Wakefield, Inc.*, 235 F. Supp. 2d 291, 294 (S.D.N.Y. 2002); *see generally Moore* § 38.52[3].

Parties insert such jury-waiver clauses in their agreements because they think a jury may be biased against them (large corporations, for example) or that a "runaway jury" will award astronomical damages. It is not clear, however, that trusting one's rights to a single judge—rather than a group of disinterested citizens who have to reach agreement on the outcome—is a better safeguard against bias. Judges may be biased too, or (in the many states in which judges must stand for election) subject to political pressure. Some studies suggest that judges, on average, will award higher damages than juries do on the same facts.

C. Selecting the Jury

Typically, a large number of potential jurors will be summoned to the courthouse for jury duty on any given day. The *venire*, or group of potential jurors summoned, will be randomly chosen from voter lists or other demographic sources. In state courts, this will likely be organized by county. In federal court, jurors will likely be drawn from a broader geographic area. This can be a significant factor in choosing between state and federal court. If Curtis brings her housing discrimination claim in a state court in an urban county, she will likely try it to a fairly diverse jury. If she brings it in federal court in the same city, the jury is likely to be less diverse and more affluent, since it will be drawn not only from the city but also from surrounding suburban and rural areas.

Twelve Angry Jurors

Moviestore Collection, Ltd. / Alamy Stock Photo

To the left, this scene from the classic movie, *Twelve Angry Men*, depicts the jury in a criminal case in the 1950s. A civil jury might have looked much the same, including neither women nor minorities. Today's typical jury would be more likely to look like the drawing below of the jury in the O.J. Simpson criminal trial (again, a civil jury would be similar).

Illustration by Bill Robles

Today's jury might also not have twelve members. Many cases are tried to juries with as few as six members. And, in many types of civil cases, parties are not entitled to jury trial at all. If they are, they frequently choose to try the case to a judge (a "bench trial") instead.

When a judge is ready to empanel a jury, a number—perhaps twenty-five to forty—potential jurors will be brought to the courtroom. The judge or the lawyers will then question the venire (the group of potential jurors) to weed out jurors who might be biased. This procedure, called *voir dire*, differs from one court to another. In some courts, the judge questions jurors, either individually or as a group, perhaps asking some questions submitted by the lawyers. In others, counsel for the parties may be allowed to ask additional questions of individual jurors.

The lawyers have the opportunity to challenge jurors *for cause* based on some information suggesting that the juror may be biased. They may also be entitled to several *peremptory challenges*, that is, to strike a few jurors without explanation. Ultimately, a full jury will be seated, with several alternates in case a juror is dismissed for some reason during the trial.

D. Racial Bias in Jury Selection

The history of Black participation in jury trials is a sordid tale of exclusion and discrimination. In the nineteenth century it was not unusual for Blacks to be excluded from jury service by state statute. For examples of such statutes, see *Neal v. Delaware*, 103 U.S. 370 (1880); *Bush v. Kentucky*, 107 U.S. 1110 (1883). Although the United States Supreme Court held such *de jure* exclusion unconstitutional in *Strauder v. West Virginia*, 100 U.S. 303 (1879), exclusion of Black jurors continued under ostensibly race neutral jury selection regulations. For example, in *Norris v. State*, 294 U.S. 587 (1935), the Court reviewed jury selection under an Alabama statute that provided:

> The jury commission shall place on the jury roll and in the jury box the names of all male citizens of the county who are generally reputed to be honest and intelligent men, and are esteemed in the community for their integrity, good character and sound judgment, but no person must be selected who is under twenty-one or over sixty-five years of age, or, who is an habitual drunkard, or who, being afflicted with a permanent disease or physical weakness is unfit to discharge the duties of a juror, or who cannot read English, or who has ever been convicted of any offense involving moral turpitude. If a person cannot read English and has all the other qualifications prescribed herein and is a freeholder or householder, his name may be placed on the jury roll and in the jury box.

Ala. Code 1923, § 8603. Jury commissioners applying such vague and discretionary criteria systematically excluded Blacks from jury service. The record in *Norris*

> tended to show that "in a long number of years no negro had been called for jury service in that county." It appeared that no negro had served on any grand or petit jury in that county within the memory of witnesses who had lived there all their lives. Testimony to that effect was given by men whose ages ran from fifty to seventy-six years. Their testimony was uncontradicted. It was supported by the testimony of officials. The clerk of the jury commission and the clerk of the circuit court had never known of a negro serving on a grand jury in Jackson county. The court reporter, who had not missed

> a session in that county in twenty-four years, and two jury commissioners testified to the same effect. One of the latter, who was a member of the commission which made up the jury roll for the grand jury which found the indictment, testified that he had "never known of a single instance where any negro sat on any grand or petit jury in the entire history of that county."

Norris, 294 U.S. at 591. The *Norris* Court reversed a Black criminal defendant's conviction based on this evidence, holding that the evidence established a clear practice of discriminatory exclusion of Blacks from the jury venire (the pool of citizens called for jury service). *See also Hernandez v. Texas*, 347 U.S. 475 (1954) (exclusion of persons of Mexican descent violates the Fourteenth Amendment Equal Protection Clause); *Neal v. Delaware*, 103 U.S. 370 (1880) (exclusion of persons of African descent violates the Equal Protection Clause).

Even where Black citizens have been included in the larger jury venire, they have often been excluded from being seated as jurors for trial by "somewhat more subtle ways" of excluding Blacks. (*Batson v. Kentucky*, 476 U.S. 79, 103 (1986) (Marshall, J. concurring)). In criminal trials both the prosecutor and the defense counsel may seek to exclude jurors "for cause" if examination suggests that the juror might not be impartial. In addition, counsel are typically entitled to a number of "peremptory challenges," that is, the right to strike a number of jurors without stating a reason. A common tactic in trials of Black defendants has been for prosecutors to use peremptory challenges to exclude Black jurors from the jury.

The United States Supreme Court sought to counter this tactic in *Batson v. Kentucky*, 476 U.S. 79 (1986). *Batson* held that the use of peremptory challenges to exclude jurors of the same race as the defendant violates the Equal Protection Clause. The Court held that a defendant may make a *prima facie* case of discrimination by showing that a prosecutor has systematically excluded Black jurors from being seated. The prosecution can rebut that prima facie showing by offering a race-neutral reason for striking each Black juror. If such a reason is offered, the court must then determine whether the defendant has established racial discrimination in the prosecution's use of peremptory challenges. This *Batson* framework for assessing discrimination has been extended to civil jury practice as well. *Edmonson v. Leesville Concrete Co., Inc.*, 500 U.S. 614 (1991). It has also been applied to jury selection procedures that exclude jurors from jury service on other discriminatory bases. *See, e.g., Hernandez v. New York*, 500 US. 352 (1991)) (use of peremptory challenges to exclude Latino jurors); *Taylor v. Louisiana*, 419 U.S. 522 (1975) (partial exclusion of women from jury service).

Unfortunately practice under the *Batson* framework has failed to eliminate racial bias in juror selection. Prosecutors (or counsel in civil cases) are usually able to articulate some non-discriminatory reason for striking a juror, whether or not that reason actually led to the decision.

> The Supreme Court has articulated that [the burden to offer a race-neutral reason] is a low burden and that the reason offered "need not be plausible, let alone persuasive." As a result, courts have accepted "race-neutral" dismissals of African American potential jurors for reasons such as: alleged lack of intelligence or low education; living in an area with a high crime rate; "look[ing] like a drug dealer"; chewing gum; wearing sunglasses in court; or having a

> child out of wedlock. Because almost any proffered explanation is accepted, the procedure does little to eliminate racial discrimination from jury selection procedures; consequently, minorities continue to be denied their constitutional right to sit on juries at alarmingly high rates.

Hilary Weddell, Note, *A Jury of Whose Peers?: Eliminating Racial Discrimination in Jury Selection Procedures*, 33 B.C. J.L & Soc. Just. 453, 459 (2013) (citations omitted).

The persistence of claims of racial bias in use of peremptory challenges has led to calls to eliminate them from the jury selection process. *See Miller-El v. Dretke*, 545 U.S. 211, 269–73 (2005) (Breyer, J. concurring). For a recent example of efforts by a state to counter race-based jury selection practices, see Wash. Gen. R. 37, adopted by the Washington Supreme Court in 2018. That rule establishes criteria for trial judges to consider in evaluating peremptory challenges for bias, provides that certain reasons for striking jurors are "presumptively invalid," and provides that certain stock reasons for peremptory strikes will not suffice unless corroborated by the judge or opposing counsel.

E. Scheduling Jury Trial

When a case is tried to a jury, it must be tried in one continuous sequence. The jury can't be convened for a while, hear some evidence, disperse to their private affairs, and reconvene a month or so later to hear more evidence. Trial will proceed from day to day from opening statements to verdict, with few if any interruptions for other judicial business. By contrast, a trial to the judge can be episodic: Parties may spend a day presenting evidence, suspend the trial for a week, spend another day at it, and so forth. In civil law systems, the evidence usually is presented in this stop-and-go fashion, giving the court more flexibility in scheduling. Jury trial means you build to a climax and have a single, unified trial.

VII. Current Perspectives on Jury Trial

A. Can Juries Try Complex Cases?

Some scholars and judges have questioned whether juries can understand the complex questions involved in sophisticated cases. Indeed, a chief justice of the United States has expressed doubts about the propriety of jury trials in such cases:

> The changes in litigation patterns in recent years boggle the mind, and numerous cases document that reality. Even Jefferson would be appalled at the prospect of a dozen of his stout yeoman and artisans trying to cope with some of today's complex litigation.

Warren E. Burger, *Thinking the Unthinkable*, 31 Loy. L. Rev. 205, 210 (1985). The description below of the dispute in *Rieff v. Evans*, 672 N.W.2d 728, 730–31 (Iowa 2003), suggests some of the problems that have fueled doubts about the adequacy of juries to accurately handle complex cases.

> In her 36-page, 104-paragraph Amended petition, Plaintiff challenges in excess of ten separate, complex financial transactions that took place over an eight-year period between 1985 and 1993. These challenged transactions include a "pooling agreement" between Allied Mutual, Allied Group, and other affiliated organizations; administration of the pooling agreement; a leveraged employee stock ownership plan (ESOP); executive equity incentive plans; stock options; the formation and acquisition of various business entities; "corporate opportunities"; and restructuring. The various complex concepts foreign to lay people encompassed in these transactions include mutual insurance company governance issues, corporate debt, funding and initial public offerings, equity, premium to surplus and gross leverage ratios, expense ratios, loss ratios, combined ratios, underwriting, pooling and inter-company operating agreements, conflicts of interest, corporate restructuring, tender offers, return on premium, risk-based capital, and preferred versus common stock. As to each of the challenged transactions, Plaintiff seeks an accounting to determine the consideration exchanged between the parties.
>
> The defendants add that, because the plaintiff seeks over $500,000,000 in damages, complex valuations at various times during an eight-year time period would be required. They estimate they alone have produced more than 100,000 pages of documents; the plaintiff has issued subpoenas to eight nonparty actuarial and accounting entities, and additional voluminous documents will be produced. They estimate the trial will last at least twelve weeks. In view of these assertions, we assume, for purposes of this appeal, this is truly a "complex" case.*

Similarly, in *In re Japanese Electronic Products Antitrust Litigation*, 631 F.2d 1069 (3d Cir. 1980), the appellate court noted that the published opinions in the proceedings below would fill an entire volume of the *Federal Supplement*, and that the record appendix filed with the appeal ran to forty volumes.

Typically, arguments that juries should not be used in complex cases cite four problems: the massive amount of evidence that must be reviewed and understood by the fact-finder, the likely duration of trial (which may be more than a year in massive cases), the complexity of the factual issues raised, and the complexity and multiplicity of legal concepts that the jury must apply to different claims and parties.

A footnote in *Ross v. Bernhard*, decided by the Supreme Court in 1970, appeared to give support to the notion that jury trial might not be appropriate in complex cases:

> As our cases indicate, the "legal" nature of an issue is determined by considering, first, the pre-merger custom with reference to such questions; second, the remedy sought; *and, third, the practical abilities and limitations of juries.*

396 U.S. at 538 n.10 (emphasis added). Several prominent court of appeals decisions take opposite positions on whether a "complexity exception" to the right

---

* Despite the sophisticated issues described here, the *Rieff* court rejected a "complex litigation" exception to Iowa's jury trial guarantee. 672 N.W.2d at 732.

to jury trial exists. In *In re Japanese Electronic Products Antitrust Litigation,* 631 F.2d 1069 (3d Cir. 1980), the Third Circuit held that requiring a jury trial might deprive litigants of due process of law under the Fifth Amendment if the case was so complex that the jury could not adequately decide it. But in *In re U.S. Financial Securities Litigation,* 609 F.2d 411 (9th Cir. 1979), the court rejected a complexity exception.

Although *Japanese Products* has never been overruled, it has seldom been followed, and the controversy seems to have abated without clear recognition of a complexity exception. Courts instead have turned their attention to ways of structuring trials, narrowing issues, and educating jurors to make complex cases more amenable to jury trial. For a discussion of various devices that may assist jurors in understanding complex cases, see Richard C. Waites & David A. Giles, *Are Jurors Equipped to Decide the Outcome of Complex Cases?,* 29 Am. J. Trial Advoc. 19, 42–58 (2005).

B. Is Jury Trial Desirable?

Jury trials take more time than trials to the court. Selecting a jury can take a considerable amount of time. Dealing with evidence and the logistics of trial is more complicated in a jury trial. Jury instructions must be drafted and delivered to the jury at the close of trial. For these and other practical reasons, it may take twice as long to try a case to a jury as to a judge.* In addition, because the jury is assembled from unrelated individuals who must interrupt their private affairs to serve, jury trial must take place in a continuous sequence, with as few interruptions as possible for the judge's other duties (such as emergency motions in other cases).

Despite these complexities, many—perhaps most—judges believe fervently in jury trial. One federal trial judge describes the American jury system as "[t]he most stunning and successful experiment in direct popular sovereignty in all history. . . ." William G. Young, *Vanishing Trials, Vanishing Juries, Vanishing Constitution,* 40 Suffolk U. L. Rev. 67, 69 (2006). The jury brings the public into the judicial process.** It submits disputes to a panel of disinterested fact-finders from outside the system who do not share its biases. It invokes the common sense consensus of a group in making sensitive decisions. The evidence suggests as well that juries generally reach the "right" decision—or, at least, the same decision that the judge would reach.*** In many ways, it is a grand institution worthy of admiration.

Despite the jury's virtues and its status as a cornerstone of American justice, other countries do not share our enthusiasm for it. No other country in the world uses juries to nearly the extent that we do. In civil law jurisdictions, virtually all civil cases are tried to the court. *See generally* Oscar Chase, *American*

* *See* Richard A. Posner, The Federal Courts: Crisis and Reform 130 n.1 (1985). An earlier study suggested that trials to the court are 40 percent shorter than jury trials. Hans Zeisel et al., Delay in the Court 75–78 (1978).

** "Judges are far more consistently white, formally educated, male, middle aged, and affluent than the broader community that sits on juries." Note, *Practice and Potential of the Advisory Jury,* 100 Harv. L. Rev. 1363, 1372 (1987).

*** Research suggests that juries reach the same decision the judge would have rendered in about 80 percent of cases. *See* Paula L. Hannaford, B. Michael Dann & G. Thomas Munsterman, *How Judges View Civil Juries,* 48 DePaul L. Rev. 247, 249 (1998) (summarizing several studies).

"Exceptionalism" and Comparative Procedure, 50 Am. J. Comp. L. 277, 288–89 (2002). Even Great Britain, where the jury evolved, has largely abandoned jury trial in civil cases.

VIII. The Right to Jury Trial: Summary of Basic Principles

- The Seventh Amendment to the United States Constitution "preserves" the right to jury trial in "Suits at common law." It does not guarantee jury trial of claims that were heard in equity or admiralty courts under traditional procedure.
- While the Seventh Amendment does not apply to trials in state courts, most states have similar provisions guaranteeing the right to jury trial in common law cases.
- The Supreme Court has applied an "historical test" to determine the right to jury trial. The test considers whether each claim in the action is analogous to a claim tried at law under traditional procedure and whether the remedy sought is one that would have been available at law or in equity. Most claims for money damages are analogous to actions at law, in which the right to jury trial applies.
- Under traditional procedure, claims that sought legal relief (usually damages) might be decided by an equity court, depending on the procedural context in which they arose. (For example, an equity court might award "clean-up damages" in an action for specific performance). Under the merged procedure of the Federal Rules, the trial should be structured so that any claims that seek legal relief are tried first to a jury if one is requested.
- If some claims in a case are equitable and others legal, the trial should be structured so that the jury determines issues common to both claims. The judge will then follow the jury's findings on those issues if they are also relevant to the equitable claims in the action.
- The Seventh Amendment may mandate jury trial of claims created by Congress even though those claims did not exist in 1791. In determining whether there is a right to jury trial, the court will consider whether the statutory claim is analogous to legal or equitable claims under traditional practice and (more importantly) the type of remedy sought.
- If there is no constitutional right to jury trial for a claim, Congress (or, for the state courts, a state legislature) may grant the right to jury trial by statute.
- If a right to jury trial attaches to a claim, either party may request it and the claim will be tried to a jury. If neither party requests a jury trial, they both waive the right and the judge will determine the factual issues in the case.

29

Judgment as a Matter of Law (Directed Verdict and JNOV)

I. Introduction

Plaintiffs who file lawsuits expecting a jury trial and verdict are often disappointed. The reality, as previous chapters make clear, is that judges frequently dismiss cases, often long before a trial. For example, judges can grant motions to dismiss under Rule 12(b)(6) if a complaint fails to state a claim. If the complaint survives, the plaintiff faces another hurdle after the completion of discovery—under Rule 56, a judge can grant summary judgment if no genuine dispute of material fact remains to be litigated. In sum, judges exercise an important gatekeeping function throughout the civil litigation process.

This judicial gatekeeping function does not end with summary judgment—it continues throughout a trial and even after a verdict. In federal court, judges exercise this late-stage gatekeeping authority through a procedure known as "judgment as matter of law."

A. Motions for Judgment as a Matter of Law Under Rule 50(a) (Directed Verdict)

A simple example illustrates this procedural device. Suppose that Penny sues Desmond, alleging in her complaint that Desmond drove through a red light and collided with Penny's car as she was making a left turn from the opposite direction.

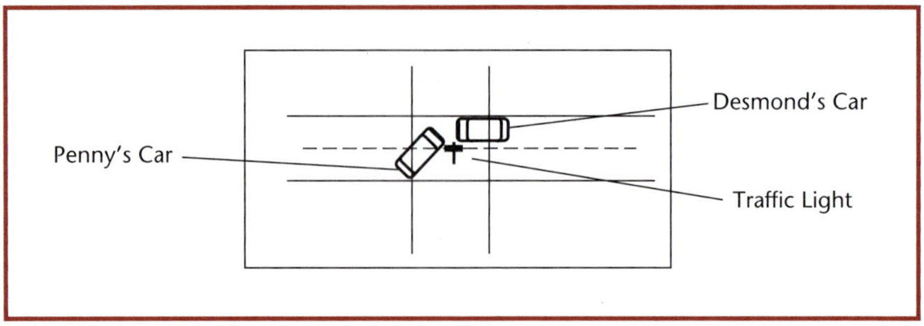

Figure 29–1: A HYPOTHETICAL CAR ACCIDENT

At trial, Penny testifies that Desmond hit her and that she suffered injuries as a result of the accident. Penny, however, does not testify about the color of the traffic light, either for her or Desmond. Moreover, Penny does not offer any evidence, such as eyewitness testimony, regarding the light's color at the relevant time, and she does not offer other evidence of Desmond's negligence.

Normally, after the plaintiff rests her case, the defendant offers evidence in support of his version of events. But wouldn't that be a waste of time here? Penny is the plaintiff and had the burden of production—the burden to produce evidence from which a reasonable jury could find that she has proven each element of her cause of action. Because Penny did not offer *any* evidence concerning Desmond's negligence (i.e., that he ran a red light), Penny did not satisfy her burden and cannot win the case.

A judgment as a matter of law exists to address this type of situation. Desmond can make a motion under Rule 50(a) of the Federal Rules of Civil Procedure, arguing that no reasonable jury could find the facts necessary for Penny to win and that judgment should therefore be entered in Desmond's favor "as a matter of law." If the judge agrees, the judge can enter a judgment for Desmond.

In many state courts and in older federal cases, this motion is called a motion for a directed verdict. That is, the moving party (in this case, Desmond) asks the judge to direct a verdict in his favor because no reasonable jury could render a verdict for the non-moving party (in this case, Penny) based on the evidence that she presented at trial. If the judge grants the motion, the judge enters a judgment for the moving party and dismisses the jury. The term "directed verdict" was used in Rule 50 until 1991, when it was replaced with the phrase "judgment as a matter of law." (Most state courts, however, still use the traditional terminology; motions for a directed verdict and Rule 50(a) motions for judgment as a matter of law are different names for the same concept.)

Rule 50(a) motions serve at least two important functions. First, they notify a non-moving party such as Penny that she has failed to offer evidence concerning a key element of her case, thus giving her an opportunity to correct the omission. That's why Rule 50(a)(2) provides that "[t]he motion must specify the judgment sought and the law and facts that entitle the movant to the judgment." For example, Desmond's motion would have to specify that Penny failed to offer any evidence to establish Desmond's negligence. After the motion is made, Penny's lawyer might request an opportunity to recall Penny to the witness stand so that she can offer this important, but omitted, testimony. A Rule 50(a) motion, therefore, helps to ensure that a case turns on its merits and not on an inadvertent omission of trial testimony. *See, e.g., Wright & Miller* § 2533.

But why would Desmond want to alert Penny that she has omitted crucial testimony? The answer turns on a second reason for these motions—Desmond might think that Penny does not actually *have* any evidence of his negligence. For example, Desmond might think that, at the time of the accident, Penny could not have observed the color of the light when Desmond drove into the intersection and that no other witness could have observed it either. If Desmond is correct, the judge might grant the motion and enter a judgment in Desmond's favor. The judgment would save Desmond the time and expense of presenting his side of the case, and Desmond would not have to risk a jury verdict in Penny's favor. Moreover, the judge and the jury would not have to hear the rest of a case for which the outcome is clear.

B. Renewed Motions for Judgment as a Matter of Law Under Rule 50(b) (JNOV)

Assume now that, although Penny does not offer any additional evidence concerning Desmond's negligence, the judge nevertheless denies Desmond's Rule 50(a) motion. Desmond subsequently presents his evidence, and the case goes to the jury, which renders a verdict for *Penny*. Can the judge exercise any gatekeeping authority at this stage of the case?

The somewhat surprising answer is "yes." If Desmond renews his motion for judgment as a matter of law, the judge can set aside the jury's verdict for Penny and enter judgment for Desmond instead. Rule 50(b) authorizes the judge to grant this "renewed" motion for judgment as a matter of law, which most state courts (and pre-1991 federal cases) refer to as a motion for judgment notwithstanding the verdict, or "JNOV" (an abbreviation of the Latin phrase judgment *non obstante veredicto*). Again, the names may differ, but they refer to the same procedural device.

These procedures highlight a fundamental tension between the role of judges and juries in the American civil justice system. As a general rule, judges are supposed to decide legal issues, and juries are supposed to determine the facts. The line, however, between "law" and "fact" is not always clear, and Rule 50 highlights just how fuzzy that line can be. When a judge grants a Rule 50 motion, the judge has determined that a party has offered so little evidence that the *facts* can be determined as a matter of *law*.

This judicial authority to determine the facts "as a matter of law" is an extraordinary power and is not exercised lightly. Rule 50 provides that a judge should do so only when a party has failed to offer a "legally sufficient evidentiary basis" to support a judgment in her favor. But when has a party offered "legally sufficient" evidence? Much of this chapter tries to answer this question. Before turning to that discussion, consider the following additional introductory points about Rule 50.

Notes and Questions: Understanding the Basics of Rule 50

Q **1. Judicial reluctance to grant Rule 50(a) motions.** The judge in Penny's case denied Desmond's Rule 50(a) motion, even though it appeared that the motion should have been granted. Why might a judge have an incentive to deny a seemingly meritorious Rule 50(a) motion? (Hint: Consider what would happen if an appellate court reverses a judge's decision to grant a Rule 50(a) motion.)

A The answer turns on pragmatic concerns about what will happen if the judge grants the Rule 50(a) motion. If the judge grants it, the losing party (in this case, Penny) is likely to appeal, arguing that the judge should have permitted her case to proceed to a jury verdict. If the appellate court agrees with Penny, the court will remand the case for a retrial. Judges prefer to avoid this risk of a time-consuming and expensive retrial and thus grant Rule 50(a) motions only when the argument for doing so is strong and the likelihood of reversal is low. *See, e.g., Unitherm Food Systems, Inc. v. Swift-Eckrich*, 546 U.S. 394, 405–06 (2006) (making a similar observation) (quoting *Wright & Miller* § 2533).

This reluctance is especially understandable in light of what will happen if the judge denies a Rule 50(a) motion, such as Desmond's. The jury will probably see the weakness in Penny's case and render a verdict for Desmond anyway. If not, Rule 50(b) gives the judge an opportunity to revisit the decision to deny the Rule 50(a) motion after the verdict. Thus, denying the first motion will lead to the "right" outcome (i.e., a verdict for Desmond) in most cases, and postponing the decision avoids the risk of a retrial, while preserving the judge's ability to revisit the denial after the jury renders its verdict.

Q **2. The Rule 50(b) safety net.** Why would a court be more inclined to grant a renewed motion under Rule 50(b) than to grant the original Rule 50(a) motion? Why don't judges have the same pragmatic concerns about Rule 50(b) motions as they do about Rule 50(a) motions?

A When an appellate court reverses a district court's decision to grant a Rule 50(b) motion for judgment as a matter of law (i.e., a judgment notwithstanding the verdict), the appellate court has determined that the jury's verdict was reasonable and should not have been set aside. Under these circumstances, the appellate court can remand the case with instructions for the trial court to enter a judgment based on the jury's original verdict. There is no need for a retrial. For this reason, most courts prefer to deny Rule 50(a) motions (motions for a directed verdict) and revisit the issue under Rule 50(b) in the event that the jury renders an unsupportable verdict.

3. The legal fiction of the "renewed" motion. Judges may have fewer pragmatic concerns about Rule 50(b) motions, but students tend to be more troubled by them. The motion comes after a jury verdict, so it appears to be asking the judge to question the jury's findings of fact. Moreover, by granting these motions, judges appear to violate the right to a jury trial under the Seventh Amendment, which provides that, "[i]n Suits at common law, where the value in controversy shall exceed twenty dollars, the right of trial by jury shall be preserved, and no fact tried by a jury, shall be otherwise re-examined in any Court of the United States, than according to the rules of the common law."

Arguably, allowing the judge to enter judgment as a matter of law *after* the verdict is an impermissible "re-examination" of a jury's verdict, barred by the Seventh Amendment. However, in *Baltimore & Carolina Line, Inc. v. Redman*, 295 U.S. 654, 659–60 (1934), the Supreme Court upheld the entry of what we now call judgment as a matter of law under Rule 50(b). The Court reasoned that if a party makes a motion for judgment as a matter of law under Rule 50(a) *before* the case goes to the jury and the judge does not grant the motion, the judge is considered to have conditionally submitted the case to the jury and can reassess the sufficiency of the evidence after the verdict. *See* Fed. R. Civ. P. 50(b) ("If the court does not grant a motion for judgment as a matter of law made under Rule 50(a), the court is considered to have submitted the action to the jury subject to the court's later deciding the legal questions raised by the motion.").

This may sound like the Rules are slicing the bologna a little thin, but there is ample historical precedent for these procedures. At the time that the Seventh Amendment was ratified, courts had used this legal fiction to grant the procedural equivalent of Rule 50(b) motions. Because the Seventh Amendment does not prohibit practices that were permissible at the time of the Amendment's ratification, Rule 50(b) has been held to be constitutional. *Baltimore & Carolina Line, Inc. v. Redman*, 295 U.S. 654, 659–60 (1934). *See also Moore* § 50.04; *Wright & Miller* § 2522 (asserting that "[t]he constitutionality of Federal Rule 50 is thoroughly settled").

There is also a policy rationale for Rule 50(b) motions. Without them, judges would have no opportunity to correct an unsupportable jury verdict. Knowing that they lack this power, judges would be more inclined to grant Rule 50(a) motions in order to avoid the possibility of an unsupportable jury verdict. But granting more Rule 50(a) motions also increases the likelihood of time-consuming and expensive retrials. The safety net of Rule 50(b), therefore, gives judges a greater incentive to permit the case to proceed to a jury verdict.

Q **4. Why not summary judgment?** If Penny had so little evidence to support her claim, why was there a trial? Why didn't the court grant summary judgment?

A There are at least two possible explanations. First, the parties might not have taken much, if any, discovery, especially if the case involved relatively limited damages. For example, without taking Penny's deposition or seeking any other discovery (e.g., through interrogatories), it would be difficult for Desmond to demonstrate that there is no genuine dispute of material fact regarding the color of the light. The absence of any evidence to support Penny's case might only become apparent at trial.

Second, even if the parties took discovery, the evidence is not necessarily presented the same way at trial. Suppose that during Penny's deposition, she said, "I think that Desmond's light was red, but I'm not sure." That statement is probably sufficient to avoid summary judgment, because there appears to be a genuine dispute regarding the light's color. At trial, however, Penny is much more uncertain and says, "I don't know what color the light was. It was so long ago." Her trial testimony is different from her deposition testimony, so although the judge properly denied the summary judgment motion, judgment as a matter of law may be appropriate at trial.

Summary judgments and judgments as a matter of law involve an examination of different information at different times in the litigation process. The standard that applies to each type of judgment, however, is identical. *Anderson v. Liberty Lobby*, 477 U.S. 242, 251–52 (1986). In both situations, a judge tries to determine whether any reasonable jury could render a verdict in favor of the non-moving party (usually the plaintiff). Of course, the standard simply begs the key question: When would it be reasonable for a jury to render a verdict for the non-moving party? We now turn to that critical question.

II. Defining a "Legally Sufficient Evidentiary Basis"

Rule 50(a)(1) provides that a judge may grant a judgment as a matter of law when "a reasonable jury would not have a legally sufficient evidentiary basis to find for... [that] party...." But when has a party failed to provide a "legally sufficient evidentiary basis" to support a verdict in its favor? Rule 50 does not offer much guidance, so it is necessary to look at how courts have applied the Rule in particular cases. The following two cases may help.

A. Granting a Judgment as a Matter of Law: An Example

Many casebooks include the following case, and for good reason. It discusses the standard for what the Federal Rules of Civil Procedure now call a judgment as a matter of law, and it includes an interesting factual dispute about how someone died. (Note that the case uses the pre-1991 federal court terminology of "directed verdict.")

READING *PENNSYLVANIA RAILROAD CO. v. CHAMBERLAIN.* Consider the following questions as you read *Chamberlain*.

- Which particular fact is in dispute in this case?
- Why does the Court conclude that the evidence presented was inadequate to support a verdict for the plaintiff?
- Does the Court consider the defendant's evidence when assessing the reasonableness of the plaintiff's theory?

PENNSYLVANIA RAILROAD CO. v. CHAMBERLAIN

288 U.S. 333 (1933)

Mr. Justice SUTHERLAND delivered the opinion of the Court.

This is an action brought by respondent [Chamberlain] against petitioner [Pennsylvania R.R. Co.] to recover for the death of a brakeman, alleged to have been caused by petitioner's negligence. The complaint alleges that the deceased, at the time of the accident resulting in his death, was assisting in the yard work of breaking up and making up trains and in the classifying and assorting of cars operating in interstate commerce; that in pursuance of such work, while riding a cut of cars, other cars ridden by fellow employees were negligently caused to be brought into violent contact with those upon which deceased was riding, with the result that he was thrown therefrom to the railroad track and run over by a car or cars, inflicting injuries from which he died.

At the conclusion of the evidence, the trial court directed the jury to find a verdict in favor of petitioner. Judgment upon a verdict so found was reversed by the Court of Appeals, Judge Swan dissenting. 59 F.(2d) 986.

That part of the yard in which the accident occurred contained a lead track and a large number of switching tracks branching therefrom. The lead track crossed a "hump," and the work of car distribution consisted of pushing a train of cars by means of a locomotive to the top of the "hump," and then allowing the cars, in separate strings, to descend by gravity, under the control of hand brakes, to their respective destinations in the various branch tracks. Deceased had charge of a string of two gondola cars, which he was piloting to track 14. Immediately ahead of him was a string of seven cars, and behind him a string of nine cars, both also destined for track 14. Soon after the cars ridden by deceased had passed to track 14, his body was found on that track some distance beyond the switch. He had evidently fallen onto the track and been run over by a car or cars.

The case for respondent rests wholly upon the claim that the fall of deceased was caused by a violent collision of the string of nine cars with the string ridden by deceased. Three employees, riding the nine-car string, testified positively that no such collision occurred. They were corroborated by every other employee in a position to see, all testifying that there was no contact between the nine-car string and that of the deceased. The testimony of these witnesses, if believed, establishes beyond doubt that there was no collision between these two strings of cars, and that the nine-car string contributed in no way to the accident. The only witness who testified for the respondent was one Bainbridge; and it is upon his testimony alone that respondent's right to recover is sought to be upheld. His testimony is concisely stated, in its most favorable light for respondent, in the prevailing opinion below by Judge Learned Hand, as follows:

> "The plaintiff's only witness to the event, one Bainbridge, then employed by the road, stood close to the yardmaster's office, near the 'hump.' He professed to have paid little attention to what went on, but he did see the deceased riding at the rear of his cars, whose speed when they passed him he took to be about eight

> or ten miles. Shortly thereafter a second string passed which was shunted into another track and this was followed by the nine, which, according to the plaintiff's theory, collided with the deceased's. After the nine cars had passed at a somewhat greater speed than the deceased's, Bainbridge paid no more attention to either string for a while, but looked again when the deceased, who was still standing in his place, had passed the switch and onto the assorting track where he was bound. At that time his speed had been checked to about three miles, but the speed of the following nine cars had increased. They were just passing the switch, about four or five cars behind the deceased. Bainbridge looked away again and soon heard what he described as a 'loud crash,' not however an unusual event in a switching yard. Apparently this did not cause him at once to turn, but he did so shortly thereafter, and saw the two strings together, still moving, and the deceased no longer in sight. Later still his attention was attracted by shouts and he went to the spot and saw the deceased between the rails. Until he left to go to the accident, he had stood fifty feet to the north of the track where the accident happened, and about nine hundred feet from where the body was found."

The [U.S. Court of Appeals], although regarding Bainbridge's testimony as not only "somewhat suspicious in itself, but its contradiction . . . so manifold as to leave little doubt," held, nevertheless, that the question was one of fact depending upon the credibility of the witnesses, and that it was for the jury to determine, as between the one witness and the many, where the truth lay. The dissenting opinion of Judge Swan proceeds upon the theory that Bainbridge did not testify that in fact a collision had taken place, but inferred it because he heard a crash, and because thereafter the two strings of cars appeared to him to be moving together. It is correctly pointed out in that opinion, however, that the crash might have come from elsewhere in the busy yard and that Bainbridge was in no position to see whether the two strings of cars were actually together; that Bainbridge repeatedly said he was paying no particular attention; and that his position was such, being 900 feet from the place where the body was found and less than 50 feet from the side of the track in question, that he necessarily saw the strings of cars at such an acute angle that it would be physically impossible even for an attentive observer to tell whether the forward end of the nine-car cut was actually in contact with the rear end of the two-car cut. The dissenting opinion further points out that all the witnesses who were in a position to see testified that there was no collision; that respondent's evidence was wholly circumstantial, and the inferences which might otherwise be drawn from it were shown to be utterly erroneous unless all of petitioner's witnesses were willful perjurers. "This is not a case," the opinion proceeds, "where direct testimony to an essential fact is contradicted by direct testimony of other witnesses, though even there it is conceded a directed verdict might be proper in some circumstances. Here, when all the testimony was in, the circumstantial evidence in support of negligence was thought by the trial judge to be so insubstantial and insufficient that it did not justify submission to the jury."

We thus summarize and quote from the prevailing and dissenting opinions, because they present the divergent views to be considered in reaching a correct determination of the question involved. It, of course, is true, generally, that where there is a direct conflict of testimony upon a matter of fact, the question must be left to the jury to determine, without regard to the number of witnesses upon either side. But here there really is no conflict in the testimony as to the facts. The witnesses for petitioner flatly testified that there was no collision between the nine-car and the two-car strings. Bainbridge did not say there was such a collision. What he said was that he heard a "loud crash," which did not cause him at once to turn, but that shortly thereafter he did turn and saw the two strings of cars moving together with the deceased no longer in sight; that there was nothing unusual about the crash of cars—it happened every day; that there was nothing about this crash to attract his attention except that it was extra loud; that he paid no attention to it; that it was not sufficient to attract his attention. The record shows that there was a continuous movement of cars over and down the "hump," which were distributed among a large number of branch tracks within the yard, and that any two strings of these cars moving upon the same track might have come together and caused the crash which Bainbridge heard. There is no direct evidence that in fact the crash was occasioned by a collision of the two strings in question; and it is perfectly clear that no such fact was brought to Bainbridge's attention as a perception of the physical sense of sight or of hearing. At most there was an inference to that effect drawn from observed facts which gave equal support to the opposite inference that the crash was occasioned by the coming together of other strings of cars entirely away from the scene of the accident, or of the two-car string ridden by deceased and the seven-car string immediately ahead of it. . . .

That Bainbridge concluded from what he himself observed that the crash was due to a collision between the two strings of cars in question is sufficiently indicated by his statements. But this, of course, proves nothing, since it is not allowable for a witness to resolve the doubt as to which of two equally justifiable inferences shall be adopted by drawing a conclusion, which, if accepted, will result in a purely gratuitous award in favor of the party who has failed to sustain the burden of proof cast upon him by the law.

And the desired inference is precluded for the further reason that respondent's right of recovery depends upon the existence of a particular fact which must be inferred from proven facts, and this is not permissible in the face of the positive and otherwise uncontradicted testimony of unimpeached witnesses consistent with the facts actually proved, from which testimony it affirmatively appears that the fact sought to be inferred did not exist. This conclusion results from a consideration of many decisions, of which the following are examples: *Wabash R. Co. v. De Tar* (C.C.A.) 141 F. 932, 935; *George v. Mo. Pac. R.R. Co.*, 251 S.W. 729, 732 [numerous additional citations omitted]. A rebuttable inference of fact, as said by the court in the *Wabash Railroad* Case, "must necessarily yield to credible evidence of the actual occurrence." And, as stated by the court in *George v. Mo. Pac. R.R. Co.*, supra, "It is well settled that, where plaintiff's case is based upon an inference or inferences, the case must fail upon proof of undisputed facts inconsistent with such inferences."

. . .

Not only is Bainbridge's testimony considered as a whole suspicious, insubstantial, and insufficient, but his statement that when he turned shortly after hearing the crash the two strings were moving together is simply incredible, if he meant thereby to be understood as saying that he saw the two in contact; and if he meant by the words "moving together" simply that they were moving at the same time in the same direction but not in contact, the statement becomes immaterial. As we have already seen he was paying slight and only occasional attention to what was going on. The cars were eight or nine hundred feet from where he stood and moving almost directly away from him, his angle of vision being only 3°33′ from a straight line. At that sharp angle and from that distance, near dusk of a misty evening (as the proof shows), the practical impossibility of the witness being able to see whether the front of the nine-car string was in contact with the back of the two-car string is apparent. And, certainly, in the light of these conditions, no verdict based upon a statement so unbelievable reasonably could be sustained as against the positive testimony to the contrary of unimpeached witnesses, all in a position to see, as this witness was not, the precise relation of the cars to one another. The fact that these witnesses were employees of the petitioner, under the circumstances here disclosed, does not impair this conclusion.

We think, therefore, that the trial court was right in withdrawing the case from the jury. It repeatedly has been held by this court that before evidence may be left to the jury, "there is a preliminary question for the judge, not whether there is literally no evidence, but whether there is any upon which a jury can properly proceed to find a verdict for the party producing it, upon whom the onus of proof is imposed." *Pleasants v. Fant*, 22 Wall. 116, 120, 121. And where the evidence is "so overwhelmingly on one side as to leave no room to doubt what the fact is, the court should give a peremptory instruction to the jury." *Gunning v. Cooley*, 281 U.S. 90, 94. . . . Such a practice, this court has said, not only saves time and expense, but "gives scientific certainty to the law in its application to the facts and promotes the ends of justice." *Bowditch v. Boston*, 101 U.S. 16, 18. The scintilla rule has been definitely and repeatedly rejected so far as the federal courts are concerned.

Leaving out of consideration, then, the inference relied upon, the case for respondent is left without any substantial support in the evidence, and a verdict in her favor would have rested upon mere speculation and conjecture. This, of course, is inadmissible.

The judgment of the Circuit Court of Appeals is reversed and that of the District Court is affirmed.

Notes and Questions: When Judgment as a Matter of Law Is Appropriate

Q **1. The plaintiff's evidence.** Which fact was in dispute, and what evidence supported the plaintiff's version of events?

A

The factual dispute was whether the brakeman died as a result of a train collision between two strings of railroad cars or whether he simply fell from the car that he was piloting. The railroad would be liable only if a collision caused the accident.

The plaintiff's only evidence of a collision was Bainbridge's testimony. He saw the two strings of cars—one piloted by the deceased and one following the deceased's string—traveling in close proximity to each other, and he subsequently heard a loud crash. When Bainbridge looked up, he saw the two strings of cars moving in tandem, but because of his vantage point and the distance, he could not tell whether the two strings of cars had come into contact with each other. He also was not sure whether the loud crash had come from those two strings of cars or from some other source in the rail yard.

A Legally Sufficient Evidentiary Basis?

© Ted Horowitz / Corbis

The *Chamberlain* case considers whether the testimony of Bainbridge, the plaintiff's only witness, was strong enough to support a jury verdict in the plaintiff's favor. The view here is not taken from the record in *Chamberlain*, but offers some perspective on Bainbridge's difficulty in seeing events nine hundred feet away along the tracks.

Q

2. Considering all of the evidence. Did the Court consider the defendant's evidence when it concluded that the plaintiff's version of events was unreasonable?

A

Yes. The Court concluded that there was not a legally sufficient evidentiary basis to support a verdict for the plaintiff, but only after considering the substantial evidence that the defendant had offered.

In most cases, the federal courts (and a majority of state courts) follow this approach today. They examine both the defendant's and plaintiff's evidence when deciding whether to grant a judgment as a matter of law, *Reeves v. Sanderson Plumbing Products, Inc.*, 530 U.S. 133, 150 (2000), but they will typically consider the moving party's evidence (in this case, the defendant's evidence) only to the extent that it is uncontradicted and unimpeached. *Id.* at 150–51.

3. The test for sufficiency. One way to determine whether the evidence is "legally sufficient" is to ask "whether the evidence is such that, *without weighing the credibility of the witnesses or otherwise considering the weight of the evidence*, there can be but one conclusion as to the verdict that reasonable . . . [persons] could have reached." *Wright & Miller* § 2524 (emphasis added) (quoting *Simblest v. Maynard*, 427 F.2d 1, 4 (2d Cir. 1970)). The Supreme Court has articulated a similar test:

> [I]n entertaining a motion for judgment as a matter of law, the court should review all of the evidence in the record.
>
> In doing so, however, the court must draw all reasonable inferences in favor of the nonmoving party, and it may not make credibility determinations or weigh the evidence. "Credibility determinations, the weighing of the evidence, and the drawing of legitimate inferences from the facts are jury functions, not those of a judge." *Anderson v. Liberty Lobby, Inc.*, 477 U.S. 242, 255 (1986). Thus, although the court should review the record as a whole, it must disregard all evidence favorable to the moving party that the jury is not required to believe. *See Wright & Miller* § 299. That is, the court should give credence to the evidence favoring the nonmovant as well as that "evidence supporting the moving party that is uncontradicted and unimpeached, at least to the extent that that evidence comes from disinterested witnesses." *Id.*, at 300.

Reeves v. Sanderson Plumbing Products, Inc., 530 U.S. 133, 150–51 (2000) (internal citations omitted).

4. Determining sufficiency without weighing? The prohibition against "weighing" the evidence can be confusing. In general, it means that courts are not supposed to determine which side's case is more credible. A court, however, has to consider the strength of the non-moving party's evidence relative to the moving party's, at least to some degree, in order to determine whether the evidence is "sufficient" to justify a verdict in the non-moving party's favor.

Consider *Chamberlain*. It involved a modest, yet permissible, kind of evidentiary weighing. The railroad's employees testified that they saw the incident and that no collision occurred. In contrast, Bainbridge offered only circumstantial evidence of what *might* have happened. Specifically, Bainbridge was not looking in the relevant direction at the time of the alleged incident, and his location near the "hump" made it impossible for him to have seen a collision. Accordingly, the plaintiff did not impeach the defendant's evidence or directly contradict it. (*See* Figure 29–2 on the following page.)

The Court did not weigh this evidence in the sense of finding Bainbridge less credible than the defense witness, though its reference to Bainbridge's testimony being "simply incredible" sounds suspiciously close to doing so. Rather, the Court concluded that Bainbridge's testimony was insufficient to rebut the substantial and contrary direct testimony that the railroad had offered. Of course, this is really just another way of saying that the defendant's evidence was so much more compelling than the plaintiff's that no reasonable jury could find for the plaintiff. The case, therefore, illustrates that there is a fine line between an impermissible weighing of the evidence and a determination (like the one in *Chamberlain*) that the non-moving party's evidence is legally insufficient to warrant a jury verdict.

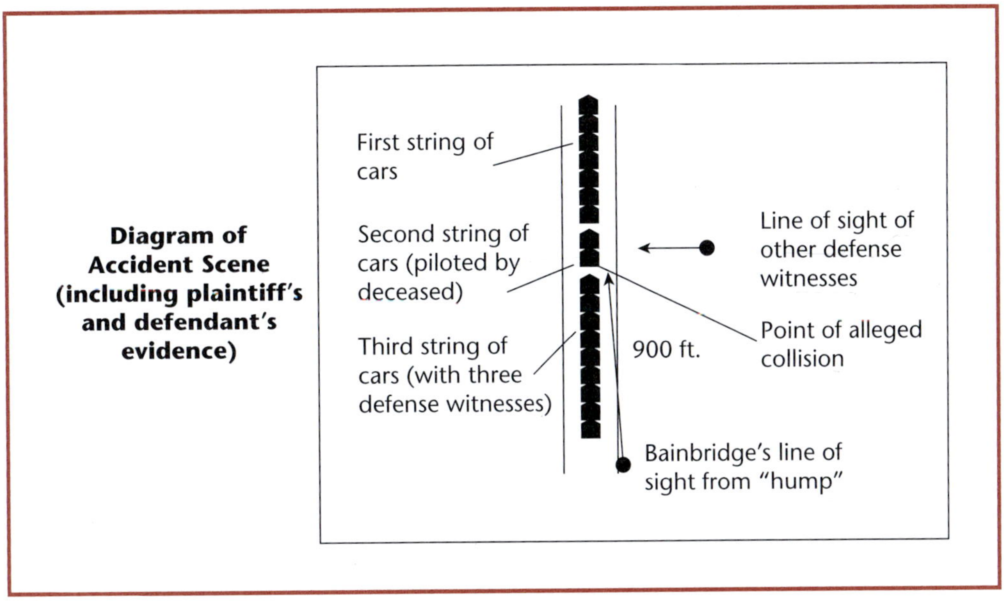

Figure 29–2: AN ILLUSTRATION OF THE ACCIDENT IN *CHAMBERLAIN*

5. Picturing the court's task. To illustrate the line between a permissible and an impermissible weighing of the evidence, many books offer some variant of the diagram below.*

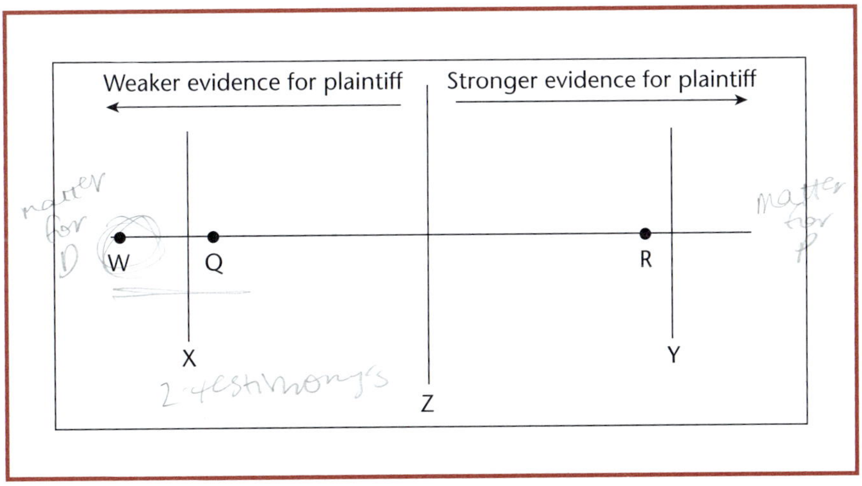

Figure 29–3: PICTURING THE JUDGE'S ROLE

* A similar diagram originally appeared in Jonathan H. Landers & James A. Martin, *Civil Procedure* (1981).

Line Z indicates the point at which the plaintiff's and defendant's evidence are evenly balanced. If a plaintiff must prove her claim by a preponderance of the evidence, she must produce enough evidence to cross this line as to each element of the claim.

The practical problem is that reasonable minds often disagree about whether proof of an element crosses line Z. For this reason, judges defer to juries as long as the evidence falls somewhere between line X and line Y. If the evidence falls somewhere in that zone, a judge will conclude that the jury's verdict—whether for the plaintiff or the defendant—is reasonable. For example, even if the judge believes that the evidence reaches only point Q, the judge will defer to a jury because the evidence is within the debatable range.

In other cases, the evidence may be so far to one of the extremes that a judge should not defer to the jury. For example, if the evidence is so lopsided that it reaches only point W (as in *Chamberlain*), the court can determine the relevant issue as a matter of law and grant a judgment for the defendant, because there is so little evidence supporting the plaintiff's case that no reasonable jury could find for the plaintiff.

On occasion, a plaintiff may offer such overwhelming evidence in favor of liability (past line Y in the diagram) that a court can enter judgment as a matter of law for the *plaintiff*. Such cases arise less frequently, but Rule 50 does not preclude this possibility.

The diagram illustrates when judgment as a matter of law is appropriate, but it does not offer much practical guidance as to how to make that determination. Put simply, knowing that there is (and should be) a line X and a line Y is easy, but knowing where those lines should be drawn in any particular case is quite a bit more difficult.

6. Burdens of persuasion and production. The diagram in the note above helps to illustrate the burdens of persuasion and production, which are concepts that arise in many procedural contexts, including when a party makes a motion for judgment as a matter of law.

The party with the burden of persuasion is the party who must persuade the fact-finder, to the necessary degree of certainty, that it should prevail in the case. For example, in criminal cases, the government has the burden of persuasion to convince the fact-finder that the defendant committed a crime "beyond a reasonable doubt." In civil cases, the plaintiff typically has the burden of persuasion to convince the fact-finder by a "preponderance of the evidence" (i.e., that it is more likely than not) that the defendant is liable. *See Moore* § 132.02[4][A]. Put another way, the plaintiff in the typical civil case has the burden to convince the fact-finder that the evidence crosses line Z in the above diagram. (In some civil cases, such as in some libel cases, the plaintiff has a heavier burden of persuasion and must prove her case by "clear and convincing evidence," approximately represented by point R in the above diagram.)

A distinct burden is the burden of production, which refers to a party's burden to produce sufficient evidence to avoid an adverse judgment as a matter of law on a particular matter. For example, when a defendant moves for summary judgment, the defendant has the initial burden of production and must demonstrate that there is no genuine dispute of any material fact. *See Moore* § 56.13. If the defendant fails to meet this burden, the judge will deny the motion. Similarly, a defendant moving for judgment as a matter of law under Rule 50(a)(2) has the initial burden of production, that is, the burden to "specify the judgment sought and the law and facts that entitle the... [defendant] to the judgment." If the defendant fails to satisfy that burden, the motion is denied. The burden of *persuasion*, however, remains at all times with the party whose claim or affirmative defense is being litigated. For instance, throughout an ordinary civil case, the plaintiff always has the burden of persuasion to prove the case by a preponderance of the evidence, but the defendant might have the initial burden of *production* in certain circumstances, such as when moving for judgment as a matter of law.

7. One witness against many.

Suppose that, instead of standing near the "hump," Bainbridge had stood a few feet from the location where the alleged collision occurred. He subsequently testifies at trial that, from this vantage point, he actually saw a collision. Assume that the rest of the evidence is largely the same—six employees with a clear view of what happened testify that there was *no* collision. Should a federal court grant the defendant's motion for a directed verdict (Rule 50(a) motion) at the close of all of the evidence?

A. Yes, because no reasonable jury could render a verdict for the plaintiff in light of this evidence.
B. Yes, because the weight of the evidence favors the defendant.
C. No, because a reasonable jury could render a verdict for the plaintiff.
D. No, because a jury is supposed to determine the relative strength of the evidence, not the judge.

Remember that a judge is not supposed to grant a motion for judgment as a matter of law simply because the weight of the evidence favors one party. B, therefore, offers a clearly incorrect statement of the Rule 50(a) standard.

It is also inaccurate to say, as suggested in answer D, that only juries assess the relative strength of the evidence. To determine whether a non-moving party has offered "sufficient" evidence to avoid a judgment as a matter of law (e.g., whether there is enough evidence to cross line X), a federal judge necessarily has to engage in some evaluation of the moving party's evidence relative to the non-moving party's evidence. For example, in *Chamberlain*, the insufficiency of Bainbridge's circumstantial evidence was apparent only in light of the substantial and contrary direct testimony that the railroad had offered.

The question boils down to whether a reasonable jury could render a verdict for the plaintiff in this case. Here, the plaintiff has offered one witness who testified that there was a collision, and the defendant has offered six witnesses who testified that there was no such collision. Can a reasonable jury find for the plaintiff under these circumstances?

The Court said in *Chamberlain* that, in general, "where there is a direct conflict of testimony upon a matter of fact, the question must be left to the jury to determine, without regard to the number of witnesses upon either side." This quote suggests the answer to the question. The defendant may have offered more witnesses, but a reasonable jury could conclude for any number of reasons that Bainbridge is a more credible witness. (For example, the jury might think that the other witnesses are more concerned about keeping their jobs than testifying truthfully.) Because judges are not supposed to weigh the credibility of the witnesses, the best answer here is C, not A. In other words, this case requires the kind of evidentiary weighing that is supposed to be left to the jury.

In contrast, in *Chamberlain,* there was not a direct conflict between Bainbridge's testimony and that of the defense witnesses. The Court explained that "[t]he witnesses for petitioner flatly testified that there was no collision between the nine-car and the two-car strings. Bainbridge did not say there was such a collision. What he said was that he heard a 'loud crash,' which did not cause him at once to turn, but he did so shortly thereafter, and saw the two strings together, still moving, and the deceased no longer in sight." As a result, the actual case did *not* require the kind of weighing (e.g., an assessment of witness credibility) that is supposed to be left to the jury.

8. The "scintilla" alternative. The *Chamberlain* Court considered all of the evidence (both the plaintiff's evidence and the defendant's uncontradicted and unimpeached evidence) when it decided that a directed verdict was appropriate. The federal courts continue to employ the same approach today, at least in most cases. *Reeves v. Sanderson Plumbing Products, Inc.*, 530 U.S. 133, 150 (2000) (resolving a circuit split on the issue).

A few states, however, have taken a different tack, concluding that a court should consider only the non-moving party's evidence. In these states, a court will deny a motion for judgment as a matter of law if the non-moving party (usually the plaintiff) has offered a mere "scintilla" of evidence in support of its position. These courts refuse to consider the quantity or quality of the *moving* party's (usually the defendant's) evidence, even when that evidence is uncontradicted and unimpeached. Thus, the motion succeeds or fails in these courts based only on a consideration of the non-moving party's evidence.

This standard has the benefit of being less intrusive into the jury's fact-finding function, and it effectively eliminates any judicial weighing of the evidence. The judge need only determine whether the non-moving party offered *any* evidence to support a jury verdict in its favor. For example, if the plaintiff reaches point W in the earlier diagram, a judge would deny the defendant's motion for a judgment as a matter of law.

The downside to this approach is that it undermines a court's ability to prevent a patently unreasonable jury verdict. *Moore* § 50.62. For this reason, lawyers who trust juries tend to prefer the scintilla approach, and lawyers who distrust juries tend to prefer the federal approach.

Q **9. The outcome under the scintilla standard.** Suppose that the *Chamberlain* Court had adopted the scintilla standard and had refused to consider the railroad's evidence. Would the Court have reached a different conclusion? Why?

A The outcome probably would have been different. Consider the following revised diagram, which reflects the more limited evidence that the court would have been able to consider under the scintilla standard.

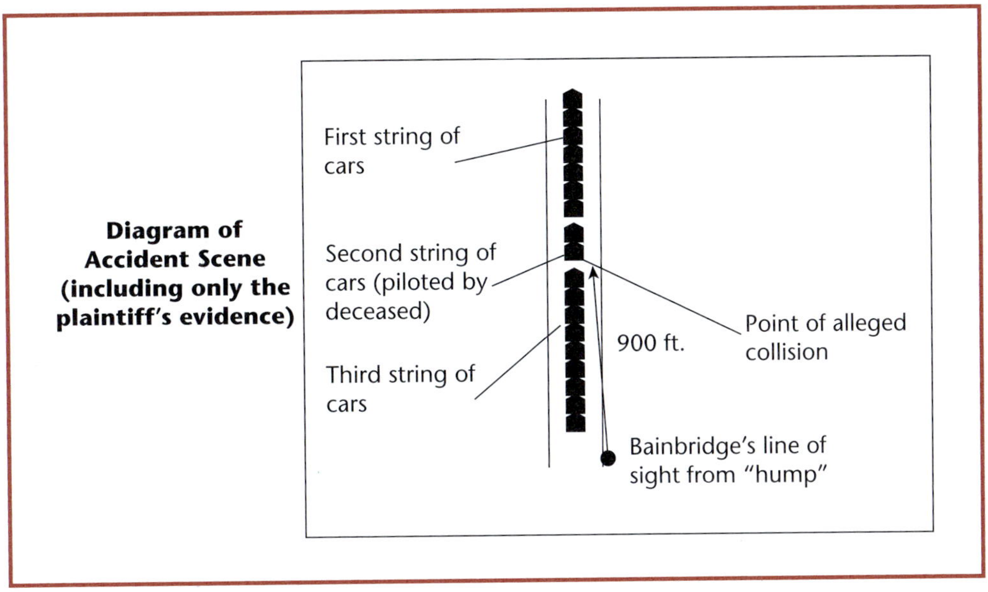

Figure 29–4: THE PLAINTIFF'S EVIDENCE IN *CHAMBERLAIN*

Unlike Figure 29–2, this diagram does not include the testimony of the numerous defense witnesses who had a clear view of the incident. The only evidence that the court would be entitled to consider under the scintilla standard is Bainbridge's testimony. He said that he had seen the third string of cars pass him at a higher rate of speed than the deceased's string of cars. Bainbridge also said that he had heard a loud crash shortly thereafter and that, when he looked up, he had seen the trailing string of cars and the deceased's string moving in tandem. That testimony would not be powerful evidence of a crash, but it is *some* evidence of a crash. Under the scintilla standard, therefore, the court would likely deny the defendant's motion.

In contrast, under the federal approach, a court considers the moving party's evidence (to the extent it is uncontradicted and unimpeached) and has to determine whether a reasonable jury could find for the non-moving party. In this case, that means that a court would have to consider the testimony of the defense witnesses (which was neither contradicted nor impeached) and ask whether, in light of that additional evidence, a reasonable jury could find for the plaintiff. When the defense's evidence is thrown into the mix and the line for "sufficiency" is moved from point W (scintilla standard) to line X (the federal standard), judgment as a matter of law is appropriate. The standard makes a significant difference.

Q **10. The Rule 50(b) standard.** Imagine that the district judge in *Chamberlain* had denied the motion for a directed verdict, perhaps hoping that the jury would get the verdict "right." Assume that, on the evidence described in *Chamberlain*, the jury nevertheless returned a verdict for the plaintiff, awarding damages of $50,000. If the railroad moved for a judgment notwithstanding the verdict—that is, a renewed motion under Rule 50(b)—should that motion be granted? Why?

A Yes. Motions for a directed verdict (Rule 50(a) motions) and motions for a judgment notwithstanding the verdict (Rule 50(b) motions) are made at different times, but the analysis of the two motions is essentially the same. *Moore* § 50.63 (explaining that the standard for the two motions is "identical"). Remember that the Rule 50(b) motion is simply a "renewed" Rule 50(a) motion, so it stands to reason that courts will employ the same analysis in both instances.

One difference between the two motions is that they implicate distinct pragmatic concerns. As explained earlier, a judge has a stronger incentive to deny a Rule 50(a) motion than a renewed motion under Rule 50(b), because a reversal of the decision to grant the Rule 50(a) motion will necessitate a new trial. In sum, a judgment notwithstanding the verdict is appropriate here for the same reason that it would have been appropriate for the judge to have granted a directed verdict: There is insufficient evidence for a reasonable jury to render a verdict for the plaintiff.

Another difference is that the motions may be made on different records. If the Rule 50(a) motion is made at the close of the plaintiff's evidence, then it will be judged against a less complete record than a renewed motion under Rule 50(b) made within 28 days after entry of judgment. The court ruling on the Rule 50(b) motion will have the benefit of the defendant's evidence, which it would not have had in ruling on the prior Rule 50(a) motion.

B. Denying a Judgment as a Matter of Law: An Example

To get a better feel for the location of line X, it is helpful to read some cases that warrant a jury verdict and some that don't. *Chamberlain* offers an example of the latter sort, and the following offers an example of the former.

READING *LANE v. HARDEE'S FOOD SYSTEMS, INC.* Consider the following questions as you read *Lane*:

- Which fact is being challenged as having inadequate evidentiary support?
- Why does the court conclude that the jury should have had an opportunity to render a verdict in this case?
- Is the case consistent with *Chamberlain*? Why?

LANE v. HARDEE'S FOOD SYSTEMS, INC.

184 F.3d 705 (7th Cir. 1999)

Flaum, Circuit Judge.

Donald Lane slipped and injured himself on the restroom floor of a Hardee's restaurant in Harrisburg, Illinois. Claiming that his fall was the result of water negligently left by a restaurant employee, Lane sued its owner, Hardee's Food Systems, Inc. ("Hardee's"). At the close of plaintiff's case-in-chief, the district court granted judgment as a matter of law in favor of the defendant holding that Lane had failed to produce sufficient evidence that Hardee's was responsible for creating the dangerous condition in its restroom. Because a jury could reasonably have found for Lane on the facts presented, we reverse the court's decision and remand for a new trial.

BACKGROUND

At some point soon after 10:00 A.M. on November 2, 1995, Donald Lane stopped at the Harrisburg Hardee's, ordered a drink, smoked a cigarette, and then entered the restroom. On his way out, Lane slipped on what he says was standing water near a drain, and sustained injuries to his head and neck when he hit the restroom floor.

Lane sued Hardee's in state court claiming the restaurant had negligently left the water on the restroom floor, failed to warn customers of it, and failed to maintain its restroom in a reasonably safe condition. Hardee's had the suit removed to federal district court and then moved for summary judgment. The motion was denied and the case proceeded to trial before a jury.

During his case-in-chief, Lane presented the testimony of Judy Rochford and Kim Thompson, both managers of the Harrisburg Hardee's, who each stated that the restaurant had a policy of cleaning (including mopping) the restroom everyday after breakfast ended at 10:30 A.M. Thompson also stated it was her habit to put out warning signs when the floor was being mopped, and that she periodically checked the restroom throughout the day. Lane testified that he arrived at Hardee's either between 10:16 A.M. and 10:26 A.M. or between 10:25 A.M. and 10:35 A.M. He estimated that it took him about ten minutes to drink his beverage and smoke a cigarette. Thus he entered the restroom at some point between 10:26 A.M. and 10:45 A.M. (but claims he saw no warning signs). Based on this, he was prepared to argue to the jury that he slipped in the restroom soon after a Hardee's employee mopped the restroom and that the restaurant was responsible for its agent's negligence in leaving the water and failing to warn customers of its presence.

The court disagreed. After hearing Lane's case, Judge Gilbert concluded that the plaintiff had failed to produce evidence that Hardee's had actually left water on the restroom floor prior to Lane's fall. Without such evidence, the court decided that Lane could not prevail on his negligence claim and that Hardee's was entitled to judgment as a matter of law. Lane now challenges that decision.

DISCUSSION

Standard of Review

The district court may grant judgment as a matter of law when "a party has been fully heard on an issue and there is no legally sufficient evidentiary basis for a reasonable jury to find for that party on that issue." Fed. R. Civ. P. 50(a)(1). The district court may not resolve any conflicts in the testimony nor weigh the evidence, except to the extent of determining whether substantial evidence could support a jury verdict: "[A] mere scintilla of evidence will not suffice." *Von Zuckerstein v. Argonne*

National Laboratory, 984 F.2d 1467, 1471 (7th Cir. 1993) (quoting *La Montagne v. American Convenience Products, Inc.,* 750 F.2d 1405, 1410 (7th Cir. 1984)). We review the district court's decision de novo, asking whether the evidence presented, combined with all the reasonable inferences permissibly drawn therefrom, is sufficient to support the verdict when viewed in the light most favorable to the party against whom the motion is directed. We will reverse the judgment "only if enough evidence exists that might sustain a verdict for the nonmoving party." *Continental Bank N.A. v. Modansky,* 997 F.2d 309, 312 (7th Cir. 1993).

Issue

The issue on appeal, therefore, is whether the plaintiff presented sufficient evidence of the defendant's negligence to allow the case to go to the jury. Specifically, it is whether Lane had come forward with evidence that Hardee's, rather than another customer, spilled the water on the restroom floor.

Illinois Negligence Law and Premises Liability Law

While we review the grant of judgment as a matter of law according to the federal standard described above, the parties agree that Illinois law supplies the elements Lane must prove to prevail in this diversity suit. Under Illinois law, a business owes the public "the duty of exercising reasonable care in maintaining the premises in a reasonably safe condition." *Donoho v. O'Connell's Inc.,* 148 N.E.2d 434, 437 (1958); *see* Illinois Premises Liability Act, 740 ILCS 130/2 (1995) ("The duty owed [invitees and licencees] is that of reasonable care under the circumstances regarding the state of the premises or acts done or omitted on them."). The law relating to business liability for slip and fall injuries is well established. If the plaintiff is injured by slipping on a foreign substance placed or left on the premises by the proprietor or its agent, the defendant business can be liable whether it knows of the dangerous condition or not. *See Olinger v. Great Atlantic and Pacific Tea Company,* 173 N.E.2d 443, 445 (1961). If the offending substance was on the premises through acts of a third person, or if there is no showing of how it got there, the business will normally only be liable if it had actual or constructive knowledge of its presence or if "the substance was there a sufficient length of time so that in the exercise of ordinary care its presence should have been discovered." *Olinger,* 173 N.E.2d at 445.

To prove that the defendant business, as opposed to a third person, created the hazard (and therefore whether actual notice by the defendant is required), Illinois courts have required the plaintiff to 1) show that the foreign material was related to the defendant's business, and 2) produce some evidence that makes it more likely than not that the defendant was responsible for its existence.

Assessment of the Evidence Presented

Based on Illinois law and the evidence Lane has presented, we conclude that a reasonable jury could have found in the plaintiff's favor on the question of negligence. The district court held that Lane lacked sufficient evidence to establish his claim that Hardee's had negligently created the dangerous condition. The court was simply not convinced that Lane had shown that Hardee's had acted improperly. While we understand the district court's doubts about the quantity of Lane's evidence, and share the court's concern about its strength,[3] once the plaintiff has presented the minimum evidence necessary to support a verdict, the court may not weigh it. Viewing the evidence and all reasonable inferences therefrom in a light most favorable to the plaintiff, we believe Lane has, though minimally, met the elements set out in Illinois case law and had, at least at the close of his case, a right not to have the negligence question taken from the jury.

First, the parties do not dispute that the substance at issue—water in a public restroom—was related to the defendant's business. Lane even took the precaution of eliciting testimony from Rochford that clean (including presumably mopped) restrooms are an important part of running the restaurant. Second, Lane has presented the kind of substantial evidence this court has identified as sufficient to support a jury finding of negligence. *See Howard,* 160 F.3d at 359 (verdict in favor of grocery shopper who slipped on a patch of spilled liquid soap upheld based on evidence that spill was near area where store employee could have been shelving the product and the fact that no broken container was ever found, which suggested that an employee rather than another customer was responsible). A jury could reasonably infer from the restaurant's daily practice of cleaning the restroom floor after breakfast at 10:30 A.M. that the floor was indeed mopped at around that time on the day of the accident. The most favorable reading of Lane's time line put the plaintiff in the restroom soon after the inferred mopping. From the fact that spilled water or residual dampness is not an unusual by-product of mopping and from the alleged mopping's proximity to the accident, a jury could reasonably conclude that Hardee's, rather than another customer, was responsible for the dangerous condition. *See id.; see, e.g., Donoho,* 148 N.E.2d at 440–41 (verdict in favor of restaurant patron who slipped on an onion ring was sustained by evidence that busboy had recently cleaned the area of the accident and had a practice of clearing the tables in a way that could allow food particles to drop on the floor). This is by no means the only—nor even the most—reasonable conclusion a jury could reach, but so long as it is permissible, the case should have been allowed to proceed.

CONCLUSION

Because Lane has met his burden of presenting sufficient evidence on which a reasonable jury could base a verdict in his favor, the district court's judgment in favor of Hardee's was improper. We therefore REVERSE and REMAND the case for proceedings consistent with this opinion.

---

3. Of particular concern to the district court was the fact that Lane was depending on Hardee's having fulfilled part of its routine policy (mopping the bathrooms around 10:30 A.M.) but not the other part (putting out warning signs). The lack of signs in violation of restaurant policy obviously makes the inference that Hardee's actually mopped prior to Lane's fall less strong, and should appropriately be weighed by the jury.

Notes and Questions: When Judgment as a Matter of Law Is Inappropriate

Q **1. The plaintiff's evidence.** Which fact did Hardee's challenge as having inadequate evidentiary support, and what evidence did the plaintiff offer in support of his version of events?

A The key factual dispute was whether the water on the restroom floor was caused by a Hardee's employee or by a patron. If an employee caused it, the plaintiff was entitled to recover for his injuries.

The plaintiff offered the testimony of two employees who said that the floor was typically mopped at 10:30 A.M. The plaintiff also offered his own testimony that he probably entered the restroom shortly after 10:30 A.M.

2. Issue analysis: Consistency with *Chamberlain*? The *Lane* court concluded that the plaintiff had offered sufficient evidence to warrant a jury verdict. Is this conclusion consistent with the analysis in *Chamberlain*? Why?

Before reading the analysis below, take a few minutes to write out an answer. In what ways are the two cases similar? How are they different? Explain whether the two cases are ultimately distinguishable (and thus consistent with each other) or whether the two cases are essentially the same (and thus inconsistent with each other).

A suggested analysis. In one respect, the two cases are indistinguishable and appear to be inconsistent. The plaintiffs in both cases offered only circumstantial evidence in support of their cases. The plaintiff in *Chamberlain* did not offer testimony from a witness who saw an actual collision. Similarly, the plaintiff in *Lane* did not offer any testimony from a witness who saw a Hardee's employee mopping the floor at 10:30 A.M.

Circumstantial evidence, however, can be sufficient to justify a verdict for the plaintiff. Thus, to determine whether the cases are inconsistent, it is necessary to examine the strength of the *defendant's* evidence (or at least the defendant's uncontradicted and unrebutted evidence).

Recall that the defendant's evidence in *Chamberlain* was quite strong. Numerous defense witnesses testified that they had been at the location in question and had not seen a collision, and the plaintiff's witness did not directly contradict this testimony.

In contrast, the court in *Lane* did not hear the defendant's evidence because the court granted judgment as a matter of law at the close of the plaintiff's case in chief. Accordingly, the court could only consider the plaintiff's circumstantial evidence that the floor had been mopped at around 10:30 A.M. That evidence alone was legally sufficient for a reasonable jury to conclude that the floor had been mopped just before Lane entered the restroom.

Put another way, in *Lane*, the plaintiff presented sufficient evidence to cross line X, and the defendant had not yet been heard. In contrast, in *Chamberlain*, the plaintiff's case may have crossed line X on its own, but the defendant's uncontradicted evidence conclusively negated the plaintiff's case, pushing it back to the other side of line X. For these reasons, the *Lane* case falls just to the right of line X, whereas the *Chamberlain* case falls to the left of line X. Accordingly, the court's decision in *Lane* appears to be distinguishable from (and thus consistent with) the Supreme Court's decision in *Chamberlain.*

3. Compelling contrary evidence.

Recall Penny's case against Desmond. Imagine that Penny offers eyewitness testimony from Widmore, a bystander who says that Desmond's light was red. In rebuttal, Desmond offers video footage from a nearby security camera, which shows him passing through the intersection when his light was green. Assume that Penny does not impeach the video's reliability or the accuracy of what is depicted in it. If Desmond moves for judgment as a matter of law after he offers this evidence and if the court adopts the federal standard for assessing the motion, the court should

A. grant the motion, because no reasonable jury could render a verdict for the plaintiff in light of this evidence.
B. grant the motion, because Penny's case was entirely circumstantial.
C. deny the motion, because a reasonable jury could render a verdict for the plaintiff.
D. deny the motion, because Penny has offered some evidence in support of her position.

B is wrong for two reasons. First, as explained above, circumstantial evidence can be sufficient to prove a case. Indeed, in *Lane,* the plaintiff's evidence was entirely circumstantial, but the court concluded that a reasonable jury could find for the plaintiff. B, therefore, offers an incorrect statement of the law.

B is also incorrect for a second reason: Penny's evidence was not circumstantial! Circumstantial evidence is evidence from which one can infer what happened, but is not direct evidence of what happened. For example, in *Lane,* the plaintiff did not offer testimony from anyone who saw an employee mopping the floor at 10:30 A.M. Rather, the plaintiff offered circumstantial evidence that the mopping occurred at that time. Similarly, in *Chamberlain,* Bainbridge did not see a collision; he *inferred* that there had been a collision. In contrast, in the question above, Penny has offered the testimony of someone who claims to have seen the traffic light when Desmond went through the intersection. That is direct testimony, not circumstantial evidence.

D also offers an incorrect statement of the law, at least in courts that have adopted the federal standard. In these courts, the non-moving party has to offer more than "some" evidence in support of her position. She must offer "sufficient" evidence from which a reasonable jury could find in her favor. D would be the right answer in the small minority of state courts that have adopted the scintilla rule, but the question states that the court has adopted the federal standard.

The difficulty here is deciding between C and A. On the one hand, there appears to be a factual disagreement—whether the light was red—that should be left to the jury. Nevertheless, the video seems conclusive, especially given that Penny did not impeach the video's reliability in any way.

If you chose A because the video seems overwhelmingly persuasive, there is some authority for your position. In *Scott v. Harris*, 550 U.S. 372 (2007), the United States Supreme Court determined that, under some circumstances, video evidence can be so persuasive that a trial is unnecessary, even when the plaintiff intends to offer her own testimony that would directly contradict the video.

There is considerable disagreement, however, about the scope of the *Scott* decision and whether it gave too much deference to video evidence. *See* Dan M. Kahan, David A. Hoffman & Donald Braman, *Whose Eyes Are You Going to Believe?* Scott v. Harris *and the Perils of Cognitive Illiberalism,* 122 HARV. L. REV. 837 (2009) (offering empirical evidence that the video in the *Scott* case is perceived differently depending on one's ideological or cultural perspective). *See also Scott v. Harris*, 550 U.S. 372 (2007) (Stevens, J., dissenting). At present, it appears that A would reflect the approach of many courts, but there is a good argument for C, especially if the video is impeached on the grounds that it is not a complete depiction (or offers a possibly inaccurate depiction) of what actually happened.

4. The district judge's gamble. Recall that if a district judge grants a Rule 50(a) motion, the judge risks the possibility of a retrial if the dismissal is reversed on appeal. In *Lane*, the appellate court ordered "proceedings consistent with this opinion," which means that, in the absence of a settlement, the parties will have to retry the case. Thus, this case illustrates the risk associated with granting a Rule 50(a) motion (a motion for a directed verdict).

So why did the judge take the risk? It turns out the risk was comparatively low. The original trial involved small stakes, little evidence, and few witnesses. Thus, the district judge might have guessed that the plaintiff was unlikely to appeal. Moreover, even though the plaintiff did appeal and the ruling was reversed, the judge may have thought that the case could be retried easily or that, in light of the relatively minor injuries involved, the case was likely to settle before retrial. Correspondence with one of the lawyers in the case reveals that the parties did, in fact, settle before a retrial.

In sum, the threat of a reversal and retrial may dissuade judges from granting the Rule 50(a) motion, but judges will not be dissuaded if the motion's merits are particularly strong or (as here) there is little reason to fear a retrial.

III. Procedural Technicalities of Rule 50

Rule 50 contains several procedural nuances. Some of those technicalities are explored in the questions below, which you should be able to answer after a careful reading of Rule 50.

Notes and Questions: Rule 50 Technicalities

Q **1. A general, oral motion.** Imagine that Penny presents her case but fails to offer evidence that Desmond ran a red light or was otherwise negligent. Immediately after Penny rests her case, Desmond's lawyer leaps from her chair and says, "Your honor, we move for judgment as a matter of law under Rule 50(a)." Why is the motion insufficient?

A Rule 50 does not require the motion to be in writing, so the motion is not insufficient for that reason. The problem here is that the motion fails to satisfy Rule 50(a)(2), which requires the moving party to "specify... the law and facts that entitle the movant to the judgment." Here, the motion was generic and did not specify Penny's failure to offer evidence regarding the color of the light. Accordingly, the motion should be denied.

This requirement is not a mere technicality. It exists to ensure that cases are decided on their merits, not on inadvertent omissions of trial testimony. This objective would be undermined if a party could make (and the court could grant) a Rule 50 motion without putting the non-movant on notice about the nature of her omission and giving her an opportunity to correct it. If a judge could grant Desmond's generic motion, Penny would be deprived of the opportunity to know why her case was deficient and to present additional evidence to correct that deficiency before the case is submitted to the jury or the motion is granted.

Q **2. Multiple Rule 50(a) motions.** At the close of Penny's case, Desmond makes a Rule 50(a) motion for judgment as a matter of law, arguing that Penny failed to offer any evidence regarding the color of the light when Desmond entered the intersection. The judge denies the motion, and Desmond subsequently presents his case. After Desmond offers his evidence, but before the case is submitted to the jury, may Desmond now make a second Rule 50(a) motion?

A Rule 50(a) does not prohibit making two Rule 50(a) motions. Rather, Rule 50(a)(2) provides that "[a] motion for judgment as a matter of law may be made at any time before the case is submitted to the jury." The only limitation is that the motion cannot be made until "a party has been fully heard on an issue...." Rule 50(a)(1).

Taken together, those two subsections mean that a Rule 50(a) motion can typically be made either: (1) after the non-moving party (usually the plaintiff) "has been fully heard on an issue," (2) after both parties have presented all of their evidence, or (3) at *both* times. (See the timeline below.)*

---

* There is even some authority for the idea that a court can grant a judgment as a matter of law after opening statements and before the plaintiff has presented any evidence, *see, e.g., Baden Sports, Inc. v. Molten USA, Inc.*, 541 F. Supp. 2d 1151 (D. Wash. 2009), *rev'd on other grounds*, 556 F.3d 1300 (9th Cir. 2009), but a motion is only proper at such an early stage if it is clear that no question exists for the jury to consider. *See Moore* § 50.20[b].

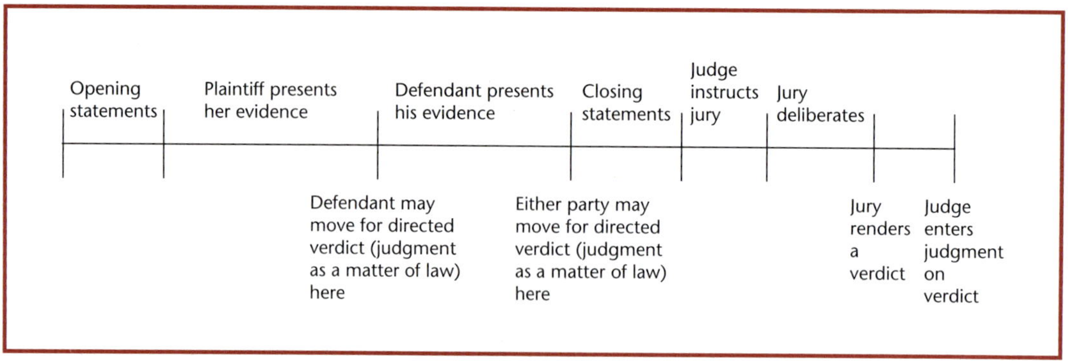

Figure 29–5: **THE TIMING OF RULE 50(a) MOTIONS**

Q **3. The meaning of "fully heard."** Imagine that Penny offers her own testimony about the accident, but she fails to offer any evidence that Desmond was at fault. Her pretrial witness list reveals that she does not intend to call any other witnesses regarding what happened at the time of the accident. Rather, Penny intends to have several doctors testify about the extent of her injuries. After Penny has finished presenting her evidence on liability, but before she has offered the doctors' testimony, Desmond moves for judgment as a matter of law. Can the judge grant Desmond's motion at this stage of the case?

A Although the typical timeline in Figure 29–5 above suggests that a party has to wait until the non-moving party has finished presenting her entire case in order to make a motion for judgment as a matter of law, Rule 50(a)(1) says that a court can grant a judgment as a matter of law after "a party has been fully heard *on an issue*..." (emphasis added). This means that a party can make a motion after the non-moving party has had an opportunity to present all of her evidence *on the issue that is the subject of the motion*, which may or may not be at the end of the non-moving party's entire case. Because Penny had finished offering her evidence on liability, Desmond could move for judgment as a matter of law on that issue without having to wait for Penny to offer evidence about her damages.

This approach makes good sense as a matter of efficiency. There is little reason to ask the parties, the court, and the jury to sit through extensive testimony on damages if Penny has failed to offer legally sufficient evidence to warrant a verdict in her favor on liability. One court has made the point this way:

> Common practice may be to wait until a party has concluded her case-in-chief to ensure that she has been "fully heard" on the issue, but the Rule provides that "[a] motion for judgment as a matter of law may be made at any time before the case is submitted to the jury." Fed. R. Civ. P. 50(a)(2). It would be a foolish rule that guaranteed a party the right to present all of its evidence when the effort would clearly be futile. It is proper to enter judgment as a matter of law prior to the close of a plaintiff's case-in-chief so long as it has become apparent that the party cannot prove her case with the evidence already submitted or with that which she still plans to submit.

Greene v. Potter, 557 F.3d 765, 768 (7th Cir. 2009).

Q

4. A better outcome for a later-filed motion? In courts that adopt the federal standard, why is a defendant's Rule 50(a) motion more likely to succeed when it is made at the close of all of the evidence than when it is made just after the plaintiff has finished presenting her case? (Hint: Why would the answer to this question be different in a state that adopts the scintilla rule?)

A

If a defendant makes a Rule 50(a) motion after the plaintiff has presented her evidence, but before the defendant has offered his, the court only has the plaintiff's evidence to consider. The plaintiff's evidence alone may suffice to cross the all-important line X. But if the defendant makes a Rule 50(a) motion at the close of *all* of the evidence, the federal court has the benefit of having heard the defendant's side as well. If this additional evidence is uncontradicted and unimpeached, it may be sufficient to push the evidence back to the other side of line X, as happened in *Chamberlain*.

In contrast, in states that have adopted the scintilla rule, the outcome should be the same regardless of the motion's timing, because these courts should consider only the non-moving party's evidence no matter when the motion is made.

Q

5. Prerequisites for a renewed motion under Rule 50(b). Suppose that the case is tried, but Desmond never makes a Rule 50(a) motion for judgment as a matter of law. If the jury returns a verdict for Penny, can Desmond make a motion for judgment as a matter of law under Rule 50(b)?

A

No. You cannot "renew" a motion that has never been made in the first place. Rule 50(b) specifies that "[i]f the court does not grant a motion for judgment as a matter of law made under Rule 50(a), the court is considered to have submitted the action to the jury subject to the court's later deciding the legal questions raised by the motion." This means that if a party fails to make a Rule 50(a) motion, the party has waived the opportunity to make a Rule 50(b) motion.

This requirement, like the requirement to specify the basis for a Rule 50(a) motion, serves the important purpose of ensuring that the cases are decided on their merits. If parties could make Rule 50(b) motions without first making Rule 50(a) motions, parties would rarely make Rule 50(a) motions. Parties would let the case go to a jury and raise the adversary's omission only if the adversary wins, at which time the adversary has no opportunity to correct the omission. To prevent this kind of sandbagging and ensure that cases do not turn on inadvertent omissions of trial testimony, Rule 50(b) requires a party to alert her adversary to the problem at a time when the adversary can fix it, i.e., by making a Rule 50(a) motion before the case is submitted to the jury. *See Moore* § 50.02 (citing cases making a similar point).

Rule 50(b) used to require a Rule 50(a) motion "at the close of all the evidence." This requirement was a common trap for the unwary litigator. There were numerous cases where defendants were precluded from making Rule 50(b) motions because they had made Rule 50(a) motion at the conclusion of the *plaintiff's* case, but had neglected to make another Rule 50(a) motion *at the conclusion of all of the evidence.* Because of the confusion, the requirement was eliminated in 2006. Parties can now make a Rule 50(b) motion as long as they previously made a Rule 50(a) motion *at some point* after the nonmoving party had been fully heard on the relevant issue and before submission of the case to the jury.

Q **6. Lost and found: Changing the basis for the motion.** Assume that Desmond makes a Rule 50(a) motion at the close of all of the evidence, arguing that Penny failed to offer any evidence that Desmond's traffic light was red. The judge denies the motion, and the jury returns a verdict for Penny for $50,000. Desmond renews his motion under Rule 50(b), arguing that Penny not only failed to offer any evidence that the light was red, but she also neglected to offer any evidence of her damages. Desmond moves for judgment as a matter of law, both with regard to the jury's determination of liability and the damages award. Should the court consider Desmond's renewed motion on the issue of damages?

A Once again, focus on Rule 50(b). It specifies that, when a court denies a Rule 50(a) motion, "the court is considered to have submitted the action to the jury subject to the court's later deciding the *legal questions raised by the motion*" (emphasis added). This language makes clear that a party can make a Rule 50(b) motion only when that party previously made a Rule 50(a) motion *that raised the same defect in the opponent's case*.

Here, Desmond's Rule 50(b) motion raises an evidentiary omission—an omission regarding damages—that was not mentioned in his Rule 50(a) motion. Accordingly, the court must deny Desmond's Rule 50(b) motion on that issue. The court is free, however, to consider Desmond's motion on the issue of the traffic light's color, because Desmond raised that argument in his Rule 50(a) motion.

This answer is consistent with the goal of notifying non-moving parties of the defects in their cases. If parties were permitted to make one argument in a Rule 50(a) motion and a different argument in a Rule 50(b) motion, as Desmond has done here, this important objective could be easily undermined.

7. Prerequisites for appeal. Assume that Desmond makes a Rule 50(a) motion at the close of all of the evidence, arguing that Penny failed to offer any evidence that Desmond's traffic light was red. The judge denies the motion, and the jury returns a $50,000 verdict for Penny. Instead of making a renewed motion under Rule 50(b), Desmond appeals the verdict, arguing that the judge should have granted the Rule 50(a) motion. Can the appellate court review the district court's decision to deny the Rule 50(a) motion?

Rule 50 does not expressly answer this question, but the United States Supreme Court has made clear that "a party's Rule 50(a) motion . . . cannot be appealed unless the motion is renewed pursuant to Rule 50(b)." *Unitherm Food Systems, Inc. v. Swift-Eckrich, Inc.*, 546 U.S. 394, 404 (2006). The Court reasoned that a post-verdict motion is necessary because such motions call "for the judgment in the first instance of the judge who saw and heard the witnesses and has the feel of the case which no appellate printed transcript can impart." *Id.* at 401 (quoting *Cone v. West Virginia Pulp & Paper Co.*, 330 U.S. 212, 216 (1947)). Thus, if a party fails to ask the district judge to make that determination in a post-verdict motion, the party waives the issue on appeal.

Q **8. The standard of review on appeal.** Appellate courts apply a *de novo* standard of review to questions of law. This means that an appellate court decides legal issues without any presumption that the lower court resolved them correctly. For example, if a party appeals a trial court's interpretation of a state statute, the appellate court does not defer to the lower court's decision; the appellate court interprets the statute for itself and reverses the decision if it concludes that the trial court's interpretation was incorrect.

In contrast, an appellate court gives substantial deference to a trial court's factual findings, typically adopting them unless they are "clearly erroneous." The rationale for this approach is that a trial court has a much better feel for the evidence and is therefore in a better position to resolve factual issues than the appellate court. Which of these standards of review should apply to an appellate court's review of a district court's decision regarding a motion for judgment as a matter of law?

A The motion's name reveals the answer. A motion for judgment as a matter of *law* asks a trial judge to decide whether a reasonable jury could find in favor of the non-moving party as a legal matter. The judge is not supposed to take into account the demeanor of witnesses or other intangible courtroom factors, so the trial judge is not in any better position to resolve the motion than an appellate court. *See Reeves v. Sanderson Plumbing Products, Inc.*, 530 U.S. 133, 150 (2000). Because the appellate court's task is to resolve a legal question based on the record, the appellate court employs a *de novo* standard of review when reviewing the trial court's ruling on a Rule 50 motion. *Wright & Miller* § 2540.

IV. Judgment as a Matter of Law: Summary of Basic Principles

- Rule 50(a) authorizes a judge to grant a motion for judgment as a matter of law after the non-moving party (usually the plaintiff) has been fully heard on an issue at trial. State courts and older federal opinions refer to this motion as a motion for a directed verdict.
- Rule 50(b) permits a party to renew a Rule 50(a) motion for judgment as a matter of law after the jury has rendered its verdict. State courts and older federal opinions refer to these motions as motions for judgment notwithstanding the verdict (JNOV).
- The standard for applying Rule 50 is essentially the same as the standard that courts employ when deciding a motion for summary judgment under Rule 56. In both situations, a court has to determine whether the

non-moving party's case is legally sufficient for a reasonable jury to reach a verdict in favor of the non-moving party.

- To determine whether the non-moving party has offered legally sufficient evidence, a federal court will consider the non-moving party's evidence along with any of the moving party's uncontradicted and unimpeached evidence. The court will then determine whether, in light of this evidence, a reasonable jury could render a verdict for the non-moving party.
- At least one state uses the "scintilla" standard and denies a motion if there is a scintilla of evidence to support the non-moving party's case. Under this approach, courts will not consider the moving party's evidence, even when it is uncontradicted and unimpeached.
- Rule 50(a) requires the moving party to specify the basis for the motion, and the motion cannot be made until the non-moving party has been fully heard on the issue that is the basis for the motion.
- A party cannot renew a motion for judgment as a matter of law under Rule 50(b) unless the party previously made a Rule 50(a) motion that raised the same issue.
- A party cannot appeal a denial of a Rule 50(a) motion unless that party renewed the motion under Rule 50(b) after the jury's verdict. An appellate court will apply a *de novo* standard of review when determining whether the non-moving party offered legally sufficient evidence to withstand a motion for judgment as a matter of law.

30

Controlling the Jury

I. Introduction

The old federal (and still current state) nomenclature, "directed verdict," and "judgment notwithstanding the verdict," made it clear that the motion for judgment as a matter of law is a method of controlling the jury by preventing it from making decisions without sufficient evidence or by overriding verdicts returned without sufficient evidence. But it is not the only control. The court's rulings on the admissibility of evidence are another, because they are primarily intended to protect the jury from misusing evidence. We discuss this control device only briefly in section II because Evidence is a separate course. Instructions to the jury are another means of controlling the jury. We discuss them in section III. Finally, verdict forms are a fourth control, inasmuch as they are templates for juries to record their work. We discuss them in section IV.

II. Rulings on the Admissibility of Evidence

While rules of evidence apply both in jury trials and bench trials, most of them were developed to protect the jury from bias and confusion "to the end that the truth may be ascertained. . . ." Fed. R. Evid. 102. Limits on admissibility of evidence in jury trials are based on the assumption that a lay jury is less able than an experienced judge to separate the probative from the unreliable or inflammatory. (In bench trials, by contrast, the judge may accept problematic evidence "for what it's worth" and then (theoretically) ignore the inadmissible or problematic evidence in reaching a decision.) Perhaps no rule of evidence more clearly reflects this presumption than Federal Rule of Evidence 403, which provides that a court may exclude even "relevant evidence . . . if its probative value is substantially outweighed by a danger of unfair prejudice, confusing the issues, [or] misleading the jury. . . ." This rule, for example, has been invoked to exclude gruesome photos in tort cases tried to the jury.

A successful objection, however, does not always exclude evidence; it may instead result in admission with a "limiting instruction" to the jury. *See* Fed. R. Evid. 105. Recall, for example, that evidence of a subsequent repair of a product is discoverable in a products liability case. Federal Rule of Evidence 407 excludes such evidence if it is offered "to prove negligence, culpable conduct, a defect in a product or its design, or a need for a warning or instruction." Yet, such evidence can be admitted if it is offered "for another purpose, such as impeachment or—if disputed—proving ownership, control, or the feasibility of precautionary measures." If the manufacturer disputes the feasibility of a product enhancement that might have prevented the injury, evidence of a subsequent product change could be offered to prove feasibility, with a limiting instruction to the jury to consider it for that purpose only and not for the forbidden purposes. *See United States v. McClain*, 440 F.2d 241, 246 (D.C. Cir. 1971) ("As long as we continue to have rules of evidence which admit testimony for some purposes but not for others, we must guard against its misuse by the jury."). Of course, you might well question the efficacy of such limiting instructions, but the point here is that evidentiary rulings are sometimes tied to jury instructions, themselves a method of controlling the jury.

III. Jury Instructions

Even in the most basic Pedestrian versus Driver lawsuit, the jury cannot just shuffle out to deliberate after the close of the evidence. Deliberate about what? To be sure, it could guess that it has to make some decision about whether the driver struck the pedestrian, but even if it did, that decision would hardly suffice to decide the case. The law does not premise liability on the driver striking the pedestrian. It depends on what duty the driver owed at the time of the accident, whether he breached it, what duty the pedestrian himself owed, if any, to avoid the accident, whether the accident "proximately caused" the pedestrian's damages, and so on. A jury needs to be instructed on what factual disputes the law requires it to resolve. It also must be instructed on what "proximately caused" means and on the standard of proof (preponderance of the evidence, not beyond a reasonable doubt, as most of the jurors might think from TV crime shows) it must apply.

The court does not need to instruct the jury unaided, however. Rule 51(a) provides that a party may make written requests for jury instructions at the close of the evidence or at an earlier reasonable time the court orders. Some courts, for example, ask for such requests at the final pretrial conference. The court then decides on the instructions, sometimes cutting and pasting from each party's submissions and sometimes adopting so-called pattern jury instructions from form books. *See, e.g.*, Kevin F. O'Malley, Jay E. Grenig, & William C. Lee, Federal Jury Practice & Instructions Civil Companion Handbook (2019–2020). The judge then informs the parties which instructions she will use before giving them to the jury and before final arguments. This advance notice gives the parties time to object to an instruction or failure to give an instruction while there is still time for the court to change the instructions. Fed. R. Civ. P. 51(c).

READING *HARDIN v. SKI VENTURE, INC.* Hardin was severely injured when he skied into a tree. He sued the ski resort operator for negligence. The judge gave the jury general instructions in negligence and assumption of the risk—explaining the generic elements that you learned in Torts—and also provided an instruction that quoted the West Virginia Skiing Responsibility Act. After the jury returned a verdict for the ski resort, Hardin appealed, challenging the jury instructions.

- Were the jury instructions accurate on the law?
- If jury instructions are accurate on the law, can they nevertheless be flawed? How?
- Suppose the court had found the jury instructions either inaccurate or otherwise flawed in some respect. Does it follow that it then must reverse the judgment on the verdict?
- Why does Judge Butzner dissent?

Hardin and the Snowmaking Machine

© Grafton Smith / Getty Images

Blinded by snow from a snowmaking machine like the one shown here, Hardin skied directly into a tree. He sued the ski slope, not because it was using snowmaking machines, but because, he alleged, it pointed them uphill instead of downhill, used artificial snow that was too wet, and left insufficient room for downhill skiers to avoid the snow plume. Was he entitled to have the judge instruct the jury as to these details of his negligence claim?

HARDIN v. SKI VENTURE, INC.

50 F.3d 1291 (4th Cir. 1995)

WILKINSON, Circuit Judge:

In this diversity tort action, a jury found that the appellee, Ski Venture, Inc., was not guilty of negligence for the injuries that appellant Henry Hardin suffered in a skiing accident at the Snowshoe Ski Resort. Hardin now contests various rulings by the trial court. Specifically, he complains about the trial court's jury instructions. . . . Because we find no error in the trial proceedings, we affirm the judgment entered on the jury's verdict.

I.

[EDS.—Hardin alleged that the artificial snow from the snowmaking machines froze on his goggles, blinding him and causing him to run off the trail and into a tree, where he sustained severe injuries. He alleged that the defendant was negligent in the placement and operation of the snowmaking machines, by pointing them uphill instead of downhill, using snow that was too wet for safety on the trail, and not leaving sufficient room for "good skier flow" past the plume. The defendant resort owner denied negligence and pleaded the affirmative defense of assumption of the risk, arguing that the West Virginia Skiing Responsibility Act made the skier responsible for exercising due care. The Act provides that there are certain "inherent risks" in skiing that cannot serve as a basis for resort owner liability. These inherent risks are distinguished, however, from the duty of a ski area operator to maintain its ski slopes in a reasonably safe condition. If injury arises from a violation of this duty as opposed to an inherent risk, the owner may be held liable. W. Va. Code §§ 20-3A-1 et seq. (1989).

The jury returned a verdict for the defendant, finding that the defendant had not been negligent in its maintenance of the ski trail. This appeal followed.]

II.

We first consider appellant's challenge to the district court's jury instructions. Hardin raises two distinct claims of error in this context. First, he argues that the trial court erred when it failed to include his two instructions on his specific theory of the case. These proposed instructions summarized his contentions about wet snow and the direction of the snow gun. Second, appellant claims that the instructions as a whole were weighted in favor of the ski resort, containing extraneous material that could have confused the jury. These instructions failed to fairly and adequately instruct the jury, Hardin argues, thereby prejudicing his case.

While the content of jury instructions in a diversity case is a matter of state law, the form of those instructions is governed by federal law. District courts are necessarily vested with a great deal of discretion in constructing the specific form and content of jury instructions. By no means are they required to accept all the suggested instructions offered by the parties. So long as the charge is accurate on the law and does not confuse or mislead the jury, it is not erroneous. A set of legally accurate instructions that does not effectively direct a verdict for one side or the other is generally adequate. On review, jury instructions must also be viewed as a whole. When the jury charge here is considered in its entirety, it is clear that the trial court provided an accurate overview of the pertinent legal principles and achieved an adequate degree of balance and fairness.

A.

First, neither side was granted the specificity that plaintiff argues he was unfairly denied. Rather, the district court discussed each party's theory of the case in general terms. The court initially noted that Hardin's cause of action alleged that Snowshoe "negligently failed to maintain the Grabhammer trail in a reasonably safe condition." The court then proceeded to explain that defendant owed plaintiff "the duty of every person to exercise ordinary care in conduct toward others." It stated that in order to decide whether ordinary care was used, "the conduct in question must be viewed in the light of all surrounding circumstances." Moreover, the court explained that the West Virginia Skiing Responsibility Act imposed a statutory duty on the defendant to "[m]aintain the ski areas in reasonably safe condition." It further stated that defendant could be found negligent if it "failed to exercise ordinary care in the operation of its snow making equipment." It also reviewed the concepts of proximate cause and canvassed the rules of damages.

The instructions for the defendant were likewise general in tone and content. The trial court discussed the duties imposed on skiers by the Act, as well as those areas where the Act exempted ski resorts from liability, quoting directly from the statute as it did so. It also reviewed the defendant's affirmative defenses. First, it noted that defendant asserted contributory negligence, which the court defined in the same general terms as negligence. The court also stated that "the burden of proving that [defense] . . . is upon the defendant." Second, the court defined the defense of assumption of risk and noted that defendant had to prove "[t]hat a hazardous condition existed at the time Mr. Hardin skied the Grabhammer trail . . . , [t]hat Mr. Hardin had actual knowledge of the hazardous or dangerous condition, appreciated the risks involved, but proceeded to take some action" such as the failure "to ski within the limits of his ability [or] to maintain reasonable control of speed and course at all times while skiing." Nowhere did the court go into great detail about defendant's evidence or contentions, just as it did not discuss plaintiff's evidence or contentions in great depth.

That was not error. A court is not required to comment on specific evidence in the course of giving a jury instruction, and indeed often is well-advised not to. It is of course open to the trial judge to comment on such evidence in the course of an instruction, but it is also reasonable for a court to believe that such comments may carry unacceptable risks of removing from the jury its critical task of assigning weight to the evidence presented. *See Quercia v. United States,* 289 U.S. 466, 470 (1933) (stating that judges must be careful in instructions to limit comments on evidence so as not to sway or mislead jury); *see also* 9A *Wright & Miller* § 2557 (1995) (noting that courts are never required to comment on evidence). Similarly, courts must have the flexibility in instructions to avoid confusing or prejudicial statements that might arise from a discussion of the specific contentions in a case. Different trial judges may have different preferences in this regard, and we decline to elevate any one preference to the status of circuit law. So long as the jury instructions are not merely statements of abstract principles of law with no relation to the facts, the choice of generality versus specificity in the charge is a matter left to the sound discretion of the trial courts.

Moreover, it is accuracy, not specificity, that is the critical question with respect to jury instructions. Where, as here, the instructions accurately covered all the issues in the case, the failure to reference specific aspects of a party's contentions, such as the direction of the snow gun or the wetness of the snow, cannot serve as a basis for a finding of error. This is not a case where the court failed to instruct the jury on an entire issue or claim presented by plaintiff's evidence. *Cf. Carvel Corp. v. Diversified Management Group, Inc.*, 930 F.2d 228, 230 (2d Cir. 1991) (finding error in failure to instruct on issue of implied duty of good faith). The substance of plaintiff's theory of the case—that the defendant failed to maintain the trail in a reasonably safe condition—was adequately conveyed to the jury. The fact that plaintiff did not also receive more specific instructions in the exact form he requested is no basis for throwing out the jury's verdict.

B.

Second, the instructions here were not weighted impermissibly in favor of the defendant. In fact, the plaintiff received several individual instructions that were helpful to his side. For example, the court mentioned several times that plaintiff was alleging that defendant had failed to maintain the trail in a reasonably safe condition, and that this could be a basis for a finding of negligence. The court also carefully explained each element of the negligence cause of action, and dwelt at length on the concepts of damages.

Plaintiff complains about the "extra" information in the instructions relating to assumption of risk by skiers under the West Virginia Skiing Responsibility Act. He points to the court's mention of the fact that ski area operators are not liable for injuries resulting from

> [v]ariations in terrain; surface or subsurface snow or ice conditions; bare spots, rocks, trees, other forms of forest growth or debris; collisions with pole lines, lift towers or any component thereof; or, collisions with snowmaking equipment which is marked by a visible sign or other warning implement in compliance with [the requirements of the West Virginia Skiing Responsibility Act].

See W. Va. Code § 20-3A-3 (quoted in jury instructions). Because these factors were not directly at issue, Hardin argues that this discussion unbalanced the instructions and could only serve to confuse the jury.

It is clear, however, that a district court is allowed to cite a relevant statute in its instructions. Indeed, it would be truly bizarre if it could not. To the degree that the instructions reflected any lack of balance, that is due to the content of state law, not to the misstatement of relevant legal principles by the court. Furthermore, the statutory reference was not extraneous. In fact, the Act was one of the central elements of state law in this case. The West Virginia statute indicates the extent of both the resort's duty and the limits of its liability with respect to skiing accidents. It reflects the relevant fact that the maintenance of a trail in a reasonably safe condition does not mean that every natural feature of the terrain must be removed. Likewise, the statutory list of the inherent risks of skiing could have been relevant to jury deliberations on whether plaintiff had in fact assumed the risk of his collision with the tree. At any rate, an objection by plaintiff to extraneous material on assumption of risk was largely moot because the jury never reached that issue, but rather decided the threshold question that defendant had not been negligent.

Even when jury instructions are flawed, there can be no reversal unless the error seriously prejudiced the plaintiff's case. It is not the function of an appellate court to nit-pick jury instructions to death. Here, there may well have been some surplusage in the instructions, but nothing that rose to a level of error, let alone prejudicial error. The instructions, taken as a whole, were accurate and balanced. They were neither too scant on details nor too expansive on irrelevancies. At the end of the day, the fact is that this case went to a fair and impartial jury, and the jury simply found in favor of the defendant. An appellate court should respect that result. . . .

V.

For the foregoing reasons, the judgment in this case is
AFFIRMED.

BUTZNER, Senior Circuit Judge, dissenting:

I respectfully dissent because the district court's refusal to instruct the jury on Hardin's theory of recovery was prejudicial error.

Hardin proved Snowshoe's snowmaking policies, which read in part: "When making snow on trails that are open, the following steps should be taken. 1. Make snow dry and skiable. . . . 3. Point gun, if possible, the same direction as skiers are skiing. . . . 5. Select snowmaking areas that are wide enough to allow good skier flow." There is no suggestion that Snowshoe's snowmaking policies did not conform to industry standards.

Both Hardin and Mrs. Cindy Jacob testified that the snow coming from the machine was wet and froze on their goggles. Hardin testified that the snow gun was pointed uphill. There is no claim that it was impossible to point the gun downhill. Mrs. Jacob testified that the snowmaking plume obscured the trail on which they were skiing.

The relevant portion of Hardin's instruction, which the court refused, was as follows:

Specifically, the plaintiff claims that the defendant [Snowshoe], was negligent in the following ways:

1. The defendant did not follow its own snowmaking policies.
2. The defendant was making wet snow.
3. The snowmaking equipment was pointed uphill, rather than in the direction the skiers, including the plaintiff, were skiing.
4. The snowmaking area was too narrow to avoid; that is, it was not wide enough to allow good skier flow.

The court instructed the jury generally on the law of negligence. The court instructed that the defendant had a duty to maintain the ski area in a reasonably safe condition. It defined negligence as a failure to exercise ordinary care.

Snowshoe does not assert that Hardin's instruction was incorrect. It argues that the district court's instructions on negligence were accurate, fair, and complete. Snowshoe's argument is just plain wrong.

Three cases, from among many of similar import, illustrate the district court's error. A court must instruct the jury on the law with due regard to the specific facts of the case at hand. *See Merchants National Bank of Mobile v. United States,* 878 F.2d 1382, 1388 (11th Cir. 1989). A failure to give proffered instructions is error when the proposed instructions are accurate and the instructions actually given to the jury fail to explain the law adequately or tend to confuse or mislead the jury. *See Sullivan v. National Football League,* 34 F.3d 1091, 1106–07 (1st Cir. 1994).

In *Baxter v. Ainsworth,* 288 F.2d 557 (5th Cir. 1961), the trial court instructed the jury on negligence in general terms but refused to instruct regarding specific acts by the defendant that could support a finding of negligence. The appellate court found the trial court's general instruction on negligence insufficient because "in no part of the charge did the court present to the jury, as plaintiffs were entitled to have him do, plaintiffs' theory of their right to recover as the facts presented it." 288 F.2d at 559.

By refusing to give Hardin's proffered instruction, the district court departed from a well-established principle of law governing the trial of cases in federal courts. While a court is not required to comment on the evidence, it must recognize that a litigant "is entitled to have its legal theories on controlling issues, which are supported by the law and the evidence, presented to the jury." *Sullivan,* 34 F.3d at 1107. There can be no doubt that Hardin suffered prejudice, for it was on the basis of faulty instructions that the jury found Snowshoe was not negligent.

Notes and Questions: Jury Instructions

1. Accurate on the law. It is axiomatic that jury instructions must be accurate on the law. In *Hardin*, that meant explaining the elements of the negligence claim that Hardin made, the elements of defendant's assumption-of-the-risk defense, and the burden of proof cast on each party. Because West Virginia had enacted a special statute that distinguished "inherent risks" of skiing from the ski resort's duty to maintain its slopes (and was probably intended to limit the resorts' liability), it also meant explaining, paraphrasing, or quoting the statute. Of course, it takes an entire Torts course for law students to comprehend the nuances of negligence law and related defenses, so the judge necessarily has a large measure of discretion in explaining the law clearly and concisely in a twenty- or thirty-minute charge to a lay jury. *See Moore* § 51.20[1][a] (urging that instructions avoid "legalistic terms" and should generally take no more than twenty or thirty minutes).

2. Pattern jury instructions. Explaining complex legal concepts in a clear and short jury instruction is no mean feat. Inevitably, therefore, parties and judges look for guidance in prior jury instructions on the same law that survived challenge on appeal. In many jurisdictions, the most common such instructions are collected in form books of *pattern jury instructions* organized by subject (simple negligence, assumption of the risk, contributory negligence, preponderance of the evidence, etc.). Most of these form books are put together by scholars or the local bar based on instructions that were upheld in reported cases. The following description of pattern jury instructions for criminal cases in the Ninth Circuit is equally true of instructions for civil cases:

> Jury instructions are only judge-made attempts to recast the words of statutes and the elements of crimes into words and terms comprehensible to the layperson. The texts of "standard" jury instructions are not debated and hammered out by legislators, but by ad hoc committees of lawyers and judges. Jury instructions do not come down from any mountain or rise up from any sea. Their precise wording, although extremely useful, is not blessed with any special precedential or binding authority. This description does not denigrate their value, it simply places them in the niche where they belong....
>
> Our own Ninth Circuit Manual of Model Jury Instructions stands on a similar footing. It begins with this caveat:
>
>> "It should be emphasized that the instructions in this Manual are models and are not intended to be pattern instructions. They must be reviewed carefully before use in a particular case. They are not a substitute for the individual research and drafting that may be required in a particular case, nor are they intended to discourage judges from using their own forms and techniques for instructing juries." 9th Cir. Man. of Model Jury Instr., Introduction (West 1996) (emphasis added).

McDowell v. Calderon, 130 F.3d 833, 840–41 (9th Cir. 1997).

So what is the chief advantage and disadvantage of a pattern jury instruction? It provides a statement of the law that was presumably good enough to be used successfully in a prior case. Using it again may be safer than winging it: trying to cast the law in a party's own language. On the other hand, a pattern instruction is not binding precedent. It may, in fact, be obsolete, and it is not tailored to the particular facts of your case. Using it may be erroneous, or even if it is still good law, not very useful for *your* jury. Yet, tailoring it too much risks getting the law wrong. And, of course, if your case charts new paths in the law, there may be no pattern instructions on point.

Q **3. Accuracy is not enough.** Even a legally accurate instruction may confuse or mislead the jury. The jury may be flummoxed by legalisms and jargon or overwhelmed to a degree that unfairly favors one side (try explaining "proximate causation" or "*res ipsa loquitur*" to a layman). The jury instructions in *Hardin* were not inaccurate. So what was Hardin's complaint?

A It was that the judge's instructions failed to particularize the duty to the facts of the case.

The Instruction Given	The Instruction Hardin Wanted
"[The ski resort owed Hardin] the duty of every person to exercise ordinary care in conduct toward others . . . in light of all surrounding circumstances."	"Specifically, the plaintiff claims that the defendant [Snowshoe], was negligent in the following ways: 1. The defendant did not follow its own snowmaking policies. 2. The defendant was making wet snow. 3. The snowmaking equipment was pointed uphill, rather than in the direction the skiers, including the plaintiff, were skiing. 4. The snowmaking area was too narrow to avoid; that is, it was not wide enough to allow good skier flow."

Figure 30–1: THE *HARDIN* INSTRUCTIONS

A Hardin thus wanted the court to explain his several theories of *how* the resort was negligent. He essentially argued that by stating the law too generally, the court confused the jury about how specific acts could support a finding of negligence.

This objection, however, runs afoul of the rule that "a set of legally accurate instructions that does not effectively direct a verdict for one side or the other is generally adequate." Jury instructions must also be considered as a whole, and an error in one instruction may be counterbalanced by the rest. Here, the majority found that the instructions for the defendant "were likewise general in tone and content." Thus, both sides suffered equally from the lack of specificity, and the instructions as a whole did not unfairly tilt to either side. Judge Butzner dissented because, he argued, a party has the right to have the jury instructed "with due regard to the specific facts of the case at hand"—that is, the jury should be instructed on issues "supported by the law *and* the evidence" (emphasis added).

Q **4. Reversing for flawed jury instructions?** Of course, even if Judge Butzner was right, and the jury instructions did not relate with sufficient specificity to the evidence, it does not follow that the judgment on the verdict should be reversed. What else must Hardin show?

A Prejudice. The requirement is codified in Rule 61, "Harmless Error," which provides that mere error will not justify setting aside a verdict, "unless justice requires otherwise." The court must disregard errors that do not affect "any party's substantial rights," or what the *Hardin* majority more prosaically called "nit-picking errors." More specific instructions might have improved Hardin's chances (or not, since they might also have improved the ski resort's chances on its affirmative defense of assumption of the risk), but "litigants are not entitled to the best possible instruction ...." *Moore* § 51.20[1][a]. Here, the instructions as a whole remained both accurate and balanced, and it couldn't be said that the jury did not understand the basic issues. Under such circumstances, "[an] appellate court should respect that result."

Q **5. Objections and waiver.** Rule 51 governs objections to jury instructions. When did Hardin have to object in order to preserve his objections for appeal?

A Essentially, at his first opportunity, which would ordinarily be when the judge informed the parties of the proposed instructions before giving them to the jury. Fed. R. Civ. P. 51(c)(2)(A). If the court had not refused in advance to give the instruction, then his first opportunity would be when the court actually instructed the jury and omitted his requested instruction. Fed. R. Civ. P. 51(d)(1)(B). The obvious lesson is to request the instruction *and* object at the time it is omitted from the instructions in order to preserve the objection for appeal.

Rule 51 provides an escape hatch, however, for *plain error*. The Rule permits a court to consider an error in instructions, even if a party did not make a timely objection, if the error "affects substantial rights." Fed. R. Civ. P. 51(d)(2). But the standard has been stringently interpreted: The error must be obvious and clear under current law, affect substantial rights, and threaten a miscarriage of justice. One circuit cites cases in which "'the failure to raise the claim below deprived the reviewing court of helpful factfinding; ... the issue is one of constitutional magnitude; ... the omitted argument is highly persuasive; ... the opponent would suffer special prejudice; ... and perhaps most importantly, ... the issue is of great importance to the public.' " *Romano v. U-Haul Int'l*, 233 F.3d 655, 664 (1st Cir. 2000) (internal citations omitted) (alterations in original). Had Hardin failed to make a timely objection, therefore, the plain error doctrine would not have saved him on appeal unless the court found that the failure to give his instructions fit one of these restrictive categories of "plain error."

6. Judicial comments on the evidence. One virtue of general jury instructions is that they avoid or minimize judicial comment on the evidence, as the court in *Hardin* noted. Federal judges are not prohibited from commenting on the evidence, but their influence on juries is such that they should be cautious about saying too much, lest they unduly influence the jury and thus usurp its function. There is unfortunately no bright line rule to test judicial comments on the evidence, but the Supreme Court has stressed that the judge "may not either distort it or add to it." *Quercia v. United States*, 289 U.S. 466, 469–70 (1933). Another popular standard is "whether the judge has made 'it clear to the jury that all matters of fact are submitted to their determination.'" *United States v. Kelm*, 827 F.2d 1319, 1323 (9th Cir. 1987) (quoting *Quercia*, 289 U.S. at 469). The theory is that the judge mitigates the influence of her comments by reassuring the jurors that the question is, after all, theirs alone to decide.

These standards give us very little to go on, but try to apply them—with a dollop of common sense—to the following comments. Which is improper?

A. "Now you heard Mr. Banbridge say that the intersection was not busy at the time of the accident. Well, I drive by there every day at about that time, and I can tell you it sure seems busy to me."
B. "And now I'm going to tell you what I think of the defendant's testimony. You may have noticed, Mr. Foreman and gentlemen, that he wiped his hands during his testimony. It is a rather curious thing, but that is almost always an indication of lying. Why it should be so we don't know, but that is the fact. I think that every single word that man said, except when he agreed with the Government's testimony, was a lie."
C. In a tort suit arising from injuries from an exploding tire, the judge asks a few questions of witnesses, and then tells the jury, "Well, I have put air in a lot of tires, but I never had one blow up on me."
D. "In deciding the credibility of the defendant, you may consider that he testified differently on these events in the prior hearing from which you were read excerpts, and he gave a different account of these events to Mr. Jameson, according to that witness. You may also consider that although the defendant testified under oath in this trial, he was also under oath in the prior hearing and not under oath when he spoke with Mr. Jameson."

A is clearly improper, because the judge is not just commenting on the evidence, but adding to it. The trouble with his "testimony" is not so much that it is not under oath, as that it is not subject to cross-examination. And, of course, coming from the judge, it carries extra weight. A "the-decision-is-yours" instruction does nothing to undo the potential damage, because the jury may still think that the judge's "testimony" is part of the record on which they decide.

B is also improper, though not exactly for the same reason. This judge is not so much supplementing the record as she is sharing her own general experience with the jury. We use juries for *their* experience. In fact, their common life experience is thought to be most effective in deciding credibility—a decision each juror makes every day. It might well be that a "the-decision-is-yours" instruction can counterbalance a judge's comments from her experience, but this particular experiential conclusion is also wrong. Witnesses wipe their hands because they sweat, and they may sweat as much from anxiety as from any guilty knowledge. In *Quercia*, the Supreme Court reversed because of this comment, though it may have made a difference that the comment was made in a criminal case.

C doesn't supplement the record; the judge is not saying that he saw this tire or that tires can't blow up. He is also sharing his experience, but less definitively than the judge in *Quercia*. Moreover, the comment is not wrong, like the one in *Quercia*; tires usually don't explode on inflation. The appellate court let this one go by, stating:

> Each case must turn on its own facts. The single comment in this case is not sufficient for reversal. The comment was a minor incident in a lengthy trial and is not the type of egregious conduct that alone would require reversal....
>
> ... With [this] ... single exception ..., the district judge did not communicate his opinions to the jury. Further, the judge carefully instructed the jury at the conclusion of the trial that his questioning was to "bring out facts not then fully covered in the testimony, that his questioning did not indicate that he held an opinion on the matters to which [his] questions may [be] related," and that the jury could "disregard all comments of the court in arriving at [its] findings as to the facts."

Hale v. Firestone Tire & Rubber Co., 756 F.2d 1322, 1330–31 (8th Cir. 1985).

Finally, **D** seems proper. The court is not adding to the record, but reminding the jury of it. In a long, complicated trial, it may be appropriate for the judge to help the jury by pointing to the relevant parts of the record or even by impartially summarizing the evidence, if, in doing so, she does not push them toward a particular finding. That said, perhaps the better part of wisdom is to withhold even this level of comment. Some state courts therefore take a much narrower view of the judge's authority to comment on the evidence, effectively limiting judges to instructions on the law. *See* Robert O. Lukowsky, *The Constitutional Right of Litigants to Have the State Trial Judge Comment Upon the Evidence*, 55 Ky. L.J. 121, 125 (1967).

IV. Jury Verdicts

It is not enough to instruct the jury in what they need to decide; a judge must also tell them how to report their findings. Even in the Pedestrian v. Driver example, this can be more complicated than returning a guilty or not-guilty verdict in a criminal case, because if the jury finds the driver liable, it must also report how much the driver must pay in damages. Furthermore, given the ease of claim and party joinder in modern civil litigation, the jury must often make and report decisions for each claim with respect to each party. "Three things, taken two at a time ..."—well, we don't remember that formula from high school either, but you get the drift—in a multi-claim lawsuit, even a general verdict may look like a spreadsheet.

The verdict form provides a template for the jury's report and thus functions as an instruction that the jury takes with it to the jury room. The usual verdict in civil cases is a *general verdict*. Rule 49 alludes to the general verdict, but does not define it. As the next case explains, general verdicts "simply ask the jury to answer the question 'who won' ["We find for the plaintiff"], and if the winning party is entitled to a monetary award, to answer the question 'how much.' " *Turyna v. Martam Constr. Co., Inc.*, 83 F.3d 178, 181 (7th Cir. 1996). Rule 49 also provides two complicated alternatives to the general verdict: the special verdict, consisting of fact questions for the jury, and the general verdict with written questions, which is a hybrid of the general and special verdicts.

READING *TURYNA v. MARTAM CONSTRUCTION CO.* The issue in the following case is what kind of verdict the trial court used. The three-page verdict form used in the case is reproduced in the opinion.

- What kind of verdict was this? Why isn't it a special verdict or a general verdict with interrogatories?
- How was the verdict inconsistent?
- What phrasing, if any, of the verdict form might have prevented the inconsistency?
- Had the lawyers been present when the jury returned the verdict, what could they have done to save the trial by sending the jury back again?

TURYNA v. MARTAM CONSTRUCTION CO.

83 F.3d 178 (7th Cir. 1996)

Diane P. Wood, Circuit Judge.

Murphy's Law was in full operation when the district court submitted this case to the jury, when the jury considered it, when the court received the verdict, and when judgment was rendered. Because the verdict as returned appears to be internally inconsistent, and the form itself is hopelessly confused, we reluctantly reverse and remand for a new trial.

I

The underlying lawsuit was relatively straightforward. Brad Turyna went to work for Martam Construction (Martam) as a truck driver in January 1986. He worked there until September 26, 1989, when he was fired. Almost two years later, Turyna filed this lawsuit against Martam, Tamas Kutrovacz (owner and president of Martam), and Claude Koenig (a vice-president of Martam), claiming (1) that Martam owed him overtime pay from September 19, 1988, through September 26, 1989, under the Fair Labor Standards Act (FLSA), 29 U.S.C. § 201, and (2) that his firing violated the public policy of Illinois and FLSA, 29 U.S.C. § 215(a)(3), because it was retaliatory in certain respects. The case went to trial in May 1994 before a jury. At the close of Turyna's case, the court entered a judgment as a matter of law on a supplemental claim of breach of an oral contract, but the overtime and retaliatory discharge claims were allowed to proceed.

The case was submitted to the jury on a form that wasn't quite a general verdict form, but it wasn't special verdicts under Federal Rule of Civil Procedure 49(a) or a general verdict with interrogatories under Rule 49(b) either. **[Eds.—The restyled Rule 49(b) uses the term "questions" instead of "interrogatories," but the terms are often still used interchangeably to refer to the specific findings that a jury may be asked to make either by a Rule 49(a) special verdict or by a Rule 49(b) general verdict with answers to written questions.]** For ease in understanding what follows, we have attached the three-page form to this opinion as Appendix A. It asks the jury to indicate for each Count whether it ruled for plaintiff or against plaintiff, with respect to each defendant. The word "Damages" then appears in the middle of the second page, with blanks for the jury to complete with amounts for compensatory damages and punitive damages. With respect to damages, the court instructed the jury as follows:

> Now, if you find in favor of defendants on both Counts I and II, then you, of course, need not consider the issue of damages. If, however, you find in plaintiff's favor on Count I and/or on either or both parts of Count II, then you will need to consider the issue of damages . . . .

[Eds.—The lawyers chose not to wait for the jury to return their verdict and left the courtroom.] Thus, no one with any incentive to take action was present when the next events occurred, with the exception of the district judge. . . .

When the jury returned with its verdict, the court confronted a situation that was confusing at best.

[Eds.—We have moved the actual verdicts below to show the situation that confronted the judge. To see how it was confusing, compare the jury's verdict on Count II (the second page of the jury verdict) with its verdict on damages for that Count (page 3 of the verdict).]

attachment ORIGINAL

[redacted]

IN THE UNITED STATES DISTRICT COURT
FOR THE NORTHERN DISTRICT OF ILLINOIS
EASTERN DIVISION

MAY 25 1994

H. STUART CUNNINGHAM, Clerk
UNITED STATES DISTRICT COURT

BRAD J. TURYNA,	:	CIVIL ACTION
Plaintiff,	:	
v.	:	
MARTAM CONSTRUCTION, INC., TAMAS KUTROVACZ and CLAUDE KOENIG,	:	
	:	
Defendants.	:	NO. 91 C 5965

VERDICT

We, the jury, unanimously find with respect to the claims of Plaintiff, Brad Turyna, as follows:

(Place an "X" on the appropriate line for each Defendant and each count.)

COUNT I - FAIR LABOR STANDARDS ACT

As to:	For Plaintiff	Against Plaintiff
Defendant, Martam Construction, Inc.	X	
Defendant, Tamas Kutrovacz	X	
Defendant, Claude Koenig	X	

COUNT II - RETALIATION UNDER FAIR LABOR STANDARDS ACT

As to:	For Plaintiff	Against Plaintiff
Defendant, Martam Construction, Inc.	________	X
Defendant, Tamas Kutrovacz	________	X
Defendant, Claude Koenig	________	X

COUNT [illegible] - RETALIATION UNDER PUBLIC POLICY OF ILLINOIS

As to:	For Plaintiff	Against Plaintiff
Defendant, Martam Construction, Inc.	________	X
Defendant, Tamas Kutrovacz	________	X
Defendant, Claude Koenig	________	X

DAMAGES

(a) Plaintiff, Brad Turyna, is awarded $ 3,105.32 in compensatory damages, itemized as follows:

Unpaid overtime wages	3,105.32
Lost Wages, accruing from the date of discharge to the date of trial	0

(b) Do you award Plaintiff, Brad Turyna, punitive damages under Count II, and if so, in what amount? (As to each defendant, either (1) place an "X" on the YES line and fill in the amount or (2) place an "X" on the NO line.)

2

COUNT II - RETALIATORY DISCHARGE UNDER FLSA:

Defendant, Martam Construction, Inc. YES ✓ $ [illegible]

NO ______

Defendant, Tamas Kutrovacz YES ______ $ 0

NO ✓

Defendant, Claude Koenig YES ______ $ 0

NO ✓

SO SAY WE ALL.

May 23, 1994
Date

[illegible]
Foreperson

[illegible]

[illegible]

[illegible]

[illegible]

[illegible]

[illegible]

[EDS.—The handwritten number next to the "YES" check mark against Martam Construction, Inc., is $35,618.01.]

Faced with this document, the district court entered judgment on the verdict, awarding Turyna $3,109.22 in compensatory damages, liquidated damages of $3,109.22 as required by the FLSA, and punitive damages against Martam in the amount of $35,618.01. The court then discharged the jury. A few days later, Martam filed a timely post-trial motion under Rule 59(e), seeking to amend the judgment on Count II to set aside the award of punitive damages. The court denied that motion, and this appeal followed.

II

Before this Court, Martam argues strenuously that there can be no award of compensatory or punitive damages to a plaintiff where the jury has found the issue of liability in favor of the defendant—an unexceptional enough proposition, if we could be sure that was what happened. In the alternative, Martam argues that in the absence of compensatory damages for the retaliation claim, it is error to award punitive damages, if perchance the jury meant to indicate that the discharge was wrongful under federal law but did not inflict any actual damages. Turyna retorts that the judgment was correctly entered because the verdict was, in substance, a general verdict accompanied by interrogatories under Rule 49(b) and thus the court was entitled to enter judgment in accordance with the specific answers notwithstanding the inconsistent general verdict. Turyna also argues that his judgment should stand because Martam waived its objections to inconsistencies in the verdict by its waiver of presence when the verdict was returned. Finally, Turyna disputes Martam's claim that punitive damages must rest on an award of compensatory damages.

The first, and as it turns out the last, question for us is whether this verdict is salvageable. There are only three logical possibilities: it is a general verdict for someone; it is several special verdicts pursuant to Rule 49(a); or it is a general verdict accompanied by answers to interrogatories pursuant to Rule 49(b). As noted before, Martam argues that the verdict is "really" a general verdict for the defendant, accompanied by surplusage on the issue of damages that must be disregarded, while Turyna urges that we should treat it as a Rule 49(b) verdict in which the judge exercised his discretion to give primacy to the answers to the interrogatories. We consider each of the three logical possibilities in turn.

It seems most likely that the court intended to submit a general verdict form to this jury. General verdicts simply ask the jury to answer the question "who won," and if the winning party is entitled to a monetary award, to answer the question "how much." The verdict form reproduced in Appendix A does precisely those two things. Read one way, the jury gave inconsistent answers to those two questions: it said that Martam won (on Count II), but that it had to pay Turyna punitive damages. Read another way, the verdict is even more confused: asked the first time who won on Count II, the jury responded "Martam," but asked the second time it responded "Turyna."

When a jury returns a factually inconsistent general verdict, the verdict cannot stand. When Martam raised its objection to the verdict in the Rule 59(e) motion, thereby calling the court's attention to the problems with the verdict, assuming for the moment that the court considered this to be a general verdict form, the court should have ordered a new trial on Count II. The problem with Martam's suggestion that the court should have simply disregarded the jury's response to the punitive damages question is that we do not know which part of the jury's verdict should control. It would do just as much violence to the jury's factual findings to give primacy to its answer on the liability issue, ignoring its response on damages, as it would to do the reverse. If this is a general verdict, it is fatally inconsistent.

Neither party argues seriously that this verdict complied with the requirements of Rule 49(a), and for good reason—it does not. Rule 49(a) contemplates a "special written finding upon each issue of *fact*." (Emphasis added.) In this case, the jury might have been asked whether Turyna worked overtime for the year in question (and how many hours), or whether he was asked to haul inappropriate materials, or maybe even whether Martam's decision to fire him was retaliatory in nature. The jury here was asked no such things, as the form makes clear. Thus, nothing in Rule 49(a) can save the verdict.

Rule 49(b) blends the devices of the general verdict and the special verdict, by allowing the court to give the jury both the general verdict form and written interrogatories on particular issues of fact. Because this almost invites contradictory and inconsistent answers, the rule also addresses what the court should do when the general verdict and the answers to the interrogatories are not harmonious. If the answers are internally consistent, but one or more is inconsistent with the general verdict, the court has a choice among entering judgment in accordance with the answers (and disregarding the general verdict), returning the case to the jury for further deliberation, or ordering a new trial. When the answers are not internally consistent, and one or more also conflicts with the general verdict, the court has only two choices: return the case to the jury, or order a new trial. When faced with interrogatories that might conflict with a general verdict, the court must take the view of the case that reconciles the interrogatories with the general verdict.

Here, of course, the middle option of returning the case to the jury was, as a practical matter, not available because all parties waived their right to be present when the verdict was returned. This decision was regrettable, because it seems plain that one if not both parties would have called the inconsistencies to the court's attention and tried to obtain further clarification from the jury that heard the case. It is also regrettable that the district judge did not spot the problems with the verdict on his own motion. Once the jury was discharged, the opportunity to correct the error promptly was forever lost. Martam's Rule 59(e) motion was adequate to raise the problem with Count II before the district court for purposes of appellate review, but it was no substitute for being present while the jury could still serve. The consequence has been wasted time for everyone, if we assume that the jury might have reconsidered either its answer on liability or its answer on damages.

Nevertheless, there is an even more fundamental problem with the hypothesis that the district court was using Rule 49(b), which flows directly from our discussion of Rule 49(a). This jury was never asked any particular factual questions about the case, and Rule 49(b) plainly states that the written interrogatories must be "upon one or more issues of fact the decision of which is necessary to a verdict." Although the amount of damages is an issue of fact, this fact is specifically determined by the jury even under a general verdict form. Asking only this question cannot transform a general verdict into one under Rule 49(b). No particular issues of facts about the case were before the jury, and thus there was nothing upon which the court could rely as "interrogatories" that were consistent with one another but not with the general verdict. We cannot infer answers to issues of fact from the verdict form as a whole because of the inconsistencies noted before. Thus, nothing in Rule 49(b) eliminates the need for a new trial here.

III

Even if we have somehow overlooked a way of reading this verdict that might, at a stretch of the imagination, support a verdict for one side or the other of this case, we are convinced that it is sufficiently confused that a new trial on Count II is necessary. We therefore REVERSE and REMAND for further proceedings.

Notes and Questions: Verdicts

Q **1. Why wasn't it a special verdict?** The verdict in *Turyna* was not a *special verdict* because such a verdict contemplates "a special written finding on each issue of fact." Fed. R. Civ. P. 49(a)(1). "With a special verdict, the jury's sole function is to determine the facts; the jury needs no instruction on the law because the court applies the law to the facts as found by the jury." *Mason v. Ford Motor Co.*, 307 F.3d 1271, 1274 (11th Cir. 2002). Of course, the court still must give "instructions and explanations necessary to enable the jury to make its findings on each submitted issue," sometimes explaining terms used in the questions. Fed. R. Civ. P. 49(a)(2). The only issue of fact on which the jury made a finding in *Turyna* was damages. But, as the court explains, this is a finding that a jury makes even on a general verdict when they have found for the claimant. By itself, it does not make the verdict a special verdict.

If the court *had* decided to use a special verdict in *Turyna*, what kinds of factual issues would it have submitted to the jury?

A The questions could include whether the decision to fire the plaintiff was retaliatory; whether he worked overtime and, if so, how many hours; whether a particular defendant participated in the decision to fire the plaintiff; and whether that defendant had retaliatory intent. It's not hard to see where these issues came from: Turyna's claims are for overtime pay and for retaliatory firing. The issues of fact are those disputed facts that are material to claims or defenses in the case.

An excerpt from a special verdict in *Turyna* might look like this, depending on the applicable law and factual allegations:

QUESTIONS	ANSWERS
1. Did Tamas Kutrovacz or Claude Koenig orally agree to pay the plaintiff Brad Turyna overtime for his work as a truck driver for Martam Construction at the time they hired him?	1. Yes.
2. If you answered yes to Question #1, what hourly rate did Tamas Kutrovacz or Claude Koenig agree to pay Brad Turyna for overtime?	2. $12 an hour.
3. Did plaintiff Brad Turyna work overtime as a truck driver for Martam Construction?	3. Yes.
4. If you found that plaintiff Brad Turyna worked overtime as a truck driver for Martam Construction, how many hours did he work overtime?	4. 30 hours.
5. On what date was Brad Turyna fired from Martam Construction?	5. Sept. 26, 1989.
6. Prior to the date you gave as an answer to Question #5, did Tamas Kutrovacz or Claude Koenig know that Brad Turyna had filed a complaint against Martam Construction with the Department of Labor for failing to pay him overtime?	6. No.
7. If your answer to Question #6 is yes, did Tamas Kutrovacz or Claude Koenig cause Brad Turyna to be fired because he had filed a complaint against Martam with the Department of Labor? . . .	7. ______.

Figure 30–2: A SPECIAL VERDICT FOR *TURYNA*

On these answers, a judge would have to enter judgment for the defendants on the retaliation counts, though it might enter judgment for the plaintiff on the contract count (if defendants did not contest non-payment). The applicable law might well require additional or different questions.

2. Why use special verdicts? Courts often use special verdicts for complicated cases because asking the jury to answer specific questions of fact can help the jury navigate the complications. Special verdicts relieve the jury of the burden of applying the law and leave it with the often easier task of answering fact questions about what happened.

Special verdicts have the added virtue that when the jury's answers supply more than one basis for the judgment entered by the court, an error by the court in instructing on or applying the law to some of them is not necessarily fatal to the verdict. In *Nowell By and Through Nowell v. Universal Elec. Co.*, 792 F.2d 1310 (5th Cir. 1986), for example, it was not clear from a general verdict whether the jury had concluded that the plaintiff was not contributorily negligent, or whether, because of an erroneous jury instruction, the jury thought that his contributory negligence did not matter. The court of appeals remarked:

> Had a special interrogatory on contributory negligence been submitted, the error in the charge might have been localized permitting the verdict to stand. . . .
>
> Special interrogatories under Fed. R. Civ. P. 49(a) are helpful to a jury because they reduce an otherwise complex trial to its simplest and most important issues. The genuine issues are distilled and an appellate court is often aided immeasurably when it is called on to review the case. In short, special interrogatories make both a jury and a reviewing court so much the wiser and so much less confused. *See Ware v. Reed,* 709 F.2d 345, 355 (5th Cir. 1983). We encourage the district court to consider the use of special interrogatories with an appropriate general charge in submitting this case to the jury on retrial.

Id. at 1316–17.

If the jury in *Nowell* had been asked by a special interrogatory whether the plaintiff had been negligent and had answered "No," that answer would have "localized," or walled off, the error in the jury instruction by making it immaterial. That is, if the jury in a special verdict found that the plaintiff was not contributorily negligent, it wouldn't matter that the jury instructions had erroneously ignored the plaintiff's possible contributory negligence. The judgment on the verdict could therefore have been upheld.

On the other hand, special verdicts pose their own complications because they require the drafting of questions "susceptible of a categorical or other brief answer" that avoid ambiguity and provide the court with the factual basis on which to apply the law in order to reach a judgment. Fed. R. Civ. P. 49(a)(1)(A). They also run the risk of inconsistent answers, as we discuss below. The drafting challenge is heightened by the proviso that a party waives the right to a jury determination of any issue of fact omitted from the special verdict unless she has requested that it be submitted to the jury. Rule 49(a)(3). When a party fails to demand the submission of an issue to the jury in the special verdict, the judge can decide the issue herself, or if she does not, the court is "considered to have made a finding consistent with its judgment on the special verdict." Rule 49(a)(3). In other words, if you opt for a special verdict, you must not only draft the proposed questions with unusual care, but make sure you include all of them.

Q **3. Why wasn't the *Turyna* verdict a general verdict with answers to written questions (formerly, interrogatories)?** Rule 49(b) combines the questions of a special verdict with the general verdict. Thus, at the end of the special verdict questions we identified above in question 1, the verdict form might include this general verdict:

> On Count I, the Fair Labor Standard Act claim, we the jury unanimously find for [check one]:
>
> ☐ the plaintiff Brad Turyna
> ☐ the defendants, Martam Construction, Inc., Tamas Kutrovacz or Claude Koenig.
>
> [If you have found for the plaintiff on Count I, complete the next line.] We award $__________ for the plaintiff on Count I.

The written questions help guide the jury in reaching the general verdict and therefore presumably make the general verdict more reliable.

So why didn't the court of appeals treat the *Turyna* verdict as this kind of hybrid?

A The verdict included a general verdict, but it failed as a Rule 49(b) hybrid verdict for the same reason it failed as a Rule 49(a) special verdict: It contained no factual questions except for the damages question.

Q **4. Inconsistent verdicts in *Turyna*.** All three kinds of verdicts can result in inconsistent jury findings. What was the inconsistency in *Turyna* and how could it have been resolved?

A The jury found for defendants on Count II (retaliation under the FLSA), but then, under the damages part of the verdict, found for the plaintiff against defendant Martam Construction on Count II and awarded $35,618.01. There was no way to harmonize these findings: The jury must either find for the plaintiff on Count II or for the defendant; it obviously can't find for both. Moreover, the court couldn't just disregard one finding because it had no way of knowing which one the jury ultimately intended. The court therefore concluded that "[i]t would do just as much violence to the jury's factual findings to give primacy to its answer on the liability issue, ignoring its response on damages, as it would to do the reverse."

Rule 49 does not address the solutions to inconsistent general verdicts, but the court's discussion in *Turyna* suggests some. The court says that had the parties been present when the verdict was returned, one of them might have called the court's attention to the problem and the court could have tried "to obtain further clarification from the jury. . . ." We assume that this might entail polling the jury—asking each member whether he or she joined in the verdict—which could, perhaps, have disclosed an error in recording. Or perhaps it could involve sending the jury back to revisit the form with a clarifying instruction. But when the jury was discharged, these opportunities were lost. The only solution that was left was a do-over: a new trial before a new jury.

Q **5. Other inconsistent verdicts.** The same options described above could be used to deal with inconsistent answers in a special verdict. Inconsistencies in the Rule 49(b) general verdict with answers to written questions are more complicated because of the several ways such verdicts can be inconsistent. Why did Turyna argue that the verdict was a Rule 49(b) verdict?

A If the jury's answers in a Rule 49(b) verdict are consistent with each other, but inconsistent with the general verdict, the court may enter a judgment consistent with the answers, notwithstanding the general verdict. Fed. R. Civ. P. 49(b)(3). But because the *Turyna* verdict did not put factual interrogatories to the jury, "there was nothing upon which the court could rely as 'interrogatories' that were consistent with one another but not with the general verdict." 83 F.3d at 182.

6. The duty to harmonize the answers. Before a court sets aside a jury verdict for inconsistency, "it is the duty of the court[] to harmonize the answers, if it is possible under a fair reading of them." *Gallick v. Baltimore & Ohio R.R. Co.*, 372 U.S. 108, 119 (1963). In *Gallick*, the plaintiff had lost a leg to complications arising from an insect bite he suffered while working next to a stagnant pool on defendant's property. In a special verdict, the jury found that the defendant was negligent in permitting the accumulation of stagnant water on its premises, that the defendant knew that the stagnant water would attract insects, and that the plaintiff's injuries were proximately caused by the defendant's acts or omissions. But it also found that there was no reason for the defendant to foresee that maintaining the stagnant water "would or might probably result in a mishap or injury," and that it was not foreseeable that the water would lead to the insect bite and the plaintiff's present condition. *Id.* at 111 (quoting special verdict).

No matter. The Supreme Court found that these answers "might mean simply that while an insect bite was foreseeable, there was no reason to anticipate a 'mishap' or 'injury' from such bite." *Id.* at 120. But a defendant does not have "to foresee the particular consequences of his negligent acts: assuming the existence of a threshold tort against the person, then whatever damages flow from it are recoverable." *Id.* The dissenters rejected this "Procrustean exercise" in harmonization, charging that "[b]y undertaking to reconcile irretrievably conflicting findings of the jury, the Court, we think, ... has invaded the province of the jury under this federal statute." *Id.* at 125, 127. The dissenters would have ordered a new trial.

V. Controlling the Jury: Summary of Basic Principles

- In a jury trial, a party must file proposed jury instructions at the close of the evidence or such other time as the court directs.
- Before the court instructs the jury, it must inform the parties of its proposed jury instructions, and a party must make any objection on the record to an instruction or the failure to give an instruction.
- A trial court has broad discretion in deciding the form and content of jury instructions and verdict forms and is not required to accept instructions offered by the parties.
- A reviewing court will not set aside a jury verdict and order a new trial unless the jury instructions, viewed as a whole, inaccurately state the law or confuse or mislead the jury, *and* the error was prejudicial to the verdict loser.
- A general verdict form asks the jury to answer, for each claim, "Who won?," and if it finds for the plaintiff in an action for damages, "how much?"
- A special verdict requires the jury to make special written findings on each issue of fact instead of returning a general verdict. Special verdicts are useful to guide the jury's deliberations in complicated cases and for making

the jury's work clear, sometimes enabling a court to salvage a verdict by "localizing" an error in the jury instruction or in the verdict itself.

- A general verdict with answers to written questions (sometimes still called "interrogatories") is a hybrid verdict, combining the questions of the special verdict with a general verdict. It is not used as often as general or special verdicts because it poses a greater risk of inconsistencies among the answers, or between them and the general verdict.
- Courts have a duty to harmonize inconsistent verdicts, if possible. When it is not possible, the court's options depend on the kind of verdict and the nature of the inconsistency.

31

New Trial and Relief from Judgment

I. Introduction

Alice Chapman sued Bob Haster for negligence when Haster's car brushed her while she was crossing the street in a crosswalk. The evidence at trial was that Chapman staggered back from the brush-by, but she showed no visible injury at the time and did not subsequently go to the doctor. She lost no time from work. The only testimony about her injuries was her own, that "my leg throbbed." After trial, the jury returns a verdict of $1.6 million in compensatory damages.

In Chapter 29, we saw that if Chapman had produced insufficient evidence of liability or injury for a reasonable jury to return a verdict in her favor, the court can grant a motion for judgment as a matter of law (JMOL) for Haster. This would be true even after a verdict against Haster, as long as Haster had moved for JMOL before the case was submitted to the jury, and he renews his motion after the verdict. When a party with the burden of production is unable to produce enough evidence to support a jury verdict, she loses and her opponent wins. JMOL is a zero-sum game.

But Chapman *did* testify that she was brushed by Haster's car and that, as a result, her leg throbbed. There is evidence from which a jury could find both liability and injury. Yet suppose the trial judge could still reasonably conclude that a verdict of $1.6 million was wrong—excessive in light of Chapman's testimony. Or suppose that the trial judge decides in retrospect that she improperly instructed the jury or even that some jurors acted improperly. Such errors in the process of trial may cast doubt on the verdict.

On a proper challenge to the verdict in such cases, the solution is *not JMOL*. The problem is not that the evidence was insufficient to reach the jury. Chapman met her burden of production; she passed the X point on Figure 29–3 in Chapter 29. *Chapman provided legally sufficient evidence, so the trial judge cannot declare that Haster won.* In the X-Y area of the figure, the trial judge has no power to declare a winner; only the jury can do that.

In such cases, instead, the court may give the case to a new jury by granting a new trial. Granting a new trial does not give Haster a win (yet). And it doesn't mean that Chapman gets a loss (yet) either. They both simply get a do-over. While this takes away Chapman's verdict, it does not take away a jury trial; she just has to try her case to a new jury.

Unfortunately, Federal Rule of Civil Procedure 59 is coyly unhelpful in telling us when a new trial may be granted. It says that a court may grant a new trial "for any reason for which a new trial has heretofore been granted" in a jury case.* It thus simply incorporates the reasoning of all prior federal cases in which new trial was granted. The cases, at first glance, are hardly more helpful. They say that the trial judge has the discretion to grant a new trial in a jury case if she finds that the verdict is "clearly erroneous," would result in a "manifest injustice," or leaves her with "a definite and firm conviction of error." Wrested from their specific contexts, they don't tell us a lot. But at second glance, the new trial cases fall into three categories that help illuminate the standards.

In one category, the judge finds that the verdict is clearly wrong because it is not supported by "the weight of the evidence." This can mean that the jury made an erroneous finding of liability or gave an erroneous answer to a material question, or that its dollar verdict was too large or too small, according to the judge's view of the evidence. As the "weight of the evidence" phrase suggests, in these cases, the judge actually weighs the evidence, something she is not allowed to do on a motion for JMOL. We will call the errors in these cases "weight-of-the-evidence errors" and discuss them in section II.

In the second category of cases, the judge finds that an error occurred in the conduct of trial or the jury's deliberations. In these cases, the verdict may be supported by the weight of the evidence, and the judge may even think that it is correct, but she also believes the error could have affected the verdict. To assure the parties a fair trial, the court may then order a new trial. We will call these "process errors" for lack of a better term and discuss them in section III.

Finally, in a third category of cases, a losing party finds new evidence after the trial that would have materially affected the outcome. New trials for newly discovered evidence, however, are exceedingly rare, because the courts have insisted that the new matter be evidence that could not have been discovered by due diligence in time for trial, and because Rule 59(b) requires the motion for a new trial

---

* It also says that a new trial may be granted in a nonjury trial for "any reason for which a rehearing has heretofore been granted in a suit in equity in federal court." Within the twenty-eight-day period after entry of a judgment that the Rule allows for filing a motion for a new trial (Rule 59(b)) or to alter or amend judgment (Rule 59(e)), a judge in a nonjury trial can correct her own error, or simply re-open the record to take more evidence to cure the error. *See* Fed. R. Civ. P. 59(a)(2). Consequently, granting a new trial is less significant as a post-trial device in nonjury cases than in jury cases, and we focus on the latter in the rest of this chapter.

to be filed no later than twenty-eight days after entry of judgment, creating a very small window for such motions.

Suppose, however, that six months after a judgment against him based on the jury's verdict, Chapman discovers new evidence that might have changed the outcome, or learns that Haster secretly lobbied one of the jurors at home to reach that verdict. It's then too late for a motion for new trial. Is there any other way Chapman can now obtain relief from the judgment? Rule 60 authorizes her to ask the trial judge for relief from a judgment for a discrete number of listed reasons, including "newly discovered evidence that, with reasonable diligence, could not have been discovered in time to move for a new trial under Rule 59(b)" and "fraud." The Rule 60 option is discussed in section IV.

II. New Trials for Weight-of-the-Evidence Errors

In our hypothetical case, the trial judge thought that the $1.6 million verdict was excessive in light of Chapman's evidence—that her leg throbbed. In such circumstances, a court may grant a new trial on the ground that "the verdict is against the weight of the evidence." The following decision by a trial judge presents a weight-of-the-evidence issue and suggests a special solution.

READING *TRIVEDI v. COOPER*. Trivedi sued his employer and his supervisor for employment discrimination based on separate claims of a hostile workplace, failure to promote, and retaliation. The jury returned a $700,000 verdict for Trivedi, and defendant moved for JMOL on two claims or for new trial, in the alternative.

- Why did the trial court deny the motion for JMOL on two claims?
- Why, given Trivedi's bizarre behavior and unfounded allegations of obstructionism, did the court not grant new trial on the hostile environment claim?
- How did the court decide that the size of the verdict was against the weight of the evidence?
- What option did the court afford the plaintiff with respect to the verdict?
- If the plaintiff refuses the court's offer, why doesn't the court order a new trial only on damages?

TRIVEDI v. COOPER

1996 U.S. Dist. LEXIS 18715 (S.D.N.Y. 1996)

Denise Cote, District Judge:

In response to a jury verdict awarding $700,000 in compensatory damages, plus an additional award of back pay, for an employment discrimination case brought under 42 U.S.C. §§ 1981, 1983, defendant Thomas Cooper moves for judgment as a matter of law pursuant to Fed. R. Civ. P. 50(b). In the alternative, defendant moves for a new trial pursuant to Fed. R. Civ. P. 59(a), or for a remittitur pursuant to Fed. R. Civ. P. 59(e). Plaintiff, Vipin Trivedi, asserts that defendant's motions for judgment as a matter of law and for a new trial were not timely filed, contests the substance of these motions, and requests an award of back pay. . . .

BACKGROUND

Mr. Trivedi, who is of East Asian Indian national origin, began work as a research scientist at the New York State Office of Mental Health in 1982. On March 28, 1995, Mr. Trivedi filed a claim in federal court under 42 U.S.C. §§ 1981, 1983 and N.Y. Exec. Law § 296 (McKinney 1996), alleging that because of his race or national origin, his supervisor Mr. Cooper harassed Mr. Trivedi, failed to promote him, and retaliated against him for seeking legal assistance in connection with the discrimination. . . . This Court conducted a jury trial from October 7–16, 1996.

At the trial, Mr. Trivedi asserted that Mr. Cooper assigned him menial tasks in the lab, prevented him from collaborating with other researchers, did not give him work that would lead to publication, prevented him from attending professional seminars and conferences, barred him from using the computer, and prevented him from using the library. The evidence showed that the menial tasks (e.g., packing samples for shipment) took about two hours a week and that the professional staff in the office were the only people normally available to perform the work. While others as well as Mr. Trivedi performed the work he described as menial, Mr. Trivedi was the only research scientist doing it on a regular basis during substantial periods of time. Taken in the light most favorable to the plaintiff, the evidence also established that the kind of research work Mr. Trivedi performed was important, but not highly creative and was unlikely to lead to publication or career advancement. Trivedi did not travel as much as some co-workers to seminars or conferences, however, such travel was funded by grants the researchers obtained for themselves. Finally, Mr. Trivedi's contentions regarding the computers and library were unsupported by any of the other evidence. The computers and library were available for anyone to use and Mr. Trivedi did not need permission to use them. The most potent evidence of a hostile work environment, however, was Mr. Cooper's use of racial slurs from 1986 onward in speaking to the plaintiff. Mr. Cooper denied making such statements.

Mr. Trivedi also maintained that Mr. Cooper refused on four occasions in the spring of 1994 to sponsor him for promotion—a sponsorship that Mr. Trivedi stated was essential to receiving the promotion. Mr. Trivedi testified that in two of these conversations Mr. Cooper ridiculed his request by referring to him as a "brown nigger."

Mr. Cooper testified that Mr. Trivedi did not ask Mr. Cooper in 1994 for his support for a promotion and that, in any event, there were two avenues to promotion: sponsorship by a supervisor and self-nomination, where an individual directly approaches the director of the facility to seek a promotion. It was fair to conclude, however, that without a supervisor's support, self-nomination was futile.

Finally, Mr. Trivedi contended that Mr. Cooper retaliated against him for seeking legal assistance to redress his discrimination claims after Mr. Cooper learned of this action in January 1993. Mr. Trivedi claimed that Mr. Cooper retaliated by giving Mr. Trivedi a poor evaluation in mid-1993.

Mr. Cooper denied this allegation, stating that Mr. Trivedi's work performance declined prior to 1993. In his 1991–92 evaluation of Mr. Trivedi, signed in August 1992, Mr. Cooper rated him as only "effective," not "highly effective" as Mr. Trivedi had earned in previous evaluations. Mr. Trivedi's deteriorating performance in 1992 was dramatically demonstrated by his bizarre behavior at two counselling sessions in 1992, as described below.

In addition to denying all of Mr. Trivedi's allegations and presenting evidence to show that Mr. Trivedi's work performance was declining, Mr. Cooper also introduced evidence to demonstrate that Mr. Trivedi suffered from mental illness, specifically, a paranoid delusion that he was being persecuted by Mr. Cooper. Most telling in this regard, he introduced evidence of Mr. Trivedi's behavior during two counselling sessions conducted in July and December 1992 to discuss Mr. Trivedi's deteriorating performance. At the first meeting, Mr. Trivedi taped his mouth shut with gauze he wrapped around his head and refused to speak. At the second meeting Mr. Trivedi wadded his ears with cotton, wore a wool hat, pretended he could not hear, and displayed a sign with directions in case of fire.

Mr. Trivedi explained these actions by saying that he did not want to say anything in the meetings because he no longer trusted Mr. Cooper, and he felt that anything he did say would be misrepresented in later accounts of those meetings. He felt that if he engaged in the behavior described, the other participants to the meetings would have to make a note of the behavior and therefore no one could allege that Mr. Trivedi had made a statement. . . .

[Eds.—Defendant Cooper called two psychiatric experts. They testified that Trivedi was mentally ill, suffering from "magical thinking" making him unable to distinguish fact from fantasy, and that he demonstrated manifestations of paranoid schizophrenia. Trivedi introduced no psychiatric evidence to dispute the psychiatrists' testimony.]

At the close of plaintiff's case, defendant moved for a directed verdict on two of the three claims, retaliation and failure to promote. In this motion, he moves for judgment as a matter of law as to all three claims.

On October 15, 1996, the jury rendered a verdict in favor of Mr. Trivedi. The jury found that Mr. Cooper created a racially hostile work environment, failed to promote the plaintiff, and retaliated against the plaintiff. The jury awarded Mr. Trivedi $700,000 in compensatory damages for pain and suffering for the hostile work environment claim, determined that Mr. Trivedi was entitled to back pay for the failure to promote claim, and awarded $1 in nominal damages for the retaliation claim. On October 16, 1996, the jury concluded that Mr. Trivedi was not entitled to punitive damages for Mr. Cooper's actions.

DISCUSSION

. . .

B. Judgment as a Matter of Law

Defendant moves for judgment as a matter of law as to all three claims. Defendant has waived his right to make such a motion for the hostile work environment claim as he did not preserve this right during trial by moving for a directed verdict at the end of plaintiff's case. Indeed, "the rule is well established that a motion for directed verdict at the close of all the evidence is a prerequisite" for judgment as a matter of law. *Cruz v. Local Union No. 3 of the Int'l Bhd. of Elec. Workers,* 34 F.3d 1148, 1155 (2d Cir. 1994) (quoting *Hilord Chemical Corp. v. Ricoh Electronics, Inc.,* 875 F.2d 32, 37 (2d Cir. 1989) (internal quotations omitted)). **[Eds.—A motion for a directed verdict (now called a motion for judgment as a matter of law) at the close of all the evidence is no longer a prerequisite for renewing the JMOL. It is sufficient if the prior JMOL was made "any time before the case is submitted to the jury" and then renewed no later than twenty-eight days after the entry of judgment. Fed. R. Civ. P. 50(a)(2) & (b).]**

With respect to the retaliation and failure to promote claims, defendant has preserved his right to renew the motion, since a party who moved for and was denied a judgment as a matter of law may renew such a motion after the judgment is entered. Fed. R. Civ. P. 50(b). . . .

To determine liability in this case, the jury had to make credibility findings, in particular between the plaintiff and defendant. The jury's verdict indicates that it concluded that the plaintiff was credible. The jury having found the plaintiff credible, there was sufficient basis for the verdict. As a consequence, I do not find that the verdict was the result of sheer surmise or conjecture, nor do I find that no reasonable person could have arrived at it, and, therefore, will not grant judgment as a matter of law on either the failure to promote or retaliation claim.

C. Motion for a New Trial

[Defendant] . . . also requests a new trial on all three claims, pursuant to Rule 59, Fed. R. Civ. P. The Court may grant a new trial if it is convinced that the jury's verdict was "against the weight of the evidence" or that the jury has reached a "'seriously erroneous result.'" *U.S. East Telecommunications, Inc. v. U.S. West Communications Services, Inc.,* 38 F.3d 1289, 1301 (2d Cir. 1994) (quoting *Mallis v. Bankers Trust Co.,* 717 F.2d 683, 691 (2d Cir. 1983)); *see also Piesco v. Koch,* 12 F.3d 332, 344 (2d Cir. 1993) ("seriously erroneous" standard reaffirmed as the standard of Second Circuit). The Second Circuit has also characterized this standard as one of determining whether "the verdict is a miscarriage of justice." *Smith v. Lightning Bolt. Prod., Inc.,* 861 F.2d 363, 370 (2d Cir. 1988).

Under this standard, the Court "'is free to weigh the evidence [itself] and need not view it in the light most favorable to the verdict winner.'" *Song v. Ives Laboratories, Inc.,* 957 F.2d 1041, 1047 (2d Cir. 1992) (quoting *Bevevino v. Saydjari,* 574 F.2d 676, 684 (2d Cir. 1978)). Even if there is substantial evidence to support the jury verdict, a new trial may be warranted. Nevertheless, the Court must bear in mind that

> where the resolution of the issues depended on assessment of the credibility of the witnesses, it is proper for the court to refrain from setting aside the verdict and granting a new trial.

Piesco, 12 F.3d at 345 (quoting *Metromedia Co. v. Fugazy,* 983 F.2d 350, 363 (2d Cir. 1992), *cert. denied,* 508 U.S. 952 (1993)).

In the instant case, I find that the jury verdicts on the failure to promote and retaliation claims were not against the weight of the evidence and, therefore, will not disturb those determinations. The issue of whether the verdict on the hostile work environment claim is against the weight of the evidence is a much closer question.

The evidence strongly suggested that the plaintiff suffered from mental illness and fabricated or imagined the discrimination. The testimony presented by Drs. Rubin and Russakoff about Mr. Trivedi's mental state was not rebutted. Both doctors testified that Mr. Trivedi suffered from a delusional disorder or paranoia. The plaintiff did not present expert testimony to rebut the assertion that he was paranoid or delusional, relying instead on the arguments that the experts had insufficient contact with the plaintiff to form a reliable conclusion or that the experts' opinion depended on the assumption that the discriminatory acts had not occurred. There was, however, strong evidence in the record that confirmed the experts' opinions. The most dramatic such evidence was the plaintiff's aberrational behavior at the two counselling sessions—taping his mouth and covering his ears. The plaintiff did not deny that he had behaved as described, but rather sought to explain the behavior as a rational response to his belief that he could no longer trust the defendant not to distort his words. In addition to this bizarre behavior, the nature and content of plaintiff's handwritten writings attached to his annual evaluation forms were additional powerful evidence that the experts were correct in their evaluation that the plaintiff was a seriously disturbed person. Finally, the experts' opinions that the plaintiff was suffering from delusion and paranoia are confirmed by the nature of the allegations of the plaintiff made at the trial. For instance, the plaintiff contended that the defendant, who was his supervisor, used demeaning racial epithets for years in speaking to him in public work places, and yet was unable to identify any witness to this conduct. In addition, Mr. Trivedi's allegations of obstructionism by Mr. Cooper—such as blocking access to computers and the library—were entirely unfounded. As noted above, Mr. Trivedi had unrestricted access to the library and to computers.

It is somewhat ironic that the plaintiff's most compelling argument offered to rebut the evidence of his mental condition was the defendant's own actions, specifically the fact that the defendant did not take steps to terminate plaintiff's employment during the years that his behavior deteriorated. The defendant explained that the loss of Mr. Trivedi would have meant the loss of funding for his research slot. In light of the seriously disruptive nature of Mr. Trivedi's mental condition, at least as described by the defendant, it was not surprising that the jury found this explanation inadequate.

Nonetheless, I find that the evidence at trial strongly supports the defendant's claim that the jury's verdict was against the weight of the evidence and a seriously erroneous result. Since the resolution of whether the defendant created a hostile work environment for the plaintiff depended critically on the jury's assessment of the credibility of these two parties, however, it would be inappropriate for the Court to grant a new trial on this claim.

D. Remittitur

Remittitur is the "process by which a court compels a plaintiff to choose between reduction of an excessive verdict and a new trial." *Earl v. Bouchard Transp. Co.,* 917 F.2d 1320, 1328 (2d Cir. 1990) (quoting *Shu-Tao Lin v. McDonnell Douglas Corp.,* 742 F.2d 45, 49 (2d Cir. 1984)) (internal quotation marks omitted). Before I order plaintiff to make this choice, I must first determine whether the verdict is excessive. If I determine the award shocks the judicial conscience, I should remit the jury's award to the maximum amount that would not be excessive. *Earl,* 917 F.2d at 1330. *See also Pescatore v. Pan American World Airways, Inc.,* 97 F.3d 1, 18 (2d Cir. 1996) (citation omitted) (in federal question case, district court has discretion to find award excessive if it "shock[s] the judicial conscience").[2]

While it is properly within the province of the jury to calculate damages, there is "an upper limit, and whether that has been surpassed is not a question of fact with respect to which reasonable [persons] may differ, but a question of law." *Mazyck v. Long Island R. Co.,* 896 F. Supp. 1330, 1336 (E.D.N.Y. 1995) (quoting *Dagnello v. Long Island R.R. Co.,* 289 F.2d 797, 806 (2d Cir. 1961)) (internal quotations omitted). Moreover, although a jury has broad discretion to award damages as it feels appropriate, "it may not abandon analysis for sympathy for a suffering plaintiff and treat an injury as though it were a winning lottery ticket." *Scala v. Moore McCormack Lines, Inc.,* 985 F.2d 680, 684 (2d Cir. 1993) (citation omitted). A jury verdict cannot stand if it is the result of a miscarriage of justice and represents a windfall to the plaintiff without regard for the actual injury.

To determine whether the award is excessive, it is appropriate to examine awards in similar cases. *Lee v. Edwards,* 1996 U.S. App. LEXIS 29378, F.3d ___, 1996 WL 692403, *7 (2d Cir. Oct. 31, 1996) (quoting *Ismail v. Cohen,* 899 F.2d 183, 186 (2d Cir. 1990) (regarding damages, "whether compensatory or punitive")). A court should determine whether the award is "within reasonable range," not just "balance the number of high and low awards and reject the verdict in the instant case if the number of lower awards is greater." *Ismail,* 899 F.2d at 187. Additionally, in reviewing a damage award, it is important to examine the particular facts and circumstances of other cases and compare them to the current case. *Scala,* 985

2. Since this Court had federal question jurisdiction pursuant to 28 U.S.C. § 1331, I will apply federal law in determining the excessiveness of the award. If this was a diversity case, I would apply New York law. . . .

F.2d at 684. Finally, a district court should not limit its comparison of awards to Section 1983 claims. . . .

An examination of . . . cases . . . demonstrates that upholding a $700,000 award for compensatory damages for emotional distress would be unprecedented. . . .

In addition to comparing the present award with other awards, a court should also look to whether there is adequate evidentiary support for the emotional distress award. It is appropriate for a trial court to reduce an award where there is "sparse evidence with respect to the magnitude and duration of emotional injury or mental distress" in order to guard against awards based on speculation. [*McIntosh v. Irving Trust Co.,* 887 F. Supp. 662, 665 (S.D.N.Y. 1995).] An examination of similar cases . . . reveals that Mr. Trivedi did not present either the quality or quantity of evidence to support a $700,000 award. . . .

. . . There was no evidence of psychological counselling, physical manifestations of distress, or other actions consistent with emotional distress. The only evidence presented to prove emotional distress was Mr. Trivedi's testimony that he felt he was "starved of professional growth" and that the discrimination made him feel "like how a woman would feel if her child were lost. On the emotional side I felt insulted, I felt indignant, I felt unhappy, I felt emotionally upset."

These conclusory statements, with nothing more, are patently insufficient to uphold the $700,000 award. Indeed, Mr. Trivedi could not point to any compelling effect of the discrimination, and certainly nothing along the lines of the plaintiff in [*Marfia v. T.C. Ziraat Bankasi, New York Branch,* 903 F. Supp. 463, 467, 471 (S.D.N.Y. 1995)], where the extraordinary circumstances only warranted an award of $100,000 for the emotional distress.

Given the facts presented at trial, I find that $50,000 is a generous award, represents the maximum that does not shock the judicial conscience, and is not out of line with other cases.

E. New Trial on All Issues Versus Damages

When a court grants a new trial as an alternative to remittitur, it must determine whether to grant a new trial on all issues, or a discrete issue, such as damages but not liability. The standard set by the Second Circuit is that

> a partial new trial may not properly be resorted to unless it clearly appears that the issue to be retried is so distinct and separable from the others that a trial of it alone may be had without injustice.

In re Joint E. Dist. & S. Dist. Asbestos Lit., 995 F.2d 343, 346 (2d Cir. 1993) (quoting *Bohack Corp. v. Iowa Beef Processors, Inc.,* 715 F.2d 703, 709 (2d Cir. 1983) (internal quotation marks and citation omitted)). In that case, the Second Circuit determined that since

> the same jury heard the liability and damage phases of the trial, [it makes] partial reversal more problematic than it would be if separate juries had been impaneled.

Id. The determination, therefore, rests on the separability of the issues.

Plaintiff cites *Wheatley v. Beetar,* 637 F.2d 863 (2d Cir. 1980), to support his argument that this Court should not order a new trial on all issues merely because of the excessiveness of the award. In *Wheatley,* the court conducted a bifurcated trial on a case of excessive police force in violation of the plaintiff's constitutional rights. The Second Circuit held that there should be a new trial on damages because the jury's award of nominal damages, after having found through its verdict on liability that the plaintiff had been beaten by the police, indicated that the jury had acted "on the basis of impermissible considerations." *Id.* at 867.

In *Wheatley,* unlike here, the jury's liability decision was supported by substantial evidence, including a witness who heard the beating and the plaintiff's brother who the police prevented from photographing the plaintiff after the beating. *Id.* at 864. The defendants in *Wheatley* did not even challenge the verdict on liability in their appeal. The instant case is different since Mr. Trivedi did not introduce comparable evidence to demonstrate uncontroverted liability.

In this case, it is not possible to hold a new trial on damages without also retrying the issue of liability because the amount of damages is integrally linked to the liability and actions of Mr. Cooper. A jury would need to consider the causation between Mr. Cooper's actions and Mr. Trivedi's injuries, as well as the extent of the harassment and what amount of recovery it warrants. Put another way, liability is not a separate issue in this case. A jury will need to determine the extent of Mr. Cooper's liability in order to determine the extent of Mr. Trivedi's injuries, and award damages for those injuries.

For these reasons, I find that a new trial on damages cannot be separated from a new trial on liability and determine that a new trial must encompass both issues. . . .

. . . For the reasons stated above, it is hereby

ORDERED that plaintiff's attorney may file with the Clerk of the Court on or before December 30, 1996, an acceptance of a remittitur of $650,000, for a final judgment of $50,000 for all damages connected with this case.

IT IS FURTHER ORDERED that in the event plaintiff's attorney does not file an acceptance of the remittitur on or before December 30, 1996, a new trial on liability and damages for the hostile work environment claim will commence on a date to be set by the Court.

SO ORDERED.

Notes and Questions: Post-Trial Motions in *Trivedi*

A. Standards for New Trial and JMOL

Q **1. Why deny JMOL?** Defendant's motion for a directed verdict (now called a motion for JMOL) on the hostile work environment claim came after the jury returned its verdict. It was therefore what the Rule now helpfully calls a "renewed motion for [JMOL]." Why was that motion denied?

A

A party cannot "renew" a motion that it has not previously made; there is nothing to renew. Here defendant failed to move for directed verdict on the hostile work environment claim at "any time" before the action was submitted to the jury. *See* Fed. R. Civ. P. 50(a)(2).

In contrast, he did make such a motion—and thus preserved his right to renew it after the verdict—with respect to the retaliation and failure to promote claims. But, if the jury believed Trivedi, there was evidence from which the jury could find for him on those claims. Of course, the defendant denied it, creating a swearing contest, but it was a contest that a reasonable jury could find that Trivedi won. The court concluded, "I do not find that the verdict [on the retaliation and failure to promote claims] was the result of sheer surmise or conjecture, nor do I find that no reasonable jury could have arrived at it. . . ."

Q

2. Why was the motion for new trial preserved? Defendants did not move for a new trial before the case was submitted to the jury. Why did the court entertain this motion after the verdict?

A

There is no requirement that a party move for a new trial before the case is submitted to the jury. Rule 59 does not speak of a "renewed" motion for new trial either. In fact, the Rule even authorizes new trial on the court's own initiative, within twenty-eight days after entry of judgment, for any reason for which a party could have sought new trial. Fed. R. Civ. P. 59(d). It also would make no sense to seek a new trial on the grounds that the verdict is against the weight of the evidence *before* the jury has returned a verdict. (It is possible, however, to seek new trial at that point for a process error by asking the court to declare what is sometimes called at common law a "mistrial.")

3. Deciding the new trial motion. As the *Trivedi* court states, the verbal formulae for the new trial standard vary, from "against the weight of the evidence," and "seriously erroneous" or "clearly erroneous," to "miscarriage of justice." But one way to understand the standard, whatever it is called, is to contrast it with the standard for JMOL.

The motion for JMOL tests the sufficiency of the evidence to support a jury verdict by the reasonable jury standard. The court does not weigh the evidence. It does not judge the credibility of the witnesses. It construes all reasonable doubts against the movant. If the court grants a motion for JMOL, the court takes the case from the jury and decides it—grants judgment—"as a matter of law."

A motion for new trial assumes that there was sufficient evidence to reach the jury and that the jury verdict is reasonable, but tests whether that verdict is nevertheless clearly erroneous, either because it is against the weight of the evidence or because it was (or could have been) the product of a flawed trial process. The court can weigh the evidence and assess credibility. It does not have to resolve doubts against the movant. If the court grants a new trial, it rejects the first jury's verdict, but it does not decide the case as a matter of law. Instead, it affords the parties the opportunity to present the case to a new jury. A grant of new trial is therefore said to be consistent with the Seventh Amendment on the theory that a new trial for a weight-of-the-evidence error does not deny the verdict winner a jury trial; it only makes him try the case again to a new jury.

Of course, the judge's scrutiny of the verdict should take into account the complexity of the evidence and the relative fact-finding abilities of jurors compared to the judge's own.

> When the trial is lengthy and complicated and involves subject matters outside the ordinary knowledge of jurors, the court should more closely scrutinize the verdict; when the subject matter of the trial is simple and easily comprehended by intelligent laypersons, the court should use less demanding scrutiny.

Moore § 59.13[2][f][iii][A].

Trivedi proves the point. The trial court denied JMOL for several reasons, but, on the new trial motion, said that whether the verdict on the hostile environment claim was against the weight of the evidence was "a much closer question." This was mainly because *it was a different question*. Given the relative simplicity of the claims and the mainly testimonial evidence, the court was not prepared to find that the jury erred in finding liability. On the other hand, it found the amount of the $700,001 verdict to be against the weight of the evidence, requiring a new trial. Simply said, even a verdict that has substantial supporting evidence can be clearly wrong or appear to be a miscarriage of justice, in this case because of its size.

4. Judging the jury. The foregoing discussion raises what may seem like razor-thin differences in the way judges evaluate jury verdicts. So let's think more systematically and colloquially about "judging the jury."

Assume that a motor vehicle accident case was tried to the jury. There was sharply conflicting evidence about whether the defendant was negligent, but the parties had no objection to the trial process. The defendant moves for JMOL at the close of the evidence, but the motion is denied. The jury returns a verdict finding the defendant negligent. You are the trial judge. If the defendant files a renewed motion for JMOL or, in the alternative, for a new trial, how would you rule if you had the following view of the evidence?

A. I agree with the verdict.
B. I would not have decided the case that way, but I can't say that the verdict was wrong.
C. I think the verdict was clearly wrong, but I can't say that the jury was unreasonable.
D. I think the verdict was unreasonable; no reasonable jury could have reached this verdict.

In case **A**, you should obviously let the verdict stand. There is no basis for new trial, let alone JMOL.

In case **B**, you should also let it stand. If the court doesn't think the verdict was wrong, it can hardly think it was unreasonable, so there is no basis for granting JMOL. To grant a new trial in this case would be to substitute the judge's decision for the jury without the justification of correcting some error. Doing so would be a serious invasion of the right to jury trial. A party is entitled to the collective wisdom of her peers instead of just the lone wisdom of the judge acting like a "thirteenth juror." "What courts cannot do ... is to grant a new trial simply because [the court] would have come to a different conclusion than the jury did." *Peterson v. Wilson*, 141 F.3d 573, 577 (5th Cir. 1998) (internal citation omitted).

In case **C**, you would have decided the case differently, but you don't think the jury was unreasonable. That forecloses JMOL—which, after all, is decided by a reasonable jury standard.

But you also believe that the jury clearly erred. Granting a new trial in this case can be said to *promote* the right to jury trial, by preventing a clear jury error and submitting the case to a new jury. Still, you should not be quick to assume that the multi-member jury was wrong and that you alone are right. We assume that six, or twelve, heads are better than one on fact questions. We therefore crank up the new trial standard by insisting that a judge must find the verdict *clearly* erroneous, or be left with a *definite and firm conviction* of error, in light of the complexity and length of trial. On the other hand, we don't insist that the judge find the verdict unreasonable; otherwise there would be no difference between JMOL and new trial. This distinction may not be intuitive, but think about it: Haven't you often heard an argument that you thought was wrong without thinking it unreasonable? Thus, if you think the verdict clearly wrong, you should grant a new trial.

In case **D**, you've taken this next step: from wrong to unreasonable. When the difference between judge and jury is this wide, the judge is empowered to give JMOL to the verdict loser on a timely motion, on the theory that the verdict winner failed to meet his burden to produce sufficient evidence for a reasonable jury to find for him.

5. Why wasn't the verdict on Trivedi's hostile environment claim "clearly erroneous"? As noted, the court found this to be a difficult question. The court believed that the evidence of Trivedi's mental problems "strongly support[ed]" the defendant's case. Yet, the discrimination claim ultimately turned in substantial part on a swearing contest between Cooper and Trivedi. Juries are thought to be especially good at deciding credibility, chiefly because every juror does it every day. Thus, even though the judge appeared to believe that Cooper's evidence was stronger, she could not say that the jury's contrary conclusion was clearly erroneous.

B. Excessive (or Insufficient) Verdicts

As *Trivedi* shows, weight-of-the-evidence challenges can be made not just to what you might call the jury's substantive verdict (or, in the case of a special verdict, its answers to fact questions), but also to the amount of the verdict. The court asks whether the amount of the verdict "shocks the judicial conscience."

1. Applying the standard. The judge may personally be outraged by the verdict, but naked outrage is rarely cited by itself to justify setting aside a verdict as grossly excessive. Instead, as in *Trivedi*, the court will look for support in cases involving comparable claims. The court there surveyed multiple reported cases (only the conclusions of that survey were left in our case edit), and the court concluded that the $700,001 verdict "would be unprecedented." Against these benchmarks, Trivedi could point to nothing more than his own weak testimony that he "felt insulted, . . . indignant, . . . unhappy, . . . emotionally upset." Thus, even though the court could not find that the liability verdict for Trivedi was against the weight of the evidence, the amount of the verdict was excessive, justifying a new trial.

Q **2. Excessive verdicts and remittitur.** When the basis for a new trial is that the verdict was excessive and against the weight of the evidence, a federal court (and most state courts) have another option. What was it in *Trivedi*?

A The court in effect blackmailed Trivedi by asserting that it would grant a new trial unless he agreed to give back—"remit"—the excess of the verdict to the defendants, which in this case was all but $50,000 of the $700,001 verdict. Trivedi does not have to accept that option, but if he does not, then there will be a new trial. If he accepts the option, and remits the $650,001, then the court enters judgment for $50,000 and the case is over. Trivedi cannot appeal the remittitur order. (Cooper can still appeal, as the court would have denied his motion and entered judgment against him.) *See Moore* § 59.13[2][g][iii][E].

The Supreme Court has reasoned that the *remittitur* option does not offend the Seventh Amendment right to jury on the somewhat dubious theory that the verdict after remittitur was "part" of the original jury verdict—the part supported by the weight of the evidence. *See Dimick v. Schiedt*, 293 U.S. 474, 482–83 (1935).

Why would Trivedi ever accept a remittitur of $650,001 and go home with the relatively paltry check for $50,000, after he had successfully convinced a jury to award $700,001? The blackmail is the risk of the new trial, where he may get *nothing*. The first jury gave him $700,001, but the next jury may view the evidence as the judge did and conclude that he "could not point to any compelling effect of the discrimination." 1996 U.S. Dist. LEXIS 18715, at *25. Sometimes, a bird in the hand—the original verdict less the remittitur—is worth more than the bird in the bush—the possible verdict in the new trial, less the costs of trying the case again.

Q **3. Finding the right number.** Federal courts have taken three different approaches to deciding the "right" verdict with remittitur:

- awarding the lowest amount supported by the record (the "minimum recovery" rule).
- awarding the highest legal amount of damages (the "maximum recovery" rule).
- awarding an amount the court deems reasonable.

Moore § 59.13[2][g][iii][D]. Which did the *Trivedi* court choose?

A The second approach. After surveying verdicts in similar cases and considering the evidence, the court found that $50,000 was not just "generous," but "represents the maximum that does not shock the judicial conscience." Indeed, some have argued that anything less than the maximum recovery may violate the Seventh Amendment. *Id.*

4. Insufficient verdicts and *additur*. OK—you may well be asking yourself the next logical question. Suppose a jury comes back with a $250 verdict in a case in which the plaintiff has lost a leg as a result of the defendant's negligence. Can the judge now blackmail the *defendant* to sweeten the pot (*additur*) or suffer a new trial? The answer in federal courts is no, on the theory that the *additur*—the amount by which the verdict would need to be increased to be supported by the weight of the evidence—is not part of the jury's original verdict. *Dimick*, 2932 U.S. at 474. Because an additur is not part of the original verdict, but a judge-made add-on, it is said to be inconsistent with the right to jury trial. Or so goes the not very convincing reasoning of the Supreme Court. The better answer is simply that remittitur existed at common law, while additur did not. *See Moore* § 59.13[2][g][ii][B]. Because the Seventh Amendment "preserved" the right to jury trial at common law, it can be said to have preserved the common law remittitur feature of jury trial as well.

Some state courts have held that additur is available under state law. *See, e.g., Fisch v. Manger*, 24 N.J. 66 (N.J. 1957). In Massachusetts, for example, a rule provides:

> A new trial shall not be granted solely on the ground that the damages are excessive until the prevailing party has first been given an opportunity to remit so much thereof as the court adjudges is excessive. A new trial shall not be granted solely on the ground that the damages are inadequate until the defendant has first been given an opportunity to accept an addition to the verdict of such amount as the court adjudges reasonable.

Mass. R. Civ. P. 59(a). In federal courts, however, the only solution for a verdict that is against the weight of the evidence because the damages are inadequate is a new trial.

C. Partial New Trials

If a weight-of-the evidence challenge is to the verdict succeeds on one of several claims or defenses, a new trial could be limited to that claim or defense. *See* Fed. R. Civ. P. 59(a)(1) ("new trial on all or some of the issues—and to any part . . ."). Thus, had the court agreed in *Trivedi* that the jury verdict on the hostile environment claim was clearly erroneous quite apart from its size, it could have ordered a new trial on just that claim. Similarly, when the challenge is to the amount of the verdict on a claim, the new trial can be limited to damages on that claim.

Q **1. Severability of issue for new trial.** What is the defendants' argument against limiting new trial to damages in *Trivedi*?

A That the damages are so inseparable from liability that both must be retried together. They were originally tried together to the jury, and the court reasoned that damages turned on the same evidence as liability for a hostile work environment: evidence of causation between the supervisor's actions and Trivedi's injuries, "as well as the extent of the harassment and what amount of recovery it warrants." When a new trial of damages would cover the same evidentiary ground as liability, and the issues are interlinked, it would be unfair to defendants to limit the new trial to damages. Courts have also reasoned that when insufficient damages suggest that the jury's uncertainty about liability led them to compromise damages, the only fair remedy is a new trial on all issues. *See Wright & Miller* § 2814.

In other cases, liability and damages are clearly separable. In *Wheatley v. Beetar* (cited in *Trivedi*), for example, the jury first found defendants liable for beating the plaintiff, but then, in a separate trial of damages, awarded him only $1 in damages, notwithstanding medical evidence of fresh welts on his neck and side and a perforated ear drum. The court found that the damages verdict was unsupported by the evidence and ordered a new trial on damages alone, reasoning that there was no reason to deprive the plaintiff of the separate verdict he had won on liability.

Q **2. Slicing the new trial bologna thinly.** Suppose that in the *Wheatley* case, discussed immediately above, one defendant was a company that employed the defendants who beat the plaintiff and had been sued on a theory of *respondeat superior* (roughly speaking, that the employer is liable for torts committed by the employee in the "scope of his employment"—in the course of his assigned duties as an employee). If the jury returned a special verdict finding that the employees beat the plaintiff, that the employees were acting within the scope of their employment, and that the plaintiff was entitled to $100,000 in damages, but the court thought the scope-of-employment finding was clearly erroneous, what could it do on a motion for new trial?

A Since the liability finding is clearly erroneous, it looks like the court could order a new trial on liability. Yet, the jury found that defendants' employees beat plaintiff, and that finding was not clearly erroneous. And the scope-of-employment finding may be separable, to the extent that it turns on a job description and time and place. Depending on any actual evidentiary overlap, this may be a case in which the new trial could be limited to the scope-of-employment issue. Rule 59(a) is quite clear that a new trial can be ordered "on all or some of the issues." *See Wright & Miller* § 2814 (listing cases involving new trial limited to the issues of attempt-to-monopolize, causation, vicarious (as opposed to individual) liability, joint liability, and plaintiff administrator's capacity to sue). Partial new trial, therefore, can be very partial indeed, although the court must be careful to decide whether an issue to be retried can be truly and fairly separated from the remaining issues.

D. Mechanics of New Trial Practice

Q **1. Timing and appeal.** Cooper didn't even wait for a final judgment to file his motion for new trial. Why was it still timely?

A Rule 59(b) requires only that the motion for a new trial be filed *no later than* twenty-eight days after the entry of final judgment. When a Rule 59 motion is timely, moreover, the motion tolls the usual thirty-day time limit for filing a notice of appeal in federal courts. The time limit for appeal does not start running until the court rules on the motion for a new trial and enters final judgment. Fed. R. App. 4(a)(4).

In *Trivedi,* the court granted the new trial motion, conditional on Trivedi's refusal of the remittitur it proposed. If Trivedi accepted the remittitur, he would waive the right to appeal the remittitur order. But if he refuses the remittitur, and the new trial is ordered, can he *now* appeal?

A

No, because there is no final judgment yet from which an appeal can be taken. As we will see, appeals are ordinarily allowed only from final judgments (with several exceptions that we will discuss). The grant of the new trial continues the case, and Trivedi will have to wait until the final judgment is entered on the second verdict to appeal the court's grant of a new trial. As strange as it may seem, appellate courts have sometimes ruled that a new trial should never have been granted and reinstated the original verdict on appeal of the second verdict. *See, e.g., Peterson v. Wilson,* 141 F.3d 573 (5th Cir. 1998) (finding that trial judge improperly granted new trial based on juror misconduct, and, after perusing record, concluding that original verdict should stand).

2. Filing a renewed motion for judgment as a matter of law first. The Supreme Court has held that a party who fails to renew its motion for judgment as a matter of law cannot appeal to seek a new trial on the basis of insufficiency of the evidence. *Unitherm Food Sys., Inc. v. Swift-Eckrich, Inc.,* 546 U.S. 394, 404 (2006). Although *Unitherm* includes language suggesting that a pre-verdict motion is always a predicate for appeal, courts have read it as limited to challenges to sufficiency of the evidence. *Linden v. CNH Am., LLC,* 673 F.3d 829, 832–33 (8th Cir. 2012) ("in addressing whether [*Unitherm's*] language extends to all post-trial appeals, appeals courts have uniformly limited it to sufficiency of the evidence challenges where parties fail to file a postverdict motion under Rule 50(b) after the denial of a Rule 50(a) preverdict motion.").

But the safe rule of thumb is easy. To preserve your appellate options in a jury case, move for judgment as a matter of law before the verdict, and, after an adverse verdict, renew the motion and move for new trial in the alternative. In a nonjury case, if you lose, move for a new trial.

3. Appellate standard of review. The safest generalization about the scope of review of new trial decisions is that "[t]he trial court has very broad discretion and the appellate courts will defer a great deal to its exercise of this discretion." *Wright & Miller* § 2818. Even in reviewing questions of law in the trial process (such as whether a jury instruction correctly stated the law) that an appellate court decides *de novo*—independently without deference to the trial judge—the appellate courts are deferential to the trial court's determination of *the harm the error caused.* This is because the trial judge was present and often better able to appraise that harm than the appellate judges who have only the cold written record for review.

E. Making Combined Motions

1. Moving in the alternative. Because motions for JMOL and for new trial evoke different tests, losing parties often move for both in the alternative, as Rule 50(b) expressly allows. In *Trivedi,* the new trial motion was made alternatively as a fall-back or "even if" motion: Even if the court found sufficient evidence to support the verdict and therefore denied JMOL, it should still order a new trial because the verdict shocked the court's conscience.

These alternative motions pose a possible dilemma. If the trial court grants JMOL, there seems to be no reason to decide the motion for new trial. But suppose that, on appeal, the court of appeals reverses the JMOL. The movant might still be entitled to new trial (remember, new trial poses a different question), and the court of appeals would have to remand to the trial judge for a belated ruling on the new trial (because the trial judge has the comparative advantage of having heard all the evidence).

Rule 50(c) solves this dilemma by forcing the trial court to "conditionally rule on any motion for new trial by determining whether a new trial should be granted if the judgment is later vacated or reversed." If the judgment is reversed, the new trial proceeds (unless the Court of Appeals orders otherwise). If it is denied, then the movant can assert that error on its appeal.

Finally, if the trial court *denies* a motion for JMOL, there is obviously no reason for the verdict winner to ask for a new trial. The winner has the verdict and no reason to undermine it. But if the court of appeals reverses the judgment, Rule 50(c) allows the verdict winner on appeal to "assert grounds entitling it to a new trial should the appellate court conclude that the trial court erred in denying the motion." The appeals court then has the choice whether to order a new trial and direct entry of judgment.

2. Combined motions and appellate review. Try applying the foregoing logic to the following question.

Assume that Pasterini sues Duke for breach of contract and wins a verdict for $125,000. Duke unsuccessfully moved for JMOL at the close of all the evidence. After the jury verdict, Duke now timely renews his motion for JMOL on the theory that there was insufficient evidence to support a reasonable jury verdict, and, in the alternative, moves for a new trial on the ground that the judge mistakenly excluded material evidence that could change the outcome. Assume that the trial court decides the motions as shown below, and that on a timely appeal by Duke, the appeals court agrees or disagrees as also shown below. What should the appeals court do?

Trial court	Appeals court
A. Grants Duke's motion for JMOL and his conditional motion for new trial.	A. Agrees that JMOL is proper, but not new trial.
B. Grants Duke's motion for JMOL and his conditional motion for new trial.	B. Agrees with both decisions.
C. Denies Duke's motion for JMOL and grants his conditional motion for new trial.	C. Agrees on denial of JMOL, but disagrees on new trial.
D. Grants Duke's motion for JMOL and denies his conditional motion for new trial.	D. Disagrees on both.
E. Denies Duke's motion for JMOL. Neither party files a motion for new trial.	E. Disagrees with denial of JMOL.

First, note that Duke protected his options by filing the appropriate motions in the trial court.

In **A**, *if* the appellate court agrees with the grant of JMOL, it affirms judgment for Duke and that's the end of the case. The trial court's grant of a new trial was only conditional on its JMOL being reversed; since it was affirmed, the new trial ruling is now moot whether or not the Court of Appeals agrees. Any error in excluding evidence was harmless to Duke; the last thing he wants is a new trial.

The same is true of **B**. Even though now the appeals court would also have granted a new trial, that grant is still conditional on reversal of the JMOL. When the JMOL stands, the new trial ruling is again moot. Duke has won; he surely prefers the JMOL to a new trial.

C takes some thinking. First, the court denies JMOL but grants new trial. As we saw in *Trivedi*, this is not uncommon, because the standards for JMOL and new trial differ, and the clearly erroneous/manifest injustice standard for new trial is less rigorous then the no-reasonable-jury standard for JMOL. But the grant of the new trial means that there no longer is any final judgment from which to appeal. This order is "interlocutory" because the case continues. Thus, the trial court's ruling does not present "an appropriate time" for appeal. The parties must wait to appeal until the new trial produces a final judgment.

If Pasterini loses the second trial, she can assert error on appeal in the grant of a new trial. Since the appellate court agrees that this was an error and also agrees that JMOL was properly denied after the first trial, it can set aside the verdict in the second trial and restore and affirm the verdict in the first trial. Of course, everybody has wasted the time and resources spent in the second trial, but such are the costs of delaying appeal until a final judgment.

D should now be easy. The appellate court disagrees with the grant of JMOL, but it also disagrees with the conditional denial of new trial. Rule 50(c)(2) provides that "[i]f the motion for a new trial is conditionally denied, the appellee may assert error in that denial; if the judgment is reversed, the case must proceed as the appellate court orders." It would therefore reverse the JMOL and remand with an order for the district court to conduct a new trial in which the excluded evidence must be admitted.

E is subtle. When the trial court denies Duke's motion for JMOL, the prevailing party, Pasterini, has no reason or right to appeal. But when Duke appeals, Rule 50(e) provides that "the prevailing party may, as appellee, assert grounds entitling it to a new trial should the appellate court conclude that the trial court erred in denying the motion [for JMOL]." When the appellate court reverses the denial of JMOL, it may then "order a new trial, direct the trial court to determine whether a new trial should be granted, or direct entry of a judgment."

III. New Trials for Process Errors

Trivedi involved only weight-of-the-evidence challenges to the verdict. But in a substantial number of cases, the challenge is based instead on an error in the process of trial. These process-error challenges pose three issues for the court.

First, did an error occur? For example, did the court erroneously exclude evidence? Or did the plaintiff's attorney make an improper closing argument to the jury (e.g., by appealing to racial or religious prejudice)? Or did a juror conduct an experiment at home about something she heard during the trial, and then report the results to the jury during its deliberations?

Second, did the error probably or to a substantial degree affect the right to a fair trial or the jury verdict? Recognizing that few trials are completely error-free, the Supreme Court has long said that a litigant is entitled only to a fair, not a perfect, trial. *McDonough Power Equip. Co. v. Greenwood*, 464 U.S. 548, 553 (1984). Rule 61 therefore states that "[u]nless justice requires otherwise, no error in admitting or excluding evidence—or any other error by the court or a party—is ground for granting a new trial. . . ." Justice requires a new trial only if the error "affect[ed] any party's substantial rights." Fed. R. Civ. P. 61. The courts have variously asserted that the party claiming error must show that it is "highly probable" that the error affected the right to a fair trial, that the error affected the right "to a substantial degree," or that the verdict was "more probably than not" tainted. *See Moore* § 61.02.

Q **Affecting substantial rights?** Suppose Trivedi offered evidence that other persons in his office had been promoted, while he was not. The judge permitted five witnesses to testify to that effect and admitted employment records from twenty more showing their promotion. But she erroneously excluded three other records of promotion on the grounds of hearsay, over Trivedi's timely objection. If Trivedi lost, could he claim on appeal that this error affected his substantial rights?

A It is always hard to answer a question like this without the actual record in front of you, but the answer is probably no. Even though the exclusion of these three records was an error, they were merely cumulative evidence, consistent with a larger volume of evidence that was admitted. The exclusion is therefore likely to be viewed as harmless error by an appeals court.

On the other hand, suppose, over Trivedi's timely objection, that the trial court erroneously excluded Trivedi's psychiatrist's testimony that Trivedi's mental state was normal, though stressed. If Trivedi lost, could he claim on appeal that this error affected his substantial rights?

A Almost certainly. Defendants presented two doctors who testified that Trivedi suffered a delusional disorder or paranoia. Although some of his own testimony tended to support their conclusions, his attending psychiatrist's diagnosis would be powerful rebuttal testimony.

Third, did the party affected make a timely and specific objection to the error? *See* Fed. R. Civ. P. 46 (requiring party to state "grounds" for a request or objection); Fed. R. Civ. P. 51(c)–(d) (permitting a party to raise error in jury instructions only if objection or request was made as provided in the Rule, subject to court's authority to consider "plain errors").

Rule 61 suggests that errors can be made both by the court and by a party. As the following case suggests, an error can also be committed by a jury. Consider how the requirement for prejudicial error applies in this case.

READING *WILSON v. VERMONT CASTINGS, INC.* The plaintiff sued Vermont Castings after her clothing caught fire when she was lighting a woodburning stove sold by defendant. In order to light the stove, she had to leave the door partly open. Plaintiff alleged that this feature of the stove was a product defect that proximately led to her injuries. The jury returned a special verdict finding a defect, but finding that it did not proximately cause her injuries. During post-trial conversations with the jurors, however, plaintiff's counsel learned that one of them who owned a Vermont Castings stove looked at the manual to see what warnings it gave. She then reported them to the jury. She also told the jury that she had to leave the stove door open to start a fire. The motion for a new trial based on jury misconduct followed.

- A juror *owned* a Vermont Castings stove? Why wasn't this fact alone a ground for new trial?
- Why could the court at the hearing on the motion for new trial consider information that the juror read the stove manual and told the other jurors?
- Why did this information not warrant a new trial?
- Why did the court at the same hearing on the motion for new trial *refuse* to consider information that the juror told the other jurors of her own experience with the Vermont Castings stove?

WILSON v. VERMONT CASTINGS, INC.

977 F. Supp. 691 (M.D. Pa. 1997)

McClure, District Judge.

BACKGROUND

Plaintiffs Anne Wilson and Oliver J. Larmi filed this diversity action to recover for injuries sustained by Wilson on November 16, 1991 while she was lighting a fire in a woodburning stove sold by defendant Vermont Castings, Inc. (Vermont Castings). Wilson suffered severe burns when her clothing caught fire. Plaintiffs alleged causes of action in strict liability (Count I) and negligence (Count II) and asserted claims for loss of consortium (Count III) and punitive damages (Count IV). . . .

Trial commenced on February 12, 1997 and concluded on March 7, 1997 with a verdict in favor of defendant Vermont Castings.

Plaintiffs proceeded to trial on a strict liability theory of liability only. The jury found that the stove was defective but that such defectiveness was not a substantial factor in causing injury to plaintiff Anne Wilson.

Before the court is a motion for a new trial filed by the plaintiffs. For the reasons which follow, the motion will be denied.

DISCUSSION

Allegations of Juror Misconduct

Plaintiffs raise allegations of juror misconduct. They assert that during conversations post-trial between plaintiffs' counsel and jurors, counsel learned that: 1) a juror who owns a Vermont Castings stove reviewed the instruction manual to see what warnings were given and told other jurors what she had found; and 2) that the same juror told the other jurors, that she, like Wilson, found it was necessary to leave the door open slightly to get the fire going.

We start with the general rule that jurors may not impeach their own verdict and are not competent to testify about any aspect of their thought processes or deliberations. *In re Beverly Hills Fire Litigation,* 695 F.2d 207, 213 (1982). Any inquiry into the deliberative process or juror's mental process is impermissible under Federal Rule of Evidence 606(b). With one exception, Rule 606(b) precludes jurors from testifying about what occurred during deliberations. Rule 606(b) provides:

> Upon an inquiry into the validity of a verdict or indictment, a juror may not testify as to any matter or statement occurring during the course of the jury's deliberations or to the effect of anything upon that or any other juror's mind or emotions as influencing the juror to assent to or dissent from the verdict or indictment or concerning the juror's mental processes in connection therewith, *except that a juror may testify on the question whether extraneous prejudicial information was improperly brought to the jury's attention or whether any outside influence was improperly brought to bear upon any juror.* Nor may a juror's affidavit or evidence of any statement by the juror concerning a matter about which the juror would be precluded from testifying be received for these purposes.

general rule for juries:

Fed. R. Evid. 606(b) (emphasis supplied).

The exception is, as stated in the rule, that a court may inquire as to whether "extraneous prejudicial information was improperly brought to the jury's attention." There has been much debate as to what constitutes "extraneous information."

Some courts and commentators have favored a definition that focuses on the physical location of the juror, stating that any influence which comes to bear outside the jury room door may be inquired into, and any influence which comes to bear inside the jury room is sacrosanct. Others have focused, not on the physical location, but on the importance of barring any inquiry into the jury's deliberative process.

The debate is reflected in the Advisory Committee Notes for Rule 606 with the House and Senate favoring different versions of proposed amendments to Rule 606(b) in 1974. The version ultimately adopted favors drawing the dividing line between permissible and impermissible inquiry at the point where the jury's mental processes during deliberation would be revealed. That is, jurors may be asked whether any extraneous material or information was brought to their attention. Whether the extraneous material or information originated inside or outside the jury room is immaterial.

If jurors indicate that extraneous information was brought to their attention, the court cannot then inquire as to whether and to what extent such information affected their deliberations. Under Rule 606(b), jurors are competent to testify as to external influences upon them.

> This exception permitting inquiry into external influences upon the jury, however, is limited to identification of those extraneous sources of information—*once the existence of external influences upon the jury has been established, neither the Court nor counsel may inquire into the subjective effect of these external influences upon particular jurors. Rather, the Court must determine whether such extraneous information was prejudicial by determining how it would effect* [sic] *an objective "typical juror."*

Urseth v. City of Dayton, 680 F. Supp. 1084, 1089 (S.D. Ohio 1987), citing, *inter alia*, *Owen v. Duckworth*, 727 F.2d 643, 646 (7th Cir. 1984).

Rather, it is the court's obligation then to determine whether there was reversible error, by deciding whether such information would have affected an objective "typical juror" and led him or her to a verdict based even in part on impermissible considerations or inadmissible evidence.

Here, we will accept for purposes of deciding the motion before us that the representations made by counsel as to statements obtained from a juror are correct. We further find, for purposes of resolving plaintiffs' objection, that the information relayed to the jury by a particular juror about her Vermont Castings instruction manual was extraneous to the jury's deliberations, since it was not part of the evidence in the case.[4]

The testimony as to how this particular juror routinely operated her stove was, however, not extraneous to the process. Jurors bring with them to deliberations their life experiences. When such information becomes part of the deliberative process, it becomes sacrosanct under Rule 606(b). This is not a situation in which a juror went out on his or her own, performed an experiment for the express purpose of testing the evidence, then relayed the results to the other jurors. This was simply a matter of a juror drawing upon prior life experiences and using them in the course of deliberations. It would, therefore, be improper for us to inquire further into the matter.

We do find, however, that a limited inquiry permitted under Rule 606(b) is appropriate with respect to the statement that the same juror took it upon herself to review the instruction manual and report what she found to the jury. This was not simply a prior life experience she simply drew upon in deliberating, but rather something she did expressly, using materials available to her only outside the courtroom, for the purpose of testing or evaluating the evidence.

Plaintiffs' theory of product defect was twofold: 1) that the stove was defectively designed because users had to leave the door slightly ajar to keep the fire going and 2) that the stove was defective because there were no warnings placed

4. Evidence as to the contents of the manual was excluded on grounds of relevancy. The testimony indicated that Anne Wilson had never seen the Vermont Castings manual. As we discuss *infra*, the evidence was, in fact, excluded upon motion of defendant Vermont Casting, not at plaintiffs' urging.

on the stove itself telling users not to leave the door ajar because it posed a risk to those nearby.

Jurors were asked to answer two questions on liability:

1. Was the Defiant wood-burning stove defective when manufactured and sold by defendant Vermont Castings?; and
2. Was the defectiveness of the stove a substantial factor in bringing about harm to plaintiff Anne Wilson? They answered the first question "yes" and the second "no."

The information in the manual went only to the issue of defect. It had no bearing on the issue of causation. Unlike issues of product defect, all causation issues in this case turned on facts relating to plaintiffs' actions and other events the day of her tragic accident. Nowhere in the case was there any suggestion that plaintiff Wilson looked at the manual that day or any other day prior to the accident. Thus, whatever the manual said was irrelevant to the issue of causation, the only liability issue on which plaintiffs did not prevail.

More to the point, plaintiffs suffered no prejudice even if the jurors' consideration of information in the manual was improper. As we have stated, plaintiffs prevailed on the question of product defect. That was the only issue in the case on which information in the manual had any bearing. Thus, even if we assume, *arguendo,* that the verdict was improperly influenced by information on the manual not admitted into evidence, plaintiffs suffered no prejudice as a result. Parties are not entitled to a reversal or a new trial on grounds that caused them no prejudice.

Although Rule 606(b) allows the court to hold an evidentiary hearing, no purpose would be served by holding a hearing on this issue. We have before us, and will accept, the information obtained by plaintiffs regarding what the juror did and what she told her fellow jurors about the manual. If we were to hold a hearing, the information obtainable could not go beyond those facts without violating Rule 606(b). Rule 606(b) allows only an inquiry as to what extraneous information was before the jury. Any inquiry beyond such facts into what effect the information had on deliberations remains barred.

Further, if there are shown to have been extraneous influences on the jury, it becomes the obligation of the court to apply an objective test and assess for itself whether the information would have affected an objective "typical juror." As we stated above, inquiry into the mental processes of a particular juror or jurors during deliberations remains improper. *Urseth v. City of Dayton,* 680 F. Supp. 1084, 1089 (S.D. Ohio 1987) (collecting cases). "The court's questioning of a juror who is the recipient of extraneous information is limited to the circumstances and nature of the improper contact." *United States v. Simpson,* 950 F.2d 1519, 1521 (10th Cir. 1991), quoting *United States v. Hornung,* 848 F.2d 1040, 1045 (10th Cir. 1988), *cert. denied,* 489 U.S. 1069 (1989).

"Where an extraneous influence is shown, the court must apply an objective test, assessing for itself the likelihood that the influence would affect a typical juror." *Id.* at 1522, citing *United States v. Bassler,* 651 F.2d 600, 603 (8th Cir. 1981).

Here, it was plaintiffs' contention that the warnings should have been on the stove itself. The jury apparently agreed with the plaintiffs on that point in finding the stove defective....

For all of these reasons, plaintiffs are not entitled to the relief which they seek.

Notes and Questions: *Wilson v. Vermont Castings*

Q **1. *Voir dire* and challenges.** At first glance, you may have done a double take. A plaintiff sues the manufacturer for a product defect, and a juror *owns the very same product* that injured the plaintiff? Doesn't this conflict alone require a new trial?

A First, if most people own the product, then perhaps it would be impractical to exclude jurors for this reason alone. Though it's hard to think of a brand product that is so ubiquitous, maybe Vermont Castings woodburning stoves qualify in rural Pennsylvania? Second, and more seriously, if the plaintiff was concerned that prospective jurors owned the defendant's stoves, her lawyer should have asked them (or asked the judge to ask them) in *voir dire* whether they did, and then challenged Vermont Castings-owners for cause or exercised her three peremptory challenges to strike the owners from the jury panel. *See* Fed. R. Civ. P. 47. If she failed to do so, she probably cannot complain now—which is presumably why the opinion says nothing about this "conflict."

Q **2. Looking into the black box: Impeaching jury verdicts.** You may also have done a double take when you read that the plaintiff's lawyers talked to the jurors after the case. If so, your reaction reflects the intuition that jurors should be shielded to a significant degree from having to explain themselves in court and describe their deliberations, which, after all, are held privately. Why should they be shielded?

A Partly to encourage uninhibited discussion among themselves. Partly to "keep jurors from being harassed by the losing party in efforts to snatch victory from the jaws of defeat by turning up facts that might show misconduct serious enough to set aside the verdict" and require a new trial. Christopher B. Mueller & Laird C. Kirkpatrick, Evidence § 6.10 (6th ed. 2018). Partly to promote finality by protecting verdicts from the losers' nit-picking the deliberations that produced the verdict. Otherwise, judges "would become Penelope, forever engaged in unraveling the webs they wove."* *Jorgensen v. York Ice*

* For those who lack grounding in Greek mythology, Penelope was the wife of the absent Ulysses. She held off suitors in his absence by saying she could not decide about their proposals until she finished weaving a robe, which she secretly unraveled every night. This was before the era of "just say no."

> *Mach. Corp.*, 160 F.2d 432, 435 (2d Cir. 1947) (Hand, J.). And, truth to tell, partly to conceal ordinary human imperfections in the jury's deliberations. Prohibiting evidence of the jury's deliberations provides "an easy escape from embarrassing choices." *Id.* Just as trial is not perfect, jury deliberations may look ugly on close scrutiny, so the Rules aim at some measure of opacity for deliberations in order to make jury verdicts more credible.

Consequently, although lawyers can ask jurors what went on, *see* Model Rule of Professional Conduct 3.5(c), the common law included a blanket evidentiary rule that jurors may not impeach (discredit) their own verdict by their testimony: the "no impeachment rule." *See Peña-Rodriguez v. Colorado,* 137 S. Ct. 855, 861 (2017). It did not even allow testimony from non-jurors about jury misconduct. But Federal Rule of Evidence 606(b) took a more nuanced view, creating an exception for juror testimony about whether "extraneous prejudicial information was improperly brought to the jury's attention or whether any outside influence was improperly brought to bear upon any juror." The theory was that as long as a juror's testimony was confined to such extraneous information or outside influences, it did not violate the sanctity of the jury's deliberations.

3. The racial bias exception to the no impeachment rule. In *Peña-Rodriguez,* the jury convicted the defendant of unlawful sexual contact and harassment. After the trial, two jurors voluntarily reported to the defendant's lawyers that another juror had expressed "anti-Hispanic bias" against the defendant in a series of remarks to fellow jurors during their deliberations. For example, he told them, "'I think he did it because he's Mexican and Mexican men take whatever they want,'" and that, in his experience, "nine times out of ten Mexican men were guilty of being aggressive toward women and young girls." *Peña-Rodriguez,* 137 S. Ct. at 862. Invoking the no impeachment rule, the lower courts refused to consider the jurors' affidavits describing these remarks and declined to order a new trial.

The Supreme Court reversed. It held that the unique history of racial bias ("a familiar and recurring evil that, if left unaddressed, would risk systemic injury to the administration of justice in this country") required it to create an exception under the Sixth Amendment (guaranteeing the right in criminal cases to a public trial "by an impartial jury") to the no impeachment rule. *Id.* at 868. "[W]here a juror makes a clear statement that indicates he or she relied on racial stereotypes or animus to convict a criminal defendant, the Sixth Amendment requires that the no-impeachment rule give way in order to permit the trial court to consider the evidence of the juror's statement and any resulting denial of the jury trial guarantee." *Id.* at 869. The Court did not decide the standard for determining when evidence of racial bias is sufficient to require that the verdict be set aside and a new trial be granted. *Id.* at 870–71 (comparing *Shillcutt v. Gagnon*, 827 F.2d 1155, 1159 (7th Cir. 1987) (inquiring whether racial bias "pervaded the jury room") with *United States v. Henley*, 238 F.3d 1111, 1120 (9th Cir. 2001) ("One racist juror would be enough")." *Id.* at 870–71.

The Chief Justice and Justices Thomas and Alito dissented, noting, *inter alia*, that no such exception existed at the time the Sixth Amendment was ratified (1791) and that reform was best left to the political process.

Q **4. Identifying "extraneous prejudicial information" and "outside influences."** Under Rule 606(b), it seems reasonably clear that testimony that the juror in *Wilson* told her fellow jurors about the instruction manual was extraneous to the case. Why?

A The principal problem with extraneous information is that it is outside the record and has therefore neither been tested by the rules of evidence or by cross-examination, nor subjected to rebuttal. In fact, in *Wilson*, the court had actually excluded the manual on grounds of relevancy, since the plaintiff admitted that she had never seen it. This makes it crystal clear that the juror has improperly supplemented the record.

If it was so clear that the information about the manual was extraneous, why didn't its disclosure by one juror to the jury warrant a new trial?

A Because, as we have seen, a court will not order a new trial just because a juror committed an error. The error must have been prejudicial, in that it more probably than not affected the verdict. But the information in the manual went only to the issue of a defect, *on which the plaintiff got a favorable finding*. It was irrelevant to causation, on which the jury ruled against the plaintiff. "[A] court must disregard all errors and defects that do not affect any party's substantial rights." Fed. R. Civ. P. 61. This jury error doesn't matter. Under Rule 606(b) the court must also employ an objective test and "assess for itself whether the information would have [or probably did?] affect an objective 'typical juror.'" Here the court decides that the information had no effect.

Why were the juror's statements to the jury about her experiences using the stove not extraneous?

A This is a closer call. Her account also seems to supplement the record without affording the parties an opportunity to test it by cross-examination. But invariably, jurors will fall back on their experience in assessing the evidence and often talk about it with each other. Isn't that exactly why we use juries as fact-finders? We *want* them to use their common experiences. The issue then is whether lighting a stove is truly part of a juror's common experience, or something that she did because of the case—a juror experiment. In rural Pennsylvania, it may well be common experience to use woodburning stoves, and this juror's experience antedated the case. She did not go home, after hearing the plaintiff's testimony, and conduct an experiment in lighting the stove—which would qualify as extraneous information. *Compare In re Beverly Hills Fire Litig.*, 695 F.2d 207 (6th Cir. 1982) (considering, as extraneous information, evidence that juror went home and conducted an experiment with his electrical outlets, which he reported to the jury in a case in which plaintiffs claimed that fire originated in the electrical wiring).

5. More extraneous information, outside influences, and biased remarks.

About which of the following may a judge take testimony on a motion for a new trial in deciding whether the jury has acted improperly?

A. The jury misunderstood the judge's instruction on proximate causation when the foreman insisted that it meant the same thing as direct causation.
B. The jury consulted *Webster's Dictionary* to decide what proximate causation meant.
C. The jury speculated on whether awarding a large verdict would impact insurance rates.
D. A juror read a passage from the Bible about money-lending to the jury in an action on a debt.
E. During recesses at trial, several jurors imbibed substantial quantities of alcohol, others regularly smoked marijuana, and one ingested cocaine two or three times, with the apparent effect that some of the jurors fell asleep during the trial, and one of them described himself as "flying."
F. In the criminal trial of a Russian immigrant for assault, one juror tells the rest, "Did you see the star tattoos on that guy's neck? I've seen where they are always gang emblems that you get in Russian prisons."

A is pretty clearly not extraneous. It occurred during deliberations and it bears on the jurors' processes. This kind of evidence pierces the heart of deliberations, and if it could be admitted to impeach the verdict, many verdicts would be subject to challenge, and post-trial harassment of jurors would surely increase. Courts have therefore routinely excluded juror testimony about jury confusion in understanding instructions, interrogatories, or the evidence. *Mueller & Kirkpatrick, supra*, § 6.11.

B is just as clearly extraneous, an item of information outside the record. On the other hand, dictionary definitions are part of a jury's common experience. If a juror just recited what he remembered of the definition, this example of juror misconduct would be no different from **A**. And even if a dictionary is extraneous information, a court may well conclude that it was not prejudicial because it was not inconsistent with the jury instruction or would probably not influence a reasonable juror.

C certainly sounds improper. If a jury either cuts back on an award of damages or declines to give one altogether because of concern about the jurors' own insurance rates, the conflict is obvious. Yet, this is again an event that occurred during deliberations and concerned the jury's mental processes. Courts have therefore held that considering evidence of such general speculation is barred by Rule 606(b). *Id.* (citing cases and noting same result for speculation about impact on fees or taxes). One could say that such speculation is part of a jury's common experience as well, although this kind of experience is irrelevant to the jury's fact-finding. The Rule gives a broad protection for the jury's mental processes, which may take them right up against and even well past the rigid boundaries of evidentiary relevancy. Maybe we should put it another way: This is another probably common imperfection that the Rule helps conceal.

D sounds awfully like **B**, but, in the United States, the Bible is still part of the common experience of many jurors, and it is not uncommon for some to carry it with them. Moreover, in hard cases (and, especially, on the criminal side of the aisle, in death penalty cases),

> [i]t is hard to conceive jurors . . . *not* consorting to moral codes that carry meaning in their lives, whether drawn from the Bible, from Kant or for Shakespeare, or from other sources in philosophy or literature, or for that matter film and television and popular culture, and hard to imagine jurors who are in sympathy with the values they glean from such sources ignoring them when they reach the jury room.

Id. § 6.12. Courts have split on this one. Some refuse to consider such evidence on the grounds that Bible verses are common knowledge. But at least one considered the evidence as extraneous prejudicial information, like a dictionary meaning of a legal term or an Internet description of a drug, and therefore admissible. *Id.*

E is harder. Your casebook authors would have admitted juror evidence of this wholesale intake of mind-altering substances on the theory that the substances were outside influences improperly brought to bear on the jurors. (And their objective effect on a juror seems pretty obvious.) A sharply divided Supreme Court held otherwise in *Tanner v. United States*, 483 U.S. 107 (1987), from which these facts were drawn. (The real facts were actually even worse.) The majority reasoned that drugs or alcohol are no more outside influences than a "virus, poorly prepared food, or a lack of sleep." *Id.* at 141. It apparently feared the slippery slope: that holding such influences admissible to impeach the verdict would open the door to many other kinds of evidence of mental or physical impairments for the same purpose. But the result—affirming a criminal conviction by a drug-addled jury—is hard to swallow (no pun intended).

F pretty clearly shows that the juror believes in a stereotype of Russian immigrants, which likely biased him against this defendant. But it is not a "*racial* stereotype" within the meaning of the *Peña-Rodriguez* exception. The jury could hardly avoid seeing the tattoo when the defendant took the stand, but this juror's comment about "gang emblems" is extraneous. Without more information about the evidence at trial, however, it is unclear that it was prejudicial. We doubt that this juror's statements will be admitted to impeach the verdict.

6. Other process errors. Jury misconduct is a particularly riveting kind of process error that may warrant new trial, but there can be many others in the course of trial. These have included:

- errors in jury instructions;
- errors in evidentiary rulings;
- improper argument to the jury;
- lying by a juror during voir dire;
- witness misconduct; and
- inconsistent verdicts that the court cannot reasonably harmonize.

Remember, however, that no process error is ground for new trial unless it was timely, specifically called to the court's attention, and prejudicial, in that it affected substantial rights of the complaining party.

IV. Relief from Judgment

When the time for a post-trial motion or an appeal has passed, the last remaining recourse for a party who wants to challenge the judgment is a Rule 60 motion for relief from a judgment or an order. Unlike the former motions, however, a Rule 60 motion "does not affect the judgment's finality or suspend its operation." Fed. R. Civ. P. 60(c)(2). Rule 60 is applied ungenerously; the courts construe it narrowly and enforce its time limits. The finality provisions provide a hint of why. A party has already had multiple bites at the apple of litigation: trial, post-trial motion practice, and appeal. At some point enough is (almost) enough, and there is a need for finality. People, after all, act on judgments, money changes hands, and parties (and sometimes others who hear of the judgment) alter their conduct. The resulting reliance interests deserve protection.

How does Rule 60 protect such interests? First, it limits the bases for relief from judgment; they are narrower in scope than the grounds for new trial, JMOL, or appeal. That the verdict on which the judgment rests was against the weight of the evidence or even unsupported by sufficient evidence is not one of them, nor are most process errors, unless they involve fraud, misrepresentation, or misconduct by an opposing party. Jury misconduct, for example, is notably missing from the list unless it was a product of party conduct or fraud. Second, even the listed grounds will warrant relief only if the Rule 60(b) motion is brought within a "reasonable time," and no later than one year after entry of judgment for the first three grounds.

The court has broad discretion in granting relief from judgment. In exercising it, courts repeatedly emphasize that Rule 60(b) is not a substitute for appeal, that finality should not be lightly disturbed, that they must consider and protect good faith reliance on the judgment, and that the movant who asks the court to set aside the judgment in order to litigate again must show that it has a meritorious claim or defense. *Moore* § 60.22[2]. The deck is stacked against the motion.

In *Pease v. Pakhoed Corp.*, 980 F. 2d 995 (5th Cir. 1993), for example, the plaintiff had unsuccessfully sought relief under Rule 60(b) from a judgment against him on his retaliatory firing claim, arguing that his lawyer had essentially abandoned his case without telling him. While this might have constituted a ground for relief from judgment under the "excusable neglect" prong of Rule 60(b)(1), the court of appeals stated that "[i]t is well established that Rule 60(b) requires the movant to demonstrate that he possesses a meritorious cause of action." *Id.* at 998. It agreed with the trial court that "[t]he record before us demonstrates that [the plaintiff/appellant] has failed to satisfy this seminal requirement." *Id.*

An exception is the motion for relief from a default judgment. These are often challenged on the grounds that the rendering court lacked personal jurisdiction over the defendant or that service was never properly made. Either defect would render the judgment void, as we saw in earlier chapters, and this is expressly made a basis for relief under Rule 60(b)(4). But even in such cases, where the usual discretionary factors weighing against relief are counter-balanced by the principle that the law disfavors judgment by default, the movant must show that she has a meritorious defense and, often, that she did not contribute to the default by knowing or inexcusable inaction.

V. New Trial and Relief from Judgment: Summary of Basic Principles

- A motion for a new trial must be made no later than twenty-eight days after entry of judgment, but there is no requirement for a motion before the jury deliberates, in contrast to motions for JMOL.
- On a motion for new trial made on the grounds that the verdict is against the weight of the evidence, the court may weigh the evidence and even assess credibility, and it need not resolve reasonable doubts against the movant, unlike motions for JMOL.
- In exercising its discretion to grant the motion, the court should consider the length and complexity of the trial, the importance of credibility determinations, and the jury's comparative fact-finding capacity. The simpler and shorter the trial, and the more important credibility is, the more reluctant a court should be to second-guess the jury.
- When the court concludes that the size of a verdict was against the weight of the evidence and shocks the judicial conscience, it can give the verdict winner the choice of remitting the excess amount of the verdict and accepting instead what the court finds to be a reasonable verdict, or having the verdict set aside and undertaking a new trial. Remittitur is constitutional in federal courts, but additur—making the verdict loser sweeten the damages pot or undergo new trial—is not.
- A court may order a new trial on just damages or liability, or even just on an element of liability, provided that the issue to be retried is distinctly and fairly separable from the remaining issues.
- New trials can also be ordered for an error in the trial process, if the error probably or to a substantial degree affected the right to a fair trial or the jury verdict, and if it was timely and specifically raised by the moving party.
- Process errors based on jury misconduct implicate the rule of evidence that excludes juror testimony to impeach their verdicts. A juror's testimony is inadmissible to show what was said or what occurred during the course of deliberations or what influenced the juror's mental processes, except that it is admissible to show that extraneous prejudicial information was improperly brought to the jury's attention or that any outside influence was brought to bear on any juror.
- If all else fails—meaning post-trial motions for JMOL or new trial and appeal—a party can seek relief from judgment under Rule 60. But Rule 60 motions are not a substitute for these motions or for appeal and are granted only under limited circumstances, such as fraud or misconduct.

PART X

After Final Judgment

32

Appeals

I. Introduction

In American courts, cases are typically litigated in a *trial court*, that is, a court of original jurisdiction where the case is filed, pleadings are submitted, the factual evidence and legal arguments are gathered, pretrial motions are argued and decided, the case is tried, and a judgment is entered for one party or the other. In the course of processing a case from beginning to final judgment, the trial court judge makes many decisions that affect the parties' rights. It is not uncommon for the losing party to have objections to some of those decisions. This chapter introduces basic concepts concerning appellate review of such trial court decision making.

American court systems generally provide litigants who lose in the trial court a right to appeal. This right to appeal almost never includes a chance to retry the case.*

* A common state court exception to this generalization is for appeals from small claims courts or other courts of limited jurisdiction. In such courts, the rules of evidence are not rigorously applied and sometimes no record is made. Appeal is therefore sometimes *de novo*—that is, the cases are retried in a court of broader jurisdiction, often a court of general subject matter jurisdiction that sits at the county level. *See, e.g.*, Md. R. Cir. Ct. 7-112.

Rather, appellate courts review objections to the trial judge's processing of the case below. For example, an appeal might assert that the trial judge had wrongly denied access to important information in discovery, so that the plaintiff could not prove an element of her claim. If this is true, the appellant would not have had a full opportunity to prove her case, and the appellate court could remand the case to the trial court with orders to allow the discovery and retry the case. Or assume that the judge gave the jury an inaccurate instruction on the effect of an affirmative defense. Here again, the error may have affected the jury's verdict—after all, they evaluated the evidence under the wrong legal rules—and the appellate court can correct the error by remanding for a retrial with the proper instruction.

Q **Where is it writ?** You move to the state of Emporia and open a law practice. You lose a case and want to take an appeal. Where would you look to find which appellate courts exist in Emporia and which appellate court has jurisdiction over your appeal? Where would you look for provisions governing the structure and jurisdiction of the federal appellate courts?

A Typically, the structure and jurisdiction of the state appellate courts are governed by state statutes. You would search the Emporia statutes and would find one or more chapters of the Emporia statutory code that set forth the structure, procedures, and jurisdiction of the Emporia appellate courts. These provisions may change from time to time. For example, at one time, appeals from state courts of general jurisdiction were to the highest court in the state. Due to the increase in appellate caseloads, however, many legislatures have created intermediate appellate courts to handle most appeals. The statutes creating these courts define their jurisdiction, as well as the avenues for taking further appeal to the state's highest court. State appellate courts also often issue rules of appellate procedure to which you should look for guidance in handling an appeal.

The statutes governing the federal appellate courts are, naturally, in the United States Code. *For example,* 28 U.S.C. § 41 specifies the geographic composition of the federal circuits; § 44 governs appointment, tenure, residence, and sessions of the federal circuit courts, and §§ 1291 and 1292 govern circuit court jurisdiction over appeals. While the United States Supreme Court is created by the Constitution itself (*see* Article III, Section 1), its structure, sittings, and jurisdiction are regulated by federal statute as well. *See, e.g.,* 28 U.S.C. §§ 1254 and 1257 (specifying cases that may be appealed to the Supreme Court from the lower federal courts and from state courts). Federal courts also have their own Federal Rules of Appellate Procedure, issued (like the Federal Rules of Civil Procedure) pursuant to the Rules Enabling Act.

While appellate courts correct legal errors made by the trial court, they do not generally reevaluate the evidence and overturn findings of fact. For example, if Carlson believes that the jury was wrong in concluding that she ran a red light before an accident, she will not likely get the appellate court to reverse that finding. Appellate courts are created to police the fairness of the trial court process, not to retry cases. For this reason, appellate judges give wide deference to findings of fact by either judges or juries. These findings are not reviewed except at the margins, as Chapter 29 on judgment as a matter of law explains.

This chapter addresses basic issues concerning the appellate process. We start in section II with a short description of the process for presenting and deciding an appeal. In section III, we consider *what* can be appealed: the question of *reviewability*. Section IV then takes up *when* it can be appealed: the question of *appealability*. In the federal courts and most state courts, the question of appealability is dominated by the *finality principle*, by which appeal is ordinarily postponed until there is a final judgment in the case. However, all court systems also entertain some exceptions to this principle, which we survey in section V. Finally, section VI considers the question of the intensity of appellate review or what is often called the *standard or scope of review*.

II. The Process of Presenting and Deciding an Appeal

Assume that Hardin sued Snowbowl, a ski resort operator, for injuries sustained when he was temporarily blinded by a snowmaking machine on Snowbowl's ski slopes. *See Hardin v. Ski Venture, Inc., supra*, p. 1086. Snowbowl pleaded an affirmative defense based on the state's "Skiing Responsibility Act," which protects ski resort operators in the state from liability for "inherent risks." Before the case went to the jury, the judge instructed the jurors that Hardin "would be barred from recovery if he knew of the risk from snowmaking machines." Snowbowl makes a timely objection to the instruction on the grounds that the concept of "inherent risks" also includes risks of which Hardin was unaware. Both the objection and the court ruling are recorded by the court reporter and are thus preserved in the trial transcript.

The jury then renders a verdict for Hardin, and the court enters judgment on the verdict, as neither party files any post-trial motions challenging the verdict. Snowbowl concludes, however, that the judge's instruction was erroneous and that it has prejudiced Snowbowl's case. Specifically, the jury could have found that snowmaking on the slopes posed an inherent risk of skiing, even if Hardin did not know of it. If it had done so, the judge's instruction would have required a verdict for Snowbowl under the state law. Snowbowl therefore decides to appeal. It will begin the appellate process by filing a notice of appeal in the trial court within thirty days after the final judgment, designating "the judgment, order, or part thereof being appealed." *See* Fed. R. App. P. 3(a) (appeal taken in federal courts by filing a notice of appeal with the district court clerk). Note that the process for pursuing an appeal is not governed by the Federal Rules of Civil Procedure. Another set of rules—the Federal Rules of Appellate Procedure—governs appeals in the federal courts. These Rules also provide that had Snowbowl filed a motion for a new trial or for judgment as a matter of law, the time for noticing an appeal would have begun on the date of the court order ruling on that motion. Fed. R. App. P. 4(a)(4)(A). States have separate sets of rules governing appeals.

After filing the notice of appeal, Snowbowl, with the help of the trial court clerk, will compile a documentary record of the proceedings in the trial court relevant to the appeal. These are compiled in a "record appendix," a bound set of documents submitted to the appellate court along with the parties' briefs on the appeal. *See* Fed. R. Civ. P. 30. The record appendix should include all the documents and transcript excerpts necessary for the appellate court to understand the proceedings below relevant to the appellant's claim of error by the trial judge, which are typically fewer than all of the documents in the case. In Snowbowl's appeal, for example, the record appendix would likely include at least the docket entries in the case, the pleadings, a transcript of the argument before the judge about the jury instruction (which would show that Snowbowl's counsel had objected to it), a transcript of the jury instruction the judge actually delivered, the jury's verdict slip, and the judgment entered on the verdict. With these documents before it, the appellate court can understand the context of the decision to which Snowbowl objects and how that decision may have affected the outcome of the case, without having to search the entire record.

Along with the record appendix, Snowbowl will file a brief, which will set forth a statement of the proceedings below, the facts giving rise to the case, a statement of the issue or issues it claims were wrongly decided by the trial judge, a statement of the proper standard of review, and an argument explaining its position on the legal issues it raises on appeal. Hardin will file an appellee's brief in opposition to Snowbowl's legal arguments, and Snowbowl will likely file a "reply brief" trying to refute Hardin's arguments. The length, contents, and even the type size of briefs are governed in excruciating detail by the rules of appellate procedure. *See, e.g.,* Fed. R. App. P. 28–34.

Once the briefs have been filed in the appeals court, that court will assign a panel of judges to decide the appeal. Unlike trial proceedings, which are almost always conducted by a single judge, appeals are typically heard by a panel of three or more judges. (The number varies from court to court.) The three-judge panel may include a district court judge "sitting by designation" to make up for the shortage of appellate judges. Sometimes when different panels of the federal court of appeals for a circuit have reached inconsistent conclusions about a legal issue, the court will grant a *rehearing en banc*—that is, a rehearing by all of the judges of the circuit court (twelve to seventeen judges in most circuits, but theoretically as many as twenty-nine in the Ninth Circuit Court of Appeals).

In this era of crowded dockets, not all cases are granted oral argument. For cases that appear straightforward, the court may decide the case based solely on the record appendix, the briefs, and the court's own research, without granting oral argument. For more complex cases, oral argument would be scheduled, and the parties' lawyers would have a chance to present their positions in person and answer questions from the judges about the appeal.

After the case has been argued, the panel will discuss it, reach a decision on the legal question posed by Snowbowl's appeal, and assign one of the panel judges to write the opinion. Once that opinion has been circulated and approved by the full panel, it will be issued and sent to the parties. It may also be published in the relevant case reporter. In cases the court considers routine or unexceptional, however, it may issue an "unpublished opinion." For a good discussion of all aspects of the appellate process, see Daniel John Meador, Appellate Courts in the United States 47–62 (2d ed. 2006).

Note several things about this process. First, it is not a retrial. No witnesses are heard in person. The judges have a paper record, which (where appropriate) includes a transcript of testimony from the trial. Second, with limited exceptions (e.g., subject matter jurisdiction), the judges don't go looking for problems in the trial process: They consider only issues raised by the appellant. Thus, the appellant shapes the scope of the appeal by the issues she raises on appeal and identifies in her brief, and the court's opinion largely consists of a response to each of those issues. Finally, appellate courts use different standards of review for different types of trial court rulings. These standards of review are analyzed further in section VI of this chapter.

III. What to Appeal: Reviewability

As we said, appellate courts do not search the trial record for error. Life is too short, trial records are too long, and the number of judges are too few to indulge litigants by such efforts. Appellate courts don't sit to assure perfect trials either. They are content to let errors go unless they harmed the appellant. The burden therefore falls on the loser (the "aggrieved party") to object to an error in the trial court—giving the trial judge the first opportunity to cure the error and thereby possibly make an appeal unnecessary—and then to present and argue the error to the appellate court—sparing it the burden of searching the record. In short, for an error in the trial court to be reviewable on appeal, it must ordinarily have been prejudicial, preserved below, and presented above—the "Three Ps."

These issue-specific requirements for reviewability sound easy enough to satisfy, and they are reflected in the Federal Rules. Rule 61 insists that courts disregard all errors that do not affect substantial rights—that is, that were not prejudicial. Called "Harmless Error," this Rule could just as well have been called the "Prejudicial Error Rule." Rule 51 does not ordinarily allow a party to "assign as error" (appeal) an error by the trial court in giving a jury instruction unless the party objected to the error in the trial court (an instance of the preservation requirement).

But though the reviewability requirements seem easy to satisfy, they are still often invoked at the appellate court door to deny judicial review. Insisting on these requirements helps the appellate court to control its own workload and reinforce the authority of the trial courts.

READING *MacARTHUR v. UNIVERSITY OF TEXAS HEALTH CENTER AT TYLER*. In the following case, the plaintiff Cassandra MacArthur violated both the preservation below and presentation above requirements in her appeal. She had filed an employment discrimination action against the University of Texas Health Center and co-workers Painter and Wilson, asserting five claims against the defendants. The jury eventually returned a verdict only against defendant Painter on an intentional infliction of emotional distress claim, and the district court granted a judgment for plaintiff on this claim and dismissed the others. Plaintiff appealed the dismissals, and Painter "cross-appealed"—an appeal filed by the appellee in the same case (he becomes the "appellee/cross-appellant")—the judgment against him. As you read the case, consider the following questions.

- MacArthur clearly included in her notice of appeal and then briefed and argued an error in the dismissal of the Title VII retaliation claim. Why did the court of appeals refuse to consider that claim of error?

- The court of appeals also found that MacArthur "effectively" raised challenges *in her notice of appeal* to the dismissal of her sex discrimination and First Amendment retaliation claims. Why didn't it reach these challenges?
- Can you describe the dilemma in which MacArthur placed herself?

MACARTHUR v. UNIVERSITY OF TEXAS HEALTH CENTER AT TYLER

45 F.3d 890 (5th Cir. 1995)

E. GRADY JOLLY, Circuit Judge. . . .

[EDS.—Plaintiff MacArthur asserted five claims against the defendants:

- **retaliation under the First Amendment**
- **sex discrimination**
- **intentional infliction of emotional distress**
- **violation of Equal Protection Clause**
- **retaliation under Title VII**

She eventually presented only the first three claims to the jury, which returned a verdict for her only on the intentional infliction of emotional distress claim against defendant Painter.

The district court entered judgment for $65,000 on that claim and dismissed the rest. After it also denied MacArthur's motion for new trial, she filed a timely notice of appeal challenging the dismissal of her claims. Painter cross-appealed, attacking the judgment against him on the intentional infliction claim.]

We now turn to examine the underlying judgment to determine what claims and issues are before us—especially focusing on MacArthur's Title VII retaliation claim. The procedural facts concerning this claim are simple. MacArthur pleaded in her complaint a cause of action for retaliation under Title VII, together with First Amendment retaliation, sex discrimination, intentional infliction of emotional distress, and a violation of the Equal Protection Clause. Each of these claims appeared in the pretrial order. It is clear, however, that MacArthur ultimately argued and presented for the jury's determination only three claims: the First Amendment retaliation claim, the sex discrimination claim, and the intentional infliction of emotional distress claim. In her closing argument, MacArthur argued evidence that she contended supported retaliation generally; she did not refer to retaliation based on Title VII at any point during this argument. It is further clear that the district court did not instruct the jury on Title VII retaliation; the court instructed the jury extensively on the law concerning First Amendment retaliation, as well as on the other two claims, but did not say a single word with respect to Title VII retaliation. At the close of the instructions, when given an opportunity to object, MacArthur did not object to the court's failure to instruct on Title VII retaliation. Neither did she object to the omission of any interrogatory to the jury with respect to her Title VII retaliation claim. Her failure to lodge an objection to these omissions of Title VII retaliation is all the more indicative of her intent to abandon the claim because she specifically objected to the omission of an Equal Protection Clause claim, which the court overruled; in other words, her failure to object was not inadvertent as though she were asleep at the switch. In sum, MacArthur failed to argue this claim, failed to have the jury instructed on this claim and failed to submit this claim for the jury's determination and verdict. Under these circumstances, the jury failed to return any verdict with respect to her Title VII retaliation claim. The court specifically stated in the final judgment "*pursuant to the verdict* returned by the jury, the Court enters the following judgment." The court then dismissed, with prejudice, all claims against the defendants, except the claim for intentional infliction of emotional distress, with respect to which it entered judgment for MacArthur. Neither in post-trial motions, nor on appeal, does MacArthur raise as error the district court's failure to instruct the jury or submit an interrogatory on Title VII retaliation. Our review of the record, therefore, demonstrates that MacArthur abandoned her Title VII claim and choose [sic] to travel with her First Amendment claim for retaliation based on the exercise of her right to speak freely.

B

In appealing the final judgment, MacArthur effectively raised her claims of sex discrimination and First Amendment retaliation. She also effectively raised in her notice of appeal, the denial of her motion for a partial new trial. She has abandoned each of these claims on appeal, however, by her failure to argue any of these claims to this court—her brief arguing only error with respect to the Title VII retaliation claim. Although some confusion arose between the parties as to whether MacArthur was appealing her sex discrimination claim, MacArthur clarified this point in her reply brief when she stated that the sole issue on appeal was that of retaliation. Throughout her briefs, this claim of retaliation was consistently referred to as "a discrimination/retaliation case." She explained that she used this label "because the anti-retaliatory provision of Title VII refers to retaliation as another prohibited form of discrimination." Furthermore, MacArthur's sole argument for admissibility of the evidence at the center of this appeal is that its exclusion prevented her from proving pretext as required under Title VII. In her briefs, MacArthur does not refer to her First Amendment retaliation claim a single time. In sum, the only conclusion that can be drawn from the foregoing facts is that MacArthur does not appeal her claim that the retaliation at issue was for exercising her First Amendment rights. *See* Fed. R. App. P. 28(a)(5) [now 28(a)(9)(A)] ("The argument must contain the contentions of the appellant on the issues presented, and the reasons therefor"); *Yohey v. Collins,* 985 F.2d 222, 225 (5th Cir. 1993) (holding that appellant abandoned argument by failing to argue it in body of brief). Instead, on appeal MacArthur apparently made a strategic determination that in retrospect a Title VII retaliation claim was a stronger basis for her sole argument on appeal that the district court erred in excluding comparative evidence to establish disparate treatment.

Thus, in conclusion, we must dismiss this appeal. We do so on the basis that the one claim that she raises—Title VII retaliation—was abandoned at the district court, thus is not embodied in the district court judgment, and consequently is not before this court on appeal. With respect to the claims that were presented to the jury and that are embodied in the district court's final judgment, she has abandoned these claims on appeal by failure to brief and argue. MacArthur's appeal is therefore dismissed....

III

[Eds.—On Painter's cross-appeal, the court found that there was insufficient evidence to support the jury's finding for MacArthur on the emotional distress claim and therefore reversed and rendered judgment for defendant Painter.] ...

IV

In sum, we dismiss MacArthur's Title VII retaliation claim because she failed to argue or present it to the jury. As to the jury's verdict on the claim of intentional infliction of emotional distress, we REVERSE and RENDER judgment in favor of defendant Painter. For the foregoing reasons, this appeal is DISMISSED and the judgment of the district court is REVERSED and RENDERED....

Notes and Questions: *MacArthur* and the Three Ps

Q **1. Prejudice and harmless error.** "It is more than well-settled that a party cannot appeal from a judgment unless 'aggrieved' by it." *In the Matter of Sims*, 994 F.2d 210, 214 (5th Cir. 1993). MacArthur was clearly aggrieved by the dismissal of all but one of her claims.

Suppose, however, that her claim of error was that the trial court had erroneously admitted evidence against her that was cumulative and duplicative and therefore should have been excluded under the Federal Rules of Evidence.

A If it was cumulative and duplicative, what harm could it have caused? By her own argument, there was already sufficient properly admitted evidence against her; this was just more of the same. Rule 61—the Rule of "Harmless Error"—teaches that "[u]nless justice requires otherwise, no error in admitting or excluding evidence—or any other error by the court or a party—is ground for ... vacating, modifying, or otherwise disturbing a judgment or order."

The requirement of prejudice, therefore, goes not only to the result below—the judgment or order of the trial court—but also to specific claims of error made in challenging that result on appeal. Harmless errors are not just common, but very possibly ubiquitous. Still, perfect trials are not necessary to give substantial justice.

Q **2. Preservation below: Making timely objections or arguments in the trial court.** MacArthur's brief argued that the trial court erred in entering judgment against her on the Title VII retaliation claim. Why did the court of appeals refuse to review that claim of error?

A Because she effectively abandoned it at trial and therefore failed to preserve it for appeal. She never mentioned it in her closing argument to the jury; she never asked the trial court to instruct the jury about it; and she then failed to object to the omission of any instruction on it. *See* Fed. R. Civ. P. 51(d) (allowing a party to assign errors to jury instructions only if the party properly objected or requested an omitted instruction). Nor did she object to the omission of any interrogatory about the Title VII retaliation claim in the special verdict, an omission the court of appeals deemed "not inadvertent" because she *did* object to another omission. *See* Fed. R. Civ. P. 49(a)(3) (a party waives the right to jury trial for issues omitted from a special verdict). The record thus showed conclusively that she abandoned her Title VII retaliation claim at trial and chose to put all her retaliation eggs in the First Amendment basket. In sum, a party must preserve a claim of error by timely objection in the trial court—"making a record"—or it cannot raise the objection on appeal. Moreover, the objection or request must be sufficiently clear and timely that the trial court can understand and decide it. *See Keelan v. Majesco Software, Inc.*, 407 F.3d 332, 340 (5th Cir. 2005) ("An argument must be raised 'to such a degree that the district court has an opportunity to rule on it.'"). By failing to follow these procedures, MacArthur failed to preserve her objections and requests concerning the Title VII retaliation claim.

Q **3. The reasons for the preservation requirement.** The reasons for the "preservation below" requirement are suggested by *MacArthur*. What would have happened had MacArthur requested an instruction and an interrogatory on the Title VII retaliation claim?

A The trial court might have included them, and the claim would therefore properly have gone to the jury. If the jury returned a verdict for MacArthur on that claim, she would have had no reason to appeal it (as she would not have been aggrieved by a favorable judgment on that verdict). In fact, she might not have appealed at all, content with recovering on two of her claims and therefore willing to let the others go. Alternatively, had the trial court denied her requests, it might have explained why, providing a more complete record (and possibly a persuasive argument) for the court of appeals. Either way, the defendants would have been on notice of her request and thus had an opportunity to respond.

Thus, the preservation below requirement "eases appellate review 'by having the district court first consider the issue'" and "ensures fairness to litigants by preventing surprise issues from appearing on appeal." *Scottsdale Ins. Co. v. Flowers*, 513 F.3d 546, 552 (6th Cir. 2008) (internal citation omitted). It reduces the likelihood of sandbagging by MacArthur—holding the claim of error in reserve to see what happens. Without such a requirement, MacArthur could simply hold her tongue while she knows that the trial judge has misinstructed the jury on a point of law, reserving her objection for appeal in case she loses the case. But such sandbagging is a waste of judicial resources, because, had she instead objected at the time, the trial court might have fixed its instruction, curing the error and making an appeal, reversal, and remand for a new trial unnecessary.

Q **4. Exceptions to the preservation requirement.** The rule of preservation below is not absolute, however. There are several narrowly construed exceptions:

> First, an appellate court will consider an issue not raised in the district court if it involves a pure question of law, and if refusal to consider it would result in a miscarriage of justice. Second, the rule may be relaxed where the appellant raises an objection to an order which he had no opportunity to raise at the district court level. Third, the rule does not bar consideration by the appellate court in the first instance where the interest of substantial justice is at stake. Fourth, a federal appellate court is justified in resolving an issue not passed on below . . . where the proper resolution is beyond any doubt. Finally, it may be appropriate to consider an issue first raised on appeal if that issue presents significant questions of general impact or of great public concern.

Narey v. Dean, 32 F.3d 1521, 1526–27 (11th Cir. 1994) (footnotes and citations omitted).

The third exception noted here is also sometimes called *the plain error doctrine*. The doctrine is expressly codified for claims of error in jury instructions by Rule 51(d)(2), but it has been applied to other errors as well. *Wright & Miller* § 856.

Did MacArthur's claim of error in excluding the evidence of pretext fall under any of these exceptions?

A No. First, most evidentiary rulings do not present pure questions of law, but merely questions of abuse of discretion. Second, MacArthur had multiple opportunities to preserve her claim of Title VII retaliation to which the evidence was allegedly relevant, but passed on them. Third, it's hard to argue that intentionally self-inflicted wounds cause substantial injustice or raise issues of public concern. Her apparently intentional omission of the Title VII retaliation claim to which this evidence was relevant undercuts all of the exceptions. Fourth, even had her abandonment of her claim been inadvertent, the error she claims—the improper exclusion of some evidence of pretext—seems to have no great public impact or public interest. The plain error doctrine and the related exceptions to the preservation requirement are narrow escape hatches, and MacArthur can't fit through them.

Q **5. Presentation above: Raising preserved issues in the appellate court.** The court of appeals properly refused to hear MacArthur's claim of error in excluding evidence relevant to the Title VII retaliation claim that MacArthur briefed, because she failed to preserve that claim below. But why did it then also refuse to consider her arguments concerning the sex discrimination and First Amendment claims that *were* preserved below in the trial court?

A

She abandoned these on appeal by failing to brief them to the appellate court. The only argument she briefed and argued was the Title VII retaliation claim. It is not enough to list an error as an "issue presented" in the brief, if the brief then completely fails to develop it. "The argument . . . must contain the appellant's contentions and the reasons for them. . . ." Fed. R. App. P. 28(a)(8)(A). In other words, you usually can't ask the court of appeals to hear a claim of error and then fail to give it any guidance in your briefs for ruling on the claim.

Requiring the issue to be "presented" on appeal serves another purpose as well: Providing notice to the appellee of the issue and related arguments so that it can brief counter-arguments. Indeed, courts of appeals have held that raising a claim of error for the first time in the appellant's last brief (usually the *reply brief*, to which the appellee does not usually get to respond) is too late for just this reason.

6. MacArthur's self-imposed dilemma. MacArthur's dilemma is crisply described by the court of appeals:

> [T]he only claim that she raises—Title VII retaliation—was abandoned at the district court. . . . With respect to the claims that were presented to the jury and that are embodied in the . . . judgment, she has abandoned these claims by failure to brief and argue.

That is, the claim she raised in her appeal was waived by her failure to present it to the trial court, while the claims she did present to the trial court were waived by her failure to present them (by argument) to the appeals court. Ironically, then, the only issue properly before the court of appeals was Painter's cross-appeal on the one claim that MacArthur won, which the court then reversed for insufficient evidence. Talk about a comedy of errors.

Q

7. Attacking or supporting the judgment on alternative grounds. Suppose Painter had not cross-appealed. In responding to MacArthur's appeal, could he ask the court to reverse the judgment against him?

A

No, because the requirement for presentation above applies to Painter as well. As the appellee, Painter cannot *attack* the judgment by asking the court to change or enlarge the judgment without filing a cross-appeal. However, he is free to make any argument that is supported by the record to *support* the judgment (e.g., to argue for affirmance), even if he did not make the argument below and has not cross-appealed. For example, suppose the judgment on appeal was for the defendant Neighbor in a trespass case, based on the trial court's finding that the plaintiff Blackacre had given Neighbor an easement. But the trial record also includes evidence that Blackacre had given defendant Neighbor permission to go on the property, even though the trial court did not rely upon this ground in ruling for Neighbor. On Blackacre's appeal, Neighbor, as appellee, can argue that the court of appeals should affirm the judgment either on grounds of the easement *or,* in the alternative and without his having to file a cross-appeal, on grounds of permission.

A Generally, "a cross-appeal is required to support modification of a judgment, but . . . arguments that support the judgment as entered can be made without a cross-appeal." *Wright & Miller* § 3904.

Why the difference? Perhaps because an important systemic goal is finality, and each principle in its own way promotes this goal. Forbidding a party to *attack* a judgment unless it has cross-appealed promotes finality by reducing the number of judgments that are reversed. Allowing a party to make alternate arguments to *support* a judgment, on the other hand, promotes finality by increasing the number of judgments that are affirmed. *See Richison v. Ernest Group, Inc.*, 634 F.3d 1123, 1130 (10th Cir. 2011) ("Because of the cost and risk involved anytime we upset a court's reasoned judgment, we are ready to affirm whenever the record allows it. So it is that appellants must always shoulder a heavy burden—they must come ready *both* to show the district court's error and, when necessary, to explain why no other grounds can support affirmance of the district court's decision."). In our hypothetical, this principle gives the court of appeals an alternate basis on which to affirm the judgment. It thus also saves the cost of remanding for the trial court to consider the alternate grounds.

Q **8. Reviewability.** Which of the following claims is reviewable in the court of appeals? If your answer depends on action by the appellant in the trial court or on appeal, what action?

A. The appellant asserts that the judge committed error by failing to instruct the jury on the defense of assumption of the risk.

A Jury instructions have their own rule, and their own exacting requirements for preservation below. Rule 51(d)(1)(B) requires that a party may assign error to the failure to give an instruction only if the party properly requested it *and* also properly objected. (The Rule makes an objection unnecessary when the court has rejected the request in a "definitive ruling on the record," since then the ruling itself preserves the record.) Thus, **A** is not reviewable if the defendant failed to comply with these requirements. Nor does the omission look like a plain error affecting substantial rights.

B. The appellant asserts that the judge committed error by refusing to admit a documentary exhibit it offered.

A **B** is reviewable only if the proponent of the exhibit objected at the time to its exclusion and if the exclusion was prejudicial in light of all the other evidence. Often, this kind of evidentiary error is found harmless in light of the full record.

C. The appellee argues in its opposition brief on appeal that the judgment should be increased because the district court improperly disallowed attorneys' fees.

A **C** is an argument to modify the judgment, not just to affirm it on some alternate theory. Modification requires an appeal, or in the case of the appellee, a cross-appeal. This claim is not reviewable.

D. The appellant, who was the losing defendant below, argues that the lawyer for the plaintiff in an action for damages based on a car accident, repeatedly (and without objection by defendant's lawyer) identified the defendant as a "wetback" and an "illegal immigrant," who "uses public services without paying his fair share."

A

D looks like an error that was waived by the failure to object. But it also looks like an egregiously improper argument to the jury that is highly likely to have inflamed prejudices and influenced the jury verdict. This may be the rare case in which the plain error exception will bail out the defendant; a court of appeals is unlikely to leave this ugly blemish on the judicial process by refusing to hear the claim of error.

E. The appellee argues in its brief on appeal that the judgment below is supported by a legal theory that it had not previously advanced and that the lower court did not discuss.

A

E differs from **C** in that now the appellee is simply trying to *affirm* the judgment below with an alternate legal theory. Provided that the theory is supported by the record, it does not matter that it was never presented below and is not the subject of a cross-appeal. Affirming on any legal theory supported by the record serves the interests of finality and does not prejudice the appellant, who, after all, could have offered a rebuttal when the requisite record was made in the trial court and who will still be able to oppose the alternate argument for affirmance in a reply brief in the appeals court.

IV. When to Appeal: Appealability and the Finality Principle

A reviewable matter is not necessarily appealable. Appealability refers to *when* a matter can be appealed, one of the most vexing issues of any appellate system. Allow appeal too soon and you not only interrupt the trial court, but potentially inundate the appeals courts with many appeals that would have been mooted had the trial court been allowed to complete its work.

For example, suppose Penders's motion to compel discovery from Desmond is denied on the grounds that the documents are irrelevant. If we allow Penders to appeal the discovery ruling immediately, not only could it disrupt the litigation in the trial court (it might stop the case by issuing a "stay" until the appeal was decided), but it would occasion an appellate decision that could have been avoided if the case were allowed to go to trial and Penders won. Furthermore, this discovery ruling is probably just one of many. Any dilatory consequences of allowing interlocutory appeal are multiplied by the number of interlocutory decisions that can be appealed. *See Mohawk Indus., Inc. v. Carpenter*, 558 U.S. 100, 112 (2009) (asserting that "piecemeal appeals of all adverse attorney-client rulings would unduly delay the resolution of district court litigation and needlessly burden the Courts of Appeals" and citing *Wright & Miller* § 3914.23 ("Routine appeal from disputed discovery orders would disrupt the orderly progress of the litigation, swamp the courts of appeals, and substantially reduce the district court's ability to control the discovery process.")). Finally, most appeals fail. In 2019, the federal courts of appeals affirmed (in whole or in part) approximately 65 percent and reversed only approximately 8.2 percent of the total number of appeals that were terminated on the merits.* The figures suggest that the majority of interlocutory appeals would fare no better, so allowing more of them would not contribute much to better judicial outcomes.

On the other hand, if the appeal is not permitted until later, irreversible harm can sometimes befall a party during the delay. For example, suppose the trial court refuses Penders's motion for a preliminary injunction to stop Desmond from releasing wastewater that Penders claims is ruining his crops. If the validity of this denial is not reviewed until after trial and a final judgment in the case, Penders's crops may be destroyed.

In subsection A, we explore the *finality principle*—also commonly called *the final judgment rule*—which usually requires that appeal be postponed until there has been a final decision in the federal court. In subsection B, we see that even "final decision" is a flexible concept that has been interpreted to allow appeals of certain "collateral" decisions that are effectively unreviewable on appeal from a final judgment because delayed review would imperil important interests. Subsection C also shows that some otherwise non-final decisions can be declared final by the trial court.

A. The Finality Principle (a/k/a "The Final Judgment Rule")

Suppose that in the *MacArthur* litigation, the trial court had granted the defendants' Rule 12(b)(6) motion to dismiss the intentional infliction claim for failure to state a claim, but denied it as to her other claims. Could she immediately appeal the dismissal of the one claim?

For the federal courts, the answer to this question is provided, in most cases, by 28 U.S.C. § 1291: "The courts of appeals . . . shall have jurisdiction from all final decisions of the district courts of the United States. . . ." The term "final decision" in § 1291 has generally been interpreted to mean a final decision *of the case*, the conclusion of the litigation in the federal district court, leading to entry of judgment for one party or the other. A final decision "is one which ends the litigation on the merits and leaves nothing for the [trial] court to do but execute the judgment." *Catlin v. United States*, 324 U.S. 229, 233 (1945). "The statutory requirement of a 'final decision' means that 'a party must ordinarily raise all claims of error in a single appeal following final judgment on the merits.'" *Richardson-Merrell, Inc. v. Koller*, 472 U.S. 424, 429–30 (1985) (quoting *Firestone Tire & Rubber Co. v. Risjord*, 449 U.S. 368, 374 (1981)). In this variant on MacArthur's case, final judgment has not been entered in the trial court—her other claims still have to be litigated and the trial court will enter no final judgment in the case until they are resolved.

* *See* Table B-5, U.S. Courts of Appeals Statistical Tables for the Federal Judiciary (Dec. 31, 2019) ("*Statistical Tables*"), https://www.uscourts.gov/statistics/table/b-5/statistical-tables-federal-judiciary/2019/12/31. The totals exclude cases in the Federal Circuit.

Thus, under § 1291, MacArthur could not, without more, appeal the dismissal of her intentional infliction claim *at this point*. Instead, she could "save it up" to assert (perhaps alongside other claims of error) in her appeal from an eventual final judgment on all of the remaining claims.

Decisions like the hypothetical grant of defendants' Rule 12(b)(6) motion to dismiss one of MacArthur's claims are *interlocutory* (falling between the beginning and end of the lawsuit). Appeals from interlocutory decisions are called, sensibly enough, *interlocutory appeals*.

READING *IN RE RECTICEL FOAM CORP.* In this complex, mass disaster litigation, the court issued an ambitious case management order to regulate the protracted, wide-ranging, and expensive discovery that you would expect in any litigation involving two thousand plaintiffs and two hundred defendants. The order required the defendants to share some of the considerable expense of reproducing certain videotapes. Codefendant Recticel Foam Corp. (RFC) objected and sought an interlocutory appeal.

- Why wasn't the cost-sharing order a final decision within the meaning of 28 U.S.C. § 1291?
- Why wasn't the order appealable under the collateral order doctrine?
- How is the collateral order doctrine consistent with 28 U.S.C. § 1291?

San Juan Hotel Fire

AP Photo

The Dupont Plaza Hotel fire occurred in San Juan, Puerto Rico on New Year's Eve, December 31, 1986. The fire was set by three disgruntled hotel employees who were in the middle of a labor dispute with the owners of the hotel. Claiming ninety-six lives and causing approximately one hundred and forty injuries, it is considered the most catastrophic hotel fire in Puerto Rican history.

The fire gave rise to suits by nearly two thousand plaintiffs against roughly two hundred defendants. The federal suits were consolidated for discovery purposes, resulting in the following decision, among others.

IN RE RECTICEL FOAM CORP.

859 F.2d 1000 (1st Cir. 1988)

Selya, Circuit Judge.

There are two consolidated matters before us at this juncture. They are an odd couple: an interlocutory appeal and a petition for writ of mandamus [discussed *infra* at p. 1178]. Because we find that the challenged orders (1) are not "final" within the purview of 28 U.S.C. § 1291 (1982), (2) do not come within the encincture of our jurisdiction under any recognized exception to the finality principle, and (3) are not suitable grist for the rarely-used mandamus mill, we pretermit the present proceedings shy of the merits. **[Eds.—The court means that, by finding that the issues are not yet appealable, it avoids deciding their merits.]**

I. BACKGROUND

[Eds.—The San Juan hotel fire caused ninety-six deaths and resulted in lawsuits pitting nearly two thousand plaintiffs against two hundred defendants. The cases were consolidated for discovery purposes in a single district court, which issued an elaborate case management order (CMO) to handle discovery, appointed liaison counsel for plaintiffs and defendants, established a document depository, and formed a joint discovery committee (JDC) of lawyers on both sides.

With the blessing of the JDC, a codefendant moved to compel production of various videotapes and photographs. The holder of the images initially objected on work product grounds. But it eventually agreed to waive the work product immunity in exchange for reimbursement of one-half the $600,000 cost of generating the images. The district court ratified the agreement, ordering all served defendants to share in the expense. Codefendant RFC objected. It unsuccessfully sought reconsideration of the cost-sharing order and then appealed the ensuing denial.]

II. THE APPEAL

It is too elementary to warrant citation of authority that a court has an obligation to inquire sua sponte into its subject matter jurisdiction, and to proceed no further if such jurisdiction is wanting. As we recently stated: "No matter how tantalizing a problem may be, a federal appellate court cannot scratch intellectual itches unless it has jurisdiction to reach them." *Director, OWCP v. Bath Iron Works Corp.*, 853 F.2d 11, 13 (1st Cir. 1988). In this instance, we are persuaded that jurisdictional constraints preclude us from inquiring into the merits of RFC's appeal.

A. The Finality Principle.

Our jurisdiction over appeals stems primarily from 28 U.S.C. § 1291, which provides that the courts of appeals may review "final decisions of the district courts of the United States." An order is usually considered "final" only when it "resolv[es] the contested matter, leaving nothing to be done except execution of the judgment." *United States v. Metropolitan Dist. Comm'n,* 847 F.2d 12, 14 (1st Cir. 1988).

Discovery orders, in general, are not final. Short of electing not to comply and being adjudged in criminal contempt, a party may ordinarily obtain review of such an order only after judgment has entered. Although pretrial cost-sharing orders can validly be characterized as case management orders rather than as "pure" discovery orders, the characterization is not dispositive. Federal jurisdiction cannot be dictated by the simple expedient of artful labelling.

The similarity between discovery orders and case management orders is, we suggest, striking. In both instances, the main litigation continues to pend in the district court, as to all parties. In both instances, the orders deal with preliminary matters, leading up to—but not comprising—the main event. In both instances, the activities to which the orders relate tend to be frequent, repetitive, fragmentary, and bound up in the progress of the suit as a whole. Whether or not case management orders are discovery orders in the conventional sense, they are sufficiently akin to discovery orders to warrant precisely the same treatment under the finality principle.

Having determined that, in the usual case, orders issued incident to a CMO are on a par with discovery orders vis-à-vis finality concerns, we now discuss those considerations which, in this instance, weigh against appellate jurisdiction. In the first place, the cost-sharing orders do not seem "final." Not only does the pot continue to boil furiously below, but the rights of the parties are not settled by the disputed orders in any relevant sense. Although the orders require some temporary shifting of funds, they do not purport to resolve any party's rights in any definitive way. Given the district court's continued exercise of jurisdiction, the orders remain subject to modification. *See* Fed. R. Civ. P. 26(f) (orders relating to "proper management of discovery . . . may be altered or amended"). The district court can reassess their content, and make adjustments as it thinks best. The orders work less than an immutable rejection of Recticel's position because no *irreversible* legal consequences flow from them, as they presently stand.

Nor are the orders "final" in a monetary sense. The costs in question continue to mount, and further orders will doubtless be forthcoming. The fact that we are being asked to review what are admittedly the first flurry of a potential blizzard of similar orders argues strongly against their finality. Here, as with discovery orders generally, interruption of the ongoing process carries with it a potentially high price in terms of diminished efficiency. Moreover, to the extent that an inquiry into finality requires "some evaluation of . . . competing considerations," *Eisen v. Carlisle & Jacquelin,* 417 U.S. 156, 171 (1974), we believe that the dangers inherent in piecemeal review of cost-sharing orders[3] far overbalance any realistic possibility of denying justice by a delay in appellate oversight. As we said in *Bath Iron Works,*

3. We need not recite chapter and verse as to these dangers. We have warned, time and again, of the perils inherent in leaving "the way clear for the four horsemen of too easily available piecemeal appellate review: congestion, duplication, delay, and added expense." *Spiegel v. Trustees of Tufts College,* 843 F.2d 38, 46 (1st Cir. 1988).

> ... [M]erely saying that it would be "practical" to hear an appeal at an earlier time does not make it so. The kind of practical consideration which would warrant a departure from so well settled a principle [as finality] requires, at the least, some specialized showing of out-of-the-ordinary circumstances. These might include, say, a demonstration that what remained to be done was self-executing, or that cognizable harm of an unusual sort would result from delay, or that blind adherence to the letter of the finality principle would work some great injustice or grave systemic diseconomy. A petitioner, we think, has the burden of making the specialized showing needed to complete the arduous climb over the jurisdictional threshold.

Director, OWCP v. Bath Iron Works Corp., at 14. Having stated the task, it is readily evident that RFC's jeremiad is entirely inadequate to it. The cost-sharing orders are nonfinal, hence nonappealable, unless appellate jurisdiction attaches in some other fashion.

B. The Collateral Order Exception.

The only detour around the finality principle which could conceivably make ends meet in this instance is the so-called "collateral order" exception. *See Cohen v. Beneficial Industrial Loan Corp.*, 337 U.S. 541, 545–47 (1949). Collaterality, in the *Cohen* sense, demands conformity to certain hard-and-fast essentials:

> The order must involve: (1) an issue essentially unrelated to the merits of the main dispute, capable of review without disrupting the main trial; (2) a complete resolution of the issue, not one that is "unfinished" or "inconclusive"; (3) a right incapable of vindication on appeal from final judgment; and (4) an important and unsettled question of controlling law, not merely a question of the proper exercise of the trial court's discretion.

United States v. Sorren, 605 F.2d 1211, 1213 (1st Cir. 1979); *accord* [*Boreri v. Fiat S.P.A.*, 763 F.2d 17, 21 (1st Cir. 1985)]. We have styled the four requisites as comprising "separability, finality, urgency and importance." *In re Continental Investment Corp.*, 637 F.2d 1, 4 (1st Cir. 1980). Not surprisingly, discovery orders rarely satisfy all four of these criteria. By analogy, the same can be said of case management orders and CMO derivatives.

It is at least arguable that the particular cost-sharing orders of which Recticel complains meet *none* of these four requirements. In multi-party, multi-case litigation, the district court's success is largely dependent upon its ability to uncomplicate matters. In that endeavor, the case management order is one of the court's trustiest tools. It is central to, and in a sense inextricably intertwined with, the main case. Flinging sand in the finely-tuned case management gears has the unhappy potential for bringing the entire litigation to a grinding halt. Then, too, the issue of how to defray aggregate costs is not finished business: the costs are ongoing, the district court retains jurisdiction, and further orders can (and doubtless will) be forthcoming. Lastly, although we express no firm opinion on the subject, we are skeptical that a district court's authority to impose reasonable cost-sharing orders in multi-district litigation is much in doubt. *See, e.g.,* Fed. R. Civ. P. 26(f) (court's order following discovery conference may "includ[e] the allocation of expenses" anent discovery). The interposition of a jurisdictional defense seems to us flimsy armor against the force of that authority.

We need not dredge these waters too deeply, for this circuit has long held to the view that "urgency"—the likelihood of irreparable harm from a delay in obtaining review of the dispute—is the "central focus," if not the "dispositive criterion" in the *Cohen* equation. *Boreri,* 763 F.2d at 21 (quoting *In re San Juan Star Co.,* 662 F.2d 108, 112 (1st Cir. 1981)). Because RFC cannot swim this channel, it fails the *Cohen* test. Detailed discussion of the remaining criteria becomes, therefore, supererogatory.

We think this appeal not "urgent" within the usage of that term in our jurisprudence for several reasons. First, if the district court eventually denies RFC's motion to dismiss, petitioner-appellant's position with respect to the cost-sharing orders is then virtually indistinguishable from that of a swarm of other parties. In that event, the power of the district court to issue those orders, the extent of its discretion to utilize various allocation methods, and a myriad of like issues, will be appealable after final judgment. Nothing will be lost: money wrongfully paid by one party to another can be restored by judicial decree. Conversely, much will be gained: series of inchmeal attacks on successive cost-sharing orders will be avoided, and an appeal at the end of the litigation will permit resolution of the issue with the participation of *all* interested parties—not merely Recticel alone. This appears to us a fairer, more expedient, and more efficient procedure than RFC's scattershot approach.

Placing the shoe on the other foot does not alter the fit. Should the district court eventually grant the dismissal motion, petitioner-appellant's rights pertaining to these orders would not be irretrievably lost. A district court which has the power to allocate litigation costs retains continuing control over the allocation of those costs during the entire pretrial period (and beyond). Wholly apart from the adjudication of Recticel's dismissal motion, we believe that the district court can reshape and refashion its cost-sharing orders as new information comes to light, or as information already known takes on added significance. *See* Fed. R. Civ. P. 26(f) (discovery order "may be altered or amended whenever justice so requires"). That being so, it is certain beyond peradventure that the district court can—and, in materially changed circumstances, should—entertain motions for the reallocation of expenses. If RFC prevails on jurisdictional grounds, such a motion will be available to it. If the motion to reallocate is granted, the problem disappears. If denied, any error could presumably be rectified on appeal from the eventual final judgment in the case, or RFC could apply for the entry of a judgment under Fed. R. Civ. P. 54(b), so as to pave the way for an earlier appeal. In any event, the right to efficacious review would not be lost.

Because petitioner-appellant's claim is fully capable of vindication on appeal from final judgment in the usual course, and Recticel would suffer no irreparable harm from waiting its turn, the urgency prong of *Cohen* has not been met. Thus, we have no jurisdiction over this appeal under the collateral order doctrine. *See Van Cauwenberghe v. Biard,* 486 U.S. 517 (1988) (if claim "is effectively reviewable on appeal from final judgment, [it] is not an immediately appealable collateral order under *Cohen*")....

IV. CONCLUSION

We prize strict adherence to the rules which define and delimit our jurisdiction. The finality principle, in particular, should be accorded great deference. The Court has termed it "crucial to the efficient administration of justice." *Flanagan v. United States,* 465 U.S. 259, 264 (1984). Moreover, the importance of the finality requirement is at its zenith in large cases such as this. The finality rule, after all, was designed to conserve judicial energy and eliminate the "delay, harassment and cost" that would result from a barrage of interlocutory appeals. *Manual for Complex Litigation 2d* § 25.1 (1985). The disruptive potential of successive interlocutory appeals is magnified in complex cases such as the one before us, where the district judge has made—and must yet make—numerous pretrial rulings, all of which are interrelated and tied into an integrated case management scheme. It follows ineluctably that "[w]e should not rush to deviate from [the final judgment rule], nor should we do so lightly." *Director, OWCP v. Bath Iron Works Corp.,* at 16.

In the circumstances of this case, we abjure premature intrusion into precincts which are, for the present, reserved to the district court. It would disserve the proper relationship between trial and appellate courts in the federal system, and wreak havoc with the taxing demands of modern-day case management, were the court of appeals gratuitously to inject itself as a super-navigator of sorts, second-guessing the district court from turn to turn as that tribunal wended its way through the thickets and brambles of complex litigation. To do so, we suggest, would be to concentrate on the trees at the expense of a balanced vision of the forest.

We need go no further. The cost-sharing orders are not final within the intendment of 28 U.S.C. § 1291; the *Cohen* exception to the finality principle does not apply; and there is no other hook upon which appellate jurisdiction may suitably be hung.... The merits of the cost-sharing controversy are not properly before us in this proceeding.

In No. 88-1298, the appeal is dismissed without prejudice for want of appellate jurisdiction....

Notes and Questions: The Finality Principle

Q **1. Subject matter jurisdiction again?** The court of appeals begins by reciting the dog-eared truism that a court must "inquire sua sponte into its subject matter jurisdiction." Yet, it does not discuss diversity jurisdiction (on which the original litigation was premised) or federal question jurisdiction. What subject matter jurisdiction is it talking about?

A Diversity and federal question go to the federal courts' original subject matter jurisdiction generally, but an appeals court must also inquire into its *appellate* subject matter jurisdiction. Section 1291 is the chief grant of federal appellate jurisdiction. It is not enough that the parties agree that a matter is appealable. The court of appeals must satisfy itself. Thus, whether or not the plaintiffs raised the point, the court of appeals must find that the cost-sharing order qualifies as a "final decision" under § 1291, some other statutory grant of jurisdiction, or a recognized exception. Most appellate decisions therefore appropriately start with an examination of their appellate subject matter jurisdiction over the case, although this portion of the decision is typically edited out of the ones you read in your casebooks.

Q **2. Why isn't the cost-sharing order final?** The question of cost-sharing came before the trial judge, he decided the question and he issued his decision in an order. Why isn't that enough to allow appeal under 28 U.S.C. § 1291?

A The order was made early in the case to help manage discovery. Discovery orders are preliminary—they deal with a pretrial phase of the case. Even if this order is characterized as case management, rather than discovery per se, it is surely part of events "leading up to—but not comprising—the main event." These preliminary events, as the court notes, tend to be "frequent, repetitive, fragmentary, and bound up in the progress of the case as a whole," the intuitive antithesis of a culminating final decision and the apotheosis of an interlocutory decision. (Judge Selya's affinity for language is catching.)

Moreover, this order is not even final in the sense that it is the last directed to the issue. The court can revisit it and make adjustments if the expenses get too high. Its rejection of RFC's position is neither "immutable," nor likely to carry irreversible consequences.

Finally, it is also not final because we don't yet know what the total cost will be. The court of appeals says that "[t]he costs in question continue to mount," and their size may affect the fairness of the order; making RFC pay $1,200 poses a different question than making it pay $120,000.

Q **3. What are the costs of allowing interlocutory appeal?** Because of the fragmented and repetitive nature of many preliminary litigation activities and orders, interlocutory review would inevitably be piecemeal review, threatening to bring pieces of the case up to the court of appeals repeatedly. Why does the court of appeals in *Recticel* say that the "four horsemen of too easily available piecemeal appellate review [are] congestion, duplication, delay, and added expense"?

A *Congestion*. The more pieces that can be appealed, the more appeals there will be. This could lead to congestion in appellate dockets. In 2019, more than 49,000 appeals were commenced in the federal courts of appeals,* the vast majority of which were appeals from final judgments. Every interlocutory appeal permitted from decisions in preliminary matters would increase this figure (indeed, it is quite likely that there would be one or more interlocutory appeals for every appeal of a final judgment).

* *Statistical Tables*, *supra*, Table B.

> *Duplication.* To the extent that some of these interlocutory appeals raise issues that overlap with the merits, they would also pose costs of duplication, because the appellate courts could end up revisiting the overlapping matter on an appeal of the final judgment.
>
> *Delay.* Some interlocutory appeals could also bring the district court proceedings to a standstill, either because the appellant obtained a stay of the trial court proceedings from the court of appeals or just because the trial court might say, "Let's wait and see so we don't have to retrace our path." If trial court proceedings are suspended pending the appeal, a year could well go by for the briefing, argument, and decision of the appeal.
>
> *Expense.* Finally, all of this adds expense. Instead of a single set of briefs collecting all of the errors in a single appeal of the final judgment, we'd have one set for every interlocutory appeal, not to mention the investment of appellate resources reading them and deciding the issues they present. The real expense, however, is that of one or more unnecessary appeals. This is because interlocutory appeals would raise issues that would *never be taken up on appeal of a final judgment.* A very large number of cases settle, so no appeal is taken, even if parties believe the trial judge made erroneous rulings. If the case does not settle, one party will win. As we have seen, because she won, she will not be allowed to appeal, even when she believes the judge made some mistakes. Indeed, this fact suggests that maybe half of the mistakes fall along the way, because they only hurt the winning party who does not appeal.

There is a fifth horseman, too. As the court of appeals finally observes, "It would disserve the proper relationship between trial and appellate courts . . . were the Court of Appeals gratuitously to inject itself as a super-navigator of sorts, second-guessing the district court" even as that court manages a case toward a conclusion. Trial courts are generally allocated the business of bringing the case to trial and a conclusion, and appellate courts are generally allocated the business of reviewing alleged harmful errors in the result. An interlocutory appeal is like a short-circuit in the system and therefore should generally be disallowed.

Q **4. Examples: Deciding what is a final judgment.** *Recticel* is better at explaining what is not final than at explaining what is. But the cases have not improved much on the definition that a decision is final only when it "resolv[es] the contested matter, leaving nothing to be done except execution of the judgment." *Coopers & Lybrand v. Livesay*, 437 U.S. 463 (1978). Consider the following examples. Which are appealable final decisions? (The point of these examples is not to teach you the specific answers, but to help you recognize how treacherous the final judgment rule can be.)

A. Asanti sues Cornwall, Tremain, and Janowitz. Tremain moves to dismiss the claim against her for failure to state a claim upon which relief can be granted. The court grants the motion. Asanti appeals the decision.

A Assuming that a judgment is not final until all claims are resolved, this is not a final judgment. The dismissal resolves the claim against Tremain, but leaves claims still pending against the other defendants. Absent some exception to the final judgment rule, Asanti would have to wait until she fully litigates those claims and they are resolved before she could appeal the dismissal of the claim against Tremain. (We will see below, however, that Fed. R. Civ. P. 54(b) gives the district judge in a federal case the option to order entry of final judgment in this situation, thus allowing earlier appeal.)

B. Mafridge sues American Butane Corporation for damages arising from a contract dispute. American Butane counterclaims for damages as well. American then moves for summary judgment on Mafridge's claim. The judge grants summary judgment, stating that "judgment is granted to the Defendant American Butane Corporation, and Plaintiff Mafridge shall take nothing against Defendant."

A The judge's order sounds rather grimly final. But in fact it only resolves the claim that was before the judge on the motion: Mafridge's primary claim. It presumably does not resolve the counterclaim, so the case is not truly over in the trial court, and the court's ruling is not a final decision.

C. Abbas sues Tolliver in federal court for damages and recovers a verdict. The judge orders judgment entered on the verdict. Two days later, Tolliver files a motion for a new trial under Fed. R. Civ. P. 59(c). Rule 59(b) allows motions for new trial to be filed "no later than 28 days after entry of the judgment," so the motion is timely. But the district judge may not decide the motion before the thirty-day period for filing an appeal lapses. Should Tolliver also file a notice of appeal, or does the motion for a new trial undo the finality of the judgment?

A To answer this, you'll need to look at another set of rules of civil procedure. Rule of Appellate Procedure 4(a)(4)(A) provides that, where a new trial motion is filed, time for appeal runs "from the entry of the order disposing of the ... motion." Tolliver's Rule 59 motion has suspended the finality of the judgment. She cannot appeal from it until her new trial motion is decided.

D. Quan recovers from Morretti on a federal civil rights claim. Under 42 U.S.C. § 1988, he is entitled to recover his attorneys' fees since he has prevailed on the claim. The judge orders judgment entered on the verdict in Quan's favor, although attorneys' fees have not been assessed.

A The Supreme Court has held that a federal judgment is final even if attorneys' fees have not been assessed. *Budinich v. Becton Dickinson & Co.*, 486 U.S. 196, 202–03 (1988). State courts could view the matter differently, however.

In short, some judgments that don't appear to be final may be treated as such, and others that appear final may not be. Every court system must decide how to treat such ambiguous cases, and the result may vary among the states or between states and the federal courts. The goal is to develop an acute sensitivity to the issue, so that, whenever a judgment might be ripe for appeal, you think about it, research it, and preserve your client's rights accordingly.

Q **5. Why so neurotic about all this?** Why is it so crucial to know whether a judgment is final? In the second example, Mafridge's case, what will happen if the appellate court views the trial judge's decision as final, and American fails to appeal? What will happen if American views it as final and takes an appeal, but the appellate court holds that the judgment was not final?

A If the appellate court treats this as a final judgment, and American does not file a notice of appeal from it within the brief window for doing so (thirty days after final judgment or after a court order disposing of a post-trial motion), *it will waive its right to appeal.* Courts are very sticky about filing deadlines for appeals and highly unlikely to relieve a party from its failure to file in time. Rights will be lost, and legal malpractice claims may follow.

If American filed its notice of appeal, but the appellate court concluded that the judgment was interlocutory, it would dismiss the appeal as premature. This is certainly a less drastic ruling than in the first situation. Surely, this suggests a rule of thumb for lawyers: If in doubt, file the notice of appeal. Better to be told you're too early than too late. Yet, this tactic includes a risk as well: If the appeal was filed too soon, a court may view it as a nullity. If American assumes its rights to appeal are protected by the early notice and fails to file a *second* notice of appeal once the case is really over in the trial court (i.e., after resolution of its counterclaim as well), it might waive its right to appeal! This is all very tricky. The lesson for a first-year student is that it merits very careful thought and research when your time comes to perfect an appeal.

B. Final by Effect: The Collateral Order Doctrine

RFC made an alternative argument for appeal in *Recticel* by claiming that the cost-sharing order was appealable under a judge-made theory called *the collateral order doctrine*. The court of appeals describes this as a "detour" around the finality principle and an "exception," but the Supreme Court has said that it "is best understood not as an exception to the 'final decision' rule laid down by Congress in § 1291, but as a 'practical construction' of it." *Digital Equip. Corp. v. Desktop Direct, Inc.*, 511 U.S. 863, 867 (1994) (internal citation omitted). The Supreme Court originally suggested that, to be appealable under this doctrine, an order had to be collateral to the merits, too important to be denied review, conclusive of the issue, and effectively unreviewable on appeal of a final judgment because such review would come too late. *Cohen v. Beneficial Industrial Loan Corp.*, 337 U.S. 541, 545–47 (1949).

Notes and Questions: The Collateral Order Doctrine

1. Collateral. To qualify under this doctrine, an issue must be "collateral" to the merits; it must "resolve an important issue completely separate from the merits of the action." *Coopers & Lybrand v. Livesay*, 437 U.S. 463, 468 (1978). If the issue is intertwined with the merits, the judge's decision might be revisited as the litigation of the merits proceeds. In contrast, when an issue is really collateral, permitting an immediate appeal will not result in duplication, because the court of appeals will not revisit the collateral issue on an eventual appeal of a final judgment on the (separate and unrelated) merits, should one be necessary.

For example, the common law defense of qualified immunity protects an official from personal liability for conduct that "does not violate clearly established statutory or constitutional rights of which a reasonable person would have known." *Harlow v. Fitzgerald*, 457 U.S. 800, 818 (1982). If Citizen sues Roberts, a government official, for an official act, and the trial court denies Roberts's motion to dismiss because, on Citizen's well-pleaded facts, Roberts's act violated clearly established law, the ruling is separate from the merits because the court need not consider the correctness of Citizen's factual allegations in order to decide the legal question of whether Roberts's act violated clearly established law. *See supra* pp. 518–19. The ruling could therefore be appealed as a collateral order. *See Moore* § 202.07[2][a]. In contrast, if the trial court denies Roberts's motion for summary judgment because of a factual dispute about what Roberts did, the ruling would not be collateral to the merits. What Roberts did *is*, in part, the merits of Citizen's claim. The ruling would therefore not qualify for immediate appeal as a collateral order. *Id.* § 202.07[2][b][iii][A] (citing cases).

2. Important. Importance is in the eye of the beholder, so even though this requirement has sometimes been teased out of *Cohen*, its application is uncertain. But some circuits have said that the question must be "serious and unsettled." The "unsettled" part of the equation should at least be easily determinable: Is it an issue of first impression or one that has sharply divided the courts? The appellate courts have found the importance requirement satisfied, for example, by these questions: whether a state security requirement was applicable to a diversity action in federal court; whether a President is entitled to absolute immunity from civil liability for acts he took in office; and whether a criminal prosecution exposes the defendant to double jeopardy. *See Wright & Miller* § 3911.5. Roberts's issue of qualified immunity is not unsettled and therefore would probably fail this requirement.

3. Conclusive. The order appealed must conclusively determine the disputed question. This requirement emphasizes that the litigation of the *particular* issue must be concluded even if the litigation of the *case* is not. The trial court will not revisit the issue and change its order. The court of appeals must be convinced that "the district court has clearly said its last word on the subject." *Bradshaw v. Zoological Soc'y of San Diego*, 662 F.2d 1301, 1306 (9th Cir. 1981). In *Cohen v. Beneficial Industrial Loan Corp.*, 337 U.S. 541 (1949), the trial court had refused to make plaintiffs post a security for the payment of defendant's litigation expenses should defendant prevail. This was not the kind of decision that the trial court would revisit as the litigation unfolded, and therefore the Supreme Court viewed it as "conclusive" of the security question. In contrast, an order denying class certification is inherently tentative by the very terms of Rule 23(c)(1)(C) ("An order that grants or denies class certification may be altered or amended before final judgment."). *See Coopers & Lybrand v. Livesay*, 437 U.S. 463, 469 (1978) (so holding). The Court therefore found it unsuitable for collateral order review. (Federal Rule 23(f) now permits such an appeal. *See* 28 U.S.C. § 1292(e) (providing the Supreme Court with rulemaking power to provide for interlocutory appeal).)

4. Now or never: Effectively unreviewable on appeal from a final judgment. This is the key requirement, driving the doctrine. It recognizes that some decisions are, *as a practical matter*, final and carry such immediate consequences that review in the normal course—on an appeal from a final judgment—comes too late to prevent or to undo harm to a party. To deny early review of such a decision is basically to deny *any* meaningful review. But this question, whether a right is "effectively unreviewable," "cannot be answered without a judgment about the value of the interests that would be lost through rigorous application of a final judgment rule." *Digital Equipment Corp. v. Desktop Direct, Inc.*, 511 U.S. 863, 878–79 (2006).

> The crucial question, however, is not whether an interest is important in the abstract; it is whether deferring review until final judgment so imperils the interest as to justify the cost of allowing immediate appeal of the entire class of relevant orders.

Mohawk Indus., Inc. v. Carpenter, 558 U.S. 100, 108 (2009).

A classic example of this is *Abney v. United States*, 431 U.S. 651, 655 (1977), in which the defendant claimed that a prosecution was barred by the Double Jeopardy Clause of the United States Constitution. In *Abney*, the Court recognized that the Double Jeopardy Clause protects against a second prosecution, not just against a second conviction. That right would be completely undermined if Abney were required to actually stand trial before he could appeal the denial of his motion.

Similarly, in *Nixon v. Fitzgerald*, 457 U.S. 731 (1982), President Richard Nixon was permitted to appeal an order denying his motion to dismiss on grounds of absolute presidential immunity, even though the denial would otherwise have led to a continuation of the litigation in the trial court. Absolute immunity spares a defendant not only from ultimate liability, but also from having to stand trial at all. *See Moore* § 202.07[2][b][i]. If the President were forced to wait until appeal from a final judgment against him, he would have suffered the harm of standing trial, which even a reversal of the final judgment would not alleviate. Thus, on the claim of an immunity not just from liability but from trial itself, it was appeal now or never.

Q **5. Applying the collateral order doctrine to the cost-sharing order in *Recticel*.** It should now be pretty easy to decide whether RFC could appeal the cost-sharing order under this doctrine. How would you apply the doctrine?

A First, the order does seem "collateral" from the merits, notwithstanding the court of appeals' analysis. It is "inextricably intertwined with the main case" only in the sense that it is a necessary part of the discovery leading up to trial, but so are many preliminary matters. However, the order is also not very important to anyone but the parties. It is not the kind of order that is likely to be cited again; it has no broader social significance. Nor is it clearly "conclusive." In the course of what will undoubtedly be lengthy discovery, a trial court could revisit this more than once. Indeed, in a complex case, discovery typically requires multiple court orders (either from the trial judge or a magistrate), adjusting or even reversing prior decisions as circumstances may require. Many discovery or case management orders are quintessentially non-conclusive for these reasons.

> Most important, the cost-sharing order is reviewable upon appeal from a final judgment, and any harm that RFC suffers from its imposition can then be undone. "Nothing will be lost: money wrongfully paid by one party to another can be restored by judicial decree." *Recticel*, 859 F.2d at 1004. Even if the cost-sharing order somehow satisfies the other requirements for a collateral order appeal, its failure on this one is fatal. When a challenge to an interlocutory order is "fully capable of vindication on appeal from a final judgment in the usual course," there is no need or justification for allowing an early appeal under the collateral order doctrine.

It is no answer to this analysis that there may be a chance that something could be lost should the other parties in *Recticel* have insufficient funds left to repay RFC at the end of the case. Whether or not that might happen in this particular case, the "focus [of the collateral order analysis] is on 'the entire category to which a claim belongs,'" not just the claim in the particular case. *Mohawk Indus.*, 558 U.S. at 107. In most cases, parties will be able to repay other parties at the end of the case if the cost-sharing order is overturned on appeal. There is therefore no interest at stake in the *category* of pretrial cost-sharing orders to justify the cost of allowing immediate appeal of the entire class of such orders.

Q **6. How is the collateral order doctrine consistent with 28 U.S.C. § 1291?** Congress creates the courts of appeals and defines their jurisdiction. And it has provided, in 28 U.S.C. § 1291, that the courts of appeals may only review "final decisions" of the district courts. So how can the Supreme Court carve out an exception for collateral orders under the doctrine?

A Section 1291 does not say that there must be "final judgments" before review is authorized, just "final decisions." The logic of *Cohen* and the line of following cases is that these categories of decisions are separate from the merits of the dispute and *are* "final," in the sense that they will immediately impact the party and that the immediate impact cannot be undone by a later appeal. "[I]t is a final decision that Congress has made reviewable. . . . While a final judgment always is a final decision, there are instances in which a final decision is not a final judgment." *Stack v. Boyle*, 342 U.S. 1, 12 (1951) (Jackson, J., concurring).

7. Now or later? The policies that favor interlocutory review of various types of decision cannot be neatly categorized or definitively described.

Which of the following federal trial court decisions presents the strongest case for immediate appeal under the *Cohen* doctrine? The weakest?

A. Denial of a motion to dismiss for lack of personal jurisdiction.
B. Denial of a motion to intervene (become a party in a case) as a matter of right (without needing permission from the court).
C. Denial of a motion to dismiss for lack of subject matter jurisdiction.
D. Denial of a motion to dismiss a claim for failure to state a claim upon which relief can be granted.

A does not present a strong case for an interlocutory collateral order appeal. While this decision may be conclusive, it is not necessarily collateral to the merits if the contacts on which personal jurisdiction rests gave rise to the claim. *See S & Davis Int'l, Inc. v. Yemen*, 218 F.3d 1292, 1297–98 (11th Cir. 2000) (stating that "[t]he denial of a motion to dismiss for lack of personal jurisdiction is not, in itself, immediately appealable under the 'collateral order doctrine'"). More important, this is not an error that would be effectively unreviewable on appeal from the final judgment. An appeals court could correct it by reversing the judgment. The federal courts therefore almost universally disallow appeal of this kind of decision. Not all state courts agree. Some states authorize interlocutory appeal of decisions to deny motions to dismiss on personal jurisdiction grounds. *See, e.g., World-Wide Volkswagen Corp. v. Woodson*, 585 P.2d 351 (Okla. 1978) (allowing appeal by *writ of prohibition*).

B presents a better case for immediate appeal. But it depends on the nature of the intervention. If the movant tries to intervene as of right (without needing permission from the court), courts of appeals have allowed collateral order appeal. Although the basis for the sought-after intervention may not be entirely collateral to the merits, the order is conclusive and the party denied intervention is deprived of any further role in the litigation. Even if he can appeal the denial at the end of the case, he has lost what he was seeking: a role in the now completed litigation. *See Brotherhood of R.R. Trainmen v. Balt. & Ohio R.R. Co.*, 331 U.S. 519, 524–25 (1947).

C looks like **A**, in that the lack of subject matter jurisdiction can be asserted on appeal from the final judgment and the judgment set aside if the claim is upheld.

D is the weakest argument. While it is conclusive, and surely important to the parties (and perhaps others if it involves an issue of first impression or involves a change or extension of the law), it is hardly collateral. *It's part of the merits.* Finally, and decisively, it is classic error that can be asserted on appeal of a final judgment. Nothing is lost by waiting but the normal costs of litigation; and the damage of a final judgment is reversible on appeal of that judgment. The federal courts therefore do not allow collateral-order appeals in this context. *See Spiess v. C. Itoh & Co.*, 725 F.2d 970, 974 (5th Cir. 1984).

B thus seems to present the strongest case for an appeal under the collateral order doctrine.

C. Final by Direction: Rule 54(b)

Consider *Recticel* again. RFC was but one of almost two hundred defendants in *Recticel*. Suppose it successfully moved for summary judgment on the grounds that plaintiffs had found no evidence that it produced the foam insulation that was allegedly implicated in the hotel fire. Would that summary judgment be immediately appealable by plaintiffs? Consider Rule 54(b) in answering this question.

> Be careful on this one. Certainly, a summary judgment on the merits can be a final, appealable judgment when it decides the only claim in a case. But given that RFC is one of multiple defendants, and that claims remain pending against the rest, there is no final judgment yet. The case is not over.

> Rule 54(b) articulates this truism: "[A]ny order or decision . . . that adjudicates fewer than all the claims or the rights and liabilities of fewer than all the parties does not end the action as to any of the claims or parties. . . ." Without more, the summary judgment is not yet appealable.
>
> That might not matter much to the *Recticel* plaintiffs, since they have about 199 defendants left. But, ironically, it might matter to RFC. While it seems to be out of the case, *it will not know for certain until the grant of summary judgment is affirmed on appeal from an eventual final judgment.* If, at the end of the case, plaintiffs claim error in the grant and the court of appeals agrees, RFC would be back in the soup, perhaps several years later, and all by itself! In the meantime, it is in suspense, a frustrated spectator to the litigation, waiting for certainty.

If that seems unfair to RFC, it seemed that way also to the drafters of the Federal Rules. Rule 54(b) therefore provides a way out. It allows the federal district court to "direct entry of a final judgment as to one or more, but fewer than all, claims or parties . . . if the court expressly determines that there is no just cause for delay." What does this mean?

> The "delay" refers to the postponement of appeal that would result if the finality principle is applied to the grant of summary judgment for RFC. There is no just cause for that delay—that is, no reason to wait until a final judgment on *all* the claims—if the summary judgment for RFC is factually or legally separable from the other claims, because then an immediate appeal of that judgment would not overlap with the eventual appeal of a final judgment in the entire case. Allowing appeal now would not cause the duplication that the finality principle tries to avoid. *See* 19-202 *Moore* § 202.06[2]. On the other hand, if the summary judgment on the claim against RFC is not legally separable from the claims remaining for adjudication, then the court of appeals might have to consider the same issues twice—once if an immediate appeal is allowed of the RFC summary judgment, and again on appeal of the final judgment in the remaining claims at the end of the case. Once is enough—and the finality principle usually places that "once" at the end of the case on appeal of a final judgment on all the claims.

Assuming sufficient separateness, therefore, RFC could make a motion for the court to direct entry of a final judgment on its partial summary judgment under Rule 54(b). RFC would argue that the absence of evidence that it produced the foam insulation is a fact unique to it, such that treating the judgment as final now would not cause duplication in the court of appeals. If the court grants the motion, and the summary judgment is entered as a final judgment, then the thirty-day period for the plaintiffs to appeal begins to run. RFC does not have to wait years to determine whether its summary judgment is good; if plaintiffs appeal, it will know when the appeal is decided; if they don't, the suspense (and the case for RFC) is over. The same motion is available to plaintiffs, if they want to appeal the grant of summary judgment to RFC immediately. Conversely, should a court deny a motion for entry of a final judgment under Rule 54(b), the plaintiffs can be confident that they don't have to file a notice of appeal within thirty days after the grant of summary judgment.

But there is a catch. The courts have construed Rule 54(b) to apply only to trial court decisions that, standing alone (without regard to the other claims to which they were joined), would have satisfied the finality requirement and thus would have been appealable final judgments. RFC's summary judgment certainly qualifies; if plaintiffs' claim had been against it alone, and the court granted summary judgment for it, there would be nothing left to litigate. But suppose the court granted partial summary judgment for the plaintiffs on RFC's liability. Can the trial court direct entry of final judgment on the partial summary judgment under Rule 54(b)?

> No. If a party has sued for damages, a partial summary judgment on liability is only a step in the right direction, not the end of the journey. The summary judgment holds it liable, but it doesn't know for how much. Damages still have to be litigated and decided. Ordinarily, therefore, a court will not direct entry of final judgment as to liability alone.

More confusingly, the courts also have held that a trial court cannot enter final judgment on its disposition of one of a party's multiple requests for relief, or one of the party's alternative legal theories, on a single claim. In *Liberty Mutual Ins. Co. v. Wetzel*, 424 U.S. 737 (1976), for example, the plaintiff sued for employment discrimination, seeking both injunctive relief and damages. The trial court granted the plaintiff partial summary judgment on liability only. It then directed entry of final judgment under Rule 54(b) on the issue of liability, after which the defendant appealed. The Supreme Court held that the trial court had not properly directed entry of final judgment, because it had only decided liability and had not yet decided whether the plaintiffs were entitled to damages, injunctive relief, or both. Until the trial court decided the remedy, it had not finally decided a "claim." Rule 54(b), however, only permits direction of a final judgment as to "one or more, but fewer than all, *claims or parties*. . . ." Fed. R. Civ. P. 54(b) (emphasis added). A "complaint asserting only one legal right," the Supreme Court explained, "even if seeking multiple remedies for the alleged violation of that right, states a single claim of relief." *Liberty Mutual Ins. Co. v. Wetzel* was in reality a single claim broken into piecemeal final judgments. Identifying what constitutes the claim for relief, however, is no easy task, as we shall see when we get to claim preclusion.

V. Some Exceptions to the Finality Principle: Interlocutory Appeal

We have explored the finality principle and two extensions of the principle to certain collateral orders, because they are effectively final, and to dispositions of fewer than all the claims or parties as to which the trial court directs entry of final judgment under Rule 54(b). Although some might treat these extensions as exceptions, their rationale is still based on a pragmatic understanding of finality.

Now we turn to true exceptions to the finality principle for indisputably interlocutory decisions by the trial court. New York law permits a broad range of interlocutory appeals. *See* N.Y. C.P.L.R. § 5701(a)(2)(iv) (allowing appeal of a decision that "involves some part of the merits"), § 5701(a)(2)(v) (authorizing appeal of an interlocutory decision that "affects a substantial right"). The federal courts apply the final judgment rule more stringently, with narrower exceptions. No American court system, however, either permits unlimited interlocutory appeals or forbids them altogether. All follow the finality principle to some extent, with more or less liberal exceptions. Perhaps it is too strong to say (as one court said of another categorical rule) that the finality principle serves primarily "as a prelude to the catalogue of its exceptions." *Pacific Fire Ins. Co. v. Kenny Boiler & Mfg. Co.*, 327 N.W. 226, 228 (1937). But you should understand that even systems that generally apply the finality principle will have various mechanisms for interlocutory appeal of some decisions, through common law writs or statutory exceptions.

Federal law provides a number of such exceptions, situations in which interlocutory review is allowed because the argument for early review is particularly strong. Some of these exceptions have been developed through case law and some by statute. In subsections A and B below, we take a brief look at two statutory exceptions under 28 U.S.C. § 1292. In subsection C, we pick up *Recticel* once again to explore a common law exception that has also been codified under the All Writs Act, 28 U.S.C. § 1651(a).

A. Orders Concerning Injunctive Relief Under 28 U.S.C. § 1292(a)

Section 1292(a)(1) expressly gives the federal courts of appellate jurisdiction to hear appeals from "interlocutory orders" affecting injunctions. Suppose, for example, that the trial court issues a preliminary injunction stopping the defendant Acme Company from making widgets, which it has been selling nationwide as its main product. An injunction can be granted only if, among other factors, the party seeking it may suffer irreparable harm without it and that harm outweighs the harm to the opposing party from its issuance. Why did Congress enact the § 1292(a)(1) exception to the finality principle?

> A ruling on an injunction carries a high probability of causing one party or the other immediate harm. In our example, Acme will lose the sales from its widgets during the pendency of the injunction and attendant market share and momentum, from which it may never recover. An appeal from an eventual final judgment against it may come too late to avoid or reverse that harm. This won't always be true, of course, but Congress seemingly thought that it might be true in enough cases to adopt a general exception to the finality principle for interlocutory orders involving such relief.

B. Discretionary Review of Certified Questions Under 28 U.S.C. § 1292(b)

Not all interlocutory decisions are created equal. Some have more impact on the litigation than others. Some involve novel issues of law. Some are likely to sound the "death knell" of the litigation if not reviewed. For example, the plaintiffs may give up because the interlocutory decision made it too costly for them to proceed, even though the decision did not formally dispose of their claim. Given this diversity of interlocutory decisions, one approach to the problem of interlocutory review is to let the judges—either the trial judge or the appeals court judges or both—decide on an ad hoc basis whether to allow a particular interlocutory decision to be reviewed. 28 U.S.C. § 1292(b) provides this option for interlocutory review in federal courts:

> When a district judge, in making in a civil action an order not otherwise appealable under this section, shall be of the opinion that such order involves a controlling question of law as to which there is substantial ground for difference of opinion and that an immediate appeal from the order may materially advance the ultimate termination of the litigation, he shall so state in writing in such order. The court of appeals which would have jurisdiction of an appeal of such action may thereupon, in its discretion, permit an appeal to be taken from such order, if application is made to it within ten days after the entry of the order. . . .

Notes and Questions: Discretionary Review Under 28 U.S.C. § 1292(b)

Q **1. Appealability of another discovery order in *Recticel*?** The same day that the court of appeals declined to hear the interlocutory appeal of the cost-sharing order in *Recticel*, it heard another appeal in the very same litigation also concerning an interlocutory discovery order that ordered the parties to reveal their questions for a deponent before the deposition. The parties argued that this order improperly invaded work product protection. *See In re San Juan Dupont Plaza Hotel*, 859 F.2d 1007 (1st Cir. 1988). The difference was that the second appeal was brought under 28 U.S.C. § 1292(b).

Assume that in this later appeal, the party raising the work product argument convinced the trial judge that there "was substantial ground for difference of opinion" and that immediate appeal would "materially advance" the litigation. The trial court therefore certified a § 1292(b) appeal. Does it follow that the party can now appeal?

A No. This statute provides for a discretionary "two-key" procedure for allowing an interlocutory appeal of a "controlling question of law." The district court turns the first key by certifying the question for appeal. The court of appeals turns the second key by accepting the certification. Both keys must be turned for the appeal to be heard.

Q **2. Convincing the trial judge.** You represent the plaintiff in a suit in federal district court. The federal judge has just ruled against you on an issue in the case. Because the decision is interlocutory, you can only get immediate appellate review if you can get the judge to certify the issue under § 1292(b). What would you have to demonstrate to convince the judge to certify the issue for interlocutory review?

A

- First, that the issue for interlocutory appeal involves a "controlling question of law." A question is "controlling" if its disposition would dispose of a claim or defense. Section 1292(b) interlocutory appeals should not be used to raise fact-bound issues; they are intended primarily "for abstract legal issues that can be decided quickly and cleanly without having to study the record." 19-203 *Moore* § 203.31[2]. Thus, they are not available to challenge mere exercises of discretion by the trial judge. Apparently, the trial judge in *Recticel* found that the work product issue was such a controlling question of law. In contrast, the earlier question of cost-sharing would not have qualified for § 1292(b) review because it did not seem to involve a controlling question of law, so much as one of judicial discretion in case management.
- Second, that the issue is one on which there is a substantial ground for difference of opinion. This might be because it is a difficult question of first impression, or because, on the facts, it is close. When the trial judge has changed her mind, there is often good cause to find that there is such a ground. *See Securities and Exchange Comm'n v. National Student Marketing*, 538 F.2d 404 (D.C. Cir. 1976) (trial judge changed his mind three times before certifying question under § 1292(b)).
- Third, that an immediate appeal may materially advance resolution of the case. If the issue is an important one holding up discovery, or likely to recur during discovery, deciding it now may actually speed things up. In other words, the trial court concludes that interlocutory appeal of this issue is the exception, in that it does not saddle the horseman of delay, who usually rides with piecemeal appeals.

3. Picking and choosing.

Baskin sues Beta Corporation after she is discharged from her position as vice president for sales. She asserts claims for breach of contract, misrepresentation, and bad faith discharge. Beta moves to dismiss the bad faith discharge claim, arguing that Emporia law, which applies to this diversity case, does not allow recovery for bad faith discharge. The federal district judge agrees—though she acknowledges that it is a close question of law. Consequently, she dismisses the bad faith discharge claim.

If Baskin makes a motion for the judge to certify the dismissal for immediate review under § 1292(b) the court will likely

A. grant the motion because the issue is a closely contested issue of law. Appellate courts are particularly equipped to decide such issues.
B. deny the motion because it is governed by state law, not federal law, and is not subject to review by the federal court of appeals.
C. grant the motion because the claims can be litigated together if the judge's dismissal is reversed on an interlocutory appeal.
D. deny the motion because immediate review would not be likely to lead to an early resolution of the case.

A is not wrong; it's just not enough. Section 1292(b) has three requirements, not just one. While there may be substantial ground for difference of opinion on the validity of this claim, that just gets you part way to an interlocutory appeal. It must also be shown that the issue is "controlling" and is likely to advance the resolution of the case.

B is wrong. The federal courts of appeals can and frequently do review federal district court judges' rulings on the meaning of state law. Although these are issues of state law, they are issues of *law*, as to which the courts of appeals have special expertise. Nothing in § 1292(b) suggests that the reference to a "controlling question of law" must be a question of *federal* law.

C fails to impress as well. It suggests that efficiency may be gained if the dismissal is appealed early and reversed, since the reinstated claim could then be litigated along with Baskin's other claims. That isn't sufficient for § 1292(b) certification either. Otherwise, trial court dismissals of fewer than all the claims would always satisfy § 1292(b). Section 1292(b) requires more.

D is the best answer here. It seems unlikely that immediate review would "materially advance the ultimate termination of the litigation." Baskin's other two claims remain pending and will presumably proceed through discovery to trial whether the dismissal of the bad faith claim is reversed or not. If the dismissal were reversed, the bad faith claim could be litigated with the others, but such a reversal is not likely to lead to an early end to the case.

Q **4. Convincing the appellate court.** Suppose you convince the judge that the issue meets the § 1292(b) standard for immediate review, and the judge enters the certification to that effect. What would you do next?

A You would then file a petition in the court of appeals seeking permission to take the interlocutory appeal. Under § 1292(b), the petition must be filed with the court of appeals within ten days after the district court's entry of the order certifying the question. (Note a trap for the unwary: The § 1292(b) petition filed in the court of appeals is not the same as a notice of appeal from a final judgment, which is filed in the district court. *See Wright & Miller* § 3929.)

What standard do you have to satisfy to convince the appellate court to take your § 1292(b) appeal?

A Well, it can't simply be enough that you convinced the trial judge, because the statute expressly requires the discretionary approval of the court of appeals as well. It does not state a standard for exercise of that discretion, and the appellate rule on "appeal by permission" is hardly more helpful, stating only that the petitioner shall state "the reasons why the appeal should be allowed and is authorized by . . . [§ 1292(b)]." Fed. R. App. P. 5(b)(1)(D). Presumably, you will stress the same factors that you stressed to the trial court. Note that this introduces a new layer of litigation effort: briefs and moving papers concerning the request for interlocutory review, in effect requiring litigation about litigation.

The panel of the court of appeals that allowed a § 1292(b) appeal of the work product issue in the same litigation as *Recticel* stressed the novelty and importance of the certified issue:

> Only rare cases will qualify for the statutory anodyne; indeed, it is apodictic in this circuit that interlocutory certification of this sort "should be used sparingly and only in exceptional circumstances, and where the proposed intermediate appeal presents one or more difficult and pivotal questions of law not settled by controlling authority." *McGillicuddy v. Clements*, 746 F.2d 76, 76 n.1 (1st Cir. 1984). Although the call is close, we believe the work product issue in this matter to be sufficiently novel and important, and the circumstances sufficiently out of the ordinary, as to fulfill the statutory requisites. But we warn the parties and the district court that, in this case and any others, we will hew carefully to the *McGillicuddy* line—for we continue to believe that the instances where section 1292(b) may appropriately be utilized will, realistically, be few and far between.

859 F.2d at 1010 n.1.

As these grumpy comments suggest, the courts rarely turn both keys to allow § 1292(b) interlocutory appeals. Relatively few cases are certified by district judges, and few of these are accepted by the courts of appeals.

C. Extraordinary Interlocutory Review by Mandamus

Suppose the trial court makes an outrageously bad interlocutory decision, such as assigning trial of a major case to a special master (a lawyer specially appointed to help the court under Rule 53, who is not a magistrate judge) over the parties' objections because the trial court is too busy. (We're not making this up. *See La Buy v. Howes Leather Co.*, 352 U.S. 249 (1957).) Must the parties really try the case to a private lawyer before they can appeal this assignment as a violation of their right to have it tried by an Article III judge? (We can probably reliably assume that the trial judge would not certify the question of the propriety of this ruling under § 1292(b).)

The answer is no, not necessarily, because the federal courts have retained a safety valve for interlocutory appeal in extraordinary circumstances: a petition for a writ of mandamus under the All Writs Act, 28 U.S.C. § 1651(a), codifying an ancient common law writ. The respondent in mandamus cases challenging an action by the lower court is the trial judge himself: La Buy was the judge in *La Buy*; Woodson was the trial judge in *World-Wide Volkswagen v. Woodson*, 444 U.S. 286 (1980). A writ of mandamus issued by a court of appeals is an order to the respondent to do his duty—thus in *La Buy*, an order from the higher court to the trial judge to try his cases himself.

READING *IN RE RECTICEL FOAM CORP.* (AGAIN). The facts of this mass disaster litigation are briefly summarized earlier in this chapter (p. 1183). Recall that RFC failed to show that the cost-sharing order entered by the trial court was final or that it qualified for review under the collateral order doctrine. RFC therefore tried another alternative—the petition for the writ of mandamus.

- What are the requirements for mandamus?
- Why is it rarely granted? Why do the cases frequently emphasize that mandamus is no substitute for appeal?
- Why did the court of appeals deny the petition in this case?

IN RE RECTICEL FOAM CORP.

859 F.2d 1000 (1st Cir. 1988)

SELYA, Circuit Judge.

[EDS.—In addition to attempting to appeal, Recticel Foam Corp. (RFC) filed a petition in the court of appeals for a writ of mandamus to challenge the cost-sharing order.] There are two consolidated matters before us at this juncture. They are an odd couple: an interlocutory appeal and a petition for writ of mandamus.[1] . . .

III. THE MANDAMUS PETITION

We need not dawdle over RFC's request that we invoke mandamus to address its grievances anent the district court's cost-sharing orders. To be sure, the mandamus power is not some vestigial remnant of a bygone era, to be wrapped in cellophane and left untouched by human hands. Though ancient in its origins and potent in its effect, mandamus may be a permissible—sometimes necessary—vehicle for obtaining immediate judicial review of nonfinal orders that would otherwise escape timely scrutiny. But, "the remedy of mandamus is a drastic one, to be invoked only in extraordinary situations." *Allied Chemical Corp. v. Daiflon, Inc.,* 449 U.S. 33, 34 (1980) (per curiam); *accord Will v. United States,* 389 U.S. 90, 107, (1967); *Boreri,* 763 F.2d at 26; *Acton Corp. v. Borden, Inc.,* 670 F.2d 377, 382 (1st Cir. 1982). A valuable asset when appropriately employed, mandamus has the potential, if promiscuously used, to spawn piecemeal litigation and disrupt the orderly processes of the justice system. Therefore, we have guarded against the too-free availability of the writ: its "currency is not profligately to be spent." *Boreri,* 763 F.2d at 26. Mandamus should be dispensed sparingly and only in pursuance of the most carefully written prescription, not made available over the counter, on casual demand. It is not a substitute for interlocutory appeal.

Mandamus entreaties are generally subject to a pair of prophylactic rules, which together require that a petitioner show (a) some special risk of irreparable harm, and (b) clear entitlement to the relief requested.[4] Illustrating the first of these rules, the Court has written that a party seeking mandamus must "have no other

---

1. The petition, No. 88-1204, is brought under the All Writs Act, 28 U.S.C. § 1651(a) (1982), which empowers the courts of appeals to "issue all writs necessary or appropriate in aid of their respective jurisdictions and agreeable to the usages and principles of law." For ease in reference, we call the mode of relief sought in this action "mandamus." Technically, however, the writ of mandamus lies to *compel* action by an inferior court, whereas the writ of prohibition is used to *prevent* such action. The instant petition sounds more in the nature of prohibition. Nevertheless, we need not split fine hairs; the two are counterpart remedies for which the same grounds must be established, and they are frequently used in concert.

4. We recognize that, within limits not yet precisely defined, mandamus may also be appropriate—albeit rarely—to resolve issues which are both novel and of great public importance. We need not plumb these murky depths, however, for it is abundantly clear that here, where interstitial matters of case administration are involved, the exceptional circumstances necessary to trigger what has been termed "advisory mandamus" are utterly lacking. As [*United States v.*] *Sorren* teaches: "Invocation of our advisory mandamus power is not to be used as a bootstrap device to circumvent the limits on our jurisdiction to review discretionary interlocutory rulings of district judges." 605 F.2d 1211, 1216 (1st Cir. 1979).

adequate means to attain the relief he desires. . . ." *Allied Chemical Corp.,* 449 U.S. at 35. Because interlocutory orders are reviewable on appeal from final judgment, a mandamus petitioner who attacks such an order must ordinarily demonstrate that something about the order, or its circumstances, would make an end-of-case appeal ineffectual or leave legitimate interests unduly at risk. *Compare Boreri,* 763 F.2d at 26 (mandamus inappropriate where petitioner "not in unavoidable danger of forfeiting its perceived rights . . . [and] . . . not unable to appeal the issues under other (more propitious) circumstances") *with United States v. Christian,* 660 F.2d 892, 897 (3d Cir. 1981) (mandamus appropriate where, otherwise, district court's failure to act would be forever shielded from appellate review). In the case at bar, petitioner-appellant has advanced no thesis which would warrant a departure from the usual practice. There is no irremediable harm,[5] and RFC's rights vis-à-vis the cost-sharing orders (such as they may prove to be) are susceptible of full vindication during an appeal taken in the ordinary course.

The second rule, too, comes into play here. As a general matter, mandamus will not issue to control exercises of discretion. Rather, a petitioner's right to the writ must be "clear and indisputable." *Bankers Life & Casualty Co. v. Holland,* 346 U.S. 379, 384 (1953). Where an action is committed to judicial discretion, it cannot often be said that a party's claim of entitlement to a particular result meets this benchmark. *Allied Chemical Corp.,* 449 U.S. at 36. For that reason, mandamus has customarily been granted only when the lower court was "clearly without jurisdiction," *Sorren,* 605 F.2d at 1215, or exceeded its discretion "to such a degree that its actions amount[ ] to a 'usurpation of power.' " *In re Puerto Rico Elec. Power Auth.,* 687 F.2d 501, 503 (1st Cir. 1982) (quoting *DeBeers Consolidated Mines, Ltd. v. United States,* 325 U.S. 212, 217 (1945)). Interlocutory procedural orders, particularly case management orders of the type here in issue, rarely will satisfy this precondition for mandamus relief. Trial courts enjoy a broad measure of discretion in managing pretrial affairs, including the conduct of discovery. Decisions regarding the scope of discovery, the allocation of expenses, the most appropriate areas for enforced economy, and the protections to be afforded parties in the discovery process, are ordinarily left to the informed judgment of the district judge, who is in a unique position to gauge and balance the potentially conflicting interests at stake. That, we think, is the case in this situation.

Further discussion of the point would serve no useful purpose. Recticel—as the party seeking issuance of the writ—had the burden of showing us that its right to extraordinary relief was "clear and indisputable," *Acton Corp.,* 670 F.2d at 382, and that other available means of redress were inadequate. It has failed to do so. Thus, without reaching the merits of the district court's allocative orders, we decline petitioner's invitation to review the matter here and now, in the context of an application for mandamus. . . .

In No. 88-1204, the petition for writ of mandamus is denied, as improvidently brought.

---

5. We have earlier "rejected the general burdensomeness of litigation as a basis for assuming mandamus jurisdiction." In re Justices of the Supreme Court of Puerto Rico, 695 F.2d 17, 20 (1st Cir. 1982). We unabashedly reaffirm that view today.

Notes and Questions: Mandamus

Q **1. The requirements for mandamus.** It is not enough that the trial court committed error. What else must the petitioner show?

A First, the petitioner must show that the trial court's decision created some special risk of irreparable harm for which there is no other adequate remedy. This sounds a lot like the "effectively unreviewable" prong of collateral order appeals. Second, however, the petitioner must also show that it is *clearly* entitled to issuance of the writ. It is therefore not granted simply to correct an error in a close case or an exercise of discretion; it is generally confined to decisions by the trial court that are clearly beyond its discretion or jurisdiction—"usurpations of power," the court of appeals calls them in *Recticel*, or abdications of power as in *La Buy*. Courts of appeals have permitted review by the extraordinary writ of mandamus, for example, for claims of clear error by a trial judge in ordering disclosure of materials protected by the attorney-client privilege, assigning an entire case to a master, and refusing to recuse herself on non-frivolous grounds of conflict of interest or bias. *See Moore* § 204.06 (listing cases).

There is also a narrow exception for a writ of mandamus that is issued to guide the lower courts on a recurring and important question of case management, sometimes called "advisory" or "supervisory" mandamus. *See Schlagenhauf v. Holder*, 379 U.S. 104 (1964) (issuing writ of mandamus to instruct the trial court in the construction and proper application of its authority to order physical examinations under Rule 35, addressing a recurring issue of discovery in the district courts).

2. A substitute for appeal? The foregoing requirements help explain why mandamus is decidedly *not* a substitute for appeal. It will not issue to correct ordinary errors, which are the grist of ordinary appeal from final judgments. It is an extraordinary remedy for extraordinary abuse or abdication of power in the trial court, not just mistakes. It is available only when ordinary appeal will not avoid or repair the serious harm.

More prosaically, it is a sharp rap on the trial judge's knuckles, which can't make for pleasant luncheons in the judges' cafeteria. The issuance of a writ of mandamus to a trial judge, in effect, says, "You have not just made an error, but utterly abused your office and acted beyond clearly marked boundaries of your authority." Indeed, so harsh may it appear, that even when the requirements for its issuance are satisfied, courts of appeals have been known to conditionally *deny* the writ with a mildly scolding opinion that they expect the trial court will take to heart within a stated time period, thus sparing the petitioner from harm without insulting the trial court.

Q **3. Denying mandamus in *Recticel*.** Why didn't the petition in *Recticel* meet either of the requirements for mandamus?

A As the court of appeals already concluded in deciding against the collateral order appeal, petitioners were unable to point to any harm from the cost-sharing order that could not be remedied in the course of any ordinary appeal. It was also doubtful that the mere harm of discovery costs would qualify. The court of appeals "unabashedly" reaffirmed its oft-stated view that the "general burdensomeness of litigation" (which in a complex litigation includes substantial discovery costs) is an insufficient harm to qualify for mandamus.

In any case, a trial court clearly has some authority to regulate costs of discovery, *see* Fed. R. Civ. P. 26(b)(2), 26(c)(1), and to manage the case. *See* Fed. R. Civ. P. 16(c)(2)(F) & (L). For this reason, the court of appeals observes that interlocutory discovery or case management orders rarely will satisfy the clear entitlement prong of the mandamus standard. Ultimately, RFC's complaint was not that the trial court clearly acted beyond its discretion, but that it made a mistake within it. In fact, the court of appeals even doubted that it *was* a mistake. (Recall that in the earlier part of its opinion, the court admitted that "we are skeptical that a district court's authority to impose reasonable cost-sharing orders in a multi-district litigation is much in doubt.")

Q **4. A better rule (or statute) for interlocutory appeal?** Congress has authorized the Supreme Court to issue rules providing for appeals of interlocutory orders to the courts of appeals that are not otherwise provided for by statute. 28 U.S.C. § 1292(e). Consider the following suggested rule or statute as a means of solving the problem of interlocutory review: "A court of appeals may grant interlocutory review of any district court decision upon a finding that immediate review will advance the efficient resolution of the case."

What practical problem would you see if the Supreme Court promulgated this rule under its § 1292(e) authority or if Congress enacted this as a statute?

A This rule or statute would lead to a huge number of applications for interlocutory review. It would be an open and unrestricted invitation to litigants to ask for interlocutory review. Lawyers would accept that invitation if they thought it was in their clients' interest, and courts of appeals would have to divert significant resources to screening requests for review. As noted earlier, many interlocutory decisions that seem crucial when they are made by the trial judge end up not affecting the outcome of the case. The final judgment rule acts as a very efficient screening device in most cases, without the investment of resources by the appellate courts that the proposed statute would require. The final judgment rule also limits the possibility that an appellate judge's political views will influence the availability of appellate review.

VI. Standards of Appellate Review

We've left for last the question of the standard or scope of appellate review. In order to decide an issue, an appeals court has to decide how hard it will look at the issue—in effect, how much deference it will give to the decision maker (judge or jury) below. The standard of deference is so important that the parties to an appeal must include "a concise statement of the applicable standard of review" in their briefs. Fed. R. App. P. 28(a)(9)(B), (b)(5).

Appellate courts have assigned various labels to gradations of deference: *de novo*, clearly erroneous, reasonableness, substantial evidence, abuse of discretion, etc. But they are also divided about whether the labels make much difference.

> One school of thought holds that the verbal differences in standards of judicial review . . . mark real differences in the degree of deference that the reviewing court should give the findings and rulings of the tribunal being reviewed. The other school holds that the verbal differences are for the most part merely semantic, that there are really only two standards of review—plenary and deferential—and that differences in deference in a particular case depend on factors specific to the case, such as the nature of the issue, and the evidence, rather than on differences in the stated standard of review.

Morales v. Yeutter, 952 F.2d 954, 957 (7th Cir. 1991) (citations omitted).

To bridge this divide, it is useful to consider the verbal labels not as precise degrees of deference, but rather as approximate points on a continuum of deference running from none to complete deference, as depicted in the following figure.*

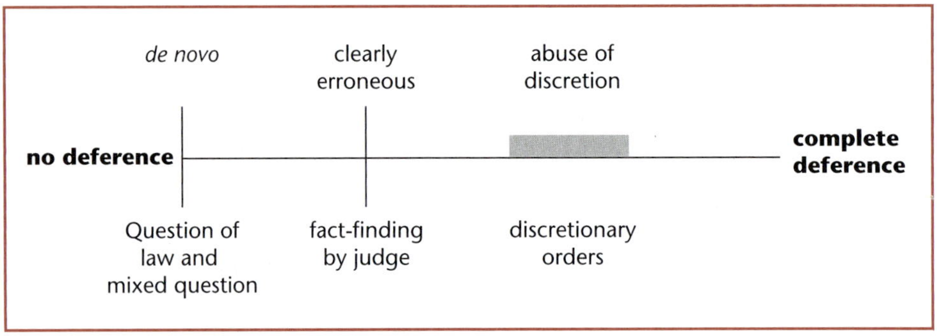

Figure 32–1: STANDARDS OF APPELLATE REVIEW

The location of a standard of review on the continuum turns in part on the comparative advantage of the decision maker (trial judge or jury) and the court of appeals in deciding a particular kind of issue on the record available to each. A trial judge and a jury usually have the advantages of hearing (and, for witnesses, seeing) all the evidence, including demeanor evidence that is not preserved in a written transcript. Juries, of course, also have the advantage of their collective experience. These advantages logically counsel a large measure of deference to fact-finding by a judge or jury. Trial judges are also usually experienced in managing litigation and trial. They not only do it day in and day out for large dockets, but they are usually steeped in the procedural course and managerial challenges of the particular cases before them. Many appellate judges never served in a trial court, and even when they have, they cannot know the ins and outs of a particular

* The table is drawn from *Shreve, Raven-Hansen & Geyh* § 13.09[1].

case as well as the trial judge who presided over it. These facts also counsel a measure of deference to the trial judge's discretionary calls in managing a case from filing to final judgment. Such calls are therefore not reversed for a mere error in the exercise of lawful discretion; they are only reversed if they reflect an abuse of discretion.

In contrast, appellate judges have an advantage over a single trial judge in deciding the law. Not only do they outnumber the trial judge in a particular case (usually sitting in panels of three or more), have the advantage of collegial decision making, and often have more law clerks, but they also don't have to do anything else—they don't conduct trials, let alone manage lengthy pretrial litigation. They only opine on the law. These advantages counsel appellate judges to decide questions of law for themselves, or *de novo* (roughly translated, anew, or even more roughly, from scratch), although they may well be influenced by the trial judge's reasoning.

But comparative advantage is not the entire answer to standard of review, because every judicial system also aims for finality and efficiency. Too much second-guessing threatens both. These objectives therefore give further impetus to deferential review and mean that on close calls, the appellate court will often let the decision below stand in the interests of finality.

A. The *De Novo* Standard of Review

Appellate courts decide questions of law without deference to the trial judge's decision (although they may be persuaded by it). Such *de novo* (also called "plenary" or "independent") review of questions of law makes good sense in light of their comparative advantage in deciding the law. It also promotes uniformity in the law.

The *de novo* standard thus applies to appellate review of dismissals for failure to state a claim, summary judgments, or judgments as a matter of law (JMOL), for example, because they are all decisions that the trial judge makes as a matter of law. See *supra* p. 1029. Assuming that the appellant has complied with any applicable requirements of Rule 50, the appellate court therefore asks the same question that the trial court asked on original and renewed motions for JMOL: Could a reasonable jury have returned the verdict? *See Federal Standards* § 3.01 ("[I]t is clear that what the federal courts are doing is testing the *sufficiency of the evidence*, by whatever test. And the *appellate* court, technically, is only reviewing the district court's own response for an error of law."). *Id.* n.10. This review is quite deferential to the jury's assessment, consistent with the Seventh Amendment.

While *de novo* appellate review of questions of law is hornbook law, the line between law and fact is not always clear.

> To be sure, at its outer limit the line is both clear and uncontroversial: when the appeals court is examining a "purely legal" conclusion, such as whether the First Amendment can broadly protect gestures or applies to the states, it is not hard to recognize that the court acting in a lawmaking role is deciding purely legal issues, free from lower court opinion (though, of course, the earlier reasoning or history may be partly persuasive on its merits). The other end also may be neat: what Alice did yesterday is regarded as a pure fact and is usually delegated to the trial court.

> [T]he area in between these "pure" examples gets increasingly sticky. . .
>
> . . . Justice Brennan offered . . . that fact questions are those for which resolution is "based ultimately on the fact-finding tribunal's experience with the mainsprings of human conduct." This appears to give some meaning to what is analytically fact rather than law—a test for the concept itself of fact-finding that is not wholly dependent on institutional competency—to guide courts in specific contexts in characterizing a certain finding.
>
> In a somewhat contrasting approach, Judge Friendly observed that "what a court can determine better than a jury is perhaps about the only satisfactory criterion for distinguishing 'law' from 'fact.'"

1 *Federal Standards of Review* § 2.13 (2019) (*"Federal Standards"*).

To complicate matters further, the courts have sometimes applied *de novo* review to what they have called *mixed questions of fact and law,* "questions in which the historical facts are admitted or established, the rule of law is undisputed, and the issue is whether the rule of law as applied to the established facts is or is not violated." *Pullman-Standard v. Swint,* 456 U.S. 278, 289–90 n.19 (1982). In 2018, the Supreme Court said that the standard of review for a mixed question depends on the mix:

> Mixed questions are not all alike. [S]ome require courts to expound on the law, particularly by amplifying or elaborating on a broad legal standard. When that is so—when applying the law involves developing auxiliary legal principles of use in other cases—appellate courts should typically review a decision de novo. [O]ther mixed questions immerse courts in case-specific factual issues—compelling them to marshal and weigh evidence, make credibility judgments, and otherwise address what we have (emphatically if a tad redundantly) called "multifarious, fleeting, special, narrow facts that utterly resist generalization." *Pierce v. Underwood,* 487 U.S. 552, 561–562 (1988) (internal quotation marks omitted). And when that is so, appellate courts should usually review a decision with deference. In short, the standard of review for a mixed question all depends—on whether answering it entails primarily legal or factual work.

U.S. Bank Nat'l Ass'n ex rel. CWCapital Asset Mgmt. LLC v. Vill. at Lakeridge, LLC, 138 S. Ct. 960, 967 (2018).

B. The Clearly Erroneous Standard of Review

In a bench trial, the judge "must find the facts specially and state its conclusions of law separately." Fed. R. Civ. P. 52(a)(1). Even in a jury trial, a judge may make findings of fact to rule on motions to dismiss for lack of personal jurisdiction, improper venue, insufficient service of process, and similar non-merits defenses. Rule 52(a)(6) provides that such

> [f]indings of fact, whether based on oral or other evidence, must not be set aside unless clearly erroneous, and the reviewing court must give due regard to the trial court's opportunity to judge the witnesses' credibility.

The clearly erroneous standard therefore "clearly" requires a measure of deference to the trial judge, based on the comparative advantage we described above—an advantage that the Rule expressly singles out where credibility determinations are concerned. That advantage is pronounced where credibility turns on demeanor evidence that only the trial judge can observe.

Does it also apply where the credibility determination and other fact-finding turns strictly on written evidence, which, at least in theory, is as available to an appellate court as it is to the trial court? Many appellate judges persisted in thinking no, until the Supreme Court decided *Anderson v. City of Bessemer City*, 470 U.S. 564 (1985). There the court of appeals had overturned the district court's fact-findings in a gender discrimination case. The Supreme Court reversed, explaining the clearly erroneous standard of review as follows:

> Although the meaning of the phrase "clearly erroneous" is not immediately apparent, certain general principles governing the exercise of the appellate court's power to overturn findings of a district court may be derived from our cases. The foremost of these principles, as the Fourth Circuit itself recognized, is that "[a] finding is 'clearly erroneous' when although there is evidence to support it, the reviewing court on the entire evidence is left with the definite and firm conviction that a mistake has been committed." *United States v. United States Gypsum Co.*, 333 U.S. 364, 395 (1948). This standard plainly does not entitle a reviewing court to reverse the finding of the trier of fact simply because it is convinced that it would have decided the case differently. The reviewing court oversteps the bounds of its duty under Rule 52(a) if it undertakes to duplicate the role of the lower court. "In applying the clearly erroneous standard to the findings of a district court sitting without a jury, appellate courts must constantly have in mind that their function is not to decide factual issues de novo." *Zenith Radio Corp. v. Hazeltine Research, Inc.*, 395 U.S. 100, 123 (1969). If the district court's account of the evidence is plausible in light of the record viewed in its entirety, the court of appeals may not reverse it even though convinced that had it been sitting as the trier of fact, it would have weighed the evidence differently. Where there are two permissible views of the evidence, the factfinder's choice between them cannot be clearly erroneous.
>
> This is so even when the district court's findings do not rest on credibility determinations, but are based instead on physical or documentary evidence or inferences from other facts. . . . Rule 52(a) [now 52(a)(6)] "does not make exceptions or purport to exclude certain categories of factual findings from the obligation of a court of appeals to accept a district court's findings unless clearly erroneous." *Pullman-Standard v. Swint*, 456 U.S., at 287.
>
> The rationale for deference to the original finder of fact is not limited to the superiority of the trial judge's position to make determinations of credibility. The trial judge's major role is the determination of fact, and with experience in fulfilling that role comes expertise. Duplication of the trial judge's efforts in the court of appeals would very likely contribute only negligibly to the accuracy of fact determination at a huge cost in diversion of judicial resources. In addition, the parties to a case on appeal have already been forced to concentrate their energies and resources on persuading the trial judge that their account of the facts is the correct one; requiring them to

> persuade three more judges at the appellate level is requiring too much. As the Court has stated in a different context, the trial on the merits should be "the 'main event' .... rather than a 'tryout on the road.' " *Wainwright v. Sykes*, 433 U.S. 72, 90 (1977). For these reasons, review of factual findings under the clearly-erroneous standard—with its deference to the trier of fact—is the rule, not the exception.

Anderson, 470 U.S. at 573–75.

C. The Abuse of Discretion Standard of Review

A trial judge has the discretion to make multiple decisions in the management of a case, including scheduling, discovery management, and trial management. For example, in *Beeck v. Aquaslide 'N' Dive Corp.*, 562 F.2d 837 (8th Cir. 1977), the trial judge exercised discretion in allowing the defendant to amend its answer and in bifurcating the issues for trial. The trial judge likewise exercises discretion deciding whether and how to sanction a party for violating Rule 11 or deciding whether to order a new trial.

The abuse of discretion standard of review that is used to review such exercises of trial court discretion is perhaps the hardest standard to explain and to locate on a continuum, because the range of discretion is so wide. This is why we used a highlight bar rather than a vertical line to locate it on the continuum of deference in Figure 32–1. It is impractical to identify a more precise point on the scale because discretion involves "multifarious, fleeting, special, narrow facts that utterly resist generalization." *Pierce v. Underwood*, 487 U.S. 552, 560–62 (1988). "Many courts define their abuse of discretion standard as falling somewhere between unreasonableness and simple error." *Federal Standards* § 4.21. But this generalization does not hold in all cases.

An appellate court will ordinarily give great deference to a case management or scheduling decision by the trial court. On the other hand, it might be far less deferential in reviewing the trial court's discretion in entering a default judgment because of its severity. *See Moore* § 206.05[1]. The trial court's discretion in ruling on a new trial motion falls somewhere in between. When the trial court denies such a motion in a jury case, the deference owed the trial court under the abuse of discretion standard is reinforced by the deference owed the jury verdict that the denial left standing. When the trial court grants new trial (and the claim of error is preserved on appeal of a final judgment after the new trial), its decision merits less deference because it overturns the jury's verdict.

D. Applying the Spectrum

Having now surveyed the standards of judicial review, consider which standards go with which issues in the following multiple choice question.

> A. The amount of attorneys' fees that the trial court orders a party to pay its opponent pursuant to Rule 37(f) for the party's failure to participate in formulating a discovery plan.

B. The jury's award of compensatory damages for the plaintiff in a negligence suit.
C. The trial court's refusal to admit into evidence graphic victim photos in a tort suit for assault.
D. The trial court's finding that the plaintiff resided in Virginia with an intent to remain indefinitely, which is required to establish domicile, in dismissing a case seeking to collect a tax based on domicile.
E. The trial court's decision to apply a particular test for deciding an individual's domicile, in the same case as D.

A, like most sanctions under the Rules, falls within the discretion of the trial court. The court has discretion not only to decide whether to impose sanctions for this failure, but how much the recalcitrant party should pay. Rule 37(f) itself says that the court "may" require payment of fees, probably a sufficient, though not necessary, hallmark of the court's discretion. The standard of review is abuse of discretion.

B is part of a jury verdict. It can only be set aside for insufficiency of the evidence if no reasonable jury could reach this verdict. If the losing party preserved this challenge below by filing a motion for judgment as a matter of law, and then renewed the motion after trial, the court of appeals will decide *de novo* whether a reasonable jury could have reached this verdict. Note that it does not matter whether this award was part of a general verdict, or just a finding in a special verdict. It is the fact that it was a decision by the jury that entitles it to this highly deferential standard of review.

C may, at first glance, look like a pure question of law: whether an exhibit satisfies a rule of evidence. But evidentiary rulings are not this cut and dried, as they may turn in part on other evidence in the record, the purpose of the proffer, and other factors. Moreover, this particular evidentiary ruling will turn significantly on prejudice (the applicable evidentiary rule calls on the judge to balance probative value against possible prejudice). The appellate courts have therefore reviewed most evidentiary rulings using an abuse of discretion standard.

D is a fact found by the trial judge. Don't make the mistake of thinking that Rule 52's clearly erroneous standard applies only to fact-finding by the judge in a bench trial. It contains no such limitation.

E looks like **D**, but there is a crucial difference. In **D**, the court found the facts necessary to decide domicile for purposes of a tax claim. But here the court chose a legal test for domicile, which presents a question of law, subject to *de novo review.*

VII. Appeals: Summary of Basic Principles

- A claim of error is reviewable if it was prejudicial to the appellant, preserved in the lower court by timely objection or request (except for plain error), and presented to the appeals court by proper briefing and argument.

- A party may make any argument on appeal that is supported by the record to affirm a judgment, but the party must formally appeal or cross-appeal to change a judgment.
- The finality principle embodied in 28 U.S.C. § 1291, and in most state appellate schemes, postpones appeal until a final judgment. A final judgment is one that resolves a contested matter, leaving nothing to be done except execution of the judgment. A party must therefore ordinarily "save" its claims of error until the appeal of the final judgment, when they are presented together.
- The collateral order doctrine treats as final a decision that is collateral to the merits, presents an important and unresolved question, conclusively decides the disputed question, and is effectively unreviewable on appeal from a final judgment, so that appellate review is now or never. The now-or-never requirement is the most important requirement for a collateral order to be appealable.
- Rule 54(b) authorizes the trial court to direct entry of a final judgment as to one or more claims or parties, but not as to parts of claims (such as liability only on a claim for damages).
- 28 U.S.C. § 1292 authorizes the appeal of non-final interlocutory orders that affect injunctive relief, as well as questions that are certified for immediate appeal by the trial court *and* accepted for appeal by the court of appeals.
- The All Writs Act, 28 U.S.C. § 1651(a), authorizes a party to petition a court of appeals for a writ of mandamus directed to the trial court to do its duty or abide by its jurisdiction. It is an extraordinary remedy requiring a showing both of a special risk of harm and a clear entitlement to relief, usually based on the trial court's usurpation or abdication of authority.
- The standard of review expresses how much deference the court of appeals should pay the decision maker below. Questions of law, and some of mixed law and fact, are reviewed *de novo*. Questions of fact found by the trial judge are reviewed for clear error under the clearly erroneous standard, even when the fact-finding was based only on documentary evidence.
- Jury verdicts challenged for insufficiency of the evidence are reviewed under the same standard as original and renewed motions for JMOL: whether a reasonable jury could have reached the verdict.
- Most other decisions by the trial court, including the vast majority of decisions made managing the case and the trial, are reviewed for abuse of discretion.

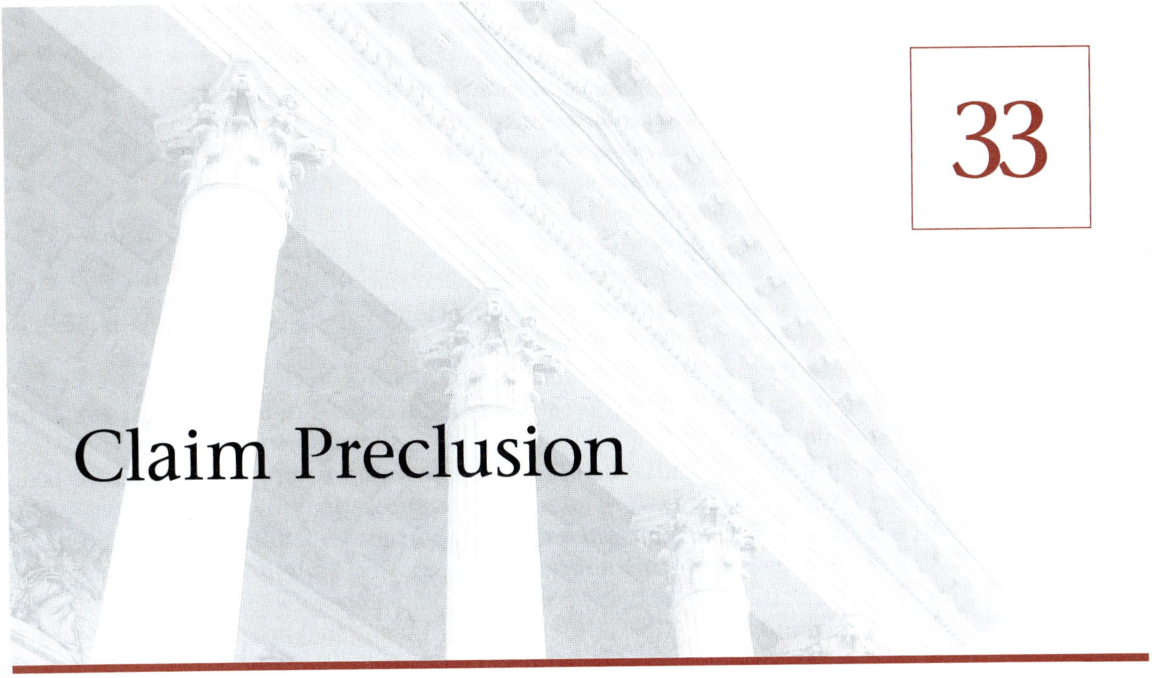

33

Claim Preclusion

I. Introduction

"Preclusion" refers to two related doctrines—claim preclusion and issue preclusion. Claim preclusion, which is also known by the Latin phrase *res judicata,* is a doctrine that prevents parties from relitigating claims that they fully litigated in a previous case. In contrast, issue preclusion, which is also called *collateral estoppel,* prevents parties from relitigating *issues* that they previously litigated in another case. Despite the simplicity of these definitions, claim and issue preclusion are often difficult to apply in practice. This chapter focuses on the complexities of claim preclusion, and the next chapter addresses issue preclusion.

A. Claim Preclusion's Importance

To see why claim preclusion is such an important doctrine, consider a simple case. Imagine that, while driving her car, Doris collides with Preetha. Preetha sues Doris in state court, alleging that Doris's negligence caused Preetha to suffer a broken leg. The jury concludes that Preetha is not entitled to any recovery because Doris was not negligent. Shortly after the verdict, Preetha files a new lawsuit against Doris, this time alleging that the same accident that gave rise to Preetha's broken leg also caused Preetha to suffer a broken hand. In this second suit, Preetha seeks to recover damages only for her broken hand.

The problem with Preetha's second case is that she is alleging the same claim that she alleged against Doris in the first case. Preetha's alleged damages may be slightly different in the second case (a broken hand instead of a broken leg), but most courts would find that the underlying claim—that Preetha suffered personal injuries due to Doris's negligent driving—is identical. Accordingly, most courts would grant a motion to dismiss Preetha's second case on claim preclusion grounds.

Claim preclusion makes good sense here for several reasons. First, it would be unfair to allow a plaintiff like Preetha to get a second chance to recover against Doris. Claimants should have only one opportunity to litigate, and in this case, Preetha is trying to have two. The second case is particularly unfair to Doris, who will have to incur the time, expense, and worry of defending against repetitive lawsuits. Moreover, if the second case proceeds, Doris might have to pay damages for an accident that the first jury concluded Doris did not cause. Such a contradictory result would add to the sense that Doris was treated unfairly.

Claim preclusion also helps to preserve the public's confidence in the judicial system. Consider what would happen if the jury in the second case concludes that Preetha is entitled to recover damages. Not only does the result seem unfair to Doris, but the second verdict gives the public the impression that the courts cannot reliably determine truth or dispense justice. After all, how reliable could the courts be if they reach opposite conclusions regarding the same claims? Claim preclusion keeps the public from developing this negative impression by barring the litigation of the second case.

Finally, and perhaps most importantly, claim preclusion promotes efficiency. Without claim preclusion, plaintiffs could ask multiple courts to hear the same claim, and each court would have to hear the same facts and try essentially the same cases. In the absence of claim preclusion, claimants might even have an incentive to relitigate claims, hoping to improve the presentation of the claim in each subsequent case. For example, plaintiffs could try one approach in one case and a different approach in a second case just to see which one is more effective. Claim preclusion prevents this waste of judicial resources by giving plaintiffs a powerful incentive to allege all of their claims—and to assert their best theories in support of those claims—in a single case.

In sum, claim preclusion advances several important values, including fairness, protecting the public's perception of the justice system, and efficiency. But as this chapter reveals, the doctrine has many complexities.

B. Distinguishing Claim Preclusion from Other Doctrines

One common mistake is to confuse claim preclusion with other procedural concepts. To avoid this error, keep an eye out for the presence of multiple lawsuits. Look for a lawsuit that reaches a final judgment, which is not necessarily the first lawsuit filed. Call this "lawsuit #1." Next, decide whether a claim (or issue) decided in lawsuit #1 seems to arise again in "lawsuit #2." If so, you may have a claim or issue preclusion problem.

Preclusion problems can be easy to confuse with retrials, collateral proceedings, and double jeopardy. With regard to retrials, a trial court can order one for a number of reasons, such as the court's determination that it erroneously excluded a key piece of evidence. Similarly, an appellate court can remand a case for a new trial when it concludes that the trial court committed certain types of errors during the original proceeding, such as giving improper jury instructions. Claim preclusion does not apply to these kinds of situations because a *retrial is simply a continuation of the original case*. Claim preclusion applies when the plaintiff files a *new, second* case against the defendant.

Claim preclusion is also inapplicable to a collateral proceeding. For example, a plaintiff may win a default judgment in one court and seek to enforce that judgment in a court in another state, perhaps where the defendant has substantial assets. To do so, the plaintiff has to initiate an enforcement action (i.e., a collateral proceeding) in that state. As with a retrial, this action is not a new, second case that re-alleges the same claim against the same defendant. Rather, the enforcement action is collateral to the *original* proceeding, making claim preclusion inapplicable.

Finally, the Double Jeopardy Clause in the Fifth Amendment to the United States Constitution "precludes" the government from re-prosecuting a criminal defendant for the same offense. Although double jeopardy functions a lot like claim preclusion, the doctrines differ in several respects. First, double jeopardy applies only to criminal cases, while claim preclusion applies to civil cases. Second, double jeopardy is a constitutional doctrine, and claim preclusion is usually a common law doctrine. Finally, double jeopardy applies only after an acquittal and thus only benefits the defendant; in contrast, civil judgments have preclusive effect regardless of who wins the case.

II. Defining a Claim: *River Park, Inc. v. City of Highland Park*

Typically, three elements must be satisfied before a claim will be barred under the claim preclusion doctrine. First, the claim must be the same as one that was litigated in a previous case. Second, the previously litigated claim must have resulted in a valid, final judgment on the merits. And third, the parties who litigated the previous claim must typically be the same parties who are litigating the current claim. *See, e.g., Federated Department Stores, Inc. v. Moitie*, 452 U.S. 394, 399 (1981). This section focuses on the first element—how to determine whether a claim is the same as one from a previously litigated case.

Courts often struggle to determine whether two claims are the same, primarily because there is no consensus on the proper definition of a "claim." Consider, for example, Preetha's claim against Doris for injuries to Preetha's leg. Why exactly should we view her second case, which alleges a hand injury, as raising the same claim as the first case? Is it because the legal theory (negligence) is the same? Is it because the cases arose out of the same incident? Should it matter that Preetha suffered different sorts of injuries or that she might need different evidence to win her second case than she needed to win her first case?

READING *RIVER PARK, INC. v. CITY OF HIGHLAND PARK.* Consider the following questions as you read this case:

- How does the Illinois Supreme Court define a "claim"?
- Why does the court reject the alternate definition of a claim?
- Why does the outcome of this case turn on the definition that the court adopts?

RIVER PARK, INC. v. CITY OF HIGHLAND PARK

703 N.E.2d 883 (Ill. 1998)

Justice McMorrow delivered the opinion of the court:

. . .

BACKGROUND

. . . [Plaintiff] River Park, Inc. (River Park), had an ownership interest in a 162-acre piece of land in the City of Highland Park known as the Highland Park Country Club (Country Club). Plaintiff Spatz & Company (Spatz) was a builder and had purchased the capital stock of River Park. . . . In July 1988, Spatz petitioned defendant on behalf of River Park to obtain approval for its plans to develop the Country Club property. . . .

. . . On November 14, 1989, the commission approved . . . the planned development. . . . The city council did not, however, communicate to Spatz that . . . [the City of Highland Park] was interested in purchasing the property [for itself].

For Spatz to obtain final approval, defendant's zoning ordinance required . . . [River Park, Inc.] to provide the commission and the city council with final engineering plans. . . .

[Eds.—According to the complaint, the City of Highland Park intentionally undermined Spatz's efforts to provide the necessary engineering plans, knowing that delays would cause a bank to foreclose on the property and allow the City of Highland Park to buy the land at a discount. The bank ultimately did foreclose, and the City of Highland Park purchased the property.]

. . .

Based on these alleged events, on February 23, 1993, plaintiffs filed a . . . complaint against defendant in the United States District Court for the Northern District of Illinois. In this complaint, plaintiffs asserted that defendant was liable pursuant to 42 U.S.C. § 1983 for depriving them of their property rights without due process of law in violation of the United States Constitution. According to plaintiffs, they had a legal entitlement to approval of their engineering plans and to the rezoning they requested. They alleged that defendant's failure to act on the plans and vote on their second petition deprived them of this property right without due process of law. The complaint alleged no claims under state law.

... On July 22, 1993, the district court issued a written order in which it found that plaintiffs had failed to allege a violation of due process. The court therefore granted defendant's motion and dismissed plaintiffs' complaint with prejudice. On April 25, 1994, the United States Court of Appeals for the Seventh Circuit affirmed the dismissal of plaintiffs' federal complaint.

Having failed in their attempt to obtain a remedy for defendant's actions in federal court, plaintiffs filed a six-count complaint against defendant in the circuit court of Lake County [an Illinois state trial court] on November 21, 1994.... [After a motion to dismiss, only three counts remained:] (1) tortious interference with business expectancy, (2) breach of implied contract, and (3) abuse of governmental power. In the tortious interference with business expectancy count of the amended complaint, plaintiffs alleged that they had a reasonable expectation of entering into profitable sale and development contracts and that defendant had intentionally interfered with this expectancy by delaying the rezoning and plat approval process in order to acquire the property at a price less than market value. With respect to their claim for breach of implied contract, plaintiffs alleged that, by accepting the fee they paid for processing their zoning petition, defendant entered into an implied contract to process this petition in good faith. They alleged that defendant breached this agreement by prolonging the zoning process, by failing to review the engineering plans within a reasonable period of time, and by deeming their application withdrawn. In the abuse of power count of their amended complaint, plaintiffs alleged that, by forcing them into bankruptcy and foreclosure in order to acquire their land at a reduced price, defendant abused its power under the Illinois Constitution to acquire private property for public use in exchange for just compensation. In each of these counts, plaintiffs requested damages of $25 million. They requested an additional $25 million in punitive damages for their abuse of governmental power claim.

... [D]efendant moved to dismiss the ... three counts of plaintiffs' amended complaint. Defendant requested that these claims be dismissed ... on the basis that ... plaintiffs' claims were barred under the doctrine of *res judicata* by the dismissal of plaintiffs' federal complaint.... The circuit court granted this motion and dismissed plaintiffs' complaint with prejudice.

... The appellate court found that ... the doctrine of *res judicata* did not apply because the cause of action asserted in plaintiffs' federal complaint differed from the cause of action alleged in the complaint they filed in state court....

... [W]e reverse the judgment of the appellate court.

ANALYSIS

... Under the doctrine of *res judicata,* a final judgment on the merits rendered by a court of competent jurisdiction acts as a bar to a subsequent suit between the parties involving the same cause of action. The bar extends to what was actually decided in the first action, as well as those matters that could have been decided in that suit. For the doctrine of *res judicata* to apply, the following three requirements must be satisfied: (1) there was a final judgment on the merits rendered by a court of competent jurisdiction, (2) there is an identity of cause of action, and (3) there is an identity of parties or their privies. . . .

Having found that . . . [the first and third] elements for the applicability of the *res judicata* doctrine are present in this case, we turn to a discussion of the third requirement: identity of cause of action. Recently, in *Rodgers v. St. Mary's Hospital,* 597 N.E.2d 616 (1992), we explained that Illinois courts have adopted two tests for determining whether causes of action are the same for purposes of *res judicata.* Under the "same evidence" test, a second suit is barred "if the evidence needed to sustain the second suit would have sustained the first, or if the same facts were essential to maintain both actions." *Rodgers,* 597 N.E.2d at 621. The "transactional" test provides that "the assertion of different kinds of theories of relief still constitutes a single cause of action if a single group of operative facts give rise to the assertion of relief." *Id.*

In almost all cases in which Illinois courts have discussed these two tests, the courts have found that the result of the analysis was the same, regardless of which test was applied. Courts, including this court, either have found that an identity of cause of action exists under either test or they have found that there is no identity of cause of action under either test. As a result, it has been unnecessary for this court to decide which test is controlling if there is a conflict between the results.

In this case, however, the question of which test prevails when the results differ is presented by the parties' arguments. Although the parties argue that we may decide the *res judicata* issue in their favor under either test, they clearly disagree as to which is the appropriate test. Plaintiffs rely on the same evidence test to show that their federal and state suits are not the same causes of action for purposes of *res judicata.* According to plaintiffs,

> "A federal 1983 cause of action requires proof of facts (i.e., a federally protected property interest and violation of due process) which are not necessary for the plaintiffs to prove to entitle them to succeed in their state action for . . . breach of [implied] contract (Count II), or violation of the Illinois Constitution (Count IV). Thus the facts in the federal 1983 action and this state action are not identical and the same evidence would not sustain both actions."

In support of their argument plaintiffs cite . . . [several older Illinois cases]. In these cases, the courts do not acknowledge the transactional test. Instead, these courts based their findings that the suits at issue did not involve the same cause of action exclusively on the same evidence test.

Defendant responds that plaintiffs' reliance on these older appellate court cases is inconsistent with recent decisions of this court adopting the transactional test. Defendant also notes that the adoption of the transactional test is in accordance with the modern trend of court decisions, as well as the approach contained in the Restatement (Second) of Judgments. See Restatement (Second) of Judgments § 24, Comment *a,* at 197 (1982).

Based on these arguments by the parties, we find it appropriate in this case to address whether the transactional or same evidence test should be applied in cases involving issues of *res judicata.*

Although Illinois courts have generally reached the same result under either the transactional test or the same evidence test, it is important to note that these tests are not the same. As the language used to describe these tests in *Rodgers* indicates, under the same evidence test the definition of what constitutes a cause of action is narrower than under the transactional test. As explained in the Restatement (Second) of Judgments, the same evidence test is tied to the theories of relief asserted by a plaintiff, the result of which is that two claims may be part of the same transaction, yet be considered separate causes of action because the evidence needed to support the theories on which they are based differs. By contrast, the transactional approach is more pragmatic. Under this approach, a claim is viewed in "factual terms" and considered "coterminous with the transaction, regardless of the number of substantive theories, or variant forms of relief flowing from those theories, that may be available to the plaintiff; . . . and regardless of the variations in the evidence needed to support the theories or rights." Restatement (Second) of Judgments § 24, Comment *a,* at 197 (1982).

This court has recognized the validity of the transactional test. Like other Illinois courts, however, we have also continued to use the standards contained in the same evidence test in our analysis of *res judicata* cases. Not only has this resulted in courts having to engage in lengthy analyses of claims under both tests, it has also created confusion as to the proper application of these tests. In this case, defendant suggests that the continued application of the same evidence test is inconsistent with our adoption of the transactional test. We agree.

Having adopted the more liberal transactional test for determining whether claims are part of the same transaction, it makes little sense to perform the identity-of-cause-of-action analysis under the more stringent standards of the same evidence test. If these stricter standards are indeed controlling, our acceptance of the transactional test would be meaningless. Consequently, our approval of the transactional test necessitates a rejection of the same evidence test. Accordingly, we hold that the same evidence test is not determinative of identity of cause of action. Instead, pursuant to the transactional analysis, separate claims will be considered the same cause of action for purposes of *res judicata* if they arise from a single group of operative facts, regardless of whether they assert different theories of relief. . . .

Our adoption of the transactional test *in lieu* of the same evidence test is consistent with the approach proposed in the Restatement (Second) of Judgments, as well as the trend of decisions in other jurisdictions. In 1982, the Restatement abandoned the same evidence test in favor of the transactional test. The current version of the Restatement advances the transactional test:

> "Dimensions of 'Claim' for Purposes of Merger or Bar—General Rule Concerning 'Splitting'
>
> (1) When a valid and final judgment rendered in an action extinguishes the plaintiff's claim pursuant to the rules of merger or bar . . . , the claim extinguished includes all rights of the plaintiff to remedies against the defendant with respect to all or any part of the transaction, or series of connected transactions, out of which the action arose.
>
> (2) What factual grouping constitutes a 'transaction,' and what groupings constitute a 'series,' are to be determined pragmatically, giving weight to such

considerations as whether the facts are related in time, space, origin, or motivation, whether they form a convenient trial unit, and whether their treatment as a unit conforms to the parties' expectations or business understanding or usage." Restatement (Second) of Judgments § 24, at 196 (1982).

. . .

Like the Restatement, a majority of federal courts, as well as numerous courts in other states, have applied a transactional analysis when determining whether there is an identity of cause of action for purposes of *res judicata.* [Numerous citations omitted.] Our decision in this case that the transactional test should control is in accordance with these authorities, as well as this court's existing recognition of this analysis.

We now turn to an application of the transactional test to the case before us. Under this test, we find that plaintiffs' claims for breach of implied contract and abuse of governmental power are the same cause of action as the section 1983 claim alleged in their federal complaint. Plaintiffs' federal and state claims are the same cause of action for purposes of *res judicata* because they arise from the same core of operative facts. Like their section 1983 action, plaintiffs' state law claims are based on defendant's alleged refusals to timely process and approve their rezoning petition in an effort to deprive plaintiffs of their rightful use of their property. Plaintiffs themselves concede in their brief that "both the federal action and the present state action in the case at bar arise out of the processing of the plaintiffs' applications for plan approval by the defendant and both actions seek damages for the wrongful acts of the defendants in processing those applications."

. . . As our previous description of the facts contained in plaintiffs' state complaint demonstrates, the facts on which they base their claim for relief under state law are virtually identical to the facts on which their federal claim was based.

In arguing that their federal and state claims are not the same causes of action, plaintiffs rely on differences in the theories of relief asserted in these suits. This is contrary to the principles of the transactional analysis, which we have explained before and reaffirm in this case. As we stated in *Torcasso v. Standard Outdoor Sales, Inc.,* 626 N.E.2d 225 (1993), suits involving different theories of relief may constitute the same cause of action:

> "Although a single group of operative facts may give rise to the assertion of more than one kind of relief or more than one theory of recovery, assertions of different kinds or theories of relief arising out of a single group of operative facts constitute but a single cause of action."

. . .

In the case before us, our review of the pleadings convinces us that there is no material difference between plaintiffs' federal and state causes of action. Plaintiffs' assertion of state law claims for breach of implied contract and abuse of governmental power after their section 1983 action was dismissed was merely a "substitution of labels." Restatement of Judgments 2d § 25, Comment *e,* at 213 (1982). We hold that the breach of implied contract and abuse of governmental power claims contained in the amended complaint plaintiffs filed in state court are the same cause of action as the section 1983 claim alleged in plaintiffs' federal complaint. Accordingly, the three requirements for the application of the doctrine of *res judicata* are satisfied in this case.

. . .

The judgment of the appellate court is affirmed in part and reversed in part, and the judgment of the circuit court, dismissing plaintiffs' complaint, is affirmed.

Notes and Questions: Definition of a Claim

Q **1. Defining a claim.** Which definition of a claim did the Illinois Supreme Court adopt in this case, and why did the court reject the alternative?

A The court adopts the transactional definition of a claim. According to this definition, different theories of recovery constitute a single claim if they arise out of the same "group of operative facts" or arise out of the same underlying transaction or occurrence.

The court rejected the narrower "same evidence" test, which some Illinois courts had used prior to the *River Park* decision. Under the same evidence test, two suits involve the same claim only "if the evidence needed to sustain the second suit would have sustained the first, or if the same facts were essential to maintain both actions." *River Park,* 703 N.E.2d at 891.

The court rejected the same evidence test for two reasons. First, the court concluded that its own precedents revealed a preference for the transactional approach and that the narrower same evidence test conflicted with those precedents. Second, the court was influenced by the trend in favor of the transactional test. Although the original *Restatement of Judgments* adopted the same evidence test, *see Restatement (First) of Judgments* § 61, the subsequent *Restatement* adopted the transactional test in 1982. *See Restatement (Second) of Judgments* § 24 (1982).

Since 1982, a growing number of state and federal courts have adopted the transactional definition of a claim. In fact, the United States Supreme Court recently endorsed the transactional definition for purposes of federal preclusion doctrine, *Lucky Brand Dungarees, Inc. v. Marcel Fashions Group, Inc.,* 590 U.S. __, __, 140 S. Ct. 1589, 1595 (2020).

Note 5 below describes several additional benefits of the transactional test that the Illinois Supreme Court did not mention.

Q **2. Applying the tests.** If the Court had adopted the same evidence test in this case, the Court might have held that claim preclusion did not apply here. Why does the transactional test preclude the plaintiffs' claims, whereas the same evidence test might not?

A *The transactional test.* Under the transactional test, the question is whether the two cases arise out of the same "group of operative facts." In the federal litigation, the plaintiffs alleged that the City of Highland Park violated the plaintiffs' due process rights. That claim relied on a group of related factual allegations, specifically that the City engaged in a conspiracy to delay the permitting process so that the City could buy the plaintiffs' property.

In the state case, the plaintiffs offered different theories of recovery—tortious interference, breach of implied contract, and abuse of governmental power—but those theories relied on the same factual allegations as the federal due process claim. In particular, all of the state claims arose out of the City's alleged tardy processing of the permit and the City's purchase of the property for itself. In short, the federal cause of action and all three state causes of action arose out of the same group of operative facts and thus constituted the same "claim" for preclusion purposes.

The same evidence test. The analysis is subtly different under the same evidence test, under which two cases give rise to the same claim only "if the evidence needed to sustain the second suit would have sustained the first, or if the same facts were essential to maintain both actions." *River Park, Inc.*, 703 N.E.2d at 891 (quoting *Rodgers v. St. Mary's Hospital of Decatur*, 597 N.E.2d 616, 621 (Ill. 1992)). The problem with applying this test is that, in many cases, some of the evidence will be identical, so it is difficult to determine whether the evidence is sufficiently similar to consider the claims to be the "same."

Here, for example, the plaintiffs had to prove in the federal case that they had a federally protected property interest and that the City violated the plaintiffs' due process rights in that property. That claim might have required evidence showing which City officials had engaged in the wrongful conduct and whether those officials were state actors. In addition, the claim might have required evidence of the City's processing procedures and how those procedures violated the plaintiffs' due process rights.

The evidence required to win the federal case arguably would not have sufficed to sustain the plaintiffs' state law causes of action. Consider, for example, the claim for implied breach of contract. The plaintiffs alleged that, by accepting the plaintiffs' processing fee, the City implicitly agreed to process the plaintiffs' application in good faith. This claim required evidence of the plaintiffs' payment of the fee and how the City handled the processing of the plaintiffs' application. Although the federal and state claims both required evidence of how the City processed the plaintiffs' application (i.e., there is some overlapping evidence), the type of evidence necessary to show how the City's procedure violated the plaintiffs' due process rights might not have proved the existence of a breach of an implied contract and vice versa. Indeed, the Illinois Appellate Court reached this very conclusion. *River Park v. City of Highland Park*, 692 N.E.2d 369, 372 (Ill. App. Ct. 1998). The Illinois Supreme Court subsequently reversed the appellate court, but only because the appellate court should have applied the transactional test, not because it applied the same evidence standard incorrectly.

In sum, it is arguable that the evidence necessary to prove the state law claims would not have sufficed to prove the federal due process claim. As a result, the court's adoption of the same evidence test might have led to the conclusion that claim preclusion was inapplicable. The tentativeness of this conclusion highlights one of the problems with the same evidence test: It is difficult to determine just how much of the evidence needs to be the same in order for two causes of action to constitute the same claim for preclusion purposes.

3. Another possible definition: Primary rights. Some state courts previously adopted a "primary rights" definition of a claim. According to this definition, a plaintiff has a separate claim for each type of injury that the defendant has incurred. *See, e.g., Carter v. Hinckle*, 52 S.E.2d 135 (Va. 1949).

Consider the *River Park* case. The plaintiffs alleged several distinct harms, such as those resulting from the tortious interference claim (e.g., the lost profits from the failure to sell the property) and the abuse of power claim (e.g., the acquisition of the plaintiffs' property for public use without just compensation). Under the primary rights approach, each of those harms would constitute a separate claim for preclusion purposes.

Q **4. Testing the tests.** Imagine that Piers is in a two-car accident while he is driving his taxi and suffers a broken leg and damage to his taxi. Piers believes that Dirk, who was driving the other car, might have caused the crash intentionally, because Dirk was angry that Piers had cut Dirk off a few moments earlier. Because Piers is not sure whether Dirk caused the crash intentionally or negligently, Piers sues Dirk for negligence as well as battery (an intentional tort). Piers's complaint seeks to recover damages for his personal injuries, lost profits from his inability to use his taxi while it was being repaired, and compensatory damages for the cost of the insurance deductible that he had to pay to get his taxi fixed. How many different claims does Piers have under the transactional test, the same evidence test, and the primary rights test?

A Under the transactional test, all of Piers's claims and injuries arose out of a single event—the car accident. Thus, using the transactional test, Piers has only one "claim" for claim preclusion purposes. He would have to assert all of his theories of recovery and all of his allegations of damages in a single case or risk that claim preclusion would bar subsequent litigation.

Under the same evidence test, it appears that Piers could bring two separate lawsuits. To prove the negligence claim, Piers would have to offer evidence that Dirk drove in a manner that was unreasonable under the circumstances. In contrast, the battery claim would require evidence that Dirk *intended* to cause the accident. That claim would require evidence about the earlier near-miss and what Dirk's reaction was to it. Did Dirk curse at Piers? Perhaps Dirk gave Piers the middle finger and yelled, "I'll get you for that!" To prove the intentional tort, Piers would have to offer evidence of this sort to demonstrate that Dirk intended to cause the accident. The evidence to prove the negligence claim, therefore, would not suffice to prove the intentional tort and vice versa.

Students sometimes think that Piers has more than two claims under the same evidence test because Piers would have to prove different types of damages (personal injury, property, and economic) using different evidence. For example, evidence of Piers's bodily injuries (e.g., a doctor's report) is quite different from the evidence establishing his lost profits (e.g., receipts reflecting his typical weekly earnings). Most courts, however, have concluded that these differences do not give rise to different claims, because the same evidence test focuses on the evidence needed to prove liability, not damages. *Freer* § 11.2.3.

Finally, the primary rights definition focuses on how many rights were alleged to have been violated. In this case, Piers arguably had three separate violations of his rights: his right to be free from bodily injury (his claim for personal injuries), his right to be free from property damages, and his right to pursue his livelihood (his claim for lost profits from the taxi). Thus, under the primary rights definition, Piers could probably bring three separate lawsuits without fearing that they would be barred under the claim preclusion doctrine: one for his personal injuries, one for property damage, and one for lost profits. *See, e.g., Carter v. Hinckle,* 52 S.E.2d 135 (Va. 1949).

Q **5. Evaluating the tests.** Which test best serves the values of efficiency, fairness, and protecting the public's perception of the justice system? Why?

A One important function of claim preclusion is to promote the efficient resolution of controversies. The doctrine accomplishes this goal by encouraging claimants to bring all related causes of action in a single case or risk losing the opportunity to litigate those causes of action later. The transactional test, as the broadest test, poses the greatest risk that claim preclusion will bar a later-filed action, so plaintiffs are more likely to combine their causes of action in a single case in jurisdictions that have adopted the transactional definition of a claim. Given that supplemental jurisdiction and liberal joinder rules make it quite easy for plaintiffs to join all related causes of action in a single case, the transactional test does not impose any unreasonable burdens.

Second, by adopting the broadest definition of a claim and limiting the relitigation of related causes of action, the transactional test also reduces the likelihood of conflicting results and arguably protects the public's image of the justice system most effectively.

Finally, the transactional test does the best job of promoting the interests of fairness to defendants because the test offers the broadest protection against serial lawsuits.

For these reasons, the transactional test has become the most commonly used definition of a claim. That test, however, is not without its problems. For example, because the transactional test is so broad, some plaintiffs may not realize that claim preclusion will prevent subsequent litigation of an omitted cause of action. Thus, the transactional test puts a plaintiff at the greatest risk of inadvertently losing the opportunity to pursue a legitimate cause of action, causing some unfairness. Indeed, the *River Park* case may be such an example.

6. Different courts and different claims?

Penny believes that Demotion, Inc. fired her because of her gender, so she brings a federal law gender discrimination claim in the federal court for the Northern District of New York. Demotion wins the case at trial, and the court enters judgment in favor of Demotion. Penny subsequently files a state law *age* discrimination claim against Demotion in New York *state* court, alleging that her firing was due to her age. Demotion's answer raises the affirmative defense of claim preclusion, and Demotion later moves for summary judgment on that basis and includes a copy of the prior judgment. If the court applies the transactional definition of a claim, the court should

A. grant the motion.
B. deny the motion because age and gender discrimination are different types of discrimination.
C. deny the motion because the evidence that Penny would need to prove her gender discrimination cause of action is different from the evidence she would need to prove her age discrimination cause of action.
D. deny the motion because claim preclusion does not bar the claim unless the previous lawsuit was litigated in the same court; in this case, the first lawsuit was resolved in federal court, not state court.

D is incorrect because claim preclusion applies to claims that were previously litigated in a different court system. *River Park* is such a case. The original lawsuit was filed in federal court, but the Illinois Supreme Court nevertheless concluded that claim preclusion barred the state court litigation. Some complexities associated with intersystem preclusion are discussed in more detail in the next chapter,* but it suffices to note here that a state court judgment can be given preclusive effect in federal court and vice versa.

C is wrong because the transactional test does not turn on whether the two claims rely on the same evidence. The transactional test asks whether the two causes of action arose out of the same operative facts.

The key question, then, is whether the two causes of action arose out of the same event. Here, they did, because both claims arose out of Demotion's firing of Penny. Do not focus on the labels of the claims—gender and race discrimination—and conclude that they rely on different theories and are therefore different claims. The focus is on the event that gave rise to those theories, and in this case, both claims arise out of the same event—the firing of Penny. Thus, the gender and age discrimination claims are part of the same "claim" for preclusion purposes, making **B** incorrect and **A** the best answer. *See Havercombe v. Department of Education of the Commonwealth of Puerto Rico*, 250 F.3d 1 (1st Cir. 2001) (finding claim preclusion to apply under similar circumstances).

This question illustrates how the transactional test is similar in scope to the "common nucleus of operative fact" concept in supplemental jurisdiction. It is not entirely clear whether the concepts are identical in scope, but substantial overlap makes good sense. Recall that supplemental jurisdiction and the joinder rules promote efficiency by allowing claimants to join related causes of action in a single case. Claim preclusion also promotes efficiency by *requiring* claimants

* One such complexity concerns choice of law. For example, when the second suit is litigated in a different court system (e.g., state court) from the first suit (e.g., federal court), does the court where the second suit is filed (e.g., the state court) apply its own preclusion law (e.g., state preclusion law) or the preclusion law of the jurisdiction that entered the first judgment (e.g., federal preclusion law)? In general, the answer is the latter, which means that the Illinois Supreme Court probably should have applied federal, not Illinois, preclusion law in the *River Park* case. Put another way, and as noted in the next chapter, the entire discussion of Illinois preclusion law in *River Park* was probably unnecessary!

to join their related claims, as the Rules permit, or risk preclusion later. In sum, although the definition of a claim does not necessarily have to correspond to the scope of joinder or supplemental jurisdiction, symmetry reinforces the goal of efficiency. *See Freer* § 11.2.2 (noting the overlap between the scope of the joinder rules and the scope of claim preclusion under the transactional test).

III. Valid, Final Judgments on the Merits

A judgment has preclusive effects only if it is valid, final, and on the merits. In the absence of such a judgment, the claimant would not have had an opportunity to litigate her claim fully, and claim preclusion would be unfair. The difficult task is figuring out when a prior court's judgment is "valid," when it is "final," and when it is "on the merits."

A. Validity of the Judgment

Historically, a judgment was considered "invalid" and not entitled to claim preclusive effect if the court issuing the judgment lacked personal or subject matter jurisdiction or if the defendant did not receive proper notice of the lawsuit. David L. Shapiro, Civil Procedure: Preclusion in Civil Actions 23 (2001).

There are, however, some exceptions to the general rule that judgments lacking in subject matter or personal jurisdiction are invalid. Such exceptions generally apply when the defendant responded to the lawsuit and both parties litigated the case without raising the jurisdictional problem. For example, imagine that Perry sues Devorah in federal court, and Perry loses at trial. Perry does not appeal. Perry subsequently learns that Devorah's citizenship was the same as Perry's, so subject matter jurisdiction was lacking in the trial court. Arguing that the court lacked subject matter jurisdiction and that the first judgment was invalid, Perry asserts an identical claim against Devorah in state court. Devorah contends that Perry's lawsuit should be barred on claim preclusion grounds. Should the court grant the motion?

Nearly all of the elements of claim preclusion are satisfied here. The two claims are identical, and the two cases involve the same claimant suing the same defendant. Moreover, the Michigan federal court issued a final judgment, and as discussed below, a jury verdict is clearly "on the merits." The only issue is whether the original judgment was "valid."

It is important to see why this judgment should be construed as valid, even though subject matter jurisdiction was lacking in the trial court. Both parties actively litigated this case and could have raised subject matter jurisdiction at any time, including on appeal. There have to be *some* limits on when parties can raise subject matter jurisdiction or else a judgment could be subject to attack forever. For this reason, the courts have concluded that, unless the district court's decision to hear the case "was a manifest abuse of authority" or would "substantially infringe the authority of another tribunal," claim preclusion should apply to a judgment, even where the court lacked subject matter jurisdiction (such as the Perry example). *Restatement (Second) of Judgments* § 12 cmt. d (1982). *See also*

Travelers Indem. Co. v. Bailey, 557 U.S. 137, 152–53 (2009) (citing the *Restatement* in a similar context); *Chicot County Drainage Dist. v. Baxter State Bank*, 308 U.S. 371, 376–77 (1940); David L. Shapiro, Civil Procedure: Preclusion in Civil Actions 25–29 (2001).

B. Finality of the Judgment

A judgment does not have claim preclusive effect until it is "final." For example, suppose that Paolo files a breach of contract claim against Dina in a New York state court, and on the same day, Paolo files an identical claim against Dina in a Florida state court. (Paolo might file these duplicative lawsuits for a number of reasons, such as a concern that the preferred court may lack personal jurisdiction over the defendant.)

Claim preclusion does not yet apply in either case, even though Paolo has filed the same claim in two different courts. One of the courts may decide to stay the proceedings—essentially, put the case on hold—until the other court has resolved the matter, but a court will not dismiss a claim on preclusion grounds until another court has issued a *final* judgment. This finality requirement makes sense, because (among other reasons) there is no concern that a court will enter a judgment that is inconsistent with a prior judgment until a prior judgment actually exists.

The primary ambiguity here concerns the meaning of the word "final." Is a judgment "final" when the trial court completes its handling of the case? Or is it "final" only after the parties have exhausted all of their opportunities to appeal? The majority of courts, including the federal courts, have concluded that a judgment is final for claim preclusion purposes when the trial court enters a judgment, even if the losing party might subsequently file a post-trial motion, such as a motion for a new trial, and even if the losing party appeals. *Restatement (Second) of Judgments* § 13 cmt. f. Again, this conclusion is consistent with the courts' growing emphasis on efficiency, because the result is that a judgment has a claim preclusive effect—and thus bars subsequent litigation—at an earlier point in time.

But suppose the judgment that gave rise to preclusion is later reversed on appeal. Does the second court have to reopen the case? As a practical matter, the issue does not arise often. If a judgment is on appeal and the same claim is pending in another court, the other court will typically await the completion of the appeal in the original case before determining whether claim preclusion applies. *Restatement (Second) of Judgments* § 13 cmt. f. But if the other court grants a dismissal on claim preclusion grounds while the appeal of the original judgment is pending and the original judgment is subsequently reversed, a party can usually set aside the second court's dismissal by filing a post-judgment motion or timely appeal. *See* Fed. R. Civ. P. 60(b)(5); *Restatement (Second) of Judgments* § 16 cmt. c.

C. A Judgment on the Merits

A judgment must also be "on the merits" for it to have claim preclusive effect. In general, courts have interpreted this requirement expansively to include not only jury verdicts, but summary judgments, judgments as a matter of law, and even (in most courts) default judgments. All of these dispositions suggest that a claimant has had an opportunity to litigate her claim and address the merits of the case, at least in some respects.

In contrast, a claimant has not had an opportunity to litigate her claim when the court dismisses it for lack of subject matter jurisdiction, personal jurisdiction, or venue. Such dismissals typically occur before a court has had an opportunity to examine the merits of a claimant's contentions and are thus not "on the merits" for preclusion purposes.

There are a few dispositions that fall into a gray area. For example, suppose that a plaintiff files a claim in California, and the claim is dismissed on statute of limitations grounds. Now assume that the plaintiff subsequently files the same claim against the same defendant in Maryland, which has a longer statute of limitations. Was the dismissal of the California action "on the merits" so that it is subject to claim preclusion in the Maryland action? Rule 41(b) suggests that such dismissals are "on the merits," at least for purposes of refiling the same action in the same court, but does such a dismissal have claim preclusive effect in cases filed elsewhere?* Although there is some disagreement, the trend has been in favor of giving statute of limitations dismissals claim preclusive effect. *See, e.g., Semtek Int'l Inc. v. Lockheed Martin Corp.,* 531 U.S. 497, 502 (2001) (observing the trend). This trend, like the trend in favor of finding judgments to be final even though they are on appeal, reflects the increasingly widespread view that claimants should have fewer opportunities to relitigate claims.

The trend also suggests that the "on the merits" requirement is misnamed. If a claim is dismissed on statute of limitations grounds (for example), a claimant has not had an opportunity to reach the merits of her claim in any meaningful sense. For this reason, the *Restatement (Second) of Judgments* has dropped the phrase "on the merits." *Restatement (Second) of Judgments* § 19 cmt. a (1982) (explaining that "judgments not passing directly on the substance of the claim have come to operate as a bar"). Courts, however, continue to use the term and have simply interpreted it expansively to include a wide range of dispositions.

D. This Requirement Is Like Rhode Island

There is an old Saturday Night Live skit where the audience is instructed: "Rhode Island is neither a 'road' nor an 'island.' Discuss amongst yourselves."

The "valid, final judgment on the merits" requirement has a similar comedic quality. Courts today will give preclusive effect to judgments that are not truly final (e.g., they can be on appeal), not really on the merits (e.g., a dismissal on

* Federal Rule 41(b) raises an interesting ambiguity regarding the meaning of "on the merits." That Rule provides that all involuntary dismissals other than dismissals for personal jurisdiction, subject matter jurisdiction, and venue are dismissals "on the merits," unless the court explicitly states otherwise. Does this mean that all such dismissals pursuant to Rule 41(b) are "on the merits" for preclusion purposes? Or does the Rule's reference to a dismissal being "on the merits" have a different meaning? The Supreme Court, in *Semtek Int'l Inc. v. Lockheed Martin, Inc.*, 531 U.S. 497, 502 (2001), held that it has a different meaning and that a dismissal under Rule 41(b) is not necessarily "on the merits" for preclusion purposes. Rather, the Rule's reference to "on the merits" means that the claimant is unable to bring the same claim in the same federal district court. The Rule does not *necessarily* preclude the claimant from litigating the same claim in another federal district court or in a state court.

statute of limitations grounds), and not valid (e.g., the court issuing the judgment did not have subject matter jurisdiction). Now try discussing *that* amongst yourselves.

IV. Non-Party Preclusion: *Taylor v. Sturgell*

Typically, a judgment does not preclude non-parties from litigating identical claims. For example, consider a three-car accident involving Peter, Paul, and Mary. Peter sues Mary, claiming that Mary caused the accident. The case goes to trial, and the jury concludes that Mary was not negligent. Subsequently, *Paul* sues Mary, claiming that Mary caused the same accident that was at issue in Peter v. Mary. Because Paul was not a party to Peter's case against Mary, Paul's claim is not subject to claim preclusion.

This conclusion—that Paul can litigate his claim against Mary—seems somewhat unfair to Mary. Mary will have to defend herself against the same claim of negligence that Peter had alleged in his case. Nevertheless, it would be even more unfair to preclude Paul's claim, because Paul has not yet had his day in court. He did not participate in Peter's case and may have better evidence against Mary than Peter offered. Moreover, Paul may have a better incentive to litigate the case vigorously. For example, Paul's injuries may be more serious than Peter's. For these reasons, a judgment in one case (e.g., Peter v. Mary) does not—and should not—preclude a non-party such as Paul from litigating his own claim in a subsequent proceeding.

There is one type of exception to the general rule that a judgment does not have preclusive effects on non-parties. A judgment can preclude non-parties, like Paul, if that non-party was in "privity" with one of the parties who actually litigated the original case or had some other legal relationship with a party such that it would be fair to conclude that the non-party's interests were fairly represented. This type of exception is explored in detail in the case below.

READING *TAYLOR v. STURGELL.* In *Taylor,* the plaintiff (Brent Taylor) filed a lawsuit under the Freedom of Information Act seeking documents from the Federal Aviation Administration that related to a vintage airplane that Taylor wanted to restore. Taylor's friend, who also was an airplane enthusiast, had previously filed an unsuccessful suit seeking the same records. The issue in the case is whether Taylor should be precluded from bringing the same lawsuit that Herrick had previously filed and lost. Consider the following questions as you read *Taylor*:

- According to the Court, what types of non-party preclusion are permissible?
- What type of non-party preclusion did the lower court adopt in this case, and how is it different from the recognized categories of non-party preclusion?
- Why does the Court hold that the form of non-party preclusion adopted by the appellate court in this case should not be permissible?

TAYLOR v. STURGELL

553 U.S. 880 (2008)

Justice GINSBURG delivered the opinion of the Court.

"It is a principle of general application in Anglo-American jurisprudence that one is not bound by a judgment *in personam* in a litigation in which he is not designated as a party or to which he has not been made a party by service of process." *Hansberry v. Lee*, 311 U.S. 32, 40 (1940). Several exceptions, recognized in this Court's decisions, temper this basic rule. In a class action, for example, a person not named as a party may be bound by a judgment on the merits of the action, if she was adequately represented by a party who actively participated in the litigation. In this case, we consider for the first time whether there is a "virtual representation" exception to the general rule against precluding nonparties. Adopted by a number of courts, including the courts below in the case now before us, the exception so styled is broader than any we have so far approved.

The virtual representation question we examine in this opinion arises in the following context. Petitioner Brent Taylor filed a lawsuit under the Freedom of Information Act seeking certain documents from the Federal Aviation Administration. [EDS.—**At the time of the appeal, Sturgell was the acting administrator of the FAA, so any lawsuit seeking the disclosure of FAA records would have to name Sturgell as the defendant.**] Greg Herrick, Taylor's friend [and fellow airplane enthusiast], had previously brought an unsuccessful suit seeking the same records [and lost on the grounds that the requested records were considered a trade secret and were therefore not covered by the Freedom of Information Act]. . . .

We disapprove the doctrine of preclusion by "virtual representation," and hold, based on the record as it now stands, that the judgment against Herrick does not bar Taylor from maintaining this suit.

I

. . .

The record before the District Court in Taylor's suit revealed the following facts about the relationship between Taylor and Herrick: Taylor is the president of the Antique Aircraft Association, an organization to which Herrick belongs; the two men are "close associate[s]"; Herrick asked Taylor to help restore Herrick's F-45 [an antique aircraft], though they had no contract or agreement for Taylor's participation in the restoration; Taylor was represented by the lawyer who represented Herrick in the earlier litigation; and Herrick apparently gave Taylor documents that Herrick had obtained from the FAA during discovery in his suit. [EDS.—**Relying on these facts, the D.C. Circuit held that Taylor's lawsuit was precluded by the judgment against Herrick because Herrick qualified as Taylor's "virtual representative."**]

. . .

II

. . . Our inquiry . . . is guided by well-established precedent regarding the propriety of nonparty preclusion. We review that precedent before taking up directly the issue of virtual representation.

A

. . . Under the doctrine of claim preclusion, a final judgment forecloses "successive litigation of the very same claim, whether or not relitigation of the claim raises the same issues as the earlier suit." *New Hampshire v. Maine,* 532 U.S. 742, 748 (2001). Issue preclusion, in contrast, bars "successive litigation of an issue of fact or law actually litigated and resolved in a valid court determination essential to the prior judgment," even if the issue recurs in the context of a different claim. *Id.,* at 748–749. By "preclud[ing] parties from contesting matters that they have had a full and fair opportunity to litigate," these two doctrines protect against "the expense and vexation attending multiple lawsuits, conserv[e] judicial resources, and foste[r] reliance on judicial action by minimizing the possibility of inconsistent decisions." *Montana v. United States,* 440 U.S. 147, 153–154 (1979).

A person who was not a party to a suit generally has not had a "full and fair opportunity to litigate" the claims and issues settled in that suit. The application of claim and issue preclusion to nonparties thus runs up against the "deep-rooted historic tradition that everyone should have his own day in court." *Richards v. Jefferson County,* 517 U.S. 793, 798 (1996). Indicating the strength of that tradition, we have often repeated the general rule that "one is not bound by a judgment *in personam* in a litigation in which he is not designated as a party or to which he has not been made a party by service of process." *Hansberry,* 311 U.S., at 40.

B

Though hardly in doubt, the rule against nonparty preclusion is subject to exceptions. For present purposes, the recognized exceptions can be grouped into six categories.[6]

First, "[a] person who agrees to be bound by the determination of issues in an action between others is bound in accordance with the terms of his agreement." 1 *Restatement (Second) of Judgments* § 40, p. 390 (1980) (hereinafter Restatement). For example, "if separate actions involving the same transaction are brought by different plaintiffs against the same defendant, all the parties to all the actions may agree that the question of the defendant's liability will be definitely determined, one way or the other, in a 'test case.' " D. Shapiro, Civil Procedure: Preclusion in Civil Actions 77–78 (2001) (hereinafter Shapiro).

Second, nonparty preclusion may be justified based on a variety of pre-existing "substantive legal relationship[s]" between the person to be bound and

6. The established grounds for nonparty preclusion could be organized differently. The list that follows is meant only to provide a framework for our consideration of virtual representation, not to establish a definitive taxonomy.

a party to the judgment. Qualifying relationships include, but are not limited to, preceding and succeeding owners of property, bailee and bailor, and assignee and assignor. These exceptions originated "as much from the needs of property law as from the values of preclusion by judgment."[8] 18A Wright & Miller § 4448.

Third, we have confirmed that, "in certain limited circumstances," a nonparty may be bound by a judgment because she was "adequately represented by someone with the same interests who [wa]s a party" to the suit. *Richards,* 517 U.S., at 798. Representative suits with preclusive effect on nonparties include properly conducted class actions, and suits brought by trustees, guardians, and other fiduciaries.

Fourth, a nonparty is bound by a judgment if she "assume[d] control" over the litigation in which that judgment was rendered. *Montana,* 440 U.S., at 154. Because such a person has had "the opportunity to present proofs and argument," he has already "had his day in court" even though he was not a formal party to the litigation. *Restatement* § 39 cmt. a.

Fifth, a party bound by a judgment may not avoid its preclusive force by relitigating through a proxy. Preclusion is thus in order when a person who did not participate in a litigation later brings suit as the designated representative of a person who was a party to the prior adjudication. And although our decisions have not addressed the issue directly, it also seems clear that preclusion is appropriate when a nonparty later brings suit as an agent for a party who is bound by a judgment.

Sixth, in certain circumstances a special statutory scheme may "expressly foreclos[e] successive litigation by nonlitigants ... if the scheme is otherwise consistent with due process." Examples of such schemes include bankruptcy and probate proceedings and *quo warranto* actions or other suits that, "under [the governing] law, [may] be brought only on behalf of the public at large." *Martin v. Wilks*, 490 U.S. 755, 762 n.2 (1989).

III

Reaching beyond these six established categories, some lower courts have recognized a "virtual representation" exception to the rule against nonparty preclusion.... [For example, the district court in this case adopted a seven-factor test for virtual representation. That test requires an "identity of interests" between the person to be bound and a party to the judgment. If that requirement is met, the court weighs six additional factors, none of which are conclusive: (1) the existence of a "close relationship" between the present party and a party to the judgment alleged to be preclusive; (2) "participation in the prior litigation" by the present party; (3) the present party's "apparent acquiescence" to the preclusive effect of the judgment; (4) "deliberat[e] maneuver[ing]" to avoid the effect of the

8. The substantive legal relationships justifying preclusion are sometimes collectively referred to as "privity." The term "privity," however, has also come to be used more broadly, as a way to express the conclusion that nonparty preclusion is appropriate on any ground. To ward off confusion, we avoid using the term "privity" in this opinion.

judgment; (5) adequate representation of the present party by a party to the prior adjudication; and (6) a suit raising a "public law" rather than a "private law" issue. *Tyus v. Schoemehl,* 93 F.3d 449, 454–56 (1996).]

The D.C. Circuit, [and] the FAA . . . have presented . . . [several] arguments in support of . . . [the concept] of virtual representation. We find none of them persuasive.

. . .

B

. . . [The FAA] asks us to abandon the attempt to delineate discrete grounds and clear rules altogether. Preclusion is in order, they contend, whenever "the relationship between a party and a non-party is 'close enough' to bring the second litigant within the judgment." Courts should make the "close enough" determination, they urge, through a "heavily fact-driven" and "equitable" inquiry. Only this sort of diffuse balancing, . . . [they] argue, can account for all of the situations in which nonparty preclusion is appropriate.

We reject this argument for three reasons. First, our decisions emphasize the fundamental nature of the general rule that a litigant is not bound by a judgment to which she was not a party. Accordingly, we have endeavored to delineate discrete exceptions that apply in "limited circumstances." Respondents' amorphous balancing test is at odds with the constrained approach to nonparty preclusion our decisions advance.

. . .

Our second reason for rejecting a broad doctrine of virtual representation rests on the limitations attending nonparty preclusion based on adequate representation. A party's representation of a nonparty is "adequate" for preclusion purposes only if, at a minimum: (1) the interests of the nonparty and her representative are aligned, and (2) either the party understood herself to be acting in a representative capacity or the original court took care to protect the interests of the nonparty. In addition, adequate representation sometimes requires (3) notice of the original suit to the persons alleged to have been represented. In the class-action context, these limitations are implemented by the procedural safeguards contained in Federal Rule of Civil Procedure 23.

An expansive doctrine of virtual representation, however, would "recogniz[e], in effect, a common-law kind of class action." *Tice v. American Airlines, Inc.,* 162 F.3d 966, 972 (1998). That is, virtual representation would authorize preclusion based on identity of interests and some kind of relationship between parties and nonparties, shorn of the procedural protections prescribed in . . . [our earlier cases] and Rule 23. These protections, grounded in due process, could be circumvented were we to approve a virtual representation doctrine that allowed courts to "create *de facto* class actions at will." *Id.* at 973.

Third, a diffuse balancing approach to nonparty preclusion would likely create more headaches than it relieves. Most obviously, it could significantly complicate the task of district courts faced in the first instance with preclusion questions. An all-things-considered balancing approach might spark wide-ranging, time-consuming, and expensive discovery tracking factors potentially relevant under seven- or five-prong tests. And after the relevant facts are established, district judges would be called upon to evaluate them under a standard that provides no firm guidance. Preclusion doctrine, it should be recalled, is intended to reduce the burden of litigation on courts and parties. "In this area of the law," we agree, " 'crisp rules with sharp corners' are preferable to a round-about doctrine of opaque standards." *Bittinger v. Tecumseh Products Co.,* 123 F.3d 877, 881 (1997). . . .

The FAA next argues that "the threat of vexatious litigation is heightened" in public-law cases because "the number of plaintiffs with standing is potentially limitless." FOIA does allow "any person" whose request is denied to resort to federal court for review of the agency's determination. 5 U.S.C. § 552(a)(3)(A), (4)(B) (2006 ed.). Thus it is theoretically possible that several persons could coordinate to mount a series of repetitive lawsuits.

But we are not convinced that this risk justifies departure from the usual rules governing nonparty preclusion. First, *stare decisis* will allow courts swiftly to dispose of repetitive suits brought in the same circuit. Second, even when *stare decisis* is not dispositive, "the human tendency not to waste money will deter the bringing of suits based on claims or issues that have already been adversely determined against others." Shapiro 97. This intuition seems to be borne out by experience: The FAA has not called our attention to any instances of abusive FOIA suits in the Circuits that reject the virtual-representation theory respondents advocate here.

IV

For the foregoing reasons, we disapprove the theory of virtual representation on which the decision below rested. The preclusive effects of a judgment in a federal-question case decided by a federal court should instead be determined according to the established grounds for nonparty preclusion described in this opinion.

Although references to "virtual representation" have proliferated in the lower courts, our decision is unlikely to occasion any great shift in actual practice. Many opinions use the term "virtual representation" in reaching results at least arguably defensible on established grounds. In these cases, dropping the "virtual representation" label would lead to clearer analysis with little, if any, change in outcomes.

In some cases, however, lower courts have relied on virtual representation to extend nonparty preclusion beyond the latter doctrine's proper bounds. We now turn back to Taylor's action to determine whether his suit is such a case, or whether the result reached by the courts below can be justified on one of the recognized grounds for nonparty preclusion.

A

It is uncontested that four of the six grounds for nonparty preclusion have no application here: There is no indication that Taylor agreed to be bound by Herrick's litigation, that Taylor and Herrick have any legal relationship, that Taylor exercised any control over Herrick's suit, or that this suit implicates any special statutory scheme limiting relitigation. . . .

It is equally clear that preclusion cannot be justified on the theory that Taylor was adequately represented in Herrick's suit. Nothing in the record indicates that Herrick understood himself to be suing on Taylor's behalf, that Taylor even knew of Herrick's suit, or that the Wyoming District Court took special care to protect Taylor's interests. Under our pathmarking precedent, therefore, Herrick's representation was not "adequate."

That leaves only the fifth category: preclusion because a nonparty to an earlier litigation has brought suit as a representative or agent of a party who is bound by the prior adjudication. Taylor is not Herrick's legal representative and he has not purported to sue in a representative capacity. He concedes, however, that preclusion would be appropriate if respondents could demonstrate that he is acting as Herrick's "undisclosed agen[t]."

Respondents argue here, as they did below, that Taylor's suit is a collusive attempt to relitigate Herrick's action. The D.C. Circuit considered a similar question in addressing the "tactical maneuvering" prong of its virtual representation test. The Court of Appeals did not, however, treat the issue as one of agency, and it expressly declined to reach any definitive conclusions due to "the ambiguity of the facts." We therefore remand to give the courts below an opportunity to determine whether Taylor, in pursuing the instant FOIA suit, is acting as Herrick's agent. Taylor concedes that such a remand is appropriate.

We have never defined the showing required to establish that a nonparty to a prior adjudication has become a litigating agent for a party to the earlier case. Because the issue has not been briefed in any detail, we do not discuss the matter elaboratively here. We note, however, that courts should be cautious about finding preclusion on this basis. A mere whiff of "tactical maneuvering" will not suffice; instead, principles of agency law are suggestive. They indicate that preclusion is appropriate only if the putative agent's conduct of the suit is subject to the control of the party who is bound by the prior adjudication.

. . .

For the reasons stated, the judgment of the United States Court of Appeals for the District of Columbia Circuit is vacated, and the case is remanded for further proceedings consistent with this opinion.

Notes and Questions: Non-Party Representation

Q **1. A creative form of non-party preclusion.** In what way does the concept of "virtual representation" differ from the six recognized categories of non-party preclusion?

A The six existing categories of non-party preclusion involve either an express or implied legal relationship between the non-party and the party who litigated the original case. In contrast, virtual representation subjects a non-party to preclusion in the absence of such a relationship.

To the extent that virtual representation is similar to any of the existing categories, it is the most similar to the Court's third category, which gives preclusive effect to non-parties who were adequately represented by the named party in the original suit. For example, in the class action context, one named party can represent the interests of a class of people who are not directly before the court. In such cases, a class member—someone who was not a named party—is precluded from bringing the same claim that the class representative previously litigated on the class's behalf.

Virtual representation is similar to, but ultimately distinct from, this category of non-party preclusion. Class actions require procedural safeguards to protect the non-party class member, such as close court supervision of the litigation and the detailed notice requirements described in Rule 23 of the Rules of Civil Procedure. Moreover, non-party class members are normally given the opportunity to "opt out" of a damages class so that they can pursue their own claims, if they so choose. By contrast, the *Taylor* Court says that "virtual representation would authorize preclusion based on identity of interests and some kind of relationship between parties and non-parties, shorn of the procedural protections prescribed in ... [the case law], and Rule 23." 553 U.S. at 901. In short, virtual representation is more problematic than the recognized categories of non-party preclusion, because virtual representation does not give non-parties key procedural protections, such as notice that their rights might be affected in the pending litigation or that they have the right to "opt out" of the litigation and pursue claims on their own.

Q **2. Other reasons for rejecting virtual representation.** What reasons does the Court offer for its rejection of virtual representation other than the need to protect the absent party's procedural rights? For example, how might the doctrine of virtual representation lead to an increase in litigation?

A The Court explains that the "amorphous balancing test" for virtual representation potentially applies to a broad range of cases and thus conflicts with the notion that non-party preclusion should apply in narrowly defined circumstances.

The Court also argues that virtual representation undermines one of claim preclusion's key objectives: the promotion of efficiency.

> [A] diffuse balancing approach to nonparty preclusion would likely create more headaches than it relieves. Most obviously, it could significantly complicate the task of district courts faced in the first instance with preclusion questions. An all-things-considered balancing approach might spark wide-ranging, time-consuming, and expensive discovery tracking factors potentially relevant under seven- or five-prong tests. And after the relevant facts are established, district judges would be called upon to evaluate them under a standard that provides no firm guidance. Preclusion doctrine, it should be recalled, is intended to reduce the burden of litigation on courts and parties. "In this area of the law," we agree, " 'crisp rules with sharp corners' are preferable to a round-about doctrine of opaque standards."

553 U.S. at 901. This passage illustrates why it is so important to understand a doctrine's premises. Courts frequently look to those premises to determine how the doctrine should be applied in a new, ambiguous context. In this case, one of the reasons why the Court rejected virtual representation was that it would be inconsistent with an important rationale for the claim preclusion doctrine: the efficient resolution of controversies. Specifically, parties might spend so much time litigating whether virtual representation applies to a case that the doctrine would ultimately produce more litigation, not less.

3. The passenger as privy?

Perriwinkle collided with another vehicle while driving a co-worker, Parra, home from work. Perriwinkle sued Drazen (the driver of the other vehicle), alleging that Drazen caused the accident. The jury concludes that Drazen was not negligent, and the court enters a judgment in favor of Drazen. Subsequently, Parra sues Drazen for his own injuries from the accident. Drazen raises the affirmative defense of claim preclusion and moves for summary judgment on these grounds. The court should

A. deny the motion because Parra was not a party to the first case.
B. grant the motion, because Parra had a sufficient relationship with Perriwinkle to give rise to non-party preclusion.
C. deny the motion, but only if Parra's injuries were more severe than Perriwinkle's and Parra had a greater incentive to litigate the case zealously.
D. grant the motion because it would be unfair to require Drazen to defend this case again.

The Court made clear in *Taylor* that a mere friendship between a claimant and non-party is insufficient to establish non-party preclusion. Here, Perriwinkle knew Parra, but there is no evidence that Perriwinkle litigated the first case on Parra's behalf or that Perriwinkle and Parra had any other kind of relationship that would preclude Parra from litigating his own claim. Thus, **B** is wrong.

D sounds plausible. It does seem unfair for Drazen to have to defend himself again. But as the Peter, Paul, and Mary example (at the beginning of section IV of this chapter) demonstrates, it would be even more unfair if Parra was not able to litigate his claim. Parra has never had his day in court and is entitled to have one. Indeed, suppose that you were Parra, and you were preparing to sue Drazen for your injuries only to discover that you were barred from doing so because Perriwinkle had already sued Drazen. If that sounds unfair, then you understand why **D** is wrong.

For similar reasons, a disparity between Parra's and Perriwinkle's injuries is irrelevant to the preclusion analysis. Parra is entitled to his day in court, even if his injuries were minor and Perriwinkle's were severe. C, therefore, is wrong.

That leaves **A**. Non-parties are typically not precluded from subsequently litigating their own claims, and none of the acceptable forms of non-party preclusion apply here.

4. The new property owner. Reread the *Taylor* Court's discussion of the six categories of non-party preclusion before trying this question.

> Phillip sued Danko Corp., alleging that Danko Corp. constructed a facility that was located partially on Phillip's land. The dispute turned on the precise boundaries of Phillip's property. The court granted summary judgment in Danko's favor, concluding that the facility was built entirely on Danko's property. Phillip subsequently sold his land to Bob, and Bob now sues Danko Corp., alleging that the same facility that was at issue in Phillip's case was built on Bob's (formerly Phillip's) property. Danko raises the affirmative defense of claim preclusion and moves for summary judgment on those grounds. The court should
>
> A. deny the motion because Bob was not a party to the first case.
> B. grant the motion, because all of the elements of claim preclusion are satisfied.
> C. deny the motion because there was never a final judgment on the merits in Phillip's case.
> D. None of the above.

Phillip's case was resolved by summary judgment, which is typically considered to be on the merits. Thus, **C** is wrong.

The question ultimately turns on whether any of the recognized categories of non-party preclusion apply here. One of them—the Court's second category—does. As the Court explains, "nonparty preclusion may be justified based on a variety of pre-existing 'substantive legal relationship[s]' between the person to be bound and a party to the judgment. Qualifying relationships include, but are not limited to, preceding and succeeding owners of property. . . ." 553 U.S. at 894. Here, there is a "qualifying relationship" between Phillip and Bob in that they are "preceding and succeeding owners of property" respectively.

It stands to reason that this relationship should qualify for non-party preclusion. Prior to buying the property, Bob could have determined that Phillip had litigated this claim. Thus, Bob could have decided not to buy the property or could have changed his purchase price accordingly. Because Bob should have had notice that this claim had already been litigated when he bought the property, it is fair to preclude him from litigating the claim again. **B**, therefore, is the answer, not **A** or **D**.

5. The counterclaim problem. The parties to the second action must not only be the same as the parties to the original judgment (or fall under one of the non-party preclusion categories), but the claimant in the second action usually needs to be the same as the claimant from the first case. In other words, for claim preclusion to apply, the plaintiff from the first case needs to be the plaintiff in the second case, and the defendant from the first case needs to be the defendant in the second case.

For example, suppose that Pritchard sues Danielle for causing a car accident. The case goes to trial, and Danielle is found not to be negligent. Subsequently, Danielle sues Pritchard for her own injuries arising from the same car accident. Pritchard's claim has been fully litigated, and the court has issued a final judgment on the merits. Nevertheless, claim preclusion does not apply here, because the defendant in the original case (Danielle) is now the claimant, and the claimant in the original case (Pritchard) is now the defendant. Because the claimants in the two cases are different, claim preclusion typically does not bar Danielle's claim against Pritchard. *See, e.g., Cambria v. Jeffery*, 29 N.E.2d 555 (Mass. 1940). The claims are different.

Although claim preclusion does not generally bar Danielle's claim against Pritchard, most states (and the federal courts) have a compulsory counterclaim rule that has the same effect. Federal Rule of Civil Procedure 13(a) requires a party to "state as a counterclaim any claim that . . . the pleader has against an opposing party if the claim: (A) arises out of the transaction or occurrence that is the subject matter of the opposing party's claim; and (B) does not require adding another party over whom the court cannot acquire jurisdiction." Here, Danielle failed to bring a compulsory counterclaim in the original case and is thus barred from bringing it in a separate case later. So even though claim preclusion does not typically apply to these facts, "rule preclusion" does. As a result, the compulsory counterclaim rule can produce the same outcome as claim preclusion.

Q **6. A challenge: Claimants vs. plaintiffs.** Pavlov sues Duchovny, alleging breach of contract. Duchovny asserts a permissive counterclaim, alleging that Pavlov engaged in an unlawful conspiracy under state law that undermined Duchovny's business. Specifically, Duchovny asserts that Pavlov conspired with other companies to deprive Duchovny of customers, thus driving Duchovny out of business.

Duchovny loses her counterclaim and subsequently sues Pavlov in a separate proceeding, alleging state antitrust violations arising from the same facts as Duchovny's earlier state law conspiracy claim. In particular, Duchovny asserts that Pavlov's conspiracy with other companies constituted unlawful activity under the state antitrust laws. Assuming the jurisdiction adopts the transactional definition of a claim and that the antitrust claim would have been a permissive counterclaim in the original lawsuit, will the court dismiss Duchovny's antitrust claim?

A The test is not whether the plaintiff and the defendant are the same in the two cases, but whether the *claimant* and the defendant are the same. Duchovny was the claimant and Pavlov was the defendant with regard to *Duchovny's state law conspiracy claim,* and Duchovny is the claimant and Pavlov is the defendant regarding a cause of action—the state antitrust claim—that arose out of the same events as Duchovny's earlier state law claim. Specifically, Duchovny's antitrust claim is based on the same set of facts as the earlier conspiracy claim; Duchovny is simply asserting a different legal theory. Thus, claim preclusion applies here. *See Freer* § 11.2.1.

V. Exceptions to Claim Preclusion

Even when all of the elements of the claim preclusion doctrine are satisfied, courts will nevertheless refuse to apply the doctrine when:

(a) The parties have agreed in terms or in effect that the plaintiff may split his claim, or the defendant has acquiesced therein; or

(b) The court in the first action has expressly reserved the plaintiff's right to maintain the second action; or

(c) The plaintiff was unable to rely on a certain theory of the case or to seek a certain remedy or form of relief in the first action because of the limitations on the subject matter jurisdiction of the courts or restrictions on their authority to entertain multiple theories or demands for multiple remedies or forms of relief in a single action, and the plaintiff desires in the second action to rely on that theory or to seek that remedy or form of relief; or

(d) The judgment in the first action was plainly inconsistent with the fair and equitable implementation of a statutory or constitutional scheme, or it is the sense of the scheme that the plaintiff should be permitted to split his claim; or

(e) For reasons of substantive policy in a case involving a continuing or recurrent wrong, the plaintiff is given an option to sue once for the total harm, both past and prospective, or to sue from time to time for the damages incurred to the date of suit, and chooses the latter course; or

(f) It is clearly and convincingly shown that the policies favoring preclusion of a second action are overcome for an extraordinary reason, such as the apparent invalidity of a continuing restraint or condition having a vital relation to personal liberty or the failure of the prior litigation to yield a coherent disposition of the controversy.

Restatement (Second) of Judgments § 26(1) (1982).

READING *RIVER PARK, INC. v. CITY OF HIGHLAND PARK.* Below is a portion of the *River Park* opinion that was omitted from the earlier excerpt. Which exception to the claim preclusion doctrine does the Illinois Supreme Court address, and why did the court conclude that it did not apply in this case?

RIVER PARK, INC. v. CITY OF HIGHLAND PARK

703 N.E.2d 883 (Ill. 1998)

. . . [P]laintiffs contend that the doctrine of *res judicata* should not bar their state claims because they could not have asserted these claims in federal court. According to plaintiffs, the district court would have lacked subject matter jurisdiction over these claims after it dismissed their section 1983 action. This argument is unavailing.

While it is true that the doctrine of *res judicata* does not bar a claim if a court would not have had subject matter jurisdiction to decide that claim in the first suit involving the same cause of action, Restatement (Second) of Judgments § 26(1) (1982), we cannot say in this case that the district court would have lacked jurisdiction over plaintiffs' state law claims. Federal courts are entitled to exercise supplemental jurisdiction over claims that are part of the "same case or controversy" as a claim over which they have original jurisdiction. 28 U.S.C. § 1367(a) (1994). Plaintiffs do not argue that their state claims would not have been considered part of the same case or controversy of their section 1983 claim. Instead, they contend that the district court would have dismissed these state claims for lack of subject matter jurisdiction when it dismissed their section 1983 claim. Contrary to plaintiffs' assertion, a district court is not required to dismiss pendent state claims after dismissing the claim from which its original jurisdiction stems. Instead, a district court has the discretion to exercise supplemental jurisdiction over pendent state claims under these circumstances. *See* 28 U.S.C. § 1367(c) (1994).

In this case, we cannot agree with plaintiffs that, had they attempted to bring their state claims in federal court, the district court would have dismissed them for lack of subject matter jurisdiction after it dismissed their section 1983 claim. First, plaintiffs filed no state claims in federal court. Consequently, we do not know whether the district court would have refused to exercise supplemental jurisdiction over these claims. In addition, federal courts have chosen to exercise supplemental jurisdiction under circumstances similar to those in this case. Plaintiffs' state claims are, therefore, claims that "could have been decided" in their federal suit. As such, they are barred under the doctrine of *res judicata* by the dismissal of the federal suit.

Plaintiffs argue that it is unfair to bar their state claims under the *res judicata* doctrine. They profess that they are caught in a "Catch-22" situation: the federal courts directed them to seek relief in state court, but the Circuit Court of Lake County held that their state claims were barred by the dismissal of their federal action. We observe, however, that any "Catch-22" situation was created by plaintiffs themselves when they chose not to assert their state causes of action in their suit in federal court. "The purpose of *res judicata* is to promote judicial economy by requiring parties to litigate, in one case, all rights arising out of the same set of operative facts and also [to] prevent[ ] the unjust burden that would result if a party could be forced to relitigate what is essentially the same case." *Heinstein v. Buschbach*, 618 N.E.2d 1042 (1993). This purpose would be undermined if plaintiffs were permitted to pursue their state claims after bringing the same cause of action against defendant in federal court. . . .

Notes and Questions: Claim Preclusion Exceptions

Q **1. Which exception to claim preclusion?** Review *Restatement (Second) of Judgments* § 26(1), which appears before the case. Which exception is at issue, and why do the plaintiffs believe that the exception applies here?

A The plaintiffs rely on *Restatement (Second) of Judgments* § 26(1)(c) (1982), which says that claim preclusion does not apply if the claimant "was unable to rely on a certain theory of the case . . . in the first action because of the limitations on the subject matter jurisdiction of the courts. . . ."

The plaintiffs argue that when the federal court dismissed the federal claim, the court would have dismissed the state claims as well. Accordingly, the plaintiffs argue that they would have been unable to assert their state claims in federal court and that the Restatement exception should apply.

Q **2. The scope of the subject matter jurisdiction exception.** Why does the court reject the plaintiffs' argument?

A The court cites two reasons. First, although the federal court *might* have dismissed the state law claims, the court was not bound to do so. 28 U.S.C. § 1367(c) (giving a court the discretion to retain the remaining claims under these circumstances). The problem is that the plaintiffs never asserted their state law claims in federal court, so there is no way to know if the federal court would, in fact, have declined jurisdiction to hear the state claims.

Second, not only did the federal court have the discretion to retain the remaining claims, but it likely would have done so. The court points out that federal courts have exercised supplemental jurisdiction over similar claims under nearly identical circumstances.

Q **3. Write your own hypothetical.** The subject matter jurisdiction exception to claim preclusion did not apply to the *River Park* case. Can you create a hypothetical that would trigger the exception?

A There are many possible examples. Assume, for instance, that a state statute requires all employment discrimination claims to be filed with a specialized state agency whose subject matter jurisdiction is limited to employment discrimination claims. A plaintiff, who was recently fired from her job, files a discrimination claim with that state agency, as the statute requires. After the agency dismisses her claim on the merits, she sues in state court for breach of contract, alleging that her termination constituted a breach.

All of the elements of claim preclusion are satisfied here. Under the transactional test, the contract and discrimination causes of action constitute the same claim because they both arise out of the plaintiff's termination. Moreover, the two cases involve the same claimant suing the same defendant, and the earlier claim involved a valid final judgment on the merits. Administrative agency determinations are often accorded preclusive effect if the agency provides litigants with an opportunity to present their claims in a manner that is equivalent to judicial procedures. *Restatement (Second) of Judgments* § 83(2).

Nevertheless, the subject matter jurisdiction exception applies to these facts. The plaintiff had no choice but to bring the discrimination claim in the administrative tribunal, and that tribunal lacked jurisdiction to hear the breach of contract claim. Without this exception, the plaintiff might not have an opportunity to assert her breach of contract claim in any tribunal. The subject matter jurisdiction exception is designed to prevent this sort of unfairness.

4. All together now. This question is similar to a question that appeared earlier in the chapter, but with a few additional nuances.

Penny, a New York citizen, believes that Demotion, Inc. (a company incorporated in New York and with its principal place of business there) fired Penny because of her gender and age. Penny sues Demotion in the federal court for the Northern District of New York, alleging a federal law gender discrimination claim and a state law age discrimination claim. The court grants Demotion's motion to dismiss the federal law claim under Rule 12(b)(6) because Demotion does not have the requisite number of employees to be subject to the federal statute. At the same time, the court declines to exercise supplemental jurisdiction over the state law claim under 28 U.S.C. § 1367(c) and thus dismisses that claim as well.

Penny subsequently files a new lawsuit against Demotion in New York state court. She raises the same federal gender discrimination claim and the same state law age discrimination claim as the earlier suit. Demotion asserts that the suit is barred by claim preclusion and makes a motion for summary judgment on those grounds. Assuming the transactional definition of a claim applies here, how should the court resolve the motion?

A. The court should grant it. All of the elements of claim preclusion are satisfied with regard to both claims.
B. The court should grant the motion only as to the federal claim. The motion should be denied as to the state claim because the federal court's judgment on that claim was not on the merits.
C. The court should grant the motion only as to the federal claim. The motion should be denied as to the state claim because the federal court's judgment on that claim is subject to claim preclusion's "subject matter jurisdiction" exception.
D. The court should deny the motion with regard to both claims.

The federal court's dismissal of the federal claim under Rule 12(b)(6) should be considered a dismissal on the merits. The dismissal turned on the substance of the claim itself (the statute's requirements) and not on a procedural problem like personal jurisdiction. The other elements of claim preclusion are also satisfied with regard to the federal claim: The new federal discrimination claim is identical to the original federal discrimination claim, and the same claimant is suing the same defendant. Claim preclusion, therefore, is appropriate regarding this claim, making **D** incorrect.

The state law cause of action is a bit trickier. It arises out of the same facts as the federal cause of action, so it is part of the same claim for preclusion purposes. The court's rationale for dismissing the state law cause of action, however, was different from its reason for dismissing the federal cause of action. Namely, the court dismissed the federal cause of action for substantive reasons relating to the applicable statute, but the state law cause of action was dismissed because the court declined to exercise subject matter jurisdiction over that claim. It appears, therefore, that the dismissal of the state law cause of action does not have claim preclusive effect, making **A** incorrect.

It is not entirely clear, however, *why* the dismissal of the state law cause of action does not have claim preclusive effect. Is it because the dismissal falls under the subject matter jurisdiction exception to the claim preclusion doctrine? Or is it because the dismissal was not "on the merits" and thus not subject to claim preclusion?

The subject matter jurisdiction exception to the claim preclusion doctrine applies in a case where a plaintiff *did not allege* a cause of action because it would have been jurisdictionally improper to do so. *Restatement (Second) of Judgments* § 26(1)(c) (1982). The previous note illustrates such a scenario. This case, however, presents a different situation, because the plaintiff *did* allege the claim. The federal court dismissed the claim because it declined to exercise subject matter jurisdiction over it. Such a dismissal is not considered to be "on the merits," making **B** a better answer than **C**.

5. Waiver. "Res judicata" (the older name for preclusion) is an affirmative defense under Federal Rule of Civil Procedure 8(c). This means that most courts will refuse to apply claim preclusion if a party fails to raise the defense in the manner specified in Rule 8(c). Waiver is thus a critical and fairly common exception to the claim preclusion doctrine.

VI. Claim Preclusion: Summary of Basic Principles

- The claim preclusion doctrine prevents claimants from relitigating claims that they fully litigated in a previous case. The doctrine is intended to promote fairness, the public's positive perception of the justice system, and efficiency.
- Typically, three elements must be satisfied before a court will give claim preclusive effect to an earlier judgment. First, the claim must be the same as the claim that was litigated in a previous case. Second, the previous case must have resulted in a valid, final judgment on the merits. And third, the parties who litigated the previous claim must typically be the same parties who are litigating the current claim, and they must be in the same configuration (the claimant in the second case is the same as the claimant in the first).
- The federal courts and most state courts apply the transactional definition of a claim. According to this definition, two claims are the same if they arose out of the same transaction or occurrence. Some state courts employ a narrower "same evidence" test, which defines two causes of action as the same claim "if the evidence needed to sustain the second suit would have sustained the first, or if the same facts were essential to maintain both actions." *River Park,* 703 N.E.2d at 891. A much smaller number of courts employ the primary rights test, which defines each violation of a right as giving rise to a separate claim.
- Most courts consider a judgment to be final for claim preclusion purposes when the trial court has entered a judgment in favor of one of the parties.

In these jurisdictions, a judgment will be considered final even if the case is on appeal.

- A judgment is on the merits when a claimant has had an opportunity to litigate her claim and a court has addressed the merits of the case in some respect. The requirement is generally interpreted broadly to include most dispositions other than dismissals for lack of personal jurisdiction, subject matter jurisdiction, and venue. For example, the trend has been in favor of giving preclusive effect to dismissals on statute of limitations grounds.
- Typically, a judgment only has preclusive effect for the parties who litigated the case. A judgment, however, can preclude non-parties in certain narrowly defined circumstances, such as members of a class action and purchasers of property that was the subject of prior litigation.
- There are several exceptions to the claim preclusion doctrine, such as when a party could not have brought a cause of action in the original court because of the court's limited subject matter jurisdiction.
- Claim preclusion is an affirmative defense, so if the defense is not raised in the manner specified in Rule 8(c), most courts will consider it to be waived.

34

Issue Preclusion: Further Limits to Relitigation

I. Introduction: The Logic and Elements of Issue Preclusion

Billy Bulger fell behind on his car loan. When he missed his monthly payments for January through March, First Bank sued him in a Maryland state court for non-payment, seeking to repossess his car. Bulger answered, denying non-payment and asserting that the loan agreement was invalid for failure to include certain required disclosures. After a jury trial in which the parties put on evidence going both to payment and the validity of the loan agreement, the jury returned a verdict for the Bank. The court then entered a judgment on the verdict in favor of the Bank.

Bulger, however, scraped together enough money to bring his loan payments up to date, and the Bank therefore agreed to continue the loan and let him keep possession of the car. (Clearly, this is a *hypothetical* bank.) Bulger made his April through July payments, but then fell behind again. Sure enough, the Bank went back to court and sued him for repossession again, this time based on his failure to make the August to December payments. Bulger's defenses were that the Bank was precluded by claim preclusion by the judgment in the first lawsuit and that the loan agreement was invalid for failure to include the required disclosures.

Q Why is the first defense no good?

A In the first lawsuit, the Bank sued for non-payment of the *January-March* payments. Having litigated that claim to a final judgment, the Bank can't litigate it again. But it isn't trying to. Instead, it is litigating a claim based on Bulger's failure to make the *August-December* payments. Not only has the Bank never before litigated this claim, but it could not have litigated it in lawsuit #1, for the simple reason that the August-December payments were not even due at any time during the first lawsuit. Thus, the Bank is not claim-precluded under even the most expansive application of the doctrine.

But the second defense stands on a different footing.

First, even though the claim in lawsuit #2 is different from the claim in lawsuit #1, the issue of the invalidity of the loan agreement for failure to make disclosures is the *same issue* in both lawsuits (it's the same loan agreement, after all).

Second, this is an issue that Bulger and the Bank *actually litigated* when they presented evidence in lawsuit #1. This is arguably the key requirement for issue preclusion, because it is litigation of the issue—the adversarial submission of evidence—that makes it likely (though not certain) that it was correctly decided. It is also a requirement that differentiates claim preclusion from issue preclusion. Claim preclusion reaches not only claims that were asserted, but also transactionally related claims *that could have been asserted*. In contrast, issue preclusion only reaches those issues that were actually litigated and not those that could have been litigated but weren't.

Third, lawsuit #1 ended in a *valid final judgment*.

Fourth, the issue of the loan agreement's validity was *necessarily decided* for the Bank in lawsuit #1, because if the jury had found the loan agreement to be invalid, it would have been required (under the judge's jury instructions) to find for Bulger. To put it differently, the Bank was entitled to a verdict and judgment in lawsuit #1 only if the jury found not just that Bulger had failed to make the January-March payments, but also that the underlying loan agreement was valid.

Fifth, Bulger was a *party to lawsuit #1*. Had he not been a party (or in privity with a party) in that lawsuit, then he would not have had any chance to contest the issue in lawsuit #1. It would deny him due process to preclude him by a decision he never had the opportunity to contest.

Finally, Bulger had a *full and fair opportunity to litigate* the validity of the agreement in lawsuit #1. Lawsuit #1 did not decide the issue using arbitrary procedures (it wasn't decided by flipping a coin or by hearing only from his opponent). It was conducted in a court that apparently followed the same procedures as the court in lawsuit #2, and there is no indication that Bulger lacked an incentive to litigate in lawsuit #1 or suffered any other unfairness.

For all of these reasons, Bulger is not entitled to litigate the issue again. The doctrine of *issue preclusion* (also called *collateral estoppel*) precludes him from doing so.

All U.S. jurisdictions apply the issue preclusion doctrine in these kinds of circumstances. Although the phrasing and ordering of these requirements varies widely from jurisdiction to jurisdiction, many opinions cite and quote the *Restatement (Second) of Judgments* § 27, which expressly or impliedly combines the first five requirements discussed above:

> When an issue of fact or law is actually litigated and determined by a valid and final judgment, and the determination is essential to the judgment, the determination is conclusive in a subsequent action between the parties, whether on the same or a different claim.

The last requirement (i.e., that a party had a full and fair opportunity to litigate the matter in lawsuit #1) is reflected in *Restatement* § 28, which asserts that even when the first five requirements are satisfied, issue preclusion should be disallowed if:

> (3) A new determination of the issue is warranted by differences in the quality or extensiveness of the procedures followed in the two courts or by factors relating to the allocation of jurisdiction between them; or (4) The party against whom preclusion is sought had a significantly heavier burden of persuasion with respect to the issue in the initial action than in the subsequent action; the burden has shifted to his adversary; or the adversary has a significantly heavier burden than he had in the first action; or (5) There is a clear and convincing need for a new determination of the issue ... (c) because the party sought to be precluded, as a result of the conduct of his adversary or other special circumstances, did not have an adequate opportunity or incentive to obtain a full and fair adjudication in the initial action.

In section II, we examine the difference between claim and issue preclusion. In section III, we explore the elements of issue preclusion. In section IV, we turn to a complication involving the traditional, but increasingly discarded, requirement that issue preclusion be "mutual"—that a party may only invoke issue preclusion if the opposing party could do so as well. Finally, in section V, we explore the effect of a judgment when lawsuit #2 is brought in a different court system than that which decided lawsuit #1.

II. Claim vs. Issue Preclusion: How Are They Different?

READING *FELGER v. NICHOLS.* *Felger* involves a common fact pattern. Professional sues client or patient for fees. Defendant argues that the services were lousy and therefore not worth the fees. The court enters a judgment. Now client or patient sues professional for malpractice based on the same services.

- Why isn't client Felger claim-precluded by the judgment in lawsuit #1 from litigating lawsuit #2? Note that Maryland has no compulsory counterclaim rule.
- How do we know whether the issue in lawyer Nichols's lawsuit for fees is the same as the issue in Felger's lawsuit for malpractice?
- Lawsuit #1 was for just $345. Suppose lawsuit #2 was for $250,000 to compensate for the injuries resulting from Nichols's alleged malpractice. Would this affect your determination whether Felger should be issue-precluded by the judgment in lawsuit #1?

FELGER v. NICHOLS

370 A.2d 141 (Md. Ct. Spec. App. 1977)

DAVIDSON, Judge.

On 21 June 1974, the appellee, Zane G. Nichols, filed suit against the appellant, Milton R. Felger, in the District Court of Maryland for Anne Arundel County for $345 in unpaid legal fees. On 12 November 1974, trial was held before Judge Raymond G. Thieme. The appellant defended on the ground that the legal services were inadequately performed and, therefore, the fee was unreasonable. The court entered judgment for the appellee in the amount of $345. . . .

[EDS.—Client Felger then sued lawyer Nichols for legal malpractice based on the same legal services from Nichols. Nichols moved for summary judgment, arguing that the final judgment for him in the fee suit precluded Felger from contesting the adequacy of the legal services in the legal malpractice suit—that is, using the terminology of Maryland common law, that Felger was "collaterally estopped" by the judgment in the first lawsuit. The court granted the motion and this appeal followed.]

In Maryland, the doctrine of *res judicata,* or estoppel by judgment, consists of two branches: direct estoppel by judgment, and collateral estoppel by judgment. The doctrine of direct estoppel by judgment **[EDS.—the court's term for claim preclusion]** establishes that in a subsequent action between the same parties upon the same cause of action, claim or demand, or subject matter, a judgment rendered on the merits constitutes an absolute bar, not only as to all matters which were actually raised, litigated and determined in the former proceeding, but also as to all matters which could have been raised and litigated. . . . The doctrine of collateral estoppel by judgment **[EDS.—the court's term for issue preclusion]** establishes that where a second action between the same parties is upon a different "cause of action," the judgment in the previous action operates as a bar only as to those matters actually litigated and determined in the original action and is not conclusive as to matters which might have been but were not litigated and determined in the previous action. Under this doctrine, as under the doctrine of direct estoppel, the matters actually determined in the previous proceeding may have been raised directly or as a matter of defense. . . .

In a suit for counsel fees, the court must consider, among other things, the skill requisite properly to conduct the case, and the fidelity and diligence of the attorney. A client, by way of defense, may produce evidence to show that he did not receive competent legal representation. In a legal malpractice suit, the court must consider, among other things, whether the attorney either lacked or failed to exercise the requisite professional diligence, knowledge and skill. In such a suit, the client must produce evidence to show that he did not receive competent legal representation. Thus, assuming that both actions involve the same legal service, the matter of the adequacy of the client's legal representation would be raised in both, either directly or by way of defense, and would be litigated and determined in both. Accordingly, a court's determination that a lawyer is entitled to a legal fee, made after a client has, as a matter of defense, produced evidence to show inadequate legal representation, would be a bar in a malpractice suit alleging inadequate legal representation . . . .

Here, the record shows that the appellant testified at the District Court trial that four other attorneys had advised him that, contrary to the appellee's opinion, he had no legal grounds for a limited divorce. He testified that the appellee misrepresented to him that his wife was about to file a complaint for divorce against him, and prodded him to file for divorce first. The appellant also testified that thereafter the appellee gave him bad advice when he said he should dismiss his divorce complaint and cross-file on his wife's complaint. The appellant testified that the appellee was unprepared for an alimony *pendente lite* hearing. Finally, at the close of the trial, the appellant moved to dismiss the suit "on the grounds that Mr. Nichols did not faithfully and fully discharge the business entrusted to him in the manner a client has the right to expect. . . ."

The record here shows that, as a matter of defense in the legal fee suit, the client did present evidence as to the inadequacy of his attorney's performance. Under these circumstances, the appellant's contention that he had no opportunity to "litigate the issue of professional malpractice in the District Court suit," because he was precluded by Maryland District Rule 314 from filing a counterclaim in excess of that Court's jurisdictional amount, is without merit. Similarly, his contention that the trial court prevented him from litigating that issue by sustaining an objection to a single question is also without merit.[10]

The adequacy of the attorney's performance in the client's divorce proceedings having been litigated and determined, the District Court's final judgment in the legal fee suit bars that matter from being litigated in the present legal malpractice suit between the same parties. The trial court correctly granted the appellee's motion for summary judgment. We shall affirm.

JUDGMENT AFFIRMED. COSTS TO BE PAID BY APPELLANT.

Notes and Questions: *Felger v. Nichols*

1. Why no claim preclusion? The claim for fees in lawsuit #1 arose out of Nichols's representation of Felger in his divorce. So did the claim that Nichols did not represent Felger competently or faithfully. In fact, both would involve evidence about the legal services Nichols provided. Claim preclusion (which the court calls "direct estoppel") applies not just to claims that were litigated—here the lawyer's fee claim—but also to claims that could have been litigated based on the same transaction (the prevailing rule) or same evidence (the minority rule, but not very different in most cases). At first glance, it might seem, therefore, that Felger could have counterclaimed for malpractice in lawsuit #1 and should therefore be claim-precluded.

However, the malpractice claim belongs to client Felger, not to his attorney Nichols. And Felger did not choose the time or place for lawsuit #1; he was haled into the court that Nichols chose when Nichols chose. Partly to protect a

10. Any alleged error in the District Court's rulings on the admissibility of evidence should have been determined on an appeal in the Circuit Court. Here, the appellant's appeal to the Circuit Court was dismissed.

defendant's right to assert his own claims in a forum and at a time of his own choosing, the common law did not require him to file a counterclaim in lawsuit #1, even if it arose from the same transaction as the plaintiff's claim.

Of course, this generosity was inefficient, as it invited multiple lawsuits over the same transaction. Many jurisdictions have therefore overruled the common law by adopting a compulsory counterclaim rule like Federal Rule of Civil Procedure 13(a). Had Maryland done so, Felger would have been compelled to file his transactionally related counterclaim for malpractice in lawsuit #1, or find himself "rule-precluded" thereafter from suing Nichols for that malpractice. But Maryland has not adopted such a rule.

There is another reason why claim preclusion may not apply. The court notes that in lawsuit #1, Maryland District Court Rule 314 prevented Felger from counterclaiming in excess of that Court's low jurisdictional limit. If his counterclaim was for more than this amount, then he had an argument that he could not have brought the full counterclaim in the district court.

2. How is issue preclusion different? The doctrine of claim preclusion precludes relitigation of *claims* that were litigated to judgment or could have been, based on the same transaction. The doctrine of issue preclusion precludes relitigation of *issues*—smaller pieces of lawsuits than claims—often the findings required to establish some element of a claim, like ownership of property, validity of an instrument, family relationship, or sometimes broader elements of a claim or defense like a party's negligence or contributory negligence.

But this obvious difference has a consequence that may be less obvious. By and large, a claimant can foresee when she might assert additional transactionally related claims against the same party (or someone in privity with it). Relitigation would be truly more of the same, at least more dispute about the same transaction. But an issue like ownership of property, validity of an instrument, or existence of a family relationship can arise in multiple settings—including some that have no relationship to the transaction that spawned lawsuit #1 and that are therefore less foreseeable. In lawsuit #1 for $2,500 for personal injuries in a pedestrian accident, for example, the fact-finder might need to decide the issue of who owned the Rolls Royce that struck the pedestrian. But the same issue might also decide an estate dispute about who inherits the $250,000 car, an action by the United States to enforce a tax lien, or an action for bankruptcy. That is why the most common historical term for issue preclusion was "*collateral* estoppel" because the preclusion applies even to lawsuits that are completely "collateral" to—have nothing to do with—the transaction that gave rise to lawsuit #1. A litigant's exposure to issue preclusion is therefore potentially much broader than its exposure to claim preclusion. As a result, "[a]lmost all of the modern expansions of [preclusion law] ... involve issue preclusion." *Wright & Miller* § 4416.

To counterbalance this broader exposure, the common law added a requirement for issue preclusion that does not apply to claim preclusion: that the issue must actually have been litigated and decided. That is, issue preclusion—unlike claim preclusion—does not apply to issues that *could* have been litigated but weren't. This not only limits the otherwise broader exposure the litigant faces, but also makes it more likely that the issue was reliably decided, to the extent that the adversarial process improves the quality of fact-finding.

Q **3. Was the issue in lawsuit #1 the same issue?** The threshold inquiry in issue preclusion is whether an issue decided in lawsuit #1 is the same as an issue in lawsuit #2. How did the court in *Felger* decide this question?

A It looked at the record from the trial in lawsuit #1. During that trial, Felger defended against Nichols's fee demand by testifying that the legal services he supplied were inadequate. In lawsuit #2, Felger raised the same argument in pressing his malpractice claim for the same services.

Q **4. Was this issue actually litigated in lawsuit #1?**

A Felger testified that Nichols gave him bad advice in multiple respects in connection with his divorce, and at the conclusion of the trial, Felger even moved to dismiss the suit "on the grounds that Mr. Nichols did not faithfully and fully discharge the business entrusted to him in the manner a client has the right to expect." This submission and related arguments were clearly sufficient to show that the adequacy of Nichols's legal representation was actually litigated in lawsuit #1.

Q **5. Was the issue necessarily decided in lawsuit #1?**

A The court in lawsuit #1 decided that Nichols was entitled to his fee. "[A] court's determination that the lawyer is entitled to a fee, made after a client has, as a matter of defense, produced evidence to show inadequate legal representation," necessarily means that the court rejected the defense and found Nichols's legal representation to have been adequate. Thus, we can logically infer from the outcome of litigation #1 that the adequacy of Nichols's representation was necessarily decided. The *Restatement (Second) of Judgments* § 27 calls such findings "essential" to the decision.

Q **6. Did Felger have a full and fair opportunity to litigate the issue?** *Felger* seems like a pretty straightforward case for issue preclusion: Felger has already litigated the issue of the adequacy of Nichols's services; the second suit is between the same parties about the same issue; and the lawsuits are in courts with similar judicial procedures. If preclusion means anything, it means no do-overs, right? But this is fair only if Felger had a reasonable opportunity and incentive to litigate the issue the first time. Did he?

A Maybe not.

First, Felger argues that he could not have brought a counterclaim in excess of the first court's jurisdictional amount. But, while this may be a good reason to deny claim preclusion (remember, claim preclusion extends to transactionally related claims a party *could have brought*), it did not prevent him from actually litigating the sufficiency of Nichols's legal services. And litigate he did—with much testimony about how bad they were.

But suppose lawsuit #1 was litigated in a small claims court that permitted little or no discovery or that required parties to represent themselves. Such restrictions are imposed in some small claims courts to simplify and expedite the resolution of the dispute given the definitionally small stakes;

the emphasis is on speed and convenience for lay litigants, more than on accuracy. These kinds of procedural differences could have prevented Felger from developing evidence of Nichols's alleged malpractice. Under these circumstances, it may make sense to allow the issue to be relitigated. *Restatement (Second) of Judgments* § 28(3) explains that "[a] new determination of the issue is warranted by differences in the quality or extensiveness of the procedures followed in the two courts or by factors relating to the allocation of jurisdiction between them."

Second, the fee claim was only for $345 in lawsuit #1. Even in 1977, this seems like chump change. It might have cost Felger more to hire a lawyer to defend the fee claim (talk about adding insult to injury) than it would cost simply to pay the fee. If a party reasonably lacks the incentive to aggressively litigate an issue in lawsuit #1, then it may be unfair to preclude him from relitigating that issue in a subsequent lawsuit with far larger stakes. We don't know the stakes in lawsuit #2, but the record reflects that Felger actively defended lawsuit #1.

Third, we don't know whether Felger had a lawyer in lawsuit #1 or whether, having been burned once, he represented himself. If he represented himself, then maybe he wasn't competent to represent himself effectively. (But wouldn't this be a problem of his own making, unless the first court required parties to represent themselves?)

So, though it's a closer call to us than it seemed to the court, Felger seemingly had a full and fair opportunity to litigate in lawsuit #1, and it's not unfair to preclude him from relitigating the issue of the adequacy of the legal services he received from Nichols.

Q **7. But what if it was wrongly decided?** If Felger *did* represent himself, maybe he had a fool for a client and just blew the case, failing to present the right evidence and running afoul of the rules of evidence, as a layman is likely to do, with the result that the court wrongly decided the issue of Nichols's services. What if the malpractice issue was decided incorrectly in lawsuit #1?

A It doesn't matter for purposes of issue preclusion. In preclusion law, "the first lesson one must learn . . . is that judicial findings must not be confused with absolute truth." Brainerd Currie, *Mutuality of Collateral Estoppel: Limits of the Bernhard Doctrine*, 9 Stan. L. Rev. 281, 315 (1957). Issue preclusion was devised to promote finality, not accuracy in fact-finding. We have a different check on accuracy. It's called appeal. As the court observes in *Felger*, "Any alleged error in the District Court's rulings on the admissibility of evidence should have been determined on an appeal in the Circuit Court."

But the law of issue preclusion is not entirely hard-hearted in this respect. As we have seen, the requirement that the precluded party had a full and fair opportunity to litigate lawsuit #1 helps to assure the reliability of the decision in lawsuit #1. In addition, the unavailability of appeal is a factor that most courts will consider in deciding whether to allow issue preclusion. *See Restatement (Second) of Judgments* § 28(1) (barring preclusion when "[t]he party against whom preclusion is sought could not, as a matter of law, have obtained review of the judgment in the initial action").

III. Applying the Elements of Issue Preclusion

READING *OTHERSON v. DEP'T OF JUSTICE, INS.* *Otherson* involves another common fact pattern, in which lawsuit #2 raises an issue of a party's misconduct for which the party was criminally convicted in lawsuit #1. Here, border patrol agent Otherson was convicted of abusing aliens (lawsuit #1), and then fired for his misconduct. He appealed his firing to the Merit Systems Protection Board (MSPB) (lawsuit #2). (Lawsuit #2 actually involved two steps. In step one, a hearing officer conducted an evidentiary hearing in which she found Otherson issue-precluded by his criminal conviction. In step 2, the full MSPB agreed, denying Otherson's petition for review.) His appeal to the court of appeals followed.

The common issue involved Otherson's alleged misconduct. Lawsuit #1 resulted in a judgment of conviction against Otherson on that issue, and the court of appeals assumed that the issue of Otherson's abuse of aliens was the same in lawsuit #2. It then discussed the remaining requirements for issue preclusion that we identified in Part I of this chapter, although the court found it easier in this case to address the "necessarily decided" requirement before the "actually litigated" requirement.

- The INS and the MSPB both applied a statutory standard for the firing: whether it promotes the efficiency of the federal service. *Was* the issue in that criminal case and the MSPB proceedings the same?
- The judge in the criminal trial rendered a general verdict of guilty on the two misdemeanor counts. How, absent specific factual findings, do we know what issues were necessarily determined?
- Otherson stipulated that the MSPB could use the testimony and cross-examination of government witnesses from his felony trial in his misdemeanor trial. Usually when a party stipulates to a fact *instead* of litigating it, the stipulation is not given issue-preclusive effect. How was Otherson's stipulation different?
- Ultimately, the stakes for Otherson were much lower in the criminal misdemeanor trial than they had been in the deadlocked felony trial, which might have impacted his incentive to litigate. Why should his incentive to litigate the misdemeanor charges matter to the fairness of precluding him?

OTHERSON v. DEP'T OF JUSTICE, INS

711 F.2d 267 (D.C. Cir. 1983)

Before EDWARDS, Circuit Judge, and McGOWAN and MACKINNON, Senior Circuit Judges.

McGOWAN, Senior Circuit Judge:

Jeffrey Otherson formerly worked as a border patrol agent for the Immigration and Naturalization Service (INS). INS discharged him after he and a co-worker received criminal convictions for physically abusing aliens according to a prearranged scheme they carried out during working hours with apparent zest. When Otherson appealed his discharge, the Merit Systems Protection Board (MSPB) held that the doctrine of issue preclusion, also known as collateral estoppel, forbade him from relitigating the facts established at the criminal trial....

On review of this order, we are asked to resolve [*inter alia*] ... whether the MSPB properly found preclusion appropriate in the particular circumstances of this case. We answer ... in the affirmative and thus deny Otherson's petition for review.

I.

[Eds.—After an eight-day criminal trial of Otherson on felony charges of conspiracy and deprivation of civil rights, resulting in approximately 1,500 pages of transcript and six days of jury deliberation, the jury deadlocked eleven to one in favor of conviction, and the judge granted a mistrial. The government then agreed to drop felony charges and to retry Otherson just for misdemeanor federal offenses. In return for this concession, Otherson agreed to proceed without a jury on the basis of a stipulated record of the government's evidence at the first trial. Specifically, he stipulated that if six of the government's witnesses were recalled, they would testify on both direct and cross-examination as they had at the first trial, and he agreed not to introduce any of the defendants' testimony or evidence.

The case was then retried on these terms, and the trial judge found Otherson guilty of the two misdemeanor counts in what the court calls a "general verdict." In other words, the judge did not make specific factual findings. He fined Otherson $1,000 and gave him a suspended sentence, subject to three years' probation and community service. The court of appeals affirmed the conviction and the Supreme Court denied *certiorari*.

Thereafter, the INS fired Otherson for his misconduct in order to "promote the efficiency of the service," the relevant statutory standard. He appealed his firing to the MSPB. As noted above, the MSPB ultimately upheld his firing, finding that he was precluded from relitigating the issue of his misconduct.

Otherson then brought the instant appeal, in part challenging this application of issue preclusion.]...

III

... Along with the doctrine of claim preclusion or res judicata, issue preclusion aims to avert needless relitigation and disturbance of repose, without inadvertently inducing extra litigation or unfairly sacrificing a person's day in court. As the Supreme Court has explained,

> "a party who has had one fair and full opportunity to prove a claim and has failed in that effort, should not be permitted to go to trial on the merits of that claim a

> second time. Both orderliness and reasonable time saving in judicial administration require that this be so unless some overriding consideration of fairness to a litigant dictates a different result in the circumstances of a particular case."

Blonder-Tongue Laboratories, Inc. v. University of Illinois Foundation, 402 U.S. 313, 324–25 (1971) (quoting *Bruszewski v. United States*, 181 F.2d 419, 421 (3d Cir.), *cert. denied*, 340 U.S. 865 (1950)).

Issue preclusion establishes in a later trial on a different claim identical issues resolved in an earlier trial, if certain conditions are met. First, the issue must have been actually litigated, that is, contested by the parties and submitted for determination by the court. Second, the issue must have been "actually and necessarily determined by a court of competent jurisdiction" in the first trial. *Montana v. United States*, 440 U.S. 147, 153 (1979). *See also Parklane Hosiery Co. v. Shore*, 439 U.S. 322, 326 n.5 (1979) ("necessary to the outcome of the first action"); RESTATEMENT (SECOND) OF JUDGMENTS § 27 ("essential to the judgment"). Third, preclusion in the second trial must not work an unfairness. Preclusion is sometimes unfair if the party to be bound lacked an incentive to litigate in the first trial, especially in comparison to the stakes of the second trial. We now consider each factor with respect to preclusion at Otherson's MSPB hearing.

A. Necessarily Determined in the First Action

We can dispose of one element without much difficulty: whether the criminal trial necessarily determined the facts the government sought to establish preclusively at the MSPB hearing. Otherson notes that each count against him and his co-defendant included either conspiracy, or aiding and abetting, as a source of liability. He also notes that the judge rendered no special findings of fact. Perhaps, he argues, the judge's general verdict did not decide in the government's favor on every fact the government alleged and to which the government's witnesses testified. Perhaps the court found Otherson's own involvement to be less direct and substantial than alleged, illegal only on grounds of conspiracy or aiding and abetting.

We find this argument unconvincing. Otherson has not shown that " 'a rational [factfinder] could have grounded its verdict upon an issue other than that which the [party] seeks to foreclose from consideration.' " *Ashe v. Swenson*, 397 U.S. 436, 444 (1970) (effect of prior acquittal). [T]he MSPB presiding official examined the record of the prior trial in detail to see if the judge might have disbelieved some aspects of the acts charged. The MSPB examination was not to be "hypertechnical," but to be conducted "with realism and rationality." *Ashe*, 397 U.S. at 444. The only grounds the judge at the criminal trial had for doubting the government's version of events was Otherson's cross-examination, which made general attacks on the witnesses' credibility. The MSPB official concluded that the judge must have found the government's witnesses credible, and thus that "it was necessary and essential for the court to find that the defendants did commit the acts listed in the pleadings." We find this conclusion to be perfectly reasonable and thus reject Otherson's contention that the general verdict at the criminal trial did not necessarily determine against him the facts preclusively established at the MSPB hearing.

B. Actually Litigated

Otherson next contends that, because the criminal trial was conducted on the basis of a stipulated record, the issues were not actually litigated. His contention, however, misconstrues the sort of stipulations that bring issues outside the actual litigation requirement. Generally speaking,[1] when a particular fact is established not by judicial resolution but by stipulation of the parties, that fact has not been "actually litigated" and thus is not a proper candidate for issue preclusion.[2] [C]*f.* *United States v. International Building Co.*, 345 U.S. 502 (1953) (consent judgment); *Tutt v. Doby*, 459 F.2d 1195, 1199–200 (D.C. Cir. 1972) (default judgment). The reasoning behind this rule is apparent from the *Restatement*'s articulation of the actual litigation requirement:

> The interests of conserving judicial resources, of maintaining consistency, and of avoiding oppression or harassment of the adverse party are less compelling when the issue on which preclusion is sought has not actually been litigated before. And if preclusive effect were given to issues not litigated, the result might serve to discourage compromise, to decrease the likelihood that the issues in an action would be narrowed by stipulation, and thus to intensify litigation.

RESTATEMENT (SECOND) OF JUDGMENTS § 27 comment e.

Otherson, however, did not stipulate to the truth of the government's allegations. He simply stipulated that the government's witnesses would testify in the second trial as they had at the first. When a stipulation merely helps to shape the record a factfinder will use to determine the truth of a fact, rather than to establish the truth of the fact itself, that fact may be preclusively established in a later trial if the other requirements for issue preclusion are met. Otherson contested the allegations against him through his attorney's cross-examination, and the parties left it to the trial judge to evaluate the witnesses' testimony and determine whether the government established its allegations beyond a reasonable doubt. Therefore, the factual basis of the charges was actually litigated and those facts are appropriate for issue preclusion at later proceedings.

C. Incentive to Litigate

Fears that a party might have litigated less than fully because the stakes in the first action were low in relation to those in the second inhere in the justification for not preclusively establishing issues not actually litigated. See RESTATEMENT (SECOND) OF JUDGMENTS § 27 comment e (party may choose not to raise an issue because the "action may involve so small an amount that litigation of the

---

1. Preclusion is appropriate when the stipulation clearly manifests the parties' intent to be bound in future actions.

2. Under the doctrine of claim preclusion (res judicata), by contrast, even issues determined by stipulation may not be reopened in later actions upon the same claim.

issue may cost more than the value of the lawsuit"). Courts, however, have considered potential unfairness from a lack of incentive to litigate even when some litigation actually took place in the first trial. In the *Restatement*'s formulation, lack of incentive to litigate is one consideration for possible exception from preclusion even in cases where the other requirements for preclusion are met. *See* RESTATEMENT (SECOND) OF JUDGMENTS § 28(5)(c).

We now consider and reject two arguments that Otherson's lack of incentive to litigate fully in the first trial makes preclusion inappropriate even though the facts were contested and submitted for judicial determination. The first argument is that the stakes in the first trial were quite low in relation to the stakes at the MSPB hearing. Otherson was fined $1,000 and was at risk for only six months in jail. This is arguably much less than the stakes of a proceeding concerning a discharge from employment. Indeed, one circuit that has found preclusion generally appropriate for issues determined by verdicts entered upon guilty pleas has suggested that facts inhering in a guilty plea to a misdemeanor may not similarly be established preclusively in later trials. Yet Otherson's case is one good example of a defendant who took the first trial quite seriously even though he was at risk for only a small amount. Although he did withhold some of his evidence, he obviously thought the charge a serious one, for he pursued his appeal on the legality of his conviction all the way to the Supreme Court. Therefore, preclusion is much more appropriate here than in a case where a defendant put up no resistance at all because the misdemeanor was too trivial to worry about.

A second argument for an exception to preclusion is that the bargain with the prosecution created an actual disincentive to litigate these particular issues, above and beyond the fact that Otherson was at risk for only a misdemeanor. Had Otherson insisted on presenting his full factual defenses to the allegations, he presumably would have faced felony charges rather than misdemeanors....

Under the circumstances we think there is no great unfairness in holding Otherson to the determinations from his prior criminal conviction. Even without the full evidentiary presentation Otherson made at the felony trial, the misdemeanor conviction does provide an extra margin of reliability that dispels some of the worries about using the conviction at the MSPB hearing. The court found Otherson guilty beyond a reasonable doubt. It did so after considering the testimony of witnesses subjected to full cross-examination. Given that the government must prove misconduct at the MSPB hearing by a mere preponderance of the evidence, it is not likely that preclusive use of the conviction will work an unfairness at the later hearing....

V

For the foregoing reasons, we deny Otherson's petition for review.

It is so ordered.

Notes and Questions: Elements and Exceptions

A. The Issue in Lawsuit #1 and #2 Was the Same

The identity of the issues is the threshold inquiry in issue preclusion, although in many opinions it is so obvious that it is simply assumed by the analysis.

Q **1. Same issue?** What issues of fact were posed in lawsuit #1, Otherson's misdemeanor trial?

A Whether Otherson and his co-defendant physically abused aliens.

Q **What issues were posed in lawsuit #2, Otherson's challenge to his firing?**

A The central issue was whether firing Otherson promoted the efficiency of the service (the statutory standard for firing him). That clearly was *not* the subject of lawsuit #1. However, Otherson's abuse of aliens was an issue in lawsuit #1 and also the factual reason that the INS thought his firing met the efficiency-of-the-service standard. Two issues can be the same for preclusion purposes even when the issue is not the "ultimate" issue in the case. "An issue on which relitigation is foreclosed may be one of evidentiary fact, of 'ultimate fact' (i.e., the application of law to fact), or of law." *Restatement (Second) of Judgments* § 27, cmt. c. Here, Otherson's misconduct is an evidentiary fact in both lawsuits.

Deciding whether the issues in two lawsuits are identical is sometimes harder. For example, in *Pastre v. Weber*, 717 F. Supp. 987 (S.D.N.Y. 1988), Pastre sued police officers for using excessive force when arresting him. Pastre had been previously convicted of resisting those officers during Pastre's arrest, after a trial where the state had the burden of proving that the force used by the arresting officers was justified. The police officers in lawsuit #2, the civil case, sought to preclude Pastre from arguing that the officers used excessive force in light of Pastre's conviction for resisting arrest in the earlier criminal case. The district court found that the criminal trial involved the officers' use of force *before* Pastre was placed in custody, while his civil rights claim also raised the issue of whether the officers used excessive force *after* Pastre was placed in custody. The court held that Pastre was estopped by his conviction from arguing that the pre-custody use of force was excessive (because the judgment of conviction necessarily decided that this use of force was justified), but that the issue of force used afterwards was different. The criminal conviction therefore carried "only partial collateral estoppel effect." *Id.* at 991.

2. Same issue: *Bank v. Bulger* again. Recall that in this chapter's opening hypothetical, the Bank sued Bulger for past due payments on his loan, and he defended on the grounds that the loan agreement was invalid for failing to make certain disclosures required by law. The Bank won; its disclosures were found to be adequate.

Now suppose it sues him again for non-payment of later installments, and he defends on the same ground, as well as on the ground that the Bank procured the loan agreement by fraud. Which of the following is true?

A. The Bank is claim-precluded from bringing lawsuit #2.
B. Bulger is issue-precluded from raising either defense.
C. Bulger is issue-precluded only from raising the non-disclosure defense.
D. Bulger is not precluded from raising either defense.

A is incorrect. A party is claim-precluded from relitigating the same claim, as well as any claim it could have litigated based on the same transaction (according to the modern view of claim preclusion). The claim for non-payment of later installments is neither the same claim as the one for prior installments nor one the Bank could have brought before the later installments became due.

B is not right either. Unlike claim preclusion, issue preclusion applies only to issues that were actually litigated, not to issues that could have been but were not, regardless of whether they are part of the same transaction. The issue of fraud was not litigated in lawsuit #1. That it could have been makes no difference to issue preclusion.

Conversely, the issue of the invalidity of the loan agreement for non-disclosures *was* litigated in lawsuit #1 and necessarily must have been decided for the Bank in order for it to have won. Therefore, **C** is correct and **D** is wrong. *See Restatement (Second) of Judgments* § 27, cmt. a, illus. 2.

B. The Issue Was Actually Litigated

Q **1. Was the issue of abuse of aliens actually litigated in lawsuit #1 in *Otherson*?**

A At one level, this seems easy. Otherson's first trial (the felony trial) focused on his alleged abuse of aliens, lasted eight days, featured at least six live witnesses and extensive cross-examination by his counsel, and produced 1,500 pages of transcripts. "When an issue is properly raised, by the pleadings or otherwise, and is submitted for determination, and is determined, the issue is actually litigated." *Restatement (Second) of Judgments* § 27, cmt. d. Moreover, a full trial is not always necessary to actually litigate an issue. Issues can also be submitted and determined on motions to dismiss for failure to state a claim, summary judgment, judgment on the pleadings, directed verdict, judgment as a matter of law, or judgment notwithstanding the verdict. *Id.*

That said, there is a problem with lawsuit #1. The eight-day felony trial did not result in any decision because the jury deadlocked. Otherson was therefore tried again on lesser, misdemeanor charges. That misdemeanor trial (still lawsuit #1 for preclusion purposes) was tried in large part on the record of the government witnesses' testimony (and their cross-examination by Otherson's lawyer) in the prior felony trial. Otherson had agreed to let the government use that prior testimony in his retrial in lieu of live testimony in return for the government's agreement to pursue misdemeanor instead of felony chanrges. It's the issues decided in the *misdemeanor trial* on which the MSPB seeks to preclude Otherson.

Q **2. But what if the parties stipulated to the fact for which preclusion is sought?**

A Otherson correctly argued that issue preclusion does not ordinarily apply to stipulated facts. They have not been actually litigated, or therefore tested by the adversarial process. Parties may stipulate to facts for reasons other than their truth (to bargain for some concession, to reach some other issue more expeditiously, to save money, etc.). Consent judgments (essentially, judgments to which the parties have mutually agreed) ordinarily do not carry issue-preclusive effect for the same reason. Parties may consent for reasons other than their admission of liability (to avoid the cost of defending, to defer defending until the judgment creditor seeks to collect the judgment, etc.). Moreover, as the court notes, giving preclusive effect to stipulated facts or consent judgments might discourage stipulations and consent judgments, which could have the inefficient consequence of causing more litigation.

The problem for Otherson, however, is that he "did not stipulate to the truth of the government's allegations. He simply stipulated that the government's witnesses would testify in the second trial as they had at the first." His stipulations simply identified the record for the judge in the misdemeanor trial, and that record included not only the witnesses' prior testimony, but also the cross-examination by Otherson's lawyer. The stipulation simply avoided making the witnesses come back and give their testimony again, but it decided no facts. The issue of Otherson's conduct was therefore still actually litigated and submitted to the judge in the misdemeanor trial on the testimonial record made at the felony trial.

3. Preclusive effects of other dispositions.

Which of the following events can have issue-preclusive effects, in light of the central requirement that an issue must have been "actually litigated"?

A. A written stipulation by a party that the party owns Blackacre?
B. An admission under Rule 36 that a party owns Blackacre? (Hint: Read Rule 36.)
C. A default judgment against a non-appearing party in a nuisance suit based in part on the allegation that the party owns Blackacre?
D. A confession to the police by Smith that he hit Jones?
E. None of the above.

A concerns a stipulation of fact, unlike Otherson's stipulations. For the reasons stated above, it does not have issue-preclusive effect unless the parties have agreed between themselves to give it that effect.

B does not seem to have issue-preclusive effect for the same reasons (although an admission under Rule 36 is arguably less voluntary than a stipulation because it is made in response to a request for admission). But the Rule itself answers the question by providing that an admission made "under this rule is not an admission for any other purpose and cannot be used against the party in any other proceeding."

C does not have issue-preclusive effects on the issue of liability either, because by defaulting, the party chose not to litigate this issue. Again, a party may default for many reasons other than its belief in its own liability.

Finally, **D** is the annoying red herring. A confession is not an issue decided by a court or any comparable adjudicative tribunal, no matter how reliable it is. It has no preclusive effect. But it *has* evidentiary value; it can be admitted as evidence of Smith's guilt. But then it is just that—evidence that the jury or judge can take into account in deciding guilt, not a determination that is conclusive of the matter. A decision that is subject to issue preclusion, by contrast, is not evidence; it is conclusive of the issue decided. In a jury trial, the jury is not left to decide a precluded issue for itself, but would be instructed to take the issue as established.

So **E** is right.

C. The Issue Was Necessarily Decided

1. Inferring what was decided by a general verdict. In *Otherson*, the trial judge rendered a general verdict of guilty in Otherson's misdemeanor trial. Otherson argued that without specific findings of fact, it was not clear whether the trial judge found that he directly abused aliens or found that his involvement was more tangential. But the misdemeanor charges depended entirely on whether Otherson had abused aliens, and there was extensive testimony that he had. To render a general verdict of guilty, the court must have believed the government's witnesses, rejected Otherson's attacks on their credibility, and decided that he had abused aliens.

So, just because a general verdict does not list the facts on which it rests, it does not mean that we can't ascertain them by logical inference. Suppose, for example, that a jury renders a general verdict for $1,000 for Peter in a suit for negligence, in which defendant Danny has defended by offering evidence of Peter's own negligence in a jurisdiction in which such "contributory negligence" would defeat a plaintiff's claim for negligence. When the parties have actually litigated each other's negligence in these circumstances, we can logically infer from the general verdict for Peter that the jury found that:

(a) Danny was negligent,
(b) Peter was not contributorily negligent,
(c) Danny's negligence proximately caused Peter's injuries, and
(d) Peter's compensatory damages were $1,000.

Each of these findings is legally necessary for a verdict for Peter. Without making each of these findings, a properly instructed jury would not have been able to render that general verdict for Peter. Thus, we can say that each of these determinations was *necessarily* decided by the jury when it returned the general verdict, even though it did not spell them out expressly.

Q **2. Unnecessary findings?** Suppose that instead of a general verdict, the jury renders a special verdict that expressly states each of its findings. *See* Rule 49(a). But this time, assume that it finds *both* parties negligent. On that special verdict, the court would enter a judgment for Danny in lawsuit #1, because Peter's contributory negligence defeats his claim.

In lawsuit #2 involving the same accident and the same negligence but another driver who was not a party to lawsuit #1, would Danny be issue-precluded from disputing his negligence?

A No. While Danny's negligence was actually litigated and decided by the special verdict in lawsuit #1, the issue of his negligence was not *necessarily decided*. It was not only unnecessary to support the judgment for Danny in lawsuit #1; it actually seems to cut the other way.

Once the jury found Peter contributorily negligent, it had to go no further. Its finding that Danny, too, was negligent was gratuitous, like dictum or an aside. Perhaps the jury considered Danny's negligence as carefully as it considered Peter's negligence, but perhaps it didn't. We don't have the same confidence in gratuitously decided issues as we have in necessarily decided issues.

Moreover, Danny could not appeal the jury's finding that he was negligent in lawsuit #1 because *he won*. If he tried to appeal, the appellate court would likely refuse to hear the appeal, reasoning that "you won the case, so what have you got to complain about?" (Recall from Chapter 32 that a party can ordinarily only appeal *prejudicial* error. The error, if any, was harmless.) The appellate court would likely dismiss the appeal since, even if it reversed the finding of the employee's negligence, the outcome of the case would remain the same. *See Restatement (Second) of Judgments* § 27 cmt. h (non-essential issue "determinations have the characteristics of dicta, and may not ordinarily be the subject of an appeal by the party against whom they were made.").

Q **3. Changing the hypothetical again.** Suppose that lawsuit #1 was tried to the judge, who found that *neither* Peter nor Danny was negligent? Who would have won the case? Which party would be issue-precluded in lawsuit #2?

A On these findings, Danny would win again because he was not negligent. This outcome does not turn on whether *Peter* was negligent. Here, the finding that Peter was not contributorily negligent is again *dictum*; it does not affect the result in the case, which would have been the same if the judge had made *no* finding about Peter's negligence. Peter lost lawsuit #1 because Danny was not negligent.

It follows that only Danny's non-negligence was necessarily decided, so only this finding could be given issue-preclusive effect in lawsuit #2 against someone who was a party to lawsuit #1.

4. Applying the essential-to-the-judgment requirement.

Fortes sues Berrier for breach of an alleged oral contract to share Berrier's winnings at all his poker tournaments during a given year. He claims that Berrier won $50,000 at the Vegas Texas Hold'Em tournament that year, but refused to pay half to Fortes.

Berrier raises several defenses: He argues that he did not make the contract. He also claims that the contract was an illegal contract for the division of gambling winnings and therefore void. Last, he argues that he did not agree to split his winnings for any tournament if Fortes failed to provide the "stake" (funds needed to enter) and that Fortes had failed to stake him for the Vegas tournament.

Before trial, both parties move for summary judgment on the first two defenses, that the parties did not make the contract, and that the contract is illegal. The judge grants summary judgment to Fortes on these two defenses, finding as a matter of law that they did make the contract and that the contract is valid. The case goes to trial, and Fortes loses, because the jury finds that Fortes had agreed to provide the stake but failed to do so.

Subsequently, Fortes sues Berrier for a later breach of the same contract, claiming that Berrier won $100,000 at the World Series of Poker, but failed to split the winnings with him. Berrier argues as a defense that they never made the contract and that the contract is illegal. Which of the following statements is correct?

A. Berrier should be precluded from asserting either defense, since the judge found against him on those issues in the prior case.
B. Berrier is not precluded from relitigating either issue, since neither was essential to the judgment in the prior case.
C. Berrier is not precluded on either issue, since they were not "actually decided" in the first case.
D. Berrier is not precluded from litigating either issue, because these issues were not decided by the jury in the prior action.

D suggests that issue preclusion does not apply because the judge ruled on these issues rather than the jury. Generally, decisions by judges as well as by juries are given issue-preclusive effect if the various requirements are met. *See Parklane Hosiery Company Inc. v. Shore,* 439 U.S. 322, 334 (1979). The grant of summary judgment represents a finding that "there is no genuine issue of material fact" on the issue and one party is entitled to judgment. So **C** fails as well.

So, the issues were litigated and decided in the prior action. However, they were not *necessarily decided* (essential to the judgment). Berrier did not win the case because the contract was made and was enforceable; he won *in spite of* these two findings, because the jury found that Fortes had not provided the stake, a condition precedent to recovering his half of the winnings. If Berrier believed that these two rulings by the judge were erroneous, he would not be able to get them corrected on appeal, since he won the case. Thus, **B** is right; Fortes will have to relitigate both issues even though they were fully litigated and resolved in the prior action. Since **B** is right, **A** is wrong.

Q **5. The most puzzling variation.** Suppose that the judge in lawsuit #1 found that Peter was negligent and that Danny was not. He enters judgment for Danny. Is Peter now issue-precluded on the issue of his negligence should it arise in lawsuit #2 by another driver in that accident?

A Hold onto your hats; this one is tough. Here, *either* of the judge's findings would have led to a judgment for Danny. The basis for Peter's suit was that Danny was negligent; if he wasn't, Danny wins. But Danny would also win, *even if he was negligent*, as long as Peter's negligence also contributed to the accident. So Danny wins lawsuit #1 in this hypothetical for two reasons; either alternative holding supports a denial of recovery.

So is Peter issue-precluded in lawsuit #2? The answer here is not clear. The *Restatement (Second) of Judgments* takes the position that issue preclusion should not apply to either holding. Here's its reasoning for this conclusion:

> First, a determination in the alternative may not have been as carefully or rigorously considered as it would have if it had been necessary to the result, and in that sense it has some of the characteristics of dicta. Second, and of critical importance, the losing party, although entitled to appeal from both determinations, might be dissuaded from doing so because of the likelihood that at least one of them would be upheld and the other not even reached. If he were to appeal solely for the purpose of avoiding the application of the rule of issue preclusion, then the rule might be responsible for increasing the burdens of litigation on the parties and the courts rather than lightening those burdens.

Restatement (Second) of Judgments § 27 cmt. i.

Courts, however, have not taken a uniform position on this subtle problem. Some, following the *Restatement (Second)*, have denied preclusive effect to either finding. *See, e.g., Society of Separationists, Inc. v. Herman*, 939 F.2d 1207, 1213–14 n.25 (5th Cir. 1991). Others have scrutinized the prior litigation to determine whether both findings were given full consideration in the prior suit and applied issue preclusion to both findings if they were. *See, e.g., Jean Alexander Cosmetics, Inc. v. L'Oreal USA, Inc.*, 458 F.3d 244, 249–57 (3d Cir. 2006).

D. There Was a Valid and "Final Judgment"

This seems like the same requirement for claim preclusion, but it is, in fact, more lenient for purposes of issue preclusion. "[F]or purposes of issue preclusion (as distinguished from [claim preclusion], 'final judgment' includes any prior adjudication of an issue in another action that is determined to be sufficiently firm to be accorded conclusive effect." *Restatement (Second) of Judgments* § 13 (1982). In other words, the requirement is more accurately phrased as "final enough."

E. The Party Against Whom Preclusion Is Sought Was a Party to, or in Privity with a Party to, Lawsuit #1

The requirement is the same for claim preclusion. *See supra* pp. 1205–15.

F. The Party Against Whom Preclusion Is Sought Had a Full and Fair Opportunity to Litigate

This requirement involves a few considerations.

Q **1. Procedural and jurisdictional differences.** Suppose lawsuit #1 was the MSPB proceedings, which found that Otherson abused aliens. If the abused aliens then sued Otherson for assault and battery or deprivation of civil rights, would he be estopped from denying that misconduct?

A Leaving aside (for the moment) that this would be using preclusion to help establish rather than to defeat a claim, the answer would depend on the procedures afforded by the MSPB. (Recall that *Restatement (Second) of Judgments* § 28 invites an exception to issue preclusion for "differences in the quality or extensiveness of the procedures followed in the two courts or by factors relating to the allocation of jurisdiction between them."). What discovery, if any, did the MSPB proceeding afford Otherson? What rules of evidence did it apply and how did they impact his case? Was Otherson permitted to be represented by counsel? Etc. The full-and-fair-opportunity inquiry is quite flexible and pragmatic; there is no fixed formula for when a proceeding can be said to meet this standard.

Many modern administrative agencies are "quasi-adjudicative," in that they use many of the same procedures as courts, such as written pleadings, oral hearings, rules of evidence, and cross-examination. The Supreme Court has therefore long since approved giving issue-preclusive effect to appropriate administrative findings. *See University of Tenn. v. Elliott*, 478 U.S. 788, 797–98 (1986) (collecting cases). Of course, the procedures are usually not completely the same. But "[r]ather than focusing on whether procedural differences exist—they often will—the correct inquiry is whether the procedures used in the first proceeding were fundamentally poor, cursory, or unfair." *B & B Hardware, Inc. v. Hargis Indus., Inc.*, 575 U.S. 138, 149 (2015).

Q **2. Incentive to litigate.** *Otherson* identifies another factor in this inquiry. When the stakes of lawsuit #1 are low, so may be a party's incentive to litigate, casting serious doubt on whether the issue was *actually* litigated. Why did the court find that Otherson had sufficient incentive to actually litigate the issue of his misconduct?

A Given that Otherson was ultimately given just a $1,000 fine and a suspended sentence, it might sound like he had little incentive to fight hard in his misdemeanor trial. But if this seems incredibly lenient to us (for "physically abusing aliens ... with apparent zest" by a "prearranged scheme"!), the risk of punishment may have looked different to Otherson. First, he could have been sentenced to up to a year in prison on one misdemeanor count. Second, he could presumably foresee an adverse job action coming if he was convicted. In any case, his actual defense belies his post hoc claim of disincentive. In his defense, he submitted his lawyer's presumably vigorous cross-examination from the felony trial; he then appealed the misdemeanor conviction; and when he lost that appeal, he petitioned for *certiorari*. These steps all suggest that he put up a vigorous fight and that he had a strong incentive to litigate this issue.

However, his second claim of disincentive is a bit harder to reject. The government agreed to drop the felony counts only if Otherson agreed to letting the government use testimony from the felony trial (including Otherson's lawyer's cross-examination). In other words, he bargained for the lesser misdemeanor charges by giving up his full opportunity to defend. Still, the court reasons that the preservation of the cross-examination was enough to make the opportunity he did get sufficient.

Q **3. Burdens of proof.** The court added that, "[g]iven that the government must prove misconduct at the MSPB hearing by a mere preponderance of the evidence, it is not likely that preclusive use of the conviction will work an unfairness at the later hearing." Why not?

A Because in lawsuit #1, the government had to prove the misdemeanors *beyond a reasonable doubt*, a much higher standard of proof than "mere preponderance." In other words, in this respect, lawsuit #1 provided Otherson *more* procedural protection than lawsuit #2.

But now flip the order of lawsuits. Suppose the INS fired Otherson, and in lawsuit #1, the MSPB found that he had abused aliens and upheld the firing. Assume that he was able to put on all his evidence in lawsuit #1 after a sufficient opportunity for discovery, that his misconduct was actually litigated and decided, and that the determination of his misconduct was necessary to the decision to uphold his firing. If the government now charges him with a crime for that same misconduct in lawsuit #2, is Otherson precluded from contesting the finding by the MSPB that he abused aliens?

A All systems are go—that is, all of the requirements for issue preclusion are satisfied—*except one*. In lawsuit #1, the government only proved his misconduct by the preponderance standard. But in lawsuit #2, it would have to prove it beyond a reasonable doubt. Precluding Otherson would unfairly let the government make an end run around this traditional high criminal standard of proof and convict him under the easier-to-establish preponderance standard. (Some courts might reach the same result—denying preclusion—by saying that the issue whether a preponderance of the evidence establishes that Otherson abused aliens is different from the issue whether he did so beyond a reasonable doubt.)

IV. Non-Mutual Issue Preclusion

A. Non-Mutual *Defensive* Issue Preclusion

In most of the cases analyzed above, a plaintiff and defendant litigated an issue in lawsuit #1. Then, the same issue came up again in another suit *between the same parties or persons in privity with them*, and the party who prevailed on the issue in the prior action argued that there was no need to relitigate it. As the materials explain, courts will usually apply issue preclusion in such cases as long as the requirements identified *supra* at pp. 1224–25 are established.

The argument for issue preclusion may also be raised, however, in cases that involve new parties. For example, in *Blonder-Tongue Laboratories v. University of Illinois Foundation*, 402 U.S. 313 (1971), the University of Illinois Foundation sued Blonder-Tongue for infringing its patent on an antenna. Blonder-Tongue claimed that the Foundation's patent was invalid. The Foundation had previously sued a different laboratory for infringing the patent, but the jury in that case had found the Foundation's patent invalid. So Blonder-Tongue asserted issue preclusion to prevent the Foundation from claiming that the patent was valid. The Supreme Court approved this use of issue preclusion by someone in lawsuit #2 who was not a party to lawsuit #1 against someone who was a party in lawsuit #1.

Notes and Questions: The Meaning of Non-Mutual Defensive Issue Preclusion

Q **1. Parsing "non-mutuality."** Why was Blonder-Tongue's assertion of issue preclusion "non-mutual"?

A Blonder-Tongue was not a party to lawsuit #1, which involved the Foundation's prior lawsuit against a different laboratory. It is hornbook due process law that Blonder-Tongue was therefore not bound by the judgment in lawsuit #1 and could not be precluded by it. The Foundation, in contrast, *was* a party to lawsuit #1. It was therefore bound by the judgment in lawsuit #1. In lawsuit #2, Blonder-Tongue argued that the Foundation was therefore precluded by the finding in lawsuit #1 from relitigating the issue of the validity of its patent in lawsuit #2.

Thus, Blonder-Tongue asserted that the Foundation was stuck with the finding in lawsuit #1 that the patent was invalid, even though Blonder-Tongue itself would *not* have been stuck with a contrary finding from lawsuit #1. Blonder-Tongue was, in effect, saying, "Heads you lose, tails I win." This is one-way preclusion or what the cases call "non-mutual" preclusion, because the parties to lawsuit #2 are not *each* able to use the judgment from lawsuit #1 to establish an issue in lawsuit #2.

Q **2. Is this fair?** Why does it seem fair to estop the Foundation from relitigating validity, even against a new defendant?

A As long as the Foundation had a full incentive to litigate the issue in lawsuit #1, it has had its chance to prove its patent valid and failed. Why should it be able to keep relitigating the same issue "as long as the supply of unrelated defendants holds out"? *Blonder-Tongue*, 402 U.S. at 329.

Q **3. "Defensive" non-mutual issue preclusion.** Why is this use of issue preclusion characterized as non-mutual "defensive" issue preclusion?

A

Here, Blonder-Tongue, a stranger to lawsuit #1, raises issue preclusion to prevent the Foundation from establishing an element of its claim that it failed to establish in the prior action. The stranger uses issue preclusion as a shield to prevent the prior party from establishing its claim — to defend against the Foundation's claim. Visually, it looks like this:

#1 Foundation —> Able
(Foundation loses on validity)

#2 Foundation —> Blonder-Tongue
(B-T asserts issue preclusion on validity to avoid liability)

Q

4. Precluding Blonder-Tongue? Change the facts. Suppose that the Foundation won its first case for infringement of the patent, because the jury found the patent is valid. The Foundation now sues Blonder-Tongue Labs for infringing the same patent, and Blonder-Tongue claims the patent is invalid. The Foundation pleads issue preclusion: "Your Honor, we already litigated the validity issue, and we won. No need to relitigate that!" Would Blonder-Tongue be precluded from relitigating validity?

A

This case would be significantly different from that in question 3. There, the party being estopped had litigated and lost on the issue. It had its "bite at the apple," and it seems fair to deny it another. But in this case, Blonder-Tongue has never litigated the issue of validity. Some other defendant did, and lost, but maybe it had less at stake or weaker representation. Blonder-Tongue would naturally feel that it deserved a chance to prove that the patent was invalid. "[L]itigants . . . who never appeared in a prior action may not be collaterally estopped without litigating the issue. They have never had a chance to present their evidence and arguments on the claim." *Blonder-Tongue Labs., Inc. v. Univ. of Illinois Found.*, 402 U.S. 313, 329 (1971). Under the Due Process Clause, issue preclusion should not bar Blonder-Tongue here.

5. Acceptance of non-mutual defensive issue preclusion. In *Blonder-Tongue*, the Supreme Court approved the use of defensive non-mutual issue preclusion in cases where it is clear that the party being estopped had fully and fairly litigated the common issue in the earlier litigation:

> In any lawsuit where a defendant, because of the mutuality principle, is forced to present a complete defense on the merits to a claim which the plaintiff has fully litigated and lost in a prior action, there is an arguable misallocation of resources. To the extent the defendant in the second suit may not win by asserting, without contradiction, that the plaintiff had fully and fairly, but unsuccessfully, litigated the same claim in the prior suit, the defendant's time and money are diverted from alternative uses—productive or otherwise—to relitigation of a decided issue. And, still assuming that the issue was resolved correctly in the first suit, there is reason to be concerned about the plaintiff's allocation of resources. Permitting repeated litigation of the same issue as long as the supply of unrelated defendants holds out reflects either the aura of the gaming table or "a lack of discipline and of disinterestedness on the part

> of the lower courts, hardly a worthy or wise basis for fashioning rules of procedure." *Kerotest Mfg. Co. v. C-O-Two Co.*, 342 U.S. 180, 185 (1952). Although neither judges, the parties, nor the adversary system performs perfectly in all cases, the requirement of determining whether the party against whom an estoppel is asserted had a full and fair opportunity to litigate is a most significant safeguard.

Blonder-Tongue, 402 U.S. at 329.

6. Non-mutual defensive issue preclusion in the state courts. Traditionally, courts held that "issue preclusion must be mutual," that is, that only a litigant who was a party to the action in which the issue was first decided could assert issue preclusion to prevent relitigation of an issue. However, some state courts have accepted the argument that a litigant in the Foundation's position should not be free to relitigate the common issue against new defendants. A classic example (and one of the first cases recognizing defensive non-mutual issue preclusion) was *Bernhard v. Bank of America*, 122 P.2d 892 (Cal. 1942). Relatives of a deceased woman challenged an accounting of her estate, insisting that Cook, the executor of the estate, had taken money from the deceased's bank account before she died. Cook maintained that the account had been a gift to him and refused to include the funds in the estate. The court rejected the relatives' claim, concluding that the account was a gift to Cook and therefore not part of the estate. Subsequently, one of the same relatives sued the bank that had handled the account, arguing that the Bank had improperly paid out the money to Cook. Though the bank had not been a party to lawsuit #1, it asserted non-mutual defensive issue preclusion to prevent the relative from relitigating the ownership of the funds, since she *had* litigated and lost on the issue in lawsuit #1. In a path-breaking decision, the Supreme Court of California approved the defense, opening the intellectual door to many (but not all) other courts abrogating mutuality on the same reasoning.

B. Non-Mutual *Offensive* Issue Preclusion

Non-mutual defensive issue preclusion typically involves a defendant fending off liability by asserting issue preclusion based on a finding from a prior action. (For example, in *Otherson*, the INS used nonmutual defensive issue preclusion to help defeat Otherson's appeal of his firing.) In other cases, plaintiffs have sought to invoke issue preclusion to *establish* facts to prove its claim. As the *Parklane* case explains, this use of issue preclusion raises other concerns that have made courts cautious about allowing it.

READING *PARKLANE HOSIERY CO. v. SHORE*. In the following case, the government sought an injunction against Parklane, alleging that its proxy statement was false and misleading. In a separate action, Shore, a private plaintiff, sued the company as well, seeking damages on behalf of shareholders who had allegedly relied on the proxy statement and lost money as a result. Both the government and Shore had to prove that the proxy statement was false and misleading in order to win their cases. In the government's case, the judge found that it *was* false and misleading and issued a judgment for the government. Shore then moved in its case (now lawsuit #2 by our terminology, because the government's case went to judgment first) to preclude Parklane from relitigating this factual issue.

In reading the case, first sort out the procedural sequence and the nature of the problem.

- What is the issue decided in lawsuit #1 that arises again in lawsuit #2?
- Why does the case involve "non-mutual offensive issue preclusion"?
- Why is the argument for allowing offensive issue preclusion weaker than the argument for non-mutual defensive issue preclusion?
- Did the Court approve use of non-mutual offensive issue preclusion in all cases?

PARKLANE HOSIERY CO. v. SHORE

439 U.S. 322 (1979)

Mr. Justice Stewart delivered the opinion of the Court.

This case presents the question whether a party who has had issues of fact adjudicated adversely to it in an equitable action may be collaterally estopped from relitigating the same issues before a jury in a subsequent legal action brought against it by a new party.

The respondent brought this stockholder's class action against the petitioners in a Federal District Court. The complaint alleged that the petitioners, Parklane Hosiery Co., Inc. (Parklane), and 13 of its officers, directors, and stockholders, had issued a materially false and misleading proxy statement in connection with a merger. The proxy statement, according to the complaint, had violated §§ 14(a), 10(b), and 20(a) of the Securities Exchange Act of 1934 . . . as well as various rules and regulations promulgated by the Securities and Exchange Commission (SEC). The complaint sought damages, rescission of the merger, and recovery of costs.

Before this action came to trial, the SEC filed suit against the same defendants in the Federal District Court, alleging that the proxy statement that had been issued by Parklane was materially false and misleading in essentially the same respects as those that had been alleged in the respondent's complaint. Injunctive relief was requested. After a 4-day trial, the District Court found that the proxy statement was materially false and misleading in the respects alleged, and entered a declaratory judgment to that effect. . . . The Court of Appeals for the Second Circuit affirmed this judgment. . . .

The respondent in the present case then moved for partial summary judgment against the petitioners, asserting that the petitioners were collaterally estopped from relitigating the issues that had been resolved against them in the action brought by the SEC.[2] The District Court denied the motion on the ground that such an application of collateral estoppel would deny the petitioners their Seventh Amendment right to a jury trial. The Court of Appeals for the Second Circuit reversed, holding that a party who has had issues of fact determined against him after a full and fair opportunity to litigate in a nonjury trial is collaterally estopped from obtaining a subsequent jury trial of these same issues of fact.... The appellate court concluded that "the Seventh Amendment preserves the right to jury trial only with respect to issues of fact, [and] once those issues have been fully and fairly adjudicated in a prior proceeding, nothing remains for trial, either with or without a jury." ... Because of an inter-circuit conflict, ... we granted certiorari....

The threshold question to be considered is whether, quite apart from the right to a jury trial under the Seventh Amendment, the petitioners can be precluded from relitigating facts resolved adversely to them in a prior equitable proceeding with another party under the general law of collateral estoppel. Specifically, we must determine whether a litigant who was not a party to a prior judgment may nevertheless use that judgment "offensively" to prevent a defendant from relitigating issues resolved in the earlier proceeding.[4]

A

Collateral estoppel, like the related doctrine of res judicata,[5] has the dual purpose of protecting litigants from the burden of relitigating an identical issue with the same party or his privy and of promoting judicial economy by preventing needless litigation. *Blonder-Tongue Laboratories, Inc. v. University of Illinois Foundation*, 402 U.S. 313, 328–29. Until relatively recently, however, the scope of collateral estoppel was limited by the doctrine of mutuality of parties. Under this mutuality doctrine, neither party could use a prior judgment as an estoppel against the other unless both parties were bound by the judgment.... Based on the premise that it is somehow unfair to allow a party to use a prior judgment when he himself would not be so bound,[7] the mutuality requirement provided a

2. A private plaintiff in an action under the proxy rules is not entitled to relief simply by demonstrating that the proxy solicitation was materially false and misleading. The plaintiff must also show that he was injured and prove damages. . . . Since the SEC action was limited to a determination of whether the proxy statement contained materially false and misleading information, the respondent conceded that he would still have to prove these other elements of his prima facie case in the private action. The petitioners' right to a jury trial on those remaining issues is not contested.

4. In this context, offensive use of collateral estoppel occurs when the plaintiff seeks to foreclose the defendant from litigating an issue the defendant has previously litigated unsuccessfully in an action with another party. Defensive use occurs when a defendant seeks to prevent a plaintiff from asserting a claim the plaintiff has previously litigated and lost against another defendant.

5. Under the doctrine of res judicata, a judgment on the merits in a prior suit bars a second suit involving the same parties or their privies based on the same cause of action. Under the doctrine of collateral estoppel, on the other hand, the second action is upon a different cause of action and the judgment in the prior suit precludes relitigation of issues actually litigated and necessary to the outcome of the first action. . . .

7. It is a violation of due process for a judgment to be binding on a litigant who was not a party or a privy and therefore has never had an opportunity to be heard. Blonder-Tongue Laboratories, Inc. v. University of Illinois Foundation, 402 U.S. 313, 329; Hansberry v. Lee, 311 U.S. 32, 40.

party who had litigated and lost in a previous action an opportunity to relitigate identical issues with new parties.

By failing to recognize the obvious difference in position between a party who has never litigated an issue and one who has fully litigated and lost, the mutuality requirement was criticized almost from its inception. Recognizing the validity of this criticism, the Court in *Blonder-Tongue Laboratories, Inc. v. University of Illinois Foundation, supra,* abandoned the mutuality requirement, at least in cases where a patentee seeks to relitigate the validity of a patent after a federal court in a previous lawsuit has already declared it invalid. The "broader question" before the Court, however, was "whether it is any longer tenable to afford a litigant more than one full and fair opportunity for judicial resolution of the same issue." . . . The Court strongly suggested a negative answer to that question:

> "In any lawsuit where a defendant, because of the mutuality principle, is forced to present a complete defense on the merits to a claim which the plaintiff has fully litigated and lost in a prior action, there is an arguable misallocation of resources. To the extent the defendant in the second suit may not win by asserting, without contradiction, that the plaintiff had fully and fairly, but unsuccessfully, litigated the same claim in the prior suit, the defendant's time and money are diverted from alternative uses—productive or otherwise—to relitigation of a decided issue. And, still assuming that the issue was resolved correctly in the first suit, there is reason to be concerned about the plaintiff's allocation of resources. Permitting repeated litigation of the same issue as long as the supply of unrelated defendants holds out reflects either the aura of the gaming table or 'a lack of discipline and of disinterestedness on the part of the lower courts, hardly a worthy or wise basis for fashioning rules of procedure.' *Kerotest Mfg. Co. v. C-O-Two Co.,* 342 U.S. 180, 185 (1952). Although neither judges, the parties, nor the adversary system performs perfectly in all cases, the requirement of determining whether the party against whom an estoppel is asserted had a full and fair opportunity to litigate is a most significant safeguard." *Id.,* at 329.

B

The *Blonder-Tongue* case involved defensive use of collateral estoppel—a plaintiff was estopped from asserting a claim that the plaintiff had previously litigated and lost against another defendant. The present case, by contrast, involves offensive use of collateral estoppel—a plaintiff is seeking to estop a defendant from relitigating the issues which the defendant previously litigated and lost against another plaintiff. In both the offensive and defensive use situations, the party against whom estoppel is asserted has litigated and lost in an earlier action. Nevertheless, several reasons have been advanced why the two situations should be treated differently. . . .

First, offensive use of collateral estoppel does not promote judicial economy in the same manner as defensive use does. Defensive use of collateral estoppel precludes a plaintiff from relitigating identical issues by merely "switching adversaries." *Bernhard v. Bank of America Nat. Trust & Savings*, 19 Cal. 2d, at 813, 122 P.2d, at 895.[12] Thus defensive collateral estoppel gives a plaintiff a strong incentive to join all potential defendants in the first action if possible. Offensive use of collateral estoppel, on the other hand, creates precisely the opposite incentive. Since a plaintiff will be able to rely on a previous judgment against a defendant but will not be bound by that judgment if the defendant wins, the plaintiff has every incentive to adopt a "wait and see" attitude, in the hope that the first action by another plaintiff will result in a favorable judgment. Thus offensive use of collateral estoppel will likely increase rather than decrease the total amount of litigation, since potential plaintiffs will have everything to gain and nothing to lose by not intervening in the first action.

A second argument against offensive use of collateral estoppel is that it may be unfair to a defendant. If a defendant in the first action is sued for small or nominal damages, he may have little incentive to defend vigorously, particularly if future suits are not foreseeable. [C]*f. Berner v. British Commonwealth Pac. Airlines*, 346 F.2d 532 (CA2) (application of offensive collateral estoppel denied where defendant did not appeal an adverse judgment awarding damages of $35,000 and defendant was later sued for over $7 million). Allowing offensive collateral estoppel may also be unfair to a defendant if the judgment relied upon as a basis for the estoppel is itself inconsistent with one or more previous judgments in favor of the defendant.[14] Still another situation where it might be unfair to apply offensive estoppel is where the second action affords the defendant procedural opportunities unavailable in the first action that could readily cause a different result.[15]

C

We have concluded that the preferable approach for dealing with these problems in the federal courts is not to preclude the use of offensive collateral estoppel, but to grant trial courts broad discretion to determine when it should be applied.[16]

---

12. Under the mutuality requirement, a plaintiff could accomplish this result since he would not have been bound by the judgment had the original defendant won.

14. In Professor Currie's familiar example, a railroad collision injures 50 passengers all of whom bring separate actions against the railroad. After the railroad wins the first 25 suits, a plaintiff wins in suit 26. Professor Currie argues that offensive use of collateral estoppel should not be applied so as to allow plaintiffs 27 through 50 automatically to recover. [Currie, Mutuality of Estoppel: Limits of the Bernhard Doctrine, 9 Stan. L. Rev. 281, 304 (1957).] See Restatement (Second) of Judgments § 88(4), supra.

15. If, for example, the defendant in the first action was forced to defend in an inconvenient forum and therefore was unable to engage in full scale discovery or call witnesses, application of offensive collateral estoppel may be unwarranted. Indeed, differences in available procedures may sometimes justify not allowing a prior judgment to have estoppel effect in a subsequent action even between the same parties, or where defensive estoppel is asserted against a plaintiff who has litigated and lost. The problem of unfairness is particularly acute in cases of offensive estoppel, however, because the defendant against whom estoppel is asserted typically will not have chosen the forum in the first action. See id., § 88(2) and Comment d.

16. This is essentially the approach of id., § 88, which recognizes that "the distinct trend if not the clear weight of recent authority is to the effect that there is no intrinsic difference between 'offensive' as distinct from 'defensive' issue preclusion, although a stronger showing that the prior opportunity to litigate was adequate may be required in the former situation than the latter." Id., Reporter's Note, at 99.

The general rule should be that in cases where a plaintiff could easily have joined in the earlier action or where, either for the reasons discussed above or for other reasons, the application of offensive estoppel would be unfair to a defendant, a trial judge should not allow the use of offensive collateral estoppel.

In the present case, however, none of the circumstances that might justify reluctance to allow the offensive use of collateral estoppel is present. The application of offensive collateral estoppel will not here reward a private plaintiff who could have joined in the previous action, since the respondent probably could not have joined in the injunctive action brought by the SEC even had he so desired.[17]

Similarly, there is no unfairness to the petitioners in applying offensive collateral estoppel in this case. First, in light of the serious allegations made in the SEC's complaint against the petitioners, as well as the foreseeability of subsequent private suits that typically follow a successful Government judgment, the petitioners had every incentive to litigate the SEC lawsuit fully and vigorously.[18] Second, the judgment in the SEC action was not inconsistent with any previous decision. Finally, there will in the respondent's action be no procedural opportunities available to the petitioners that were unavailable in the first action of a kind that might be likely to cause a different result.[19]

We conclude, therefore, that none of the considerations that would justify a refusal to allow the use of offensive collateral estoppel is present in this case. Since the petitioners received a "full and fair" opportunity to litigate their claims in the SEC action, the contemporary law of collateral estoppel leads inescapably to the conclusion that the petitioners are collaterally estopped from relitigating the question of whether the proxy statement was materially false and misleading. . . .

Affirmed.

Notes and Questions: *Parklane*

Q **1. Why is issue preclusion "non-mutual" in *Parklane*?**

A Issue preclusion in *Parklane* is non-mutual because Shore, the party who wishes to apply issue preclusion, was not a party to the action in which the issue was decided and therefore is not bound by its findings. Shore has not

17. SEC v. Everest Management Corp., 475 F.2d 1236, 1240 (CA2) ("[T]he complicating effect of the additional issues and the additional parties outweighs any advantage of a single disposition of the common issues"). Moreover, consolidation of a private action with one brought by the SEC without its consent is prohibited by statute. 15 U.S.C. § 78u(g).

18. After a four-day trial in which the petitioners had every opportunity to present evidence and call witnesses, the District Court held for the SEC. The petitioners then appealed to the Court of Appeals for the Second Circuit, which affirmed the judgment against them. Moreover, the petitioners were already aware of the action brought by the respondent, since it had commenced before the filing of the SEC action.

19. It is true, of course, that the petitioners in the present action would be entitled to a jury trial of the issues bearing on whether the proxy statement was materially false and misleading had the SEC action never been brought. . . . But the presence or absence of a jury as factfinder is basically neutral, quite unlike, for example, the necessity of defending the first lawsuit in an inconvenient forum.

litigated the false-and-misleading issue yet; instead, he seeks to "borrow" this finding from the government's suit. "Your Honor," he argues, "we don't have to litigate the issue of whether the proxy statement was false and misleading. The parties already did that in the government's case, and the issue was decided there. It would be a waste of everyone's time to litigate it again."

If the court accepts Shore's argument and precludes Parklane from relitigating the false-and-misleading issue, Shore will save the time and expense of litigating that issue. Of even greater value to Shore, he will establish an essential fact in his case *without taking the risk of losing on it*. In *Parklane*, whether the proxy statement was false and misleading is the central issue in the case. How nice to win on the issue without even having to try it!

2. Three questions: Non-mutual non-estoppel. Change the *Parklane* case slightly. Assume that the government's case goes to trial first and that Parklane wins on the false-and-misleading issue: The judge finds that the proxy statement was accurate. Now, Shore's case is ready for trial.

Q **Who will want to invoke non-mutual issue preclusion?**

A Parklane will, of course. It will argue that the false-and-misleading issue was litigated and decided in the government's suit, that they won on it, and that there is no reason to waste time relitigating the issue in Shore's case.

Q **Would this be mutual or non-mutual issue preclusion?**

A Non-mutual again. Parklane is invoking issue preclusion against Shore, a party to a different case who has not yet litigated the issue decided in the earlier case.

Q **Will the court estop Shore from relitigating the issue?**

A No, no, no, a thousand times, no! In this example, Shore is in a fundamentally different position than Parklane was in the actual case: Shore has never litigated and lost on the false-and-misleading issue. As a matter of constitutional due process, Shore cannot be precluded from litigating the issue just because someone else litigated it and lost on it. Each litigant gets one bite at the apple—one opportunity to prove her case. No party can be precluded by issue preclusion because *someone else* litigated an issue, except in very limited situations involving privity or close legal relationships.

3. So, what's the answer? Should federal courts apply non-mutual issue preclusion or not? Parklane does not give a simple "yes" or "no" answer. Instead, it offers a qualified "yes." The Court suggests that offensive non-mutual issue preclusion is appropriate in some circumstances and authorizes federal trial judges to exercise discretion in deciding whether to bar relitigation.

First, the Court appropriately expresses concern that, before applying non-mutual offensive issue preclusion to an issue, a trial court must have confidence that the issue was fairly determined in the prior action. Thus, it might be unfair to preclude a party if it did not have an adequate *incentive* to litigate the issue aggressively in the prior action. (This might be the case if the prior action involved much lower stakes than the later action in which issue preclusion is sought.) It could also be unfair if the *result* in the prior action was somehow brought into question, because, for example, it was inconsistent with findings in other actions on the same issue. Finally, it would be unfair if the losing party did not have a full *procedural opportunity* to litigate the issue in the prior action. This is the same full-and-fair-opportunity requirement that most courts now apply generally to issue preclusion.

Second, the *Parklane* Court suggested that issue preclusion might also be denied if the plaintiff had waited in the wings for another litigant to litigate a common issue, hoping to ride on that other party's coattails if the outcome is favorable and to relitigate (as the plaintiff would be entitled to do) if it is not. Permitting such strategic behavior would promote inefficiency, the Court reasoned.*

Q **4. The "multiple plaintiff" scenario.** Imagine a railroad accident in which one hundred passengers are injured. In the first passenger's action against the railroad the jury concludes that the accident resulted from the railroad's negligence. Who would later seek to invoke issue preclusion?

A Presumably, the next ninety-nine passengers will invoke non-mutual offensive issue preclusion, arguing that they can all show negligence of the railroad because the first plaintiff had already established it. If they can do that, it is easy to see that the railroad's exposure in lawsuit #1 is very great. In large part, the railroad is at risk of losing one hundred cases if it loses the first one, since the crucial issue in all the cases will be whether it was negligent. The *in terrorem* effect of non-mutual preclusion can be pretty impressive: that is to say, the pressure to settle the first case to avoid the downstream consequences of non-mutual preclusion.

---

* Much of the Court's reasoning is captured by *Restatement (Second) of Judgments* § 29:

A party precluded from relitigating an issue with an opposing party, in accordance with §§ 27 and 28, is also precluded from doing so with another person unless the fact that he lacked full and fair opportunity to litigate the issue in the first action or other circumstances justify affording him an opportunity to relitigate the issue. The circumstances to which considerations should be given include those enumerated in § 28 and also whether:
(1) Treating the issue as conclusively determined would be incompatible with an applicable scheme of administering the remedies in the actions involved;
(2) The forum in the second action affords the party against whom preclusion is asserted procedural opportunities in the presentation and determination of the issue that were not available in the first action and could likely result in the issue being differently determined;
(3) The person seeking to invoke favorable preclusion, or to avoid unfavorable preclusion, could have effected joinder in the first action between himself and his present adversary;
(4) The determination relied on as preclusive was itself inconsistent with another determination of the same issue;
(5) The prior determination may have been affected by relationships among the parties to the first action that are not present in the subsequent action, or apparently was based on a compromise verdict or finding;
(6) Treating the issue as conclusively determined may complicate determination of issues in the subsequent action or prejudice the interests of another party thereto;
(7) The issue is one of law and treating it as conclusively determined would inappropriately foreclose opportunity for obtaining reconsideration of the legal rule upon which it was based;
(8) Other compelling circumstances make it appropriate that the party be permitted to relitigate the issue.

There will be many situations in which non-mutual issue preclusion may decide an issue for many cases. Imagine, for example, cases involving an alleged design defect in the transmission of a car. If the first jury finds the design defective, the manufacturer might be precluded from contesting the issue in all later cases involving that transmission. The same might be true in a case alleging a dangerous side effect of a widely used medication and in many other situations involving widely used products.

In favor of allowing preclusion in such situations, consider the potential savings for the courts. Instead of litigating that transmission defect five thousand times, the courts may litigate it once. That's quite a savings.

The Multiple Plaintiff Anomaly

The Birmingham News

Plaintiff #1 sues a drug manufacturer for negligently producing a drug that causes an adverse effect. The plaintiff wins; the jury finds by special verdict that the manufacturer was negligent in making and marketing the drug that caused the plaintiff's side effect. It doesn't take much imagination to foresee other plaintiffs who suffered the same side effect lining up at the courthouse doors to bring their own negligence cases against the same defendant and invoking non-mutual offensive issue preclusion to preclude the defendant from denying negligence. While the doctrine thus has great promise for avoiding duplicative litigation, it also threatens drastic consequences for defendants. If the jury finds negligence in lawsuit #1, the defendant drug manufacturer may lose not just that case, but potentially hundreds or even thousands of similar cases brought by other consumers. Should that prospect give courts pause in allowing non-mutual offensive issue preclusion?

Q **5. The multiple plaintiff "anomaly."** In footnote 14, the Court describes a case in which the first twenty-five plaintiffs in a mass accident sue and lose on the common issue of negligence. (Remember, even though the railroad won on negligence in each case, the other plaintiffs all get to relitigate, as a matter of due process.) In the suit by Number Twenty-Six, however, the jury finds that the railroad was negligent. So Numbers Twenty-Seven to Fifty all invoke non-mutual issue preclusion. How should the court rule?

A We can't imagine a court in these circumstances applying issue preclusion. The *Parklane* Court suggested that a judge should consider contrary findings on the issue in deciding whether to invoke issue preclusion. Here there is not one contrary finding, but twenty-five. It is the finding in lawsuit #26 that is the anomaly. (Hence, academics refer to this reason for denying offensive non-mutual issue preclusion as the "multiple plaintiff anomaly.") But the situation is different if the plaintiff wins the first case, since there is no reason (yet) to doubt the accuracy of the jury's finding.

Q **6. Contrary arguments.** The Supreme Court's cautious embrace of offensive non-mutual issue preclusion has not been accepted in all quarters. One problem that the doctrine is said to have created is "a litigation strategy that might be called *plaintiff shopping*. The attorneys for numerous potential claimants might agree to have the strongest case go to judgment first, so the subsequent claimants can 'ride' the successful judgment through nonmutual offensive issue preclusion." *Freer* § 11.3. What answer, if any, does the Court in *Parklane* give to this concern?

A The majority would say look to whether the "free-ride" "wait-and-see" plaintiffs "could easily have joined in the earlier action." If the plaintiffs' attorneys have collaborated, their very agreement may suggest that their clients could just as well have joined (although the Court is silent on whether the convenience of joining can be considered in deciding whether they could "easily" have joined). It is hard to find cases, however, in which a court has denied issue preclusion to punish a plaintiff for hanging back. If all the other factors favor preclusion, courts have a large incentive to apply it despite strategic behavior by plaintiffs.

Another dissenting view is that "nonmutuality destroys the equivalence of litigating risk by weighting the scale against the common party, and so changes the most basic of the procedural system's rules, namely, procedure must provide a level playing field." Kevin Clermont, Principles of Civil Procedure 386 (3d ed. 2012). If this is true, the first plaintiff will have enormous bargaining leverage to force the "common party"—the railroad or stock company, for example—to settle. *Id.*

7. Non-mutual offensive issue preclusion in the state courts. *Parklane* holds that federal courts may invoke non-mutual offensive issue preclusion in their discretion under certain circumstances. However, the courts of each state are free to establish their own rules on procedural issues like issue preclusion. While the "emerging trend" of the cases is to accept nonmutual offensive issue preclusion, some states have rejected it. *Freer* § 11.3.5. For example, the Florida Supreme Court explained, "We are not convinced that any judicial economies which might be achieved by eliminating mutuality would be sufficient to affect our concerns over fairness for the litigants." *Stogniew v. McQueen*, 656 So. 2d 917, 919–20 (Fla. 1995).

V. Another Confusing Problem: Inter-System Preclusion

Suppose McEnroe seeks to preclude Connors in lawsuit #2 from relitigating an essential finding in lawsuit #1. Lawsuit #1, however, was in a Maryland state court, and lawsuit #2 action is in an Illinois state court. The very real possibility that the court that issued the judgment (the *rendering court*) will be in a different judicial system than the court that is asked to give effect to the judgment (the *enforcing court*) raises the question of which court's law of preclusion controls the effect of the judgment. This doesn't matter, of course, if the preclusion rules of the two judicial systems (here Maryland and Illinois) are the same, but we have seen that often they are not. The federal common law of preclusion permits non-mutual offensive issue preclusion; most states do not (although many—not all—allow non-mutual defensive issue preclusion). Some states give issue-preclusive effect to guilty pleas in criminal cases; some do not, requiring first a conviction after trial, in their interpretation of the "actually litigated" requirement. Some give no issue-preclusive effect to alternate findings (following the *Restatement (Second) of Judgments*), while some give that effect to both alternatives.

This is so difficult that we will not hold you in suspense. As a *general* rule, American courts give the same preclusive effect to a judgment that the rendering court would give it. Thus, in our example, in lawsuit #2, the Illinois court will apply Maryland law to decide the preclusive effect of the Maryland judgment. Keeping this straight is not impossible, but it requires keeping your eye on the ball: *the preclusion law that the rendering court would apply.*

A. Interstate Application of Preclusion Principles: Variations on a Theme

Hypothetical #1. Altieri sues Quigley in the state courts of West Dakota for his personal injuries suffered in an auto accident. He recovers a judgment. Later he brings a second action, also in the state courts of West Dakota, for the property damage to his car in the same accident. Quigley pleads *res judicata.* If the West Dakota courts apply a transactional approach to claim preclusion, this second action will be barred, since it arises from the same events as the prior suit. *Restatement (Second) of Judgments* § 24.

Hypothetical #2. Vary the hypothetical a little. Suppose the second action is brought in the state courts of another state—say, East Dakota—which takes a different approach to claim preclusion. It allows the parties to bring separate actions to recover for different "primary rights" and views personal injuries and property damage as different "primary rights." So, if Altieri's first case had been brought in the state courts of East Dakota, the judgment in that action for personal injuries would not bar the second for property damage. Should the East Dakota court in lawsuit #2 apply the preclusion rules of the West Dakota courts (which decided lawsuit #1) or its own?

A The answer that courts have given to this interesting problem derives from the Full Faith and Credit Clause of the United States Constitution (Art. IV. § 1), which provides that "Full faith and credit shall be given in every state to the records, acts and judicial proceedings of every other state...." The Supreme Court has held that this language requires the court in which a second action is brought to apply the preclusion rules of the state court that rendered the judgment. *Durfee v. Duke*, 375 U.S. 106, 111 (1963). So, the East Dakota court must ask itself, "if this second case had been brought in the courts of West Dakota, would those courts have barred it under West Dakota preclusion rules?" Since they would have, then the East Dakota court will do so as well. *See also* 28 U.S.C. § 1738.

Hypothetical #3. Consider the converse case: Altieri's first case is brought in an East Dakota state court, the state that applies the "primary rights" approach to claim preclusion. He sues for his personal injuries in the accident and recovers. He then brings a second action in a West Dakota state court for property damage to his car. Quigley pleads *res judicata*.

A Under the Full Faith and Credit Clause and § 1738, the West Dakota court must consider whether Altieri's second action would have been barred by claim preclusion if he had brought it in East Dakota. It would not have been barred, since East Dakota courts view the claim for property damage as a different "primary right" than the action for personal injuries. Since the action would not be barred in East Dakota, the West Dakota court will allow the second action, even though its own preclusion rules would bar it.

This approach to interstate preclusion has a very significant practical advantage: As soon as the judgment is rendered, the parties will know the extent to which it will bar further litigation. They need not wait to see where the second action is brought, since the court that hears that action will apply the preclusion rules of the rendering court. This discourages parties from forum shopping. Since all courts will look back to the rules applied by the courts of the rendering state, there will be no advantage from bringing the second action in a state that has less restrictive rules of *res judicata*.

Hypothetical #4. Issue preclusion poses similar Full Faith and Credit scenarios. Suppose that Altieri brought his first suit against Quigley in the state courts of West Dakota, which has never accepted the concept of non-mutual issue preclusion. He loses, because the jury finds that he was contributorily negligent, which bars recovery under West Dakota law. Subsequently, Altieri sues Romanoff, another driver involved in the accident, in an East Dakota state court for his injuries in the accident, and Romanoff asserts as a defense that Altieri was contributorily negligent. Romanoff moves for summary judgment, arguing that Altieri litigated the issue of his negligence in causing the accident against Quigley, and lost, so Altieri should be barred from litigating that issue against him. This is an argument for non-mutual defensive issue preclusion, since Romanoff was not a party to the prior action, and East Dakota (unlike the rendering court of West Dakota), authorizes trial judges to apply non-mutual issue preclusion in appropriate cases. Following the reasoning of *Parklane,* should Altieri be barred from relitigating the issue of his negligence?

A If the East Dakota court is to give the prior judgment "the same Full Faith and Credit" (28 U.S.C. § 1738) that it would have in West Dakota, it should allow Altieri to relitigate the issue of his negligence. If he had sued Romanoff in West Dakota, that court would not have barred him from relitigating, since it does not apply non-mutual preclusion. So, if it takes the phrase, "the same Full Faith and Credit" literally, the West Dakota court should allow Altieri to relitigate the issue.

Though this is tidy logic, the case law is less clear. Wouldn't the East Dakota court properly respect the West Dakota judgment if it gave it *more* effect than it would have in the courts of West Dakota, by using the negligence finding to estop Altieri in his second action, even though West Dakota

A

courts would not? Arguably, this is consistent with the command of the Full Faith and Credit Clause, and some courts have approved this "more Full Faith and Credit" approach. *See, e.g., Goodson v. McDonough Power Equipment, Inc.*, No. 80-CA-34, 1981 WL 2886, at *5–8 (Ohio Ct. App. Aug. 18, 1981) (holding that Full Faith and Credit did not prohibit an Ohio court from applying non-mutual issue preclusion even though the rendering Florida court required mutuality), *rev'd on other grounds*, 443 N.E.2d 978 (Ohio 1983). Others have required the second court to treat the judgment exactly the same way that the courts of the rendering state would.

B. Inter-System Preclusion: State Courts Honoring Federal Judgments and Federal Courts Honoring State Judgments

Hypothetical #5. Similar problems arise when lawsuit #1 is brought in a state court, and the state court judgment is used to preclude issues or claims in a later federal action. Consider the last example, in which Altieri sued Quigley in a West Dakota state court and lost because he was found negligent. If he sues Romanoff in a second action in federal court, Romanoff might plead non-mutual issue preclusion, citing *Blonder-Tongue* to prevent Altieri from recovering against him.

The Full Faith and Credit Clause does not apply here. By its terms, it only commands *states*, not the federal government, to respect judgments of other states. This variation is instead governed by the full faith and credit *statute*, 28 U.S.C. § 1738. That statute commands that federal courts give "the same full faith and credit" to state judgments that they would be given in the state where rendered. The cases hold that this language means what it says: In the Altieri example, the federal court should apply non-mutual issue preclusion if the West Dakota courts would, but allow Altieri to relitigate if the West Dakota courts would. *See Shreve, Raven-Hansen & Geyh* § 15.10[2].

Hypothetical #6. Consider the converse situation, in which Quigley brings the lawsuit #1 in the federal court for East Dakota and lawsuit #2 in state court. Here, neither the Full Faith and Credit Clause, nor § 1738, the Full Faith and Credit statute, dictate the results, because they dictate the effect given *state court* judgments. The cases have uniformly held, however, that the preclusive effect of a federal judgment must be determined under federal common law, but when the judgment is issued in a diversity case that law adopts the forum state's preclusion law as the rule of decision. *See, e.g., Semtek International Inc. v. Lockheed Martin Corp.*, 531 U.S. 497, 508–09 (2001). Thus, the state court considering Quigley's second case would apply federal common law preclusion principles to determine whether Quigley's claim or issues adjudicated in his federal action would be precluded, unless Quigley's first suit was based on diversity. In the latter case, the state court would apply the preclusion law of East Dakota to decide the effect of the federal judgment. *Erie* rears its ugly head.

Interestingly, this analysis suggests that, in the *River Park* case discussed in the previous chapter, the Illinois Supreme Court engaged in an unnecessary effort to define a "claim" under Illinois law. According to existing precedents, the Court should have looked to *federal* law for this definition, because the original judgment was entered by a federal district court and concerned a federal cause of action, not a claim under its diversity jurisdiction.

And last. There is, of course, one last scenario, in which both the first and second cases are brought in federal courts. In this variation, the preclusive effect of the earlier judgment will be governed by federal preclusion principles, except that, once again, the effect of a federal judgment based on diversity jurisdiction is decided by the preclusion rules of the state in which the rendering court sits. *See Shreve, Raven-Hansen & Geyh* § 15.10[3].

Keeping it straight. We repeat, keeping this straight is not impossible, but it requires keeping your eye on the ball: *the preclusion law that the rendering court would apply.*

A Final Exercise: A Memo to the Partner

The partner for whom you are working has brought an action for malpractice on behalf of his client, Elisabeth Tayler, against her former divorce lawyer, Gail Chase. He explains to you that a year ago, after Tayler complained to the Maryland Bar Association, the Bar Grievance Committee filed a complaint against attorney Gail Chase in an action styled *In re Chase*, brought under the original jurisdiction of the Maryland Court of Appeals pursuant to the special jurisdictional provision of an attorney discipline statute. The complaint sought disciplinary sanctions against Chase for her failure to represent Tayler adequately. Chase pled a general denial, and the case was tried by Bar Counsel for half a day before a special master, who was appointed to take evidence and make fact findings. Chase's lawyer defended her in this proceeding.

After the trial, the special master found the following facts. Chase had accepted $1,000 as a fee to obtain a divorce for her client, Elisabeth Tayler. Chase had then duly filed a complaint for divorce in a Maryland court, to which defendant interposed a counterclaim for divorce and custody. Trial of the complaint had been set for March 20, 1982, and Chase had been so advised by the clerk.

Chase, however, never told Tayler of the trial date and failed to return Tayler's phone calls inquiring about the case. Moreover, Chase failed to show up for trial. Accordingly, judgment had been entered against Tayler by default in the divorce action, granting the divorce, but denying her custody of the children, her share of the marital property, and her attorney's fees and expenses.

Accepting the special master's report, the Maryland Court of Appeals issued an opinion concluding that Chase had failed to keep her client informed of the progress of matters entrusted to her and failed to represent her client adequately, in violation of the Maryland Rules of Professional Conduct. It issued a judgment against Chase, ordering her to repay the $1,000 attorneys' fee and suspending her license to practice for 30 days.

Thereafter, Tayler brought the instant action against Chase for malpractice in the United States District Court for the Eastern District of Virginia, properly invoking diversity jurisdiction. The partner would now like to use the judgment in *In re Chase* against Chase in the malpractice action. He asks you, as someone who took Civil Procedure much more recently than he did, for your best top-of-the-head judgment on (a) whether he can, and, if so, (b) how. (If your answer is yes, then he'll presumably ask you to do some library research to follow this up.)

You should assume that the Maryland Rules of Professional Conduct say nothing about the relevancy, if any, of a rule violation to the standard of care in malpractice cases.

Memorandum to Partner re: Possible Issue Preclusion of Chase in Tayler v. Chase

(You've asked for my top-of-the-head judgment, without my researching the relevant law. My tentative conclusions are thus subject to verification by further research in Maryland law.) It appears that Tayler would like to establish Chase's malpractice in the instant lawsuit by issue preclusion based on the issue decided in the disciplinary proceeding. Whether she can depends on the preclusion law of Maryland, because it was a Maryland court that issued the judgment that she would like to use. The enforcing court—the federal court for the E.D. Virginia—must therefore apply the preclusion law that the Maryland court would apply to its own judgment.

Assuming that Maryland follows the basic *Restatement (Second) of Judgments* rule of issue preclusion, the first requirement is that the issue in *In re Chase* and *Tayler v. Chase* has to be the same. The complaint against Tayler in the disciplinary proceeding was that she "failed to represent Tayler adequately." The issue in the instant malpractice lawsuit is whether Chase breached a duty of reasonable care in representing Tayler in her divorce. While these issues are not phrased identically, they appear to be substantially the same. However, whether Chase's inadequate representation proximately caused Tayler's injuries (notably the adverse relief awarded against her in the divorce case), and what those injuries are worth, are new issues, not presented in the disciplinary proceeding. Accordingly, even if issue preclusion is permitted in the malpractice case, it will not fully establish Tayler's malpractice claim (though it may advance it far enough to induce settlement). This would at best be a case for partial issue preclusion.

Second, it appears that the issue of the adequacy of Chase's services was actually litigated. The evidentiary hearing in the disciplinary proceeding lasted half a day, and the special master's fact findings reflected some presentation and consideration of the evidence.

Third, the court of appeals issued a valid and final judgment against Chase in the disciplinary proceedings.

Fourth, the special master's specific fact findings were necessarily decided: They were adopted by the Maryland Court of Appeals as the basis for its judgment and order for sanctions. (The court also found that Chase failed to keep her client informed, but this seems, at best, just an instance of the broader finding.)

However, there may be a serious question whether Chase had a full and fair opportunity to litigate the issue. On one hand, we need more facts about the quality of the disciplinary proceeding and its rules. While the decisions of arbitration hearings and other quasi-adjudicative administrative proceedings have been given issue-preclusive effect in many jurisdictions, this depends very specifically on the litigation opportunity they afford. For example, I don't know whether the burden of persuasion is less in a disciplinary proceeding than in a tort action (if it is higher, this difference would not prevent issue preclusion). On the other hand,

I doubt that there is any question here of Chase's incentive to litigate the disciplinary proceeding. After all, her license to practice was on the line, and, indeed, she lost it for thirty days. On balance, especially inasmuch as the special master's findings are recommendations to an established court, which accepted them here, I'd venture the guess that Chase had a full and fair opportunity to litigate and that the essential findings therefore do carry issue-preclusive effect, but this will require confirmation.

Finally, the issue preclusion here is non-mutual offensive issue preclusion because Tayler (who was not a party to the disciplinary proceeding and therefore cannot be bound by it) is using the judgment against Chase (who was a party to establish part of her claim). Even if Maryland has abandoned mutuality for purposes of defensive issue preclusion, it may not have gone the whole way to allow offensive issue preclusion. If it has, and uses the same discretionary standard that the Supreme Court adopted as federal common law in *Parklane Hosiery Company, Inc. v. Shore*, 439 U.S. 322 (1979), this would seem an appropriate case in which to allow offensive preclusion. Tayler is obviously not a wait-and-see plaintiff, because she probably had no right to join as a party in the disciplinary proceeding. Please see above for my best guess as to whether that proceeding gave Chase a full and fair opportunity to litigate.

Should you decide to proceed (after confirming my top-of-the-head judgment), we will need certified copies of the complaint, trial record, findings, and the order in *In re Chase*, as the basis of a motion for partial summary judgment, or an instruction to the jury in *Tayler v. Chase* that it must take as established that Chase failed adequately to represent her client.

VI. Issue Preclusion: Summary of Basic Principles

- Issue preclusion, or collateral estoppel, bars a party from relitigating an issue that was decided in an earlier action.
- A party seeking to invoke issue preclusion must establish that: (1) the issue is the same issue that was decided in lawsuit #1; (2) the issue was actually litigated in lawsuit #1; (3) the decision in lawsuit #1 was a valid final judgment or "final enough"; (4) the issue was necessarily decided in lawsuit #1; (5) the party against whom preclusion is invoked was a party to, or in privity with a party to, lawsuit #1; and (6) that party had a full and fair opportunity to litigate. Courts vary widely in how they phrase, order, and acknowledge these requirements, although many now cite *Restatement (Second) Judgments* §§ 27 & 28.
- In most cases, issue preclusion is "mutual": The party asserts it against a party who would also be entitled to invoke it. Ordinarily, a person who was not a party to lawsuit #1 cannot be precluded by the judgment in that lawsuit; due process entitles him to his day in court. However, a stranger to lawsuit #1 can sometimes use issue preclusion to preclude someone who was a party to lawsuit #1. The federal law of issue preclusion and many

states allow such "non-mutual" issue preclusion to be asserted *defensively,* to defeat a claim by a party to lawsuit #1.

- The federal law of issue preclusion and some states also allow non-mutual issue preclusion to be asserted *offensively,* to help a stranger to lawsuit #1 establish an element of its claim against a party to lawsuit #1. Non-mutual offensive issue preclusion, however, is discretionary in federal courts and depends on such factors as the party's full and fair opportunity to litigate lawsuit #1, any inconsistency between the issues found in lawsuit #1 and findings on the same issues in other lawsuits, and the stranger's opportunity to join in lawsuit #1.
- Constitutional and statutory full faith and credit principles generally require that the enforcing court—the court in which issue preclusion is invoked—give the same preclusive effect to a judgment that the rendering court would. However, if the rendering court is a federal court sitting in diversity, then the enforcing court applies the preclusion law of the state in which the rendering court sits.

TABLE OF CASES

Principal cases are in italics.

TABLE OF STATUTES AND RULES

Federal Statutes

Federal Rules of Civil Procedure
(Fed. R. Civ. P.)

Federal and State Constitutions

INDEX